The Economics of Labor Markets

Bruce E. Kaufman
Georgia State University

Julie L. Hotchkiss
*The Federal Reserve Bank of Atlanta
and Georgia State University*

THOMSON

SOUTH-WESTERN

D0022743

Australia · Canada · Mexico · Singapore · Spain · United Kingdom · United States

The Economics of Labor Markets, Seventh Edition
Bruce E. Kaufman, Julie L. Hotchkiss

VP/Editorial Director:
Jack W. Calhoun

Editor-in-Chief:
Alex von Rosenberg

Acquisitions Editor:
Michael W. Worls

Sr. Developmental Editor:
Susanna C. Smart

Sr. Marketing Coordinator:
Jennifer Garamy

Production Editors:
Elizabeth A. Shipp and Brian Courter

Manager of Technology, Editorial:
Vicky True

Production Technology Project Manager:
Peggy Buskey

Web Coordinator:
Karen L. Schaffer

Sr. Manufacturing Coordinator:
Sandee Milewski

Production House:
Interactive Composition Corporation (ICC)

Printer:
RRD Crawfordsville
Crawfordsville, IN

Art Director:
Michelle Kunkler

Cover and Internal Designer:
Christy Carr Design

Cover Images:
© DIOMEDIA/Alamy

For more information about our products, contact us at:

Thomson Learning Academic Resource Center
1-800-423-0563

Thomson Higher Education
5191 Natorp Boulevard
Mason, OH 45040
USA

To Diane, Lauren, and Andrew
Bruce Kaufman

To Bob, Roberta, and Nathan
Julie Hotchkiss

BRIEF CONTENTS

CONTENTS

CHAPTER 3 Labor Force Participation 114

CHAPTER 4   The Demand for Labor in the Short Run   172

CHAPTER 5   The Demand for Labor in the Long Run   219

CHAPTER 6 The Determination of Wages   260

CHAPTER 7 Education, Training, and Earnings Differentials: The Theory of Human Capital 326

CHAPTER 10   The Economics of Human Resource Management   505

CHAPTER 11 Union Membership and Collective Bargaining   558

CHAPTER 12 The Economic Impact of Unions 626

CHAPTER 13 Unemployment 666

In *The Economics of Labor Markets*, we present many of the important factors affecting the market for labor, and the ever-present changes that move in tandem with our expanding global economy. One of the things students will learn from this text is to become better informed—to know what are the major events, trends, and developments in the world of work. Another is to be able to explain these real-world outcomes. Why, for example, did annual hours of work decline in the twentieth century? What factors are responsible for the earnings gap between men and women? Because these questions often have more than one answer, students should also learn why economists disagree and be able to critically evaluate alternative theories. Finally, students should learn how to apply economic theory to analysis of current events and current public policy issues.

The Economics of Labor Markets is intended as the basic text for a one-semester or one-quarter course at the undergraduate level in labor economics, or labor economics and labor relations. It is also suitable as a survey or reference text for a graduate level course. The level of exposition is relatively nontechnical and the main text eschews all mathematics except for present value and elasticity formulas. Although the only prerequisite for this text is a one-semester principles course in microeconomics, students with some exposure to statistics and intermediate level theory will be able to master the material more quickly.

Distinctive Features

The text has a number of new and unique features that distinguish it from other texts:

Pedagogical Approach An innovative feature of the text is the pedagogical approach to presenting the chapter material. Each chapter begins with a brief look at the empirical facts concerning a particular subject. For example, Chapter 2, on hours of work, begins with a review of the cross-sectional and time-series patterns of hours of work. Similarly, Chapter 7 begins the discussion of human capital by first looking at the shape of age/earnings profiles.

This approach has several advantages. For one, it helps fulfill the first criterion noted above—to inform students about events or trends in the labor market. A second advantage is that it provides motivation for studying the chapter material students know why they are studying the theory and what it is meant to explain. A third benefit is that students have more interest in the course if they can see that it has some application to real-world behavior.

Balanced Presentation of Theory A second distinctive feature of the book is that it presents a balanced and well-rounded presentation of labor market theory.

Chapter 1 argues that every labor market outcome is the product of three forces: market forces of supply and demand; institutional forces in the form of government, union, and corporate power; and sociological forces emanating from factors such as family background, cultures, class, custom, and so on. We also stress that much of the controversy in labor economics stems from differences in opinion over the extent to which imperfections and defects exist in the market mechanism. With this framework, it is possible to distinguish between the two major schools of thought in labor economics—the neoclassical school and the institutional school—based on the different weight each gives to the roles of market, institutional, and sociological forces and on the importance of imperfections in the market process.

This approach has several advantages. First, it provides students a balanced presentation of labor market theory. Paul Samuelson and William Nordhaus said, "A conscientious textbook must present all views fairly. . . . Textbook authors must be neither prosecuting attorneys nor defense counsels. They must be friends in the court of truth." We firmly agree with this standard and have written the text in that spirit. A number of existing labor texts, in our opinion, do not provide students with a representative cross section of thought in labor economics. While the neoclassical model is presented in great detail, alternative theories or points of view are given little, if any, treatment. The approach here provides the best exposition of the neoclassical model, but also introduces the student to more institutionally oriented theories.

A second advantage of this more balanced theoretical perspective is that it illustrates to students why economists disagree, particularly about issues of public policy. Finally, a third advantage is that a certain amount of controversy stimulates student interest and discussion. At the same time, we endeavored not to overdramatize theoretical disputes or to give excessive weight to unorthodox theories.

Unique Topic Coverage   This text was the first among labor texts to cover a number of topics that were not the standard in most labor texts. Examples of these topics include technological change and labor demand, discrimination in promotion, human resource management, bargaining theories of household labor supply, the minimum wage debate, and the Beveridge curve. A number of other topics are also given a much expanded treatment compared with other texts—examples are the neoclassical household model of labor supply, union wage concessions, occupational segregation, and bargaining models of wage determination. In choosing topics for the text, we deliberately tried to include issues that would be of interest to students outside of economics.

Empirical Evidence   We made the text as real-world oriented as possible by illustrating the theory with numerous empirical examples. Each chapter has at least one entire section devoted to a review of empirical research or evidence on one of the topics under consideration. Chapter 2, for example, contains a discussion of labor supply curves estimated from cross-sectional data; in Chapter 5 the relationship between productivity growth and employment in agriculture and telephone communications is reviewed. Empirical examples from scholarly research and periodicals such as *Business Week* and *The Wall Street Journal* are also presented throughout the text, often in the form of short footnotes.

Policy Applications Each chapter also contains at least one section devoted to an application of the theory to some public policy issue or current events topic. In Chapter 4, for example, the theory of labor demand is used to analyze the impact of trade liberalization on the employment and wage rates of American workers. Chapter 12 considers the pros and cons of the Davis–Bacon Act.

Current Events A third way we link theory to real-world events is by including in each chapter one or more boxed examples called "In the News." Each example contains a brief discussion of a relevant magazine or newspaper article that supplements or illustrates a particular subject contained in the chapter. Chapter 2 ("Hours of Work"), for example, contains an "In the News" section devoted to the evidence on whether Americans are overworked, while the "In the News" section in Chapter 13 ("Unemployment") discusses the difficulties some cities have in attracting businesses to their designated enterprise zones.

International Features One cannot open a newspaper today without recognizing how much more globally focused the United States is becoming. Because of this, almost every chapter contains at least one internationally-focused example, illustration, or application. For example, Chapter 4 explores how growing imports affect employment in the United States; Chapter 7 compares social and private rates of return from around the world; Chapter 9 compares the degree of occupational segregation in many different countries; and Chapter 13 compares and evaluates the experience of different countries with unemployment.

Mathematical Modeling Appendices A unique feature of the text is appendices to each of the core chapters on labor supply and labor demand (Chapters 2–5). Each of these appendices presents the mathematical representation (using simple calculus) of the major theoretical outcome contained in the chapter. For example, the appendix to Chapter 2 derives the equilibrium condition for utility maximization in the labor/leisure choice model, showing mathematically that in equilibrium the wage is equal to the marginal rate of substitution; and the appendix to Chapter 5 derives the long-run equilibrium for the demand for labor, showing that the input price ratio is equal to the marginal rate of technical substitution between capital and labor.

Linear Regression Appendices Another unique feature of the text is the series of three appendices that illustrate the use of linear regression techniques to estimate economic relationships. An appendix to Chapter 2, for example, first explains how linear regression is used to estimate a labor supply curve and then presents regression results from an empirical study to illustrate the theory.

Data and Reference Appendix The appendix to Chapter 6 contains a detailed list of data and reference sources in labor economics, including Internet sources, to aid students in writing research reports and term papers.

Organization and Course Outline

We organized the chapters in a logical progression so that one subject smoothly flows into another. Chapter 1 provides an overview of the major labor market outcomes examined later in the text; a detailed discussion of the role of market, institutional, and sociological forces in the labor market; and a review of the evolution of labor market theory. Chapters 2 and 3 are devoted to labor supply (hours of work and labor force participation), and Chapters 4 and 5 to labor demand (in the short run and long run). We prefer to discuss labor supply before labor demand, although instructors who prefer the opposite approach can easily change the chapter sequence. In Chapter 6 demand and supply are combined to show the process of wage determination. Although wage determination is probably the central issue in labor economics, few texts give this topic adequate coverage, and none that we know of examine the extent to which the predictions of the competitive model accord with real-world behavior. These topics are considered in detail in this book.

Chapters 7 through 10 discuss the causes of wage differentials in nonunion labor markets. Chapter 7 is devoted to human capital theory, Chapter 8 examines occupational wage differentials, Chapter 9 looks at the causes and consequences of discrimination, and Chapter 10 examines the wage structure in the context of human resource management.

Chapters 11 and 12 are devoted to the economics of unions and labor relations. Chapter 11 describes why workers join unions and examines the process of collective bargaining. Chapter 12 analyzes the impact of unions on wages, fringe benefits, productivity, income inequality, and profits. Since courses in labor economics differ considerably with respect to the amount of attention given to unions and collective bargaining, it was difficult to decide the amount of space to devote to this topic in the text. Some authors devote as little as one chapter, others use half the book. We tried to strike a balance at about 15 percent—a figure approximating the size of the organized sector in the labor market. The material on unions in Chapters 11 and 12, along with the extensive treatment of human resource management in Chapter 10 (as well as material in Chapters 2, 4, and 9), is extensive enough to make the text suitable for a course that includes a significant emphasis on labor relations, without detailed discussion of labor history, labor law, and the administration of the labor agreement.

The final chapter of the text is devoted to the one macroeconomic issue that probably receives the most attention from the press and from policy makers: unemployment. Both the causes and consequences of unemployment receive considerable attention.

One consequence of the extensive topical coverage, the in-depth treatment of most subjects, and the presentation of alternative theories is that the text is relatively comprehensive. We believe, however, that most instructors will find this to be a virtue, not a vice. Some topics that appeal to one instructor may not appeal to another. With this text, instructors can structure the content of the course to match their needs and interests. Each chapter is written so that one or more sections can be deleted without loss of continuity. In addition, the nontechnical style of exposition allows the instructor to assign sections in each chapter as outside reading, making it possible to cover more of the book than could be covered in class discussion alone.

New Features of the Seventh Edition

In addition to updating statistics, data, and policy/institutional details, this edition's revision includes updated applications and the new "In-the-News" boxes. It is important to keep the applications of the theory relevant to what the student is reading about in the newspaper and seeing on the TV news.

Some of the major changes in this edition include **a completely rewritten** section on the evolution of labor market theory in Chapter 1, a new policy application on the earned income tax credit in Chapter 3, a new empirical example about the wage impact of immigration in Chapter 6, and updated Empirical Evidence 6.2 with more recent example of job losses, and a revised section on the "Firm's Demand for HRM Services" model in Chapter 10.

Additional changes include the many updated "**In the News**" features: In **Chapter 2,** two new boxes cover a comparison of hours of work in the United States and Europe, and another evaluates the success of, and problems with, welfare reform. Chapter 3 includes an "In-the-News" box discussing the implications of retiring baby boomers on the next generation. In other chapters, news features cover concerns of the middle-class, and the rising costs of health and other fringe benefits; how American manufacturers are faring in a growing global, low-wage economy; the living wage; anti-discrimination based on sexual orientation; union health benefits, and the relatioship between job growth and the unemployment rate.

Ancillary Materials

A comprehensive *Instructor's Manual and Test Bank* (ISBN 0-324-28880-8), prepared by the authors, is available in print version and electronically on the text website. The manual includes an overview of each chapter and answers to the end-of-chapter review questions, as well as Internet-based assignments relevant to the topics in each chapter.

In addition, the test bank portion for each chapter contains ten multiple choice questions, ten true/false/uncertain questions requiring explanations, and a detailed answer key.

The website at http://kaufman.swlearning.com is valuable resource for instructors and students, and contains the following:

- **PowerPoint slides** of key tables and figures
- **Additional readings** list to accompany each chapter
- **e-con @pps Economic Applications**—EconNews Online, EconDebate Online, EconData Online, and EconLinks Online help to deepen students' understanding of theoretical concepts through hands-on exploration and analysis of the latest economic news stories, policy debates, and data. An access card is provided with each new text.

Acknowledgments

In writing this edition of the text, we have benefited greatly from the comments and suggestions of a number of people. We would particularly like to thank Susan Averett, Lafayette College; Christopher Geller, Deakin University; Jill Gunderson, Economic Research Services; and Sabrina Pabilonia, Bureau of Labor Statistics, for their detailed comments for this revision. We also thank the reviewers who contributed many good ideas and suggestions to previous editions of *The Economics of Labor Markets*: Steve G. Allen, North Carolina State University; John Antel, University of Houston; Thomas R. Arnold, King's College; John Barron, Purdue University; Brian Becker, State University of New York, Buffalo; Mary Ellen Benedict, Bowling Green State University; Sherrilyn M. Billger, Illinois State University; Richard Bryant, University of Missouri, Rolla; Carol Clark, Guilford College; Marie D. Connolly, Chatham College; Donald A. Coffin, Indiana University, Northwest; Betsy Crowell, University of Michigan, Dearborn; Laurence Fisher, Our Lady of the Lake University; Donald E. Frey, Wake Forest University; Paul Grimes, Mississippi State University; Wallace Hendricks, University of Illinois; Stephen M. Hills, Ohio State University; Barry T. Hirsch, Florida State University; David C. Huffman, Bridgewater College; Jerry Kingston, Arizona State University; Andrew I. Kohen, James Madison University; Anil Kumar, Syracuse University; Joseph Lee, Mankato State University; Michael A. Leeds, Temple University; Stuart Low, Arizona State University; John G. Marcis, Francis Marion University; Jorge Martinez, Georgia State University; Nan Maxwell, California State University, Hayward; Robert Moffitt, Johns Hopkins University; Edward Montgomery, University of Maryland, College Park; Robert E. Moore, Georgia State University; Roger D. Morefield, University of St. Thomas; Kevin J. Murphy, Oakland University; Peter Orazem, Iowa State University; Bruce Pietrykowski, University of Michigan, Dearborn; Solomon Polachek, State University of New York, Binghamton; Lidija Polutnik, Babson College; Jonathan F. Pingle, University of North Carolina, Chapel Hill; Elton Rayack, University of Rhode Island; John W. Ruser, Bureau of Labor Statistics; John F. Schnell, University of Alabama, Huntsville; Bruce Seaman, Georgia State University; Paula Stephan, Georgia State University; Peter von Allman, Moravian College; Susan Vroman, Georgetown University; Jennifer L. Warlick, University of Notre Dame; William W. Wilkes, Athens State University; Donald R. Williams, Kent State University.

In addition, valuable assistance was provided by John Stavick and Velma Zahirovic-Herbert.

Bruce E. Kaufman
Julie L. Hotchkiss
Atlanta, Georgia
March 2005

Bruce E. Kaufman is Professor of Economics, and Senior Associate of the W. T. Beebe Institute of Personnel and Employment Relations at Georgia State University. He received his Ph.D. in Economics from the University of Wisconsin, Madison. Professor Kaufman has authored several dozen articles on labor markets, industrial relations, and human resource management in scholarly journals and has written or edited fifteen books. His book, *The Origins and Evolution of the Field of Industrial Relations in the United States,* won the "Best Book in Labor Economics and Industrial Relations" award in 1992; his most recent book (2004) is *Theoretical Perspectives on Work and the Employment Relationship.* Professor Kaufman's research interests include wage determination, the economics of firm employment practices, labor law, collective bargaining, behavioral and institutional economics, and the history of thought in labor economics.

Julie L. Hotchkiss is Research Economist and Policy Advisor at the Federal Reserve Bank of Atlanta, and adjunct Professor of Economics in the Andrew Young School of Policy Studies at Georgia State University. She received her B.A. degree from Willamette University and her Ph.D. in Economics from Cornell University in 1989 and has published numerous articles on a variety of topics including the relationship among state-level unemployment rates, wage differentials in Jamaica, labor supply behavior and welfare of two-earner families, the impact of unemployment insurance programs on individual job search behavior, and wage determination of part-time workers. She has written one book, *The Labor Market Experience of Workers with Disabilities: The ADA and Beyond.* Current research projects include the impact of intermittent labor force participation of lifetime earnings and wealth accumulation, successful transition from welfare to work, and the dynamics of jobs and workers across the business cycle.

The Labor Market

Economics is concerned with the general question of resource allocation and the determination of prices and levels of production in the economy. Labor economics focuses on one particular aspect of this process, the determination of wages and employment in the labor market and the resulting distribution of income among individuals and households.

Labor economics is both an interesting and a useful subject. One reason is that the topics and issues addressed in labor economics are of direct and immediate relevance to each of us. The focus of labor economics is on the world of work—who is working, what types of jobs are available, and why people are being paid what they are. These issues are not of purely academic interest, because the availability, financial remuneration, and psychological gratification of work are central to the lives of most of us.

Labor economics is also a popular course because it deals with a subject with which many students have firsthand experience. Not many of us have been involved with the intricacies of foreign exchange markets, central banking, or government tax and expenditure programs. Most students do have some previous experience with finding employment, the advantages and disadvantages of particular types of jobs, planning careers, and possibly the operation of labor unions.

Finally, a third factor that makes labor economics an interesting subject is that it has so many applications to current social issues and public policy debates. Should the minimum wage be raised? Should it be abolished? Why is the unemployment rate for blacks twice that for whites? Do unions cause inflation? Will technological change lead to greater unemployment? While labor economics will not provide definitive answers to all of these questions, it can provide a very useful framework in which to analyze them more intelligently.

The Labor Market and the Economy

At the present time, about 137 million people in the United States are employed either part- or full-time, and approximately 25 million business firms provide jobs for these people. How do all of these individual workers and firms get matched up with one another? What determines the rates of pay that go with these jobs?

The central analytic device that economists use to answer these questions is the concept of a **labor market.** A market exists whenever there is a good or service for which there are buyers (demanders) and sellers (suppliers) who engage in mutual exchange or trade of the item. This exchange or trade is typically consummated when there is common agreement on the price per unit that the buyer must pay the seller.

Just as there are readily observable markets for wheat, steel, and automobiles, so too is there a readily observable market for labor, or more correctly, the services of labor (slavery is illegal). Wheat, steel, and other goods are traded in commodity or product markets. Labor, on the other hand, is a factor of production that is owned by individuals and, in effect, is rented to business firms for a period of time (for instance, an hour or a year) to be combined with other factor inputs such as land and capital to produce a good or service. Labor is traded in what economists call a **factor market,** just as the other factors of production are land and capital.

The relationship between the labor market and the product market is illustrated in more detail by the circular flow diagram in Figure 1.1. It depicts in a highly simplified form the manner in which the market forces of demand and supply connect the product market in the top half of Figure 1.1 and the labor market in the bottom half. In this simplified economy there are two sets of economic agents, households (the left-hand box) and business firms (the right-hand box). The goal of business firms is to make a profit, and to do so they produce goods and services to be sold in the product market. This supply of goods and services is represented in the product market by the supply curve S_G. On the other side of the product market, households desire as high a material standard of living as possible, leading to a flow of consumer expenditure on goods and services, represented by the demand curve D_G. The interaction of demand and supply in the product market gives rise to an equilibrium price (P_1) and quantity (Q_1).

The lower half of Figure 1.1 shows how purchases of labor by firms and sales of labor by individual household members interact in the labor market to determine the level of wages and employment in the economy. To produce the goods and services demanded by households, firms must obtain sufficient amounts of land, capital, and labor. The desire by firms to supply goods and services in the product market thus gives rise to a demand for workers in the labor market, represented by the labor demand curve D_L. Similarly, for households to purchase the goods and services they desire requires that individual household members seek work in order to earn incomes. The demand for goods and services by households thus gives rise to a supply of labor to firms, represented by the labor supply curve S_L. As in the product market, the interaction of demand and supply in the labor market determines the wage rate (W_1) and the level of employment (L_1). The average rate of hourly compensation times the number of people employed determines, in turn, the total amount of labor earnings that households have to spend. In 2003, the total compensation received by American workers amounted to $6.2 billion, 64 percent of total personal income created in the United States.

FIGURE 1.1   A CIRCULAR FLOW MODEL OF THE ECONOMY

The household sector gives rise to a demand for goods (D_G) in the product market and supply of labor (S_L) in the labor market. The business sector gives rise to a supply of goods (S_G) and a demand for labor (D_L). The interaction of demand and supply in the product market determines the level of prices and production (P_1, Q_1); the interaction of demand and supply in the labor market determines the level of wages and employment (W_1, L_1).

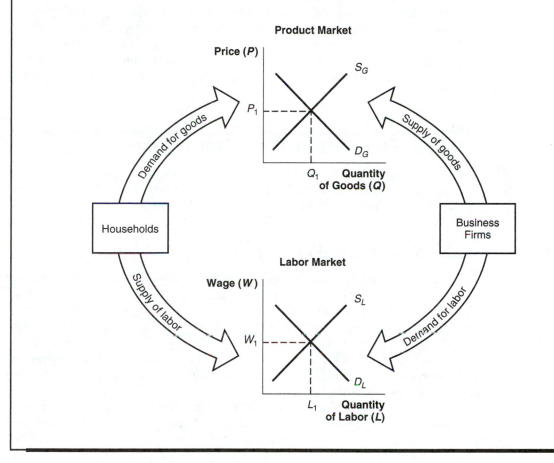

Microeconomics and macroeconomics focus on the determination of price and quantity in the product market, either at the level of the individual firm or for the aggregate economy. Labor economics, on the other hand, focuses on the bottom half of Figure 1.1, the labor market. Although labor economics deals with a separate set of questions and issues, the circular flow diagram in Figure 1.1 suggests that labor economics and microeconomic and macroeconomic analysis are closely linked because of the important feedback effects that events in one sphere of the economy have on the other. An increase in consumer expenditure in the product market, for example, will feed back into the labor market in the form of a greater demand for labor as firms attempt to increase production. Likewise, higher wages in the labor market feed back into the product market as they affect both business costs and consumer income.

Labor economics and general economic analysis are also closely linked at the conceptual or theoretical level. As Figure 1.1 illustrates, while the product market and labor market are quite distinct, economists use the same theoretical apparatus to analyze each market, namely, the theory of demand and supply in competitive markets. Just as in microeconomics, where changes in price bring demand and supply in the product market into a state of balance or equilibrium, so too in labor economics attention is focused on the role of wages as the "balancing wheel" in the labor market.

Unique Features of the Labor Market

There are several ways in which the labor market differs from product markets in its structure or characteristics. These differences, in turn, have a large impact on both the theory and the actual operation of the labor market.

Labor Is Embodied in the Seller

Probably the most important feature of the labor market that distinguishes it from all other markets is that the item being exchanged is embodied in a human being.[1] The ownership and possession of a commodity such as wheat is completely transferable between buyer and seller and, thus, neither party has any interest in the personal characteristics of the other (for instance, age, gender, color, or personality); the only interest of each party is to secure the most advantageous price possible. Likewise, the wheat, since it is an inert commodity, does not have any preference as to where and to whom it is sold.

The same conditions are not true in the labor market. Labor as a service is inseparable from the person providing it and, thus, the worker supplying labor and the firm buying it must have a direct, personal relationship with each other. This, and the fact that human beings have definite preferences with respect to the conditions they work under, causes the exchange in the labor market to be determined not only by the price of labor but also by a host of noneconomic factors that are largely absent in commodity markets. These noneconomic factors are partly physical in nature, such as the risk of injury on the job or the pleasantness of the work environment, and partly social in nature, such as the prestige of the job, the race or

---

1   Eli Ginzberg, *Understanding Human Resources: Perspectives, People, and Policy* (Cambridge: University Press of America, 1985)

gender of workmates, and the attitude of the management. The importance of these factors for labor economics is that the decision of workers concerning whom to work for and the decision of firms regarding whom to hire are based on a complex package of considerations, including not only the wage but all the nonpecuniary advantages and disadvantages associated with the job or worker.

The Long-Term Nature of the Employment Relationship

A second significant feature of the labor market is the long-term nature of the employment relationship. With many goods and services, such as automobiles, clothing, or airline travel, buyers and sellers may switch from one to another on a daily basis in pursuit of the most attractive price. Such shopping around occurs in the labor market, but in a more attenuated form due to the costs to both workers and firms of frequent job changing. Employers, for example, find it to their advantage in normal times to cultivate stable workforces, since they make substantial investments in workers in the form of costs of hiring and, more important, training and experience. Likewise, individual workers often find it to their advantage to remain with one employer for a considerable time, particularly as they get beyond their teens and early 20s. One reason for this is economic in nature, since wages and fringe benefits normally increase with tenure on the job; another, more psychological reason is related to the value people place on security and familiar surroundings. How long do most people stay on one job? One study found the typical worker can expect to have ten jobs between ages 18 and 65, two-thirds in the first ten years of work life. Thus, the average duration of a job for a teenager is generally quite short—about three months—while 40 percent of workers over the age of 40 hold jobs for 20 years or more.[2]

The most important implication of the long-term employment relationship between workers and firms is that it reduces the sensitivity of wages to changes in demand and supply and, thus, the ability of wages to clear the market. The classic type of auction market where prices rise and fall daily exists for commodities, such as wheat, or financial issues, such as stocks and bonds. In the wheat market, an excess supply of wheat quickly leads to a drop in its price as sellers underbid each other to attract a buyer; buyers, in turn, have little reason not to switch from one seller to another since all bushels of wheat are exactly the same. In the labor market, however, an excess supply of labor typically does not lead to a fall in money wage rates. While workers who are unemployed and want a job might offer to work for a firm at lower wages, most firms would find it unprofitable to hire them because the costs of hiring and training, as well as the disruptive influence on morale, would far outweigh the savings in lower wages. Thus, while in commodity markets prices fluctuate up and down to restore a balance between demand and supply, in

---

2   See Robert H. Topel and Michael P. Ward, "Job Mobility and the Careers of Young Men," *Quarterly Journal of Economics* 107 (May 1992): 439–79. The average job duration for teenagers is provided in Kim B. Clark and Lawrence H. Summers, "Labor Market Dynamics and Unemployment: A Reconsideration," *Brookings Papers on Economic Activity* 1 (Washington, D.C.: Brookings Institution, 1979): 13–60.

the labor market wages change more slowly (particularly in the downward direction) due to the costs imposed on firms and workers by frequent turnover. Because of this sluggishness of wages, an imbalance between the demand and supply of labor may persist for a considerable length of time before wages rise or fall enough to bring about the necessary adjustments in the labor market to restore equilibrium. However, in labor markets where the employment relationship is short-term and turnover costs are negligible, as for day laborers or migrant farm workers, wages exhibit a flexibility similar to that in commodity markets.[3]

Heterogeneity of Workers and Jobs

A third feature of the labor market that distinguishes it from most product markets is the extreme diversity in the characteristics of the good being traded. For agricultural commodities, raw materials, or semifinished products like steel, each unit is identical and the decision to buy or sell is made strictly on the basis of price. Other products, particularly consumer goods such as automobiles, cereals, and so on, are differentiated from each other by their physical appearance, quality, and brand. The decision to buy and sell these products is influenced not only by price, but also by these nonprice factors.

The same consideration holds true in the labor market except that the degree of differentiation in the characteristics of jobs and workers is frequently much greater. Individual workers differ by age, race, gender, education, experience, skills, and complex personality factors, such as motivation and congeniality. While a firm may have several types of machinery to choose from in making its product, every single worker it interviews is in some way unique. In choosing between employers, workers face the same diversity in characteristics of jobs. Employers and jobs, for example, differ in the type and difficulty of the work, commuting distance, fringe benefits, and quality of employee relations, as well as wages.

This extreme diversity in the characteristics of workers and jobs has two consequences for the operation of the labor market. The first is to make exchange in the labor market a function not only of wage rates but also of the many nonwage characteristics that differentiate workers and jobs from one another. Workers do not choose between jobs solely on the basis of pay, but also take into account a wide range of nonpecuniary factors; likewise, employers hire workers partly with an eye to the wage each will work for, but also with regard to many noneconomic factors. The second way in which the differentiation of jobs and workers affects the labor market is by complicating the acquisition and evaluation of information that both buyers and sellers must have before an exchange can take place.[4] In the wheat market, for example, each bushel of wheat is alike and the buyer need only acquire information about the price that various sellers are demanding. In the labor market, however,

---

3   See Carl M. Campbell III, "The Variation in Wage Rigidity by Occupation and Union Status in the US," *Oxford Bulletin of Economics and Statistics* 59 (February 1997): 133–47.

4   See George Stigler, "Information in the Labor Market," *Journal of Political Economy* 70, part 2 (October 1962): 94–105.

both buyers and sellers must invest much more time and effort in evaluating the many nonpecuniary and hard-to-measure characteristics that differentiate each worker and job. The result is that exchange in the labor market is both more costly to undertake and less likely to result in the most efficient match of buyer and seller compared to markets where the product is more nearly standardized.

The Multiplicity of Markets

A fourth characteristic that distinguishes the labor market is the multiplicity of individual submarkets. A labor market is the area over which demand and supply determine the going wage rate for labor. While the concept of one national labor market, as shown in Figure 1.1, is a useful conceptual device, in reality there is a multiplicity of markets separated by geographic location, occupation, skill, and so on. In analyzing the determination of wages, it is obvious that a distinction should be made between the market for plumbers, teachers, and bankers, for example, since the supply and demand for each occupation is likely to be quite distinct. Likewise, geographical location gives rise to distinct labor markets; the demand and supply for legal secretaries in Los Angeles is likely to be distinct from that in Boston. For some occupations, such as college professor, lawyer, or baseball player, the labor market may be national or even international in scope. Although many product markets are also less than national in scope, few are as fragmented as the labor market.

The boundaries between many of the individual labor markets are relatively porous, so workers can flow from one market to another in response to changes in wages; a teacher can become a flight attendant, or a plumber in Michigan can move to California. This movement between markets becomes progressively more difficult the greater the disparity in skills or geographic distance. For example, a truck driver may be able to compete for an auto assembly job, but would not be in competition in the market for orthopedic surgeons.

Labor Market Outcomes

There is a useful distinction between **labor market outcomes** and the **labor market process.** Labor market outcomes are the observed events, behavior, or developments in the labor market we are trying to understand and explain; the outcomes represent the end product or final result of the operation of the labor market. To understand the cause of the outcomes, however, it is necessary to understand the process that gave rise to them, that is, the mechanics of how the labor market works.

A great number of labor market outcomes are examined in this book. Of these, five are of particular interest to labor economists.[5]

---

5   These and other important outcomes in the labor market are examined in more detail in "Benefits of a Strong Labor Market," *Economic Report of the President, 1999* (Washington, D.C.: Government Printing Office, 1999), Chapter 3. For an analysis of earlier years, see Richard Freeman, "The Evolution of the American Labor Market," in Martin Feldstein, ed., *The American Economy in Transition* (Chicago: University of Chicago Press, 1980), 349–414.

The Changing Level and Composition of Labor Supply

Labor is a factor input into the production of goods and services and, thus, the quantity and quality of labor that individuals are willing to supply for market work is an important determinant of the economy's level of production and rate of growth. In calculating the amount of labor input available to the economy, it is important to realize that there are several different dimensions of labor supply. The quantity of labor supply depends, for example, on the size of the population, the proportion of the population that desires to work, and the hours of work per year; the quality of labor supply depends on such factors as the level of education, skill, and health of the workforce.

During the post-World War II period, dramatic changes in the size and composition of labor supply have taken place. Some of these are illustrated in Figure 1.2. Graph (a) shows the trend over time in the average number of hours worked per year by all workers between 1900 and 2004. In 1900, average hours worked per year were 2,766; by 1980 they had fallen to 2,002, a 27.6 percent decline. During the 1980s and 1990s, on the other hand, annual work hours increased modestly. Thus, one important trend in labor supply has been the long-term decline in annual hours of work, interrupted by a short-run increase in work hours between 1980 and 2000.

Graph (b) illustrates the trend over time in two other dimensions of labor supply. The first, the labor force participation rate, represents the fraction of the non-institutionalized population (persons not in a prison or mental hospital) 16 years of age or over who were either employed or looking for work. The graph shows that in 1950, 86 percent of men but only 34 percent of women were participating in the labor force. Between 1950 and 2004, these percentages changed rather noticeably; the labor force participation rate for men declined to 73.3 percent, while that for women increased to 59.2 percent. A second important trend in labor supply, then, is that a somewhat smaller proportion of men are in the labor force today, counterbalanced by a much larger proportion of women.

Also shown in the bottom part of graph (b) is the trend in one measure of the quality of labor supply—the percentage of the population having a college degree. Between 1940 and 2003, the proportion of the population (25 years and older) who had four or more years of a college education increased more than fivefold, from 4.6 percent to 27.2 percent. A third important trend in labor supply, therefore, is the rapid increase in the educational attainment of the workforce. Taken together, these three trends in labor supply have led to a fundamental shift over the past three decades in who is working, the hours devoted to work, and the skills that individual workers bring to the job.

The Changing Level and Composition of Labor Demand

Just as the number and characteristics of people wanting to work have changed significantly over the last 50 years, so have the number and the characteristics of jobs that employers have to offer. One important feature of employers' demand for labor is the growth over time in the total number of jobs made available. As the labor force has grown year after year, has the number of new jobs created been able to keep pace?

FIGURE 1.2   TRENDS IN THREE DIMENSIONS OF LABOR SUPPLY

(a) Annual Hours of Work, All Workers

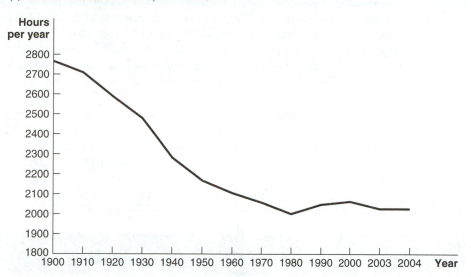

(b) Labor Force Participation Rate (LFPR) of Men and Women, Percent of Population with 4 Years of College Education

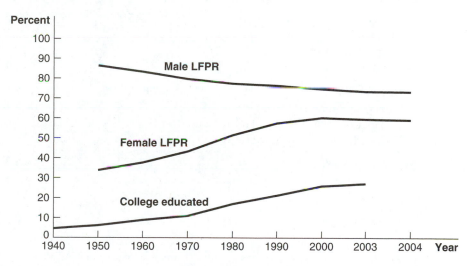

SOURCE: Annual hours of work were estimated by the authors based on data obtained from the Bureau of Labor Statistics, Employment and Earnings (January 1981, 1991, 2001, 2005); and G. Moore and J. Hedges, "Trends in Labor and Leisure," *Monthly Labor Review* 94, no. 2 (February 1971): 5. Labor force participation rates (16 years and older) from the Bureau of Labor Statistics, *Employment and Earnings* (January 2005): Historical A tables. Education data from U.S. Bureau of the Census, http://www.census.gov/population/www/socdemo/education.html.

In general, the answer is yes, witnessed by the large-scale expansion of employment in the economy from 60 million to 139 million between 1950 and 2004.

A second equally significant feature of labor demand is the types of jobs that are available in the economy. Demand for the goods and services produced in the product market of the economy shifts over time. In reaction to this, the demand for labor expands in some occupations and industries while it contracts in others, leading to large changes in the skills, education, and geographic locations required of workers. One particular aspect of the changing composition of labor demand is illustrated by the data in Table 1.1, which show the distribution of employment in the economy among ten occupational groups for the years 1950 and 2004. Since 1950, the proportion of white-collar jobs in the economy has grown tremendously, expanding from one-third of total employment in 1950 to over 60 percent in 2004. Among these white-collar occupations, two have grown exceptionally quickly—professional and technical occupations (such as engineers and teachers) and clerical occupations (such as secretaries). As the proportion of white-collar jobs grew, the share of blue-collar jobs shrank significantly, from 39.1 percent of total employment in 1950 to

TABLE 1.1	CHANGES IN THE COMPOSITION OF LABOR DEMAND, 1950–2004		
		Percentage Share of Total Employment	
Occupation		1950	2004
White Collar		37.50%	60.32%
Management			10.5
Professional and Technical			20.32
Sales and Office			25.47
Blue Collar		39.1	23.4
Construction and Extraction			6.1
Installation, Maintenance and Repair			3.6
Production and Transportation			12.9
Service Workers		11	16.3
Healthcare and Personal Service			5.3
Other Services			11.0
Farm Workers		12.4	0.71

The 2004 data were adjusted by the authors to correspond roughly to the 1950 occupational classification system.

SOURCE: Bureau of the Census, *Statistical Abstract of the United States* (1970), Table 334; Bureau of Labor Statistics, *Employment and Earnings* (January 2005), Table 9.

only 23.4 percent in 2004. The decline has been particularly rapid among jobs in the "operatives" occupation (including assemblers, machine operators, and truck drivers), reflecting in part the relative decline of manufacturing as an important source of jobs in the economy. Also shown in Table 1.1 are two other major occupational groups, service workers and farm workers. Not unexpectedly, the proportion of service-related jobs outside of private household work (such as waitresses, dental hygienists, and guards) has grown over time while farm-related jobs have plunged from 12.4 percent of total employment in 1950 to only 0.71 percent in 2004.

The Structure of Earnings

A third labor market outcome of considerable importance concerns the structure of earnings (differences in earnings) among individual workers, occupations, industries, and geographic areas. The concept of earnings may relate to average hourly earnings, weekly earnings, annual earnings, or even lifetime earnings; whichever concept is focused on, a central task of economic analysis is to explain what gives rise to the observed differential in earnings among workers at a point in time and why these differentials change over time.

Some of the issues involved here are illustrated in Table 1.2. The left-hand portion contains data on the average weekly earnings in 2003 of full-time workers in

TABLE 1.2   THE STRUCTURE OF EARNINGS

Occupation	Median Weekly Earnings, 2003[a]	Industry	Percentage Change in Average Hourly Earnings, 1993–2003[b]
Pharmacists	$1,477	Gas stations	69.5%
Chemical Engineer	1,250	Leather Footwear	50.4
Registered Nurse	899	Hospitals	43.8
Police Officer	784	Newspapers	32.2
Electrician	748	Trucking	30.1
Telephone Installer	713	Knitting Mills	28.7
Truck Driver	603	Carpentry	23.2
Bank Teller	395	Meatpacking	22.1
Child-care Worker	330	Data Processing	21.7

[a]Full-time wage and salary workers.
[b]Production workers.

SOURCES: Bureau of Labor Statistics, *Employment and Earnings* (January 2005): Table 39 (March 1994 and March 2004): Table B-15.

ten different occupations. There is a considerable range or dispersion in earnings among these occupations; the weekly earnings of pharmacists, for example, were five and a half times as large as those of child-care workers, while truck drivers earned one and a half as much as bank tellers. One of the tasks of labor economics is to identify the factors responsible for this particular spread in earnings. To what extent are these earnings differentials related to the educational qualifications needed for each occupation? What about the role of unionization? Does the fact that the occupation employs predominantly men or women make a difference?

A second important aspect of the structure of earnings concerns the change in earnings differentials over time—why the earnings of some workers grow relatively rapidly while the earnings for others lag behind. This issue is illustrated in the right-hand portion of Table 1.2, which contains data on the percentage change in average hourly earnings between 1993 and 2003 for workers in ten different industries. Much as with the structure of earnings at a point in time, the change in earnings exhibits a wide dispersion among different groups of workers. Workers in hospitals, for example, gained an increase in average hourly earnings (43.8 percent) that was more than twice as large as that received by data processors (21.7 percent). A central focus of economic research in recent years has been to identify the factors responsible for this pattern of earnings growth.

Labor–Management Relations and Collective Bargaining

Even though the degree of unionization in the United States continues to decline, labor economists are still fascinated by all aspects of the relationship between workers and their employers in the context of collective bargaining. Many studies are concerned with the relative balance of power between workers and firms and how strikes serve to enhance the power of labor unions.[6] Other studies focus on the internal operation of the union itself, such as the union's goals and the political process by which decisions are made.[7]

Two union-related outcomes of particular interest concern the number of workers unionized and the impact unions have on wage and other labor market outcomes. Figure 1.3 shows the wage premium earned by union members (holding all other characteristics, such as type of job, constant) and the percentage of workers that are union members, from 1930 to 2000. By the beginning of the twenty-first century the wages of union workers are estimated to be 19 percent higher than those of comparable nonunion workers. This wage premium was as high as 38 percent between 1930 and 1935, and dipped as low as 2 percent during the postwar boom of the late 1940s.

---

6   For a survey of this literature, see Daniel Gallagher and Cynthia Gramm, "Collective Bargaining and Strike Activity," in David Lewin et al., eds., *The Human Resource Management Handbook*, vol. 2 (Greenwich, Conn.: JAI Press, 1997), 65–94. Also see Peter Crampton and Joseph Tracy, "Unions, Bargaining, and Strikes," in John Addison and Claus Schnabel, eds. *International Handbook of Trade Unions* (Edward Elgar, 2003), 86–117.

7   See, for example, Bruce E. Kaufman, "Models of Union Wage Determination: What Have We Learned Since Dunlop and Ross?" *Industrial Relations* 41 (January 2002): 110–58; and Robin Naylor, "Economic Models of Union Behavior," in Addison and Schnabel, op. cit., 44–85.

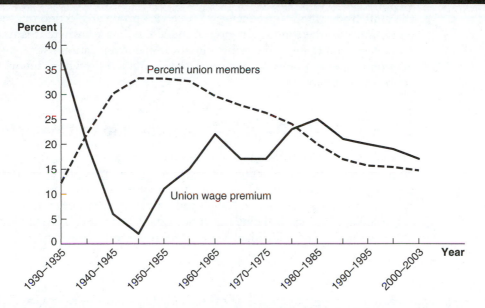

SOURCE: Barry T. Hirsch and David A. Macpherson, *Union Membership and Earnings Databook 2004* (Washington, D.C.: Bureau of National Affairs, Inc.): Table 1a, 2004; George E. Johnson, "Changes over Time in the Union-Nonunion Wage Differential in the United States," in Jean-Jacques Rosa, ed., *The Economics of Trade Unions: New Directions* (Boston, Kluwer Nijhoff, 1984), 5; Barry T. Hirsch and Edward Schumacher, "Private Sector Union Density and the Wage Premium: Past, Present, and Future," *Journal of Labor Research* 22 (Summer 2001): Figure 6.

While the union wage premium has shown a fair amount of volatility over time, there is little dispute that unionized workers, on net, receive higher wages and more fringe benefits than workers in nonunion firms. The reason for this fact is controversial, however. Some theorize that union members earn more because they are more productive, either because of the skills and abilities they possess or because of the positive production environment created by the presence of a union. Others have found evidence that the higher pay and benefits of union workers are due to the union's bargaining power, which allows it to redistribute some of the firm's revenues from profits to wages.

The percentage of the workforce belonging to unions has also not been constant over time, showing a steady decline since the 1950s.[8] In 1950, approximately

---

8   As will be seen in Chapter 11, as the percentage unionized began its decline in the 1950s, the total number of workers belonging to unions continued to grow until the late 1970s.

35 percent of the nonagricultural workforce belonged to a union; by 2003, the proportion had dropped to 12.9 percent. Many factors important in explaining this pattern will be discussed in Chapter 11. Some that deserve brief mention here include the shift from a goods-producing to a service-producing economy; the shift in employment to the southern region of the United States, where it is traditionally more costly to organize; the growth in government regulation of the employment environment and protection of worker rights; and the growth in union avoidance activities by employers.

Changes in the Level and Composition of Unemployment

Few labor market outcomes gain more public attention and concern than does unemployment. A person is defined as *unemployed* when he or she does not have a job and has made an active effort in the previous four weeks to find one. (A person who has a paying job is classified as "employed"; a person who does not have a job and is not looking for one is defined as "not in the labor force.") Unemployment entails costs both to the individual worker because of the consequent loss of earnings

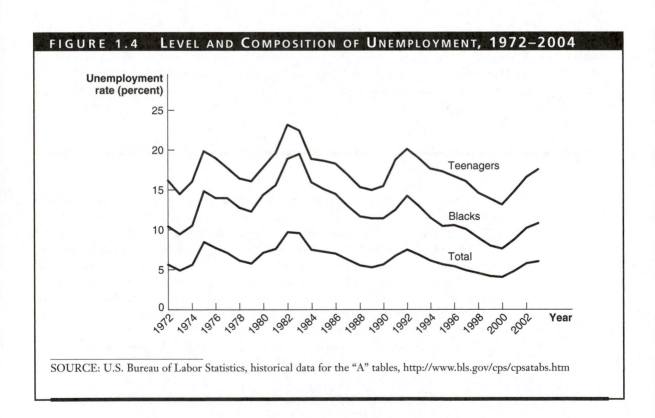

FIGURE 1.4   LEVEL AND COMPOSITION OF UNEMPLOYMENT, 1972–2004

SOURCE: U.S. Bureau of Labor Statistics, historical data for the "A" tables, http://www.bls.gov/cps/cpsatabs.htm

and to society because of the loss of the goods and services that could have been produced with that labor input.

Two aspects of unemployment are of particular importance. The first is the overall level of unemployment and its change over time. This is illustrated in Figure 1.4 by the line marked "Total," which shows the annual unemployment rate for workers of all demographic groups for the years between 1972 and 2004. It is apparent that the movement in the unemployment rate has two dimensions: a short-term cyclical movement connected with the rise and fall of the business cycle, and a longer-term secular trend. During periods of recession (such as 1974 through 1975, 1980 through 1982, 1990 through 1991, and in 2001), for example, the unemployment rate temporarily increases as firms lay off workers as a result of the decline in their sales; with the end of the recession, unemployment falls again as economic activity recovers.

Figure 1.4 also points out an area of public concern regarding unemployment, which is its unequal distribution among different groups in the labor force. In addition to the unemployment rate for all workers, Figure 1.4 also shows the unemployment rate for two particular demographic groups, black workers and teenaged workers. Both groups experience much higher levels of unemployment: the unemployment rate for black workers is generally double the unemployment rate for all workers, and the teenaged unemployment is even greater, often three times higher than the average. Thus, while all groups in the labor force are hurt by unemployment, some groups bear a much larger burden than others.

The Labor Market Process

The five developments outlined above represent the most important labor market outcomes covered in this book. The question that immediately follows is, what caused these labor market outcomes? Why have annual hours of work declined? Why does the level of unemployment differ across demographic groups? To answer these questions, it is necessary to study the labor market process—how the labor market works, the nature of the cause-and-effect relationships in the labor market, and the major actors or institutions in the market. The labor market process involves three broad forces that together determine each of the outcomes. These three forces are, respectively, market forces, institutional forces, and sociological forces.

Market Forces

The first process to consider in the determination of the price and allocation of labor is the **market forces** of supply and demand in the labor market. While a number of important noneconomic factors influence the pricing and distribution of labor, most economists would agree that the interaction of the market forces of supply and demand in the labor market is the single most important determinant of labor market outcomes.

On the demand side of each labor market are all the business firms, plus various nonprofit organizations such as government, which all actively compete for workers of a particular skill or trade. The demand for labor on the part of business firms is a **derived demand**—derived from the demand for the good or service produced by the firm. The business firm has as its primary goal the maximization of profit, and its demand for labor arises only to the extent that labor as a factor input is necessary to the production of the firm's product. This goal of profit maximization motivates the business firm to economize on labor as much as possible and to seek out those workers who are likely to be the most productive and efficient and who will work for the least remuneration. Given the wide range of products and services produced in the American economy, and the great diversity in skills and training that such production requires, the demand for labor among business firms is quite heterogeneous.

The supply side of each labor market comprises all the individuals who are working or looking for work. Just as the demand for labor is derived from the demand for the business firm's product, the supply of labor is derived from the individual's or household's demand for income to purchase the goods and services produced by the business firms. Much as with the business firm, the individual worker is motivated by self-interest and the desire to maximize his or her well-being to seek out the type and location of work that yields the highest return. Given the diverse backgrounds, education, skills, and preferences of the American labor force, the supply of labor is likely to be as variegated as is the demand for labor.

Because it happens more or less routinely, the efficiency with which a market system allocates labor in the economy is often taken for granted. It is, however, a monumental task. How do all the different jobs and all the diverse individuals in any one of our larger cities get matched up? How is it that there are enough truck drivers to deliver food to grocery stores, enough tellers to wait on customers at banks, and enough telephone repairers to keep the phone system working?

A market system solves this problem through two related mechanisms—*changes in wage rates* and the *mobility of labor*. This process is illustrated in Figures 1.5 and 1.6, which show, respectively, the determination of the equilibrium wage rate for a particular type of labor by demand and supply, and how changes in demand and supply lead to a corresponding change in the equilibrium wage.

Figure 1.5 shows a representative demand curve D_1 on the part of employers and supply curve S_1 on the part of workers in some particular labor market, say the market for truck drivers in New York City. The vertical axis of Figure 1.5 measures the money wage rate W, while the horizontal axis measures the number of workers L. The **labor demand curve** D_1 depicts the relationship between the quantity of labor demanded by firms in this market and the wage rate they have to pay if other things are held constant, such as the state of the economy. The demand curve slopes downward to the right, illustrating the inverse relationship that exists between wages and firms' demand for labor—the higher the wage firms must pay for labor, the fewer the workers they will demand. Thus, at the wage W_1, firms in this

FIGURE 1.5 **THE DETERMINATION OF WAGE RATES BY DEMAND AND SUPPLY**

Equilibrium in the labor market occurs at the wage W_E (point E) where labor demand and supply are equal. At the wage W_1, labor demand (point V) is greater than labor supply (point X). In this situation, competition among firms for scarce labor will cause wages to rise to W_E, leading firms to cut back on their desired level of employment from L_1 to L_E, while inducing $L_E - L_2$ additional people to supply labor in this market. At the wage W_2, supply is greater than demand, and competition will force the wage to W_E.

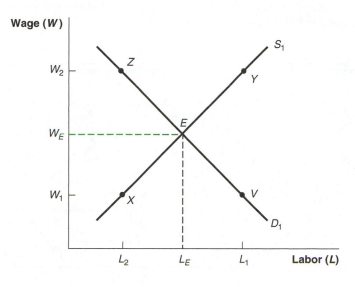

market would want to hire L_1 truck drivers (point V); should the wage rise to W_2, however, the demand for truck drivers would decline to L_2 (point Z).

The **labor supply curve** S_1 depicts the relationship between the wage rate and the number of people willing to work in this market. The supply curve slopes upward to the right on the presumption that at higher wage rates more people would want to work as truck drivers. Thus, at a wage of W_1, the quantity of labor supplied would be L_2 (point X); a rise in the wage to W_2 would increase the number of people wanting to be truck drivers in the New York City market to L_1 (point Y).

The central focus in labor economics is on how changes in wages and the process of labor mobility serve to allocate labor efficiently among different markets. To see how this works, assume that the wage rate for truck drivers in New York City is only W_1. At this relatively low wage, delivery companies in New York City would find it profitable to hire L_1 workers (point V), but only L_2 (point X) people would offer to work at this low wage. In this situation demand is greater than supply, and the competition among delivery companies to hire drivers should

FIGURE 1.6   THE MARKET ADJUSTMENT TO SHIFTS IN DEMAND AND SUPPLY

Graph (a) shows the adjustment of the labor market to an increase in the demand for labor. The initial equilibrium wage/employment level is W_1/L_1 (point X). The increase in labor demand shifts the demand curve to the right from D_1 to D_2, creating an excess demand for labor of $L_3 - L_1$. The result is that the wage rises until a new equilibrium is established at the wage/employment level W_2/L_2 (point Z).

Graph (b) illustrates the market adjustment to an increase in labor supply. The wage/employment level is initially W_1/L_1 (point X). The increase in labor supply shifts the supply curve to S_2, resulting in an excess supply of labor of $L_3 - L_1$. The result is a decline in the wage until a new equilibrium is reached at the wage/employment level of W_2/L_2 (point Z).

(a) A Demand Increase

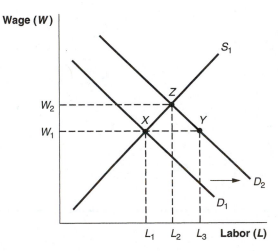

(b) A Supply Increase

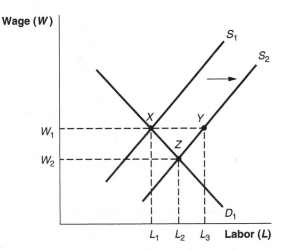

result in wages being bid up. This rise in wages would continue until enough new workers were attracted into this occupation and enough firms decreased their desired employment level until a balance or **market equilibrium** is reached where demand just equals supply. In Figure 1.5 this is at point E, with a wage of W_E and a level of employment of L_E.

   This process also works in reverse. What if the wage rate is W_2 and supply (point Y) is greater than demand (point Z) in Figure 1.5? The excess supply of people wanting to be truck drivers should put downward pressure on wages as delivery firms find they have many qualified applicants willing to work. In such a situation, wage rates in the truck drivers' market will decline, if not through actual cuts in wage rates by employers, then at least in relative terms as wages in other occupations continue to grow while wages for truck drivers remain stagnant.[9] This decline in wages will eventually bring the market back to equilibrium as firms are motivated to increase hiring and some workers leave this market for higher-paying jobs elsewhere. This process of changes in wages and labor mobility will continue until demand and supply are again in balance.

Another way to see the essential role that wages and labor mobility play in the labor market process is to examine how the market adjusts to a shift in the labor demand or supply curve. This is illustrated in graphs (a) and (b) of Figure 1.6.

The demand curve D_1 and supply curve S_1, reproduced from Figure 1.5, each show how the quantity of labor demanded or supplied varies with changes in the wage rate, *other things held constant*. In real-world labor markets, however, various outside events, such as the rise and fall of the economy over the business cycle, continually shift the labor demand curve to the right or left, while the labor supply curve undergoes similar shifts due to changes over time in the size of the population, the number of graduates of educational institutions, and other such factors.

How does the labor market adjust to shifts in demand and supply? Graph (a) of Figure 1.6 illustrates the case of a demand increase. Given the labor demand curve D_1 and the supply curve S_1, the equilibrium wage in this market (again assumed to be truck drivers in New York City), is W_1 (point X). Assuming the economy of the New York City area now experiences a boom, at any given wage, such as W_1, trucking companies will want more drivers to handle the increased business. This event is illustrated by shifting the labor demand curve to the right, from D_1 to D_2. At the wage W_1 the demand for truck drivers has risen from L_1 (point X) to L_3 (point Y). It is evident that the labor market is now out of equilibrium, for, at the wage W_1, supply (point X) is less than demand (point Y). What will happen?

The sequence of events will be exactly the same as for the situation of excess demand depicted in Figure 1.5. The wage rate will rise from the original equilibrium of W_1 (point X) to a new equilibrium of W_2 (point Z) where demand and supply are again equal. A necessary second step is that this rise in the wage also induces individuals in different occupations (such as shipping clerks) or different geographic locations (such as Philadelphia) to quit their jobs and move to take the now higher-paying jobs in the New York City truck drivers market. As a result, equilibrium employment rises from L_1 to L_2 (but not all the way to L_3).

Graph (b) of Figure 1.6 illustrates the market adjustment to a rightward shift of the labor supply curve, say because of a liberalized immigration law. At the original equilibrium wage of W_1, the number of people willing to work as truck drivers in New York City is L_1 (point X) on the labor supply curve S_1. Assume now that because of the change in the law, a large number of persons from foreign countries immigrate to the New York City area. At the wage W_1 trucking companies now have L_3 (point Y) people who want a driver's job, an outcome that is represented by the rightward shift of the labor supply curve from S_1 to S_2. At the wage

---

9   If changes in relative wages bring about equilibrium in the market, then the vertical axis of Figure 1.5 needs to be changed from W (the wage rate of truck drivers) to W/W_A, the wage of truck drivers relative to wages of all other occupations (W_A).

W_1 a situation of excess supply has emerged that, as demonstrated earlier, should cause a decline in the wage until a new equilibrium is reached at W_2 (point Z).

The examples in Figures 1.5 and 1.6 illustrate how changes in wages and the resulting flow of people from one occupation or area to another bring about a balance in the labor market between demand and supply. In this regard, it is important to point out that the process of labor mobility not only helps achieve an efficient allocation of labor, but also acts as an important check on the employment practices and working conditions offered by employers. Because workers are free to quit one employer and find another, a trucking company that requires excessive work hours, uses unsafe equipment, or treats employees in an arbitrary or authoritarian manner will find that it is unable to attract and keep a workforce. The competition among employers for labor and the existence of labor mobility, therefore, automatically police the social conditions of labor.

This discussion of the labor market process is not a new observation; it was perhaps best analyzed over 200 years ago by Adam Smith. In describing the labor market, Smith said:

> The whole of the advantages and disadvantages of the different employments of labour and stock must, in the same neighborhood, be either perfectly equal or continually tending to equality. If in the same neighborhood, there was any employment evidently more or less advantageous than the rest, so many people would crowd into it in the one case, and so many would desert it in the other, that its advantages would soon return to the level of other employments.[10]

This is as clear a statement as possible of how the forces of supply and demand determine wages and how, in reaction to these wage rates, people flow from one employment to another seeking their highest advantage. An illustration of this process can be found in Empirical Evidence 1-1. Smith's second brilliant insight was to realize that this process not only resulted in each individual maximizing his or her own economic rewards, but also brought about, as if by an "invisible hand," the most efficient allocation of labor for the society as a whole.

➲ SEE

Empirical Evidence 1-1: The Market for Teachers, p. 40.

Institutional Forces

The second determinant of labor market outcomes is what economists call **institutional forces.** Institutional forces represent the influence of various organizations such as unions, governments, and corporations on the pricing and distribution of labor.

Institutions affect labor outcomes in two different ways. First, they fragment or "balkanize" the labor market into a number of segmented, loosely connected submarkets. As described by Clark Kerr, institutions introduce structure, artificial

---

10   Adam Smith, *The Wealth of Nations* (Chicago: University of Chicago Press, 1976), 111.

boundaries, and rigidities into the labor market.[11] In the classical labor market of Adam Smith, wages change automatically in response to changes in demand and supply, and workers in turn flow from occupations or areas of excess supply to those experiencing shortages. The boundaries of this "natural" market are defined only by the limits placed on the sphere of competition by the flow of information, the transferability of skills, and the willingness of workers to travel. Institutions, however, introduce rules and regulations that further define the dimensions of the labor market. These rules and regulations may be either formal (written) or informal (customary). In either case, they effectively delineate who can compete for particular jobs, who is most preferred, and which business firms can compete in the bidding. These rules are established in the form of corporate personnel policies, union contracts, and government legislation, among other influences.

Perhaps the best example to illustrate how institutions can segment the labor market is the concept of the internal labor market. Business firms often have a policy of promoting people from within the firm rather than hiring new people from the outside. Such a seniority or in-house bidding system creates an internal labor market in that the effective sphere of competition is limited to individuals already employed in the firm. Thus, when workers who have been with the company for some time retire or leave to work for another employer, vacancies are created on the firm's internal "job ladder." Rather than hiring workers from the outside to fill these jobs, the firm limits the competition to workers already employed with the company, since they are the ones most likely to have the required skills and knowledge. As these workers move up the job ladder, vacancies then appear at the bottom—the "port of entry." It is at the port of entry where the sheltered, internal market is connected to the external labor market. Individuals in the external market are in competition with each other to win the jobs at the port of entry; once having done so, they can then move up the company job ladder.

This balkanization of the labor market is a consequence not only of corporate personnel policies but also of union and government policies. Union contracts often contain detailed seniority provisions that specify which individual or group of individuals have first bidding rights for a new job vacancy. Similarly, the operation of union hiring halls in such trades as construction and longshoring restricts the sphere of competition for work largely to union members. Finally, government legislation in the form of occupational licensing and protective labor laws that limit the ability of people, such as the self-trained, teenagers, or immigrants to compete for certain types of work also establishes barriers to enter that segment of the labor market.

By delineating and narrowing the effective area over which the forces of demand and supply can interact, institutions diminish the role of market forces as determinants of wages and employment. This does not mean, however, that the operation of the labor market is necessarily any less efficient. Internal labor markets, seniority provisions, and other such rules often have a positive impact on the

---

11   Clark Kerr, "The Balkanization of Labor Markets," *Labor Markets and Wage Determination* (Berkeley: University of California Press, 1977), 21–37.

operation of the labor market by giving firms a method to train workers in the idiosyncratic tasks of the job and as a means to promote on-the-job experience and continuity of employment.[12]

The second way in which institutions affect labor market outcomes is through their independent effect on wage rates. In the classical market of many buyers and sellers, no one employer or worker can independently affect the going market wage; individual firms and workers are what economists call "price takers." The same is not true, however, in real-world labor markets populated by large corporations, powerful unions, and firms regulated by the government.

The best example of how institutions can independently affect wage rates is the labor union. In a competitive market, an individual worker has little or no power to raise the wage above the going market rate, since the firm can easily let one worker go and hire someone else. But what if the workers band together to form a union? The power of a union to raise wages comes from its threat of a strike. While the firm may be able to replace individual workers, if all workers walk off the job together the company faces a potentially long shutdown and loss of profits. The strike threat, then, gives trade unions an institutional influence on rates of pay (and other forms of compensation) that originates outside of the market forces of supply and demand. Market forces do impinge on the process of union wage determination, however, since if a union pushes up wages too far it risks causing substantial layoffs among its members. Empirical evidence suggests that unions are able to raise the wages of their members above the going market rate quite substantially, often on the order of 15 to 20 percent.[13]

Large business firms and government also have an institutional influence on wages. In competitive theory, any firm with labor costs higher than its competitors' will suffer the ultimate penalty of bankruptcy. In today's economy, however, some firms operate in oligopolistic or regulated markets where the forces of competition are attenuated, allowing some discretion to such companies in setting their wage policies. Government also has a wide influence on wages that transcends market forces. Examples are minimum wage floors, prevailing wage standards in government construction, and legislated wage increases for government employees.

Sociological Forces

The third determinant of labor market outcomes is **sociological forces,** which represent the influence of social groups and norms on the determination of wages and the allocation of labor. Important factors include family background, class, culture, discrimination, and custom.

Analogously with institutional forces, sociological forces influence the labor market process in two distinct ways—first, through their influence on who can

---

12   See Oliver E. Williamson, *The Economic Institutions of Capitalism* (New York: The Free Press, 1985).

13   David G. Blanchflower, "Changes over Time in Union Relative Wage Effects in Great Britain and the United States," in Sami Daniel et al., eds., *The History and Practice of Economics* (Northampton, Mass.: Edward Elgar, 1999), 3–32.

compete in particular labor markets and second, through their influence on the determination of wage rates in the market.[14]

With respect to the first influence, sociological considerations such as family background, parents' occupations, and socioeconomic class may have an important effect on an individual's range of choice and mobility in the labor market. This is clearly stated in the following passage written over 100 years ago by J. E. Cairnes in describing his theory of **noncompeting groups.**

> No doubt various ranks and classes fade into each other by imperceptible gradations, and individuals from all classes are constantly passing up or down; but while this is so, it is nevertheless true that the average workman, from whatever rank he be taken, finds his power of competition limited for practical purposes to a certain range of occupations, so that, however high the rates of remuneration in those which lie beyond may rise, he is excluded from sharing them. We are thus compelled to recognize the existence of noncompeting industrial groups as a feature of our social economy.[15]

The labor market described by Cairnes is balkanized much like the one discussed by Kerr, but for quite different reasons. Here the stratification between labor market groups stems from one's class and background as well as from specific labor market skills.

To better appreciate the extent to which family background and socioeconomic class create noncompeting groups in the labor force, consider a current-day example. At present strong competition exists for admission to medical school because of the high income and status that it leads to. Do family background and social class have any bearing on the individuals who are ultimately accepted? To be more specific, is the fact that an applicant is the son of a construction worker or the daughter of a bank executive likely to have any independent influence on who eventually becomes a doctor and who does not? Some economists would argue that family background has relatively little impact, pointing to numerous examples of people who have risen from very humble beginnings to positions of great wealth. Others, however, would argue that family background is quite important, admitting that while there is some movement between broad socioeconomic groups, individuals as a rule do not move far from their parents' occupational and social position.

This question is obviously quite complex, subject to considerable debate.[16] It is also quite important because one's position on this issue is likely to significantly influence one's view of the social merits of relying on market forces as the distributor

---

14 This distinction is made by Henry Phelps Brown, who argues that sociological factors affect labor market outcomes "before the market" and "within the market." See *The Inequality of Pay* (Berkeley: University of California Press, 1977), particularly Chapters 1 and 10. On the role of sociological factors, also see Neil Smelser and Richard Swedberg, eds., *The Handbook of Economic Sociology* (Princeton, N.J.: Princeton University Press, 1994).

15 J. E. Cairnes, *Political Economy* (New York: Harper, 1974), 67–68.

16 See, for example, Janet Currie and Duncan Thomas, "The Intergenerational Transmission of 'Intelligence': Down the Slippery Slopes of the Bell Curve," *Industrial Relations* 38 (July 1999): 297–330.

of economic rewards in society. The greater the opportunity of individuals (and their sons and daughters) to move up and down the occupational ladder as a consequence of their own efforts and decisions, the greater the argument for relying on the market. If, however, one's station in life is largely determined by the accidents of birth and inheritance, then the market merely passes on the status quo from one generation to another.[17]

The second way in which sociological factors affect labor market outcomes is through their influence on the supply of labor and the determination of wage rates and earnings in the labor market. In some cases sociological factors influence wages independently of the market forces of supply and demand; in other cases these sociological factors work through market forces as they influence the supply of labor to the economy or to specific occupations and industries. With respect to the latter, an individual's decision about the amount of work versus the amount of leisure, or the choice of occupations, for example, involves not only a consideration of market opportunities such as wage rates and employment prospects, but also the individual's psychological feelings about which choice is valued more. Economists have always recognized this psychological aspect of choice and include it in economic theory under the rubric of "preferences" or "tastes." Thus, whether a person chooses to become a teacher or a lawyer, for example, depends not only on the wage rate that can be earned in each occupation, but also on the individual's preference or taste for each line of work.

In order to focus on the role of economic factors such as wage rates, income, and prices as determinants of labor market outcomes, and because the determinants of tastes and preferences have generally been thought to lie outside the domain of economics, most economists assign a passive role to these variables, assuming that they are either given or, alternatively, that they vary among individuals in some unsystematic fashion. While such an assumption is both useful and empirically correct in certain labor market contexts, in other contexts the tastes and preferences of individuals not only vary systematically over time and by age, race, culture, and work group, but also influence their choices regarding education, occupational attainment, and labor force participation, to give a few examples.

An illustration of this influence is the dramatic increase over the past two decades in the proportion of working women in the economy. Research finds that part of the rise in female labor force participation can be explained by economic factors such as the rise in real-wage rates and the greater number of job opportunities for women. A second influence, however, has been more noneconomic in nature, and that is the revolution in attitudes regarding the appropriateness for married women of working outside the home.[18] The influx of millions of women into the job market has caused, in turn, a large expansion in labor supply to those occupations that traditionally employ a large number of women (such as secretary and

---

17   As one piece of evidence on this, a survey of the 400 richest Americans (*Forbes*, October 12, 1998) found that 88 had obtained their wealth through either inheritance or divorce, while 312 had largely earned it themselves. By contrast, however, a survey of the Forbes 400 in 1984 found that 146 had inherited their wealth.

18   Ronald R. Rindfuss et al., "Women, Work, and Children: Behavioral and Attitudinal Change in the United States," *Population and Development Review* 22 (September 1996): 457–82.

schoolteacher), depressing wage rates for those jobs below what they would have otherwise been.

Culture is another sociological factor that affects the wage determination process. Culture inculcates in people a set of values or beliefs common to the larger social group. These cultural values may have an important effect on the earnings and economic success of different ethnic groups in the labor market, as they shape the attitudes of individuals concerning the work ethic, entrepreneurship and risk-taking, occupational choice, the importance of education, and the desirability of getting ahead in a materialistic society. Are cultural differences important in explaining wage and income differences among people? In several influential books, economist Thomas Sowell argues that they are.[19] In terms of average family income, the two ethnic groups that have experienced the greatest success in America are Jewish Americans and Japanese Americans. The great majority of people of both groups came to America penniless and often suffered intense discrimination here. Despite these roadblocks, both groups worked their way up the economic ladder, passing by other ethnic groups such as the Irish and the Italians. Why have other ethnic groups not succeeded economically to the same extent? One reason is that some groups came to America later than others and are several generations behind in the economic race.[20] Sowell argues, however, that some groups are also penalized by cultural attitudes that conflict with the demands of a highly techno-cratic, rationalistic society. Native Americans are perhaps the best example of this conflict. Despite being the first group to settle in America, they still have the lowest average family income of all ethnic groups.

Sociological factors also influence wages in ways that are independent of supply and demand conditions in the labor market. One example is discrimination. Discrimination occurs whenever one person is treated preferentially over another even though both individuals are equal except for some characteristic such as gender, race, religion, or nationality. While each of us has individual likes and dislikes, discrimination typically involves a common taste or preference on the part of one social group against another, making discrimination a sociological phenomenon. Does discrimination play a role in the wage determination process? The answer is surely yes. One issue this book examines in considerable detail, for example, is the causes of the earnings gap between men and women. In 2003, women who were year-round full-time workers earned only 79 percent as much as their male counterparts. The existence of an earnings differential between two groups does not, of course, prove that discrimination is the cause. Research shows that half or more of the male/female earnings gap is due to legitimate market-related factors, such as length of work experience, college major, and number of career interruptions for family reasons.[21] There is, however, incontrovertible evidence that some

---

19   For example, see Thomas Sowell, *Race and Culture: A World View* (New York: Basic Books, 1994).

20   Dating the beginning point for when black Americans started the economic race is more difficult than for most other groups. Was it the early 1800s, when most blacks were brought to America; 1865, when slavery was abolished; or the 1950s, when segregation was outlawed?

21   For example, see Garey Durden and Patricia Gaynor, "More on the Cost of Being Other Than White and Male: Measurement of Race, Ethnic, and Gender Effects on Yearly Earnings," *American Journal of Economics and Sociology* 57 (January 1998): 95–103.

employers systematically reward women differently than men (and blacks differently than whites) with respect to pay and promotions.[22] To the extent that discrimination occurs, therefore, wages and other market outcomes are determined by factors that are separate from the market forces of supply and demand. This is not to say that market forces are irrelevant, for the employers that desire to discriminate are constrained in the exercise of their prejudice by the need to hire the most qualified, productive employees possible for the firm to make a profit.

Custom is a second example of an independent sociological influence on the labor market. Custom is a practice or belief that has gained acceptance and legitimacy simply because it has been followed for a long time. Some economists argue that custom has a strong influence on wages, particularly relative wage differences between groups of workers.[23] Such pay differences, for instance those between firefighters and police officers or between locomotive engineers and conductors, are regarded by the workers involved to be as much a matter of social standing and equity as economics, and often become a major criteria in the wage determination process.

The Evolution of Labor Market Theory

Most economists would readily agree that each of the market, institutional, and sociological forces has some role in shaping labor market outcomes. Over the years, however, debate and disagreement has arisen concerning the relative importance of each force and how these forces work to bring about specific labor market outcomes. These debates and different points of view led to the emergence of alternative schools of thought in labor economics during the twentieth century. Historically viewed, the two most important have been the neoclassical and institutional schools, although other smaller schools of thought also exist.[24] To provide some perspective on the development of labor economics, as well as heightened appreciation for why labor economists disagree on fundamental issues of theory and policy, a brief overview of the neoclassical and institutional schools

---

22   See U.S. Department of Labor, *Working Women Count! A Report to the Nation* (1994).

23   Michael J. Piore, "Fragments of a Sociological Theory of Wages," in Michael J. Piore, ed., *Unemployment and Inflation: Institutionalist and Structuralist Views* (White Plains, N.Y.: M. E. Sharpe, 1979): 134–43, and David Marsden, *The End of Economic Man? Custom and Competition in Labor Markets* (New York: St. Martin's Press, 1986).

24   Other, smaller schools of thought include Marxist or "radical" economics, feminist economics, and economic sociology. See James Rebitzer, "Radical Political Economy and the Economics of Labor Markets," *Journal of Economic Literature* 31 (September 1993): 1394–1434. On feminist economics, see Gillian Hewitson, *Feminist Economics: Interrogating the Masculinity of Rational Economic Man* (Northampton, Mass.: Edward Elgar, 1999). A good introduction to the literature of economic sociology is Neil Smelser and Richard Swedburg, eds., *The Handbook of Economic Sociology* (Princeton: Princeton University Press, 1994). All three schools of thought share a number of common elements with the institutional school.

is provided.[25] Their possible synthesis and reconciliation in what is today often called "modern labor economics" is then considered.

The Neoclassical School

The **neoclassical school** is by all accounts the dominant paradigm in labor economics today. The word *neoclassical* in economics means derived from or an extension of the classical economics of Adam Smith, David Ricardo, and other early nineteenth-century economists. The two principal founders of neoclassical economics are the French economist Léon Walras (1834–1910) and English economist Alfred Marshall (1842–1924). Walras pioneered mathematical economics and general equilibrium theory; Marshall pioneered partial equilibrium analysis and rigorously developed and popularized the graphical model of supply and demand in competitive markets. The model for economics that inspired Walras (but less so Marshall) was physics.[26] After Walras and Marshall, neoclassical economics received its next big boost in the late 1920s and 1930s from two economists, Nobel laureate John R. Hicks of Oxford University and Paul Douglas of the University of Chicago. Hicks developed a number of crucial theoretical concepts relating to labor demand and labor supply; Douglas's major contribution was to show how these theoretical concepts (such as the supply curve of labor) could be estimated from available statistical data.[27]

Beginning in the 1930s and extending into the 1950s, the neoclassical school fell out of favor in the United States, largely because the events of the Depression seemed to discredit it. From about the mid-1950s, however, the neoclassical school staged a remarkable comeback, primarily as a result of the writing and research of a highly influential group of economists associated with the University of Chicago.

---

25 A detailed history of thought in labor economics is provided in Paul McNulty, *The Origin and Development of Labor Economics* (Cambridge, Mass.: MIT Press, 1980). See also Bruce E. Kaufman, "The Evolution of Thought on the Competitive Nature of Labor Markets," in Clark Kerr and Paul Staudohar, eds., *Labor Economics and Industrial Relations: Markets and Institutions* (Cambridge, Mass.: Harvard University Press, 1994): 145–88; and George Boyer and Robert Smith, "The Development of the Neoclassical Tradition in Labor Economics," *Industrial and Labor Relations Review* 54 (January 2001): 199–223.

26 Walras states in *Elements of Pure Economics* (1874: 73), for example, "Our task then is to discover the laws to which these purchases and sales tend to conform automatically. To this end, we shall suppose that the market is perfectly competitive, just as in pure mechanics we suppose, to start with, that machines are perfectly frictionless." Illustrative of the universalistic domain of demand/supply analysis in neoclassical economics is Marshall's statement in *Principles of Economics* (1961, 9th ed.: 526), "The normal value of everything, whether it be a particular kind of labour or capital or anything else, rests, like the keystone of an arch, balanced in equilibrium between the contending pressures of its two opposing sides; the forces of demand press on the one side, and those of supply on the other."

27 See John R. Hicks, *The Theory of Wages* (New York: Macmillan, 1932), and Paul H. Douglas, *The Theory of Wages* (New York: Macmillan, 1934), Chapters 11 and 12. Although Douglas's work on labor supply and production functions is solidly in the neoclassical tradition, he also gave considerable stress in his writings to the importance of labor market imperfections and the benefits of labor unions, themes associated with the institutional school discussed shortly.

These economists included Nobel laureates Milton Friedman, George Stigler, Theodore Schultz, Gary Becker, and James Heckman, as well as H. Gregg Lewis, Jacob Mincer, Melvin Reder, Albert Rees, and Sherwin Rosen.

The neoclassical school of economics of labor economics is distinctive in terms of both its theoretical framework and its methodological approach to research. Some of these features have, however, significantly evolved over time. With respect to theory, in years past, the neoclassical school gave primary attention to the operation of markets and how market forces determine wages and the allocation of labor. This was the original "price theory" (or "market") version of neoclassical economics. In this version, since market forces were being highlighted, other factors, such as the nature of legal and business institutions, sociological considerations of culture and class, the distribution of property and wealth, and the pattern of tastes and preferences, were generally abstracted from or treated as a given. This is not because neoclassical economists necessarily viewed these factors as unimportant, but because these factors lay outside of what was perceived as the labor economist's area of expertise.

In more recent years, the focus of neoclassical economics has shifted to a more inclusive approach. Whether this new approach is still neoclassical, at least as this term was originally conceived, is a matter of debate, however. This movement is particularly associated with the many pioneering studies of Gary Becker.[28] As Becker frames it, the essence of modern economics (or what he calls "the economic approach") is not the study of markets per se but, rather, the application of a model of rational economizing behavior to all aspects of human life. In this "choice theory" version of neoclassical economics, the object of attention shifts from the noun *economy* (or market) to the verb *economizing*.[29] The choice theory version assumes people desire to maximize utility and they rationally weigh the benefits and costs of alternative courses of action and choose the one that maximizes satisfaction. Mathematically, the foundation of this version of neoclassical theory is constrained optimization. Becker has used this model to examine a wide range of diverse behaviors, including fertility, crime, drug addiction, marriage, and fads and fashions, and it has been applied to a host of interesting issues in labor economics as well as in sociology, demography, and political science.

The neoclassical theory of the labor market (including Becker's) has two important parts that heavily influence the conclusions and predictions derived from it. The first concerns the nature of human behavior. Neoclassical theory makes several simple but very important assumptions about human behavior, assumptions that collectively give rise to what is called the **rational actor model** (or, the model

---

28 See Gary S. Becker, *The Economic Approach to Human Behavior* (Chicago: University of Chicago Press, 1976), 3–14, and "Nobel Lecture: The Economic Way of Looking at Behavior," *Journal of Political Economy* 101 (June 1993): 385–409.

29 The distinction between the price theory and choice theory versions of neoclassical economics is made in Bruce E. Kaufman, "The Institutional and Neoclassical Schools in Labor Economics," in Dell Champlin and Janet Knoedler, eds., *The Institutionalist Tradition in Labor Economics* (Armonk: M.E. Sharpe, 2004), pp. 13–38.

of economic man). One key assumption concerns human motivation.[30] The model of economic man holds that individuals seek to *maximize* their level of well-being, always striving for the best or optimal outcome, given the constraints they face. A second key assumption is that human beings have the cognitive ability to exercise rational choice. This implies that the human brain is powerful enough to calculate the value of alternative outcomes and rank them in a consistent manner so that the optimal outcome can be chosen. Finally, a third assumption of traditional neoclassical economics is that human beings are individualists in that their behavior and preferences are largely independent of what others outside the family think or do. This assumption, however, has also been extensively modified in work by Becker and associates.[31]

The second important part of neoclassical theory concerns the nature and operation of markets. While neoclassical economists recognize the labor market has certain unique features, they do not perceive these differences to be so great as to preclude analyzing the labor market with the same theoretical model used to study other product and factor markets. Furthermore, in the original price theory version of neoclassical economics it is usually assumed that the labor market is competitive, having a large number of buyers and sellers and relatively unobstructed opportunities for moving between jobs. The importance of these assumptions is that they ensure that demand and supply determine a stable equilibrium, that impersonal market forces are the major determinant of wages and the distribution of labor, and that market outcomes result in an efficient allocation of resources.[32] In the more recent choice theory version of neoclassical economics, labor markets are less often presumed to be competitive. A principal task of this theory is to explain, using constrained optimization techniques and the theory of rational behavior, why markets may have imperfections (e.g., rigid wages) and the effect of these imperfections (e.g., incomplete and asymmetric information gives rise to frictional unemployment and wage dispersion for otherwise identical jobs). Nonetheless, a hallmark of neoclassic economics in either price theory or choice theory guises is adherence to a general version of the *invisible hand idea*—the hypothesis originally advanced by Adam Smith that individual pursuit of self-interest in a market economy leads to well-coordinated and efficient use of resources.[33]

30　A comparison of the model of human behavior in neoclassical and institutional theory is presented in Bruce E. Kaufman, "Models of Man in Industrial Relations Research," *Industrial and Labor Relations Review* 43 (October 1989): 72–88, and "Expanding the Behavioral Foundations of Labor Economics," *Industrial and Labor Relations Review* 52 (April 1999): 361–92.

31　See Gary Becker, *Accounting for Tastes* (Cambridge, Harvard University Press, 1996) for a description of the traditional neoclassical approach to modeling preferences. An expanded approach to modeling preferences that incorporates relative comparisons and other social features of behavior is given in Gary Becker and Kevin Murphy, *Social Economics: Market Behavior in a Social Environment* (Cambridge: Harvard University Press, 2000).

32　Melvin Reder, "Chicago Economics: Permanence and Change," *Journal of Economic Literature* 20 (March 1982): 1–38, and Robert Solow, "How Did Economics Get That Way, and What Way Did It Get?" *Daedalus* 126 (Winter 1997); 39–58.

33　See Edward Lazear, "Economic Imperialism," *Quarterly Journal of Economics* 115 (February 2000): 99–145.

In addition to its theoretical framework, the methodology of neoclassical economics is also noteworthy. The word *methodology* means the methods and processes by which economists seek to explain real-world behavior. The first feature of methodology that distinguishes neoclassical economics is the reliance on *deductive* reasoning to derive theoretical predictions and testable hypotheses. Deductive reasoning is logic that progresses from the general to the specific; its opposite is *inductive* reasoning, which progresses from the specific to the general.

Either method can be employed to predict what will happen to a firm's desired level of employment if it is forced to pay a higher wage. One method is to study a number of individual firms in which the wage has gone up and, based on the change in employment in each, formulate a general law or prediction. This is an example of inductive reasoning. A second method is to start with several general assumptions about the goals of business firms and the determinants of revenues and costs, and from this deduce the likely employment effect of a wage increase. This is a case of deductive reasoning. Neoclassical economists make heavy use of the deductive method, believing it is both more general and more fruitful than an inductive, case-study approach. The benefit of the deductive method is that, given only a few rather general assumptions, it is possible to derive a very elegant and sophisticated model of labor market behavior. The drawback is that the model and its predictions may be seriously in error if the assumptions do not accord with real-world labor markets.

The second noteworthy aspect of methodology is the heavy reliance on *marginal* decision rules in neoclassical theory. Given that the goal of individuals is to maximize some objective such as profits or utility, the golden rule is always the same: Whatever the activity, continue to do more of it as long as the marginal increase in benefit exceeds the marginal increase in cost; when the two become equal, the optimal amount has been reached.

And, finally, a third distinctive aspect of neoclassical methodology is a commitment to a uni-disciplinary, heavily formalistic (mathematical), and imperialistic approach to theorizing.[34] As neoclassical labor economists seek to explain and understand new behaviors or empirical puzzles, they always start with the standard microeconomic model (rational behavior, competitive markets, equilibrium) and then expand or revise it until the predictions of the theory fit the facts. In this effort, they generally do not look to other disciplines and fields, such as history, psychology, sociology, or business, for new theoretical concepts. Rather, the direction of trade is the reverse in that neoclassical economists are continually seeking to enter these other disciplines and demonstrate the explanatory power and superiority of the economic approach. In the eyes of neoclassical economists, another virtue of the economic approach is that it lends itself to mathematical representation, leading to models that are very general, abstract, and sophisticated.

---

34   Ibid.

The Institutional School

The main rival to the neoclassical school in labor economics is the **institutional school.** Institutional economics emerged in the United States in the early twentieth century. Institutional economics was in part an outgrowth of German and British historical-social economics (a nineteenth-century movement that sought to build economic theory through a melding of insights from economics, history, sociology, and law) and partly as a reaction against the perceived narrowness and laissez-faire orientation of neoclassical economics. It is generally considered that institutional economics had three founders: Thorstein Veblen (1857–1929), John Commons (1862–1945), and Wesley Mitchell (1874–1948).[35]

The history of institutionalism in labor economics is a complicated one, involving four separate phases. The first phase, dating from the early 1900s to the late 1930s, is associated with Commons and his students at the University of Wisconsin. This branch of institutionalism largely eschewed formal models or quantitative analysis of the labor market, preferring instead to conduct painstaking historical studies of the labor movement and investigative studies of current-day labor problems. The second phase is associated with the "neoinstitutionalists" of the 1940s and 1950s.[36] The neoinstitutionalists dominated labor economics over this twenty-year period and included many names that remain well known in the field today, such as John Dunlop, Lloyd Reynolds, Clark Kerr, Arthur Ross, and Richard Lester. The neoinstitutionalists were different from Commons and the Wisconsin school in placing more emphasis on the study and theory of how labor markets actually work. While this moved them closer to the position of the neoclassical economists, the case studies of labor markets conducted by the neoinstitutionalists convinced them that the neoclassical theory was quite unrealistic as a description of how wages and employment are actually determined. With the revival of neoclassical theory by the Chicago school in the 1960s, the influence of the neoinstitutionalists in labor economics waned, although their presence remained considerably stronger in the related field of industrial relations. In the late 1960s, a third phase of institutionalism emerged under the rubric of "dual" and "segmented labor market" (SLM) theory. SLM economists include Michael Piore,

---

35   See Joseph Dorfman, *Institutional Economics: Veblen, Commons, and Mitchell Reconsidered* (Berkeley: University of California Press); Yuval Yonay, *The Struggle for the Soul of Economics: Institutional and Neoclassical Economics in America between the Wars* (Princeton: Princeton University Press); Dell Champlin and Janet Knoedler, eds., *The Institutionalist Tradition in Labor Economics* (Armonk: M.E. Sharpe); and Bruce E. Kaufman, *The Global Evolution of Industrial Relations: Events, Ideas, and the IIRA* (Geneva: International Labour Organization, 2004).

36   See Glen G. Cain, "The Challenge of Segmented Labor Market Theories to Orthodox Theory: A Survey," *Journal of Economic Literature* 14, no. 4 (December 1976): 1215–57. Not all economists agree that this second phase was actually a continuation of the institutional school. For alternative points of view on this subject, see Clark Kerr, "The Neoclassical Revisionists in Labor Economics (1940–1960)—R.I.P."; Bruce E. Kaufman, "The Postwar View of Labor Markets and Wage Determination," in Bruce E. Kaufman, ed., *How Labor Markets Work: Reflections on Theory and Practice by John Dunlop, Clark Kerr, Richard Lester, and Lloyd Reynolds* (Lexington, Mass.: Lexington Books, 1988), 1–46, 145–203; and Boyer and Smith, "The Development of the Neoclassical Tradition in Labor Economics."

Peter Doeringer, and Barry Bluestone.[37] Like the neoinstitutionalists before them, these economists emphasize how the policies of unions and corporations, as well as the effect of social forces such as discrimination and class, segment the labor market, preventing the operation of competitive forces as envisioned in neoclassical theory. An example is models of dual labor markets that posit that the economy is composed of two types of labor markets—one with high-wage jobs, employment security, and good promotion opportunities and a second with low-wage jobs, high rates of turnover, and few prospects for advancement.

The fourth phase of institutionalism in labor economics began in the mid-1980s. Research in the "old institutional" tradition of the first three phases continued, albeit on a relatively modest scale, while under the leadership of Oliver Williamson a "new institutional" school of economics emerged and grew in popularity in the 1990s.[38] The foundation concept in new institutional economics is *transaction cost* (the *ex ante* and *ex post* costs of contracting in economic exchange), an idea first broached by Commons in the early 1930s and shortly thereafter independently developed in more detail by Nobel laureate Ronald Coase (also from the University of Chicago).[39] Like the old institutional economists, Williamson and colleagues also replace the neoclassical rational actor model with a model that emphasizes the limited and sometimes biased decision-making ability of human beings. The new institutional economists are closer to the neoclassical school, however, in that they downplay the role of market imperfections and unequal resources. They have used these theoretical concepts to analyze a number of interesting labor market phenomena, such as the existence of internal labor markets and employment-at-will policies.[40]

Although the institutional school of labor economics includes a number of diverse people and strands of thought, there are certain common features in terms of both theory and methodology that unite institutionally-oriented economists. One issue of theory concerns the appropriate model of human behavior. Institutionalists do not reject out of hand the mathematical model of constrained optimization, but do feel its operationalization in the rational actor model of neoclassical economics often leads to inaccurate predictions or caricatured descriptions about how people behave in labor markets (just as a Picasso painting captures a real but caricatured aspect of human life). The neoclassical model of utility maximization, for example, presumes that what motivates people is the pursuit of self-interest and the desire to

---

37   See, for example, Peter B. Doeringer and Michael J. Piore, *Internal Labor Markets and Manpower Analysis* (Lexington, Mass.: Heath Lexington Books, 1971), and Peter Doeringer, "Internal Labor Markets and Noncompeting Groups," *American Economic Review* 76 (May 1986): 48–52.

38   Oliver Williamson, *The Economic Institutions of Capitalism* (New York: The Free Press, 1985).

39   See Bruce E. Kaufman, "The Organization of Economic Activity: Insights from the Institutional Theory of John R. Commons," *Journal of Economic Behavior and Organization* 52 (1, 2003): 71–96; Williamson, op. cit.; and Ronald Coase, "The Nature of the Firm," *Economica* 4 (November 1937): 386–405.

40   See Gregory Dow, "The New Institutional Economics and Employment Regulation," in Bruce E. Kaufman, ed., *Government Regulation of the Employment Relationship* (Madison: Industrial Relations Research Association, 1997), 57–90.

get the "most," and that these psychological drives are shaped and guided largely by externally given incentives and constraints as represented by prices, incomes, and other economic variables. While admitting that this model captures a portion of reality, institutionalists point out that research in psychology strongly suggests that human motivation is also characterized by non-egoistic concern for others (e.g., altruistic acts that benefit another person without any expectation of a personal utility gain), "satisficing" behavior (people do not maximize but sometimes pursue a goal only until an acceptable or satisfactory level is reached), and internally generated drives not related to economic benefits and costs (e.g., working hard at a job may arise not from expectation of higher pay or promotion but from pride in a job well done, known as "intrinsic motivation"). Likewise, institutionalists also believe that people's choices are less rational and consistent than the rational actor model presumes. The major problem, as they see it, is that the human brain is too limited, and in some cases too clouded by emotions, to assimilate all the data and to make all the complex calculations required to arrive at optimal and consistent choices. Nobel laureate Herbert Simon calls this feature of human decision making *bounded rationality*.[41] Finally, institutionalists also place great stress on two aspects of preferences. The first is that people's preferences or tastes are interdependent; what one person or group does has a large influence on the behavior and preferences of others. As one example, institutionalists place considerable emphasis on the role of equity or "fairness" as a determinant of human behavior.[42] The second aspect of preferences emphasized by institutionalists is that preferences are not *exogenous* or a "given," but are *endogenous*, meaning that they are shaped by and change with the economic system.

Institutionalists also hold a different view concerning the structure and operation of labor markets. While neoclassical economists emphasize the competitive nature of labor markets and the primacy of market forces in determining wages and employment, institutional economists tend to emphasize just the opposite.[43] As they see it, institutional forces, such as internal labor markets and unions, and sociological factors, such as class and discrimination, segment or stratify the labor market into noncompeting groups, preventing the free flow of labor from one sector to another. Institutionalists also do not believe that market forces work as efficiently or strongly as neoclassical economists maintain. In part, institutionalists

41   See, for example, Herbert Simon, "Rationality as Process and as Product of Thought," *American Economic Review* 68, no. 2 (June 1978): 1–16, and Bruce E. Kaufman, "Emotional Arousal as a Source of Bounded Rationality," *Journal of Economic Behavior and Organization* 38 (February 1999): 135–44.

42   On the role of fairness in labor markets, see David Levine, "Fairness, Markets, and Ability to Pay," *American Economic Review* 83 (December 1993): 1241–59; Albert Rees, "The Role of Fairness in Wage Determination," *Journal of Labor Economics* 11 (January, part 1, 1993): 243–52; and Truman Bewley, "Fairness, Reciprocity, and Wage Rigidity," IZA Working Paper 1137 (Bonn, Germany: 2004).

43   See, for example, Bruce E. Kaufman, "Labor Markets and Employment Regulation: The View of the Old Institutionalists," in Bruce E. Kaufman, ed., *Government Regulation of the Employment Relationship* (Madison, Wis.: Industrial Relations Research Association, 1997), 11–56; James Annable Jr., *The Price of Industrial Labor* (Lexington, Mass.: Lexington Books, 1984); and Peter Dorman, *Markets and Mortality: Economics, Dangerous Work, and the Value of the Human Life* (New York: Cambridge University Press, 1996).

place far more emphasis on the unique features of the labor market and how these features impede or diminish the role of supply and demand. Institutionalists also do not believe that market forces work as efficiently or strongly as neoclassical economists maintain, thus invalidating the invisible hand idea. In part, institutionalists place far more emphasis on the unique features of the labor market and how these features impede or diminish the role of supply and demand. Another factor is that institutionalists give more weight to the importance of market imperfections such as rigid wages, persistent unemployment, barriers to labor mobility, and poor information. Because market forces are attenuated and incomplete in many labor markets, institutionalists give a correspondingly larger role in their theories and analyses to the role of non-market institutions, such as large corporations, human resource management practices (e.g., wage setting by management decision rather than the impersonal forces of supply/demand), labor unions, and the forces of culture and custom. Finally, with regard to policy, while neoclassical economists are generally critical of unions and laws for minimum wages and affirmative action institutional economists are more likely to believe these interventions in labor markets are (within limits) both necessary and beneficial.

Institutional economists also approach research methodology in a different way than their neoclassical counterparts. Institutionalists tend to emphasize a holistic, interdisciplinary approach that seeks to capture the full range of reality and import into economics useful concepts and theories from other fields of study. They thus decry the neoclassical economic approach as too narrow and fixated on using mathematics and mimicking the physical sciences. Institutionalists also place considerable emphasis on the idea that the assumptions of labor economic theories must be *realistic*—that is, abstractions or generalizations that are nonetheless a good first-approximation to actual practice. To build realistic theories, institutionalists emphasize an inductive, hands-on style of research where the model-builder first gains familiarity with the subject through case studies, field investigations, and immersion in the empirical literature and then builds the theory from the "ground up." Institutionalists also claim that the marginal decision rules of neoclassical theory often unrealistically describe how decisions are actually made. In their view, decisions are more often made on the basis of average values rather than on the basis of marginal values. One reason for this, according to institutionalists, is that organizations such as unions typically make policy decisions on the basis of a majority vote of the membership rather than on some type of marginal calculation of benefit and cost. A second reason is that the standard accounting data available to firms provides ready information on average cost, average output per worker, and so on, but very little information on the marginal value of such variables.

Modern Labor Economics: A Pragmatic Blend?

The boundaries and key features of the institutional and neoclassical schools have tended to blur over time and many labor economists today are less persuaded that these distinctions remain valid or useful. In reaction to the criticisms of the institutionalists, neoclassical economists have broadened their theories to take into account factors such as interdependent preferences and imperfect information and have sought to explain deviant observations (e.g., occupational concentration of men and women, rigid wages) and the origins and practices of institutions such as business firms. On their part, the institutionalists have moved closer to the neoclassical school by adopting more of the techniques and tools of neoclassical economics (e.g., constrained optimization, marginal analysis) and giving greater recognition to the virtues as well as flaws of labor markets.

The result is that modern labor economics is less explicitly neoclassical or institutional and more a theoretical blend that emphasizes understanding reality in all its forms and shapes through the practice of model-building and empirical hypothesis-testing. There remains an often-submerged but fundamental dividing line in labor economics, however, that still separates the more neoclassical from the more institutional-oriented economists. At the level of theory, the dividing line is centered on the continuing debate over the degree to which labor markets are self-coordinating and give rise to efficient (and equitable) outcomes; at the level of method it turns on the institutional commitment to a plura-disciplinary, social science perspective and the neoclassical commitment to a uni-disciplinary, imperialistic approach that builds on and expands the standard theoretical core of orthodox microeconomics.

The Importance of Theory and Hypothesis Testing

Given the different theories and schools of thought in labor economics, how does an individual as a policymaker, economist, or just an interested student go about deciding which explanation of labor market behavior best fits the facts? As an example, consider the decline that took place over the twentieth century in average hours of work per week. What factors were responsible for this trend? Was it the result of government legislation requiring overtime pay after 40 hours of work per week, or does it reflect the bargaining success of unions in lowering hours of work? Was it reflective of changing shift and production patterns of employers or was it a consequence of the growing demand by workers for more hours of leisure time?

Here are four different explanations for the same event. Which one is correct? Are they all correct? To decide this question involves the use of both theory and empirical hypothesis testing.[44]

The first requirement in explaining a particular labor market outcome is to have a theory or model showing the logical cause-and-effect relationships between some original Event A and the resulting outcome in the labor market, Event B. Without such a theory we have no way of knowing why Event A caused Event B

---

44 For a more detailed discussion of methodological issues in economics see Mark Blaug, *The Methodology of Economics*, 2d ed. (Cambridge, Eng.: Cambridge University Press, 1992).

Different Views on the Merits of Ergonomics Standards

In November 2000 the Occupational Safety and Health Administration (OSHA) issued ergonomics standards for the workplace. Ergonomics is the science of designing workplaces so they fit the physical limitations of workers. Poorly designed work environments lead to a variety of injuries. While improper ergonomics has plagued the meatpacking, poultry processing, and other industries for some time, the problem has received fresh attention as widespread computer use means that many white-collar workers began suffering from similar repetitive-action injuries known to assembly-line workers for years.

The OSHA standards took effect January 2001, but Congress immediately passed a resolution of disapproval making them invalid as of April 2001. The controversy continues, however, as the U.S. Secretary of Labor holds hearings to determine what ergonomic standards might meet with the approval of Congress.

Are the injuries caused by poorly designed workplaces serious enough to warrant the cost of imposing additional regulation on business? Do policymakers, and more important, OSHA, have enough information to implement useful, meaningful guidelines? Given below are two perspectives on these questions. The first excerpt, from a press release issued by the U.S. Chamber of Commerce, argues that the standards proposed by OSHA are vague, and that we really don't know enough about the extent of the potential injuries to pass any legislation dictating ergonomic designs. The second excerpt, from a press release issued by the AFL-CIO, argues that these injuries have plagued workers long enough and it is about time the government did something about it. Note how the different policy conclusions reached by each side reflect fundamentally different assumptions about the source of the evidence and the importance of ergonomics.

The U.S. Chamber of Commerce: Ergonomics Edict Out of Joint

"What's wrong with the ergonomics standard? It is overreaching and prohibitively costly. The standard, which OSHA claims will alleviate musculoskeletal disorders (MSDs) caused by workplace activity, consumes more than 600 pages of fine print in the Federal Register, covers 102 million employees, 18 million jobs, and 6.1 million businesses of all types and sizes, and will cost businesses nearly $100 billion a year, resulting in higher consumer prices for products and services. It is, in no sense, limited to jobs involving repetitive motion.

"A regulation of this breadth might be justifiable if it was based on sound science and common sense, but the ergonomics standard clearly is not. In its rush to please labor union bosses, the Clinton Administration issued the rule despite agreement by leading scientists and medical practitioners that not enough is known about ergonomics injuries—what causes them and how to prevent them—to warrant a regulation of this size and scope. Even the American College of Occupational and Environmental Medicine (ACOEM) does not support OSHA's standard, noting that 'the final standard appears to require neither a medical diagnosis nor a causal assessment.'

"The regulation completely undermines state workers' compensation laws. It overrides well-established state standards in determining whether a condition is work-related. It even supersedes state standards establishing levels of compensation for injured workers. If a condition is determined to be work-related within the meaning of the OSHA standard, the employer must provide full benefits and 100% of the employee's pay for up to three months while he or she is in a light-duty job, or 90% of pay and full benefits while not working.

"Finally, one must question the need for such a sweeping, one-size-fits-all regulation. Evidence shows that business is voluntarily and effectively dealing with real ergonomic issues. MSDs in the workplace are declining. According to the federal government, repeated trauma injuries such as carpal tunnel syndrome have declined 24% since 1994. Many businesses have successfully implemented commonsense ergonomics programs that address real, identifiable workplace problems and achieve measurable results. OSHA's ergonomics rule will undermine these highly successful, custom-designed programs. The business community is willing and prepared to work with OSHA on reasonably and effectively addressing the ergonomics issue, but this regulation is unacceptable. Congress should exercise its authority to repeal this egregious standard. If they don't, we'll see OSHA in court."

The AFL-CIO: Good Ergonomics Is Good Economics

"Ergonomics programs not only protect workers from crippling work-related repetitive strain injuries, but they also improve the bottom line. This is the experience of hundreds of employers, large and small, the finding of independent studies and experts and the conclusion of OSHA's rulemaking process.

"Musculoskeletal disorders are a major national problem costing the economy—by conservative estimates—more than $50 billion every year, according to OSHA and confirmed by the recent report by the National Academy of Sciences. Every year employers pay between $15 billion and $18 billion in workers' compensation costs alone.

"According to OSHA, its now-defunct ergonomics standard would have cost businesses $4.5 billion annually, but would have generated benefits of more than $9 billion in each of the first 10 years it was in effect by preventing 4.6 million MSDs. Savings from improved productivity were estimated to save another $700 million each year.

"Business associations, as expected, dispute OSHA's conclusions, estimating that the rule could cost more than $100 billion dollars each year, with little or no benefits. These industry estimates are nothing new. Over the past 30 years, business associations have grossly inflated projected compliance costs and have predicted widespread bankruptcy as a result of almost every standard OSHA has issued proposed.

"But the real bottom line is that without ergonomic protections, workers pay the highest costs. Witness after witness at the OSHA hearings told of how workers were often afraid to file for workers' compensation because they or their co-workers had been fired, disciplined or lost money after reporting MSDs. Even when they were successful in receiving workers' compensation, benefits often took many months or even years to receive. Many never received workers' compensation at all. And workers who eventually receive workers' compensation still suffer significant economic loss as a result of their injuries because of initial waiting periods for which compensation may or may not be paid, inadequate benefits that fail to provide adequate wage replacement, and caps on permanent partial disability benefits. Some workers have successfully been awarded disability payments, but these also fall far short of making up workers' lost wages and future earnings capacity.

"The financial burdens created by MSDs result in workers losing their homes and health insurance. Injured workers are often unable to lead a normal life and experience great difficulty performing routine activities such as writing, cleaning, caring for children, bathing and driving a car. The effects of these injuries on injured workers' well-being is also significant. Workers suffering MSDs report high levels of depression, anxiety and stress at home. These are the monetary and non-monetary costs paid by workers when businesses refuse to address ergonomic hazards in their workplaces."

SOURCES: Thomas J. Donohue, "Ergonomics Edicts Out of Joint," *Washington Times* (7 March 2001), as reproduced on http://www.uschamber.org; "Good Ergonomics Is Good Economics," AFL-CIO Fact Sheet (March 2001), http://www.aflcio.org/yourjobeconomy/safety/ergo/ergo_infopack_goodergo.cfm

nor can we predict what will be the effect if Event C takes place instead of Event A. Such a theory can be verbal, graphical, or mathematical; the major requirements are that it be logically consistent and generate predictions or conclusions that can at least potentially be refuted from examination of actual labor market events or experience. An additional requirement of most theory is that it be an abstraction from real life so that the main cause-and-effect relationships are not obscured by the complexity of the labor market.

Having constructed one or several theories to explain a particular event, how does a person then choose among them? The next step involves the role of empirical research and hypothesis testing. To be useful, a theory has to yield a prediction or hypothesis in the form of "if A, then B." The role of empirical research is to test this hypothesis by examining actual empirical data gathered in the labor market and seeing whether the predictions of the theory reasonably fit the facts. If the predictions do not fit the facts, the theory can be rejected as incorrect; if they do coincide, then we can infer support for the theory, but not its final proof.

This two-step process of theory and empirical research is crucial to understanding how the labor market works and why events occur as they do. In the terminology of economics, this process involves **positive economics**—the study of how and why things are the way they are. Positive economics involves questions of fact—why is the unemployment rate for blacks twice that of whites, or why did productivity growth boom in the 1990s? The answers to these questions are varied and not always in agreement, but through scientific investigation and examination of empirical data it should be possible to reject competing hypotheses and accept the one that best fits reality. In practice this process is not as clear-cut as it sounds because of the complexity of human behavior and the limitations and shortcomings in the available data.

It is a short step from questions of fact—positive economics—to questions of how things *ought* to be—**normative economics.** Normative economics involves value judgments; for example, women should earn as much as men, or the minimum wage should be abolished. While facts alone cannot answer these or other normative debates encountered in labor economics, theory and empirical evidence are usually (but not always) a crucial input in shaping decisions on such issues.

The Importance of Theory for Public Policy

Since the New Deal of the 1930s, government regulation and intervention in the labor market have expanded tremendously. Before that time, the minimum wage, Social Security, overtime pay requirements, health and safety regulations, and affirmative action and equal opportunity laws were unknown. There has always been a vigorous debate as to the proper role of government in the economy and, in particular, whether the economic and social welfare of the country would be better promoted by dismantling or expanding some of the legislative and regulatory programs enacted over these years.

The two sides to this debate start out with different normative assumptions about what ought to be the goals and direction of society. The important point, however, is that both sides attempt to buttress their public policy programs on an appeal to the "facts," that is, on a positive analysis of how the labor market works and the effect of government intervention on it. The fact that each side reaches a diametrically opposite conclusion concerning the desirability of a minimum wage law or equal opportunity requirements, to give two examples, stems from their different assumptions about the labor market process and in particular the relative roles of economic, institutional, and sociological forces in the labor market.

As Ray Marshall, former U.S. Secretary of Labor, has argued, every proposed or actual piece of government labor legislation is based or justified on either an explicit or an implicit theory of the labor market.[45] As a rule, economists and policymakers who believe in the primacy of market forces and the competitive model of demand and supply favor a minimal amount of government intervention in the labor market.[46] Others who give greater weight to the defects of the market system, as well as to the role of institutional and sociological considerations, favor a greater intervention by government in the labor market.[47] In either case, the normative public policy proposals of what ought to be done are based directly on a positive theory of how the labor market works.

Seen in this light, it is clear that the theory of the labor market process is much more than just an interesting economic debate; the outcome of this debate has profound implications for the direction of economic and social policy in the country. The resolution of this debate (if there ever is one) will come from the weight of empirical evidence for and against each point of view as citizens and policymakers observe the labor market outcomes generated by the respective programs of one side or the other. Thus, the interaction between theory and empirical evidence not only guides economists in their search for *the* answer to how the labor market works, it also provides the basic tool for policymakers and the average voter to judge the relative merits of particular labor market programs and the broader issues of government and society.

---

45 F. Ray Marshall, "Implications of Labor Market Theory for Employment Policy," in Gordon Swanson and Jan Michaelson, eds., *Manpower Research and Labor Economics* (Beverly Hills, Calif.: Sage, 1979), 18.

46 See, for example, Morgan O. Reynolds, "A New Paradigm: Deregulating Labor Relations," *Journal of Labor Research* 17 (Winter 1996): 121–28, and Gary Becker, "Let's Put Deregulation to Work in Labor," *Business Week* (July 14, 1986).

47 For an example of this point of view, see Sar A. Levitan, Frank Gallo, and Isaac Shapiro, *Working but Poor: America's Contradiction* (Baltimore: Johns Hopkins University Press, 1993).

The Market for Teachers: 1971–2001

Do market forces really work as described previously, or is this just theory? For some evidence on this issue, consider the market for teachers over the thirty year period 1971–2001. Graph (a) of Figure 1.7 illustrates data on the growth in the employment of elementary and secondary school teachers and the growth in the number of new college graduates qualified to teach. The growth in employment is a measure of the strength of labor demand; the growth in the number of new college graduates qualified to teach is a measure of labor supply.[1] Graph (b) shows data on the relative earnings ratio of teachers, measured as the annual earnings of teachers as a percentage of the median income of women employed year-round full-time in the economy.

Graph (a) shows that while the growth in employment has remained fairly steady, with a slight upward trend since the early 1980s, the growth in the supply of teachers went through distinct boom and bust cycles over this 28-year period. The late 1960s and early 1970s saw the supply of teachers growing at a faster rate than employment. This was likely the leftover residual growth required to educate the baby boom children. This supply growth also likely reflects the tremendous growth of the numbers of women in the labor market during this time period.

Given the excess supply of teachers in the 1970s that resulted from this growth, the model of demand and supply predicts that two things should have happened to restore equilibrium. First, relative wages for teachers should have fallen, and second, this should have caused a decline in the number of people choosing to be teachers. Both of these events clearly took place in the teachers' market. From 1970 to 1980, the earnings ratio of teachers fell precipitously, from 162 percent to 143 percent. Likewise, in the space of 10 years (from 1970 to 1980) the number of college graduates with majors in education declined nearly in half (from 20 percent to 12.6 percent), resulting in the negative growth in supply depicted in panel (a).

Panel (a) shows that the buyer's market for teachers ended in the late 1980s. In response to the upward trend in demand growth, the growth in teacher supply began to rapidly expand and in the early 1990s overshot demand. The growth spurt in teacher supply in the first half of the 1990s put new downward pressure on teacher relative wages, indicated by the downward movement in the relative wage line commencing in the mid-1990s. In the last part of the 1990s and early 2000s, demand and supply regained an approximate balance, and the relative wage of teachers also stabilized.[2]

---

1   The employment growth depicted in panel (a) of Figure 1.7 does not strictly represent demand for teachers, as it does not take into account replacement demand, but employment in any given year should be very closely related to overall demand. Demand projections (growth *and* replacement) are calculated for detailed occupations and by the Bureau of Labor Statistics and can be found at http://www.bls.gov/emp. Regrettably, these overall demand statistics are not retained historically.

2   In representing this sequence of events, it is important to distinguish clearly between movements along a labor supply curve and shifts in the curve. At any one point in time, there is an upward-sloping supply curve for teachers, illustrating that, for the given stock of people trained to be teachers, a higher salary will induce more of them to offer to work. Over time, however, this higher salary will also lead more people to obtain teaching certificates, which will then shift the supply curve for teachers to the right, showing that at any given salary more people will now offer to work. Thus, excess demand for teachers in the late 1980s caused a rise in salaries, which, in turn, brought about two types of supply adjustments: a movement up a given labor supply curve and, somewhat later, a rightward shift of the supply curve. The rightward shift in the supply curve will continue until teachers' salaries fall back to a level just competitive with other occupations.

FIGURE 1.7   DEMAND AND SUPPLY IN THE MARKET FOR TEACHERS

(a) Growth in Employment and Growth in Supply of Teachers

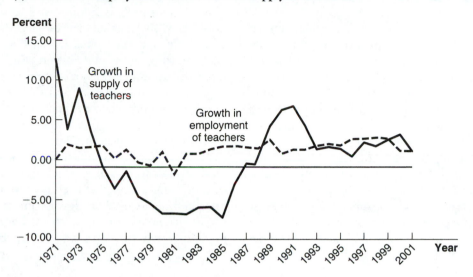

(b) Relative Earnings Ratio

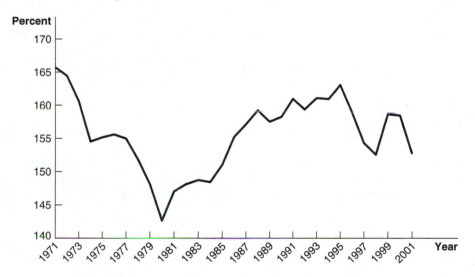

SOURCE: National Center for Education Statistics, *Digest of Education Statistics, 2002*, tables 65, 77, and 283 http://nces.ed. gov/pubs2004/digest; U.S. Census Bureau, *Historical Income Tables*, tables P-38 http://www.census.gov/hhes/income/histinc/ p38.html.

Summary

The science of economics is concerned with the allocation of resources in the economy and the determination of prices and levels of production. For a capitalist economy, the primary theoretical construct used to understand these issues is the market model of supply and demand. In labor economics, one particular market, the labor market, is studied. Labor is a service that households supply to business firms in order to earn an income and that business firms demand in order to produce their product. It is this interaction of the demand and supply of labor that determines wage rates, the level of employment, and the distribution of income in the economy. Market forces of supply and demand are not the only determinants of these market outcomes, however; institutional and sociological forces also play roles. Institutional forces affect labor market outcomes through the influence of organizations such as labor unions, large corporations, and government; sociological forces exert their influence through such factors as culture, class, discrimination, and custom. There is no one model or paradigm in labor economics that weaves these market, institutional, and sociological forces into a universally accepted theory of how the labor market works. Rather, there are different schools of thought that give varying degrees of emphasis to the relative importance of these forces in the labor market and the degree to which the market forces of supply and demand efficiently work to set wage rates and allocate labor. To discriminate between these alternative theories, therefore, requires a process of hypothesis testing and empirical validation of competing theoretical predictions.

Review Questions

1. Where do the other factor markets for capital and land (natural resources) belong in the circular flow model depicted in Figure 1.1? Can you draw them in? Are there any connections or feedbacks between one factor market (such as labor) and another (such as capital)? How would you represent them in Figure 1.1?

2. If human beings could be bought and sold like commodities such as wheat, how would it change the operation of the labor market? Would the supply of labor become more or less sensitive to the nonpecuniary aspects of employment (such as working conditions)? Would market forces still be able automatically to police the social conditions of labor?

3. Are there any differences between the labor market for day laborers or migrant workers and the market for teachers or pilots? What are these differences, and how do they affect the pricing and allocation of labor?

4. Why is the role of labor mobility crucial if market forces of demand and supply are to efficiently allocate labor in the economy? What role does labor market information have in this process? Do you think people move from one labor market to another in search of the highest wages, as economic theory assumes? Why or why not?

5. What is the difference between an external and an internal labor market? How are they connected? Can a firm decide on its own what wages to pay in the internal labor market, or do the market forces of supply and demand have some influence?

6. In 2003, the average weekly earnings of truck drivers was $603 while average weekly earnings of bank tellers was only $395. How might market, institutional, and sociological forces, respectively, be responsible for the higher earnings of truck drivers?

7. Describe the major differences between the neoclassical and institutional schools of labor economics.

8. Labor market outcomes for men and women show marked differences along a number of dimensions. Men, for example, are on average paid higher hourly earnings, work longer hours, and are more likely to be employed in occupations such as investment banker, sales, construction, and auto repair. Conversely, women on average earn less per hour, work fewer hours (including more part-time jobs), and tend to cluster in occupations such as school teacher, human resource manager, nurse, and retail trade. Give an explanation for these differences that reflect, respectively, market, institutional, and sociological forces.

Hours of Work

This chapter and the next deal with the subject of labor supply. Labor supply has several dimensions encompassing both the quantity and the quality of the labor input made available for market work. This chapter begins the analysis of labor supply by focusing on one of the quantity dimensions—hours of work. The first part of the chapter develops the basic neoclassical theory of labor supply, known as the labor/leisure model. This is followed by an examination of empirical evidence on the determinants of work hours. The theory and empirical evidence are then used to analyze two public policy debates. These are the impact on labor supply of income tax cuts and of welfare programs such as Temporary Assistance for Needy Families. The following section analyzes two more institutionally oriented aspects of labor supply, the impact of employer-mandated work schedules and the time and money costs of working. The final part of the chapter examines the causes of the long-term decline in average work hours per week in the economy.

The Pattern of Hours of Work

Before the theory of labor supply is introduced, it is important to point out the real-world behavior that the theory is meant to explain. This is done in Figure 2.1. Graph (a) shows the distribution of people employed in 2003 by their hours of work per week. This is an example of **cross-sectional data**—it shows a "snapshot" at one point in time of the distribution of hours of work across individuals. Graph (b), on the other hand, provides an illustration of time-series data, showing the change over time in average hours worked per week for all workers as a group.

Three features of the cross-sectional distribution of hours are noteworthy. The first is the wide diversity among individuals in the hours worked per week. At one extreme are the 4.8 percent of the employed who worked 14 hours or less per week; at the other are the 7.6 percent who worked 60 hours or more. The second feature is the sharp peak in the hours distribution at 40 per week. Although a great many Americans work either relatively few or many hours, the single

(a) Cross-Sectional Pattern

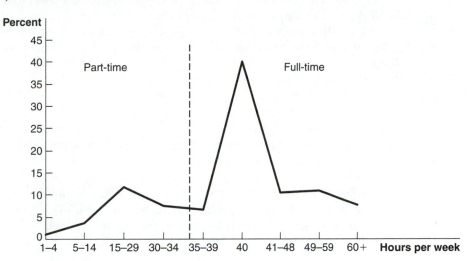

(b) Time-Series Pattern

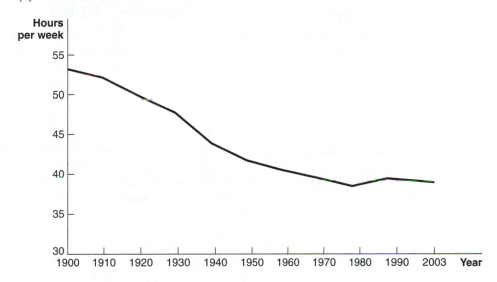

SOURCE: Bureau of Labor Statistics, *Employment and Earnings* (January 1981, 1991, 2004); G. Moore and J. Hedges, "Trends in Labor and Leisure," *Monthly Labor Review* 94 no. 2 (February 1971): 5; and http://www.bls.gov/webapps/legacy/cesbtab2.htm.

greatest number in 2003 (41.3 percent) worked exactly 40 hours per week. Finally, also shown is the proportion of people who were *full-time* or *part-time* workers. To be classified as a full-time worker, a person must work 35 or more hours a week, depicted in graph (a) by the broken vertical line. Despite the growing proportion of part-timers in the workforce, they continue to account for fewer than one-fourth of all the persons employed in the economy.

Graph (b) shows the change in average hours worked per week in the economy from 1900 to 2003. At the turn of the century the average workweek was 53 hours; for many workers a 9- or 10-hour day was standard, with time off only on Sunday. Over the course of the twentieth century, however, the workweek declined significantly until by 2003 the average workweek was 42.9 hours for full-time workers and 39 hours for all workers. A second interesting feature of the long-term decline in hours of work is the marked difference in the trend in hours of work before and after World War II. Most of the decline in hours of work occurred between 1900 and 1945; since then there has been some further decline, but it has not been nearly as sharp as before.

In the terminology of Chapter 1, the cross-sectional and time-series patterns of hours of work are the labor market outcomes we wish to explain. To do so, we need a theory that can identify the major influences on people's choices concerning work versus leisure.

The Theory of the Labor/Leisure Choice

There is wide diversity in the hours per week that people choose to work. Why do some individuals work only part-time while others moonlight on two or three separate jobs? Presumably both the part-time worker and the moonlighter have made a conscious choice to find jobs that provide the work schedule they want. This section analyzes how this choice is made.

There are 168 hours in a week, and each individual decides how to allocate those hours among various activities. A certain number of hours per week are not really discretionary, however, since there are fixed biological needs for sleeping, eating, and so on. Assuming, for simplicity, that these fixed needs require 68 hours per week (or a little less than 10 hours per day), 100 hours remain about which choices can be made. This chapter assumes that there are two possible uses for this discretionary time—work and leisure. Work is all hours devoted to a paying job; leisure is the remainder of time used for all other activities. Leisure is used here in a very broad sense to cover nonmarket activities as diverse as watching a movie, going to school, or working in the home. This somewhat artificial definition of leisure keeps the analysis at a relatively simple level; in the next chapter, the theory is made more realistic by distinguishing among three possible uses of time: market work, nonmarket work, and leisure.

Since the amount of time not working is by definition the amount of time spent at leisure, it is possible to treat the demand for leisure and the supply of labor as one and the same decision. Since economics has a well-developed theory of demand, the choice between labor and leisure is analyzed in terms of the demand for leisure; the supply of labor can then be found by subtracting hours of leisure from total discretionary time.

According to the theory of consumer demand, the demand for a specific good or service depends on a number of variables: in particular, the price of the good or service, the amount of income that potential buyers have, and tastes or preferences for the good or service. The theory predicts that the higher the price of a good is, holding all other things constant, the lower the quantity of it demanded will be. Similarly, this theory predicts that if income should increase, the demand for the good will increase, assuming that it is what economists call a *normal* good. (A normal good is one that individuals want more of as their incomes rise. The opposite is an *inferior* good.) Finally, the demand for a good may also change simply because of a change in the preferences or tastes concerning it.

This theory of demand can be used to analyze an individual's decision about how much leisure time he or she desires. While it may seem strange to talk about a "demand for leisure," leisure time provides utility or satisfaction much like any other good or service, and it also has a definite price attached to its use. Given these parallels, the following sections analyze first the role of preferences in shaping the labor/leisure choice and second the role of price and income in this decision.

Preferences and Indifference Curves

Preferences represent an individual's psychological feelings or perceptions about an item's desirability vis-à-vis other goods and services. They are inherently subjective in nature and potentially influenced by a host of factors related to one's ethnicity, socioeconomic class, and occupation, as well as individual personality factors. Although preferences are subject to considerable variation among people, research shows that at a point in time individuals possess a clear notion of how they rank the desirability of competing goods or services and how much they would trade of one to get more of another. In some complex situations, however, such as choice over items embodying risk or uncertainty, research also finds that people's preferences may not be entirely consistent.[1]

The theory developed here assumes that individuals have to rank and choose between two goods: leisure and income earned from work. Leisure is desired for its own intrinsic qualities; income is desired for the goods and services it can buy. Figure 2.2 graphically represents the process of ranking and choosing among alternative combinations of leisure time and income.

In Figure 2.2 the horizontal axis measures hours of leisure per week ranging from zero to the hypothetical maximum of 100 hours. The vertical axis measures money income (Y) and ranges from zero to $1,000 per week. Point A is an arbitrary

1   See Robin Hogarth and Melvin Reder (eds.), *Rational Choice* (Chicago: University of Chicago Press, 1987); and Theo B.C. Poiesz, "The Free Market Illusion: Psychological Limitations of Consumer Choice," *Tijdschrift voor Economie en Management 49* (April 2004): 309–38.

FIGURE 2.2   A SET OF INDIFFERENCE CURVES

Points A, B, and C represent successively higher levels of utility since the person gains more of both leisure and income. For each level of utility, an indifference curve may be constructed that shows all the other combinations of income and leisure that the person regards as equally satisfying. Points A, D, and E on indifference curve I_1, for example, all yield the same level of utility. Each indifference curve is convex, giving rise to a diminishing marginal rate of substitution (MRS) between income and leisure. The MRS at point A is given by the slope of the dashed line.

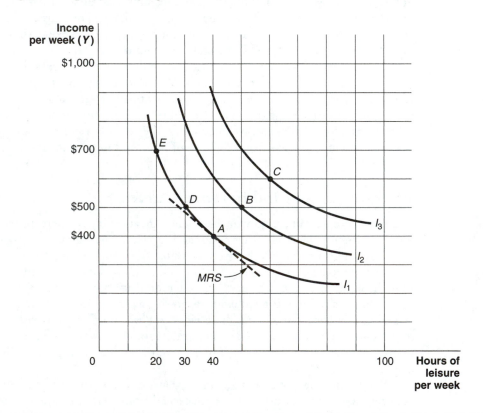

combination of leisure and income. At point A the individual has 40 hours of leisure and $400 of income per week, yielding some particular level of utility. A basic assumption of utility theory is that given the initial combination of leisure and income at point A, any other combination, such as point B, that provides more income or leisure or more of both income and leisure will lead to a higher level of satisfaction and will be clearly preferred to point A. By the same reasoning, point C will clearly be ranked as superior to point B.

The next step in the analysis is to derive what is known as an **indifference curve.** The derivation of an indifference curve is based on an individual's answer to the following question: "What other combinations of leisure and income besides that at point A would leave you just as well off as before?" (Or, put another way, "Are there other combinations of leisure and income besides those at point A that you would just be indifferent to?") The answer typically will trace out a curve much like the one labeled I_1 in Figure 2.2.[2] On an indifference curve, every point represents a combination of income and leisure that yields exactly the same level of utility.

Indifference curves have several important properties. First, as a matter of logic, they have to have a negative slope—that is, they slope down and to the right. The reason is that if we are to find some new combination of income and leisure that has just the same utility level as point A, clearly the person must receive more of one but at the same time lose some of the other. Such a new combination might be point D on indifference curve I_1, with an income of \$500, but leisure of only 30 hours.

The second important property of indifference curves is that they are convex to the origin. At point A, how much income would this person have to be given to compensate for the loss of 10 hours of leisure time? Point D gives the answer, which is \$100. To keep utility constant, how much income would have to be given to induce this person to give up *another* 10 hours of leisure (that is, to have only 20 hours of leisure)? Would he or she be willing to trade away that 10 hours of leisure for another \$100? The answer is most likely no—with fewer and fewer hours of leisure time, each remaining hour of leisure becomes increasingly valuable. Thus, to persuade the person pictured in Figure 2.2 to reduce leisure from 30 hours to 20 would require not an additional \$100 but, it is assumed, an additional \$200. This combination of income (\$700) and leisure (20 hours) is shown as point E on indifference curve I_1.

This convex shape reflects what economists call a diminishing **marginal rate of substitution (MRS).** The *MRS* measures the rate at which a person is willing to trade income for leisure; a diminishing *MRS* implies that a person will give up successive units of leisure only in exchange for larger and larger increments of income, and vice versa. Graphically, the *MRS* is given by the slope of the indifference curve at any point on it. The *MRS* at point A in Figure 2.2, for example, is given by the slope of the broken tangent line. (The slope of a line is given by the rise over the run, measured here as Δincome/Δleisure.) As leisure hours decrease from points A to D to E, the slope becomes steeper and steeper, illustrating the diminishing rate at which the person is willing to trade leisure for income.

A third property of indifference curves is that there is a whole set of separate curves, such as I_1, I_2, and I_3, for each level of utility. Having derived one indifference curve such as I_1, for example, it is then an easy matter to increase both income

2   See L. F. Dunn, "An Empirical Indifference Function for Income and Leisure," *Review of Economics and Statistics* 60, no. 4 (November 1978): 533–40.

and leisure, move to a new point such as *B*, and at this higher level of utility derive an entirely new indifference curve, such as I_2. Every point on I_2 represents a higher level of utility than I_1, and every point on I_3 corresponds to a higher level of satisfaction than on I_2.

A fourth property of indifference curves is that they never intersect or cross each other for any one person, at any one point in time. If they did it would imply illogical preferences. This is illustrated in graph (a) of Figure 2.3. From the definition of an indifference curve, a person would be indifferent between point *V* or point *X* on indifference curve I_1; likewise he or she would be indifferent between

---

FIGURE 2.3

INCONSISTENT PREFERENCES AND DIFFERENCES IN PREFERENCES FOR INCOME VERSUS LEISURE

One property of indifference curves is that they never intersect one another. If they did, as shown in graph (a), preferences would no longer be consistent. Thus, points *V* and *X* are of equal utility as are points *Z* and *X*. Logic implies that points *V* and *Z* should also be of equal utility, but clearly they are not since *Z* provides more of both income and leisure. A second property of indifference curves is that their shape and degree of convexity will vary from person to person depending on individual preferences regarding income versus leisure. The indifference curve I_A represents a "workaholic" person who willingly trades off an hour of leisure for only a small increase in income. The curve I_B represents a "laid-back" person who will give up an hour of leisure only in exchange for a relatively large increase in income.

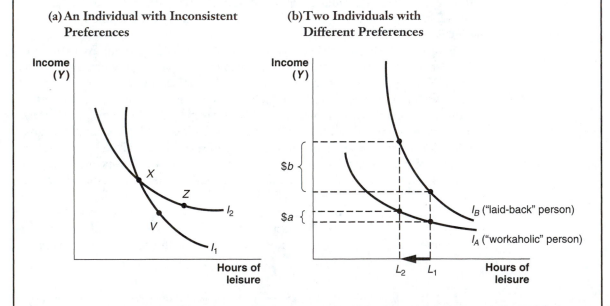

(a) An Individual with Inconsistent Preferences

(b) Two Individuals with Different Preferences

---

points Z and X on indifference curve I_2. Logic implies that if points V and X and points Z and X, respectively, yield the same level of utility, then points Z and V should also be equal. But in Figure 2.3, points V and Z are not equally desirable, since Z gives more of both income and leisure than V. Hence, for a given set of preferences to be consistent, the indifference curves can never intersect.

The final point concerning indifference curves is that their shape (slope and degree of convexity) differs for each individual, to the extent that people have different preferences or attitudes regarding the desirability of work versus leisure. The two indifference curves in graph (b) of Figure 2.3 illustrate this. The indifference curve of person A (I_A) is relatively flat; that for person B (I_B) is relatively steep. The flat curve, I_A indicates that person A would not require as much additional income ($\$a$) as person B requires ($\$b$) to be persuaded to give up one hour of leisure and remain just as happy when leisure decreases from L_1 to L_2.

There are at least three possible sources of these differences in tastes. One may simply be innate personality differences. Person A may be a "workaholic" by nature, requiring little monetary inducement to work extra hours; person B, on the other hand, may possess a "laid-back" personality and place a high value on every hour of leisure. A second reason is related to the type of work people do. The basic assumption that gives the indifference curves their negative slope is that work is a source of disutility—a person has to be paid before he or she will do it. [This assumption is explored in more detail in Appendix 2A.] The amount of disutility associated with each hour of work depends, however, on the type of job a person has. Person B, for example, may have a relatively disagreeable job, such as assembly-line worker or janitor, while person A may have an agreeable job, such as airline pilot or college professor. Since each hour of work for person B involves a greater amount of disutility, he or she would require a larger increase in income before willingly giving up another hour of leisure, making I_B steeper than I_A is.[3] Finally, a third factor that might make person B's indifference curve steeper is if he or she has a relatively more valuable use for leisure time than person A, such as attending school or caring for children.

Wages, Income, and the Budget Constraint

The demand for a good or service is shaped not only by preferences, but also by economic factors such as price and income. Consider first the price of leisure.

An hour of leisure has no necessary explicit cost—it is possible to sit under a tree and daydream without spending a cent. There is a definite cost to that hour of

---

3   In recent research, Linda Bell and Richard Freeman have found that the more a worker expects to gain in the future from working an extra hour, the more hours he/she will work. As discussed in more detail in Appendix 2A, this difference in individual labor supply behavior may be modeled as reflecting differences in preferences (some people have a greater psychological willingness to sacrifice leisure today for future income), but it also can be interpreted as reflecting differences in budget constraints (some people gain a greater monetary return in the future from giving up an hour of leisure today). See "Incentive for Working Hard: Explaining Hours Worked Differences in the U.S. and Germany," *Labour Economics* 8 (2001): 181–202.

leisure, however, in the sense of an *opportunity cost*. Every hour spent in leisure is an hour that could have been devoted to market work; the opportunity cost of an hour of leisure, therefore, is equal to the wage rate per hour of work. The higher the wage is, the higher is the price of leisure.

The wage earned per hour multiplied by the number of hours worked per week yields total weekly earnings from work. This relationship between the wage rate, hours worked, and total income is known as the **budget constraint;** it shows all the various combinations of income and hours of work (and thus of leisure) that are available to an individual, given the wage he or she can earn in the market.

Figure 2.4 shows a graph of the budget constraint. It again has income on the vertical axis and leisure (up to the assumed maximum of 100 hours per week) on the horizontal axis. What is different here is that the horizontal axis represents *both*

FIGURE 2.4 A SET OF BUDGET CONSTRAINTS

The budget constraint *AB* shows all the attainable combinations of income and leisure given a wage rate of $8 per hour and zero nonlabor income. An increase in the wage rate to $10 rotates the budget constraint to *AC*. The addition of $200 of nonlabor income per week

would then cause a parallel shift to the right in the budget constraint to *ADE*. The slope of the budget constraint *AB* is equal to −8 (the negative of the wage rate), showing that each additional hour of leisure results in a reduction of income of $8.

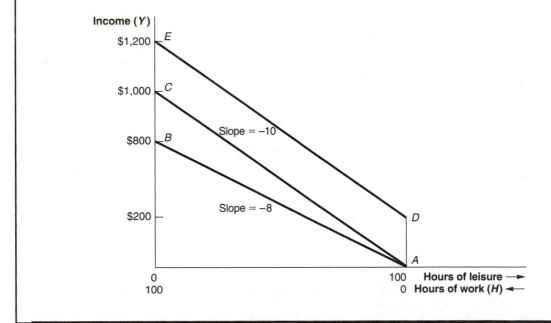

hours of leisure and hours of work (*H*). Hours of leisure are read from left to right; hours of work are read in the opposite direction. When leisure is zero, hours of work are 100, and when leisure is 100, hours of work are zero.

Each person, based on education, experience, occupation, and so on, can earn some particular wage rate in the market. Here it is assumed to be $8 per hour. The budget constraint can be derived by plotting in Figure 2.4 all the various combinations of hours of work and levels of income available to this person. If zero hours are worked (100 hours of leisure), and assuming for the moment no other sources of income, total weekly income is also zero. This is shown as point *A*. Likewise, if all 100 hours are worked at $8 per hour, weekly income will be $800, shown as point *B*. It is possible to plot every other combination of income and hours worked; doing so yields a straight line or budget constraint shown as line *AB*.[4]

The budget constraint has several important properties. First, its slope is negative, reflecting the fact that income falls as hours of leisure rise. Second, the slope of the budget constraint equals the negative of the wage rate. In this example the slope is equal to −8, the amount of income lost for each extra hour of leisure.

A third property of the budget constraint concerns the effect upon it of a change in the wage rate. For example, what would happen to the budget constraint in Figure 2.4 if the wage increased from $8 to $10 per hour? Point *A* would remain the same, since no matter how high the wage became, income would still be zero if hours of work were zero. If all 100 hours were devoted to work, however, total weekly income would become $1,000, or point *C*. Thus, a change in the wage rate *rotates* the budget constraint, making it steeper for a rise in the wage and flatter for a fall in the wage.

A fourth feature of the budget constraint concerns the impact upon it of a change in nonlabor income. Assuming a wage of $10 and zero nonlabor income, how does the budget constraint *AC* change if the person receives $200 per week of nonlabor income in the form of, say, rental income from property? If hours of work are zero, total weekly income will be $200, or point *D* in Figure 2.4, representing zero dollars of earned (labor) income and $200 of rental income. If all 100 hours are devoted to work, total income will be $1,000 of earned income plus $200 of

---

4   It is assumed for the sake of simplicity that each hour of work pays a constant $8 per hour. There are several other possibilities, however. One is the presence of an overtime law that requires time and a half to be paid after 40 hours. The effect of such a law on the budget constraint is left as an exercise for the student (see Review Question 1 at the end of the chapter). A second possibility is that the wage varies with the number of hours a person is willing to work. One study [Robert Moffitt, "The Estimation of a Joint Wage–Hours Labor Supply Model," *Journal of Labor Economics* 2, no. 4 (October 1984): 550–66] found the budget constraint actually had an inverse S-shape—the wage rate rose by about 22 cents (in 2004 dollars) for each 5 additional hours worked until 35 hours per week, after which it leveled off and then began to decline. Also see Shelly Lundberg, "Tied Wage–Hours Offers and the Endogeneity of Wages," *Review of Economics and Statistics* 67 (August 1985): 405–11; and Susan L. Averett and Julie L. Hotchkiss, "Female Labor Supply with a Discontinuous, Nonconvex Budget Constraint: Incorporation of a Part-Time/Full-Time Wage Differential," *Review of Economics and Statistics* 79 (August 1997): 461–70.

nonlabor income for a total of $1,200 per week (point *E*). This yields a new budget constraint *ADE* in Figure 2.4. The addition of nonlabor income results in a *parallel* shift of the budget constraint, from *AC* to *ADE*, not a change in its slope since, by assumption, the wage remained constant at $10 per hour.

The Equilibrium Hours of Work

An individual's decision concerning hours of work is the result of the interaction of preferences, wages, and income. To demonstrate this, Figure 2.5 brings together in one diagram both the series of indifference curves I_1, I_2, and I_3 from Figure 2.2 and the budget constraint *AB* from Figure 2.4.

It is assumed that the person's objective is to maximize utility—in other words, to reach the highest indifference curve possible. The level of utility that is obtainable is constrained by the wage rate and the amount of nonlabor income. Given this, it is clear, for example, that point *Z* on I_3 is not an attainable combination of income and leisure since it lies to the right of the budget constraint. Conversely, point *V* on I_1 is attainable, but it does not maximize utility. By moving down the

FIGURE 2.5   EQUILIBRIUM HOURS OF WORK

The equilibrium hours of work is 50 per week (point *X*), where the indifference curve I_2 is tangent to the budget constraint *AB*. Point *Z* would yield a higher level of utility, but it is unobtainable since it lies to the right of the budget constraint. Point *V* is obtainable, but would not maximize utility since it is on a lower indifference curve.

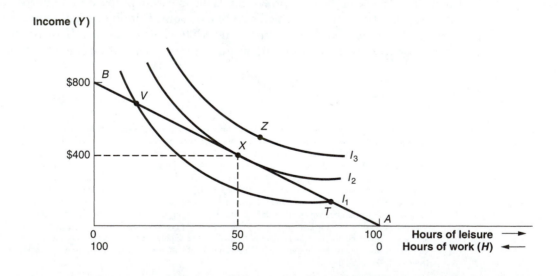

budget constraint, it is possible to reach successively higher indifference curves until point X is reached, where the indifference curve I_2 and the budget constraint AB are just tangent. Point X is therefore the point of maximum utility, yielding an equilibrium combination of 50 hours of work, 50 hours of leisure, and $400 of income.

The equilibrium at point X has the unique property that it is the only point where the slope of the budget constraint is equal to the slope of the indifference curve. Since the slope of the indifference curve is given by the marginal rate of substitution, and the slope of the budget constraint is the wage (neglecting the minus sign), the equilibrium hours of work is given by the condition:

$$MRS = W \qquad\qquad (2.1)$$

This equality has a special economic interpretation that further demonstrates why point X is the optimal level of hours of work.

The slope of the budget constraint measures the wage rate, the dollars that are obtainable from an additional hour of work. The slope of the indifference curve measures the number of dollars that the individual psychologically feels each hour of leisure is worth. To maximize utility, the appropriate decision rule is to keep on working additional hours as long as the wage earned exceeds the psychological valuation of that hour of leisure; when the two become equal, utility will be at its highest. At point T, the MRS (slope of the indifference curve), or the individual's psychological value of time, is less than the wage rate, or the *market's* value of the individual's time. Thus, utility could be increased by working additional hours. Utility would continue to increase until hours of work reached point X, where the two slopes are equal. At point V, the individual values his or her time more than the market does ($MRS > W$). Thus utility could be increased by working fewer hours.

Hours of Work and Changes in Nonlabor Income

The tangency between a budget constraint and an indifference curve yields the highest level of utility and the optimal number of hours of work. The next question to consider is how the number of hours supplied to the market changes when either nonlabor income or the wage rate changes. First the effect of a change in nonlabor income is considered.

Before the addition of any nonlabor income, the budget constraint in Figure 2.6 is AB, and the equilibrium hours of work are H_1 per week at point X. Should this individual now receive Y_1 in nonlabor income, the budget constraint becomes ACD. Because the budget constraint has shifted up, it is possible to reach a higher indifference curve and level of utility. The optimal combination of leisure and income is given at point Z, where the new budget constraint is just tangent to the higher indifference curve I_2.

The addition of $\$Y_1$ nonlabor income shifts the budget constraint from AB to ACD. Since leisure is assumed to be a normal good, equilibrium hours of work fall from H_1 (point X) to H_2 (point Z).

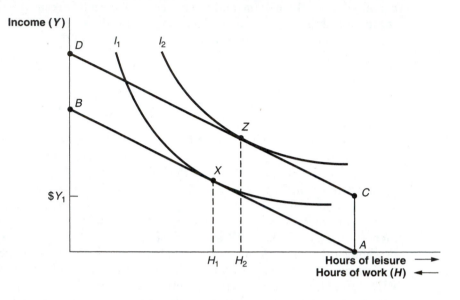

With the addition of nonlabor income, what happens to hours of work? Like most goods and services, leisure is assumed to be a normal good—that is, as income increases, so does the demand for leisure, other things equal. This is reflected in Figure 2.6 by the movement from point X to point Z. At point Z, hours of leisure are now greater, while hours of work have fallen from H_1 per week to H_2 per week.

This relationship between changes in income and changes in hours of work leads to one of the most important concepts in the theory of labor supply. This concept is known as the **income effect,** defined as the change in hours of work (ΔH) resulting from a change in income (ΔY), keeping the wage rate constant ($\overline{W}$). If leisure is a normal good, the sign of the income effect must be negative:

$$\text{Income effect} = \frac{\Delta H}{\Delta Y}\bigg|_{\overline{W}} < 0 \tag{2.2}$$

The income effect attempts to capture only the pure, isolated influence of changes in income (the income may be from any source), netting out the influence of possible changes in the price of leisure.[5] Graphically, the income effect is given by the change in hours of work resulting from a *parallel* shift of the budget constraint as a result of changes in income, such as from *AB* to *ACD* in Figure 2.6. The income effect, therefore, gives rise to a change in the level of utility as the person moves from one indifference curve to another. In Figure 2.6, the income effect is $H_1 - H_2$ (point X to Z). To measure accurately the pure effect of income on hours of work, the slope of the budget constraint cannot change as it shifts from one position to another. To change the slope causes a change not only in income, but also in the wage, violating the very definition of the income effect.

Hours of Work and Changes in the Wage Rate

The next issue to analyze is the effect of a change in the wage rate on hours of work. This is illustrated in Figures 2.7 and 2.8, for two different scenarios.

The wage rate is assumed to be W_1 per hour, giving rise to the budget constraint *AB* and, accordingly, an equilibrium number of hours of work of H_1 per week (point V) in both figures. What would happen to hours of work if the wage rate were to increase from W_1 to W_2 per hour? For both scenarios, the budget constraint would rotate upward to become the new line *AC*. As before, the new point of maximum utility is where the new budget constraint *AC* is just tangent to the highest indifference curve. In Figure 2.7 this occurs at point X on indifference curve I_2; in Figure 2.8 this occurs at point X' on indifference curve I_2'.

What happens to hours of work as a reaction to this increase in the wage rate? In Figure 2.7, the new equilibrium at point X shows that hours of work have *increased* from H_1 per week to H_2 per week. Conversely, in Figure 2.8 the new equilibrium at point X' indicates a *decrease* in hours worked from H_1 per week to H_2' per week. These diagrams indicate that it is possible for hours of work to go either up or down as a result of a change in the wage rate. The next question to consider is why this is so.

The reason for this discrepant outcome is that a change in the wage rate sets off two conflicting and opposing influences on the demand for leisure. First, a rise in the wage rate means that if the person works the same number of hours as before, the total amount of weekly income will be higher. A rise in income motivates a person to demand more leisure and less work. This is the income effect.

<hr>

5   A good example of the income effect in action is the labor supply response of people who have won a multimillion-dollar prize in a state lottery. A study of 1,000 people who won $1 million or more found that a year afterward, 23 percent had at least temporarily quit working, 17 percent had permanently retired, and 30 percent of the winners' spouses had quit working. The study concluded that while labor supply is responsive to changes in income, many people's attachment to work is quite strong. See "What Lottery Winners Prove about the Work Ethic," *Business Week* (October 7, 1985): 21. A more recent survey confirmed this strong work ethic. Sixty-four percent of workers surveyed in 1994 said they would keep working if they won $1 million in the lottery. See "Take the Pizza, Shove the Job," *Money* (March 1994): 82. Also see Imbens et al., "Estimating the Effect of Unearned Income on Labor Earnings, Savings, and Consumption: Evidence from a Survey of Lottery Players," *American Economic Review* 91 (September 2001): 778–94. They find, based on a sample of Massachusetts lottery winners, that the marginal propensity to consume leisure out of lottery winnings is −.11, a relatively small response.

FIGURE 2.7   A WAGE CHANGE LEADING TO INCREASED HOURS OF WORK

A rise in the wage rotates the budget constraint from AB to AC. Equilibrium hours of work increase from H_1 (point V) to H_2 (point X). The rise in the wage to W_2 sets off both an income and a substitution effect. The income effect causes a reduction in desired work hours from H_1 (point V) to H_3 (point Z). The substitution effect causes an increase in desired work hours from H_3 (point Z) to H_2 (point X). In this example, the substitution effect outweighs the income effect, and hours of work rise by the net amount of $H_2 - H_1$.

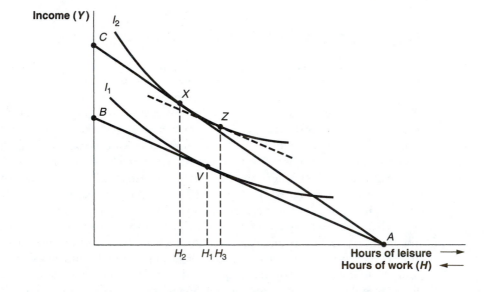

There is a second force that works in the opposite direction, however. Not only does a rise in the wage rate cause an increase in income, it also causes an increase in the opportunity cost or price of leisure. The theory of demand predicts, in turn, that when the price of leisure increases, the demand for leisure should decline, causing an individual to work more hours per week. This is called the **substitution effect.**

The essence of the substitution effect is that when the price of leisure goes up, the individual is motivated to substitute away from the now more expensive leisure toward additional hours of work. The sign of the substitution effect must be positive, therefore. To measure the substitution effect, it is necessary to let the relative price of leisure (the wage) change while everything else is held constant, particularly the person's level of income or, more precisely, the level of utility associated with that income. Thus, the substitution effect is defined as:

$$\text{Substitution effect} = \left. \frac{\Delta H}{\Delta W} \right|_{\bar{Y}} > 0 \qquad (2.3)$$

FIGURE 2.8   A WAGE CHANGE LEADING TO DECREASED HOURS OF WORK

In this case the rise in the wage causes the person to reduce desired hours of work from H_1 (point V) to (point X'). The income effect causes a decline in desired work hours from H_1 to (point V to Z'); the substitution effect causes an increase in desired work hours from to (point Z' to X'). Because the income effect is quantitatively larger, the rise in the wage results in a net decrease in desired hours of work from H_1 to H_2'.

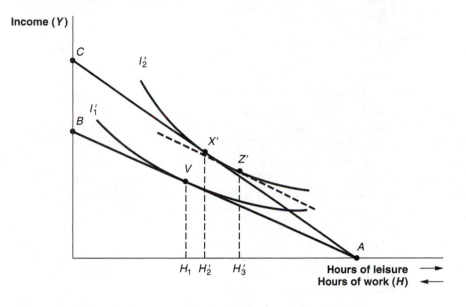

where $\bar{Y}$ signifies that all other things such as income that affect a person's level of utility are being held constant.[6] Graphically, the substitution effect is shown as the change in hours of work, resulting from the *rotation* of the budget constraint along a given indifference curve.

A change in the wage rate engenders *both* an income effect and a substitution effect. At a higher wage rate income is also greater, leading a person to "buy" more leisure and less work. Simultaneously, however, this higher wage rate also means each hour of leisure costs more, causing a substitution away from leisure and toward more work. The income effect from a wage increase tugs the individual toward less work; the substitution effect pulls him or her toward more work.

---

6   An intuitive example of the substitution effect is the following: Consider a person working 40 hours at $8 per hour, yielding a weekly income of $320. Allow the wage to increase to $9 per hour, but also charge this person a $40 lump-sum tax in order to keep income at the original level of $320. The prediction of the theory is that the person will decide to work more hours now that the price of leisure is higher.

Whether hours of work actually increase or decrease depends on the relative strength or size of the substitution effect versus the income effect.

A Graphic Derivation of Income and Substitution Effects

Hours of work change due to the wage increase from H_1 to H_2 in Figure 2.7 and from H_1 to H_2' in Figure 2.8. It is possible to graphically decompose this change in hours of work into two parts: the part due to the change in income (the income effect) and the part due to the change in relative prices (the substitution effect).

To isolate the income effect in both diagrams, the following hypothetical experiment can be done. Starting from point V and the original budget constraint AB, increase each individual's income just enough to reach the higher level of utility associated with the indifference curve I_2 or I_2'. Doing so causes the budget constraint (shown as the broken line in each figure) to shift upward in a parallel direction until it just touches I_2 at point Z in Figure 2.7 and I_2' at point Z' in Figure 2.8. In essence, the question being asked is what would happen to hours of work if the wage (the slope of the budget constraint) is held constant but the income is increased enough to provide the individual with the same level of utility as obtained at points X and X'? The answer is that hours of work would decline from H_1 to H_3 (point V to Z) in Figure 2.7, and from H_1 to H_3' (point V to Z') in Figure 2.8. This decrease in hours measures the pure income effect.

Points Z and Z' are not the actual utility-maximizing combinations of income and leisure; points X and X' are. What accounts for the disparity? The answer is the substitution effect.

The rise in the wage from W_1 to W_2 per hour increased both income and the price of leisure. The movement in each diagram from point V to points Z and Z', respectively, represented the income effect, holding the wage at W_1. The substitution effect can be isolated by returning to points Z and Z' and raising the price of leisure (the wage) but holding constant the level of utility that the person's income could purchase. This can be accomplished graphically by the following hypothetical exercise: beginning at points Z and Z', rotate the broken line along indifference curves I_2 and until the slope increases from $-W_1$ to $-W_2$, which gives rise to a new tangency point at points X and X'. (When the slope of the broken line becomes $-W_2$, it will coincide with the slope of the solid line AC.) The increase in hours of work from H_3 to H_2 (point Z to X) in Figure 2.7, and H_3' to H_2' (point Z' to X') in Figure 2.8, measures the pure substitution effect from the change in the wage.[7]

In Figure 2.7 the higher wage rate led to a net increase in labor supply from H_1 to H_2 hours. In Figure 2.8, however, the wage increase caused a reduction in

---

7   It is possible to derive the income and substitution effects in reverse order, doing the substitution effect first and then the income effect. To do so, start at point V and rotate a broken line along I_1, until it has the slope of AC, then shift the broken line in a parallel direction to point X (X').

hours of work from H_1 to H_2'. In each scenario the increase in the wage rate set off both an income and a substitution effect; in Figure 2.7 the positive substitution effect (H_3 to H_2) was quantitatively larger than the negative income effect (H_1 to H_3), and hours of work increased. In Figure 2.8, however, the income effect dominated the substitution effect, and hours of work declined. The reason for this divergent outcome is attributable entirely to the different shapes of the indifference curves, reflecting different preferences regarding the trade-off between income versus leisure. Since preferences vary from one person to another, it is impossible to say *a priori* which effect will dominate for a given individual.

The Supply Curve of Labor

A **supply curve of labor** represents the relationship between the wage rate and the hours of labor supplied to the market. The derivation of a labor supply curve is illustrated in graphs (a) and (b) of Figure 2.9. Each diagram has the wage rate (W) on the vertical axis and hours of work per week (H) on the horizontal axis (note that H goes from left to right in this graph). Point V in Figures 2.7 and 2.8 indicates that at a wage of W_1 per hour, labor supply is H_1 hours per week. This combination of the wage rate and hours of work is plotted as point V in graphs (a) and (b) of Figure 2.9. If the wage should go up to W_2, what will happen to hours of work? This is a question whose answer can spark debates on appropriate government policies (see Policy Application 2-1). Points X and X' in Figures 2.7 and 2.8 give the answer: in Figure 2.7, hours of work increase to H_2 hours per week, and in Figure 2.8 hours of work decline to per week. In graph (a) of Figure 2.9, plotting point X and then connecting points V and X with a straight line yields the supply curve of labor S_1. (Other points on S_1 can be derived in a similar manner.) In graph (b) of Figure 2.9, plotting point X' and then connecting points V and X' yields the labor supply curve S_2. In the first scenario the supply curve S_1 slopes upward and to the right, indicating that person 1 is willing to work more hours at a higher wage rate. This, in turn, reflects the fact that the substitution effect dominates the income effect. In the second scenario, however, the supply curve S_2 is negatively sloped, indicating that the person works fewer hours at higher wages. This is due to the larger size of the income effect relative to the substitution effect.

Although not shown here, it is possible that the supply curve of labor could contain *both* a positively and a negatively sloped portion. One example is what economists call a **backward-bending supply curve** of labor. A backward-bending supply curve is positively sloped at low wage rates but negatively sloped at high wage rates. The presumption behind a backward-bending supply curve is that at low wages the desire for additional income is so great that the substitution effect will outweigh the income effect; beyond a certain wage rate, however, the person's income is sufficiently high that he or she would react to a still higher wage by buying more leisure and reducing hours of work. For evidence on the existence of a backward-bending supply curve, see Empirical Evidence 2-1.

➲ **See**

Policy Application 2-1:
Supply-Side Economics and Labor Supply, p. 87.

➲ **See**

Empirical Evidence 2-1:
Labor Supply Curves Estimated from Cross-Sectional Data, p. 91.

FIGURE 2.9 | **A POSITIVELY SLOPED AND NEGATIVELY SLOPED LABOR SUPPLY CURVE**

The supply curve of labor may have either a positive or negative slope. In graph (a), a rise in the wage rate from W_1 to W_2 causes an increase in desired work hours from H_1 to H_2. In this graph the substitution effect outweighs the income effect. In graph (b), a rise in the wage rate from W_1 to W_2 causes a decline in desired work hours from H_1 to H_2. In this case the income effect outweighs the substitution effect, causing the supply curve to have a negative slope.

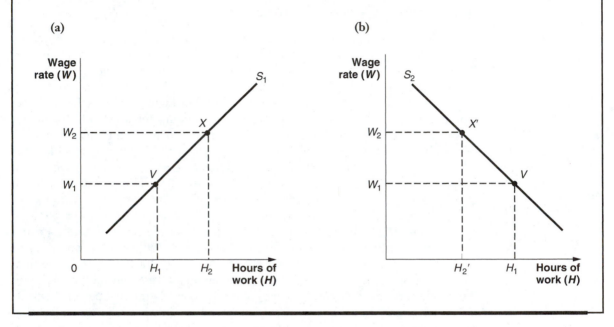

Income Maintenance Programs and Labor Supply

The discussion in a later section of this chapter concerning the labor supply effects of supply-side economics (see Policy Application 2-1) points out one important way in which the concept of income and substitution effects, and the labor/leisure model in general, can be of considerable relevance in analyzing questions of public policy. This section focuses on another application of the labor/leisure model to public policy, the question of how income transfer programs affect hours of work and labor supply.

Types of Income Transfer Programs

One of the fastest-growing components of government expenditures in the past 30 years has been various income transfer or "entitlement" programs. Table 2.1 shows the major income transfer programs in the United States and the public expenditure on each program for 1965, 1985, 1995, and 2002.[8] Expenditures on transfer programs have expanded at a rapid rate, increasing from 4.8 percent of GDP in 1965 to 10.1 percent in 2003.

Income transfer programs fall into two basic groups: **social insurance programs** and **income maintenance programs** (or "welfare" programs). These programs have two basic objectives—to replace income lost from events that are largely outside an individual's control and to assure a minimum level of economic support to those with little other income.

The first objective is largely served by social insurance programs. Under these programs the receipt of benefits is conditioned on the loss of labor market earnings from some identifiable problem, such as old age, illness, disability, or unemployment. To receive benefits, an individual does not have to show financial need; eligibility and level of benefits are tied to the amount of past contributions into the program (as in Social Security). The second objective is served by public assistance or welfare programs. Welfare benefits are not conditioned on contributions into the program, but rather are determined by a demonstration of "need" under the eligibility guidelines. One characteristic of most welfare programs in the United States is that they are *categorical* in nature; that is, to be eligible the individual not only has to fall under the asset and income cutoffs, but also must possess certain characteristics (such as single mother with children, blind, or disabled) that determine which program the individual qualifies for.

With the rapid growth in income transfer programs has come a growing debate on the effects of these programs on such matters as labor supply, savings, and economic growth. One particular income maintenance program, Temporary Assistance for Needy Families (TANF), serves to illustrate some of the issues involved.

TANF: The Successor to AFDC

Aid to Families with Dependent Children (AFDC) originated with the Social Security Act of 1935 and was set up to provide federal grants to states to help families with children who are in need because of the death, incapacitation, or absence of one of their parents. On August 22, 1996, President Clinton signed the Personal Responsibility and Work Opportunity Reconciliation Act of 1996, which, among

---

8   The Social Security Administration compiles the statistics contained in Table 2.1 from many different departments, resulting in a significant lag in current statistics.

Program	Public Expenditures (Billions of Dollars)				
	1965	1985	1995	2002	
Social Insurance					
Social Security (OASDI)	$18.1	$186.2	$331.6	$457.8	
Unemployment Insurance	2.4	18.3	26.3	42.1	
Workers' Compensation	1.2	22.3	43.4	49.4[a]	
Veterans' Pension and Disability Compensation	3.0	14.3	18.0	—	
Railroad Retirement, UI, and Disability	1.1	6.5	8.1	—	
Veterans' and Black Lung Benefits	—	—	—	6.6	
Medicare	—	71.4	164.7	265.7	
Income Maintenance					
Public Assistance	5.9	66.2	187.2	180.2[b]	
Supplemental Security Income (SSI)[c]	2.7	11.8	30.1	34.6	
Food Stamps	0.03	12.5	25.3	18.3	
Total Expenditures	$34.43	$409.5	$834.7	$1,054.7	
US Gross Domestic Product	$719.1	$4,220.3	$7,397.6	$10,487.0	
Expenditures as a Percentage of GDP	4.8%	9.7%	11.3%	10.1%	

[a]2001 data.
[b]Includes TANF, Medicaid, and Home Energy Assistance.
[c]Aid to the Blind, and to the Permanently and Totally Disabled, and Old Age Assistance in 1965.

SOURCE: U.S. Department of Health and Human Services, *Social Security Bulletin, Annual Statistical Supplement, 2003* (Washington, D.C.: Government Printing Office, July 2004); http://www.ssa.gov/policy/docs/statcomps/supplement/2003/#editions.

other things, replaced AFDC with **TANF (Temporary Assistance for Needy Families).** In 2002 $10.1 billion was spent on 2.04 million families (5.1 million persons, about 3.8 million of whom were children). The monthly payment per family averaged $411. The typical TANF family is a single mother with two children; 32 percent of the adult recipients are white.[9] The TANF program is financed jointly by the federal government and the states, with each state determining the specific eligibility criteria and benefit levels.

TANF falls into the category of **block grant** funding, which essentially means that states are given a fixed sum of money based on the *projected* welfare needs of the state, and it is the state's responsibility to use that money to administer their welfare program in the way they see fit.[10] The AFDC program was funded by open-ended federal grants that matched the cash amounts provided by the state to poor children and their caretakers. Unlike AFDC, receipt of welfare through TANF requires that the head of each family be working within two years after cash benefit payments begin. In addition, a five-year lifetime limit on payments is placed on TANF recipients. These requirements are mandated by the federal government as a condition for receiving the block grant funding. Each state may place more stringent work requirements on their cash welfare recipients. For example, as of August 2003, 7 states have lifetime limits on cash welfare benefits shorter than five years and 37 states have work requirements shorter than two years.

TANF and Hours of Work

The benefit payments individuals receive through most social insurance and income maintenance programs are dictated by formulas that alter a person's budget constraint and, thus, are likely to influence that person's labor supply decision.[11] In the context of TANF, the first feature of a state's benefit formula is the **income guarantee (G),** the amount of money per month paid to the family if the family has zero income from work. In 2003 the maximum weekly benefit level for a family with two children and one adult ranged from $164 in Alabama to $923 in Alaska.[12]

The second feature of TANF and other welfare programs is the **level of disregard (D),** which is the amount of income a family can earn without having its benefit reduced. For example, the state of California allows a family to earn $225 dollars per week without having its cash welfare benefit reduced at all; $225 of

---

9   Department of Health and Human Services, *Social Security Bulletin, Annual Statistical Supplement 2003* (Washington, D.C.: Government Printing Office), Table 9.G1.

10 The legislative authority for the TANF block grant program expired in September 2002. Since then the program has been operating under a series of short-term extensions.

11 Also see Alan B. Krueger and Bruce D. Meyer, "Labor Supply Effects of Social Insurance," in *Handbook of Public Economics*, Vol. 4 (London: Elsevier, 2002): 2327–92, for an analysis of Unemployment Insurance and Workman's Compensation programs on labor supply.

12 http://www.stateline.org

earnings is *disregarded* in the calculation of the family's benefit. Until the family's earnings reach the level of disregard, its total income increases by the full amount of the earnings.

The third feature of the TANF program is the existence of an **implicit tax rate** (*t*) on earnings. The idea is that if the family has zero income, then the guarantee provides them with an income floor of $*G*. If a family member should go to work, however, and bring in extra income, then family need is presumably less and the TANF payment is reduced once those earnings surpass the level of disregard. Under AFDC, the family's income guarantee was reduced by $1 for every dollar of earned income. This reduction was in essence an implicit tax on earnings; in this case $t = 1.00$, and the family's *net* income remained the same for every dollar that was earned. Under TANF, each state has complete discretion about the rate at which benefits are reduced for every dollar of earned income. For example, the implicit tax rate for the state of Arizona is 0.30; for every $1 a TANF recipient in Arizona earns, beyond the level of disregard, his or her total income goes up by 70¢.

The fourth feature of TANF is the **break-even point (*BE*)**, the level of earned income for the family where it no longer receives any welfare payment. It can be determined by the formula $BE = D + G/t$. For a family with two children in the state of Michigan, for example, it would be approximately $773.75 = $200 + $459/.8. For every additional dollar the family earned beyond $200 (the level of disregard *D*), the family's guarantee *G* of $459 is reduced by 80¢ for every additional dollar earned until the guarantee *G* has been reduced to zero at an earnings level of $773.75. Beyond the break-even point, the family no longer qualifies for the program and is affected by neither the income guarantee *G*, the level of disregard *D*, nor the tax rate *t*.[13]

Effect of TANF on Labor Supply   Figure 2.10 illustrates the effect of a welfare program such as TANF on the labor supply decision of individual adults. It assumes that the mother, if she works, can earn $6.50 per hour. Her budget constraint, in the absence of a TANF program, is *AB*. If she works zero hours, total income is zero; if she works all 100 hours that are possible per week, her income is $650. Given the budget constraint *AB*, and the individual's preferences for income versus leisure as represented by the indifference curve, I_1, she will choose to work 45 hours per week (point *V*) and will earn $292.50.

With a simplified version of a TANF program in which the disregard level of earnings is zero, the budget constraint becomes *ACDB*. At zero hours of work, total family income is $200 (point *C*), comprising zero labor income and a hypothetical income guarantee of $200 (*G* = $200), in this example. If the TANF program has

---

13   In many income transfer programs, such as Unemployment Insurance, benefit payments are discontinued at some arbitrary level of earnings, which further changes the budget constraint. See Raymond Munts, "Partial Benefit Schedules in Unemployment Insurance: Their Effects on Work Incentives," *Journal of Human Resources* 5 (Spring 1970):160–76, for an example of the marked impact a state's unemployment insurance formula can have on the budget constraint.

FIGURE 2.10   HOURS OF WORK WITH A TANF PROGRAM

Prior to the introduction of a TANF program, the budget constraint is *AB*, and the person chooses to work 45 hours per week (point *V*). With a TANF program, the budget constraint becomes *ACDB*. As a result, equilibrium hours of work fall from 45 to 15 (point *V* to *X*). The income effect from the TANF program causes a reduction in desired work hours from 45 to 30 hours (point *V* to *Z*); the substitution effect causes a further reduction in desired work hours from 30 to 15 (point *Z* to *X*).

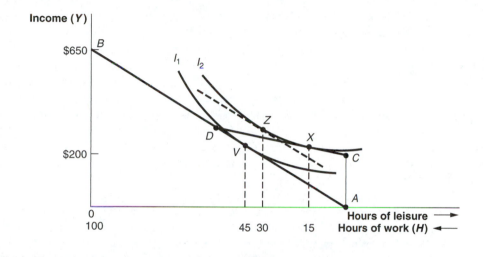

a zero level of disregard ($D = \$0$), meaning that welfare payments are reduced as soon as an adult in the family starts earning money, and if the implicit tax on earnings is .60, one hour of work will increase total family income by a net amount of $2.60 as labor earnings rise by $6.50, but the guarantee (*G*) is reduced by $3.90.[14] The budget constraint between point *C* and the break-even point (point *D*) will have a slope of only -2.6. The break-even point will occur in this example at $333.33 = \$0 + \$200/.6$. Beyond the break-even point of $333.33, the family is no longer on the TANF program, and the budget constraint thus coincides with the original one from point *D* to point *B*.

Given the new budget constraint *ACDB*, the individual maximizes utility at point *X*, where indifference curve I_2 is just tangent to the budget constraint. At point *X*, hours of work have been reduced to 15 per week. The prediction of the theory, then, is that the introduction of an income maintenance program, such as TANF, will cause a net reduction in hours of work among the recipient population.

---

14   A nonzero level of disregard will be illustrated in Chapter 3.

Welfare Reform: Success with Trouble Spots

In 2004 Secretary of Health and Human Welfare Tommy Thompson announced that the nation's welfare rolls had once again declined over the previous year—an event that continued the sharp downward trend initiated by the historic TANF welfare reform legislation of 1996. Thompson noted that since 1996 the welfare rolls have shrunk an amazing 60 percent as the number of people receiving welfare assistance dropped from 12.2 million to 4.4 million. He remarked, "American families are improving their lives by leaving public assistance and entering the workforce. . . .Thanks to welfare reform, millions more children and families are self-sufficient today than they were 8 years ago." A less sanguine assessment was offered in an editorial in the *New York Times,* however. The editors concluded, "If the goal was to get people off the welfare rolls and save the government money in the short run, then the 1996 welfare reform law was a great success. If the goal was to help our fellow citizens out of poverty and toward lives of greater dignity, then it has failed miserably."

The truth appears to be somewhere in the middle, although it seems fair to say that most economists and news analysts rate the welfare reform legislation as an overall success. Yet there also remain a number of worrisome trouble spots.

Under the old AFDC program the number of people receiving welfare payments gradually rose until in the mid-1990s nearly 15 percent of the American families with children were receiving cash assistance. Investigation showed that many of these families, once on the welfare rolls, tended to stay on welfare for an extended time.

The central object of welfare reform was to reverse the upward climb in the welfare rolls, end welfare dependency, and encourage welfare recipients to move to self-supporting and higher paying jobs. In broad outline, all three goals were accomplished.

Evidence reveals, for example, that 40–50 percent of the mothers who left welfare since 1996 are working regularly at full-time jobs. The rate of pay is modest—usually between $6 and $8 dollars an hour—which leaves a family close to the poverty line ($7 an hour times 2,000 hours of work per year yields an income of $14,000, which is roughly the poverty line for a family of three). But other government programs augment the income of these families and in some cases provide additional incentives to work. For example, a single mother with two children earning a poverty level income would be eligible for nearly $4,000 from the Earned Income Tax Credit (money available only if a person is working), up to $2,700 in food stamps, up to $1,200 in subsidized school meals, an average of $2,500 in Medicaid health insurance payments, and various amounts of assistance for child care and transportation. Thus, one analyst concludes, "This combination of earnings and government benefits is not enough for a life of middle-class comfort, but it is much better than being on welfare. And this is probably why the majority of those surveyed invariably say that they are better off after having left welfare."

Based on previous empirical research, one study concluded that AFDC caused recipients to reduce labor supply by an average of 600 hours of work per year.

Income and Substitution Effects   The income and substitution effects set off by the program help explain why an income maintenance program such as TANF

continued

But the picture turns considerably gloomier for two other parts of the welfare population. One of these groups is the 50–60 percent of the former welfare recipients who do not successfully transition to self-supporting gainful employment. Perhaps a third of this group work at part-time jobs, while two-thirds appear to have no employment. Cut off from welfare by the TANF time limits, these people typically have suffered a significant decline in income and benefit payments. One statistic that reflects this trend is that the number of families living in "severe poverty" (a family with an income level less than half the poverty line) has increased by over one-half million in the early 2000's.

The second group comprises the people who remain on welfare, for the maximum time limit, or cycle in and out of welfare, and thus tend to comprise the "hard core" among the poverty population. Most lack a high school education and have few if any job skills or work experience. Although the TANF program has increased spending on job training in order to increase these people's employability, budget pressures have kept the training programs of modest size. In the early 2000's, for example, only about 5 percent of TANF families included an adult receiving education or training. Likewise, the people who remain on welfare often have a variety of other problems and handicaps that make it difficult to transition to gainful employment, such as mental illness, drug dependency, and poor personal work habits and social attitudes. Solving these problems is difficult and expensive and, accordingly, not much addressed in the welfare reform legis-

lation. According to one news analyst, women in this category are "trapped in lives of gloom" and rather than successfully transition out of poverty through regular paying work more often sink into a deeper pit of homelessness, drug use, dependency on abusive and exploitative boy friends, and deteriorating health.

Overall, welfare reform legislation—in combination with other government programs and a strong economy in the 1990s—has been notably successful in substantially reducing the proportion of American families on welfare. A significant portion of the women and children who have left welfare have been net gainers with a modest increase in living standards and economic independence. Another sizable segment, however, has not made a successful transition to regular paid work and in many cases are marginally or substantially worse off. The size of the latter group has increased noticeably since 2000 because of the abrupt end of the strong labor market of the 1990s— witnessed by a steady upward creep in the number of families in poverty between 2000 and 2004. Thus, while welfare reform has so far been an overall success its gains and future prospects would be substantially improved by the return of a strong job market.

Sources: "Secretary Thompson Announces TANF Caseloads Declined in 2003," *Regulatory Intelligence Database* (August 23, 2004), p. 1; "Are Those Leaving Welfare Better Off Now?: Yes and No," *New York Times* (October 20, 2003), p. 1; Douglas Besharov, "The Past and Future of Welfare Reform," *The Public Interest* (Winter, 2003), pp. 4–22; "Welfare Reform Failure," *New York Times* (September 18, 2002), p. 30.

reduces labor supply. In Figure 2.10, the observed change in hours of work due to the TANF program is from point V on indifference curve I_1 to point X on indifference curve I_2. To determine the income effect, income for the individual is increased just enough to reach the higher indifference curve I_2, but the wage rate is kept constant. This is represented as a parallel shift of the original budget constraint AB to the broken line just tangent to I_2 at point Z. At point Z, hours of work have been reduced from 45 to 30 hours per week, which represents the income effect stemming from the addition of nonlabor income in the form of the income guarantee payment of $\$G$.

The TANF program also gives rise to a substitution effect. Because of the implicit tax rate t, the net hourly wage is reduced from $\$6.50$ to $\$2.60$ per hour under the program, reducing the price of leisure and leading the individual to substitute leisure for work. This substitution effect is represented by keeping the individual on indifference curve I_2 but rotating the budget constraint from a slope of -6.5 to a slope of -2.6. The resulting change in hours of work from point Z (30 hours) to point X (15 hours) represents the substitution effect.

Under an income maintenance program, *both* the income and the substitution effects lead to a reduction in hours of work. The income effect on hours of work arises from the addition of extra nonlabor income in the form of the income guarantee G. Assuming leisure is a normal good, additional income motivates the individual to consume more leisure and work less. This negative income effect on hours of work is reinforced by a further reduction in hours worked due to the substitution effect. Because of the implicit tax rate under the TANF program, the take-home wage from an hour of work is reduced by 60 percent. Since each hour of leisure now has a lower opportunity cost, the individual is motivated to substitute from work towards more leisure, further reducing total hours of work.

Issues in Welfare Reform

Three general goals are associated with any welfare program: income provision, work incentives, and cost minimization. First, to the extent that protecting people from the indignities of poverty is a social goal, the welfare program should provide a relatively high income floor or guarantee. Second, if encouraging people to find work and be self-supporting is also a social goal, the program should have a relatively low implicit tax rate t so as not to penalize the rewards from work. Third, it is also likely to be a social goal that the costs of the program be held to "reasonable" levels.

The fundamental dilemma facing policymakers is that the three goals are impossible to achieve simultaneously. Achieving the first two goals expands the cost of the program dramatically, as both the sizes of payments and the number of people eligible for payments increase. On the other hand, holding down costs of the welfare program requires either an income guarantee so low it may not provide a minimum standard of living, or a tax rate high enough to remove any incentive on the part of recipients to find work.

The Personal Responsibility and Work Opportunity Reconciliation Act of 1996 is an attempt to compromise on the satisfaction of these three goals. Theory and empirical evidence have shown that AFDC recipients were not inclined to work; between 1965 and 1987 the percent of AFDC recipients who worked *at all* never exceeded 18 percent. In addition, research shows that the labor supply behavior of welfare recipients is very insensitive to changes in benefit formula parameters. For example, experiments show that lower values of the implicit tax rate *t* do not encourage much of an increase in the supply of labor.[15] The 1996 welfare reform was the culmination of a sentiment that what welfare recipients needed was some "tough love." Policymakers believed that AFDC had created a segment of society dependent on public welfare, and while they wanted to make sure that the safety net is available for those who need it, a genuine work effort should be required for the receipt of such assistance. Early results from welfare reform anlaysis shows a dramatic drop in welfare recipients since 1993. Caseloads declined 21 percent in Hawaii to 94 percent in Wyoming between 1993 and 2000. Most research, however, has attributed the bulk of this dramatic decline to the strength of the economy over this time period.[16]

Qualifications to the Labor/Leisure Model

The neoclassical theory of the labor/leisure choice developed in the preceding sections is relatively simple, yet it provides a number of important insights regarding the determinants of labor supply. In some respects, however, the assumptions of the labor/leisure model do not always accord with actual conditions facing individual workers in the labor market. In particular, three important assumptions of the model are frequently violated in the real world. The first has to do with fixed work schedules mandated by employers. The second concerns the existence of time and money costs of working. The third, discussed in an appendix to this chapter, concerns employees who are paid a lump-sum salary rather than a wage per hour.

Employer-Mandated Work Schedules

The labor/leisure model emphasizes the role of individual choice as the major determinant of work hours. The data presented in Figure 2.1 suggest that other factors are also important. While there is a great diversity in hours of work among individuals, the single greatest percentage of workers just happened to "choose" 40 hours per week as their work schedule. How is it that 40 hours per week is so popular?

---

15 A review of much of this literature can be found in Robert Moffitt, "Incentive Effects of the U.S. Welfare System: A Review," *Journal of Economic Literature* 30 (March 1992): 1–61.

16 See, for example, Julie L. Hotchkiss, Peter Mueser, and Christopher King, "Determinants of Welfare Exits and Employment," in King and Mueser, Ed. *Welfare Reform in Six Metropolitan Areas* (Kalamazoo, Mich: W.E. Upjohn Institute for Employment Research, 2005); and Rebecca M. Blank, "Evaluating Welfare Reform in the United States," *Journal of Economic Literature* 40 (December 2002): 1105–66.

The answer has to do with employer preferences and *fixed work schedules*.[17] A common feature of the majority of jobs in the labor market is that the employers set the hours of work, with respect to both the starting and ending times each day and the total number of hours each week. Only 29 percent of full-time workers in 2001 had some flexibility about when they started or stopped work.[18] For the majority of full-time jobs, however, 40 hours per week is the standard workweek set by employers. This standard reflects the influence of such things as the necessity of paying overtime for work over 40 hours per week and the fact that continuous-process industries such as steel or chemicals can divide the workweek into three 8-hour-per-day shifts.[19]

Employer-set work schedules represent an institutional constraint on individual choice that may prevent some workers from reaching their most preferred combination of hours of work and leisure. This situation is illustrated in Figure 2.11. The budget constraint is AB, assuming a wage rate of W_1 per hour. Also shown are two indifference curves, I_A for person A, and I_B for person B. If free to choose his or her optimal work schedule, person A would choose 50 hours per week (point V), and person B would choose 30 hours per week (point X). What if each person's employer requires a workweek of 40 hours? This combination of income and hours of work is shown as point Z.[20] The effect of the fixed 40-hour-per-week work schedule is to reduce the level of utility for both persons below what they could have obtained if left free to choose—point Z is on a lower indifference curve for both individuals (neither of these indifference curves is drawn in). Individual A is made worse off because he or she desires to work longer hours and would willingly sacrifice 10 more hours of leisure to obtain the additional income.[21] Person B is also made worse off, but for the opposite reason, since he or she would gladly sacrifice some income to have 10 more hours of leisure.

In this situation both individuals have several courses of action open to them. One option is to find a new occupation that allows flexibility in working hours. A person who feels dissatisfied with the rigid 9-to-5 schedule of an office job for example, can quit and enter a different line of work such as sales or self-employment

17 Yoram Weiss, "Synchronization of Work Schedules," *International Economic Review* 37 (February 1996): 157–79, offers a theoretical alternative for observing a clumping of hours derived from *worker* preferences, based on psychological considerations of daily cycles and networking externalities. Also see John P. Robinson, et al. "Measuring the Complexity of Hours at Work: the Weekly Work Grid," *Monthly Labor Review* 125 (April 2002): 44–54, for an alternative, more accurate, way to determine hours spent at work, rather than just asking for a worker to recall those details.

18 "Workers on Flexible and Shift Schedules in 2001," *BLS News Release* USDL 02-225 (18 April 2002).

19 Competing explanations for observing hours constraints are explored in Shulamit B. Kahn and Kevin Lang, "The Cause of Hours Constraints: Evidence from Canada," *Canadian Journal of Economics* 28 (November 1995): 914–28.

20 With an employer-mandated work schedule of 40 hours per week, the budget constraint in Figure 2.11 degenerates from AB to two points, point Z and point A.

21 An international comparison finds that hours constraints vary considerably across countries. In all countries, however, the proportion of workers wanting to work more hours exceeded the proportion wanting to work fewer hours. See Alfonso Sousa-Poza and Fred Henneberer, "Work Attitudes, Work Conditions and Hours Constraints: An Explorative Cross-National Analysis," *Labour* 14 (September 2001): 351–72.

FIGURE 2.11   FIXED WORK SCHEDULES AND DESIRED HOURS OF WORK

If left free to choose, person *A* would maximize utility by working 50 hours (point *V*), and person *B* would maximize utility by working 30 hours (point *X*). Should the employer require a fixed work schedule of 40 hours (point *Z*), however, both persons suffer a decline in utility since point *Z* is on a lower

indifference curve for each. Note that the indifference curves I_A and I_B represent the preferences of two different people and, thus, it is possible for the two curves to intersect, whereas indifference curves for one individual never cross each other.

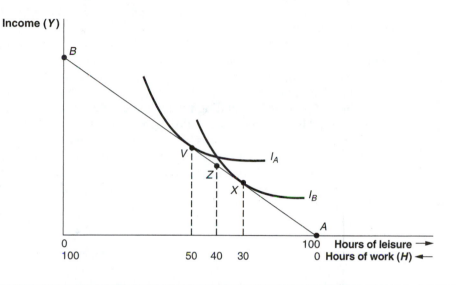

where there is the freedom to set one's own hours. Many people cannot switch to an entirely new occupation, but they do have a second option—to quit their present employer and search for another firm that does provide the desired work schedule.[22] In certain fields with large numbers of alternative employers and types of work that do not require rigid production shifts this is a viable option. Examples are dental hygienist, store clerk, bookkeeper, and carpenter. Flexible hours are particularly important for working women with children, helping to explain why women are concentrated in certain occupations, such as the first three listed above.

While labor mobility offers a solution to rigid work schedules for many workers, there are also a large number who cannot easily change employers, either because similar jobs with the desired work schedules are not available at other firms

---

[22]   One arrangement popular with many working mothers is called job sharing, where two workers coordinate their hours to make up one full-time job. See Maria Mallory, "Job Share: It's a Creative Plan to Keep Workers Who Want More Balanced Lives," *Atlanta Journal and Constitution*, 3 September 2000: R1. Rene Boheim and Mark P. Taylor, "Actual and Preferred Working Hours," *British Journal of Industrial Relations* 42 (March 2004): 149–66, find that movement between employers greatly facilitates the alignment of preferred and actual working hours.

in the area, or because factors such as seniority or pension rights inhibit mobility. In this case, the constraints on choice in the labor market confine workers, at least in the short run, to a disequilibrium situation. In the long run, however, this situation may be alleviated if the dissatisfaction with existing work schedules is strong enough and is felt by a sufficient number of people. In that case, a firm would find that it could increase its profits by changing from the 40-hour work schedule, since the dissatisfied workers would presumably be willing to work for somewhat lower wages in order to gain their desired hours of work.

A third option that is available at least to individual A (the underemployed worker) is to *moonlight* by taking on a second job. Although the primary employer may provide only 40 hours of work per week, a 10-hour part-time job during the weekend or before or after regular hours would allow person A to reach the desired income/hours of work position (point V). In 2003, 7.1 million wage and salary workers, 52 percent of whom were men, held multiple jobs.[23]

Moonlighting has several drawbacks, however, that may limit its use by some workers. One drawback is that the second part-time job frequently pays less than the primary job, in effect rotating the budget constraint to the left after point Z in Figure 2.11. The option of moonlighting may, therefore, overcome part of the disequilibrium caused by fixed hours of work, but it still may not allow the worker to completely reach the most preferred income/hours of work combination. Another drawback is that the additional commuting costs and irregular hours of the second job may make it much less preferable to the alternative of additional hours on the primary job.

The option of moonlighting is not relevant for individual B, whose problem is having to work more hours than he or she wants to.[24] If there are no alternative employers offering work schedules with fewer hours, is there a way for the overemployed worker to obtain the preferred hours of work? One answer is deliberate tardiness or absenteeism on the worker's part. Although the employer in Figure 2.11 mandates a 40-hour workweek, by calling in sick or coming to work late person B can still reduce hours of work toward the desired level at point X. Such a course of action is not free of cost for the employee, who risks disciplinary action including loss of the job. Absenteeism also imposes clear-cut costs on the firm due to lost production and inflated labor cost. Should the cost of absenteeism become sufficiently large, the firm will be motivated by its desire to maximize profits to change its work schedule to meet more closely the preferences of its employees.

---

23   http://www.bls.gov/cps/home.htm. Using longitudinal data, Christina H. Paxson and Nachum Sicherman, "The Dynamics of Dual Job Holding and Job Mobility," *Journal of Labor Economics* 14 (July 1996): 357–93, find that moonlighting is primarily a response to hours constraints on the main job and that over 50 percent of working men moonlight at some point in their careers. Jean Kimmel and Karen Smith Conway, "Who Moonlights and Why," *Industrial Relations* 40 (January 2001): 89–120, come to the same conclusion that hours constraints play an important role in the decision to moonlight. Linda Bell, "Differences in Work Hours and Hours Preferences by Race in the U.S.," *Review of Social Economy* 56 (Winter 1998): 481–500, finds that black workers are less likely to be satisfied with their hours of work than white workers. Also see Susan Averett, "Moonlighting: Multiple Motives and Gender Differences," *Applied Economics* 33 (September 2001): 1391–1410.

24   Workers have lamented for years the difficulties of finding meaningful careers with part-time hours. See "Employees Are Seeking Fewer Hours; Maybe Bosses Should Listen," *Wall Street Journal* (21 February 2001): B1.

Work Hour Differences between the United States and Europe: Economic, Legal, or Cultural Explanations?

According to recent data published by the International Labour Organization, in 2002 the average American worked 1,815 hours per year while in France average annual work hours were 1,545 and in Germany an even lower 1,444. The difference between the United States and Germany is 371 hours per year, which when evaluated against the standard 40-hour workweek in America means the Germans work more than 9 weeks less than the Americans!

Analyzed in terms of the labor-leisure model, this substantial difference in labor supply between the United States and Europe arises from either (or a combination of) differences in preferences (indifference curves), relative prices (budget constraints), or legal mandates (restrictions on the size of the opportunity set).

Some articles in the press attribute these work hour differences to cultural and lifestyle differences between the two groups of people—factors economists would consider part of "tastes." A frequently quoted expression, for example, is "Americans live to work and Europeans work to live," while one American magazine article declared "We value more money and more stuff; they value more leisure time." Echoing this second quotation, European critics say that Americans are caught up in a rat race fueled by excessive materialism and consumerism, whereas American critics say that the Europeans are addicted to *la dolce vita*—the Italian expression for "the sweet life," the notion that life is meant to be enjoyed and not endured.

A second possible explanation for these large work hour differences is the influence of national laws and collective bargaining agreements. In France, for example, national law mandates a 35-hour workweek and a minimum of 5 weeks of paid vacation for all full-time employees. Similarly, in Germany the major unions have negotiated a 35-workweek, and German law gives employees extended holidays for a host of religious events related to feast days and the birth of various saints. In the United States, by comparison, the standard work week is 40 hours, American labor law does not mandate any minimum vacation time, and union coverage is much smaller and very few contracts call for less than 40 hours of standard work.

A third possible explanation is economic. In particular, the large difference in work hours may reflect substantial differences in the relative price of leisure or, conversely, the relative reward that workers in the United States and Europe receive for working an extra hour. One prime factor in this regard, argue some economists, is differences in tax rates. According to one estimate, the effective tax rate on an extra dollar of earnings from work in France and Germany is 59 percent, while it is only 40 percent in the United States. Italy is even higher at 64 percent. Thus, a person in Europe gets to keep (approximately) only forty cents of every dollar earned from work, while the average American gets to keep sixty cents. Given these differences in incentives, not unexpectedly Americans choose to work more than the Europeans.

Sorting out the relative importance of the three explanatory factors is very difficult. The fact that most European governments have decided in recent years to reduce marginal income tax rates suggests, however, that they think incentives are certainly a significant part of the story.

Sources: "European Vacation," Federal Reserve Bank of Minneapolis, *The Region* (December, 2003): 1–9; "Give This Policy the Guillotine," *Business Week* (October 27, 2003): 58; "Europe's Shorter Work Hours," *Monthly Labor Review* (February, 2004): 106; "Vacation Laws and Annual Work Hours," Federal Reserve Bank of Chicago *Economic Perspectives* (Third Quarter, 2003): 2–18.

A final option is available to workers who are either overemployed or underemployed because of fixed work schedules. Rather than individually searching elsewhere for a firm with a more desirable work schedule, workers could collectively join together at their present place of work and form a union. Through the threat of a strike they could induce the firm to change the work schedule toward that preferred by the workers.

How serious a problem are fixed work schedules? One survey finds that 18 percent of workers are required to work overtime when they would rather not.[25] Another survey found that rigid work schedules are a much larger constraint on women's work hours than men's, since women are more likely to prefer a part-time job and there are not enough such jobs available in the labor market.[26] The 2002 National Study of the Changing Workforce confirms that workers with more control over their work schedule have much greater overall life satisfaction.[27] The same study shows that the ability of workers to exercise some control over their work schedule has grown over the past 10 years. In 1992, 44 percent of workers said they had very little or no control; this percent dropped to 39 percent in 2002. Over the same time period, the percentage of workers with complete or a considerable amount of control grew from 30 percent to 36 percent.

To respond to these demands, companies have tried several innovations. One is a system of "flextime," giving employees a range of hours from, for example, 7:00 a.m. to 9:00 a.m. when they can report for work, and a similar range when they can leave work. Another tactic, tried by firms in the chemical and petroleum industries, is to provide workers with bigger *blocks* of leisure time by switching from 8-hour shifts to 12-hour shifts.[28] These longer shifts allow 3 to 4 days off from work at one time, rather than the typical 2-day weekend. Some firms are also experimenting with job-sharing—splitting one full-time job among two part-time workers.

Time and Money Costs of Working

The labor/leisure model assumes that every hour not spent consuming leisure translates into an income-generating work activity. In reality, a decision to work 40 hours per week, for example, likely means that leisure is reduced by more than 40 hours; it takes time to get to and from work. In addition, total income does not likely increase by the full amount of 40 hours times the hourly wage rate; the worker incurs some monetary costs associated with working, such as hourly child care costs and/or monthly parking fees. These time and monetary costs associated

---

25 See Lonnie Golden and Helene Jorgensen, "Time after Time: Mandatory Overtime in the U.S. Economy," *Economic Policy Institute Briefing Paper* (January 2002).

26 Marin Clarkberg and Phyllis Moen, "The Time Squeeze: Married Couples' Work-Hour Patterns and Preferences," *Proceedings of the 51st Annual Meeting, Vol.1.* Madison: Industrial Relations Research Association: 15–23.

27 James T. Bond, et al., *Highlights of the National Study of the Changing Workforce* (New York: Families and Work Institute, 2003).

28 See Herbert Northrup, James Wilson, and Karen Rose, "The Twelve-Hour Shift in the Petroleum and Chemical Industries," *Industrial and Labor Relations Review* 32, no. 3 (April 1979): 312–26.

FIGURE 2.12   COSTS OF WORKING AND DESIRED HOURS OF WORK

A person's desired hours is affected by the presence of time and/or monetary costs of working. Graph (a) shows that time cost reduces the amount of time available to work; both leisure time and hours of work may decline. Graph (b) shows that fixed monetary costs will act as a decrease in income, increasing desired hours if the person continues working. Graph (c) shows that variable monetary costs will act as a decrease in the wage; change in desired hours will be determined through both an income and a substitution effect.

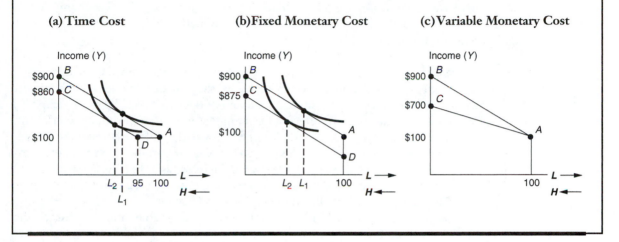

(a) Time Cost   **(b) Fixed Monetary Cost**   **(c) Variable Monetary Cost**

with working affect the shape of the budget constraint, thus influencing the number of hours a person chooses to work.[29]

Fixed Time Costs   In the absence of any costs of working, and given a wage rate of $8 per hour, the budget constraint in Figure 2.12 would be the line *AB*. If it takes someone 30 minutes to get to work, the total amount of time available for working is reduced to 95 hours per week (one hour of commuting per day, for five days).[30] This is illustrated in graph (a) of Figure 2.12. The introduction of this time cost of working may either increase or decrease hours of work. For individuals who keep working, the increase in fixed time costs has essentially the same effect as shifting the budget constraint downward, in much the same way as if the

---

29 Early work determining the impact of costs of working on desired hours was done by John F. Cogan, "Fixed Costs and Labor Supply," *Econometrica* 49, no. 4 (June 1981): 945–63. More recently Bradley T. Heim and Bruce D. Meyer, "Work Costs and Nonconvex Preferences in the Estimation of Labor Supply Models," *Journal of Public Economics* 88 (September 2004): 2323–38, explore the empirical implications of ignoring work costs in labor supply estimations for policy analysis.

30 Average time spent commuting to work was roughly 19 minutes per day in 2001. See "Highlights of the 2001 National Household Travel Survey," http://www.bts.gov; average commute times were obtained from the help center (answers@bts.gov).

individual had experienced a reduction in nonlabor income. While this downward shift in the budget constraint will reduce the demand for leisure (through the income effect), it will not necessarily translate into an increase in hours of work. If the difference between L_2 and L_1, in graph (a) of Figure 2.12, is less than 5 hours, then actual hours have decreased ($95 - L_2$ is smaller than $100 - L_1$); if the difference between L_2 and L_1 is greater than 5 hours, then work hours have increased for this person.[31] The complication in evaluating the labor supply response of the introduction of time costs comes for those people who desire to work just a few hours per week. For example, if someone really only wants to work just 5 hours per week (one hour per day for five days per week) and faces a 30-minute commute to the job, the decision to work 5 hours results in a 10-hour reduction in leisure time.

Monetary Costs   Monetary costs can either be fixed (a lump-sum cost incurred each time one goes to work, such as a parking fee) or they can be variable (a per-hour cost whose total increases with the number of hours worked, such as child care). Graph (b) of Figure 2.12 illustrates the effect of fixed monetary costs on the budget constraint. If this person faces a weekly fixed cost of $25 for parking, for example, the budget constraint becomes line *ADC*. If this person chooses to continue working in the presence of this fixed monetary cost, he or she will increase his or her chosen work hours; the budget constraint has shifted down, resulting in an income effect. [The person may choose not to work at all, a topic explored in Chapter 3.]

Graph (c) of Figure 2.12 illustrates the effect of a variable monetary cost on the budget constraint. If this person faces a $2-per-hour fee for child care, his or her income increases by only $6 for every hour worked; for every hour worked income goes up by the $8 market wage minus the $2 that has to be spent on child care. Since the introduction of variable costs of working essentially has the effect of reducing the person's net wage, desired hours will either increase or decrease, depending on whether the income or the substitution effect is strongest.

The effect of the costs of working can be important in the evaluation of the impact of certain social policies. For example, the federal tax credit for child-care expenses reduces the variable monetary costs of working, and has been shown to substantially increase the desired hours of working women.[32] The decision to

---

31   For a sample of working women from four U.S. metropolitan areas, a 5-minute reduction in one-way commute time (which amounts to a 22 percent reduction in the average commute time for workers in the sample) was estimated to increase work hours by an average of 9.6 percent (or an average increase of almost 3 hours per week). For details of the study see Mark Alan Thompson, "The Impact of Spatial Mismatch on Female Labor Supply," Ph.D. dissertation, Georgia State University, 1994.

32   See Susan L. Averett, Elizabeth H. Peters, and Donald M. Waldman, "Tax Credits, Labor Supply, and Child Care," *Review of Economics and Statistics* 79, no. 1 (February 1997): 125–35. In addition, David Blau and Erdal Tekin, "The Determinants and Consequences of Child Care Subsidies for Single Mothers," *NBER Working Paper No. 9665* (2003), find evidence of a positive impact of employment of child care subsidies. Patricia Anderson and Phillip Levine, "Child Care and Mothers' Employment Decisions," in David E. Card and Rebecca M. Blank, eds. *Finding Jobs: Work and Welfare Reform* (New York: Russell Sage, 2000): 420–62, find that low-skilled workers' labor supply is more sensitive to the costs of child care.

construct a high-speed mass transit system may in part take into consideration the impact of reducing time costs on desired hours of workers.[33] Even simply raising the gasoline tax (which increases the fixed monetary costs of working for those who drive to work) might be expected to have an impact on desired hours.

Employers might also consider adopting certain employment policies that would impact their workers' desired hours. For example, providing subsidized child care would reduce the variable monetary costs of working; subsidizing an in-house cafeteria would reduce fixed monetary costs of working; and providing an in-house exercise facility would ease the conflict between work and leisure hours, freeing up more time available to work.[34]

The Time-Series Pattern of Hours of Work

Figure 2.1 shows that average hours of paid work in the United States have declined substantially over the twentieth century, from approximately 53 hours per week in 1900 to slightly under 40 hours per week in 2003. The labor/leisure model provides a consistent explanation for the cross-sectional pattern in hours of work. Can the same be done for the time-series pattern?

In general the answer is yes, although with a few qualifications. The application of the labor/leisure model to the **time-series** pattern of hours of work is relatively straightforward.[35] Figure 2.13 shows the budget constraint facing the average working person in 1900 as *AB*, the slope of which reflects the real wage rate earned per hour of work in 1900. Individuals in 1900 also had certain preferences regarding income versus leisure, represented by the indifference curves I_1 and I_2. Given the budget constraint and the indifference curves, the equilibrium hours of work in 1900 for the average working person would be 53 hours, where the budget constraint *AB* is just tangent to the indifference curve I_1 at point *V*.

Between 1900 and 2003 the average level of real wages in the economy increased by more than 700 percent, causing the budget constraint to rotate sharply to the right, from *AB* to *AC*. Assuming people in 2003 had the same general preferences for income versus leisure as in 1900 (admittedly a big assumption), and thus

---

33   See Joseph S. DeSalvo and Mobinul Huq, "Income, Residential Location, and Mode Choice," *Journal of Urban Economics* 40, no. 1 (July 1996): 84–99.

34   In addition to benefiting employees, one firm estimated they save $3 (in lower absenteeism, in lower medical claims, and in increased productivity) for every $1 spent on maintaining their in-house exercise facility. See Nicole Wise, "Employers See Benefits in Workplace Workouts," *New York Times*, CN1 (12 May 1991). Among the least conventional ideas about how to ease work and leisure conflicts is to provide workers nap time. A survey conducted by NASA found that an average 26-minute nap improved the performance of airline pilots by 34 percent and improved their alertness by 54 percent. Another study found that 60–90 minutes of rapid-eye movement sleep improved visual learning by as much as six hours of sleep. See Jared Sandberg, "As Bosses Power Nap, Cubicle Dwellers Doze Under Clever Disguise," *Wall Street Journal* (23 July 2003): B1.

35   See H. G. Lewis, "Hours of Work and Hours of Leisure," *Proceedings of the Ninth Annual Meeting* (Madison, Wis.: Industrial Relations Research Association, 1956): 196–206.

FIGURE 2.13   THE LONG-TERM DECLINE IN HOURS OF WORK

The figure for equilibrium hours of work in 1900 was 53 per week (point V). The rise in real wages between 1900 and 2003 is represented by the rotation of the budget constraint from AB to AC. Given the indifference curve I_2, hours of work per week in 2003, fall to 39 (point X), suggesting that the income effect engendered by the rise in wages outweighed the substitution effect. The amount of income given up to purchase extra leisure is $Y_3 - Y_2$.

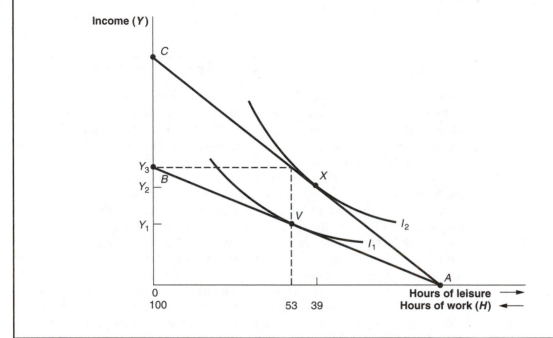

the same set of indifference curves, the new equilibrium level of hours of work would occur where the budget constraint AC is tangent to the indifference curve I_2 at point X. As a result of the rise in real wages, hours of work per week fall from 53 to 40, but weekly income rises from Y_1 to Y_2.

The increase in real wages over time will cause both an income effect and a substitution effect; the income effect from higher wages leading to a reduction in hours of work, and the substitution effect leading to an increase in hours of work. Since hours of work have declined substantially in the past 100 years, the inference is that for the average person, the income effect has dominated the substitution effect as people have, on balance, used part of their higher income to purchase more leisure as well as more market goods. The exact amount of income forgone to buy additional time off from work is readily identifiable in Figure 2.13. If workers in 2003 continued to work 53 hours per week, weekly income would have been Y_3; the difference of $Y_3 - Y_2$, therefore, represents the amount of goods and services sacrificed to obtain additional leisure. One study estimated $Y_3 - Y_2$ to be 15 percent of the growth in potential income per person.

This time-series conclusion dovetails with the empirical evidence found in cross-sectional studies. Cross-sectional studies have found that the labor supply curve for men is negatively sloped as the income effect from higher wages dominates the substitution effect. Since men have historically been the largest group in the labor force, the decline in hours of work in the past 100 years suggests that over time the income effect for males has also been stronger than the substitution effect, a result entirely consistent with the cross-sectional evidence.

While the labor/leisure model thus provides a consistent and appealing explanation for the long-term decline in hours of work, three important questions remain about this process. The first concerns the mechanism by which preferences for greater leisure have actually been translated into shorter working hours; the second issue concerns the sharp difference between the reduction of work hours prior to World War II and that which has taken place since; the third issue concerns the observed rise in work hours since the early 1980s.

The Process of Hours Reduction

As real wages have increased over time, the labor/leisure model suggests that people have chosen to take part of this gain in income in the form of additional leisure. How has this preference for additional leisure been realized? This question again involves the institutional constraint placed on individual choice by employers' fixed work schedules.

At the turn of the century, the working day was frequently 9 or 10 hours; in the steel industry a 12-hour day was standard. While workers may desire shorter working hours, employers—then and now—typically resist a reduction in working hours because it typically raises costs as capital is less efficiently utilized, hiring costs are increased and, frequently, the demand for shorter hours is accompanied by a demand for higher wages in order to maintain the same level of weekly income. What force or forces induced employers to reduce the workweek from 53 hours in 1900 to 40 or so in 2003?

The Role of Market Forces One answer is the market forces of demand and supply. Economic theory suggests that employers will continue to require long working hours as long as the monetary benefits from doing so exceed the costs. Maintaining longer work schedules than desired by employees will, however, raise costs for firms in several ways. First, employees who remain with the firm will likely be less productive because of factors such as low morale, increased fatigue, and greater absenteeism.[36] Second, the process of labor mobility will penalize firms with longer-than-desired work hours since workers will quit those firms and seek work elsewhere, making it necessary for these firms to pay higher wages to attract

---

36   In 2003, 3.3 percent of all workers were absent from their jobs during an average week http://www.bls.gov/cps.

a sufficient supply of labor. In this way, if the outcome dictated by institutional forces (employer preferences) diverges too far from that desired by individual workers, market forces are set in motion that raise costs to employers until they find it serves their own self-interest to reduce hours of work.[37]

There is historical evidence that part of the long-term decline in hours of work is a result of this process. The 8 percent reduction in hours of work achieved during the labor shortages of the World War I period is one example. Other historical examples indicate, however, that the competitive pressures caused by individual labor mobility were not strong enough to overcome the institutional power of employers. One such case is the steel industry, which adopted the 8-hour day in 1924 only after massive strikes, public boycotts, and the personal intervention of President Harding.[38]

The Role of Institutional Forces   Market forces are effective in inducing employers to cut hours of work only during periods of near full employment, because only then are firms' costs of production threatened by inability to attract workers. During periods of significant unemployment, however, the shortage of available work leads workers to prefer a job with longer-than-desired hours to no job at all, short-circuiting the competitive pressure on the employer to reduce hours of work. In these situations, the preference of workers for shorter hours has been expressed in a *collective* form through the countervailing institutional force of union bargaining demands and government legislation.

A collective decision to say no to long hours of work (that is, to strike) may raise costs sufficiently that the employer finds it more profitable to avoid the strike and reduce hours of work. While the proportion of the work force that was unionized remained relatively small (about 10 percent) up to the mid-1930s, historical evidence suggests that unions had a significant effect in reducing hours of work in the industries that they organized as well as among unorganized employers through the threat of unionization.[39] Likewise, paid holidays and vacations were first won in unionized industries in the 1940s and then later adopted by nonunion employers. In the postwar period, unions have continued to push for shorter hours, primarily as a means to create additional jobs.[40]

---

[37]   Some evidence has been provided that workers can become more productive when they are allowed to work fewer hours per week or have some flexibility in their work arrangements. See Amy Saltzman, "When Less Is More," *U.S. News and World Report* (27 October 1997): 79; Karen Hohl, "The Effects of Flexible Work Arrangements," *Nonprofit Management and Leadership* 7 (Fall 1996): 69–86; and Organization for Economic Co-operation and Development, *OECD Employment Outlook: Towards More and Better Jobs*, (Paris: OECD, 2003).

[38]   Marion Cahill, *Shorter Hours* (New York: Columbia University Press, 1932): 206–16.

[39]   See Paul Douglas, *Real Wages in the United States, 1890–1926* (Boston: Houghton Mifflin, 1930), 112–18, and Richard L. Rowan, "The Influence of Collective Bargaining on Hours," in Clyde Dankert et al., eds., *Hours of Work* (New York: Harper and Row, 1965), 17–35.

[40]   Sar Levitan and Richard Belous, *Shorter Hours, Shorter Weeks: Spreading the Work to Reduce Unemployment* (Baltimore: Johns Hopkins University Press, 1977). Also see Jennifer Hunt, "Hours Reductions as Work-sharing," *Brookings Papers on Economic Activity* 0(1) (1998): 338–69; and Matthieu Bunel and Stephane Jugnot, "35 Heures: Evaluations de l'effet emploi," *Revue Economique* 54 (May 2003): 596–606.

A second institutional force leading to a reduction in hours of work has been government legislation.[41] Government legislation, like union bargaining demands, represents a collective expression of preferences for shorter hours of work. Rather than through the strike threat, however, government legislation induces employers to reduce hours in two ways. It can require under penalty of law that hours of work shall not exceed a certain number. This approach was used in 1912 in the Eight Hours Act, which required the 8-hour day in government contract work. Legislation can also raise the cost of long work schedules through such requirements as overtime pay. This approach was used in the **Fair Labor Standards Act (FLSA)** passed in 1938. The FLSA is the most important piece of protective labor legislation in the United States, establishing for the first time nationwide overtime and minimum wage standards. The FLSA requires that employers pay a worker covered under the act one and one-half times the employee's base wage rate for all hours worked over 40 per week.

These three factors, one economic and two institutional, have in combination brought about the long-term decline in hours of work. Most economists would give primary emphasis to market forces as the major impetus inducing employers to reduce hours of work, although unions and government legislation have also played a role.

The Slower Decline of Work Hours in the Postwar Period

The second issue concerning the long-term decline in the workweek that deserves closer examination is that hours of work declined more slowly in the post-World War II period than earlier in the century and have actually risen slightly since the early 1980s. Between 1900 and 1940, for example, the workweek was reduced by about 10 hours; from 1950 to 2001, hours of work declined by only another 4 hours. It has been argued that even this 4-hour decline in the reported workweek is largely a statistical artifact due to the growing number of part-time and female workers in the labor force, a fact which by itself would result in a long-term decline in the reported average hours of work. As an example of this downward bias, John Owen found that when work hours of only nonstudent males were considered, the workweek changed little over the post-1945 period, from 42.7 hours in 1948 to 42.8 hours in 1986.[42]

How can this divergent pattern in hours of work be reconciled? If rising real wages led to a decrease in the workweek prior to World War II, why hasn't this same trend continued in the postwar years? There are several possible explanations.

---

41 F. Ray Marshall, "The Influence of Legislation on Hours," in Dankert et al., eds., *Hours of Work*, 36–53, and Claudia Goldin, "Maximum Hours Legislation and Female Employment: A Reassessment," *Journal of Political Economy* 96, no. 1 (February 1988): 189–205.

42 John D. Owen, "Work-Time Reduction in the U.S. and Western Europe," *Monthly Labor Review* 111, no. 12 (December 1988): 41–45.

The Growth of Paid Time Off According to some economists, leisure time has continued to grow as in the past—the problem is that there is a growing gap between *scheduled* or paid hours of work, and *actual* hours that employees are on the job.[43] The primary cause of this gap is the growth in paid time off from work. Before 1940, paid holidays and vacations were practically unknown. Over the intervening 60 years, they have come to account for a sizable block of leisure time. In 2003, a survey conducted by the Society for Human Resource Management found that workers who had been with their firms between 5 and 10 years received about 15 days of paid vacation.[44] Thus, while the number of hours per week that workers are paid for has not declined much in recent years, there has been a significant reduction in actual hours on the job. In addition, a new term has developed to describe a more informal way that workers attain more leisure without working fewer hours: undertime. As opposed to over time, undertime is time spent running errands while away from the office or shopping on the Internet at work, for example. There is no hard evidence of trends in these types of activities, but access to technology at work likely facilitates the growth of this phenomenon.[45]

Increase in Leisure over the Life Cycle Broadening the focus to annual hours of work still understates the true growth of leisure time. The more accurate measure is *lifetime* hours of work. For example, the life expectancy of men increased from 46.3 years in 1900 to 74.4 years in 2001, an increase of 28.1 years. These extra years of free time have been used primarily to delay entrance into the labor force to allow continued schooling and at the end of the life cycle for retirement.[46] For women, life expectancy increased by 31.8 years between 1900 and 2001, when it reached 79.8 years. Unlike men, however, women have devoted 74 percent of these additional years to market work. These trends have resulted in two different changes in the pattern of work and leisure. The first is that work histories of men and women are converging; in 1900 men worked 32.1 years on average, while women worked, on average, 6.3 years. In 1980, the gap had narrowed considerably, to 38.8 years and 29.4 years, respectively, and shrank even further by the year 2003. The second change is that for both men and women, total leisure time over the life cycle has grown quite substantially, dwarfing the gains in leisure from a shorter workweek and more paid time off.

Other Factors A variety of other factors have also been suggested as a possible cause of the leveling off of the workweek. According to one analyst, the Depression

---

43 Herbert Northrup and Theresa Greiss, "The Decline in Average Annual Hours Worked in the United States, 1947–1979," *Journal of Labor Research* 4, no. 2 (Spring 1983): 95–114.

44 "Weekly Poll—vacation days" (5 August 2003), http://www.shrm.org.

45 See Sue Shellenberger, "Why You Can Hit the Gym—but not get a manicure—on Company Time," *The Wall Street Journal* (18 April 2002): D1.

46 Details of retirement trends among U.S. workers can be found in Patrick J. Purcell, "Older Workers: Employment and Retirement Trends," *CRS Report for Congress*, Order Code RL30629 (26 October 2001).

and World War II forced people to forgo a variety of consumption needs; after the war, therefore, workers were far more interested in catching up on purchases of consumer goods and housing than in further reductions of work time.[47] This catching-up process also had a longer-run dynamic to it because of the baby boom that followed the war. Children impose financial costs on a family for 20 years or more; thus, the costs of raising and educating the baby-boom children made further reductions in work hours and income unattractive for most American households.

Two other reasons for the stability in weekly hours of work have been advanced. The first is that the increase in benefits and coverage of the Social Security program led workers to change their life cycle pattern of labor supply by retiring earlier, but working more hours during their prime earning years.[48] A second and quite different explanation is that after World War II the preferences for income versus leisure changed among the American work force. Prior to the 1940s, preferences were such that rising wages led to a dominant income effect, leading in turn to a decline in desired work hours. Some economists have argued, however, that the development of the modern "consumer society," with its emphasis on the acquisition of material goods, has led to a shift in preferences that gives more weight to income and less to leisure.[49] In this view the stability of weekly hours in the postwar period is explained by a change in the shape of the indifference curves in Figure 2.13 such that the income and substitution effects engendered by the continuing rise in wages just happen to offset each other.

The Recent Increase in Work Hours

Although growth in paid time off and longer expected lifetimes may mean that leisure has increased by a greater amount than the slower decline in hours suggests, it is hard to ignore the recent upward trend in average hours worked per week. Average hours per week bottomed out in 1982 at 38.0 and have increased by 1 hour per week to 39 in 2003. In addition, at least one economist has pointed out that the ratio of the number of persons at work to the number employed has also been rising since the early 1970s. This means that among those employed, fewer people are taking time away from work for vacation, sickness, and other reasons.[50] Together, these indicators suggest that the trend toward more leisure time has at least been halted, and may have reversed itself. A number of explanations have been offered to account for this trend reversal.

---

47   Owen, *Hours of Work*.

48   Richard V. Burkhauser and John Turner, "A Time-Series Analysis on Social Security and Its Effect on the Market Work of Young Men," *Journal of Political Economy* 86, no. 4 (August 1978): 701–15.

49   Levitan and Belous, *Shorter Hours, Shorter Weeks: Spreading the Work to Reduce Unemployment*, and Juliet Schor, *The Overworked American: The Unexpected Decline of Leisure* (New York: Basic Books, 1991).

50   Brian Motley, "Long-Run Trends in Labor Supply," *Federal Reserve Bank of San Francisco Economic Review* No. 3 (1997): 22–33.

Changing Age Profile   One source of the rise in hours of work is purely demo-graphic. By the mid-1990s baby boomers (those born between 1946 and 1964) had all reached their prime working ages of 25 to 54. Since people typically work the longest hours they will ever work during these years of their lives, it follows that the average number of hours would rise. The average hours of work per week for persons between the ages of 25 and 54 is about 41, whereas the average hours of work for persons younger than 25 and older than 54 is about 35. As this baby-boom cohort starts to retire, the statistics will show a new decline in the average hours per week.

Decline in Real Wage and Changes in Consumption Patterns   Between 1980 and 2003, real average weekly earnings for nonagricultural workers declined 1.07 per-cent. Referring to Figure 2.13, this would amount to a (small) rotation of the bud-get constraint from *AC* to *AB*. If the income effect outweighed the substitution effect, then hours would increase as a result of this wage decrease. This would be consistent with the domination of the income effect between 1900 and 1940, when hours declined as real wages rose.

In spite of the decline in real wages, there is some evidence that the taste for material possessions has continued to increase. Between 1990 and 2003, for exam-ple, per capita personal consumption expenditures increased by one-third faster than per capita disposable income. Clearly, some upward adjustment in work hours must be made to accommodate these rising expenditures, which otherwise must be financed from savings or capital gains on assets.

Moonlighting   As explained in Figure 2.11, a worker may have more flexibility in increasing hours of work than in decreasing them. If workers face fixed (employer-mandated) work schedules, the worker who desires more hours of work can simply take an additional job, or moonlight. The percent of employed persons holding multiple jobs rose from 4.9 percent in 1980 to 5.3 percent in 2003 (the rate be-tween 1970 and 1980 held steady at about 5 percent).[51] So it appears as though workers have been able to use moonlighting as a way to accommodate their in-creased desire for hours.

---

51   John F. Stinson Jr., "New Data on Multiple Jobholding Available from the CPS," *Monthly Labor Review* 120 (March 1997): 3–8.

Supply-Side Economics and Labor Supply

During the 1960s and 1970s, the twin forces of economic growth and inflation, together with the progressive nature of the income tax system, pushed the average wage earner into successively higher income tax brackets. In 1961, for example, only 10 percent of income tax returns had a marginal tax rate (the tax rate on the last dollar of earnings) exceeding 22 percent; by 1979, this proportion had more than tripled, to 35 percent.[1] This increase in tax rates was particularly great for high-income families; families with twice the median income experienced a rise in marginal tax rates from 22 percent in 1960 to 43 percent in 1980. The top tax bracket for married couples in 1980 had risen to 70 percent.

An income tax system forms a wedge between a worker's *gross* wage and *net* or "take-home" wage; for a given gross wage, the larger the marginal tax rate is, the lower is the additional net income earned from working one more hour. A number of economists and policymakers (most notably, President Reagan) believed that the rise in marginal income tax rates noted above caused a serious decline in work effort and labor supply precisely because the growing tax wedge stifled individuals' incentives to work. For this reason, the centerpiece of the Reagan economic program in his first term was a 25 percent cut in personal income tax rates over 3 years. The major purpose of the cut was to stimulate more work, saving, and investment. The theory that lowering tax rates will induce people to supply more labor, resulting in greater output, is referred to as "supply-side economics." In 1986, income tax rates were lowered further as part of the Reagan tax reform package. Altogether, the two pieces of legislation reduced the top marginal tax rate on income from 70 percent to 28 percent.

Having different priorities than President Reagan, President Bill Clinton implemented a tax reform that resulted in an increase in the top marginal tax rate to 39.6 percent in 1993. With the White House changing parties once again in 2000, President George W. Bush listed "tax relief" as one of his top priorities; by the year 2006, the top marginal tax bracket will be lowered to 35 percent. Like President Reagan, President Bush is sold on the idea that lower taxes will make people work harder and result in greater economic growth.

Although it seems reasonable that lower tax rates, by increasing the net earnings from an hour of work, will cause people to work more, the answer is by no means that simple. A number of economists have argued that the Reagan tax cuts may, in fact, have caused people to work *less*, not more.[2] What effect does an income tax have on labor supply? The labor/leisure model is used to answer this question for the case of an individual worker, and then the implications are considered for labor supply in the aggregate economy.

Graphic Analysis

Figure 2.14 depicts the labor supply decision of a representative individual before and after the imposition of a progressive income tax on earnings. By definition of a progressive income tax, the marginal tax rate t increases with the level of earnings. To begin, assume there is no income tax ($t = 0$), the person's wage is W_1, and he or she has zero nonlabor income. These assumptions give rise to the budget constraint AB in Figure 2.14; with zero hours of work, earned income is zero (point A). With each additional hour of work, income rises by

---

1   Charles R. Hulten and June A. O'Neill, "Tax Policy," in John L. Palmer and Isabel V. Sawhill, eds., *The Reagan Experiment* (Washington, D.C.: Urban Institute, 1982), 97–128 and Table A–6. Also see Joel Slemrod and Jon Bakija, *Taxing Ourselves: A Citizen's Guide to the Great Debate over Tax Reform* (Cambridge, Mass.: The MIT Press, 2000).

2   James Tobin, "Supply-Side Economics: What Is It? Will It Work?" *Economic Outlook USA* 8, no. 3 (Summer 1981): 51–53.

FIGURE 2.14 THE EFFECT OF AN INCOME TAX ON HOURS OF WORK

With the imposition of a progressive income tax, the budget constraint rotates from *AB* to *AC*. The equilibrium hours of work decline from H_1 (point *V*) to H_2 (point *X*). The income tax sets off an income effect that causes the person to desire more hours of work (point *V* to *Z*) and a substitution effect that causes the person to desire fewer hours of work (point *Z* to *X*). In this example, the substitution effect outweighs the income effect, and the net result is a decrease in labor supply. The opposite could also happen, however.

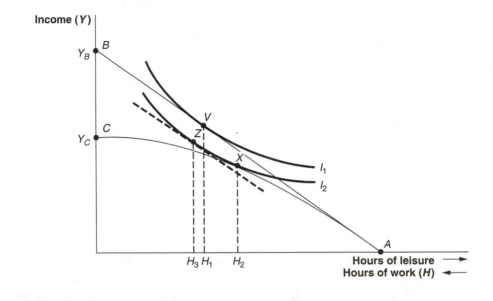

W_1 dollars up to a maximum of *YB* amount (point *B*). Given the budget constraint *AB*, and assuming the person has the indifference curve I_1, the tangency between the two at point *V* yields the equilibrium number of hours of work of H_1.

Next consider the impact on hours of work if a progressive income tax is imposed on labor earnings. Although the gross wage paid the worker remains W_1, the net wage received by the individual for each additional hour of work is reduced to $(1 - t)\,W_1$. The effect of the income tax, then, is to give rise to the new, curved budget constraint *AC*. For zero hours of work, total income is still zero (point *A*); with each additional hour of work, however, the net increase in earnings is no longer W_1 but the lesser amount $(1 - t)\,W_1$, causing the budget constraint to rotate to the left from *AB* to *AC*. The slope of the budget constraint *AC* also becomes progressively flatter as additional hours are worked, since the marginal tax rate *t* rises with additional earnings.[3] The maximum amount of earnings available to the individual even if all 100 hours are worked is reduced to *YC* dollars (point *C*); the area between *AB* and *AC* thus shows the total wedge between gross and net earnings caused by the income tax.

---

3   For ease of exposition the budget constraint *AC* is drawn as a smooth, continuous line. It actually should be drawn as a series of linear segments corresponding to each discrete tax bracket.

Given the new budget constraint, utility is maximized at point X, where the indifference curve I_2 is just tangent to AC. The key issue is whether hours of work at this new equilibrium will be more or less than they were before the imposition of the tax. The answer depends on the size of the income and substitution effects. The income tax results in a substitution effect that motivates the person to work less. Instead of receiving W_1 for each hour of work, the person now receives a smaller amount $(1 - t) W_1$. The tax reduces the return on work and makes leisure less expensive, providing an incentive for the person to substitute from the former to the latter. The tax also, however, sets off an income effect that pulls in the direction of more work. At the original level of hours of work, the person brings home less income than before. This drop in income leads to a decrease in the demand for all normal goods, including leisure. Which effect will dominate? The answer depends on the shape of the indifference curves, or more generally, the preferences of each individual regarding income versus leisure. Some people who have a dogged determination to maintain or increase their standard of living will work longer in reaction to the tax; others, however, will respond more strongly to the disincentive effects of the tax and will cut back their hours of work. In the example shown in Figure 2.14, the income tax leads to a net reduction in hours of work from H_1 to H_2 (point V to X), implying that the substitution effect outweighed the income effect.

The income effect can be identified by beginning at point V and decreasing income just enough to reach the new indifference curve I_2, holding the price of leisure constant. This is represented by the broken line tangent to I_2 at point Z. Assuming leisure is a normal good, the reduction in disposable income due to the tax should cause an increase in hours of work, shown by the increase in weekly hours from H_1 to H_3 (point V to Z). The substitution effect can be determined by rotating the broken line along I_2 until it has the same slope as the budget constraint AC. The result of doing so is a reduction in hours of work of $H_3 - H_2$ (point Z to

X). The income effect, therefore, leads to an increase in hours from H_1 to H_3, and the substitution effect leads to a decrease in hours from H_3 to H_2. The observed result is the net decrease in hours from H_1 to H_2.

The outcome shown in Figure 2.14 is only one of several possibilities. A different set of indifference curves can be drawn in Figure 2.14 that results in a net increase in hours of work. In this case, the income effect would dominate the substitution effect.

Income Taxes and Aggregate Labor Supply

The basic conclusion of the labor/leisure model is that in reaction to a tax cut a person may either work more or work less, depending on the relative sizes of the income and substitution effects. What implication does this have for verifying the prediction of supply-side economics? The traditional approach to answering this question is explained first.

As discussed earlier, the estimated labor supply elasticity for men is -0.1, implying that their labor supply curve has a slight negative slope. For men, then, a tax cut would increase the net take-home wage, causing a movement up the supply curve and a small reduction in hours of work. If men were the only group in the labor force to receive the tax cut, the critics of supply-side economics would be right; it would lead to less labor supply, not more. It was also shown earlier, however, that women's estimated labor supply elasticity is quite different, being both positive and much larger ($+0.9$). Since the labor supply curve of women is forward-sloped and more responsive to wages, the rise in the after-tax wage would lead to a significant increase in hours of work for women, particularly married women who would be drawn from work at home to market work by the rise in potential earnings. For women, then, the supporters of supply-side economics are right; it would lead to more labor supply in the economy.

What would be the net impact? Based on elasticity estimates such as those cited above, Michael Evans concluded that a 1 percent cut in the marginal tax rate would raise labor supply by an average of 0.2 percent.[4] Given that in 1980 the median-income family was in a 24 percent marginal tax bracket, the Reagan 3-year, 25 percent cut in tax rates should have lowered the marginal tax rate by a total of 6 percentage points, leading to a 1.2 percent increase in hours of work. A second study estimated that the Reagan tax cut should have resulted in a 1.2 to 2.9 percent increase in labor supply.[5]

The traditional approach to estimating the impact on aggregate supply of an income tax cut has been challenged, however, by James Gwartney and Richard Stroup.[6] They claim that economists such as Evans have committed the fallacy of composition, that is, they have assumed that what holds true for an individual also holds true for the economy as a whole. Gwartney and Stroup argue that with respect to taxes and labor supply, this is not a valid assumption.

For an individual worker, a cut in income tax rates causes both a substitution effect and an income effect since it simultaneously increases the price of leisure and the amount of goods and services the person can buy, given his or her current level of work hours. The net impact of the tax cut on labor supply is, therefore, indeterminant.

If income tax rates are reduced for all individuals in the economy, however, the result is quite different, say Gwartney and Stroup. An aggregate cut in income tax rates produces a substitution effect because the opportunity cost of leisure is greater for each person in the economy. To generate an income effect, the tax cut would also have to increase people's level of real income (i.e., the amount of goods and services they can buy). The crux of Gwartney and Stroup's argument is that this can not happen at the economy-wide level. They reason that the total amount of goods and services (GNP) available to people is determined by the state of technology and the amount of the factor inputs land, capital, and labor utilized in production. Holding these determinants of the level of production constant, it is clear that a tax cut, by itself, cannot increase everyone's level of real income since it will have produced no corresponding increase in GNP.

All a tax cut does in the aggregate is change the relative share of GNP that goes to households versus government. The paychecks and purchasing power of workers increase with a tax cut, but the amount of goods and services that can be provided by the government (e.g., defense, interstate highways) necessarily diminish. Since the extra goods and services households gain from a higher after-tax income are just offset by the loss of government-produced goods and services, the net impact on total real income in the country is zero. The net impact on labor supply of an aggregate tax cut, therefore, must *unambiguously* be positive, according to Gwartney and Stroup, because the substitution effect motivates people to work more hours. This conclusion implies, in turn, that estimates such as Evans's probably understate the increase in labor supply that was expected from the Reagan tax cuts.[7]

---

4   Michael K. Evans, *The Truth about Supply-Side Economics* (New York: Basic Books, 1983), Chapter 9.

5   Robert Haveman, "How Much Have Reagan Tax and Spending Policies Increased Work Effort?" in Charles R. Hulten and Isabel Sawhill, eds., *The Legacy of Reaganomics: Prospects for Long-Term Growth* (Washington: The Urban Institute, 1984).

6   James Gwartney and Richard Stroup, "Labor Supply and Tax Rates: A Correction of the Record," *American Economic Review* 93, no. 3 (June 1983): 446–51.

7   If the substitution effect is sufficiently large, it is possible that a cut in income tax rates, by engendering more labor supply, production, and income, may actually *increase* the total dollars of tax revenue collected by the government. This would occur if the economy is to the right of the peak of the Laffer curve (the hypothesized U-shaped relationship between the size of tax collections and the size of the marginal tax rate). Although some supply-side economists believe this to be the case, empirical evidence suggests that aggregate labor supply is not sufficiently responsive to tax rate changes for a tax cut to "pay for itself." See Don Fullerton, "On the Possibility of an Inverse Relationship between Tax Rates and Government Revenues," *Journal of Public Economics* 15 (October 1982): 3–22.

Gwartney and Stroup's position has not gone unchallenged. Several sets of economists have argued that their conclusions rest on special or highly restrictive assumptions.[8] When these are taken into account, it turns out that it is still possible for a tax cut such as those in the Reagan years to lead to a reduction in aggregate labor supply. The bottom line appears to be, therefore, that at the economy-wide level, a tax cut will *probably* lead to a net increase in hours of work. This prediction is supported by the findings of a recent empirical study that concluded after a careful weighing and sifting of the evidence that the Reagan tax cuts led to a net increase in labor supply, albeit of relatively modest proportions.[9]

For example, assume government transfer payments go to disabled persons who cannot work, while the taxes to pay the transfer payments come from able-bodied workers. A tax cut decreases the income of the former group and increases the income of the latter group by offsetting amounts, but the change in hours of work will not net out—the decreased labor supply of the able-bodied engendered by the income effect will not be offset by any increase in labor supply on the part of the disabled. It is possible, therefore, for the tax cut to lead to a reduction in hours of work to the extent that a negative income effect remains. For a general review and critique of the literature on this subject, see Arthur Snow and Ronald Warren Jr., "Tax Rates and Labor Supply in Fiscal Equilibrium," *Economic Inquiry* 22, no. 3 (July 1989): 511–20.

9 Barry Bosworth and Gary Burtless, "Effects of Tax Reform on Labor Supply, Investment, and Saving," *Journal of Economic Perspectives* 6 (Winter 1992): 3–25. Also see Nada Eissa, "Tax Reforms and Labor Supply," in *Tax Policy and the Economy*, vol. 10, James M. Poterba, ed. (Cambridge, Mass.: National Bureau of Economic Research and MIT Press, 1996), who also finds a small but positive labor supply response in hours worked among highly educated men after the 1986 tax reforms. The debate continues, however, as Robert Moffitt and Mark Wilhelm find no evidence of a significant labor supply response to lower marginal tax rates; see their paper, "Taxation and the Labor Supply Decisions of the Affluent," in *Does Atlas Shrug? Economic Consequences of Taxing the Rich*, Joel Slemrod, ed. (Cambridge, Mass.: Harvard University Press and the Russell Sage Foundation, 2000).

---

8 David Betson and David Greenberg ["Labor Supply and Tax Rates: Comment," *American Economic Review* 76 (June 1986): 551–56] show that a tax cut may still lead to a reduction in labor supply if some groups in the population cannot adjust their hours of work.

EMPIRICAL EVIDENCE 2-1

Labor Supply Curves Estimated from Cross-Sectional Data

Economists have conducted extensive empirical research in an attempt to determine the actual shape of the labor supply curve. Is it positively sloped, negatively sloped, or backward-bending? To answer this question, economists typically use cross-sectional data on hours of work, wages, income, and other variables collected in large surveys of individuals to estimate the labor supply curve and the underlying income and substitution effects.

Although a number of complex theoretical and empirical issues are involved, the process of estimating a labor supply curve from cross-sectional data is fairly straightforward.[1] The basic idea is first to obtain data on the wage rate, hours of work, age, sex, education, occupation, and other such variables for a large number of individuals. Then the

---

1 For a nontechnical discussion of some of these issues, see Cynthia Lloyd and Beth Niemi, *The Economics of Sex Differentials* (New York: Columbia University Press, 1979), 61–66. The more advanced student might consult Mark Killingsworth, *Labor Supply* (Cambridge, Eng.: Cambridge University Press, 1983).

individuals are sorted or standardized into homogeneous groups to eliminate the influence of differences among them in nonlabor income and preferences for income versus leisure. Next the data on hours of work and wage rates for each individual in a group are plotted. Passing a line through this scatter of points will then trace out the supply curve of labor. This entire process is done today by means of a computer and the statistical technique of *linear regression*.[2]

Given the mechanics of estimating a labor supply curve, what are the results from cross-sectional studies? For adult men, nearly all studies find the labor supply curve to be negatively sloped or backward-bending. Figure 2.15 shows the labor supply curve for men estimated in five different cross-sectional studies.[3] Three of the studies (Hill; Cohen, Rea, and Lerman; and Greenberg and Kosters) found the labor supply curve to be negatively sloped throughout; the other two (Hall; Kalachek and Raines) found a positively sloped segment at low wage rates, which then became backward-bending as the wage rate increased.

Because the labor supply curve for men is negatively sloped over all or most of its range, the implication is that the negative income effect from higher wages dominates the positive substitution effect.[4] This has been the result found by nearly all cross-sectional studies. For example, a recent survey reports that the labor supply *elasticity* for men is about −0.04, meaning that an increase of 10 percent in the wage rate for men will, on average, cause a net reduction in hours of work of about 0.4 percent.[5] This reflects, in turn, the combined influence of a negative income effect from higher wages of −0.13 and a positive substitution effect of +0.09.

Although hours of work for men decrease with higher wages, this decrease is, quantitatively speaking, not very large, particularly for prime-age males (age 25 to 54). Thus, a 10 percent wage increase (for a given level of prices and all other factors) would cause a male working 2,000 hours a year (40 hours per week for 50 weeks) to cut back on work only 8 hours a year, on average.

In contrast with these average results from a combination of earlier studies, recent analyses of the labor supply of physicians suggest that the labor supply curve is upward-sloping for at least one group of high-income men. One study estimates that a substantial negative income effect from a wage increase of −0.26 is overwhelmed by an even larger substitution effect of 0.51 to yield a total labor supply elasticity of 0.25.[6] This means that a 10 percent increase in a physician's wage would result in a 2.5 percent *increase* in hours. Separating physicians into even smaller comparison groups, another study found that self-employed physicians were much more sensitive to wage

---

2   See Appendix 2C for a more in-depth discussion of linear regression and an example of its use in estimating a labor supply curve.

3   The supply curve for the Cohen, Rea, and Lerman study, for example, is for men aged 22 to 54 in 1966 who had $2,000 per year in nonlabor income, were neither ill nor at school, worked one or more weeks, had completed 12 years of school, were married with spouse present, had two children under 18, neither lived in a poverty tract nor in the South, were white, and were not self-employed. If persons with $3,000 per year of nonlabor income had been analyzed, the labor supply curve would shift to the left, showing that in any given wage rate fewer hours would be supplied, assuming leisure is a normal good.

4   See Chung-Cheng Lin, "A Backward Bending Labor Supply Curve Without an Income Effect," *Oxford Economic Papers* 55 (April 2003): 336–43, for how a backward bending labor supply curve can arise when effort is endogenous and there is no income effect.

5   Labor supply elasticity is defined as the percentage change in hours supplied divided by the percentage change in the wage rate. These figures are an average from 19 different studies as reported by Derek Hum and Wayne Simpson, "Labour Supply Estimation and Public Policy," *Journal of Economic Surveys* 8 (March 1994): 57–81, Table 1. These estimates are from nonexperimental data sources. A second source of labor supply elasticities is from the negative income tax experiments sponsored by the federal government in the 1970s. These data yield income effects that are of the same magnitude as found in nonexperimental studies; the substitution effects, however, are generally smaller. See Robert Moffitt and Kenneth Kehrer, "The Effect of Tax and Transfer Programs on Labor Supply: The Evidence from the Income Maintenance Experiments," in Ronald G. Ehrenberg, ed., *Research in Labor Economics*, vol. 4 (Greenwich, Conn.: JAI Press, 1981), 103–50.

6   John A. Rizzo and David Blumenthal, "Physician Labor Supply: Do Income Effects Matter?" *Journal of Health Economics* 13 (December 1994): 433–53. Also see K. Smith Conway and T. J. Kniesner, "How Fragile Are Male Labor Supply Function Estimates?" *Empirical Economics* 17 (1992): 169–82.

FIGURE 2.15 ESTIMATED LABOR SUPPLY CURVES IN FIVE STUDIES

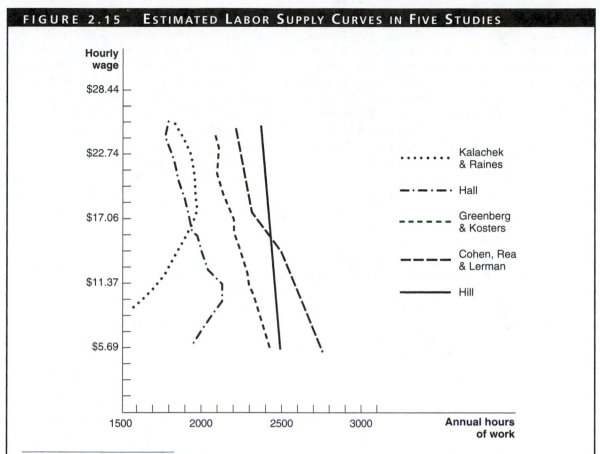

SOURCE: Robert E. Hall, "Wages, Income and Hours of Work in the U.S. Labor Force," in Glen G. Cain and Harold W. Watts, eds., *Income Maintenance and Labor Supply* (Madison, WI: Institute for Research on Poverty; 1973): 102–162. The wage rate figures on the vertical axis are expressed in 2003 dollars.

changes than physicians employed by hospitals or HMOs (health maintenance organizations).[7] This makes sense, given that self-employed physicians have greater flexibility to adjust their hours in response to wage changes than do physicians whose hours are dictated by their employer. The results of this study also indicate that grouping all workers together to evaluate labor supply responses to policy changes that affect wages may produce an inaccurate picture.

The labor supply curves estimated from cross-sectional data for women have been substantially different than those for men in two important respects. First, empirical studies have found that the labor supply curve is positively sloped; women, on average, work *more* hours at higher wage rates, not

---

7   Mark H. Showalter and Norman K. Thurston, "Taxes and Labor Supply of High-Income Physicians." *Journal of Public Economics* 66 (October 1997): 73–97.

less as typically found for men. This increase in hours comes from two sources: the entrance of women into the labor force to begin work, and longer hours of work by women who already hold jobs. An average estimate derived from a large group of studies of adult women is that the labor supply elasticity for females is about 0.9; that is, for a 10 percent increase in wages, women will increase hours of work by about 9 percent, reflecting a negative income effect of -0.2 and a positive substitution effect of $+1.1$.[8] Thus, while the negative income effect for women is about the same size as for men, the positive substitution effect is about twelve times larger. The second important difference between men and women, therefore, is that female labor supply not only increases with higher wages but the response is also quantitatively much larger.

What accounts for this discrepant behavior between men and women? Although a full discus-sion of this issue must be postponed until the next chapter, the basic explanation can be briefly stated here. Since over 90 percent of adult men work full time, additional hours of work must come primarily from one source: leisure. A different situation exists for adult women, however. Many women devote a considerable amount of time to work in the home. These women, therefore, have *three* alternative uses of time: market work, home work, and leisure. A rise in the market wage induces a substitution not only from leisure to market work, but also from home work to market work. It is this substitution from home work to market work that accounts for the large, positive labor supply elasticity for women.

---

8   Hum and Simpson, "Labor-Supply Estimation and Public Policy," Table 2. These estimates are based on 22 studies.

Summary

Hours of work in the economy exhibit both a distinct cross-sectional and a time-series pattern. At a point in time, there is a considerable variation in weekly hours, ranging from the 5 percent of the work force who work less than 15 hours a week to the 8 percent who work more than 60 hours a week. The greatest proportion of people, however, work exactly 40 hours per week. Over time, average work hours have declined significantly in the economy, from about 53 hours per week in 1900 to slightly under 40 hours per week in 2003.

The pattern of hours is influenced by individual choice and institutional constraints. The role of individual choice is explicated by the labor/leisure model, which shows that the individual maximizes utility by choosing the hours of work where the wage rate is equal to the marginal rate of substitution. The labor/leisure model also shows that, in response to a change in the wage rate, a person may either increase or decrease hours of work, depending on whether the income effect or the substitution effect is larger.

The long-term decline in hours of work in the twentieth century is explicable in terms of a dominant income effect arising from the long-term rise in wages. While individual choice is an important determinant of work hours, so too are fixed work schedules mandated by employers. If such schedules conflict too greatly with individual preferences, then market forces are set in motion that induce employers to change their scheduled hours. In times of less than full employment, however, market forces may prove ineffective in this task, and workers will then turn to collective action in the form of union bargaining power or government legislation to achieve the desired change in work hours.

The concept of income and substitution effects has many applications to issues of public policy. For example, a decrease in the income tax rate sets off a substitution effect that pulls a person toward more work and an income effect that pulls toward less work. Whether tax cuts lead to more or less labor supply in the economy depends on whether the substitution or the income effect is quantitatively larger. A second public policy example is the labor supply impact of a welfare program such as TANF. In this case both the income and the substitution effects work together to cause a reduction in desired hours of labor supply, a factor which led to the recent welfare reforms.

Review Questions

1. Use the labor/leisure model to analyze the effect on hours of work of a law requiring employers to pay time and a half for hours worked over 40 per week.

    a. First, draw a budget constraint for someone earning $8 per hour who receives $100 a week in nonlabor income. What now happens to the budget constraint with the time-and-a-half requirement?

    b. Given your answer to (a), draw an indifference curve so that, given the original budget constraint, the person is working 40 hours per week. What now happens to hours of work given the new budget constraint? Draw an indifference curve to show this. Have hours of work increased or decreased as a result of the overtime law? Explain why.

    c. In words, define the income and substitution effects. Next, use the graph to identify the income and substitution effects. Which is stronger?

    d. If the wage had been increased for all hours worked rather than just for those after 40 per week, would the change in hours of work be any different? Show this in the graph and explain why or why not.

2. Use the labor/leisure model to analyze the effect on labor supply of a lump-sum tax (a tax that is independent of income, such as a property tax) and a proportional income tax (the tax rate t is constant regardless of earnings). Identify the income effect and the substitution effect (if any) caused by each tax.

3. If every employer in the labor market mandates a fixed work schedule, is there still room for choice by individuals concerning their hours of work per week? What economic forces would induce employers over the long run to change fixed work schedules to match more nearly the preferences of workers? Does this result depend at all on how competitive the labor market is, say as measured by the number of employers in the market?

4. Use the labor/leisure model to illustrate the impact of increasing the implicit tax rate t in a TANF program from $t = .50$ to $t = 1.00$ on the labor supply decision of the following three groups: (a) those people working zero hours; (b) those people who are receiving some benefits, but who are also working in the market a few hours per week; and (c) those people who are receiving some benefits from the program, but who are also earning a sufficient amount to put them close to the break-even point.

5. Use the labor/leisure model to explain the long-term decline in hours of work per week during the twentieth century. What role, if any, did institutional forces have in this process?

6. In order to reduce the fixed cost of working, an employer is trying to decide whether to offer its workers an at-rate subsidy for parking or to compensate workers for the amount of time they are having to spend to get to work. Illustrate and compare the impact each of these policies would have on desired hours of the workers.

7. The following labor supply model for 8,274 women was estimated by Averett and Hotchkiss (*RESTAT* 1997). Use the estimates and Slutsky's equation to derive the gross wage elasticity, the compensated wage elasticity, and the income elasticity for this sample of women.

DEPENDENT VARIABLE = WEEKLY HOURS OF WORK (AVERAGE = 36.39)

These regressors were coded as =1 if the description was true, 0 otherwise

	Constant	Age	Education	Non-labor Income	No. of Children less than 6	Weekly Wage	Single	Black	Enrolled in School
Coefficient Estimate	1.433	−0.0312	0.1284	−0.000215	−0.832	0.024	0.278	0.196	−1.747
Standard Error of the Regression Estimate	0.192	0.0027	0.0192	0.000008	0.046	0.014	0.064	0.089	0.156
Mean of the Variable	—	37.29	13.15	$2,760	0.31	$8.88	0.33	0.10	0.04

a. Using the concept of marginal rate of substitution, explain why the coefficients on *No. of Children Less than 6* and on *Enrolled in School* are negative.

b. Calculate the gross wage elasticity, the total income elasticity, and the compensated wage elasticity for the average woman in the sample.

c. Does the income or substitution effect dominate for this sample of women?

APPENDIX 2A

The Hours of Work Decision for Salaried Workers

This appendix considers an additional qualification to the standard labor/leisure model: the decision made by salaried workers concerning hours of work. This analysis also provides an interesting contrast between an economic and a sociologically oriented explanation of human behavior.

Salaried workers are most likely to be employed in white-collar occupations, particularly professional workers such as lawyers, engineers, and teachers, as well as persons in a wide range of managerial occupations. The hours of work decisions for an hourly worker and a salaried worker, respectively, are illustrated in Figure 2A.1. It is assumed both individuals have the same set of indifference curves, I_1, I_2. The major difference between them is the budget constraint. The budget constraint for the hourly worker is AB, the slope of which is equal to the marginal change in

FIGURE 2A.1 HOURS OF WORK FOR AN HOURLY AND A SALARIED WORKER

The budget constraint for the hourly worker is AB, and the desired hours of work are H_2 (point V). Should this person be converted to a salaried worker earning Y_S, the budget constraint becomes CDE. Below H_1 hours of work, the person loses the job and income is zero; above H_1, the person receives Y_S weekly income regardless of how many hours are worked. Since the marginal wage is zero, the salaried worker maximizes utility by working the least number of hours possible, H_1 (point D).

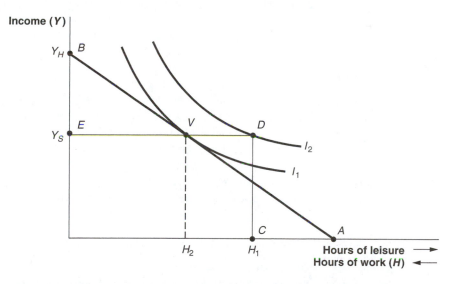

income for each additional hour worked, that is, the wage rate W_1. Income for the hourly person can thus range from zero at zero hours of work to a maximum of $\$W_1 \times 100 = Y_H$ if all possible hours are worked (again assuming 100 maximum work hours per week). The budget constraint for the salaried worker, on the other hand, is shown by the right-angle line CDE. Below some minimum hours of work per week, for instance H_1, the individual would be fired by the employer, and earnings would be zero (point C). Above this minimum level of work effort, the worker receives a weekly salary of Y_S regardless of how many hours are worked, even up to the maximum possible of 100 (point E). Because income is invariant to the number of hours worked above the minimum H_1, the salaried worker faces a zero marginal wage rate—an additional hour of work results in no change in income.

The equilibrium level of hours of work for the hourly worker is H_2, and income earned is Y_S (point V), where the budget constraint AB and indifference curve I_1 are just tangent. If this worker were now to be converted to a salaried worker and guaranteed the same income of Y_S as he or she had been earning, what would happen to the optimal level of hours of work? The individual would maximize utility by selecting the point on the budget constraint that touches the highest indifference curve possible, in this case I_2. Hours of work for the salaried person, therefore, would be predicted to fall from H_2 to H_1 (point V to D). Since each extra hour of work results in no additional income for the salaried worker, it is not surprising that the optimal level of work effort is the minimum amount necessary to preserve the job.

Empirical evidence shows just the opposite for most salaried professional and managerial workers, however. Instead of working fewer hours than the standard 40-hour week, many of these salaried workers put in quite long hours. Data from the March 2004 Current Population Survey indicates that salaried workers average 45.5 hours per week and hourly workers average 33.7 hours per week. In addition, 32 percent of salaried workers work 45 hours per week or more. What can account for this apparent discrepancy between theory and fact? Economists have advanced two possible explanations, one more sociological in nature, the other more economic.[1]

Differences in Tastes

The first explanation for salaried professional and managerial workers' longer than average work hours is that they have a greater "taste" for work. According to this view, professional and managerial jobs offer a wide range of opportunities for creativity, self-expression, and ego gratification. Work in this case is no longer a source of disutility that a worker must be offered extra money to perform, but an activity willingly taken on by the individual to obtain these psychic rewards.[2] Several pieces of evidence can be marshaled in support of this view. In one national

---

1 This discussion is drawn from Bevars Mabry, "Income–Leisure Analysis and the Salaried Professional," *Industrial Relations* 8, no. 2 (February 1969): 162–73. The reasons why some workers are paid on an hourly basis while others receive a salary is discussed in Chapter 10.

2 For an elaboration of this theme, see Mark Lutz and Kenneth Lux, *The Challenge of Humanistic Economics* (Menlo Park, Calif.: Benjamin/Cummings, 1979).

One explanation for why salaried workers put in long hours on the job is because they enjoy their work. If work is not a source of disutility, then the indifference curves I_1, I_2, and I_3 are horizontal (up to a maximum hours of work of H_2). Utility is maximized where the indifference curve I_2 is tangent to the budget constraint ABC. Equilibrium hours of work are between H_1 and H_2. If work is actually preferred to leisure up to H_2 hours, the indifference curve will resemble the broken line I_2'. In this case, the salaried worker will choose to work exactly H_2 hours (point X).

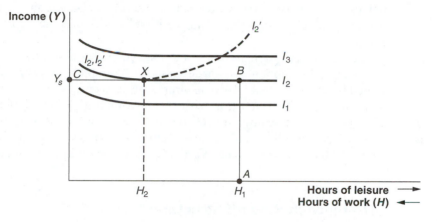

survey, 87 percent of workers in management positions stated that they liked their job very much, while only 59 percent of hourly workers stated such a view.[3] Also of interest are the observations of a bank economist who recently completed several years of service with an agency of the federal government. He noted that as a result of the temporary nature of the positions held by many upper-level political appointees and the limited opportunity for bonuses or promotions in the civil service system, there is frequently little financial incentive to work long hours. Despite this, in his words, "the top people work long and intensely because of a genuine liking for their jobs. They are attracted by the public service opportunities and the excitement present in the political policymaking process."[4]

The influence on labor supply of these positive tastes for work is illustrated in Figure 2A.2. The budget constraint is assumed to be ABC; below H_1 hours of work,

3   Cited in "Workers Today Sacrifice Less for Job," Jackson, Mich., *Citizen Patriot* (October 14, 1984): E1.

4   Robert Dederick, "A Primer on Surviving in Washington," *Business Economics* 19, no. 5 (October 1984): 7. Other examples of people finding complete fulfillment in their jobs can be found in Hank Ezell, "It's a compulsion that can destroy lives, but some people are addicted to . . . work, work, work," *Atlanta Journal Constitution* (5 September 1994): E1.

income is zero; above H_1 hours, the person is paid a straight salary of Y_S. Two different sets of indifference curves are also shown. The first is the set of three curves labeled I_1, I_2, and I_3. The distinctive aspect of these indifference curves is that they have a horizontal segment up to H_2 hours of work. This implies that work is no longer a source of disutility—the individual considers work and leisure to be perfect substitutes and will voluntarily work additional hours (up to H_2) for no additional compensation. The object of the worker is to maximize utility, and to do so he or she seeks to reach the highest indifference curve possible, which is I_2 given the budget constraint ABC. There is no unique tangency point; rather, a series of tangency points extend from point B to X. The equilibrium hours of work is thus indeterminate; the person could work as many as H_2 hours or as few as H_1. To induce him or her to work more than H_2, however, would require additional compensation, since beyond that point work really does become "work" (a source of disutility).

It would be possible to obtain a unique equilibrium number of hours of work if a stronger assumption were made about the desirability of work. Work may be so valued by the individual relative to alternative uses of time that over some range of hours it is actually *preferred* to leisure. This would give the indifference curves a U shape, as illustrated by the broken curve I_2' (beyond point X, I_2' merges into the upward-sloping solid line I_2). The tangency point between I_2' and the budget constraint ABC occurs at H_2 (point X), giving rise to long hours of work for the salaried worker.

Difference in Reward Structures

A second explanation for the long hours worked by salaried professional and managerial workers rests on a more economic argument that stresses the difference in reward structures facing hourly and salaried workers. In this view, it is not love of work that induces professional and managerial workers to put in 50- or 60-hour weeks, but rather the financial rewards they hope to receive in the form of future salary increases and job promotions. On the surface, hourly workers appear to have more incentive to work longer hours since they generally receive overtime pay (150 percent of the usual hourly wage) for all hours worked over 40 per week, unlike the salaried worker who often receives zero additional compensation for each extra hour. The fallacy of this view is that it neglects the long-run nature of the reward system for salaried workers. Additional hours of work this year may not affect *this year's* income for the salaried worker, but there is a definite link in the reward structures of most companies between work effort this year and *future* earnings and promotions. The reason many people are attracted to these salaried jobs, it is argued, is precisely because the potential for earnings growth far outdistances what an hourly worker can hope to make even at overtime rates.

The nature of this argument is illustrated in Figure 2A.3. Shown there is the horizontal budget constraint ABC; below H_1 hours of work, income is zero, and above H_1 hours of work, the person's salary in the current year is Y_1, regardless of hours worked. Also shown are two representative indifference curves, I_1 and I_2.

A second explanation for why salaried workers work long hours is that of the anticipation of future economic rewards. Focusing only on current year income, the budget constraint for the salaried worker is ABC, yielding equilibrium hours of work of H_1 (point B). If additional hours of work in the current year result in salary increases in future years,

however, the budget constraint becomes ABD. At H_2 hours, for example, total compensation received for this level of work effort is Y_2, made up of Y_1 income in the current year and $Y_2 - Y_1$ income in future years in the form of salary increases. Given the budget constraint ABD, equilibrium hours of work are H_2 (point X), an amount higher than H_1.

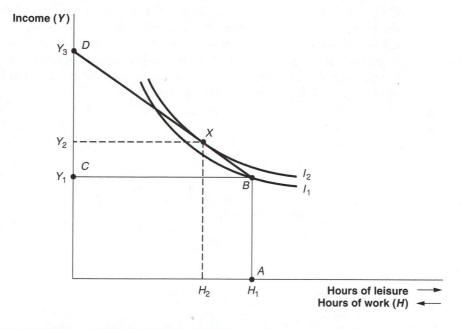

Based on this simple model, it would seem, as was shown in Figure 2A.1, that the salaried person's equilibrium hours of work would be the minimum amount H_1 (point B), where the indifference curve I_1 and the budget constraint ABC just touch each other. In fact, the salaried person works much longer hours than this, say H_2. The key to this paradox is that while additional hours of work in the current year will not, by assumption, result in any increase in earnings above Y_1, these extra hours of work will lead to an increment in income in future years, making the budget constraint no longer ABC but ABD. Thus, if hours of work are H_2, total income received by the salaried worker over the life of the job for these H_2 hours comprises two components: the Y_1 amount that is received in the current year, and the salary increases of $Y_2 - Y_1$ amount received in future years as a result of this year's work effort.[5] Similarly, if all 100 hours were worked, total income earned would rise to Y_3 (point D), composed of Y_1 current income and $Y_3 - Y_1$ income received in the future.

Given the new budget constraint ABD, it is now obvious why, in this view, salaried professional and managerial workers work long hours. The equilibrium in Figure 2A.3 occurs at point X where the indifference curve I_2 and budget constraint ABD are just tangent, giving rise to an observed level of work of H_2 hours, not H_1. In this case, it is not because salaried workers prefer to work any more than hourly workers do; rather, they consciously trade off current work for the expectation of higher future income.

Which of these competing explanations is correct? Economists would most likely emphasize the second one; sociologists would probably tend to emphasize the first. The empirical evidence cannot clearly show one view or the other to be correct. The two views do show that market and sociological forces work together to give rise to the pattern of hours of work observed in the labor market, and that there is considerable room for controversy regarding the exact role and importance of each of these factors in the labor market.

---

5   Since the $Y_2 - Y_1$ income is received in future years, it should be discounted to express it in present-value terms. Because we have not yet introduced the concept of present value, this consideration is abstracted from in the present discussion.

Constrained Optimization and the Labor/Leisure Choice Model

The slope of an indifference curve at any number of hours, the equilibrium hours of work, and the relationship between the *MRS* and the market wage at that equilibrium can all be derived mathematically.[1]

Equilibrium Hours of Work

Mathematically, indifference curves are derived by determining all combinations of income and leisure that generate a single level of utility (*U*) through a mathematical function that satisfies certain properties:

$$U = U(Y, L), \tag{2B.1}$$

where *U* reflects the level of utility generated by specific levels of income (*Y*) and leisure (*L*). The individual's goal is to select that combination of *Y* and *L* which yields the maximum value of the utility function, keeping in mind that the choice of *Y* and *L* is constrained by the individual's budget and time constraints:

$$Y = (T - L)W \quad \text{or} \quad Y - (T - L)W = 0 \tag{2B.2}$$

$$T \geq L. \tag{2B.3}$$

The budget constraint (2B.2) shows the trade-off that exists between income and leisure in attaining higher levels of utility, and that the market wage rate (*W*) limits the extent to which leisure can be translated into income. The time constraint (2B.3) merely recognizes that one cannot consume more hours of leisure than are available in a given time period (*T*).

The constrained optimization problem is set up by constructing a new function (called a *Lagrangian function*). The new function is formed by multiplying the budget constraint by what is called a *lagrange multiplier* (λ) and adding the product to the utility function:

$$F(Y, L, \lambda) = U(Y, L) + \lambda[Y - (T - L)W]. \tag{2B.4}$$

The values of *Y*, *L*, and λ at which utility is maximized are found by partially differentiating *F*(.), setting each of the partial derivatives equal to zero, then solving the three partial derivatives simultaneously.[2]

---

[1]   A good reference for the mathematical representation of many economic models is Edward T. Dowling, *Introduction to Mathematical Economics*, Schaum's Outline Series (New York: McGraw-Hill, 1980).

[2]   This formulation of the Lagrangian function assumes that the individual works a positive amount (*T* > *L*). The possibility of choosing not to work at all will be explored in the text and appendix to Chapter 3.

Setting the partial derivatives of $F(.)$ equal to zero yields the following *first-order conditions*:

$$\partial U/\partial Y + \lambda^* = 0 \tag{2B.5}$$

$$\frac{\partial U}{\partial L} + \lambda^* W = 0 \tag{2B.6}$$

$$Y^* - (T - L^*)W = 0. \tag{2B.7}$$

The asterisk (*) denotes the values of the variables at which these conditions hold their "optimal" values. Equations 2B.5 and 2B.6 can be rewritten as follows:

$$\lambda^* = -\partial U/\partial Y \tag{2B.5'}$$

$$\lambda^* = \frac{-\partial U/\partial L}{W} \tag{2B.6'}$$

Setting these two expressions for λ equal to one another, one obtains:

$$\frac{\partial U/\partial L}{\partial U/\partial Y} = W, \tag{2B.8}$$

or:

$$MRS = W. \tag{2B.8'}$$

The combination of leisure and income that satisfies this condition will yield the greatest value of utility possible given the market wage and time constraint. This is the same condition for equilibrium hours of work as stated in Equation 2.1 in the text. This also illustrates how the *MRS* reflects the rate (in utility terms) at which a person is willing to trade income for leisure.

$$\frac{\partial U/\partial L}{\partial U/\partial Y}$$

indicates how much additional utility a person receives for one more hour of leisure relative to the additional utility lost by giving up one more dollar of income.

The Slope of the Indifference Curve

The text indicates that the *MRS* at a particular point on the indifference curve is equal to the negative of the slope of the line tangent to the indifference curve at that point. In other words, the *MRS* at a point is (negative) the slope of the indifference curve at that point. This can be illustrated mathematically by *totally differentiating* the utility function:

$$dU = \frac{\partial U}{\partial Y}dY + \frac{\partial U}{\partial L}dL, \tag{2B.9}$$

where $\partial U/\partial Y$ is the partial derivative of the utility function with respect to income (Y) and $\partial U/\partial L$ is the partial derivative of the utility function with respect to leisure (L). Since utility does not change as one moves along an indifference curve ($dU = 0$), the total derivative can be rewritten as:

$$0 = \frac{\partial U}{\partial Y}dY + \frac{\partial U}{\partial L}dL. \tag{2B.10}$$

Rearranging the terms in (2B.10):

$$\frac{\partial U/\partial L}{\partial U/\partial Y} = \frac{dY}{dL}, \tag{2B.11}$$

or:

$$MRS = -[\text{slope of the indifference curve}]. \tag{2B.12}$$

Equations 2B.89 and 2B.12 can be combined to reflect the equilibrium illustrated as point X in Figure 2.5:

$$W = MRS = -[\text{slope of the indifference curve}]. \tag{2B.13}$$

The Income and Substitution Effects

Solving the utility maximization problem for the optimal levels of leisure and income also, necessarily, indicates what the optimal number of hours, H, is (since $H = T - L$, where T is the maximum number of hours available for both leisure and work). An individual's labor supply function can be expressed as a function of the market wage and income:

$$H = h(W, Y). \tag{2B.14}$$

Differentiating this labor supply function with respect to the wage results in

$$\frac{\partial H}{\partial W} = \frac{\partial h}{\partial W} + \frac{\partial h}{\partial Y}\frac{\partial Y}{\partial W}, \tag{2B.15}$$

Given that $Y = HW$, $\frac{\partial Y}{\partial W} = H$, (2B.15) can be rewritten as:

$$\frac{\partial H}{\partial W} = \frac{\partial h}{\partial W} + H\frac{\partial h}{\partial Y}. \tag{2B.15'}$$

The first expression on the right-hand side of (2B.15′) reflects the change in hours that results from a wage change, *while holding income constant*. This is the substitution effect. The second term on the right-hand side of (2B.15′) is the income effect; the change in hours that results from a change in income, *holding the wage constant*. Given that the substitution effect is a positive number and the income effect is assumed to be negative (leisure is a normal good), one can see the ambiguity that results in determining the total impact on hours that results from a change in the wage.

It is standard practice to transform the total absolute effect of a wage change in (2B.15′) into an elasticity so that comparisons across people earning different wage levels can be made. Multiplying both sides of (2B.15′) by the ratio (W/H) yields:[3]

$$\frac{\partial H}{\partial W}\frac{W}{H} = \frac{\partial h}{\partial W}\frac{W}{H} + W\frac{\partial h}{\partial Y}. \qquad \textbf{(2B.16)}$$

The term on the left-hand side of (2B.16) is the *gross* or *uncompensated wage* elasticity. The uncompensated wage elasticity is the percentage change in H for a given percentage change in W. The change may be either positive or negative, depending on whether the substitution effect is less than or greater than the income effect. The first term on the right-hand side of (2B.16) is the *compensated wage* elasticity; it measures the percentage change in H for a given percentage change in W, holding income constant. The second term on the right-hand side of (2B.16) is the *total income* elasticity; it measures the percentage change in H for a given percentage change in Y, holding the wage constant.

3   See Mark Killingsworth, *Labor Supply* (Cambridge: Cambridge University Press, 1983), Chapter 3.

Estimating a Labor Supply Curve with Linear Regression

Chapter 2 gives a brief, heuristic explanation of how economists estimate a labor supply curve from cross-sectional data. This appendix provides a deeper look at this subject, albeit at a very nontechnical level.

The Regression Line

A supply curve of labor shows the relationship between the wage rate and hours of work, holding other factors constant. To estimate such a supply curve, economists typically use cross-sectional data obtained from surveys of several thousand people. These surveys provide a wide range of information on each person, such as hours of work per year, wage rate, annual income, spouse's income, race, sex, years of schooling, occupation, and so on. One approach to estimating the labor supply curve is to plot in a scatter diagram the combination of annual hours of work H and wage rate W for each person in the survey. This is illustrated by the hypothetical scatter of points in graph (a) of Figure 2C.1.[1] To derive the supply curve of labor,

FIGURE 2C.1 ESTIMATING A LABOR SUPPLY CURVE WITH LINEAR REGRESSION

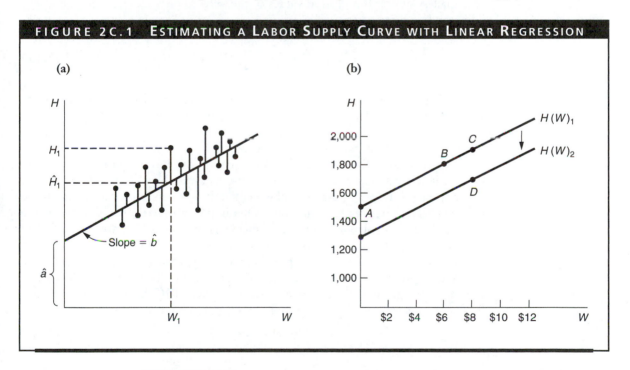

---

1   For expositional convenience, H is measured on the vertical axis and W on the horizontal axis rather than the reverse, as is usually done in drawing a labor supply curve (as in Figure 2.9).

the next step is to pass a straight line through this scatter of points so that it fits the data as closely as possible.

Given that H is the dependent variable in the labor supply function and W is the independent variable, the equation for such a straight line can be written as:

$$H = a + bW. \tag{2C.1}$$

The coefficient a is the *intercept* term; it shows that when $W = 0$, $H = a$. The coefficient b is the *slope* term; it shows the change in H for a one-unit change in W, that is, $b = \Delta H / \Delta W$. The survey data provide the values for H and W; the job of the researcher is to estimate the values of the coefficients a and b. Let $\hat{a}$ and $\hat{b}$ stand for these estimates. With the estimates $\hat{a}$ and $\hat{b}$, it is possible to draw a straight line through the scatter of points, such as the one illustrated in graph (a). The equation for this line is:

$$\hat{H} = \hat{a} + \hat{b}W \tag{2C.2}$$

where $\hat{H}$ is the predicted value of H, given the actual value of W. Thus, as shown in graph (a), if $W = W_1$, the actual value of H is H_1, and the predicted value given by the labor supply function is $\hat{H}_1$.

The statistical technique used by economists to obtain the coefficients a and b is known as *linear regression*. Linear regression calculates the a and b that result in the smallest sum of the squared values of the vertical distance between H and $\hat{H}$.[2] This can be expressed as:

$$\sum_{i=1}^{N} (H_i - \hat{H}_i)^2 = \sum_{i=1}^{N} (H_i - \hat{a} - \hat{b}W_i)^2 \tag{2C.3}$$

where N is the number of observations. The deviations between H and $\hat{H}$ are squared; otherwise, distances above the line would be canceled by distances below the line. Minimizing the sum of squared deviations results in a line that passes through the scatter of points as closely as possible.

The regression line estimated from Equation 2C.3 is a bivariate regression; that is, it is a relationship between only the two variables H and W. Economic theory predicts, however, that an individual's desired hours of work are influenced by other factors besides the wage rate. One important factor, for example, is the person's level of nonlabor income Y_0. Since it is of interest to know the effect of changes in both W and Y_0 on hours of work, economists typically estimate labor supply curves with an expanded regression technique known as *multiple* regression. Multiple regression estimates the linear relationship between the dependent variable and a group of independent variables. Thus, if W and Y_0 are the only two independent variables, the labor supply function to be estimated is:

$$H = a - bW - cY_0, \tag{2C.4}$$

---

2   A detailed description of linear regression is provided in Damodar Gujarati, *Essentials of Econometrics* (New York: Irwin/McGraw-Hill, 1999).

where the coefficient c shows the effect on H of a one-unit change in Y_0, *holding the value of W constant* ($c = \Delta H / \Delta Y$). Multiple regression estimates the coefficients $\hat{a}$, $\hat{b}$, and $\hat{c}$ that minimize the sum of squared deviations between H and $\hat{H}$:

$$\sum_{i=1}^{N} (H_i - \hat{H}_i)^2 = \sum_{i=1}^{N} (H_i - \hat{a} - \hat{b} W_i - \hat{c} Y_0)^2. \tag{2C.5}$$

An example of such a regression line might be:

$$\hat{H} = 1{,}500 + 50W - .1Y_0. \tag{2C.6}$$

This regression line is shown in graph (b) of Figure 2C.1 as $H(W)_1$. If $W = 0$ and $Y_0 = 0$, annual hours of work would be 1,500 (point A). Keeping $Y_0 = 0$, each dollar increase in the wage W would cause annual hours of work to increase by 50 hours. Thus, if $W = \$6.00$ and $Y_0 = 0$, predicted hours of work would be $\hat{H} = 1{,}500 + 50(6.00) - .1(0) = 1{,}800$ (point B). An increase in the wage to $8.00 would cause hours of work to increase further to 1,900 (point C). What happens to annual hours of work if nonlabor income Y_0 is no longer $0 but $2,000? From Equation 2C.6, $\hat{H} = 1{,}500 + 50(8.00) - .1(2{,}000) = 1{,}700$ (point D), yielding a new regression line $H(W)_2$. A change in the wage rate causes a *movement along* the labor supply function, while a change in nonlabor income causes a *shift* in the labor supply function.

There are a number of other factors besides the wage rate and level of non-labor income that affect hours of work and, accordingly, should be included in the regression equation. Let the letter Z stand for this list or vector of variables. The complete labor supply function to be estimated, therefore, can be represented as:

$$H = a + bW + cY_0 + dZ, \tag{2C.7}$$

where d is the vector of regression coefficients that correspond to the variables in Z.

The Standard Error of the Regression Coefficient

Once estimates of $\hat{b}$ and the other regression coefficients are obtained, there is next a question about their reliability. The reliability of the regression coefficient b is measured by the *standard error of the regression coefficient $\hat{\sigma}_b$*. The standard error provides an idea of the precision with which the regression coefficient $\hat{b}$ is able to estimate the true value of b. The following concrete example may make this concept clearer.

In Equation 2C.6 it is assumed that $\hat{b} = 50$. If $\hat{\sigma}_b = 3.0$ there is (roughly speaking) about a 68 percent chance that the true value of b will be in the interval $\hat{b} \pm \hat{\sigma}_b$ that is, within 47 and 53. Likewise, there is about a 95 percent chance that b will be in the interval $\hat{b} \pm 2\hat{\sigma}_b$ (44 to 56). This range is fairly narrow, suggesting that $\hat{b}$ is a very reliable estimate of b. If, on the other hand $\hat{\sigma}_b = 75$, this implies that there is about a 95 percent chance that the interval -100 to 200 contains the true value of b. In this case $\hat{b}$ is a very unreliable estimate of b, so unreliable, in fact, that it is quite possible that $b = 0$ (implying no relationship between W and H).

A common way to judge whether $\hat{b}$ is sufficiently reliable that it can be assumed that $b \neq 0$ is to calculate a *t-ratio*. The *t*-ratio is measured by dividing the regression coefficient by its standard error. For $\hat{b}$ the *t*-ratio is $t_b = \hat{b}/\hat{\sigma}_b$. As a handy rule of thumb, whenever the *t*-ratio equals two or more it can be concluded with a 95 percent degree of confidence that $\hat{b}$ is "statistically significant," meaning that the true value of b is indeed different from zero. Thus, in the example above, for $\hat{b} = 50$ and $\hat{\sigma}_b = 3.0$, $t_b = 16.6$; if $\hat{\sigma}_b = 75$, however, $t_b = .66$. In the latter case, although $\hat{b} = 50$, the *t*-ratio indicates that this estimate is sufficiently unreliable that we cannot reject the possibility that $b = 0$. Finally, although the discussion has been in terms of the regression coefficient $\hat{b}$ it is possible to calculate a standard error and *t*-ratio for each of the other regression coefficients estimated using Equation 2C.7.

The Coefficient of Determination

Another statistic frequently encountered in regression analysis is *the coefficient of determination*, R^2. It measures the proportion of the overall variation in the dependent variable that is explained by the regression equation. The R^2 can range in value from 0 (the regression explains none of the variation in H) to 1.0 (all the variation is explained). The coefficient of determination is often used as a measure of the explanatory power or "goodness of fit" of the regression. While a low R^2 means that much of the variation in the dependent variable is unaccounted for by the independent variables in the model, this does not mean that the regression equation is fundamentally flawed. Particularly in studies using cross-sectional data, much variation in behavior is random or a result of factors incapable of being measured. In this case, the R_2 may be quite low, although the estimated regression coefficients on the independent variables may all be statistically significant.

Calculating Labor Supply Elasticities

One of the major objectives of estimating a labor supply function is to determine the size of the income and substitution effects. As given in Equations 2.2 and 2.3, the substitution effect is $\left.\dfrac{\Delta H}{\Delta Y}\right|_{\bar{Y}_0}$ and the income effect is $\left.\dfrac{\Delta H}{\Delta Y}\right|_{\bar{W}}$. These expressions relate the absolute change in H to the absolute change in W or Y_0. For many purposes, it is more convenient to express these in percentage terms, or what are called *elasticity* estimates. From the labor supply function Equation 2C.7 and from the derivation illustrated in Appendix 2B, the income and substitution effects are reflected in terms of an elasticity as follows:[3]

$$\frac{\partial H}{\partial W}\frac{W}{H} = \frac{\partial b}{\partial W}\frac{W}{H} + W\frac{\partial b}{\partial Y}, \tag{2C.8}$$

---

3 See Mark Killingsworth, *Labor Supply* (Cambridge: Cambridge University Press, 1983), Chapter 3.

where $h(.)$ corresponds to the labor supply function itself. Each of the terms in (2C.8) can be obtained from the estimation of Equation 2C.7 through regression techniques. The gross or uncompensated wage elasticity of labor supply is calculated as $e_{H,W} = \hat{b}(\overline{W}/\overline{H})$, where $\hat{b}$ is the estimated regression coefficient from Equation 2C.7 (recall that $\hat{b} = \partial H/\partial W$)) and $\overline{H}$ and $\overline{W}$ are the sample means of the variables H and W. The total income elasticity (the second term on the right-hand side) is calculated as $e_{H,\overline{Y}_0}|_W = \hat{c}(\overline{Y}_0/\overline{H})$, where $\overline{Y}_0$ is the sample mean of the nonlabor income variable. The compensated wage elasticity (the first term on the right-hand side) is calculated as $e_{H,W}|_{Y_0} = e_{H,W} - e_{H,Y_0}|_W$.

An Example of a Labor Supply Function

To illustrate the concepts discussed above, an actual example of a labor supply function estimated with linear regression is examined. The study was done by Jane Leuthold. The dependent variable was the annual desired hours of work in 1969 of white married women with husband present. The independent variables are briefly described below and are listed in Table 2C.1.

Table 2C.1 also reports the estimated regression coefficients, t-ratios, and the coefficient of determination.[4] The data used by Leuthold to estimate the regression came from the National Longitudinal Survey (NLS). The number of women in her sample was 1,543.

In estimating a labor supply function, the first task is to decide what independent variables should be included in the regression. Economic theory suggests what these variables might be. Based on the labor/leisure model, differences in annual hours of work among married women would be expected to be related to the after-tax wage, the family's nonlabor income, and the wife's preferences for work versus leisure. As discussed in Chapter 3, the husband's earnings, the number of children in the family, the wife's level of education, and the husband's attitudes toward his wife working, among other things, should also have an influence on the desired hours of work of married women. Table 2C.1 shows that Leuthold has included variables for all of these factors in her regression model, although some (particularly the attitude variables) do not totally capture their theoretical counterpart in the theory.

The interpretation of the regression results in Table 2C.1 is relatively straightforward. The regression coefficient on the wife's wage rate, for example, is 104.97. This means that the desired hours of work of the married women in the sample increased, on average, by about 105 hours per year for each dollar increase in the after-tax wage rate. This increase would indicate that for these workers the substitution effect outweighed the income effect, making the labor supply curve upward sloping. The uncompensated wage elasticity $e_{H,W}$, therefore, would be positive. (Leuthold did not report the sample means $\overline{H}$ and $\overline{W}$ so the exact value of $e_{H,W}$ and

---

4   To save space, not all of the independent variables included in the regression are reported in Table 2C.1. Some of the variable names have also been altered slightly.

TABLE 2C.1 AN EXAMPLE OF A LABOR SUPPLY FUNCTION ESTIMATED WITH LINEAR REGRESSION

Dependent Variable	Constant	Wife's Wage Rate	Husband's Earnings	Age	Education	Independent Variables				R^2
						A(1)	A(2)	C(1)	C(2)	
Wife's hours	1286 (4.67)	104.97 (3.70)	−.026 (−3.80)	1.20 (.24)	.69 (.08)	−19.47 (−.40)	266.06 (6.94)	−118.64 (−3.04)	−110.61 (−6.14)	.383

NOTE: *t*-ratios are in parentheses.

Variable Description

Hours: Wife's annual desired hours of work, calculated as usual work hours per week times weeks worked per year plus weeks looking for work.

Wife's wage rate: After-tax real average hourly earnings of wife.

Husband's earnings: Husband's previous year after-tax real annual earnings.

Age: Wife's age in years.

Education: Years of school completed by wife.

A(1): Attitude variable. Coded = 1 if "respondent felt it was all right for a woman to work if she desired and her husband agrees." Coded 0 otherwise.

A(2): Attitude variable. Coded = 1 if "the respondent's husband favored his wife's working." Coded 0 otherwise.

C(1): Number of children less than 6 years of age.

C(2): Number of children in age group 6 to 13.

SOURCE: Jane Leuthold, "The Effect of Taxation on the Hours Worked by Married Women," *Industrial and Labor Relations Review* 31, no. 4 (July 1978): 520–26.

the other labor supply elasticities cannot be calculated.) Since the t-ratio is 3.70, the regression coefficient is statistically significant from zero.

The second variable of interest is the husband's after-tax earnings. The coefficient is $-.026$, indicating that for each additional $1,000 of the husband's earnings, the wife's desired hours of work fall by 26 per year. Since additional earnings by the husband increase the income available to the wife but do not change her wage rate, this should lead to a pure, negative income effect on the wife's desired labor supply. The negative sign on the regression coefficient, and the fact that the coefficient is statistically significant, supports this prediction of the theory.

Several other aspects of the regression results also deserve mention. Some of the regression coefficients have t-ratios less than 2 and, thus, are not statistically significant. The regression coefficient on the age variable, for example, is 1.20, meaning that desired hours of work increase by an average of 1.2 per year with each additional year of age. This estimate is so imprecise, however, that the true value may actually be zero. A second feature of interest is the regression coefficients on the attitudinal variables $A(1)$ and $A(2)$. These are *dummy* variables that take on only one of two possible values: 0 or 1. The second attitudinal variable $A(2)$ is "respondent's husband favored his wife's working." If the answer was "no," the variable $A(2)$ was given a value of 0; if the answer was "yes," it was given a value of 1. The regression coefficient on this variable is approximately 266. What this means is that women who answered yes to this question worked, on average, 266 more hours per year than women who answered no. For a no answer, the effect of this variable on labor supply is $266(0) = 0$, and for a yes answer it is $266(1) = 266$.

A third point of note is that the R^2 statistic is .383, meaning that the regression equation was able to account for 38 percent of the variation in the desired work hours among the women in the sample.

Labor Force Participation

A second dimension of labor supply is labor force participation. Not only do individuals have to make a choice of how many hours to work, they make a simultaneous decision of whether to work at all. As with hours of work in the previous chapter, this chapter first highlights recent trends in labor force participation, then examines theoretical explanations for these trends, and finally turns to a review of empirical evidence on labor force participation.

Definition and Measurement of the Labor Force

Before examining the trends in labor force participation, it is necessary to understand some of the concepts to be discussed in this and later chapters and how labor force data are collected.

Prior to and during most of the Depression, the federal government did not regularly and systematically collect data on employment, unemployment, and other vital economic conditions. Without these data it was difficult for policymakers to gauge either the extent of economic hardship or the direction of change in the economy. As a consequence of this difficulty, Congress authorized a joint program administered by the Census Bureau and the Bureau of Labor Statistics (BLS) to collect and analyze labor force statistics. A major source of such data is the **Current Population Survey (CPS),** commonly referred to as the "household" survey. The CPS is conducted each month to obtain comprehensive data on the labor force, the employed, and the unemployed. The information is collected by a special group of 1,500 highly trained interviewers who sample about 60,000 households across all 50 states.[1] Even though only 1 out of every 1,600 American households is interviewed, the figures obtained from the CPS on national employment and unemployment

---

[1] A detailed discussion of the sample design, interview process, and accuracy of the CPS is given in *How the Government Measures Unemployment*, prepared by John F. Stinson Jr. for the Bureau of Labor Statistics, U.S. Department of Labor (Report 864, Feb. 1994). Also see the "Explanatory Notes" in any issue of *Employment and Earnings*.

are quite accurate. The chances are 9 out of 10, for example, that the unemployment rate calculated from the survey will be within one-tenth of one percentage point of the true rate.

Table 3.1 shows several key measures of labor force activity collected from the CPS for various years between 1950 and 2004. The basic purpose of the labor force data is to measure the amount of labor input available for production in the economy. Thus, of the total population of more than 295 million in 2004, people who were less than 16 years of age or were confined to prisons, mental hospitals, or other institutions were immediately excluded from consideration as potential labor force participants, since they are presumed to be unable to work.[2] Subtracting this group from the total population yields the *noninstitutional population*, shown in the far left column of Table 3.1. Those 223.3 million people were potentially available for work, but not all decided to work or look for work; some chose instead to go to school, stay at home and care for children, or retire, for example. All individuals who were neither working nor looking for work are counted as *not in the labor force*. In 2004, 75.9 million people were included in this category.

The remaining part of the population comprises the *labor force*. These people were either working or looking for work. In 2004, there were 147.4 million people in the labor force. One of the most important labor force statistics is the **labor force participation rate;** it measures the people in the labor force as a percentage of the noninstitutionalized population. In 2004, the labor force participation rate was 66 percent.

The labor force itself comprises two groups: the *employed* and the *unemployed*. The employed group includes anyone working for pay at least one hour a week who is not in an institution or the armed forces. Also counted as employed are two other groups of people: those who work 15 hours or more a week without pay in a family business, and those who have a paying job but are not currently at work because of illness, bad weather, a strike, or personal reasons. The unemployed group is counted in the labor force because even though these people are not working, they are seeking work and are thus available as labor input for the economy. The **unemployment rate** in 2004 was 5.5 percent; it is measured as the number of unemployed persons divided by the total labor force.

The most recent modifications to the way in which data are collected and in which some statistics are calculated were made in 1994. Modifications made prior to 1994 took place in 1979 based on recommendations made by the National Commission on Employment and Unemployment. As currently defined, to be counted as unemployed an individual has to satisfy three criteria: he or she must be out of work, looking for work, and able to take a job if it is offered. The criteria for "looking for work" is defined as making some effort (for example, answering a want ad, going for a job interview, or asking friends for job leads) to find work in the previous *four* weeks. If the person is out of work and desires a job, but has made no overt effort in the last four weeks to find employment, the CPS interviewer no longer counts the person as unemployed, but as not in the labor force. If a person

---

2   Prior to 1967 the lower age limit for inclusion in the labor force was 14.

	Noninstitutional Population	Civilian Labor Force		Employed			Unemployed		Not in Labor Force
	Number	Number	Percentage of Population	Total	Agricultural Industries	Nonagricultural Industries	Number	Percentage of Labor Force	
1950	104,995	62,208	59.2	58,918	7,160	51,758	3,288	5.3	42,787
1960	117,245	69,628	59.4	65,778	5,458	60,318	3,852	5.5	47,617
1970	137,085	82,771	60.4	78,678	3,463	75,215	4,093	4.9	54,314
1980	167,745	106,940	63.8	99,303	3,364	95,938	7,637	7.1	60,805
1985	178,206	115,461	64.8	107,150	3,179	103,971	8,312	7.2	62,745
1990	189,164	125,840	66.5	118,793	3,223	115,570	7,047	5.6	63,324
1995	198,584	132,304	66.6	124,900	3,440	121,460	7,404	5.6	66,280
2000	209,699	140,863	67.2	135,208	3,305	131,903	5,655	4.0	68,836
2001	211,864	141,815	66.9	135,073	3,144	131,929	6,742	4.8	70,050
2002	217,570	144,863	66.6	136,485	2,311	134,174	8,378	5.8	72,707
2003	221,168	146,510	66.2	137,736	2,275	135,461	8,774	6	74,658
2004	223,357	147,401	66	139,252	2,232	137,020	8,149	5.5	75,956

Note: Numbers are in thousands.

SOURCE: Bureau of Labor Statistics, *Employment and Earnings* (January 2005): Tables A-1 and 15. Also see, http://www.bls.gov/cps/cpsatabs.htm.

The Work Force in the Twenty-First Century: The Challenge Facing Employers

Three labor force developments promise to make the work force in the early twenty-first century a special challenge for U.S. companies. One of these developments is the dramatic slowing in the rate of labor force growth. In the 1980s the labor force grew by 2–2.5 percent a year, fueled in large part by the entrance into the labor market of the last part of the baby-boom generation. By the early 2000s, however, labor force growth fell to only half this level as the "baby-bust" generation of the 1970s trickled into the work force. Labor force growth is projected to fall even further in the future, reaching 0.8 percent a year by 2010. Although the recession and slow economic recovery during the 2000–2004 period has led to a temporary surplus of job seekers and rise in unemployment, over the longer run the big concern of employers is not labor surpluses but labor shortages. Their fear is that the combination of few new labor market entrants, a flood of people exiting the labor market as baby boomers retire from the work force, and resumption of healthy economic growth will leave them unable to find enough employees to meet production goals.

The second labor force development that will have a significant impact on employers is the growing gender, cultural, and racial diversity of the work force. White males, traditionally the mainstay of the work force, will comprise only three out of every ten new entrants into the labor force after the year 2000. Their share of the total labor force has shrunk from 51 percent in 1980 to 45 percent in 2003. The other seven out of ten new entrants will be women, members of minority groups such as blacks and Hispanics, and new immigrants from a variety of third-world countries. Hispanics, for example, will comprise 25 percent of the work force in 2020, compared to only 12 percent today. The new corporate buzzword for recruiting, training, and promoting this disparate group of new employees is "managing diversity."

The third challenge will be a work force not trained to meet the skill demands of an increasingly high-tech economy. A top executive in the North Central Massachusetts Chamber of Commerce estimates that one-third of the workers in the state are not equipped to meet the demands of employers. With workers lacking basic math and language skills, employers need to face the possibility that further general education beyond school will fall on their shoulders.

A number of companies have begun to implement proactive policies to meet the challenges of the work force in the twenty-first century. Examples include:

- improving child-care arrangements to attract working mothers.
- stepping up recruitment efforts among minorities.
- instituting aggressive policies to combat discrimination.
- increasing expenditures on in-company training programs.
- promoting a corporate culture receptive to cultural diversity
- implementing of flexible work hours.
- upgrading jobs and improving the work environment.
- providing drug and alcohol counseling services.
- providing adult education opportunities.
- recruiting overseas for high-tech workers.

SOURCES: "Get Ready for the New Work Force," *Fortune* (23 April 1990): 165–81; "Work Force Lacking Skills: Workers Falling behind Fast-Changing Economy," *Telegram and Gazette* (15 February 2001): E1; "Davos: The Brainstorming Retreat for World Leaders," *Business Times* (28 January 2000): 4; "Coming Soon: The Vanishing Work Force," *New York Times* (August 29, 2004), p. BU-1, "Hispanic Nation," *Business Week,* (March 15, 2004), p. 58; "The Business Impact of Diversity," *Personnel Today* (September 2, 2003), p. 18.

is not in the labor force, wants a job, is available for work, and has looked for work sometime in the past 12 months (but not recently), he or she is called a **discouraged worker,** implying that he or she has given up even looking for work because of poor job prospects. In fact, the person must also indicate that the reason for not recently looking for work is the impression that job prospects are poor. In 2004 there was an average of 466,000 discouraged workers. A number of critics of the current BLS definition of unemployment argue that by excluding discouraged workers, the BLS biases the unemployment rate significantly downward. If discouraged workers had been included as part of the unemployed group in 2004, the unemployment rate would have been 5.8 percent instead of 5.5 percent.

A major argument against counting discouraged workers as unemployed is that to be reliable, the data on unemployment have to be based on objective differences in behavior (such as whether a person has made a recent explicit effort to find a job) rather than on the subjective desire of wanting a job. This debate is what led to a new definition of discouraged workers in 1994. Prior to 1994, to be considered discouraged, a person not in the labor force merely had to indicate a desire for a job. Now that person must indicate that some effort has been made to find a job in the past year, although the effort has not been recent enough to classify that person as unemployed.

Patterns in Labor Force Participation

The labor force participation rate measures the percentage of the eligible population that is working or seeking work. It is clearly an important dimension of labor supply to the economy.

Shown in Figure 3.1 for the years 1950 through 2004 is the labor force participation rate for three groups: men, women, and all demographic groups together. In 1950, 59.2 percent of the noninstitutional population was in the labor force; by 2004 this rate had increased to 66 percent. During the first two-thirds of this period, the total labor force participation rate was constant, hovering around 60 percent. In the 1970s, however, the participation rate moved upward fairly noticeably. Since the year 2000, however, the labor force participation rate has shown a decline.

The constancy in the total participation rate in the 1950s and 1960s masked significant developments in participation for men and women, respectively. In 1950, there was a clear division of labor between the sexes—the great proportion of men (86.4 percent) were in the labor force, while only one-third (33.9 percent) of women were. This disparity has shrunk considerably in the intervening 50 years; the male labor force participation rate had declined to 73.5 percent by 2004 while the participation rate of women had risen to 59.2 percent.

It is evident from Figure 3.1 that the most dynamic change in labor force participation in the post-World War II era is the dramatic increase in the proportion of women working in the labor market. In a 50-year period, the labor participation rate for women increased by two-thirds, with the result that today three of every five women are working or seeking work. This development has had profound social and economic consequences and is a central focus of this chapter.

FIGURE 3.1   TRENDS IN LABOR FORCE PARTICIPATION RATES, 1950–2004

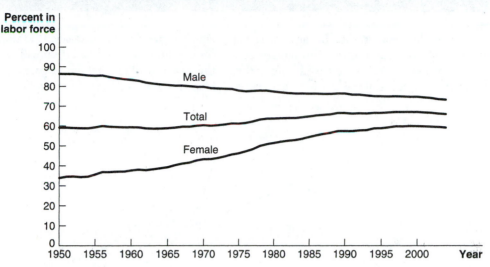

SOURCE: Bureau of Labor Statistics, *Employment and Earnings* (January 2005): Historial A tables. Also see http://www.bls.gov/webapps/legacy/cpsatab1.htm.

The Decision to Work

As with hours of work, each individual is faced with a choice of how to allocate time: Should he or she work in the market or spend time in nonmarket activities? As a first step in analyzing the labor force participation decision, it is assumed that total discretionary time can be used for one of two mutually exclusive activities, work or leisure. The next section, however, introduces a more realistic three-way use of time, distinguishing among market work, nonmarket work, and leisure.

The labor/leisure model presented in Chapter 2 to analyze hours of work can also be used to analyze the labor force participation decision, as shown in Figure 3.2. It is assumed there are 100 hours of discretionary time per week that can be allocated between work and leisure. The budget constraint *ABC* represents the possible combinations of income and leisure available to the individual, given both the wage rate of W_1 and Y_1 nonlabor income. Finally, there is a series of indifference curves I_1, I_2, and I_3 that represent the individual's preferences for income versus leisure. To maximize utility, the individual should choose the combination of income and leisure that allows him or her to reach the highest indifference curve possible. Chapter 2 (Figure 2.5) shows this occurring where the budget constraint and an indifference curve are just tangent, an outcome economists call an *interior solution*, since the point of tangency occurs within the end points of the budget constraint. If the indifference curves are relatively steep, or the budget constraint is

FIGURE 3.2   A CORNER SOLUTION AND NONPARTICIPATION IN THE LABOR FORCE

Given the budget constraint *ABC* and the shape of the indifference curves, utility is maximized by working zero hours (point *B*). As long as the slope of the budget constraint is less than or equal to the reservation wage (the slope of the broken line), a corner solution will occur and the person will choose not to participate in the labor force.

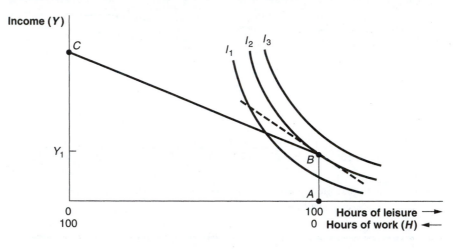

relatively flat, however, no interior solution may be possible. This situation is illustrated in Figure 3.2. Given the budget constraint *ABC*, the highest level of utility is reached at point *B*, where the budget constraint and the indifference curve I_2 intersect. Point *B* is called a *corner solution*. At point *B*, the person maximizes utility by working zero hours and is classified as not in the labor force. This person devotes the entire amount of discretionary time to nonmarket activities, whether school, housework, or pure leisure.

Why did the individual depicted in Figure 3.2 decide not to participate in the labor force? Recall that the slope of the budget constraint reflects the value of the wage rate—the value of this person's time *to the market*. The slope of the indifference curve, on the other hand, measures the marginal rate of substitution, the subjective value this person places on his or her time. The slope of the indifference curve at the point of zero hours of work is of particular significance and is called the **reservation wage;** it measures the amount of money the person would have to be given to be induced to work the *first* hour. The value of the reservation wage is shown in Figure 3.2 by the slope of the broken line, which is just tangent to I_2 at point *B*, where hours of work are zero. At point *B* the value of this person's time is greater than the amount the market is willing to pay him or her to work ($MRS_B > W_1$). Therefore, this person chooses not to work. Whenever the market wage (the slope of the budget constraint) is less than the reservation wage (the *MRS* at zero hours of work), hours of work will be zero since the utility loss from giving up even one hour of leisure to participate in the labor force would be greater than the utility gained from the income earned from market work. For a person to participate in the labor force, therefore, the fundamental requirement is that the market wage exceed the reservation wage.

➲ **SEE**

Policy Application 3-1: The Earned Income Tax Credit: A Way to Help the Poor *and* Encourage Labor Force Participation, p. 153.

As pointed out in Chapter 2, one of the main goals of welfare reform in the mid-1990s was to encourage (create incentives for) greater labor force participation among the poor. While welfare time limits and work requirements take the "stick" approach to encouraging labor force participation, there are other programs, such as the Earned Income Tax Credit (EITC) that take the "carrot" approach to encouraging labor force participation. Policy Application 3-1 explores the effectiveness of the EITC in encouraging labor force participation.

Participation and Changes in the Market Wage Rate

Figure 3.3 illustrates how the decision to participate in the labor force is influenced by changes in the market wage rate. The initial equilibrium is at point *B*, where the indifference curve I_1 intersects the budget constraint *ABC*, and the individual opts not to participate in the labor force. What happens to labor force participation if the wage rate rises to W_2? The rise in the wage rotates the budget constraint from *ABC* to *ABD*, and a new equilibrium point is reached at H_1 hours of work (point *X*), where *ABD* is just tangent to the indifference curve I_2. Because the person is now working at a paying job, he or she is classified as in the labor force. The reason for this switch in behavior is that the market wage (the slope of *BD*) now exceeds the person's reservation wage (the *MRS* at zero hours of work on I_2), and the monetary gain from working that first hour exceeds the utility loss from giving up that hour of leisure. Each extra hour of work continues to increase utility until point *X* is reached, where the wage W_2 is equal to the marginal rate of substitution.

It is evident that an increase in the wage rate has a different impact on labor force participation and hours of work, respectively. Chapter 2 shows that a rise in the wage rate may cause a person already working in the market to either work more hours or fewer hours, depending on the relative size of the income and substitution effects. If a person is not in the labor force, however, a rise in the wage rate will unambiguously increase the probability of entering the labor force to seek market work. The reason is that a rise in the wage cannot give rise to a negative income effect as long as hours of work (and earnings from work) are zero. A rise in the market wage will continue to give rise to a positive substitution effect, however, since every hour of nonmarket time now becomes more expensive. For a person who is out of the labor force, a sufficiently large increase in the market wage must at some point make the market wage greater than the reservation wage, leading the individual to seek gainful employment. One prediction of the labor/leisure model, therefore, is that labor force participation should be more sensitive to changes in

FIGURE 3.3   THE EFFECT ON PARTICIPATION OF A CHANGE IN THE WAGE RATE

The original value of the wage rate is W_1, giving rise to the budget constraint ABC and a corner solution with the indifference curve I_1 at point B. At point B the person is out of the labor force. An increase in the wage to W_2 rotates the budget constraint to ABD, and an interior solution occurs at point X on indifference curve I_2. The person now chooses to participate in the labor force and work H_1 hours.

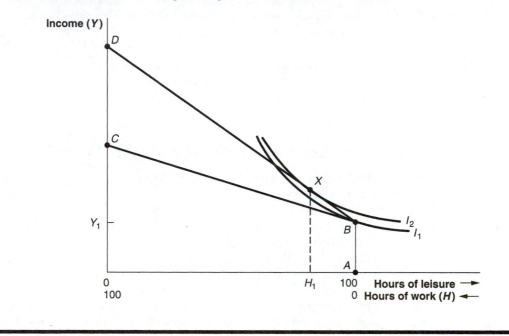

wage rates than should hours of work, a prediction that is confirmed by most empirical studies.[3]

Participation and Changes in Nonlabor Income

The next issue concerns the effect of changes in nonlabor income on the decision to participate in the labor force. This case is illustrated in Figure 3.4. It is assumed that the person has zero nonlabor income and the market wage is W_1, giving rise

3   Michael C. Keeley, *Labor Supply and Public Policy* (New York: Academic Press, 1981): 24; Lisa M. Powell, "The Impact of Child Care Costs on the Labour Supply of Married Mothers: Evidence from Canada," *Canadian Journal of Economics* 30 (August 1997): 577–94; and Jean Kimmel and Thomas J. Kniesner, "New Evidence on Labor Supply: Employment Versus Hours Elasticities by Sex and Marital Status," *Journal of Monetary Economics* 42 (October 1998): 289–301.

With zero nonlabor income, the budget constraint is *AB*, and hours of work are H_1 (point *V*). The person chooses to participate in the labor force since the market wage (the slope of the budget constraint) is greater than the reservation wage (the slope of the dashed line drawn tangent to I_1). With nonlabor income of Y_1, the budget constraint becomes *ACD*, and

hours of work decline to H_2 (point *X*). Since the market wage still exceeds the reservation wage, the person chooses to remain in the labor force. When nonlabor income is increased to Y_2, the budget constraint becomes *AEF*, and the person drops out of the labor force. At this point the market wage no longer exceeds the reservation wage.

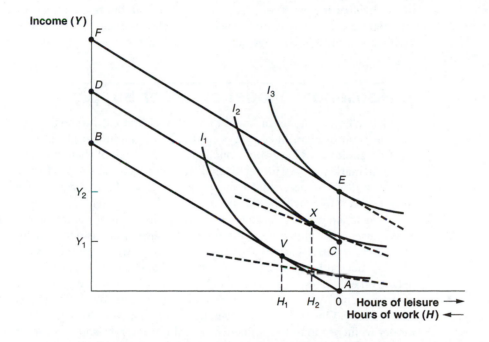

to the budget constraint *AB* and equilibrium hours of work of H_1 (point *V*), where the budget constraint *AB* is tangent to the indifference curve I_1. Since the value of the market wage (the slope of *AB*) exceeds the reservation wage (the slope of the broken line tangent to I_1), the person chooses to participate in the labor force.

An increase in nonlabor income of Y_1, holding the wage rate constant, shifts the budget constraint to *ACD*, giving rise to a new equilibrium at point *X*, where the budget constraint *ACD* is tangent to I_2. Hours of work fall from H_1 to H_2, consistent with the assumption that leisure time is a normal good. The person still chooses to participate in the labor force, however, since the market wage (the slope of CD) exceeds the reservation wage (the slope of the broken line tangent to I_2). If nonlabor income is increased further, the person will at some point finally decide to work zero hours in the market and will drop out of the labor force. Given Y_2 nonlabor income, for example, the budget constraint is AEF and the equilibrium is at point E, where there is a corner solution between the budget constraint and the indifference curve I_3. At zero hours of work (point E), the market wage is exactly equal to the reservation wage, and the individual finds it optimal to drop out of the labor force.

The conclusion is that the probability of labor force participation decreases with the amount of nonlabor income, other things equal. The reason for this can be seen in Figure 3.4. Given the assumption that leisure is a normal good, it is evident by comparing the respective slopes of the broken lines that the reservation wage of the individual increases as successively greater amounts of nonlabor income are attained. At a sufficiently high level of nonlabor income the reservation wage will finally equal the market wage, and the person will drop out of the labor force.

A Household Model of Labor Supply

The labor/leisure model of hours of work was first used to analyze the participation decision of men, since they were by far the largest group in the labor force. Because adult males have traditionally spent the bulk of their time in continuous, full-time market work with relatively little time spent on various forms of nonmarket work (for instance, child rearing and housework), it did not seem to stretch reality too far to couch the time allocation decision in terms of work and leisure.

As married women became a growing proportion of the labor force, however, economists realized that the simple labor/leisure model is deficient in two important respects. First, it ignores the family context in which the labor supply decisions of husbands and wives are made. The husband and wife do not independently decide on each person's allocation of time to work and leisure, but rather pool their resources and make a joint labor supply decision to maximize the utility of the entire family. One needed improvement, therefore, is to broaden the labor/leisure model to incorporate the influence that the wage rate and income of one family member has on the labor supply decisions of other family members.

The second deficiency of the labor/leisure model is that it does not realistically represent the set of choices open to men and women with respect to their use of time. Rather than a strict dichotomy between labor and leisure, married women have traditionally had three alternative uses of time: market work, nonmarket or home work, and leisure. Given the gradual evolution in the social perception of family roles, this three-way allocation of time has become increasingly relevant for men as well in recent years. Thus, to adequately explain trends in labor supply it is necessary to expand the theory to take into account not only shifts in time between labor and leisure, but also between market work and nonmarket work.

Studies by Jacob Mincer and Marvin Kosters were among the first to broaden the labor/leisure model to take into account both of these objections to the simpler theory.[4] The decision-making unit in this household model is the family, composed of a husband, wife, and possibly one or more children. Both the husband and wife (and children who are old enough to work) have three uses of their time: market work, nonmarket work (household or school), and leisure. The objective of the family is to allocate the time of each family member to these three activities to maximize the total utility of the group. The attainable combination of market goods, nonmarket or home goods (such as home-cooked meals, a clean house, and child rearing), and leisure are constrained by the wage rate that each family member can earn, the family's level of nonlabor income, and the total amount of time per week over which the family has discretion.

The first issue to consider is the effect of changes in nonlabor income on the family's allocation of time. As before, leisure is assumed to be a normal good. An increase in the amount of nonlabor income available to the family will, therefore, set off a negative income effect, leading to a reduction in hours of work on the part of all or some of the family members. A large inheritance or a substantial amount of capital or property income, for example, might lead the husband to work fewer hours of overtime or the wife or teenaged son or daughter to withdraw from the labor force altogether. In this three-way household model a greater demand for leisure does not necessarily imply an equal decrease in hours of market work as in the two-way labor/leisure model; more hours of leisure could be obtained by reducing work in the home instead of work in the market.

The allocation of time of each family member is also influenced by the wage rate each person can earn in the market. A change in the wage of person i in the family will affect both the individual's own labor supply decision and the labor supply decision of another family member, person j, through three different and conceptually distinct channels. First, a change in the wage of person i (W_i) will lead to a positive substitution effect on the hours of work of person i (H_i). The change in W_i will also affect H_i through a countervailing, negative income effect. Both of these are exactly the same concepts as were developed in Chapter 2. In the household model there is also a third effect not found in the simple labor/leisure model—the "cross-substitution" effect. This measures the effect of a change in the wage of person i on the hours of work of person j in the family.

To make the discussion more concrete, assume the family is composed of only a husband and wife, and that initially the husband works in the market full-time while the wife devotes her time to work in the home. Also assume that, due to economic growth, the market wage that the wife can earn increases. This will have several repercussions on the family's allocation of time. With respect to the wife's own labor supply decision, the rise in the wage increases the opportunity cost of each

---

4   Jacob Mincer, "Labor Force Participation of Married Women," in H. Gregg Lewis, ed., *Aspects of Labor Economics* (Princeton, N.J.: Princeton University Press, 1962): 63–105; Marvin Kosters, "Income and Substitution Effects in a Family Labor Supply Model," P-3339 (Santa Monica, Calif.: Rand Corporation, 1966). Alternative household models are described in Marjorie B. McElroy, "Empirical Content of Nash Bargained Household Behavior," *Journal of Human Resources* 25 (Fall 1990): 559–83. Also see Shelly Lundberg, et al., "The Retirement-Consumption Puzzle: A Marital Bargaining Approach," *Journal of Public Economics* 87 (May 2003): 1199–1218.

hour spent in home work and leisure, pulling the wife toward participation in the labor force. Only when the market wage rises enough to exceed her reservation wage, however, will she seek employment outside the home.

When the wife was out of the labor force, the rise in her market wage led to a positive substitution effect that motivated her to substitute from nonmarket uses of time to market work. Once she is in the labor force, a further increase in the wage sets off both an income effect and a substitution effect for the wife. For a given number of hours of work, a rise in her wage leads to a higher amount of income and a negative income effect pulling her toward additional hours of leisure. A rise in the wage also raises the price of nonmarket time, leading to a positive substitution effect that pulls her towards market work and away from home work and leisure. The net effect of this increase in the wife's wage on her hours of work, therefore, is indeterminant—it depends on the relative sizes of the income and substitution effects.

The increase in the wife's wage also leads to a second income effect in the household model that was not present in the simple labor/leisure model. When the wife decides to work, not only her income increases, but also the income available to her husband, leading to a negative income effect on *his* labor supply. Assuming his wage rate remains constant, higher earnings of the wife are equivalent to an increase in nonlabor income for the husband, causing him to demand greater leisure and, thus, to offer less time to market work and home work.[5] This result is symmetric: if the earnings of the husband increase, the greater is the income available to the wife, and the lower is the probability that she will participate in the labor force. (This corresponds to the situation illustrated in Figure 3.4.) This prediction accords with the observed tendency for married women's labor force participation rate to fall as the income of the husband becomes greater.

Finally, a rise in the wife's wage also leads to a **cross-substitution effect** on her husband's supply of labor.[6] As stated earlier, the cross-substitution effect is the change in hours of work of person j given a change in the wage rate of person i, holding income of the family constant.

$$\text{Cross-substitution effect} = \left.\frac{\Delta H_j}{\Delta W_i}\right|_{\overline{Y}} \gtreqless 0 \qquad \textbf{(3.1)}$$

The sign of the cross-substitution effect can be either positive or negative. Just as a rise in the price of good X will cause consumers to change the quantity they demand of good Y, so too will a rise in the price of leisure for the wife cause a change in the quantity of market work offered by the husband (and vice versa),

---

5   The validity of this prediction was clearly attested to in remarks made by the president of the American Society for Personnel Administration. He said, "When a family had a single wage earner, that man often had to accept many kinds of unattractive work obligations. Now men are saying no to overtime, to heavy travel, to unpleasant working conditions. But the freedom to put lifestyle first comes only with the fact that the man has a second income, namely his wife's." Quoted in "Men Lose Freedom If Women Lose Ground," *Wall Street Journal* (February 2, 1987): 24.

6   See Orley Ashenfelter and James Heckman, "The Estimation of Income and Substitution Effects in a Model of Family Labor Supply," *Econometrica* 42, no. 1 (January 1974): 73–85. More recent estimates of own- and cross-wage elasticities can be found in Paul J. Devereux, "Changes in Relative Wages and Family Labor Supply," *Journal of Human Resources* 39 (Summer 2004): 696–722.

quite independent of any change in family income. The effect of a rise in the price of good X on the demand for good Y depends on whether the two goods are substitutes (apples and oranges) or complements (cameras and film). The same is true in the theory of labor supply. Holding income constant, a rise in the wife's wage leads her to work more through the substitution effect. If the wife's and husband's time in the market are substitutes, as she works more he will work less (for example, he will spend more time cooking and cleaning at home), leading to a *negative* cross-substitution effect. It is possible, however, that her market work and that of her husband may be complements—as she works more in the market so does he (for example, leisure time is only enjoyed if they share it together and, thus, as the wife reduces her amount of time devoted to leisure so does the husband). In the case of complements, the cross-substitution effect is *positive*.

Theory cannot predict whether the cross-substitution effect will be positive or negative. Several studies on the subject found that for husband–wife couples with no children, the cross-substitution effect was zero or positive, while for couples with children, the cross-substitution effects were negative (or at least less positive)—an increase in the husband's (wife's) wage and labor supply, holding family income constant, causes the wife (husband) to work less.[7]

The household model illustrates the complex interrelationships that exist between a change in one person's wage rate and income and the resulting change in the individual's own hours of work and the hours of work of other family members. The household model of labor supply also provides several key insights into different facets of labor force participation.

The Division of Labor by Gender

The household model helps explain the clear division of labor between husband and wife in the "traditional" family of 40 or 50 years ago. It suggests that the specialization of men in market work and women in home work reflected a rational allocation of time by the family to those activities for which each person had a comparative advantage. For the husband and wife to achieve an optimal allocation of time, each should work an additional hour in the market as long as the wage rate exceeds the value of that hour devoted to work in the home. In the context of the economic and social environment of 1950, the great majority of married women did not participate in the labor force because, in this view, the wage rate they could get from market work was relatively low while the value of their time at home was much higher due to factors such as the large number of children in the family and the unavailability of time-saving household appliances and ready-to-eat food.

7   Shelly Lundberg, "Labor Supply of Husbands and Wives: A Simultaneous Equations Approach," *Review of Economics and Statistics* 70, no. 2 (May 1988): 224–35. Julie Hotchkiss, Mary Mathewes Kassis, and Robert Moore, "Running Hard and Falling Behind: A Welfare Analysis of Two-Earner Families," *Journal of Population Economics* 10 (Fall 1997): 237–50; Shelly Lundberg and Elaina Rose, "Parenthood and the Earnings of Men and Women," *Labour Economics* 7 (November 2000): 689–710; and Daniel Hamermesh, "Timing, Togetherness, and Time Windfalls," *Journal of Population Economics* 15 (November 2002): 601–23.

Married men, on the other hand, found it economically worthwhile to devote their time to market work, reflecting the relatively high wage that they could earn and their actual or perceived low productivity at child care, housework, and so on.

The Convergence in Participation Rates

The household model also explains why this traditional division of labor between the sexes has been breaking down. As shown in Figure 3.1, over the past 40 years the labor force participation rates of men and women have slowly converged. Why has the labor force participation rate for females risen so sharply and that for men fallen?

In terms of the household model, the key to understanding the rise in female labor force participation is the increase in labor market opportunities for women. Over the postwar period, real wages earned by women have risen considerably, giving rise to a positive substitution effect for women as the relative price of time spent in nonmarket activities becomes greater. A major insight of the household model is to show that this substitution effect for women takes two different forms. A rise in the wage rate makes leisure more expensive, motivating a substitution from leisure to market work. A rise in the wage *also* makes time devoted to home work more expensive, motivating a substitution from nonmarket to market work. If the woman is already working, this rise in the wage also sets off a negative income effect, pulling her toward more leisure and less work.

The household model predicts that the potential for substitution not only from leisure to market work but also from home work to market work should make the substitution effect for married women much larger than that for men. Evidence from time-budget studies does reveal just such a substitution. One study found that women who were full-time homemakers devoted more than one and one half times as many hours per week to household work as did women who held paying jobs.[8] Part of the rise in female labor force participation, therefore, has taken the form of replacing home work with market work. These studies have also found that women who choose to work also reduce their leisure time as well, particularly for passive leisure activities such as sleeping, reading, and watching television. The same survey mention above estimates that the working women have about 16 hours less leisure time per week than the full-time homemaker.[9]

If women's labor force participation has increased over time as a reaction to rising wages, why has the participation rate for men declined at the same time? The household model also offers an explanation for this apparent inconsistency. The rise in wages over time leads to an income effect and a substitution effect on the labor supply of men, the income effect pulling men toward more leisure and

---

[8]   Bureau of Labor Statistics, "Time-Use Survey—First Results Announced by the BLS," *NEWS*, USDOL 04–1797 (14 September 2004).

[9]   Also see Mohammed Alenezi and Michael L. Walden, "A New Look at Husbands' and Wives' Time Allocation," *Journal of Consumer Affairs* 38 (Summer 2004): 81–106.

the substitution effect pushing men toward additional work. The crucial difference is that the size of the substitution effect for men is likely to be much smaller than for women. Since men have traditionally devoted little time to home work, they cannot substitute from nonmarket work to market work as women can, and, thus, the substitution effect for men is limited to a trade-off of leisure for market work.

The secular decline in male labor force participation rates reflects the fact that for men the negative income effect from higher wages has outweighed the substitution effect, a substitution effect that was considerably smaller than that for women. Part of the decline in male labor force participation rates may also have been due to a negative cross-substitution effect between the rise in women's wages and husbands' hours of work. As women work more, assuming that the time of husbands and that of wives in home work are substitutes, part of the decline in male labor force participation would reflect a reallocation of time for men from market work to home work. Is this what has happened?

The evidence is contradictory on this point. One study found that between 1969 and 1987 employed women increased their annual hours of market work by 305 hours and decreased hours of housework by 145 hours, resulting in a net increase in work hours of 160. Over the same period, men increased their hours of housework by only 68 per year (this amounts to less than 15 minutes per workday).[10] A more recent survey, however, found that between 1977 and 1997, married men with children increased their average number of hours spent on child care and chores by 1.5 hours per workday, while employed married women decreased their hours spent on the same activities by 0.4 hours. So, while men may not have appeared to be doing their share through the eighties, they seem to have been making up for lost time in the nineties.[11]

SEE

Empirical Evidence 3-1:
Age/Participation Profiles, p. 159.

Further details about labor force participation over a worker's lifetime can be found in Empirical Evidence 3-1.

Time Allocation: An Extension to the Household Model

The household model represents a significant generalization of the theory of choice. This generalization is carried one step further in an important study by Gary Becker.[12] According to Becker, leisure time does not yield utility in and of itself; rather, time is best viewed as an input that is combined with purchased goods

---

10 Juliet Schor, *The Overworked American* (New York: Basic Books, 1991), Table 2.3. Also see F. Thomas Juster and Frank P. Stafford, "The Allocation of Time: Empirical Findings, Behavioral Models, and Problems of Measurement," *Journal of Economic Literature* 29 (June 1991): 471–522.

11 James T. Bond, Ellen Galinsky, and Jennifer E. Swanberg, *The 1997 National Study of the Changing Workforce* (New York: Families and Work Institute, 1998), Chapter 3. These statistics correspond to married men and women with children working 20 hours or more per week. As additional years of the U.S. Census Bureau's American Time Use Survey are collected (the first release was September 2004), more current statistics about changes in time use will be readily available.

12 Gary Becker, "A Theory of the Allocation of Time," *Economic Journal* 75 (September 1965): 493–517. Also see Reuben Gronau, "Home Production—A Survey," in Orley Ashenfelter and Richard Layard, eds., *Handbook of Labor Economics*, vol. 1 (New York: North-Holland, 1986), 273–304.

and services to produce various activities or experiences. Whether such an experience is watching a movie, eating a meal, or raising children, each activity requires some combination of time and market goods.

The important insight from Becker's theory is that as the cost of time changes, so will the way in which people produce the experiences that yield utility. In particular, as wage rates increase, individuals are motivated not only to substitute time from nonmarket uses to market work, but also to substitute away from activities that are relatively time-intensive, such as cooking a meal at home, to less time-intensive but more income-intensive activities, such as dining out at a restaurant.

Becker's model has considerable relevance to explaining the long-term rise in women's labor force participation. The household model explained the increase in women's participation in terms of a substitution from home work (and possibly leisure) to market work. This shift has been made possible, however, only by a fundamental change in family lifestyle, ranging from having fewer children to the use of labor-saving appliances such as microwave ovens and dishwashers.[13] Becker's model can be used to analyze the reasons for this change in lifestyle. The rising wage rate for women over the past 40 years gave a natural incentive to substitute goods purchased in the market for time in producing a particular activity (for instance, to substitute nursery school for mother's time in child care). Thus, Becker's model points out an *additional* substitution effect neglected by the household model, the substitution of market goods for the time of the wife in household production. It is this substitution effect that has allowed married women to substantially reduce home work and increase market work. Changes in labor force participation rates across marital status are highlighted in Empirical Evidence 3-1.

Changes in Participation over Time

One of the most important labor supply developments of the past 40 years has been the gradual convergence in the labor force participation rates of men and women due to the long-term decline in male participation rates and the sharp long-term increase in female participation rates. The basic economic explanation for this phenomenon was discussed previously in the development of the household theory of labor supply. Several additional facets of the time-series change in male and female

---

[13] One study has shown that the purchase of a microwave oven was almost two times more likely in married households with a full-time employed wife than in households with a full-time homemaker wife. See R. S. Oropesa, "Female Labor Force Participation and Time-Saving Household Technology: A Case Study of the Microwave Oven from 1978–1989," *Journal of Consumer Research* 19 (March 1993): 567–79. More evidence on the tradeoffs between time and goods and the differences and similarities in those tradeoffs between men and women can be found in Reuben Gronau and Daniel S. Hamermesh, "Time vs. Goods: The Value of Measuring Household Production Technologies," *Mimeo, Hebrew University of Jerusalem* (April 2003); and Mohammad Alenzi and Michale L. Walden, "A New Look at Husbands' and Wives' Time Allocation," *Journal of Consumer Affairs* 38 (Summer 2004): 81–106.

participation rates deserve further attention, however. The decline in male participation rates is discussed first, followed by the rise in female participation rates.

The Decline in Male Participation Rates

Between 1950 and 2004 the real hourly wage rate among private workers increased by 50 percent. Over the same period the labor force participation rate of men declined from 87 percent to 73.3 percent. The long-term decline in male participation rates would suggest, therefore, that the negative income effect from this increase in the wage rate has dominated the positive substitution effect, leading men to cut back on market work and increase their hours of nonwork, leisure time.

Further insights into this process are provided in Figure 3.5, which shows age/participation profiles for men for the years 1950 and 2004. The decline in male labor force participation over the past 50 years is largely concentrated in three groups. The first is young men (ages 16 to 24), the second is prime-age males in the 45-to-64 age bracket, and the third, and most important, is among men at retirement age (65 plus). Among men age 65 and over, for example, the decline in participation was quite dramatic, from 46 percent in 1950 to 19.1 percent in 2004.

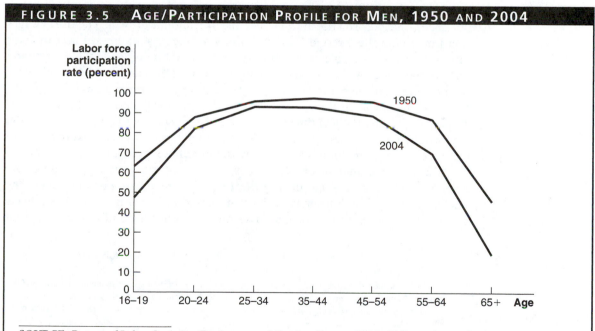

FIGURE 3.5 AGE/PARTICIPATION PROFILE FOR MEN, 1950 AND 2004

SOURCE: Bureau of Labor Statistics, *Employment and Earnings* (January 2005): Table 3, also see http://www.bls.gov/cps/cpsatabs.htm; and *Handbook of U.S. Labor Statistics*, 1997.

Economists have advanced several reasons to account for the long-run decline in the participation rates of these groups of men. Three of the most important are considered here.

The Life Cycle Allocation of Time   One defect of the labor/leisure model and the expanded household model is they are static or "one-period" models—they do not consider the optimal timing of labor, leisure, and nonmarket activities over the multiperiod life cycle of an individual. Economists, therefore, have broadened the theory of labor supply even further by constructing dynamic models of labor supply that are capable of predicting the optimal allocation of time over the entire adult life of an individual.[14] While these models tend to be highly mathematical and beyond consideration here, they do yield some commonsense insights into the reasons behind the decline in male participation rates.

Why, for example, are fewer men working beyond age 65? Two related facts seem to explain this in a life cycle context. The first is that the life cycle pattern of men's real wage rates is typically an inverted U, rising rapidly from midlife to later life and then declining as skills become obsolete and on-the-job training slackens. Because of this pattern of earnings, the opportunity cost of additional hours of leisure in the prime work years (ages 24 to 54) is much higher than in later years in life. The implication is that an individual has a strong economic incentive to substitute work for leisure during midlife when the rewards from work are greatest, postponing leisure until later in life when the opportunity cost is lowest.[15] The second fact of importance is the long-run rise in real wages due to economic growth. The rise in wages over time causes the inverted U **age/earnings profile** to shift upward over time for successive cohorts (people of the same age group), setting off an income effect and substitution effect on lifetime labor supply much as in the static household model.[16] Assuming that for men, the income effect of this wage increase outweighs the substitution effect, when is the optimal time to take additional leisure? Life cycle models predict that the optimal time is at the *end* of a person's working years, when the opportunity cost is lowest. Earlier retirement, therefore, is the rational response to the increased demand for leisure, which arises out of the income effect.

Life cycle considerations also help explain the decline in the labor force participation rate among young men in the 18-to-24 age group. For these men, the smaller amount of time spent at work has little to do with leisure; rather, it reflects a reallocation of time from work to investment in education and training, or what

---

14   The most accessible introduction to dynamic labor supply models is Mark Killingsworth, *Labor Supply* (Cambridge, Eng: Cambridge University Press, 1983), Chapter 5.

15   Empirical evidence in support of this prediction is presented in an interesting study by Frank Stafford and Greg Duncan, "The Use of Time and Technology by Households in the United States," in Juster and Stafford, eds., *Time, Goods, and Well-Being* (Ann Arbor, Mich.: Institute for Social Research, 1985), 245–88, particularly Figure 10.1.

16   As discussed in Killingsworth, *Labor Supply*, a wage change due to a *shift* in the age/earnings profile gives rise to both an income effect and a substitution effect, while a wage change due to a movement *along* a given profile gives rise only to a substitution effect since total lifetime remains unchanged. An important implication is that cross-sectional estimates of income and substitution effects may be seriously biased because they confuse these two sources of change in wages.

economists call *human capital*. In 2003, 27.2 percent of those 25 years and older had completed four or more years of college, compared with just 6 percent of the non-institutional population in 1950. As compared to 1950, today's jobs require a much higher level of education. Since education is often a full-time activity, the worker faces the question of when in the life cycle to schedule work and when to schedule time out of the labor force for education.

Not unexpectedly, the optimal time to invest in human capital is at the beginning of the life cycle for two important reasons.[17] The first is that the opportunity cost of devoting time to education is lowest when an individual is young. Since wage rates rise as a person ages because of experience and on-the-job training, it makes economic sense to invest in additional human capital at a young age when the earnings penalty is the lowest. A second consideration is that the return on an investment in education is also greater the earlier in the life cycle it is made. The direct monetary outlay for a college education will be the same for a person whether he or she is 25 or 45. The younger person, however, will have 20 more years over which to recoup the costs of the education, making the rate of return on the human capital investment much greater.

Social Security and Private Pension Plans   A second important reason for the decline in participation rates among older men is the growth in the coverage and benefits from Social Security and private pension plans.

The Social Security program was instituted in 1935. Although the legislation originally provided only for retirement benefits for workers at age 65, over the years it has been broadened considerably to provide other forms of income protection, principally in the form of disability insurance, survivors' benefits, and hospital and medical insurance for the elderly. Both the number of people eligible for Social Security retirement benefits and the dollar amount of the benefits have increased substantially in the past two decades. In 2002, 86 percent of the population aged 65 or over received Social Security payments, compared to 64 percent in 1970. Likewise, between 1970 and 2002 the average monthly benefit received by a retired worker increased by 67 percent in real terms.[18]

Most research on the subject has found that the availability of Social Security benefits is an important influence leading workers to retire earlier.[19] The reasons for this are illustrated in Figure 3.6. The budget constraint for a worker in the absence of a Social Security law is assumed to be *AB*, reflecting a wage rate of W_1 and zero nonlabor income. Under the Social Security program the budget

---

17   See Karl E. Ryder, Frank P. Stafford, and Paula E. Stephan, "Labor, Leisure, and Training over the Life Cycle," *International Economic Review* 17, no. 3 (October 1976): 651–74; and Susumu Imai and Michael P. Keane, "Intertemporal Labor Supply and Human Capital Accumulation," *International Economic Review* 45 (May 2004): 601–41.

18   Social Security Administration, *Social Security Bulletin: Annual Statistical Bulletin, 2003* (Washington, D.C.: Government Printing Office, 2003).

19   See Gary Burtless and Robert A. Moffitt, "The Effect of Social Security Benefits on the Labor Supply of the Aged," in Henry J. Aaron and Gary Burtless, eds., *Retirement and Economic Behavior* (Washington, D.C.: Brookings Institution, 1984), 135–71; Helmuth Cremer, et al., "Social Security, Retirement Age, and Optimal Taxation," *Journal of Public Economics* 88 (September 2004): 2259–81.

FIGURE 3.6 THE EFFECT OF SOCIAL SECURITY ON LABOR FORCE PARTICIPATION

Before Social Security, the budget constraint is AB, and hours of work are H_1 (point V in both graphs). With Social Security, the budget constraint can take on one of two transformations, represented by the two graphs. Graph (a) represents the budget constraint for a retired worker who has not yet achieved the full age of retirement. These workers are subject to an earnings test, and the budget constraint

becomes $ACDEB$. Graph (b) represents the budget constraint for a retired worker who has achieved the full age of retirement and is not subject to an earnings test; the budget constraint becomes ACD. As drawn, both scenarios lead to reduced hours of work, from H_1 to H_2. It is possible, however, that a corner solution would occur at point C and the person in either case would drop out of the labor force.

(a) Social Security budget constraint for a person who has not reached the full age of retirement

(b) Social Security budget constraint for a person who has reached the full age of retirement

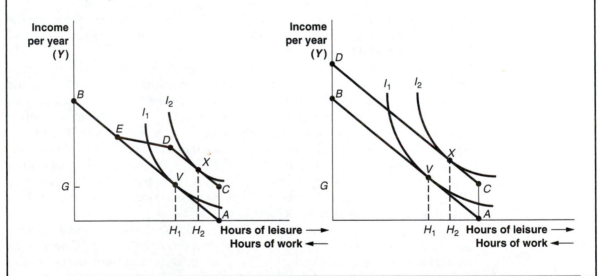

constraint takes on one of two transformations, depending on whether the retiree has reached what is termed the full age of retirement.[20] For a worker who has *not* reached the full age of retirement, the budget constraint becomes $ACDEB$ (see Figure 3.6, graph a). A worker will qualify for an annual payment of $\$G$ (point C) if he or she decides to retire. (The exact amount depends on previous contributions into the program.) Just as with Temporary Assistance for Needy Families, there is

20   The full age of retirement is defined as age 65 for beneficiaries who attain age 62 before 2000, and gradually increasing to age 67 for beneficiaries who attain age 62 in 2022 or later (see Social Security Administration's web site, http://www.ssa.gov).

also an implicit tax rate t on additional labor earnings. For those who have not yet reached the full age of retirement, the Social Security program has an *earnings test* that results in a reduction of the annual payment by 50 cents for each dollar of earnings over a specific amount (the "level of disregard" discussed in Chapter 2). As of 2004, the level of disregard was $11,640. The implicit tax rate is $t = .50$ and the break-even point where an individual receives zero payments is $BE = 11,640 + G/.50$ (point E). Between points C and D the new budget constraint has the same slope as the original constraint AB, since the first $11,640 of earnings are not subject to the implicit tax rate.[21] For workers who *have* attained the full age of retirement, no earnings test is applied; benefits are not reduced based on earnings. The catch, of course, is that the full age of retirement is gradually increasing. The effect of no earnings test on the labor supply can be seen in Figure 3.6, graph (b). When a worker qualifies for a Social Security payment regardless of his or her earnings, it amounts to a pure increase in nonlabor income of the amount G.

What impact does the Social Security program have on desired hours of work? Not surprisingly, the provision of additional nonlabor income provides strong incentives for older workers to reduce their supply of labor. Without the Social Security program, the equilibrium hours of work is H_1 (point V), given by the original budget constraint AB and the indifference curve I_1. With the program, the budget constraint becomes $ACDEB$ (in graph a) or ACD (in graph b) and a new equilibrium occurs at H_2 (point X), where I_2 is tangent to the new budget constraint. The impact of the program is to reduce hours of work from H_1 to H_2. Although the new equilibrium hours of work in Figure 3.6 occurs at point X, there are several other possibilities. One would be for the indifference curve to be tangent to the segment ED (in graph a); another would be for the new equilibrium to be a corner solution at point C. In the latter case, the person would retire from work altogether and drop out of the labor force. Evidence shows that about one-half of new Social Security recipients do completely withdraw from the labor force, while the other half continue to work at a paying job, generally for fewer hours than before.[22]

While it might appear that elimination of the earnings test would provide even stronger incentives to reduce hours of work (since it affects all workers, not just those earning below a certain level), the evidence is not so clear. Jonathan Gruber and Peter Orzag find the structure of an earnings test does not impact older men's decisions to work but does impact the decision of women.[23]

In general, however, Social Security is one important cause of earlier retirement. The growth in private pension plans since the Revenue Act of 1942, which

---

[21] For retirees who *do* attain the full age of retirement during the year in which they choose to retire, the program parameters adjust so that by the time someone wants to retire in the year 2004, the earnings disregard is equal to $31,080 and the implicit tax rate, t, is .33. See http://www.ssa.gov.

[22] Further evidence of the impact of Social Security on retirement decisions can be found in Courtney Cole and Jonathan Gruber, "Social Security Incentives for Retirement," in *Themes in the Economic of Aging* (Chicago: University of Chicago Press, 2001): 311–41.

[23] Jonathan Gruber and Peter Orzag, "Does the Social Security Earnings Test Affect Labor Supply and Benefits Reciept?" *National Tax Journal* (December 2003).

granted tax incentives to firms to establish pension plans, has also likely contributed to earlier retirements. In 2001, roughly 40 percent of persons aged 65 or over were receiving income from pensions, compared to only 17 percent of men and 5 percent of women in 1962.[24] Research has found that private pension plans have a stronger impact on the retirement decision of workers than does Social Security.[25] Two factors account for this. The first is that private pension plans generally condition the provision of benefits on a complete cessation of work at the firm, unlike Social Security, which allows a person to work and draw benefits simultaneously. The second reason is that the benefit structures of most private pension plans contain stronger incentives for early retirement than does Social Security. Under Social Security, a person can retire at age 62 or 65 or later. The incentive to retire at age 62 is the three years of additional benefits that can be obtained; the drawback is that the monthly payment is smaller. Whether the worker is financially ahead by retiring early at age 62 or waiting until age 65 depends on two factors: the degree to which the monthly Social Security payment is larger at age 65, and the life expectancy of the recipient.[26] Studies that have examined this issue reach contradictory conclusions, although the evidence indicates that there is a large financial penalty to postponing retirement *beyond* age 65.[27]

What about private pension plans? Here too the worker must balance the benefits of retiring earlier against the cost of a smaller monthly payment. In the case of private pensions, the evidence is unambiguous—the total value of pension benefits declines as the worker postpones retirement. One study estimated that a worker who postpones retirement from age 64 to age 65 sacrifices from $1,200 to $1,400 in pension benefits.[28] One reason private pension plans may be structured this way

---

24   *Income of the Aged Chartbook, 2001* http://www.ssa.gov/policy/docs/chartbooks/income_aged/2001/#toc.

25   Robin L. Lumsdaine, James H. Stock, and David A. Wise, "Retirement Incentives: The Interaction between Employer-Provided Pensions, Social Security, and Retiree Health Benefits," in *The Economic Effects of Aging in the United States and Japan* (Chicago: University of Chicago Press, 1997): 261–93; Dora L. Costa, "Pensions and Retirement: Evidence from Union Army Veterans," *Quarterly Journal of Economics* 110 (May 1995): 297–319; and Monika Butler, et al. "What Triggers Early Retirement? Results from Swiss Pension Funds," *CEPR Discussion Paper 4394* (2002).

26   See Robert Hutchens, "Social Security Benefits and Employer Behavior: Evaluating Social Security Early Retirement Benefits as a Form of Unemployment Insurance," *International Economic Review* 40 (August 1999): 659–78; and Olivia Mitchell and John Phillips, "Retirement Responses to Early Social Security and Benefit Reductions," *NBER Working Paper No. W7963* (October 2000).

27   See Alan S. Blinder, Roger H. Gordon, and Donald E. Wise, "Reconsidering the Work Disincentive Effects of Social Security," *National Tax Journal* 33, no. 4 (December 1980): 431–42; Richard V. Burkhauser and Joseph F. Quinn, "The Effect of Pension Plans on the Pattern of Life Cycle Compensation," in Jack E. Triplett, ed., *The Measurement of Labor Cost* (Chicago: University of Chicago Press, 1983), 395–415; and Olivia S. Mitchell and Gary S. Fields, "The Economics of Retirement Behavior," *Journal of Labor Economics* 2 (January 1984): 57–83. James E. Pesando and Moreley Gunderson, "Does Pension Wealth Peak at the Age of Early Retirement?" *Industrial Relations* 30 (Winter 1991): 79–95; Erik Hernaes et al. "Early Retirement and Economic Incentives," *Scandinavian Journal of Economics* 102 (June 2000): 481–502; and J. Ignacio Conde-Ruiz and Vincenzo Galasso, "The Macroeconomics of Early Retirement," *Journal of Public Economics* 88 (August 2004): 1849–69.

28   Burkhauser and Quinn, Table 12.2. Also see Lawrence Kotlikoff and David Wise, "The Incentive Effects of Private Pension Plans," in Zvi Brodie, John Shoven, and David Wise, eds., *Issues in Pension Economics* (Chicago: University of Chicago Press, 1987), 283–336.

is because most employers can no longer mandate at what age their workers will retire (as of 1986, the Age Discrimination in Employment Act prohibits mandatory retirement policies for most employers).

The Growth in Disability Benefits The third group of men for whom participation rates have declined noticeably is prime-age men between the ages of 45 and 62. This phenomenon is primarily concentrated among black men. The participation rate for black males aged 45 to 54, for example, fell from 93 percent in 1954 to 77.4 percent in 2004, more than twice the decline for white males.

The factors responsible for this trend are not entirely understood. One possible reason is that poor employment prospects for older, less-educated black males cause a greater proportion to drop out of the labor force as discouraged workers. A second factor found to be important in several studies is the greater incidence of health problems among older black males.[29] A third factor, identified by Donald Parsons as a major explanation, is the rather substantial expansion and liberalization of coverages and benefits in the disability insurance program of Social Security.[30] In addition, Jonathan Gruber finds sizable labor supply responses to changes in disability programs.[31] Between 1975 and 2002, for example, the number of recipients grew from 2.5 to 5.5 million while average benefits per month increased by 10.4 percent in real terms. Given that older black workers have a greater incidence of health problems, the expansion and liberalization of the disability program would be expected to cause the greatest decline in participation among that group. Parsons also argues that older, less-educated black males have the most incentive to attempt to qualify for disability benefits since the level of benefits relative to their potential earnings from work is frequently much higher than for white workers with better-paying jobs. His statistical analysis of labor force participation rates for black and white workers found considerable evidence that a significant portion of the relative decline in the participation rate of black males is due to the greater availability of disability benefits. A more recent study on this subject also found a positive link between the generosity of disability benefits and the probability of nonparticipation in the labor force by prime-age males, although the magnitude was far smaller than that estimated by Parsons.[32]

---

29 L. Wayne Plumly, "The Declining Labor Force Participation Rate of Prime-Age Males," Ph.D. dissertation, Georgia State University, 1983. Olivia Mitchell and John Phillips report that blacks are twice as likely to retire with disability benefits than with either early or normal Social Security benefits. See "Retirement Responses to Early Social Security Benefit Reductions," *NBER Working Paper No. 7963* (October 2000).

30 Donald O. Parsons, "Racial Trends in Male Labor Force Participation," *American Economic Review* 70, no. 5 (December 1980): 911–20.

31 Jonathan Gruber, "Disability Insurance Benefits and Labor Supply," *Journal of Political Economy* 108 (December 2000): 1162–83.

32 Robert Haveman, Barbara Wolfe, and Philip DeJong, "Disability Transfers and the Work Decision of Older Men," *Quarterly Journal of Economics* 106 (August 1991): 939–49. For further evidence on this point, see Brent Kreider, "Social Security Disability Insurance: Applications, Awards, and Lifetime Income Flows," *Journal of Labor Economics* 17 (October 1999): 784–827. Also see Jonathan Gruber, "Disability Insurance Benefits and Labor Supply," *Journal of Political Economy* 108 (December 2000): 1162–83 for further evidence of the link between greater disability program generosity and reduced labor for participation.

Decreased Demand for Low-Skilled Workers One study points to declining labor market opportunities for less-skilled workers as an additional explanation for the continuing decline in labor force participation among older males.[33] In just a short period of time, jobs requiring more education and training (e.g., managerial and professional jobs) have increased by three percent (from 2000 to 2003). Over the same time period, production jobs have decreased by twelve percent.[34] The increased openness of the U.S. economy and technical advances in production are often identified as the reasons that demand for low-skilled workers has declined. Some of the impact of this decrease in demand for low-skilled workers can be seen in the faster rate at which older low-skilled workers have retired over this time period relative to more highly skilled workers. Peracchi and Welch estimate that between 1969 and 1989, the probability of a low-skilled older man retiring from his full-time job increased by 17.3 percent, whereas a highly skilled older man increased his probability of retiring by only 10.5 percent over the same time period.[35]

The Increase in Female Participation Rates

The most dramatic change in labor supply in the United States has been the tremendous increase in the number of working women. At the turn of the twentieth century only 5 million of the 28 million Americans in the labor force were female. One-quarter of these women were teenagers; only 15 percent were married. As recently as 1950, fewer than 19 million of the 64 million labor force participants were women. Over the past 50 years, however, women, and in particular married women, entered the labor force at an unprecedented rate. Between 1950 and 2004, for example, six out of ten additions to the labor force were women, with the result that women now compose 46.4 percent of the labor force. Equally significant, almost two-thirds of married women are now working, including a majority of mothers with preschool children.

The dynamics of change in the pattern of female labor force participation are apparent from the age/participation profiles for women for the years 1940, 1960, and 2004, as shown in Figure 3.7. Two features stand out. The first is that the rise in female participation has been widespread across all age groups up to age 65, reflected in the general upward shift in the age/participation profile for 2004 relative to 1940. The second feature of note is the changing pattern of participation for women in the childbearing years. In 1940, the age/participation profile had a single peak in the age

---

33 Franco Peracchi and Finis Welch, "Trends in Labor Force Transitions of Older Men and Women," *Journal of Labor Economics* 12 (April 1994): 210–42. Also see Ann P. Bartel and Nachum Sicherman, "Technological Change and Retirement Decisions of Older Workers," *Journal of Labor Economics* 11 (January 1993): 162–83. Also see Leora Friedberg, "The Impact of Technological Change on Older Workers: Evidence from Data on Computer Use," *Industrial and Labor Relations Review* 56 (April 2003): 511–29; and Bart L.W. Cockx and Muriel Dejemeppe, "Do Higher Educated Unemployed Crowd Out the Lower Educated Ones in a Competition for Jobs?" *IZA Discussion Paper No. 541* (August 2002).

34 Occupations were reclassified in 2000 so a longer comparable comparison is not possible, but rough estimates indicate that the increase in professional jobs and the decrease in production jobs are continuations of a much longer trend.

35 Peracchi and Welch, "Trends in Labor Force Transitions of Older Men and Women," Table 8.

FIGURE 3.7   AGE/PARTICIPATION PROFILES FOR WOMEN, 1940, 1960, AND 2004

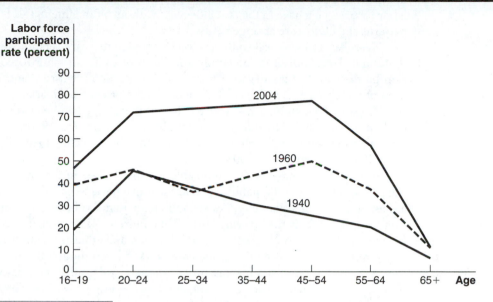

SOURCE: Bureau of Labor Statistics, *Employment and Earnings* (January 2005): Table 3, also see http://www.bls.gov/cps/cpsatabs.htm; *Handbook of U.S. Labor Statistics* 1997; and Department of Commerce, *Historical Statistics of the United States: Colonial Times to 1970*, Part 1 (Washington, D.C.: Government Printing Office, 1975): 132.

group 20 to 24 followed by a sharp and continuous decline that coincided with the time of marriage and childbearing. By 1960, the age/participation profile had changed considerably, and began to resemble an inverted *W*. Women still dropped out of the labor force with marriage and childbearing, but the difference between 1960 and 1940 was that many of the women in 1960 were *reentering* the labor force once their children were older and in school. This pattern in 1960, while revolutionary at the time, was only a milepost in an ongoing transformation. By 2004, the sharp dip and rebound in female participation rates had itself disappeared, replaced by a pattern of stable participation rates even during the childbearing years.

The household model of labor supply pointed out the important role that the rise in real wages available to women played in bringing about this secular increase in labor force participation. Several other developments have, however, also played crucial roles in this process.[36]

---

36   A thorough review of the causes of the increase in female labor force participation over the twentieth century is provided in Smith and Ward, "Time-Series Growth in the Female Labor Force," in *Women in the Labour Market*, Marianne Ferber, ed. (Williston, Vt.: Elgar, 1998), 33–64. They conclude that 60 percent of the secular increase in female participation rates is due to the rise over time in the real wage (and the induced decline in fertility), with other factors accounting for the rest.

Fertility   For biological and cultural reasons, childbirth and child rearing have been the primary responsibility of the female parent. Given the tremendous time demands that raising children entails, married women could not have entered the labor force as they have in the past 3 decades without a fundamental shift in fertility patterns and child-care arrangements.

Nearly every empirical study has found a strong negative relationship between the number of children in the family and the probability of labor force participation by the wife.[37] This negative relationship is particularly pronounced for children of preschool age. A powerful influence leading to greater market participation on the part of women in the United States, therefore, has been the significant decline in the birth rate and average family size. In the mid-1950s, women gave birth to an average of 3.5 children, a figure that then declined steadily, reaching 1.9 children per woman in 2002.

Several factors have been responsible for the decline in fertility rates. One is the greater number and reliability of contraceptive devices, as well as greater social acceptance of family planning.[38] A second factor that has been given much attention by economists is the growing "price" of children.[39] The price or cost of a child for the family is the direct cost of food, clothing, and education, and the opportunity cost of the wife's time if she does not work.[40] Even though the real wage that can be earned at work has increased over the past 3 decades, the relative price of time-intensive activities such as raising children has also grown, causing families to consciously cut back on the number of children they plan to have. In this view, the decline in fertility and the rise in female labor force participation reflect a simultaneous response to the ever-growing economic rewards from market work.

A second shift in fertility patterns is the postponement of childbirth by many women until they are past their mid-20s. The number of first births per 1,000 women aged 15–29 has fallen from 28.5 in 1980 to 26.7 in 2000, whereas for women aged 33–44, first births per 1,000 women has risen over the same time period from 6.3 to 12.5.[41] The impetus behind this trend is an attempt by women to accommodate both careers and children. As documented in an interesting study by Marianne Ferber and Bonnie Birnbaum, a woman in her 20s who desires both a career and children faces a significant time squeeze—there is not enough time

---

37   See, for example, Julie L. Hotchkiss and M. Melinda Pitts, "Female Labor Force Intermittency and Current Earnings: A Switching Regression Model with Unknown Sample Selection," *Applied Economics* (2005): forthcoming.

38   See, for example, Martha J. Bailey, "More Power to the Pill: The Impact of Contraceptive Freedom on Women's Labor Supply," *Mimeo*, Vanderbilt University (April 2004).

39   Gary S. Becker, "An Economic Analysis of Fertility," in Universities-National Bureau Committee for Economic Research, *Demographic and Economic Change in Developed Countries* (Princeton, N.J.: Princeton University Press, 1960): 209–31; and, more recently, T. Paul Schultz, "The Fertility Transition: Economic Explanations," *Economic Growth Center Discussion Paper No. 833* (August 2001).

40   See Lawrence Olson, *Costs of Children* (Lexington, Mass.: Lexington Books, 1983). Also see Jin-Long Li and Ching-chun Hsu, "Economies of Scale, Gender Discrimination, and Cost of Children," *Applied Economics Letters* 11 (May 2004): 377–82.

41   U.S. Census Bureau, *Statistical Abstract of the United States* (2003): Table No. 98.

available to do both simultaneously.[42] One option is to have children first and then seek a job. Another is to reverse the order and begin a career first, postponing children until later, even if this means dropping out of the labor force for a period of time. Research shows that the second option is the superior one in that it promises higher future earnings than the first.[43] As women move into upper management and professional positions, even the second option (postponing children until several years of job experience are accumulated) is perceived by many as prohibitively expensive in terms of career advancement. A 1992 survey of over 2,000 women executives found that almost 40 percent of the women had no children. By comparison, a 1989 study of executive men found only 5 percent who had no children.[44] In addition, 34.4 percent of the women responding to the survey say they postponed or decided not to have children because of their careers.[45]

A third aspect of the fertility/participation relationship that has changed dramatically over time is the greater propensity of women to continue working when there are small children in the family. While married couples are having fewer children and having them later in life, childless couples are still a distinct minority in the population. According to survey results, 80 percent of women between the ages of 18 and 34 say they expect to have between one and three children.[46] A fundamental shift has occurred, however. When these women do have children, they are less likely than before to drop out of the labor force and to remain out of the labor force as long.[47]

This is vividly illustrated by comparing the participation rate for married women with respect to the ages of their children. It remains true today as in the past that the younger the children in the family are, the less likely the wife is to participate in the labor force. In 2002, 76.8 percent of married women whose youngest child was over 6 were in the labor force, compared to only 58 percent for married women whose youngest child was under 3 years of age. What is remarkable, however, is how many of these mothers with preschool children are remaining in the

---

42 Marianne Ferber and Bonnie Birnbaum, "One Job or Two Jobs: The Implications for Young Wives," *Journal of Consumer Research* 7, no. 3 (December 1980): 263–71; and Elizabeth M. Caucutt, et al., "Why do Women Wait? Matching, Wage Inequality, and the Incentives for Fertility Delay," *Review of Economic Dynamics* 5 (October 2002): 815–55.

43 See Ellen Van Velsor and Angela M. O'Rand, "Family Life Cycle, Work Career Patterns, and Women's Wages at Midlife," *Journal of Marriage and Family* 46, no. 2 (May 1984): 365–73; and Caucutte, et al. (2002).

44 Korn/Ferry International and UCLA Anderson Graduate School of Management, *Decade of the Executive Woman* (New York: Korn/Ferry International, 1993), Table 90. More recent evidence on these details has proven to be elusive.

45 *Decade of the Executive Woman*, Table 97.

46 See Kristin A. Moore and Sandra L. Hofferth, "Women and Their Children," in Ralph Smith, ed., *The Subtle Revolution*, 125–57. According to the National Center for Health Statistics, women's average expected family size in 1995 was 2.2 children per woman. (The National Survey of Family Growth has not been updated since that time.)

47 See Shapiro and Shaw, "Growth in the Labor Force Attachment of Married Women"; Bureau of Labor Statistics, *Families at Work: The Jobs and the Pay*, Bulletin 2209 (Washington, D.C.: Government Printing Office, 1984); Lisa Barrow, "An Analysis of Women's Return-to-Work Decisions Following First Birth," *Economic Inquiry* 37 (July 1999): 432–51; and Charles L. Baum, II, "The Effects of Maternity Leave Legislation on Mothers' Labor Supply after Childbirth," *Southern Economic Journal* 69 (April 2003): 772–99.

labor force compared with before. In 1970, only 30 percent of married women with children under the age of 6 were in the labor force. This growth in the participation rate of mothers with preschool-age children has necessitated fundamental shifts in child-care arrangements. The number of preschoolers primarily cared for in organized child-care facilities grew from 13 percent in 1977 to 22.3 percent in 1999.

Education   A second factor often cited as a cause of greater labor force participation among women is the rise over time in educational attainment.[48] At a point in time there is a strong, positive relationship between years of education completed and probability of participation in the labor force. In 2003, the participation rate of women with less than a high school education was 32.7 percent, compared to 73.1 percent for college graduates. Since the median years of schooling completed by women have risen steadily over time, the logical inference is that there should be a concomitant increase in the participation rate of women.

There are several reasons for the positive correlation between education and labor force participation. First, higher education is often undertaken as an investment in the sense that a person willingly suffers the large direct costs (tuition) and opportunity cost (forgone earnings from work) of a college education with the anticipation that these costs will be recouped in the form of higher earnings and occupational attainment after graduation. To reap this return on education, however, requires a sustained period of participation in the labor force. A second reason why education is positively correlated with labor force participation is that earnings from work progressively rise with educational attainment, increasing the cost of time spent in nonmarket activities.[49] Finally, education may increase the probability of participation as it changes an individual's tastes or attitudes with respect to the desirability of home work versus market work.

Not only have increased years of education among women encouraged greater labor force participation, so too has the shift over time in the fields of study pursued by women in high school and college. Twenty years ago, the majority of women in college majored in fields such as English, history, or education, while men were more likely to choose subjects such as engineering, business, or pre-law. Although there is still a marked difference between men and women in the choice of a college major, it has certainly narrowed.[50] In 1971, for example, only 1 percent

---

48   For example, see Claudia Goldin, "The U-Shaped Female Labor Force Function in Economic Development and Economic History," in *Investment in Human Capital*, T. Paul Schultz, ed. (Chicago: University of Chicago Press, 1995).

49   Increased years of schooling could also increase the productivity of time spent in home work and leisure, making it less likely that a person would participate in the workforce. Shapiro and Shaw, "Growth in the Labor Force Attachment of Married Women," find that once the higher wage derived from additional schooling is controlled for, women with more education have a lower probability of being on the labor force. This finding is reinforced by the study by Derek Neal, "The Measured Black-White Wage Gap Among women is Too Small," *NBER Working Paper #9133* (2002).

50   See Linda Loury, "The Gender Earnings Gap among College-Educated Workers," *Industrial and Labor Relations Review* 50 (July 1997): 580–93; Catherine Weinberger, "Race and Gender Wage Gaps in the Market for Recent College Graduates," *Industrial Relations* 37 (January 1998): 67–84; and Sarah E. Turner and William G. Bowen, "Choice of Major: The Changing (unchanging) Gender Gap," *Industrial and Labor Relations Review* 52 (January 1999): 289–313.

of undergraduate engineering degrees and 9 percent of business degrees were awarded to women; by 2000 these figures had risen to 20 percent and 50 percent, respectively.[51] Young women, therefore, are increasingly pursuing fields of study in school that prepare them for full-time jobs in the labor market.

A final factor is the influence that the sharp rise in divorce rates has on the motivation of women to invest in additional education. Marriage encourages a division of labor, with each spouse specializing in certain activities in which he or she has a comparative advantage. The benefit of specialization is that the total amount of market and nonmarket goods that can be obtained by the family is larger than if both persons shared these activities equally.[52] For instance, in years past it was not unusual for the wife to work to put her husband through school, with the expectation that he would then support her as she raised the children full-time. In a world without divorce, this type of specialization works to the benefit of both partners, since each shares the other's "production." The greater the probability of divorce, however, the less incentive either partner has to invest in the other because of the danger of suffering a capital loss should the marriage fail.[53] Why are more young women obtaining additional schooling and majoring in marketable fields such as business or law? Given the probability that over 40 percent of all first marriages end in divorce within 15 years, it is increasingly important for both spouses to have an independent source of earnings as insurance against marital dissolution.

Advancement in Living Standards   During the 1970s the greatest increase in labor force participation was among women in the 25–34 age group. Women continued to increase their labor force participation rates during the 1980s and 1990s, but at a much slower rate, with the greatest increases coming in the 35–54 age group during the 1980s and the 55–64 age group during the 1990s. Many economic and social factors spurred these women into the labor force. One of the most important was the attempt by married couples to maintain and advance their standard of living in the face of two economic squeezes.[54]

One squeeze on married couples, particularly in the 1970s and 1980s, was the stiff competition for jobs as the baby-boom generation poured out of school and into the labor market. Between 1960 and 1980, the number of people aged 18 to 35 nearly doubled, as a result of the rise in birthrates after World World II. A natural outcome of this rather large and sudden increase in labor supply was a depressed labor market in the 1970s and early 1980s, particularly for entry-level

---

51   National Center for Education Statistics, *Digest of Educational Statistics, 2002.*

52   This is shown in Gary S. Becker, "A Theory of Marriage: Part I," *Journal of Political Economy* 81, no. 4 (July/August 1973): 813–46.

53   See Alan King, "Human Capital and the Risk of Divorce: An Asset in Search of a Property Right," *Southern Economic Journal* 49, no. 2 (October 1982): 536–41.

54   See Valerie Kincaid Oppenheimer, *Work and the Family* (New York: Academic Press, 1982), and Rose M. Rubin and Bobye J. Riney, *Working Wives & Dual-Earner Families* (Westport, Conn.: Praeger, 1995). Evidence provided by Dora Costa suggests that living standards may be rising twice as fast as previously thought. She argues that using expenditures on recreation is a better measure than the per capita income measure typically used. See "American Living Standards: Evidence from Recreational Expenditures," *NBER Working Paper No. 7148 (May 1999).*

positions. One study estimated that the growth in cohort size between 1967 and 1975 depressed the weekly earnings of college graduates 13 percent.[55]

Although the number of new labor force entrants slowed in the 1990s as the "baby bust" generation came of working age, for families with low levels of education and skill the competition for jobs—particularly good-paying jobs—remained intense. The second squeeze on married couples was that in many years, from 1970 to the present, the rate of inflation has exceeded the rate of increase in wages and salaries. Even as earnings were held down by the sharp competition for jobs, the level of consumer prices rose by 142 percent between 1973 and 1985. Since the mid-1980s, the inflation rate has dropped considerably, yet so has the rate of growth in workers' wages. Consequently, instead of growing steadily year after year, real median male income has declined noticeably since its peak in 1973. Real median income for men (in 2001 dollars) was $30,445 in 1970 and $29,101 in 2001. The most dramatic decline in real median income for men occurred in the early 1980s, reaching a low point in 1982 of $22,895.

Additional evidence that families are feeling financial pressure is offered by Joanne Sandberg and Daniel Cornfield, who investigated the reasons why women return to work after a leave of absence. The reason given by 53 percent of the sample studied was: "Could not afford to take any more time off."[56]

The impact of these two economic events on the labor supply decision of married couples can be analyzed with the household model of labor supply. If only the husband worked, the slow growth in his earnings, coupled with the substantial rise in prices, would have resulted in a sharp decline in the family's standard of living, particularly in comparison to two-earner families. This decline in real income would have caused a pure income effect on the nonworking wife, leading her to cut back on leisure in favor of market work. The entrance of women into the labor force, however, also increased the competition for jobs and further depressed wage rates in entry-level positions. The fact that a record number of women did enter the labor force during this period suggests, therefore, that the desire to advance family income dominated the adverse effect on female participation of a lower real wage per hour of work.

The substantial increase in the number of working women not only provided the means for many families to increase their standard of living, it also had a far-reaching effect on the distribution of income among families. Twenty-five years ago, there was a strong inverse relationship between the husband's income and the wife's probability of participation in the labor force. Because women from low-income households were the most likely to work, this helped to equalize family income—poorer families had two earners whose combined income would more nearly match the income of the single earner in the more well-to-do family. More recently, however, this equalizing effect is not as strong. One reason is that the

---

55   Finis Welch, "Effects of Cohort Size on Earnings: The Baby Boom Babies' Financial Bust," *Journal of Political Economy* 87, no. 5, pt. 2 (October 1979): 565–97.

56   Joanne Sandberg and Daniel Cornfield, "Returning to Work: The Impact of Gender, Family, and Work on Terminating a Family or Medical Leave," in *Work and Family*, Toby Parcel and Daniel Cornfield, eds. (Thousand Oaks, Calif.: Sage, 2000), 161–87.

negative relationship between the husband's income and the wife's probability of being in the labor force has diminished as a greater proportion of wives from high-income families are now working. A second is that these wives, like their husbands, tend to have above-average earnings.[57]

Increased Job Opportunities for Women A fourth factor cited by many analysts as an important cause of the increase in female participation rates is the rapid expansion of job opportunities for women.[58] One form this has taken is the substantial growth in the number of jobs in traditionally "female" occupations in the economy. It remains true today that women workers are concentrated in relatively few occupations. In 2003, for example, over 65 percent of women were employed in six occupational categories: administrative support, food preparation services, sales clerks in retail trade, elementary and secondary school teachers, secretaries and typists, and nurses. While this range of occupations is fairly narrow, many of them have grown rapidly in size in the postwar period. Perhaps the best example is in the clerical field, where employment more than doubled between 1960 and 2003.

The second source of greater job opportunities for women is the gradual opening up of a wide range of male-dominated occupations. Due to a combination of factors, including increased job commitment on the part of women, affirmative action and antidiscrimination laws, and changes in social attitudes, employment of women in many of these occupations has increased significantly. In 1960, for example, only 3 percent of lawyers and 15 percent of managers were women. By 2003 the proportion of women lawyers and managers had risen to 28 percent and just over 50 percent, respectively.

Changing Social Attitudes A final consideration in explaining the rise in female labor force participation is the evolution of social attitudes concerning the appropriateness for married women of working outside the home, particularly when they have small children. Prior to World War II, there were quite strong social taboos against married women working outside the home. In a poll taken in 1937, only 18 percent of the respondents answered in the affirmative to the question, "Do you approve of a married woman earning money in business or industry if she has a husband capable of supporting her?" By the early 1960s, attitudes had softened to the extent that only 46 percent of husbands said they disapproved when asked the question, "Do you think it is a good thing for a wife to work or a bad thing?"[59] Probably the greatest transition in social attitudes concerning married women and work took place during the 1970s. In 1968, only 14 percent of women aged 20 to 24 felt it was all right for a woman to work "if she prefers to work, but her husband doesn't particularly like it." Ten years later, the response to this same question

---

57   See John Pencavel, "Assortive Mating by Schooling and the Work Behavior of Wives and Husbands," *American Economic Review* 88 (May 1998): 326–29; and Robert A. Nakosteen and Michael A. Zimmer, "Spouse Selection and Earnings: Evidence of Marital Sorting," *Economic Inquiry* 39 (April 2001): 201–13.

58   This factor is given particular stress in Valerie Kincaid Oppenheimer, *The Female Labor Force in the United States* (Berkeley, Calif.: Institute of International Studies, 1970).

59   Oppenheimer, *The Female Labor Force in the United States*, 39–52.

gained a 53 percent yes response.[60] Attitudes continued to change in the 1980s. In 1977, 68 percent of the total population agreed with the statement, "A preschool child is likely to suffer if his or her mother works." In 1991, the number agreeing with the statement had fallen to 48 percent (only 34 percent of *women of childbearing age* agreed).[61] The 1990s also saw a continuation of this trend. The percent of people agreeing with the statement, "All in all, family life suffers when the woman has a full-time job," dropped from 25 percent in 1990 to 19 percent in 1998.[62]

These statistics suggest that social attitudes have changed significantly regarding women and work outside the home. There is a considerable controversy, however, over the extent to which this change in social attitudes is a *cause* or a *consequence* of the movement of women into the workforce. Some researchers argue that the underlying determinants of the rise in female participation are economic in nature, and changing attitudes (for example, the women's movement) simply provide an ideological rationale for a process that is already in motion.[63] Others have found evidence in statistical studies that changes in attitudes do play an important, independent role in explaining why more women are entering the labor force.[64] One study found that men growing up in a family model in which the mother worked contributed significantly to the later rise in female labor force participation, suggesting that social attitudes are a important contributor.[65]

Perhaps the clearest evidence that social attitudes influence family labor supply decisions comes from a comparison of labor force participation trends in foreign countries. Figure 3.8 shows the trend in the female labor force participation rate between 1960 and 2003 for four countries: Sweden, the United States, Germany, and Japan. The participation rate of women in Sweden and the United States increased sharply over this period (from 46.1 percent to 57.2 percent in Sweden between 1960 and 2003 and from 35.5 percent to 56.1 percent in the United States between 1960 and 2003), while in Germany and Japan the female participation rate either registered a net decline or remained essentially unchanged. In Japan, the participation rate for women declined from 51.8 percent in 1960 to 44 percent in 1975, after which it began to rise slowly, reaching 45.3 percent in 2003. In Germany, the female participation rate fell from 40.4 percent in 1960 to 38.2 percent in 1970, and then it too began to rise modestly, reaching 44.4 percent in 2003.

---

60   Frank L. Mott, "Women: The Employment Revolution," *The Employment Revolution* (Cambridge, Mass.: MIT Press, 1982), 14–17.

61   Ronald R. Rindfuss, Karin L. Brewster, and Andrew L. Kavee, "Women, Work, and Children: Behavioral and Attitudinal Change in the United States," *Population and Development Review* 22 (September 1996): 457–82, Table 3.

62   "General Social Survey, 1972–2000 Cumulative Codebook" (Survey performed by the National Opinion Research Center at the University of Chicago), accessed at http://webapp.icpsr.umich.edu/GSS/.

63   Oppenheimer, *Work and the Family*, 28–31; and Bowen and Finegan, *The Economics of Labor Force Participation*; Rindfuss et al., "Women, Work, and Children: Behavioral and Attitudinal Change in the United States."

64   Mott, "Women: The Employment Revolution"; Marianne Ferber, "Labor Market Participation of Young Married Women: Causes and Effects," *Journal of Marriage and the Family* 44, no. 2 (May 1982): 457–68; and David I. Levine, "The Effect of Nontraditional Attitudes on Married Women's Labor Supply," *Journal of Economic Psychology* 14 (December 1993): 665–79.

65   Raquel Fernandez, et al., "Preference Formation and the Rise of Women's Labor Force Participation: Evidence from WWII," *NBER Working Paper #W10589* (June 2004).

FIGURE 3.8

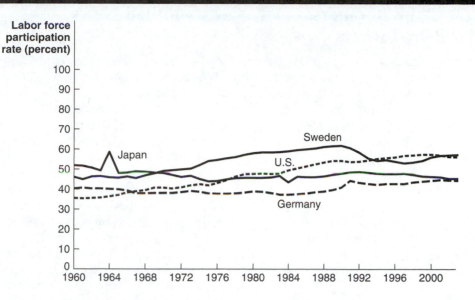

SOURCE: Bureau of Labor Statistics, Office of Productivity and Technology, http://www.bls.gov/fls, Comparative Civilian Labor Force Statistics, Ten Countries, 1959–2003, Table 4.

Economists have explained the sharp rise in female participation in the United States as a result of the positive substitution effect on women's labor supply set off by the secular rise in real wages. Since real wages have increased considerably in Germany and Japan over the past 30 years, why haven't female participation rates also increased as much in these countries? There are several explanations. One is that the aggregate data mask conflicting trends among demographic subgroups.[66] In Japan, part of the drop in the female participation rate was due to the decline of agriculture, a sector in Japan that had traditionally employed a large number of women. Similarly, in Germany much of the decline in labor force participation has been among young single women, while the participation rate among married women has risen significantly.

Although these factors explain part of the divergent behavior in participation rates among these four countries, they cannot explain it all. An additional factor that must be considered is the social attitudes in each country concerning the appropriateness for women of engaging in paid work outside the home. While

66   See Wolfgang Franz, "An Economic Analysis of Female Work Participation, Education, and Fertility: Theory and Empirical Evidence for the Federal Republic of Germany," and Haruo Shimada and Yoshio Higuchi, "An Analysis of Trends in Female Labor Force Participation in Japan," *Journal of Labor Economics* 3, no. 1, pt. 2 (January 1985), S218–S234 and S355–S374.

Exit the Baby Boomers: Good News and Bad News for the Baby Busters

During the Depression years of the 1930s and the war years of the early 1940s young adults postponed marriage and having children. After the war, they made up for lost time on both fronts. The result was the baby-boom generation of 1946–1964. The number of births per adult woman jumped from .6 in the 1930s to 3.5 in the 1950s. Suddenly the nation was awash with tens of millions of new children. In the 1970s and 1980s, these millions of baby boomers were now graduating from high school and college and entering the labor force. Suddenly labor force growth, which had been roughly 1 percent a year, ratcheted upwards to 2.5–3.0 percent and the labor market was flooded with new workers, all looking to get started with careers. One thing the baby boomers did not do, however, was marry or procreate as prolifically as their parents. Among boomers, a small but growing proportion chose not to marry, while the large bulk of married couples chose to have fewer children, and in a number of cases no children at all. Thus, the birth rate among adult women of the boomer generation fell to 2.0. The result was the emergence of a baby bust in the 1970s and 1980s and far fewer Gen Xers in the 1990s and Gen Yers in the early 2000s. Predictably, after 1990 labor force growth slowed considerably, falling back to the 1 percent range. After 2010 it is forecast to fall to only 0.8 percent.

Between 2005–2010 the leading edge of the baby-boom generation will reach retirement age. Then in the next decade the stream of retirements will turn into a flood, with 77 million baby boomers exiting the work force at some point. Remaining behind will be a much smaller number of baby busters. One statistic that captures this demographic shift is the *dependency ratio*—the number of people aged 20–64 relative to the number aged 65 and over. In 2000 the ratio was five to one, in 2030 it will be less than three to one.

This dramatic demographic shift will have huge economic and social reverberations, particularly in labor markets. Some of these repercussions are likely to be positive for the baby busters and still-younger cohorts of workers who will populate the workforce of the 2010–2030 period, while others will be negative.

On the positive side, the retirement of the baby-boom generation is forecast to create a significant labor shortage in the years after 2010. According to the Bureau of Labor Statistics, for example, by 2010 there could be a shortfall of as many as ten million workers relative to the available jobs. Although this number seems huge (too huge in the view of some labor economists), it may nonetheless at least capture the main trend. An indication is given in one news article that examined the workforce at several companies in the Pittsburgh area. The reporter found that at Duquesne Light (the local electric utility) half of the line workers will be eligible to retire by 2010. Similarly, half of the 6,500 nurses at University of Pittsburgh medical center will reach retirement age in 2010, while the average age of engineers at the Westinghouse Corporation is the late 40's. The conclusion was that by 2012 southwestern Pennsylvania could face a shortage of 125,000 workers—about one-tenth of today's labor force.

As the baby-boom generation retires, therefore, the remaining baby busters and Gen Xers and Gen Yers should face a robust labor market with lots of job opportunities and rising wages. In this respect the situation will be the exact opposite of the 1970s when the baby-boom generation substantially increased the supply of labor in the market. In real (inflation

continued

adjusted) terms, the expansion of labor supply is estimated to have depressed wages by 15 percent. During the 2010s the opposite should happen—the labor supply will shrink and real wages will rise.

There is also a dark side to the retirement of the baby-boom generation. The largest problem area is financing the Social Security and Medicare programs in the next several decades. The Social Security program promises monthly benefits to eligible workers and their families who have retired from the workforce, financed by payroll taxes levied on firms and their workers. The Medicare program (part of Social Security) provides subsidized or free health care and prescription drugs to the elderly, also financed from current tax revenues.

A person who retires now at age 65 can expect to live nearly another twenty years. With this fact in mind, and recalling that 77 million baby boomers are set to retire in the years ahead, one can understand the statement in one recent news, article, "You don't need to be a mathematician to see the trouble ahead." The size of the trouble is staggering. According to estimates released by the Social Security Administration in 2004, the gap between projected tax revenues to finance Social Security and Medicare and the projected expenditures under current laws totals a whopping $32 trillion over the next seventy-five years. This may be compared to the size of the current national debt, which is now 4 trillion. Certainly seventy-five years is a long time from now, but even in the nearer term a crisis may be lurking.

Currently the Medicare and Social Security programs generate more tax revenue than expenditures, but this situation will reverse in the year 2019, according to the most recent estimates. Because the federal government is already running a sizable budget deficit, adding a large and growing deficit from Social Security and Medicare would only further unbalance the government's fiscal position. What are the options? If the deficits are allowed to build, they become so large that interest rates would skyrocket and the government could face the prospect of bankruptcy. To avoid this calamity, two other courses of action are open—one is to shift the burden of adjustment to the baby boomers by reducing the payments they receive. This could be done by raising the retirement age to 70 (or more) or reducing the monthly retirement benefits of Social Security; Medicare expenditures could be reined in by limiting eligibility, putting a cap on reimbursable medical expenses, or eliminating prescription drug reimbursements. The other option is to shift the burden of adjustment to the baby busters by increasing the taxes they pay. For example, one estimate is that tax rates would have to rise by one-third to keep Social Security and Medicare solvent.

If this last option is pursued, the baby busters will be in the paradoxical situation of having great job opportunities and rising wages in the years ahead but quite possibly smaller net pay as taxes rise to cover the obligations owed the baby boomers. Or, will the baby busters try to shift the burden to their parents by reducing benefits? We do not know the answer, but clearly a battle of the generations could lie ahead.

SOURCES: "Time to Touch the Third Rail," *U.S. News & World Report* (September 13, 2004), p. 45; "Coming Soon: The Vanishing Work Force," *New York Times* (August 29, 2004), p. C1; "A Future Meltdown?" *The Economist* (September 4, 2004), p. 72; "Our Kids will Pay the Bill," *Newsweek* (January 12, 2004), p. 41; "The Coming Labor Shortage," *The Futurist* (September/October, 2003), p. 24.

these attitudes have undergone a virtual revolution in the United States in the post-war period, in Germany and Japan they have historically remained more rigid and uncompromising. In Japan, for example, many companies have had a formal or informal policy that a female employee must resign when she marries.[67] Similarly, social attitudes in Germany have always discouraged women from working outside the home. Unlike the United States, even during the height of World War II Germany did not utilize married women for work in defense plants.[68] Rising wages in Germany and Japan did not, therefore, result in a large-scale movement of married women into the labor force, in part because social attitudes regarding women's place in society would not accommodate it. This conclusion, however, merely confirms what was learned from the labor/leisure model—the decision to participate in the labor force is determined *both* by preferences (the indifference curves) *and* by market opportunities (the budget constraint).

A Bargaining Model of Family Labor Supply

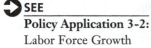

SEE
Policy Application 3-2:
Labor Force Growth during Recessions, p. 156.

Although the household model is the theoretical tool used by most economists to explain the pattern of family labor supply, it is not the only one. An alternative, more institutionally-oriented model emphasizes the role of bargaining power and social norms in the labor supply decision of family members. The way in which labor supply decisions are made in a family context during recessionary times is explored in Policy Application 3-2.

The household model explained the division of labor in the traditional family of 40 to 50 years ago as a rational response to the different productivities and rewards available to the husband and wife, respectively, in market work and home work. Some economists have argued that social norms and women's inequality in bargaining power in the family were a more important cause of women's low involvement in market work than were rational considerations of comparative advantage.[69] In this view, the reason relatively few women participated in the labor force in the years prior to World War II was not through choice, but *lack of choice*. This lack of choice emanated from several sources. One was custom and tradition, which made it socially unacceptable for married women to pursue careers outside the home. A second was discrimination on the part of educational institutions, employers, and unions, which prevented women from acquiring training and employment outside the narrow range of low-wage female occupations. A third cause of lack of choice was women's unequal legal and economic position in the family vis-à-vis their husbands. As described in a classic work by John Stuart Mill, these three

67 See Alice H. Cook and Hiroko Hayashi, *Working Women in Japan: Discrimination, Resistance, and Reform* (Ithaca: New York State School of Industrial and Labor Relations, Cornell University, 1980), and "Japan's Secret Economic Weapon: Exploited Women," *Business Week* (March 4, 1985): 54–55.

68 See George Katona et al., *Aspirations and Affluence* (New York: McGraw-Hill, 1971), 135–44.

69 Marianne Ferber and Bonnie G. Birnbaum, "The 'New Home Economics': Retrospects and Prospects," *Journal of Consumer Research* 4, no. 1 (June 1977): 19–28; Clair Brown, "An Institutional Model of Wives' Work Decisions," *Industrial Relations* 24, no. 2 (Spring 1985): 182–204; and Barbara Bergman, *The Economic Emergence of Women* (New York: Basic Books, 1986).

factors kept most married women at home, not for reasons of comparative advantage, but because it preserved the hegemony (monopoly position) of men in the job market and the family.[70]

This explanation for the sexual division of labor is far different from that offered by the household model. Several pieces of evidence can be marshaled to support it, however. One is the experience of working women in World War II. During the war, millions of women entered the labor force to fill jobs left vacant by men who had been inducted into the armed forces. When the war ended in 1945, many of these women voluntarily resumed their roles as mothers and housewives. Many others, however, desired to keep their jobs, since the level of earnings was much higher than in the jobs traditionally open to women. Despite this desire, a large portion were forced to quit, and the jobs were given to men.[71]

A second, more recent piece of evidence concerns the division of labor in households where the wife has a higher level of education than the husband. One study looked at 49 families where the wife had a Ph.D. but the husband had less than four years of college.[72] Based on considerations of comparative advantage, it would be hypothesized that the wife would specialize in market work and the husband would specialize in home production. None of the men, however, were found to be "house husbands."

A bargaining model of family labor supply also offers quite a different perspective on the reasons for the large increase in the female participation rate over the past 40 to 50 years. The bargaining power of each spouse in the family is a function of his or her dependency on the other: the greater the degree of dependency of spouse X on Y, the less bargaining power X has to influence decision making and the allocation of income and consumption in the family.[73] In this view, married women in the family of 1950 were at a distinct disadvantage in bargaining power in the family because they were far more dependent on their husbands than their husbands were on them. One important reason was economic—the range of jobs and relatively high rates of pay open to the husband gave him more financial independence than the wife.[74] A second factor was the near inevitability of children because of the unreliable birth control methods available at the time. Why, then, did so many married women enter the labor force in the 1960s and 1970s? The answer is that employment afforded women the opportunity to achieve positions of equality in the family. One

---

70 John Stuart Mill, *The Subjection of Women* (London: Longmans, Green, Reader, and Syer, 1869).

71 At Ford Motor Co., for example, women composed 25 percent of the workforce during the war, but only 4 percent in 1946. See Mary M. Schweitzer, "World War II and Female Labor Force Participation Rates," *Journal of Economic History* 15, no. 1 (March 1980): 89–95. On this subject, also see Ruth Milkman, *Gender at Work: The Dynamics of Job Segregation by Sex during World War II* (Champaign, Ill.: University of Illinois Press, 1987).

72 Cited in Ferber and Birnbaum, "The New Home Economics," 21.

73 The link between bargaining power and dependency is developed in Samuel B. Bacharach and Edward J. Lawler, *Bargaining, Power, Tactics, and Outcomes* (San Francisco: Jossey-Bass Publishers, 1981). A formal bargaining model of family labor supply is given in Marilyn Manser and Murray Brown, "Bargaining Analysis of Household Decisions," in Cynthia Lloyd, Emily Andrews, and Curtis Gilroy, eds., *Women in the Labor Market* (New York: Columbia University Press, 1979), 3–26.

74 See Roberta M. Spalter-Roth, "Differentiating between the Living Standards of Husbands and Wives in Two Wage-Earner Families, 1968 and 1979," *Journal of Economic History* 18, (March 1983): 231–40.

factor facilitating this trend was the growing number of white-collar and "pink-collar" jobs available to women. A second was the improvement in contraceptive devices that allowed women to both limit and time the birth of children.[75] A third was the rather marked shift in social attitudes toward working women, coupled with the passage of antidiscrimination and affirmative action laws.

A variant on the bargaining model, perhaps best classified as a competitive market model, considers the impact of the marriage market on a woman's reservation wage through her valuation of marriage. Shoshana Grossbard-Schechtman argues that when the ratio of marriageable men to women is low (more women than men), the security of the marriage is threatened, reducing the expected value of the marriage, lowering the woman's reservation wage, and driving women into the labor market.[76] Grossbard-Schechtman shows that her theory is consistent not only with the overall increase in labor force participation among young married women in recent years in the U.S.[77] but also with the noticeable increase in home-based work[78] and the higher labor force participation rate of black married women relative to that of white married women.

In the household model it was largely the rise in real wages over time that pulled married women into the labor force. From a bargaining perspective, these women were attracted into the labor force not only by rising wages but also by the opportunity to establish personal independence and equality in marriage, and, in the case of early baby-boom women, by the lack of opportunities to be supported as homemakers in marriage.

The bargaining model offers an intriguing alternative for explaining the rise in female labor force participation. In addition, it performs fairly well in explaining the allocation of leisure time within a family (leisure that, according to the model, family members have won through implicitly threatening to leave the family).[79] The bargaining model, however, does not allow one to ascertain the common well-being that accrues to a family through joint decision making. It is up to the household model to allow for the possibility that family members make labor supply decisions based on the "common good" of the household (total family utility) rather than solely on what promotes their self-interest (individual utility).

---

75 See David M. Heer and Shoshana Grossbard-Schectman, "The Impact of the Female Marriage Squeeze and the Contraceptive Revolution on Sex Roles and the Women's Liberation Movement in the United States, 1960–1975," *Journal of Marriage and Family* 43, no. 1 (February 1981): 49–66.

76 Shoshana Grossbard-Schechtman, "A Theory of Allocation in Time in Markets for Labour and Marriage," *Economic Journal* 94 (December 1984): 863–82; and Shoshana Grossbard-Schechtman, "A Model of Labor Supply and Marriage," Mimeo, San Diego State University (January 2001).

77 Shoshana Grossbard-Schechtman and Clive W. J. Granger, "Travail des Femmes et Mariage: Du baby-boom au baby-bust," *Population* (December 1998): 731–52; Shoshana Grossbard-Schechtman and Shoshana Neuman, "Marriage and Work for Pay," in *Marriage and the Economy*, Shoshana Grossbard-Schechtman, ed. (Cambridge: Cambridge University Press, 2003).

78 Elizabeth Field-Hendrey and Linda Edwards, "Marriage and Home-Based Work for Pay," in *Marriage and the Economy*, Shoshana Grossbard-Schechtman, ed. (Cambridge: Cambridge University Press, 2003).

79 See Bernard Fortin and Guy Lacroix, "A Test of the Unitary and Collective Models of Household Labor Supply," *The Economic Journal* 107 (July 1997): 933–55; and Urvashi Dhawan Diswal, "Testing the Family 'Common Preference' Model for Immigrant and Nonimmigrant Women's Labor Supply," *Canadian Public Policy* 25 (Supplement November 1999): S95–S114.

The Earned Income Tax Credit: A Way to Help the Poor *and* Encourage Labor Force Participation?

A major criticism of cash transfer welfare programs, such as Temporary Assistance for Needy Families (TANF), is that they provide a strong disincentive to work. Indeed, this disincentive effect was the most important motivation behind the 1990s reform of the Aid to Families with Dependent Children (AFDC) welfare program in the United States. As described in Chapter 2, the Personal Responsibility and Work Opportunity Reconciliation Act of 1996 replaced AFDC with TANF, and sought to encourage more work through strict payment limits and mandatory work requirements.

An alternative to the "stick" approach of payment limits and work requirements in TANF is the "carrot" approach contained in another government program, the Earned Income Tax Credit (EITC). A number of economists believe the EITC is more effective in helping reduce poverty and also in promoting work.[1]

Rather than a direct cash transfer program, the EITC works as an income supplement; a person must be working to qualify. The supplement (a form of a wage subsidy) is administered through the Internal Revenue Service and one applies by filing an income tax return. The program was first written into the tax code on a temporary basis in 1975, but became permanent in 1978. There are several requirements for workers to qualify for the EITC. In addition to actually filling out a tax return (even if the recipient owes no income tax), the worker must earn an adjusted gross income below some threshold amount (which varies by year and family size). Until 1994 the worker needed to also house a "qualifying" child. Today there is a small subsidy available to childless couples. Further-

more, married individuals cannot separately receive the credit; they must file a joint tax return. Figure 3.9 illustrates in graphical form what the EITC benefit schedule looks like for a representative single worker with two or more children in the year 2003.

In 2003, single taxpayers with two or more children could receive a credit of 40 percent of income, up to $10,500 (this is shown by the upward sloping portion of the line in Figure 3.9). This would result in a maximum credit of $4,200. Between the earnings of $10,500 and $13,750, the worker would receive the maximum credit (thus, the flat portion of the benefit profile). Then, between $13,750 and $33,650 of earnings, the benefit is reduced by 21.11 percent for every dollar of additional earnings beyond $13,750. Once earnings reach $33,650, the EITC has completely phased out and the taxpayer no longer qualifies. The primary difference between the structure of the EITC and TANF is that EITC payments *increase* as a percentage of earned income (up to a point). The EITC and TANF affect the budget constraint differently and this is why the EITC is expected to have solved the work disincentive concern, as will be illustrated in the discussion that follows.

Work Incentives of EITC vs. TANF

Figure 3.10 depicts three budget constraints. One is the budget constraint a worker faces with a given market wage and in the absence of any welfare program or non-labor income (line segment *AB*). The second is similar to that depicted in Figure 2.10

---

[1] A comprehensive, detailed treatment of the EITC (its history, behavioral impact, and further controversies in the early 2000s) is found in V. Joseph Hotz and John Karl Scholz, "The Earned Income Tax Credit," *NBER Working Paper #8078* (January 2001). The relationship of the EITC to its intellectual predecessor, the Negative Income Tax, is examined in detail by Robert A. Moffitt, "The Negative Income Tax and the Evolution of U.S. Welfare Policy," *NBER Working Paper #W9751* (June 2003).

FIGURE 3.9   THE BENEFIT SCHEDULE OF THE EARNED INCOME TAX CREDIT
IN 2003

A single taxpayer with two or more children earns a credit equal to 40% of income, up to $10,500 (shown by the upward sloping portion of the line). Between the earnings of $10,500 and $13,750, the worker receives the maximum credit of $4,200 (thus, the flat portion of the benefit profile). Between $13,750 and $33,650 of earnings, the benefit is reduced by 21.1 percent for every dollar of additional earnings beyond $13,750 (the slope of the downward-sloping line is equal to −0.211). Once earnings reach $33,650, the EITC has completely phased out and the taxpayer no longer qualifies.

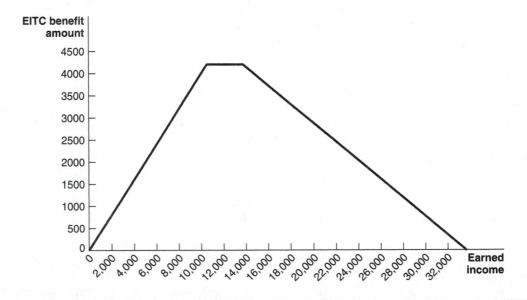

and reflects the budget constraint under the TANF cash transfer program (line segment *ACDB*). The third reflects the presence of an EITC program (line segment (*AEFGB*).

There are several differences to point out in the construction of the TANF and EITC budget constraints. First, the level of guarantee in the TANF program is typically lower than the maximum EITC benefit (although one must be working to get *any* payment from EITC). Secondly, the EITC always has a level of earnings over which the benefit is not reduced, whereas the TANF payment can be reduced in some states with the first dollar of earnings (i.e., the disregard is zero). And, lastly,

the break-even point (level of income at which the benefit is discontinued) typically occurs at a much higher level of income for the EITC recipient than the for the TANF recipient.

The next point of comparison is the source of enthusiasm for the EITC: the differential impact of these two programs on labor force participation. Recall that a person will participate in the labor force if the market wage (or market wage adjusted by some subsidy, such as EITC) exceeds the person's reservation wage. Given the preferences depicted by the indifference curves in Figure 3.10, this person works zero hours under the TANF program (I_1), but works 30 hours under the EITC

FIGURE 3.10   LABOR FORCE PARTICIPATION: EITC VERSUS TANF

The TANF cash transfer program results in a budget constraint represented by the line segment *ACDB* (see Figure 2.10 for its construction; this depiction assumes a level of $0 disregard). The EITC program results in a budget constraint *AEFGB*. The segment *AE* represents a subsidy to earnings, meaning that the benefit increases as earnings increase; the segment *EF* is the amount by which income can go up without any reduction in the subsidy; and at point *G* is where the subsidy phases out and becomes zero. Under the preferences depicted here, the worker chooses not to participate in the labor market under the TANF program but will work *H** number of hours under the EITC program.

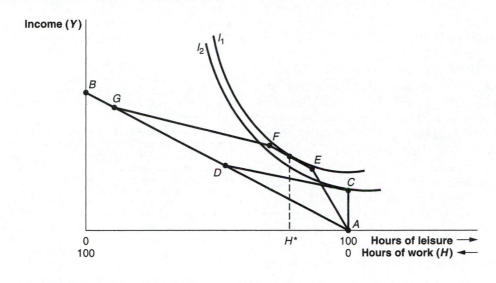

program (I_2). Does the person reach a higher level of utility under the EITC program? Yes, the indifference curve I_2 is further out from the origin than indifference curve I_1. Of course, one caveat to this rosy scenario is that a job is actually available for this worker.

Research Evidence of the Impact of EITC on Poverty and Labor Force Participation

A major purpose of all welfare programs is to reduce poverty. Empirical research shows that the EITC appears to be successful in this mission. One analysis has found that over 60 percent of EITC payments go to taxpayers with pre-EITC incomes below the poverty line.[2] Another study finds that 95 percent of EITC benefits go to workers earning less than the median wage ($13.53 in 2003). Furthermore, the Council of Economic Advisors estimated that the EITC program lifted 4.3 million people from poverty in 1997 and 1998. It is widely believed that the EITC program raises more children out of poverty than other government-funded

2   John K. Sholz and Kara Levine, "The Evolution of Income Support Policy," *Mimeo*, University of Wisconsin (May 2000).

welfare program.[3] This success comes at a cost, however. The Center for Budget and Policy Priorities estimates that the total cost of EITC in 2002 to have been over $32 billion.[4] By comparison, the federal government spent half that ($15 billion) on TANF in the same year.[5]

One of the most popular selling points of the EITC program, over other welfare programs such as TANF, is the theoretical conclusion (as seen in Figure 3.10) that the EITC encourages labor force participation among the poor. How well does it succeed in this goal? Many studies make use of the natural experiment that was created when the EITC program underwent major expansions in 1986 and 1993. By doing a before-and-after comparison, these studies have found that increased generosity of the EITC program tends to increase labor force participation among single women and married men, but has a negative effect on the labor supply of married women.[6] The result that married men increase their labor supply and that married women are more likely to stay home in the wake of an expansion of the EITC program is a good example of the joint decision making within the household. This result suggests that EITC families view non-market time of each adult member as substitutable and an increase in the

effective market wage allows members of the family to specialize in that activity in which they have a comparative advantage.

3   Nancy K. Cauthen, *Earned Income Tax Credits*, Research Findings About Increasing Family Income Through Employment, Policy Brief No. 2 (New York: National Center for Children in Poverty, Columbia University, June 2002). David Neumark and William Wascher, "Using the EITC to Help Poor Families: New Evidence and a Comparison with the Minimum Wage," *National Tax Journal* 54 (June 2001): 281–317, find that the EITC is more effective in raising families out of poverty than is the minimum wage.

4   Center on Budget and Policy Priorities, "Estimating the Cost of a State Earned Income Tax Credit," (28 April 2003), http://www.cbpp.org/11-11-99sfp.htm.

5   U.S. Department of Health and Human Services, Administration for Children and Families, "TANF Financial Data," http://www.acf.dhhs.gov/programs/ofs/data/overview_2002.html accessed 15 October 2004.

6   See Nada Eissa and Jeffey B. Liebman, "Labor Supply Response to the Earned Income Tax Credit," *Quarterly Journal of Economics* (May 1996): 605–37; David Ellwood, "The Impact of the EITC on Work and Social Policy Reforms on Work Marriage, and Living Arrangements," *Mimeo*, John F. Kennedy School of Government, Harvard University (November 1999); and Nada Eissa and Hilary Williamson Hoynes, "Taxes and the Labor Market Participation of Married Couples: The Earned Income Tax Credit," *Journal of Public Economics* 88 (2004): 1931–58. Also see V. Joseph Hotz and John K. Scholz, "The Earned Income Tax Credit," *NBER Working Paper #8078* (January 2001) for a review of many more analyses of the impact of the EITC on labor supply behavior among the poor.

POLICY APPLICATION 3-2

Labor Force Growth during Recessions

The growth in the labor force exhibits both a steady, long-term upward trend and a short-term, cyclical movement associated with the business cycle. This cyclical aspect of labor force growth raises an important question that has been a source of debate in labor economics for over 50 years—whether the size of the labor force will expand or contract during periods of recession and depression.[1] The answer to this question depends on the strength of what has become known as the **added**

worker effect and the **discouraged worker effect.** The issues involved in this debate can be readily understood using the household model of labor supply.

The Added Worker Effect

The added worker effect leads to a temporary *increase* in the size of the labor force during

1   Jacob Mincer, "Labor Force Participation and Unemployment: A Review of Recent Evidence," in Robert A. Gordon and Margaret S. Gordon, eds., *Prosperity and Unemployment* (New York: John Wiley and Sons, 1966), 73–112.

recessions and depressions. The reasoning is relatively simple. Consider a family where the husband works while the wife and teenaged children are engaged solely in nonmarket activities (such as housework and school). Next, assume the economy enters a recession and the husband is laid off from his job. Since the unemployed are counted as part of the labor force, as long as the husband actively searches for work, his movement from the employed group to the unemployed group does not cause any net change in the size of the labor force.

The household model predicts, however, that the unemployment of the husband will have a definite impact on the labor supply decisions of the wife and teenaged children. The loss of the husband's earnings results in a large decrease in income for the entire family, setting off a pure negative income effect for the other family members. Assuming that leisure is a normal good, the reduction in family income will lead to a decreased demand for leisure and a greater supply of labor as the wife or teenaged children seek work to supplement the family income. From the wife's point of view, for example, the situation is exactly the opposite of that shown in Figure 3.4; as her nonlabor income is reduced her reservation wage declines, and at some point she finds it advantageous to join the labor force. The added worker effect, therefore, represents the temporary entrance into the labor force of "secondary" workers (the wife or teenaged children) in response to the unemployment of the primary head of household. If the added worker effect were the only development to take place, the labor force would grow more rapidly during economic downturns, further exacerbating the imbalance between labor demand and supply.[2]

The Discouraged Worker Effect

The positive impact on labor force growth of the added worker effect is offset by the simultaneous occurrence during recessions of the discouraged worker effect. Figure 3.11 illustrates the discouraged worker effect. Suppose the individual earns a wage of W_1 per hour, the budget constraint is AB,

and hours of work per week are H_1 (point X). Assume now that a recession begins and the person is laid off from his or her job. Even though hours of work temporarily fall to zero (point A), it is a disequilibrium position—given the wage rate of W_1 and the preferences for income versus leisure, the individual desires H_1 hours of work and will search for new employment offering those hours. As long as the worker does continue to search for new employment, there is again no net change in the labor force.

Does it pay to keep searching for work, however? To answer this, the unemployed worker compares the financial return obtained from devoting an hour of time to job search relative to the value of time in nonmarket activities. These activities might include, for example, painting the house, looking after the children, or just consuming leisure. When this person had a job, the wage W_1 was high enough that it exceeded the reservation wage, and he or she chose to work in the market rather than pursue these other nonmarket activities. Now that the person is unemployed, however, each hour spent in the labor force does not pay W_1, but some lesser amount. In statistical terms, this lesser amount is equal to $E(W)$, the *expected value* of the wage. In equation form, this expected value is equal to:

$$E(W_1) = pW_1, \tag{3.2}$$

where p is the probability of finding another job paying W_1. If $W_1 = \$8$ and there is a 50 percent chance of obtaining such a job ($p = 0.5$), the average return the unemployed worker can expect from this hour in the labor force is only 0.5 ($\$8$) = $\$4$. For someone without a job, the opportunity cost of not working is only $E(W_1)$, not W_1. This is represented in Figure 3.11 by rotating the budget constraint downward to AC, with a slope of $-pW_1$. If the probability of finding a job is sufficiently low, the expected value of the wage will fall below the person's reservation wage, and he or she will give

---

2   For empirical evidence on the added worker effect, see James R. Spletzer, "Reexamining the Added Worker Effect," *Economic Inquiry* 35 (April 1997): 417–27.

FIGURE 3.11   THE DISCOURAGED WORKER EFFECT

Given the wage W_1, the budget constraint is AB and the person chooses to participate in the labor force, working H_1 hours (point X). Should the person be unemployed, the monetary return from an hour spent in the labor force falls to pW_1, where p is the probability of finding another job. Assuming $p < 1.0$, the budget constraint rotates to the left from AB to AC. If the probability of finding another job is small enough, the person's reservation wage will exceed the expected value of the market wage (the slope of AC) and he or she will drop out of the labor force as a discouraged worker (point A).

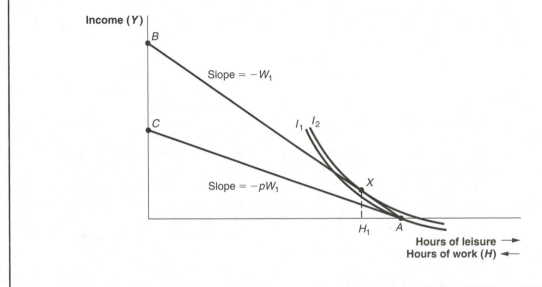

up the job search altogether and drop out of the labor force, shown in Figure 3.11 by the corner solution at point A, where the budget constraint AC and indifference curve I_1 intersect. The person pictured in Figure 3.11 is a discouraged worker because he or she desires to work at the wage of W_1 but has given up any job search because of the low probability of finding such a job. This discouraged worker effect causes the labor force to contract during recessions as unemployed workers temporarily (or in some cases permanently) withdraw from the labor force. This withdrawal causes the published unemployment rate to actually lower (ceteris paribus) and thus understate the true amount of joblessness during recessions.

The added worker effect leads to an expansion in the labor force during periods of recession, and the discouraged worker effect leads to a contraction of the labor force. Is the impact of one larger than the other? Empirical research has consistently found that the discouraged worker effect dominates in quantitative terms the added worker effect, causing the labor force to shrink in recessions and to grow in periods of economic recovery.[3] While both occur simultaneously during a period of recession, the added worker effect occurs only in a relatively small percentage of families in which

3   William Bowen and T. A. Finegan, *The Economics of Labor Force Participation* (Princeton, N.J.: Princeton University Press, 1969).

both the primary earner is laid off and other family members are able to work, but are not currently in the labor force. In addition, the presence of unemployment insurance benefits makes the entrance of other family members into the labor force less financially crucial.[4] The discouraged worker effect, on the other hand, is likely to be more widespread, since the probability of finding work will decrease for *all* the unemployed. Rising unemployment will also cause some people, such as students or housewives, to postpone entry into the labor force until better economic conditions return, further slowing the growth of the labor force. Finally, it should be noted that discouraged workers are most likely to be found in labor force groups that either have alternative uses of their time in nonmarket pursuits that are relatively productive (for example, housewives) or face particularly poor job prospects in the labor market (such as less-educated black males).

---

4   Julie Cullen and Jonathan Gruber, "Does Unemployment Insurance Crowd Out Spousal Labor Supply?" *Journal of Labor Economics* 18 (July 2000): 546–72. Researchers have found that the added worker effect dominates the discouraged worker effect among married women in Turkey; see Cem Baslevent and Ozlem Onaran, "Are Married women in Turkey More Likely to Become Added or Discouraged Workers?" *Labour* 17 (September 2003): 439–58.

EMPIRICAL EVIDENCE 3-1

Age/Participation Profiles

The household model of labor supply can explain a number of important patterns or trends in the labor force participation rates of various demographic groups in the population. In this section, attention focuses on the cross-sectional pattern of labor force participation rates among persons classified by sex, race, and marital status.

Several facets of the cross-sectional pattern in labor force participation rates are illustrated in Figure 3.12. Both diagrams present what is known as an **age/participation profile**—a snapshot at a point in time of the labor force participation rates of individuals of different ages. Graph (a), for example, shows the age/participation profiles for men and women, respectively, classified by marital status, for the year 2003. Several features stand out in the data shown there. First, both for married and single groups, men have a higher overall labor force participation than do women. In 2003, 68.7 percent of single (never married) men 16 years of age and over were in the labor force, while 57.9 percent of single women were. Similarly, 77.3 percent of married men (spouse present) and 61.0 percent of married women were in the labor force.

A second feature is that marriage accentuates the divergence in the participation behavior of men and women. For the single group, men's and women's labor force participation rates are fairly close together; for the married group, women's labor force participation rates fall considerably from those of single women, while participation rates for married men rise considerably relative to those of single men.

A third feature of the participation rates shown in graph (a) is their pattern over the life cycle of each group. The pattern for single men and women is nearly identical, with participation rising sharply from the teenage years to a peak in the midlife years, followed by an accelerating decline

FIGURE 3.12

AGE/PARTICIPATION PROFILES BY SEX, MARITAL STATUS, AND RACE, 2003

(a) By Sex and Marital Status

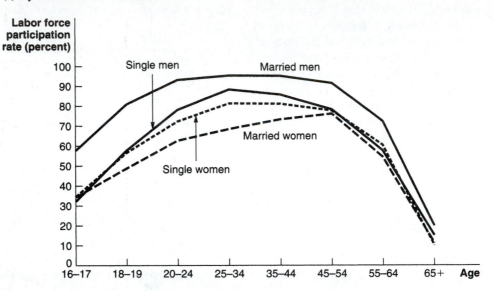

(b) By Sex and Race

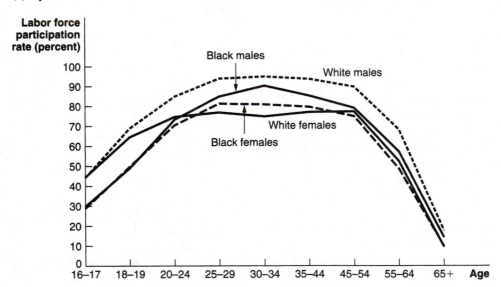

SOURCE: Bureau of Labor Statistics, unpublished data and January 2004 Employment and Earnings Table 3, http://www.bls.gov/cps/cpsatabs.htm.

as the individuals approach age 65.[1] The life cycle pattern of married men and women, however, differs markedly in several respects. The pattern for married men is much flatter over the life cycle than for single men; even in their teenage years, 81 percent of married men participate in the labor force, and not until the 55- to 64-year-old age group do participation rates fall much. Much the same pattern is evident in a comparison of the profiles for single women and married women. While the participation rate for single women increases sharply up to the age group of 25 to 34, reaching a peak of 81.3 percent, the participation rate for married women doesn't peak-out until the late 30s (after the prime childbearing years), where it reaches 76.2 percent.

Graph (b) of Figure 3.12 shows the age/participation profiles in 2003 for men and women classified by race. Several interesting features of participation stand out. First, white men participate more in the labor force than do black men, and this relationship is true for every age group. Second, much the opposite situation is true for women, with black women having an overall participation rate of 61.9 percent compared to 59.1 percent for white women. Finally, the life-cycle patterns of participation rates for white and black women differ significantly; white women's participation rates decline during the prime childbearing years (ages 25 to 34) while the participation rate for black women continues to rise until the ages 40 to 44.

The household model of time allocation offers several explanations for this marked contrast in the labor force participation of these various demographic groups.

Marital Status

The household model suggests that each person should allocate an additional hour to home work as long as its value exceeds the monetary value received from an hour of work at a paying job. Why, as shown in Figure 3.12, is there a much greater division of labor between market and nonmarket work for married people than for single people?[2]

Perhaps the most fundamental difference between the average single, never-married person and the family unit of husband and wife is the presence of children. One important reason for the division of labor by a married couple is that the presence of children substantially increases the value of an hour of time spent at home work relative to market work. Children, particularly preschoolers, require substantial amounts of time for caring, feeding, and training and, thus, an hour of time devoted to home work will increase the individual and family's well-being by more, on average, than the same hour devoted to home work by a single person.

The second aspect of the time allocation decision for a married couple is to choose the combination of husband's time and wife's time to allocate to home work. Traditionally, the husband specialized in market work and the wife specialized in home work. The household model suggests that this decision reflected, first, the higher wage rate the husband could earn from an hour of market work relative to the wife and, second, the greater actual or perceived productivity of the wife at various home tasks, particularly child care. Thus, marriage causes a more pronounced difference in male and female labor force participation because, on one hand, marriage leads to activities (for example,

---

[1] It is important to realize that the actual age/participation profile of persons in relatively young cohorts in 2003 (say 20 to 24 years old) will probably look quite different from those shown in Figure 3.12, which are based on the experience of cohorts born in much earlier years. This is particularly true for women. Evidence on this point is given in James P. Smith and Michael P. Ward, "Time-Series Growth in the Female Labor Force," *Journal of Labor Economics* 3, pt. 2 (January 1985): 559–90.

[2] These issues are discussed in Sandra L. Hofferth and Kristin A. Moore, "Women's Employment and Marriage," in Ralph E. Smith, ed., *The Subtle Revolution* (Washington, D.C.: The Urban Institute, 1979): 99–124. Issues impacting on the labor supply decisions of married women are empirically investigated in Daniela Del Boca et al., "Employment Decisions of Married Women: Evidence and Explanations," *Labour* 14 (March 2001): 35–52.

bearing and raising children) that enhance the value of time spent at home work while, at the same time, allowing a degree of specialization in market and nonmarket work unavailable to the single person.

This dual consideration of returns from work versus productivity in the home also helps to explain another feature of married women's labor force participation. As noted in Figure 3.12, the life cycle pattern of participation for married women is much lower than that for single women and does not exhibit the peak in participation rates in the 25-to-29 age group. This pattern is clearly associated with the timing of the birth of children, as well as the total number of children. The household model predicts that the labor supply of the wife should decrease as her time becomes more valuable in the home, and it is no accident that (white) married women's participation falls during the prime childbearing years.

Race

The household model also provides a logical explanation for the differences in labor force participation rates among whites and blacks in the population. The two features of most importance noted in Figure 3.12 are the smaller participation rates for black men relative to white men, but higher participation rates for black women relative to white women.

Because of differences in quantity and quality of education, geographic location, and discrimination, among other reasons, the average wage rate available to black men is significantly less than that for white men. The household model predicts that, given their smaller return for an hour's work, black men would substitute toward relatively more nonmarket work, and possibly leisure, than white men, leading to lower labor force participation. Particularly for black men with low levels of schooling, this prediction seems to accord with observed behavior. Studies of black men living in urban ghetto areas, for example, find a much lower attachment to the labor force (as officially defined), both because they are more likely to engage in work in the "underground" economy and because they show a tendency to move into and out of jobs on a fairly frequent basis.[3]

Black women, on the other hand, have a higher labor force participation rate for several reasons.[4] One reason is that in black married couples, given that the husband's income is on average lower than his white counterpart's, there is less of a negative income effect on the wife's decision to work than for a white woman. Second, it is often observed that the forces of discrimination in the job market fall less heavily on black women than on black men, making the return from work outside the home relatively greater for black women. Finally, the labor force participation of black women does not decrease during the childbearing years as it does for white women. One explanation for this is that a greater proportion of black mothers are single parents (51 percent of black children in 2003 were living only with their mother, compared to 18 percent of white children) and, thus, fewer black women than white women can specialize in child rearing since fewer have husbands present. A second reason is the greater proportion of extended families among blacks, resulting in better access to relatives to help with child care.[5] A third factor is economic necessity—given the lower income of the husband (or absence of a husband), the black mother has little choice but to work.

---

[3] See, for example, Elliot Liebow, *Tally's Corner* (Boston: Little, Brown and Co., 1967); Ken Auletta, *The Underclass* (New York: Vintage Books, 1983); and Rebecca M. Blank, *It Takes A Nation: A New Agenda for Fighting Poverty* (New York: Russell Sage, 1997).

[4] See Phyllis A. Wallace, *Black Women in the Labor Force* (Cambridge, Mass.: MIT Press, 1980).

[5] Thirteen percent of black children in 2003 had a grandparent living with them, compared with only six percent of white children ("America's Families and Living Arrangements, 2003," http://www.census.gov see "children").

Summary

Labor force participation involves the question of whether or not to work in the market. The labor/leisure model shows that work in the market is optimal only if the market wage exceeds the individual's reservation wage. The person's reservation wage is determined, in turn, by factors such as the preferences for work and leisure and productivity in nonmarket activities. The labor/leisure model shows that the probability of labor force participation increases with the wage rate. This insight is further developed by the household model of labor supply. This model shows that a wage increase for one spouse affects not only that person's labor supply, but also that of the wife or husband. One channel through which this occurs is the cross-substitution effect.

The most important trend in labor force participation in the last 50 years has been the rapid increase in the proportion of women working outside the home. This development has many origins, including the rise in real wages, greater educational attainment, expanded job opportunities, the desire to advance family living standards, changing social attitudes, and the desire of women for equal bargaining power within the family. Concomitant with the rise in female labor force participation has been the gradual decline in the participation rate of men. This was traced to several factors such as the desire for earlier retirement brought on by the secular increase in incomes, the greater coverage and benefits from Social Security and private pension plans, and the declining participation rate among prime-age black males due to poor health and discouragement over job prospects.

Review Questions

1. Why might a married woman with children have a higher reservation wage than a single woman with no children?

2. According to the household model, why is the substitution effect for women likely to be larger than the substitution effect for men? What should be the relationship between the husband's income and the wife's probability of labor force participation according to this model?

3. The household model suggests that the division of labor in the traditional family where the husband engages in market work and the wife engages in home work is the result of rational decision making based on considerations of comparative advantage. Critics of this theory argue that the division of labor between the sexes has little to do with the innate productivities of men and women in market versus home work, but rests on the forces of tradition and male dominance in the family. Briefly discuss the arguments for and against each point of view.

4. Why does the added worker effect cause the labor force to grow during recessions? Why does the discouraged worker effect cause it to shrink? Which effect is likely to be more important?

5. Under the Social Security law, until the year 2000, every dollar of earnings over $15,500 was subject to an implicit tax rate of $t 5 0.33$ because benefits were reduced by 33¢ for every dollar of additional wage income. What should be the effect on labor supply of Congress eliminating the earnings test and allowing recipients to earn as much as desired from work with

no reduction in benefits ($t = 0$)? Show this in a graph using the labor/leisure model.

6. Use the labor/leisure model to analyze the impact of child-care costs on the decision of a married woman with children to participate in the labor force.

a. First, draw a budget constraint assuming the wage is $6 per hour and the woman has $200 per week of nonlabor income. Then draw in an indifference curve so that her equilibrium hours of work are 20 per week.

b. Next, assume that if the woman works she must pay child-care costs. These costs are of two kinds. The first is a lump sum or *fixed* cost of $50 per week for, say, transportation of the child to a day-care facility. The second is a *variable* cost of $2 for each hour the child is at the day-care facility. Given these two types of costs, draw the new budget constraint for this woman.

c. Without child-care costs, the woman maximized utility by working 20 hours; with child-care costs, will this woman continue to work or will she drop out of the labor force? To determine this, draw an indifference curve so that it has a tangency point with the new budget constraint. Is this level of utility higher or lower than if she did not work at all? Show this in the graph. Would the effect of child-care costs be different if she had originally been working 50 hours per week? Show this and explain why.

7. Nearly 3.2 million people in the United States work full-time "graveyard" shifts. Some common experiences of working nights include not feeling "quite as aggressive and rested [compared to] working the day shift," and feeling "dysfunctional as a parent." In fact, one study has shown that night workers are more susceptible to heart attacks, gastrointestinal disorders, and depression. Given that working during the night is less desirable than working during the day, illustrate the implied reservation wages (the minimum wage that would induce someone to take a job) for night-shift jobs and day-shift jobs. Which is higher? Why?

8. In a recent story in the *Atlanta Journal–Constitution*, entitled "Mommy Wars," one stay-at-home mom laments, "Lots of career women think the only reason I'm staying home is that I'm not capable of doing anything else." Evaluate this criticism in the context of the household model of labor supply. In other words, is it true that the only reason women don't enter the labor market is because the market doesn't value her skills?

The Allocation of Time to Market Work, Home Work, and Leisure: A Graphic Exposition

The labor/leisure model was extended in Chapter 3 to incorporate a three-way allocation of time to market work, home work, and leisure. To keep the exposition relatively simple, this model was explained solely in verbal terms. This appendix develops the same model using a graphic approach for those students who want a more in-depth treatment of this subject.[1]

In the labor/leisure model, an individual's utility is assumed to be a function of goods (purchased with labor earnings and nonlabor income) and leisure time. Gary Becker has argued, however, that goods and time are better treated as inputs that people use to produce various "commodities" that are the direct source of utility.[2] As an example, a box of fried chicken does not yield any utility until it is combined with an hour of time to create a commodity called a picnic lunch.

To develop this line of reasoning more formally, assume a single-person household. This person seeks to maximize the amount of commodity Z, which is a combination of goods and services (X) and consumption time (L),

$$Z = Z(X, L). \tag{3A.1}$$

The goods can be either purchased in the market (X_M) or produced at home (X_H), implying:

$$X = X_M + X_H \tag{3A.2}$$

Market goods and home goods are assumed to be perfect substitutes for each other, and both are measured in terms of their dollar value.

Home goods are produced by work at home, according to the production function:

$$X_H = f(H), \tag{3A.3}$$

where H is hours of work in the home. (Note that this definition of H is different from that in Chapters 2 and 3.) Since the capital stock and technology of production in the household are assumed constant, additional hours of home work increase the amount of home goods produced, but at a diminishing rate (i.e., the factor input H is subject to declining marginal productivity).[3]

---

[1]   This appendix is drawn from Reuben Gronau, "Leisure, Home Production and Work—The Theory of the Allocation of Time Revisited," *Journal of Political Economy* 85 (December 1977): 1099–1124.

[2]   See Gary Becker, "A Theory of the Allocation of Time," *Economic Journal* 75 (September 1965): 493–517.

[3]   Students unfamiliar with the concepts of a production function and marginal product can find both terms defined in the next chapter.

In attempting to maximize utility, this person is bound by two constraints. The first is the budget constraint:

$$X_M = WN + V \tag{3A.4}$$

where W is the person's wage rate (assumed to be constant), N is hours of market work, and V is nonlabor income. The second constraint is the time constraint:

$$T = L + H + N, \tag{3A.5}$$

where T is total time available per period (e.g., week, month).

Given this framework, the issue to be determined is how the person will allocate his or her time to the three activities: market work, home work, and consumption time or "leisure." The answer is given in Figure 3A.1. The concave curve $ABCD$ depicts the relationship between hours of time devoted to home work and the value of home goods produced, as given by the home production function in Equation 3A.3. At point A, all time is devoted to T_6 hours of leisure, implying $H = 0$ and $X_H = 0$. At point B, hours of leisure have fallen to T_4 and hours of home work have increased to $T_6 - T_4$. The slope of the curve $ABCD$ measures $\Delta X_H / \Delta H$, the marginal product of home work or the "shadow wage" (i.e., the implicit dollar value received from an hour of home work). The curve becomes progressively flatter, illustrating that home work is subject to declining marginal productivity.

The next step is to incorporate market work into the diagram. The relationship between goods and market work is given by Equation 3A.4. Assume initially that $V = 0$ (no nonlabor income) and $W = W_1$. Starting at point A, if the person works successive hours in the market instead of at home, the value of goods available is given by the dashed straight line budget constraint (only a portion of which is drawn in). The slope of the budget constraint is $\Delta X_M / \Delta N = W_1$. Since the return to home work (the shadow wage) is assumed at point A to be greater than the return to market work (the market wage), a person who decides to work should initially start out in the home. Next consider point B. If the person chooses to work one more hour, should it be in the market or at home? It should be at home, since the slope of the curve $ABCD$ at point B still exceeds the return to market work, given by the slope of the dashed straight line at point B. As still more hours are devoted to home work, at some point, such as at C, it is likely that market work will begin to yield a bigger increment of goods than home work. This is illustrated by the fact that beyond point C, the slope of the solid straight line CF exceeds the slope of the curve CD. The relevant opportunity set for this person, therefore, is ACF.

If it is assumed that the person also has nonlabor income of, say, V_1, the effect is to shift out the opportunity locus to $AGJM$. The addition of nonlabor income does not affect the point at which market work is more productive than home work since neither the value of the market wage nor that of the shadow wage is affected.

The slope of the dashed lines at points A and B reflects the values of the market wage; the slope of the concave curve $ABCD$ reflects the marginal product of time devoted to home production. Given zero nonlabor income, the person's opportunity set is $ABCF$. If the person's indifference curve is I_1 utility is maximized at point B and $T_6 - T_4$ hours of time are devoted to home production, zero hours to market

work, and $T_4 - T_0$ hours to leisure. Given a different set of preferences as represented by indifference curve I_2, utility is maximized at point E with $T_6 - T_3$ hours of home work, $T_3 - T_1$ hours of market work, and $T_1 - T_0$ hours of leisure. An increase in nonlabor income shifts the opportunity set to $AGJM$, resulting in a new allocation of time.

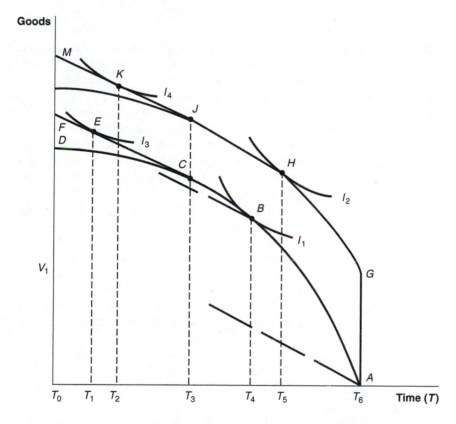

The opportunity set ACF or $AGJM$ shows the combinations of goods and leisure that are available. To determine the person's actual allocation of time, it is also necessary to know his or her preferences for the two items. This information is given by Equation 3A.1, which can be used to derive a set of indifference curves.

For purposes of exposition, two alternative sets of indifference curves are represented in Figure 3A.1, I_1 and I_2, along with I_3 and I_4.

The person's optimal allocation of time can now be determined. Assume first that the opportunity set is ACF. If the person's indifference curve is I_1, utility is maximized at point B. This person will devote $T_6 - T_4$ hours to home work, zero hours to market work, and $T_4 - T_0$ hours to consumption time or "leisure." If the person's indifference curve is I_3, however, a different allocation of time results. In this case, utility is maximized at point E and $T_6 - T_3$ hours are devoted to home work, $T_3 - T_1$ hours are devoted to market work, and $T_1 - T_0$ hours are spent on leisure.[4]

Next consider how the allocation of time to these three activities is affected by changes in nonlabor income and the market wage rate. Figure 3A.1 illustrates the impact of changes in nonlabor income. Increasing nonlabor income from $V = 0$ to $V = V_1$ shifts the opportunity set from ACF to $AGJM$. If the person had been at point E, the new equilibrium will be at point K. The result is a decline in market work from $T_3 - T_1$ to $T_3 - T_2$, an increase in leisure, and no change in home work. Alternatively, the new equilibrium for the person at point B is point H. In this case, hours of home work fall from $T_6 - T_4$ to $T_6 - T_5$, while leisure time increases and hours of market work remain unchanged at zero.

The impact of a change in the market wage rate on the allocation of time is illustrated in Figure 3A.2. The initial opportunity set is ADG. An increase in the market wage changes the opportunity set to ABK. The line segment BK has a steeper slope than DG and is tangent to the home production curve further to the right. Assume first that the person is initially working in the market, such as at point F. Hours of home work are $T_6 - T_3$, hours of market work are $T_3 - T_1$, and hours of leisure are $T_1 - T_0$. The increase in the wage leads to a new equilibrium at point J. One unambiguous prediction is that hours of home work will decline, from $T_6 - T_3$ to $T_6 - T_5$.[5] The impact on hours of market work and leisure is indeterminant, however, just as in the simple labor/leisure model. Hours of market work will increase only if the increase in leisure time from $T_1 - T_0$ to $T_2 - T_0$ is more than outweighed by the decrease in home production time from $T_6 - T_3$ to $T_6 - T_5$. This condition is more likely to occur as the rate of substitution increases between goods and consumption time in the person's utility function and as the income elasticity of leisure declines.

A second possibility to consider is a situation where the person initially engages only in home production (point C). An increase in the market wage in this case results in a new equilibrium at point H. The net result is that hours of market

---

4   If the market wage is greater than the shadow wage at point A, the diagram becomes, in effect, the traditional labor/leisure model. In this case, the person would devote zero hours to home work.

5   Empirical evidence in support of this prediction is presented in Peter Kooreman and Arie Kapteyn, "A Disaggregated Analysis of the Allocation of Time within the Household," *Journal of Political Economy* 95 (April 1987): 223–49. Also see Larry E. Jones, et al., "Why Are Married Women Working so Much?" *Federal Reserve Bank of Minneapolis Staff Report #317* (2003).

The original opportunity set is *ADG*. With the indifference curve I_3 (point *F*), the person's original allocation of time would be $T_6 - T_3$ hours of home work, $T_3 - T_1$ hours of market work, and $T_1 - T_0$ hours of leisure. An increase in the wage rate changes the opportunity set to *ABK*, giving rise to a new equilibrium at point *J*, where leisure hours increase, hours of market work increase, and time spent on home work declines.

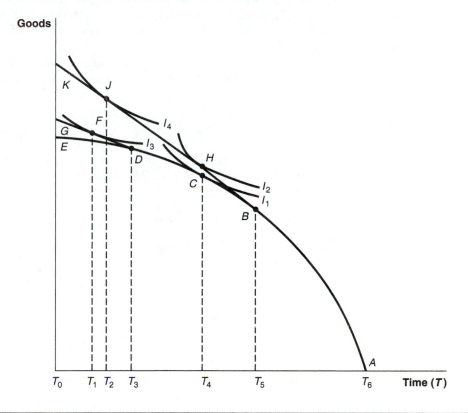

work increase from zero to $T_5 - T_4$, reflecting the decision of this person to begin to participate in the labor force. At point *H*, hours of home work have declined by a like amount, while hours of leisure time have remained the same. Leisure time could also increase or decrease, however, depending on the shapes of the indifference curves. Finally, note that if the original tangency point at *C* had instead occurred to the right of point *B*, the increase in the market wage would have no impact at all on the allocation of time.

Constrained Optimization and the Participation Decision

The mathematical representation of the optimization decision within the context of the labor/leisure choice model presented in Appendix 2C did not allow for the possibility that not participating in the labor market might be the optimal choice. In other words, the first-order conditions in equations (2C.5)–(2C.7) hold only for *interior solutions*. This appendix presents the mathematical representation of a *corner solution*, or the condition under which supplying zero hours of work (not working) maximizes utility.

To show the condition for a corner solution, it is instructive to rewrite the utility function as a function of hours of work, H, instead of leisure, L, and to allow this individual some nonlabor income, Y_0:

$$U = U(Y,H). \tag{3B.1}$$

So, instead of utility increasing in both its arguments, it now is an increasing function of income (Y) and a decreasing function of (H); as hours of work increase, utility decreases. The budget and time constraints become:

$$Y = Y_0 + HW \quad \text{or} \quad Y - Y_0 - HW = 0 \tag{3B.2}$$

$$T \geq H. \tag{3B.3}$$

Assuming that this individual does not work the entire time that is available (allowing, say, some time for sleep), constraint (3B.3) become $T > H$.

The *Lagrangian function* becomes:

$$F(Y,H,\lambda) = U(Y,H) + \lambda[Y - Y_0 - HW]. \tag{3B.4}$$

Allowing for a corner solution, the first-order conditions become:

$$\partial U/\partial Y + \lambda^* = 0 \qquad \text{if } Y^* > 0 \tag{3B.5}$$

$$\partial U/\partial H - \lambda^* W \leq 0 \qquad \text{if } H^* \geq 0 \tag{3B.6}$$

$$Y - Y_0 - H^* W = 0 \qquad \text{if } \lambda^* > 0. \tag{3B.7}$$

$$\text{Note that if } \partial U/\partial H - \lambda^* W < 0, \text{ then } H^* = 0.[1] \tag{3B.8}$$

---

[1] These conditions are formally known as Kuhn-Tucker conditions and, as written here, assume that $Y > 0$ and that utility is maximized *on* the budget constraint $[Y = Y_0 + HW]$. See A. K. Dixit, *Optimization in Economic Theory*, 2d ed. (New York: Oxford University Press, 1990).

The asterisk (*) denotes the values of the variables at which these conditions hold, their "optimal" values. The interpretation of condition (3B.8) can be seen by a number of manipulations. First, rewriting Equation 3B.5:

$$\lambda^* = -\partial U/\partial Y. \qquad\qquad\qquad (3B.5')$$

Second, using this expression to replace in Equation 3B.6:

$$\partial U/\partial H + (\partial U/\partial Y)(W) \leq 0 \qquad\qquad\qquad (3B.6')$$

and, rewriting the condition in Equation 3B.7:

$$H^* = 0 \text{ if } W < \frac{-\partial U/\partial H}{\partial U/\partial Y}. \qquad\qquad\qquad (3B.7')$$

Since the marginal value of working is the negative of the marginal value of leisure $(-\partial U/\partial H = \partial U/\partial L)$, Equation 3B.7′ can be rewritten as:

$$H^* = 0 \text{ if } W < \frac{\partial U/\partial L}{\partial U/\partial Y} = MRS. \qquad\qquad\qquad (3B.7'')$$

So, if the market value of leisure (W) is less than the marginal value of leisure to the individual (MRS), that person will not work $(H^* = 0)$. This is the same condition stated in the text that in order for someone to participate in the labor market, that person's reservation wage (value of time) must be less than the market is willing to pay that person for his or her time (W).

4

The Demand for Labor in the Short Run

In this and the following chapter, attention is focused on the demand for labor. The demand for labor is concerned with the level of employment desired by business firms. Important issues to be analyzed are the factors that determine a firm's optimal level of employment and how this desired level of employment responds to changes in wages, the costs of capital and other inputs, the level of sales of the firm, and improvements in the state of technology.

The analysis of the demand for labor is broken into two parts. This chapter examines the demand for labor in the short run, reserving for the next chapter a consideration of labor demand in the long run. The distinction between the short run and long run is of fundamental importance. In its attempt to maximize profits, a business firm will adjust its use of labor, capital, energy, and other factor inputs to achieve the lowest costs of production. If the relative price of labor should increase, the firm is motivated to cut back on the use of labor and substitute capital and other factor inputs in its place. Every business firm, however, needs time to order and put in place new machinery or build a new, more automated plant. The length of time during which the firm is locked into a fixed amount of plant and equipment is defined as the *short run*. The *long run* is defined as the period of time over which the firm can change not only labor, but the amounts of capital and all other factor inputs. The distinction between the short run and the long run is a conceptual one. In practice, the actual length of the short run varies considerably from industry to industry. A textile firm, for example, could quite possibly purchase and put in place new, more technologically advanced dyeing and weaving machines in a few months; a new integrated steel plant, on the other hand, might take five years or more to complete.

The first objective of this chapter is to derive the firm's demand curve for labor, showing, in the process, the reason for the inverse relationship between the wage rate and the firm's desired level of employment. The next topic is the elasticity of demand for labor. The importance of this concept is illustrated by an analysis of wage concessions in the auto industry and the employment effects of a wage subsidy program. The final section analyzes the link between the firm's level of sales and its desired level of employment, focusing on issues such as the impact of the business cycle on employment and the employment effects of foreign trade.

The Pattern of Employment

The demand for labor is reflected in the level of employment among business firms and nonprofit organizations such as government. Several key features of the pattern of employment in the United States are illustrated in Figure 4.1. Shown there are the annual levels of employment in the entire economy for the years 1950 through 2004 and the levels of employment in four major sectors: agriculture, other goods-producing industries (mining, construction, and manufacturing), government, and other service-producing industries (transportation and communications, trade, finance, and services).

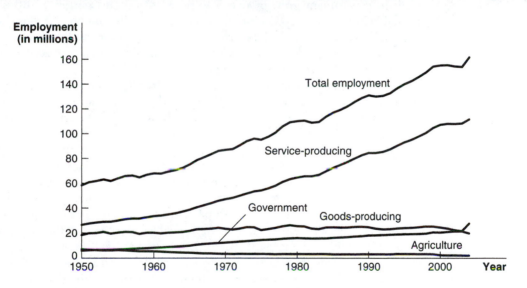

FIGURE 4.1   THE PATTERN OF EMPLOYMENT GROWTH IN THE U.S. ECONOMY, 1950–2004

NOTE: Employment figures do not correspond to those reported in Chapter 3 since those in Chapter 3 are from a household survey, and these figures were obtained from an establishment survey (except Agriculture). These figures are more reflective of the total number of *jobs*, as opposed to the total number of people employed; for example, one person may hold more than one job.

SOURCE: Bureau of Labor Statistics, *Establishment Data*, http://www.bls.gov/ces/cesbtabs.htm; Agriculture employment obtained from the Current Population Survey.

Several aspects of the pattern of employment depicted in Figure 4.1 are particularly noteworthy. The first is the trend over time in the total level of employment in the economy. To keep unemployment from rising, the economy must generate nearly 2 million new jobs each year, both because of the entrance of additional people into the labor force and because productivity growth allows firms to produce the same level of output with less labor. How has the American economy done? Since 1950, employment growth has been quite remarkable, the total number of jobs having increased from 60 million in 1950 to 154 million in 2003. To put this fact in perspective, consider that while the American economy added more than 17 million new jobs during the expansion between 1993 and 2003, the four largest European countries had a net job gain of barely more than 6 million.

A second important feature of this employment pattern is the relative decline of agriculture and the goods-producing industries as a major source of jobs in the economy. In 1950, 44 percent of jobs were in agriculture or industries that produced a physical good of some type. Over the next 50 years, however, employment in agriculture was cut by more than half, while employment in the goods-producing industries managed a scant increase of 6.6 million. This performance stands out in stark contrast with employment in government and other service-producing industries. Employment in government grew by over 246 percent over this period, and the service-related industries in the private sector generated over 80 million new jobs. As a result of these disparate trends, by 2003, roughly eight out of every ten jobs in the American economy were in government or private sector industries that produced a service.

A third feature that deserves attention is the rise and fall of employment over the business cycle. Even as employment increased steadily from one decade to another, this upward march was temporarily interrupted by ten recessions between 1950 and 2003. During each recession, the decline in business activity caused some firms to slow their hiring; others closed plants and laid off workers. The result was a significant slowdown in employment growth or, when the recession was quite severe, as in 1981 and 1982, an actual decline in the number of jobs in the economy. Figure 4.1 shows, however, that the effect of recession on employment is not spread evenly through the economy. In government and service-related industries, it is difficult to discern recession years from years of prosperity, since employment in these sectors is not very cyclically sensitive. Goods-producing industries, on the other hand, are quite vulnerable to the cyclical swings in economic activity, as revealed by the declines in employment in recession years such as 1971, 1975, 1982, 1991, and 2001.

These are some of the most important aspects of employment on which these two chapters focus. First, however, it is necessary to develop the basic theory of labor demand.

The Marginal Productivity Theory of Labor Demand

The optimal level of employment for a business firm is contingent on a number of factors, such as the cost of labor, the productivity of the workforce, the level of production, and the price the business firm can charge for its product. The theory of labor demand developed here organizes these diverse considerations into a model of employer decision making which, though relatively simple, nevertheless has considerable ability to explain real-world behavior.

The Model

The standard model of labor demand in economics is the neoclassical *marginal productivity theory of demand*. To develop this model, several simplifying assumptions must be made. First, it is assumed that the goal of business firms is to maximize dollar profits. Second, in order to simplify the graphic analysis, it is assumed that the firm uses only two factors of production, capital and labor, to produce its product. Third, it is initially assumed that the business firm operates in perfectly competitive product and labor markets. The substantive importance of this assumption is that both the price the firm can get for its product and the wage rate it has to pay for labor are unaffected by changes in its individual production and hiring decisions, and thus both variables can be treated as given. Finally, it is assumed that wages represent the only cost of labor and that labor is completely *homogeneous*, meaning that each worker is identical. Each of these assumptions is then relaxed or critically examined in either this or the next chapter.

How many workers should a business firm hire? Economic theory suggests a simple answer: hire additional workers as long as each one adds even so much as $1 of extra profit to the business firm. This solution is one specific example of the basic marginal decision rule found throughout economics—continue to do something as long as the marginal increase in the benefit exceeds the marginal increase in the cost from that activity. Thus, the firm that wants to maximize profits (profits are the difference between revenue and cost) should determine the marginal increase in revenue from hiring one more worker and compare it with the marginal increase in labor cost of that last worker. As long as additional workers bring in more revenue than the cost of hiring them, the firm adds to its profit by increasing employment; when the last worker added by the firm brings in revenue no greater than the labor cost, hiring should stop and profits will be at a maximum.

In deriving the short-run demand for labor, the first task is to determine the increase in revenue to the firm from hiring an additional worker. This involves several steps, the first of which is to determine worker productivity.

The Production Function   The relationship between the amount of capital inputs (K) and labor inputs (L) used in production and the resulting output (Q) is determined by the firm's production function:

$$Q = f(K, L). \tag{4.1}$$

The production function represented in Equation 4.1 states that the amount of output produced Q is a function f of the amount of capital K and labor L used by the firm, given the current state of technology. While the production function given in Equation 4.1 is simply an abstract mathematical representation, economists can determine the actual statistical relationship between inputs and outputs for a particular firm or industry, given the appropriate data.

TABLE 4.1 — DATA NECESSARY TO DERIVE A HYPOTHETICAL FIRM'S LABOR DEMAND CURVE

Labor Input L (1)	Quantity of Output Q (2)	Average Product AP_L (3)	Marginal Product MP_L (4)	Marginal Revenue MR (5)	Marginal Revenue Product MRP_L (6)	Wage Rate W (7)
0	0	—	—	$2	—	$40
1	10	10	10	2	$20	40
2	34	17	24	2	48	40
3	66	22	32	2	64	40
4	100	25	34	2	68	40
5	130	26	30	2	60	40
6	150	25	20	2	40	40
7	154	22	4	2	8	40
8	136	17	−18	2	−36	40

Note: The production function that generates these data is $Q = L + 10L^2 - L^3$. The marginal product of labor would more precisely be calculated according to the following formula, which is simply the first derivative of the total product curve: $MP_L = 1 + 20L - 3L^2$.

Since the amount of capital is fixed in the short run, additional output can be produced by the firm only by hiring additional workers. Holding capital constant, the production function in Equation 4.1 can be used to predict the increase in output that would result from these extra workers. Such data for a hypothetical firm are shown both in tabular form in Table 4.1 and in graphic form in Figure 4.2. Graph (a) of Figure 4.2 depicts the total product curve TP_L for the firm; it shows the total amount of output produced at each level of employment.

The Marginal and Average Product of Labor Two measures of productivity can be calculated from the data on total product and labor input. The first and most important is the **marginal product of labor (MP_L)**. The MP_L measures the increment in production contributed by each additional worker hired. The marginal product of labor is defined as the increase in total production (ΔQ) from adding one more unit of labor (ΔL), that is:

$$MP_L = \frac{\Delta Q}{\Delta L}.$$

Geometrically, the marginal product of each worker is given by the slope of a line drawn tangent to the total product curve at each level of labor input.

The marginal product of each worker is given by the slope of a line drawn tangent to the total product curve TP_L. Up to L_1 the tangent lines become steeper, indicating that production is in the area of increasing returns; after L_1, however, the tangent lines become flatter, indicating that diminishing returns have set in. Beyond L_2 the marginal product of labor becomes negative. Plotting the slope of the tangent lines in graph (b) yields the marginal product schedule MP_L. After point A, labor is subject to diminishing marginal productivity. The maximum of the average product of labor is at point C, where the slope of a ray from the origin to the total product schedule is the greatest.

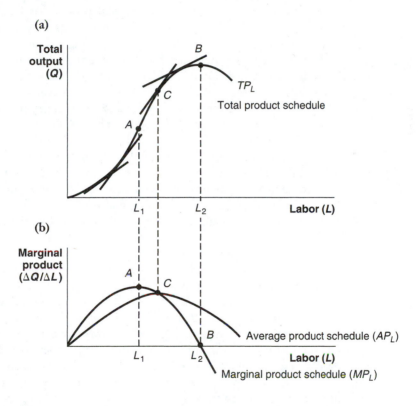

The shape of the total product curve in Figure 4.2 shows that production in this firm is first characterized by increasing marginal productivity of labor (compare the slope of the first two tangent lines) and then, beyond the employment level of L_1 (point A), by diminishing marginal productivity of labor (compare the slope of the last two tangent lines). Starting from a zero level of output, the marginal product of each additional worker at first increases, as only a larger workforce can efficiently use and operate the plant and equipment of the firm. From the origin to L_1, therefore, is known as the area of *increasing returns* in production. Beyond L_1, however, production enters the area of *diminishing returns* as the marginal product of each additional worker becomes smaller and smaller. The **law of diminishing returns** states that, holding one factor of production constant, adding additional units of another factor will increase production, but eventually only at a diminishing rate. In this particular case, diminishing returns arise because the fixed amount of plant and equipment of the firm is gradually spread among an ever greater number of workers, leaving a smaller amount of capital for each one. While diminishing returns set in at an employment level of L_1, if labor is increased beyond L_2 (point B), efficiency will suffer so greatly that total output will actually decline. Beyond point B, therefore, the marginal product of labor is negative.

It is possible to directly graph the marginal product of labor, as shown in graph (b) of Figure 4.2. The horizontal axis measures units of labor; the vertical axis measures the additional output produced by each worker. The curve MP_L is called a *marginal product schedule*; it shows the addition to output of each successive worker. It is derived from graph (a) of Figure 4.2 by plotting the value of the slope of the tangent lines at each level of labor input. The marginal product schedule rises while production is in the area of increasing returns; beyond point A, diminishing returns set in and the marginal product schedule begins to decline, becoming negative after point B.

The same relationships are depicted by the hypothetical data given in Table 4.1. Column 1 in Table 4.1 shows the number of workers L employed by the firm. Column 2 shows total production Q per hour for each level of employment. Given these data, it is then possible to calculate the marginal product of labor MP_L, shown by the data in column 4. The marginal product of the fourth worker, for example, is 34 units per hour—the increase in production from 66 to 100 units attributable to hiring him or her. The data in column 3 show that production is subject to increasing returns up to the fourth worker, and to diminishing returns thereafter.

The second productivity measure is the **average product of labor.** It is defined as $AP_L = Q/L$, which means the average amount of output produced per worker. It can be measured geometrically in Figure 4.2 by the slope of a ray emanating from the origin and intersecting the total product curve at a particular level of output, such as point A or point B (not drawn, in order to keep the diagram uncluttered). The maximum level of the average product is reached at point C in Figure 4.2, where the hypothetical ray's slope is greatest. Note that as long as the marginal product is greater than the average product, the latter continues to rise, and when the marginal product is less than the average the latter falls. This merely illustrates the mathematical fact that as one adds a number (marginal product) that is above the current average of that total (average product), it will pull up the average. Adding numbers less than the average will pull the average down. This relationship between average and marginal product is also shown in Table 4.1.

Marginal Revenue Product   The marginal product data in column 4 of Table 4.1 do not yet tell the firm the extra revenue it will gain from employing an additional worker. The marginal product of labor is expressed in terms of physical units of production. To determine the dollar worth to the firm of the marginal product of each worker, those units of production have to be multiplied by their *marginal revenue (MR)*. Marginal revenue is defined as the change in total revenue (*TR*) received by the firm from producing one more unit of output; that is, $MR = \Delta TR/\Delta Q$. For a perfectly competitive firm, as assumed here, the price (*P*) received for the product and its marginal revenue are the same. Since a competitive firm can sell every additional unit of production at the same price, the increment in revenue from selling one more unit (the marginal revenue) is exactly equal to the price it is sold for.

The marginal revenue received from each unit of production for this hypothetical firm is shown in column 5 of Table 4.1. It is assumed here that the product price, and hence the marginal revenue, is $2 per unit. The marginal increase in revenue for this firm from hiring additional workers can now be calculated, which is done in column 6 of Table 4.1. Column 6 contains data on the **marginal revenue product (*MRP$_L$*)** of labor, calculated by multiplying the marginal product of labor MP_L by the marginal revenue *MR*. How much extra revenue does the firm get from hiring the third worker? The third worker produces an extra 32 units of production per hour, and each unit sells for $2. The increase in revenue for the firm, then, is $MP_L \times MR$, or (32)($2) = $64. Similarly, the marginal revenue product of the fourth worker is (34)($2) = $68. Note that the marginal revenue products of the fifth through eighth workers in Table 4.1 decline in value. The reason is not that the last worker hired is intrinsically any less productive, efficient, or capable than the previously hired workers. The decline is tied directly to the law of diminishing returns and the fact that additional workers have less capital to work with.

The Marginal Cost of Labor   The marginal revenue product data express the marginal benefit to the firm from hiring additional workers. The decision rule to maximize profits is to continue to hire workers as long as the marginal benefit exceeds the marginal cost. The final piece of information needed to determine the firm's demand for labor, then, is the cost of hiring an additional worker.

The cost per hour to the firm of hiring each worker is equal to the wage rate, assumed here to include all sources of labor cost to the employer, such as employee benefits and government-mandated tax contributions. It is assumed here that the wage rate (*W*) is $40 per hour, shown in column 7 of Table 4.1. Because this firm is assumed to operate in a competitive labor market, its marginal wage costs per worker are the same no matter how many workers it hires.

The Equilibrium Level of Employment   It is now an easy task to determine the optimal level of employment for this firm. Should it hire the third worker? The answer is yes, since the third worker produces $64 worth of output and costs only $40 per hour to hire, resulting in $24 of extra profit for the firm. What about the seventh worker? The answer is clearly no, since the wages paid to the seventh worker ($40) exceed the value of his/her production ($8). Hiring the seventh worker would reduce profits by $32. Obviously, then, the optimal level of employment in this example is six workers. The sixth worker contributes just as much to revenue as he or she costs and should be hired; beyond that level of employment, however, additional employment would reduce profits.

The equilibrium condition for a firm's labor demand can thus be stated as:

$$W = MRP_L, \text{ or } W = MR \cdot MP_L. \tag{4.2}$$

For a competitive firm, Equation 4.2 can also be written as:

$$W = P \cdot MP_L, \text{ or } W/P = MP_L. \tag{4.3}$$

Equation 4.2 states that the firm should continue to hire labor as long as the marginal revenue product of each successive worker exceeds the money wage rate; when the marginal revenue product of the last worker just equals the wage, the optimal level of employment has been reached, and hiring should stop. For the special case of a competitive firm, the product price P can be substituted for the marginal revenue MR, as in Equation 4.3, and after rearranging terms yields an equivalent statement of the firm's optimal employment level—hire workers as long as the marginal product of labor is greater than or equal to the real wage (W/P).

The Short-Run Demand Curve for Labor

The equilibrium condition given in Equation 4.2 can be used to derive the firm's **short-run demand curve for labor,** as shown in Figure 4.3. The short-run labor demand curve depicts the relationship between the wage rate and the firm's desired level of employment, holding capital and all other factors constant.

The horizontal axis of Figure 4.3 measures employment (L); the vertical axis measures the wage rate per hour (W). The first step in deriving the demand curve is to plot in Figure 4.3 the data on marginal revenue product (MRP_L) from column 6 of Table 4.1. Since MRP_L is measured in terms of dollars, as are wages, these data can be plotted in the same diagram. The line labeled MRP_L is the marginal revenue product schedule. It shows the marginal revenue product of each worker: the fourth worker's MRP_L is $65, the fifth worker's MRP_L is $60, and so on.

It turns out that the downward-sloping portion of the MRP_L schedule in Figure 4.3 (the solid part of the line) *is* the firm's demand curve for labor (D_L). The equilibrium condition in Equation 4.2 says to hire each additional worker as long as the increase in revenue (MRP_L) is greater than or equal to the increase in wage cost (W). At a wage of $40 per hour, how many workers have a MRP_L greater than or equal to $40 per hour? The answer is that the first through sixth workers do and, thus, the optimal level of employment is six (point A). Given the market wage rate, then, the MRP_L curve can be used to determine the firm's demand for labor.[1]

A second example demonstrates this in a slightly different way. What would happen to this firm's demand for labor if the wage rate were to increase from $40

---

1 If the wage were $64 in Figure 4.3, the firm would maximize profits by expanding employment to five workers rather than just three, since the fourth worker's MRP_L is greater than the wage rate. It is only the downward-sloping portion of the MRP_L schedule, therefore, that is used by the firm as its labor demand curve.

The marginal revenue product schedule MRP_L shows the additional revenue the firm obtains from hiring each worker. The fifth worker brings in $60, the sixth worker $40, and so on. The downward-sloping portion of the MRP_L schedule is also the firm's short-run demand curve for labor (shown by the solid portion of the line). Thus, if the wage W is $40, the firm would maximize profit by hiring five workers (point A) since each of these workers has an MRP_L at least as great as the wage. At a wage of $60, the optimal employment level is five workers (point B).

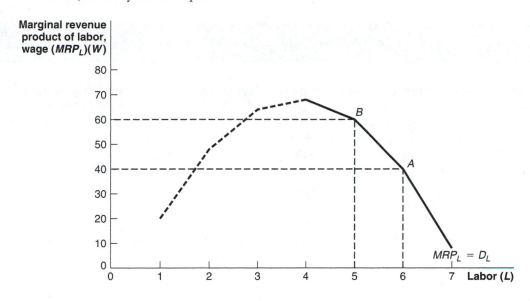

to $60 per hour? At $60 per hour it no longer pays to hire the sixth worker, since the marginal revenue product is less than the wage rate. Employment will be reduced to five workers, where the equality $W = MRP_L$ again holds (point B).

Two points should be stressed about the demand curve for labor. First, a change in the wage rate causes a movement *along* one particular demand curve. Thus, if the wage rate the firm has to pay for labor rises from $40 to $60 per hour, the change in employment is represented graphically by moving up the demand curve D_L in Figure 4.3 from point A to point B; conversely, if the wage were to decrease to $8, the firm would move down the demand curve until the marginal revenue product of the last worker hired was just equal to the wage rate of $8 (this occurs where $L = 7$). The second point is that a change in the firm's demand for labor for any other reason will cause a *shift* in the demand curve to the left or right. Two different events illustrate this.

An Increase in Product Demand What will happen to the firm's demand for labor if the demand for its product increases? An increase in product demand in a competitive industry will cause the price of the product to rise in the market as the product demand curve shifts to the right along a given upward-sloping supply curve. This immediately affects the demand for labor on the part of each individual firm, since price P (and thus marginal revenue MR in column 5 of Table 4.1) is part of the marginal revenue product calculation. At a higher price (say, $3 in Table 4.1), the MRP_L of each worker increases and, as shown in graph (a) of Figure 4.4, results in a shift to the right in the demand curve from D_1 to D_2. At the prevailing wage of W_1, employment can be expanded from L_1 (point A) to L_2

FIGURE 4.4   **THE IMPACT ON THE LABOR DEMAND CURVE OF CHANGES IN PRODUCT DEMAND AND MARKET STRUCTURE**

Graph (a) shows that an increase in the firm's product demand will cause the labor demand curve to shift to the right, from D_1 to D_2. At the prevailing wage of W_1, the firm's optimal level of employment would increase from L_1 to L_2. Graph (b) shows that the labor demand curve for an imperfectly competitive firm D_I will lie to the left and be steeper than the demand

curve for a competitive firm (D_C). At the prevailing wage of W_1, the imperfectly competitive firm will hire fewer workers (L_I) than the competitive firm (L_C). It will also expand employment by a smaller amount than would a perfectly competitive firm in response to a decrease in the wage.

(a) An Increase in Product Demand

(b) Perfect and Imperfect Competition in the Product Market

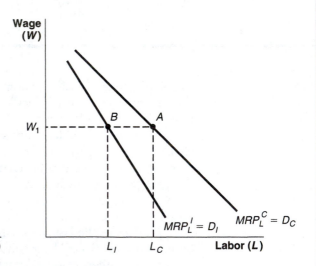

(point B) since, at the higher product price, the MRP_L of additional workers hired beyond L_1 will now exceed the wage cost W_1 until employment reaches L_2. A decrease in product demand would cause the labor demand curve to shift to the left for the opposite reasons.

Imperfect Competition in the Product Market   The data in Table 4.1 and the derivation of the demand curve for labor in Figure 4.3 assume the firm is only one among many firms operating in a perfectly competitive product market. What happens to the demand curve for labor if this firm is in an imperfectly competitive product market (such as monopolistic competition, oligopoly, or monopoly)?

A competitive firm has a horizontal product demand curve and can sell all its output at a constant price. This is reflected in Table 4.1 by the same price and marginal revenue of $2 per unit in column 5 no matter how much the firm produces. An imperfectly competitive firm, however, faces a downward-sloping product demand curve, implying that to sell more output it has to lower the price. In this situation, the marginal revenue from selling a unit of output is less than the price it is sold for.[2] Equally important, if the imperfectly competitive firm desires to sell additional units of output, it has to further lower the price, causing marginal revenue to decline further.

The fact that price is greater than marginal revenue for the imperfectly competitive firm has two separate effects on its demand curve for labor. First, since P is always greater than MR, the marginal revenue product $(MR \cdot MP_L)$ of the last worker hired in a competitive firm (worker L_C in graph b) will be more than that of the same worker in an imperfectly competitive firm (worker L_I). This would cause the labor demand curve for the imperfectly competitive firm, shown as D_I in graph (b) of Figure 4.4, to lie to the left of that of the competitive firm, D_C, at the prevailing wage. At W_1, therefore, employment in the imperfectly competitive firm would only be L_I (point B) compared to L_C (point A) for the competitive firm.[3] The second effect of imperfect competition in the product market is to not only reduce the demand for labor but to also make the demand curve D_I steeper relative to D_C.[4] The reason for this is that the MRP_L schedule for the imperfectly competitive firm declines for *two*

<table>
<tr><td>

➡ SEE

Policy Application 4-1:
Wage Subsidy Programs,
p. 205.

</td><td>

reasons—first, because the MP_L of each worker declines due to diminishing returns in production, as for the competitive firm, and, second, because its marginal revenue from extra production also declines, unlike that of the competitive firm. Policy Application 4-1 illustrates how the shape of the demand curve for labor can be affected by government policy.

</td></tr>
</table>

---

2   As an example, assume a firm can sell 10 units at $10 apiece, yielding a total revenue of $100, or by lowering the price to $9, it can sell 12 units, bringing in $108. Even though the price of the 12th unit is $9, its marginal revenue is only $4 (i.e., $MR = \Delta TR / \Delta Q = \$8/2 = \$4$); thus, $MR < P$.

3   At a given wage, one can compare the demand for labor in a competitive product market (D_C) with the demand for labor in an imperfect product market (D_I). Since $P > MR$ in the imperfect market:

$$D_C = MRP_L^C = (P)(MP_L) > (MR)(MP_L) = MRP_L^I = D_I$$

4   A more precise term than *steeper* is *more inelastic*, a term to be defined shortly.

FIGURE 4.5 DERIVATION OF THE MARKET LABOR DEMAND CURVE

The lines D_A and D_B in graphs (a) and (b) show the labor demand curve for each individual firm. At the wage W_1, total employment in the market—graph (c)—is $L_{1A} + L_{1B} + \cdots + L_{1N} = L_{1M}$ (point X). A fall in the wage from W_1 to W_2 in any *one* firm would cause a movement down its MRP_L schedule, increasing employment from L_{1A} to L_{2A} in Firm A, for example. If the wage falls to W_2 for *all* firms, however, the resulting expansion in employment and output will cause a decline in the price of the product, shifting each firm's MRP schedule to the left, such as D'_A and D'_B. At the wage W_2, therefore, total labor demand is $L'_{2A} + L'_{2B} + \cdots + L'_{2N} = L'_{2M}$ (point Z). Connecting points X and Z yields the market labor demand curve, D_M.

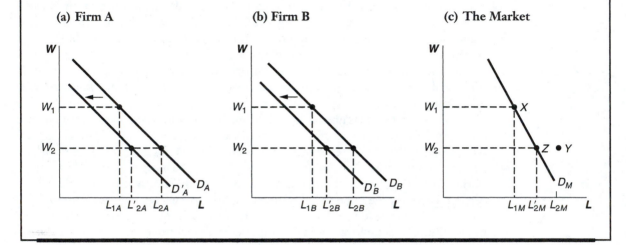

The Market Demand Curve for Labor

For many purposes it is important to know not only the individual firm's demand curve for labor, but also the demand for labor on the part of *all* firms in the labor market. The labor market in question may encompass a local area, an industry, or the nation as a whole, depending on the type of labor being analyzed. The derivation of the market demand curve for labor is illustrated in Figure 4.5.

It is assumed there are N individual perfectly competitive firms in an industry. Graphs (a) and (b) in Figure 4.5 show the labor demand curves D_A and D_B for two of these firms, Firm A and Firm B. At the wage of W_1, the demand for labor in each individual firm can be determined from its respective marginal revenue product schedule; employment in Firm A would be L_{1A}, in Firm B it would be L_{1B}, and so on for the other $N - 2$ firms. The total demand for labor by all the firms in the market could then be found by adding up the employment demand of each individual firm—$L_{1A} + L_{1B} + \cdots + L_{1N} = L_{1M}$, shown as point X in graph (c).

If the wage were to fall to W_2, it would be tempting to repeat the same exercise. Employment in Firm A, given the demand curve D_A, would be L_{2A}, employment in Firm B would be L_{2B}, and so on for the other firms, yielding a total market demand for labor of $L_{2A} + L_{2B} + \cdots + L_{2N} = L_{2M}$, shown as point Y in graph (c). Connecting points X and Y would, presumably, trace out the market demand curve for labor. Unfortunately, however, this reflects an error in reasoning. It was implicitly assumed in deriving point Y that the price of the product and, thus, the marginal revenue of each additional unit of output are constant. This is a correct assumption for an individual competitive firm, since its level of output is so small relative to the entire product market that it can expand or contract employment and output with no effect on the product price. What is true for an individual firm will not be true, however, if the wage drops to W_2 for *all* N firms. As all N firms expand employment, total output in the product market will increase, and to sell this extra output the price will have to fall. As the price falls, the marginal revenue product of each worker is reduced, causing the MRP_L schedule of each individual firm to shift to the left, such as from D_A and D_B to D'_A and D'_B. Consequently, given a decline in the wage to W_2 in the entire market, the total market demand for labor is $L'_{2A} + L'_{2B} + \cdots + L'_{2N} = L'_{2M}$, shown as point Z in graph (c). Connecting points X and Z yields the *true* market demand curve D_M.

This analysis shows that wages and employment are inversely related at the level of both the individual firm and the market. An important insight, however, is that a wage change isolated to only one firm will have a proportionately bigger impact on employment than if the wage change occurs in all the firms in the labor market.

Criticisms of the Theory of Labor Demand

The marginal productivity theory of labor demand outlined previously can predict both the optimal level of employment for a firm and how this employment level will change in reaction to various economic events. The theory has, nevertheless, been the subject of much controversy and criticism through the years, especially by more institutionally oriented economists. The critics contend that it rests on a number of assumptions that are unrealistic or incorrect. Five of these criticisms are briefly discussed here.

Limits to Human Cognition   One objection is that the information and computations necessary to operationalize the theory generally exceed the mental or cognitive ability of most employers and managers.[5] For example, while the concept of marginal productivity is clear in theory, can the typical manager of a firm actually

---

5   Richard Lester, "Shortcomings of Marginal Analysis for Wage–Employment Problems," *American Economic Review* 36, no. 1 (March 1946): 63–82. Also see Julian L. Simon, "Unnecessary, Confusing, and Inadequate: The Marginal Analysis as a Tool for Decision-Making," in *Economics against the Grain* (Northampton, Mass.: Elgar, 1998): 93–104.

Rise in Benefit Costs Leads to Job Growth Slowdown

The labor demand curve shows how employment changes with respect to changes in the price of labor. Often economists talk about the price of labor as equivalent to the *wage rate* per hour (or salary per hour). But, as noted earlier in this chapter, the wage rate is really a simplified or shorthand way of saying "total compensation cost per hour for labor"—a concept that includes not only the wage (or salary) per hour but also expenditures for other outlays, such as hiring, training, and employee benefits. It is the total of all of these costs that represent the true price of labor and upon which firms make their hiring decisions.

Often these wage and non-wage labor costs change in approximately equal proportion from year to year, so for purposes of analyzing trends in labor demand no great error is made by focusing largely on wages. This practice is frequently done, in turn, for the practical reason that the wage rate is the most easily measured and available part of labor cost in government data sets. In recent years, however, the sharp rise in the cost of employee benefits has made this practice increasingly problematic. Of more practical importance, the sharp rise in benefit costs has been one of the major factors behind the lack of employment growth experienced by the United States during the early 2000s.

From 2000 to 2004, wage cost rose 13.4 percent but the cost of benefits to companies went up 24.9 percent—nearly twice as fast. At the same time, employment growth from 2000 to 2004 was negative, reflecting the net decline in jobs of more than 2 million over this period. Part of this job loss was due to factors that shifted the labor demand curve to the left, such as the recession of 2001 and process of globalization (the outflow of jobs to China and other low-wage countries). But another part stems from the substantial rise in the cost of employee benefits—a factor that increased the price of labor and moved American firms up their labor demand curves.

Two components of benefit cost have been the main culprits. The first is health insurance. Health insurance costs the nation's employers an average of about $3,000 per year. The expense is often double and triple for medium-large companies that provide extensive company-financed medical and dental packages for employees and their families. The big three U.S. automakers, for example, spent $8.5 billion on health-care costs in 2003 for current and retired workers—an amount that added $1,400 to the price of each car sold by General Motors. Not only are health care costs high, they are also the most rapidly rising component of labor cost. In 2003, health care costs went up more than triple the rate of wage cost and the expected rate of increase in 2005 is a whopping 13 percent.

The other component of employee benefits that is dragging down employment growth is the cost of

measure or even approximate the likely increase in production from hiring a new employee? For small businesses or firms with fairly simple production processes, the answer may be yes, but the difficulties, in the critics' view, of measuring the marginal product in large-scale organizations with highly interdependent production processes preclude the use of marginal calculations. Even if a marginal product can be calculated, the critics would then ask how the firm can meaningfully compare a worker's marginal revenue product with the wage, when product prices and output levels (and thus the MRP_L) are constantly changing. Finally, the critics

continued

pensions. American companies have promised future and current retirees financial payments estimated at over one trillion dollars. When the baby boom generation was far from retirement age two and three decades ago, the generous retirement plans corporate America offered to its workers did not seem too financially onerous. But now that the baby boomers are starting to near retirement age, the cost obligations facing many companies are staggering. For example, United Airlines must cough up over $4 billion in pension payments between 2004 and 2008. Not only are these expenses huge, many foreign rivals of American firms—particularly in China and other less developed countries—have little or no pension obligations, thus allowing them to underprice American firms and gain market share.

The rise of benefit costs has chilled the job market, according to many economists and corporate leaders. One predictable result from the theory of labor demand is a slowdown in hiring and faster rate of layoff and plant-closing as firms move up their labor demand curves with the rise in the cost of labor. But American companies have also responded in other ways to slow the increase in labor cost. Many firms, for example, are significantly increasing the co-payment and deductible levels for health insurance. A large number of others are not offering health insurance benefits at all. Indeed, the latest government estimate is that over 20 million full-time

workers have no health insurance coverage. On the pension front, the number of companies offering the traditional "defined benefit" pension plan (where the company promises to pay the retiree a certain dollar amount each year until death) has plummeted, replaced by new and less expensive "defined contribution" plans (where the company contributes a fixed payment to the worker's financial retirement account). Also, a growing number of financially hard-pressed companies are substantially reducing their pension obligations by declaring bankruptcy. The most publicized example is the American steel industry where in 2002 Bethlehem, LTV, and National Steel went to bankruptcy court and unloaded over $7 billion of pension commitments.

These examples highlight fundamental conflicts and trade-offs in both positive and normative economics. In terms of positive economics, one sees a prime illustration of the trade-off between higher labor cost and reduced number of jobs; in terms of normative economics one also sees a sharp debate about fundamental issues of fairness and, in particular, the degree to which companies should be required to honor their past promises to employees.

SOURCES: "Cost of Benefits Cited as Factor in Slump in Jobs," *The New York Times* (August 19, 2004): A1, C-2; "Will the Bough Break," *Business Week* (April, 14, 2003): pp. 62–63.

argue that case studies and interviews reveal that the actual process of business decision making does not follow the marginal calculations assumed in the theory.[6]

Proponents of the theory respond to these criticisms in several ways. First, although managers may not consciously use marginal calculations, the decisions they reach must approximate those predicted by the theory if the firm is to survive

---

6   Herbert Simon, "Rational Decision Making in Business Organizations," *American Economic Review* 69, no. 4 (September 1979): 493–513.

in a competitive business world. Second, proponents argue that while managers may not be able to identify the marginal contribution of an individual worker or adjust employment one employee at a time as the theory presumes, they can identify the revenues and costs associated with particular lines of activity (e.g., the baggage-handling department or the night shift) and they do adjust employment in these activities in light of their contributions to profit.[7]

Nonmaximizing Behavior   A second criticism of the marginal productivity theory deals with the assumption of profit maximization. The impetus driving the firm to make the calculations of marginal revenue product versus marginal cost of labor is the goal of maximizing profits. The critics of the theory argue, however, that business firms, particularly in oligopolistic markets or in corporations where ownership and control are separated, are more accurately characterized as *"satisficing"* with respect to profit.[8] In this view, the managers of business firms strive to achieve a minimum level of profit in order to protect their survival and that of the firm; once this minimum goal is satisfied, the managers tolerate some "slack" in the operation of the firm and no longer strive to fully minimize production costs. One important way firms exhibit satisficing behavior, the critics say, is by employing more people than are really needed, as evidenced by the bloated ranks of middle management and the inefficient organization of production on the factory floor in some large American companies.

The defenders of marginal productivity theory would probably admit that other goals besides maximizing profits do enter into business decision making. They would argue, however, that the ultimate goal of each firm is survival and that survival in a competitive economy requires keeping costs and employment down and profits up. Thus, while it may not be literally true that management squeezes out of the business every last dollar of profit possible, the pressure on the firm to survive is sufficiently strong that all other goals, in the long run, are subordinated to the single goal of maximizing profits. The necessity of making a profit, in turn, assures that business firms will be induced to economize on labor and make hiring decisions that broadly accord with the predictions of the marginal productivity theory. The defenders would argue that this is true even for regulated firms or not-for-profit organizations, since their survival and growth requires conscious efforts to minimize cost.

Fixed Capital/Labor Proportions   A third criticism of the theory asserts that the nature of technology makes it impossible to derive a continuous marginal product (MP_L) schedule as drawn in Figure 4.2.[9] The derivation of the marginal product schedule assumes that the fixed stock of capital is divisible in the sense that it can

7   Fritz Machlup, "Marginal Analysis and Empirical Research," *American Economic Review* 36, no. 4 (September 1946): 519–41.

8   Simon, "Rational Decision Making in Business Organizations." For a theoretical treatment of satisficing and other approximations to optimizing behavior, see Henke Norde et al., "Characterizing Properties of Approximate Solutions for Optimization Problems," *Mathematical Social Sciences* 40 (November 2000): 297–311.

9   Alan M. Cartter, *Theory of Wages and Employment* (Homewood, Ill.: Irwin, 1959), 45–47.

be "spread" among greater and greater numbers of workers as employment is increased. According to critics of the theory, however, many types of production processes require labor and capital in relatively fixed proportions. One hypothetical example is a small commuter airline with, say, three planes, each of which requires two pilots. Given the stock of capital of three planes, is it possible to calculate the marginal product of each pilot? The marginal product of the first pilot would be zero, since with only one pilot no plane could fly. With a second pilot, one plane could fly, and both pilots *together* would yield a positive increment in production. The addition of yet a third pilot, however, would not lead to any further increase in production since the second plane could not fly. The result is that it is impossible either to attribute a unique marginal product to each individual worker or to derive a continuous marginal product schedule.

The proponents of the marginal productivity theory discount the seriousness of these objections. They contend that in nearly all real-world production situations there is no fixed, necessary relationship between capital and labor. In the previous example, one pilot could, it would be argued, fly the plane if she or he had to. The first pilot would have a nonzero marginal revenue product and the second pilot would also have an identifiable marginal revenue product—the increase in safety and efficiency with which the flight is operated. The proponents of the theory would also argue that more often than not, fixed capital/labor requirements stem from union work rules or regulatory constraints (such as FAA requirements concerning flight crew size), rather than from technology itself. In any case, the proponents of the theory argue that employers usually are able to attribute to each individual worker the net contribution to production.[10]

Increasing Returns to Labor A fourth criticism of the marginal productivity theory is that labor may be subject to increasing returns in the short run, not diminishing returns as the theory assumes. According to the law of diminishing returns, as a firm expands employment, the marginal product of labor should decline as the fixed stock of capital is spread over more workers. It is precisely this fact that causes the MRP_L schedule and the labor demand curve to slope downward for a competitive firm. Numerous empirical studies have found, however, that labor productivity (output per hour) actually varies directly with the level of employment in the firm—when employment rises on a business cycle upswing, output rises more than proportionately.[11] Since labor productivity is nothing but the average product of labor, Q/L, some economists have reasoned that if the average product rises with increased employment, this suggests that the marginal product of labor, $\Delta Q/\Delta L$, also increases, implying that the marginal revenue product schedule is actually

---

10   Casey Mulligan derives a theoretical equivalence between models assuming indivisible labor inputs and divisible labor inputs, allowing, at least, for the consideration of production processes requiring bulky labor inputs within the context of a continuous optimization framework. See "Microfoundations and Macro Implications of Indivisible Labor," *NBER Working Paper No. 7116* (May 1999).

11   See Jon A. Fay and James L. Medoff, "Labor and Output over the Business Cycle: Some Direct Evidence," *American Economic Review* 75 (September 1985): 638–55; and Michele Vecchi, "Increasing Returns, Labor Utilization and Externalities: Procyclical Productivity in the United States and Japan," *Economics* 67 (May 2000): 229–44.

upward sloping.[12] (Remember that when the marginal rises it pulls up the average.) If this result is true, the critics ask, doesn't it invalidate one of the marginal productivity theory's basic assumptions?

Proponents of the theory have attempted to account for the paradox of increasing returns in several ways. One is to argue that it is a statistical illusion caused by faulty data on the level of production. During a recession, for example, firms may have employees work on deferred maintenance projects or the completion of unfinished assemblies. Since these activities are not counted as part of output, their omission causes measured labor productivity to vary procyclically, in apparent conflict with the predictions of marginal productivity theory. Second, proponents also note that the marginal productivity theory assumes that workers put in a constant level of effort, while in reality effort is likely to slacken in bad times and increase in good times. This fact also makes labor productivity behave procyclically. Finally, defenders of the theory argue that the paradox of increasing returns is due in part to the tendency of firms to "hoard" labor during recessions by consciously keeping more workers than they really need given the current level of production. As explained later in this chapter, firms are motivated to do so by their desire to avoid additional hiring and training costs, factors the simple version of the marginal productivity theory overlooks.

Interdependence between the Wage and Worker Productivity A final criticism of the marginal productivity theory concerns the relationship between the wage rate the firm pays and the level of productivity of its workers. The theory assumes that the marginal product schedule is determined solely by the technology of production, as represented by the production function in Equation 4.1 and the size of the firm's capital stock. One important implication of this assumption is that, regardless of whether the firm pays $2 or $20 per hour for labor, the MRP_L schedule will maintain its position and shape; that is, a change in the wage will cause the firm to move up or down the MRP_L schedule, but the schedule itself will not change. Critics of the theory argue, however, that in real life the level of worker productivity is likely to be directly related to the wage the firm pays.[13] One reason is that higher pay allows workers to improve their physical ability to work through improved nutrition and health; a second is that a wage increase is likely to stimulate greater work effort and higher morale among employees. The implication, then, is that there is a separate MRP_L schedule for *each* level of the wage—the higher the wage, the greater will be each employee's work effort and marginal product and the further to the right the entire MRP_L schedule will lie. Because of this, whether employment will increase or decline in response to a wage change can no longer be

---

12   See Arthur M. Okun, "Inflation: Its Mechanics and Welfare Costs," *Brookings Papers on Economic Activity* (Washington, D.C.: Brookings Institution, 1975): 378, and Ben Bernanke and Martin Parkinson, "Procyclical Labor Productivity and Competing Theories of the Business Cycle," *Journal of Political Economy* 99 (June 1991): 439–59.

13   See George Akerloff and Janet Yellen, *Efficiency Wage Models of the Labor Market* (Cambridge, Eng.: Cambridge University Press, 1986).

unambiguously predicted. A higher wage will cause the firm to reduce employment due to the higher cost per unit of labor, counterbalanced by an increase in employment because each worker becomes more productive.[14] It is conceivable that a wage increase could actually lead the firm to hire *more* labor, not less, if the higher wage stimulates a sufficiently large increase in worker productivity.

Proponents of the marginal productivity theory respond to this criticism in several ways. First, they admit that, realistically, it is probably true that the level of worker productivity depends to some degree on the rate of pay. This is likely to be most true in underdeveloped countries, however, where higher pay could significantly improve nutrition and health conditions of workers. In developed economies, on the other hand, modest adjustments in wage rates will probably have small to negligible impacts on employee work performance, particularly at the industry or national level. Proponents of the theory also note that there is considerable disagreement among specialists in organizational behavior over the extent to which pay really influences performance at the firm level. Some studies find a positive relationship between wages and employee performance, others find no relationship, and still others find a negative relationship.[15] These results suggest, in the view of the theory's supporters, that it is safe to continue assuming that labor demand curves slope downward, just as marginal productivity theory predicts.

Conclusion   Despite these criticisms, the great majority of economists continue to subscribe to the marginal productivity theory for several reasons. First, most economists remain convinced that the objections outlined above do not invalidate marginal productivity theory. They argue that some objections (e.g., limited cognition) have little substantive merit, while others (e.g., increasing returns) can be adequately handled by expanding the theory to take into account additional real-world complications that the simple version of the theory neglects. Also, most economists believe the theory's basic predictions are supported by the available evidence. It does seem to be true, as the theory predicts, that as the cost of labor rises, firms react by cutting employment. Finally, most economists are reluctant to throw out an existing theory until a better one is developed to take its place. So far the critics of marginal productivity theory have not succeeded in this task.

The Elasticity of Demand for Labor

The downward slope of the labor demand curve shows that the wage rate and the level of employment are inversely related. For many issues, however, it is important to know more than this. In particular, economists and policymakers need to know *how sensitive* employment is to changes in the cost of labor. This involves the concept of the elasticity of labor demand.

---

14   For a diagrammatic analysis, see Richard Perlman, *Labor Theory* (New York: John Wiley and Sons, 1969), 50–56.

15   See Andrew Szilagy and Marc Wallace, *Organizational Behavior and Performance*, 5th ed. (New York: Harper-Collins, 1990).

FIGURE 4.6   THE FIVE CATEGORIES OF DEMAND ELASTICITY

There are five different classifications of demand elasticity. Graph (a) illustrates labor demand curves that are perfectly inelastic ($E_D = 0$), perfectly elastic ($E_D = \infty$), and unit elastic ($E_D = 1$). Graph (b) illustrates labor demand curves that are inelastic ($E_D < 1$) and elastic ($E_D > 1$).

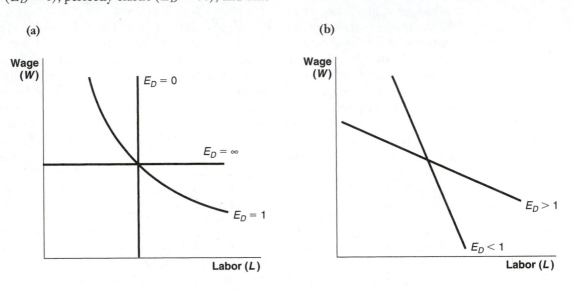

The **elasticity of labor demand (E_D)** is defined as:

$$E_D = \frac{\% \Delta L}{\% \Delta W}, \tag{4.4}$$

where $\% \Delta L$ is the percentage change in employment and $\% \Delta W$ is the percentage change in the wage rate. Since the wage rate and the firm's desired level of employment are inversely related, the elasticity of labor demand must be a negative (or at least a nonpositive) number. For convenience, however, economists usually neglect the minus sign in discussing the elasticity of demand, a practice followed here.

The more responsive is the firm's demand for labor to changes in the wage rate, the greater will be the numerical value of the elasticity of demand. It is possible to distinguish five different cases. Each case is defined below and is illustrated in Figure 4.6, graphs (a) and (b).

1. $E_D = 0$. If an increase in the market wage rate of, say, 10 percent ($\% \Delta W = 10\%$) causes no change in the demand for labor ($\% \Delta L = 0$), the elasticity of demand will equal zero. The demand for labor is known in this case as *perfectly inelastic* and is represented by the vertical demand curve in Figure 4.6, graph (a).

2. $E_D < 1$. If the elasticity of demand is less than one but greater than zero, demand is called *inelastic*. This would be the case, for example, if a 10 percent reduction in the wage rate led to only a 5 percent increase in labor demand ($E_D = 0.5$). An inelastic demand curve implies that labor demand is relatively insensitive to labor cost, a notion that is represented graphically by the steep demand curve drawn in Figure 4.6, graph (b).

3. $E_D = 1$. If the percentage change in labor demand is just equal to the percentage change in the wage rate, then $E_D = 1$, and demand is known as *unit* elastic. A unit elastic demand curve is shown in graph (a) of Figure 4.6. It has the shape of a rectangular hyperbola, for reasons that are explained below.

4. $E_D > 1$. If the percentage change in labor demand exceeds the percentage change in the wage rate, the elasticity of demand will be greater than one, and demand is *elastic*. An elastic demand curve implies that labor demand is highly responsive to changes in the wage rate, indicated in graph (b), by the flat demand curve.

5. $E_D = \infty$. If the firm is willing to hire all the additional employees it can at the prevailing wage, but will hire no employees at any higher wage, demand is known as *perfectly elastic*. A perfectly elastic demand curve is illustrated by the horizontal line in Figure 4.6, graph (a).

Special Relationships

There are several important points to note about the elasticity of demand. The first, rather technical in nature, concerns the relationship between elasticity and the slope of a linear demand curve. While flat demand curves such as those depicted in Figure 4.6, graph (b), are said to be elastic, strictly speaking, this is incorrect—any straight-line, downward-sloping demand curve will have *both* an elastic and an inelastic portion, as shown in Figure 4.7. If the wage should fall from $8 to $7, for example, employment would rise from 20 to 30 workers. What is the elasticity of demand? $E_D = 50\%/-12.5\% = 4$ (neglecting the minus sign); demand is very elastic. If the wage begins at $2, and falls by a dollar to $1, employment will rise from 80 to 90 workers. The elasticity of demand is $E_D = 12.5\%/-100\% = 0.125$; demand is quite inelastic.

For the same $1 change in the wage, demand on the top half of the curve is elastic, on the bottom half it is inelastic, and at the midpoint it is unit elastic. The reason is that elasticity is measured in terms of *percentage* changes, while a linear curve shows *absolute* changes in wages and employment.[16] The same dollar decrease in the wage

---

16 To avoid this problem, in empirical work labor demand curves are usually estimated in double logarithmic form: $\ln L = \ln a + b \ln W$. The coefficient b yields the elasticity of demand since:

$$b = \frac{d(\ln L)}{d(\ln W)} = \frac{dL/L}{dW/W} = \frac{\%\Delta L}{\%\Delta W}.$$

Although steep demand curves are usually labeled inelastic and flat demand curves are labeled elastic, technically this is incorrect. Along any straight-line, downward-sloping demand curve, the top half is elastic, the midpoint is unit elastic, and the bottom half is inelastic.

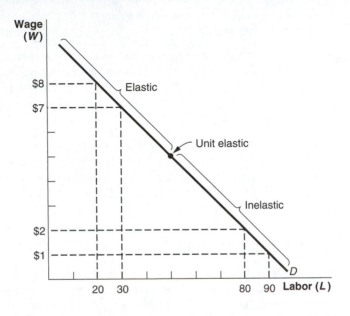

is a small percentage change at $8 but a large percentage change at $2, thus leading to different elasticity estimates along one straight-line demand curve. For a demand curve to have a constant elasticity along every point, it has to be a curved line such as the unit elastic demand curve in graph (a) of Figure 4.6. Given this caveat, for ease of exposition flat demand curves are referred to as elastic and steep demand curves as inelastic in the remainder of this book. This convention is extremely convenient and does not affect any major conclusion concerning the theory of labor demand.[17]

A second important consideration with respect to the elasticity of demand is the firm's wage bill. The **wage bill** is defined as the firm's total money outlay for

---

[17] The mathematical relationship between the slope of the demand curve for labor and the elasticity can be seen as follows:

$$E_D = \frac{\%\,\Delta L}{\%\,\Delta W} = \frac{\Delta L/L}{\Delta W/W} = \frac{\Delta L}{\Delta W}\frac{W}{L} = \frac{1}{\text{slope of } D_L}\frac{W}{L}.$$

So, the flatter the demand curve (at a given wage and labor locus)—which means the slope is relatively small in absolute value—the larger is the elasticity of demand. Also, given a particular demand curve, the elasticity will be greater at higher wage levels (the top part of the demand curve).

labor. It is calculated by multiplying the average wage rate per hour times the total number of workers employed—the wage bill is equal to $W \times L$. If labor demand is inelastic, a rise in the wage rate will result in a net increase in the total wage bill, since the percentage increase in the wage W will exceed the percentage decline in employment L, making the product $W \times L$ greater than before. The opposite holds true for a wage decrease. Conversely, if labor demand is elastic, a rise in the wage rate will cause the wage bill paid for labor to decline, since the percentage decrease in employment will be greater than the percentage increase in the wage rate.[18]

A third consideration is what determines the elasticity of demand. Why is it that in some cases labor demand is elastic while in others it is inelastic? The key consideration is the ease of substitution available both to consumers in their choice of what firm to buy from and to business firms in their choice of labor, capital, and other inputs to use in producing the product. A rise in the wage rate in the market raises the costs of production for firms, leading to a reduction in employment for two reasons. First, firms will be forced to raise their product price, resulting in fewer sales, less production, and a smaller demand for labor. Second, higher costs of labor will motivate firms to substitute capital and other inputs for labor in the long run, leading to a further reduction in labor demand. Thus, the easier it is for consumers to find a substitute good (such as an imported car) to replace the one whose price has gone up (such as a domestic car) or, alternatively, the easier it is for the firm to substitute capital for labor, the greater will be the reduction in employment in those firms where wages have increased—that is, the more elastic will be the demand for labor. This subject is treated in much more detail in the next chapter.

Estimates of the Elasticity of Labor Demand

The marginal productivity theory predicts that the demand curve for labor slopes downward to the right. The most fundamental implication of this prediction is that wage rates and levels of employment are inversely related—the higher the wage rate, other things equal, the lower will be the level of employment in the firm or industry.

Economists have conducted numerous empirical studies to test this prediction of the theory. Daniel Hamermesh has surveyed much of this literature and arrived at several conclusions.[19] Every study finds that, as predicted, the demand curve for labor slopes downward to the right. Whether measured across

---

18 This relationship can be seen mathematically as follows. Since the wage bill equals $W \times L$, whenever $(\%\Delta L < \%\Delta W)$, $\%\Delta W$ (as in the case of inelastic demand), the change in the wage bill will be driven by the change in the wage. Thus, if the wage increases, the wage bill increases. Analogously, when demand is elastic $(\%\Delta L > \%\Delta W)$ the change in employment (L) will drive the direction of the change in the wage bill.

19 Daniel Hamermesh, "Econometric Studies of Labor Demand and Their Application to Policy Analysis," *Journal of Human Resources* 11, no. 4 (Fall 1976): 507–25. For updates of this study, see his article "The Demand for Labor in the Long Run," in Orley Ashenfelter and Richard Layard, eds., *Handbook of Labor Economics* (Amsterdam: North-Holland, 1986): 429–71, and his book *Labor Demand* (Princeton, N.J.: Princeton University Press, 1993).

occupations, industries, or demographic groups, higher wages lead to less employment, holding all other things constant. A second conclusion from Hamermesh's survey is that, in general, demand curves in the economy are inelastic. Based on the estimates presented in his most recent survey, Hamermesh calculated a consensus estimate for the elasticity of demand of −0.30, meaning that for every 1 percent increase in the wage rate, labor demand would decline by three-tenths of 1 percent.[20]

A related conclusion concerning the elasticity of demand was that it increases on average as the particular type of employment becomes narrower or more disaggregated. Thus, the elasticity of labor demand for manufacturing was generally estimated in studies as larger than for the entire economy but still inelastic, while for a demographic group such as teenagers it was much higher, possibly greater than 1.0 and, thus, elastic.[21] This result reflects the fact that the narrower the type of employment and product considered, the greater the substitution possibilities in both production and consumption.

Finally, evidence suggests that the elasticity of demand is greater for unskilled and blue-collar workers than for skilled and white-collar workers.[22] The reason is that capital and blue-collar or unskilled workers are generally substitutes for each other in production, while capital and skilled or white-collar workers tend to be complements. A good example is television manufacturing. In response to rising wages and greater import competition, television manufacturers automated the production process to reduce labor cost. The workers most adversely affected were unskilled assemblers, whose jobs were largely displaced by computer-controlled automatic inserting equipment. Employment among more-skilled machine operators declined only slightly and actually increased for other skilled workers such as computer programmers and electronic technicians.[23]

➦ SEE

Empirical Evidence 4-1:
Union Wage Concessions, p. 214.

The importance of the elasticity of demand for labor in determining employment levels and bargaining strategies of unions is illustrated in Empirical Evidence 4-1.

---

20 Hamermesh points out that the estimates reported in his Table 3.2 reflect an aggregate elasticity for the demand of labor; any individual firm's demand is likely to be more sensitive to wage movements than reflected by the aggregate statistic reported here.

21 Further evidence on the elasticity of labor demands for teenagers can be found in Kenneth Couch and David Wittenberg, "The Response of Hours of Work to Increases in the Minimum Wage," *Southern Economic Journal* 68 (July 2001): 171–77.

22 Daniel Hamermesh and James Grant, "Econometric Studies of Labor–Labor Substitution and Their Implications for Policy," *Journal of Human Resources* 14, no. 4 (Fall 1979): 518–42; Villy Bergstrom, "How Robust Is the Capital–Skill Complementarity Hypothesis?" *Review of Economics and Statistics* 74 (August 1992): 540–45; and Martin Falk and Bertrand Koebel, "A Dynamic Heterogenous Labour Demand Model for German Manufacturing," *Applied Economics* 33 (February 2001): 339–48.

23 See Bureau of Labor Statistics, *Technology and Labor in Four Industries*, Bulletin 2104 (Washington, D.C.: Government Printing Office, 1982), 34–44. Another good example of how technology has impacted employment is in the banking industry. The rise in the use of ATMs and telephone and computer banking has meant lower employment for bank tellers. See Teresa Morisi, "Commercial Banking Transformed by Computer Technology," *Monthly Labor Review* (August 1996): 30–36.

The Relationship between Product Demand and Labor Demand

Up to this point the chapter has focused on the relationship between the wage rate and the firm's short-run demand for labor, a relationship represented diagrammatically as a movement along a given labor demand curve. However, a number of factors besides the wage rate influence a firm's desired level of employment. One of the most important is the strength of the demand for its product. As emphasized in Chapter 1, the demand for labor by a firm is a *derived* demand. The business firm has as its primary goal the maximization of profit. Its demand for labor rises only to the extent that labor is necessary to produce the level of output desired by the firm's customers. The fact that labor is derived from the demand for the product implies that changes in the level of sales and production of the firm will necessarily cause a concomitant change in the firm's desired level of employment, represented graphically by a *shift* in the labor demand curve. This section examines more closely three aspects of this relationship: the cyclical fluctuation in employment over the business cycle, the pattern of interindustry employment growth due to long-run shifts in consumer expenditure patterns, and the impact of imports on domestic employment.

The Demand for Labor over the Business Cycle

An enduring feature of a capitalist economy is the business cycle. The business cycle is the wavelike pattern that occurs in general business activity as spending and production increase during the expansion phase of the cycle and then contract during periods of recession. From the end of World War II through 2003, there were ten recessions in the U.S. economy. These are illustrated in Figure 4.8 by the bars denoting the beginning of each recession and the end of the recession. Given the derived nature of labor demand, it would be expected that employment in the economy would also rise and fall with the business cycle. This is clearly confirmed by the line showing nonagricultural employment in Figure 4.8. From 1947 through 2003, nonagricultural employment increased from 43.5 million to 137 million. This secular increase in employment was temporarily interrupted ten times, however, by the sharp contraction in employment that occurred during each recession. In the 2001 recession, for example, employment fell from 136.7 million in February 2001 to 136.3 in November 2001.

The cyclical expansion and contraction of total spending in the economy give rise, therefore, to a similar cyclical fluctuation in employment. Two additional facets of this relationship are important to consider.

Industry Sensitivity to the Business Cycle The first issue is the much greater impact that recession has on employment in certain cyclically vulnerable industries in the economy, particularly in durable manufacturing.[24] This is illustrated in

---

[24] Jay Berman and Janet Pfleeger, "Which Industries Are Sensitive to Business Cycles?" *Monthly Labor Review* 118 (February 1997): 19–25, explore expected industry sensitivities through the year 2005.

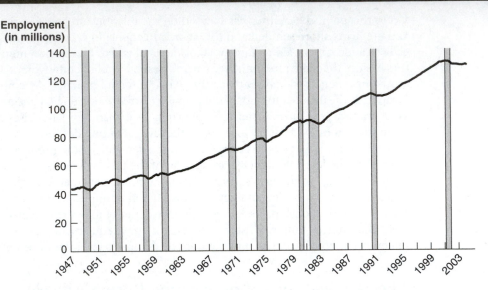

SOURCE: Department of Commerce, *Survey of Current Business* (Washington, D.C.: Government Printing Office) and Bureau of Labor Statistics, http://www.bls.gov/webapps/legacy/cesbtab1.htm.

Table 4.2. Table 4.2 shows the percentage decline in real gross national product and nonfarm payroll employment, respectively, in the goods-producing and service-producing sectors of the economy in each of the nine postwar recessions. Employment in the goods-producing sector of the economy is subject to much greater cyclical volatility than is employment in the service sector. Over all ten recessions, the average percentage decline in employment in the goods-producing sector was 7.5 percent, while employment in the service-producing sector actually *increased* by 0.3 percent. Within each sector, the extremes in the cyclical responsiveness of employment are illustrated by the durable manufacturing industries and government, respectively. Government employment continued to expand in all but the last two recessions, while employment in durable manufacturing declined an average of 10.1 percent in each recession.

    The markedly different cyclical behavior of employment in the goods-producing and service-producing sectors reflects the difference in expenditure patterns for the products of each sector. Expenditures for durable goods (for example, new homes and factories, automobiles, and capital equipment) tend to be quite volatile because often the purchase can be postponed, involves a very large lump-sum payment, or is financed by borrowing. Expenditures on service-type goods (such as purchases

TABLE 4.2

PERCENT DECLINE IN INDUSTRY EMPLOYMENT DURING RECESSIONS

		Percentage Change in Payroll Employment				
Recessions	Percentage Change in Real GDP	Total Nonfarm	Total Goods Sector	Durable Manufac-turing	Total Service Sector	Govern-ment
Nov. 1948–Oct. 1949	−1.7	−5.0	−10.7	−16.2	−0.9	1.7
July 1953–May 1954	−2.6	−3.0	−7.2	−10.5	0.0	2.0
Aug. 1957–Apr. 1958	−3.2	−4.0	−8.0	−11.8	−1.4	1.6
Apr. 1960–Feb. 1961	−1.0	−2.2	−5.6	−8.1	−0.1	0.7
Dec. 1969–Nov. 1970	−0.6	−1.2	−6.8	−11.2	1.7	2.8
Nov. 1973–Mar. 1975	−3.1	−1.8	−10.9	−11.2	2.5	5.2
Jan. 1980–July 1980	−2.2	−1.3	−5.8	−6.8	−0.6	0.8
July 1981–Nov. 1982	−2.7	−3.5	−11.0	−12.9	0.0	−1.6
July 1990–Mar. 1991	−1.3	−1.9	−5.2	−5.3	−0.9	0.0
Mar. 2001–Nov. 2001	−0.04	−0.5	−4.2	−7.2	0.4	−1.5

SOURCE: Percentage change in real GDP calculated as the percentage change in real quarterly seasonally-adjusted annualized GDP from peach to trough (http://www.bea.gov/bea/dn/gdplev.xls). Employment changes calculated using data from U.S. Bureau of Labor Statistics, *Employment and Earnings* (various months).

from department stores, grocery stores, and insurance companies) tend, on the other hand, both to be more divisible and to involve smaller outlays on the part of the purchaser.

One might expect that since the service-producing sector has grown so much as a percentage of total nonfarm employment (see Figure 4.1), and since employment in that sector is relatively stable, cyclical swings in the economy should have dampened over time. However, as one can see from the percentage change in real GNP in Table 4.2, the depth of recessions in the 1980s, 1990s, and 2000s is no less severe than in the 1950s, 1960s, and 1970s.[25]

Layoffs versus Cuts in Hours So far the demand for labor has been discussed solely in terms of persons employed as if labor input were available only in discrete "lumps" of 40 hours per week per person. In actuality, firms are able to adjust either the number of persons employed or the hours per week each person works. During an unanticipated recession, which dimension of labor demand are firms more likely to change—hours or jobs?

---

[25] Additional evidence that recessions are not growing less severe or infrequent can be found in Andrew J. Filardo, "Cyclical Implications of the Declining Manufacturing Employment Share," *Federal Reserve Bank of Kansas City Economic Review* 82 (Spring 1997): 63–87.

Worries about Middle Class Jobs and Upward Economic Mobility

A recent magazine article declared that a person in the American upper-middle class had the enviable position of being ahead of 99 percent of the rest of the world's population in terms of income, health, and quality of life. Another noted that the reason so many people from around the world want to emigrate to the United States is because the American labor market provides unparalleled opportunity for upward economic mobility from poor to affluent.

These positive features of the American labor market still hold true, but worries are growing among significant parts of the workforce that middle-class jobs and upward mobility are getting progressively more difficult to attain and hold on to. A number of writers have talked about the "middle-class squeeze," others have framed the proliferation of lower-wage jobs as the "Wal-Martization" of the labor market and, even more starkly, others have framed recent events as "the downward escalator" of economic opportunity and the appearance of "two Americas"—one rich and the other poor. Others argue that all of this doom and gloom is over-hyped, not supported by the statistics, and/or too focused on temporary or short-run problems.

Evidence can be found to support both sides of this debate. Take the case of the worriers, for example. The most up-to-date government statistics, for example, show that real (inflation adjusted) median family income has basically been stagnant since 1998. Although definitions of "middle-class"

vary, one common yardstick is a family with an annual income between $25,000 and $75,000. Using this definition, the proportion of American families in the middle-class has fallen from 52 percent in 1980 to 45 percent in 2003. Likewise, income inequality continues to grow, with most of the income gains generated by the economy going to the families in the top one-tenth of the income distribution while the number of people in poverty and without health insurance continues to grow. The problem confronting the middle-class, according to the worriers, is that the middle of the job distribution is gradually eroding. Between 1998 and 2004 over two million manufacturing jobs disappeared, and hundreds of thousands of good-paying white-collar, technology, and service jobs were either eliminated through downsizings or shifted overseas through outsourcing. As a result, job insecurity and lowered economic expectations afflicted many college-educated and high-skilled technical workers who in earlier years thought these problems only affected blue-collar workers. Emblematic of the new anxiety in the labor market is the title of a recent cover story in *Business Week:* "Is Your Job Next?"

The optimists say all these concerns are either overblown or are short-run adjustment problems. Over the long-term, they note, the American economy continues to outperform most foreign rivals. True, they say, employment growth has been

A partial answer is provided in Figure 4.9, which shows the average length of the workweek for production workers in manufacturing from 1948 through 2003. Hours of work per week scheduled by firms exhibit a clear cyclical pattern as does employment, rising during cyclical upswings and falling during recessions. A second and more interesting point concerns the relative timing of changes in hours and employment. A comparison of the cyclical turning points of employment in Figure 4.8 and the average workweek in Figure 4.9 reveals that changes in hours of work precede changes in employment at both the beginning and the end of recessions.

sluggish in the early 2000s and the unemployment rate is higher than in the boom years of the late 1990s, but relative to Europe things still look much better in the United States. Consider that from 1991 to 2003 job growth in the United States was 17 percent, compared to just 1 percent in France and Germany. Likewise, the unemployment rate in both European countries is roughly double the American level. So why the anxiety in the United States about the disappearance of middle-class jobs and upward economic mobility? The optimists claim these fears originate in several factors that have recently come together to cause an unusual amount of change and dislocation in the labor market. One such factor is globalization and, in particular, the dramatic rise of the economies of China and India. Suddenly it seems half the goods we buy say "Made in China" while newspapers are full of stories about call center and computer programming jobs being transferred to India. A second factor is the continued record of strong productivity growth in America. As explained in the next chapter, rapid productivity growth allows firms to produce the same output with less labor— a factor the optimists point to as a reason why the U.S. GDP has grown every quarter since the end of the 2001 recession, yet employment growth has remained worryingly anemic. The optimists say even though these factors cause short-run problems, the American economy will benefit in the long run, partly because productivity growth makes American firms more competitive. Thus they will grow and add jobs in the future, in part because rapid growth in foreign economies translates into extra demand for American-made goods and services. Once these things sort out the American labor market will start to create more good-paying jobs as in the past, making the current anxiety about the "disappearing middle class" seem like another over-hyped social trend.

The truth, as in most matters, probably lies somewhere in the middle. For twenty years the income distribution in the United States has become noticeably more unequal, reflecting the rise of both an increasingly affluent segment of the workforce at the top end and several tens of millions of "working poor" at the lower end who are trapped in dead-end, low-paying jobs. This is one reality. The other reality is that the American economy remains one of the most vibrant and adaptive in the world and out-performs most foreign rivals in creating new jobs and economic opportunities, even if considerable dislocation and uncertainty for individual families and workers accompanies the process. The pressures on the American middle-class could well be viewed as a case of: is the glass half empty or half full?

SOURCES: "Economic Squeeze Plaguing Middle-Class Families," *The New York Times* (August 28, 2004): A11; "Is Your Job Next?," *Business Week* (February 3, 2003): 50–60; "How Real is the 'Squeeze'?", *Time* (July 19, 2004): 41–43.

When faced with the prospect of declining sales and production, why do firms choose to cut hours before jobs? An important reason has to do with various **fixed costs of employment**.[26] Firms make substantial investments in workers in the form of recruitment and hiring costs and in the form of substantial expenditures on

---

[26]   See Walter Oi, "Labor as a Quasi-Fixed Factor," *Journal of Political Economy* 70, no. 6 (December 1962): 538–55, and Robert A. Hart, *The Economics of Non-Wage Labour Costs* (Boston: Allen and Unwin, 1984). Also see Francis Kramarz and Marie-Laure Michaud, "The Shape of Hiring and Separation Costs" *CEPR Discussion Paper No. 3685* (January 2003).

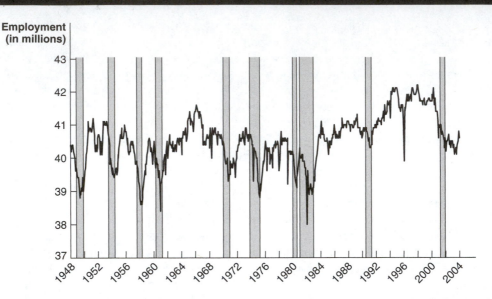

SOURCE: Department of Commerce, *Survey of Current Business* (Washington, D.C.: Government Printing Office); and Bureau of Labor Statistics, http://www.bls.gov/webapps/legacy/cesbtab2.htm.

training. According to one estimate, for example, a firm's cost of hiring or firing a white-collar worker is between two weeks' and two months' pay, and between two days' and two weeks' pay for a blue-collar worker.[27] Both hiring and training costs are fixed or "sunk" costs to the firm in that they do not vary proportionately with the number of hours the employee works. Having made this investment in the worker, the firm obviously has a financial incentive to avoid worker turnover, since these fixed costs would be lost should the worker leave the firm. For this reason, firms react to a decline in labor demand by first chopping hours and only later, if the recession persists or deepens significantly, by instituting layoffs. One implication of this theory is that the greater a firm's investment in fixed hiring and training costs in a worker, the lower is the probability that he or she will be laid off. This helps explain the tendency for firms to "hoard" their skilled workers during cyclical downswings while permitting layoffs for the less skilled.[28] This also may help

27   See S. J. Nickell, "Dynamic Models of Labour Demand," in Ashenfelter and Layard, eds., *Handbook of Labor Economics*, 517. Also see John Abowd and Francis Kramarz, "The Cost of Hiring and Separation," *Labour Economics* 10 (October 2003): 499–530.

28   See, for example, Farrell E. Bloch, "Labor Turnover in U.S. Manufacturing Industries," *Journal of Human Resources* 14, no. 2 (Spring 1979): 236–46.

explain the growing attractiveness of flexible work arrangements and temporary workers to firms. Having fewer permanent and rigidly scheduled employees means a greater ability to adjust to demand fluctuations.[29]

Overtime Hours   The data in Figure 4.9 also show that during cyclical upswings of the economy the average workweek begins to increase above 40 hours per week as employers schedule overtime hours. If all labor costs were variable, employers would find it profitable to hire a new part-time worker rather than pay an existing employee time and a half for overtime. The greater the proportion of fixed costs of employment in a firm's compensation package, however, the more likely it is that paying an employee even at a rate of time and a half will be cheaper to the firm than hiring a new worker and paying the initial hiring and training costs.[30] One economist notes that during the expansion that followed the recession of the early 1990s, firms were even more likely to increase overtime hours than to hire new workers than they had been after previous recessions. By 1997, average overtime hours had reached 4.9 hours per week, the highest since the initial publication of that statistic in 1956.[31]

An important consideration in this regard is the effect of fringe benefits on the demand for labor. Fringe benefits include a variety of nonwage forms of compensation such as paid vacations, life and health insurance and government-required contributions to Social Security, workers' compensation, and other such programs. Fringe benefits have become an increasingly large share of a firm's total cost of labor, averaging 27 percent of total compensation in 2000.

Fringe benefits frequently represent a fixed cost in the sense that once a worker is hired, the expense of health insurance or a paid vacation, for example, does not vary with the number of hours worked. The larger the ratio of fringe benefits to total compensation, therefore, the greater is the inducement for the firm to use overtime as a means of meeting an increased demand for labor rather than hire a new worker.

Fringe benefit costs may also have an impact on the firm's layoff decision during a recession. If a worker's marginal revenue product is likely to fall permanently below the variable cost of labor (the straight-time wage) because of a slowdown in sales, the firm would find it profitable to let him or her go even if it means losing the sunk costs of hiring and training. Given this, which worker would the firm be most likely to lay off? In a number of instances the answer is the older worker, since the firm thereby avoids or minimizes the future expense of pension benefits. Preventing this practice is a major factor in the insistence of labor unions on strong seniority systems that require layoffs to begin with the least-senior worker. This practice has also been circumscribed by the provisions of the Employee Retirement

---

29   See Susan Houseman, "Why Employers Use Flexible Staffing Arrangements: Evidence from an Establishment Survey," *Industrial and Labor Relations Review* 55 (October 2001): 149–70.

30   See David J. Smyth and Stephen H. Karlson, "The Effect of Fringe Benefits on Employment Fluctuations in U.S. Automobile Manufacturing," *Review of Economics and Statistics* 73 (February 1991): 40–49. Higher fixed costs of employment also cause firms to have a greater demand for full-time employees relative to part-timers. For empirical evidence, see Mark Montgomery, "On the Determinants of Employer Demand for Part-Time Workers," *Review of Economics and Statistics* 80, no. 1 (February 1988): 112–17.

31   See Ron Hetrick, "Analyzing the Recent Upward Surge in Overtime Hours," *Monthly Labor Review* 123 (February 2000): 30–33.

Income Security Act of 1974 (ERISA), which mandate that a worker's right to pension benfits must be guaranteed or "vested" after a certain length of service with the firm, regardless of whether he or she later quits or is laid off.

Consumer Expenditure Patterns and the Demand for Labor

Table 4.3 shows data on the percentage change in employment in 10 consumer goods industries over the period 1980 to 2002. The growth rates range from a 61 percent decline in employment in the apparel industry to a 246 percent increase in employment in Internet Service Providers and Web Search Portals. What factor or factors account for this disparate behavior of labor demand among these industries?

One important explanation has to do with the pattern of consumer expenditures. As consumers' income grows, a relatively small fraction of the additional income is devoted to savings, and the remainder of the increase is spent on additional purchases of goods and services. Consumer expenditures do not increase equally for all goods and services however; the exact proportion depends on the product's *income elasticity of demand*.[32] If the income elasticity of demand is negative, the good in question is an inferior good, meaning that the quantity of it demanded declines as consumers' income increases. A product that has a positive income elasticity is a normal good. Goods that are staples or necessities, such as potatoes, bread, household supplies, and paint, generally have low or even negative income elasticities, as do certain services such as shoe repair. Higher-priced durable goods such as cameras and jewelry, services such as education and health care, and retail products such as restaurant meals, on the other hand, tend to have high income elasticities.

As income grows over time, the product demand curve in those industries or occupations with a high income elasticity of demand should shift to the right quite rapidly, causing a similar rightward shift in the labor demand curve. This prediction is borne out in the data shown in Table 4.3. Employment in industries such as air transportation, ISP services, and education experienced quite sizable increases in employment between 1990 and 2002. Conversely, industries with low income elasticities should experience slow or even declining growth in product demand and, thus, in labor demand. This is also evident in Table 4.3 from the decline in employment that took place in the paper products, apparel, power supply industries.[33]

SEE
Policy Application 4-2:
Imports and the
Demand for Labor,
p. 209.

Policy Application 4-2 illustrates how "labor" and consumers can be at odds over certain policies, such as free trade, in which one contingency gains and the other loses.

---

32   The income elasticity of demand is measured as the percentage change in quantity demanded of the good (Q) divided by the percentage change in income (Y), i.e., $\%\Delta Q/\%\Delta Y$.

33   Part of the decline in employment in these industries is also due to productivity growth. This topic is discussed in the next chapter.

Industry	Percentage Change in Employment 1990–2002	Industry	Percentage Change in Employment 1990–2002
Apparel	−61%	ISPs and Web Search Portals	+246%
Power Generation and Supply	−21	Education Services	+57
Paper and Paper Products	−16	Eating and drinking establishments	+29
Primary Metal Manufacturing	−26	Finance and Insurance	+17
Beverage and Tobacco Products	−6	Air Transportation	+6

SOURCE: U.S. Department of Commerce, *Statistical Abstract of the United State: 2003*, Chart 631 http://www.census.gov/statab/www/.

POLICY APPLICATION 4-1

Wage Subsidy Programs

Even in the best of times a significant number of persons face great difficulty finding employment, persons sometimes identified as the *structural* or "hard-core" unemployed. Prominent among the hard-core unemployed are people in three problem groups: low-skilled adults, disadvantaged youth, and residents of economically depressed areas. The most glaring example of hard-core unemployment in today's labor market is black teenagers, a group whose unemployment rate in 2003 (33 percent) was five times the national average (6 percent).

Why can't the hard-core unemployed find work? One answer is a combination of discrimination and a shortage of jobs in the economy. A number of economists argue, however, that these factors are of secondary importance; the more important explanation is that firms simply do not find it profitable to hire these people. The fundamental proposition of the marginal productivity theory is that a profit maximizing firm will hire a worker only if the extra revenue he or she produces exceeds the wage the firm has to pay. Why would a firm not find it profitable to hire the hard-core unemployed? One reason is that these workers have a very low level of productivity. Many disadvantaged youths, for example, are high school dropouts who have neither the basic educational skills nor the good work habits that are necessary in today's job market. The second reason, in this view, is that the minimum wage law prevents employers from lowering their rate of pay enough to make it profitable to hire the hard-core unemployed.

From the perspective of marginal productivity theory, therefore, policymakers have two alternative ways to attack the problem of hard-core unemployment. One is manpower training programs such as the Job Corps (to be discussed in Chapter 13) that provide the hard-to-employ with specific job skills. This has the effect of increasing a worker's marginal product, thus increasing employment of that type of worker at any given wage. A second route is to lower the cost to the firm of hiring the hard-core unemployed. One option advocated by a number of economists to reduce black teenage unemployment, for example, is a teenage subminimum wage (to be discussed in Chapter 6). A second option is a wage subsidy program. The next section analyzes this type of program in more detail.

The Employment Effect of a Wage Subsidy Program

A wage subsidy program aims to create additional jobs in the economy by subsidizing the employer's cost of labor. Unlike public-service–type programs that create new jobs through expanded government employment, wage subsidy programs focus on employment in the private sector. A variety of wage subsidy programs have been either adopted or proposed. In recent years, income tax credits have been used to subsidize the wages of the handicapped, welfare recipients, ex-convicts, disadvantaged youths, and Vietnam veterans. Subsidized employment has become a major component of each state's attempt to comply with the employment requirements for TANF recipients set forth in the Personal Responsibility and Work Opportunity Reconciliation Act of 1996 (welfare reform).

The federal government has enacted several different wage subsidy programs over the years. Some examples are the New Jobs Tax Credit and the Targeted Jobs Tax Credit (both programs had expired by 1994), which provided direct subsidies to private employers for new jobs created for a targeted group of workers. More recently, the Work Opportunity Tax Credit and the Welfare-to-Work

Tax Credit were short-lived (18 months) similar programs.

Recent efforts by the federal government are directed towards providing training to improve employment opportunities for targeted workers. The Workforce Investment Act (WIA) of 1998 was implemented in September 2000. The WIA superseded another long-standing training program, the Job Training Partnership Act (JTPA), which began in 1983.

The employment effect of a wage subsidy program is illustrated in Figure 4.10. Shown in graph (a) as $D_0 D_1$ is the "before-subsidy" demand curve.[1] This curve shows that at a market wage of W_1, in lieu of any subsidy, a typical firm would be willing to hire L_1 workers (point A); at a wage of W_2, employment would be L_2 (point C). Now assume that Congress attempts to stimulate employment by providing a wage subsidy to employers for every additional worker hired.

In designing a wage subsidy program, policymakers are faced with the same conflict in goals as those for the income transfer programs analyzed in Chapter 2. In particular, they must weigh the trade-off between program costs and the size of the financial incentive offered to firms to increase employment. One approach to solving this dilemma involves the following type of wage subsidy program. First, the program is "categorical" in that the wage subsidy applies only to workers of some identifiable low-skill group, such as teenagers or welfare recipients. This provision serves to target the program at the hard-core unemployed. Second, the firm receives a wage subsidy only for people newly hired, not for existing employees. This provision limits the program costs by excluding payments to workers the firm has hired anyway. This type of program is known as a "marginal" or "incremental" wage subsidy. A third feature is that only those new workers who earn a wage less than a target wage

---

1 This graphic analysis is adapted from Robert I. Lerman, "A Comparison of Employer and Worker Wage Subsidies," in Robert Haveman and John L. Palmer, eds., *Jobs for Disadvantaged Workers: The Economics of Employment Subsidies* (Washington, D.C.: The Brookings Institution, 1982), 159–79.

FIGURE 4.10   THE EFFECT OF A WAGE SUBSIDY PROGRAM ON LABOR DEMAND

A wage subsidy program gives rise to the kinked labor demand curve $D_1 TD_2$. At the wage W_1, employment increases from L_1 to L_1' in graph (a). The cost of the wage subsidy program is shown by the rectangle in graph (b).

The more inelastic the presubsidy demand curve, the larger the size of the subsidy payment S must be to stimulate an increase in employment of $L_2 - L_1$.

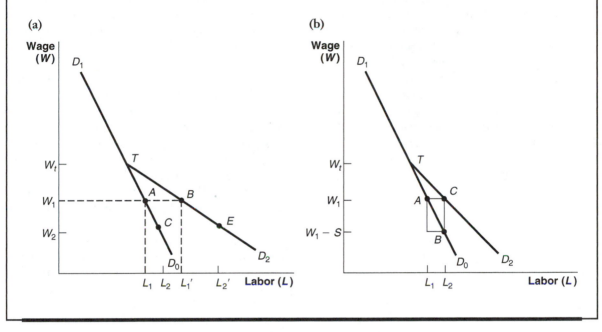

rate of W_t qualify for a subsidy. This restriction excludes all but the lowest-wage workers, targeting the benefits to those who are likely to have the most difficulty obtaining employment owing to a lack of experience or training, physical impairment, or other such limiting factor. Fourth, for every worker hired the employer receives a subsidy payment per hour S equal to some percent r of the *difference* between the target wage W_t and the presubsidy, hiring wage of, say, W_p. The subsidy payment is given by the formula:

$$S = r(W_t - W_p). \qquad (4.5)$$

The subsidy payment received by the firm will be greater for higher values of the subsidy rate r or the greater the difference between W_t and W_p.

This type of wage subsidy program has both positive and negative aspects. One advantage is that the program provides the largest subsidy and stimulus to employment for those workers who are the lowest paid or most marginal in the labor market. A second advantage is that the subsidy payment is reduced as the worker's wage increases with experience and training, gradually weaning the worker from the program. One negative feature is that the program encourages employers to replace full-time workers with part-time workers. Although the actual hours of work performed might not change, the firm's employment would significantly increase, qualifying it for subsidy payments. A second drawback is that employers may "churn" their labor force by replacing experienced, higher-wage employees with inexperienced, low-wage workers from the target group in order to maximize the amount of subsidy per worker. To the extent that the subsidy program causes the employer to substitute one type of worker for another, the net increase in jobs will be diminished. Finally, a third negative outcome of the wage subsidy program is that it may reduce employment prospects for the very group of people it is meant to help. Evidence indicates that eligibility for a subsidy has a stigmatizing effect on disadvantaged workers because employers regard it as a clear signal that they are "problem cases" and, thus, too big a risk to employ even at the reduced wage per hour.[2]

The effect of this wage subsidy program is to create the kinked "after-subsidy" demand curve $D_1 T D_2$ in graph (a). The before-subsidy demand curve $D_0 D_1$ shows that at a wage of W_1 the firm would hire L_1 workers. After enactment of the wage subsidy program, however, the employer's demand for labor at W_1 would no longer be L_1 (point A) but rather L'_1, shown as point B on the kinked demand curve $D_1 T D_2$. Had the employer's before-subsidy hiring wage been even lower, say at W_2, a wage subsidy program would lead to a correspondingly larger increase in employment from L_2 to L'_2 (point C to E) due to the larger subsidy payment per worker hired.

Derivation of the After-Subsidy Demand Curve

The derivation of the kinked demand curve $D_1 T D_2$ is illustrated in graph (b) of Figure 4.10. If the employer pays a wage equal to or greater than the target wage W_t, then by Equation 4.5 the subsidy payment S is zero. In this case the employer's demand for labor is unaffected by the subsidy program and the after-subsidy demand curve remains D_1 above point T. If the employer is paying a wage below W_t, say W_1, the firm qualifies for a subsidy $S = r(W_t - W_1)$ for each additional worker hired. The subsidy lowers the employer's *net* cost of labor for each additional worker from W_1 to $(W_1 - S)$ per hour. At W_1 the firm's demand for labor before

the subsidy was L_1 (point A); what will it now be with the subsidy?

While the actual wage paid by the firm continues to be W_1, with the subsidy it acts *as if* the before-subsidy wage were only $W_1 - S$, leading it to increase employment from L_1 (point A) to L_2 (point B). Plotting the combination of the wage W_1 and new level of employment of L_2 yields point C, which is one point on the kinked, after-subsidy demand curve. Other points could be obtained in a similar manner for different before-subsidy wage rates, in the process tracing out the demand curve $D_1 T D_2$. This kinked demand curve is derived for a particular value of the subsidy rate r. A higher value of r gives rise to an entirely new after-subsidy demand curve that lies to the right of $D_1 T D_2$.

As hoped for by the program's designers, the wage subsidy resulted in an increase in employment, represented in graph (b) by the increase in employment at W_1 from L_1 to L_2. The benefit of the program is the extra $L_2 - L_1$ workers hired by the employer. The cost of the program can also be shown in graph (b); it is the rectangle determined by the amount of the subsidy payment per worker S (the difference between W_1 and $W_1 - S$) times the $L_2 - L_1$ additional workers hired by the employer.

The benefits and costs of a wage subsidy program depend critically on the elasticity of demand for labor. The more inelastic is labor demand, the smaller will be the net increase in employment for any given amount of subsidy per worker. For example, if the before-subsidy demand curve $D_0 D_1$ in graph (b) were redrawn to be more inelastic, the decline in the employer's net cost of labor from W_1 to $W_1 - S$ would result in an increase in employment not to L_2 but to some lesser amount. This

2   See Gary Burtless, "Are Targeted Wage Subsidies Harmful? Evidence from a Wage Voucher Experiment," *Industrial and Labor Relations Review* 39 (October 1985): 105–14; John Bishop and Suk Kang, "Applying for Entitlements: Employers and the Targeted Jobs Tax Credit," *Journal of Policy Analysis and Management* 10 (Winter 1991): 24–45; and Stacy Dickert-Conlin and Douglas Holtz-Eakin, "Employee-Based versus Employer-Based Subsidies to Low-Wage Workers: A Public Finance Perspective," in *Finding Jobs: Work and Welfare Reform* (New York: Russell Sage Foundation 2000): 262–95.

would be reflected, in turn, by a smaller gap between D_0D_1 and the kinked demand curve D_1TD_2. If labor demand is relatively inelastic, a wage subsidy program will yield less "bang for the buck" in terms of increased employment, resulting in a high ratio of program cost to jobs created. (If the before-subsidy demand curve D_0D_1 was more inelastic in graph (b), what would have to happen to the size of the subsidy payment S to generate the same $L_2 - L_1$ increase in jobs?)

Estimating the Benefits and Costs of a Wage Subsidy Program

In deciding whether or not to implement a wage subsidy program, considerations of jobs created versus dollar cost to the government are quite important to policymakers. There is typically some debate about how cost effective a wage subsidy program is. A study by John Bishop concluded from a detailed statistical analysis that the *New Job Tax Credit* (NJTC), a wage subsidy program enacted in 1977, was responsible for generating as many as one-third of all new jobs in the construction and retailing industries in 1977 and 1978.[3] A much more pessimistic assessment was reached in a study by Robert Tannenwald.[4] Based on telephone and personal interviews with employers, he found that the NJTC stimulated relatively few jobs—for a 10 percent reduction in wages due to the wage subsidy, firms increased their hiring of new workers by only 0.4 percent. This implies that the elasticity of demand was quite low: $E_D = -0.04$. When asked why they added

so few jobs in response to the wage subsidy, employers cited several reasons. The most important was that they were reluctant to hire additional workers without a prior increase in sales. Other deterrents were the complexity of the program regulations and its temporary two-year lifetime. Because the elasticity of demand was so low, the cost per job created by the wage subsidy program was also much higher than Bishop and Lerman anticipated—estimated at $19,000 to $23,000 per job.

Recent evaluations of a variety of wage subsidy programs conclude that programs which include a training component are the most successful in elevating the labor market experiences of the economically disadvantaged.[5]

---

3   John Bishop, "Employment in Construction and Distribution Industries: The Impact of the New Jobs Tax Credit," in Sherwin Rosen, ed., *Studies in Labor Markets* (Chicago: University of Chicago Press, 1981), 209–46. The NJTC was replaced by the *Targeted Jobs Tax Credit* (TJTC) in 1979 and remained in effect until 1994.

4   Robert Tannenwald, "Are Wage and Training Subsidies Cost Effective? Some Evidence from the New Jobs Tax Credit," *New England Economic Review* (September/October 1982): 25–34.

5   The strongest positive impact appears to accrue to women; see David H. Greenberg, et al., "A Meta-analysis of Government-sponsored Training Programs," *Industrial and Labor Relations Review* 59 (October 2003): 31–53. Also see Lawrence F. Katz, "Wage Subsidies for the Disadvantaged," in *Generating Jobs: How to Increase Demand for Less Skilled Workers* (New York: Sage, 1998), 21–53; Brian Bell et al., "Getting the Unemployed Back to Work. The Role of Targeted Wage Subsidies," *International Tax and Public Finance* 6 (August 1999): 339–60; and Timothy Bartik, "Aggregate Effects in Local Labor Markets of Supply and Demand Shocks," W. E. Upjohn Institute for Employment Research Staff Working Paper No. 99-57 (July 1999).

POLICY APPLICATION 4-2

Globalization and the Demand for Labor

One of the most hotly debated subjects facing economic policymakers is the issue of imports and, in particular, the threat of foreign competition to

American jobs. Economic theory demonstrates that both sides gain from international trade because of the specialization and division of labor that trade allows. In spite of this theory, however, several arguments are frequently made in order to justify restricting trade, or limiting imports. One justification is to protect a weak or new industry from competition until it has developed the strength and experience to compete with more experienced foreign producers (the infant-industry argument). A second justification is to make sure that industries important for national defense (petroleum and steel, for example) do not become import industries—that we are not dependent on another country for supplying materials that may be needed in times of conflict. A third justification often given for imposing import restrictions is to affect the behavior of other countries; a country can use stricter import restrictions as a threat and relax import restrictions as a reward for eliciting some kind of action from the affected foreign country.[1]

Trade restrictions result in both winners and losers. Firms in the industry in which a trade restriction is placed are typically identified as clear winners of trade restrictions; the restriction protects the firms from competition, which increases their profits. American workers are also frequently identified as winners; as will be seen below, trade restrictions are often equated with protection of American jobs. American consumers, however, bear the burden of trade restrictions; the lack of competition drives up prices for those goods in the protected industry.

Policymakers have a real dilemma. They must weigh the interests of individual business owners and the welfare of workers against the interests of consumers and the overall economic gains economists can unambiguously show would result from eliminating trade restrictions.

Import Restrictions and Employment

The marginal productivity theory of labor demand can be used to illustrate why American workers are often identified as winners from import restrictions. Regardless of the reason for restricting imports, the impact of these restrictions on the affected labor markets is the same. Reducing competition in any market drives up the price. When the price for a final product is higher, the marginal

revenue product of labor in that industry is higher, leading to higher levels of employment. Using the auto industry as an example, Figure 4.11 illustrates the impact on both the product and the labor markets that results from imposing a restriction on imported automobiles. This restriction might take the form of a *tariff*, which essentially charges foreign producers a tax for the right to sell their automobiles in the United States. The United States might also set a numerical limit on the number of automobiles a foreign producer is allowed to sell in the United States; such a restriction is called a *quota*. Again, regardless of the form of the trade restriction, the impact on the auto industry labor market will be the same.

Shown in graph (a) of Figure 4.11 is the market for American-made automobiles. Without import restrictions, the demand curve for domestically produced cars is assumed to be D_1, and the industry's supply curve is S_1. The equilibrium price for American-made cars is P_1, and the level of production is Q_1 (point A). Graph (b) shows the industry's demand curve for labor $D(Q_1)$. Given the prevailing wage of W_1 and the level of production of Q_1, the level of employment in the auto industry is L_1 (point X). The imposition of import restrictions on foreign cars would be predicted to have several effects on the domestic auto industry. By either artificially restricting the availability of foreign cars through quotas or artificially raising the price of foreign cars through tariffs, demand for American-produced autos would increase, shown in graph (a) by the rightward shift of the demand curve from D_1 to D_2. (The size of this increase in demand hinges crucially on the degree to which foreign and American cars are substitutes in consumption.) At the new equilibrium (point B), output of American cars increases from Q_1 to Q_2, and their price rises from P_1 to P_2. Given the increase in sales from Q_1 to Q_2, the industry's demand for labor would also

---

1 These arguments (and their counterarguments) as well as other arguments often given for restricting trade are dealt with in great detail in Beth V. Yarbrough and Robert M. Yarbrough, *The World Economy: Trade and Finance* 6th ed. (Mason, Ohio: South-Western/Thomson, 2003), Chapter 8.

FIGURE 4.11   THE EFFECT OF IMPORT RESTRICTIONS ON AUTO EMPLOYMENT

An import restriction on foreign-made cars shifts the demand curve for American autos from D_1 to D_2 in graph (a), leading to a rise in price to P_2 and in level of sales to Q_2. The increase in production in the domestic auto industry results in a rightward shift of the industry's labor demand curve from $D(Q_1)$ to $D(Q_2)$ in graph (b). At the prevailing wage of W_1, auto employment increases from L_1 to L_2.

(a) Product Market

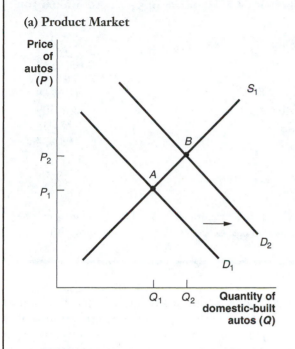

(b) Labor Market

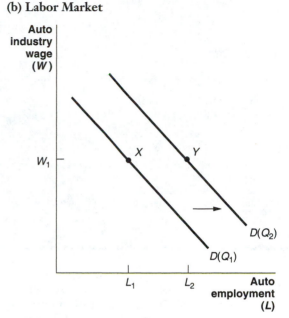

increase, illustrated in graph (b) by the rightward shift of the labor demand curve from $D(Q_1)$ to $D(Q_2)$. At the prevailing union wage of W_1, employment in the auto industry would increase from L_1 to L_2 (point X to Y).

This simple model predicts that import restrictions would lead to higher output, higher prices, and higher employment in the domestic auto industry. Gary Hufbauer and Kimberly Ann Elliott have estimated the impact that import restrictions had on employment and prices in a variety of U.S. industries, based on trade restrictions that were in place in 1990.[2] Table 4.4 shows how much higher prices are (column 1) and how much higher employment is (column 3) as a result of the trade restrictions in place for each industry listed. For example, if Figure 4.11 depicted the sugar industry, $P_2 = (1.66) \times P_1$ (i.e., sugar prices are 66 percent higher as a result of import restrictions)

---

2   The cost of trade restrictions in Japan and China tell a similar story and can be found in Yoko Sazanami et al., *Measuring the Costs of Protection in Japan* (Washington, D.C.: Institute for International Economics, January 1995), and Zhang Shuguang et al., *Measuring the Cost of Protection in China* (Washington, D.C.: Institute for International Economics, November 1998).

	IMPACT OF IMPORT RESTRICTIONS ON PRICE AND EMPLOYMENT IN SEVEN INDUSTRIES (IN 2003 DOLLARS)			
TABLE 4.4				
Industry	Percent Price Increase Resulting from Import Restrictions (1)	Total Cost of Import Restrictions to Consumers (millions) (2)	Additional Employment Resulting from Import Restrictions (3)	Cost to Consumers of Each Additional Job (4)
Sugar	66%	$1,968	2,261	$870,411
Canned Tuna	12	106	390	271,794
Costume Jewelry	9	150	1,067	140,581
Women's Footwear	10	545	3,702	147,218
Orange Juice	30	407	609	668,309
Dairy Products	50	1,717	2,378	722,035
Peanuts	50	78	397	196,474

Note that these figures are based on trade restrictions that were in place in 1990.

SOURCE: Constructed from information contained in Gary Clyde Hufbauer and Kimberly Ann Elliott, *Measuring the Costs of Protection in the United States* (Washington, D.C.: Institute for International Economics, January 1994): Appendix I.

and $L_2 = L_1 + 2,261$ (i.e., there were 2,261 more jobs in the sugar industry as a result of import restrictions). So, clearly, the evidence bears out that both prices and employment will be higher in the presence of trade restrictions. Table 4.4 tells another story as well, however. Column 2 sums up the total cost to consumers of the import restrictions in each industry (price increase times the number of consumers plus the loss to those who don't buy the product at the higher price). Dividing this total cost to consumers by the number of additional jobs present as a result of the import restriction yields how much each of those additional jobs is costing the U.S. consumers (reported in column 4). For example, each additional job gained in the sugar industry as a result of import restrictions in that industry would have cost U.S. consumers $870,411. Since the median annual salary of an agricultural worker was approximately $16,000 in

2003, one could easily argue that the import restrictions in the sugar industry are just too costly as a jobs program; it costs more (to consumers) per job gained through import restrictions than workers would lose in the absence of import restrictions.

NAFTA: The Impact

January 1, 2004 marked the ten-year anniversary of the North American Free Trade Agreement (NAFTA). By 2009, NAFTA is supposed to eliminate virtually all tariff and nontariff restrictions among the United States, Canada, and Mexico. The Free Trade Area that NAFTA created is equal in population and production to the European Economic Union. It has merged into one market two of the United States' most important trading partners. (America's largest trading partners are—in terms of dollar value of exports and imports—Canada, Japan, and Mexico.) Not only has the elimination of import restrictions in the United States led to the predicted negative impact on employment in importing sectors detailed in the previous section, but elimination of import restrictions in Canada and Mexico has caused expansion (greater employment) in exporting sectors within the United States. Increasing the possibilities of exporting goods to Canada and Mexico has increased the number of potential consumers, increasing demand for those products, and, in turn, increasing demand for labor in production of those goods. A recent OECD report found that "an increase of 10 percentage points of trade exposure (an adjusted average of exports and imports as percentages of GDP) raises output per person by 4 percentage points."[3] The expected impact of a multieconomy elimination of trade restrictions will differ across each of the economies involved—the impact will necessarily vary by industry, depending on whether the industry is primarily an import-competing industry (an industry competing with products that are imported to the United States), or an export industry (an industry that exports its product). There will be greater overall output which typically translates into greater overall employment levels. Furthermore, the greater competition in the product market will cause an unambiguous drop in prices consumers pay.[4]

So what impact has NAFTA had on the economies of these three countries? The highest estimates of job losses in the United States as a result of NAFTA have been 110,000 per year between 1994 and 2000. During this same time period, however, the United States has created more than two million jobs per year. Much of the job loss is concentrated in manufacturing, but NAFTA is only part of the reason for job losses in that industry—productivity growth is mostly to blame.[5] The jobs that have been created in the United States, at least since the mid 1990s, have been at above-median wages.

The primary concern of Canadians regarding NAFTA was that increased competition would threaten their generous social welfare system. The fear was that, for example, high unemployment insurance benefits would prove to be non-competitive and erode corporate and personal incomes to the degree that popular social programs would no longer be viable. Canadians, however, seem to have resolved the issue through their willingness to pay enough higher taxes to support their social programs. The Canadian labor market has also appeared to withstand greater competition from the South.[6]

The impact of NAFTA was expected to be the greatest for Mexico, a much smaller and more closed economy than either the United States or Canada in the 1980s. Unfortunately, the financial system in Mexico collapsed in the mid-1990s (for reasons unrelated to NAFTA), and the peso (Mexico's currency) lost half of its value against the dollar. This crisis makes it difficult to disentangle any impact of NAFTA on the Mexican economy. In spite of this difficulty, however, most people agree that NAFTA and the source of external markets helped Mexico recover much more quickly than it would have in pre-NAFTA protectionist days. Over the past 10 years, $12 billion have flowed to Mexico, exports grew from $56 billion to $161 billion, and per capita income has risen by 24 percent.[7]

---

3   See Martin Neil Baily, "The Sources of Economic Growth in OECD Countries: A Reveiw Article," *International Productivity Monitor* 7 (Fall 2003): 66–70.

4   Arguments both in favor and against NAFTA are summarized in Mary Burfisher et al., "The Impact of NAFTA on the United States," *Journal of Economic Perspectives* 15 (Winter 2001): 125–44.

5   "Free Trade on Trial Ten Years of NAFTA—Has NAFTA been a success?" *The Economist* (3 January 2004).

6   See Mary Burfisher, "The Impact of NAFTA on the United States," and Michael R. Smith, "What Have the FTA and NAFTA Done to the Canadian Job Market?" *Forum for Social Economics* 30 (Spring 2001): 25–50.

7   Geri Smith and Cristina Lindblad, "Mexico: Was NAFTA Worth it? A Tale of What Free Trade Can and Cannot Do," *BusinessWeek* (22 December 2003): 66. Other research not willing to blame NAFTA for Mexico's economic woes include, Aaron Tornell, et al. "NAFTA and Mexico's Less-than-stellar Performance," *National Bureau of Economic Research Working Paper No. 10289* (2004). For a rather critical editorial on NAFTA and what it should grow up to be, see Jeff Faux, "NAFTA at 10" *The Nation* (2 February 2004).

For Mexico, being involved with NAFTA may have been like learning to swim by jumping into the deep end of a pool, but it is clear that they are learning and have reaped some benefits in the process.

The complete elimination of trade barriers between Canada, the United States, and Mexico will occur in January 2009. By then we should have an even clearer picture of the overall gains to each country from opening their border to the free flow of goods and services.

EMPIRICAL EVIDENCE 4-1

The Motivation behind Union Wage Concessions

A long-standing union policy is "no backward step" on wages and benefits. But there are many examples where unions have nonetheless agreed to some type of cut in compensation. In a sample of negotiated contracts between 1987 and 1991, for example, 38 percent contained wage concessions and 61 percent contained benefit concessions.[1] The reason unions agree to cuts in pay and benefits is because they also care about another important variable—preserving jobs for their members. For example, if demand for the union's labor becomes more elastic, then long-term wage increases will result in greater employment losses than when the contract was originally negotiated. The reason for this is that when labor becomes more elastic, a wage increase of a certain percentage will be accompanied by a decrease in employment by an even larger percentage than originally projected (see footnote 18 in this chapter). In addition, if the demand curve for labor experiences a leftward shift, less labor will be demanded at each wage level, so a union might agree to a lower wage in order to maintain original employment levels.

A study by Linda Bell confirms that an increase in the elasticity of demand and leftward shifts in the demand curve are associated with a greater incidence of contracts that contain wage concessions.[2]

Greater Elasticity of Demand for Labor

One important reason for greater elasticity of demand for labor is increased competition for the sales of a firm's product. As we will see in greater detail in the next chapter, the greater the elasticity of demand for the final product, the greater will be the elasticity of demand for labor. Basically, if the firm faces a highly competitive product market, it cannot as easily pass wage increases on to the consumer; it must reduce employment more severely than if the product market were less competitive and could absorb the higher cost of production. Graphically, the more elastic demand curve D_1 in Figure 4.12 reflects a product market that is more competitive (and

---

1   Joel Cutcher-Gershenfeld, Patrick McHugh, and Donald Power, "Collective Bargaining in Small Firms: Preliminary Evidence of Fundamental Change," *Industrial and Labor Relations Review* 49 (January 1996): 195–212.

2   Linda A. Bell, "Union Wage Concessions in the 1980s: The Importance of Firm-Specific Factors," *Industrial and Labor Relations Review* 48 (January 1995): 258–75. An examination of wage concessions in the auto industry during the late 1970s and early 1980s can be found in Bruce E. Kaufman and Jorge Martinez-Vazquez, "Voting for Wage Concessions: The Case of the 1982 GM–UAW Negotiations," *Industrial and Labor Relations Review* 41 (January 1988): 183–94. Alan B. Krueger and Alexandre Mas, "Strikes, Scabs and Tread Separations: Labor Strife and the Production of Defective Bridgeston/Firestone Tires," *NBER Working Paper* #9524 (February 2003), find that wage concessions themselves can have a demoralizing impact on workers, thus affecting worker productivity.

FIGURE 4.12   THE DEMAND FOR LABOR AND WAGE CONCESSIONS

Empirical evidence shows that unions are more likely to agree to wage concessions when the demand for their labor becomes more elastic and when they face a decrease in overall demand for their labor. A wage increase from W_1 to W_2 results in much greater employment loss when the demand for labor is more elastic (from A to C) as opposed to less elastic (from B to C). In addition, if the demand curve for labor shifts to the left (which could result from a decrease in demand for the firm's final product), the firm demands fewer workers at every wage level (from C to E), leading unions to be much more likely to agree to wage concessions.

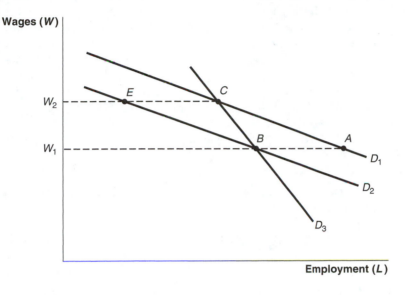

more likely to lead to wage concessions) than the relatively inelastic demand curve D_3, which reflects a product market that is less competitive. A wage increase from W_1 to W_2 will result in a much greater employment loss when the union faces D_1 (from point A to point C) than when the union faces D_3 (from point B to point C). So, a union that finds itself in an industry which is becoming more competitive is more likely to agree to wage concessions.

Leftward Shift in the Demand Curve

If a firm faces a decline in demand for its final product (measured by Bell as a decline in the firm's stock price), the firm's demand for labor will fall as well. The union now faces lower employment at each wage level than before. Graphically, this can be illustrated as a movement from point C to point E in Figure 4.12. In the face of a leftward shift in demand, therefore, not only must the union agree to wage concessions to get employment levels back up, but it is now operating on a more elastic portion of the demand curve (recalling that elasticity increases as one moves up a linear demand curve), which provides additional incentive for wage concessions as explained above.

Summary

This chapter examines the firm's demand for labor in the short run. The most important concept developed here is the demand curve for labor. The demand curve has a negative slope, illustrating that there is an inverse relationship between the wage rate and the number of employees a firm will desire to hire, other things held constant. Based on the marginal productivity theory, the demand curve for labor is shown to be the firm's marginal revenue product schedule. For many economic and public policy issues, the elasticity of the demand curve is also of vital importance. The more elastic is demand, the greater will be the decrease in employment in response to a rise in wage rates.

The demand for labor is affected by more than just wage rates, of course. A second key influence on a firm's desired level of employment is its level of sales. On a year-to-year basis, employment exhibits a distinct cyclical movement associated with the business cycle. Over the longer run, employment among particular industries or sectors of the economy is also heavily influenced by shifting patterns of consumer expenditures. A final consideration is the impact that foreign trade has on domestic employment. Although most attention is focused on the displacement of jobs by imports, the United States also gains thousands of jobs because of exports. Specifically, the multilateral relaxation of import restrictions through NAFTA has resulted in a modest net increase in jobs.

Review Questions

1. Use the marginal productivity theory of labor demand to predict the impact on the firm's employment level of the following events. Explain why the change in employment occurs and show it in a graph.
   a. A decrease in the wage rate
   b. An increase in the demand for the firm's product
   c. A lower tariff on imported goods
   d. The conversion of the firm from a perfectly competitive firm to a monopolistically competitive firm

2. State whether items a–d are true, false, or uncertain, and briefly explain why.
   a. Diminishing marginal productivity of labor begins when the total product curve reaches a peak and then declines.
   b. If the labor demand curve is inelastic, lowering the wage rate will result in a decrease in the firm's wage bill.
   c. Since skilled workers are paid a higher wage than the less skilled, the firm has an incentive to lay off the skilled workers first during a recession.
   d. Whether or not a college student had been elected to office in the student government is a useful screening device for employers.

3. Employers urge labor unions to accept wage concessions as a means to increase jobs. For a union to do so, however, usually requires approval by a majority of the membership. Given this situation, if a layoff caused 30 percent of the membership to lose their jobs, would the union vote for a wage concession? How large would the layoff have to be before the union would accept a concession? What influence does the elasticity of demand have on the size of the wage concession that the union would have to agree to in order to preserve the jobs of its members? If demand were highly

inelastic, how would this affect the union's attitude toward a concession?

4. Employment in the government sector grew by roughly 140 percent between 1960 and 2003. Can you explain this rapid growth based on what you think is the likely elasticity of the labor demand curve for government workers, the income elasticity of demand for government services, and the cyclical sensitivity of government employment?

5. Until recently, the only manufacturer of large motorcycles in the United States was the Harley-Davidson Company. The company's market share dropped precipitously in the late 1970s and early 1980s due to greater competition from Japanese producers. After several years of losses, the company announced it would soon close down, with the loss of several hundred jobs. In response, Congress passed a bill that significantly raised the tariff on large motorcycles imported from other countries. What effect would this bill have on employment at Harley-Davidson? Show this in a graph. Who were the winners and losers from this legislation?

6. Some city governments require that all city employees live within the city limits. What impact does this have on the elasticity of demand for employees of a city government with such a requirement?

7. The production function that generated the data in Table 4.1 is $Q = L + 10L^2 - L^3$. One can imagine that technological advancements might alter how much output is generated by each unit of labor, essentially increasing the productivity of workers. Suppose the production function becomes $Q = 5L + 10L^2 - L^3$.

a. Reconstruct Table 4.1 using this new production function. At a wage rate of $40, the optimal amount of labor to hire was 6 workers. These workers produced 150 units of output. Suppose the firm still want to produce 150 units of output.

b. How many workers does the firm have to hire to produce 150 units?

c. What wage rate would the firm be willing to pay? How did you figure this out?

d. Use what you've learned in answering a–c to provide a potential explanation for why employment in manufacturing (which has experienced an annual 4.3 percent increase in worker productivity between 1995–2000) has declined and why employment in educational services (which experienced a 0.5 percent annual decrease in productivity) has increased.

The Short-Run Equilibrium Level of Employment

The equilibrium condition for employment given in the text as Equation 4.2 can be derived mathematically. In the short run, it is assumed that labor (L) is the only variable input. So the firm's problem is to choose the level of L that will maximize profit. Profit is given by:

$$\pi = P \cdot Q - W \cdot L \qquad (4A.1)$$

where π represents profit, P is the product price (assumed fixed because of competition in the product market), Q is output, w is the wage rate (assumed fixed because of competition in the labor market), and L is the level of employment. Replacing Q with the production function (remembering that K is fixed because this is the short run):

$$\pi = P \cdot f(K, L) - W \cdot L \qquad (4A.2)$$

The level of employment that maximizes profit is found by partially differentiating Equation 4A.2 and then solving the resulting first-order condition:

$$P \frac{\partial f}{\partial L} - W = 0 \qquad (4A.3)$$

The term $\partial f / \partial L$ indicates how much additional output is generated by an additional worker. Thus, it represents the *marginal product of labor* (MP_L). Since the product market is assumed to be competitive, P is equal to the *marginal revenue* (MR). And, since the labor market is assumed to be competitive, W is the additional cost of a labor unit, regardless of how much labor is hired.

Rearranging the terms of the first order condition (4A.3) and rewriting based on the definitions of MR, MP_L and MRP_L:

$$P \frac{\partial f}{\partial L} = W, \text{ or} \qquad (4A.3')$$

$$MR \cdot MP_L = W, \text{ or} \qquad (4A.3'')$$

$$MRP_L = W. \qquad (4A.3'')$$

Therefore, the level of employment that equates MRP_L with the wage rate is the level of employment that will maximize profit.

The Demand for Labor in the Long Run

This chapter examines the demand for labor in the long run. The distinctive feature of the long run is a sufficiently long period of time for the firm to vary the amounts of *both* labor and capital in response to changes in factor prices, product demand, and technology. This ability to substitute between capital and labor raises a number of important issues with respect to the demand for labor. One that has received wide attention is the impact that capital/labor substitution has on the elasticity of labor demand. Not surprisingly, it can be shown that an increase in the cost of labor will lead to a much larger decline in employment in the long run than in the short run, when capital is fixed. A second important issue is the impact that technological change and productivity growth have on the level of employment in the economy. Over time technological change and productivity growth continuously reduce the amount of labor needed to produce a unit of output. Does this mean that new technology will lead to growing unemployment as robots and computers replace humans? Fortunately, the answer is no, for reasons that are explained in this chapter.

The Pattern of Capital/Labor Substitution

A business firm can use many different combinations of capital and labor in producing its product. Which combination will it choose? This is the central issue that the theory presented in this chapter attempts to answer. Before developing this theory, it is important first to gain a better perspective of the facts to be explained.

Figure 5.1 shows data on the *capital/labor ratio* for 10 industries in 1970 and 2001. The capital/labor ratio measures the dollar amount of capital (plant and equipment) used in production relative to each employed worker. The capital/labor ratio varies tremendously among industries. Petroleum refining and communications, for example, are highly capital intensive, while apparel and construction are quite labor intensive. One important reason for this difference is

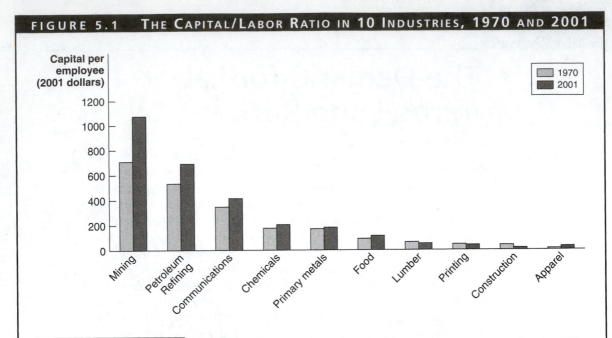

FIGURE 5.1 THE CAPITAL/LABOR RATIO IN 10 INDUSTRIES, 1970 AND 2001

Capital per employee (2001 dollars)

1970
2001

Industries: Mining, Petroleum Refining, Communications, Chemicals, Primary metals, Food, Lumber, Printing, Construction, Apparel

SOURCE: Bureau of the Census, *Statistical Abstract of the United States* (Washington, D.C.: Government Printing Office, 2003 [table 766] and Bureau of Labor Statistics, *Employment and Earnings* (2002, table 18); Bureau of Labor Statistics, *Employment and Earnings* (March 1971, table B-2). Dollar figures are in 2001 dollars.

the technology of production. The current state of technology in petroleum refining requires gasoline to be produced with large amounts of capital in the form of oil crackers and distillers. The production of a woman's dress, on the other hand, requires large amounts of hand labor for cutting, stitching, and fitting.

While technology places important constraints on the proportions of capital and labor used in production, it would be a mistake to conclude that a firm has no choice in this matter. In general, quite the opposite is true. This is most starkly revealed by comparing how particular products are made in the United States relative to other countries, particularly third-world countries, where the cost of labor is much lower. Whether in a capital-intensive industry such as petroleum refining or a labor-intensive industry such as apparel, producers in less-developed countries adapt to the high costs of capital and low price of labor by conserving on the use of machinery and utilizing additional labor. Thus, on a Chinese construction site, bricks and dirt are carried by hand or pushcart, while in the United States bulldozers and forklift trucks do the same tasks. Likewise, cars produced in the United States are welded by robots, while cars produced in Mexico are welded by humans.

Since technology generally affords a firm a "menu of choice" as to the proportion of capital and labor it uses, the exact proportion chosen will be significantly influenced by the relative prices of the two inputs. Over time, wages in the United States have risen faster than the costs of capital, causing firms to substitute capital for labor. This process is revealed in Figure 5.1 by the rise in the capital/labor ratio between 1970 and 2001. The shift was most pronounced in petroleum refining, where the amount of capital per employee hour more than doubled.

This discussion points out two central issues that the theory of labor demand must address: first, what determines at a point in time the optimal mix of capital and labor in production, and second, how does this optimal mix of capital and labor change over time as wages and the cost of capital change? These questions are answered in the next several sections of this chapter.

The Theory of Labor Demand in the Long Run

The previous chapter derived the firm's short-run demand curve for labor under the assumption that the amount of capital was fixed. In this section the theory is extended to cover the long run when both capital and labor are variable.

The Technology of Production: Isoquants

The goal of the firm is to produce the level of output that maximizes profits. To accomplish this, the firm must decide on the least-cost production method and, in particular, on the appropriate combination of capital and labor. This decision is influenced by two considerations: the first is the constraints that technology places on the mix of capital and labor, and the second is the relative prices of the factor inputs.

The technology of production is embodied in the firm's production function. As discussed in the previous chapter, each firm has a production function of the form:

$$Q = f(K, L), \tag{5.1}$$

which expresses the relationship between the level of capital and labor inputs and the maximum obtainable level of output, given the current state of technology. It is possible to use the production function to illustrate graphically the alternative production processes that current technology makes available to the firm. This is shown in Figure 5.2.

The production function states, for example, that if K_1 amount of capital and L_1 amount of labor are used by the firm, the resulting level of output will be Q_1 (point A). Similarly, if capital and labor are increased to K_2 and L_2, respectively, output would increase to Q_2 (point B). A further increase to K_3 and L_3 would yield Q_3 (point C). The production function thus shows the relationship between increases in capital and labor and increases in output, represented by the movement from point A to B to C. It can also be used to answer a different type of question, however. Returning to point A, if K_1 units of capital and L_1 units of labor can

FIGURE 5.2   A SET OF ISOQUANTS

The curves Q_1, Q_2, and Q_3 are isoquants. Each curve shows the alternative combinations of capital and labor that can produce a given level of output. The slope of an isoquant measures the marginal rate of technical substitution (*MRTS*)—the rate at which labor can be substituted for capital while keeping output constant.

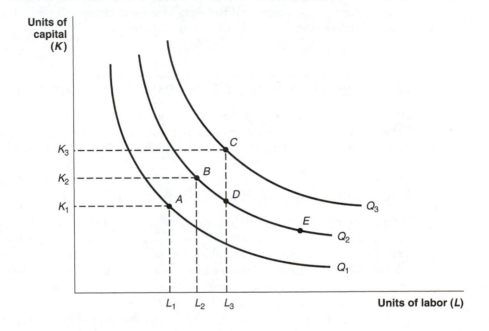

produce Q_1 units of output, could any *other* combinations of capital and labor also produce Q_1? In general the answer is yes, as illustrated by Q_1, the curve that passes through point A. The curve is called an **isoquant;** it shows all the various combinations of capital and labor that are just able to produce a given level of output.

An important feature of isoquants is that they are convex to the origin. The reasoning is much the same as for indifference curves. In moving from point B to point D along isoquant Q_2, labor must be increased by $L_3 - L_2$ and capital decreased by $K_2 - K_1$. This process of substitution could be repeated, but the question is: To reduce capital usage by the same amount as before but still keep output constant at Q_2, how much more labor would be needed? The answer is that more than an additional amount $L_3 - L_2$ (see point E) will be needed since each worker now has less capital to work with. In general, then, isoquants are convex, giving rise to a diminishing **marginal rate of technical substitution (*MRTS*).** The marginal rate of technical substitution measures the additional amount of capital that is required if labor is changed by one unit and output is kept constant. The *MRTS* is given by the negative of the slope of the isoquant. Moving down an isoquant, the *MRTS* becomes progressively smaller.[1]

For most goods, the technology of production allows at least some room for choice in the exact proportion of capital and labor that is used in production. In some cases, however, the technology is such that capital and labor must be used in strict proportion to each other, allowing one and only one capital/labor ratio in production. Examples include airplanes that require a fixed crew size, or manufacturing equipment (such as a drill press) that requires a fixed number of operators. This type of technology gives rise to right-angled, L-shaped isoquants.[2] This is illustrated in Figure 5.3.

It is assumed that each unit of output requires 0.2 units of labor and 0.1 units of capital. Thus, to produce $Q_1 = 100$ units of output requires $K = 10$ and $L = 20$ (point A); to produce $Q_2 = 200$ units requires the same proportion of capital and labor, but twice as much, $K = 20$ and $L = 40$ (point B). There are several important features about these isoquants. First, for a given level of output there are *zero* substitution possibilities between capital and labor ($MRTS = 0$). Since capital and labor are required in fixed proportions, it is impossible to produce a given level of output with more of one but less of the other. Second, if one factor is held constant, adding more of the other will not increase output at all, as can be seen by starting at point A, and keeping K at 10, but increasing L to 40. The result is no increase in output (point D), since the additional labor has no capital to work with. Finally, also drawn in Figure 5.3 is a ray from the origin through the kink points of the isoquants. The slope of this ray defines the capital/labor ratio necessary for production. In this example, the slope is 0.5.

---

1   Observe that the convexity of the isoquants also gives rise to diminishing marginal productivity of labor in the short run. This can be shown in Figure 5.2 by drawing a horizontal line beginning at K_1 capital and zero labor; to reach each successive isoquant takes ever larger increases in labor.

2   A concept known as the *elasticity of substitution* ($\sigma_{K,L}$) measures the relative curvature of the isoquants and, thus, the degree of substitution possibilities between capital and labor. It is defined (where R is the cost of capital) as:

$$\sigma_{K,L} = \frac{\%\Delta\left(\dfrac{K}{L}\right)}{\%\Delta\left(\dfrac{W}{R}\right)}$$

The greater the curvature of the isoquant, the greater will be the change in the ratio of capital to labor (the numerator) for a given percentage change in relative factor prices (the denominator). If the isoquant is L-shaped (fixed proportions and no curvature), $\sigma_{K,L} = 0$. Yu Hsing, "An Empirical Estimation of Regional Production Functions for the U.S. Manufacturing Industry," *Annals of Regional Science* 30 (December 1996): 351–58, estimated an elasticity of substitution of 1.56, indicating a large degree of substitution possibilities between capital and labor in the manufacturing industry. Antonio Ciccone and Giovanni Peri, "Long Run Substitutability Between More and less Educated workers: Evidence from U.S. states 1950–1990," *Mimeo, Universitat Pompeu Fabra* (June 2004), estimate that substitutability between different types of labor is pretty high ($\sigma_{K,L} = 1.5$ in the long run).

FIGURE 5.3

A PRODUCTION TECHNOLOGY WITH ZERO SUBSTITUTION POSSIBILITIES

The L-shaped isoquants Q_1, Q_2, and Q_3 represent a production technology with zero substitution possibilities between capital and labor. In this example, a unit of output requires labor and capital in the proportion of 2:1.

Thus, to produce $Q_1 = 100$, production requires $L = 20$ and $K = 10$. Any less of either L or K means that production would necessarily fall to a lower level, no matter how much of the other input is provided.

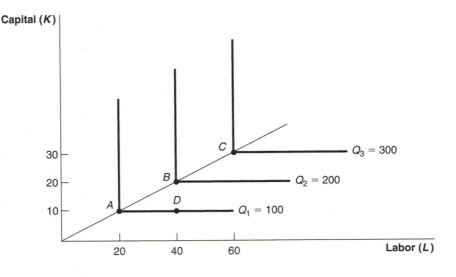

Factor Prices: Isocost Lines

The isoquants show all the possible combinations of labor and capital that a firm could choose to produce a particular level of output. Before the firm can choose the particular combination that would maximize profits, it also has to know what the relative prices of labor and capital are.

At a particular point in time, a going price or "rental rate" will exist for a unit of capital of R_1 dollars and a wage rate for labor of W_1 dollars per hour that the firm must pay for its capital and labor inputs.[3] Given these factor prices, an **isocost line** shows all the various combinations of capital and labor that the firm could purchase with a particular amount of money expenditure. A series of isocost lines AB,

---

[3]   Since the price of labor (the wage) is measured per hour, the price of capital should be similarly measured. To do so, economists assume the hourly cost of capital (R) to be the amount per hour a firm would have to pay to rent the plant and equipment.

FIGURE 5.4 A SET OF ISOCOST LINES

Each isocost line shows all the combinations of capital and labor that can be purchased for a fixed dollar expenditure, given the prices of the two inputs. The slope of an isocost line is equal to the negative of the ratio of factor prices, W/R. An increase in the wage rate will cause an isocost line to rotate to the left, such as from the solid CD to the dashed line AD.

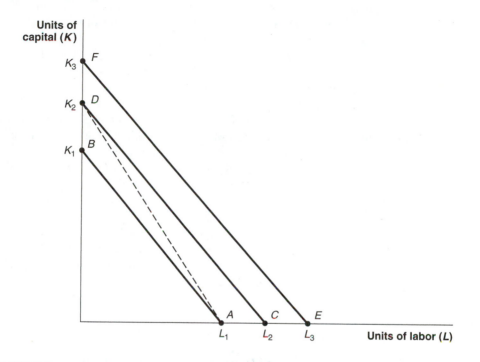

CD, and EF are shown in Figure 5.4. The derivation of the isocost line AB is straightforward. For a given level of expenditure by the firm of E_1 dollars, the total amount of labor that could be hired, given the wage W_1, is $E_1/W_1 = L_1$ workers, shown as point A. Similarly, if the firm spent all E_1 dollars on capital, it could purchase $E_1/R_1 = K_1$ units, shown as point B. Connecting these two points yields a straight line that shows all the other combinations of capital and labor that could just be purchased with E_1 dollars of expenditure.

Several features of isocost lines are important. First, the slope of an isocost line is constant and equal to the (negative) ratio of the factor prices $-W_1/R_1$.[4] Thus, if

---

4 This is shown by using the formula for slope. Slope = rise/run. For an expenditure of E_1, the rise of line AB is $K_1 = E_1/R_1$ and the run is $-L_1 = -E_1/W_1$. The slope, then, is $\dfrac{E_1/R_1}{-E_1/W_1} = \dfrac{-W_1}{R_1}$.

the wage is $10 and the cost of capital is $20, the slope of the isocost line is -0.5, reflecting the fact that to purchase one more unit of capital, two units of labor have to be given up. The slope of an isocost line is constant, reflecting the assumption that the firm can buy as much labor or capital as it desires at the going market prices of W_1 and R_1.

Second, for given factor prices, a higher level of expenditure by the firm on capital and labor will give rise to an entirely new isocost line that is parallel and to the right of the original one. Thus, if the number of dollars budgeted for labor and capital were increased from E_1 to E_2, the total amount of labor that could be purchased would increase to $E_2/W_2 = L_2$ (point C), and total capital purchased could increase to $E_2/R_1 = K_2$ (point D). A still higher expenditure level of E_3 would give rise to the isocost line EF. The isocost lines are parallel to each other since, for a given wage rate and cost of capital, each has the same slope of $-W_1/R_1$.

Finally, if either the price of capital or the wage rate should change, it will give rise to an entirely new set of isocost lines. Given the factor prices W_1, R_1, and an expenditure level of E_2, for example, the isocost line is CD. What would happen to the isocost line, however, if the wage rate rises from W_1 to W_2? Given the same cost of capital, R_1, the firm could still purchase $E_2/R_1 = K_2$ units of capital (point D). At the higher wage of W_2, however, only a smaller $E_2/W_2 = L_1$ units of labor (point A) could be purchased. Connecting points D and A by the broken line gives a new isocost line that is steeper and to the left of the original isocost line DC. The slope of the isocost line DA is steeper, reflecting the higher ratio of factor prices, $-W_2/R_1$. A rise in the wage, therefore, causes the isocost line to *rotate* to the left; a decrease in the wage would cause it to rotate to the right. (How would a decline in the cost of capital change the isocost line?)

The Equilibrium Level of Employment

The isoquants Q_1, Q_2, and Q_3 from Figure 5.2 are combined in Figure 5.5 with the isocost lines AB, CD, and EF from Figure 5.4. To determine its optimal level of employment, the firm has two related decisions or calculations to make. The first decision concerns the optimal level of production for the firm. To maximize profits, should it produce Q_1, Q_2, or Q_3? Given the factor prices of W_1 and R_1, microeconomic theory shows that the profit-maximizing level of output for a competitive firm is where the product price (P) equals the marginal cost of production (MC). For the sake of exposition, assume that $P = MC$ at the output level of Q_2 in Figure 5.5.

Given the choice of Q_2 as the rate of output, the second decision facing the firm is *how* to produce Q_2. This decision involves the following question: What combination of capital and labor would produce Q_2 at *minimum* cost? The answer is given by the tangency between the isocost line CD and the isoquant Q_2 at point X. At point X the firm minimizes the cost of production, since no other combination of capital and labor would allow it to reach a lower isocost line. Point Z, for example, is an alternative way to produce Q_2, but it lies on the higher isocost line

FIGURE 5.5   THE PROFIT-MAXIMIZING COMBINATION OF CAPITAL AND LABOR

The firm must choose the level of output that maximizes profits, and then the combination of capital and labor that produces that level of output at least cost. Assuming that Q_2 is the optimal output level, the least-cost combination of capital and labor is K_1 and L_1, where the isoquant Q_2 and isocost line CD are tangent (point X).

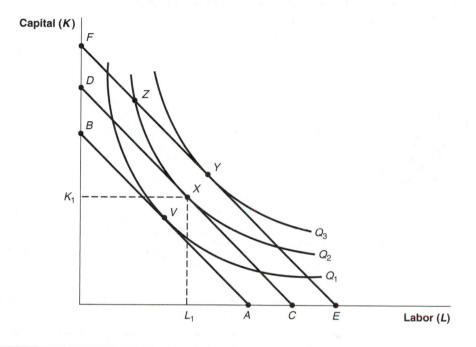

EF. Points V and Y represent the respective cost-minimizing input combinations for producing output levels Q_1 and Q_3 although, by assumption, neither would be the profit-maximizing point of production.[5]

At the tangency of the isoquant Q_2 and the isocost line CD, the slopes of the two lines are just equal. Since the slope of the isocost line is given by the ratio of factor prices W/R (neglecting the minus sign) and the (negative) slope of the isoquant is given by the marginal rate of technical substitution, $MRTS$, the minimum-cost combination of capital and labor is given by the following equilibrium condition:

$$MRTS = \frac{W}{R} \tag{5.2}$$

---

[5]   Connecting points V, X, and Y yields the firm's *expansion path*. The expansion path shows all the combinations of capital and labor that minimize the cost of producing alternative levels of output such as Q_1, Q_2, and Q_3.

The rise in the wage causes the firm's demand for labor to fall from L_1 to L_2 (point X to Y) in the short run due to the scale effect as the firm cuts back its production level from Q_1 to Q_2. In the long run, the firm is able to substitute capital for labor in the production of Q_2, leading to a further decline in labor demand from L_2 to L_3 (point Y to Z) due to the substitution effect.

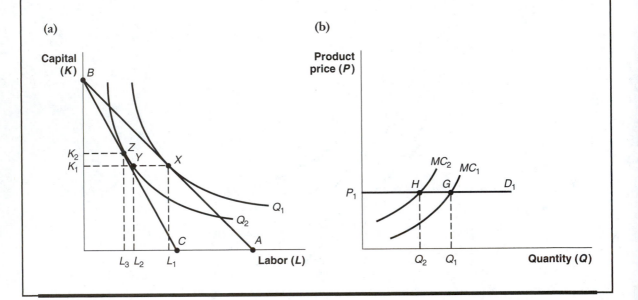

(a)

(b)

Using this equilibrium condition, the firm in Figure 5.5 would minimize cost by employing L_1 workers and K_1 amount of capital.

A Change in the Wage Rate

The next issue concerns how the firm's desired level of employment will change if the cost of labor should change. This is illustrated in Figure 5.6, graphs (a) and (b). To make the graphic presentation simpler, only the conditions for cost minimization (rather than profit maximization) are analyzed.

To begin, assume that the wage rate is W_1 and cost of capital is R_1, giving rise to the isocost line AB in graph (a). The tangency point between the isoquant Q_1 and the isocost line AB (point X) yields the firm's least-cost level of employment L_1. Graph (b) shows the horizontal product demand curve of a perfectly competitive firm D_1 and its marginal cost curve MC_1. As stated before, the competitive firm will produce the output where $P = MC$; in graph (b), this occurs at the output level Q_1 (point G), given the prevailing price in the market of P_1.

Assume now that the wage rate increases from W_1 to W_2, the cost of capital remaining constant at R_1. What will be the impact on the firm's demand for labor? In answering this question, the adjustment process is broken into two discrete steps: the initial change in labor demand when capital is fixed in the short run, and the further change in labor demand when capital becomes a variable input in the long run.

A rise in the wage rate from W_1 to W_2 rotates the isocost line to the left in graph (a), from AB to CB. Given the higher cost of labor, the firm has to reconsider what its optimal level of output is. Assuming the wage increase is isolated to this particular firm, the impact on the firm's level of output is shown in graph (b). A rise in the wage will increase the firm's costs of production, shifting its marginal cost curve to the left, from MC_1 to MC_2. At the going market price of P_1, this rise in production cost causes the firm to lower its level or "scale" of production from Q_1 to Q_2 (point G to H), where $P_1 = MC_2$.

The initial impact of an increase in the wage rate, therefore, is to reduce the firm's level of output, in this case from Q_1 to Q_2. Reduction in the level of production also leads to a decline in the firm's demand for labor. This is illustrated in graph (a). The original level of labor demand was L_1 (point X). By increasing production costs, the higher wage of W_2 makes this firm less competitive in the product market, forcing it to reduce output to Q_2. In graph (a), therefore, the isoquant Q_2 becomes the new level of production. Given this, the firm must then decide on the least-cost combination of capital and labor to produce Q_2. In the short run, this decision is constrained by the fact that the amount of capital is fixed at K_1. Thus, in the short run, the firm's optimal level of employment falls from L_1 (point X) to L_2 (point Y), where the input combination of K_1, L_2 is just able to produce the new output level Q_2.

Point Y is *not* a long-run equilibrium point, however, because it does not produce the output level Q_2 at minimum cost (it is not on the isocost line CB). Given the higher wage of W_2, the cost-minimizing combination of capital and labor to produce Q_2 is given by the condition $MRTS = W_2/R_1$. This occurs at point Z, where the isoquant Q_2 and the isocost line CB are tangent. In the short run the firm is constrained to use K_1 amount of capital and thus cannot reach point Z. In the long run, however, the higher price of labor will induce the firm to substitute capital for labor in producing Q_2, increasing capital to K_2 but reducing labor still further to L_3.[6]

The decrease in labor demand from L_1 to L_3 in graph (a) can be decomposed conceptually into two separate parts. The first impact of a rise in the wage is to

---

6   Point Z represents a position of long-run cost minimization, but it is not the firm's ultimate point of profit maximization. This is because the movement from point Y to Z reduces the firm's marginal costs of production, making the profit-maximizing level of output greater than Q_2 (but still less than Q_1). After all adjustments are complete, therefore, the scale effect will be smaller than indicated in Figure 5.6.

cause the firm to reduce its level or scale of production from Q_1 to Q_2 and, thus, its demand for labor. This decline in labor demand due to the decrease in the level of production is known as the **scale effect.** Graphically, the scale effect is measured as the *shift* from one isoquant to another. In graph (a), the scale effect is measured by the decline in labor demand from L_1 to L_2 (point X to point Y).

An increase in the wage rate also leads to a second adjustment in the firm's demand for labor. For any given level of output such as Q_2, the change in relative factor prices will cause the firm to substitute capital for labor in the long run. The resulting change in labor demand due to capital/labor substitution is known as the **substitution effect.** Graphically, the substitution effect is measured by the *movement along* an isoquant, such as from point Y to point Z on Q_2. It shows that even if the scale of production did not change, a wage increase would cause a decrease in labor demand $L_2 - L_3$ from the decision of the firm to utilize more capital and less labor in the production process.

The Long-Run Demand Curve for Labor

Figure 5.6 can be used to derive the firm's short-run and long-run demand curves for labor. At the original equilibrium (point X), the wage rate was W_1 and the level of employment in the firm was L_1. This combination of wage rate and level of employment is plotted as point X in Figure 5.7. By increasing the wage to W_2, Figure 5.6 shows that in the short run the scale effect causes the firm to reduce employment to L_2 (point Y). This combination of W_2 and L_2 is then plotted in Figure 5.7 as point Y. Connecting points X and Y yields the firm's *short-run* demand curve for labor D_S.

In the long run, the rise in the wage to W_2 provides an incentive for the firm to reduce its employment even further by substituting capital for labor. This was shown in Figure 5.6 by the substitution effect as labor demand declined from L_2 to L_3. In Figure 5.7, at W_2 the short-run demand for labor is L_2 (point Y), but in the

➲ **SEE**

Policy Application 5-1:
Employment
Forecasting, p. 246.

long run the demand for labor is only L_3 (point Z). Connecting points X and Z yields the **long-run demand curve for labor** D_L. It shows that in response to the rise in the wage from W_1 to W_2, the demand for labor in the long run declines from L_1 (point X) to L_3 (point Z). This decline in employment is made up of two components: the short-run decrease from L_1 to L_2 because of the scale effect, and the additional decline from L_2 to L_3 because of the substitution effect. Consideration of both scale and substitution effects is crucial for projecting employment into the future, as is discussed in Policy Application 5-1.

The most important point to notice from Figure 5.7 is that the long-run demand curve is more elastic than the short-run demand curve. In the short run the firm's ability to adjust to a wage increase is limited because it is locked into a fixed amount of capital. In the long run, however, the ability to change not only the level of production but also the amount of capital provides the firm with much more

FIGURE 5.7   THE LONG-RUN AND SHORT-RUN DEMAND CURVES FOR LABOR

The long-run labor demand curve D_L is more elastic than the short-run demand curve D_S. A rise in the wage from W_1 to W_2 leads to a decline in labor demand in the short run from L_1 to L_2 (point X to Y) due to the scale effect. In the long run, however, labor demand declines further from L_2 to L_3 (point Y to Z) due to the substitution effect.

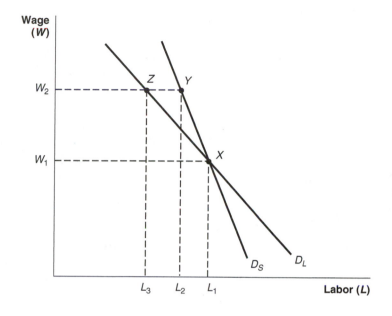

flexibility in adapting to higher or lower wages, resulting in a demand curve for labor that is more sensitive to changes in wage costs in the long run than in the short run.

Economists Martin Falk and Bertrand Koebel estimate a short-run elasticity for the demand for labor in German manufacturing of −0.09; a 10 percent increase in the wage of manufacturing workers results in a 0.9 percent decrease in employment.[7] They estimated a larger −0.21 long-run elasticity of demand, more than double the short-run elasticity.[8]

7   Martin Falk and Bertrand Koebel, "A Dynamic Heterogeneous Labor Demand Model for German Manufacturing," *Applied Economics* 33 (February 2001): 339–48.

8   Timothy Dunne and Mark J. Roberts, "The Long-Run Demand for Labor: Estimates from Census Establishment Data," Center for Economic Studies, U.S. Bureau of the Census Working Paper #CES93-13 (September 1993).

The Determinants of the Elasticity of Labor Demand

The elasticity of labor demand is one of the most important concepts in labor economics because it is at the center of so many economic and public policy issues. For example: How much will an increase in the minimum wage cause firms to cut back on employment? To what extent will a wage subsidy program stimulate new jobs? If unions push up wages, how many of their members will lose their jobs as a result? The answer to all of these questions depends on the sensitivity of employment to wage rates.

Economists have identified four specific factors known as the **four laws of derived demand** that determine the relative size of the elasticity of labor demand.[9] These four laws state that the demand for labor, other things equal, will be *more* elastic:

1. The larger the price elasticity of demand for the product being produced.

2. The greater the share of labor cost as a percentage of the total cost of production.

3. The greater the ease of substitution in production between labor and other factor inputs such as capital.

4. The greater the elasticity of supply of other competing factors of production.

The reasoning behind each of these four laws is briefly explained below.

Demand for the Final Product

Will the demand for labor in a particular industry or occupation be elastic or inelastic? In answering this question, the price elasticity of demand for the product is of crucial importance. The reason is that an increase in wages immediately results in higher costs of production, causing firms to raise the price of their product in order to maintain profit margins. As the price of the product goes up, consumers buy less of it. If the demand for the product is very elastic, the result of this price increase will be a large decrease in sales and hence a relatively large decrease in the demand for labor.

This first law of derived demand affects the elasticity of labor demand through the scale effect, because, in this case, the impact of a wage change is felt through a change in the level of production. The more elastic the demand curve for the product, the greater will be the decrease in employment due to an increase in the wage rate. In terms of Figure 5.6, this means that the short-run decrease in employment

---

9   See John R. Hicks, *The Theory of Wages*, 2d ed. (New York: St. Martin's Press, 1963), 241–47.

from point X to point Y will be relatively large as the firm is forced by the substantial decline in sales to produce on a much lower isoquant. In Figure 5.7, in turn, the larger the scale effect, the more elastic will be both the short-run and long-run demand curves for labor.

This law of derived demand has several important implications. The first is that the demand curve for labor for the individual firm will be more elastic, other things equal, the more competitive the product market in which it operates. The reason is that the greater the number of firms selling a particular product, the greater the ability of consumers to switch their purchases from one company to another, making each company's product demand curve more sensitive to the price it charges. This is why, as shown in Chapter 4, the labor demand curve for an imperfectly competitive firm is more inelastic than that of a perfectly competitive firm.

This result helps explain, for example, why unions in the 1970s were able to push up wages more rapidly in oligopolistic industries such as autos and steel and in regulated industries such as trucking and airlines.[10] In both situations, either large economies of scale or government restrictions on entry resulted in only a relatively small number of firms in each industry or market, reducing consumers' substitution possibilities and, as a result, making the demand curve for labor in each industry more inelastic. The more inelastic the labor demand curve, in turn, the smaller will be the employment loss for a union as it raises wages.

A second implication of this law of derived demand is that, as shown in Chapter 4, the labor demand curve for an entire industry should be less elastic than the labor demand curve for any one individual firm in the industry. A rise in wages by one tire manufacturer, for example, would increase its production costs, forcing it to raise tire prices. Since one brand of tire is a close substitute for another brand, the tire manufacturer with higher prices would suffer a significant decline in sales and employment as customers switched to its lower-cost rivals. Should all tire producers increase wages, however, the resulting rise in tire prices would have a much smaller impact on sales, since consumers now have few viable substitutes. Thus, because there are fewer substitutes for tires in general than for one particular brand of tire, a wage increase throughout the industry will have a smaller relative effect on employment than if the wage increase were isolated to one individual firm.

The Share of Labor in Total Cost

The second law of derived demand concerns the share of labor cost as a percentage of the total cost of production. It also influences labor demand through the scale effect. A rise in wages, as discussed previously, causes production costs and the price of the product to rise, reducing sales and the demand for labor. The actual impact of

---

10   This is shown in Bruce E. Kaufman and Paula E. Stephan, "The Determinants of Interindustry Wage Growth in the Seventies," *Industrial Relations* 26 (Spring 1987): 186–94. This result also helps explain the positive relationship estimated between growth in firm profits and wage growth; see Steven G. Allen, "Updated Notes on the Interindustry Wage Structure, 1890–1990," *Industrial and Labor Relations Review* 48 (January 1995): 305–21.

a rise in wages on production costs depends on how high labor costs are relative to other costs of production. In capital-intensive industries such as petroleum refining, labor cost is a small fraction of the total cost of refining a barrel of oil. In this case, a 20 percent increase in wages for refinery workers would have a relatively small impact on the level of employment since total production costs and the price of refined oil would not be much affected. In labor-intensive industries such as apparel, however, the demand for labor is likely to be much more elastic, since the same 20 percent increase in wages would boost total costs considerably more, resulting in much higher prices, lower sales, and a relatively large decrease in employment.[11]

One implication of this second law of derived demand is that the firm's labor demand curve for a narrowly defined occupation or craft will be more inelastic than that for all employees in general. As an example, consider the case of movie and television actors. Movie and television actors are represented by the Screen Actors Guild, a craft union that limits its membership to actors.[12] While labor costs in general represent a sizable share of total costs for studios and television networks, the cost of actors themselves relative to total costs is much smaller. As a result, the impact on the employment of actors from a wage increase will be much smaller than if the guild were an industrial union that bargained the same wage increase for *all* studio and network employees. It is thus to the advantage of the guild and the actors it represents to restrict its membership to a narrowly defined occupation so that the disemployment effect of raising wages is reduced. (This is sometimes called the "importance of being unimportant.") The same conclusion applies to other craft unions such as airline pilots, painters, carpenters, and plant guards.

Substitutability of Other Factor Inputs

An increase in the wage rate causes a reduction in the short-run demand for labor because of the scale effect. In the long run, the demand for labor will decline even more as capital is substituted for labor. The greater this substitution effect is, in turn, the more elastic will be the long-run labor demand curve.

The ease of substitution between capital and labor is determined by both technological and institutional constraints. The technological ability to substitute between capital and labor in production is reflected in the relative curvature of the isoquants; the more sharply curved the isoquant, the less able the firm is to substitute one factor input for another. Thus, if the technology of production is such that only one combination of capital and labor is able to produce a particular level of output, such as that pictured by the L-shaped isoquants in Figure 5.3, there will be a scale effect but no substitution effect from a wage increase, causing the long-run

---

11   J. R. Hicks (*The Theory of Wages*) has shown that this prediction may not always hold. In particular, this prediction is reversed when there are small substitution possibilities in consumption, but large substitution possibilities in production.

12   A craft union organizes workers who have a particular skill or occupation (such as plumbers); an industrial union organizes workers of all skills in a particular industry (such as autoworkers).

demand curve for labor to be relatively inelastic (but *not* completely inelastic). On the other hand, because of the greater ease of substitution between low-skilled workers and capital (as opposed to high-skilled workers and capital), the elasticity of demand for low-skilled workers is estimated to be greater than that estimated for high-skilled workers.[13]

An excellent example of how differences in the ease of substitution between capital and labor can affect the elasticity of labor demand is provided by farm laborers and movie actors. A wide range of possible combinations of capital and labor can be used by a landowner to produce a crop such as wheat. When wages are low relative to the price of capital, planting and harvesting will be done by hand, with only the simplest of tools. Should wages of farm laborers rise, the farmer is motivated to mechanize farm production, replacing labor with machinery. The ease of substitution between capital and labor in agriculture thus makes the long-run demand curve for farm labor relatively elastic. The opposite case is provided by movie actors. As wages rise for actors, movie production studios would like to replace labor with capital much as wheat growers have done. Are they able to do so? While animation (mechanically produced images) may provide some substitution for the entertainment provided by actors, that substitution possibility is limited. What would be expected, therefore, is that an equal increase in wages for farm laborers and actors, other things being equal, would result in a much larger decline in employment for the farm laborers because of the easier substitution possibilities in agriculture.

Substitution possibilities between capital and labor and between different types of labor (for example, union versus nonunion labor) are also constrained by institutional rules such as union work rules, and government safety regulations. As one example, railroads switched from steam to diesel locomotives partly because of the potential savings in labor; diesel locomotives do not need firemen. The railway craft unions, however, successfully bargained for work rules that required the railroads to keep firemen on the trains, preventing the substitution of capital for labor.

A second example concerns union work rules. If wages of unionized workers increase relative to those of nonunion workers, firms have an incentive to substitute from the former to the latter. To limit the disemployment effect on their members, therefore, unions have frequently negotiated contracts mandating the firm to operate a "union shop." A union shop clause mandates that upon 30 days from being hired a worker must join the union as a condition of continued employment, diminishing the ability of employers to substitute nonunion labor for union labor. Substitution possibilities under a union shop agreement are still not zero, however, since in the long run the firm can build new plants in less-unionized states or states with "right-to-work" laws (laws that make union shop requirements illegal). Unions can also limit substitutability by negotiating contracts that specify the number of workers assigned to operate specific equipment.[14]

---

13   See Martin Falk and Bertrand Koebel, "A Dynamic Heterogenous Labour Demand Model for German Manufacturing," *Applied Economics* 33 (February 2001): 339–48.

14   See Jurgen Jerger and Jochen Michaelis, "On the Employment Effect of Manning Rules," *Journal of Institutional and Theoretical Economics* 153 (September 1997): 545–68.

Government safety regulations can also reduce the firm's ability to substitute between capital and labor. One example is in the airline industry. Before airlines could fly the new generation of jets (the Boeing 757 and the McDonnell Douglas DC-9 Super 80) that required only two pilots, the planes had to obtain safety certification from the Federal Aviation Administration (FAA). While certification was ultimately granted, the Airline Pilots Association actively lobbied against it, delaying certification for several years.[15]

The Elasticity of Supply of Other Factor Inputs

The fourth law of derived demand concerns the elasticity of supply of factors of production besides labor. This fourth law also affects the elasticity of labor demand through the substitution effect. As discussed previously, a rise in the wage rate relative to the price of capital motivates the business firm to substitute capital for labor. As the demand for capital increases, this may itself set off a large increase in the price of capital, negating the original desire on the part of the firm to make the substitution of capital for labor. The extent to which the price of capital rises in response to an increase in demand depends on the elasticity of its supply curve; the more inelastic the supply curve, the higher will be the rise in the price of capital and the less strong will be the firm's incentive to substitute away from labor. Thus, the more inelastic are the supply curves of other competing factors of production, the smaller will be the substitution effect for a given wage increase and the smaller the long-run elasticity of labor demand.

The importance of this fourth law is illustrated by the example of airline pilots. Some senior pilots for major carriers earn as much as $300,000 a year. Given the high cost of pilots, airlines have a strong incentive to substitute capital for labor by purchasing new two-pilot planes such as the Boeing 757. The supply curve of these new planes, however, is fairly inelastic, since increases in production are heavily constrained by long lead times for parts and components, as well as by the relatively fixed supply of certain highly skilled workers. If all airlines attempt to purchase these new planes, the large increase in demand will result in a substantial bidding up of the price, eliminating part of the incentive to buy them.

Technological Change and Labor Demand

Over time, the demand for labor is influenced not only by changes in relative factor prices but also by changes in technology. Improvements in the state of technology arise from advances in basic knowledge (for example, genetic engineering) and improved techniques of production (such as robots, word processors, and jumbo jets). Particularly during the 1960s, there was widespread concern over whether the

---

15 This is described in "Do Three Pilots Make a Crowd?" *Business Week* (July 21, 1980): 179–80.

process of technological change, or "automation," would result in rising levels of unemployment in the economy. This concern about automation has given way to a similar concern in the 1990s regarding computers and information technology.[16]

The impact of technological change on employment can be analyzed with the long-run theory of labor demand. Most often, improvements in the state of technology can be incorporated into the production process only through the addition of new capital in the form of more up-to-date plants and equipment. Thus, in the short run the employment of a firm is largely unaffected by technological change because, by definition, the amount of capital is fixed. In the long run, however, the firm has the opportunity not only to substitute between labor and capital but also to replace older, technologically outdated capital with the technologically most advanced capital.

The impact of technological change on the demand for labor is best illustrated in terms of its effect on employment within an industry rather than within a single firm. Assume that each firm in the industry has an identical production function of the form $Q = f(K, L)$ that expresses the relationship between capital and labor inputs and the maximum amount of output that can be obtained, *given the current state of technology*. This production function can be used to generate a series of isoquants, one of which is pictured in Figure 5.8 as $Q_{1,t}$. It represents a level of industry output of Q_1 produced in the current time period t. Given the ratio of factor prices W_1, R_1 in the industry and the resulting isocost line AB, firms minimize costs by producing $Q_{1,t}$ with K_1 units of capital and L_1 units of labor, shown as point X.

Technological change has a two-pronged effect on the demand for labor. The initial effect is to *reduce* the demand for labor as better technology allows firms to produce a given level of output with fewer workers. The second effect is that improved technology results in lower production costs and, thus, lower product prices, increased sales, and a *greater* demand for labor.[17]

The Displacement of Labor by Technological Change

The essence of technological change is that it opens up new, more efficient ways to produce a product with less labor or capital. This effect is represented in Figure 5.8 by the shift toward the origin of the isoquant $Q_{1,t}$ to $Q_{1,t+1}$. The isoquants $Q_{1,t}$ and

---

16   See Chris Freeman and Luc Soete, *Work for All or Mass Unemployment: Computerised Technical Change into the Twenty-First Century* (London: Pinter; New York: St. Martin's Press, 1994).

17   The two-pronged effect of the technological advancements of computers and their widespread integration into almost every occupation in the U.S. economy is illustrated through a series of articles in the *Monthly Labor Review* 119 (August 1996). Specifically, see William C. Goodman, "The Software and Engineering Industries: Threatened by Technological Change?" (pp. 37–45), and Laura Freeman, "Job Creation and the Emerging Home Computer Market" (pp. 46–56). Also see Catherine J. Morrison Paul and Donald S. Siegel, "The Impacts of Technology, Trade, and Outsourcing on Employment and Labor Composition," *Scandinavian Journal of Economics* 103 (June 2001): 241–64; Bruce Weinberg, "Computer Use and the Demand for Female Workers," *Industrial and Labor Relations Review* 53 (January 2000): 290–308; and Martin Falk and Bertrand M. Koebel, "The Impact of Office Machinery, and Computer Capital on the Demand for Heterogeneous Labour," *Labour Economics* 11 (February 2004): 99–117.

FIGURE 5.8   THE EFFECT OF TECHNOLOGICAL CHANGE ON LABOR DEMAND

Technological change shifts the isoquant $Q_{1,t}$ inwards to $Q_{1,t+1}$, illustrating that the same Q_1 level of output can now be produced with less capital and labor (compare points X and Y). The lower costs of production this makes possible, however, result in a lower price and an increase in sales to $Q_{2,t+1}$. The net result is an increase in the demand for capital and labor from point X to Z.

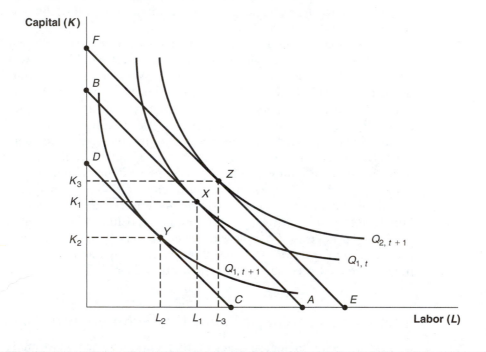

$Q_{1,t+1}$ represent exactly the *same* level of output; the difference is that with the advance in the state of technology, Q_1 can now be produced in period $t+1$ with less labor and capital. If factor prices remained at W_1, R_1, firms in this industry would minimize the costs of producing Q_1 by using only K_2 units of capital and L_2 units of labor, given by the tangency of the isoquant $Q_{1,t+1}$ and the isocost line CD (point Y).

The first impact of technological change, then, is to reduce the demand for labor in the industry from L_1 to L_2 (point X to Y) as firms build new labor-saving plants or install more advanced labor-saving equipment. Although it may seem counterintuitive at first, technological change is also capital saving in many cases, as shown by the decline in capital inputs from K_1 to K_2. One example is the railroad industry. When railroads switched from steam to diesel locomotives, the same number of ton miles of freight service could be produced with less capital since diesels required less time for repairs and could operate over much greater distances without refueling. Similarly, computers have resulted in substantial savings in capital in the trucking industry, since more efficient scheduling permits fewer trucks to haul the same amount of freight. While technological change frequently reduces both the absolute level of capital and labor needed to produce a particular product, the *ratio* of capital to labor may change if technological change has a factor "bias," that is, if it proportionately reduces the use of one input more than the other.

If the only effect of technological change was to continually shift the isoquants in Figure 5.8 toward the origin, over time the economy would need fewer and fewer workers to produce a given level of output. Despite the revolution in technology in the twentieth century, however, the number of jobs in the economy has not decreased but rather has increased by many millions. How can this be accounted for?

Technological Change and Product Demand

It is true that if firms were to produce the level of output of 1900 with the technology of the twenty-first century, only a fraction of the work force would be employed today. However, even as technological change reduces the amount of labor needed *per unit* of output, it also leads to a large expansion of *total* output demanded and thus of labor demanded in the economy.

Technological change leads to an increase both in the sales of the individual industry and in total product demand in the entire economy. Consider first the level of sales in the industry. Beginning microeconomics shows that the average total cost of production puts a floor under the product price that firms can charge if they are to earn a "normal" profit and remain in business in the long run. The effect of technological change, however, is to reduce the unit costs of production, since the same level of output can now be produced with less labor and capital. In a competitive industry, as costs per unit of production fall, competition among firms leads to downward pressure on the price of the product until the price is again just equal to average total cost.[18] This fall in the price is quite important for employment, since it leads to expanded sales in the industry. The extent to which output demand increases depends on the elasticity of the industry's product demand curve; the more elastic it is, the greater will be the increase in sales in response to the fall in price. The effect on labor demand is illustrated in Figure 5.8. The initial impact of technological change shifts the isoquant from $Q_{1,t}$ to $Q_{1,t+1}$, causing a decrease in employment in the industry of $L_1 - L_2$. The fact that Q_1 can now be produced at

---

18 Perhaps the best example of this is the computer industry, where prices per unit of memory have fallen 15 percent to 20 percent a year.

a lower cost, however, leads to a lower price and greater sales in the industry. If the product demand curve is relatively elastic, the increase in sales may be enough to make the isoquant $Q_{2,t+1}$ the new profit-maximizing level of production. Given the same ratio of factor prices, the tangency of the isocost line EF and isoquant $Q_{2,t+1}$ (point Z) yields a new demand for labor of L_3 units and demand for capital of K_3 units. While $L_1 - L_2$ workers initially lost their jobs due to the more efficient technology, the lower prices this made possible resulted in the end in a net *increase* of employment in the industry of $L_3 - L_1$.

It is also possible, however, that employment may decrease. If the elasticity of product demand is relatively low, or alternatively, if, due to a lack of competition in the industry, the cost savings are not passed on in the form of lower prices, the decline in the product price may not generate enough new sales to provide jobs for all the $L_1 - L_2$ workers initially laid off. In this case, the new profit-maximizing isoquant $Q_{2,t+1}$ in Figure 5.8 would lie somewhere in between $Q_{1,t+1}$ and $Q_{1,t}$, and the level of employment would likewise lie somewhere between L_1 and L_2, resulting in a net decline over time in industry employment. Where will these workers who are permanently displaced by the technological change find jobs?

The answer is that technological change, by reducing the price of the industry's product, stimulates more sales not only in the industry itself, but also in many other industries in the economy. A fall in the product price of one good has the effect of increasing the *real* income of every worker in the economy. For a given level of dollar income, a decline in the price of one product means that the consumer can now buy not only more of it, but also more of other products as well, leading to an expansion of sales and in labor demand across numerous industries. The extent to which employment expands in each industry as a result of the higher level of real income depends, as shown in the previous chapter, on the income elasticity of the industry's product demand curve.

The Combined Effect

The net result is that in a particular industry, technological change may or may not lead to a long-run decline in the demand for labor. This is illustrated in Figure 5.9, which shows the long-run industry labor demand curve. At the wage of W_1, assuming the level of output is Q_1, the demand for labor in period t is L_1 (point A). The first impact of technological change is to reduce the labor requirements per unit of output, represented by a leftward shift of the long-run demand curve to $D_{t+1(Q_1)}$. At the same level of output of Q_1, in period $t + 1$ the demand for labor is reduced to L_2 (point B). The second impact of technological change is to reduce per unit costs of production and the price of the industry's product, leading to an increase in sales and the demand for labor. This is represented by the rightward shift of $D_{t+1(Q_1)}$ to $D_{t+1(Q_2)}$, resulting in an increase in employment from L_2 (point B) to L_3 (point C). Whether this subsequent increase in labor demand of $L_3 - L_2$ is enough to offset the initial displacement of labor of $L_1 - L_2$ depends on the extent to which the savings in production cost are passed on to buyers in the

FIGURE 5.9

THE IMPACT OF TECHNOLOGICAL CHANGE ON THE LONG-RUN DEMAND FOR LABOR

Given the wage W_1, the first impact of technological change is to displace labor as better technology enables the firm to produce the same Q_1 units of output with less labor. This shifts the long-run labor demand curve to the left, from $D_{t(Q_1)}$ to $D_{t+1(Q_1)}$. The resulting decline in the production price,

however, stimulates an increase in sales to Q_2, leading to a rightward shift of the labor demand curve to $D_{t+1(Q_2)}$. In this example, sales do not increase enough to offset the original displacement of labor, and employment suffers a net decline of $L_1 - L_3$. The opposite could also occur.

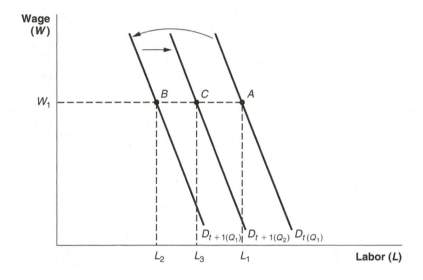

form of lower prices and on the price and income elasticity of the industry's product demand curve. Figure 5.9 assumes a net *decrease* of $L_1 - L_3$ jobs in the industry. Due to higher real incomes of consumers, however, labor demand curves in other industries will also shift to the right, providing jobs in other sectors of the economy to replace those lost because of technological change.

The scenario of events traced out here has a real-world counterpart. As shown in Chapter 4, employment in the goods-producing sector of the economy has grown only slightly over time, while employment in the service sector has boomed. One reason is that the pace of technological change has been greatest in the goods-producing sector, resulting in a significant decline in unit labor requirements. The resulting gains in real income have been disproportionately spent by consumers on services, causing large gains in employment there. The combination of high rates of technological change in goods production and a high income elasticity of

How American Manufacturers Survive the Low-Wage Global Challenge

In 1998 the United States had 17.5 million people employed in the manufacturing sector; six years later, in 2004, the number stood at 14.4 million. Thus, over this brief time span three million jobs in the heartland of the American economy disappeared.

One must first note that manufacturing employment has been on a downward trend in the United States since the end of the 1970s, so the loss of factory jobs in the early 2000s is not a completely new and unprecedented event. What is new, however, is the size and speed of the drop in manufacturing employment. For example, the decline in manufacturing jobs from 1998 to 2004 was almost one-third larger than occurred in the preceding twenty years!

What is going on in American manufacturing? Two things figure quite prominently. The first is the outflow of manufacturing jobs to other countries with lower labor costs. The average wage in American manufacturing is nearly $16 an hour and the total hourly compensation cost is over $21 (counting benefits and other employer payments). Compensation cost per hour in Singapore, by comparison, is 34 percent of the American level, whereas in Mexico it is 12 percent and in Sri Lanka only 2 percent. As a result, American companies have been shifting production overseas at a rapid rate. Nike may be an American company, but most of its shoes are foreign-made.

Although outsourcing of American jobs to foreign countries has garnered considerable news coverage (and criticism from commentators, such as Lou Dobbs on CNN's MoneyLine), most economists consider outsourcing a distinctly secondary cause of the decline in American manufacturing employment. Far more important, they claim, is a central topic of this chapter—the decline of employment that frequently accompanies rapid productivity growth.

The only way American companies can keep manufacturing operations in the United States, when labor costs are ten times (or more) higher than low-wage countries in Asia, Latin America, and Africa, is to get at least ten times as much productivity from every American employee. In this case, the high wage earned by American workers is more than offset by the high output they produce, thus keeping unit production cost of goods "Made in America" competitive with products from overseas.

Because the cost of labor in the United States keeps rising year after year, American companies find themselves in a never-ending race to keep productivity growing just as fast (or faster). Of course, the essence of higher productivity is getting more output per worker, so frequently higher productivity translates into figuring out ways to produce the same output with less labor. In the early 2000s, labor productivity has been rising at an unusually brisk 3–3 1/2 percent rate—about a percentage point higher than many economists expected. While this is extra good news for American companies threatened by low-cost foreign competition, one downside is that higher productivity growth, at least in the short run, translates into lower employment. One estimate, for example, is that a one percentage point gain in productivity means an employment loss of 1.3 million jobs.

How have American manufacturing companies kept labor productivity growing so strongly? One approach is through continued capital investment in new plants and equipment. New information technology is particularly important. One recent news story, for example, showcased how one American factory equipment maker reduced its employment by several thousand workers in just four years, gaining a 14 percent productivity boost. This feat was accomplished, in part, by building several new highly automated plants in which computers control most of the production process—one group of seven machines needs just three workers to run them. Another news article highlighted the role of information technology in allowing companies to reduce inventories to the bare minimum through "just-in-time" procurement practices. Every part bought from outside suppliers is bar-coded and tracked by computers in the production process. When the stock of parts gets to the minimum target level for the current production run, a computer generates a purchase order and sends it electronically to the parts supplier.

A second approach is new "high-performance" work systems and human resource management practices. Companies have organized workers into self-managed teams, thus eliminating one or more layers of supervisors and middle management. Also, the team's duties are expanded to include things such as quality inspection, ordering new supplies, and interviewing job applicants. Another closely related high-performance practice is employee-involvement. Instead of the old tradition of having employees "check their brains at the door," companies today empower workers by giving them more opportunity to voice their opinions and suggestions on ways to make the company more efficient. At a paper mill, for example, the company now has front-line employee representatives meet on a regular basis with the mill's management to make recommendations on all aspects of plant performance and policy. A third example is new forms of compensation that go from the simple wage-per-hour scheme that only rewards employees for the time they put in to different forms of gain-sharing pay plans (e.g., making a portion of the self-managed team's compensation depend on reduction of quality defects) and pay-for-knowledge systems that reward workers for working not only harder but smarter.

A third approach is to use "just-in-time" employment practices to gain extra flexibility and lower cost. Manufacturers, for example, will have a core workforce of full-time employees and then a "buffer" of temporary and contingent workers they can quickly expand or contract as sales and production fluctuate.

These and other innovative practices allow American manufacturing companies to keep their domestic plants competitive with foreign-based operations. The price of competitiveness, however, is a continual search for ways to produce more with less labor. Although this quest for higher productivity frequently means fewer jobs in the short term, the upside is that without productivity growth even *more jobs* would be threatened over the long term.

SOURCES: "The Price of Efficiency," *Business Week* (March 22, 2004): 38–42; "The Bright Side of Sending Jobs Overseas," *New York Times* (February 15, 2004): 3; "The Flexible Factory," *Business Week* (May, 5, 2003): 90–91; "Information Technology and Productivity: Where Are We Now and Where Are We Going?" *Federal Reserve Bank of Atlanta Economic Review* (Third Quarter 2002): 15–44.

demand for services has resulted, therefore, in a fundamental shift in the locus of employment in the economy.

In the long run, technological change is a positive force leading to higher real incomes and growing employment opportunities.[19] Society, therefore, gains from technological progress. Not all of these gains are equally shared, however, and for some workers there are significant costs.[20] The plight of displaced workers and policies designed to assist them are examined in Policy Application 5-2. Several articles detail how technological change in the U.S. manufacturing industry has resulted in a shift in demand away from low-skilled workers toward more highly skilled workers.[21] Workers who are displaced from their jobs by new technology may have to seek work in a completely different industry or occupation. For older workers or workers with families, this transition process may be a difficult one. Many of the new jobs created in service-related industries, for example, pay considerably lower wages than the jobs in manufacturing eliminated by new technology.[22] An additional aspect of technological change is that it frequently imparts a *skill twist* to labor demand, decreasing labor demand for unskilled or semiskilled workers (such as assembly line workers, telephone operators, and stenographers), while increasing the demand for skilled, highly educated workers (for example, robot maintenance workers, computer programmers, and information technology support). One researcher estimates that increased use and adoption of information technology accounted for 40 percent of the acceleration in demand for educated workers since the 1970s.[23] To effectively compete for these new jobs, displaced workers must invest in a new vintage of "human capital" in the form of additional education or vocational training. While younger workers can frequently undertake the financial and emotional burdens of this transition, older workers often cannot, resulting in a serious unemployment problem for this labor force group.[24]

➡ SEE

Policy Application 5-2: Displaced Workers, p. 250.

---

19   See Richard Belous, "Technological Change and Its Effects on Labor Markets," in *Proceedings of the 1986 Spring Meeting* (Madison, Wis.: Industrial Relations and Research Association, 1986): 494–501.

20   See Michael Handel, "Computers and the Wage Structure" *Levy Economics Institute Working Paper No. 285* (October 1999), and Richard Nahuis and Sjak Smulders, "The Skill Premium, Technological Change and Appropriability," *Journal of Economic Growth* 7 (June 2002): 137–56. Also see Joseph R. Meisenheimer II, "The Services Industry in the 'Good' Versus 'Bad' Jobs Debate," *Monthly Labor Review* (February 1998): 22–47, for a more favorable view of the shift toward service industry employment.

21   For example, see Eli Berman, John Bound, and Zvi Griliches, "Changes in the Demand for Skilled Labor within U.S. Manufacturing: Evidence from the Annual Survey of Manufacturers," *Quarterly Journal of Economics* 109 (May 1994): 367–97, and Dominique Goux and Eric Mauin, "The Decline in Demand for Unskilled Labor: An Equilibrium Analysis Method and Its Application to France," *Review of Economics and Statistics* 82 (November 2000): 596–607.

22   See John T. Addison, ed., *Job Displacement: Consequences and Implications for Policy"* (Detroit: Wayne State University Press, 1991).

23   Hyunbae Chun. "Information Technology and the Demand for Educated workers: Disentangling the Impacts of Adoption versus Use," *Review of Economics and Statistics* 85 (February 2003): 1–8.

24   See Leora Friedberg, "The Impact of Technological Change on Older Workers: Evidence from Data on Computer Use," *Industrial and Labor Relations Review* 56 (April 2003): 511–29.

Productivity Growth and the Demand for Labor

The discussion of capital/labor substitution and technological change leads to a third subject—the effect of productivity growth on the demand for labor. The term "productivity" usually refers to **labor productivity,** defined as the amount of output produced in the firm, industry, or economy per employee hour. There are other productivity measures, however, such as *capital productivity* (output per unit of capital input) and *multifactor productivity* (output per unit of a composite of factor input).[25]

An increase in labor productivity means that firms are able to produce each physical unit of output with less labor input. The discussion of the long-run demand for labor provides insight into two of the most important causes of the secular increase in labor productivity. The first is the process of capital/labor substitution that has taken place as wage rates have risen relative to the costs of capital. The price of capital equipment (producer's durable equipment) rose by 248 percent between 1970 and 2003, for example, while wage rates in manufacturing rose by 390 percent. Business firms responded by trying to hold down production costs as much as possible by substituting from labor to capital in production.[26] By doing so the firm produces the same level of output with fewer employee hours, giving rise to an increase in labor productivity. A second important factor leading to increases in labor productivity is technological change. As shown in Figure 5.8, technological change allows the firm to produce the same level of output with less labor, leading to an increase in output per worker and, thus, in labor productivity.

The initial impact of the rising relative price of labor and the continual advance in the state of technology, therefore, is to increase labor productivity and reduce the demand for labor. Since labor productivity has grown on average by 2.3 percent a year since 1950, does this mean that the economy offers 2.3 percent fewer jobs each year? The answer is no for reasons already discussed. Although the initial impact of productivity growth is to reduce the demand for labor, it also leads to greater employment because lower product prices and higher real incomes stimulate additional sales in the economy.[27] Rather than destroying jobs, therefore,

---

25 These are described in more detail in J. A. Mark and W. H. Waldorf, "Multifactor Productivity: A New BLS Measure," *Monthly Labor Review*" 106, no. 12 (December 1983): 3–15. Also see Ziaul Z. Ahmed and Patricia S. Wilder, "Multifactor Productivity Trends in Manufacturing Industries, 1987–96," *Monthly Labor Review* (June 2001): 3–12; and Tarek M. Harchaoui et al., "Information Technology and Economic Growth in Canada and the U.S.," *Monthly Labor Review* 125 (October 2002): 3–12.

26 Further evidence of firms responding to high wages by substituting capital is provided by George J. Borjas and Valerie A. Ramey, who find that industries that pay higher than average wages at a given point in time experience greater subsequent growth in capital/labor ratios. See "Market Responses to Wage Differentials." *UC-San Diego Working Paper No. 2000/18* (2000).

27 Capital/labor substitution in response to rising wages does not reduce production costs; rather, it minimizes the *rise* in per unit cost. The continuing process of technological change in the capital goods industries, however, reduces the price of capital and gives rise to capital/labor substitution, which does result in higher productivity and lower per unit costs of production.

productivity growth is actually the wellspring of higher per capita incomes and more jobs in the economy.[28]

What is true at the economywide level may not be true for an individual industry, however. If an industry's product has a low price elasticity and income elasticity of demand, rapid productivity growth may lead to a net decline in employment as the additional sales resulting from lower prices do not offset the displacement of labor from capital/labor substitution and labor-saving technological change. The increase in real income resulting from the higher productivity growth in the one industry, however, will create additional jobs in other industries as that income is spent by consumers. Empirical Evidence 5-1 illustrates just how different two industries' experiences can be in the face of similar productivity growth.

➲ SEE

Empirical Evidence 5-1: Productivity Growth and Employment in Agriculture and Telephone Communication, p. 252.

---

28 Edmund S. Phelps, "The Boom and the Slump: A Causal Account of the 1990s/2000s and the 1920/1930s," *Journal of Policy Reform* 7 (March 2004): 3–19, documents that this addition of jobs can take some time, however.

POLICY APPLICATION 5-1

Employment Forecasting

What industries and occupations will offer the best job prospects for college graduates in the year 2010? How many new jobs are created by an increase in defense spending? What region of the country gains the most jobs from American exports to other countries? These are some of the questions for which policymakers in Congress and state and local governments need answers and that economists are trained to provide. How do economists make such employment projections? Employment forecasting is an application of the theory of labor demand. One frequently used approach utilizes the *input–output* model.[1]

The input–output model was first developed by the Harvard economist Wassily Leontief, an accomplishment that earned him the Nobel prize. The heart of the input–output model is the concept of the production function, symbolically represented here as $Q = f(K, L)$. The traditional use of the production function is to predict the level of output that will result from a given level of factor inputs. Leontief's key insight was to realize that the production function could also be used in reverse to predict, given a certain level of output, the labor and capital requirements necessary to produce it.

Using the production function to forecast future employment trends is more complicated than it might sound, however. The reason is illustrated in Figure 5.10. Assume the current level of employment is L_1, given by the tangency between the isocost line AB and the isoquant Q_1 (point X). The first step to employment forecasting is to estimate how much the level of output will rise between the current period and the forecast date. In some cases one or more estimates may be supplied to the forecaster; for example, Congress might ask for projections of the number of new jobs created

---

1 A description of how the Bureau of Labor Statistics makes use of the input–output model to make employment projections can be found in *The Handbook of Methods, Chapter 13* http://www.bls.gov/opub/hom/homch13_a.htm.

Given the existing employment of L_1 (point X), to forecast the future level of employment it is necessary first to predict the level of output. Assuming the level of output to be Q_2, if isoquants are convex allowing substitution possibilities between K and L, it is also necessary to predict the change in relative factor prices and the curvature of the isoquants. If factor prices do not change, future employment would be L_2 (point Y); if wages increase relative to the cost of capital, however, the future level of employment might be only L_3 (point Z).

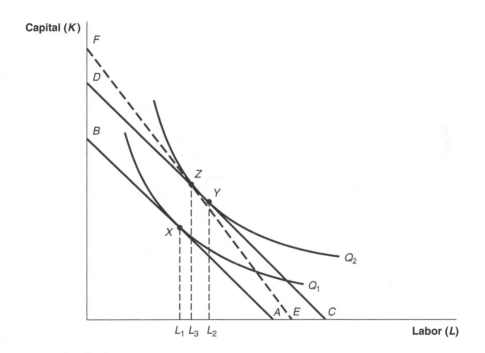

by three alternative defense budgets of $300 billion, $350 billion, and $400 billion. In other cases the forecaster has to project the future level of output (such as the level of GNP in 2010) based on historical trends and current developments. Whatever the method, the example considered here assumes that the future level of output at the forecast date is predicted to be Q_2.

With the convex isoquants pictured in Figure 5.10, even if output is correctly predicted to be Q_2 it is still impossible to predict the level of employment without additional information. In particular, it is also necessary to predict, first, the change in relative factor prices between the current date and the forecast date and, second, the relative curvature of the isoquants. If relative factor prices remain the same, for example, the isocost line CD would be parallel to AB and the predicted level of employment would be L_2 (point Y). If wages increase faster than the cost of capital, the slope of the isocost line would become steeper, such as the broken line *EF*. In this case, at the same output level of Q_2 employment would only be L_3 (point Z). The extent to which changes in factor prices affect the predicted level of employment depends on the curvature of the isoquants. The greater the substitution possibilities between capital and labor, the greater will be the sensitivity of labor demand to changing factor prices (that is, the greater the distance $L_2 - L_3$).

The assumption that isoquants are convex as in Figure 5.10 places a considerable burden on the forecaster, who has to predict not only the future level of output but also the future level of wages and capital costs and the convexity of the isoquants. These informational demands are, in fact, so large and the resulting computational work is so complex that the traditional production function can generate employment forecasts only at a very aggregated level, such as for the manufacturing sector.

By way of contrast, the input–output model is capable of generating employment forecasts for several hundred detailed industries or occupations. How is it able to do this?

The Input–Output Model

The key to the input–output model is the assumption that the technology of production allows zero substitution possibilities between capital and labor, giving rise to a "fixed proportions" type of production function. Such a production function was illustrated in Figure 5.3. Each isoquant is L-shaped, implying that a given level of production requires capital and labor in one and only one proportion.

Given the assumption of fixed proportions, the crucial step in using the input–output model is to calculate the **input–output coefficients.** The input–output coefficient for labor (a_L) is defined as $a_L = L/Q$ and the coefficient for capital (a_K) is defined as $a_K = K/Q$ where *L*, *K*, and *Q* are measured at the time of the forecast. The labor input–output coefficient is the amount of labor required per unit of output. For the technology

illustrated in Figure 5.3, and assuming Q_1 is the initial level of output, $a_L = 20/100 = 0.2$, and $a_K = 10/100 = 0.1$. Since the labor/output ratio is, by assumption, the same for all levels of output, the demand for labor can be written as:

$$L = a_L Q, \tag{5.3}$$

and the demand for capital as:

$$K = a_K Q. \tag{5.4}$$

Thus, if the projected level of output in Figure 5.3 is $Q_3 = 300$, the forecast of employment in that year would be $L = 0.2(300) = 60$ workers.

The demand for labor function in Equation 5.3 can be used to predict the total amount of labor required to produce a given level of output. For many purposes, it is also desirable to be able to forecast labor requirements for detailed industry and occupational groups. This can be accomplished by defining a more disaggregated input–output coefficient $a_{L,i} = L_i/Q$, where L_i equals the amount of labor in the *i*th occupation or industry (machinists or basic steel) needed to produce one unit of output (an automobile).

Forecasting with the Input–Output Model

The following example illustrates how the input–output model can be used. One of the burning questions as the North American Free Trade Agreement (NAFTA) was being negotiated in Congress was what impact the resulting liberalization of trade would have on employment levels. States, too, were concerned with the local impact, since the effects were likely to be concentrated in certain industries, some of which might be heavily represented in the state. In 1994 researchers at Georgia State University and the Georgia Institute of Technology undertook the task of predicting what impact NAFTA would have on employment within the state of Georgia; they used an input–output model to estimate the impacts.[2]

The first step was to estimate how NAFTA would impact demand, and thus output, across industries. The researchers estimated that overall output in the state would increase by $582 million. This overall output increase was not spread evenly across industries. For example, output in the carpet-manufacturing industry was projected to increase by $147 million, whereas output in the apparel-manufacturing industry was projected to *decrease* by $142 million. The second step was to calculate the labor input–output coefficient (a_L). For overall production in Georgia, the ratio L/Q was estimated to be 10 persons per $1 million of output. The input–output coefficient was estimated to be 11 persons per $1 million of output in the carpet industry and 18 persons per $1 million of output in the apparel industry. The final step is to plug the estimate of 0.000010 (for all of Georgia) into Equation 5.3. The predicted increase in the number of jobs in Georgia as a result of NAFTA is 5,667. Since total employment in Georgia was roughly three million (in 1994), this amounts to a 0.2 percent increase in employment.[3] The change in carpet and apparel employment, specifically, can be calculated in a similar manner.

The input–output model offers a relatively simple method for forecasting future employment levels.[4] The input–output model's simplicity, however, is also its weakness. In particular, there are three potential sources of error in making employment projections with it. The first, and the one the Bureau of Labor Statistics (BLS) has found to be the most serious, is inaccurate estimates of the input–output coefficients themselves.[5] Obviously, if the data used to construct the coefficients are inaccurate due to measurement error, the projections derived from the model will also be inaccurate.

The second most serious source of error found by the BLS is caused by changes over time in the value of the input–output coefficients. The "naive" version of the input–output model, as in Equation 5.3, assumes that the input–output coefficient is a constant. For this to be true, over the forecast period there must be no improvement in technology and no capital/labor substitution due to changing factor prices. Studies that have used the input–output model to explain historical trends in employment have found, however, that the input–output coefficients actually change a good deal over a period of a decade or more, causing the forecasts from a naive version of the model to have a large amount of error.[6] In its forecasts, therefore, the BLS adjusts the input–output coefficients to take into account secular trends in productivity, technological change, and other such factors.

Finally, the BLS found that the least important source of error in its employment forecasts involves incorrect estimates of the future level of output (the assumed value of Q in Equation 5.3). These three factors do not invalidate the usefulness of the input–output model, but they do suggest that users of employment forecasts be aware of the uncertainties involved in the forecasting process.

---

2   Keith Ihlanfeldt, William Riall, and Peter Terrebonne, "Globalization and the Georgia Economy," Research Report No. 48, Policy Research Center, Georgia State University (November 1994).

3   This projection is clearly a short-run projection that does not take into account long-run technological change impacts or structural adjustments as a result of NAFTA or other policies.

4   Another application of the input–output model illustrates how product demand growth in labor intensive industries (i.e., in industries with high a_L) leads to more growth in labor demand than the same amount of product demand in industries with a lower a_L. The research also shows that a simultaneous growth in product demand and technological advancement (advancement that lowers a_L) can actually reduce employment levels. See Mark S. Leclair, "Export Composition and Manufacturing Employment in the U.S. during the Economic Downturn of 1991–92," *Economic Systems Research* 14 (June 2002): 147–56.

5   See Betty W. Su, "The U.S. Economy to 2010," *Monthly Labor Review* (November 2001): 3–20.

6   This is shown in Richard B. Freeman, "Manpower Requirements and Substitution Analysis of Labor Skills: A Synthesis," in Ronald G. Ehrenberg, ed., *Research in Labor Economics*, vol. 1 (Greenwich, Conn.: JAI Press, 1977): 151–84.

Displaced Workers

Even though the overall level of employment can be growing in an economy, that growth is not typically spread evenly across industries and occupations. As was seen in Chapter 4, the service-producing sector has grown at a tremendous pace, while the goods-producing and farm industries have been declining. While the economy and labor market continually adjust to changes in technology, trade policy, and product demand, there could easily arise a "mismatch" of workers and jobs. For example, job growth may be concentrated in one region of the country while population growth is concentrated in another; this would result in a geographic mismatch. Rapid technological change in a production process (say, a shift to computer-controlled manufacturing) may result in increased demand for a new type of skill that the current work force does not possess, leading to a mismatch of skills. Also, demand for items produced by one industry, say oil-drilling equipment, may fall off and items produced by another industry, say health care services, may become more attractive; here one will see an industrial mismatch. Any of these adjustments will lead to the displacement of workers—workers who lose their jobs with small probability of regaining them or even of finding jobs similar to those lost.

The federal government categorizes workers as "displaced" if they are at least 20 years old and have lost their jobs as the result of a plant closing or a relocation, insufficient work, or because the jobs were abolished. The government has been collecting information on displaced workers since 1984. This information is collected biannually as a supplemental questionnaire to the Current Population Survey.[1] Between January 2001 and December 2003, 5.3 million workers who had held their jobs for at least three years were displaced. Forty-three percent of these workers were displaced as a result of a plant shutdown or move. Of the displaced workers

men comprised 56 percent and blacks 13 percent. Manufacturing workers made up 32 percent of the displaced workers in 2001. This was the largest percentage among industries, but roughly equivalent to the percentage of displaced workers from manufacturing during the late 1990s.[2]

Impact of Displacement

The concern about whether a person who loses his or her job is displaced lies in the fact that these workers' job losses have resulted from a structural change in the labor market, and therefore it is more difficult for them to find a new job or to regain the losses in earnings. Displaced workers face greater amounts of nonemployment (time unemployed or out of the labor force) than nondisplaced workers. The length of nonemployment is higher the longer someone has been on the job before displacement. This could be either because those who have been on their job a longer period of time limit their job searches to jobs similar to the ones they have lost, or because their skills have depreciated or for some other reason are no longer needed.[3] In addition, not only are wages initially lower for displaced workers than for nondisplaced workers once they have found new jobs, but the lower

---

1   Statistics related to the 2003 Displaced Worker Survey were obtained from Bureau of Labor Statistics, *Displaced Workers Summary USDOL04-1381* 30 July 2004). Also see http://www.bls.gov/news.release/disp.nr0.htm.

2   Evaluation of displacement trends can be found in Ryan T. Helwig, "Worker Displacement in a Strong Economy," *Monthly Labor Review* (June 2001): 13–28. Also see Ryan Helwig, "Worker Displacement in 1999–2000," *Monthly Labor Review* 127 (June 2004): 54–68.

3   See Robert G. Valletta, "Job Tenure and Joblessness of Displaced Workers," *Journal of Human Resources* 26 (Fall 1991): 726–41; Paul Swaim and Michael Podgursky, "Displacement of the Unemployed," in John T. Addison, ed., *Job Displacement: Consequences and Implications for Policy* (Detroit: Wayne State University Press, 1991); and Bruce C. Fallick, "The Industrial Mobility of Displaced Workers," *Journal of Labor Economics* 11 (April 1993): 302–23.

wages of displaced workers persist over time.[4] Older and less educated workers also appear to suffer greater and more persistent losses than younger or more educated workers.[5] In other words, displacement has what appears to be a permanent negative impact on lifetime earnings, but to varying degrees depending on the displaced worker's age.

Among workers who were displaced between January 2001 and December 2003, 65 percent were reemployed by January 2004, 20 percent were unemployed, and 15 percent had dropped out of the labor force. Workers displaced from the durable manufacturing industry were the least likely, and workers in the professional and technical services industry the most likely, to be reemployed by 2004. Women were less likely to be reemployed than men; 70 percent of displaced men but only 62 percent of women were reemployed by 2004. This lower reemployment level for women reflected that they were twice as likely as men to leave the labor force after being displaced.

Among reemployed workers who were displaced from full-time jobs, 24 percent were reemployed in jobs paying at least 20 percent less than their previous job. Thirty percent of the reemployed displaced workers were earning the same or more than they had previously been earning; this was a significantly greater loss in earnings compared with workers displaced in 1999. Forty-three percent of those workers got a new job paying at or above their previous job; 32 percent of workers reemployed in 2002 earned at least as much as on their previous job.

As a result of the difficult experience of many displaced workers and what has been perceived as a growing problem, a number of government policies have been put into place to assist this group of workers.

Policies to Assist Displaced Workers

The Federal **Unemployment Insurance (UI) program** clearly benefits displaced workers. It is in place to assist all workers who have lost their jobs for reasons other than their own behavior; workers who have been fired for poor job performance, for example, are not eligible for assistance through the UI program. There are several programs, however, that are in place to specifically assist those classified as "displaced." Federal laws designed along these lines include the Trade Adjustment Assistance (TAA) Act, the Workforce Investment Act (WIA), and the Worker Adjustment and Retraining Notification (WARN) Act. These programs are distinguishable from general unemployment insurance programs in having some provision for (re-)training and job-search assistance. WARN is unique in that it was specifically designed with the displaced worker in mind.

WARN, which became effective on February 4, 1989, requires employers to provide 60 days' notice to workers of a plant closing (shutdown for at least 30 days of a site employing at least 50 workers) or of a mass layoff (layoff for 30 or more days of at least 500 workers, or 33 percent of the employer's work force). All employers who employ 100 or more workers are covered under WARN. The TAA and WARN are provisions under the broader Economic Dislocation and Worker Adjustment Assistance Act (EDWAA), which amended Title II of the Job Training Partnership Act (JTPA). Each state has a Dislocated Worker Unit (DWU) created exclusively to assist workers who have been dislocated.

---

4   See Christopher J. Ruhm, "Are Workers Permanently Scarred by Job Displacements?" *American Economic Review* 81 (March 1991): 319–24; Louis Jacobson, Robert LaLonde, and Daniel Sullivan, "Earnings Losses of Displaced Workers," *American Economic Review* 83 (September 1993): 685–709; and Ann Huff Stevens, "Long-Term Effects of Job Displacement: Evidence from the Panel Study of Income Dynamics," *NBER Working Paper No. 5343* (November 1995).

5   Lori G. Kletzer and Robert W. Fairlie, "The Long-term Costs of Job Displacement for Young Adult Workers," *Industrial and Labor Relations Review* 56 (July 2003): 682–98; and Madeline Zavodny and Daniel Rodriguez, "Changes in the Age and Education Profile of Displaced Workers," *Industrial and Labor Relations Review* 56 (April 2003): 498–510.

In terms of improving the outcome of being displaced, there is some evidence that providing workers with advance notice of their impending displacement reduces the chance that they experience nonemployment.[6] In addition, there is also some evidence that postdisplacement earnings are higher and workers are more successful in finding jobs for which they are well suited when they have been given plenty of warning about their upcoming displacement.[7] These improved outcomes stem, in part, from workers being able to begin their job search prior to the actual job loss, affording them more time to find a better-fitting job. So the evidence seems to indicate that giving the worker some warning about his or her job loss can improve the outcome of displacement.

---

6   Pietro Garibaldi, "Search Unemployment with Advance Notice," *Macroeconomic Dynamics* 8 (February 2004): 51–75. The effectiveness of WARN, however, is dependent on the disclosure of accurate information regarding pending closures; see Oren M. Levin-Waldman, "Plant Closings: Is WARN an Effective Response?" *Review of Social Economy* 56 (Spring 1998): 59–79.

7   Christopher J. Ruhm, "Advance Notice, Job Search, and Postdisplacement Earnings," *Journal of Labor Economics"* (January 1994): 1–28; Stephen Nord and Yuan Ting, "The Impact of Advance Notice of Plant Closings on Earnings and the Probability of Unemployment," *Industrial and Labor Relations Review* 44 (July 1991): 681–91; and John T. Addison and Douglas A. Fox, "Job Changing after Displacement: A Contribution to the Advance Notice Debate," *Southern Economic Journal* 60 (July 1993): 184–200.

EMPIRICAL EVIDENCE 5-1

Productivity Growth and Employment in Agriculture and Telephone Communication

The relationship between productivity growth and labor demand is vividly illustrated by the different patterns of employment change in two industries, agriculture and telephone communication. Both industries have experienced a virtual revolution in the technology of production over the past 40 years. In 1960, for example, a long-distance telephone call was handled with mechanical switching equipment, long-distance operators, and cable transmission systems; four decades later the same long-distance call is made with direct dialing equipment, computers, and satellites. A similar transformation has taken place in agriculture with the introduction of high-yielding hybrid grains, modern tilling and harvesting machinery, and computerized egg and cattle production.

The process of technological change and capital/labor substitution in both industries has resulted in dramatic increases in labor productivity. These productivity gains are illustrated by the data in columns (a) and (d) of Table 5.1, which show the growth in output per worker in each industry between 1960 and 1999. The productivity gains were dramatic. Between 1960 and 1999 output per worker in agriculture increased by slightly over 345 percent and in telephone communication by over 700 percent. Such rapid gains in productivity substantially reduced the amount of labor needed per unit of output. Given the state of technology and the level of capital in 1999, for example, firms in both industries could have produced 1960's output with roughly less than 20 percent as many workers.

The previous section shows, however, that productivity growth also leads to forces that increase employment in the industry. First, productivity growth leads to declining unit costs of production, which should lead to lower product prices, greater sales, and greater employment. This process has clearly been operative in both agriculture and

TABLE 5.1

THE RELATIONSHIP BETWEEN PRODUCTIVITY GROWTH AND EMPLOYMENT IN AGRICULTURE AND TELEPHONE COMMUNICATION, 1960–1999

	Agriculture			Telephone Communications		
	Index of Output per Employee Hour (a)	Relative Price of Agricultural Goods (b)	Total Farm Employment (thousands) (c)	Index of Output per Employee Hour (d)	Relative Price of Telephone Service (e)	Total Telephone Employment (thousands) (f)
1960	100.0	100.0	5,458	100.0	100.0	706
1999	445.8	56.8	3,281	815.0	30.6	1043

SOURCES: 1960 statistics: *Statistical Abstract of the United States* (Washington, D.C.: U.S. Bureau of the Census), 1974 Table 566 (telephone employment); Table 5-3; *Handbook of U.S. Labor Statistics, 1975* (Washington, D.C.: Government Printing Office), Table 128 (1960 telephone productivity).

1999 statistics: Table B-99, *Economic Report of the President, 2004* Table B-99 (farm productivity data), Table B-67 (Agricultural Price Index); *Employment and Earnings* (January 2000) Table 17 (agricultural employment). *Statistical Abstract of the United States, 2004* Table 684 (telephone employment), Table 713 (CPI), Table 719 (PPI). *Handbook of U.S. Labor Statistics, 2004*, Table 5-2 (telephone productivity). *Statistical Abstract of the United States, 2001*, Table 694 (telephone price).

telephone communication, as revealed by the data in columns (b) and (e). The figures in each column are a ratio of two price indexes: the numerator is the respective price index for the industry's product or service (1960 = 100.0), and the denominator is an index of consumer prices in the economy (the Consumer Price Index, 1960 = 100.0). Both ratios have declined over time, meaning that the level of prices in both agriculture and telephone communication increased less rapidly than all prices in general or, to put it another way, the *relative* price of agricultural goods and telephone service declined over time.[1] By 1999, for example, the *relative* price of agricultural products and telephone service had been cut in half. This decline in the relative product price should have led to greater sales and employment in both industries, the amount of increase depending on how price elastic each industry's product demand curve was.

The second source of employment growth from increases in productivity comes from increased product demand as a result of the rise in the real income of consumers. Because productivity growth leads to lower product prices (or at least to a slower rate of increase), the rise in wage rates over time will outstrip the rise in product prices, leading to an increase in real income for consumers. This increase in real income has led to greater consumer expenditures and product demand for agricultural goods and telephone service, as well as for many other goods and services.

The net effect of productivity growth on industry employment depends on whether the initial displacement of labor because of productivity growth is less than or greater than the subsequent increase in employment because of greater industry sales. For agriculture, column (c) of Table 5.1 shows that the initial displacement effect of productivity growth has far outweighed the effect of increased sales from lower prices and higher incomes. Between 1960 and 1999, for example, agricultural employment fell by 40 percent. The reason is that agricultural products have both a very low price elasticity and income elasticity of product demand. Even though relative prices of agricultural goods

have fallen and the real incomes of consumers have risen, demand for agricultural goods such as bread, milk, and meat has increased only modestly. For agriculture, then, productivity growth has led to a sharp decline in agricultural employment because the savings in labor per unit of agricultural goods have outweighed the increase in labor demand due to greater levels of production.[2]

In marked contrast to agriculture, employment in the telephone communication industry actually increased by 48 percent between 1960 and 1999. Technological change and capital/labor substitution significantly reduced unit labor requirements in the telephone industry, but the demand for telephone service has grown so rapidly that the net effect has been a rise in total employment. In this situation, then, the price and income elasticities of demand for the product have been sufficiently high that productivity growth has resulted in a net increase in industry employment.

The telephone industry also offers a prime illustration of the skill twist that technological change imparts to labor demand. A study of a large Canadian telephone company, for example, found that technological change reduced the demand for labor in inverse relation to the skill level of the occupation—the least-skilled category, telephone operators, suffered a sharp relative decline in employment while more highly skilled white-collar workers increased their share of employment.[3] Similar trends have been projected to continue in future years.

---

1   Further price reductions in the early 2000s have resulted from increased competition through deregulation. See Almar Latour, "Telecom Companies Are Invading One Another's Turf Like Never Before. Here's a Guide to Cutting Through the Confusion," *Wall Street Journal* (13 September 2004): R1.

2   See Patricia A. Daly, "Agricultural Employment: Has the Decline Ended?" *Monthly Labor Review* 104, no. 11 (November 1981): 11–17.

3   Michael Denny and Melvyn Fuss, "The Effect of Factor Prices and Technological Change on the Occupational Demand for Labor: Evidence from Canadian Telecommunications," *Journal of Human Resources* 18, no. 2 (Spring 1982): 161–76.

Summary

In the long run, the firm has more flexibility in adjusting its employment needs to the relative prices of capital and labor, since it is free to vary both factor inputs. One result of this greater flexibility is that the long-run labor demand curve is more elastic than the short-run labor demand curve. A rise in the wage rate, for example, leads to a reduction in employment in the short run because of the scale effect as the firm cuts its level of production, and a further reduction in the long run because of the substitution effect as the firm replaces labor with capital.

A second influence on labor demand in the long run is technological change and productivity growth. The initial effect of technological change is to displace labor as more efficient techniques of production allow firms to produce a unit of output with less labor. Over the longer run, technological change and productivity growth also lead to more jobs in the economy, because they result in lower prices and greater real income, fueling an increase in product demand and labor demand. Technological change may have an adverse impact on workers in certain occupations by making their particular skills obsolete.

An additional topic considered in this chapter is employment forecasting. To make employment forecasts, economists frequently use the input–output model of labor demand. The most important assumption of the input–output model is that the technology of production allows zero substitution possibilities between capital and labor. Research shows that changes in factor prices and the state of technology do cause the input–output coefficients to change over time, requiring that the forecaster adjust the projections for these potential biases.

Review Questions

1. Demonstrate in a graph that if the production technology is of the fixed proportion type (L-shaped isoquants), an increase in the wage rate will cause only a scale effect on labor demand and no substitution effect. Will there be any difference between the short-run and long-run labor demand curves?

2. Before the airline industry was deregulated, the Airline Pilots Association (ALPA) was generally regarded as one of the most successful unions in raising the wages of its members; the International Ladies Garment Workers Union (ILGWU), on the other hand, has had only limited success in raising wages. First, use the four laws of derived demand to explain this difference. Second, after deregulation of the airline industry, over 40 new airlines began business. What was the likely effect of this on the elasticity of demand for airline pilots? Which law of derived demand does this involve?

3. The United Automobile Workers Union has lobbied heavily for a "domestic content" bill that would require American cars be produced with parts and components made in the United States. What effect would passage of this bill have on the demand for labor in the auto industry? Consider both the scale and the substitution effects.

4. One of the demands of railroads in recent labor negotiations has been to eliminate the caboose from trains, cutting train crews from four workers to three. The unions have resisted this because of the loss of jobs. Are the unions right? Would removing the caboose cause a decline in total employment? Consider

the short-run and long-run effects. What factors does the answer depend on?

5. "If productivity growth occurs more rapidly than expected, then an employment forecast using an input–output model will underestimate the actual level of future employment." Is this statement true, false, or uncertain? Why?

6. Consider the capital/labor ratios in the mining and communication industries below. Assuming that over this period of time, the cost of labor increased relative to the cost of capital in both of the industries by approximately the same amount, which industry can you conclude

faced a technology with the higher elasticity of substitution in 1970? Depict the relative shape of the isoquant that likely prevailed for these industries in 1970.

Capital/Labor Ratios

Year	Petroleum Refining	Mining
1970	502	667
2001	690	1075

7. Explain how the introduction of distance learning technology can be expected to affect the elasticity of demand for college professors.

The Long-Run Equilibrium Level of Employment

The long-run equilibrium condition for employment, where the marginal rate of technical substitution (*MRTS*) is equal to the cost ratio of labor and capital, can be derived mathematically.

Mathematically, isoquants are derived by determining all combinations of capital and labor that generate a single level of output (*Q*) through a mathematical production function that satisfies certain properties:

$$Q = f(K,L), \tag{5A.1}$$

where *Q* reflects the level of output generated by specific levels of capital (*K*) and labor (*L*) inputs. The firm's goal is to select that combination of *K* and *L* which yields the maximum profit, given that *K* and *L* are costly to purchase. It is assumed that capital may be purchased at a price of "*R*" per unit of capital, and that labor may be purchased at a price of "*W*" per unit of labor. Profit is defined as total revenue minus total cost. Total revenue is calculated by multiplying the product price by the level of output (*P* · *Q*). Total cost is calculated by adding the cost of capital (amount of capital times its price, *K* · *R*) and the cost of labor (amount of labor times its price, *L* · *W*). So, profit is given by:

$$\pi = P \cdot f(K,L) - K \cdot R - W \cdot L. \tag{5A.2}$$

The amounts of capital and labor that maximize profit (given the product price and input prices) are found by partially differentiating Equation 5A.2 with respect to *K* and *L* and solving those first-order conditions for *K* and *L*. Partially differentiating Equation 5A.2 yields the following first-order conditions:

$$P \cdot (\partial f/\partial K) - R = 0 \tag{5A.3}$$

$$P \cdot (\partial f/\partial L) - W = 0 \tag{5A.4}$$

Equations 5A.3 and 5A.4 can be rewritten as follows:

$$P = \frac{R}{\partial f/\partial K} \tag{5A.3'}$$

$$P = \frac{R}{\partial f/\partial L} \tag{5A.4'}$$

Setting these two expressions for *P* equal to one another, one obtains:

$$\frac{\partial f/\partial L}{\partial f/\partial K} = \frac{W}{R}, \tag{5A.5}$$

or:

$$MRTS = \frac{W}{R}. \tag{5A.5'}$$

It is the combination of capital and labor that satisfies this condition which will yield the greatest profit possible given the product price and the input prices. This is the same condition for the equilibrium level of employment as stated in Equation 5.2 in the text. This also illustrates how the *MRTS* reflects the rate at which a firm can substitute capital for labor and still maintain the same level of output. The ratio

$$\frac{\partial f / \partial L}{\partial f / \partial K}$$

indicates how much additional output a firm receives from one more unit of labor relative to the additional output lost by giving up one more unit of capital.

The Slope of the Isoquant

The text indicates that the *MRTS* at a particular point on the isoquant is equal to negative of the slope of the line tangent to the isocost curve at that point. In other words, the *MRTS* at a point is (negative) the slope of the isoquant at that point. This can be illustrated mathematically by *totally differentiating* the production function:

$$df = \frac{\partial f}{\partial K} dK + \frac{\partial f}{\partial L} dL. \tag{5A.6}$$

Since output does not change as one moves along an isoquant ($df = 0$), the total derivative can be rewritten as:

$$0 = \frac{\partial f}{\partial K} dK + \frac{\partial f}{\partial L} dL. \tag{5A.7}$$

Rearranging the terms in 5A.7:

$$\frac{\partial f / \partial L}{\partial f / \partial K} = -\frac{dK}{dL}, \tag{5A.8}$$

or:

$$MTRS = -[\text{slope of the isoquant}]. \tag{5A.9}$$

Equations 5A.5′ and 5A.9 can be combined to reflect the equilibrium illustrated as point X in Figure 5.5:

$$\frac{W}{R} = MTRS = -[\text{slope of the isoquant}] \tag{5A.10}$$

The Scale and Substitution Effects[1]

Solving the profit maximization problem for the optimal levels of capital and labor yields a demand function for labor that is a function of input prices, R and W, and the level of output demanded, Q:

$$L = l(R, W, Q). \tag{5A.11}$$

---

1   This section is based on Daniel S. Hamermesh, "Econometric Studies of Labor Demand and Their Application to Policy Analysis," *Journal of Human Resources* 11 (Fall 1976): 507–25.

Writing output demand as a function of the product price, P, which in turn is determined by the cost of production, (5A.11) becomes:

$$L = l(R, W, Q[P(R, W)]).$$ (5A.11′)

Totally differentiating this labor demand function results in

$$dL = \frac{\partial l}{\partial R} dR + \frac{\partial l}{\partial W} dW + \frac{\partial l}{\partial Q} \frac{\partial Q}{\partial P} \frac{\partial P}{\partial R} dR + \frac{\partial l}{\partial Q} \frac{\partial Q}{\partial P} \frac{\partial P}{\partial W} dW.$$ (5A.12)

Holding the cost of capital constant, the total derivative becomes:

$$dL = \frac{\partial l}{\partial W} dW + \frac{\partial l}{\partial Q} \frac{\partial Q}{\partial P} \frac{\partial P}{\partial W} dW.$$ (5A.13)

Dividing both sides of Equation 5A.13 by dW, the total change in employment that results from a wage change can be seen to comprise two pieces:

$$\frac{dL}{dW} = \frac{\partial l}{\partial W} + \frac{\partial l}{\partial Q} \frac{\partial Q}{\partial P} \frac{\partial P}{\partial W}.$$ (5A.14)

The second expression on the right-hand side of Equation 5A.14 reflects the change in employment that results from a change in output (Q). As the wage goes up, the cost of production increases, raising the price in the product market and reducing the quantity demanded, thus lowering employment levels. This is the scale effect. The first term on the right-hand side of Equation 5A.14 reflects the change in employment that results from the wage change, *while holding everything else (output level and input prices) constant*. This is the substitution effect. Empirical evidence offered by Daniel Hamermesh indicates that while both these terms have the same sign in response to a wage change, the scale effect tends to be slightly larger than the substitution effect.[2]

---

2   Hamermesh, "Econometric Studies of Labor Demand and Their Application to Policy Analysis," Table 3, p. 519.

The Determination of Wages

In this chapter demand and supply are brought together in order to analyze the process of wage determination. Wage determination is at the core of labor economics, since the structure of wages and the change in wages over time are responsible for efficiently allocating labor and maintaining a balance between demand and supply in the market. The chapter begins by focusing on the determination of wages in perfectly competitive markets. The two major issues of concern are how market forces determine an equilibrium wage rate for a particular type of labor and how the market responds to a condition of disequilibrium caused by a change in demand or supply. The chapter also considers wage determination in what economists call "imperfect markets." Two examples are monopsony labor markets (those with only one employer) and segmented labor markets. The chapter also discusses two different ways in which institutional forces affect wage rates. These are through government-mandated minimum wages and internal labor markets.

The Pattern of Wages

Industries, occupations, and geographic areas differ markedly in terms both of the levels of wage rates and in the changes in wages over time. This diversity is illustrated in Table 6.1. Shown in column (a) is the level of average hourly earnings in 2003 for production workers in the U.S. nonagricultural economy and in nine individual industries identified by their unique NAICS (North American Industry Classification System) codes. Shown in column (b) is the percentage change in average hourly earnings between 1993 and 2003 in these industries.

Before examining these data, it is useful to discuss briefly the exact meaning of average hourly earnings, how the data are collected, and the concept of NAICS numbers. To economists, the meaning of the term "wage rate" is intuitively obvious—it is the price of labor per hour of work. Measuring the actual wage rate can be difficult, however. One complication is that firms use several different types of payment schemes. While some employees are paid on

NAICS	Industry	Average Hourly Earnings, 2003 (a)	Percentage Change in Earnings, 1993–2003 (b)
—	Nonagricultural Private Economy	$15.35	42%
51419	Computing Services	30.60	87
3162	Leather Footwear	10.80	50
622	Hospitals	19.37	44
51111	Newspapers	15.68	32
23551	Carpentry	18.99	32
447	Gas stations	8.72	31
484	Trucking	16.29	30
31324	Knitting Mills	10.44	29
2121	Coal	20.85	21

SOURCE: 2003 data: http://www.bls.gov/ces/cesbtabs.htm; 1993 data: Table B-15, March 1994 Employment and Earnings.

an hourly basis, others receive salaries or are paid on a piece-rate basis. Whichever method is used, it is possible to calculate the average compensation received per hour by dividing weekly earnings by weekly hours of work. Doing so yields *average hourly earnings.* Do average hourly earnings measure the price of labor? Unfortunately, the answer is no, for the data do not capture all forms of employee compensation, particularly fringe benefits. This complication can be dealt with by calculating *total compensation costs per hour,* where total compensation includes both earnings and the dollar value of fringe benefits prorated on an hourly basis. While this measure of labor cost comes closest to the economists' notion of the price of labor, the drawback is that data on fringe benefits are often unavailable, making average hourly earnings the next best measure of the wage rate.[1]

A second issue is the source of the data on average hourly earnings. As discussed in Chapter 3, the data on employment, unemployment, and labor force

---

[1] For more detail on the measurement of labor cost, see Jack E. Triplett, ed., *The Measurement of Labor Cost* (Chicago: University of Chicago Press, 1983). Also see Nancy D. Ruggles and Richard Ruggles, "The Treatment of Pensions and Insurance in the National Accounts," in *National Accounting and Economic Policy: The United States and the UN Systems* (Northampton, Mass.: Elgar, 1999): 91–128.

participation are derived from the Current Population Survey (CPS), or "household" survey. The data on average hourly earnings, as well as data on employment, hours of work, and productivity by detailed industry, are obtained from the "establishment" survey. This survey, conducted monthly by the Bureau of Labor Statistics (BLS), is done by mail questionnaire and includes in its sample establishments (industrial plants or places of business) that employ over 40 percent of all workers in the nonagricultural economy. The data from both the household and the establishment surveys are presented in the monthly BLS publication *Employment and Earnings*.

In 2003, the United States began to report industry statistics using a revised method called the **North American Industry Classification System (NAICS)**.[2] This new classification system, shared by the United States, Canada, and Mexico, replaced the **Standard Industrial Classification** (SIC), which had been in place since the early 1930s and had last been revised in 1987. The old SIC system was heavily oriented to traditional manufacturing industries; the new classification system includes many new information technology and service industries and has been designed to be flexible enough to allow for the emergence of new industries and production processes in the future.

Each establishment in the United States is put into a two-digit sector based on the process the establishment uses to produce its good or service. For example, a construction establishment is placed in NAICS 23 and a restaurant is placed in NAICS 72, Accommodation and Food Services. Any establishment producing anything related to information (including data processing, publishing, and telecommunications) is classified as NAICS 51. The advantage of NAICS over SIC is its flexibility and that it is based on a more detailed six-digit classification structure, as opposed to the four-digit structure of the SIC system.

The data in Table 6.1 show the great diversity in the behavior of wages among these various industries. In 2003, the level of average hourly earnings varied among these industries from a low of $8.72 in gasoline service stations to a high of $30.60 in computing services. The average of hourly earnings in the entire nonagricultural economy was $15.35. Likewise, between 1993 and 2003, wages grew much more rapidly in some industries than in others. While the average rate of (real) wage growth in the economy was about 12 percent, the rate varied from a low of negative five percent in coal mining to 47 percent in computing services.

What can account for the fact that average hourly earnings in computing services were 351 percent higher than in gas stations? Why did hourly earnings grow far more rapidly in hospitals than in the newspaper industry? There is no single answer to these questions, since wages are influenced by a host of factors—the strength of product demand, the capital intensity of production, the extent of unionization, the skills and training required of the workforces, the nature of the

---

2   See James Walker and John Murphy, "Implementing NAICS at BLS," *Monthly Labor Review* 124 (December 2001): 15–21; and U.S. Census Bureau, "Development of NAICS," http://www.census.gov/epcd/www/naicsdev.htm.

working conditions, and many others. Despite the complexity of the subject, economic theory can explain much of this disparate behavior, as this and succeeding chapters attempt to show.

Wage Determination in Competitive Markets

The starting point in developing the theory of wages is the model of perfect competition. This model best illustrates how market forces, operating through labor demand and labor supply, interact to determine the level of wages and employment. There are five key assumptions in the model of perfect competition:

1. Business firms seek to maximize dollar profits, and workers seek to maximize utility.

2. Workers and firms have perfect information about wages and job opportunities in the labor market.

3. Workers in the labor market are identical with respect to skills and productivity; jobs offered by firms are identical with respect to working conditions and other nonwage attributes.

4. The labor market is composed of many individual firms on the buyer's side of the market and many workers on the seller's side. The workers do not belong to unions, and firms do not collude.

5. All jobs in the labor market are open to competition by workers, no institutional barriers (for instance, seniority provisions and internal hiring rules) inhibit mobility of workers from one job to another. Costs of mobility are zero.

The Law of One Wage

Given these assumptions, the perfectly competitive model gives rise to one of the most important predictions in labor economics—the **law of one wage.** The law of one wage states that in a competitive labor market the competition between buyers and sellers will result in the establishment in the market of one uniform "going" wage rate that will be paid by all the firms and received by all the workers.[3]

The determination of wages in a perfectly competitive market and the reasoning behind the law of one wage are illustrated in Figure 6.1. Represented in graph (a) is the market for some particular type of labor; graph (b) represents one

---

3   The law of one wage is the labor market analog of the more familiar law of one price in competitive product markets. The reasoning behind the law of one wage is discussed in Alfred Marshall, *Principles of Economics*, 9th ed. (New York: Macmillan, 1961), 546–50.

FIGURE 6.1   THE DETERMINATION OF WAGES IN A PERFECTLY
COMPETITIVE MARKET

If the labor market—graph (a)—is perfectly competitive, the equilibrium wage will be W_E, where demand and supply are equal. At a wage of W_1, demand (point A) is greater than supply (point B), and competition will force the wage up. At a wage of W_2, there is an excess supply of labor (point C − point D) and the wage will fall until W_E is reached. Given the wage W_E in the market, the individual firm—graph (b)—can hire all the labor it wants at that wage, as illustrated by its perfectly elastic supply curve S_1. If it pays a wage less than W_E (point G), it will lose all its workers; if it pays more than W_E, the competitive firm will lose profits and be forced out of business.

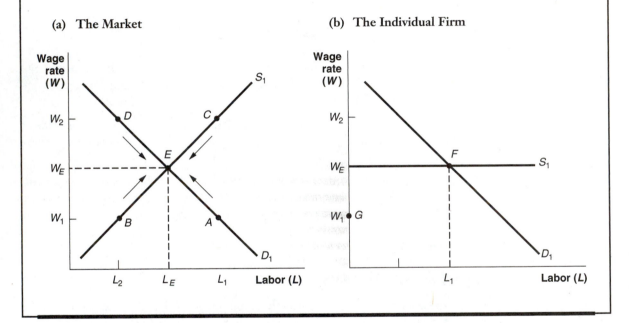

(a) **The Market**   (b) **The Individual Firm**

individual firm in the market. The wage rate is determined by the interaction of demand and supply in the overall market.[4] As shown in Chapter 1, at any wage higher than the equilibrium wage W_E (say W_2) a surplus of labor will occur (point C − point D), resulting in a bidding down of wages until demand and supply are equal. Likewise, at any wage below W_E (say W_1) a shortage of labor occurs

---

4   Chapter 2 showed that the labor supply curve for a demographic group may be positively or negatively sloped. In an individual labor market, however, the supply curve is always positively sloped. A rise in the wage for truck drivers in Chicago, for example, will induce a greater supply of truck drivers as persons move from other cities or switch occupations in order to obtain these higher-paying jobs.

(point A − point B), and wages will be bid up as companies compete for additional workers. Only at W_E will the labor market be at an equilibrium or state of balance.

The process of wage determination for one individual firm in the market is illustrated in graph (b). What wage does the firm have to pay for labor? The answer is W_E, given by the intersection at point F of the firm's downward-sloping demand (marginal revenue product) curve D_1 and the horizontal or perfectly elastic supply curve S_1. The reason is that the wage W_E is determined by the overall competition between the aggregate of firms and workers in the market graph (a). The individual competitive firm, because it is so small relative to the entire market, cannot pay less than W_E and still attract labor, nor does it have to pay more than W_E to obtain all the labor it needs. In the language of economics, the competitive firm is a "wage taker"; it has to pay the going wage, but can hire as much labor as it needs without paying more. This is shown in graph (b) by the horizontal or perfectly elastic supply curve of labor to the firm, S_1. Given its downward-sloping demand curve D_1 and the market-determined wage of W_E, the firm's optimal level of employment is L_1.

According to the law of one wage, in equilibrium all workers in this labor market will receive and all firms will pay the same wage of W_E. It is important to understand why. What would happen in the labor market pictured in Figure 6.1, for example, if one firm decided to pay only W_1 (less than W_E), while a second firm decided to pay W_2 (more than W_E)?

Given the assumptions of perfect information, maximizing behavior, and free mobility, competitive pressure will cause both firms to ultimately change their rates of pay to W_E. At the wage of W_1 the supply of labor to the low-wage firm will be zero, shown as point G in graph (b). All of that firm's workers would quit and seek employment at other firms that are paying more for the same job. To attract and keep its workforce, the low-wage firm would be forced by the pressure of labor mobility to raise its wage to W_E.

An opposite situation faces the high-wage firm paying W_2. This firm will have a long line of job applicants wanting to work there. The problem for this firm is that by paying a higher wage its labor costs are also higher than those of other firms, and it will earn less profit. While this situation may be tolerable in the short run, in the long run in a perfectly competitive product market this firm will eventually be forced out of business by its lower-cost rivals. The pressure to maximize profits in order to survive will thus force this high-wage firm to reduce its wage from W_2 to W_E. Thus, as predicted by the law of one wage, competition will ensure that in equilibrium only one going wage is observed in each particular market for labor.

The Law of One Wage Put to the Test: Secretaries

To what extent do wages in the labor market correspond to the predicted one wage of competitive theory? Evidence on this issue is presented in Figure 6.2 for workers in a highly competitive labor market, the market for clerical workers. The data show the distribution of annual earnings for workers

FIGURE 6.2

THE DISTRIBUTION OF WORKERS IN THE UNITED STATES BY ANNUAL EARNINGS IN TWO SECRETARY OCCUPATIONS, 2003

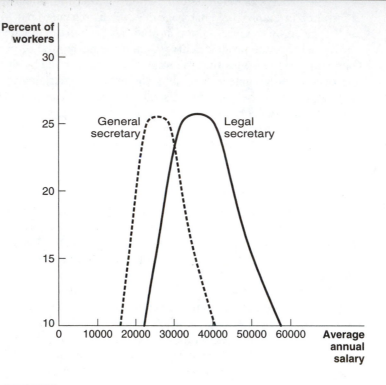

SOURCE: Occupational Employment Statistics Survey, Bureau of Labor Statistics http://www.bls.gov/oes. Probability distributions constructed from data provided on earnings percentiles.

classified as General Secretaries and Legal Secretaries in the United States in 2003.[5]

These data seem to offer only partial support for the predictions of the competitive model. For each occupation, the earnings distributions trace out a distinct bell-shaped curve, showing that earnings for each occupation are centered around a specific level of pay. Thus, in the General Secretary occupation, the greatest number of workers earned between $20,000 and $30,000 per year; for the Legal Secretary occupation, the largest group of workers earned between $35,000 and $45,000. This

---

5   Figure 6.2 was generated using data on earnings by quintiles. The distributions, therefore, do not strictly correspond to figures produced by density functions. Earnings data for secretaries within individual metropolitan areas are not available.

result suggests that rates of pay in each occupation are not randomly determined, but rather are shaped by forces such as those envisioned in the competitive model.

Given this, it is also evident from Figure 6.2 that the earnings for workers in each occupation exhibit a good deal of dispersion about the mean.[6] In the General Secretary occupation, the mean level of annual earnings was $26,508, but 50 percent of the workers received either below $19,000 or above $30,000. A similar pattern exists for the Legal Secretary occupation, although the amount of dispersion is modestly greater.

These data suggest that the labor market gives rise to clear differences in average rates of pay *among* occupations, but *within* occupations a good deal of dispersion in earnings separates individual workers. From this it must be concluded that the law of one wage is refuted if literally interpreted as requiring a single rate of pay for each worker in the market; as a description of the central tendency for wages in each occupation to be grouped about a common rate, however, the law serves as a good approximation for competitive markets such as those for secretaries.

Market Imperfections

It is worthwhile to pursue the example of secretaries further and ask why the labor market did not give rise to the predicted one wage. One possible reason is that the law of one wage describes a situation of long-run equilibrium, while real-world labor markets are in a constant state of change. A second reason is that the market for secretaries violates one or more of the five assumptions of the perfectly competitive model. A factor or circumstance that causes a market to diverge from the perfectly competitive ideal is called a **market imperfection**. The more serious the imperfections in a labor market, the more the outcome of the wage determination process will diverge from the predicted outcome of competitive theory.

Nonmaximizing Behavior   The perfectly competitive model assumes that firms always act to maximize profits. Given this, a firm will never pay workers a wage higher than the minimum necessary to attract a sufficient supply of labor, since to do so would raise labor costs and reduce profits. This motivation to maximize profits is reinforced not only by the quest for pecuniary gain on the part of the owners

---

6   Part of the dispersion in weekly earnings may be due to differences in hours worked. A detailed study by Francine Blau, *Equal Pay in the Office* (Lexington, Mass.: Lexington Books, 1977), that used data on hourly earnings of clerical workers also found large wage dispersion among firms, however. Further evidence of occupational wage dispersion among firms can be found in Erika L. Groshen, "Sources of Intra-industry Wage Dispersion: How Much Do Employers Matter?" *Quarterly Journal of Economics* 106 (August 1991): 869–84, and Madelyn Young and Bruce Kaufman, "Interfirm Wage Differentials in a Local Labor Market: The Case of the Fast-Food Industry," *Journal of Labor Research* (Summer 1997): 463–80. Also see M. G. Coles, "Equilibrium Wage Dispersion, Firm Size, and Growth," *Review of Economic Dynamics* 4 (January 2001): 159–87.

of the firm, but also by the threat of bankruptcy in the long run if the firm allows its labor costs to exceed those of its rivals in a highly competitive industry.

While the maximization assumption is central to economic theory, some economists argue that firms frequently do not maximize profits, but rather *satisfice* with respect to profits.[7] Proponents of the theory of satisficing behavior provide two reasons why firms do not always maximize profits. The first involves the **principal–agent problem**. The "principal" is the stockholders of the corporation who hire managers as their "agents" to operate the firm. The stockholders desire that the managers maximize profits, but managers often are insulated to some degree from effective stockholder control and thus can pursue other goals (for example, paying above-average wage rates and salaries or avoiding confrontation with unions) that may be at the expense of maximum profits as desired by the shareholders. A second reason is that firms in oligopolistic or regulated industries may not face heavy competitive pressure and do not have the incentive to hold down wages and other costs to a minimum in order to survive.

The consequences of satisficing behavior are that some firms may consciously pay wages higher than the minimum going rate, giving rise to a dispersion of wage rates in the market. In a classic study of 50 manufacturing firms in the New Haven, Connecticut area, for example, Lloyd Reynolds found that firms had a considerable latitude in their pay policies and that the larger, more profitable firms paid substantially higher wages for a given grade of labor relative to their smaller, less profitable counterparts.[8] Reynolds's explanation for this dispersion in wage rates was in part that the companies with high profits were generally those having **barriers to entry** in the product market. A barrier to entry is some factor that impedes the ability of new firms to enter a market, usually resulting in a high level of *market concentration* (few firms in the market). In oligopolistic industries in manufacturing, the main barrier to entry is large capital requirements; in nonmanufacturing industries such as trucking or airlines (prior to deregulation in 1979), the principal entry barrier was the difficulty firms had in gaining regulatory permission to compete in new markets. In either case, barriers to entry allow firms in concentrated or regulated industries to pay wages higher than the market level, since higher labor costs can more easily be passed on in the form of higher prices without precipitating the entry of new, lower-cost rivals. These high-wage firms will also be able to attract the "highest quality" workers in the labor market, making **productivity-adjusted wages** more equal than money wage rates. Whether the increased productivity of workers employed by high-wage firms completely offsets their higher rates of pay has been investigated in a number of studies. While evidence has been found on both sides of this issue, a number of studies find that workers in concentrated and regulated

---

7   Herbert Simon, "Rational Decision Making in Business Organizations," *American Economic Review* 69, no. 4 (September 1979): 493–512. Also see Philippe Aghion et al., "Competition, Financial Discipline, and Growth," *Review of Economic Studies* 66 (October 1999): 825–52, for a more recent application of the assumption of satisficing.

8   Lloyd G. Reynolds, *The Structure of Labor Markets* (New York: Harper & Row, 1951), Chapter 9.

industries do receive a wage premium that cannot be totally accounted for by higher worker productivity.[9]

Imperfect Information   Another departure from the perfectly competitive model is imperfect information, which can lead to a dispersion in wage rates in two ways. The first has to do with the job search process. If workers in the General or Legal Secretary occupations knew the wages paid by all firms in any one location, they would flock to the high-wage firms and shun the low-wage firms, driving wages to equality in the market just as the theory predicts. As emphasized by Nobel laureate George Stigler, however, information about wages, working conditions, and job openings is not announced to workers like prices at an auction; rather, acquiring information about these factors requires a process of job search by workers as they sequentially contact one employer and then another in the labor market.[10]

The theory of job search is examined in Chapter 13. The essential point to note here is that the acquisition of information in the labor market through job search is costly, in terms of both direct out-of-pocket costs and the opportunity cost of the time devoted to it. While each worker would like to obtain the highest-paying job possible, beyond some point the additional search costs from contacting yet another firm will surpass the probability of finding a higher wage offer. Rather than searching in the labor market until the highest wage is found, the worker will find it profitable to search only until he or she finds a job paying a wage equal to or greater than some minimum acceptable wage. With imperfect information, in an otherwise perfectly competitive market, two identical workers may be paid different wage rates. Part of the dispersion in earnings of secretaries in Figure 6.2, therefore, reflects the fact that imperfect information and search costs prevent the process of labor mobility from fully competing away differences in wages among similar jobs in the labor market.

Imperfect information can also lead to a dispersion of wages by affecting the pay policies of employers. In a world of perfect information, a firm would know the performance level of each secretary it employs and could set the wage in proportion to his or her productivity. In the real world, however, firms can only imperfectly monitor an employee's job performance, both because supervisory staff is costly and because many aspects of job performance (e.g., effort and diligence) are difficult to measure. The problem posed for employers in this situation is that both hourly and salaried workers are faced with the temptation to work at less than peak efficiency since the employer cannot fully detect loafing or malfeasance. How can

---

9   See John S. Heywood, "Labor Quality and the Concentration–Earnings Hypothesis," *Review of Economics and Statistics* 68 (May 1986): 342–46; S. Nickell, J. Vainiomaki, and S. Wadhwani, "Wages and Product Market Power," *Economica* 61 (November 1994): 457–73; and Kare Johansen et al., "Firm Profitability, Regional Unemployment and Human Capital in Wage Determination," *Applied Economics* 33 (January 2001): 113–21. Besides being able to obtain higher-quality workers, high-wage firms will also incur lower search costs and lower costs from turnover, further reducing the dispersion in hourly labor cost.

10   George J. Stigler, "Information in the Labor Market," *Journal of Political Economy* 70, pt. 2 (October 1962): 94–105.

the employer combat this problem? One solution is to deliberately pay a wage above the market level. The higher the wage, the more a secretary stands to lose from being fired for poor job performance and, thus, the harder he or she will work. A dispersion in wages for a specific occupation such as General Secretary will emerge, in turn, if firms differ either in their ability to monitor employee performance or in the amount of profit that is at risk from acts of malfeasance by workers. This partially explains the fact that workers in any given occupation generally tend to be paid more in large-sized plants or companies than in smaller ones.[11] The management in large-size organizations finds it more difficult to detect shirking on the job and, accordingly, pays a higher wage as a means to increase the incentive for employees to work diligently.[12] In this case, both efficiency wages and money wages will systematically differ across employers.

Heterogeneity of Workers and Jobs   Competitive theory predicts that a single going wage will prevail in the market for a set of *homogeneous* jobs and workers. It is reasonably certain, however, that workers and jobs in the secretary's market are *heterogeneous* or "differentiated," introducing an imperfection into the market. One source of heterogeneity is with respect to the supply of labor offered to firms. Despite the fact that our empirical example examines earnings for two narrowly defined occupations, not all workers classified as General Secretaries or Legal Secretaries are likely to be of the same skill and productivity level, reflected by differences among them in years of education, experience, job skills, and innate ability, for example. Part of the dispersion in earnings in Figure 6.2, therefore, may reflect the fact that employers pay different wages to workers of different productivity. This result is quite consistent with the law of one wage if the law is slightly reinterpreted; that is, in terms of productivity-adjusted wages (wage rates per unit of work performed) the labor market may still give rise to equality of earnings once differences in worker productivity are taken into account.[13] One study, for example, found that workers who use computers on their jobs earn a wage 2 percent higher than that of workers who do not use computers.[14]

---

11   Numerous studies find that wage rates vary positively with the size of the plant or company, other things being equal. See Charles Brown and James Medoff, "The Employer Size Wage Effect," *Journal of Political Economy* 97, no. 5 (October 1989): 1027–59; Christoph M. Schmidt and Klaus F. Zimmermann, "Work Characteristics, Firm Size, and Wages," *Review of Economics and Statistics* 73 (November 1991): 705–10; Sebastien Ringuede, "An Efficiency Wage Model for Small Firms: Firm-Size and Wages," *Economics Letters* 59 (May 1998): 263–68; Robert W. VanGietzen, "Occupational Pay by Establishment Size," *Compensation and Working Conditions* (Spring 1998): 28–36; and Erica Groshen, "Five Reasons Why Wages Vary Among Employers," in *Income Distribution*, Vol. 2, ed. Michael Sattinger (Northampton, Mass: Elgar, 2004): 453–84.

12   See Lawrence Katz, "Efficiency Wage Theories: A Partial Evaluation," in Stanley Fischer, ed., *NBER Macroeconomics Annual 1986* (Cambridge, Mass.: MIT Press, 1987): 235–76.

13   Although "productivity-adjusted wages" are sometimes referred to as "efficiency wages," the first term is preferred in this context in order to avoid confusion when the term "efficiency wage" is used later in this chapter (and in Chapter 12) to denote the idea that employee work effort or "efficiency" is positively related to the wage rate paid by the firm.

14   Horst Entorf et al., "New Technologies, Wages, and Work Selection," *Journal of Labor Economics* 17 (1999): 464–91.

A related reason for the dispersion in earnings is that not all jobs in the General or Legal Secretary occupations are identical. Some jobs will have more pleasant working conditions, shorter commuting distances, or more fringe benefits than other jobs. As shown in more detail in Chapter 8, workers presumably would accept a lower wage, or "compensating differential," to obtain the job with good working conditions, but would demand a higher wage to take the same secretarial job with poor working conditions, leading to the pattern of earnings shown in Figure 6.2.

Albert Rees and George Shultz, in a detailed study of 12 different occupations in the Chicago area, attempted to determine to what extent these factors could account for the apparent discrepancy between the prediction of the theory and the actual observed pattern of wages.[15] In their study they controlled for differences among workers with respect to age, sex, race, seniority, experience, education, commuting distance, type of neighborhood (where the job was located), and type of industry. They found for typists and keypunch operators that differences in these variables among individual workers could account for, respectively, 47 and 55 percent of the difference in the wage rates these workers were paid, substantially reducing the actual dispersion in earnings.[16]

If the wage data for secretaries in Figure 6.2 could be standardized as Rees and Schultz did in their study, the variance (relative spread) of wage rates around the mean of each frequency distribution would be narrowed considerably, perhaps by 50 percent or more. Decreasing the variance of each distribution by even one-half still leaves a dispersion in wage rates for individual workers that hardly fits the predicted one wage of competitive theory. What else can explain this apparent deviation between theory and fact?

Unions and Employer Collusion   The assumption that neither employers nor workers collude or act as a collective unit in their operation of the market could be violated in a number of ways. For example, the presence of unions violates this assumption. Through a union, the many workers act as if they are one, providing the workers some monopoly power in the sale of their labor. Since clerical workers are not highly unionized as an occupation, this is not likely to be a major source of the observed wage dispersion. Another example of collusion is when employers get together to set the wage for an occupation, like secretaries. Since the net result of employers colluding is a single wage (albeit lower than the competitive outcome), it would be difficult from wage data alone to determine whether a single wage was

---

15   Albert Rees and George P. Shultz, *Workers and Wages in an Urban Labor Market* (Chicago: University of Chicago Press, 1970).

16   Although controlling for sex and race reduces measured wage dispersion, these variables may reflect discriminatory differences in wages rather than productivity differentials. Evidence on this point is provided in Blau, *Equal Pay in the Office*. Also see Barry Hirsch and David Macpherson, "Wages and Gender Composition: Why Do Women's Jobs Pay Less?" *Journal of Labor Economics* 13 (July 1995): 426–71; and Hirsch and Macpherson, "Wages, Sorting on Skill, and the Racial Composition of Jobs," *Journal of Labor Economics* 22 (January 2004): 189–210.

the result of competitive pressure or employer collusion. In addition, the greater the number of employers, the more difficult it is for them to collude. Since we do not observe one wage in the market for secretaries and since there exists a very large number of employers of secretaries, it is not likely that employers are colluding to set the wage.

Costly Mobility   When evaluating a national market for any occupation, the costs of mobility clearly come into play. It is not costless to pack up and move from Atlanta to Chicago in search of the highest secretarial wage. One could argue, however, that the availability of secretarial jobs at one geographic location is such that mobility across firms is not likely to be much of an obstacle to competition. Another source of mobility cost is the presence of strict seniority provisions or in-house promotion rules. If these features are important in the determination of secretarial wages, wage dispersion will persist. While promotion may be more important at the Legal Secretary level, the competition for General Secretary positions is fairly wide open (not restricted to in-house candidates). An additional cost of mobility—loss of employer-provided fringe benefits—is highlighted in Policy Application 6-1.

➡ SEE

Policy Application 6-1:
Job Lock, p. 305.

A More Realistic Model

This discussion of the wages of secretaries suggests that a more realistic representation of the wage determination process would resemble that given in Figure 6.3. If the labor market satisfied all five assumptions of the perfectly competitive model, the equilibrium wage in the market would be W_E, and this wage rate would be the one and only wage paid by each firm in the market. Most real-world labor markets, however, feature imperfections such as nonmaximizing behavior, limited information, and heterogeneous workers and jobs, that prevent the forces of competition and labor mobility from completely eliminating all wage differentials. The dispersion of wage rates that results is illustrated in Figure 6.3 by the band of wage rates bounded on the top by an upper limit W_U and on the bottom by a lower limit W_L. The firm cannot pay more than W_U because to do so would lower its profits below the minimum necessary level; likewise it cannot pay below W_L because it would not be able to attract or keep a workforce. Within the band, however, is an **area of indeterminacy** where the imperfections in the competitive process allow some room for discretion by individual firms with respect to their pay policies.[17]

---

17   See Richard A. Lester, "A Range Theory of Wage Differentials," *Industrial and Labor Relations Review* 5, no. 4 (July 1952): 483–500. The existence of an area of indeterminacy in wage rates in a nonunion labor market was well accepted by the neoinstitutional labor economists of the 1950s. With the ascendancy of the neoclassical school in the 1960s and 1970s, the idea largely dropped from sight in economic research. That the concept is of real-world importance, however, is suggested by the prominent role it still retains in the more applied field of compensation management. See George T. Milkovich and Jerry M. Newman, *Compensation* 8th ed. (Columbus, Ohio: McGraw-Hill, 2005).

FIGURE 6.3 THE AREA OF INDETERMINACY IN WAGE RATES

The area of indeterminacy in wages is represented by the band extending from the upper limit W_U to the lower limit W_L. Most firms will pay close to the going market wage W_E, but some will be in either tail of the wage distribution as high-wage or low-wage firms. The more closely the labor market fits the perfectly competitive ideal, the smaller will be the area of indeterminacy.

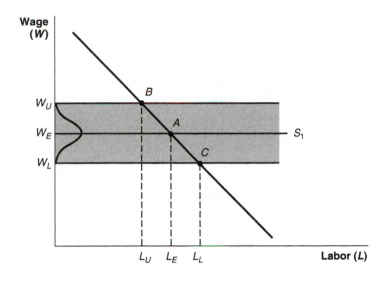

As shown by the bell-shaped curve in Figure 6.3, most firms will pay close to the average market wage W_E. Others, however, will be in either tail of the distribution as high-wage or low-wage firms, depending on their size, industry, profitability, and management attitude toward employee compensation. Of these factors, research has found that a firm's industry affiliation is a particularly important determinant of its position in the wage hierarchy.[18] A good illustration of this point is provided in a well-known study by John Dunlop in which he examined the wage rates paid to truck drivers by various firms in Boston in 1953.[19] Since driving a truck is a fairly standard type of job, it might be thought that all truck drivers

---

18   See Alan B. Krueger and Lawrence H. Summers, "Efficiency Wages and the Interindustry Wage Structure," *Econometrica* 56 (March 1988): 259–93; Erdil Erkan and Hakan Yetkiner, "A Comparative Analysis of Inter-industry Wage Differentials: Industrialized versus Developing Countries," *Applied Economics* 33 (October 2001): 1639–48.

19   John Dunlop, "The Task of Contemporary Wage Theory," in George Taylor and Frank Pierson, eds., *New Concepts in Wage Determination* (New York: McGraw-Hill, 1957), 117–39.

would earn a similar wage per hour. He found, however, that truck drivers' wages not only had a wide dispersion, but also varied systematically by the industry of the particular firm. The lowest-paid drivers worked for scrap metal firms and earned only $1.27 per hour, while the highest-paid drivers delivered magazines and earned $2.49 per hour. He concluded that firms in a labor market are arrayed along a series of distinct "wage contours" within the area of indeterminacy, with a separate contour for firms in each industry. In Figure 6.3, the horizontal line at W_U would be the wage contour for magazine delivery firms; the line at W_L would be the contour for scrap metal firms. According to Dunlop, the position of each contour in the area of indeterminacy is largely determined by product market characteristics of the industry such as degrees of competition, firm size, profitability, and so on.

The size of the area of indeterminacy in market wage rates will vary from one labor market to another depending on the degree to which the market conforms to the assumptions of the perfectly competitive model. The more closely a particular labor market approximates an auction-type market, such as the stock exchange or a market for a commodity such as wheat, the smaller will be the dispersion in wage rates. Perhaps the best example of this was documented in a study by Melvin Reder of the starting salaries of MBA graduates from the University of Chicago.[20] This market was found to have many of the characteristics of an auction market (the buying and selling took place through one centralized exchange, buyers and sellers had considerable information about each other, and the product was fairly homogeneous) and thus competition resulted in a very small dispersion in starting salaries, once productivity differences among students (for example, differences in grade point average) were accounted for. Many other labor markets, however, diverge in one or several respects from a true auction market; the more they do so, the greater will be the area of indeterminacy in wages. Several studies, for example, have found a large degree of wage dispersion among semiskilled factory workers such as machine operators.[21] One important reason for this finding (the internal labor market) is examined later in this chapter.

Wage Determination in a Monopsony Market

The discussion up to this point has focused on wage determination in competitive markets. There are a number of other types of market structures, however. This section examines the polar opposite to perfect competition—**monopsony.** Technically speaking, monopsony means a labor market with only one buyer of labor. Economists often use the term *monopsony* more broadly, however, to denote any labor market situation where employers have some discretionary control in setting the wage. If there is more than one employer in the labor market, strictly speaking

---

20　Melvin W. Reder, "An Analysis of a Small, Closely Observed Labor Market: Starting Salaries for University of Chicago MBA's," *Journal of Business* 51, no. 2 (1978): 263–97.

21　Robert Raimon, "The Indeterminateness of Wages of Semiskilled Workers," *Industrial and Labor Relations Review* 6, no. 2 (January 1953) 180–94.

other terms should be used, such as *oligopsony* (several employers and limited entry) and *monopsonistic competition* (many employers, free entry, but imperfect information and/or mobility).[22] In this section we will use monopsony in the broad sense.

To begin the discussion, note that economists distinguish two types of monopsony: static (or "structural") and dynamic. The static model was developed in the 1930s by British economist Joan Robinson and is the best known.[23] It examines the labor market in equilibrium (thus neglecting dynamic flows of labor in and out of employment) and locates the source of monopsony in structural conditions of the market that in some way create a barrier to entry and thus limit the number of employers (just as economies of scale can act as a barrier to entry in the product market and create a monopoly firm). The classic example of structural monopsony is a one-company town where the only source of jobs in the local area is a textile mill or coal mine. A situation approaching structural monopsony can also arise in other contexts. One occurs when numerous employers compete in the local labor market, but only one employer demands a specific set of skills. An example is a city fire department. Once trained, the firefighters may find few, if any, other employers in the area that could use their skills. Finally, monopsony-like conditions may arise because of factors such as seniority and pension rights, company loyalty, marriage and family obligations, or a fear of the unknown that prevent labor mobility by tying workers to a particular firm or community.[24] As explained in more detail later, the common effect of these factors is to make the labor supply curve no longer horizontal to the firm (the competitive case) but upward sloping.

The second type of monopsony is the dynamic model and is of much more recent origin.[25] It locates the source of the firm's monopsony power not in structural characteristics of the labor market that restrict the number of competitors but in the dynamic inflow and outflow of workers among the potentially many firms competing in the labor market (such as among fast-food restaurants in a large city). These factors can also create an upward-sloping supply curve to the firm. For example, at a low wage the number of people who quit a firm is high and the number of new applicants is low, resulting in a low supply of labor. As the wage offered by the firm goes up, however, quits decrease and new applicants increase, leading to a larger supply of labor to the firm, other things being equal. In this case, the cause of monopsony-like conditions is not a barrier to entry but imperfect information and non-zero mobility, hiring, and training costs.

Just as a monopolist in the product market is able to charge a higher price than it could if it were a perfectly competitive firm, so a monopsonist can pay a lower

22 See V. Bhaskar, A. Manning, and T. To, "Oligopsony and Monopsonistic Competition in Labor Markets," *Journal of Economic Perspectives* 16 (Spring): 155–74.

23 Joan Robinson, *The Economics of Imperfect Competition* (London: Macmillan, 1933).

24 See Martin Bronfenbrenner, "Potential Monopsony in Labor Markets," *Industrial and Labor Relations Review* 9 (July 1956): 577–88.

25 See David Card and Alan Krueger, *Myth and Measurement: The New Economics of the Minimum Wage* (Princeton: Princeton University Press, 1995) and *Alan Manning, Monopsony in Motion* (Princeton: Princeton University Press, 2003).

FIGURE 6.4   WAGE DETERMINATION IN A MONOPSONY MARKET

The profit-maximizing level of employment for the monopsonist is L_1. This is determined by where the firm's *MRP* schedule intersects its *MCL* schedule (point B). Given that the firm desires to hire L_1, the supply curve S_1 shows that the firm must pay a wage of W_1 (point A) to attract that many workers. If the labor market were competitive, the wage rate and level of employment would be W_2, L_2 (point C). The amount of monopsonistic exploitation is the difference between the value of what labor produces (point B) and what it is paid (point A).

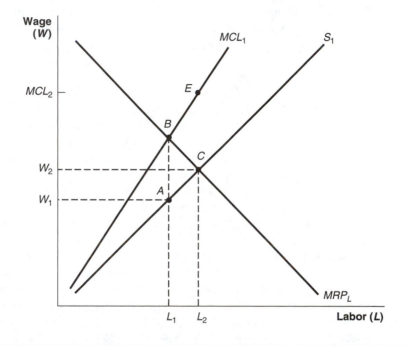

wage than if it were a perfect competitor in the labor market. The process of wage determination for a monopsonist is shown in Figure 6.4. To simplify the discussion, we assume a condition of structural monopsony in which there is only one firm (a textile mill) hiring labor in the market.

The monopsonist, like the competitive firm, has a downward-sloping marginal revenue product schedule, shown as MRP_L. What is different between the monopsonist and the competitive firm is the labor supply curve. The supply curve for a competitive firm is perfectly elastic (horizontal), meaning that it can hire as many workers as it wants at the going market wage. The supply curve facing the monopsonist is far different. Since the textile mill in the one-company town is the only firm in the market, it has the entire labor supply exclusively to itself. The supply curve facing the monopsonist is thus the upward-sloping *market* supply curve, shown as S_1 in Figure 6.4. While the competitive firm can hire all the labor it wants at the going wage, the monopsonist cannot; to hire additional workers, the supply curve S_1 shows that the monopsonist must pay a successively higher wage rate to attract additional workers. Thus, as the textile mill tries to expand employment, it must pay a higher wage to attract housewives into the labor force, for example, or to induce persons in outlying rural areas to accept employment at the plant. Conversely, if the textile mill lowers the wage it will pay, it will not lose all of its workforce, since they have few, if any, other employment opportunities.

Given the marginal revenue product curve and the supply curve for the monopsonist, how many workers should it hire? What wage rate will it have to pay? As shown in Chapter 4, the decision rule for calculating the optimal level of employment is to hire additional workers as long as the marginal increase in revenue to the firm is greater than the marginal increase in labor cost. Thus, the perfectly competitive firm in Figure 6.1 (b) hired L_1 workers (point F), since at that point the extra revenue from one additional worker as measured by the marginal revenue product is just equal to the extra cost as measured by the wage rate per hour. This decision rule holds true for the monopsonist, but the resulting level of wages and employment turns out to be considerably different than for a perfectly competitive firm. The reason has to do with the marginal cost of labor.

The Marginal Cost of Labor Schedule

To determine the monopsonist's optimal level of wages and employment, it is necessary to derive in Figure 6.4 a **marginal cost of labor (*MCL*) schedule,** shown as the line MCL_1. It shows the change in the firm's total dollar outlay for labor per hour for each additional worker hired. For the competitive firm, the marginal cost of labor schedule is horizontal and coincides with its supply curve, reflecting the fact that it can hire as many hours of labor as it wants at the going market wage. For the monopsonist, the marginal cost of labor schedule lies above the supply curve and is more steeply sloped.

Why does the marginal cost of labor schedule for a monopsonist have this shape? To explain this, assume the wage is $8.00 per hour and the firm hires 10 workers. Total labor cost is $80. If the firm has to pay $8.50 an hour to attract an additional worker, what will be the marginal increase in labor cost? Total cost of 10 workers was $80; the total cost of 11 workers is $(11 \times \$8.50) = \$93.50$. The increase in cost is $13.50, higher than the actual wage of $8.50. Why? Hiring the last worker cost $8.50, which meant paying the previous 10 workers $8.50, not $8.00, causing the total increase in labor cost to be $(\$8.50 + \$5.00) = \$13.50$.[26]

---

[26] It is assumed the firm must pay all workers a uniform wage. If it was able to limit the wage increase to only the last worker hired (a form of price discrimination), the increase in marginal labor cost would be much lower. One way firms attempt to accomplish this is by limiting the amount of information that workers have about each other's rates of pay; a second is to pay one-time hiring bonuses or other lump-sum payments such as those for moving or housing expenses (this allows the firm to pay the new worker more money without having to extend an increase to current employees).

Thus, with an upward-sloping supply curve such as S_1, to hire worker L_2 requires a wage of W_2 (point C), but the actual increase in labor cost is MCL_2 (point E).

The Equilibrium Level of Wages and Employment

How many workers should the monopsonist hire? The answer is L_1. At point B in Figure 6.4 the extra revenue brought in from hiring an additional worker (the MRP_L) is just equal to the marginal increase in labor cost (the MCL). To expand employment to L_2 would result in lower profits, since the extra cost of hiring that last worker (point E) is far greater than the revenue brought in (point C). Once the level of employment is determined, it is an easy matter to determine the wage the monopsonist will pay for labor. To hire L_1 workers, the labor supply curve shows that a wage of W_1 (point A) has to be paid.

To appreciate the implications of this outcome, it is useful to compare the wage and employment level under monopsony with what would result if the market were competitive. Under perfect competition, the wage rate and level of employment in the market would be W_2 and L_2 in Figure 6.4, determined by the intersection of the marginal revenue product schedule MRP_L and the supply curve S_1 (point C). Under monopsony, the wage and employment levels are only W_1 and L_1. The result is that *both* wages and employment are lower in a monopsonistic market than in a competitive market. If workers had alternative sources of employment, the monopsonist would not be able to take advantage of its employees by paying them less than competitive rates. Since they do not, this gives the firm power to practice **monopsonistic exploitation** of labor. The amount of exploitation is the difference between what labor is worth to the firm (shown by the MRP_L at point B) and the wage that labor receives (W_1). Note that in perfect competition there is no monopsonistic exploitation, since labor is hired up to the point where $W = MRP_L$.

➡ SEE

Empirical Evidence 6-1:
Monopsony in Baseball, p. 307.

Evidence of the existence of a monopsony market structure in the baseball industry prior to 1977 is examined in Empirical Evidence 6-1.

The Process of Market Adjustment

An important function of the labor market is to allocate labor to its most efficient use. This task is gargantuan. On the demand side of the market, the demand for labor by business firms is in a constant state of flux. Some business firms are growing rapidly and need many additional employees, while others are laying off workers because of declining sales. The supply side of the labor market is also quite dynamic. Each year over one and a half million people enter the labor force looking for work, and several million more who are already employed change jobs. Given the great heterogeneity of labor demand in terms of industry, occupation, and geographic area, and the great heterogeneity of labor supply in terms of education, skill, job preference, and desired geographic location, how does the labor

Graph (a) illustrates the market adjustment to a situation of excess demand. The original equilibrium is point A. Assuming the demand curve shifts to D_2, at the wage W_1 there is an excess demand for labor of $L_2 - L_1$ (point B – point A). As a result, wages rise to W_2 (point C), but the net increase in employment is only to L_3.

Graph (b) illustrates a situation of excess supply. Assuming the supply curve shifts to the right to S_2, at the wage of W_1, there is an excess supply of labor of $L_2 - L_1$ (point B – point A). As a result, wages fall to W_2 (point C) but the net increase in employment is only to L_3.

(a) Excess Demand

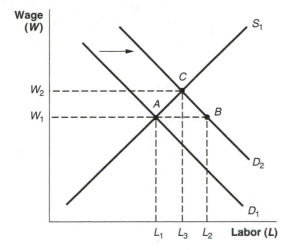

(b) Excess Supply

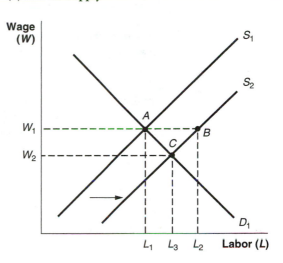

market efficiently match the job openings in firms with the individuals seeking work? As discussed in Chapter 1, the answer to this question involves two key processes: changes in wage rates and the process of labor mobility. This section first examines how these processes work to efficiently allocate labor in the absence of any restrictions. Then the section explores in detail how labor markets adjust to the imposition of a government-mandated minimum wage.

Shown in Figure 6.5 are two labor markets. The demand curve for labor in each market is D_1, and the supply curve is S_1. Assuming each market is perfectly competitive, the equilibrium wage and level of employment will be W_1, L_1 (point A). Assume that each market is perturbed by some event that shifts the demand or supply curve for labor. How will the market regain an equilibrium so that

SEE

Empirical Evidence 6-2:
Wages of Hospital and
Manufacturing Workers,
p. 307.

demand and supply are again equal? There are two cases to consider: first, the market reaction to a situation of *excess demand;* and second, the reaction to a situation of *excess supply.* Two real-world examples of the adjustment process described in this section are illustrated in Empirical Evidence 6-2.

Excess Demand

Starting from a point of equilibrium such as point A in Figure 6.5, a situation of excess demand in the labor market can arise from one of two sources: an increase in labor demand or a decrease in labor supply. The former case is illustrated in graph (a). Assume for this example that a rise in consumer spending has led to an increase in sales for firms in this labor market, with sales in other markets remaining constant. As a result, the demand curve for labor will shift to the right, from D_1 to D_2, illustrating that at the going wage of W_1 the desired level of employment by firms has increased from L_1 to L_2 (point A to B). At the wage W_1, there is now an excess demand for labor of $L_2 - L_1$, a condition that will cause firms to bid up wages as individual firms compete for scarce labor. A new equilibrium will be achieved only when the wage rate has risen to W_2 (point C), where demand is again equal to supply. This wage adjustment necessary to reach the new equilibrium is possible only if workers are free to enter the labor market (move up the supply curve) and employers face no restrictions in offering workers higher wages. At this new equilibrium, the level of employment L_3 is higher than L_1 but lower than L_2. The competitive model predicts that three things will happen in this labor market: (1) the *absolute* dollar level of the wage will rise; (2) the wage *relative* to wages in other labor markets will rise; and (3) the level of employment will rise. If the excess demand originated from a leftward shift of the supply curve instead, predictions (1) and (2) remain the same, but prediction (3) is reversed.

Excess Supply

The second form that disequilibrium in the market can take is excess supply. This may be caused by either a leftward shift of the demand curve or a rightward shift of the supply curve. The latter case is illustrated in graph (b) of Figure 6.5. Assume for this example that a sizable migration of job seekers enters this labor market. The effect is a shift of the labor supply curve from S_1 to S_2, illustrating that at the going wage of W_1 the number of people seeking work has increased from L_1 to L_2 (point A to B). At the wage W_1, there is an excess supply of labor of $L_2 - L_1$, bidding down wage rates in a competitive market as unemployed workers compete for the scarce jobs. The new equilibrium is at the lower wage of W_2, where the demand curve D_1 and supply curve S_2 intersect (point C). The level of employment increases to L_3. Again, if restrictions to mobility or wage adjustments exist, this market could not reach its new equilibrium. One important potential restriction the market might face is the presence of a minimum wage; the minimum wage places a lower bound on how far wages can fall in the market's attempt to reach a new equilibrium. The competitive model predicts that in this situation three things will happen: (1) the absolute dollar level of wages will decline; (2) the wage rate relative to the wage in other markets will decline; and (3) the level of employment will increase. If the excess supply originated from a leftward shift of the demand curve, predictions (1) and (2) remain the same, but prediction (3) is reversed.

➡ SEE

Empirical Evidence 6-3:
The Wage Effect of
Immigration, p. 313.

Empirical Evidence 6-3 investigates the impact of the change in labor supply that results from immigration.

Market Adjustment and the Minimum Wage

An issue of long-standing controversy in labor economics is the minimum wage. Ever since the minimum wage was first established, economists have been debating the benefits and costs of the law. This section evaluates the impact of the minimum wage both in the context of a perfectly competitive labor market and in the context of a labor market monopsony.

History of the Minimum Wage

The federal minimum wage was established in 1938 by the Fair Labor Standards Act (FLSA). As shown in Table 6.2, when first established the minimum wage was set at 25 cents per hour and covered only a minority (43 percent) of the workforce, primarily workers in larger firms involved in interstate commerce. Over the years the FLSA has been amended a number of times to raise both the level of the minimum wage and the number of workers covered by the law. Most recently, the minimum wage was raised in September 1997 from $4.75 per hour to $5.15. At that time, approximately 83 percent of nonsupervisory employees in private industry were covered by the law. As of August 2004, 10 states had a minimum wage higher than the federal minimum wage, ranging from $6.15 in Delaware to $7.16 in Washington. The major groups of workers not now covered under the federal minimum wage law are executive, administrative, and professional personnel, employees of small retail firms, household workers, workers in certain recreational industries, and agricultural workers.

The reason for the periodic upward adjustment of the minimum wage is illustrated in the last two columns of Table 6.2, which show the minimum wage as a percentage of the average wage in manufacturing before and after the date of each amendment to the FLSA. Since the minimum wage is stated as a fixed dollar amount per hour, the process of economic growth and inflation continually erodes the minimum wage as an effective floor on the wages and purchasing power of low-income workers. Between January 1981 and April 1990, for example, the minimum wage declined 37 percent in real terms. As a consequence, Congress periodically raises the level of the minimum wage, generally to a level of 40 to 50 percent of the average manufacturing wage. The result is to give a saw-toothed pattern to the relative value of the minimum wage.

TABLE 6.2 LEVEL AND COVERAGE OF THE MINIMUM WAGE, 1938–THE PRESENT

Date of Minimum Wage Change	Minimum Wage	Percentage of Employees Covered in Private Industry	Percentage of Minimum Wage Relative to Average Hourly Wage in Manufacturing	
			Before	After
October 1938	$0.25	43.4%	—	40.6%
October 1939	0.30	47.1	39.6%	47.6
October 1945	0.40	55.4	30.8	41.1
January 1950	0.75	53.4	28.7	53.7
March 1956	1.00	53.1	39.3	52.3
September 1961	1.15	62.1	43.1	49.6
September 1963	1.25	62.1	46.6	50.6
February 1967	1.40	75.3	44.8	50.2
February 1968	1.60	72.6	47.6	54.4
May 1974	2.00	83.7	37.8	47.3
January 1975	2.10	83.3	42.7	44.9
January 1976	2.30	83.8	41.7	45.6
January 1978	2.65	85.1	38.5	44.4
January 1979	2.90	85.1	40.8	44.6
January 1980	3.10	86.1	41.7	44.5
January 1981	3.35	86.0	40.1	43.3
April 1990	3.80	87.5	31.4	35.6
April 1991	4.25	88.4	34.2	38.3
October 1996	4.75	87.6	33.1	37.0
September 1997	5.15	83.1[a]	35.9	38.9

[a]Corresponds to 1999 annual averages; U.S. Department of Labor, Minimum Wage and Overtime Hours under the Fair Labor Standards Act (January 2001): Table 2. This number is not directly comparable with earlier years because of the use of a new data source.

SOURCE: Bureau of the Census, *Statistical Abstract of the United States, 1992; Employment and Earnings,* various issues; and U.S. Department of Labor, *Minimum Wage and Overtime Hours under the Fair Labor Standards Act* (June 1998).

Purpose of the Minimum Wage

In assessing the benefits and costs of the minimum wage, one important consideration is to what degree the minimum wage actually fulfills its intended purposes.

As stated in the Fair Labor Standards Act, the primary purpose of the minimum wage is the "maintenance of the minimum standard of living necessary for health, efficiency and general well-being of workers." The important point to note is the phrase "minimum standard of living," which pertains to annual income, not the wage rate per se. Much like other government tax and transfer programs (for example, TANF and Social Security), the minimum wage is an attempt to put a floor under the income of a particular subgroup of the population, in this case the "working poor"—people with jobs that pay very low wages.

Who are the working poor, and how many are affected by the minimum wage? In 2003, 1.6 million workers, or about 2.9 percent of workers who were paid an hourly wage, reported earning less than or equal to the minimum wage of $5.15.[27] This group of workers comprised largely young people and women; the majority worked part-time, and most were employed in service and sales occupations. It is apparent, then, that a significant group of people work, yet receive wages sufficiently low that they may still have annual incomes below the government's official poverty line. In 2003, for example, the official poverty line for a family of four—one adult with three children—was $18,725. A head of a household with three dependents who earned the minimum wage in 2003 and worked full-time (2,000 hours per year) would have earned only $10,300.

It would appear from this example that if Congress intended the minimum wage to ensure a minimum standard of living, it has failed. The minimum wage still leaves a head of a household working full-time far below an adequate level of family income. Studies have found, however, that in actuality only a small portion of the low-wage workers (earning $5.15 or less) are living in poverty households. The reason for this discrepancy is that many low-wage workers are not single-earner heads of households, but rather so-called secondary earners, such as teenagers and spouses. In this case, while the individual incomes of these low-wage workers were quite low, total family income was often above the poverty line because of earnings of other family members, particularly male heads of households.

These data point out a critical issue for Congress in deciding on the appropriate level of the minimum wage. For the minority of low-wage workers who are single-earner family heads, particularly female family heads, the minimum wage is sufficiently low that even with full-time work their annual income may still fall far below the poverty line. For these people, the minimum wage fails to fulfill its objective of ensuring a minimum standard of living. To raise the minimum wage further, however, might work to the detriment of other low-wage workers such as teenagers who do not have the minimum income requirements of a household head and who might, at the higher minimum wage, be unable to find jobs at all.

The Minimum Wage in a Perfectly Competitive Market

Given the intended purpose of the minimum wage law, the competitive model of wage determination can be used to identify the benefits and costs of the law and who the gainers and losers are likely to be in a perfectly competitive environment. This analysis is illustrated in Figure 6.6, graphs (a) and (b).

---

27   http://www.bls.gov/cps/cpsaat44.pdf.

Before the enactment of a minimum wage law, the wage rate in both the covered—graph (a)—and uncovered—graph (b)—sectors is W_1. If employers in the covered sector are required to pay a minimum wage of W_2, employment will decline from L_1 to L_2 (point A to B), but L_3 (point C) people will now want to work. If the $L_3 - L_2$ people continue to search for work in the covered sector, unemployment will rise by that amount. Some of these workers, however, will probably migrate to the uncovered sector, shifting the labor supply curve from S_U to S_{U1}. If wages are flexible downward, the wage in the uncovered sector will fall to W_3 (point F).

(a) Covered Sector

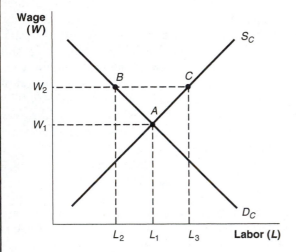

(b) Uncovered Sector

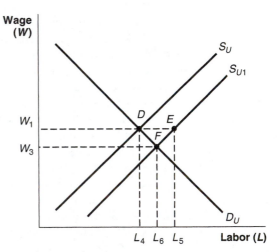

Figure 6.6 shows the market demand and supply curves for two low-wage sectors, a "covered" sector in graph (a) and an "uncovered" sector in graph (b). To begin, assume that there is no minimum wage law and that the workers and jobs in each sector are identical. Competition in the labor market would ensure that the wage rates in each sector are also equal, shown as W_1 in both graphs. Now assume that Congress passes a minimum wage law that mandates all employers in the covered sector to pay a wage of at least W_2. What will be the impact on the two sectors?

The first and most basic prediction of economic theory is that the imposition of a minimum wage above the market-determined wage will cause a decline in employment in the covered sector. In graph (a) this prediction is represented by the decline in employment from L_1 (point A) to L_2 (point B) on the demand curve D_C.

In the short run this decline in employment results from the scale effect of labor demand as the higher minimum wage forces up labor costs and product prices with a resulting decline in sales and employment. In the long run the negative employment effect is even larger, since the demand curve becomes more elastic due to the substitution effect as firms replace labor with capital.

A second, less certain prediction is that the imposition of a minimum wage will also cause a rise in unemployment in the covered sector. At the minimum wage of W_2, employment is only L_2 (point B), but the supply of people wanting to work has increased to L_3 (point C). If these workers continue to search actively for jobs, then measured unemployment in the covered sector would increase by $L_3 - L_2$. The reason this prediction is less than certain is that some or all of these unemployed workers may give up their job search in the covered sector, either by dropping out of the labor force as discouraged workers, pursuing some nonwork alternative such as school, or remaining in the labor force but moving to the uncovered sector in hopes of obtaining jobs there.[28] To the extent that any of these three events happens, measured unemployment in the covered sector will increase less, or possibly not at all, in reaction to a minimum wage.

A third predicted impact of a minimum wage involves wages and employment in the uncovered sector. Assuming that some of the workers who lose their jobs in the covered sector decide to seek jobs in the uncovered sector, the supply of labor at the prevailing wage of W_1 would increase, represented in graph (b) by a rightward shift in the supply curve from S_U to S_{U1}. At W_1 there is now an excess supply of labor of $L_5 - L_4$ (point E − point D) in the uncovered sector, resulting in downward pressure on wages. If wages are downwardly flexible in this market, the wage would decline from W_1 to W_3, leading to a new equilibrium at point F with a lower wage, but a higher level of employment (L_6) than originally. If wages do not fall, and assuming some of the unemployed workers continue to search actively for jobs in the uncovered sector, unemployment will register a net increase.

The winners from the minimum wage law are the L_2 workers in the covered sector who kept their jobs and are working at higher wages than before. There are several groups of losers. The $L_1 - L_2$ workers in the covered sector who are laid off by employers because of the increase in the wage lose most. Two other groups of losers are consumers who have to pay higher prices for the goods and services produced by firms in the covered sector, and the business firms themselves that, in the short run at least, will have lower profits. If wages should fall in the uncovered sector, a fourth group of losers would be those workers who had originally been working for the wage W_1.

Has the minimum wage law achieved its objective of raising the income of low-wage workers? The answer to this depends on the elasticity of the demand curve in the covered sector. If labor demand is *inelastic* ($E_D < 1$) the answer is yes; if it is elastic the answer is no. By definition, when demand is inelastic the percentage decline in employment is smaller than the percentage increase in the wage, causing total

28 Jacob Mincer, "Unemployment Effects of Minimum Wage Changes," *Journal of Political Economy* 84, no. 4 (August 1976): S87–S104.

A Living Wage

In 1988 Des Moines, Iowa, became the first municipality to adopt what has become referred to as a "Living Wage Ordinance" (LWO). In general terms, a LWO is a local ordinance requiring city governments and, typically, firms doing business with city governments to pay workers a "living wage." This living wage is essentially a minimum wage set at a level higher than any prevailing state or federal minimum wage. The living wage gained its name from proponents whose goal is for all workers to earn a wage on which a full-time worker could achieve a reasonable standard of living; a level generally believed not achievable at prevailing state and federally mandated minimum wages. Not only have LWOs been considered and adopted by over 100 city and county governments, several colleges, universities, and school board jurisdictions have also adopted them. Each ordinance is unique in the level of the wage, who it covers, and what other restrictions are attached.

A common thread running through LWOs is a requirement that businesses with whom the city (or county, or other jurisdiction) has contracted for provision of some service (e.g., janitorial, landscaping, security) pay their workers a wage at or above some certain minimum amount. If the contracting business also offers workers health benefits, the minimum pay required is typically lower. In addition, the state living wage is typically indexed by some price index so the required minimum will increase at the same rate as prices. The minimum pay required as of July 2004 ranged from $5.70 per hour in Madison, Wisconsin, to $14.74 ($13.00 with benefits) in Fairfax, California.

The level of the living wage is typically justified based on an estimate of the amount a full-time worker would need to be paid to earn enough money to put his/her earnings at some multiple of the poverty line. For example, in 2003, the poverty line for a family with one adult and three children was $18,725 per year. This is the amount of money the federal government has determined a family of this structure needs to live. While this is the official poverty level, the goal of the living wage movement is to raise the family well out of poverty. It is commonly agreed that a reasonable goal is to elevate families from two to four times the poverty level. This means for a family with one adult and two children to be earning two times the poverty level, it would have to earn $37,450. If the adult works 2000 hours per year, he/she would need to be paid $18.73 per hour to achieve this standard of living. None of the current LWOs require this high a wage. The living wage would need to be set at $9.36 per hour for a worker to achieve even the poverty line of earnings, working 2000 hours per year; a vast majority of the current ordinances require a wage of this level or higher.

There is much controversy over the potential and realized benefits and costs to society of adopting a LWO. The primary potential benefit of requiring payment of a living wage is the reduction of poverty.

wage income paid by firms to low-wage workers in the covered sector to increase. This increase in income is not equally shared, however, since a minority of the workers in the covered sector will lose their jobs altogether, while the majority will keep their jobs and earn more per hour. Conversely, if wages fall in the uncovered sector and demand is inelastic, total income received by workers in that sector will fall.

continued

Not only do the lowest paid workers gain from a higher minimum, but employers may raise wages of higher-paid workers, as well, in order to maintain their wage structure differentials. Indeed, a broad study of the impacts of the living wage found that the wages of primarily the lowest-paid workers increased and that measured poverty was lowered in the urban areas in which these laws were introduced. Even if the living wage is not at a level high enough for a single earner to pull its family out of poverty, many low-wage workers are not the only wage earners in the household, so that even a poverty-level living wage can be high enough to raise a multiple-earner household out of poverty.

As shown in Figure 6.6, the potential cost of an LWO is that the wage gains result in employment losses. The same study that found higher earnings and poverty reduction also found reduced employment among the lowest paid, which was partially offset by greater employment among higher-paid workers. There seemed to be some displacement of workers going on; now that employers had to pay more at the low-end, they were replacing those low-paid workers with higher-skilled, higher-paid workers. Other studies, that looked at the specific hiring patterns of firms, rather than overall employment levels, have found very little to no change in firing patterns among firms affected by an LWO.

Among other potential impacts that have been measured in various locales, one identified outcome is higher worker productivity and fewer absences among workers affected by the LWO; the higher living wage seems to have had an efficiency wage effect in some places. This may explain why small employment effects have been measured at the firm level. In addition, some studies have found contractors passing on the higher employee costs to the city in which an LWO has been enacted, reducing services that a city can provide with its limited budget. Others have found better quality contractors willing to bid on jobs because higher worker costs for all bidders made the bids from contractors who have always paid their workers a higher wage more competitive.

For every study that finds a net societal benefit of an LWO, there is another finding just the opposite. What is clear is that there are winners and losers, but how much is won and how much is lost is much less clear.

SOURCES: Living Wage Resource Center http://www. livingwagecampaign.org; Timothy J. Bartik, "Thinking about Local Living Wage Requirements," mimeo, W.E. Upjohn Institute for Employment Research (November 2003); Scott Adams and David Neumark, "Living Wage Effects: New and Improved Evidence," *NBER Working Paper #9702* (May 2003); Anonymous, "Costly 'Living Wage' Not Way to Help Low-Paid Workers," *Tampa Tribune* (16 June 2004): 12; Anonymous, "Living Wage Laws Benefit Entire Community," *The Washington Post* (5 February 2004): T04.

The Minimum Wage in a Monopsony Market

The analysis of a minimum wage can look very different if evaluated in the context of a monopsony labor market. This analysis is illustrated in Figure 6.7. In this situation a minimum wage law can come closer to unambiguously improving the labor market condition of low-wage workers.

Prior to the establishment of a minimum wage, the monopsonist would pay a wage of W_1 and hire only L_1 workers (point A). When a minimum wage is set at W_2, not only do workers earn a higher wage, but employment also increases, to L_2. The reason employment increases when the wage is increased to W_1 is that the marginal cost of labor schedule

changes from MCL_1 to W_2CDE. Up to L_2, the firm can hire each additional worker at a constant wage of W_1; past L_2, however, it must pay a successively higher wage as given by the supply curve. Should the government raise the minimum wage beyond W_3, employment would decline below the original level of L_1.

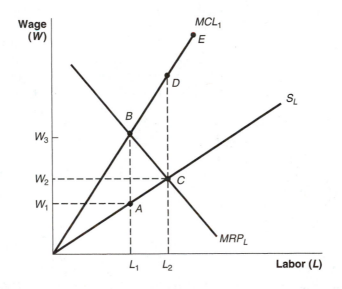

Figure 6.7 depicts the firm's marginal revenue product schedule (MRP_L) and market supply schedule (S_L) for labor and, since the market is characterized by a single employer, the upward-sloping marginal cost of labor curve (MCL_1) is also depicted. The monopsonist decides on an employment level of L_1, which is the level of employment where the marginal cost of labor equals the marginal revenue product of labor. In order to attract L_1 workers into the market, the employer pays a wage of W_1 (point A). Now assume that Congress passes a minimum wage law mandating that this employer must pay a wage of at least W_2. What happens to employment?

    The impact of the minimum wage is to flatten out the marginal cost of labor curve; the employer can hire additional workers (up to L_2) at a constant rate of W_2. Beyond L_2 (point C), the employer must pay a successively higher wage as dictated by the supply curve. In effect, the firm's marginal cost of labor schedule becomes W_2CDE. In this example, employment actually *increases* when Congress mandates a minimum wage higher than the prevailing wage; both wages *and* employment increase (from W_1, L_1 to W_2, L_2). In terms of gainers and losers, it is clear that all original low-wage workers gain; they all keep their jobs and they are all now earning a higher wage. In addition, all workers between L_2 and L_1 gain; they are working and earning a wage higher than they require to supply their labor (a wage above the labor supply curve). The losers in this scenario are consumers, who will likely pay a higher price for the product being produced, and employers who lose some of their monopsony profits. It is important to note, however, that if the government raises the minimum wage above W_3, employment will decline below the original level of L_1.

In both the perfectly competitive labor market and the monopsony labor market, therefore, raising the minimum wage beyond a certain level will almost certainly reduce employment of low-wage workers. However, there is a range within which the minimum wage can be raised in a monopsony environment and result in an *increase* in employment. While it is unlikely that most labor markets are characterized by a single employer (particularly in low-skill industries, such as fast-food restaurants), there is greater possibility that individual firms face an upward-sloping labor supply curve and thus experience a "local" monopsony. For example, while a large city may have many fast-food restaurants, they each mostly employ teenagers who are not willing (and, often, are unable) to travel across town to chase a higher wage; they will likely take what they can get at the fast-food restaurants closest to their home. It is important to point out that for local monopsony to result in an employment increase in the labor market, each restaurant must also have some control over the price it charges consumers. Otherwise, the increase in employment by restaurants who stay in the industry will be offset by the loss of employment by firms who go out of business as a result of the higher labor cost. (Increased employment results in greater output supplied in the market and a fall in product price, and firms previously just breaking even will start to operate at a loss and eventually leave the market.)

The Minimum Wage and Efficiency Wage Theory

The discussion of labor market adjustments to shifts in supply or demand, and analysis of the employment impact of institutional features such as the minimum wage, have all taken place so far under the assumption that workers' productivity levels are unaffected by the wage level. This assumption was first questioned in Chapter 4 in the discussion of criticisms of the marginal productivity theory of labor demand. In Chapter 4 it was argued that higher wages might lead to higher worker productivity either by inducing them to work harder or by improving their physical strength through improved diet and health. This hypothesis—that higher wages lead to high worker productivity—is known as **efficiency wage theory.**[29]

A positive impact of wages on employee productivity changes the analysis of the impact of a minimum wage (or any other policy that affects the wage) on employment.[30] Figure 6.8 shows the market demand and supply curves for labor in a perfectly competitive market. In the absence of a minimum wage, the market wage is W_1 and the employment level is L_1 (point A). Now assume that a minimum wage law is passed, setting the minimum wage at W_2. Under the assumption of no link between wages and productivity, the demand curve for labor remains D_1 and the firm adjusts its level of demand along the demand curve to point B. If, in light of this higher wage, workers now have greater physical strength or increase their effort on the job, the marginal product of each worker is now higher, which in turn increases the marginal revenue product of each worker, shifting the demand curve to the right.[31] The new demand curve is reflected in Figure 6.8 as $D_2 = MRP_{L2}$, and employment actually increases to L_2 (point C).

Clearly there is a limit to which workers can adjust their effort or productivity levels in response to a higher wage. Consequently, this potential positive employment impact of a minimum wage is almost certainly restricted to low wage levels in the case of improved physical strength and to modest-sized wage increases in the case of improved morale and work effort. Even if the higher wage doesn't spur any single worker to put forth greater effort, however, it surely will attract a worker of higher quality (that is, with a higher reservation wage) to the market, enhancing the overall productivity pool.

Research Findings

In an attempt to determine the benefits and costs of the minimum wage, economists have conducted considerable empirical research. Several conclusions from these studies stand out.

---

29 Harvey Leibenstein, "Underemployment in Backward Economies," *Journal of Political Economy* 65 (1957): 91–103, is credited with providing the first modern illustration of how high wages can positively impact productivity through their improved nutritional implications in the context of a developing economy. An earlier reference found in Jacob Vanderlint, *Money Answers All Things* (London, 1734), likely entitles him to recognition as the first person to suggest the positive effect of high wages on productivity. Joseph E. Stiglitz, "The Efficiency Wage Hypothesis, Surplus Labour and the Distribution of Labour in LDCs," *Oxford Economic Papers* 28 (1976): 185–207, was one of the pioneers who applied efficiency wage models to labor markets in advanced economies. An example of recent research on efficiency wages can be found in Carl M. Campbell III, "Do Firms Pay Efficiency Wages? Evidence with Data at the Firm Level," *Journal of Labor Economics* 11 (July 1993): 442–70; Arthur Goldsmith et al., "Working Hard for the Money? Efficiency Wages and Worker Effort," *Journal of Economic Psychology* 21 (August 2000): 351–85; and Peter Muhlau and Siegwart Lindenberg, "Efficiency Wages: Signals or Incentives? An Empirical Study of the Relationship Between Wages and Commitment," *Journal of Management and Governance* 7 (2003): 385–400.

30 See James B. Rebitzer and Lowell J. Taylor, "The Consequences of Minimum Wage Laws: Some New Theoretical Ideas," *Journal of Public Economics* 56 (February 1995): 245–55.

31 Recall that the demand curve actually plots workers' marginal revenue product, which is marginal revenue times the marginal product of each worker ($MRP_L = MR \cdot MP_L$). If workers' marginal product of labor is a positive function of wages, then as wages increase, MRP_L increases, yielding a new, higher demand curve.

FIGURE 6.8 **EFFICIENCY WAGE THEORY AND THE IMPACT OF A MINIMUM WAGE**

Before a minimum wage law is enacted, the wage rate in the labor market is W_1, and employment is L_1 (point A). If wages and worker productivity are assumed to be unrelated, a minimum wage set at W_2 would result in a decreased employment level (point B). If wages and worker productivity are positively related, however, the higher minimum wage results in a higher MRP_L, thus a higher demand curve (D_2). Employment actually increases to L_2 (point C).

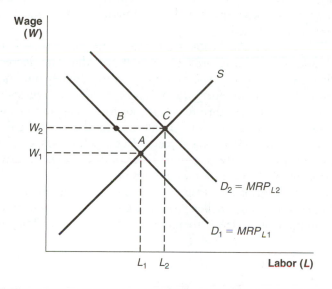

First, a significant rise in the minimum wage (or coverage ratio) does lead to a net decline in employment, as the perfectly competitive model predicts. A small to modest increase in the minimum wage, on the other hand, sometimes has little or no negative effect on employment, at least in the short run (for reasons explained shortly). Evidence indicates that the negative employment effect is greatest for teenagers and least for adult men. For teenagers, for example, a 10 percent rise in the minimum wage has been found to reduce their employment by about 2 to 4 percent, on average.[32]

32 Nicholas Williams and Jeffrey A. Mills, "Minimum Wage Effects by Gender," *Journal of Labor Research* 19 (Spring 1998): 397–414. Also see Stephen Basen and Velayoudom Marimoutou, "Looking for a Needle in a Haystack? A Re-examination of the Time Series Relationship Between Teenage Employment and Minimum Wages in the United States," *Oxford Bulletin of Economics and Statistics* 64 (August 2002): 599–725.

While the bulk of the literature indicates that a rise in the minimum wage will lower employment levels, some recent research suggests that the employment impact will actually be negligible or, in some cases, positive as might be predicted in the case of a monopsony market or in the presence of efficiency wages.[33]

Even in the perfectly competitive model, an increase in the minimum wage results in higher incomes for some workers. Higher incomes should result in greater demand for products, thus greater demand for labor to produce those products. So even if workers affected by the minimum wage experience an overall employment decline, *total* employment may rise as a result of the increased spending by those minimum wage workers who have retained their jobs. It is difficult to argue, however, that the new employment spawned by increased spending by these low-income workers would be enough to fully offset the initial employment losses.[34]

A second conclusion from the literature is that a decline in employment, should it take place, probably understates the total decrease in labor demand by firms, since the response of employers to a higher minimum wage is often to reduce the hours of work of employees. Evidence suggests that a higher minimum wage leads firms to turn full-time jobs for teenagers and adult males into part-time jobs to save on labor cost.[35] Evidence that the income gain among teenagers (that results from a higher wage) may offset any hours or employment loss, however is provided by a study that finds that youth crime is negatively correlated with the presence and level of a minimum wage.[36]

Third, firms also respond to a higher minimum wage with a combination of higher prices and smaller profit margins. There is also some evidence that a higher minimum wage leads to increased management efficiency due to attempts to

---

[33] Details of minimum wage alternative outcome models are found in Madeline Zavodny, "Why Minimum Wage Hikes May Not Reduce Employment," *Federal Reserve Bank of Atlanta Economic Review* (2d Quarter, 1998): 18–28. Also see David Card and Alan Krueger, "Minimum Wages and Employment: A Case Study of the Fast-Food Industry in New Jersey," *American Economic Review* 84 (September 1994): 772–84, and David Neumark and William Wascher, "A Reanalysis of the Effect of the New Jersey Minimum Wage Increase on the Fast-Food Industry with Representative Payroll Data," *American Economic Review* (December 2000): 1362–1420. Some international evidence of the impact of a minimum wage can be found in Stephen Machin and Alan Manning, "Minimum Wages and Economic Outcomes in Europe," *European Economic Review* 41 (April 1997): 733–42; Martin Roma, "The Consequences of Doubling the Minimum Wage: The Case of Indonesia," *Industrial and Labor Relations Review* 54 (July 2001): 864–81; Francis Kramarz et al., "The Tail of Two Countries: Minimum Wages and Employment in France and the United States," *IZA Discussion Paper* No. 203 (September 2000); and Richard Dickens et al., "The Effects of Minimum Wages on Employment," *Journal of Labor Economics* 17 (January 1999): 1–22.

[34] The potential for the increased product demand, which results from workers earning higher wages, leading to inflation is explored by Sara Lemos, "The Effect of the Minimum Wage on Prices," *IZA Discussion Paper No. 1072* (March 2004).

[35] Evidence of this is found in Rand W. Ressler, John K. Watson, and Franklin G. Mixon Jr., "Full Wages, Part-Time Employment and the Minimum Wage," *Applied Economics* 28 (November 1996): 1415–19.

[36] Andrew Kallem, "Youth Crime and the Minimum Wage," Mimeo, Harvard University (March 2004).

minimize the adverse impact of the wage hike on the firm, a reaction commonly referred to as a **shock effect**.[37] The impact of a higher minimum wage is also offset by the fact that a small minority of employers (either knowingly or unknowingly) will continue to pay wages below what is legally required. The net effect is that a modest-sized increase in the minimum wage may not result in any detectable decline in employment in the short run.

Fourth, of the workers who lose their jobs in the covered sector, only one-third or fewer remain unemployed; the majority withdraw from the labor force.[38] This effect, however, is mitigated by new entrants to the covered sector now seeking the higher-paying jobs.[39]

Fifth, a rise in the minimum wage increases the total income received by adult males and females despite the negative employment effect. For teenagers, the elasticity of demand is sufficiently high that as a group their total income may be reduced by the increase. The chief beneficiaries of the minimum wage are adult females, and the chief losers are teenagers, particularly nonwhite teenagers.[40] Adult males, because of the small number working at minimum wages, are not much affected.

Sixth, and finally, an additional cost to teenagers from the minimum wage is a decrease in job experience and on-the-job training. According to a number of economists, the most important consideration for a teenager is not the wage itself, but rather a chance to get a first job, acquire some experience and training, and then use this as a springboard to upward mobility in the job market. Because it raises labor costs to employers, critics of the minimum wage contend that it causes a reduction in job opportunities and training for teenagers and thus has a detrimental impact on their transition from school to work.[41]

Almost every other country in addition to the United States also has a minimum wage in place. Cross-country variations in minimum wage levels and other

---

[37] "Rise in Minimum Wage Spurs Some Firms to Cut Work Hours and Hiring of Youths," *Wall Street Journal* (August 15, 1978), and E. G. West and Michael McKee, "Monopsony and 'Shock' Arguments for Minimum Wages," *Southern Economic Journal* 46, no. 3 (January 1980): 883–91. The impact of a minimum wage productivity "shock" can also be traced to changes in unemployment and wage disparity. See Birthe Larsen, "Minimum Wages, Technological Progress, and Loss of Skill," *European Economic Review* 45 (August 2001): 1521–44.

[38] Mincer, "Unemployment Effects of Minimum Wage Changes." Also see Walter Wessels, "The Minimum Wage and Labor Force Participation," Mimeo, North Carolina State University Economics Department (1998).

[39] Kenneth A. Couch and David C. Whittenburg, "The Response of Hours of Work to Increases in the Minimum Wage," *Southern Economic Journal* 68 (July 2001): 171–77.

[40] An analysis of the impact of the minimum wage on low-wage teenagers is provided by Madeline Zavodny, "The Effect of the Minimum Wage on Employment and Hours," *Labour Economics* 7 (2000); 729–50.

[41] Masonori Hashimoto, "Minimum Wage Effects on Training on the Job," *American Economic Review* 72, no. 5 (September 1982): 1070–87. Darron Acemoglu and Jorn-Steffen Pischke, "Minimum Wages and On-the-Job Training," MIT Department of Economics Working Paper No. 99–25 (November 2001); and David Fairris and Roberto Pedace, "The Impact of Minimum Wages on Job Training: An Empirical Exploration with Establishment Data," *Southern Economic Journal* 70 (January 2004): 566–83, find little evidence of the minimum wage reducing training.

institutional differences provide fertile ground for exploring the employment impacts of the minimum wage. David Neumark and William Wascher compare these effects across countries and find that negative employment effects are stronger in countries with other rigid labor standards (e.g., government restrictions on work time, flexible contracts, and unionization).[42] Among countries with low employment protection laws and rigid labor standards, Neumark and Wascher found minimum wage disemployment effects for teens averaging between −0.3 to −0.5, meaning that a one percent increase in the minimum wage reduces employment among teens in these countries by 0.3 and 0.5 percent.

The evidence on the minimum wage suggests that the benefits and costs of the law vary considerably for different labor force groups—adult women gain the most and teenagers are hurt the most. In an attempt to lessen the adverse impact of the minimum wage, Congress has established a subminimum wage (currently referred to as the "Youth Minimum Wage Program") that can be used to pay employees under 20 years of age for the first 90 consecutive days of their employment. In addition, certain students, apprentices, and workers with disabilities may be paid less than the minimum wage if their employers obtain special certificates.[43] Proponents of this type of legislation argue that it leads to a large increase in job opportunities for the qualifying groups of workers. Critics argue that the subminimum wage will lead to more jobs for these workers, but only at the expense of fewer jobs for other groups.[44] The main beneficiary, in this view, would be business firms that could pay lower wages for the same work and earn more profits. Subsequent research on this issue found that the subminimum wage that was in place in the early 1990s had only a very modest positive impact on the number of job opportunities for teenagers, in large part because few employers used it.[45]

The adoption of a national minimum wage by the United Kingdom for the first time in 1999 provides a unique opportunity to assess the impact of a minimum wage on employment, training, and other outcomes.[46] In April 1999, the National Minimum Wage (NMW) came into effect at £3.60 for adults and £3.00 for eighteen- to twenty-one-year-olds and twenty-two-year-olds undergoing training (this lower level is referred to as the "Development Rate"). Both the adult and

---

42 David Neumark and William Wascher, "Minimum Wages, Labor Market Institutions, and Youth Employment: A Cross-National Analysis," *Industrial and Labor Relations Review* (January 2004): 223–48.

43 For further details on the provisions of the current minimum wage laws, see http://www.dol.gov/dol/compliance/comp-flsa.htm

44 An additional unintended consequence of greater job opportunities for teenagers is that many will drop out of school to pursue those jobs. See David Neumark and William Wascher, "The Effects of Minimum Wages on Teenage Employment and Enrollment: Evidence from Matched CPS Surveys," *Research in Labor Economics*, vol. 15 (1996): 25–63.

45 David Neumark and William Wascher, "Employment Effects of Minimum and Subminimum Wages: Panel Data on State Minimum Wage Laws," *Industrial and Labor Relations Review* 46, no. 1 (October, 1992): 55–81.

46 For details on spill-over (wage effects of a minimum wage on more highly paid workers) and wage inequality outcomes, see David Metcalf, "The Impact of the National Minimum Wage on the Pay Distribution, Employment and Training," *The Economic Journal* 114 (March 2004): C84-C86; and Richard Dickens and Alan Manning, "Spikes and Spill-overs: The Impact of the National Minimum Wage on the Wage Distribution in a Low-wage Sector," *Economic Journal* 114 (March 2004): C95-C101.

development rates have been increased on a regular basis, and as of October 2004 were at £4.85 and £4.10, respectively. These amounts are equivalent to $8.78 and $7.43 in U.S. dollars (October 2004). The rates are now indexed and will be raised in conjunction with the median wage.

Analyses find no evidence of widespread employment loss from either the introduction of or later increases in the NMW.[47] However, one study found marginally significant employment losses among home care assistants, a group of workers among the lowest paid in the United Kingdom. Prior to the introduction of the NMW, 32 percent of care assistants were paid below the minimum wage level. In care homes with 10 percent or more of their workers being paid below the new minimum wage, employment growth was 1.3 percent lower.[48] In other words, those employers who experienced the greatest increase in labor costs as a result of the NMW also added workers to their payroll more slowly than employers not as heavily affected. In addition, contrary to some predictions that the introduction of a minimum wage might reduce training among workers who might be willing to pay for training through a lower wage, research on the U.K. development minimum wage indicates that it increased training among the affected workers. The probability of training among workers previously earning below the NMW increased 8 to 11 percent relative to workers earning above the NMW when it was introduced.[49]

The Firm's Internal Wage Structure

Up to this point the process of wage determination has been examined at the market level and the level of the firm. The next topic is the determination of wages *within* the firm, or what is known as the firm's internal wage structure.[50] The internal wage structure refers to the set of wage rates paid for particular jobs and workers in the business firm and the system of wage differentials that separate each job and worker from others. The workforce of nearly every firm comprises people performing varied and distinct jobs, ranging from the waitress, cook, and cashier in a small restaurant to the hundreds and thousands of distinct jobs in a large corporation. Part of the personnel function of the management of every firm is to decide what wage rate each individual in the organization will be paid. The interesting questions for labor economics on this topic are how the internal wage structure is

---

47 For example, see Mark B. Stewart, "The Employment Effects of the National Minimum Wage," *The Economic Journal* 114 (March 2004): C110–C116.

48 Stephen Machin and Joan Wilson, "Minimum Wages in a Low-wage Labour Market: Care Homes in the UK," *The Economic Journal* 114 (March 2004): C102–C109.

49 Wiji Arulampalam, Alison L. Booth, and Mark L. Bryan, "Training and the New Minimum Wage," *The Economic Journal* 114 (March 2004): C87–C94.

50 The continued importance of established internal wage structures in determining the pay of managers is demonstrated by K. C. O'Shaughnessy et al., "Changes in Managerial Pay Structures 1986–1992 and Rising Returns to Skill," *Oxford Economic Papers* 53 (July 2001): 482–507.

established, whether it serves to efficiently allocate labor within the firm, how the structure might affect worker productivity, and the extent to which market forces of supply and demand influence the internal wage structure.

An important component of a firm's internal wage structure is the **job structure** within the firm.[51] The job structure is defined as the set of jobs in terms of skill and function required by the firm. The job structure in a particular firm is heavily influenced by the technology of production; if the company is an airline, for example, technology dictates that the firm's job structure must include pilots, flight attendants, and so on. The types of jobs in a firm are not completely determined by technology, however, for as shown in Chapter 5, one of the major long-run decisions of the firm is what proportions and kinds of labor, capital, and other factor inputs to use. Once these are decided and a specific plant is built, then the technology of production generally determines within fairly narrow bounds the job structure for which the firm will need to recruit labor.

A particular job structure is illustrated in Figure 6.9 for a chemical plant. This job structure shows one of the most fundamental features of modern technology—specialization and the division of labor. As Adam Smith pointed out two hundred years ago, production can be made more efficient by breaking the task into separate identifiable parts and assigning workers to specialize in different ones. This is reflected in the organization of modern firms into functional departments that specialize in one particular part of the production process. The chemical plant in Figure 6.9 requires five separate functions or **job clusters** (jobs related to a common activity): maintenance, quality control, operations, clerical, and management.

One additional feature of a firm's job structure has an important influence on the internal wage structure: the concept of a **job ladder.** Each job cluster contains a group of tasks that are related to a common function or activity in the production process. For many types of production, the common set of jobs in a job cluster also form a definite hierarchy of tasks extending in a vertical direction from the least-skilled job up to the most-skilled job. This vertical hierarchy of jobs, known as the job ladder, is illustrated in Figure 6.9 by the upward line of progression in jobs for both the "operations" and the "quality control" cluster.

What gives rise to these job ladders? Peter Doeringer and Michael Piore have identified three factors: the specificity of skills for the jobs, the importance of on-the-job training, and workplace custom.[52] In many firms, some jobs require specific skills or knowledge that are, at least to some degree, of use only to that one firm and can be learned only by actual training on the job. An example is a locomotive engineer who starts out as a yardman and works up to brakeman, conductor, and finally engineer for a particular railroad. An engineer with the knowledge of

---

51   The discussion in this section is drawn from George H. Hildebrand, "External Influences and the Determination of the Internal Wage Structure" in J. L. Mey, ed., *Internal Wage Structure* (Amsterdam: North-Holland, 1963): 260–99.

52   Peter B. Doeringer and Michael J. Piore, *Internal Labor Markets and Manpower Analysis* (Lexington, Mass.: Heath Lexington Books, 1971).

FIGURE 6.9   THE JOB STRUCTURE IN A CHEMICAL PLANT

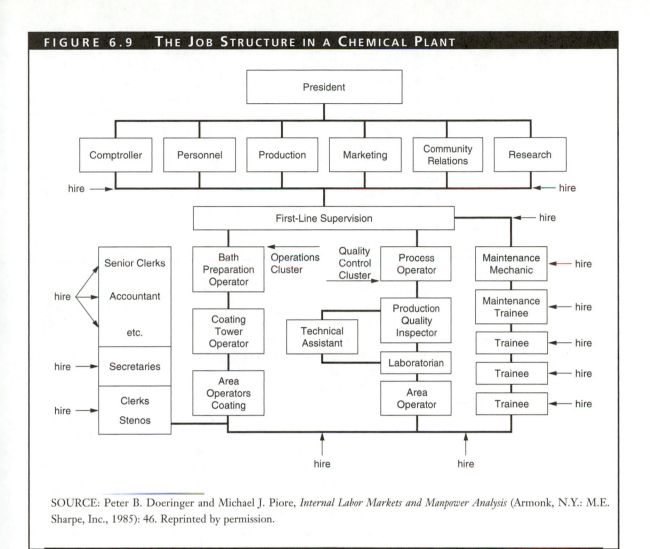

SOURCE: Peter B. Doeringer and Michael J. Piore, *Internal Labor Markets and Manpower Analysis* (Armonk, N.Y.: M.E. Sharpe, Inc., 1985): 46. Reprinted by permission.

the specific route and operating procedures of that railroad cannot be bought by the firm in the **external labor market**—the knowledge and skills have to be learned and the progression up the job ladder is the manner in which the training is accomplished. According to Doeringer and Piore, these economic reasons for job ladders are also augmented by the force of custom at the workplace as informal or unwritten practices regarding promotion to higher jobs become solidified over time into a recognized job ladder.

The effect of a job ladder, then, is to create an **internal labor market** within the firm. The internal labor market refers to those jobs in the firm for which competition to fill a vacancy is limited to workers already employed with the firm. The beginning of the internal labor market is the **port of entry,** which connects the internal job ladder to the labor market outside the firm. In Figure 6.9, the ports of entry are denoted by the word *hire* at the bottom of the operations and quality control clusters. If someone at the top of the job ladder retires, workers at each step of the ladder move up one rung, creating a vacancy at the bottom or port of entry. To fill this vacancy, the firm goes to the external market, where it competes with other firms for workers at the entry level. The decision of whom to hire to fill the entry-level positions is important for both the firm and the job applicants in the external market. It is important for the firm because the person chosen is likely to be with the firm for a considerable time, and the firm will invest much money in that person for additional training. For these reasons, firms often conduct elaborate screening processes to select workers for entry-level positions in the internal labor market (for example, management trainee), taking much more care with these positions than with secretarial or custodial positions requiring less investment in firm-specific training. The selection process for these entry-level positions is also important for the persons in the queue of job applicants because the chosen person gains a job with the potential of considerable earnings growth, promotion possibilities, and job security. Not surprisingly, these attractive features often result in intense competition, as several hundred job candidates compete for a handful of job openings at the ports of entry of large firms.

Given the structure of jobs and promotion ladders in the firm, how does the firm determine the appropriate set of wage rates for workers in each job cluster and among job clusters? One solution would be to pay workers in each job classification the going wage for that occupation and skill level as determined by supply and demand in the external labor market. This solution was pictured in Figure 6.1, where demand and supply in the market determined the equilibrium wage for each type of labor and the firm acted as a passive wage taker.

For some or all of the job clusters within a firm, the internal wage structure is, in fact, largely determined by competitive pressures in the external labor market. An example is the clerical job cluster in the chemical plant shown in Figure 6.9. For clerical jobs there is no job ladder to speak of and no internal labor market. The skills required of clerical workers are generally standardized and transferable from one employer to another. In this case, the area of indeterminacy in wages will be relatively small, and the chemical plant, if it is not to lose all of its workers, must pay a rate fairly close to the going wage in the market.

For other job clusters in the firm for which job ladders and on-the-job training are important, the area of indeterminacy in wages may be much larger.[53] This is because jobs in the internal labor market are not all standardized as the clerical jobs are; rather, each one is idiosyncratic in that it involves a specific set of skills unique to the firm that can be learned only by a process of on-the-job training as the worker moves up the job ladder. The upper limit to wages W_U for each job in the internal labor market is determined by the marginal revenue product of the

---

53   See O. E. Williamson, M. L. Wachter, and J. E. Harris, "Understanding the Employment Relation: The Analysis of Idiosyncratic Exchange," *Bell Journal of Economics* (Spring 1975): 250–78.

worker; at a wage higher than the MRP_L, the firm would find it unprofitable to fill the job. The lower limit to wages W_L that the firm must pay for each job in the internal labor market is determined by the best wage offer the worker could get if he or she quit and went elsewhere. Because of the firm-specific nature of job skills and training, the value of the worker to another firm, and thus the wage received, is likely to be considerably lower than the wage paid by the present firm. In the chemical plant in Figure 6.9, for example, a worker in the operations job cluster who quit would lose the position on that job ladder and would have to begin again at a lower position (possibly the port of entry) at another chemical firm. The consequence is that even if the firm does not pay the worker in the internal labor market a wage equal to the value of his or her productivity, the worker would still accept a range of lesser wage rates before going to some other firm. For clerical workers, on the other hand, the lack of job ladders and firm-specific job skills makes the worker equally valuable to every firm in the market. Thus this type of labor will trade at or relatively close to the going wage.[54]

Because the external labor market cannot determine a unique wage for jobs in the internal labor market, firms have to use some nonmarket device to establish an explicit wage structure. One technique that is frequently used is *job evaluation*. The primary objective of a job evaluation system is to achieve an internal wage structure that promotes equity and rewards efficiency while at the same time being consistent with competitive conditions in the external labor market. Most job evaluation systems have the same basic methodology.[55] The first step is to write a detailed description of each job. The second step is to rate or evaluate each job according to one or more "compensable factors" such as the skill and education required, degree of physical discomfort or risk, amount of supervisory responsibility, and so on. The third step is to add these ratings together in some way to create a total "job worth score." Based on the job worth score, each job in a job cluster can then be ranked from highest to lowest and assigned a wage rate or pay range. In actual practice, most job ladders contain certain "key" jobs that are closely linked to the external labor market and for which market rates of pay are readily available from surveys conducted by the federal government (such as the local area wage survey) or from surveys conducted by private consulting firms.[56] In devising an internal wage structure, the firm will take these wage rates as reference points and then use job evaluation scores to establish pay rates for the positions between the key jobs.

---

54   Further evidence on the power of internal labor markets to curb or not curb certain turnover behavior of workers is found in Laura J. Owen, "Gender Differences in Labor Turnover, and the Development of Internal Labor Markets in the United States," *Enterprise and Society* 2 (March 2001): 41–71.

55   See Richard I. Henderson, *Compensation Management in a Knowledge-Based World*, 7th ed. (Upper Saddle River, N.J.: Prentice-Hall, 1997).

56   A bibliography and description of sources (both public and private) for occupational wages and compensation schemes can be found in Julie L. Hotchkiss, "Compensation Policy and Firm Performance: An Annotated Bibliography of Machine-Readable Data Files," *Industrial and Labor Relations Review* 43 (February 1990): 274S–289S. Also see Jason Ford, "Earnings by Level of Work: Results from Pilot Studies of the National Compensation Survey Program," *Compensation and Working Conditions* (Summer 1997): 24–31, for a description of a new methodology used by the U.S. Bureau of Labor Statistics for comparing earnings across occupations.

Segmentation and Dual Labor Market Theory

The final topic considered in this chapter is segmented labor market theory. One of the basic assumptions of the perfectly competitive model is that all jobs in the labor market are open to competition. This obviously does not mean that a waitress with no medical training can quit her job and immediately become a doctor or that an unskilled laborer can effectively compete for an ironworker's job—each person's sphere of competition is limited in the short run by his or her education, job skills, geographic location, and mental and physical abilities. The presumption of competitive theory, however, is that the walls separating labor markets are relatively porous. Given enough time to acquire the training or to move to a different city, workers can effectively compete for jobs on an equal footing with persons already in that labor market.

Many economists, while recognizing that there are some barriers to mobility across individual labor markets, believe that most jobs are, in fact, relatively wide open to competition. Others disagree, believing that the labor market is segmented or balkanized into noncompeting groups.[57] The idea of **labor market segmentation** is that strong barriers to entry prevent certain groups of workers from effectively competing for jobs in a given market. These barriers may take several forms. One is the internal labor market, which prevents workers in the external market from competing for job openings above the entry level in the firm. A second is discrimination, which causes workers of certain race or sex groups to be excluded from competition for desirable jobs. A third is union hiring rules that restrict the competition for jobs to those workers who are registered with the union hiring hall or are next in line on the company seniority list. A fourth is occupational licensing laws that restrict the entry of new practitioners into an occupation by making the licensing exam difficult, by imposing lengthy residency requirements, or by requiring large licensing fees. The common effect of these entry barriers is to give a marked advantage to the persons who are the "ins" over those who are the "outs" in the competition for jobs.

There are a number of different theories of segmented markets. One that has received considerable attention is the *dual labor market* theory. Dual labor market theory was developed in the late 1960s by institutionally oriented economists such as Peter Doeringer, Michael Piore, Barry Bluestone, and Bennett Harrison to explain continuing poverty and unemployment among disadvantaged workers, particularly blacks and other minorities in the inner city.[58] From the perspective of

---

[57]   See Marcia Freedman, *Labor Markets: Segments and Shelters* (Montclair, N.J.: Allanheld, Osmun and Co., 1976), and R. Loveridge and A. L. Mok, *Theories of Labor Market Segmentation* (Boston: Martinus Nijhoff, 1979).

[58]   See, for example, Doeringer and Piore, *Internal Labor Markets and Manpower Analysis*; Barry F. Bluestone, "The Tripartite Economy: Labour Markets and the Working Poor," *Poverty and Human Resources* (July/August 1970): 15–36; and Bennett Harrison, "The Theory of the Dual Economy," in B. Silverman and M. Yanowitch, eds., *The Worker in the Post Industrial World* (New York: Free Press, 1971). For another appraisal of the state of dual labor market theory, see William T. Dickens and Kevin Lang, "The Reemergence of Segmented Labor Market Theory," *American Economic Review* 78 no. 2 (May 1988): 129–34.

competitive theory, inner-city workers have low wages and poor employment prospects because they lack the human capital (education and training) necessary for high productivity and high earnings in the labor market. The solution to the poverty problem from this perspective is improved educational systems and job training programs for inner-city residents so that these workers can leave low-wage "bad" jobs and effectively compete in markets offering higher-wage "good" jobs.

Primary and Secondary Jobs

While this approach to the poverty problem seems promising, the dual labor market theorists concluded from their case studies of inner-city labor markets that it would not succeed. To explain why, they developed the theory of dual labor markets. Dual labor market theory posits that the labor market is segmented into a **primary labor market** and a **secondary labor market.** The primary sector consists of the good jobs in the labor market, meaning those that offer high wages, good working conditions, employment stability, chances of promotion, and equity and due process in the administration of work rules. Primary jobs are typically found in firms that are large in size, unionized, or have a superior technology. A key feature of employment in these firms is their well-developed internal labor markets, owing to the substantial amount of on-the-job-training in firm-specific skills invested in the workers. These firms screen very carefully the persons hired for the entry-level positions in the internal labor market, hoping to find persons possessing traits such as reliability, discipline, company loyalty, an ability to be a member of the company "team," and an ability to learn quickly on the job.

The secondary sector consists of the jobs in the labor market considered bad or undesirable. These low-paying, "dead-end" jobs offer little in the way of promotion prospects or job security and little protection from the arbitrary or unilateral exercise of management's authority to discipline or fire workers. Secondary jobs are typically found in smaller firms that lack the capital assets to have an extended internal labor market, or in industries such as retail trade and services where the product can be produced without much firm-specific on-the-job training. Because firms in the secondary market do not offer much training or have substantial job ladders, the wages they pay are low, as are the incentives for job stability among the employees.

Limited Mobility

Given the existence of a primary and a secondary sector in the labor market, the second crucial assumption of dual labor market theory is that mobility between the two sectors is limited. Some workers in the secondary sector prefer those types of jobs and would not compete for primary jobs, even if given a chance. Examples would be teenagers who seek part-time work after school or married women who desire jobs that are easily interrupted for a period of time. According to proponents of the dual labor market theory, however, many workers in the secondary sector

Are Firms Developing Two-Tier Workforces?

Large Japanese companies are famous for their **two-tier employment systems** composed of "core" groups of permanent employees and larger groups of "contingent" workers with little or no job security. In some cases, the contingent workers are directly affiliated with the parent company, in others the contingent workers are employed by subcontractors or work at home. In either case, the result is something of a dual labor market structure, where one group of employees have "good" jobs providing high wages, extensive fringe benefits, considerable opportunities for promotion, and job security, and another group of employees have less desirable jobs, paying low wages with few fringe benefits and providing little, if any, job security.

During the 1990s it seemed as though the United States was headed in the direction of Japan as more and more American companies began to use contingent workers. Throughout most of the post-World War II period, a blue-collar or white-collar job with a large American corporation generally meant lifelong economic security, at least once the employee had established some tenure with the firm.

Driven by the need to reduce costs and increase flexibility, however, many corporations have replaced thousands of regular employees with temporary workers and part-timers, or have bid out the work to smaller subcontractor firms. This brings two advantages. One is that the contingent workers cost less, partly because their hourly pay is often only half that of regular employees and partly because they receive far fewer fringe benefits such as paid vacations and health insurance. A second benefit of using contingent employees is that they can easily be let go when the company no longer needs them, in effect turning the quasi-fixed cost of regular employees into a variable cost.

American labor law, however, also places constraints on the use of contingent workers. Some U.S. companies have gotten into trouble for continuing to pay contingent workers low wages and to deny them benefits, even when some of these workers have been with the company longer than some permanent employees; long-term temps essentially become "common-law" employees. The effect is segmentation of a firm's own labor force between those hired

desire work in primary jobs, but are effectively excluded from the competition. The major barrier to entry they face is discrimination.

Primary employers who offer good jobs have a long queue of job applicants. In making its hiring decision, the primary employer ranks the job applicants from highest to lowest based on an estimate of who will most likely possess the desired traits of trustworthiness, low turnover, trainability, and so on. The dualists argue that because employers perceive that white males are more likely to possess these traits than blacks or women, a white male will be systematically favored over an equally qualified minority worker. Owing to this type of discrimination, white males gain access to the firm's internal labor market and primary jobs, while minority groups are forced to accept jobs in the secondary sector. Thus, it is argued that improving the education or job skills of inner-city workers would not improve their economic status because these workers would still be denied access to primary jobs because of the stigmatizing effects of their race, sex, and previous employment

continued

as permanent workers and those hired as temporary workers. A ruling in January 1998 by the Supreme Court resulted in Microsoft Corp. having to provide thousands of its common-law employees (also called "permatemps") benefits, including payments for missed back years. In addition, Microsoft apparently had to pay nearly $97 million to settle two additional law suits brought by workers the company had classified as temporary.

While recent court cases mean that companies will have to rethink their contingent worker strategy, the benefits of such an arrangement mean that firms will likely continue to make use of contingent workers. A 1999 survey found that 78 percent of firms made use of contingent workers to meet work-load fluctuations. While definitions vary, contingent workers numbered 5.4 million in 2001 according to government estimates, or 4 percent of total employment. Adding independent contractors raises this number to 8.6 million, or 6.4 percent of the U.S. workforce. One researcher has estimated that between 2001 and 2003 that number has increased by another 1.5 million.

Does this mean that millions of workers are destined to live with the revolving door of contingent work while many others enjoy the security of high pay and permanent jobs? A sizable portion of contingent workers choose temporary or part-time work in order to gain job experience or more flexible work schedules. For another portion, however, contingent work is thrust upon them when their regular jobs fall victim to corporate cost cutting. For these workers the lower wages and skimpy benefits of contingent work are accepted more out of necessity than choice.

SOURCES: Jan Larson, "Temps Are Here to Stay," *American Demographics* (February 1996): 26; Robert J. Grossman, "Short-Term Workers Raise Long-Term Issues," *HRMagazine* 43 (April 1998): 80; Aaron Bernstein, "When Is a Temp Not a Temp?" *Business Week* (7 December 1998): 90; Jessica Guynn, "Microsoft Case Sets New Rules for Treating Temps," *Contra Costa Times* (18 December 2000); and Stacy A. Teicher, "Free-lancing in your Future?; Rise of Independent Workers Highlights Challenges Facing Today's US Labor Market," *Christian Science Monitor* (2 August 2004): 14.

history. The dualists argue that because minority workers are trapped in the secondary sector, they then adapt to the low wages and dead-end nature of secondary jobs by engaging in frequent job changing, tardiness, sloppy work habits, and so on. These traits reinforce the perceptions of primary employers that minority workers would not be good employees, setting off a vicious circle that confines these workers to the secondary sector.

Implications and Evidence

Dual labor market theory set off a considerable debate in labor economics because it offered a markedly different view of the wage determination process.[59] One issue

---

59   See Glen G. Cain, "The Challenge of Segmented Labour Market Theories to Orthodox Theory," *Journal of Economic Literature* 14, no. 4 (December 1976): 1215–57.

was whether or not there are identifiable primary and secondary sectors in the labor market. At an aggregate, economywide level, little evidence has been found of a bimodal distribution of earnings among individual workers, nor has a ranking of earnings among individual industries revealed any type of two-humped distribution as might be predicted from the dual model. In spite of the absence of evidence of overall duality within the economy, there are examples of pockets of its existence. For example, one economist suggests that the workers at farmers' markets are a good illustration of what a secondary labor market looks like.[60]

As several of the dualists have themselves admitted, however, a strict dichotomy of the economy into primary and secondary sectors is too much of a simplification to be analytically useful. Piore, for example, expanded the model into four sectors: a secondary sector, a primary sector divided into an upper and lower tier, and a craft sector.[61] This too may be oversimplified; as the example of the chemical plant in Figure 6.9 suggests, primary and secondary jobs often exist within the same firm. While empirical evidence does not offer a great deal of support for a dual segmentation of the labor market, the more general proposition that labor markets are segmented, albeit in finer detail, can be supported by more persuasive evidence.[62] Much of this evidence is reviewed in Chapters 8 and 9, where discrimination and differences in occupational attainment among race and gender groups are discussed.

Returns to Education   One implication of dual labor market theory is that the financial returns to years of education and experience should differ significantly depending on whether the individual is employed in the primary or the secondary sector. Two persons with identical years of education would have very different lifetime levels of income if one were hired into an entry-level position in the primary sector and another could find work only in a secondary job. Not only would the level of income differ between the two, so would the rate of increase of earnings with additional years of experience as the primary worker moved up the job ladder in the internal labor market and the secondary worker's earnings stagnated in a dead-end job. This prediction of dual labor market theory has found at least some empirical support. William Dickens and Kevin Lang found that whereas primary

60   Lisiunia A. Romienko, "Dual Labor Market Theory and the Institutionalization of Farmers' Markets: Marginalized American Workers Adapting to Inhospitable Conditions," *Economic Research* 13 (2000): 59–70.

61   Suzanne Berger and Michael J. Piore, eds., *Dualism and Discontinuity in Industrial Societies* (New York: Cambridge University Press, 1980), 1–12. Paul Osterman also distinguishes between four different types of employment systems, but calls them, respectively, the industrial, salaried, craft, and secondary sectors. See "Choice of Employment Systems in Internal Labor Markets," *Industrial Relations* 26 (Winter 1987): 46–67.

62   One statistical study of labor mobility among women, for example, found evidence of 16 distinct labor market segments. See Alisa Wilson, *Women's Interindustry and Occupational Mobility Using a Multidimensional Model of Economic Segmentation* (Ph.D. dissertation, University of Southern California, 1984). Also see Sara McLafferty and Valerie Preston, "Spatial Mismatch and Labor Market Segmentation for African-American and Latina Women," *Economic Geography* 68 (October 1992): 406–31, and William T. Dickens and Kevin Lang, "Labor Market Segmentation Theory: Reconsidering the Evidence," in William Darity Jr., ed., *Labor Economics: Problems in Analyzing Labor Markets* (Norwell, Mass.: Kluwer, 1993), 141–80.

sector workers earn about a 7 percent return on additional education, workers in the secondary sector receive no return from such investments.[63]

Firm Size and Wages For jobs characterized by a great deal of autonomy and nonquantifiable output, such as primary jobs, effort becomes more difficult to monitor as the size of the firm increases. If a job is fairly monotonous with output that can be more easily measured, such as in secondary jobs, however, the size of the firm should not substantially increase the difficulties of monitoring effort. According to the efficiency wage hypothesis, one way to increase effort without increasing monitoring is to raise the wage. Consequently, one should observe higher wages at large firms (where it is difficult to monitor effort) for primary jobs, but not for secondary jobs (whose output is generally not difficult to monitor). As additional evidence of labor market segmentation, researchers have found that indeed among primary jobs, wages are considerably higher at large firms than at small firms. And among secondary jobs, the relationship between firm size and wages is either nonexistent or very weak.[64]

---

63 William T. Dickens and Kevin Lang, "A Test of Dual Labor Market Theory," *American Economic Review* 75 (September 1985): 792–805. For additional evidence of the presence of dual labor markets, see John Baffoe-Bonnie, "Distributional Assumptions and a Test of the Dual Labor Market Hypothesis," *Empirical Economics* 28 (June 2003): 461–78.

64 See James B. Rebitzer and Michael D. Robinson, "Employer Size and Dual Labor Markets," *Review of Economics and Statistics* 73 (November 1991): 710–15, and Kenneth J. Hoffmann, "Analyzing Wage Patterns of Engineers and Secretaries," *Compensation and Working Conditions* (Fall 1997): 19–24.

POLICY APPLICATION 6-1

Job Lock

One of the most important requirements for a labor market to function competitively is that workers are able to move from one job to another in order to take advantage of any wage discrepancies that arise across jobs. There are several factors that can limit labor market mobility. Poor information about job availability is one such factor. Potential loss of employer-provided benefits is another.[1]

Prior to passage of the **Employee Retirement Income Security Act of 1974 (ERISA)**, workers were at risk of losing their private pension benefits if they were terminated or quit any time prior to "retirement," even if they had enjoyed long, productive careers with their employer. ERISA originally required that all plans covered by the law

---

1 An additional source, albeit extreme, of reduced labor mobility is the presence of a planned economy where the government tells workers what jobs they will take. Nauro Campos, "So Many Rocket Scientists, So Few Marketing Clerks: Occupational Mobility in Times of Rapid Technological Change," *CEPR Discussion Paper No. 3531* (September 2002), documents the important role labor mobility has played in the transformation of Estonia's labor market from a communist to a capitalist structure.

make employees eligible for their fully accrued benefits after 10 years of service; the Tax Reform Act of 1986 reduced that vesting period to 5 years for most workers.[2] Even though accrued benefits are still lost if a worker leaves the firm before 5 years are up, current laws protect a worker from losing accrued benefits after many years of service. Most workers participating in defined benefit retirement plans offered by medium-sized or large employers are affected by pension vesting policies, meaning that their mobility carried a cost, particularly early in their careers.

Employer-provided health insurance that excludes preexisting conditions can also increase the cost of changing jobs if it causes a worker to be denied health insurance with the new employer. For example, say a worker develops an ulcer while working for one employer. The insurance provider for a new employer may deny any claims related to that worker's ulcer since it developed prior to the worker's participation in the new company's insurance plan. The ulcer is considered a preexisting condition. The risk of losing health insurance can make a worker feel "locked in" to his or her current job; hence the term **job lock** has come to refer to the constraint placed on mobility as a result of the risk of losing health insurance. Since 61 percent of insured persons in 2002 were insured through their employers, this could be of acute concern.[3]

Over the past 20 years the cost of health care and, thus, health insurance has increased tremendously. Between 1993 and 2003, prices of all consumer goods increased 27 percent; prices for medical care increased 48 percent and prices for medical care services increased 51 percent over the same time period. Naturally concerned about the availability and affordability of health insurance, people are unwilling to undertake some action that could put their health coverage at risk. Given that most people have access to health insurance through their employers, and given that the cost of health insurance has been rising steadily, the opportunity cost of changing employers (loss of health insurance) has increased as well.

The research evidence on how important job lock is in restricting labor market mobility is mixed. One researcher finds little evidence that concerns about losing health insurance restrict movement in the labor market.[4] Several other authors, however, estimate that health insurance restrictions reduce labor market mobility by 20 to 40 percent.[5]

While the economists are still sorting out the impact of job lock on actual labor mobility, the United States Congress has acted to ensure that, regardless of the impact, job lock is even less of an obstacle to labor market competition than it was 20 years ago. In 1985 Congress passed legislation (the **Consolidated Omnibus Budget Reconciliation Act—COBRA**) requiring employers to allow workers the opportunity to continue health insurance coverage for up to 18 months after leaving their jobs. Then, in 1996, passage of the **Health Insurance Portability and Accountability Act of 1996 (HIPAA)** limited the amount of time a worker can be refused coverage on a new job due to preexisting conditions.[6] While there still may be other hindrances to competition, both of these policies certainly reduce the cost of mobility; they are doing their part in moving the labor market closer to the perfectly competitive model.

---

2   James H. Schulz, *The Economics of Aging*, 7th ed. (Westport, Conn.: Auburn House, 2001).

3   U.S. Census Bureau, *Health Insurance Coverage: 2000*, Table 1, http://www.census.gov/hhes/www/hlthin02.html.

4   Kanika Kapur, "The Impact of Health on Job Mobility: A Measure of Job Lock," *Industrial and Labor Relations Review* 51 (January 1998): 282–98.

5   Thomas C. Buchmueller and Robert G. Valletta, "The Effects of Employer-Provided Health Insurance on Worker Mobility," *Industrial and Labor Relations Review* 49 (April 1996): 439–55; Alan C. Monheit and Philip F. Cooper, "Health Insurance and Job Mobility: Theory and Evidence," *Industrial and Labor Relations Review* 48 (October 1994): 68–85; Brigitte C. Madrian, "Employment-Based Health Insurance and Job Mobility: Is There Evidence of Job-Lock?" *Quarterly Journal of Economics* 109 (February 1994): 27–54; and Scott J. Adams, "Employer-provided Health Insurance and Job Change," *Contemporary Economic Policy* 22 (July 2004): 357–69.

6   Details of HIPAA can be found at http://www.dol.gov/ebsa/consumer_info_health.html.

Monopsony in Baseball

The most important prediction of the monopsony model is that the wage rate paid to workers will be lower than if the labor market were competitive. One example that offers striking support for this prediction is the dramatic increase in player salaries in baseball following the introduction of the free agent system in 1977.[1]

Prior to 1977, a baseball player was a "free agent" (could negotiate with any club) until he signed his first contract with a major league team or its minor league affiliate. Once signed, all baseball contracts contained a renewal or "reserve" clause stipulating that thereafter the player's services were the sole property of that club for his entire career in baseball unless the club decided to sell or trade his contract. The reserve clause effectively turned the market for individual players into a monopsony by preventing them from negotiating with any but their own club.

On December 23, 1975, the reserve clause was struck down by an arbitrator ruling on a grievance brought by the Major League Baseball Players Association (MLBPA). Under a new agreement negotiated by the MLBPA and the owners, players were no longer permanently tied to a team; players who had signed contracts prior to 1976 were able to become free agents in 1977; players signing contracts after 1976 could become free agents after six years. The effect of the new contract system was to turn what had been a monopsony into a competitive market.

What effect did this development have on players' salaries? According to one study, average player compensation rose from $54,330 in 1976 to $77,292 in 1977—a 42-percent increase in one year! Opening the market to competitive bidding led to a substantial rise in salaries, as the theory would predict.

A second prediction of the monopsony model is that workers are paid less than their marginal revenue product; in a competitive market, by contrast, workers are paid wages equal to their marginal contribution. This same study also found clear evidence of this prediction; under the free agent system salaries rose an estimated 37 percent for "below average" hitters but 69 percent for the "star" hitters—the ones whose marginal contributions to the teams (and to the owners' revenues) were the greatest.

---

1   The discussion in this section is drawn from James R. Hill and William Spellman, "Professional Baseball: The Reserve Clause and Salary Structure," *Industrial Relations 22*, no. 1 (Winter 1983): 1–19.

EMPIRICAL EVIDENCE 6-2

Wages of Hospital and Manufacturing Workers

Do changes in demand and supply actually lead to changes in wages, as the competitive model predicts? Some interesting evidence on this question is provided by two examples discussed below. The first concerns the change in wages for hospital workers; the second pertains to wage changes for manufacturing workers.

Hospital Workers

A marked increase occurred in the demand for hospital workers (NAICS 622) during the 22-year period 1980 through 2003. As shown in the first row of Table 6.3, expenditures on hospital care in the United States rose by more than four times over the time period, from $102.7 billion to $451.2 billion. Because the demand for labor is derived from the demand for the product, the rapid increase in

	1980	1990	2003
Expenditures on hospital care (billions)	$102.7	$253.9	$451.2
Average hourly earnings	$6.06	$11.79	$19.37
Industry wage as percentage of total private wage	91%	118%	125%
Employees (thousands)	2,750	3,549	4,252

SOURCE: Bureau of the Census, *Statistical Abstract of the United States, 2001* (Washington, D.C.: GPO, 2001): Table 126; and Bureau of Labor Statistics, *Employment and Earnings*, various issues.

expenditures for hospital services led to a similar increase in the demand for labor, such as for medical technologists, nurses, dietitians, and hospital administrators. This increase caused the industry demand curve for labor to shift rapidly to the right.

The competitive model makes three predictions concerning the change in wages and employment in response to a situation of excess demand in the market. The first is that the absolute level of wages in the industry should rise. As shown by the data in the second row of Table 6.3, this prediction is borne out for this industry. Average hourly earnings in the hospital industry rose from $6.06 in 1980 to $19.37 in 2003, an increase of 220 percent. If the rise in prices between 1980 and 2003 is subtracted out, earnings in real terms (expressed in 1980 dollars) still advanced significantly, from $6.06 in 1980 to $8.71 in 2003.

The second prediction of the competitive model is that wages in this industry relative to wages in other industries should also increase. The data in the third row confirm this prediction. They show the ratio of average hourly earnings in the hospital industry relative to average hourly earnings in the entire private sector economy. In 1980, wages received by hospital workers were only 91 percent of that received by the average worker in the economy; by 2003 the relative wage position of hospital workers had increased markedly, so that they now earned 25 percent *more* than the average

worker in the economy. While product demand increased across nearly all industries in the 1980s, the relative increase was greater in the hospital industry, leading to a rise in relative wages as the competitive model predicts.

The third prediction of the competitive model is that the level of employment should increase in the industry. This prediction is confirmed by the data in the fourth row of Table 6.3, which show the number of workers employed in hospitals. Employment expanded sharply during this period, from 2.75 million to almost 4.3 million.

The pattern of wages and employment in this particular industry between 1980 and 2003 matches quite closely the predictions of the competitive model. This example also illustrates how changes in wages serve to efficiently allocate labor resources in the economy. Given the increased demand of the American public for health care, hospitals and other health-care providers found it to their advantage to significantly expand the level of service. Given the low pay, inconvenient hours, and highly specialized skills of many jobs in the industry, how were hospitals to obtain the 1 million extra workers needed to provide these services? The obvious, but nevertheless profound, answer is that wages rose until enough job seekers, whether new college graduates, laid-off factory workers, or persons looking to switch careers, were attracted to the industry to meet the demand for labor. Thus,

TABLE 6.4	**WAGES AND EMPLOYMENT IN MILWAUKEE, WISCONSIN, BEFORE AND AFTER THE SLUMP IN THE MANUFACTURING SECTOR**		
	2000	**2001**	**2002**
Manufacturing employment	164,500	154,200	143,700
Average hourly earnings, manufacturing	$15.55	$15.66	$15.85
Wage in Milwaukee as percentage of wage in Minnesota	103.7%	101.9%	101.2%

SOURCE: Bureau of Labor Statistics, *Employment and Earnings* (May 2003), Washington, D.C.: Government Printing Office.

without any centralized direction the operation of the labor market brought about a redistribution of labor resources that served the self-interest of both hospitals and their workers, and the social interests of the country at large.

Manufacturing Workers

The case of hospital workers illustrates the reaction of wages and employment to excess demand in the labor market. A second example, illustrating the opposite case of how wages and employment adjust to excess labor supply, is the mass layoff of manufacturing workers in Milwaukee, Wisconsin in 2001.

Milwaukee is a classic Rust Belt city with a heavy concentration of employment in manufacturing. Employment in Milwaukee grew steadily during the boom time of the 1990s and even manufacturing employment registered a net increase. But the bottom fell out in the manufacturing sector in 2001, due to both the national economic recession in 2000–2001 and much-heightened global competition. In 2001, over four dozen companies announced plant closings and large layoffs in Milwaukee. As one example, the Tower Automotive Corporation, a maker of truck frames, laid off 700 workers due to slow sales.

The adjustment of wages and employment in the Milwaukee labor market in response to the plant closings and layoffs is illustrated by the data in Table 6.4. Manufacturing employment in Milwaukee in 2000, a still-prosperous year, was 164,500 (row 1). In 2001, 10,000 manufacturing jobs disappeared, followed by another 10,000 in 2002, or a combined job loss of 13 percent. As shown in Figure 6.5, these job losses are represented by a leftward shift of the labor demand curve, illustrating that at the going wage of W_1 there was now a smaller demand for labor in the market.

The competitive model predicts that three adjustments will take place in the labor market in a disequilibrium situation such as this. The first prediction is that employment will decline. This prediction is borne out by the data in row 1, which shows that manufacturing employment declined from 164,500 to 143,700.

The second prediction is that the absolute dollar level of wages will decline. This prediction is *not* borne out by the behavior of wages in Milwaukee, as shown in row 2. Average hourly earnings in manufacturing firms in Milwaukee actually rose from $15.55 in 2000 to $15.85 in 2002, even as employment sharply declined. (If inflation is taken out, *real* wages did modestly decline.)

The third prediction of the competitive model is that the level of wages in Milwaukee relative to wages in other labor markets should also decline. This prediction is confirmed by the data in row 3 of Table 6.4. These data show the manufacturing wage in Milwaukee as a percent of the manufacturing wage in the neighboring state of Minnesota, under the assumption that Minnesota represented the most prosperous alternative labor market for Milwaukee workers. (Of all the neighboring states to Wisconsin, Minnesota's employment best weathered the hard times of 2000–2002.) In 2000, Milwaukee's wage was 103.7 percent of Minnesota's; two years later Milwaukee's had declined to only 101.2 percent, a trend consistent with the prediction of the theory.

The net result, then, is that in response to the excess supply of labor created by the slump in the manufacturing sector in Milwaukee, both relative wages and employment did decline as predicted by the competitive model. The absolute level of wages, however, not only did not decline as the theory predicts, but instead continued to increase.

The failure of money wage rates to decline in the face of an excess supply of labor represents one of the most important deviations of actual labor market behavior from the predictions of competitive theory. When President Carter imposed an embargo on grain sales to the Soviet Union in 1979 in reaction to its invasion of Afghanistan, the price of wheat received by farmers dropped precipitously in a matter of days. Why, with the mass layoffs in Milwaukee, did wages received by workers in Milwaukee not also drop to clear the market?

The answer to this question revolves around differences in the two types of markets. The wheat market is a classic example of an auction market. Prices rise and fall as buyers and sellers bid against each other in an attempt to strike the best bargain possible. The flexibility of prices is encouraged by several features of the market and the good in question. Buyers and sellers of wheat, for example, engage in constant "shopping around" in the market as they search for the best price. Likewise, since wheat is a standardized commodity, the only variable of concern to both parties is the price. Finally, since wheat is an inert commodity, it does not care at what price it is bought and sold, nor does it care who the buyer is or how many times it changes hands.

The labor market is far different.[1] If the labor market were like a commodity market, firms would auction jobs on a daily basis to the lowest bidders. Competition among unemployed workers would cause the wage to be bid down until everyone who wanted a job had one. Eighty years ago factory labor was often hired this way as a foreman standing at the plant gate would offer work to those outside at whatever wage the market would bear.[2] This type of buying and selling is seldom done in the labor market today for several reasons. One is the growing prevalence of long-term jobs in the labor market. While the plant foreman 80 years ago might hire and fire workers on a daily or weekly basis, many firms today would find this prohibitively expensive. Firms invest substantial sums of money in their employees in the form of hiring and training costs. Thus, even if an unemployed worker offers to work at a lower wage than an existing employee, the firm will generally not find it profitable to hire him or her. A second reason why money wages are downwardly inflexible is that unemployed workers frequently refuse to lower their "asking wage," preferring instead to remain unemployed until a job opening is found at the desired wage rate. This reflects the expectation of many workers that their loss of job is temporary, the psychological resistance of workers to accepting a wage lower than what they have been accustomed to, and the availability of unemployment insurance benefits. A third reason, often cited as the most important by business people, is that wage cuts damage employee morale, sometimes causing the gain from lower wage cost to be more than offset by the decline in employee work effort and productivity.

---

1   See Daniel J. B. Mitchell, "Explanations of Wage Inflexibility: Institutions and Incentives," in Wilfred Beckman, ed., *Wage Rigidity and Unemployment* (Baltimore: Johns Hopkins University Press, 1986): 43–76, Alan S. Blinder and Don H. Choi, "A Shred of Evidence on Theories of Wage Stickiness," *Quarterly Journal of Economics* 105, no. 4 (November, 1990): 1003–16; and Truman Bewley, *Why Wages Don't Fall in a Recession* (Cambridge: Harvard University Press, 1999).

2   See Sanford Jacoby, *Employing Bureaucracy: Managers, Unions, and the Transformation of Work in American Industry, 1900–1945* (New York: Columbia University Press, 1985).

The original equilibrium is at point A with the demand curve D_1 and supply curve S_1. Assuming the demand curve shifts to D_2, if wages were flexible downward they would fall to W_1, restoring equilibrium at point C. With inflexible wages, however, an excess supply of labor of $L_1 - L_2$ (point A − point B) will persist. Although the money wage remains at W_1, this wage will decline relative to wage rates in other labor markets. This decline in the relative wage restores equilibrium (point E) by causing people to move out of this labor market, shifting the supply curve leftward to S_2, and by inducing a flow of capital investment into the area, shifting the demand curve rightward to D_3.

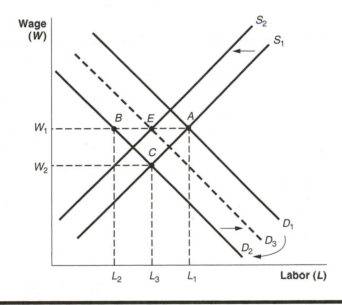

For these and other reasons, then, money wage rates typically do not fall even in the presence of considerable unemployment.

The Role of Relative Wage Adjustments

If the level of money wages does not fall in response to an excess supply of labor, is there an alternative route by which the labor market can reach a new equilibrium? The answer is yes and involves the role of relative wages and factor mobility. This process is illustrated in Figure 6.10 for the case of the Milwaukee labor market.

Before the mass layoffs, the labor demand curve in Milwaukee was D_1, the supply curve was S_1, and the equilibrium wage and level of employment were W_1 and L_1 (point A). When the layoffs occurred, the demand curve for labor in Milwaukee shifted to the left, from D_1 to D_2, leading to an excess supply of labor in the Milwaukee market of $L_1 - L_2$ (point A − point B). In a perfectly competitive market, this excess supply of labor would have been eliminated by a fall in the wage to W_2, giving rise to a new equilibrium level of employment of L_3 (point C). If wage rates are inflexible downward, however, this path to equilibrium in the labor market is blocked. How is a new equilibrium restored?

Even if the level of money wages in Milwaukee did not decline, the *relative* wage did as wages in Milwaukee grew more slowly than wages in other, more buoyant labor markets. The decline in the relative wage provided an incentive, in turn, for some of the $L_1 - L_2$ unemployed workers to migrate to other cities or states to find work. The effect of this, in Figure 6.10, is to cause a shift of the supply curve of labor to the left from S_1 to S_2, depicting that at the prevailing wage of W_1 there is less labor available in the Milwaukee market. Equilibrium will be restored when the process of relative wage decline and outmigration of labor has caused the supply curve to shift leftward until it intersects the demand curve D_2 at point B. The decline in relative wages will also restore equilibrium in the labor market through a second mechanism. The fall in the relative wage not only induces an outflow of labor from the Milwaukee market but also an *inflow* of capital as firms decide to locate new plants in the area to take advantage of the lower price of labor. The new plants shift the solid demand curve D_2 to the right, to the broken demand curve D_3. The combination of labor outflow and capital inflow works to restore equilibrium in the market, illustrated by the intersection of the demand curve D_3 and supply curve S_2 at a wage level of W_1 and employment level of L_3 (point E).

While a change in relative wages is thus able to restore equilibrium in the labor market given an initial situation of excess supply, several caveats concerning this process should be pointed out. The first is that the process of labor outflow and capital inflow can take a relatively long time to restore equilibrium. Government surveys, for example, reveal that even in prosperous economic times 3 out of 10 displaced workers remain jobless a year or more after their plants have closed, a figure that rises to nearly 5 out of 10 if the shutdown takes place during a period of recession.[3] This high rate of joblessness reflects the slow rate of outmigration of workers from local labor markets and the even slower process of attracting new firms into the area.

A second feature of the adjustment process that should not be glossed over concerns the economic and social costs suffered by individuals and families involved in plant shutdowns and layoffs. While a large majority of displaced workers eventually find new jobs, the job search process often lasts many months. Most likely to remain unemployed for extended periods of time are displaced workers who are older, have no college education, work in durable goods manufacturing industries (e.g., steel, autos), and were previously employed at much higher than average wages. During this time, family savings are often depleted, and in some cases homes are lost and marriages fall apart under the financial and emotional stress. Indicative of the emotional costs is the finding of a case study of 233 brewery workers in South Bend, Indiana, after their plant closed.[4] The mortality rate among the displaced brewery workers was *22 times* the national average. For those who do eventually find new jobs, it is common for those jobs to pay wages or salaries significantly below what was previously earned. Of the 5.3 million workers displaced from jobs between January 2001 and December 2003, for example, 63 percent of those who found new full-time jobs were working at a lower rate of pay and 29 percent had taken a pay cut of 20 percent or more.[5] On the other hand, a significant minority of displaced workers are able to find jobs that actually pay better than the ones they lost.

---

3 Diane Herz, "Worker Displacement Still Common in the Late 1980s," *Monthly Labor Review* 114, no. 5 (May, 1991): 3–9. These statistics held even in the 1990s. See Ryan T. Helwig, "Worker Displacement in a Strong Labor Market," *Monthly Labor Review* (June 2001): 13–28.

4 Charles Craypo and William Davisson, "Plant Shutdown, Collective Bargaining, and Job and Employment Experience of Displace Brewery Workers," *Labor Studies Journal* 7 (Winter 1983): 195–215.

5 Bureau of Labor Statistics, "Worker Displacement, 2001–2003," *NEWS*, USDL #04-1381 (30 July 2004).

In an attempt to lower the economic and social costs of plant shutdowns, the first President Bush signed into law in 1989 the **Worker Adjustment and Retraining Notification Act (WARNA).** The act requires employers with 100 or more employees to provide 60 days' advance notice to workers who are to be laid off due to a plant shutdown or relocation. Supporters of the act argued that advance notice should reduce the incidence and duration of unemployment among displaced workers by giving them two months to begin searching for alternative employment. Several recent empirical studies find evidence in support of this prediction, although white-collar workers appear to benefit much more from advance notice than do blue-collar workers.[6]

Finally, an interesting question to ponder, and one that is the focus of Chapter 13, is what happens to the equilibrating process if the decrease in demand for labor occurs across *all* local labor markets rather than just one as in the case of Milwaukee. While a decline in relative wages can restore equilibrium in one market through the mobility of labor to other expanding job markets, if labor demand decreases in all markets together (such as in a recession or a depression) there is an opportunity neither for changes in relative wages nor for workers to migrate to other areas in search of better job opportunities. In this case the downward rigidity of wage rates may prevent the labor market from reaching a new equilibrium, leading to the possibility of persistent unemployment.

---

6   John T. Addison and Pedro Portugal, "Advance Notice and Unemployment: New Evidence from the 1988 Displaced Worker Survey," *Industrial and Labor Relations Review* 45, no. 4 (July, 1992): 645–64; Stephen Nord and Yuan Ting, "The Impact of Advance Notice: A Rejoinder," *Industrial and Labor Relations Review* 45, no. 4 (July, 1992): 674–82; and Pietro Garibaldi, "Search Unemployment with Advance Notice," *Macroeconomic Dynamics* 8 (February 2004): 51–75.

EMPIRICAL EVIDENCE 6-3

The Wage Effect of Immigration

Another interesting empirical application of the competitive demand/supply model concerns the wage effect of foreign immigration into the United States.

The United States is a land of immigrants. In the early twentieth century, immigration reached a peak when over one million new immigrants entered the country every year. This great inflow of labor, coming predominantly from the nations of southern and eastern Europe, fed the nation's booming economy but also led to considerable criticism that it was hurting the wages and employment prospects of native-born American workers. In response to rising political pressures, the American government in the mid-1920s enacted the nation's first restrictive immigration law and effectively turned a flood of foreign-born labor into a trickle. The impact of this policy change can be seen in Figure 6.11.

In the 1950s not more than a quarter-million new immigrants entered the United States. Then in 1965 the immigration law was substantially revised and liberalized. For two more decades immigration only slowly increased, as can be seen in Figure 6.11. From 1980 onward, however, immigration has expanded greatly until in the early 2000s the flow of immigrants is again more than one million a year.[1] Perhaps one-fourth or more are illegal entrants. Although the number of immigrants is roughly similar to the early 1900s, the countries of origin have changed greatly. Today, as can be seen in Table 6.5, Europe contributes

---

1   See Vernon Briggs, Jr., *Mass Immigration and the National Interest* (Armonk, N.Y.: M.E. Sharpe, 2003).

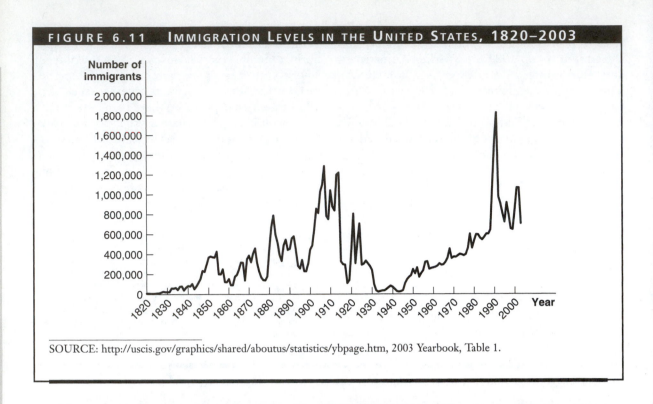

FIGURE 6.11   IMMIGRATION LEVELS IN THE UNITED STATES, 1820–2003

SOURCE: http://uscis.gov/graphics/shared/aboutus/statistics/ybpage.htm, 2003 Yearbook, Table 1.

TABLE 6.5   ORIGIN OF IMMIGRANTS AS PERCENT OF TOTAL, 1901–2002

Year Span	Percent from Europe	Percent from Asia	Percent from Mexico	Percent from other Latin America and Caribbean Countries
1901–10	91.6%	3.7%	0.6%	1.5%
1911–20	75.3%	4.3%	3.8%	3.2%
1921–30	60.0%	2.7%	11.2%	3.2%
1931–40	65.8%	3.1%	4.2%	5.5%
1941–50	60.0%	3.6%	5.9%	9.0%
1951–60	52.7%	6.1%	11.9%	10.3%
1961–70	33.8%	12.9%	13.7%	25.0%
1971–80	17.8%	35.3%	14.2%	26.1%
1981–90	10.4%	37.3%	22.6%	24.6%
1991–2000	14.9%	30.7%	24.7%	22.5%
2003	14.6%	33.4%	16.3%	24.8%

SOURCE: http://uscis.gov/graphics/shared/aboutus/statistics/ybpage.htm, 2003 Yearbook, Table 2.

roughly 15 percent of the nation's immigrants whereas the countries of Latin America (including Mexico and the Caribbean) contribute the largest share—over 40 percent of the total, with the influx being particularly heavy in California and Florida.

As it did one hundred years ago, the recent surge in immigration has led to renewed controversy and concern over the labor market effects on native-born American workers. Naturally, economists have devoted a good deal of research attention to this subject.

The place to start is with theory. The textbook model gives an unambiguous prediction. In the short-run, and assuming native and foreign-born workers are perfect substitutes, an increase in labor supply due to increased immigration shifts the labor supply curve to the right, just as shown in Figure 6.5 (b). Other things equal, the model predicts that higher immigration reduces the wages received by domestic workers (shown by the movement from point A to C in the diagram). Although total employment and production increase (higher employment leads to greater output via the production function), some domestic workers will decide to drop out of the work force at the lower wage, fueling perceptions that immigrants are taking the jobs of American workers.

The bulk of research on immigration by economists during the 1990s provided, somewhat surprisingly, only scant-to-modest empirical evidence for these predictions. Most of the research was done on the wage effect of immigration. The standard technique was to compare the change in wages across individual American cities, noting that the bulk of new immigrants cluster in certain cities and areas. Thus, if most immigrants locate in Los Angeles and Miami, holding constant other sources of wage change, we should see the wage in these two cities decline relative to the wage in, for example, Minneapolis and Seattle. But most studies that used this technique found only small negative effects on wages, and sometimes no effect at all.[2] It may be noted that similar studies in other countries experiencing high immigration, such as Australia and Israel, also found small to zero negative wage effects.[3]

The most oft-cited study of this nature was done by David Card.[4] In April, 1980, Fidel Castro declared that Cuban nationals wishing to move to the United States could freely do so from the port of Mariel. Six months later over 125,000 Cubans had immigrated to America, predominantly locating in the Miami area. The result was an expansion of the Miami labor force by 7 percent in a short period. Card found, however, practically no evidence that the large influx of Cuban immigrants had lowered the wage rate for native workers in Miami, or even for the new Cuban immigrants. Unemployment did increase, but this was attributed to the national recession then taking place. Also, Card found no evidence that the wages and employment of groups most likely to directly compete with the new immigrants, such as native African-Americans, were adversely affected—even though a three-day street riot broke out in the black neighborhoods of Miami over this issue.

What can account for this apparent deviation between theory and empirical evidence? One possibility, of course, is that the competitive model does not represent the way the labor market really works and thus gives a wrong answer. Most economists, however, are reluctant to accept this explanation. Instead, two other avenues have been explored.

The first is not to discard the competitive model but to introduce additional complexities and real-world qualifications. One qualification, for

2 Robert LaLonde and Robert Topel, "Labor Market Adjustments to Increased Immigration," in J. Abowd and R. Freeman, eds., *Immigration, Trade, and the Labor Market* (Chicago: University of Chicago Press, 1991), 167–99; Rachel Friedberg and Jennifer Hunt, "The Impact of Immigration on Host Country Wages, Employment and Growth," *Journal of Economic Perspectives* 9 (1, 1995): 23–44.

3 Rachel Freidberg, "The Impact of Mass Migration on the Israeli Labor Market," *Quarterly Journal of Economics* 116 (November): 1373–1408; Thomas Addison and Christopher Worswick, "The Impact of Immigration on the Earnings of Natives: Evidence from Australian Micro Data," *The Economic Record* 78 (March, 2002): 68–78.

4 David Card, "The Impact of the Mariel Boatlift on the Miami Labor Market," *Industrial and Labor Relations Review* 43 (January, 1990): 245–57.

example, is to consider that immigrants and domestic workers may not be perfect substitutes, or even substitutes at all. Immigrants, for example, often do not speak English, many have never completed high school, and often seek work in jobs that native workers do not want. In this case, large immigration may not have a negative effect on native workers' wages since the two groups do not, in effect, compete in the same labor market. Indeed, it is possible that large immigration could raise the wages of native workers! This result occurs if immigrants and native workers are complements in production and, thus, the expansion of production stimulated by higher immigrant employment simultaneously shifts the demand curve to the right for native workers.

Another qualification is to note that native workers may change their location in response to new immigration. In areas such as Miami and Los Angeles where immigration is heavy, native workers may respond by leaving those highly competitive labor markets and moving to other cities where competitive pressures are less. Likewise, domestic workers who were considering a move to Miami or Los Angeles may decide not to. (This is the factor that Card found helped explain the zero-wage effect in Miami from the Mariel boatlift.)

The second possibility explored by economists to account for the apparent discrepancy between theory and empirical evidence is that the empirical techniques used in past studies are not sufficiently refined and sophisticated to capture the true effect of immigration on wages. Part of the problem is that earlier studies were not able to fully take into account the theoretical qualifications just noted. Thus, if native workers move out of Miami in response to the influx of new Cuban workers, the labor supply in Miami may not change much and no negative wage effect will be observed. The true test of the theory, however, is to hold outmigration constant and then see what the wage effect would be. Similarly, past empirical studies have not been able to finely disaggregate the labor supply of immigrants and native workers by skill and experience, making it difficult to ensure that the two groups of workers being compared are indeed competing in similar labor markets.

Several recent empirical studies have been able to improve on these matters and have found stronger evidence of a negative wage effect from immigration. Perhaps the leading economic researcher in this area is George Borjas. In a detailed study covering the entire United States, he finds that a 10 percent increase in immigration, other things equal, leads to a decrease in real wage rates of 3–4 percent.[5] Likewise, another study by Orrenius and Zavodny finds clear evidence that regions of the country with the highest inflow of immigrants experience a noticeable widening in the degree of wage inequality as wages in the lower end of the labor market are depressed (where immigrants and native workers compete the most strongly), whereas wages in the top end of the labor market continue to grow.[6]

This last finding points out an additional significant effect of immigration. Just as a higher minimum wage has winners and losers, so, too, does higher immigration have winners and losers. Several groups are winners. Among them are consumers who get more output of goods and services at lower prices, firms who are able to hire workers at lower wages, and complementary high-skilled workers who have greater employment opportunities due to the expansion of output induced by an expanded immigration. The largest potential loser are native-born workers who face lower wages, benefits, and working conditions and possible longer spells of unemployment due to the expansion of immigrant labor supply. It is also possible taxpayers, at least in certain high immigrant areas, may be losers if new immigrants (such as illegal aliens) extensively use public services but pay little taxes to support them.

---

5   George Borjas, "The Labor Demand Curve *Is* Downward Sloping: Reexamining the Impact of Immigration on the Labor Market," *Quarterly Journal of Economics* 118 (November, 2003): 1335–74.

6   Pia Orrenius and Madeline Zavodny, "Does Immigration Affect Wages? A Look at Occupation-Level Data," Working Paper 0302, Federal Reserve Bank of Dallas (2003). Also see Deborah Reed, "Immigration and Male's Earnings Inequality in the Regions of the United States," *Demography* 38 (August, 2001): 363–73.

Summary

This chapter began with a look at wage determination in a perfectly competitive labor market. If real-world labor markets satisfied all the assumptions of the perfectly competitive model, demand and supply would give rise to one unique equilibrium wage for a particular type of labor. Since real-world labor markets are to one degree or another imperfect, wage rates at any one point in time are dispersed around the mean level of hourly earnings.

Wage rates change over time with shifts in the demand and supply curves of labor. In a situation of excess demand, competition causes wage rates to be bid up. While in a perfectly competitive market an oversupply of labor would result in a bidding down of wage rates, this typically does not occur because of the existence of sizable hiring and training costs and other such factors. As long as relative wages are flexible, demand and supply can be brought into balance by competitive forces.

The polar opposite of perfect competition is monopsony. In a monopsony market the firm is able to set a wage rate lower than would prevail in a competitive market, because workers lack alternative sources of employment. A degree of monopsonistic exploitation may also occur in situations of oligopsony.

Wage rates are determined not only by demand and supply but also by institutional forces, such as the presence of a minimum wage. The institution of a minimum wage in a perfectly competitive market results in misallocation of resources and economic inefficiency. In a monopsony market, however, a minimum wage may benefit workers and consumers and result in a better allocation of resources. A higher wage may also make workers work harder, changing the wage/employment relationship and resulting in greater employment.

If the labor market were perfectly competitive, the firm's internal wage structure would be dictated by demand and supply in the external labor market. Many firms have an internal labor market in which rates of pay are somewhat sheltered from outside competition. Wage rates for the port of entry jobs at the bottom of the job ladder are largely market determined, but within the internal labor market the specific nature of job skills creates an indeterminacy in wage rates.

If competitive forces are to allocate labor efficiently, there must be relatively few impediments to labor mobility. Real-world labor markets are sometimes segmented by factors such as internal labor markets, discrimination, and occupational licensing laws that create barriers to entry. One extreme version of market segmentation is dual labor market theory, which hypothesizes a primary sector of good jobs and a secondary sector of bad jobs, with little mobility between the two.

Review Questions

1. How closely does the labor market for the following type of worker approximate a perfectly competitive market? What, if any, are the major imperfections in each market?
   a. migrant farm worker
   b. steelworker
   c. nurse
   d. bank executive

2. Consider the following quotations:

   "For the general tendency for the wages of labourers of equal efficiency to become equalized in different occupations (allowances being made for the advantages and disadvantages of employment) has been a commonplace of economics since the days of Adam Smith. . . . The movement of labour from one occupation to another, which brings it about, is certainly a slow one; but there is no need to question its reality." [J. R. Hicks, *The Theory of Wages* (New York: Macmillan, 1932), 3.]

"Abundant evidence now testifies that it would, in the absence of collusion, be almost more correct to say that wages tend to be unequal rather than the other way around. . . . Occupational wage rates, locality by locality, in the absence of collective bargaining displayed no single going rate but a wide dispersion." [Clark Kerr, "Labor Markets: Their Character and Consequences," *American Economic Review* 40, no. 2 (May 1950): 280.]

Are the statements by these two prominent economists in conflict? Why? Is it possible to reconcile Kerr's statement with Hicks's? Analyze each statement in terms of the model of perfect competition, drawing graphs to illustrate your answer.

3. In recent years a large number of high-tech and Internet companies have closed. Illustrate the impact of this development on the labor market for software engineers. How, if at all, will the labor market return to equilibrium? If unemployment persists in the software engineer labor market, would this be consistent with the model of perfect competition? Why or why not?

4. What has happened to the extent of monopsony in the labor market in the past 40 years? Relate your answer to the ease of labor mobility and the slope of the supply curve of labor for the individual firm.

5. A common finding is that women's earnings increase at a slower rate with each additional year of work experience than those for men of similar educational backgrounds. How would dual labor market theory explain this?

6. What impact do you think the emergence of the Internet has had on the competitiveness of the labor market? Think about how the presence of the Internet has affected the realism of the assumptions necessary for the labor market to operate in a perfectly competitive environment.

7. Every large firm has a personnel department responsible for setting specific rates of pay for each job. In performing this function, how much discretion does the personnel department have in terms of the rates it sets? To what extent do outside market forces impinge on this decision? For what types of jobs would market forces leave little room or much room for discretion? Why?

Data, Reference, and Internet Sources in Labor Economics

Many students are required to write a paper or complete some type of research project in their labor economics class, a task that is usually begun at about this point in the course. To help the student in this process, this appendix provides a list of the major data and reference sources in labor economics.

Indexes and Abstracts: Newspapers

1. *The New York Times Index.* http://www.nytimes.com/specials/150/index.html Indexes articles from the *New York Times* from 1851 to the present in the Archives section.

2. *The Wall Street Journal Index.* New York: Dow Jones. Monthly with annual accumulations. The first half of the index is arranged by company name; the second half by subject headings.

Indexes and Abstracts: Periodicals

3. *Business Periodicals Index.* New York: Wilson. Monthly with accumulations. A subject index to articles pertaining to business and economics. List of business periodicals indexed can be found at http://www.ovid.com/site/catalog/Catalog_DataBase.jsp?top=2&mid=3&bottom=7&subsection=10.

4. *The Conference Board Cumulative Index.* New York: The Conference Board. Annual. Indexes publications of the Conference Board, an independent non-profit business research organization; covers numerous subjects in the labor area. A list of research reports can be found at http://www.conference-board.org/publications.

5. *Human Resource Abstracts.* Thousand Oaks, Calif.: Sage. Quarterly. Abstracts books, reports, and periodicals on topics such as employment and unemployment, earnings and benefits, labor force participation, and manpower policy. Abstracts are arranged by broad subject category, with author and subject indexes.

6. *Journal of Economic Literature.* Nashville: American Economic Association. Quarterly. Indexes scholarly articles in the labor area. Includes annotated listing of new books, abstracts of major articles, and a large number of book reviews.

7. *Monthly Labor Review.* Washington, D.C.: Bureau of Labor Statistics. Monthly. Indexes books and publications received. Also includes book reviews. Online index can be found at http://www.bls.gov/opub/mlr/mlrhome.htm.

8. *Work-Related Abstracts*. Detroit: Information Coordinators. Monthly with cumulative annual index. Abstracts 250 management, union, government, and academic periodicals. Arranged into 20 broad subjects such as employment, union organizing, and collective bargaining.

Bibliographies

9. *BLS Publications, 1978–1998*. Washington, D.C.: Bureau of Labor Statistics. Contains a numerical listing of bulletins with some annotations; a numerical listing of reports; and a list of BLS periodicals. Updated by quarterly report *BLS Update*. Online information about BLS publications can be found at http://www.bls.gov/opub/home.htm.

10. *Major Programs, Bureau of Labor Statistics*. Washington, D.C.: Bureau of Labor Statistics. Presents in condensed form the scope of the major programs of the BLS, the principal data-gathering agency of the federal government in the labor area. The following is given for each major program: the data available, the coverage, the source of the data, the reference period, the publications issued, and the principal use of the data. Data available from individual states are also listed. Online information about BLS programs can be found at http://www.bls.gov/bls/proghome.htm.

11. *Government Printing Office Subject Bibliographies* http://bookstore.gpo.gov/sb/sale180.html. This website contains a bibliography of government publications by subject.

Academic Journals

12. The major academic journals in the field of labor economics and industrial relations are:

Industrial and Labor Relations Review

Industrial Relations

Journal of Human Resources

Journal of Labor Economics

Journal of Labor Research

Labor History

Labor Studies Journal

Proceedings of the Industrial Relations Research Association (*Labor and Employment Relations Association* as of 2005)

Labour Economics

Nonacademic Journals

13. The articles in the academic journals listed in 12 often require technical expertise in economic theory, mathematics, and statistics. Some nonacademic journals that contain articles written for the layperson are:

    International Labour Review

    Monthly Labor Review

    Compensation and Working Conditions

    Work and Occupations

    Occupation Outlook Quarterly

Statistical Sources

14. *Statistical Abstract of the United States.* Washington, D.C.: Department of Commerce, Bureau of the Census. Annual. Provides a wealth of statistical data on labor subjects as well as many other areas. Also serves as a guide for obtaining more complete data from other sources. The most current (in addition to recent past years) edition is available in PDF format at http://www.census.gov/statab/www/.

15. *Census of the Population.* Washington, D.C.: Department of Commerce, Bureau of the Census. Every 10 years. Provides the most detailed information available on earnings, employment, occupational attainment, and other such subjects for both the nation and individual states. Detailed census tables can be found at http://factfinder.census.gov.

16. *Money Income of Households, Families, and Persons in the United States.* Current Population Report P-60. Washington, D.C.: Department of Commerce, Bureau of the Census. Annual. Presents detailed data on annual earnings and income of Americans classified by demographic, industry, and occupational characteristics. Derived from the Current Population Survey. Tables for the current version of this report can be found at http://www.census.gov/hhes/www/income.html.

17. *Historical Statistics of the United States: Colonial Times to 1970.* Washington, D.C.: Department of Commerce, Bureau of the Census, 1975. A compilation of historical statistics on the labor force, employment, earnings, and union membership, among other subjects. Many statistical series extend back to the 1800s.

18. *Employment and Earnings.* Washington, D.C.: Bureau of Labor Statistics. Monthly. Presents monthly data obtained from the Current Population Survey and the survey of business establishments. The basic source for current labor force and earnings data. Tables from *Employment and Earnings* can be accessed at http://www.bls.gov/cps.

19. *Monthly Labor Review*. Washington, D.C.: Bureau of Labor Statistics. Monthly. Also presents current labor force data, as well as data on consumer and producer prices, productivity, and strikes. Index of publications and PDF versions of the papers containing statistical information can be found at http://www.bls.gov/opub/mlr/mlrhome.htm.

20. *Handbook of U.S. Labor Statistics*. Lanham, Md.: Bernan Press. Annual. Provides a compilation of much of the statistical data gathered by the BLS. The 1975 "Reference Edition" provides complete historical data. Formerly *Handbook of Labor Statistics*, published by the Bureau of Labor Statistics.

21. *Compensation and Working Conditions*. Washington, D.C.: Bureau of Labor Statistics. Monthly. Provides details on the contract terms of major union agreements, plus statistical data on various measures of compensation. Formerly titled *Current Wage Developments*. Index of publications and PDF versions of the papers containing statistical information can be found at http://www.bls.gov/opub/cwc.

22. *Economic Report of the President*. Washington, D.C.: Government Printing Office. Annual. Appendix contains detailed information on income, employment, and production. The complete report can be found online at http://www.gpoaccess.gov.eop.

23. *Annual Report of the National Labor Relations Board*. Washington, D.C.: Government Printing Office. Annual. Presents detailed data on a number of unfair labor practice charges, their disposition, petitions for representation elections, the union win-rate by state, industry, and so on. Also see http://www.nlrb.gov.

24. *Directory of U.S. Labor Organizations*. Washington, D.C.: Bureau of National Affairs, 2000. Provides data on union membership in the United States. Also lists national unions and employee associations, their officers, and headquarters addresses. This is an annual publication.

25. *Digest of Education Statistics*. Washington, D.C.: Department of Education, National Center for Education Statistics (NCE). Annual. Contains comprehensive data on all aspects of education, including enrollment rates, tuition, and occupational attainment. A PDF version of the *Digest* and its tables can be found by searching the NCE web site for the name of the publication at http://nces.ed.gov/pubsearch.

26. Wright, John W., ed. *The American Almanac of Jobs and Salaries*. New York: Avon, 1987. Provides detailed information concerning rates of pay and employment prospects for a wide range of occupations. Updated annually.

27. *Survey of Current Business*. Washington, D.C.: U.S. Department of Commerce. Monthly. Provides macroeconomic statistics such as gross product by industry, product and income accounts, international transactions, and measures of the health of businesses. Index by issue and subject available in PDF or HTML format at http://www.bea.doc.gov/bea/pubs.htm.

28. Law, Gordon T. *A Guide to Sources of Information on the National Labor Relations Board*. New York: Routledge, 2002. The many different sources of information available from the National Labor Relations Board (from 1935 to the present) are brought together in this book. There is much institutional background and information to help provide a perspective on the Board and the statistics is collects.

Internet Sources

29. *Indexes.* These sites provide indexes to other Internet sites that contain information of interest to economists.

WebEc http://netec.wustl.edu/WebEc/WebEc.html From this site one can select an economic category, such as "Labor and Demographics," which will link up with other topics within that category.

Institute of Industrial Relations Library Internet Research Guides http://library.berkeley.edu/IIRL/iirlnet.html This site is maintained by the University of California-Berkeley Library system and provides a guide to labor-oriented Internet resources.

workindex http://workindex.com Maintained by Cornell University's School of Industrial and Labor Relations and *Human Resource Executive* magazine, this site provides access to workplace-oriented websites on the Internet.

30. *Government Agencies.* There are several government agencies whose operations impact or are impacted by the labor market. Many of these sites contain important statistical and policy information that can be crucial for labor market analysis.

The Federal Web Locator http://www.firstgov.gov This site is basically a search engine that allows one to search for the Internet address for any government (and some nongovernment) agencies. It is maintained by the Center for Information Law and Policy.

Social Security Online http://www.ssa.gov This site contains regulations, statistics, and consumer information for all programs administered by the Social Security Administration.

Bureau of Economic Analysis http://www.bea.doc.gov The BEA is an agency of the U.S. Department of Commerce and provides statistics and publications related to industry performance, national accounts, and international activity.

Economic Statistics Briefing Room http://www.whitehouse.gov/fsbr/esbr.html Maintained by the Executive Office of the President, this site contains brief statistical overviews of many aspects of the economy.

United States Congress Economic Indicators http://www.gpoaccess.gov/indicators/index.html This site contains a search engine that gives the user access to up-to-date statistical indicators of the status of the economy.

Council of Economic Advisers http://www.whitehouse.gov/cea The Council of Economic Advisers produces a number of research "white" papers on topics relevant to the labor market.

United States National Labor Relations Board http://www.nlrb.gov This site contains information on all aspects of union organization and regulation. The NLRB is an independent federal agency.

U.S. Department of Health and Human Services http://www.dhhs.gov This site contains regulations, statistics, and consumer information for all programs administered by the Department of Health and Human Services, most of which have some relationship to the labor market.

U.S. Department of Labor http://www.dol.gov This is *the* site for statistics, publications, and regulations related to all aspects of the U.S. labor market.

31. *Statistics and Data.* These sites are good sources for data related to a variety of aspects of the labor market.

U.S. Census Bureau http://www.census.gov From this site one can not only access a variety of tabulated statistics and downloadable reports related to all aspects of the labor market (indexed by subject) but can also directly access specific survey results, such as the Current Population Survey, and generate user-specified tables or data sets ready for analysis.

STAT-USA http://www.stat-usa.gov/ Selecting "State of the Nation" at this site takes the user to all sorts of domestic economic statistics.

FEDSTATS http://www.fedstats.gov/ This site provides for easy access to economic statistics from over 70 U.S. agencies.

National Center for Health Statistics http://www.cdc.gov/nchs/ This site, maintained by the U.S. Centers for Disease Control and Prevention, contains statistics related to all aspects of the health of the citizenry, including divorce rates, teen pregnancy, and mental health.

32. *Research Centers.* These research centers produce articles and papers that are frequently related to labor market issues.

Institute for the Study of Labor http://www.iza.org/ This center is located in Bonn, Germany and sponsors research on international labor issues.

Center for Economic Studies http://www.ces.census.gov/ This center is a research unit of the Office of the Chief Economist of the U.S. Census Bureau and produces research papers which may be downloaded from the Internet.

Economic Policy Institute http://epinet.org The institute is a nonprofit, nonpartisan think tank that produces research and education related to the living standards of workers.

W. E. Upjohn Institute for Employment Research http://www.upjohninst.org/ This independent, nonprofit research organization funds and publishes research that identifies, evaluates, and promotes solutions to employment related problems.

33. *Other Sources of Information on the Internet.*

Bureau of National Affairs http://www.bna.com/ The bureau has a long history of gathering and reporting information related to all aspects of the economy. In addition to reporting up-to-the-minute statistics and analyses for subscribers, it also produces in-depth reports available for purchase by the public.

Education, Training, and Earnings Differentials: The Theory of Human Capital

This chapter examines the role of education and on-the-job training as a source of earnings differentials. The analysis of the labor market effects of education and training is the province of what economists call *human capital theory*. The essence of human capital theory is that expenditures on education and training are investments individuals make in themselves to increase their market skills, productivity, and earnings. In explaining earnings differentials, therefore, human capital theory focuses on individual differences in years of schooling and length of on-the-job training, and the factors that cause some individuals to invest in more human capital than others do.

This chapter is divided into three major parts. The first part examines formal education as a type of human capital investment, develops the concept of a rate of return to human capital investment, and shows why differences in years of education among individuals lead to differences in earnings. The second part of the chapter focuses more closely on the causes of individual differences in investment in schooling, particularly with respect to factors such as individual ability, financial opportunity, and so on. The third part of the chapter is devoted to on-the-job training and the implications of different types of on-the-job training for earnings differentials.

The Pattern of Education and Earnings

Is there any truth to the old maxim, "If you want to get ahead, get an education"? Consider the evidence shown in Figure 7.1, which illustrates age/earnings profiles. Each individual profile shows the annual earnings in 2003 of males of particular ages, with the same level of education, who were year-round, full-time workers. (Age/earnings profiles for women are shown later in the chapter.) These data show that men who were high school graduates (12 years of schooling) and were 25 to 34 years of age in 2003 earned, on average, $35,509 a

FIGURE 7.1   AGE/EARNINGS PROFILES FOR MEN BY EDUCATIONAL LEVEL, 2003

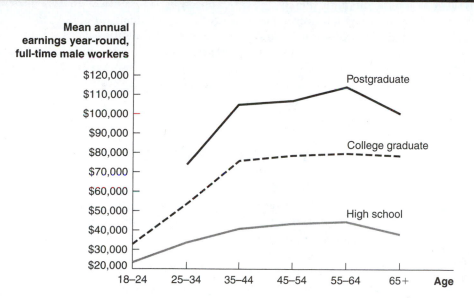

SOURCE: U.S. Census Bureau, Current Population Survey, 2004 Annual Social and Economic Supplement. (PERINC-04).

year; male high school graduates who were 35 to 44 years of age in 2003 earned $40,885, and so on.

The age/earnings profiles in Figure 7.1 provide strong evidence that education and earnings go hand in hand. Several features in particular stand out. First, men with more education make more money, as shown by the successively higher level of each age/earnings profile. The age/earnings profile for male high school graduates, for example, peaks at $44,619, while the peak for persons with four years of college is $79,764 and $114,172 for persons with an advanced degree. A second feature is that the rate of increase of earnings is more rapid for individuals with more education, as shown by the successively steeper slopes of each profile. Between the ages of 18 and 24, male high school graduates were earning an average of $23,119 per year, while males with an advanced degree did not, for the most part, have any full-time earnings from work. By age 45 to 54, however, the earnings of the latter group far exceeded the earnings of their high school graduate counterparts. A third feature is that the earnings for men with higher levels of education continue to rise until later in life and then decline more slowly. While the earnings of both high school and college graduates peak in the 55–64 age group, for example, earnings for high school graduates decline much faster after that than the earnings of college graduates.

Is education a good investment? At first glance it would certainly seem so, since the earnings a person can expect to obtain in the labor market increase rather markedly with higher levels of education. The answer to this question is more complicated, however, because it requires a comparison of both the increased earnings from additional years of education *and* the additional costs. Empirical evidence presented later in this chapter suggests that a college education does open the way to a substantially higher paying job for most people, although the return to this investment is being squeezed by the rapidly rising costs of obtaining the degree.

The Theory of Human Capital

Over two centuries ago Adam Smith observed:

> When any expensive machine is erected, the extraordinary work to be performed by it before it is worn out, it must be expected, will replace the capital laid out by it, with at least the ordinary profits. A man educated at the expense of much labour and time to any of those employments which require extraordinary dexterity and skill, may be compared to one of those expensive machines. The work which he learns to perform, it must be expected, over and above the usual wages of common labour, will replace to him the whole expense of his education, with at least the ordinary profits of an equally valuable capital.[1]

Smith's insight was largely neglected by later economists, who concentrated on investment in physical capital. In the late 1950s, however, economists such as Jacob Mincer and Nobel laureates Theodore Schultz and Gary Becker rediscovered Smith's insight and developed it into the theory of human capital. As Becker states in his classic work, *Human Capital*, any activity that entails a cost in the current period and raises productivity in the future can be analyzed within the framework of investment theory.[2] With respect to human beings, a number of activities that individuals undertake fit this conception of an investment; education, training, migration, health care, and job search are examples.

The type of human capital investment that has received the most attention from labor economists is education and training. While schooling is partly a consumption good for many people (that is, individuals pursue an education for the pleasure and satisfaction of the experience), it is also treated by most individuals as a clear investment in their future. Every college student, for example, is aware of the costs of pursuing a college degree. These include the direct costs of tuition, books, and other educational expenses, and the indirect or opportunity costs in the form of earnings from work that are forgone to attend school. Counterbalanced

1   Adam Smith, *The Wealth of Nations* (Chicago: University of Chicago Press, 1976): 113–14.

2   Gary S. Becker, *Human Capital*, 2d ed. (New York: National Bureau of Economic Research, 1975).

against these costs are the anticipated benefits of increased earnings, more attractive employment opportunities, and higher status and social prestige.

When is an additional year of education a good investment? The quotation from Adam Smith provides the answer—whenever the increased benefits both pay back the initial costs *and* yield a rate of return at least as high as alternative investments of one's time and money. A major contribution of the human capital theory developed by Becker and others is to take this insight of Adam Smith and show how it can be used to measure the private and social rate of return not only to education, but also to numerous other labor market activities. The next section explains this process.

The Investment Decision

To make the discussion more concrete, attention focuses on one particular type of human capital investment—whether or not to attend a four-year university or college. The principles outlined here apply to investments in all types of education and training, however.

Should an individual attend college? From a human capital perspective, the answer depends on the monetary benefits relative to the costs. The precise nature of these benefits and costs is illustrated in Figure 7.2, which is a stylized representation of the age/earnings profile resulting from two different investment strategies. The first strategy is to finish high school and then begin full-time work at age 18, working continuously until age 65. This results in the age/earnings profile *HS*. The second strategy is to attend college for four years from age 18 to 21, then work continuously from age 22 to retirement at age 65, resulting in the age/earnings profile *Col*.

The benefits and costs of attending college are readily identifiable in Figure 7.2. The costs of going to college are of two types. The first is the direct or out-of-pocket cost, which includes payments for tuition, books, and other fees. (The cost of room and board are not counted, since these are incurred even if the person is not enrolled in school.) In Figure 7.2, the direct costs are shown by area (1), where the age/earnings profile *Col* lies below zero on the vertical axis. The size of the direct costs depends on such factors as whether the individual attends a state-supported school or a private school, whether he or she obtains a scholarship or tuition waiver, and so on.

The second type of cost of attending college is the opportunity cost, the earnings from work received by the high school graduate that the college student could also be making. This opportunity cost is shown in Figure 7.2 by area (2). The size of this cost depends on the earnings that a high school graduate is able to make and whether or not the person in college works full-time or part-time while in school. Although not shown in Figure 7.2, the opportunity cost of attending college may extend several years beyond age 22 if the college graduate begins work at a lower salary than the high school graduate is earning at age 22. This might well be the case, since the earnings of the high school graduate will have benefitted from four years of experience and training. Finally, note from Figure 7.2 that the opportunity

FIGURE 7.2   BENEFITS AND COSTS OF FOUR YEARS OF COLLEGE EDUCATION

The lines *HS* and *Col* are the age/earnings profiles of a representative high school and college graduate, respectively. The cost of a college education is the direct cost of tuition, books, and so on (area 1) and the opportunity cost of forgone earnings (area 2). The monetary benefit of attending college is the higher earnings that a college degree makes possible (area 3).

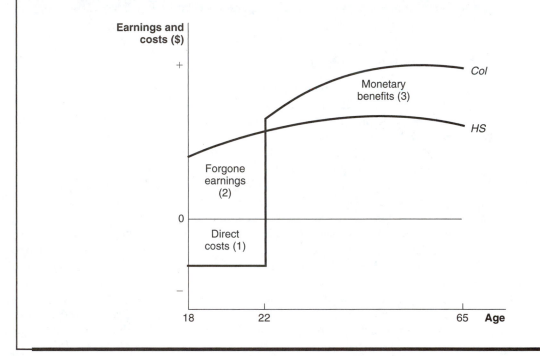

cost of attending college far outweighs the direct cost. Data for 2002 clearly reveal this. The average level of in-state tuition and fees for an academic year was $4,059 at a four-year state-supported university and $16,948 at a private university.[3] The average annual level of earnings for a male high school graduate aged 18 to 24 who worked full-time, on the other hand, was $23,119.

The monetary benefits of a college education are the higher after-tax earnings that the college graduate is able to command in the job market. In Figure 7.2, these monetary benefits are given by the difference between the age/earnings profiles *Col* and *HS* after age 21, shown in the diagram as area (3). The gap in earnings between

---

3   National Center for Education Statistics, *Digest of Educational Statistics, 2000* (Washington, D.C.: Government Printing Office, 2001), Table 313 http://nces.ed.gov/pubs2001/digest/dt313.html.

the college graduate and high school graduate gradually widens with age, reaching a maximum after midlife as the profile *HS* turns down but *Col* continues to rise. While the costs of attending college are substantial, so are the benefits. Using the data for earnings of high school and college graduates from Figure 7.1, one can estimate that a man with a college education who works year-round will earn, on average, $3,162,493 from age 18 to 65 (in 2003 dollars), compared to $1,430,667 for a man with a high school diploma.[4] The corresponding earnings figures for women were $2,135,581 for college graduates and $1,311,690 for high school graduates.

The dollar value of the costs and benefits of a college education are not yet comparable because they accrue at different points in time. The costs of acquiring the human capital are suffered immediately, but the benefits are obtained only in the future. To compare the benefits with the costs, the benefits must be calculated in terms of their present value.

Present Value   The basic economic principle behind the concept of **present value** is that the more distant in time is the receipt of a sum of money, the less is its value today. The reason is easily seen. For a given market rate of interest i, the *future value* (*FV*) in year n of a sum of money Y is given by the formula:

$$FV = Y(1+i)^n. \tag{7.1}$$

Thus, if $Y = \$100$, $i = 10$ percent, and $n = 2$ years, $FV = (\$100)(1 + 0.1)(1 + 0.1) = (\$100)(1 + 0.1)^2 = \$121$.

The formula for future value yields the amount that a sum of money invested today at a given rate of interest will be worth in the future. The formula for *present value* (*PV*) does just the opposite: it calculates what a sum of money Y received n years in the future, given the market rate of interest i, is worth today. This formula is:

$$PV = \frac{Y}{(1+i)^n}, \tag{7.2}$$

or, assuming $Y = \$121$, $i = 10$ percent, and $n = 2$, then $PV = \$121/(1 + .1)^2 = \$100$. This simply states that the promise of $121 two years from now, given the rate of interest of 10 percent, is presently worth $100. It is worth only $100 because two years of interest are forgone before the money is received. Obviously, the longer the time before the payment is received (if $n = 3$ years instead of 2) or the higher the rate of interest is (if $i = 20$ percent instead of 10 percent), the lower will be the present value of the same Y dollars. Equation 7.2 shows the present value of a sum of money to be received n years in the future. Calculating the present value of the lifetime stream of income earned by the high school graduate and college graduate is, however, more complex. Each receives income (or suffers costs) not in just one year but in each year between ages 18 and 65. What is required is the *sum* of

---

4   See Bureau of the Census, "More Education Means Higher Career Earnings," *Statistical Brief* (August 1994), for a discussion of the simple statistical technique used to obtain these estimates and the caveats associated with it.

the discounted value of each year's income. For the high school graduate, the present value of the lifetime stream of income (Y^H) is:

$$PV = Y_{18}^H + \frac{Y_{19}^H}{(1+i)} + \frac{Y_{20}^H}{(1+i)^2} + \cdots + \frac{Y_{64}^H}{(1+i)^{46}}, \tag{7.3}$$

which can be expressed more compactly as:

$$PV = \sum_{t=18}^{64} \frac{Y_t^H}{(1+i)^{t-18}} \tag{7.4}$$

where $t = 18, \ldots, 64$ indexes the person's age, and i is again the market rate of interest. For the college graduate, the lifetime stream of income (Y^C) is:

$$PV = -C_{18} + \frac{-C_{19}}{(1+i)} + \cdots + \frac{Y_{22}^C}{(1+i)^4} + \cdots + \frac{Y_{64}^C}{(1+i)^{46}}, \tag{7.5}$$

or

$$PV = \sum_{t=18}^{64} \frac{Y_t^C - C_t}{(1+i)^{t-18}}. \tag{7.6}$$

In Equation 7.6, the earnings stream of the college graduate in the first four years is equal to $-C$ dollars per year, where C is the direct cost of tuition, books, and fees. The costs at ages 19, 20, and 21 are discounted, as is the income received each year from age 22 to age 64, since these dollars (either as a payment or a receipt) all lie in the future.

Converting the income stream of the high school and college graduate into their present value has a dramatic impact on the relative benefits and costs of a college education. Equations 7.3 and 7.5 show that the more distant the receipt of income, the more heavily it is discounted and the less is its present value. This fact clearly bears on the decision of whether or not to invest in college. The high school graduate earns an income from age 18 to 22 that, because of its immediacy, is discounted relatively little. The college graduate, on the other hand, forgoes current income for the promise of higher income in the future. Because these higher earnings are not realized for 10, 20, or 30 years, they are worth considerably less in terms of their present value. For example, as mentioned earlier, a male college graduate in 2003 could expect to earn $3,162,493 over his lifetime, compared to only $1,430,667 for a male high school graduate. Using a discount rate of 5 percent $(i = 5\%)$ causes the present value of these income streams to shrink to $1,046,524 and $508,777, respectively. While both income streams are considerably reduced in value, the income stream of the college graduate shrinks by the largest dollar value since his earnings are received further in the future.

Two Investment Decision Rules Which investment strategy is the optimal one: to begin work after high school or to continue on to college? Two separate decision rules can be used to answer these questions. Both, in general, yield the same answer.[5] The first is to compare the net present value of each income stream (Equations 7.4 and 7.6) and select the one that is the highest. This choice results in the human capital investment that maximizes the discounted value of lifetime income.

The second way to decide whether college is a good investment is to calculate the **internal rate of return** and compare it with the market rate of interest: if the internal rate of return is greater than or equal to the market rate of interest, the investment is profitable. The internal rate of return is the discount rate (r) that equalizes the net present value of the income streams earned by the high school and the college graduate. To calculate the rate of return, it is necessary to solve for the value of r that makes Equations 7.4 and 7.6 equal:

$$\sum_{t=18}^{64} \frac{Y_t^H}{(1+r)^{t-18}} = \sum_{t=18}^{64} \frac{Y_t^C - C_t}{(1+r)^{t-18}}. \tag{7.7}$$

The meaning of the rate of return can be more easily grasped with the help of Figure 7.2. If the discount rate r were zero, the present value of the income stream (*Col*) of the college graduate would far exceed the lifetime income of the high school graduate (*HS*). At $r = 0$, the much higher future earnings of the college graduate are not discounted at all, and thus the present value of the income stream *Col* is quite high. As the discount rate r increases, the higher future earnings of the college graduate begin to shrink in present value terms, until at some value of r (call it r^*), the present value of the age/earnings profile *Col* and *HS* will be equal. The value r^* is the internal rate of return, and it measures the percentage yield the college graduate reaps on the investment.

Is r^* a return that justifies the investment? The answer to this depends on the market rate of interest i. If $r^* \geq i$, the investment in college is profitable and should be undertaken, since the rate of return on the investment is at least as large as the market rate of interest that has to be paid to finance the investment or that could have been earned if the money had not been spent on college. This conclusion agrees exactly with that reached by the first decision rule, since if $r^* \geq i$, the present value of income given in Equation 7.6 will exceed that in Equation 7.4. Note that the rate of return varies inversely with the costs of college education (both direct and forgone) and positively with the size of the earnings gap between college and high school graduates. As the costs and benefits of college change over time, so too will the rate of return.

The Private and Social Rate of Return

Two separate rates of return to college education are estimated by economists: the **private rate of return** and the **social rate of return.** Both are calculated using Equation 7.7. The difference between them rests on the precise definition of the cost and income variables. The private rate of return is the yield on the investment

---

5   There are exceptions, however, as discussed in Jack Hirshleifer, *Investment, Interest and Capital* (Englewood Cliffs, N.J.: Prentice-Hall, 1970), Chapter 3.

in college that is received by the person making the investment. The cost variable C in Equation 7.7, therefore, includes only those direct costs actually paid by the student. The income variable Y for both the high school and college graduate includes only after-tax income, since this is the portion of income that each person receives from the human capital investment.

The social rate of return measures the yield to society from the resources devoted to college education. From a social point of view, the cost variable C used in calculating the private rate of return significantly understates the true cost of college education to the economy. One reason is that at state-supported schools tax revenues from various levels of government cover about three-fourths of the operating costs. A second reason is that many students receive financial aid from parents or third parties. On the benefit side, to calculate the social rate of return, economists use the pretax income of high school and college graduates. Assuming that firms pay workers an income equal to their productivity, it is the difference in the pretax income of college and high school graduates that represents the additional output gained by society from its commitment of resources to education. A study by the Joint Economic Committee of the U.S. Congress, "Investment in Education: Private and Public Returns" (January 2000), has estimated that 25 percent of the U.S. economic growth since 1959 can be accounted for by higher levels of educational attainment by U.S. citizens.

A number of studies have estimated the private and social rates of return for various levels of schooling. The most recent summary of results across countries puts the private rate of return to a college education at 12 to 28 percent.[6] The Joint Economic Committee report mentioned previously reports an estimated 10 percent annual private rate of return to an additional year of schooling. The private rate of return has usually been found to be larger than the social rate of return, and the rate of return for white men is usually found to be larger than for women or blacks. Since

➡ SEE

Empirical Evidence 7-1: Estimated Rates of Return to Formal Education, p. 373.

the real rate of return from other investments such as stocks, bonds, and savings deposits has generally been lower than this, education would appear to be a very sound investment. As discussed later in this chapter, evidence points to an increase in the rate of return to education through the 1980s and 1990s, which further supports this conclusion. These rates of return are discussed in greater detail in Empirical Evidence 7-1.

Before these numbers are accepted uncritically, it is important to note that estimated rates of return are subject to many possible biases. On the one hand, there are several compelling reasons to suppose that the actual return from additional schooling is considerably less than the reported 12 to 20 percent. One is the problem of "other things equal"—the higher income that is associated with more education may actually be due to the fact that the more educated also have higher ability, for instance. The social rate of return to education is also overstated to the extent that additional education serves merely to sort or screen people in the job

---

6   See George Psacharapoulos, "Returns to Investment in Education: A Further Update," *Education Economics* 22 (August 2004): 111–34.

market rather than to raise their levels of productivity.[7] Both of these biases are considered more fully later in the chapter.

On the other hand, a variety of reasons support the view that the true rate of return to education is higher than the estimated figures suggest. One study enumerated 20 different nonwage benefits of additional education that are not included in the usual rate-of-return calculation.[8] These omitted benefits included such things as a more pleasant or prestigious job, greater fringe benefits, better health, a reduction in crime, and the fact that education is a consumption good for many people. The authors of the study concluded that the total benefits from one additional year of schooling might actually be double those suggested by earnings data alone.

Implications of Human Capital Theory

The foregoing discussion outlines two alternative decision rules by which to determine whether or not a college education is a good investment. An objection sometimes made is that people do not really make decisions in this way. Two arguments can be marshaled against this objection. The first is that prospective college students *do* seem to be quite cognizant of the monetary benefits and costs of attending college. Richard Freeman has found that college students' estimates of their forgone earnings correspond quite closely to an estimate of actual forgone earnings.[9] In his study, students were also asked to provide estimates of their expected starting salaries in their intended occupations. The ranking of these estimates correlated quite closely with the actual salaries of recent college graduates in these occupations.[10] While it is no doubt true that few prospective college students explicitly calculate the rate of return to a college education, evidence does suggest that the decision to attend college is significantly influenced by considerations of benefits and costs, as the theory suggests. The second way to judge the validity of human capital theory is to compare the predictions of the theory with actual behavior. Following are some implications of the theory.

---

7   For example, Daron Acemoglu and Joshua Angrist, "How Large Are the Social Returns to Education? Evidence from Compulsory Schooling Laws," *MIT Working Paper* 99/30 (1999), report private rates of return at 7 percent and social rates of return of less than 1 percent.

8   Robert H. Haveman and Barbara L. Wolfe, "Schooling and Economic Well-Being: The Role of Nonmarket Effects," *Journal of Human Resources* 19, no. 3 (Summer 1984): 377–407.

9   Richard Freeman, *The Market for College Trained Manpower: A Study of the Economics of Career Choice* (Cambridge, Mass.: Harvard University Press, 1971), Chapter 11. Also see Dennis L. Hoffman and Stuart A. Low, "Rationality and the Decision to Invest in Economics," *Journal of Human Resources* 18, no. 4 (Fall 1983): 480–96.

10 Additional evidence on this point is provided by Julian R. Betts, "What Do Students Know about Wages? Evidence from a Survey of Undergraduates," *Journal of Human Resources* 31 (Winter 1996): 27–56. Betts finds, not surprisingly, that upperclassmen are better at predicting earnings. A study of European college students finds that they tend to overestimate the returns to a college education. See Giorgio Brunello et al., "The Wage Expectations of European College Students," *IZA Discussion Paper* No. 299 (June 2001).

Costs   One prediction of human capital theory is that any factor that reduces the cost of a college education should lead to an increase in college enrollments. Scholarships, fellowships, and tuition waivers, for example, reduce the direct costs of college education (area 1 in Figure 7.2) and should make college attendance more attractive. A reduction in the indirect or opportunity costs (area 2 in Figure 7.2) would also raise the rate of return to education, making college more attractive to prospective students. Many colleges and universities have recognized this fact by offering more evening classes so that students may continue to work either full-time or part-time, thereby reducing the forgone costs of further education.

Research does find that college enrollments are sensitive to the costs of education. One study estimated that a $1,000 increase in the net cost of college leads to a 16 percent decline in enrollment.[11] Predictably, this response is considerably greater for young people from lower-income families, while those from middle- and upper-income families exhibit a much weaker response.

Age   The great majority of college students are in the age group 18 to 24. In 2001, only 16 percent of full-time students were 25 years of age or older. Why is college attendance concentrated among young adults? Human capital theory offers two reasons. The first is that the older a person is, the fewer are the remaining years of work life over which to recoup the costs of attending college. This consideration is of obvious importance to individuals who are contemplating a midlife career change that involves going back to college (for example, an English teacher who wants to switch to a career in business). The extension of the retirement age from 65 to 70 would counteract this consideration by allowing five more years of potential earnings to balance against the costs of college. The second reason college attendance declines with age is that the opportunity costs of college are higher. As workers age, their earnings increase because of experience, training, and seniority. To quit a job to attend college entails far larger opportunity costs for a 40-year-old than for a 20-year-old, whose earnings level is likely to be considerably lower.

Labor Force Continuity   A third prediction of human capital theory is that persons who do not expect to work continuously in the labor force should have lower enrollment rates in college. The reason is analogous to that for age—the fewer years spent in the labor force, the less time there is to recoup the costs of attending college. This prediction seems to be supported by the trend in women's labor force participation and enrollment in college. In 1961, only 38 percent of women were in the labor force, compared to 84 percent of men. Not surprisingly, men were also awarded the lion's share of bachelor's degrees—69 percent. Forty years later, a far greater proportion of young women planned to work, many in continuous, full-time careers. For these women, a college degree became a much more attractive investment, reflected in the fact that women obtained 59 percent of all bachelor's degrees awarded in 1998.

---

11   Michael S. McPherson and Morton Owen Schapiro, "Does Student Aid Affect College Enrollment? New Evidence on a Persistent Controversy," *American Economic Review* 81, no. 1 (March 1991): 309–18.

SEE
Policy Application 7-1:
Interrupted Work
Careers and Women's
Earnings, p. 369.

The impact of a career interruption on a worker's earnings is explored in greater detail in Policy Application 7-1.

Earnings Differentials A fourth prediction of human capital theory is that persons with more education should also have higher earnings in their peak work years. This prediction is supported by the age/earnings profiles shown in Figure 7.1. There are three reasons for this prediction. First, higher earnings are necessary to compensate for the costs associated with additional schooling. If the earnings of a college graduate were no greater than those of a high school graduate, there would be little financial incentive to attend college. For the same reason, the annual earnings of a physician must exceed those of a person with a four-year B.A. degree to keep the rate of return to a medical degree competitive. Second, people with more education have fewer years in the labor force in which to recoup their investment in schooling. The high school graduate, for example, has 47 years of earnings between age 18 and 65; the person with a PhD may have only 35 years or so (from age 30 to 65) in the labor force. Fewer working years plus additional costs require that actual dollar earnings be greater for persons with more years of schooling to induce them to invest in human capital. A third reason why additional education results in greater earnings is that those higher earnings are not received until relatively later in life and are heavily discounted in terms of their present value. The earnings of doctors or lawyers are received relatively far in the future compared to those of high school graduates. To make investment in education attractive, dollar earnings must be greater for persons with more years of education as a reward for postponing earnings and consumption.

The Size of Earnings Differentials The theory of human capital not only predicts that wages and average annual earnings should be greater for persons with successively more years of education, it also predicts how large these earnings differentials should be, as illustrated in Figure 7.3, graphs (a) and (b). Graph (a) shows the age/earnings profiles for college graduates (Col_1) and high school graduates (HS). Graph (b) shows the labor market for college graduates. The vertical axis measures the average wage rate of college graduates as a percentage of the average wage rate of high school graduates; the curve D_1 represents employers' demand for college graduates; the curve S_1 shows the supply of college graduates as a function of the relative college wage.

How large should the wage differential between college and high school graduates be? In equilibrium the college/high school wage differential must be just large enough to make the net present value of the two lifetime streams of income equal. If the relative wage of college graduates were greater, the higher rate of return would induce more 18-year-olds to pursue college educations, expanding the supply of college graduates and driving down wages and the rate of return of college graduates until an equilibrium is reached. Similarly, if wages of college graduates were equal to those of high school graduates, the poor rate of return would lead to a decrease in college enrollments, causing college graduates' wages and the rate of return to increase until an equilibrium differential in wages is restored.

The demand and supply curves in the college labor market—graph (b)—are D_1 and S_1, giving rise to a large relative wage of W_1 for college graduates (point A). This is reflected in graph (a) by the large gap between the age/earnings profiles Col_1 and HS. If the present value of the lifetime income is greater for college graduates than for high school graduates, more people will enroll in college, shifting the supply curve to the right, such as to S_2, and driving down the relative college wage to W_2 (point B). This causes the age/earnings profile for college graduates to shift downward, from Col_1 to Col_2. This process will continue until an equilibrium is reached where the present values of the two income streams are equal.

(a) Age/Earnings Profiles, College and High School Graduates

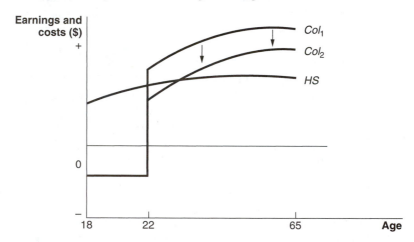

(b) Labor Market for College Graduates

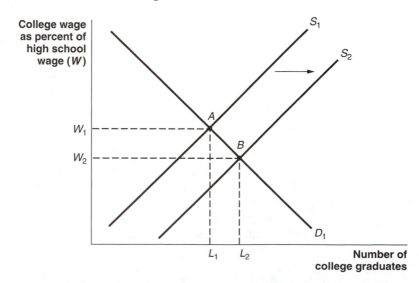

College Graduates: Too Many or Too Few?

An interesting debate continues among economists over the relative state of demand and supply in the labor market for college graduates. One group argues that there are too few college graduates; the other argues that there are too many. Since the labor market prospects of most readers of this book clearly hinge on the answer to this question, it seems worthwhile to explore the controversy in more detail.

First is the case for too few college graduates. As these economists see it, the college labor market was in a state of excess demand during much of the last two decades. The surest evidence, they say, is to look at the relative earnings of college graduates and high school graduates. In 1979, male college graduates earned 33 percent more than high school graduates, and female college graduates earned 41 percent more than female high school graduates. By 2004, these premiums had risen to 97 percent and 78 percent for males and females.

What could account for this dramatic increase in the financial payoff to a college degree? The answer, these economists claim, has two parts. The first is a large increase in the demand for college-educated labor due to the rapid growth of jobs in professional, managerial, and technical occupations that traditionally employ a disproportionate share of college graduates; the second is that the supply of college graduates increased only modestly over the decade, in part due to a decline in the number of college-aged people in the population (the lagged effect of the "baby bust" that started in the mid- to late 1960s). Since these economists expect these trends in demand and supply to continue into the first decade of the 2000s, from their point of view the outlook for college graduates is relatively bright.

Now the case for too many college graduates. These economists do not dispute that the relative earnings of college graduates rose substantially over this period; it is the explanation of this fact that they question. They first disagree with the contention that the demand for college graduates outstrips supply. One study projects that between 2000 and 2010, about 4 million total new jobs requiring a college degree will be created. During the same time period, just over one million college graduates are expected to enter the labor force each year. This surplus in college-educated workers will be absorbed in several ways, such as longer spells of job search, involuntary unemployment, and employment in jobs for which the graduate is overqualified.

If there is an excess supply of college graduates, then how is the rise in the relative earnings of college graduates explained? Easily, say this group of economists. The key to the puzzle is to look at what is happening in the labor market for high school graduates.

While the demand for college graduates is not expected to quite keep up with the supply, the disparity between demand and supply in the market for high school graduates is far greater. Over three million high-wage jobs in the goods-producing sector of the economy that provided jobs for high school graduates have disappeared due to plant closings, downsizings, and layoffs, while many of the new jobs available for high school graduates are in low-wage sectors, such as retail trade and fast food. The result is that the relative earnings of high school graduates have been severely depressed due to excess supply.

What is the bottom line? Whichever perspective is correct, the message is the same—the payoff to a college degree is high and likely to rise further. But the implications for the U.S. economy are quite different. From one point of view, the large payoff to a college degree is a sign of a healthy, growing economy that demands large numbers of highly skilled workers. From the other point of view it is a sign of a sick economy that is falling far short of providing enough decent-paying jobs for those who either do not choose to, or cannot, go to college.

SOURCES: Robert Hall, "The Remarkable Prosperity of College Graduates," http://www-hoover.stanford.edu/pubaffairs/we/current/hall_0900.html (accessed 1/19/05); Richard Rothstein, "Supply, Demand, Wages, and Myth," http://www.epinet.org/content.cfm/webfeat_lessons20001101 (accessed 1/19/05).

This process is illustrated in Figure 7.3. Assume initially that the average wage differential for college graduates is large, shown as W_1 in graph (b) where the demand curve D_1 and supply curve S_1 intersect (point A). A large wage differential is reflected, in turn, in a relatively wide gap separating the age/earnings profiles of college graduates (Col_1) and high school graduates (HS) in graph (a), and in a relatively large private rate of return to college education. From the point of view of 18-year-olds, the high wages earned by college graduates provide a clear incentive to attend college. With a lag of four years, the supply of college graduates will expand, shifting the supply curve to S_1. The larger supply of college graduates, however, depresses their relative wage in the market to W_2 (point B), which results in smaller annual earnings for college graduates, a downward shift of the college age/earnings profile to Col_2, and a lower rate of return to college education. This process continues until the relative wage differential and rate of return for college graduates fall enough just to make individuals indifferent between college and working after high school.

Schooling and the Distribution of Individual Earnings

One of the most important labor market outcomes that economists seek to explain is the distribution of income among persons in the labor force. The largest component of income for most people, in turn, is labor market earnings. In 2003, 11 percent of men aged 15 years and older who worked at full-time jobs earned less than $17,500 per year while 13 percent earned more than $85,000 per year. What can account for this wide diversity in earnings? Many factors come into play, such as occupational attainment, unionism, and pure luck. Not surprisingly, however, one of the most important (if not *the* most important) is education, the role of which is considered in this section.

The Market for Human Capital

Since persons with more education earn more money, one prerequisite to explaining the distribution of earnings is to explain the distribution of schooling—why some individuals invest in only an eighth-grade education, while others invest in a Ph.D. Human capital theory can help provide this answer. To maximize the present value of lifetime income, the decision rule is to invest in human capital up to the point where the private rate of return is equal to the market rate of interest. Given this decision rule, the reason some persons invest in more education than others do must arise from factors that either raise the rate of return they receive or lower the cost they must pay for funds.

This insight has been developed into a formal model of human capital investment by Gary Becker.[12] Becker's theory explains individual differences in years of education in terms of a person's demand curve for human capital and supply curve of investable funds.

The Demand Curve for Human Capital   A representative **demand curve for human capital** is shown in graph (a) of Figure 7.4. The demand curve D_1 shows the marginal rate of return r earned from each additional dollar spent on human capital (assumed here to be education). Thus, the H_1 dollar spent on schooling yields a rate of return of r_1, the H_2 dollar yields a rate of return of r_2, and so on. The demand curve is drawn with a negative slope, implying that the marginal rate of return declines with additional investment in schooling. There are at least two reasons for this. The first is tied to the law of diminishing returns. Since each person has a fixed mental capacity, equal dollar expenditures on additional schooling will raise a person's productivity (and thus earnings) at a diminishing rate, causing the rate of return to decline as more and more education is acquired. One thousand dollars spent on completing a bachelor's degree will provide a higher percentage yield than the same $1,000 spent on completing a PhD. A second reason is that additional schooling leaves the person with fewer working years to recoup the costs of education.

A demand curve expresses the relationship between price and quantity demanded.[13] With respect to investment in human capital, the "price" is the interest rate that has to be paid on borrowed funds or that could have been earned if the money invested in education had been put to some other use. The decision rule for human capital investment is to invest additional funds as long as the rate of return on the last dollar spent is at least as large as the cost of acquiring that dollar. Given the demand curve D_1, if the marginal interest cost of funds were i_1, the optimal level of expenditures on schooling would be (point A), since at that point $r_1 = i_1$. If the cost of funds were to drop to i_2, additional schooling expenditures up to H_2 (point B) would become profitable.

The demand curve D_1 not only shows the rate of return to additional investments in human capital, it can also be used to show (approximately) the person's annual earnings from work. For a given stock of human capital (total $ spent on schooling) of H_m, annual earnings can be expressed as:

$$Y = Y_0 + \sum_{j=1}^{m} r_j H_j \tag{7.8}$$

12   Becker, *Human Capital*, 95–144.

13   Examples of modeling and estimating the demand for education can be found in Rajindar K. Koshal and Munjulika Koshal, "Demand and Supply of Educational Service: A Case of Liberal Arts Colleges," *Education Economics* 7 (August 1999): 121–30, and Robert Quinn and Jamie Price, "The Demand for Medical Education: An Augmented Human Capital Approach," *Economics of Education Review* 17 (June 1998): 337–47. An empirical investigation of differential demand for college across race can be found in Sandra E. Black and Amir Sufi, "Who goes to College? Differential Enrollment by Race and Family Background," *NBER Working Paper No. W9310* (November 2002).

FIGURE 7.4 — THE DEMAND CURVE FOR HUMAN CAPITAL INVESTMENT AND THE SUPPLY CURVE OF FUNDS

Graph (a) illustrates a demand curve for human capital investment. It shows that the rate of return to the H_1 dollar spent on human capital is r_1, and the annual income earned is approximated by the area OD_1AH_1. The rate of return to the H_2 dollar falls to r_2; the annual income of the person is approximately OD_1BH_2. If the interest rate is i_1, the demand curve D_1 shows that H_1 is the optimal level of investment. Graph (b) illustrates a supply curve of funds for human capital investment. The first H_1 dollars are provided by parents and have no interest cost; additional funds, however, are available only at successively higher interest rates until H_4 is reached, where no more borrowed funds are available.

(a) The Demand Curve

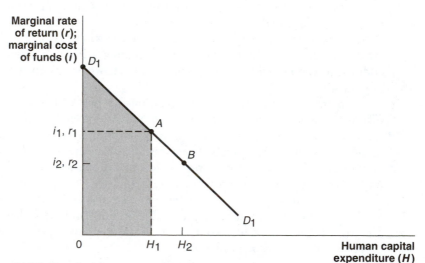

(b) The Supply Curve

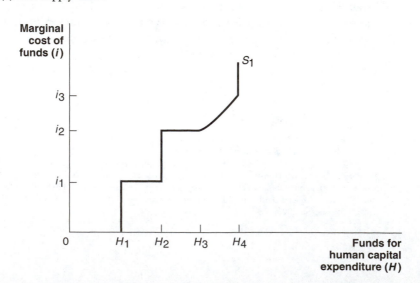

where Y is annual earnings, Y_0 is the person's earnings with zero human capital (zero \$ spent on schooling), and r_j is the marginal rate of return on the jth dollar invested. The annual income generated by the jth dollar of human capital is $r_j \cdot H_j$ (for example, 10% of \$1 = \$0.10), the annual income from the kth dollar is $r_k \cdot H_k$, and so on. Summing these up (and ignoring Y_0 since it is likely to be quite small) yields annual earnings. Graphically, the sum of these dollar earnings from the person's stock of human capital is given by the area under the demand curve up to the last H_m dollar invested. In graph (a) of Figure 7.4, for example, if the stock of human capital is H_1, annual earnings are given by the shaded area OD_1AH_1. If investment in schooling is H_2, annual earnings will increase to OD_1BH_2. Because of the law of diminishing returns, additional dollars spent on education result in successively smaller increments to annual income.

The Supply Curve of Investable Funds A representative **supply curve of investable funds** is shown in graph (b) of Figure 7.4. The supply curve S_1 shows the interest rate that must be paid to acquire each dollar invested in human capital. This interest rate is the marginal cost of funds. It was assumed in the discussion of the demand curve that the person could borrow all the funds desired at a constant rate of interest, implying a perfectly elastic supply curve. This assumption is quite unrealistic, however, because the market for lendable funds for education is imperfect.[14] A person often cannot obtain all the funds for schooling, even if the investment is economically worthwhile. The reason is that the lender cannot repossess the human capital should the student default on the debt, making it too risky to lend more than a limited amount.

For most students, therefore, the supply curve of funds is upward sloping, as represented by the supply curve S_1. For the first H_1 dollars of expenditure, the interest cost may effectively be zero if the student's parents pay the full cost of tuition, books, and other such fees. At some point, however, the student will have to acquire his or her own source of funds for further schooling. The cheapest source of funds might be low-cost student loans with an interest rate of i_1. After this $H_2 - H_1$ amount of funds is exhausted, the next cheapest source of funds may be personal savings or earnings from work, available at a rate of i_2. The interest rate i_2 is the opportunity cost of using these funds for education rather than leaving them in the bank to earn interest. After these $H_3 - H_2$ dollars of personal funds are gone, the student may have to resort to bank loans that have a high and rising interest cost. Beyond some dollar amount such as H_4, the student will find it impossible to acquire additional funds at any reasonable interest rate, causing the supply curve to become completely inelastic.

14   The importance of the availability of funds in choices between public and private colleges is highlighted in the article by Fred Thompson and William Zumets, "Effects of Key State Policies on Private Colleges and Universities: Sustaining Private Sector Capacity in the Face of Higher Education Access Challenge," *Economics of Education Review* 20 (December 2001): 517–31. Further evidence of the impact of the availability of funds on college attendance and college choice can be found in Katherine G. Abraham and Melissa A. Clark, "Financial Aid and Students' College Decisions: Evidence from the District of Columbia's Tuition Assistance Grant Program" *NBER Working Paper No. 1012* (November 2003): and Christopher Avery and Caroline Minter Hoxby, "Do and Should Financial Aid Packages Affect Students' College Choices?" *NBER Working Paper No. W9482* (February 2003).

FIGURE 7.5   THE EQUILIBRIUM LEVEL OF HUMAN CAPITAL INVESTMENT

The equilibrium level of human capital investment is H_1 dollars. At H_2, the marginal rate of return r_2 (point B) is higher than the marginal cost of funds i_2 (point C), implying that additional investment is worthwhile. When the cost of funds and the rate of return are equal, the optimal expenditure has been reached (point A).

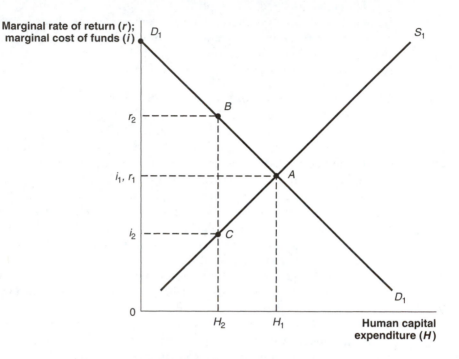

Equilibrium Investment in Human Capital

Equilibrium Investment in Human Capital   The demand curve for human capital and the supply curve of funds are combined in Figure 7.5. For ease of exposition, the supply curve has been drawn as a continuous upward-sloping line. How many dollars should the person pictured here spend on education? The answer is H_1, given by the intersection of the demand curve D_1 and supply curve S_1 (point A), where $r_1 = i_1$. At any lesser amount of expenditure, such as H_2, the rate of return from that dollar of expenditure (point B) exceeds the interest cost i_2 of financing it (point C), implying the individual could profitably increase the investment in education. Given the level of expenditure on schooling of H_1, the person's annual earnings are given by the area OD_1AH_1 (neglecting the term Y_0 in Equation 7.8).

The Distribution of Earnings

To explain the differences in education and earnings among people in the labor force, it is necessary to look at reasons the demand and supply curves may vary from one person to another.

Differences in Supply Curves   Shown in graph (a) of Figure 7.6 is a common demand curve D_1, but three individual supply curves, S_1, S_2, and S_3. The common demand curve implies that each person obtains the same financial return from a given expenditure on schooling; the three different supply curves show that the marginal cost of funds differs for each of the three individuals. The person with supply curve S_3 faces the greatest accessibility to funds for any given level of human capital investment; the person with supply curve S_1 has the least accessibility.

What might cause such differences in supply curves? An important factor is what Becker called differences in *opportunity*. Opportunity in this sense relates to the availability and cost of funds for investment in schooling.[15] For example, probably the most important determinant of an individual's financial opportunity is his or her parents' financial resources. The supply curve of funds for investment in schooling for the son or daughter of a well-to-do family, for example, may resemble the supply curve S_3. For an initial investment in schooling of H_2 (say through 4 years of college), the cost of funds may be zero if the parents pay for all tuition, books, and so on. Beyond H_2 the cost of funds may rise if the person then has to turn to student loans or savings.

The supply curve of funds for a person from a family may, on the other hand, resemble S_1. This person may not be able to count on any family financial support and may have to finance schooling with personal savings or part-time work. In either case a forgone interest cost is attached to these funds. The marginal cost of funds to this person will also rise with additional educational investment as he or she is forced to resort to bank loans and other sources of funds. Beyond some level of investment, say H_2, lenders will be unwilling to lend additional funds at any reasonable interest rate for fear of default. This causes the supply curve S_1 to become perfectly inelastic, precluding the acquisition of additional schooling.

Inequality of opportunity leads to inequality in years of schooling and labor market earnings. The equilibrium levels of human capital investment for the three individuals pictured in graph (a) of Figure 7.6 are given by points A, B, and C, where the demand curve intersects each supply curve. Individual 3 has the greatest financial opportunity and finds it profitable to invest in H_3 human capital. This level of human capital yields market earnings approximated by the area under the demand curve OD_1CH_3. Individual 1, on the other hand, has the smallest amount of financial opportunity, reflected by the relatively high cost of funds, and invests in only H_1 education. As a result, individual 1's earnings are also smaller, being approximated by the area OD_1AH_1.

---

15   See Susan M. Dynarski, "Does Aid Matter? Measuring the Effect of Student Aid on College Attendance and Completion," *American Economic Review* 93 (March 2003): 279–88.

FIGURE 7.6

INEQUALITY IN EARNINGS DUE TO DIFFERENCES IN HUMAN CAPITAL SUPPLY AND DEMAND CURVES

In graph (a) each person has the same demand curve D_1, but the supply curves differ. The person with the least access to funds (S_1) invests in only H_1 human capital (point A), yielding earnings of OD_1AH_1. The person with the greatest access to funds (S_3) invests in a greater amount H_3 (point C), yielding higher earnings of OD_1CH_3. In graph (b) each person has the same supply curve S_1 but demand curves differ. The most able person (D_3) invests in H_3 human capital (point C); the least able person invests in only H_1 (point A). The earnings of the most able person are OD_3CH_3; the earnings of the least able person are a much smaller amount OD_1AH_1.

(a) Differences in Supply Curves

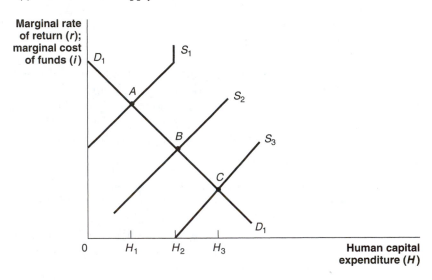

(b) Differences in Demand Curves

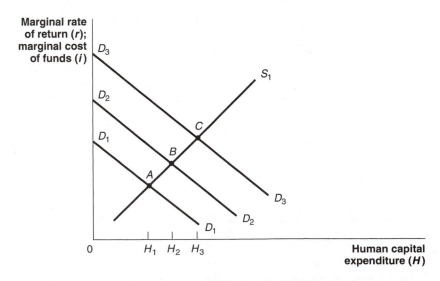

The more unequal is the distribution of opportunity in the population, the more unequal will be the distribution of earnings. This explanation for earnings inequality underlies much of American social policy with respect to education. As immigrants, farmers, and manual workers realized two centuries ago, education is the surest route to personal economic advancement. Accordingly, one of the most important political goals of these groups in the 1800s was the achievement of free public education. This goal is readily interpretable with this model as a means not only to promote more education by shifting the supply curve of funds to the right, but also to equalize incomes by reducing the dispersion in supply curves due to differences in family wealth. The same philosophical commitment to "equal opportunity" underlies many social programs today, such as federally subsidized low-interest student loans and financial aid targeted specifically to low-income families.[16]

Differences in Demand Curves   At the other end of the spectrum is the situation where supply curves are identical, but demand curves vary across individuals. This case is illustrated in graph (b) of Figure 7.6 by the common supply curve and the separate demand curves D_1, D_2, and D_3.

What might cause such differences in demand curves? One important factor identified by Becker is differences in individual *ability*. Ability in this regard is synonymous with an individual's intelligence and learning capacity. A more able person would presumably gain more from a given expenditure in schooling than a less able person, resulting in greater market productivity, earnings, and rate of return. This is illustrated by the three separate demand curves D_1, D_2, and D_3, corresponding to individual 1 (the least able), individual 2 (of average ability), and individual 3 (the most able).[17] For the same expenditure on schooling of H_1, the rate of return for the least able person is shown by the demand curve D_1 to be much lower than the rate of return from the same H_1 investment for the most able person.

Although Becker concentrated his analysis on the role of ability as a cause of differences in individual demand curves for human capital, later studies have identified other important factors as well. One such factor is *discrimination* in the labor

---

16   The G.I. Bill of 1944, which provided payments to military veterans for college tuition, has probably been one of the most important pieces of legislation promoting equality of opportunity, since veterans tend to come from lower socioeconomic groups. Empirical evidence on this point is provided in Jere Behrman, Robert Pollak, and Paul Taubman, "Family Resources, Family Size, and Access to Financing for College Education," *Journal of Political Economy* 97, no. 2 (April 1989): 398–419. More recently, the HOPE scholarship in Georgia has put a college education into financial reach of many lower-income students. See Mary Beth Marklein, "HOPE Scholarship Built on Merit, Faith," *USA Today* D11:5 (19 November 1997), and Deepa Sridhar, "Postsecondary Enrollment Effects of Merit-Based Financial Aid: Evidence from Georgia's HOPE Scholarship Program" Ph.D. dissertation, University of Georgia (2001).

17   While it is assumed here that the effect of higher ability is to shift the demand curve to the right, it is possible that the opposite could also happen. Persons of higher ability may be able to earn a considerable amount without additional education, making the forgone costs of education quite high relative to those for less able persons. Perhaps the best example is persons having a unique physical ability or talent such as Madonna or Michael Jordan. Since the definition of "ability" used here pertains only to superior intelligence, many of these cases may not apply. Consideration of forgone income may also cause the impact of discrimination on the demand curve to be the opposite of that assumed here (i.e., since persons discriminated against earn less, the opportunity cost of further education is also reduced).

market. The rate of return from a given expenditure on schooling depends on the market earnings from work after the schooling is completed. Discrimination, whether in the form of wage discrimination (lower wages for the same type of work) or occupational discrimination (segregation in certain low-paying occupations), would result in a lower rate of return for any given expenditure on schooling, shifting the demand curve to the left for the person discriminated against.

Another factor that might lead to differences in individual demand curves is variation in *school quality*. If two people of equal ability made the same dollar expenditure on schooling, but one received schooling of higher quality, presumably that person would receive higher earnings and a greater rate of return, shifting the demand curve to the right relative to that of the person with the lower-quality schooling. Differences in ability, quality of schooling, or discrimination, by causing differences in demand curves for human capital, also lead to differences in years of schooling and earnings. In graph (b), the equilibrium levels of human capital investment for the three individuals are given by points A, B, and C. The least able person has the demand curve D_1 and invests in only H_1 schooling. His or her earnings are approximated by the area OD_1AH_1. Individual 3, on the other hand, because of greater ability or some other factor, has the demand curve D_3 and finds it profitable to invest in relatively more schooling of H_3 amount, giving rise to larger earnings of OD_3CH_3.

The more unequal is the distribution of ability, the extent of discrimination, or the quality of schooling, the more variation there will be in the demand curves for human capital and in market earnings among individual workers. While this conclusion was also reached concerning variations in supply curves, the *degree* of earnings inequality caused by differences in demand curves is much greater. Graph (a) of Figure 7.6 shows that differences in supply curves lead to an inverse relationship between the marginal rate of return r and the amount of investment expenditure H; moving down the demand curve D_1 from point A to point C, the amount of capital invested increases, but the rate of return falls. Conversely, in graph (b) differences in demand curves lead to a positive relationship between r and H. Variation in demand curves, therefore, leads to much larger differences in individual earnings than variation in supply curves, since in this case, a more able person not only has more schooling but also derives a higher rate of return from that schooling—both factors work together to cause higher earnings. Since most studies have found that years of education and the rate of return are, in fact, inversely correlated in the population, variation in supply curves appears to be the dominant cause of earnings inequality.[18]

Just as public policy has worked to reduce income inequality by promoting greater equality of opportunity, it has attempted to reduce the variation in individual demand curves and earnings. Given, for example, that ability is at least partly a function of one's home environment, social programs such as Head Start (a preschool

---

18 See Robert J. Willis, "Wage Determinants: A Survey and Reinterpretation of Human Capital Earnings Functions," in Orley Ashenfelter and Richard Layard, eds., *Handbook of Labor Economics*, vol. 1 (Amsterdam: North-Holland, 1986). Also see Empirical Evidence 7-1 at the end of this chapter.

program for disadvantaged children) lead to a more equal distribution of abilities and earnings. Research has documented definite short- and medium-term benefits of early childhood education programs and demonstrated that the effects are greatest for disadvantaged children. Long-term positive effects of these programs, however, are still elusive.[19] Antidiscrimination laws, equal opportunity requirements, and other such laws also lead to a smaller dispersion in demand curves. Inequality in school quality has similarly been attacked by court-ordered busing programs, the demise of the "separate but equal" doctrine that maintained racial segregation in education until the Supreme Court's landmark decision in 1954, and state laws equalizing expenditures per pupil across low- and high-income school districts.

Correlations between Demand and Supply Curves   Differences in labor market earnings may come about from differences in either demand curves for human capital or supply curves of investable funds. In either case, the greater is the variation in demand curves or supply curves, the greater will be the variation in individual earnings in the population. Empirical Evidence 7-2 explores these differences in greater detail using some current statistics on earnings and education levels.

⮞ **SEE**
Empirical Evidence 7-2:
Schooling and Earnings,
p. 374.

Becker posed the interesting question whether there might be a systematic correlation between individual demand curves and supply curves. For example, shown in Figure 7.7 are three demand curves, D_1, D_2, and D_3, and three supply curves, S_1, S_2, and S_3. Given individuals A, B, and C, nine combinations of demand curves and supply curves might result, denoted by point P_{11} (the intersection of D_1 and S_1), P_{12} (D_1 and S_2), and so on. Person A, for example, might have demand curve D_3 (high ability) and supply curve S_3 (above-average access to funds), giving rise to H_{33} human capital investment and a rate of return of r_{33} (point P_{33}); alternatively, person A might have D_3 (high ability) but S_1 (below average access to funds), giving rise to point P_{31} (H_{31}, r_{31}).

When both demand curves and supply curves vary among individuals, the distribution of earnings will depend, in part, on whether there is a correlation between an individual's demand curve and supply curve. For example, a positive correlation would mean that the most able persons had the greatest access to funds. This would be represented by the combination of demand curve D_3 and supply curve S_3 (P_{33}). What might cause such a positive correlation? One factor would be if financial aid to higher education were awarded on the basis of test scores or a student's grade point average. Alternatively, it may be that the children of higher-income families are also, on average, more intelligent. A third possibility is that those groups in the labor force who enjoy the least discrimination or the best quality of schooling also have the most financial resources to devote to education.

---

[19]   See Janet Currie, "Early Childhood Education Programs," *Journal of Economic Perspectives* 15 (Spring 2001): 213–38; Alison Aughinbaugh, "Does Head Start Yield Long-Term Benefits?" *Journal of Human Resources* 36 (Fall 2001): 641–65; and Richard K. Caputo, "The Impact of Intergenerational Head Start Participation on Success among Adolescent Children," *Journal of Family and Economic Issues* 25 (Summer 2004): 199–223.

FIGURE 7.7   CORRELATION BETWEEN DEMAND AND SUPPLY CURVES

If there is a positive correlation among demand and supply curves, the equilibrium points will be P_{11}, P_{22}, and P_{33}. In this case, the most able persons will also have the greatest access to funds, and vice versa. If there is a negative correlation, the equilibrium points will be P_{31}, P_{22}, and P_{13}. In both situations differences in demand and supply curves cause an inequality in earnings, although the degree of inequality is much larger with a positive correlation.

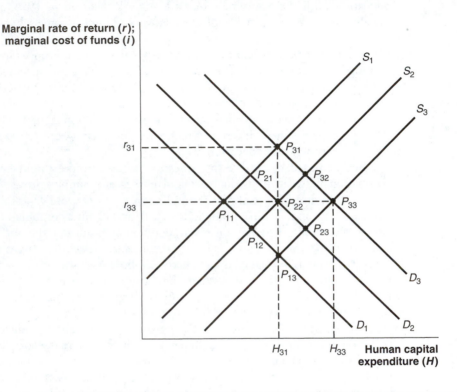

Individual demand curves and supply curves may also be negatively correlated. In Figure 7.7, this would be represented, for example, by the demand curve D_1 and supply curve S_3 (P_{13}). Such a negative correlation might result if financial aid for education were awarded primarily to individuals who have suffered the most discrimination or attended schools of inferior quality. Likewise, compensatory aid programs that sought to subsidize additional education for persons with low scholastic test scores or marginal grades would also result in a negative correlation.

For which correlation, positive or negative, would the inequality in earnings be the greatest? The answer is that a *positive* correlation between the demand for human capital and the access to funds would lead, other things equal, to a greater dispersion in individual earnings in the labor market. A positive correlation would lead to the series of points P_{11}, P_{22}, and P_{33} in Figure 7.7; a negative correlation would lead to the series of points P_{31}, P_{22}, and P_{13}. To measure the difference in earnings that results in the case of a positive correlation, the area under the demand curve D_3 at point P_{33} should be compared with the area under D_1 at point P_{11}. For a negative correlation the difference in earnings is given by the area under D_3 at point P_{31} and D_1 at point P_{13}. The comparison shows that the difference in earnings between the high-income person and the low-income person is much greater if the demand and supply curves are positively correlated, as some economists think they are.[20]

Human Capital versus Screening

The age/earnings profiles in Figure 7.1 and the review of empirical studies in the previous section represent fairly convincing evidence of the strong link between years of education and the earnings of individuals in the labor market. There remains one important issue, however, and that is *why* education leads to higher earnings.

According to advocates of human capital theory, the link between education and earnings is *productivity*. Additional schooling, in their view, enhances a person's innate intellectual ability with the "tools" needed to be more productive at work. These tools include an increased facility for logical reasoning, conceptualization, and communication as well as more specific job skills imparted in courses such as accounting or engineering. The reason a college graduate earns more than a high school graduate or why business majors earn more than history majors is no mystery to a human capital theorist—they have skills that employers are willing to pay extra to get.

Not all economists agree with this point of view. While not denying that education in some cases does enhance job skills, these economists maintain that the primary reason education and earnings go hand in hand is because employers use education as a *screening device*.[21] At the time of hiring the employer is quite uncertain about each applicant's actual level of productivity. To improve the probability that the best worker is chosen, firms use indicators or "signals" such as years of education to sort or screen prospective workers into those most likely to be high- and low-productivity employees. Screening advocates believe, therefore, that education

---

20 See, for example, Barry Chiswick, "Minimum Schooling Legislation and the Cross-Sectional Distribution of Income," *Economic Journal* 79 (September 1969): 495–507. Empirical evidence in support of this proposition is provided in Joyce R. Shackett and D. J. Slottje, "Labor Supply Decisions, Human Capital Attributes, and Inequality in the Size Distribution of Earnings," *Journal of Human Resources* 22 (Winter 1987): 82–100. Evidence of a positive correlation between supply and demand curves is provided by Dennis Epple et al., "Peer Effects, Financial Aid, and Selection of Students into Colleges and Universities: An Empirical Analysis," *Journal of Applied Econometrics* 18 (Sept–Oct 2003): 501–25.

21 See Mark Blaug, "The Empirical Status of Human Capital Theory: A Slightly Jaundiced Survey," *Journal of Economic Literature* 14, no. 3 (September 1976): 827–55, and Barry Chiswick, "Schooling, Screening, and Income," in Lewis Solomon and Paul Taubman, eds., *Does College Matter?* (New York: Academic Press, 1973), 151–58.

and earnings are positively related *not* because education itself increases a person's productivity on the job, but because employers have found that the number of years of schooling is a reliable signal concerning native intelligence and trainability on the job.

A good example of the screening view of education is provided by the *job competition model* advanced by Lester Thurow.[22] According to Thurow, most job skills are not acquired before one enters the labor market but rather are obtained through on-the-job training and learning by doing. In this case, the labor market is not primarily an auction market where workers of different educational levels sell their skills, as envisioned in human capital theory, but is instead a training market where firms have training slots to be filled at the bottom of the job ladder and workers compete to be hired.

How does a firm decide whom to hire? From the employer's perspective, a pool of applicants compete for the job opening. The decision of which worker to hire is based not on a consideration of who will work for the lowest wage but rather of who is most trainable. Because the firm is uncertain about which applicant can be trained at the least cost, it must screen or sort the applicants into a queue, from highest expected productivity to lowest based on each worker's signals and indexes. From the viewpoint of the applicants, the competition in the labor market is over obtaining access to the firm's job ladder (hence the term job competition model), setting off a race among workers to acquire the background characteristics and credentials that employers value most.

The role of education in the job competition model differs markedly from its role in the human capital model. In the job competition model, education does not in and of itself lead to greater productivity for workers; rather, it identifies for employers the workers who possess the character traits such as intelligence, perseverance, and communication skills necessary for success on the job. As in the human capital model, additional years of education result in additional earnings, but these extra earnings are *not* a payment reflecting the productivity of the person's human capital; they are a payment for the individual's preexisting ability and intelligence that education signals. From a screening point of view, an investment in education may yield a high *private* rate of return if it moves the individual up in the queue for high-paying jobs; for society, however, the *social* rate of return to devoting additional resources to education may be quite low since it generates little actual gain in productivity.

These two opposing views of schooling have led to considerable controversy and debate over the social benefits of additional expenditures on education. From the perspective of human capital theory, additional resources devoted to education are an important source of economic growth because they represent an investment in upgrading the work skills and productive capacity of the nation's workforce. From a screening perspective, the social benefits from additional expenditures on education are more dubious. At its best, education adds to productivity by enabling

---

22   Lester Thurow, *Generating Inequality* (New York: Basic Books, 1975).

firms to identify superior-quality employees; at its worst, the main effect is to set off a "paper chase" as workers invest in ever higher educational degrees in order to compete for jobs.[23] Some have even gone so far as to suggest that the government mandate entry-level skills tests to avoid the inefficiencies in hiring that arise from relying on education to signal potential performance.[24]

A number of studies have attempted to sort out to what degree the positive relationship between education and earnings is the result of screening and productivity. Since a person's productivity is uncertain not only to the employer but also to the economist doing the research, this is a difficult task.

On the basis of various types of empirical tests, in some cases years of schooling and other types of academic credentials seem to raise a person's income independent of any productivity that may have been acquired in the educational process. One study looked at the starting salaries of college graduates who majored in economics.[25] The authors hypothesized that if earnings are strictly related to productivity, then economics majors who took jobs that utilized their academic training should be paid more than those who took jobs unrelated to their field of study. They could find no difference in the starting salaries of the two groups, leading them to conclude that employers were using a college degree as a screening device. A second piece of evidence often cited as proof that education is used as a screening device is the so-called sheepskin effect. Studies typically find that the marginal rates of return to the 12th and 16th years of schooling are much higher than those to the 11th and 15th years, suggesting that acquiring the diploma has an impact on earnings that probably exceeds whatever additional knowledge was gained in that one extra year of education.[26]

This type of evidence does not mean that education has *no* productivity value. One study compared the years of schooling obtained by persons who were self-employed relative to persons who worked for salaries.[27] If education were simply a screening device, presumably those people who planned on being self-employed would invest in only the amount that could be justified from a productivity viewpoint, while the salaried workers would invest in additional schooling for its value

23 The "paper chase" point of view is given in Ivar Berg, *Education and Jobs: The Great Training Robbery* (New York: Praeger Publishers, 1970).

24 See Peter Mueser and Tim Maloney, "Ability, Human Capital and Employer Screening: Reconciling Labor Market Behavior with Studies of Employee Productivity," *Southern Economic Journal* 57 (January 1991): 676–89.

25 Paul W. Miller and Paul A. Volker, "The Screening Hypothesis: An Application of the Wiles Test," *Economic Inquiry* 22, no. 1 (January 1984): 121–27.

26 See Thomas Hungerford and Gary Solon, "Sheepskin Effects in the Return to Education," *Review of Economics and Statistics* 69 (February 1987): 175–77, and Jin Heum Park, "Estimation of Sheepskin Effects Using the Old and the New Measures of Educational Attainment in the Current Population Survey," *Economics Letters* 62 (February 1999): 238–40. Sheepskin effects show up in countries other than the U.S., as well. See Kevin J. Denny and Colm P. Harmon, "Testing for Sheepskin Effects in Earnings Equations: Evidence for Five Countries," *Applied Economics Letters* 8 (September 2001): 635–37; Norbert R. Schady, "Convexity and Sheepskin Effects in the Human Capital Earnings Function: Recent Evidence for Filipino Men," *Oxford Bulletin of Economics and Statistics* 65 (May 2003): 171–96; and Thomas K. Bauer, et al., "Sheepskin Effects in Japan," *CEPR Discussion Paper No. 3609* (November 2002).

27 Kenneth Wolpin, "Education and Screening," *American Economic Review* 67, no. 5 (December 1977): 949–58.

as a credential. The study did find that self-employed workers had a lower level of education relative to similar salary workers, but the difference was not large (13.95 versus 14.55 years). Another study found that while evidence for the screening hypothesis exists in private, nonunion labor markets it is virtually nonexistent in the public sector or unionized markets.[28] The most plausible explanation offered by the authors for this outcome is that signals *other* than education are more important in predicting productivity in the public and unionized sectors. For example, unions may rely on apprenticeship completion or seniority as the relevant signal of productivity.

Quite apart from empirical evidence, economists have a second reason for doubting that education serves only as a screening device. If screening were education's only function, both business firms and workers would have a large incentive to find some lower-cost method of identifying worker productivity. That this is not happening implies that education does enhance worker skills in a way that is of value to firms.

On-the-Job Training

Formal education is one type of human capital investment. On-the-job training (OJT) is a second. Although it is difficult to measure precisely the amount of OJT that takes place, an international survey of firms (conducted by the American Society for Training and Development) found that overall, firms spent an average of $627 per employee on training in 1998.[29] Expenditures were highest in the United States ($724 per worker) and lowest in Asia ($241 per worker). Furthermore, between 70 and 77 percent of each firm's workers received some training.

Few people are hired with the complete knowledge and experience necessary to perform the job. What typically occurs is a period of on-the-job training as the new worker learns what tasks are to be performed and how to do them. In some cases, on-the-job training takes place in a fairly structured setting that closely resembles classroom instruction in school. In many other situations, job skills are learned in a much more informal way through learning by doing or instruction from a workmate.

On-the-job training is as much a form of human capital investment as college education, for it involves both current costs and future benefits. The costs of OJT are incurred by the firm in the form of direct costs of classroom instruction or additional supervision, and indirect costs from the lesser amount of output that a new worker can produce during training. Workers may also bear some of the costs of

---

28   John S. Heywood, "How Widespread Are Sheepskin Returns to Education in the U.S.?" *Economics of Education Review* 13 (September 1994): 227–34.

29   The web page for the American Society for Training and Development is http://www.astd.org/astd.

acquiring OJT by agreeing to work at reduced wages during the training period. Juxtaposed to the costs of on-the-job training are the anticipated benefits to both the firm and workers. The benefit to the firm is that its workforce will be more productive, and this greater productivity will result in greater profits. Workers benefit because they gain additional skills and experience that increase their earning power and bargaining strength in the labor market.

General versus Specific Training

Gary Becker has pointed out that there are two conceptually distinct forms of training—general training and specific training.[30] Whether training is general or specific has a number of implications for understanding the pattern of earnings, layoffs, and other labor market outcomes.

General on-the-job training is training that increases a worker's productivity not only at the firm providing it, but also at other firms in the labor market. A clear-cut example is apprenticeship training for a craft such as electrician or carpenter where the skills imparted are of general value throughout the industry. Similarly, less-formalized types of training such as how to operate a word processor or a bulldozer also work to enhance an employee's productivity both at the firm providing the training and at other firms. General training can be obtained in other ways than through training on the job. Perhaps the classic example of general training is formal education, since the skills learned there are of value to a wide range of employers.

The opposite of general on-the-job training is specific training. **Specific on-the-job training** increases the worker's productivity *only* at the firm providing it; at other firms the training is of no net value.[31] Although few types of on-the-job training are wholly specific in nature, many job skills do have a firm-specific component. One source of skill specificity stems from unique features of the firm's production process. A telephone lineman, for example, develops skills that are, to a large degree, of use only to the telephone company. Skill specificity may also arise out of unique features of the firm's product. A computer engineer employed by IBM, for example, would develop many skills of value to IBM, but this knowledge may be of far less value to a company that manufactures computers of a different design. Finally, regardless of whether a person is a secretary, a salesperson, or a manager, each worker in the firm acquires with experience on the job a detailed knowledge of the organizational structure and operation of the firm that is itself a valuable but very firm-specific type of training.

---

30 Becker, *Human Capital*, Chapter 2.

31 Research by Alan Barrett and Philip J. O'Connell, "Does Training Generally Work? The Returns to In-Company Training," *Industrial and Labor Relations Review* 54 (April 2001): 647–62, questions the productivity gains of specific training. They do find, however, significant increases in productivity from general training.

The German Apprenticeship Program: A Model for the United States?

In an effort to increase U.S. competitiveness, American companies and policymakers naturally look to our overseas rivals for improved ways of doing business. Most often their attention is focused on Japan, particularly Japanese management methods associated with quality improvement and employee participation.

Other countries also have things to teach us about competitiveness, but often they don't receive the same attention. A case in point is Germany and its system of worker training through company apprenticeships.

On the face of it, the German economy should be experiencing significant competitive problems. For some time now, costs of production in Germany have been the highest in the world—the result of high employee wages, generous benefits, a short workweek, and stringent social regulations. Surprisingly, however, the German economy has not slumped under this weight but exhibits continued growth (albeit quite modest) in production and real income and a sizable trade surplus. How could the German economy prosper under these constraints when the same set of conditions in the United States would probably cause accelerated downsizings and layoffs?

A significant part of the explanation has to do with the quality of the German workforce. Contrary to the assertions of some critics, American employees are among the hardest-working in the industrial world. Increasingly, however, the international economic struggle turns not on intensity of work but on skills and knowledge. Here the United States is beginning to lag behind.

One segment of the American workforce continues to be world-class in skills—the college-educated—reflecting both the high quality of American colleges and universities and the fact that firms lavish two-thirds of their training on college-educated employees. Many people among the remaining 75 percent of the American workforce, however, are seriously ill-equipped to handle modern, high-technology, high-involvement jobs; their basic reading and math skills are often deficient, a problem frequently exacerbated by poor work habits and poor social skills.

What is the cause of this shortcoming? According to many analysts, the root cause has three parts: inadequate vocational education programs in high schools and community colleges, lack of a system facilitating the transition from school to work for the non-college bound, and failure of companies to make a sufficient investment in training of frontline production workers.

What do these three problems have to do with Germany and its apprenticeship program? Lots. German students at about age 15 choose between two educational tracks—college preparatory coursework or a combination of vocationally oriented

Benefits and Costs of On-the-Job Training

For on-the-job training to be undertaken, it must promise a rate of return competitive with that from other investments. The rate of return is a function of the benefits and costs of training illustrated in Figure 7.8.

Figure 7.8 shows a worker's productivity level before and after on-the-job training. For simplicity, it is assumed the worker receives one "dose" of training

continued

coursework (*Arbeitslehre*) and an apprenticeship or practicum at a company. It is the latter track that is missing in the United States; only 14 percent of all schools in the U.S. offered apprenticeship programs in 1996. It is these apprenticeship programs in Germany, according to many experts, that are a key ingredient in Germany's economic success. Here's why:

First, the German system leads to a much higher skill level among the non-college-educated part of the workforce. For students who choose the vocational track, the last three years of secondary school are strongly vocation oriented, and students learn to integrate theory and practice through their apprenticeships. Thus, German employees who have completed the vocational/apprenticeship program typically have well-developed technical skills *and* extensive knowledge of the business.

Second, the German system also provides greater incentives for non-college-bound students to stay in school and hone their basic educational skills. These students realize that an apprenticeship is a prerequisite for landing a high-paying job with career advancement potential. Because the best apprenticeship positions go to those students who have done well in grades K through 10, the link between educational achievement and economic success is clearer and, hence, the motivation to perform is stronger.

Finally, the German apprenticeship program facilitates the school-to-work transition for non-college-bound youth. In the United States one-quarter of young people never graduate from high school, while many of those who do spend several years in a fairly haphazard, unstructured search for work. In Germany, on the other hand, high school graduation rates are considerably above U.S. levels and young people tend to find a long-term match with an occupation or trade much earlier than American youth. In both cases, the apprenticeship program plays an important role by providing a more direct, immediate path from school to full-time gainful employment.

As Congress searches for ways to increase the competitiveness of the American economy, the German apprenticeship system provides one model that clearly deserves study.

SOURCES: "German Companies Find Job Training Pays Off," *Wall Street Journal* (April 19, 1993): A1, A2; Mary Joyce and David Neumark, "School-to-Work Programs," *Monthly Labor Review* (August 2001): 38–50; Robert J. Gitter and Markus Scheuer, "U.S. and German Youths: Unemployment and the Transition from School to Work," *Monthly Labor Review* (March 1997): 16–20; and Sprios Bougheas and Yannis Georgiellis, "Early Career Mobility and Earnings Profiles of German Apprentices: Theory and Empirical Evidence," *Labour* 18 (June 2004): 233–63.

and that the economic value of the training does not depreciate over time. (Both assumptions are relaxed in the next section.) Without training, this worker's marginal revenue product in each time period would be MRP_0, shown by the horizontal line EG. With OJT, the worker's time pattern of productivity resembles the step function $ABCD$. During the training period, the worker's marginal revenue product is reduced from MRP_0 to MRP_1 because he or she is spending time attending

FIGURE 7.8   BENEFITS AND COSTS OF ON-THE-JOB TRAINING

Without on-the-job training, the worker's time-pattern of productivity is *EG*; with training it is *ABCD*. If the training is general, the worker bears the cost of training by working at the reduced wage W_1 but is able to earn W_2 after training. If the training is firm specific, the firm bears the cost of training by continuing to pay the worker W_0 even though the worker's productivity is only MRP_1. The return on the firm's investment is the difference between the worker's higher productivity of MRP_2 and the wage W_0. To reduce the probability of turnover, however, the firm may pay a higher wage such as W_3.

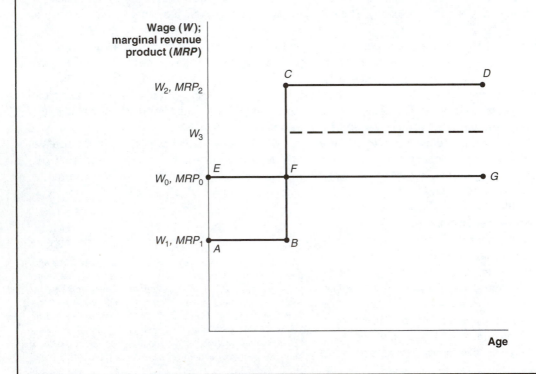

training classes, learning how to operate unfamiliar equipment, and so on. After the completion of either specific or general training, however, the marginal revenue product of the worker rises to MRP_2.[32]

---

[32] Evidence of the positive impact of training on productivity can be found in John Barron et al., "Do Workers Pay for On-the-Job Training?" *Journal of Human Resources* 34 (Spring 1999): 235–52. Pal Schone, "Why Is the Return to Training so High?" *Labour: Review of Labour Economics and Industrial Relations* 18 (September 2004): 363–78, finds that many estimates of increased productivity from training are too high.

The cost of training is the value of production forgone during the training process, shown by the area *AEFB*. The economic benefit is the increase in production that training makes possible, shown by the area *FCDG*. For training to be a good investment, the present value of the stream of output (in dollars) generated by the worker's receiving training (the profile *ABCD*) must be at least as large as that of the output stream if no training were provided (the profile *EG*).

Assuming that training is a good investment, will the firm or the worker bear the cost and reap the benefit? The answer depends on whether the OJT is general or specific in nature.

With general on-the-job training, it is the worker, not the firm, who bears the cost of training. Without training, the worker's marginal revenue product is MRP_0. Competition among firms, in turn, ensures that the worker is paid a wage W_0 commensurate with this level of productivity. If the firm were to bear the cost of training, it would continue to pay the worker W_0 even though productivity during training is only MRP_1. What inducement does the firm have to do this? With general training, the answer is none. When the worker completes the OJT, his or her productivity rises to MRP_2. If the firm were able to still pay a wage of only W_0, the difference between the value of output produced and wage paid (the distance *FC*) would provide it with a return on its investment. Because general training is transferable, however, were the firm to pay less than W_2, the worker would quit and find employment at a firm that was willing to pay a wage equal to his or her productivity. Competition for labor, in conjunction with the transferable nature of general training, makes it impossible for the firm to pay a wage less than W_2. At this wage, the firm is unable to recoup its investment, making it unwilling to underwrite the costs of general training.

Because firms have no incentive to pay for general OJT, the workers must pay for it. The cost of general training is the drop in productivity $MRP_0 - MRP_1$. A worker pays for general OJT by agreeing to work during the training period for a wage of only W_1. Workers have an incentive to bear this cost since once training is completed, the wage they can command in the market will rise to W_2, providing the return on their investment.

If on-the-job training is specific in nature, on the other hand, it is the firm, not the worker, that bears the cost. Because specific OJT is nontransferable, once training is completed the productivity of the worker at any other firm in the labor market is still only MRP_0. Even though the firm that provided the training receives a level of production worth MRP_2, it need not pay the worker more than W_0, since he or she can do no better elsewhere. In this case the worker has no incentive to work for a lower wage of W_1 during training since it is the firm that reaps the benefit. To induce workers to acquire specific OJT, the firm must bear the cost of training by paying the original unskilled wage of W_0, even though the worker's productivity is only MRP_1. The return on its investment is the difference between the worker's higher-productivity MRP_2 and the wage W_0 that it pays after training.

In practice, the post-training wage paid by the firm in the case of specific training will generally be higher than the minimum W_0. One possible wage might

General OJT: When the Employer Pays

The human capital model as it is applied to OJT predicts that an employer will bear the cost of firm-specific training and that the employee will bear the cost of general training, because the training is transportable. It appears that no one has shared this result with Dundee Mills, the nation's fourth-largest towel manufacturer, located in Griffin, Georgia. The firm instituted a program that allows employees to attend school, free of charge, in order to boost basic reading and math skills. Employees are encouraged to take their education as far as they want, including advanced technical training or college classes. Dundee Mills is not alone in offering general training at its own expense.

The 1995 Survey of Employer-Provided Training indicates that in 1994 general training accounted for 33 percent of all hours spent in training and 52 percent of all employees who received some training received some form of general training. In addition, employers spent from $41 to $76 per employee on tuition reimbursement programs. How can one explain the incidence of employers providing general training to workers at the employers' expense?

One reason is that general training (and a worker's performance in that training) may provide an employer with some valuable information about the abilities of that worker. So the firm is willing to pay for the training to the extent that the information has value in making promotions, job assignments, and other such decisions.

Another possible explanation is that the firm provides the training as a form of employee benefit. Tuition reimbursement, for example, might be attractive to workers just as is health insurance. In a competitive labor market, however, a firm that pays more in benefits will pay less in wages in order to keep total labor cost with competitors equal. Offering more valuable benefits may even attract a higher quality worker.

A third reason a firm may bear part of the cost of general OJT is if there are constraints on worker mobility and it seeks to use training as a means to boost employee morale and loyalty. Recall that in a competitive labor market if the firm pays enough to keep the newly trained worker it will never recoup the cost of training. A crucial element in this scenario, however, is that the labor market is competitive, meaning that the

be W_3, shown by the broken line in Figure 7.8. The reason is that specific training creates a situation of *bilateral monopoly* between the worker and the firm. This means that both the worker and the firm have some monopoly power over the other. Should the worker with specific training quit, the firm will lose its investment in training. To prevent this, the firm is induced to share a portion of its return ($W_3 - W_0$) with the worker. The firm also has power over the worker, however. Should the worker demand a wage so high that it eliminates the firm's return on its investment, the worker would be laid off, imposing a financial loss on the worker since he or she could only earn the lower wage of W_0 at any other firm.

continued

worker is mobile enough, or there are enough other employers valuing his or her new skills close by, for the threat of the worker's leaving to be very real.

Griffin is a rural town in Georgia that is 40 miles from Atlanta, has a population of about 22,000, and is an average of 72 miles away from other textile manufacturing plants. So one reason the company may be able to pay for general training and not lose money is that the workers' mobility is limited; the labor market is less than competitive, so although the firm may pay the trained workers a higher wage, the wage doesn't need to match the workers' *MRP*, allowing the employer to recoup its training costs. The limited worker mobility is recognized by the company's president, who estimates that 80 percent of his company's workforce will still be with the company 10 years from now.

But, if worker mobility is limited, why would a firm choose to pay the costs of general OJT if it does not have to? One possible answer is that it is using training as a means to motivate employees and instill company loyalty. This situation appears to be the case at Dundee Mills. It is clear that workers who have participated in the training program feel positively about themselves and about Dundee Mills. One

woman stated, "It's a good feeling to be able to do things for myself." Another employee noted, "For a while, things were just at a standstill. . . . Just looking at society itself, the technology, I felt I needed more education just to stay where I am. Now I can study computers and run the ones on my job if I want." A good feeling about one's employer, or company loyalty, works the same as geographic barriers to limit workers' mobility.

While there are outcomes in the real world that may appear to be in conflict with predictions from economic models, typically the source of the anomaly can be traced back to the violation of an assumption of the model. In this case, the violated assumption is that of costless mobility. Still, the model has served a valuable function by logically organizing thinking on the subject and calling attention to the important variables affecting the outcome.

SOURCES: Sonia Murray, "Sending Workers to School," *Atlanta Journal* (20 October 1990): C1; David H. Autor, "Why Do Temporary Help Firms Provide Free General Skills Training?" *Quarterly Journal of Economics* 116 (November 2001): 1409–48; and Peter Cappelli, "Why do Employers Pay for College?" *NBER Working Paper No. W9225* (September 2002).

Implications of On-the-Job Training

Investment in human capital in the form of on-the-job training has a number of implications with respect to observed labor market outcomes. Five such implications are briefly discussed below.

Employee Turnover   Specific on-the-job training provides a strong incentive to both firms and workers to reduce turnover from quits and layoffs. Employee turnover is costly to a firm because it loses its investment in specific training. Workers with specific training also stand to lose by leaving (or being forced to leave) the firm because there is no other firm at which their productivity and their wage will be as high. One prediction of the theory is that quits and layoffs will be fewer among workers who have relatively more specific training. The 1995 Survey of Employer-Provided Training reveals that establishments which provide less training also experience higher rates of turnover. Low-turnover establishments provided an average of 10.8 hours of training to workers in 1994, whereas establishments with high turnover provided only 7.2 hours of training per employee.[33]

The theory also predicts that the quit rate will decrease with the age of workers since their amount of specific training and, hence, potential earnings loss from quitting grow with tenure on the job. One study found, for example, that older workers suffered the largest drop in earnings from being displaced from their jobs and that 90 percent of the earnings loss could be traced to the decline in value of their specific job skills.[34]

The Minimum Wage   A frequent criticism of minimum wage laws is that they may lead firms to curtail the amount of general on-the-job training provided to workers, particularly younger workers. Because teenaged workers typically remain with the firm a relatively short time, an employer has little incentive to bear the costs of training them. To make training a profitable venture for the firm, the teenaged worker must invest in himself or herself by working at a relatively low wage such as W_1 in Figure 7.8. The incentive to do so is that with some experience the teenager can move up to a better job with higher earnings. A minimum wage law may prevent this process if it places a floor under wages at a level of, say, W_0. At this wage the employer no longer finds it profitable to provide general training because the cost of labor exceeds the worker's productivity.[35]

Internal Labor Markets   Specific on-the-job training is also a key factor in explaining the development of job ladders and internal labor markets within business firms. For many types of production processes, a vertical or hierarchical set of job tasks or positions build on one another and are sufficiently unique to that one firm

---

33   Also see Josef Zweimuller and Rudolf Winter-Ebmer, "On-the-Job Training, Job Search, and Job Mobility," *Swiss Journal of Economics and Statistics* 139 (December 2003): 563–76; Jonathan R. Veum, "Training and Job Mobility among Young Workers in the United States," *Journal of Population Economics* 10 (May 1997): 219–33, and Lisa Lynch and Sandra Black, "Beyond the Incidence of Employer-Provided Training," *Industrial and Labor Relations Review* 52 (October 1998): 64–81. Andrew Glenn et al. also find that the human capital predictions related to on-the-job training also hold in unconventional labor markets, like baseball; see "Firm-Specific Human Capital, Job Matching, and Turnover; Evidence from Major League Baseball, 1900–1992," *Economic Inquiry* 39 (January 2001): 86–93. David Fairris, "Internal Labor Markets and Worker Quits," *Industrial Relations* 43 (July 2004): 573–94, finds that factors *other than training* play a significant role in determining worker quits.

34   David Shapiro and Steven Sandell, "Age Discrimination in Wages and Displaced Older Men," *Southern Economic Journal* 52 (July 1985): 90–102.

35   Evidence that a higher minimum wage reduces formal training can be found in David Neumark and William Wascher, "Minimum Wages and Training Revisited," *Journal of Labor Economics* 19 (July 2001): 563–95. To the contrary, however, David Metcalf, "The Impact of the National Minimum Wage on the Pay Distribution, Employment and Training," *Economic Journal* 11 (March 2004): C84-86, finds that the national minimum wage *boosted* the probability and intensity of training.

that they can only be learned by workers starting at the bottom and working up. If all job skills were acquired through general OJT, there would be no internal labor markets since firms could readily hire a worker in the external labor market. The more important specific training is as a source of job skills, however, the less reliance the firm will put on outside recruitment of labor and the greater emphasis it will put on internal promotion and advancement as a means of filling job vacancies.

The Indeterminacy of Wages   Chapter 6 showed that specific on-the-job training leads to an area of indeterminacy in wage rates. In a perfectly competitive market the forces of supply and demand will give rise to one unique equilibrium wage rate for a particular type of labor. It is evident in Figure 7.8 that with specific training, the firm may pay a range of possible wages, bounded on the top by a wage close to (but not equal to) W_2 and on the bottom by a wage equal to W_0. Within this range the exact wage that is paid is no longer strictly determined by demand and supply, but rather by company policy, individual bargaining, or collective bargaining. Unionization, in particular, is one means by which workers have to shift the balance of bargaining power in their favor within this area of indeterminateness.

Age/Earnings Profiles   Investment in on-the-job training also helps explain several key features of age/earnings profiles, as illustrated in Figure 7.9.

The previous section pointed out that formal education can be considered as a type of general training. The direct cost of general training is borne by the individual, shown in Figure 7.9 by the area *OABC*, which represents the cost of tuition, books, and so on. After the completion of schooling at age 21, the individual's productivity and earnings rise, say to W_1 (point *E*). If the person undertook no further human capital investment, and *if* the existing stock of human capital never depreciated, the age/earnings profile would be the horizontal line *EF*. Earnings are not flat over a person's life cycle, however, but rise, reaching a peak in midlife or later and declining thereafter. This is illustrated by the parabolic line *DG*.

What can account for this parabolic shape of the age/earnings profile? Research by Jacob Mincer and others has suggested that this time pattern of earnings is due to the continuing process of on-the-job training and human capital depreciation.

Because formal schooling does not usually provide all the skills and experience necessary to successfully perform a job, a continuing process of human capital investment is necessary in the form of general and specific on-the-job training. Such investment entails lower earnings at first as the worker bears the cost of acquiring that portion of OJT that is general in nature, counterbalanced by higher earnings in the future after training is completed. With training, therefore, the worker's earnings after graduation rise at first to only W_2 (point *D*) as he or she bears the initial costs of general OJT; after the completion of training, earnings will rise along the curve *DG* as training increases the worker's total stock of human capital above the amount gained from formal schooling alone. The point *H*, where earnings with on-the-job training (line *DG*) just equal what earnings would have

A college graduate, given no training or depreciation in human capital, would have the age/earnings profile *ABEF*. With general training, earnings are initially reduced to W_2 but then rise over time with the higher productivity as a result of training. As a person ages, however, existing human capital depreciates. The net effect of declining amounts of training over the life cycle, coupled with accelerating depreciation of human capital, is to cause the line *DG* to decline after midlife.

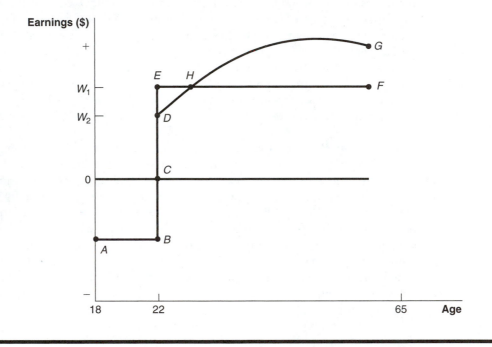

been on the basis of years of education alone (line *EF*), has been labeled by Mincer as the "overtaking year," which he estimates to be approximately the eighth year after the completion of school.[36] This gradual increase in the person's stock of human capital accounts for the similar rise in the age/earnings profile.[37] The

---

36 Mincer, *Schooling, Experience, and Earnings*, Chapter 3.

37 The assumption of the human capital model is that the upward slope of the age/earnings profile is due to the increased productivity of workers as they receive OJT. Evidence in support of human capital theory is given in Cheryl L. Maranto and Robert C. Rodgers, "Does Work Experience Increase Productivity? A Test of the On-the-Job Training Hypothesis," *Journal of Human Resources* 19, no. 3 (Summer 1984): 341–57; Wim Groot and Eddie Mekkelholt, "The Rate of Return to Investments in On-the-Job Training," *Applied Economics* 27 (February 1995): 173–81; Alan Barrett and Philip J. O'Connell, "Does Training Generally Work? The Returns to In-Company Training"; and Pal Schone, "Analysing the Effect of Training on Wages—Using Combined Survey-Register Data," *International Journal of Manpower* 22 (2001): 138–57.

greater the accumulation of on-the-job training, the more steeply will earnings rise with age. Reed Olsen and Edwin Sexton use the increased OJT that women received in the late seventies and early eighties as a partial explanation for the growth in women's wages relative to men's during this time period.[38] It is also often documented that workers with more education more often receive employer-provided training, increasing the earnings differential between college and high school graduates. This can be seen in the divergence of high school and college earnings profiles over time in Figure 7.1.[39]

The remaining feature of the age/earnings profile to explain is the declining portion after midlife. Two factors can account for this phenomenon. First, as the person ages, the investment in on-the-job training will slow and eventually stop. With increasing age fewer years remain over which to recoup the costs of OJT through higher earnings, which reduces the rate of return and the incentive to invest. The second factor is the process of human capital depreciation. Like the productivity of physical capital, the productivity of a given stock of human capital depreciates over time as acquired skills and knowledge are gradually made obsolete by scientific and technological advances. In the early part of the life cycle the combination of low rates of depreciation and high rates of investment in OJT lead to a net increase in earnings over time. After midlife, investment in OJT slows while depreciation of existing human capital accelerates, giving rise to the declining portion of the age/earnings profile DG.[40]

Alternative Explanations

Although the human capital explanation for the upward-sloping portion of the age/earnings profile is widely accepted among economists, alternative explanations have been offered for the positive relationship between earnings and work experience. Three alternative theories are briefly summarized below.

Seniority The critical assumption of the human capital model is that the increase in earnings with additional time on the job reflects a concomitant increase in the

---

38   Reed Neil Olsen and Edwin A. Sexton, "Gender Differences in the Returns to and Acquisition of On-the-Job Training," *Industrial Relations* 35 (January 1996): 59–77.

39   For example, see David S. Stern et al., "Company Training in the United States 1970–2000: What have been the Trends Over Time?" *International Journal of Training and Development* 8 (September 2004): 191–209. Evidence of this same phenomenon in other countries can be found in Kenn Ariga and Giorgio Brunello, "Are the More Educated Receiving More Training? Evidence from Thailand," *IZA Discussion Paper No. 577* (September 2002); and Pilipe Almeida-Santos and Karen Mumford, "Employee Training in Australia: Evidence from AWIRS," *Economic Record* 80 (September 2004): S53-S64.

40   One study found that real earnings of men in their 50s declined by slightly less than 1 percent per year and by 2 percent per year for men in their 60s. Although earnings for older men declined relative to men of younger cohorts, these declines were outweighed by the general increase in real wage levels due to productivity growth, so that on average the real wages of men approaching retirement did not decrease (i.e., the upward *shift* in the age/earnings profile for older men more than offset the downward movement *along* a given profile). See Geoffrey Carliner, "The Wages of Older Men," *Journal of Human Resources* 27 (Winter 1982): 25–38. More recent evidence of how technological advancement can lead to declining wages among older workers can be found in Glenn MacDonald and Michael S. Weisbach, "The Economics of Has-Beens," *Journal of Political Economy* 112 (February 2004): S289-310.

individual worker's productivity due to training. The first study to directly test this hypothesis with company-level data found, however, that the evidence did not support it. James Medoff and Katherine Abraham obtained data from the personnel files of several large companies on the earnings, years of work experience, and performance-evaluation scores of individual workers.[41] Within job classifications, they found a strong positive relationship between workers' years of experience and relative earnings, but either no relationship or a negative relationship between years of experience and performance-evaluation scores. The net result was that earnings did increase with experience in the firm, but productivity (as measured by the performance ratings) did not, a finding directly counter to human capital theory.

One obvious criticism of Medoff and Abraham's study is that the reason the performance-evaluation scores of workers within a job classification did not increase with years of experience is that the more able or hardworking employees were promoted to higher job classifications, leaving the "deadwood" behind. To determine the validity of this criticism, Medoff and Abraham and several other researchers have examined the relationship between experience, performance, and the probability of promotion.[42] It was found that performance ratings and more general considerations of merit do significantly influence a company's decision about whom to promote, but that years of experience or seniority also play a large role independent of individual ability.

Medoff and Abraham concluded, therefore, that part of the upward slope of the age/earnings profile is related not to workers' increased productivity from additional training, but rather to the institutional practice of basing pay increases and promotions on years of experience or seniority in the firm.[43] The question then posed by human capital theorists is, Why would firms base pay on seniority if seniority is not related to productivity? One answer provided by researchers in industrial relations is that workers feel they develop a growing equity position or property right in their job the longer their service with the firm.[44] As a matter of fairness, therefore, it is

---

41 James L. Medoff and Katherine G. Abraham, "Experience, Performance, and Earnings," *Quarterly Journal of Economics* 95 (December 1980): 703–36, and "Are Those Paid More Really More Productive: The Case of Experience," *Journal of Human Resources* 16 (Spring 1981): 188–216. The results of Medoff and Abraham discussed here have been replicated more recently using Italian data by Luca Flabbi and Andrea Ichino, "Productivity, Seniority, and Wages: New Evidence from Personnel Data," *Labour Economics* 8 (June 2001): 359–87.

42 Katherine G. Abraham and James L. Medoff, "Length of Service and Promotions in Union and Nonunion Work Groups," and D. Quinn Mills, "Seniority versus Ability in Promotion Decisions," *Industrial and Labor Relations Review* 38 (April 1985): 408–20, 421–25. Also see David Fairris, "Internal Labor Markets and Worker Quits," *Industrial Relations* 43 (July 2003): 573–94.

43 More recent research suggests that the relationship between training, performance, and wage growth is much stronger than suggested by Medoff and Abraham. See Ann P. Bartel, "Training, Wage Growth, and Job Performance: Evidence from a Company Database," *Journal of Labor Economics* 13 (July 1995): 401–25, and Christopher J. Ruhm, "Do Earnings Increase with Job Seniority?" *Review of Economics and Statistics* 72, no. 1 (February 1990): 143–47. Other research finds a stronger relationship between overall experience and earnings and practically no returns to seniority or tenure with a firm. See Christian Dustmann and Costas Meghir, "Wages, Experience, and Seniority," *Centre for Economic Policy Discussion Paper* No. 2077 (1999).

44 See Frederic Meyers, "Ownership of Jobs," and Daniel J. B. Mitchell, "The Ownership of Jobs: Variations on a Theme by Meyers," in Walter Fogel, ed., *Job Equity and Other Studies in Industrial Relations: Essays in Honor of Frederic Meyers* (Los Angeles: Institute of Industrial Relations, UCLA, 1982), 6–34, 99–154.

believed that earnings and promotions should increase with seniority. Firms, in turn, are induced to follow this social convention in order to avoid unionization and other costs (e.g., high turnover) that go with a dissatisfied workforce.[45]

Deferred Compensation as an Incentive Device   A second alternative explanation for the upward-sloping portion of the age/earnings profile has to do with the role of deferred compensation as an incentive device. As noted in Chapter 6, most employees are paid on a time rate, such as a wage rate per hour or salary per month. This type of payment scheme, while easy to administer, suffers from the principal–agent problem. In this case, the principal is the owner or manager of the firm who hires a worker to act as his or her agent in the workplace. The agent or worker agrees in exchange for a sum of money to follow the principal's directions regarding what to produce, how to produce it, and so on. The principal–agent problem arises from the difficulty and expense for the manager of verifying that the employee is fully living up to the terms of the implicit contract to which the two parties agreed at the time of hiring. In particular, the more difficult or costly it is for the manager to monitor the performance of the worker, the more incentive the employee has to shirk and work at the minimum required level of effort.

How can the firm provide its time-rated employees with an incentive to work hard? Edward Lazear has provided one answer.[46] He notes that because of specific OJT and other factors, many employees develop long-term employment relationships with their companies. Given this situation, Lazear argues that it is to both the firm's and the worker's interest to adopt a deferred system of compensation, paying the worker less than his or her marginal revenue product in the early years of employment with the company and then more than the marginal revenue product in later years.[47] This deferred compensation can take the form not only of higher wages or salaries later in life, but also of a pension upon retirement. It is evident that a system of deferred compensation does provide long-term employees with an incentive for hard work in their early work years, since the financial penalty for being fired for poor job performance is increased. Workers can also benefit from such a payment plan, however, because their hard work enables the firm to prosper and to pay higher wages than would otherwise be possible.

Lazear's theory also offers an alternative explanation for the rising portion of the age/earnings profile. Even if, to take an extreme case, the productivity of workers remains constant throughout their working life, a system of deferred compensation will cause earnings to increase with age. Another implication of his theory is that firms

---

45   Also see Edward P. Lazear for a new explanation for observing the positive correlation between tenure and wages. His theory, found in "Firm-Specific Human Capital: A Skill-Weights Approach," *NBER Working Paper No. W9679* (May 2003), is based on the premise that every aspect of a worker's human capital is general in that it has some value to all employers (but to some more than others).

46   Edward Lazear, "Why Is There Mandatory Retirement?" *Journal of Political Economy* 6 (December 1979): 1261–84. Also see Edward Lazear and Robert Moore, "Incentives, Productivity, and Labor Contracts," *Quarterly Journal of Economics* 99 (May 1984): 275–95.

47   Additional evidence in support of deferred compensation plans can be found in Erling Barth, "Firm-Specific Seniority and Wages," *Journal of Labor Economics* 15 (July 1997): 495–506.

will desire some method, such as a rule for mandatory retirement age, to force older workers to retire. Without such a rule, a deferred compensation scheme might not be feasible since the payment of high wages later in life would cause many older employees to continue working even though their productivity to the firm is relatively low.[48]

A final implication of Lazear's model is that firms have a substantial incentive to cheat on the implicit contract and lay off or fire older workers to avoid paying the deferred compensation. This practice is partly circumscribed by self-interest on the part of firms, because if they cheat very often the promise of deferred compensation will lose its incentive value. Other constraints on this type of cheating by firms include government legislation such as the Employee Retirement Income Security Act (ERISA), which regulates employer pension plans and the threat of unionization.

Job Matching and Worker Sorting   A third explanation for the upward-sloping portion of the age/earnings profile has to do with the process of workers finding those jobs to which their skills are best suited.[49] It is unlikely in the United States that the first job that a worker finds, say out of high school or college, will be that worker's final job. The median number of years a worker stays with his or her employer in 2004 was 4.0 years for all workers. This figure ranges from 0.7 years for workers 16–17 years old to 12.2 years for workers between the ages of 55 and 64. The median number of years for workers 25 years and older is only 5.0 years. These statistics translate into numerous job changes throughout one's working career. As workers progress in their careers, they must necessarily obtain a better vision of what jobs they are best suited for and which will yield the highest return to their human capital. In other words, a 40-year-old worker who has been in the labor market for 15–20 years has much more accumulated knowledge about which jobs will provide the greatest amount of satisfaction and return on the worker's specific set of skills than a 21-year-old fresh out of college. We would expect, then, that this 40-year-old would find a better job "match" than the 21-year-old and would be earning a higher wage partly because of this better match. One paper attributes some of the shrinkage in earnings between men and women over the past 10 years to changes in the job search process of women; the movement of women between jobs is becoming more similar to that of men, leading to better job matches and higher wages for women.[50] In the end, it is likely that the shape of the age/earnings profiles results from influences from all of the four explanations discussed here (human capital, seniority, deferred compensation, or matching).

---

48   As shown in Chapter 3, however, employers deliberately structure pension benefits so that even without a mandatory retirement law, employees still have an incentive to retire at or before age 65. Also see Edward Lazear, "Pensions as Severance Pay," in Zvi Bodie and John Shoven, *Financial Aspects of the United States Pension System* (Chicago: University of Chicago Press, 1983), 57–89.

49   See the classic article on this topic: Boyan Jovanovic, "Job Matching and the Theory of Turnover," *Journal of Political Economy* 87 (October 1979): 972–90.

50   Alan Manning, "Movin' On Up: Interpreting the Earnings–Experience Profile," *Bulletin of Economic Research* 52 (October 2000): 261–95. Also see Raqu Wang and Andrew Weiss, "Probation, Layoffs, and Wage–Tenure Profiles: A Sorting Explanation," *Labour Economics* 5 (September 1998): 359–83.

POLICY APPLICATION 7-1

Interrupted Work Careers and Women's Earnings

An interesting application of the theory of on-the-job training concerns the differences in the shape of age/earnings profiles for men and women. Figure 7.10 shows age/earnings profiles for male and female high school graduates, and male and female college graduates, who were year-round, full-time workers in 2003. Two features of these profiles stand out. First, the earnings of men of a given educational level (particularly college) are much above those of the same group of women, shown by the vertical distance between the profiles. The second distinctive difference between the age/earnings profiles of men and women is that the male profiles are steeper, meaning that earnings increase with age much more rapidly for men than for women. Among college graduates, for example, earnings in 2003 of men aged 18–24 were $32,598, while they were $79,533 (144% higher) for men 40–44. Earnings for women in the same age groups were $27,571 and $52,784 (only 91% higher), respectively.

What can account for this disparate behavior of earnings between men and women of equal educational attainment? Economists have advanced

FIGURE 7.10   AGE/EARNINGS PROFILES FOR MEN AND WOMEN BY LEVEL OF EDUCATION, 2003

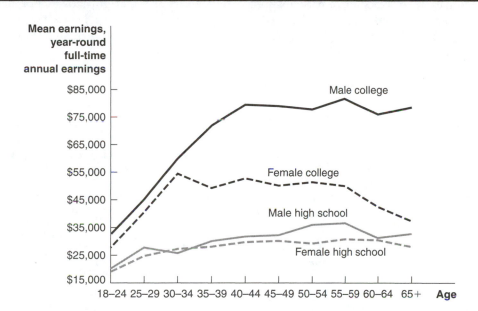

SOURCE: U.S. Census Bureau, Current Population Survey, 2004 Annual Social and Economic Supplement. PINC-04
http://www.census.gov.

at least three different (although not mutually exclusive) explanations. The first ties the gender gap in earnings to the discontinuous nature of women's work careers and its adverse impact on the accumulation of on-the-job training. A second explanation rests on the different types of occupations that men and women choose. A third explanation involves the role of discrimination as a source of unequal rates of pay for men and women. This section examines the first of these three explanations; the other two are discussed in later chapters.

The Continuity of Labor Force Attachment of Men and Women

A major characteristic that differentiates the work histories of men and women is the continuity of labor force participation. While generalizations can be treacherous, it is true that, on average, men are much more likely to exhibit a continuous, uninterrupted pattern of labor force participation; the work experience of women is more likely to be discontinuous, with one or more spells of nonparticipation associated with marriage and childbirth, in particular.

In 2004, the median number of years men 25 years and older had been with their current employer averaged 5.9 years across age groups. Women averaged 4.2 years with their current employer. In addition, as of 2002, men spent 10.5 percent of their years between the ages of 18 and 38 out of the labor force, whereas women were out of the labor force 26.3 percent of the time.[1] While this 26.3 percent is lower than the 31 percent of the time women expected to spend away from work during the 1970s, many more women than men still experience periods of nonparticipation for family and other reasons.[2]

A number of economists have argued that the greater tendency of women to have a discontinuous pattern of labor force participation is an important factor accounting for the flatter slope of their age/earnings profile. According to Jacob Mincer and Solomon Polachek, the interrupted work careers of women are likely to result in women accumulating a smaller amount of both general and specific OJT relative to men for several reasons.[3] To obtain general on-the-job training the worker must bear the cost by working at relatively low wages during the training process, recouping the investment in later years from the higher earnings the increased skills make possible. The expectation of an interrupted work career reduces the incentive to invest in such training, since fewer years will remain to repay the costs of training. Based on this reasoning, a man might find it profitable to enter a management trainee program, aware that the low earnings experienced in the first several years will be counterbalanced by relatively rapid earnings growth later in his career. This option might be unattractive for a woman who planned to drop out of the labor force for a year or two, since she would suffer the costs of training but would then fail to reap the higher earnings that go with it. For her, a more attractive choice might be to become a dental hygienist or a schoolteacher, an occupation requiring a smaller investment in general OJT. The result would be higher earnings in the first few

---

1   These statistics were obtained from the News Release USDOL 04-1678 (August 2004) and USDOL 04-1829 (September 2004).

2   Current statistics available from the U.S. Bureau of Labor Statistics http://www.bls.gov/news.release/tenure.toc.htm. Earlier evidence on men's and women's work histories can be found in Bureau of the Census, *Lifetime Work Experience and Its Effect on Earnings: Retrospective Data from the 1979 Income Survey Development Program*, Current Population Report P-23, no. 136 (Washington, D.C.: Government Printing Office, 1984).

3   Jacob Mincer and Solomon Polachek, "Family Investments in Human Capital: Earnings of Women," *Journal of Political Economy* 82, no. 2, pt. 2 (March/April 1974): 576–608. Also see Wayne Simpson, "Intermittent Work Activity and Earnings," *Applied Economics* 32 (November 2000): 1777–86, and Michelle Budig and Paula England, "The Wage Penalty for Motherhood," *American Sociological Review* 66 (April 2001): 204–25.

years of work relative to the management trainee position but slower earnings growth in the future.[4]

A second reason women's age/earnings profile may be flatter than men's is that employers have less incentive to hire women for jobs requiring large amounts of specific on-the-job training. Fearing a capital loss on its investment, a firm will be reluctant to provide specific OJT to a person it believes has a relatively high probability of quitting. This provides one explanation for why women are overrepresented in "secondary" jobs, such as secretary and store clerk, and underrepresented in "primary" jobs, such as manager and machinist. The secondary jobs require little specific training, and thus turnover does not impose large costs on the firm. When there is little specific OJT needed, job ladders are short or nonexistent, allowing little opportunity for career advancement and earnings growth. The large amount of specific training required for primary jobs causes the firm to hire only workers with strong job attachment. Once hired, these workers can then move up the job ladder in the internal labor market, steadily obtaining promotions and a relatively rapid growth in wages.

Finally, a third factor accounting for the flatter slope of women's age/earnings profile is the depreciation or "atrophy" of existing human capital during a period of nonparticipation in the labor force. Work skills and experience gradually lose their economic value the longer the person interrupts a career.

Research Evidence

These hypotheses of human capital theory have been tested in several studies. The results of one study are summarized in Figure 7.11.[5] This study examined women ages 30–65 who had completed their education and who were more or less continuously employed over a 32-month period. Some of the women in the sample had been continuously employed since completing their education (no gaps in employment); some had experienced one or more gaps lasting six months or more in their employment. Controlling for factors such as the women's educational attainment, occupation, hours of work, age, and geographic location, Figure 7.11 plots the average hourly wages calculated at the beginning of the study for women with different gap experiences. Wages are calculated for women with no gaps and for women who had an employment gap within the past year (from the time of the study), from 3 to 5 years prior to the beginning of the study, from 6 to 10 years prior to the study, and more than 20 years prior to the study.

The main conclusion from Figure 7.11 is that there is indeed a penalty for women who interrupt their work careers. For example, the average wage of women with no gaps is $7.26, but only $5.22 for women with a gap as recent as one year before. Also, the data indicate that the penalty shrinks once the women reenter employment but has not disappeared even 20 years after the gap in employment occurred (illustrated in Figure 7.11 by the rising wage as more time passes between when the gap occurred and the time of the study). This partial rebound in earnings has been interpreted by human capital theorists as reflecting the effect of human capital "restoration," as the depreciated value of human capital incurred during the employment gap is restored through renewed training

4 Additional evidence of the role expectations concerning labor force participation play in occupational choice and human capital investment decisions of women can be found in Kevin C. Duncan and Mark J. Prus, "Atrophy Rates for Intermittent Employment for Married and Never-Married Women: A Test of the Human Capital Theory of Occupational Sex Segregation," *Quarterly Review of Economics and Finance* 32 (Spring 1992): 27–37. Julie L. Hotchkiss and M. Melinda Pitts, "Female Labor Force Intermittency and Current Earnings: A Switching Regression Model with Unknown Sample Selection," *Applied Economics* (forthcoming), find that women experience a wage penalty at low levels of labor force intermittency, but this expected penalty doesn't influence their decisions to be intermittent. Other personal considerations are much more important.

5 Also see Elaine Sorensen, "Continuous Female Workers: How Different Are They from Other Women?" *Eastern Economic Journal* 19 (Winter 1993): 15–32.

FIGURE 7.11   THE EFFECT OF EMPLOYMENT GAPS FOR WOMEN, AGES 30–65

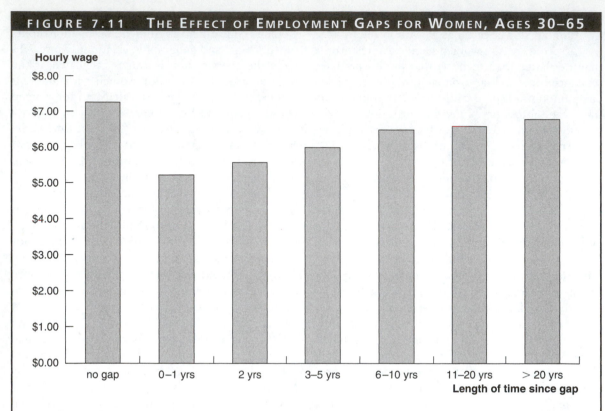

SOURCE: Predictions calculated from results reported in Joyce P. Jacobsen and Laurence M. Levin, "Effects of Intermittent Labor Force Attachment on Women's Earnings," *Monthly Labor Review* (September 1995): 14–19.

and experience on the job.[6] An alternative explanation is that new workers often start out at a low wage during an initial probationary period, and receive relatively large wage increases afterwards to bring their wage rate in line with other workers.

The earnings penalty illustrated in Figure 7.11 can also help to explain why the age/earnings profile of women is flatter than that for men, who are much less likely to interrupt their work careers. Most research on this issue has concluded, however, that career interruptions can explain at most one-third to one-half of the earnings gap between men and women.[7] And, given the greater attachment of women to the labor force today, we must look for

alternative explanations for the wage differential between men and women, a topic that will be taken up in Chapter 9.

---

6   See, for example, Jacob Mincer and Haim Ofek, "Interrupted Work Careers: Depreciation and Restoration of Human Capital," *Journal of Human Resources* 17 (Winter 1982): 3–24. Hotchkiss and Pitts, "Female Labor Force Intermittency and Current Earnings: A Switching Regression Model with Unknown Sample Selection," *Applied Economics:* forthcoming, find that women who have had intermittent activity receive a larger boost in earnings from additional years with their employer than fully continuous workers.

7   See, for example, Mary Corcoran and Greg J. Duncan, "Work History, Labor Force Attachment, and Earnings Differences between the Races and Sexes," *Journal of Human Resources* 14 (Winter 1979): 3–20.

Estimated Rates of Return to Formal Education

George Psacharapoulos, an economist at the World Bank, has calculated both private and social rates of return to investment in various levels of education across countries. His most recent compilation of estimates highlights some important features regarding investments in education.[1]

The rates of return reported in Table 7.1 result from what Psacharapoulos refers to as the "full" or "elaborate" method of estimation. It essentially amounts to calculating the internal rate of return for the level of investment being considered (see Equation 7.7). For example, the rate of return to a college education is determined by equating the lifetime stream of benefits of a college education (e.g., the income of a college graduate minus the income of a comparable high school graduate) with the lifetime stream of costs of a college education (e.g., the direct costs of tuition plus the forgone earnings while in school). An alternative method to estimating the private rate of return is detailed in Appendix 7A.

Private versus Social Rates of Return

The social rate of return calculation differs from the private rate of return because it includes all costs of education (paid by the individual or third parties). Consequently, the social rate of return will always (using this method of estimation) be lower than the private rate of return. It is of interest to

---

[1] This discussion summarizes some of the results found in George Psacharapoulos, "Returns to Investment in Education: A Further Update," *Education Economics* 12 (August 2004): 111–34. Additional rates of return for specific countries can be found in Philip Trostel et al., "Estimates of the Economic Return to Schooling for 28 countries," *Labour Economics* 9 (2002): 1–16.

TABLE 7.1   SOCIAL AND PRIVATE RETURNS TO INVESTMENT IN EDUCATION

Country	Social Rates of Return			Private Rates of Return		
	Prim.	Sec.	Higher	Prim.	Sec.	Higher
Sub-Saharan Africa	25.4	18.4	11.3	37.6	24.6	27.8
Asia (non-OECD)	16.2	11.1	11.0	20.0	15.8	18.2
Europe/Middle East/ North Africa (non-OECD)	15.6	9.7	9.0	13.8	13.6	18.8
Latin America/Caribbean	17.4	12.9	12.3	26.6	17.0	19.5
OECD[a]	8.5	9.4	8.5	13.4	11.3	11.6
World	18.9	13.1	10.8	16.6	17.0	19.0

[a]Countries that are members of the Organization for Economic Cooperation and Development include countries in North America and industrialized, market economies in Europe and the Pacific regions. Further information about the OECD can be found at http://www.sb05.com/OECDE.html.

SOURCE: Psacharapoulos, Table 1. Rates of return reflect the internal rate of return calculated by equating the net lifetime income stream resulting from the level of education compared with the next lowest level of education.

note that the social rate of return to investment in primary education is relatively high, probably exceeding in many cases what most countries can hope to earn from investing in physical capital. Although it would make sense to devote more resources to building human capital in the countries than to buying machines, this is typically not what happens. While most countries were investing between 1 and 2 percent of their GDP in the development of human capital through education, the same countries were devoting on average more than 20 percent of GDP to the enhancement of their physical capital.[2]

The Value of a Primary Education

For every region listed in Table 7.1, both the social and the private rates of return to investment in primary education are greater than the investment in either secondary or higher education. This is accounted for, according to Psacharapoulos, by the law of diminishing returns to the formation of human capital. Since the return to an investment in a specific level of education is calculated relative to not having made that investment, the return will be highest for that level of education which improves a person's productivity by the greatest amount relative to the next lowest level of education. Considering that one learns reading, writing, and arithmetic in the primary grades, the decline in estimated rates of return is not surprising. For example, the ability to perform simple mathematical functions (necessary skills for balancing a checkbook or keeping track of costs and revenues), which are learned in the primary grades, widens a person's opportunities for employment by much more than, say, learning calculus, which might be learned in secondary or higher levels of education.

The return to primary education is particularly pronounced in sub-Saharan Africa. This region is very poor, and it is clear that knowing the basics provides a great return to the investor, as well as to the region. The differences in social rates of return across different levels of investment in formal education are what Psacharapoulos argues should drive policy decisions about where countries should devote their resources. Given that the social rate of return to investment in primary education exceeds the social rate of return to investment in secondary and higher education, a country should devote more of its resources to supporting development of human capital in the primary grades rather than in colleges. Both OECD and non-OECD countries did devote slightly more resources to primary education than to higher education in 1992. OECD countries devoted an average of 1.55 percent of their gross domestic product (GDP) to primary education and an average of 1.10 percent to higher education. Non-OECD countries devoted an average of 1.77 percent of their GDP to primary education and an average of 0.75 percent of GDP to higher education.

---

2   World Bank, *World Development Indicators* (Washington, D.C.: The World Bank, 1997), Tables 2.7 and 4.15.

EMPIRICAL EVIDENCE 7-2

Schooling and Earnings

Shown in Figure 7.12 is the distribution of earnings for men and women aged 15 years and older with full-time jobs in 2003. The demand/supply model of human capital makes a major contribution in helping to account for two features of these distributions that economists were previously unable to explain satisfactorily. The first feature concerns the *skewness* in the distribution of earnings; the second concerns the large *dispersion* in earnings.

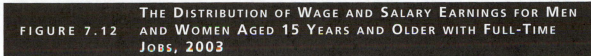

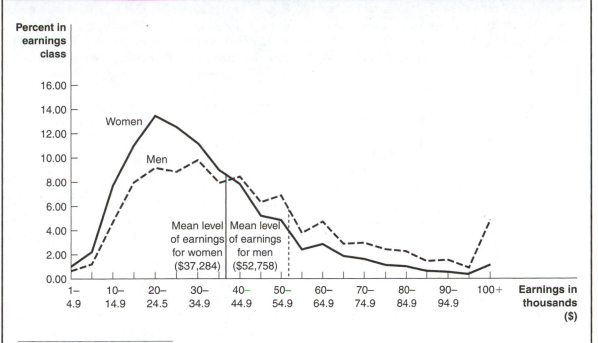

SOURCE: U.S. Census Bureau, Current Population Survey, 2004 Annual Social and Economic Supplement. PINC-10 Wage and Salary Workers http://www.census.gov.

The Skewness in Earnings

A distribution is "skewed" when one tail of the distribution is relatively bunched while the other is relatively dispersed. This is in contrast to a "symmetrical" distribution, where the left-hand side of the distribution is a mirror image of the right-hand side. The best example of a symmetrical distribution is a normal or bell-shaped curve. Figure 7.12 shows that the distribution of earnings is strongly skewed to the right. The mean level of earnings in 2003 of men aged 15 years and older with full-time jobs was $52,728. If the earnings distribution were symmetrical, as many men would be earning $10,000 less than the average as earned $10,000 more than the average. Such is not the case,

however. The bulk of earners are concentrated to the left of the mean (shown by the broken vertical line); a relatively small number of people are spread out in the high end or right-hand tail of the distribution.

The skewness of earnings presents an intriguing puzzle to economists. Most economists assume (although the evidence is not conclusive on this point) that the distribution of innate ability among individuals in the population is symmetrically distributed about the mean. If ability is reflected in productivity and earnings, the distribution of earnings should also be symmetrical. The earnings distribution is not symmetrical, however, but is highly skewed. How can this discrepancy be explained?

The demand and supply model of human capital investment offers a simple solution to this puzzle.[1] If ability were symmetrically distributed and if individuals did not invest in education and training, the earnings distribution would be symmetrical. Alternatively, if investment in human capital were symmetrically distributed but ability were the same for each person, earnings would again be symmetrical. It was argued previously, however, that ability and investments in schooling are likely to be strongly correlated—people of higher ability are able to derive more benefits from schooling and invest in more of it. The interaction of greater ability *and* greater schooling leads to substantially greater earnings for the high-ability people, causing the earnings distribution to be skewed to the right.

The Dispersion in Earnings

A second characteristic of the earnings distribution that human capital theory has helped to explain is the relatively large dispersion or variance in individual earnings. Although the average level of earnings for men aged 15 years and older with full-time jobs in 2003 was $52,758, many earned substantially above or below the mean. Less than half (41%) had earnings in the range of $25,000 to $50,000, with 7.0 percent earning below $15,000 and 13.4 percent earning over $75,000.

What factors might account for this dispersion? Human capital theory suggests a number of potentially important factors, such as years of schooling, age, mental ability, family background, quality of schooling, and discrimination. To isolate the impact of each variable on earnings, economists have used the statistical technique of linear regression to estimate *human capital earnings functions*.[2] The dependent variable in an earnings function is an individual's annual earnings; the independent or explanatory variables are all the factors thought to influence earnings.

The simplest earnings function would include years of schooling as the *only* explanatory variable. Studies of this kind have found that differences in years of schooling among individuals are able to account for only about 10 percent of the overall

dispersion in earnings.[3] This does not mean that education is relatively unimportant as a cause of earnings differentials—the problem is that the earnings function neglects a large number of other important influences on earnings. One additional factor, for example, is a person's age. As shown in the age/earnings profiles in Figure 7.1, individuals with the same level of schooling have very different levels of earnings depending on their age at the time the data are collected. By including in the earnings function variables both for years of schooling and for age, Jacob Mincer found that approximately 30 percent of the dispersion in earnings could then be accounted for.[4]

The demand and supply model of human capital investment suggests that Mincer's earning function is still incomplete. Figure 7.7 shows that three individuals may have exactly the same level of human capital investment (H_{31}) but very different earnings and rates of return to education (points P_{13}, P_{22}, and P_{31}) if their demand and supply curves differ. To more adequately explain differences in individual earnings, variables must be included in the earnings function to control for factors that cause systematic variation in demand curves and supply curves.

Of the variables that affect the demand curve, particular attention has been given to the role of ability as a cause of individual earnings differentials. If other things are equal, the demand curve for human capital of a person of higher ability will lie to the right of that for a less able person, leading the more able person to have both more schooling and higher earnings. If a measure of ability is not included in the earnings function, the higher earnings of the individual will mistakenly be

---

1   Jacob Mincer, "The Distribution of Labor Incomes: A Survey with Special Reference to the Human Capital Approach," *Journal of Economic Literature* 8, no. 1 (March 1970): 1–26.

2   See Appendix 7A for a more detailed discussion of earnings functions.

3   Barry Chiswick, *Income Inequality: Regional Analyses within a Human Capital Framework* (New York: National Bureau of Economic Research, 1974).

4   Jacob Mincer, *Schooling, Experience, and Earnings* (New York: National Bureau of Economic Research, 1974), Chapter 3.

attributed to the effect of extra schooling when, in fact, *both* the higher amount of schooling and the higher earnings are due to the individual's greater ability.

A large number of studies have attempted to disentangle the separate effects of ability and schooling on individual earnings.[5] This line of research is fraught with more than its share of controversy, however. One issue concerns the measurement of ability. Earning an income involves many different dimensions of ability, ranging from the ability of a salesperson to be a "smooth talker" to the ability of an engineer to solve complex mathematical equations. Most often, however, ability is treated as synonymous with intelligence or intellectual capacity. To obtain an empirical measure of intelligence, most studies have used intelligence quotient (IQ) test scores, or scores on various types of aptitude tests. Whether or not IQ scores are a valid measure of intelligence is open to debate, but studies have found a strong positive correlation between IQ and educational attainment—people who are "smarter" (or at least are better test-takers) also have more education. When IQ scores are included in the earnings function, however, it is generally found that this does not substantially lower the rate of return to investment in education. This implies that the higher earnings of the more educated are attributable to schooling, not to higher innate ability. Without IQ scores in the earnings function, for example, the rate of return to education is typically estimated to be in the range of 6 to 10 percent (earnings rise 6 to 10% with each additional year of schooling). Including IQ scores usually reduces the rate of return by only 1 to 2 percentage points.[6]

These results have been heavily criticized on several counts. One is that measured IQ scores fail to capture many aspects of ability, biasing downward the estimated impact of ability on earnings. Second, ability itself is a function of a third variable—family background. Family background includes such factors as parents' income, education, and occupational status. It is quite conceivable that children raised in families of a high socioeconomic position may also score better on IQ tests as a result of better care and parental instruction. In fact,

a recent study finds that family background is at least as important as IQ (and in some cases, more important) in determining economic success.[7] This possibility has led to a heated debate over the extent to which IQ scores are determined by heredity or environment ("nature versus nurture"). The more important nurture is in this regard, the more important family background becomes as a determinant of both educational attainment and earnings and, conversely, the less important inherited intelligence becomes.[8]

It is difficult to disentangle the independent effects on earnings of family background, ability, and education. The most novel approach to solving this problem has utilized data on the education and earnings of twins. Two studies deserve mention.

The first is by Paul Taubman, Jere Behrman, and other associates who examined earnings differentials for a large sample of World War II veterans who were identical or fraternal twins aged 45 to 55 in 1973.[9] The advantage of these data is that identical

---

5   For a review of this literature, see Willis, "Wage Determinants," 572–90.

6   Zvi Griliches and William Mason, "Education, Income, and Ability," and John C. Hause, "Earnings Profile: Ability and Schooling," *Journal of Political Economy* 80, no. 3, pt. 2 (May/June 1972): S108–S138.

7   Sanders Korenman and Christopher Winship, "A Reanalysis of the Bell Curve: Intelligence, Family Background, and Schooling," in *Meritocracy and Economic Inequality* (Princeton, N.J.: Princeton University Press, 2000): 137–78.

8   In 1992, students from low socioeconomic status (SES) families earned, on average, 5.5 points lower than the average on standardized achievement tests, whereas students from high-SES families earned 4.8 (9%) higher than the average. (SES is a composite measure of parental education, parental occupations, and family income used by the U.S. Department of Education to quantify economic status of students.) Also see Amy J. Orr, "Black–White Differences in Achievement: The Importance of Wealth," *Sociology of Education* 76 (October 2003): 281–304.

9   See Paul Taubman, "Earnings, Education, Genetics, and Environment," *Journal of Human Resources* 11, no. 3 (Fall 1976): 447–61; and Jere Behrman et al., *Socioeconomic Success: A Study of the Effects of Genetic Endowments, Family Environment, and Schooling* (New York: North-Holland, 1980). In addition, one study finds that a person's *effort* accounts for 40 percent of measured effect of IQ on earnings, suggesting an additional factor for which IQ is merely a proxy. See Jeffrey Zax and Daniel Rees, "IQ, Academic Performance, Environment, and Earnings," *Review of Economics and Statistics* 84 (November 2002): 600–16.

twins do not differ genetically while fraternal twins do, allowing the researcher to identify through statistical techniques the effect of differences in ability on the earnings of persons who have identical family backgrounds. Without controlling for either ability or family background among the sets of twins in the sample, the rate of return to additional education was found to be 8 percent. When the influence of family background was controlled for, the rate of return fell to 6 percent, and when both family background and genetic ability were introduced into the earnings function, the rate of return fell to 3 percent. What this means is that about two-thirds of the estimated effect of additional education on income was really due to the fact that those individuals who obtained more education were also of higher ability or were from a more favorable family background.

The second study is by Orley Ashenfelter and Alan Krueger.[10] They attended the annual "twins festival" at Twinsburg, Ohio, in 1991 and through personal interviews obtained detailed data on the earnings, education, and family background of nearly 250 sets of identical twins. Their results were quite different from Taubman and Behrman's. The statistical analysis of Ashenfelter and Krueger found that the estimated rate of return to an additional year of education was 16 percent—far higher than found by Taubman and Behrman—and that controlling for family background factors did not substantially lower this estimate. They attributed a large part of the difference in their findings to the fact that they were better able to control for measurement error in the reported levels of education of the twins, a factor that if not accounted for biases downward the estimated rate of return to education.[11]

A second variable that affects the demand curve for human capital and the rate of return from education is school quality. As with ability, there are obvious difficulties in obtaining a measure of school quality. One approach used in a study by Terrence Wales included the Gourman quality index of undergraduate colleges and universities in the earnings function.[12] Wales found that a person with a B.A. degree received, on average, $1,793 more per month (in 2004 dollars) than did a high

school graduate of equal age, ability, and so on. However, if the B.A. degree was earned from an institution in the top fifth of the Gourman quality index, the person's monthly earnings were another $68.2 higher. A second approach adopted in a recent study by David Card and Alan Krueger was to include in the earnings function three different variables that, they argued, reflect school quality: the pupil–teacher ratio, the length of the school term, and average annual teacher salaries.[13] They found that a decrease in the pupil–teacher ratio, for example, was associated with an increase in the rate of return to education of 1 percent.[14]

A third cause of differences in demand curves for human capital is discrimination. Discrimination is predicted to cause a person to invest in fewer years of schooling and to realize a lower rate of return and income from that schooling. Statistics seem to confirm this prediction. In 1940 black males earned only 47 percent as much as their white counterparts. By 2003 this ratio had risen to 79 percent. Why the large increase in relative earnings of

10   Orley Ashenfelter and Alan Krueger, "Estimates of the Economic Return to Schooling from a New Sample of Twins," *American Economic Review* 84 (December 1994): 1157–73.

11   Even more recent evidence from twin studies put the rate of return at 10 percent. See Cecelia Elena Rouse, "Further Estimates of the Economic Return to Schooling from a New Sample of Twins," *Economics of Education Review* 18 (April 1999): 149–57.

12   Terrence J. Wales, "The Effect of College Quality on Earnings: Results from the NBER-Thorndike Data," *Journal of Human Resources* 8, no. 3 (Summer 1973): 306–17.

13   David Card and Alan Krueger, "Does School Quality Matter? Returns to Education and the Characteristics of Public Schools in the U.S.," *Journal of Political Economy* 100, no. 1 (February 1992): 1–40. Also see Janet Currie and Duncan Thomas, "School Quality and the Longer-Term Effects of Head Start," *Journal of Human Resources* 35 (Fall 2000): 755–74.

14   Another study found school-quality measures to be much more important for black women than for white women. See Julian R. Betts, "The Impact of School Resources on Women's Earnings and Educational Attainment: Findings from the National Longitudinal Survey of Young Women," *Journal of Labor Economics* 19 (July 2001): 635–57. Bernt Bratsberg and Dek Terrell, "School Quality and Returns to Education of U.S. Immigrants," *Economic Inquiry* 40 (April 2002): 177–98, also find that immigrants from countries with higher school quality (measured by pupil–teacher ratio and expenditure per student) receive a greater return on their education in the U.S.

African-American males? An explanation offered by Smith and Welch is reduced discrimination in education.[15] In 1940 young black males obtained nearly four years less education than white males. James Smith and Finis Welch also found that black males earned a rate of return on education that was substantially lower than that earned by white males. Over the next five decades, however, many discriminatory policies were reduced or eliminated, such as the "separate but equal" school systems in the South, the relatively small amount of tax revenue given by states and localities to predominantly black schools, and restrictions on admittance of blacks to top-tier universities and professional schools. The results, say Smith and Welch, were predictable. The schooling gap of four years that existed in 1940 had shrunk to less than one year in 2003. Similarly, the rate of return to additional education for young black males rose substantially and by the late 1970s was actually greater than that received by similar white males.[16] Smith and Welch attribute the later finding, in part, to the fact that the relative quality of schooling received by African-American males increased significantly over time, making each new "vintage" of human capital for blacks more productive relative to that received by earlier generations.

Differences in demand curves are one factor causing a dispersion in earnings among individuals; differences in supply curves are another. The supply curve represents access to investable funds for human capital investment; the greater this access, the more schooling will be acquired and the greater the person's earnings. As suggested earlier, access to funds for education is principally related to an individual's family background, particularly the income level of the parents. It would be predicted that other things equal, persons from richer families would acquire more education and would have higher incomes as adults. In general, this is the result found by most studies. Controlling for ability and a wide range of other factors, William Sewell and Robert Hauser found that each additional $10,000 of parents' income (in 1967) was associated with slightly more than an additional half-year of

college education among their sons.[17] A more recent study on this issue found that parents' income alone was not a significant determinant of whether their children attended college, but that a broader measure of the family's socioeconomic position (parents' education, occupation, and income) was. The single most important determinant of college enrollment, however, was the student's academic ability.[18] And yet another study found that a 10 percent increase in family income is associated with a 1.4 percent increase in a child's likelihood of attending college.[19] These results suggest that persons from favorable family backgrounds are to some degree doubly advantaged—a favorable family background or good "nurture" leads to higher ability and greater education and earnings (a rightward shift in the demand curve), *and* it provides the financial resources with which more education can be purchased (a rightward shift in the supply curve).[20]

---

15 See James P. Smith and Finis R. Welch, "Black Economic Progress after Myrdal," *Journal of Economic Literature* 27 (June 1989): 519–64. Also see Robert A. Margo, "Explaining Black–White Wage Convergence, 1940–1950," *Industrial and Labor Relations Review* 48 (April 1996): 470–81.

16 A study using the 1980 Current Population Survey estimates the rate of return to college as 28 percent for white males and 33 percent for black males. See Michele C. McLennan, Susan Averett, and Megan Young, "Do Higher Returns to College Education Encourage College Enrollments? An Analysis by Race," *Research in Labor Economics* 19 (2000): 63–82.

17 William Sewell and Robert Hauser, *Education, Occupation, and Earnings* (New York: Academic Press, 1975), Chapter 7.

18 Baum, "Financial Aid to Low-Income College Students." A study by Jere Behrman and Paul Taubman, "Is Schooling 'Mostly in the Genes'? Nature–Nurture Decomposition Using Data on Relatives," *Journal of Political Economy* 97, no. 6 (December 1989): 1425–43, also found that variation in demand curves due to genetic differences among people was the most important cause of differences in educational attainment.

19 Daron Acemoglu and J. S. Pischke, "Changes in the Wage Structure, Family Income, and Children's Education," *European Economic Review* 45 (May 2001): 890–904.

20 As discussed in Chapter 9, the proportion of families headed by a female has increased dramatically among blacks from 29 percent in 1960 to 44 percent in 2000. Among whites the figures are 7 percent and 13 percent, respectively. Since female-headed households are one of the most poverty-prone groups in the labor force, this development (given the importance of parents' income for the future economic success of their children) represents one of the gravest threats to the continued economic progress of blacks.

Summary

People augment their stock of human capital in many ways. One of the most important is education. The acquisition of additional education entails both costs and benefits to the individual and to society. For the individual, the costs of education are the direct cost of tuition, books and other fees, and the opportunity cost of forgone income from work; the monetary benefit is the higher after-tax income the person earns after graduation. For society, the cost of education is the forgone goods and services that could have been obtained if the resources devoted to schooling had been invested in their next best alternative use; the economic benefit is the higher production that education makes possible. From an individual point of view, the optimal expenditure on education is where the private rate of return equals the cost of funds. For society, additional education is worthwhile as long as the social rate of return is greater than or equal to the rate of return on alternative investments. Calculating the private and social rate of return is complicated, however, by the fact that education yields many nonmonetary benefits as well.

Education is one of the most important determinants of a person's level of earnings in the labor market. The amount that a person spends on education is influenced by both the demand for human capital and the supply of funds for investment. The demand for human capital is influenced by the rate of return a person can earn from an additional dollar spent on it. This, in turn, is dependent on the person's level of ability, the quality of schooling obtained, and the extent to which he or she is discriminated against. The availability and interest cost of funds also influence the amount of human capital a person obtains. One important determinant of the supply of funds is parents' income. The interaction of demand and supply in the market for human capital determines the amount of funds invested by each person, the rate of return on the investment, and the level of earnings. If a positive correlation exists between demand and supply curves, there will be a greater inequality in earnings than if there is a negative correlation between them.

There is some debate about why education and earnings go hand in hand. According to human capital theory, the reason is that education increases a person's productivity at work. It is also possible, however, that education serves more as a screening device to distinguish the more able from the less able. Some evidence supports both points of view, although it is unlikely that education is strictly a screening device.

A second important form of human capital investment is on-the-job training. General on-the-job training increases the worker's productivity not only at the firm providing it, but also at other firms in the labor market. For this reason, the worker must bear the cost of the training in the form of a lower wage during the training period. Specific on-the-job training increases a worker's productivity only at the firm providing it. Since the skills are not transferable, the firm must bear the cost of training.

Differences in on-the-job training are hypothesized by economists to be a major explanation for the fact that earnings of women increase less rapidly than those of men with additional years of experience. Women are, on average, more likely than men to interrupt their work careers and, if they do so, to remain out of the labor force a longer time, reducing both the incentive of women to invest in general training and the incentive of firms to provide women with specific training. While important, this factor accounts for significantly less than half of the earnings gap between men and women.

Review Questions

1. What effect would a 25 percent cut in marginal income tax rates have on the private rate of return to education? Consider the effect on both the benefits and the costs of education.

2. Although an eminent labor economist calculated that the private rate of return to investment in a Ph.D. in English literature is −10 percent, hundreds of people still pursue such a degree. Is this evidence of irrational behavior? How can you explain this result in terms of human capital theory?

3. Based on a comparison of education and earnings among individuals, empirical studies have found that the rate of return declines with additional years of education. Does this suggest that the population has a relatively greater variation in demand curves or in supply curves for human capital? Draw a graph to show this.

4. People often argue that economic rewards in society should be meritocratic, that is, that everyone should have an equal opportunity to get ahead and those that do succeed because of their greater ability, hard work, and so on, should then be allowed to enjoy the full fruits of their labor. To accomplish this goal, what would have to be true about the variation in demand and supply curves for human capital among individuals in the population? What types of government policies regarding education might promote a meritocracy?

5. If screening is responsible for the higher incomes of college graduates, why might the private rate of return to college be relatively high, yet the social rate of return relatively low?

6. Under what conditions would firms find it profitable to pay for their employees to attend college to obtain MBA degrees?

7. Why would an employer be reluctant to hire a person for a job that entailed a considerable amount of specific on-the-job training if the person had a high probability of leaving the firm after a year or two? How can this help explain the flatter age/earnings profile of female workers relative to male workers?

Estimating a Human Capital Earnings Function

One of the most widely used empirical tools in labor economics is the human capital earnings function. This appendix describes in a relatively nontechnical way the theoretical derivation of the human capital earnings function. An actual example of an earnings function estimated by linear regression techniques is then presented to illustrate the empirical application of the theory.

Deriving the Earnings Function

The derivation of the human capital earnings function is relatively straightforward.[1] With zero years of education, a person's annual earnings are equal to Y_0, the value of his or her "raw" labor power. An investment in the first year of education will yield a rate of return r_1, defined as:

$$r_1 = \frac{Y_1 - Y_0}{Y_0}, \tag{7A.1}$$

where Y_1 denotes the annual earnings received after one year of education. For simplicity, it is assumed that Y_1 is constant over the life cycle, implying a zero rate of depreciation on human capital. Earnings from this investment in education can then be expressed as:

$$Y_1 = Y_0(1 + r_1). \tag{7A.2}$$

If the person invests in a second year of education, the rate of return will be:

$$r_2 = \frac{Y_2 - Y_1}{Y_1}, \tag{7A.3}$$

and, similarly, annual earnings will be:

$$Y_2 = Y_1(1 + r_2)$$
$$= Y_0(1 + r_1)(1 + r_2). \tag{7A.4}$$

Following this line of reasoning, annual income after S years of schooling will be:

$$Y_S = Y_0(1 + r_1) \cdots (1 + r_S). \tag{7A.5}$$

If it is assumed that $r_1 = r_2 = \cdots = r_S = r$, Equation 7A.5 can be simplified to:

$$Y_S = Y_0(1 + r)^S, \tag{7A.6}$$

and taking natural logarithms yields:

$$\ln Y_S = \ln Y_0 + S \ln(1 + r). \tag{7A.7}$$

---

1   See Jacob Mincer, *Schooling, Experience, and Earnings* (New York: National Bureau of Research, 1974).

The final step is to note that for "small" values of r (less than 0.2), $\ln(1 + r)$ is approximately equal to r. Making this substitution results in the human capital earnings function:

$$\ln Y_S = \ln Y_0 + rS. \tag{7A.8}$$

The value of r measures the rate of return from an investment in one more year of education. This can be shown by differentiating Equation 7A.8 with respect to S, obtaining:

$$\frac{\partial \ln Y_S}{\partial S} = r \tag{7A.9}$$

or,

$$\frac{\frac{dY}{Y}}{\partial S} = r.$$

This simply states that the proportionate change in annual earnings resulting from an additional increment of schooling is equal to r.

The earnings function in Equation 7A.8 relates annual earnings to years of formal education. It is still seriously incomplete in two major respects, however. The first is that it neglects the impact on earnings of on-the-job training. Mincer has shown that based on certain simple assumptions it is possible to express the path of earnings over the life cycle as a quadratic function of years of labor force experience (EXP). These assumptions are that the job involves T years of on-the-job training, and that the fraction of working time each year devoted to investment in OJT declines from some maximum value in the first year of work ($j = 1$) to $k_j = 0$ when $j = T$. Writing the earnings function in the form of a linear regression equation, this expanded model is:

$$\ln Y = \ln Y_0 + \alpha_1 S + \alpha_2 EXP + \alpha_3 EXP^2.$$

The coefficient α_1 is the rate of return to additional years of schooling. If $k_j = 0$ for $j = 1, \ldots, T$ (that is, the person makes no investment in OJT), then α_2 and α_3 would equal zero and the age/earnings profile after graduation from school would be horizontal (such as the line EF in Figure 7.9). The larger k_j is, however, the steeper the age/earnings profile is and the higher its peak value. The peak value also increases with additional years of training T. In this case it can be shown that the coefficient α_2 will be positive, but α_3 will be negative, giving rise to a parabolic profile (such as the line DG in Figure 7.9). Thus, the increase in earnings from one more year of work experience is:

$$\frac{\partial \ln Y}{\partial EXP} = \alpha_2 + 2\alpha_3 EXP \tag{7A.11}$$

or

$$\frac{\frac{dY}{Y}}{\partial EXP} = \alpha_2 + 2\alpha_3 EXP. \tag{7A.12}$$

Assuming α_3 is small relative to α_2, Equation 7A.12 shows that the slope of the age/earnings profile is positive over initial values of EXP, reaches a maximum when $EXP = \alpha_2/2\alpha_3$, and then declines.

The second reason the simple earnings function in Equation 7A.8 is incomplete is because it omits other factors that influence earnings such as individual ability, school quality, demographic characteristics such as race and sex, and family background variables such as parents' income. If this list or "vector" of variables is represented by the letter Z, the earnings function can be written as:

$$\ln Y = \ln Y_0 + \alpha_1 S + \alpha_2 EXP + \alpha_3 EXP^2 + \alpha_4 Z. \qquad \textbf{(7A.13)}$$

If the only variable in Z were a person's IQ score, for example, the effect on log earnings of a higher IQ score, holding the level of schooling and experience constant, would be given by the regression coefficient α_4. Based on the discussion in Chapter 7, it would be predicted $\alpha_4 > 0$. A higher IQ score, therefore, would cause an upward shift in the age/earnings profile.

Estimating the Earnings Function: An Example

Presented in Table 7A.1 are the estimated regression coefficients, t-ratios, and the R^2 for an earnings function estimated by John Akin and Irwin Garfinkel.[2] A description of the dependent and independent variables in the earnings function is also given in the table. The data were obtained from the Panel Study of Income Dynamics (PSID) and other sources. The sample was limited to white men between the ages of 30 and 55 in 1972 who were not self-employed and who had positive earnings.

The rate of return to additional education is given by the regression coefficient on the variable $EDYEARS$. It is statistically significant and shows that earnings rise approximately 13.28 percent on average for each additional year of schooling.[3] The coefficients on the experience variables $EXPER$ and $EXPE^2$ are, respectively .0965 and $-.0011$. These show (using Equation 7A.12) that earnings increase by approximately $.0965 - (2)(.0011)(1) = 9.43$ percent for the first year of experience, but only $.0965 - 2(.0011)(10) = 7.45$ percent for the tenth year. At approximately the 44th year of experience the age/earnings profile reaches its peak.[4]

---

2   For the sake of space, not all of the variables included in the earnings function are reported in Table 7A.1. The earnings function was estimated as part of a recursive system of four equations.

3   To calculate the precise percentage increase, it is necessary to compute the antilog of the regression coefficient: $e^{.1328} - 1 = 14.2$ percent. When the proportionate change in earnings is small, the regression coefficient on the education variable gives a close approximation of the actual percentage change since $\ln(1 + \%\Delta \text{ of } AVEARN) \cong \%\Delta \text{ of } AVEARN$.

4   As shown in Table 7A.1, years of work experience are measured as $EXP = [\text{age} - (\text{years of schooling} + 6)]$. A problem in empirical work is that while this is a fairly reliable measure of years in the work force for men since most are continuous workers, for many women this measure of EXP has a serious upward bias due to their discontinuous pattern of labor force participation.

TABLE 7A.1 AN EARNINGS FUNCTION ESTIMATED WITH LINEAR REGRESSION

Dependent Variable	Independent Variables								
	EDYEARS	EXPER	EXPER^2	VERAB	LNSCHEXP	FATHINC	FATHED	WKSICK	R^2
LNAVEARN	.1328 (7.09)	.0965 (4.80)	2.0011 (23.78)	.0329 (3.73)	.2038 (3.64)	.00001 (0.39)	.0049 (0.98)	2.0581 (26.08)	.38

Note: t-ratios are in parentheses.

Description of Variables

LNAVEARN—Natural log of the respondent's 5-year average annual earnings.

EDYEARS—Years of schooling completed by respondent.

EXPER—Potential years of labor force experience defined as [age − (years of schooling + 6)].

EXPER^2—(EXPER) (EXPER).

VERAB—Respondent's score on a 13-sentence completion verbal ability test.

LNSCHEXP—Natural log of average school expenditures in the state where the respondent grew up.

FATHINC—An estimate of respondent's father's income based on the father's occupation.

FATHED—Years of schooling completed by respondent's father.

WKSICK—Average annual weeks of work missed due to illness.

SOURCE: Adapted from John Akin and Irwin Garfinkel, "School Expenditures and the Returns to Schooling," *Journal of Human Resources* 12, no. 4 (Fall 1977): 460–81.

Chapter 7 shows that to obtain an unbiased estimate of the rate of return from additional investment in schooling, it is necessary to control for those variables that cause systematic variation in the demand and supply curves of human capital among individuals. These variables include such factors as ability, school quality, race, and parents' income. The regression results in Table 7A.1 show that earnings are positively related to the quality of the school the person attended (the variable *LNSCHEXP*), where quality is measured by the average school expenditures in the state where the person grew up. Earnings are also positively related to the person's mental ability (the variable *VERAB*), as measured by the score on a sentence completion test. A variable for race was not included in the earnings function since the sample was restricted to white men. Finally, the coefficient in father's income (*FATHINC*) is positive but statistically insignificant, suggesting that whether a person's father was rich or poor had no net effect on the child's earnings. This result may be due to the fact that father's income was an estimated figure and subject to considerable measurement error. Two additional variables that Akin and Garfinkel included in the earnings function were father's years of education and the weeks of work missed by the individual due to illness. The former was positive but statistically insignificant; the latter was negative and significant.

The R^2 statistic shows that the independent variables included in the earnings function were able to explain 38 percent of the variation in the dependent variable *LNAVEARN*. The remaining variation may be due to variables that Akin and Garfinkel did not include in the earnings function, or to purely random factors such as luck.

Occupational Wage Differentials

Earnings differentials among workers can be analyzed on the basis of many different characteristics, such as occupation, industry, geographic area, gender, or race. Of these different dimensions of the wage structure, occupational differentials are one of the most important because they capture the influence of several of the principal determinants of earnings in the labor market. Chief among these are differences among workers in levels of education and training and differences among jobs in terms of various noneconomic attributes such as status, prestige, and the quality of working conditions.

The first task taken up in this chapter is to broaden the theory of wage determination developed in Chapters 6 and 7 to incorporate job attributes in the consideration of why wages vary across occupations. This expanded model of wage determination is known as the *theory of compensating wage differentials*. Two important applications of the theory of compensating wage differentials are examined. The first has to do with government regulation of occupational safety and health conditions; the second concerns the factors that influence the mix of fringe benefits and wages in the compensation packages offered to workers by business firms. The second part of the chapter explores the role that the institution of occupational licensing plays in determining occupational earnings. And third, the chapter analyzes one of the most hotly debated topic in labor economics—the reasons for the widely disparate occupational earnings of men and women. The roles of market and social forces are highlighted in this analysis.

The Pattern of Occupational Earnings

Which occupations pay the most in the United States? Which pay the least? Evidence on this issue is provided in Table 8.1. The left side of the table shows the median weekly earnings in seven of the higher-paid occupations in 2004; the right side shows the same data for seven of the lower-paid occupations.[1] The data are for full-time wage and

---

1   Since these data are for wage and salary workers, persons who are self-employed are excluded. This causes the reported earnings figures for certain professional occupations such as lawyers to be significantly understated.

TABLE 8.1	MEDIAN WEEKLY EARNINGS OF FULL-TIME WAGE AND SALARY WORKERS IN SELECTED OCCUPATIONS BY GENDER, 2004						
	Higher Paid				**Lower Paid**		
Occupation	Earnings of Men	Earnings of Women	% Female	Occupation	Earnings of Men	Earnings of Women	% Female
Lawyers	1,710	1,255	33.5	Elementary school teachers	917	776	80.3
Managers, marketing	1,441	898	39.7	Bus drivers	588	440	41.5
College professors	1,162	886	41.5	Secretaries	598	550	96.7
Engineers	1,139	880	13.2	Nurses' aides	420	383	88.3
Computer systems analysts	1,092	902	30.8	Janitors	425	343	25.9
Accountants	1,016	757	60.8	Waiters and waitresses	399	327	67.3
Insurance sales people	970	615	52.7	Cashiers	380	313	75.0

SOURCE: Bureau of Labor Statistics, *Employment and Earnings* (January 2005), Table 39.

salary workers and are broken down by gender. Also shown for each occupation is the percentage of the workforce that was female.

Several features of the structure of occupational earnings stand out. First, higher-paid occupations generally are found in fields classified as professional or managerial, a characteristic that holds true for both men and women. Not surprisingly, for example, some of the top earners in the American economy are lawyers, engineers, and managers. The occupations that have lower earnings are also no surprise. These tend to be clustered in operative, clerical, and service-type occupations such as bus driver, secretary, and cashier. The gap in earnings between the highest-paid and lowest-paid occupations is quite large. A lawyer, for example, had weekly earnings in 2004 over four times those of a wait person or cashier.

While certain features of the pattern of occupational earnings are similar for men and women, the data in Table 8.1 also reveal several marked dissimilarities. The most obvious difference is that the weekly earnings of women are, as a rule, considerably less than the earnings of men. For the entire set of occupations from which the data in Table 8.1 were drawn, the average weekly earnings in 2003 of full-time female workers were only 80.4 percent of the earnings of male workers.

What factors might account for this disparity? The data in Table 8.1 suggest two reasons, which are explored in this and the next chapter. One reason has to do with differences in occupational attainment. Women are underrepresented in the top-paying professional and managerial occupations and overrepresented in the lower-paid occupations, such as services. In only one of the seven higher-paid occupations do women account for 50 percent or more of the workforce, while they represent over 65 percent of the workers in five of the seven lower-paid occupations. The second reason for the pay gap is that not only are women, on average, in lower-paying occupations than men, but even when they are in the same occupation, they earn less than men. One example is the accounting profession, where the median weekly earnings in 2004 were $1016 for male accountants but only $757 for female accountants. This relationship also holds true for most low-paying occupations, although there are exceptions.

Economists have devoted considerable effort to discover the reasons for these differentials in earnings among occupations. Perhaps the best explanation for earnings differentials among occupations was given by Adam Smith over 200 years ago. He observed:

> Pecuniary wages and profit, indeed, are everywhere in Europe extremely different, according to the different employments of labour and stock. But this difference arises partly from certain circumstances in the employments themselves, which either really, or at least in the imagination of men, make up for a small pecuniary gain in some and counterbalance a great one in others; and partly from the policy of Europe, which nowhere leaves things at perfect liberty.[2]

Smith linked occupational wage differentials to all three of the labor market forces discussed in Chapter 1 (market, institutional, and sociological). People choose among occupations partly because of their taste for one occupation versus another, a taste that is often influenced by subjective, nonmonetary considerations that heighten the appeal of some occupations and diminish the appeal of others. To the extent that occupational tastes are common to particular social groups, sociological forces have an impact on the supply of labor and, thereby, on the determination of wages. Market forces of supply and demand also play a crucial role in causing occupational wage differentials. As Smith describes, whether it is differences in people's tastes for occupations or other, more pecuniary considerations such as the skill required, the probability of success in that line of work, or the danger of injury, for equilibrium in the labor market to occur, wages must vary between occupations so that the attractiveness of one occupation just equals that of another. Finally, Smith also notes that institutional forces ("the policy of Europe") affect

---

2   Adam Smith, *The Wealth of Nations* (Chicago: University of Chicago Press, 1976), 111.

occupational wage differentials in the form of government policies that either re-strict or promote the entrance of people into certain occupations. Modern eco-nomic theory follows Smith in his attention to market, institutional, and sociolog-ical forces as the cause of occupational wage differentials as illustrated throughout this chapter.

Compensating Wage Differentials

Occupations differ one from another in terms of many characteristics, such as the education and training required, the pleasantness or unpleasantness of the work, the status and prestige in which the occupation is held, the probability of success in that line of work, and the level of wages in the occupation. Adam Smith's great insight was to realize that people choose an occupation based not on the wage alone, but on the whole package of attributes, both negative and positive. Smith postulated that each worker compares the *total of the advantages and disadvantages* of each occupation, and chooses the one yielding the highest level of net advantages.[3] Because some occupations are more desirable than others, if the wage rates were equal, workers would crowd into the desirable occupations and shun the undesir-able ones. As Smith deduced, therefore, for an equilibrium to occur in the labor market, the wage rate must rise in the undesirable occupations and fall in the de-sirable occupations until the total of advantages and disadvantages are equalized across occupations. Differences in rates of pay among occupations thus represent **compensating wage differentials** in the sense that they equalize the net attrac-tiveness of each occupation.

Job Attributes

Many factors affect the attractiveness of one occupation relative to another. Adam Smith referred to these considerations as the "agreeableness" or "disagreeableness" of the occupation. Some occupations have very agreeable features, such as high social status, flexible working hours, or room for considerable autonomy and cre-ativity. Examples are doctor, professor, and opera singer. Other occupations have very disagreeable features, such as unpleasant working conditions, monotonous or tedious work, or low social status. Examples include butcher, assembly-line worker, and janitor. While these factors do not directly affect the monetary return derived from employment in an occupation, they do nevertheless have a strong influence on its relative attractiveness to people.

Other attributes are less subjective in their valuation by workers. For example, if people could choose between a 9-month full-time (40 hours per week) job and a 12-month full-time job that both pay the same salary, they would choose the 9-month job in order to have the same income but more leisure. So, in order to

---

3   This is clearly stated in the quotation by Adam Smith in Chapter 1.

attract workers to the 12-month job, workers will require a higher salary than that being paid to 9-month workers. In addition, some occupations, such as miner, logger, or packing-house worker, are far more dangerous than others. If persons are to be induced to work in these occupations, the wages must be high enough that the differential in wages just compensates for the shorter time that the person can expect to work (because of injury), the direct costs of medical expenses, and the costs of pain and suffering.[4] And, last, a relatively large number of persons aspire to be major league baseball players or professional actors, but only a few actually succeed. The smaller the probability of success, the higher must be the wage in the occupation for the expected value of the lifetime stream of income to equal that in an occupation in which success is assured.[5]

In recent years, the U.S. Navy has implemented a compensating wage differential approach to disagreeable Navy assignments.[6] The Navy posts undesirable "job postings" on the Internet and allows qualified personnel to "bid" on them. One job was a mechanic in Italy. Someone who did not want to move to Italy, but would do so for more pay would enter a high bid. Someone who finds moving to Italy less disagreeable would enter a lower bid. The Navy, wanting to save money, would take the lowest bid. So far, this procedure of assigning jobs has been popular with sailors.

To illustrate the effect of job attributes on wage differentials, assume occupations A and B are identical in every respect except that occupation B involves work that is of low social prestige. If the wages in occupations A and B were equal, everyone would seek employment in occupation A and would refuse to consider work in occupation B. To achieve an equilibrium in the labor market, the wage must rise in occupation B relative to A until it is just high enough to compensate for the negative attribute of low prestige. The size of this compensating differential is illustrated graphically in Figure 8.1. The $W_1 - W_0$ difference represents the

---

4 In addition, compensating differentials have been found associated with other job attributes, such as stress. Michael French and Laura Dunlap, "Compensating Wage Differentials for Job Stress," *Applied Economics* 30 (August 1998): 1067–75, find a 3–10 percent wage premium attributable to mental stress on the job. Ronald Ehrenberg et al., "Do Economics Departments with Lower Tenure Probabilities Pay Higher Faculty Salaries?" *Review of Economics and Statistics* 80 (November 1998): 503–12, find that assistant professors in departments with lower probabilities of tenure earn a compensating wage differential for that lower probability. Keith Bender and Robert Elliot, "The Role of Job Attributes in Understanding the Public-Private Wage Differential," *Industrial Relations* 41(2002): 407–421, find that differences in job attributes pay a major role in explaining wage differences between public and private sector jobs. Susan Averett, et al., "Unemployment Risk and Compensating Differences in Late-Nineteenth Century New Jersey Manufacturing," *NBER Working Paper No. NOW9977* (September 2003), find some evidence that before the presence of unemployment insurance, workers in jobs with a higher probability of layoff earned a compensating wage differential. And, Jeff Desimone and Edward J. Schumacher, "Compensating Wage Differentials and AIDS Risk," *NBER Working Paper No. W10861* (November 2004), find that a 10 percent increae in the AIDS rate raises earnings for RNs by about 0.8 percent.

5 Less than 2 percent of minor league baseball players ever make it to the major leagues. In the minors they play at ramshackle ballparks, ride buses (not airplanes) between cities, and earn a relatively low salary. Why do they do it? One reason, no doubt, is love of the game and the desire to be stars. Another important reason is that the median salary in 2004 ranged between $325,000 for the Cleveland Indians to $3.1 million for New York Yankees players.

6 See Greg Jaffe, "Navy Turns Auctioneer, Lets Sailors Bid for Unpopular Posts," *Wall Street Journal* (11 Aug 2003) B1.

FIGURE 8.1

THE COMPENSATING WAGE DIFFERENTIAL FOR A DISAGREEABLE OCCUPATION

If occupation B offers low social prestige while occupation A is prestigious, the wage in occupation B must be higher to equalize the sum of advantages and disadvantages. Thus, equilibrium occurs at point X, where the demand curve D_B intersects the supply curve S_B. The compensating wage differential is

$W_1 - W_0$. The broken line at $W_0 = 1.0$ is where the wage rates in the two occupations are equal. The supply curve S_B is perfectly elastic at the wage W_1, indicating that at any wage lower than W_1, no one would be willing to work in occupation B.

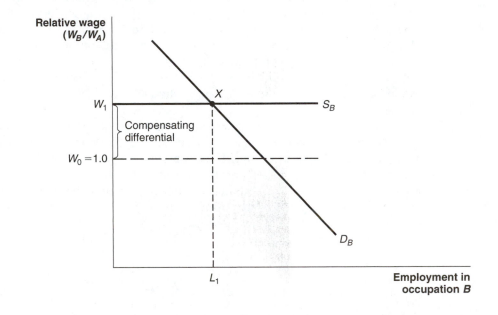

dollar value per hour necessary to just compensate for the negative utility arising from this undesirable feature of the work. While a negative attribute must be balanced by a higher money wage, an occupation that possesses a positive or agreeable attribute must pay a money wage lower than other occupations if the advantages and disadvantages are to be equalized. In this case, the supply curve S_1 in Figure 8.1 would lie below the line of equal wages.

One can think about the prestige enjoyed by workers in occupation A as a "psychic" payment or wage. In this light, one can consider the equilibrium in Figure 8.1 as occurring where the net incomes, including actual and psychic wages, for the two occupations are equalized. Evidence of a compensating wage differential existing for the reputation of one's occupation or employer is presented in Empirical Evidence 8-1.

➲ SEE

Empirical Evidence 8-1:
Compensation for
Reputation, p. 436.

With differences among people's tastes and abilities for particular occupations, the supply curve of labor to any one occupation becomes an upward-sloping line, such as S_1. The compensating differential in wages now depends on the strength of demand. If the demand curve is D_1 the compensating differential is $W_1 - W_0$ (point A); if it is D_2 the compensating differential rises to $W_2 - W_0$ (point B). Given the demand curve D_2, all persons but the last $L_{2}\text{nd}$ worker hired receive an economic rent. The amount of economic rent for person L_1 is $W_2 - W_1$.

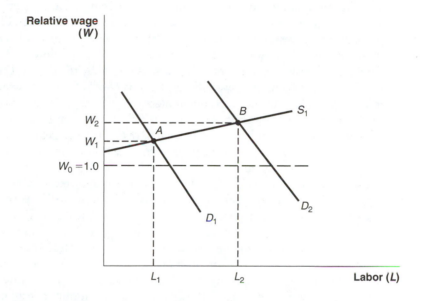

Differences in Tastes and Abilities In the previous discussion, workers were assumed to have the same occupational tastes and abilities. A more realistic treatment must allow for heterogeneity in these factors. Not everyone dislikes to an equal degree occupations that have unpleasant attributes, such as janitor or butcher, and a minority of persons may prefer such work. Likewise, not everyone has an equal mental or physical ability to practice occupations such as lawyer, ironworker, or interior decorator.

The effect of incorporating heterogeneous tastes and abilities into the theory of compensating differentials is shown in Figure 8.2. If everyone equally disliked occupations with noxious odors or if everyone had the same ability to argue a case before a jury, the supply curve to an occupation such as garbage collector or lawyer would be perfectly elastic (as in Figure 8.1). Once heterogeneity of tastes and abilities is allowed for, however, the supply curve becomes an upward-sloping line, such as S_1. The supply curve S_1 is derived by arranging workers from left to right on the basis of their intensity of preference for the attribute or their ability to master the employment. Workers with the least dislike for noxious odors would require the smallest compensating differential; each additional worker would require a larger wage premium to compensate for his or her greater distaste for the negative attribute.[7] Similarly, persons with the highest ability for jurisprudence would be willing to be lawyers for a relatively small compensating differential, since they could finish law school in the shortest time and with the smallest amount of anxiety and stress. Persons of lesser ability in the legal field, however, would require successively greater wage premiums to compensate for their higher money and psychic costs of obtaining the training.

The most important implication of introducing heterogeneity of tastes and abilities into the model is that the size of the compensating wage differential for a particular occupation depends on the *strength of labor demand*. This is illustrated in Figure 8.2, which shows two demand curves, D_1 and D_2. If there were relatively little demand for garbage collectors or lawyers, as shown by the demand curve D_1, only a relatively small compensating differential of $W_1 - W_0$ (point A) would be required in order to induce L_1 workers to voluntarily choose these occupations. Should the demand curve for labor shift to the right to D_2, a larger compensating differential of $W_2 - W_0$ (point B) would have to be paid to overcome the greater dislike of the L_2nd worker for noxious odors, or the greater costs of becoming a lawyer.

When the supply curve of labor is perfectly elastic, as in Figure 8.1, the compensating wage differential $W_1 - W_0$ is an equalizing differential for *all* the persons employed in the occupation, in the sense that at the wage W_1 each of these workers is just indifferent between this occupation and some other. When the labor supply curve is the upward-sloping line S_1 as in Figure 8.2, a wage such as W_2 is an equalizing differential for the last or *marginal* worker hired (the L_2nd) but is more than what is necessary to attract the previous workers. All the workers up to (but not including) the L_2nd receive what economists call an **economic rent.** An economic rent is a payment above the factor input's minimum asking price. If the demand curve is D_2, the economic rent received by the L_2nd worker is $W_2 - W_1$, the difference between the wage actually paid and the lowest wage the worker would have been willing to work for in this occupation. As Figure 8.2 shows, the persons with the greatest preference for the occupation or with the greatest ability for that line of work receive the largest amount of economic rent. Much of the multimillion-dollar earnings of star athletes or popular rock singers are an economic rent—the result of a limited supply of people with their talents, coupled with a large demand for their services.

Unemployment and Noncompeting Groups Competitive forces are predicted to give rise to a distinct set of compensating differentials that equalize the net

---

7   If some workers actually prefer this attribute, the supply curve will intersect the vertical axis at a wage below and then slope upward, crossing the broken line when employment reaches the worker who neither likes nor dislikes the attribute.

advantages among all occupations. Heterogeneity of tastes does not overturn this prediction but qualifies it so that the exact size of the compensating differential depends on the strength of demand. Some economists object to the theory of compensating differentials because in their view its predictions do not accord with the observed pattern of wages among occupations. This was perhaps most forcefully stated one hundred years ago by the noted economist and philosopher John Stuart Mill. He wrote:

> It is altogether a false view of the state of facts to present this [the theory of compensating differentials] as the relation which generally exists between agreeable and disagreeable employments. The really exhausting and the really repulsive labors, instead of being better paid than others, are almost invariably paid the worst of all, because they are performed by those who have no choice.[8]

Mill readily conceded that in a perfectly competitive market the disagreeable occupations would earn higher wages than the agreeable occupations, but he denied, for two reasons, that this actually occurred. The first reason discussed by Mill was a result of the general tendency for the economy to operate at less than full employment. Under full employment, firms would be forced by the scarcity of labor to pay higher wages for disagreeable occupations in order to induce workers to undertake them. With unemployment in the market, the excess supply of people looking for work short-circuits the competitive process, because firms then face a large supply of applicants who are willing to take on the disagreeable employments at wage rates that they would otherwise refuse. The second reason advanced by Mill was the influence of what he called "natural and artificial monopolies" that tended to segment the labor market into noncompeting groups, causing an oversupply of labor to low-skill, disagreeable occupations. One such factor identified by Mill was the class system that, particularly in countries such as Britain, prevented the bulk of working-class youth from acquiring the necessary education and social skills to compete for jobs in the higher-paying professional occupations.[9] A second factor that segmented the labor market in his view was the inability of unskilled workers to acquire the necessary funds for education and training in order to compete for the agreeable occupations. Finally, a third source of noncompeting groups identified by Mill was the influence of prejudice and custom, which restricted the employment of women to a relatively few lower-skill, lower-prestige occupations.

The impact of unemployment and noncompeting groups on the theory of compensating differentials is illustrated in Figure 8.3, which represents the labor

---

8   John Stuart Mill, *Principles of Political Economy*, vol. 1 (New York: D. Appleton and Co., 1902), 474–75. Mill's theory of noncompeting groups is the intellectual forefather of modern theories of segmented and dual labor markets that are discussed in Chapter 6.

9   This process in modern Britain is described in Paul Willis, *Learning to Labor* (New York: Columbia University Press, 1977). Also see William T. Dickens and Kevin Lang, "Labor Market Segmentation Theory: Reconsidering the Evidence," in William Darity Jr., ed., *Labor Economics: Problems in Analyzing Labor Markets* (Norwell, Mass.: Kluwer, 1993), 141–80.

Given full employment and free mobility among occupations, the supply curve S_1 for an undesirable occupation such as garbage collector would lie above the broken line of equal wages, resulting in garbage collectors receiving a higher wage of W_1. Unemployment or noncompeting groups, however, increase the supply of labor willing to be garbage collectors because some workers are unable to obtain other, more desirable jobs. As a result, the supply curve shifts to the right to S_2, and the wage in the undesirable occupation is only W_2, lower than in the preferred occupations.

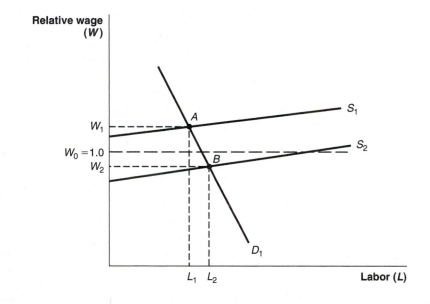

market for some disagreeable occupation such as garbage collector. With full employment and freedom of mobility between occupations, the supply curve of garbage collectors would be the line S_1. The crucial feature of the supply curve S_1 is that it lies above the broken line of equal wages, illustrating that workers would voluntarily work as garbage collectors only if they received a compensating wage premium relative to otherwise identical occupations. Given the demand curve D_1, the compensating wage differential earned by garbage collectors would be $W_1 - W_0$ (point A). If an excess supply of labor exists in the market because of either less than full employment in the economy or the segregation of certain groups of workers to low-status occupations, the supply curve for garbage collectors would no longer be S_1, but S_2. The supply curve S_2 lies much further to the right, illustrating that at any given wage a much greater number of people are willing to work as garbage collectors due to the scarcity of other, more preferred jobs. The wage for garbage collectors is now only W_2 (point B), a wage *below* that earned in more agreeable occupations.[10] Given a choice of other occupations, the L_2 workers employed as garbage collectors would not voluntarily work at the wage W_2. That they take these jobs, therefore, reflects not deliberate choice or different tastes, but economic necessity due to lack of alternative employments in the market.[11]

The Hedonic Theory of Compensating Wage Differentials

The theory of compensating wage differentials makes the basic prediction that in order to attract and keep a workforce firms offering jobs with a disamenity such as high risk of injury or unpleasant working conditions must pay a higher wage than firms with otherwise similar jobs that lack the disamenity. This section utilizes the model of hedonic prices developed by Sherwin Rosen to illustrate how wages adjust to compensate workers for job disamenities.[12] A key feature of this model is that it allows for differences in worker preferences with respect to the disamenity and for differences in the technological ability of firms to reduce the disamenity. While the general theory of compensating wage differentials predicts that workers will have to be compensated to take undesirable jobs, Rosen's extension yields additional predictions. For example, workers will sort themselves into jobs with different characteristics based on their individual preferences regarding those characteristics, and this sorting results in lower compensating wage differentials than if the market provided for one compensating differential to cover all possible disagreeable attributes of all jobs. The model is extended in the next section to explore the provision of fringe benefits (a job *amenity*) to workers. The key insight provided by Rosen's approach is the nature of the matching process between workers and firms in the labor market and the efficient allocation of labor that results.

To keep the model simple, it is assumed that all jobs under consideration are identical except for some disamenity. For the sake of concreteness, let the

---

10   It is assumed in Figure 8.3 that the wage in the undesirable occupation is flexible downward so that the market clears at W_2, although wages in other, more desirable occupations cannot adjust if there is to be unemployment in the economy. The best real-world example may be the downward pressure on wages that occurred in the harvest labor market in California during the 1930s as thousands of unemployed workers competed for jobs that in better times they would have shunned. This is vividly described in John Steinbeck, *The Grapes of Wrath* (New York: Viking Press, 1939).

11   Empirical evidence on the existence of compensating wage differentials in the labor market is reviewed in this chapter with respect to two important nonwage job characteristics, the risk of injury and the amount of fringe benefits. In both cases, evidence in support of the theory's predictions is mixed. In this vein, Charles Brown, after an in-depth review of the literature, concluded that there is "some support for the theory but an uncomfortable number of exceptions." See "Equalizing Differences in the Labor Market," *Quarterly Journal of Economics* 94 (February 1980): 113–34. For a somewhat more positive assessment, see Robert F. Elliott and Robert Sandy, "Adam Smith May Have Been Right After All: A New Approach to the Analysis of Compensating Differentials," *Economics Letters* 59 (April 1998): 127–31.

12   Sherwin Rosen, "Hedonic Prices and Implicit Markets," *Journal of Political Economy* 82 (January/February 1974): 34–55. Evidence that workers less sensitive to risks on the job will be found in more risky jobs is provided by Morley Gunderson and Douglas Hyatt, "Workplace Risks and Wages: Canadian Evidence from Alternative Models," *Canadian Journal of Economics* 34 (May 2001): 377–95.

disamenity be risk of injury on the job. Given this, the starting place in the analysis is to examine employee preferences.

Employee Indifference Curves   As was argued in the previous section, workers are generally willing to trade additional money for an increased probability of injury. This trade-off for one particular worker is represented by the indifference curves in Figure 8.4(a). Each indifference curve slopes upward to the right, illustrating

---

FIGURE 8.4   EMPLOYEE PREFERENCES FOR WAGES VERSUS RISK OF INJURY

The indifference curves in graph (a) show that a person must be compensated with a higher wage to willingly accept a job with a higher risk of injury. The indifference curve I_3 represents a higher level of utility than I_1, since for any given injury rate (R), the wage is higher on I_3 (W_3) than I_1 (W_1). Graph (b) shows the indifference curves for two people, worker A

and worker B, who differ in their degree of aversion to risk. The steeper slope of curve I_A indicates that worker A is the relatively more risk averse of the two people, since he or she must be compensated with a higher wage ($W_{2A} - W_1$) than worker B ($W_{2B} - W_1$) for any given increase in the risk of injury ($R_1 \rightarrow R_2$).

(a) One Person's Indifference Curves

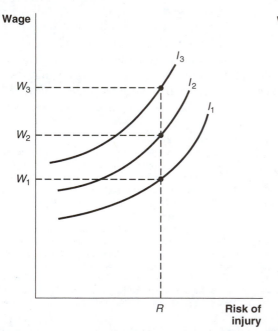

(b) Indifference Curves of Two People

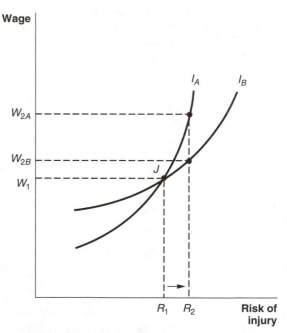

that the worker will only accept a higher risk of injury in return for a higher wage per hour. Each indifference curve is also convex, implying that the worker requires successively larger increments in money to compensate for higher levels of risk. Also, indifference curves lying further to the upper left represent higher levels of utility. Thus, I_3 would be preferred to I_1 since, for any given level of injury (R), the wage rate on I_3 (W_3) is higher than on I_1 (W_1).

Workers are likely to differ in regard to their willingness to trade additional money for an increased risk of injury. This notion is illustrated in Figure 8.4(b). The two indifference curves shown there, I_A and I_B, represent the preferences of two different workers, worker A and worker B. The flatter slope of the indifference curve I_B indicates that worker B ($W_{2B} - W_1$) is less averse to risk than worker A. Starting from point J, for example, both workers would demand an increase in the wage rate before they would willingly accept a greater risk of injury, but the increase demanded by worker B is less than that demanded by worker A ($W_{2A} - W_1$).[13]

Employer Isoprofit Curves   Technology of production generally gives employers the ability to reduce the risk of injury through the expenditure of additional funds on safer equipment, increased supervision, and so on. For firms to earn the same level of profit, however, the additional money spent to reduce the risk of injury must be counterbalanced by the payment of a lower wage rate per hour. This idea is represented in Figure 8.5(a) for one particular firm by the set of **isoprofit curves** P_1, P_2, and P_3.

Each isoprofit curve shows all the combinations of wage rates and injury rates that result in the same level of profit. Each curve slopes upward to the right because, if a firm spends less on safety (has a higher risk of injury), it can pay a higher wage, and vice versa, while profit remains constant. A second feature of the isoprofit curves is that each is concave, illustrating the diminishing returns (higher marginal cost) that a firm encounters as it lowers the injury rate. As a firm that starts with a high risk of injury adopts procedures to reduce risk, it can begin with the simplest (and least expensive) devices (such as goggles or hard hats). Reducing risk even further requires more expensive devices (such as a new ventilation system) and/or additional staff (such as a full-time safety director). This makes each incremental reduction in risk more expensive than the last. Finally, isoprofit curves lying to the lower right represent higher levels of profit. The reason is that, for any given wage rate, the risk of injury is higher on curve P_3 than on P_1, implying a lower level of expenditure on safety and a higher profit level. Thus, P_3 would represent higher profit than P_1, since for any given level of risk (R), the wage paid to workers on P_3 (W_3) on is lower than on P_1 (W_1).

---

13   One report indicates that some workers view risk or other job disamenities as a "badge of honor"; these workers will clearly have very flat indifference curves and, in some rare instances, may actually seek out the risky jobs. See "Workers with Unsavory Jobs Have a Secret: They're Proud," *Wall Street Journal* (13 October 1998): A1. Evidence that workers less sensitive to risks on the job will be found in more risky jobs is provided by Morley Gunderson and Douglas Hyatt, "Workplace Risks and Wages: Canadian Evidence from Alternative Models," *Canadian Journal of Economics* 34 (May 2001): 377–95.

FIGURE 8.5   EMPLOYER ISOPROFIT CURVES

The curves P_1, P_2, and P_3 represent isoprofit curves for a particular firm. Each curve slopes upward and to the right, showing that a firm can pay a higher wage if it spends less on safety (becoming a higher-risk place to work). The level of profit associated with curve P_3 is higher than with curve P_1, since for any given risk-of-injury rate (R), the firm pays a lower wage

($W_3 < W_1$). The steeper slope of the isoprofit curve P_Y in graph (b) shows that the marginal cost of reducing the risk of injury is greater for firm Y than firm X. For any comparable reduction in risk ($R_1 \rightarrow R_2$), wages in firm Y must be lowered by a greater amount than in firm X in order to maintain the same level of profit as at the higher risk level.

(a) One Firm's Isoprofit Curves

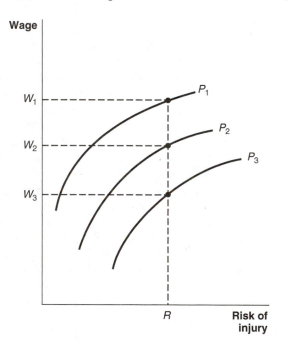

(b) Isoprofit Curves of Two Firms

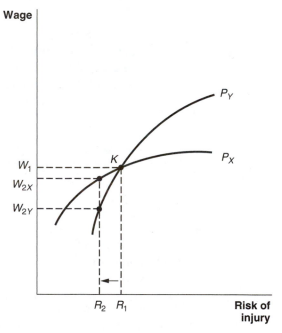

Just as workers differ in their preferences regarding wages versus risk of injury, so do firms differ in the cost required to reduce the risk of injury for their workers. This is illustrated in Figure 8.5(b) by the two isoprofit curves, P_X and P_Y, which represent two different firms, firm X and firm Y. The curve P_Y is steeper than P_X, indicating that the marginal cost of reducing the risk of injury is higher for firm Y than for firm X. Thus, starting from point K, an equal reduction in the injury rate at both firms ($R_1 \rightarrow R_2$) requires a larger decline in the wage rate at firm Y ($W_1 - W_{2Y}$) if profits are to remain constant, reflecting firm Y's higher marginal cost of increasing safety in the workplace. Factors that will influence how costly it is for a firm to reduce the risk of injury are the type of product produced, the age of the plant, and so on. Thus, if firm X is in a relatively low-risk business such as brewing, while firm Y is in a high-risk business, such as coal mining, firm Y will be able to achieve the same injury rate as firm X only with much higher dollar expenditure.[14]

Matching Workers and Firms   Figures 8.4(b) and 8.5(b) are combined in Figure 8.6. It is now possible to tell which worker will be matched with which firm and the wage rate and injury rate that will prevail for the two worker/firm combinations. Employee A maximizes utility by working for firm X (point M), while employee B maximizes utility by working for firm Y (point N). Employee B is paid the relatively high wage of W_{BY} but suffers the higher risk of injury R_{BY}. Conversely, employee A earns the lower wage of W_{AX} but enjoys the lower risk of injury R_{AX}.

This particular matchup of firms and workers occurs because worker A is more averse to the risk of injury than worker B, while firm X can achieve a low risk of injury at a smaller increment in cost than firm Y. Worker A is clearly better off with firm X since the alternative wage/injury combination of W_{BY}/R_{BY} offered by firm Y (point N) places worker A on a lower indifference curve (the dashed indifference curve I'_A). Likewise, worker B is better off with firm Y since, for this person, the additional risk of injury is more than offset by the much higher wage that can be earned. To accept employment with firm X clearly would not make sense for worker B since at the injury rate of R_{BY} the wage paid by firm X (point Q) would be much lower than W_{BY}.

This model yields three important conclusions. First, even with heterogeneous preferences and production technologies, a competitive labor market will give rise to a series of compensating wage differentials that increase directly with the risk of injury (or some other disamenity) at the workplace.[15] Second, workers with strong

---

14 According to one study, the marginal cost (in 2002 dollars) of accident reduction to firms in the fabricated metal products industry was $207,498 per disabling injury, but it was $374,468 in the electrical machinery industry. See Gal Sider, "Work-Related Accidents and the Production Process," *Journal of Human Resources* 20 (Winter 1985): Table 2. There is also evidence that increasing the cost of accidents by tying a firm's worker's compensation tax to the firm's injury rate provides a significant incentive for the firms to reduce risk. See Terry Thomason and Silvana Pozzebon, "Determinants of Firm Workplace Health and Safety and Claims Management Practice," *IILR* 55 (January 2002): 286–307.

15 Several recent studies provide evidence for this conclusion. See, for example, Joni Hersch, "Compensating Differentials for Gender-Specific Job Injury Risks," *American Economic Review* 88 (June 1998): 598–607, and Robert F. Elliott and Robert Sandy, "Adam Smith May Have Been Right After All: A New Approach to the Analysis of Compensating Differentials," *Economics Letter*, and Morley Gunderson and Douglas Hyatt, "Workplace Risks and Wages: Canadian Evidence from Alternative Models," *Canadian Journal of Economics* 34 (May 2000): 377–95.

FIGURE 8.6 MATCHING WORKERS AND FIRMS

Worker A, who is relatively risk averse, trades off a low wage of W_{AX} for the opportunity to work for firm X, with its lower probability of injury. Worker B, who is less risk averse, accepts the higher risk of injury at firm Y in return for the higher wage of W_{BY}. Through the matching process of workers and jobs, the labor market gives rise to a compensating differential for risk of injury of $W_{BY} - W_{AX}$.

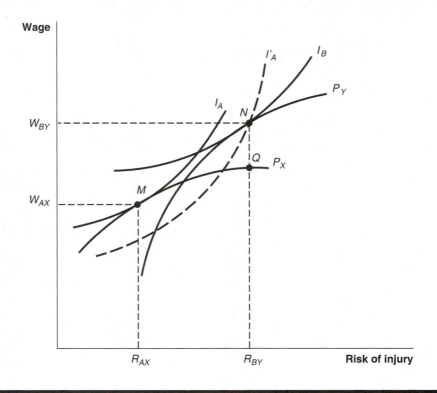

preferences for a safe work environment will take jobs in firms where safety can be provided least expensively, albeit at the cost of a lower wage.[16] Workers who are willing to accept a higher level of risk, on the other hand, find it advantageous to work for firms where it is more economical to pay a high wage than to reduce the chance of injury.

---

16   At best we can use workers' responses to risk levels as evidence for this prediction. James Robinson, "Worker Responses to Occupational Risks of Cancer," *Review of Economics and Statistics* 72 (August 1990): 531–41, found that a four-standard-deviation increase in the probability of getting cancer due to workplace health risks was associated with a 5 to 6 percent increase in quitting among employees of high-risk firms.

Finally, the size of the compensating differential for risk of injury is much smaller when workers have heterogeneous preferences than if all workers had the preferences of the risk-averse worker A. Empirical evidence has shown, for example, that individuals who signal a distaste for risk through their behavior, such as not smoking and wearing a seat belt, require (and receive) a higher compensating differential per unit of risk than workers who engage in either of the risky behaviors.[17] Individuals who engaged in the riskiest behavior category (smoking and not wearing a seat belt) received only $54,878 per lost workday injury, whereas the safest behavior category (not smoking and wearing a seat belt) received $102,552, on average.[18]

➲ SEE
Policy Application 8-1: Government Regulation of Occupational Safety and Health, p. 430.

Additional evidence of the presence of compensating wage differentials, and considerations specifically related to regulating how much risk employees should be exposed to, are evaluated in Policy Application 8-1 at the end of the chapter. The same tools developed here to derive compensating wage differentials for the risk of injury are applied in the next section to analyze the trade-off between wages and a job amenity.

The Economics of Employee Benefits

One of the most important developments in the area of compensation in recent years has been the proliferation and rapid growth in employee, or fringe, benefits. Before World War II, wage and salary workers received nearly all compensation in the form of pay for time worked. In 1929 fringe benefits or supplements amounted to only 1.4 percent of total compensation. During the war, supplements began to spread rapidly as an alternative form of compensation because firms were prevented by wage and price controls from directly raising wage rates. This trend has continued to the present time until, as shown in Table 8.2, they represented 31.96 percent of compensation in 2004.

The data in Table 8.2 also reveal the wide variety of employee benefits and their relative importance in total compensation. On average, 30 percent of the value of employee benefits paid by firms is in the form of legally required supplements. Principal among these are Social Security and unemployment insurance. The remaining 70 percent of total benefits are provided voluntarily by employers, either by unilateral decision or as a result of collective bargaining. Among the most important are paid vacations, holiday pay, life and health insurance, and pensions.

---

17 See Joni Hersch and Todd S. Pickton, "Risk-Taking Activities and Heterogeneity of Job-Risk Tradeoffs," *Journal of Risk and Insurance* 11 (December 1995): 205–17. Also see W. Kip Viscusi and Joni Hersch, "Cigarette Smokers as Job Risk Takers," *Review of Economics and Statistics* 83 (May 2001): 269–80.

18 Other research has shown that individual preferences have a lot to do with the size of the compensating differential that shift workers receive: "night owls," or those not opposed to working at night, do not receive as large a compensating wage differential. See Peter F. Kostiuk, "Compensating Differentials for Shift Work," *Journal of Political Economy* 98 (October 1990): 1054–75.

TABLE 8.2   BENEFITS IN EMPLOYEE COMPENSATION, 2004

	Dollars per Hour	Percentage of Compensation
Total compensation	**23.29**	**100.00**
Wages and salaries	16.64	71.45
Total benefits	6.65	28.55
Paid leave	1.5	6.44
Vacation	0.74	3.18
Holiday	0.52	2.23
Sick	0.18	0.77
Other	0.06	0.26
Supplemental pay	0.66	2.83
Premium pay	0.24	1.03
Nonproduction bonuses	0.06	0.26
Shift pay	0.36	1.55
Insurance	1.65	7.08
Health insurance	1.53	6.57
Retirement and savings	0.8	3.43
Defined benefit	0.37	1.59
Defined contributions	0.43	1.85
Legally required	2.01	8.63
Social security	1.12	4.81
Medicare	0.27	1.16
Federal unemployment	0.03	0.13
State unemployment	0.13	0.56
Workers compensation	0.45	1.93
Other benefits	0.04	0.17

SOURCE: Bureau of the Census, *Statistical Abstract of the United States*, 2005, Table 628.

Pensions represent a form of *deferred compensation*—compensation paid at some time after it is earned. Statistics show that employee benefits are a higher proportion of total compensation in large firms than in small ones, and in unionized firms than in nonunion ones.[19]

The total compensation per hour paid to workers could range from one extreme of zero employee benefits and all wages, to the other extreme of zero wages and all benefits. What determines the actual amount of benefits that firms will provide? This question is similar to that of how much safety firms will provide at the

---

19   See Carmen DeNavas-Walt et al., "Income, Poverty, and Health Insurance Coverage in the United States: 2003," *Current Population Reports P60-226* (August 2004) and Carl B. Barky, "Incidence Benefits Measures in the National Compensation Survey," *Monthly Labor Review* 127 (August 2004): 21–28.

FIGURE 8.7   **WAGE/FRINGE ISOPROFIT AND INDIFFERENCE CURVES**

The solid lines JK and MN in graph (a) are isoprofit curves; each represents all the combinations of the wage rate and per-hour cost of employee benefits that result in the same level of total hourly compensation cost and, thus, profit to the firm. A decrease in the relative cost of benefits would rotate the isoprofit curve from MN to the broken line GN. Shown in graph (b) are indifference curves, representing a person's willingness to substitute wages for benefits. Each curve is convex since wages and benefits are imperfect substitutes. The curve I_A is steeper than I_B, reflecting person A's greater preference for benefits, relative to person B. (Note that the indifference curves cross because they represent the preferences of two *different* individuals.)

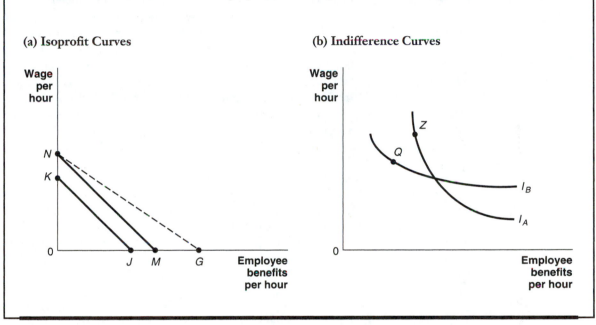

(a) Isoprofit Curves

(b) Indifference Curves

workplace. In each case, it is necessary to determine the mix between wages and some other good, whether employee benefits or increased safety. As with safety, the amount of employee benefits provided in the labor market will depend on two factors—the preferences of workers regarding the mix of wages and employee benefits, and the relative cost to firms of providing additional employee benefits.[20]

The Relative Cost of Employee Benefits   One important influence on the amount of employee benefits provided in the market is their relative cost to the employer. The central concern of the firm is to minimize the *total* compensation cost per hour

---

20   The following analysis is based on Robert S. Smith and Ronald G. Ehrenberg, "Estimating Wage–Fringe Trade-Offs: Some Data Problems," in Jack E. Triplett, ed., *The Measurement of Labor Cost* (Chicago: University of Chicago Press, 1983), 347–67.

that it pays its employees because, other things equal, the higher its compensation cost per hour, the lower its profits. This idea is illustrated in graph (a) of Figure 8.7 by the isoprofit curves JK and MN. Each isoprofit curve shows all the wage rate/employee benefit combinations that yield the same level of profit. While there are many different isoprofit curves (only two of which are shown in Figure 8.7), competition in a competitive industry will move the firm in the long run to the isoprofit curve where it just earns a normal profit. This might be the line JK.

These isoprofit curves have several properties similar to those introduced in the previous section. The first is that an isoprofit curve such as MN that lies further to the right than another such as JK implies a higher level of total compensation cost per hour (since both wages and benefits are higher) and a lower level of profit. Second, each isoprofit curve has a negative slope, reflecting the fact that higher employee benefits have to be offset by lower wages if the rate of total compensation is to remain constant. This is different from the isoprofit curves that illustrate the trade-off between wages and the risk of injury, because an increase in fringe benefits corresponds to higher cost, whereas an increase in the risk of injury corresponds (for the firm) to lower per unit labor cost. A third feature is that the steepness of an isoprofit line reflects the relative cost of employee benefits to the firm. If the cost to the firm of providing a dollar of employee benefits is the same as that of providing a dollar of wages, as might seem reasonable at first glance, the slope of the isoprofit curve would be -1.[21]

For several reasons, the relative cost of a dollar expenditure on employee benefits may be less than a dollar expenditure on additional wages. The most important is the differential treatment under the tax laws of employer expenditures for wages and employee benefits. When a firm pays a higher wage, its tax liabilities also increase, because employer contributions to Social Security and workers' compensation are calculated as fractions of total payroll. Employee benefits, on the other hand, currently are not taxed. The result is that in place of a $100 increase in salary, for example, the firm may be able to provide $110 of additional benefits for the same net increase in total compensation cost. The effect of the tax laws is to rotate each isocost line so that it has a flatter slope, as shown by the rotation of MN to the new isoprofit line GN (the broken line).

Other factors may also increase the relative attractiveness to firms of paying employee benefits in lieu of wages. Employee benefits such as pensions, health and dental plans, stock purchase options, and so on, help to bind workers to the firm, reducing costs from employee turnover. One study found, for example, that being covered by a pension increased a worker's tenure (length of time with the firm) from between 66 percent to 192 percent, depending on the size of the firm.[22] Firms

---

21 Also note that, unlike in the previous section, the isoprofit curves are not convex. This means that the first dollar of benefits provided by a firm to workers costs the same as the last dollar of benefits provided by the firm.

22 The relationship between turnover and pension coverage is much stronger in large firms. See William E. Even and David A. Macpherson, "Employer Size and Labor Turnover: The Role of Pensions," *Industrial and Labor Relations Review* 49 (July 1996): 707–28. Also see Darrell F. Parker and Sherrie L. W. Rhine, "Turnover Costs and the Wage–Fringe Mix," *Applied Economics* 23 (April 1991): 617–22, and Dan A. Black, "Family Health Benefits and Worker Turnover," Department of Economics, University of Kentucky Working Paper (April 1996).

can also structure their employee benefit plans to attract a particular type of worker. Younger workers might find liberal maternity benefits quite desirable, while older workers would be attracted by a liberal pension plan. Further, employers can often obtain significantly lower rates on employee benefits such as health insurance as a result of economies of scale in their purchase. Finally, employee benefits have an advantage over wages during periods of wage and price controls, since they are harder for government agencies to monitor and can usually be increased without violating controls programs.

While each of these considerations lowers the relative cost of employee benefits, several factors work in the opposite direction. Certain employee benefits may result in a lower level of worker productivity than if compensation were paid in the form of wages. Perhaps the best example is the greater amount of absenteeism that a firm will suffer if it provides for paid sick leave.[23] A second disadvantage of employee benefits is that they can be quite complicated to administer, especially pension and health insurance programs. Considerations such as these increase the relative cost of employee benefits and would be represented by rotating the isocost line to the left, such as from GN to MN.

The Preferences of Employees   The firm's isoprofit curve defines all the various combinations of wage rates and employee benefits that it is willing to provide. For this reason the isoprofit curve is often referred to as an "offer curve." Which combination will be chosen? The answer depends on the preferences of employees for wages versus employee benefits, as represented by the indifference curves in graph (b).[24] Point Q is one combination of wages and employee benefits, and every other point on the indifference curve I_B is another combination that is equally attractive. Similarly, every wage/benefit combination on the indifference curve I_A is equally attractive, although point Z on I_A would clearly be preferable to point Q on I_B.

Several aspects of these indifference curves are important. The first is that they are convex to the origin. This implies that wages and employee benefits are imperfect substitutes for each other; to get the worker to give up some of one, he or she has to be given ever larger increases in the other. Why might this be? From an employee's point of view, there are positive and negative aspects about both wages and employee benefits. A major advantage of wages is that they provide the worker much more flexibility in consumption—$100 of life insurance has only one use, but $100 in cash can be spent on anything the employee chooses. For young workers, an employee benefit such as life insurance may have little value at all, just as

---

23   For evidence on this see Ronald G. Ehrenberg et al., "School District Leave Policies, Teacher Absenteeism, and Student Achievement," *Journal of Human Resources* 26 (Winter 1991): 72–105.

24   Research by Michael Bucci and Robert Grant, "Employer-Sponsored Health Insurance: What's Offered; What's Chosen?" *Monthly Labor Review* (October 1995): 38–44, shows a good degree of variation in employee preferences regarding type of health insurance chosen, with 14 percent of workers with a choice electing no coverage at all. M. Kate Bundorf, "Employee Demand for Health Insurance and Employer Health Plan Choices," *Journal of Health Economics* 21 (January 2002): 65–88 finds that employer offerings of health insurance are sensitive to the preferences of their workers.

maternity benefits will be of nearly zero value to older workers. Wages also have disadvantages, however, that make employee benefits more attractive. The principal one is that wages are subject to income taxation, while compensation provided in the form of a paid vacation or a dental plan is not. The tax laws also provide an incentive for workers to save for old age through an employer-sponsored pension fund rather than personal savings from wages. Employer contributions to a pension fund are not taxed, but a worker who saves for old age from wages is taxed twice, once when the earnings are received and again on the interest earned from savings. Because wages and employee benefits have both advantages and disadvantages, workers are willing to trade some of one for more of the other. Few people would desire all of their compensation exclusively in the form of wages or employee benefits, however, and this preference gives the indifference curves in Figure 8.7 their convex shape.[25]

The second feature of the indifference curves in Figure 8.7 is that I_A is steeper than I_B. The slope of an indifference curve measures the rate at which a person is willing to trade employee benefits for wages. The indifference curve I_B is relatively flat, meaning that the worker will give up quite a bit of employee benefits to obtain additional wages. The steeper slope of I_A, on the other hand, implies that the worker values employee benefits more highly—to get him or her to give up the same amount of employee benefits as before, the increase in wages must be much greater. The reason for this is again related to the tax laws. An increase in income, such as occurs with the movement from point Q to point Z, pushes the worker into a higher marginal income tax bracket. Since every dollar of compensation in the form of wages now has a bigger tax bite taken out of it, employee benefits become relatively more attractive, a fact reflected in the steeper slope of I_A.

The Equilibrium Wage/Benefit Mix   Figure 8.8 shows the employer's isoprofit or offer curve JK together with two indifference curves, I_A for person A and I_B for person B. The optimal combination for the worker is determined by the tangency point between the indifference curve and the offer curve. For person A, the utility-maximizing wage/benefit combination is W_Z, F_Z (point Z), and for person B it is W_Q, F_Q (point Q). The reason person A chooses a compensation package with a higher proportion of employee benefits reflects a difference in preferences. This indifference curve is steeper than person B's, possibly because he or she is in a higher tax bracket or because the particular type of employee benefits is highly valued.

If the firm allows each employee to choose the desired wage/benefit package from the offer curve, no matter how diverse preferences are, each worker will be

---

25   The elasticity of substitution between wages and benefits has been calculated as between 1.7 and 3.5, suggesting that the two components of compensation are viewed by workers as close (but not perfect) substitutes. See Stephen Woodbury, "Substitution between Wage and Nonwage Benefits," *American Economic Review* 73, no. 1 (March 1983): 166–82. More recent analysis of the trade-off between pensions and wages is consistent with these earlier findings. See Edward Montgomery, Kathryn Shaw, and Mary Ellen Benedict, "Pensions and Wages: An Hedonic Price Theory Approach," *International Economic Review* 33 (February 1992): 111–28.

FIGURE 8.8   THE EQUILIBRIUM COMBINATION OF WAGES AND BENEFITS

Given the isoprofit or "offer" curve JK, person A would choose the wage/benefit combination $W_Z F_Z$ (point Z). Although any one firm may offer only one combination, such as $W_Z F_Z$, person B could nevertheless obtain the desired wage/benefit combination by quitting that firm and seeking employment at another firm that offers $W_Q F_Q$.

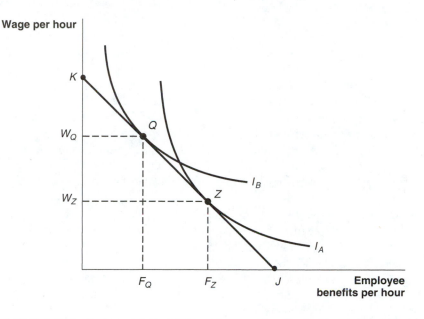

able to reach his or her equilibrium point. In general, however, most firms do not provide complete freedom of choice. Many smaller companies offer only one fixed wage/benefit package, while larger companies often provide several options for employees. (This situation is changing, however, as discussed in the accompanying In the News section.) The result is that some workers in the firm are forced to consume either a larger or smaller amount of employee benefits than they desire. If the firm chose the combination (W_Z, F_Z), for example, person B (possibly a young, unmarried person) would feel dissatisfied because he or she would prefer fewer benefits such as pensions and life insurance, but more wages. Can person B obtain the desired wage/benefit package? The answer is yes, and the method is to quit and seek employment in a firm that does offer the desired wage/benefit mix. Thus, given a diversity among firms, workers can still obtain the combination of wages and benefits they prefer. This outcome is easily represented in Figure 8.8. Instead of JK being the offer curve of one firm, assume it is the offer curve for every

Flexible Benefit Plans Grow in Popularity among Both Workers and Employers

Business firms have traditionally offered their employees a certain wage or salary and a fixed package of fringe benefits such as a company-sponsored health insurance plan, a certain number of vacation days, and so on. The traditional approach has been giving way, however, to a new type of fringe benefit package called the "flexible benefit plan." Rather than one fixed package of benefits paid by the company, a flexible benefit plan provides each employee with an amount of money with which to purchase the mix of fringe benefits desired. In some cases, the employees can even choose to take the money in the form of additional cash compensation rather than fringe benefits.

Flexible benefit plans first emerged in the late 1970s after Congress legalized them. Their popularity did not really take off until 1984, however, when the Internal Revenue Service clarified their tax status. In 1999 (the last year for which BLS statistics are available), 28 percent of workers in private industry were provided benefit plans that allowed choice over the mix and level of fringe benefits. This percentage is as high as 62 percent of workers in very large firms. White-collar workers were from 50 to 100 percent

more likely to be given choice over blue-collar workers. A survey of high-tech firms conducted in 2004 illustrates that there is a wide variety of types of flexible benefits offered by employers. Roughly 30 percent of high-tech firms offered full cafeteria-style benefit plans, and 90 to 100 percent of employers offer dependent care and medical expense reimbursement plans.

Why have flexible benefit plans grown in popularity? The reason appears to be that they offer significant advantages to both firms and workers over the traditional fixed package approach. Because of the growing heterogeneity of the workforce, firms have found it increasingly difficult to structure benefit packages that suit the needs and preferences of their employees. The traditional benefit plan was typically designed for a male wage earner with a family at home, while today the workforce is increasingly composed of people who are part of dual-earner couples with no children, are single parents, or are unmarried men. By offering flexible benefit plans, therefore, firms have a much better opportunity to attract and keep workers from diverse socioeconomic backgrounds. Employees gain, too, because

firm in the market. (In a competitive market this will be the case since competition forces each firm to pay the same level of total compensation.) The isoprofit line shows that one firm offers (W_Z, F_Z) and another offers (W_Q, F_Q). Workers with the preferences of person A will seek employment at the former; workers with the preferences of person B will seek employment at the latter.

Implications Two important predictions flow from this analysis. The first is that among equally productive workers in a competitive market, an inverse relationship should hold between the wages and employee benefits they receive. This is simply a restatement of the theory of compensating differentials—jobs that provide large employee benefits should pay lower wages (and vice versa) if the total of advantages and disadvantages is to balance out. This prediction has not, however, always found

continued

each can structure a package of benefits that more closely meets their individual needs.

A second important advantage of flexible benefit plans from the perspective of business firms is that they often yield large cost savings. In traditional benefit plans employees may bear up to 20 percent of some health-care costs, but usually only up to some specified amount. When insurance premiums rise sharply, as they have in recent years, the employer pays most of the increase. Many flexible plans function differently, however. Rather than defining the benefits it will pay for, the company states how much it will contribute toward the cost of benefits. It then allocates money to employees, who buy the benefits they want. The result is that a much larger part of the inflation in benefit costs is shifted onto employees. Firms have also used the introduction of flexible benefit plans as opportunities to raise premiums or deductible levels, further reducing their benefit costs.

Despite the greater expense, most employees say they prefer to stay with a flexible benefit plan. One important advantage from their perspective is that a flex plan spreads the cost of child care or medical expenses more equitably among the people in the company. Under the traditional system, where every worker receives the same medical coverage, workers who are young or unmarried are the least likely to use the benefit and, in effect, are subsidizing heavier users such as older employees or those with families. Under a flex plan, however, an employee with a family of four might pay $1,000 a year for medical and dental benefits while a single person would be charged only $350. Likewise, under a flex plan, childless employees would no longer have to pay for a benefit such as child care for which they have no use.

SOURCES: Del Jones, "Vacation as a Commodity: Sell It or Buy More," *USA Today* (17 July 1998): B1; "Flexible Programs Fill Needs of Many Employees," *Detroit News* (22 December 1997): F8; Steven Ginsberg, "In Today's Quest for Compensation, Money Isn't Everything; Companies Find That Flexible Benefits, Stocks, and Other Alternatives to Pay Raises Can Keep Employee Morale Up, Expenses Down," *Washington Post* (29 June 1997): H05; and Anonymous, "IRS Proposes Rules to Make 'Cafeteria' Plans Easier," *Wall Street Journal* (23 March 2000): A12; Anonymous, "Employers Choose Flexibility," *Investment Week* (11 August 2003); John B. Wollenberg, "Tax Benefits of Cafeteria Plans," *The Tax Advisor* (10 October 2004): 607; and Amy Schurr, "Flexible Benefit Plans," *NetworkWorldInfusion* (21 October 2004), http://www.nwfusion.com/newsletters/itlead/2004/1018itlead2.html.

consistent empirical support. Several case studies in the 1950s concluded that wages and employee benefits were positively related; the firms that paid the highest wage in the local labor market also offered the most employee benefits.[26] This conclusion is open to criticism, since these studies did not control for differences in worker productivity; it could be that the workers receiving more of both wages and benefits were also more productive because of greater skills or education. More recent studies have had some success in uncovering the predicted wage/benefit trade-off by controlling for productivity and job characteristics. One study estimated that a one-dollar increase in pension benefits will lower wages by 22 to

---

26   Lloyd G. Reynolds, *The Structure of Labor Markets* (New York: Harper and Row, 1951).

53 cents, depending on the size of the firm.[27] Not only does this confirm the trade-off between a benefit provision and workers' wages, it also indicates that, for pensions, that trade-off is less than one to one. In other words, firms can provide a dollar of pension coverage for less than a full dollar in expenses. A second study finds that women who are provided health benefits by their employer earned about 20 percent less than women not provided health insurance.[28]

A second prediction is that in the long run, firms in a competitive market will provide the employee benefit package that workers desire without any need for government intervention. An interesting illustration of this prediction concerns maternity leave. A survey conducted in 1984 revealed that among the 1,500 largest industrial and financial companies only 38 percent guaranteed women their jobs back if they took a leave of absence for childbirth.[29] Most smaller establishments made no provision at all. Many argued that the lack of maternity leave imposed an unfair burden on working women. As one person stated it, getting pregnant often meant looking for a new job.

Assuming more women desired maternity leave than could obtain it at their places of work, was government legislation needed? Asked to comment on this issue, a spokesperson for the Merchants and Manufacturers Association said no, that the free market would ultimately solve the problem. In his words, "Why don't women go to work for the companies with the good maternity leave policies? If companies find they can't attract the workers they need without changing their policies, they'll change them." Is he right? If the labor market is competitive (or reasonably close to it), his argument is correct, with a few important qualifications.[30] This is illustrated in Figure 8.9.

Assume that the current wage/employee benefit combination offered by all firms in the market is W_Q, F_Q (point Q), where F_Q does not include maternity leave benefits. Women workers are dissatisfied with this combination because it puts them on a lower indifference curve, I'_A than if the firm would choose point Z, where the wage is lower at W_Z but benefits have been increased to F_Z by adding maternity leave benefits. Do firms have any incentive to change their wage/employee benefit combination from W_Q, F_Q to W_Z, F_Z? The answer is clearly yes. Some firm, call it firm X, could offer a wage/employee benefit combination shown as point T that did contain maternity leave benefits. Since point T is on a higher indifference curve than point Q, women workers would quit their current employers and seek work at firm X, obtaining maternity leave benefits at the expense of a lower wage. Firm X would also benefit because point T puts it on a higher isoprofit

27   Edward Montgomery and Kathryn Shaw, "Pensions and Wage Premia," *Economic Inquiry* 35 (July 1997): 510–22.

28   Craig A. Olson, "Do Workers Accept Lower Wages in Exchange for Health Benefits?" *Journal of Labor Economics* 20 No. 2 (2002): S91–S114.

29   "Maternity Leave: Is It Leave Indeed?" *New York Times* (July 22, 1984): F1, 23. In 1978 Congress passed the Pregnancy Discrimination Act. It requires that women affected by pregnancy or childbirth be treated the same as other employees with respect to eligibility for fringe benefits such as disability pay. The law did not require that a firm either provide maternity leave or hire a woman back if she quits to have a child.

30   There is evidence that workers will choose employers somewhat based on the type of health insurance provided. See Alan Monheit and Jessica Vistnes, "Health Insurance Availability at the Workplace: How Important Are Worker Preferences?" *Journal of Human Resources* 34 (Fall 1999): 770–85.

FIGURE 8.9   THE PROVISION OF MATERNITY LEAVE BENEFITS

If firms offer a wage/benefit combination of $W_Q F_Q$ (point Q) but workers desire $W_Z F_Z$ (point Z), market forces will be set off that cause firms to voluntarily change to $W_Z F_Z$. For example, a firm could offer the wage/benefit combination at point T. Workers would prefer point T to point Q since point T is on a higher indifference curve, while the firm would benefit since its profits are higher relative to firms that offer a wage/benefit package at point Q. To avoid losing their workers and to achieve a lower labor cost, therefore, firms at point Q would be induced to adopt the wage/benefit package at point T. This process would repeat itself until workers obtained the equilibrium combination $W_Z F_Z$ (point Z).

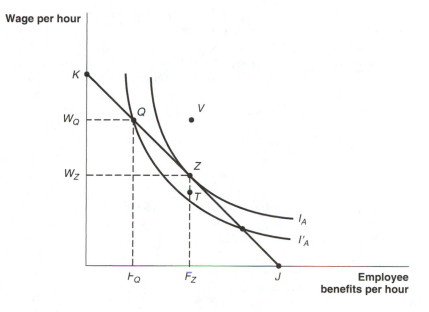

curve (in terms of dollars of profit) than its rivals. (A similar process would eventually force firm X to move from point T to point Z.) Just as the spokesperson for the Merchants and Manufacturers Association claimed, therefore, competitive pressures would eventually induce those firms without maternity leave benefits to add them, both to keep their workforces and because not doing so puts them at a profit disadvantage relative to firms that do.[31]

---

31   The First Atlanta Bank Corporation in Atlanta established a day-care program for its employees in 1987. According to a spokesperson for the bank, "The rationale for the company getting involved is that it solves a problem. . . . By meeting the needs of employees and improving the work environment, productivity would increase and they would want to stay with us." Quoted in "Day Care: A Key Concern," *Atlanta Journal* (November 9, 1987): C1, 8. Also see Madlen Read, "Companies Warm to Working Moms: Daycare, Health Facilities Lift Qualities of Life," *The Oakland Tribune* (22 September 2004).

This prediction requires a few qualifications. First, the labor market must be competitive, and workers must be well informed and able to move from one job to another without too much cost and difficulty. Second, to obtain maternity leave benefits, women have to be willing to work for a lower wage, such as W_Z in Figure 8.9. Some firms in sheltered product markets that earn above-normal profits could possibly continue to pay W_Q but also provide maternity leave benefits and fringes of F_Q (point V). While from the perspective of women workers this would be the most desirable outcome, firms in a competitive industry could not do so because they would eventually be driven out of business by their lower-cost rivals. A final difficulty is that firms that do offer the wage/employee benefit combination (W_Z, F_Z) may find that they lose their male employees. Since men do not directly benefit from maternity leave plans, they would desire to work at firms that offer fewer benefits but higher wages, such as (W_Q, F_Q). If firms could offer one wage/employee benefit combination to men and another to women, this problem could be surmounted. As it is, the Pregnancy Discrimination Act of 1978, as well as various equal pay laws, required that men and women be treated equally with respect to wage rates and types of employee benefits.

Although the number of companies offering unpaid maternity leave benefits did increase noticeably from the early 1980s to the early 1990s, as of 1991 it was still the case that only slightly more than one-third of full-time employed women in medium to large firms were covered by this benefit. (Only 2 percent were covered by plans that provided paid maternity leave.) On the belief that more rapid progress was required, one of the first legislative acts of the Clinton administration was passage of the **Family and Medical Leave Act of 1993.** It requires private employers of 50 or more employees to provide eligible employees (those employed at least one year who worked 1,250 or more hours) with up to 12 weeks of unpaid leave following the birth of a child, their own serious illnesses, or the illness of a child, spouse, or parent. As a result of this legislation, medium and large firms report that 93 percent of their employees have access to unpaid maternity leave. However, still only 2 percent of all workers are covered by *paid* maternity leave.

Occupational Licensing

It has been shown in this chapter that market forces lead to a distinct structure of occupational wage rates in the form of compensating differentials. As Adam Smith emphasized, however, occupational wage rates are also influenced by institutional forces. One institutional force that affects the structure of occupational earnings is unionism. As will be seen in Chapter 12, unions tend to follow wage policies that compress the wage differential between skilled and unskilled production workers and between white-collar and blue-collar workers, reducing the dispersion in occupational earnings. A second institutional influence on the structure of occupational earnings is government policies that either promote or restrict the supply of labor to particular occupations. This section examines one type of such a policy—occupational licensing laws.

Who Is Licensed?

The number of occupations that are licensed grew substantially from approximately 70 in the 1950s to over 700 in the latter half of the 1990s.[32] In 1996, for example, the *Professional and Occupational Licensing Directory* detailed licensing requirements in all 50 states for over 700 occupations covering over 1,040 job titles.[33] Licensed occupations include accountants, architects, barbers, dentists, funeral directors, nurses, physicians, private detectives, and used-car dealers, among others. The particular occupations that are licensed and the requirements for licensing vary from state to state. Within each state, the common practice is to create a licensing board for the occupation that administers written examinations, levies licensing fees, and sets minimum standards with regard to age, education, training, "moral character," and state residency. To obtain a barbering license in Arizona, for example, the applicant must be at least 16 years of age, have at least a tenth-grade education, pass written and practical exams, pay a $30 license fee, and pay a $75 examination fee. If the applicant is licensed in one of the 24 states with which Arizona has reciprocity agreements, he or she must pay $150 to obtain a license.[34] Many other states have additional requirements for barbers such as formal training in an accredited barber school.

Each licensing board is composed of anywhere from 3 to 12 members who are themselves licensed practitioners in the field. To become a member of a state medical board, for example, a person must typically have an MD degree, live in the state, and be nominated by the state medical association. While this practice ensures that board members are knowledgeable about the occupation, it also leads to an obvious conflict of interest, since the occupation is given considerable power to regulate itself.

The Benefits and Costs of Licensing

Occupational licensing confers both benefits and costs on society.[35] On the benefit side, the basic rationale for licensing is protection of the consumer. Three ways have been suggested in which consumers benefit from licensing. The first stems from the difficulty consumers have in differentiating the quality of the service and the competency of the practitioner, particularly when the service is infrequently

---

32   See Morris Kleiner, Robert Gay, and Karen Greene, "Barriers to Labor Migration: The Case of Occupational Licensing," *Industrial Relations* 21, no. 3 (Fall 1982): 383 for trends up to the late 1970s.

33   David P. Bianco, ed., *Professional and Occupational Licensing Directory*, 2d ed. (Detroit, Mich.: Gale Research, 1996).

34   Ibid., p. 170.

35   See Simon Rottenberg, "The Economics of Occupational Licensing," in National Bureau of Economic Research, *Aspects of Labor Economics* (Princeton, N.J.: Princeton University Press, 1962), 3–20, Morris M. Kleiner, "Occupational Licensing," *Journal of Economic Perspectives* 14 (Fall 2000): 189–202; and Marc T. Law and Sukkoo Kim, "Specialization and Regulation: The Rise of Professionals and the Emergence of Occupational Licensing Regulation," *NBER Working Paper No. 10467* (August 2004).

used (funeral services) or highly technical (medicine). A second is that even if consumers know the substandard quality of service provided, their purchase of it may harm others. This might occur if an epidemic spread as a result of the malfeasance of a poorly trained doctor to whom a patient had gone in order to save money. A third is that individuals may systematically underestimate the risks to themselves from purchasing low-quality services and, thus, society should protect the individual from such errors of judgment.

Occupational licensing also entails economic costs by raising prices and wage rates in the occupation and reducing employment. This is illustrated in Figure 8.10. Before the occupation is licensed, the equilibrium wage is W_1 and the level of employment is L_1, determined by the intersection of the demand curve D_1 and the supply curve S_1 (point A). The effect of licensing is to raise the standards

---

FIGURE 8.10   **THE EFFECT OF OCCUPATIONAL LICENSING ON WAGES AND EMPLOYMENT**

Before the enactment of occupational licensing, the wage in the labor market is W_1 and employment is L_1 (point A). With licensing, entry into the occupation is restricted, shifting the supply curve from S_1 to S_2. The effect of licensing, therefore, is to raise the wage to W_2 but to reduce employment to L_2 (point B).

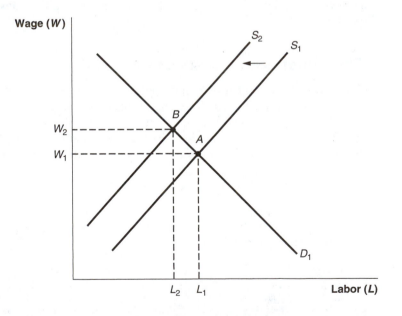

that prospective entrants into the occupation must meet. The licensing board may require two years of college or apprenticeship training, or alternatively, it might make the licensing examination more difficult to pass. All of these changes raise the costs of entry into the occupation and reduce the financial rate of return. Some individuals, as a consequence, will no longer find the occupation an attractive employment and will seek work elsewhere. As a result, the supply curve shifts to the left, from S_1 to S_2. At the new equilibrium (point B), the wage rate is now higher at W_2, but the level of employment has fallen to L_2. Although not directly shown in Figure 8.10, an additional impact is the higher price consumers pay for a reduced volume of services.[36] One study finds that tougher licensing standards for dentists does raise prices but does not improve dental outcomes of patients, suggesting the costs of licensing may be exceeding the benefits in this case.[37]

Occupational Licensing as a Source of Monopoly Rents

The higher product price and lower amount of employment and production that arise from licensing may be a reasonable trade-off for increased consumer protection. From at least the time of Adam Smith, however, many economists have had the deep-seated belief that the real purpose of occupational licensing is not protection of the consumer, but rather protection of the business interests of the practitioners of the occupation. Occupational licensing laws erect a barrier to entry that restricts the entrance of new persons into the occupation, leading to higher earnings for those already practicing the employment.[38] These higher earnings are what economists call a **monopoly rent**—a wage that is artificially higher than the competitive level because of a restriction on the supply of labor or from some other form of market power. In at least three ways, occupational licensing can lead to monopoly rents for the practitioners of the occupation.

Raising Minimum Standards Occupational licensing can lead to monopoly rents by raising standards for new entrants into the occupation, but not for existing members. This is typically done by increasing the educational requirements or

---

36   In addition, one article points out that these barriers to entry exist in many low-skilled occupations, such as taxi driving and laundry work, seriously limiting the options of welfare recipients trying to transition to the workforce. See Thomas W. Hazlett and Jennifer L. Fearing, "Occupational Licensing and the Transition from Welfare to Work," *Journal of Labor Research* 19 (Spring 1998): 277–94.

37   Morris M. Kleiner and Robert T. Kurdle, "Does Regulation Affect Economic Outcomes? The Case of Dentistry," *Journal of Law and Economics* 43 (October 2000): 547–82.

38   The state of Georgia issued 341,471 licenses to professionals and tradespeople between July 1977 and June 1998. (There were other professional organizations, such as the Georgia Bar Association, which issued additional licenses.) During this same time period, only 1,419 sanctions were issued (0.4 percent of the total licenses issued). In addition, only a small fraction of those sanctions resulted in a license being revoked. One newspaper editorial suggests that the licensing boards in Georgia are so ineffective (they do nothing but "keep out competition") that many should be disbanded. See "Too Many Boards," *Atlanta Journal* (20 January 1998): A6.

training period required of new practitioners, but exempting existing practitioners through a grandfather clause. For new entrants, the higher wage of W_2 (in Figure 8.10) just offsets the higher costs of entry, and thus the rate of return to investing in the occupation remains at a competitive level. Existing practitioners, however, earn a higher than competitive return because the increase in licensing standards raises the wage they can earn from W_1 to W_2, while at the same time they are exempted from the increase in costs imposed on new entrants.[39]

Restrictions on Interstate Mobility A second way in which licensing can lead to monopoly rents is by limiting interstate mobility of workers through **nonreciprocity clauses.** A nonreciprocity clause means that the licensing board in one state refuses to allow a person to practice with a license granted in a different state. A lawyer or teacher certified to practice in state A, for example, may not practice in state B until passing its bar exam or fulfilling its teacher certification requirements. The effect of nonreciprocity clauses is to raise the costs of entry into the occupation for nonresidents of the state and protect the incomes of existing practitioners from the full brunt of competition. One study of dentists found, for example, that the mean income of dentists was 12 to 15 percent higher in nonreciprocity states.[40]

Restrictions on Training A third way in which occupational licensing can lead to monopoly rents for practitioners is by limiting the supply of new entrants through restrictions on the availability of training and education. For a number of occupations, such as physician or lawyer, one of the licensing requirements in many states is that the applicant must have graduated from a school accredited by the professional organization that represents the occupation, such as the American Medical Association (AMA) or American Bar Association (ABA). Opponents of occupational licensing argue that these professional organizations consciously restrict the number of accredited schools in order to limit the supply of new entrants into the occupations. Milton and Rose Friedman, for example, have called the AMA "one of the most successful unions in the country" on account of its alleged ability to control the supply of doctors.[41] In a classic study, Milton Friedman and fellow

---

39   One study found that a 1 percent decrease in the pass rate of the dental examination required to practice dentistry (implying a more difficult exam) resulted in a decrease of between 0.19 and 0.32 percent in the number of new dental enrollees who plan to practice dentistry in the state. A low pass rate is particularly costly since most qualifying dental exams are offered at most twice a year. See Morris M. Kleiner and Robert T. Kurdle, "Do Tougher Licensing Provisions Limit Occupational Entry? The Case of Dentistry," *NBER Working Paper #3984* (February 1992), and Kleiner and Kurdle, "Does Regulation Affect Economic Outcomes? The Case of Dentistry." A study of midwifery found that licensing that profession does more to restrict the supply of midwives than it does to raise quality; see A. Frank Adams, III, et al., "Occupational Licensing of a Credence Good: The Regulation of Midwifery," *Southern Economic Journal* 69 (January 2003): 695–75.

40   Lawrence Shepherd, "Licensing Restrictions and the Cost of Dental Care," *Journal of Law and Economics* 21, no. 1 (April 1978): 187–201. Adriana Kugler and Robert Sauer, "Doctors Without Borders: The Returns to an Occupational License for Soviet Immigrant Physicians in Israel," *IZA Discussion Paper No. 634* (November 2002) find that relicensing requirements (or nonreciprocity provisions) in Israel generate significant positive rents for physicians.

41   Milton Friedman and Rose Friedman, *Free to Choose* (New York: Harcourt Brace Jovanovich, 1980), 231.

Nobel laureate Simon Kuznets concluded that 16.5 percent of the income of doctors in the 1930s was, on average, due to barriers to entry into the profession.[42] A later study found little evidence of monopoly rents in doctors' incomes, pointing to a diminution over time in the restrictive policies of the AMA.[43] An additional study has found that the ineffectiveness of state bar associations to restrict the supply of lawyers in recent years has eliminated any price effect of having those restrictions in place.[44]

Occupational Attainment and Earnings of Men and Women

Of all the earnings differentials in the labor market, probably none has stimulated as much debate and research in the last couple of decades as the large disparity in earnings between men and women workers. In 2004, for example, the median usual weekly earnings of women who were full-time wage and salary workers were only 79.4 percent of the earnings of men.

The discussion of the occupational earnings data in Table 8.1 identified two separate reasons for this earnings differential. One was the unequal distribution of men and women *among* occupations; men are proportionately overrepresented in high-wage professional, managerial, and craft occupations, while women are over-represented in low-wage clerical and service occupations. A second reason is that even *within* a given occupation, women tend to earn less than men. As an illustration of how, in addition to market forces, social forces can contribute to wage differentials, this section explores each of these observations in more detail, beginning with the issue of unequal occupational attainment.

Gender Differences in Occupational Attainment

A portion of the earnings gap between men and women is attributable to the fact that the majority of women are employed in a fairly narrow set of low-wage, female-dominated occupations while a significant number of men are employed in a different set of male-dominated, high-wage occupations. In 2004, 65 percent of women workers were employed in six occupational categories: nurses and health technologists, elementary and secondary school teachers, salesclerks in retail trade, administrative support, apparel and textile workers, and service workers (for example,

---

42   Milton Friedman and Simon Kuznets, *Income from Independent Professional Practice* (New York: National Bureau of Economic Research, 1945). Also see Barry J. Seldon et al., "Market Power among Physicians in the U.S., 1983–1991," *Quarterly Review of Economics and Finance* 38 (1998): 799–824, for further evidence on this point.

43   Keith B. Leffler, "Physician Licenses: Competition and Monopoly in American Medicine," *Journal of Law and Economics* 21, no. 1 (April 1978): 165–86.

44   Dean Lueck, Reed Olsen, and Michael Ransom, "Market and Regulatory Forces in the Pricing of Legal Services," *Journal of Regulatory Economics* 7 (January 1995): 63–83.

waitresses, dental assistants, and cleaning workers). Some occupations, such as secretary, consist of nearly all women (97 percent of secretaries are women). This division of the occupational structure into "female" occupations and "male" occupations is generally referred to as **occupational segregation,** although some economists prefer the less pejorative term "occupational concentration."[45]

Studies of occupational segregation have found that until the early 1970s the division of jobs in the labor market into male and female occupations was both quite pervasive and subject to little change over time. A study by Mary King, for example, found that the extent of occupational segregation between men and women declined between 1940 and 1950, yet barely changed at all between 1950 and 1970 (see Appendix 8A).[46] After 1970, however, and continuing to the present time, the degree of occupational segregation between men and women has declined rather noticeably. [The same study also found that occupational segregation between blacks and whites started its most marked decline between 1960 and 1970, the time period during which affirmative action and other antidiscrimination laws went into effect.] The decline in occupational segregation by gender is reflected in the data in Table 8.3. Table 8.3 shows the percentage of the workforce that was female in 1960, 1970, 1980, 1990, 2000, and 2004 in 12 traditionally male occupations and 9 traditionally female occupations. The male occupations include a wide range of professions such as lawyer, physician, and engineer; the broad span of management occupations; craft occupations such as carpenter and auto mechanic; and selected service occupations such as police protection. Female occupations are centered in the service, clerical, health, and teaching occupations, as noted previously.

Several trends stand out in the data in Table 8.3. First, women continue to represent a minority in all the traditionally male occupations. It is also evident that particularly in the 1980s and 1990s a growing number of women were entering many of these male fields, particularly in white-collar professional and managerial occupations. In 1960, only 3.4 percent of women were lawyers; by 2004 this had risen to 33.5 percent. In addition, women made up nearly half the number of

---

45 Occupational segregation also exists on the basis of race, although the degree of concentration of blacks and whites in different occupations is less pronounced than for men and women. This subject is illustrated in the appendix to this chapter. In addition, evidence exists to suggest that systematic segregation of male and female workers occurs in as narrow a labor market as the plant level within the manufacturing industry. See William J. Carrington and Kenneth R. Troske, "Sex Segregation in U.S. Manufacturing," *Industrial and Labor Relations Review* 51 (April 1998): 445–64, and Kimberly Bayard et al., "New Evidence on Sex Segregation and Sex Differences in Wages from Matched Employee–Employer Data," *Journal of Labor Economics* 21 (October 2003): 882–922. A study comparing occupational segregation in the United States with occupational segregation in Europe finds that the level of segregation for college graduates is greater in Europe than in the United States and that this contributes to observed earnings differentials; see Juan Jose Dolado et al., "Recent Trends on Occupational Segregation by Gender: A Look across the Atlantic," CEPR *Discussion Paper No. 3421* (June 2002).

46 Mary C. King, "Occupational Segregation by Race and Sex, 1940–88," *Monthly Labor Review* 115 (April 1992): 30–37. The appendix to this chapter provides details of how Mary King calculated the degree of segregation. Francine D. Blau et al., "Continuing Progress? Trends in Occupational Segregation in the United States over the 1970s and 1980s," *Feminist Economics* 4 (Fall 1998): 29–71, find the same results as reported by King. Also see Dawn M. Baunach, "Trends in Occupational Segregation and Inequality, 1950–1990." *Social Science Research* 31 (2002): 77–98.

TABLE 8.3 **PERCENTAGE OF FEMALE WORKERS IN TRADITIONALLY MALE AND FEMALE OCCUPATIONS IN 1960, 1970, 1980, 1990, 2001, 2004**

Traditionally Male Occupations

Occupation	Percent Female						
	1960	1970	1980	1990	2000	2001	2004
Engineers	0.8	1.7	4.5	8.0	9.7	9.7	13.2
Lawyers	3.4	4.8	13.6	26.9	34.1	34.1	33.5
Physicians	6.7	8.3	17.4	25.6	31.2	32.6	31.2
Economists	13.8	11.4	29.3	40.4	48.2	54.2	—
Clergy	2.2	2.9	5.8	8.2	13.4	11.2	13.3
Insurance agents	10	17.6	25.6	38.9	47.4	54.0	52.7
Managers and administrators	14.5	16.7	30.2	42.7	47.0	47.1	44.7
Carpenters	0.3	1.3	1.6	1.3	0.6	1.5	1.8
Auto mechanics	0.3	1.4	1.2	0.5	0.8	1.2	1.6
Telephone line installers	—	1.2	5	8.2	12.5	12.6	5.2
Bus drivers	9.8	28.3	45.8	39.4	45.1	41.3	41.5
Truck drivers	0.5	1.5	3.2	3.0	3.7	4.3	7.6
Police and detectives	2.8	3.8	7.8	13.5	14.9	17.5	12.7

Traditionally Female Occupations

Occupation	Percent Female						
	1960	1970	1980	1990	2000	2001	2004
Registered nurses	97.5	97.4	93.5	93.5	92.3	91.0	91.7
Librarians	85.5	81.5	84.2	84.2	85.5	83.0	85.5
Elem. Schoolteachers	72.7	69.3	71.3	71.3	74.4	73.1	80.3
Bank tellers	69.3	86.3	92.7	92.7	90.8	89.1	88
Secretaries	97.2	97.7	99.1	99.1	99.0	98.6	96.7
Typists	95	94.2	95.1	95.1	96.1	95.4	93.3
Sewing machine operators	96.8	96.5	88.2	88.2	79.0	72.9	76.9
Dental assistants	—	97.9	99.1	99.1	96.4	97.7	96.5
Child care workers	—	93.1	98.6	98.6	98.5	97.8	93.7

SOURCE: Bureau of the Census, *Census of the Population* (Washington, D.C.: GPO, 1960, 1970, 1980); and Bureau of Labor Statistics, *Employment and Earnings* (January 2005), Table 39.

insurance agents in 2004. Among male-dominated blue-collar occupations such as auto mechanic and carpenter, however, the proportion of women changed only very slightly.

A second trend in the data in Table 8.3 concerns the change over time in the gender composition of the nine traditionally female occupations. While increasing numbers of women are entering male occupations, there are few signs of a similar movement of men into female occupations (with the exception of sewing machine operators). The proportion of women in seven of the nine female occupations remained relatively stable between 1960 and 2004; one occupation (bank tellers), saw a shift over time toward more exclusive employment of females, and another occupation, sewing machine operators, has become less female-dominated.

➡ SEE

Empirical Evidence 8-2: Occupational Segregation and Male/Female Earnings Differentials, p. 438.

Concern over this stability in the concentration of women in certain occupations lies in the fact that this concentration typically occurs in the lower-paying occupations. The empirical relationship between the concentration of women in an occupation and the earnings in that occupation is explored in Empirical Evidence 8-2.

Reasons for Occupational Segregation

Economists and other social scientists have advanced three explanations for the pattern of occupational segregation in the labor market.[47] These explanations focus on the roles of market, institutional, and sociological forces in shaping the occupational choice of workers and the hiring decisions of firms.

The Discontinuous Pattern of Female Participation   The first explanation for occupational segregation rests on the differences in the continuity of labor force attachment of men and women. As discussed in Chapter 7, women are likely, on average, to have more frequent and longer interruptions in their life cycle pattern of labor force participation. This fact influences occupational attainment as it affects both women's choices of occupation and firms' decisions on whom to hire.

As one consequence of a career interruption, the earnings power of a person's human capital is diminished, partly because skills and training depreciate or atrophy with continued nonparticipation in the labor force, and partly because the worker will lose the value of specific on-the-job training should he or she not return to the same employer. Solomon Polachek has pointed out in several studies the implication that women, in anticipation of one or more future periods of nonparticipation, have an economic incentive to purposely choose occupations in which the earnings loss on their human capital is the smallest.[48] According to Polachek, these occupations are likely to be exactly the ones where women are disproportionately employed, such as nurse, schoolteacher, and secretary. These

---

[47]   For a general review, see Richard Anker, "Theories of Occupational Segregation by Sex: An Overview," *International Labour Review* 136 (Autumn 1997): 315–39.

[48]   Solomon W. Polachek, "Occupational Self-Selection: A Human Capital Approach to Sex Differences in Occupational Structure," *Review of Economics and Statistics* 63 (February 1981): 60–69.

occupations share the common characteristic that the skills and training are primarily general in nature, training ladders are relatively short, and job skills do not become obsolete for a lengthy period of time.

For a young man who plans to work continuously for 45 years, an occupation such as dental hygienist or elementary school teacher may be quite unattractive since it will promise limited earnings growth and meager room for advancement. To a young woman who anticipates one or several spells out of the labor force, these vices, Polachek argues, become virtues that attract her to choose these occupations. Because the skills and training required to be a nurse or secretary are general in nature, they allow her to more easily switch employers, say, after spending two years out of the labor force to raise children or because of her husband's job transfer to a different city. Short training ladders mean that a person who interrupts a career can reenter the occupation at close to the earnings and responsibility level at which he or she left. Finally, the fact that the job skills needed to be a nurse or schoolteacher do not atrophy very rapidly results in a smaller decline in the worker's earnings power during a stay out of the workforce.

One study attributes the growth (as observed in Table 8.3) of women in the traditionally male job of bank teller to the changing character of that job. The job of bank teller used to be an entry point of further advancement within the bank. As the occupation has been transformed to one with generic skills and virtually no training ladder, men exited and more women entered.[49]

The pattern of occupational attainment is also influenced on the demand side by whom business firms choose to hire into particular jobs. Even if a woman desires to be a financial analyst or an aircraft mechanic, she will not actually become one until a bank or airline hires her. Why might a person's gender influence a company's hiring decision? Human capital theory again provides an answer. In occupations that require a heavy investment by the firm in specific on-the-job training, the employer has a strong economic incentive to select job candidates who will remain with the firm for a considerable time.[50] Given the greater propensity of women to interrupt their careers, employers may rationally decide to hire only men as financial analysts and aircraft mechanics, fearing that women, once trained, might soon quit for family reasons.[51] These employers might willingly hire women into clerical or unskilled production work however, since the job skills are primarily general in nature and the

---

49   Myra H. Strober and Carolyn L. Arnold, "The Dynamics of Occupational Segregation among Bank Tellers," in Clair Brown and Joseph A. Pechman, eds., *Gender in the Workplace* (Washington, D.C.: Brookings Institution, 1987), 107–48.

50   A theoretical derivation of this result can be found in Selamah Abdullah Yosuf, "Labour Force Attachment: Explaining Gender Differences in Earnings and Employment," *IIUM Journal of Economics and Management* 6 (1) (1998): 51–68. Evidence of differences in quit behavior between men and women can be found in Nachum Sicherman, "Gender Differences in Departures from Large Firm," *Industrial and Labor Relations Review* 49 (April 1996): 484–505. Like much of the rest of the literature, this study finds that women are much more likely than men to quit their jobs early in their careers.

51   Julie L. Hotchkiss and M. Melinda Pitts, "Female Labor Force Intermittency and Current Earnings: A Switching Regression Model with Unknown Sample Selection." *Applied Economics* (forthcoming), find that women suffer an earnings penalty at very low levels of intermittency and in such a way that employer preferences figure prominently in that penalty.

firm would not suffer a capital loss from turnover. (Note the potential existence of a vicious circle here—firms fear that women are more likely to quit and, thus, provide them with only general training. Because women have only general training, they then quit more frequently, confirming the employer's original belief.) The shift in the bank teller occupation from a port-of-entry job, in which a worker could expect to receive additional training for advancement, to a dead-end job could also be used to explain women's entrance into this occupation. Banks became willing to hire more women into these jobs in which they no longer invested training dollars.

Evidence has been marshaled both for and against this explanation for occupational segregation. Some evidence supporting Polachek's theory can be found in a study by David Macpherson and Barry Hirsch.[52] In a very large national sample of men and women observed over several years, Macpherson and Hirsch conclude that the majority of observed segregation of men and women across occupations was the result of individual preferences and skills. This result suggests that men and women choose those careers for which their skills and preferences are best suited.[53] A paper by Thomas DeLeire and Helen Levy found women's different preferences for risk (women choose safer jobs than men) explain about one-quarter of the observations that men and women choose different occupations.[54] As we saw earlier in this chapter, risky jobs pay higher wages than nonrisky jobs, and women's preference for safer jobs can help explain some of the observed differential between men and women.

An additional piece of evidence that gives credence to the importance of career interruptions comes from a study that followed the lives of 80 high school valedictorians.[55] The researcher found no differences among the male and female valedictorians in their probability of graduation from college, level of academic achievement, or plans to attend graduate school, yet paradoxically, by the fifth year after high school graduation, it was already apparent that a much smaller proportion of the women would fulfill their original career goals. Why was this? According to the researcher, nearly all the women expressed concern as early as their sophomore years about merging career and family responsibilities, a consideration that left the men largely unaffected. The female valedictorians split into two nearly equal-sized groups in terms of how this issue affected their career goals, however. One group of achievers/aspirers maintained their original career goals and, to obtain them, were much more likely to delay marriage and childbearing, to seek PhD or medical degrees, and to plan for uninterrupted work. The second group of women placed more emphasis on family considerations and structured

---

52 David A. Macpherson and Barry T. Hirsch, "Wages and Gender Composition: Why Do Women's Jobs Pay Less?" *Journal of Labor Economics* 13 (July 1995): 426–71. Also see Geraint Johnes, "It's Different for Girls: Participation and Occupational Segregation in the USA," *Manchester School* 68 (September 2000): 552–67.

53 Richard A. Easterlin, "Preferences and Prices in Choice of Career: The Switch to Business, 1972–87," *Journal of Economic Behavior and Organization* 27 (June 1995): 1–34, also provides evidence that individual preferences play a strong role in occupational choice.

54 Thomas DeLeire and Helen Levy, "Gender, Occupation Choice and the Risk of Death at Work," *NBER Working Paper No. 8574* (November 2001).

55 Karen D. Arnold, *Lives of Promise: What Becomes of High School Valedictorians: A Fourteen-Year Study of Achievement and Life Choices* (San Francisco: Jossey-Bass, 1995).

their education and work lives around marriage and children. Representative of this second group, for example, were six of the female valedictorians who started college as premed majors, but later switched to another major such as nursing or physical therapy. As one of them said, "If I were a man I probably would go to med school and become a sports doctor, but I'm not. I want to have children. Is it worth it to go to med school—and come out in time to have a family?" A number of women in this second group did attend graduate school, but they appeared more likely to end their studies with master's degrees than the women in the first group.

Other researchers, however, have questioned the importance of career interruptions as a source of occupational segregation.[56] First, they argue, even if women do seek jobs that require less training, there is no reason to expect them to cluster in a select group of female-dominated occupations, since many male-dominated occupations also require little skill or training.[57] Second, several studies have shown that women who have discontinuous work histories are no more likely to be employed in predominantly female occupations than are women who have continuous work histories, nor is the atrophy rate on human capital lower in female-dominated occupations.[58]

Gender Roles　A second reason for occupational segregation is more sociological in nature, involving the influence of gender roles on the attitudes of men and women as to what is "men's" work and "women's" work. Research by psychologists and other social scientists has shown that men and women both have well-defined conceptions of occupations that are male and female. One study asked 400 male and female undergraduate college students to express their opinion regarding the personal characteristics of a variety of hypothetical women of varying maternal status (number of children), employment status, and occupational attainment. While women who were employed were viewed more favorably than unemployed women (regardless of maternal status), women in nontraditionally female jobs were more often denigrated by the undergraduate student evaluators.[59] This suggests that people have a very clear notion of what are acceptable jobs for women. Another study found that both boys and girls as young as four years old show a well-defined preference for occupations traditionally associated with their own gender.[60]

56　See Reskin and Hartmann, eds., *Women's Work, Men's Work: Sex Segregation on the Job* (Washington, D.C.: National Academy Press, 1986), and Francine Blau and Marianne Ferber, "Career Plans and Expectations of Young Men and Women," *Journal of Human Resources* 26, no. 4 (Fall 1991): 581–607.

57　See June Lapidus, "Family Structure, Flexible Employment, and Labor Market Segmentation: Evidence from a Study of the Temporary Help Industry," *International Contributions to Labour Studies* (1993): 91–100.

58　See Dina Okamoto and Paula England, "Is There a Supply Side to Occupational Sex Segregation?" *Sociological Perspectives* 452 (Winter 1999): 557–82; John M. Abowd and Mark R. Killingsworth, "Sex Discrimination, Atrophy, and the Male–Female Wage Differential," *Industrial Relations* 22, no. 3 (Fall 1983): 387–402; and Michelle J. Budig and Paula England, "The Wage Penalty for Motherhood," *American Sociological Review* 66 (April 2001): 204–25.

59　Karla Ann Mueller and Janice D. Yoder, "Gendered Norms for Family Size, Employment, and Occupation: Are There Personal Costs for Violating Them?" *Sex Roles: A Journal of Research* 36 (February 1997): 207–20.

60　Ashton D. Trice and Kimberly Rush, "Sex-Stereotyping in Four-Year-Olds' Occupational Aspirations," *Perceptual & Motor Skills* 81 (October 1995): 701–2.

How is it that occupations come to be gender-stereotyped, and how does this influence men's and women's occupational choices? The origins of gender roles and occupational gender typing are open to a good deal of controversy.[61] One view is that "male" occupations such as lawyer, miner, or auto mechanic require "masculine" attributes of aggressive, competitive behavior or large amounts of physical strength and endurance, while "female" occupations such as nurse or receptionist require patience, caring, and empathy that women allegedly possess relatively more of. Self-selection of women into "female" occupations and men into "male" occupations in this view arises from innate biological differences between the sexes.

An alternative view holds that gender stereotyping of occupations arises not from objective attributes of the occupations themselves, but rather from the *socialization process* as boys and girls are taught by parents, teachers, and the media the appropriate career goals and aspirations for men and women.[62] In this theory, the desire of men to be coal miners and women to be nurses comes from the gender roles that our culture sets up as the ideal types for persons of each gender and that people are conditioned from a young age to accept as the natural order of things. These gender roles have a powerful influence on the occupational choice of men and women because a person who violates established norms of behavior soon suffers internal stress and conflict as well as social sanctions from friends, family, and coworkers. Numerous studies have documented that women who have chosen to work in upper-level management positions suffer a good deal of mental stress, and women who enter nontraditional blue-collar fields frequently encounter hostility or harassment from male workers and foremen.[63] In the past 20 years, social attitudes regarding appropriate occupational choice for women (and to a lesser extent men) have undergone something of a revolution, with the result that a far greater number of young women today are planning to pursue nontraditional occupations.[64] Research suggests, however, that traditional gender role stereotypes continue to have an important influence on career choices of men and women.[65]

---

61 See, for example, Stephen Franzor, *Social Psychology* (New York: McGraw-Hill, 2006).

62 Tracey Idle, Eileen Wood, and Serge Desmarais, "Gender Role Socialization in Toy Play Situations: Mothers and Fathers with Their Sons and Daughters," *Sex Roles* 28 (June 1993): 679–91; Azy Barak, Shoshana Feldman, and Ayelet Noy, "Traditionality of Children's Interests As Related to Their Parents' Gender Stereotypes and Traditionality of Occupations," *Sex Roles* 24 (April 1991): 511–24; Ashton D. Trice, "Stability of Children's Career Aspirations," *Journal of Genetic Psychology* 152 (March 1991): 137–39; and Betsy Cahill and Eve Adams, "An Exploratory Study of Early Childhood Teachers' Attitudes toward Gender Roles," *Sex Roles* (April 1997): 517–29.

63 See Leonard H. Chusmir and Victoria Franks, "Stress and the Woman Manager," *Training & Development Journal* 42 (October 1988): 66–70; Judith Gains, "In Retreat, a Pause for Powerful Women: Executives Take Time to Analyze Roles, Lives," *Boston Globe* (25 June 1998): B1; and Anonymous, "Blue-Collar Blues," *Small Business Reports* 18 (August 1993): 25–26.

64 Andrew A. Helwig, "Gender-Role Stereotyping: Testing Theory with a Longitudinal Sample," *Sex Roles* 38 (March 1998): 403–23.

65 See Jan Farrington, "Who's Under the Hard Hat? Nontraditional Jobs for Women and Men," *Career World* 23 (January 1995): 22–27.

Discrimination   A third explanation for occupational segregation focuses on discrimination against women practiced by educational institutions and business firms. In this view, the segmentation of the labor market into high-paying male occupations and low-paying female occupations is not the result of market forces or worker preferences, but rather is the outcome of discriminatory policies regarding admittance of women to school and apprenticeship programs and in the hiring and promotion of women by firms.[66]

A firm's hiring policy is discriminatory if it treats two people of equal productivity differently because of some personal characteristic such as age, race, gender, or religion. As the next chapter discusses, discrimination against women in hiring can result from a variety of causes related to gender-role stereotypes on the part of the employer or the customers of the firm, prejudice against women by the employer or workers in the firm, or an inability by the employer to discern the true productivity of women. Regardless of the cause, the result is that women are systematically denied employment in certain occupations because of their gender. As an example, it is frequently alleged that one reason only 7 percent of lawyers in 1970 were female is because law firms refused to hire women, regardless of their credentials.[67] The legal profession's historically negative attitude toward female lawyers was revealed in a survey of 430 private law firms undertaken by the *Harvard Law Record* in 1963.[68] Asked to rank from least desirable (-10) to most desirable (-10) the characteristics of law school graduates, the characteristic "female" received the lowest rating (-4.9) in the poll. Women have also had difficulty being hired into a number of other occupations, two examples being firefighter and police officer. A number of city governments hired women into these jobs only after court orders, leading in some cases to public protests by the male police officers and firefighters (and their wives).[69]

Women have also been excluded from employment in certain occupations because of discrimination in training and education. University professional schools, unions, and business firms at times acted as gatekeepers to occupations because their admittance or hiring policies determined who would and would not obtain the necessary training.[70] Even as late as 1970, only 1 percent, 9 percent, and

---

66   Rudolf Winter-Ebmer and Josef Sweimüller, "Occupational Segregation and Career Advancement," *Economics Letters* 39 (June 1992): 229–34, provides empirical evidence in favor of the discrimination explanation for occupational segregation. Also see Suzanne E. Tallichet, "Barriers to Women's Advancement in Underground Coal Mining," *Rural Sociology* 65 (June 2000): 234–52.

67   See Cynthia Fuchs Epstein, *Women in Law* (New York: Basic Books, 1981).

68   Ibid.

69   See "Women Firefighters Still Spark Resentment in Strongly Macho Job," *Wall Street Journal* (February 3, 1983): 1, 18, and "Firehouse Door Opening Slowly for Women," *New York Times* (October 12, 1987): 1. Some evidence that even recently women have had difficulty being hired into police jobs can be found in Tim R. Sass and Jennifer L. Troyer, "Affirmative Action, Political Representation, Unions, and Female Police Employment," *Journal of Labor Research* 20 (Fall 1999): 571–87.

70   See Paula E. Stephan and Sharon G. Levin, "Sex Segregation in Education: The Case of Doctorate Recipients," *Journal of Behavioral Economics* 12, no. 2 (Winter 1984): 67–94.

Why More Women Managers and Executives Are Putting Their Careers on Hold

Although the proportion of women has increased in nearly all white-collar occupations in recent years, one of the biggest breakthroughs has been in corporate management. Once almost an exclusively male reserve, in 2003, nearly 50 percent of management positions were held by women. Is it safe to conclude, therefore, that occupational segregation is dead and buried? Not necessarily. A recent phenomenon that has attracted considerable attention in the press is the growing number of women who are dropping out of the managerial workforce. In a number of cases, these dropouts are the pioneering women of the 1970s who braved discrimination and economic adversity in their efforts to work up to high-level executive positions.

Recent statistics paint a revealing picture. In 2003, women comprised 50 percent of the Yale undergraduate class, 63 percent of the Berkeley Law School class, 47 percent of all medical students, and 50 percent of all undergraduate business majors. But after spending some years in the management workforce many women either throttle-back or drop out altogether. Thus, despite two to three decades of open doors, in 2003 women represented only 16 percent of corporate officers, and 14 percent of the

U.S. House of Representatives. Much of this attrition, according to recent surveys and interviews, is because women simply decide that a full-time business career and getting to the top is either not worth it or not their life goal. Reflective of this decision, while 95 percent of white men with MBAs work full-time only two-thirds of white women do so. (The ratios for black women and men are closer.) Likewise a survey of women in the Harvard Business School classes of 1981, 1985, and 1991 found that only 38 percent were working full-time.

Women are dropping out of the managerial workforce for several reasons. One is that some women managers become disillusioned because they are not promoted as fast as men, a perception that often seems to emerge when women are in their mid-30s and early 40s and are in competition with men for the middle to top positions in the organizational pyramid. A second factor is the resentment women managers feel when they are not paid as well as their male counterparts. Several studies of MBAs, for example, have shown that while women and men start out with equal salaries, five to ten years after graduation the men are outearning the women.

14 percent, respectively, of dental, medical, and PhD graduates were women. To some degree this reflected the fact that few women applied for admission to these programs; there is also evidence, however, that until the mid-1970s many professional schools explicitly limited the number of women they would admit.[71] The same situation existed in apprenticeship programs run by labor unions, where only under court order have women been admitted in significant numbers for training in the skilled construction trades. Finally, business firms can also act as gatekeepers

---

71   See Michelle Patterson and Laurie Engelberg, "Women in Male-Dominated Professions," in Stromberg and Harkess, *Women Working*, 266–92; and Epstein, *Women in Law*.

continued

Most studies conclude, however, that the most important factor causing women to give up their careers in management is the demands of raising a family. According to one executive recruiter, "We have more women than before who are having second thoughts about everything-for-the-career. When a baby comes along, the 6-week maternity leave becomes a 2-year maternity leave." Earlier in the 1980s, he says, women embarking on careers in management thought they could have it all, that they could be the "superwoman" who is a successful corporate executive, wife, and mother. More and more women, however, are discovering that it is impossible to be superwoman and, thus, they must choose between career and family. A growing proportion are apparently choosing family, either by dropping out of the managerial workforce for several years, switching to other occupations that provide more flexible hours, such as real estate agent or independent business consultant, or leaving the workforce altogether to be full-time mothers and homemakers.

How are business firms reacting to this development? It is strengthening in at least some top corporate executives' minds the traditional stereotype that women are not as devoted to their careers as men. A second reaction of many companies is to look for ways to reduce the turnover of their women managers. Probably the area receiving the most attention in this regard is child care. A growing number of companies are providing paid maternity leaves, typically ranging from six weeks to six months, while others are starting on-site day-care centers. As another line of attack, some companies have adopted more flexible work hours, sometimes including the option to work part-time at home.

At the same time, as women achieve greater heights in the decision-making echelons of firms, their ability, and apparent new desire, to make changes in the workplace itself is being felt. One executive commented, "Female executives are appearing who try and bring a little dose of humanity and sanity into the workplace." The net result is that all-or-nothing choices need no longer be the only options facing a female executive.

SOURCES: "The Out-Out Revolution," *The New York Times Magazine* (October 26, 2003): 42; "The Flight of the Managers," *Business Week* (February 22, 1993): 78–80; Jane R. Eisner, "Woman to Her Job: Enough of Too Much," *Philadelphia Enquirer* (22 March 1998): E7; and "New Page in Management: Female Executives Doing It Their Way, and Succeeding," *Newsday* (3 February 2002): F10.

through their control of who obtains on-the-job training and promotions in the firm. It is argued that one reason for occupational segregation is that firms adopt hiring policies that place men on the training ladders within the internal labor market while women are hired only into dead-end jobs that provide little room for occupational advancement.[72] This issue is examined more fully in Chapter 9.

---

[72] Evidence on this is provided in Jeffrey Waddoups and Djeto Assane, "Mobility and Gender in a Segmented Labor Market: A Closer Look," *American Journal of Economics and Sociology* 52 (October 1993): 399–412, and U.S. Department of Labor, "Working Women Count! A Report to the Nation Executive Summary." Contrary evidence of the presence of glass ceilings in the law profession is found in Joe G. Baker, "Glass Ceilings or Sticky Floors? A Model of High Income Law Graduates," *Journal of Labor Research* 24 (Fall 2003): 695–71.

Government Regulation of Occupational Safety and Health

The theory of compensating wage differentials is directly applicable to an analysis of one of the most controversial forms of government intervention in the labor market—the regulation of occupational *safety* and *health* conditions. Do competitive market forces lead business firms to voluntarily adopt sufficient safety and health protection for workers, or is additional government regulation needed in this area?

During the 1960s two events led policymakers to the conclusion that additional regulation was needed. Probably the single most important factor was the increase in the reported injury rate in American industry, an increase of nearly 29 percent from 1961 to 1970. As of 1970, 3 percent of the employed civilian labor force were injured seriously enough each year to require sick leave, causing the loss of over 100,000 worker-years of production. The National Safety Council estimated that 14,000 deaths occurred annually as a result of accidents on the job.[1]

A second consideration was the growing public concern over occupational disease. Injuries on the job are generally traceable to readily identifiable *safety* hazards associated with electrocution, fires, dangerous machinery, falls, and so on. Occupational disease, on the other hand, stems from a variety of *health* hazards that are only partially identified or understood. Examples include coal miners' pneumoconiosis (black lung), asbestos-caused cancer, textile workers' byssinosis (brown lung), vinyl chloride-caused cancer, and so on. During the 1960s the toxic nature of many workplace chemicals, metals, and other substances began to be better appreciated, causing growing alarm over the long-range effects on the health of workers. It was estimated at the time that only 25 percent of workers exposed to health hazards were adequately protected and that 390,000 new cases of occupational disease arose each year.[2]

The Occupational Safety and Health Act

In the belief that the health and safety hazards facing American workers were both unacceptably large and growing worse, Congress enacted into law the Occupational Safety and Health Act of 1970. The act imposed upon virtually every employer in the private sector a general duty to "furnish to each of his employees employment and a place of employment which was free from recognized hazards that are causing or are likely to cause death or serious physical harm to his employees." To administer the act, Congress established the **Occupational Safety and Health Administration (OSHA)** under the jurisdiction of the Department of Labor.

As the principal means to improve workplace safety and health, Congress gave to OSHA the power to issue detailed standards that specified required safety conditions (for instance, railings must be 42 inches in height and made of 3-inch steel tubing) or maximum levels of exposure to particular toxic substances (for example, 50 parts per million of vinyl chloride). Within two years of passage of the act, OSHA had issued over 4,400 standards.[3]

---

1   Robert S. Smith, *The Occupational Safety and Health Act: Its Goals and Its Achievements* (Washington, D.C.: American Enterprise Institute, 1976), 1–2.

2   Ibid. While statistics on occupational injury and fatalities have been historically unreliable, in 1992 the Bureau of Labor Statistics began compiling statistics on workplace fatalities from a number of different sources to make up the Census of Fatal Occupational Injuries (CFOI). These sources include death certificates, OSHA reports, and news media reports, among others. The most recent tabulations report 5,559 workplace fatalities in 2003. The BLS has also estimated that there were 4.7 million workplace nonfatal injuries and illnesses in 2002.

3   Nearly all of these standards were taken without modification from standards then used by various industry groups. OSHA's haste in issuing them proved to be a major mistake, since many were outdated, irrelevant, or trivial. One statute, for example, prohibited employers from serving ice water to their workers because many years previously ice was cut from unsanitary river water. In formulating its own standards, on the other hand, OSHA has been notoriously slow. For a review of OSHA, see Sar Levitan, Peter Carlson, and Isaac Shapiro, *Protecting American Workers* (Washington, D.C.: Bureau of National Affairs, 1986), Chapter 6.

To enforce the standards, OSHA was given the power to inspect, unannounced, the employer's place of business. If an inspection disclosed a violation, the employer had a specified time period in which to meet the standard or risk a possible fine of up to $1,000 per day. One of the most recent controversial efforts of OSHA have been in the area of ergonomics. On November 14, 2000, OSHA issued ergonomic standards affecting jobs that require constant handling and lifting.[4] Industries that require such activities report injury rates 2.6 times as high as other private industries.[5] The OSHA standards took effect January 16, 2001. However, under the Congressional Review Act of 1996, Congress passed a resolution of disapproval of the final standards, making them invalid as of April 23, 2001.

This whole process, and the continuing effort of the secretary of labor to resolve concerns about repetitive stress injuries, highlight how controversial and politically charged the actions of OSHA are. Central to this controversy are two related questions. The first concerns the need for government regulation in the first place. Opponents of OSHA argue, particularly in the case of safety hazards, that the competitive forces of supply and demand in the labor market will ensure that employers provide an adequate amount of protection for workers; proponents of OSHA argue that imperfections in the market mechanism require government intervention. The second issue of controversy follows from the first: If government regulation is called for, what is the optimal amount of risk to which workers should be exposed on the job? Each of these questions is briefly considered below.

The Cases for and against Government Regulation

The hedonic theory of compensating wage differentials can be used to evaluate whether government regulation of risk of injury is called for and, if so, what impact that regulation will have on workers and firms. The injury rate R_{BY} in Figure 8.6 is the optimal level of safety and health protection for firm Y, since at that point it maximizes profits. An important issue to consider is whether the injury rate R_{BY} is also optimal from the point of view of workers and society. It can be shown that it is if (1) workers have complete and accurate information about the level of risk at the firm; (2) workers have complete freedom of mobility from one employer to another; and (3) the labor market is close to full employment. The basic presumption is that if workers have complete information about the types and level of risk at the workplace, they will demand a compensating differential in wages that reflects the full value to them of both lost income from a possible injury or illness and the attendant pain and suffering. The assumptions of perfect mobility and full employment assure that firms are forced by competitive pressure to pay this compensating differential to keep their workforces from quitting and going to other firms. Given these considerations, the indifference curves I_A and I_B (in Figure 8.6) reflect fully informed preferences regarding risk. From society's point of view, therefore, forcing all firms to reduce risk below the injury rate R_{BY} (say, to R_{AX}) would reduce worker B's utility and potentially drive firm Y out of business, because the cost of reducing risk to such a low level is so expensive the firm wouldn't be able to pay high enough wages to attract any workers.

In this case, government regulations requiring an increase in safety and health expenditures beyond the level voluntarily provided by business firms would result in a net reduction in social welfare. The case for government regulation becomes stronger, however, if imperfections impair the functioning of the market mechanism—in particular, if workers have incomplete information about the risks they face, if barriers to mobility inhibit movement in the market, or if firms have a large excess supply of labor to choose from.[6] With

<hr/>

4   Details of OSHA's effort and the history of the ergonomic guidelines can be found on the Department of Labor's website, http://www.dol.gov.

5   "OSHA Tries Again to Develop Ergonomic Standards for Employers," *Wall Street Journal* (7 October 1998): A1.

6   Peter Dorman and Paul Hagstrom, "Wage Compensation for Dangerous Work Revisited," *Industrial and Labor Relations Review* 52 (October 1998): 116–35, argue that noncompetitive elements in the labor market are strong enough to overcome any tendency for compensating wage differentials for risk to arise.

incomplete information, workers would be likely to systematically underestimate the true risk of injury and illness and would not demand a large enough compensating differential in wages.[7] Likewise, if workers could not costlessly quit one employer and move to another because of specific on-the-job training and internal labor markets, or if workers were restrained from quitting due to high unemployment, then firms would not be forced by competitive pressure to pay workers the full compensating differential for risk. In either event, the labor market would give rise to compensating differentials in wages that did not incorporate the full cost to workers and society of injuries and illnesses at the workplace.

The impact of market imperfections on the welfare of workers and on the profits of firms is illustrated in Figure 8.11. Under perfect information and mobility, the equilibrium outcome for worker B and firm Y from Figure 8.11 is at point N, at a wage/risk combination of (W_{BY}, R_{BY}). If worker B is misinformed about the actual risk of injury (it is actually at a level of R'_{BY}), then his or her willingness to work at a wage of W_{BY} means greater profits for firm Y and lower utility for worker B (point Q). A similar outcome would result (lower worker utility and higher firm profits) if workers did not have any other employment options and were impelled to take a job that involved higher risk of injury without being fully compensated for that risk. In a situation with perfect information and perfect mobility, worker B would receive W_{BY} by taking on risk at a level of R'_{BY} (point M). Clearly, the more severe the market imperfections in the labor market, the greater will be the divergence between actual wages and a wage that would fully compensate workers for the risk they bear on the job.

The Size of Compensating Wage Differentials

The critical issue in the debate over the need for government regulation of safety and health conditions is whether or not market forces give rise

to compensating differentials in wages that fully reflect the monetary and psychic costs to workers of injuries and illnesses incurred on the job.

Nearly all empirical studies have found that occupations or industries that have a higher incidence of fatal accidents and injuries also pay higher wages, other things being equal. For example, Michael French and David Kendall estimate that the risk of a disabling injury in the railroad industry is worth between $48,527 and $58,925 (in 2004 dollars) in additional compensation.[8] Similar evidence of compensation for risk of injury was found in Canada.[9] Jean Michel Cousineau et al. found that a one-day increase per year in time lost per worker at a firm was associated with a 1.1 percent higher level of wages. Further evidence suggests that these figures may actually understate the actual premium, since workers tend to sort based on

7 In fact, W. Kip Viscusi and Michael J. Moore, "Worker Learning and Compensating Differentials," *Industrial and Labor Relations Review* 45 (October 1991): 80–96, find that workers who have been with a firm longer are more likely to quit their jobs when job risk increases than are their junior colleagues. This finding suggests that information, gained through learning about risk from being on the job longer, can greatly influence how workers respond to risk. Evidence that a lack of accurate information results in very little presence of compensating wage differentials is offered by J. Paul Leigh and Jorge A. Garcia, "Some Problems with Value-of-Life Estimates based on Labor Market Data," *Journal of Forensic Economics* 13 (Summer 2000): 127–43. Also, worker inexperience, as in the case of teen workers can result in workers making decisions without complete information. See "Antiquated Labor Laws Fail to Protect Young Workers," and "Teens Don't Need Sheltering," *USA Today* (12 July 2002): 8A.

8 Michael T. French and David L. Kendall, "The Value of Job Safety for Railroad Workers," *Journal of Risk and Uncertainty* 5 (May 1992): 175–85. Also see Henry W. Herzog Jr. and Alan M. Schlottmann, "Valuing Risk in the Workplace: Market Price, Willingness to Pay, and the Optimal Provision of Safety," *Review of Economics and Statistics* 72 (August 1990): 463–70, for evidence of compensating wage differentials in the manufacturing sector, and Edward Montgomery and Kathryn Shaw, "Pensions and Wage Premia," *Economic Inquiry* 35 (July 1997): 510–22, for evidence across industries. W. Kip Viscusi and Joni Hersch, "Cigarette Smokers as Job Risk Takers," *Review of Economics and Statistics* 83 (May 2001): 269–80, find comparable valuation of injury risk, but also find the compensating differential is higher for nonsmokers.

9 Jean Michel Cousineau et al., "Occupational Hazards and Wage Compensating Differentials," *Review of Economics and Statistics* 74 (February 1992): 166–69.

Given perfect information, zero costs of mobility, and full employment, workers would demand compensating differentials for risk that fully reflect the value to them of the monetary and psychic costs they might suffer from an injury or illness. This would give rise to the wage/risk equilibrium of (W_{BY}, R_{BY}), point N. In the presence of imperfect information, costs to mobility, or less than full employment, however, workers might not demand a fully

compensatory risk premium in wages and end up at a lower utility level (and firms with higher profits) than otherwise (point Q). At this higher level of risk (R_{BY}) a fully compensating wage would be W'_{BY}(point M). Some argue that OSHA goes too far in requiring employers to attain the lowest level of risk that is "feasible," say R^*. The cost to firms of attaining R^* exceeds the monetary value workers attach to this lower risk.

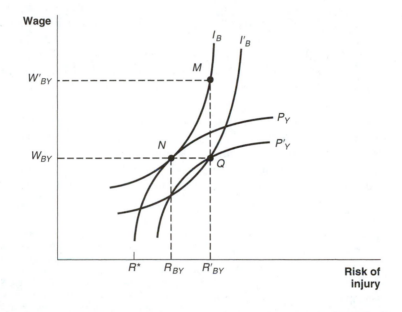

their risk tolerance.[10] In other words, if workers who don't mind risky environments are also less productive than the average worker, the wage they receive actually reflects a much greater risk premium than if they were of average productivity.

There is also evidence that workers are well compensated for the extreme incidence of a fatal injury (death) on the job. One study estimates that

workers in jobs with the median level of risk of death receive a compensating differential equal to about $22.50 per week ($1,170 per year) relative to risk-free jobs. The size of this risk premium,

10   Morley Gunderson and Hyatt Douglas, "Workplace Risks and Wages: Canadian Evidence from Alternative Models," *Canadian Journal of Economics* 34 (May 2001): 377–95.

coupled with the probability of death, implies an estimated value of life of approximately $11.7 million per worker.[11] Other studies have found different compensating wage differentials paid across race and gender groups. For example, one study found that blue-collar females earn an annual compensating wage differential of $850, while blue-collar men only receive $700 extra per year for a comparable level of fatality risk.[12]

This brief review suggests that compensating wage differentials exist, at least to some degree, particularly for risk of death. This fact clearly does not prove that government regulation is unnecessary, for it may be that the risk premiums are not fully compensatory. Because a large component of injury-related losses is the psychic costs of pain and suffering that are difficult to quantify, this issue is unlikely ever to be resolved.[13] Given the lack of conclusive data, the decision about government intervention comes to rest largely on whether workers are well informed about job-related risks and are mobile enough to avoid undesired risk.

The strongest case for government intervention is in the area of occupational disease.[14] The exact risk levels associated with benzene, vinyl chloride, coal dust, and asbestos, for example, are uncertain even to scientists and, in addition, their impact on workers' health often takes years to appear. Asbestos-related cancer and black lung disease, for example, typically take 20 to 30 years to develop. For these reasons, therefore, it is unlikely that workers are able to form accurate estimates of the risk they are exposed to.

With respect to occupational injuries the case for government intervention is less clear, as the occurrence of an injury is both immediate and visible. These facts would tend to make existing employees cognizant of the level of risk they are exposed to, reducing the problem of inadequate information. For occupational injuries, however, the more important imperfection of the market may be lack of mobility. Pension plans, seniority rights, and specific on-the-job training all make moving to another firm costly for workers and, thus, reduce the pressure on firms to pay fully compensating wage differentials.

Issues in Safety and Health Regulation

If policymakers decide that some form of government regulation of safety and health conditions is required, two additional issues arise. The first issue is to determine the *level* of safety and health protection business firms should be required to provide their workers. The second issue is to determine the *type* of regulatory mechanism that will most efficiently achieve this desired level of protection.

The Optimal Level of Regulation   The average risk of a fatal accident on the job is about 1/10,000, and the risk of a nonfatal accident is about 1/30. The creation of a regulatory agency such as OSHA suggests that Congress believes these levels of risk are too high and should be reduced. One important issue facing Congress, therefore, is to determine the optimal level of risk at the workplace.

The legislation creating OSHA mandated that every employer furnish for each employee a job "free from recognized hazards that are causing or likely to cause death or serious physical harm." The implication of this language is that the optimal level of risk is *zero*. Later in the legislative act creating OSHA, Congress wrote in a crucial, but

---

11   Since the probability of death is approximately 1/10,000, the value of life is calculated as $1,170/0.0001 = $11.7 million. See Kip Viscusi, *Risk by Choice* (Cambridge, Mass.: Harvard University Press, 1983), Chapter 6. Estimates using Australian data put the value of life in this same range: between $11.4 million and $19.4 million. See Paul Miller, Charles Mulvey, and Keith Norris, "Compensating Differentials for Risk of Death in Australia," *The Economic Record* 73 (December 1997): 363–72.

12   W. Kip Viscussi, "The Value of Life: Estimates with Risks by Occupations and Industry," *Economist Inquiry* 42 (January 2004): 29–48. Viscussi also finds that white workers receive higher compensating wage differentials than black workers. See "Racial Differences in Labor Market Values of a Statistical Life," *Harvard Law and Economics Discussion Paper No. 418* (April 2003).

13   For one attempt to put a dollar value on the psychic costs of work-related injuries, see W. Kip Viscusi and Michael J. Moore, "Workers' Compensation: Wage Effects, Benefit Inadequacies, and the Value of Health Losses," *Review of Economics and Statistics* 69 (May 1987): 249–61.

14   Smith, *The Occupational Safety and Health Act.*

ill-defined qualifier that directed OSHA to also take into account the "feasibility" of its protection standards. This qualifier led to a large debate over whether feasibility should be construed narrowly to mean technically achievable or more broadly, allowing for consideration of economic costs in judging the merits of a standard.

The promulgation and enforcement of the health and safety standards by OSHA have, in practice, adopted the narrow interpretation of technically achievable.[15] Economists have attacked this policy as a prime example of wasteful and inefficient government regulation. The reason is easy to see in Figure 8.11. Without government regulation, the free market (assuming imperfect information or some other such impediment) gives rise to an injury rate of R'_{BY} (point Q). The optimal (perfectly competitive) injury rate that government regulation should attempt to achieve is R_{BY} (point N). By requiring business firms to reduce health and safety hazards to the lowest technically achievable level, Congress has gone beyond the optimal injury rate of R_{BY} and has instead selected the injury rate $R*$, where the isoprofit curve becomes almost vertical. From an economic point of view, such a regulatory policy is ill advised since it totally neglects considerations of *cost*. The additional cost to firms and the economy of achieving the injury rate of $R*$ far exceeds the implicit monetary value that workers attach to this reduction in risk.

The principal contribution of economic analysis is to point out that even in matters of safety and health, economic resources are limited, and efficient government regulation requires an explicit balancing of benefits and costs. The benefits and costs of safety and health protection are not known with any certainty, and thus they have to be estimated. The principal means of doing so is *benefit–cost analysis*. Benefit–cost analysis attempts to compute a dollar value for both the costs and benefits from a regulatory standard. Although this procedure is fraught with many difficulties, it does provide a basis for rational decision making in the regulatory process.[16]

The Method of Enforcement If through benefit–cost analysis or some other means it has been determined that the optimal level of safety is the injury rate R_{BY} (point N) in Figure 8.11, the final question remains of how to induce firms to increase the level of safety and health protection from the current level of R'_{BY} (point Q).

OSHA chose to lower the injury rate to the desired level by issuing several thousand detailed standards that specified everything from the proper construction of a stepladder to the permissible level of noise in a plant. The advantage of written standards is that they attack specific, known causes of occupational injuries and illnesses. They also have several disadvantages. One is the sheer volume of standards that have to be issued; a second is their technical complexity. Perhaps more important, written standards are inflexible and do not allow business firms to use alternative, lower-cost methods to achieve the same safety goals. Economists have suggested that OSHA replace written standards with an "injury tax" that would assess a financial penalty on the firm for every accident or injury.[17] Such a tax would lead firms to reduce the injury rate by increasing their marginal costs of damage; the added benefit of the tax approach over written standards is that the costs of achieving the safety goal are likely to be lower since each firm is motivated to search out the least-cost method of injury prevention. Finally, an additional drawback of written standards is that they attack only one source of worker injuries—permanent, physical hazards—while as many as 75 percent of such

15   Viscusi, *Risk by Choice*, 6–7.

16   See, for example, Kenneth J. Arrow et al., "Is There a Role for Benefit–Cost Analysis in Environmental, Health, and Safety Regulation?" *Environment and Development Economics* 2 (May 1997): 196–201. A specific application can be found in "The Regulation of Vinyl Chloride: A Case Study," in Herbert R. Northrup et al., *The Impact of OSHA* (Philadelphia: Industrial Research Unit, 1978), 291–418; this study finds that the cost of saving one additional life through implementation of OSHA standards to be approximately $9 million, compared to a benefit of $1.5 million.

17   Robert S. Smith, "The Feasibility of an 'Injury Tax' Approach to Occupational Safety," *Law and Contemporary Problems* 37, no. 4 (Summer 1974): 730–44.

injuries are due to accidents off the work site, transient conditions in the workplace, and worker carelessness.

A second issue pertaining to the enforcement of safety and health standards is the number of inspectors who visit business firms and the fines levied for violations of the standards. The reduction of injuries and illnesses from R'_{BY} in Figure 8.11 to the desired level of R_{BY} imposes additional costs on business firms that they would not willingly undertake if left unregulated. To motivate firms to reduce the injury rate to R_{BY}, OSHA has to confront them with the prospect of larger costs if they do not comply with the standards than if they do. Most evidence suggests, however, that the costs of noncompliance have been, and continue to be, relatively minimal for most firms.[18] One reason for this is that firms have a small chance of being inspected. In 2003, only 1.3 percent of all workplaces were visited by an OSHA inspector. A second reason noncompliance costs tend to be minimal is the small size of financial penalties imposed on firms for violations of the OSHA standards. Although OSHA can impose a penalty of up to $7,000 per day for failure to eliminate a violation, only in a few well-publicized cases have such fines been assessed. In most cases, the financial penalties are relatively modest. For example, in 2003, the average penalty imposed for a serious violation was $985. However, in cases of

willful violation of an OSHA regulation, the fines can be as high as $70,000 per violation, and averaged $32,639 for 2003.

Given the low costs of noncompliance, it is not surprising that most statistical studies have found that the creation of OSHA has had a modest to negligible impact on the incidence of work-related injuries and fatalities.[19] The relative ineffectiveness of OSHA is also suggested by the fact that the injury rate among American workers during the 1990s has been higher than it was before the law was passed in 1970.[20]

---

18 See, for example, David Well, "If OSHA Is So Bad, Why Is Compliance So Good?" *RAND Journal of Economics* 27 (Autumn 1996): 618–40, and James C. Robinson, "The Impact of Environmental and Occupational Health Regulation on Productivity Growth in U.S. Manufacturing," *The Yale Journal on Regulation* 12 (Summer 1995): 387–434, Table III.C.1.

19 See David McCaffrey, "An Assessment of OSHA's Recent Effects on Injury Rates," *Journal of Human Resources* 18, no. 1 (Winter 1983): 131–46; William P. Curington, "Safety Regulation and Workplace Injuries," *Southern Economic Journal* 53 (July 1986): 51–72. In addition, to the evidence of low, impact overall, there is also evidence that OSHA inspections are becoming les and less effective in reducing injuries over time. See Wayne Gray and John Mendeloff, "The Declining Effects of OSHA Inspections on Manufacturing Injuries: 1979-1998," *NBER Working Paper No. W9119* (August 2002).

20 See Dino Drudi, "A Century-Long Quest for Meaningful and Accurate Occupational Injury and Illness Statistics," *Compensation and Working Conditions* (Winter 1997): 19–27.

EMPIRICAL EVIDENCE 8-1

Compensation for Reputation

One research project presents evidence that not only are workers compensated for unpleasant characteristics of their specific jobs, but they are also compensated if either their occupations or their

employers suffer a bad reputation.[1] In other words, if workers are embarrassed about what they do for a living or who they work for, they will have to

---

1 Robert H. Frank, "What Price the Moral High Ground?" *Southern Economic Journal* 63 (July 1996): 1–17.

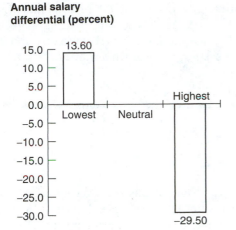

Occupational social responsibility

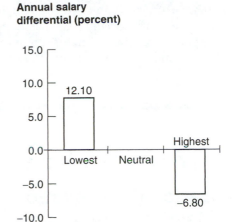

Employer social responsibility

SOURCE: Adapted from Robert H. Frank, "What Price the Moral High Ground?" *Southern Economic Journal* 63 (July 1996): 1–17, Figure 2.

receive a wage large enough to compensate them for having to tell people what they do for a living or admitting who they work for.

This study by Robert Frank measures the reputation of the occupation and the employer in terms of social responsibility. The hypothesis put forth is that the less socially responsible the occupation and the employer, the greater is the compensating wage differential (*ceteris paribus*) received. Based on surveys of students, Frank constructed a continuous measure of social responsibility for both a sample of occupations and a group of employers. The occupation ranked as the least socially responsible was stockbroker, followed by salesman; the most socially responsible occupations were emergency medical technician and teacher. The least socially responsible

employers were judged to be Drexel Burnham Lambert and Salomon Brothers, whereas Boston City Hospital and Andrus Children's Home were ranked as the most socially responsible employers.

A comparison of salaries earned by workers in the different occupation groups and employed by the different employers yielded the results summarized in Figure 8.12. Individuals whose occupations fell in the least socially responsible group earned a salary that was 13.6 percent higher than those in occupations considered neutral with respect to social responsibility. Workers whose occupations fell in the most socially responsible grouping earned 29.5 percent less than the salaries paid to those in neutral occupations. These salary comparisons were made holding other factors that may affect a worker's wage constant, such as the worker's college GPA, college major, gender, and sector of employment (e.g., government, non-profit). Also holding these factors constant, Frank found that workers employed by employers deemed as the least socially responsible earned 12.1 percent more than workers employed at neutral firms, and workers employed by the most socially responsible firms earned 6.8 percent less than at neutral firms.

This research has demonstrated that job attributes need not be highly quantitative (e.g., number of deaths on the job or the value of benefits offered) to require a compensating wage differential. In addition, workers seem to care about who they work for, not just what they do.

EMPIRICAL EVIDENCE 8-2

Occupational Segregation and Male/Female Earnings Differentials

The weekly earnings of full-time women workers are about 79.4 percent the earnings of men. To what extent is the unequal pattern of occupational attainment among men and women responsible for this differential in earnings? The answer depends significantly on how finely occupations are defined. Studies that adjust only for differences in the employment of men and women across broad occupational categories generally find that occupational segregation counts for relatively little of the earnings gap. One study found that if men and women were equally distributed across 12 major occupational groups, the gender gap in earnings would be reduced by only 10 percent or so.[1] The reason for the small reduction in the earnings gap is that even within major occupational groups, women earn substantially less than men—only 72 percent as much in managerial occupations, for example. After disaggregating the census data into 499 detailed occupations, however, this study found that the concentration of men in higher-paying occupations and women in lower-paying occupations could account for 35 to 40 percent of the gender gap in earnings.[2]

The results of this study have been replicated several times. For example, Figure 8.13 presents the estimated relationships between the hourly wages received by men and women in each of over 300 occupations and the percentage of the occupation's workforce that was female.[3] Clearly, the higher the proportion of women in an occupation, the lower, on average, was its level of pay. Though this relationship holds for both men and women, the effect is stronger for women. The results indicate that for every 10 percent increase in the

---

1 Donald J. Treiman and Heidi I. Hartmann, eds., *Women, Work, and Wages: Equal Pay for Jobs of Equal Value* (Washington, D.C.: National Academy Press, 1981), Chapter 2. Also see Randall S. Brown, Marilyn Moon, and Barbara S. Zoloff, "Incorporating Occupational Attainment in Studies of Male–Female Earnings Differentials," *Journal of Human Resources* 15, no. 1 (Winter 1980): 3–28. A more recent study, also using narrowly defined occupations and establishments, estimates that at least half of the wage gap is accounted for by occupational segregation. See Kimberly Bayard et al., "New Evidence on Sex Segregation and Sex Differences in Wages from Matched Employee–Employer Data," *Journal of Labor Economics* 21 (October 2003): 887–922.

2 Even within finely detailed occupations, jobs are often sex segregated. Although 25.2 percent of physicians in 2002 were women, women made up only 14.7 percent of surgeons, but 50.2 percent of pediatricians. See Lillian Randolph et al., *Physician Characteristics and Distribution in the US, 2004* (Chicago: American Medical Association, 2004), Tables 1.2–1.4.

3 See Michael Baker and Nicole M. Fortin, "Occupational Gender Composition and Wages in Canada, 1987–1988," *Canadian Journal of Economics* 34 (May 2001): 345–76.

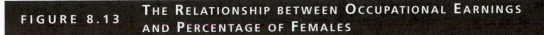

FIGURE 8.13 THE RELATIONSHIP BETWEEN OCCUPATIONAL EARNINGS AND PERCENTAGE OF FEMALES

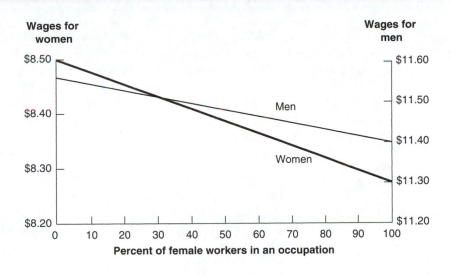

SOURCE: Authors' calculations based on results found in Michael Baker and Nicole M. Fortin, "Occupational Gender and Composition and Wages in Canada, 1987–1988," *Canadian Journal of Economics* 34 (May 2001): 345–76.

proportion of women in the occupation, women earn 1.4 percent (12¢) less per hour and men earn 0.4 percent (5¢) less per hour, on average.

The relationships reported in Figure 8.13 have already accounted for differences in age and education levels of the workers in the sample. If additional factors apply, such as the industry in which the occupation is found, the region in which the worker is employed, and whether the worker is employed by the government, the effect of percentage female on wages is reduced. With all of these controls, the study estimates that a 10 percent increase in the proportion of women in the occupation results in a 1 percent (8¢) lower wage for women and a 0.1 percent (1¢) lower wage for men, on average.[4]

So, even though job requirements and personal characteristics of workers account for some

of the measured negative impact on wages of being in a female occupation, the majority of the effect remains for women, and even some of the effect remains for men.[5]

---

4 These results are consistent with the findings of David A. Macpherson and Barry T. Hirsch, "Wages and Gender Composition: Why Do Women's Jobs Pay Less?" *Journal of Labor Economics* 13 (July 1995): 426–71.

5 Also see Elaine Sorensen, "Measuring the Effect of Occupational Sex and Race Composition on Earnings," in Robert T. Michael, Heidi I. Hartmann, and Brigid O'Farrell, eds., *Pay Equity: Empirical Inquiries* (Washington, D.C.: National Academy Press, 1989), 49–69. See Claudia Golden, "A Pollution Theory of Discrimination: Male and Female Differences in Occupations and Earnings," *NBER Working Paper No. 8985* (April 2004) for a theory of how an occupation that becomes "polluted" by women results in lower wages in that occupation.

Summary

This chapter examines the pattern of occupational earnings differentials and the factors that give rise to them. The major theoretical construct introduced in the chapter was compensating wage differentials. Given that occupations differ one from another in terms of both desirable and undesirable attributes, in order for the total of advantages and disadvantages to be equalized among occupations, wages must rise or fall by enough to form equalizing or compensating differentials. When tastes or abilities are heterogeneous, the size of these compensating differentials will depend on the strength of demand. The theory of compensating differentials rests on an assumption that the labor market is competitive. With noncompeting groups or extensive unemployment, the predictions of the theory may not hold.

The hedonic theory of compensating wage differentials plays a key role in the analysis of many different public policy issues. The one examined in this chapter is the case for and against government regulation of safety and health conditions in the workplace. If workers have complete information about the nature of job hazards and zero costs of mobility, they will demand a wage premium that fully compensates for the additional risk of injury or death. In this case, market forces will ensure that firms provide the "right" amount of health and safety protection. The more limited is information about health and safety hazards or the greater are the costs of mobility, the smaller will be the competitive pressure on firms to pay compensating differentials for risk. The greater the imperfections in the market, the stronger the case for government intervention.

A second application of the hedonic theory of compensating differentials is with respect to fringe benefits. The mix of wages and fringe benefits received by workers is determined by two factors. The first is the relative cost to the firm of providing a dollar's worth of wages versus an equivalent amount of fringe benefits. The second factor is the preferences of the workers with respect to the proportion of wages and benefits in the compensation package. One of the central predictions of the theory is that a competitive market should generate a trade-off between the amount of wages and benefits received by workers of equal productivity if the total dollar value of compensation per hour is to be equal. Only limited support was found for this prediction.

An additional source of wage differentials considered here was occupational licensing laws. The purpose of occupational licensing is to protect the consumer by ensuring that practitioners of the occupation can meet minimum competency requirements. Occupational licensing laws also erect barriers to entry into the employment, leading to monopoly rents for existing members.

The final section of the chapter examines the reasons behind the marked dissimilarity in occupational attainment and earnings of men and women. Women are concentrated in a rather narrow range of occupations, a phenomenon generally referred to as occupational segregation. Three alternative explanations seek to account for the difference in occupational attainment of men and women. One stresses the effect of interrupted work careers on women's occupational choices, the second stresses differences in tastes among men and women because of sex roles, and the third stresses discrimination. Whatever the reason, earnings in female-dominated occupations are depressed from occupational crowding as the millions of women who have entered the labor force in recent years compete for jobs in a fairly narrow segment of the labor market.

Review Questions

1. Occupations A and B are identical except that occupation B requires people to work at night. Assume that some people prefer night jobs, but others do not. Will the wage in occupation B be higher, lower, or equal to that in A?

2. According to one estimate, the musical group the Jacksons earned $30,000 for each *minute* they were on stage during their 1984 Victory tour. What combination of demand and supply in the market for pop music brought about such huge earnings for the Jacksons? Illustrate with a graph. Show in your graph the amount of economic rent (if any) earned by the Jacksons.

3. Do disagreeable jobs pay more than agreeable jobs, as Adam Smith claimed, or is it just the opposite, as John Stuart Mill claimed? What do you think, and why?

4. It has been found that the skilled/unskilled wage differential widens during recessions and narrows during boom times. Can you offer an explanation for this?

5. Only 3 percent of airline pilots are women, and only 2 percent of dental hygienists are men. What reason can you give to account for this pattern?

6. The median weekly earnings of women employed full-time are about 74 percent of the weekly earnings of men. What accounts for this earnings disparity? Is it a compensating differential that equalizes the sum of advantages and disadvantages between men's occupations and women's occupations? Why or why not?

7. Consider the following statement: "As long as even one person dies from an industrial accident there is not enough safety at the workplace." Evaluate this statement from an economic point of view. Critics charge that human life cannot be assigned a dollar value, and benefits of additional safety cannot and should not be balanced against costs as advocated by economists. What do you think about this argument?

8. Some studies have found that firms that pay high wages also offer the best employee benefits. Use isoprofit and indifference curves to represent this outcome. Why would any firm pay both higher wages and higher benefits than its rivals? If the labor market and product market are perfectly competitive and workers are of equal productivity, why would this situation not persist in the long run? What market imperfections might allow it to?

9. In most cases the political pressure to pass an occupational licensing law comes from persons employed in the occupation rather than consumers. Why might current practitioners of an occupation desire that it be licensed? Are all of these reasons necessarily inimical to the interests of consumers and society? Would society be better off to abolish occupational licensing laws? Why or why not?

10. One could argue that a long commute to work is an undesirable characteristic of any job. If most people live in the suburbs, what would the theory of compensating wage differentials predict about the relative wages of jobs in the suburbs versus wages of jobs located downtown (*ceteris paribus*)? Explain.

Measuring Occupational Segregation—The Duncan Index

Economists rely primarily on two statistical measures for evaluating the degree of occupational segregation across race and gender groups. The first measure is the representation of race and gender groups in occupations relative to the group's overall labor market presence. For example, because women comprised 43.9 percent of the labor force in 2003, any occupation in which women comprised less than 43.9 percent is said to underrepresent women. Similarly, any occupation comprised of less than 12 percent black workers in 2003 would be classified as an occupation in which blacks were underrepresented. As pointed out in the chapter text, this measure is of particular interest if certain workers are systematically overrepresented in the lowest-paying occupations.

The second measure of occupational segregation focuses on the distribution of workers across occupations. While the measure of representation tends to draw attention to particular occupations, or categories of occupations, the distribution measure yields a picture of a race or gender group's overall position in the labor market.

The Duncan Index

The statistic that is used most frequently to compare distributions of workers was developed in the 1950s by two sociologists, Otis Dudley Duncan and Beverly Duncan.[1] The Duncan index (D) is commonly referred to as a measure of dissimilarity since it indicates how similar (or dissimilar) the distributions of two groups are across occupations.[2] It is calculated according to the following formula:

$$D = \left(\frac{1}{2}\right) \sum_{j=1}^{N} |F_j - M_j|, \qquad \text{(8A.1)}$$

where N is the total number of occupations and F_j and M_j are the proportions of all females and males, respectively, in occupation j. The index is equal to one-half the sum of the absolute differences between the proportion of women and men in each occupation. An index equal to zero means that women and men have identical employment distributions across occupations. An index equal to 1 corresponds to the extreme situation of complete segregation (no men or women work in the same

---

1 Otis Dudley Duncan and Beverly Duncan, "A Methodological Analysis of Segregation Indexes," *American Sociological Review* (April 1955): 210–17.

2 Extensions of the Duncan Index that allow computing a measurement of dissimilarity among more than two groups of workers can be found in Jacques Silber, "Occupational Segregation Indices in the Multidimensional Case: A Note," *The Economic Record* 68 (September 1992), and Dale Boisso et al., "Occupational Segregation in the Multidimensional Case: Decomposition and Tests of Significance," *Journal of Econometrics* 61 (March 1994): 161–71. Also see Martin Watts, "Occupational Gender Segregation: Index Measurement and Econometric Modeling," *Demography* 35 (November 1998): 489–96.

occupation). Another way to interpret D is as the percentage of women (or men) that would have to change occupations in order to eliminate the difference in occupational distributions.

An Example: The United States

Table 8A.1 contains the distribution of male, female, black, and white workers across occupations in the United States in 2004. For 2004, and referring to Equation 8A.1, the number of occupations (N) is equal to 6, F_j for the first occupation is 0.377 and M_j is 0.324; the absolute value of the difference is 0.053. Continuing in this fashion, Equation 8A.2 provides the calculation of D for males and females for 2004. It is equal to 0.244, meaning that 24.4 percent of either men or women would have to change occupations for the distributions of men and women across to be equal. The Duncan index for comparing the distribution of black and white workers in 2004 is 0.09, meaning that black and white workers are much more equally distributed across occupations than men and women are.

$$D_{MF}^{2004} = \left(\frac{1}{2}\right)[0.053 + 0.178 + 0.067 + 0.06 + 0.122 + 0.008] = 0.244 \qquad \text{(8A.2)}$$

In order to determine in what direction occupational segregation is going, one must calculate D across different time periods. Two articles are used to construct such calculations from 1940 to 1997.[3] Using the decenniel census (and the 1988

---

3   Mary C. King, "Occupational Segregation by Race and Sex, 1940–88," *Monthly Labor Review* 115 (April 1992): 30–37. The number of occupational categories included in the calculation are known to skew the Duncan measure. The more aggregated are occupations (the fewer the categories) the smaller will be the calculated Duncan index, all else equal. Because of this, it is important to keep the number of occupational categories constant when making comparisons across labor markets or across time for one labor market.

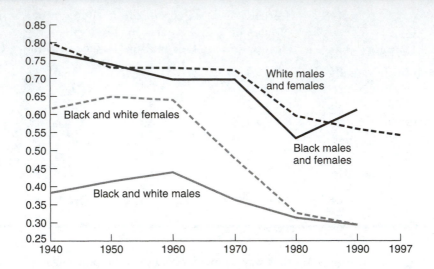

SOURCE: Mary C. King, "Occupational Segregation by Race and Sex, 1940–88," *Monthly Labor Review* 115 (April 1992): 30–7, Chart 1, published by the Bureau of Labor Statistics, Washington, D.C. (1990 data for comparisons other than white males and females actually corresponds to 1988). Data for 1980–1997 white men and women: Thomas Wells, "Changes in Occupational Sex Segregation during the 1980s and 1990s," *Social Science Quarterly*, 80 (June 1999): 370–80.

Current Population Survey), Mary King calculates the Duncan index for 159 occupations found in all surveys. Using the decennial census (and the 1997 Current Population Survey) Thomas Wells makes a similar calculation for 497 occupations. Figure 8A.1 illustrates the findings. For all race and gender comparisons, there has clearly been an increase in similarity of distributions. The dissimilarity between black and white females, however, has decreased the most. The dissimilarity between white males and females continued to decline in the 1990s, but at a slower rate than that in previous decades.

Table 8A.2 presents the Duncan index calculation across race and gender groups for 1990 and 2004. These numbers are not comparable to those reported in Figure 8A.1 since only six occupational categories were used, compared with 159 used by Mary King and 497 used by Thomas Wells; the Duncan values are smaller in Table 8A.2 across the board. The Duncan values in Table 8A.2, however, show the same pattern seen in Figure 8A.1; men and women and blacks and whites are becoming more similar in their distributions across occupations.

TABLE 8A.2	DUNCAN INDEX CALCULATIONS COMPARING RACE AND GENDER GROUPS, 1990 AND 2004		
Race/Gender Comparison		**1990**	**2004**
White males and females		0.330	0.250
Black males and females		0.366	0.267
Black and white females		0.156	0.106
Black and white males		0.227	0.152

SOURCE: Calculated from Bureau of Labor Statistics, *Employment and Earnings* (January 2005, table 10).

International Comparisons

It is of interest to see that the segregation of occupations by gender is not unique to the United States. Several authors have assembled measures of occupational segregation across the globe. Table 8A.3 shows that countries and regions can vary quite a bit regarding the degree of occupational segregation, and whereas seven of the countries in the Tzannatos study document a reduction in occupational segregation across gender (albeit by fairly small amounts for the most part), occupational segregation in five of the countries actually became more severe. The study by Dolado et al. illustrates that while European countries typically experience lower segregation of occupations across gender, both Europe and the United States are seeing even lower levels of segregation among younger cohorts than older cohorts. For example, the 0.28 index value for the European Union corresponds to 25–34-year-olds. By comparison, the index of dissimilarity among 45- to 54-year-olds is 0.42, indicating progress is being felt over time.

In the study by Hang-yue Ngo (providing the index for Hong Kong), occupational segregation between men and women remained fairly constant between 1991 and 1996. But the study also illustrates how the simple Duncan index of dissimilarity can mask a great deal of movement of men and women across occupations. Ngo refers to the movements he observed in his data as de-segregation and re-segregation. For example, between 1991 and 1996, the number of women employed in business-related occupations grew by 110 percent (outpacing overall growth of the occupation). At the same time, the percentage of women in blue-collar occupations declined from 36 percent to 19 percent. It is clear that one single index does not tell the whole story.

TABLE 8A.3 DUNCAN INDEX MEASURES OF OCCUPATIONAL SEGREGATION ACROSS GENDER FOR DIFFERENT COUNTRIES, DIFFERENT YEARS

Country	Range of years from which data were collected		
	1950s–1960s	1970s–1980s	1990s
Europe & North America[d]	0.37	—	—
European Union[e]	—	—	0.28
Latin America:			
The Region[d]	0.49	—	—
Chile[a]	0.43	0.53	—
Costa Rica[a]	0.59	0.50	—
Ecuador[a]	0.49	0.47	—
Guatemala[a]	0.62	0.57	—
Honduras[a]	0.75	0.66	—
Jamaica[a]	0.47	0.54	—
Mexico[a]	0.39	0.32	—
Panama[a]	0.53	0.59	—
Peru[a]	0.31	0.33	—
Uruguay[a]	0.42	0.43	—
Venezuela[a]	0.55	0.47	—
Asia:			
The Region[d]	0.28	—	—
India[b]	—	0.010	—
Indonesia[b]	—	0.13	—
Japan[b]	—	—	0.19
Korea[b]	—	—	0.17
Malaysia[b]	—	0.15	—
Philippines[b]	—	—	0.37
Thailand[b]	—	0.09	—
China (Hong Kong)[c]	—	—	0.40
Middle East/North Africa:			
The Region[d]	0.39	—	—
Algeria[b]	—	0.48	—
Egypt[b]	—	—	0.07
Iran[b]	—	0.01	—
Iraq[b]	—	0.02	—
Tunisia[b]	—	0.11	—
Turkey[b]	—	—	0.08

SOURCES:

[a]Zafiris Tzannatos, "The Industrial and Occupational Distribution of Female Employment," in George Psacharapoulos and Zafiris Tzannatos, eds. *Women's Employment and Pay in Latin America*, Latin America and the Caribbean Technical Department, Regional Studies Report No. 10 (Washington, D.C.: The World Bank, 1991): 3.1–3.22.

[b]Susan Horton, "Marginalization Revisited: Women's Market Work and Pay, and Economic Development," *World Development* 27 (1999): 571–82.

[c]Hang-yue Ngo, "Trends in Occupational Sex Segregation in Hong Kong," *International Journal of Human Resource Management* 11 (April 2000): 251–63.

[d]E. Boulding et al., *Handbook of International Data on Women* (New York: Sage, 1976).

[e]J. J. Dolado et al., "Female Employment and Occupational Changes in the 1990s: How Is the EU Performing Relative to the US?" *European Economic Review* 45 (2001): 875–89.

9

Discrimination in the Labor Market

The preceding chapter briefly discussed the subject of discrimination; this chapter takes a more in-depth look at both its causes and its consequences. The subject of discrimination is a complicated one because it takes many forms and occurs for a variety of reasons, ranging from pure prejudice and bigotry on one hand to the profit motive on the other. This chapter first examines several different theories that attempt to explain why discrimination takes place, what its consequences are, and finally, who gains and loses from it. The second part of the chapter looks at the empirical evidence on discrimination—how it is measured, to what extent it is responsible for the inequality in earnings among persons of different race and gender groups, and what role it plays in the economic progress or lack of progress of blacks and women in the labor market. Finally, the last portion of the chapter discusses government programs aimed at combating discrimination and their effectiveness in improving the economic status of minority groups.

The Pattern of Earnings Differentials by Race and Gender

It is well known that large earnings differentials separate workers of various race and gender groups. An idea of how large these differentials are and how they have changed over time is given in Figure 9.1. Graph (a) of Figure 9.1 shows earnings ratios for selected years between 1940 and 2003 for whites and blacks who were year-round full-time workers. One line shows the annual earnings of black males relative to those of white males; the other compares the annual earnings of black females to those of white females. Graph (b) shows the ratio of female to male annual earnings for two groups: white females compared to white males, and black females compared to black males.[1]

One interesting feature of these data is the trend in the earnings differentials between black and white workers. In 1940, black males

---

[1] Unless otherwise indicated, the statistics for blacks also include other nonwhite persons.

FIGURE 9.1   MEDIAN EARNINGS RATIOS FOR YEAR-ROUND FULL-TIME WORKERS BY RACE AND GENDER, 1940–2003

(a) Black/White

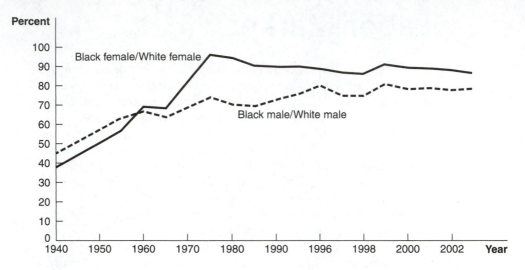

(b) Female/Male

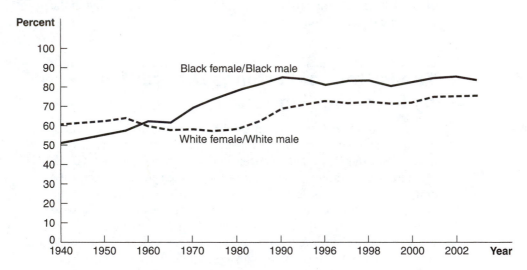

SOURCE: U.S. Bureau of the Census, *Money Income of Households, Families, and Persons*, P-60, nos. 69, 80, 105, 132, 156, 174, 193, 197, and 200. And, beginning in 2000, Table U.S. Bureau of the Census, PINC-05. Work Experience of People 15 Years Old and Over by Total Money Earnings, Age, Race, Hispanic Origin, and Sex.

• **Chapter 9** *Discrimination in the Labor Market*

who worked year-round earned only 45 percent as much as their white counterparts; black females earned only 38 percent as much as white females. By anyone's standards, the inequality of income between blacks and whites was staggering. Since World War II, however, black and white earnings have converged significantly. Black females have made dramatic gains, reaching near parity in earnings (about 90 percent) with white females;[2] black males, on the other hand, still earn only 78 percent as much as white males. Finally, in contrast, against the backdrop of a long-term convergence stands the lack of improvement in relative black incomes since 1975.

A second feature of the data in Figure 9.1 that deserves attention is the size of the gender differential in earnings and its trend over time. Until its growth starting in the mid-1980s, the earnings of white women as a percentage of earnings of white men hovered for many years around 60 percent.[3] Between 1985 and 2003, the earnings of white women grew from 63 percent to 76 percent of the earnings of white men. The data tell a significantly different story for black workers. Not only is the earnings gap between black females and black males smaller (84 percent in 2003) than for white workers, it has also narrowed at a much faster rate over the past three decades. If the earnings of black females are compared with those of white males, however, the earnings gap becomes much larger (76 percent in 2003).[4]

The persistent disparity in income revealed in Figure 9.1 between men and women and blacks and whites is a well-accepted fact; what remains highly controversial are the *causes* of the earnings differentials. One answer is race and sex discrimination. There are many other potential factors, however, such as differences among race and sex groups in years of education, on-the-job training, or innate ability. Over the past three decades, economists have devoted considerable research effort to disentangling the separate effects of these and other influences on earnings differentials in the labor market. This chapter reviews the results of this research, focusing particularly on the extent to which discrimination is responsible for the inequality in incomes noted in Figure 9.1.

Theories of Market Discrimination

The word *discrimination* has an unmistakably pejorative connotation, suggesting treatment of individuals or groups of individuals that is not only unequal, but also unfair. In various ways, people whom society holds in an inferior status are denied

---

2   Derek Neal, "The Measured Black–White Wage Gap Among Women is Too Small," *Journal of Political Economy* 112 (February 2004): S1-28 finds that when selection into the labor market is controlled for, black/white female earning ratio is actually much lower.

3   The 60 percent female/male earnings ratio apparently goes back much further than even the early 1900s. According to the Bible, "And the Lord spake unto Moses, saying, . . . and thy estimation shall be of the male from twenty years old even unto sixty years old . . . fifty shekels of silver . . . And if it be female, then thy estimation shall be thirty shekels" (Leviticus 27:3–4).

4   In 2003, the Hispanic male/white (non-Hispanic) male earnings ratio was 58 percent; the Hispanic female/white (non-Hispanic) female earnings ratio was 70 percent.

an equal opportunity to develop their potential capability, to use that capability in its most advantageous employment, and to earn a wage that is equal to what others of the same capability are paid. The lack of equal opportunity especially affects members of minority groups marked off by color, national origin, religion, or speech, as well as women, to whom certain market opportunities are denied that are open to men.

Implicit in this description of discrimination is a distinction between **premarket discrimination** and **market discrimination.** Premarket discrimination denies to those who are discriminated against an equal opportunity to develop their natural abilities and talents during their formative, preemployment years.[5] Premarket discrimination can take a number of forms, such as when children of a minority group are provided inferior schooling or poorer health services, or when parents send their sons but not their daughters to college. Market discrimination takes place when people of equal capabilities who are competing in the labor market are given unequal job assignments, promotions, or rates of pay solely on the basis of some characteristic unrelated to their performance. Discrimination, therefore, affects economic outcomes at two separate points: in the premarket acquisition of income-generating characteristics, such as education and good health, and second, in the rewards given to these characteristics within the market itself.

Most of this chapter focuses on market discrimination, not because premarket discrimination is unimportant, but because its causes are largely beyond the domain of labor economics. Three different theories of market discrimination are examined, based on (1) prejudice, (2) market power, and (3) imperfect information. For purposes of exposition, it is assumed that two groups of workers are in the labor market: a minority group B and a majority group W. These groups may represent blacks and whites, males and females, or some other ethnic or religious division.

Personal Prejudice

The first source of discrimination is personal prejudice. *Prejudice* connotes a subjective feeling of dislike for a person or group. This dislike may arise from a number of sources, such as appearance, speech, or unfamiliar customs; whatever the source, a common feature of prejudice is that the person desires *distance* from the individual or group that is the object of dislike. This distance may take two forms. One is physical distance, where the workers of the minority group are segregated in separate departments in a plant or in separate firms, for example; a second form of distance is more social in nature, where workers of the majority and minority groups mix together, but the minority workers are confined to menial or less desirable jobs that are subordinate in both status and authority to the jobs of the majority workers.

---

5   Derek A. Neal and William R. Johnson, "The Role of Pre-market Factors in Black–White Wage Differences," *Journal of Political Economy* 104 (October 1996): 869–95.

FIGURE 9.2   WAGE DIFFERENTIALS CAUSED BY EMPLOYER PREJUDICE

Arranging employers from left to right on the basis of their degrees of prejudice yields the demand curve for minority workers D_B. Up to point X employers are unprejudiced and would hire B workers as long as $W_B = W_W$ (1.0). After point X, however, employers have an increasing degree of prejudice and will only hire B workers if $W_B < W_W$. The relative wage depends on the supply of B workers; a "small" supply of S_1 results in a relative wage of 1.0 (point X) for B workers; a "large" supply of S_2 results in a lower relative wage of 0.7 (point Y).

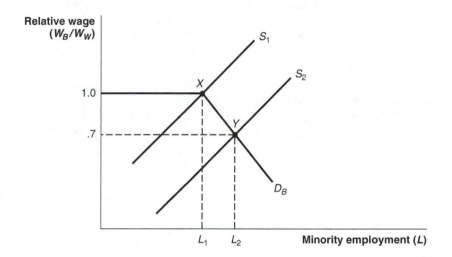

The implications of prejudice for the pattern of earnings and employment of majority and minority workers were first worked out by Gary Becker.[6] Becker observed that prejudice toward minority workers could arise from three sources within the majority group: employers, workers, or consumers.

Prejudice by Employers   According to Becker, an employer with a "taste for discrimination" will be willing to pay something, either directly or in the form of forgone income, to obtain distance from workers of the minority group. For example, prejudiced majority employers, when faced with minority workers that could be hired at the wage W_B, act *as if* the actual money cost were $W_B(1 + d_i)$ where d_i is the ith employer's **discrimination coefficient** against the minority group. The discrimination coefficient represents the employer's psychic disutility of contact with minority workers; the amount of this disutility in money terms is $W_B d_i$.

This model of employer prejudice gives rise to several predictions about earnings and employment, as illustrated in Figure 9.2. The vertical axis measures

6   Gary Becker, *The Economics of Discrimination*, 2d ed. (Chicago: University of Chicago Press, 1971).

W_B/W_W, the relative wage of minority workers compared to majority workers; $W_B/W_W = 1.0$ is the point of equal wages between the two groups. The demand curve D_B shows the total number of minority workers that will be demanded by employers at various wage rates. The shape of the demand curve D_B is determined by arranging the job offers of employers by the size of their discrimination coefficients, with those whose d_i is smallest placed furthest to the left. The horizontal portion of D_B represents the labor demand of nondiscriminating employers ($d_i = 0$) since, if majority and minority workers are assumed to be equally productive, nondiscriminators would be willing to hire minority workers whenever $W_B \leq W_W$. Beyond the kink point (point X), the remaining employers have increasing amounts of prejudice ($d_i > 0$) and would only hire minority workers at successively lower relative wages. Finally, if some minority employers (or liberal majority employers) practiced favoritism toward minority workers, their d_i would be negative, and the initial part of the demand curve would then lie above 1.0.

Becker's model suggests that the size of the wage differential between majority and minority workers depends on two factors. The first is the size of the minority group. Given the demand curve D_B in Figure 9.2, the larger the supply of minority workers in the market, the lower their relative wage is. If the supply curve were S_1, for example, minority workers could all find jobs with nondiscriminating employers and wages between the two groups would be equal (point X). With a larger supply of S_2, the relative wage of minority workers must fall to, say, 0.7 (point Y), in order to induce prejudiced employers to hire them. (The wage paid by nonprejudiced employers will also be 0.7, since that is where supply and demand are equal.) This would offer one possible explanation, for example, why the relatively few black workers in states such as Colorado and Oregon have higher earnings relative to whites than those of similar minority workers in states such as South Carolina or Michigan, which have larger minority populations.

A second factor determining the size of the wage differential between minority and majority workers is the extent of prejudice among employers. If all employers were nondiscriminators, the curve D_B in Figure 9.2 would be perfectly elastic at 1.0, and equal wages would prevail in the market regardless of the size of the minority group. The greater the number of employers who are prejudiced, the further the demand curve D_B will lie to the left, and (other things being equal) the lower the relative wage of minority workers will be.[7] The stronger legacy of prejudice against blacks in many areas of the South helps explain, for example, why the relative earnings of black workers are lower in those states. A second implication of the model is that having more minority group employers means more favorable demand conditions for minority workers and, accordingly, higher relative wages. As Thomas Sowell has noted, this prediction seems to be borne out by the experience of various ethnic groups in America. Jews and Chinese, for example, are much

---

7   It may well be that the degree of prejudice against a racial or ethnic group is positively correlated with the size of that group. This would cause the relative earnings of members of a large minority group to be depressed for two reasons: the supply curve in Figure 9.2 would lie relatively far to the right and the demand curve would lie relatively far to the left.

more likely to be independent businesspeople than Irish or Puerto Ricans, and their relative incomes are also higher.[8]

Several other implications of Becker's model should be noted. One prediction of the theory is that prejudice by employers should lead to a completely segregated workforce among firms. Assuming the supply curve of minority workers is S_2 in Figure 9.2, employers to the left of point Y would hire only minority workers, and employers to the right of point Y would hire only workers of the majority group. To the left of point Y, the lower relative wage of group B workers is more than enough to overcome the employers' prejudice, and given a choice between equally productive group B and group W workers, they would hire all group B workers. Employers to the right of point Y, however, would hire only group W workers, since the lower relative wage of group B workers is not enough to overcome their large amount of prejudice.

Although examples of completely segregated plants can be found from 40 and 50 years ago, this prediction of Becker's model does not accord with present-day reality. As noted in the preceding chapter, segregation in today's labor market is more likely to take the form of occupational segregation. This can be incorporated into Becker's model by allowing the discrimination coefficient to differ not only among the i employers in the market, but also among the j occupations in the firm. The size of the discrimination coefficient d_{ij} would be larger for more strongly prejudiced employers and in occupations such as managerial positions or skilled trades that did not fit the employer's view of appropriate positions for minority workers. Becker's model would then be consistent with integrated firms, although occupations would still be perfectly segregated. If the d_{ij} were quite large for all but a narrow range of occupations, this would result in what economists call "occupational crowding," the funneling of minority workers into a small number of occupations. The result is to further depress wages as a large number of minority workers compete for relatively few jobs.

A second implication of Becker's model is that discriminatory wage differentials should gradually disappear as prejudiced employers are driven out of business by the forces of competition. A crucial insight from Becker's analysis is that when business firms allow prejudice to enter into hiring decisions, it costs them profits because they could have hired an equally qualified group B worker at a lower wage than a group W worker.[9] Firms that do not discriminate, therefore, have a cost advantage over their prejudiced competitors and, if the economy is competitive, should be able to drive the discriminators from the market, making the demand curve D_B in Figure 9.2 perfectly elastic in the long run.

---

8   Thomas Sowell, *Ethnic America: A History*, 2d ed. (New York: Basic Books, 1981).

9   An interesting example of this comes from Japan. At one time, many Japanese companies were very reluctant to hire female college graduates because, in the words of one newspaper article, "There is a widely held belief that young women recruits look more toward hooking an eligible bachelor than to their job contribution." As a result, the article notes that "foreign companies without prejudices about employing women gain from Japanese attitudes, getting the pick of female graduates from the best schools." "Women Still Forced to Play Second Fiddle in Japan," *Hong Kong Standard* (March 22, 1986): 11.

A number of economists have questioned the validity of this prediction of the Becker model, noting that race and sex discrimination have persisted for the entire history of market economies.[10] Why don't competitive forces bring an end to discrimination more quickly? The answer involves several parts. One is that some firms operate in oligopolistic or regulated industries and are under less competitive pressure to maximize profits, giving them some slack in which to indulge their tastes for discrimination.[11] A second reason is that, owing to premarket discrimination in education and training, there is not a sufficient supply of minority workers in many higher-level blue-collar and white-collar occupations for nondiscriminators to hire. A third reason is that in periods of unemployment, firms can exercise their prejudice against minority workers at relatively little cost since many workers of the majority group are willing to work at low wages. The best example of how full employment can break down the forces of prejudice is the dramatic breakthroughs achieved by women and blacks during the labor shortages of World War II. Finally, Jim Crow laws in the states of the South that required separate locker rooms, cafeterias, and drinking fountains for blacks and whites raised the price to firms of employing black workers, removing part of the incentive to hire them.

With respect to the elimination of employer discrimination, Becker's model seems to suggest three options. One is to adopt policies that reduce the prejudicial attitudes of employers. A second is to impose financial penalties on firms that raise the costs of discrimination. A third is to increase the competitiveness of the economy so that market forces can more rapidly bring about the long-run demise of discriminatory firms. In this model, a fourth option—an equal pay for equal work law—would not benefit minority workers. In Figure 9.2, requiring employers to pay group B workers a wage equal to that of group W workers (1.0 instead of 0.7) would cause employment of minority workers to fall from L_2 to L_1. The equal pay law removes the cost to firms of discrimination, and every firm with any $d_i > 0$ would hire only group W workers.

Prejudice by Workers A second source of market discrimination may come from the prejudice of majority group workers. It is often argued that prejudice by workers is likely to be a more powerful source of discrimination because the motives are stronger; unlike employers who rarely come in contact with minority workers and for whom discrimination costs money, prejudice among workers of different races, sexes, or ethnic groups is fueled both by their competition for jobs and their close personal contact at work.

---

10   See Kenneth J. Arrow, "The Theory of Discrimination," in Orly Ashenfelter and Albert Rees, eds., *Discrimination in Labor Markets* (Princeton, N.J.: Princeton University Press, 1973), 3–33, and F. Ray Marshall, "The Economics of Discrimination: A Survey," *Journal of Economic Literature* 12, no. 3 (September 1974): 849–71.

11   One study of the banking industry, for example, found that the fewer the number of banks competing in a geographical area, the smaller was the share of female employment in each firm. See Orley Ashenfelter and Timothy Hannan, "Sex Discrimination and Product Market Competition: The Case of the Banking Industry," *Quarterly Journal of Economics* 101 (February 1986): 149–73. Additional evidence on the presence of wage discrimination in markets where firms have more market power is provided by Judith K. Hellerstein et al. "Market Forces and Sex Discrimination," *Journal of Human Resources* 37 (Spring 2002): 353–80.

In Becker's model, a worker of the majority group has a taste for discrimination if he or she, when offered a wage W_w for a job that entails working with members of the minority group, acts as if the net wage were $W_w(1 - d_k)$.[12] The variable d_k is the kth worker's discrimination coefficient and equals the amount of disutility experienced from contact with minority persons. Because of their prejudice, group W workers will agree to work with B workers only if they are paid a wage premium equal to $W_w d_k$. An employer may be unprejudiced and willing to hire both group B and group W workers; if workers are prejudiced, however, the firm will suffer a cost penalty to maintain an integrated workforce because it will have to pay a wage higher than the market level to keep its group W workers. In the long run, Becker's model predicts that two things will happen. The first is that firms will become completely segregated, having all group B workers or all group W workers in order to avoid the higher labor costs of an integrated workforce. The second prediction is that any discriminatory wage differentials will disappear, since if group W workers were paid more, firms would switch to a lower-wage, all group B workforce.

Do these predictions accord with observed behavior? With respect to the first, although firms rarely switch from all male or all white workers to all black or all female workers, on a departmental or occupational level such switches have occurred. In a study of the automobile industry, for example, Herbert Northrup observed that once a sizable number of blacks gained entrance into a formerly all-white production department, a "white flight" often occurred as prejudiced or fearful white workers no longer wanted jobs they had formerly accepted at the going wage.[13] A similar experience has occurred in occupations such as bank teller or bookkeeper that were once primarily male occupations and are now largely female dominated. With segregation by gender, however, the cause may not be so much prejudice as status.[14] One study finds that racial and ethnic segregation (even across jobs at the same firm) can account for as much as one-half the observed wage gap between these groups.[15] Other research, however, does not find widespread segregation of workers by race.[16] A final example that seems to offer some support for Becker's theory comes from organized baseball. In the 1880s, several clubs had black players

---

12   A variation on Becker's theory suggests that men may have a distaste for being supervised by women, not merely just working with them. Some evidence of the pay differences and occupational sorting that derive from this distaste is provided for the insurance industry by Marjorie L. Baldwin et al., "A Hierarchical Theory of Occupational Segregation and Wage Discrimination," *Economic Inquiry* 39 (January 2001): 94–110.

13   Herbert R. Northrup, "The Negro in the Automobile Industry," in *Negro Employment in Basic Industry* (Philadelphia: Wharton School of Finance and Commerce, 1970), 105–6.

14   See Myra H. Strober and Audri Gordon Lanford, "The Feminization of Public School Teaching: Cross-Sectional Analysis, 1850–1880," *Journal of Women in Culture and Society* 11 no. 2 (1986): 212–35.

15   Kimberly Bayard et al., "Why Are Racial and Ethnic Wage Gaps Larger for Men Than for Women? Exploring the Role of Segregation," *NBER Working Paper #6997* (March 1999).

16   See Barry T. Hirsch and David A. MacPherson, "Wages, Sorting on Skill, and the Racial Composition of Jobs," *Journal of Labor Economics* 22 (January 2004): 189–210; and Judith K. Hellerstein and David Neumark, "Workplace Segregation in the United States: Race, Ethnicity, and Skill," *Public Policy Institute of California Working Paper No. 2004.05* (April 2004). These papers find racial and ethnic segregation is mostly driven by skill differentials and complementarities.

on their teams. Despite the desire of the team managers to keep the black players, prejudiced white players forced the clubs to let them go by refusing to take the field if blacks were in the game.[17] The result was the formation of two segregated leagues, the all-white major leagues and the black Negro leagues.[18]

The second prediction—the disappearance of discriminatory wage differentials—has not been fully accomplished, and it is instructive to consider why. One possible explanation is again that firms operate in sheltered product markets where the forces of competition are sufficiently attenuated that they can continue to pay higher wages to workers of the majority group.[19] A second explanation is that competition can erode discriminatory wage differentials only if employers can find a sufficient supply of equally qualified group B workers to replace the prejudiced group W workers. In southern industry prior to the 1960s, for example, if a firm hired a black worker into some type of skilled job, it was not unusual for the white workers to stage a boycott or a strike until the black worker was let go.[20] If a large pool of trained black workers were available to the firm at a lower wage than whites, it could increase its profits by hiring them and thus breaking the strike. This rarely if ever happened, however, since one of the most important functions of premarket discrimination in schooling and training was to prevent the creation of a skilled black labor force that could challenge the job control of the white workers. Traditional gender-role stereotypes have similarly limited the supply of female workers to skilled craft and professional occupations, though whether this was a conscious ploy on the part of men (possibly in their role as employers) to preserve

---

17 Robert Peterson, *Only the Ball Was White* (Englewood Cliffs, N.J.: Prentice-Hall, 1970). Prejudice took many forms. Baseball folklore has it that a black player invented the shin guard to protect himself from white players who deliberately tried to spike him while sliding into second base. Evidence on modern-day worker discrimination in sports can be found for the National Basketball Association in Orn B. Bodvasson and Mark D. Partridge, "A Supply and Demand Model of Co-Worker, Employer, and Customer Discrimination," *Labour Economics* 8 (June 2001): 389–416.

18 Whether Branch Rickey (general manager of the Brooklyn Dodgers) acted out of altruism or the pursuit of profit when he brought Jackie Robinson into the major leagues and broke the color barrier in 1947 remains a controversial question. It is clear, however, that segregation cost the team owners a lot of money. In his first three games with the Cleveland Indians, for example, black pitching star Satchel Paige drew over 201,000 fans, breaking all-time attendance records. (Peterson, *Only the Ball Was White*, 140.)

19 Evidence on this point is provided in Martin Brown and Peter Philips, "Competition, Racism, and Hiring Practices among California Manufacturers, 1860–1882," *Industrial and Labor Relations Review* 40 (October 1986): 61–74. Because of labor shortages in the 1850s, many California employers hired low-wage Chinese immigrants. In the 1860s through the 1870s, however, the number of white workers grew rapidly, and they put considerable pressure on those firms to replace their Chinese workers with higher-cost white labor. Employers in industries such as canning that had relatively high entry barriers did switch to whites, while employers in industries with low entry barriers, such as cigar rolling, kept their Chinese workers to avoid being quickly driven out of business by new, lower-cost firms operated by the Chinese themselves. Although competition forced these white-owned firms to continue to hire Chinese, it also led to virulent anti-Chinese agitation and racial violence. As an end result, white workers resorted to an institutional device to limit competition—in 1882 Congress passed the Chinese Exclusion Act, which sharply reduced the number of Orientals that could immigrate to the United States.

20 F. Ray Marshall, *Labor in the South* (Cambridge, Mass.: Harvard University Press, 1967), 81, and "The Negro in the Paper Industry," in Northrup, *Negro Employment in Basic Industry*, 120–23.

their hegemony in the job market is open to debate.[21] Regardless of intent, a clear policy implication is that providing equal access to education and job skills to all groups of workers could significantly combat race or sex differentials in earnings due to worker prejudice.

Prejudice by Consumers   Discriminatory wage differentials between minority and majority workers may also occur because of the prejudice of consumers. A prejudiced group W consumer, when faced with an opportunity to purchase a good or service from a group B worker at a price, acts as if the price were $P_B(1 + d_m)$, where d_m is the discrimination coefficient of the mth consumer. If the group B workers are employed in jobs that require personal contact with group W customers, they must be willing to work at a lower wage than group W workers so the firm can lower its price to overcome the aversion of the prejudiced customer. This is an unstable situation, since group B workers could earn more in jobs that did not involve customer contact. In the long run, equally productive group B workers and group W workers should receive the same wages, but group B workers will be segregated in jobs that do not involve interaction with group W customers.

There are numerous historical examples of this type of discrimination in labor markets. A study of the meatpacking industry found that up to the mid-1950s, firms systematically excluded blacks from jobs that involved physical contact with finished cuts of meat and other products such as oleo so that prejudiced white customers would not worry that black hands had touched the final product.[22] In addition, evidence suggests that women and blacks have had a difficult time breaking into occupations such as stockbroker and lawyer because employers fear adverse reactions from their white male clients.[23] There is even some evidence that customer discrimination persisted into the 1990s and significantly impacted employment and wages of blacks. Harry Holzer and Keith Ihlanfeldt make use of responses from a survey administered between 1992 and 1994 to employers in Atlanta, Boston, Detroit, and Los Angeles to show that blacks are less likely to be

---

21   A persistent theme in much of the feminist and radical literature is that the traditional feminine sex role was deliberately propagated by men either to maintain their power over women or to divide and segment the workforce so as to prevent working class solidarity. See, for example, Kate Millett, *Sexual Politics* (New York: Avon, 1970), 23–58, and Richard Edwards, Michael Reich, and Thomas E. Weisskopf, *The Capitalist System: A Radical Analysis of American Society*, 2d ed. (Englewood Cliffs, N.J.: Prentice-Hall, 1978), particularly 331–41. Also see Myra A. Strober, "The Relative Attractiveness Theory of Gender Segregation: The Case of Physicians," *Proceedings of the 44th Annual Meetings of the Industrial and Labor Relations Association* (Fall 1992): 42–50. Racism, in this view, plays much the same role.

22   Walter A. Fogel, *The Negro in the Meat Industry* (Philadelphia: Wharton School of Finance and Commerce, 1970), 105.

23   See Michelle Patterson and Laurie Engelberg, "Women in Male-Dominated Professions," in Ann H. Stromberg and Shirley Harkess, eds., *Women Working: Theories and Facts in Perspective* (Palo Alto, Calif.: Mayfield, 1978), 266–92. After one day on the job as a pharmacy trainee at a Tifton, Georgia, drugstore, the owner told the worker, a black female student from the University of Georgia, that he could no longer employ her because some of his white customers objected to being served by a black. He said, "I have no prejudice at all, but it's hard for the small independent business to survive. You bend to what your customers say." Quoted in "Store Denies UGA Student Work Because She's Black," *Atlanta Journal* (August 13, 1987): 1, 13A.

hired into jobs when the degree of customer contact in those jobs is significant and when the customers being served are mostly white.[24] It is also of interest to note that whites are less likely to be hired into jobs serving mostly black customers, indicating that customer discrimination can go both ways.

Market Power

A second source of market discrimination between minority and majority workers arises from the exercise of market power in the labor market, either on the demand side by monopsonistic business firms or on the supply side by labor unions. The essence of market power is that the monopsonistic firm or the labor union is not simply a passive "wage taker" in the market, but has some discretion to set the wage independent of competitive forces. One possible use of such market power is to set wage rates that discriminate between workers of various races, sexes, or ethnic groups. The motive in this case is not prejudice, but *pecuniary gain*. Unlike the prejudice theory outlined above where it costs to discriminate, market power theories assert that discrimination takes place precisely because it *adds* to the incomes of the discriminators. In this view, the long-term persistence of discrimination is readily explained by the fact that some members of the majority groups make money from it.

Monopsonistic Discrimination   The model of **monopsonistic discrimination** was developed in the 1930s by Joan Robinson, a famous British economist, as an explanation for sex discrimination in wages.[25] As shown in Chapter 6, a monopsonist is able to pay wages below the competitive level because workers lack alternative employers to choose from. Robinson showed that under certain circumstances, a monopsonist could increase its profits even further by discriminating in the wages it pays so that some workers receive a lower wage than others. Two conditions must be satisfied for monopsonistic discrimination to take place. The first is that the firm's labor supply must be separable into distinct groups. Demographic characteristics such as race and sex offer two possible ways to do this. The second condition is that the elasticity of the labor supply curve of one group must be different than that of the other. Such a situation is illustrated in Figure 9.3.

It is assumed that the monopsonist can hire either group B workers (the left-hand part of the diagram) or group W workers (the right-hand part). It is also assumed that group B and group W workers are equally productive and, for the sake of simplicity, that each has an identical marginal revenue product. This last assumption is illustrated by the horizontal curve MRP_L. The supply curve of group B and group W workers is given by S_B and S_W, respectively, along with their

---

24   Harry J. Holzer and Keith R. Ihlanfeldt, "Customer Discrimination and Employment Outcomes for Minority Workers," *Quarterly Journal of Economics* 113 (August 1998): 835–68.

25   Joan Robinson, *Economics of Imperfect Competition* (London: Macmillan, 1933).

FIGURE 9.3   WAGE DISCRIMINATION BY A MONOPSONIST

It is assumed that each B and W worker is equally productive, shown by the horizontal MRP_L curve. To maximize profits, the monopsonist hires L_B of the B workers (point V) and L_W of the W workers (point Y).

Since the supply curve S_D is more inelastic than S_W, the firm maximizes profits by paying B workers a wage of only W_B (point X) while paying a higher wage of W_W (point Z) to W workers.

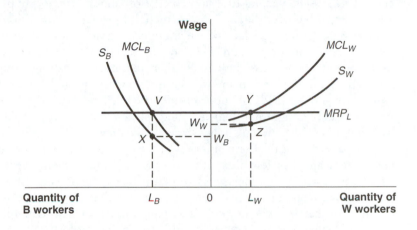

accompanying marginal cost of labor schedules MCL_B and MCL_W. The supply curve S_B is more steeply sloped than S_W, indicating that the supply of group B workers is more inelastic than that of group W workers. To maximize profits, the monopsonist should hire workers from each group as long as their marginal revenue product is greater than or equal to their marginal cost of labor. The optimal level of employment of group B workers is L_B (point V); the optimal employment of group W workers is L_W (point Y). To obtain L_B and L_W workers, the firm must pay a wage of W_B (point X) and W_W (point Z), respectively.

The monopsonist practices wage discrimination in that $W_B < W_W$, even though workers of both groups are equally productive. Group B workers receive a lower wage because their supply curve is more inelastic. The more inelastic labor supply is, the less responsive it is to changes in the wage. Thus, the curve S_B shows that the firm can pay group B workers a much lower wage than group W workers, and yet relatively few group B workers will leave the firm. Likewise, to increase employment of group B workers very far does not pay because the wage that must be paid increases rapidly, given their limited supply.

There is considerable debate over whether monopsonistic discrimination is an important source of pay differentials between minority and majority groups in the labor market.[26] A precondition for such discrimination is that the employer have some degree of monopsony power over its workers. The pure form of monopsony (the one-company town) is relatively rare, although conditions of oligopsony and monopsonistic competition may have a wider applicability. A second prerequisite is that the supply curve of labor be more inelastic for the minority group than for the majority group. This is likely to be a realistic assumption in certain situations, but unrealistic in many others. For example, in traditionally female or black occupations, occupational segregation is likely to result in a crowding of minority workers in these fields, making the supply curve of labor of these groups quite elastic and incompatible with the monopsony model. In other, nontraditional fields such as professional, managerial, or skilled craft occupations, however, occupational segregation results in a very limited supply of female and black workers. Particularly in the case of women, their limited numbers in these occupations, coupled with the geographic immobility of many women due to marriage and family ties, may give employers in these fields an opportunity to practice monopsonistic discrimination. A good example might be a female college professor or lawyer who is married and lives in a city with only one university or only a few law firms. Since she is effectively tied to the local labor market (or at least more so than are her married male colleagues), and has few alternative sources of employment, the firm can take advantage of her greater inelasticity of supply by paying her a lower wage than that received by equally productive men. In a study of the impact migration has on the earnings of married women, Felicia LeClere and Diane McLaughlin found that married women who migrate suffer an earnings loss of $918, on average, during their first year after migration.[27]

The monopsony model suggests a different set of policies to end discriminatory pay differentials than does the prejudice model. One remedy might be equal pay legislation, which would end discrimination by forcing the employer in Figure 9.3 to pay women the wage W_W instead of W_B. The law would not, however, end the monopsonistic exploitation of *both* men and women in the firm. The second legal remedy would be some sort of affirmative action law requiring the firm to increase its hiring of minority workers. This would gradually increase the elasticity of supply of minority workers by breaking down occupational segregation. A third option would be to pass laws making it easier for workers to join a union since a union's bargaining power is able to offset the firm's monopsony power.

---

26 See Janice Fanning Madden, *The Economics of Sex Discrimination* (Lexington, Mass.: D. C. Heath, 1973); Lucy Cardwell and Mark Rosenzweig, "Economic Mobility, Monopsonistic Discrimination and Sex Differences in Wages," *Southern Economic Journal* 46, no. 4 (April 1980): 1102–17; and Barry T. Hirsch and Edward T. Schumacher, "Classic or New Monopsony? Searching for Evidence in Nursing Labor Markets," Mimeo, Trinity University (November 2003).

27 Felicia B. LeClere and Diane K. McLaughlin, "Family Migration and Changes in Women's Earnings: A Decomposition Analysis," *Population Research and Policy Review* 16 (August 1997): 315–35; this loss is in 1997 dollars. Also see Haim Ofek and Yesook Merrill, "Labor Immobility and the Formation of Gender Wage Gaps in Local Markets," *Economic Inquiry* 35 (January 1997): 28–47. Additional evidence of the important role of mobility in potentially explaining labor market discrimination is found in Steven Raphael and David Riker, "Geographic Mobility, Race, and Wage Differentials," *Journal of Urban Economics* 45 (January 1999): 17–46.

Discrimination by Unions   By seeking equal pay for equal work, a union can end discrimination in the workplace. Paradoxically, a union can also be a major cause of discrimination. The determining factor in shaping a union's racial or gender policy is most often its organizational structure.[28] Industrial-type unions have typically been much more progressive on the issue of fair employment than have craft unions. Through their operation of apprenticeship programs and hiring halls in industries such as construction or longshoring, craft unions have a built-in mechanism to exclude minority workers from the trade. Discrimination is a source of pecuniary gain to their white rank and file because it preserves their monopoly on job opportunities. Industrial unions, on the other hand, typically lack a means to control whom the firm hires; in the automobile or steel industries, for example, the employer hires "off the street" and the union has little ability to influence whether whites or blacks are chosen. If the industrial union is to effectively organize the firm, it must adopt a policy of nondiscrimination in membership in order to secure a strong bargaining position. Discrimination in industrial unions is not unknown, however. Its principal form is the development of seniority systems that block the advancement of minority workers into the higher-paying jobs held by white workers.

Imperfect Information

A third explanation for market discrimination is **statistical discrimination.**[29] In this theory, discrimination is a result not of prejudice or the pursuit of pecuniary gain, but rather of the imperfect information that confronts employers in the screening process. An employer can never be sure of a worker's actual productivity at the time of hiring; as a result firms use personal characteristics of workers to sort them into productivity groups. Some of these personal characteristics are individual in nature, such as years of education, previous work experience, or test scores; others are "indices" or group characteristics, such as race, gender, or nationality. The use of group characteristics in screening gives rise to statistical discrimination.

For discrimination to take place, two workers of equal productivity must be paid different wages based on a criterion such as race or gender. How might this occur? Imagine that the employer wishes to hire a new worker. The firm's want ad in the paper has resulted in a pool of job applicants from various race and gender groups who have different levels of education and work experience. To choose the best (most productive) worker, the firm will screen the applicant pool based on

---

28   See Brigid O'Farrell and Suzanne Moore, "Unions, Hard Hats, and Women Workers," in Dorothy Sue Cobble, ed., *Women and Unions: Forging a Partnership* (Ithaca, N.Y.: ILR Press, 1993), 69–84; F. Ray Marshall, *The Negro and Organized Labor* (New York: Wiley, 1965); and Philip Taft, *Organizing Dixie: Alabama Workers in the Industrial Era* (Westport, Conn.: Greenwood Press, 1981). A theoretical treatment of the employment outcomes in unions that discriminate can be found in John R. Dobson and Anthony A. Sampson, "Labour Market Efficiency with Discriminatory Unions," *Bulletin of Economic Research* 53 (July 2001): 183–89.

29   The discussion in this section is based on Dennis J. Aigner and Glen G. Cain, "Statistical Theories of Discrimination in Labor Markets," *Industrial and Labor Relations Review* 30, no. 2 (January 1977): 175–87.

characteristics that it believes correlate with, or are related to, a worker's productivity on the job. Assume that the firm observes only two characteristics of each worker, the level of education (college degree or no college degree) and race (black or white). If years of education were a perfect predictor of productivity, the firm would hire only college graduates, and black and white workers of equal education would receive equal wages. If education is an imperfect predictor of productivity, the employer will search for additional characteristics that are correlated with job performance in order to improve the screening process. In this example, the only other observable characteristic is race. The group characteristic of race can affect who is hired in two possible ways.

Unequal Productivity   The first is if black workers, on average, have a lower level of productivity than white workers. This case is illustrated in Figure 9.4, which shows the frequency distribution of the black and white college graduates in the firm's applicant pool by their level of productivity (output per hour). The mean level of productivity of black workers, is less than that of white workers, although many black workers in the upper tail of the distribution exceed the average level of productivity of whites. The lower average level of black productivity might come from several sources. One source is premarket discrimination in the form of inferior schooling. A second possible source is if blacks have lower innate ability or

FIGURE 9.4   **HYPOTHETICAL FREQUENCY DISTRIBUTION OF WORKER PRODUCTIVITY AMONG BLACKS AND WHITES**

Each curve represents the frequency distribution of black and white workers, respectively, by their levels of productivity. It is assumed that the average productivity level of blacks, $\overline{Q}_B$, is less than that of whites, $\overline{Q}_W$.

Given that race and productivity are correlated, a B worker may suffer statistical discrimination since he or she may be more productive than a W worker, yet will not be hired by the employer because of the group affiliation.

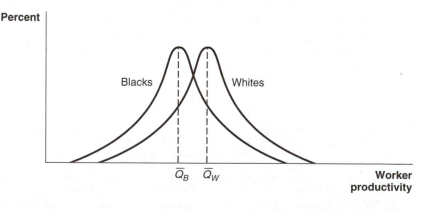

cultural values that are less attuned with the "Protestant work ethic" of whites.[30] A third possibility is that because of prejudice or ignorance, employers systematically underestimate the average productivity of black workers. Finally, if men and women were the groups being compared, the mean level of productivity of women might be lower due to interrupted work careers.[31]

If race is correlated with productivity, as assumed in this example, employers will be able to improve their selection of job candidates by considering both individual and group characteristics of workers. Since, in the example, the average productivity of black workers is lower than that of whites, this will lead employers to systematically prefer white workers over black workers of equal educational level, giving rise, in turn, to lower earnings for blacks relative to whites. Are these earnings differentials discriminatory? On a group basis, they are not, to the extent that the differences in wages reflect actual differences in productivity.[32] On an individual basis, however, they are. The reason is that the black worker, even if identical to the white worker in terms of personal qualifications, is rejected based on his or her group affiliation. This result helps to explain the complaint of black workers that they are held to higher standards than whites in hiring and promotion. As one black worker in a middle-management position put it, "You've got to take the riskier assignments and prove yourself over and over again."[33] Women of equal ability with men may also be rejected for jobs since their gender is associated with a greater probability of quitting, even if they themselves plan on uninterrupted work careers. Statistical discrimination, therefore, may lead to unequal earnings among individual workers of identical productivity because of their group affiliations.

---

30 The average IQ score of blacks in America is 15 points less than that of whites. As discussed in Daniel Seligman, *A Question of Intelligence* (New York: Birch Lane Press, 1992), there has been a spirited debate over the extent to which this racial difference in scores can be attributed to genetic differences between blacks and whites. An article in the *New York Times* ("An Emerging Theory on Blacks' IQ Scores," April 10, 1988: Educ 22–24) states that many experts on the subject now discount a genetic explanation for lower black IQ scores and emphasize instead a social/psychological explanation involving the role of social subordination and alienation. Empirical evidence shows that in nearly all countries where there is a dominant social group and a subordinated minority group the children of the minority group have lower average IQ scores. The hypothesis is that the members of the minority group perceive themselves to be inferior relative to members of the dominant group and, hence, come to believe that they either cannot do well at school or will not benefit from it. Also see Christopher Jencks and Meredith Phillips, "The Black–White Test Score Gap," *The Brookings Review* (Spring 1998): 24–27.

31 Michael Sattinger, "Statistical Discrimination with Employment Criteria," *International Economic Review* 39 (February 1998): 205–37, develops a model illustrating how employers may establish stricter employment criteria for women based on the higher quit rates observed for women as a group. Also see Harry J. Holzer, "Employer Skill Demands and Labor Market Outcomes of Blacks and Women," *Industrial and Labor Relations Review* 52 (October 1998): 82–98, for evidence of hiring outcomes in the early 1990s consistent with the presence of statistical discrimination. Joseph Altonji and Charles Pierret, "Employer Learning and Statistical Discrimination," *Quarterly Journal of Economics* 116 (February 2001): 313–50, find little evidence of statistical discrimination on race but evidence of statistical discrimination on education levels. Also see Nick Feltovich and Chris Papageorgiou, "An Experimental Study of Statistical Discrimination by Employers," *Southern Economic Journal* 70 (April 2004): 837–49.

32 If employers' lower estimate of black productivity is due to ignorance or prejudice, then even on a group basis any wage differential is discriminatory.

33 Quoted in "Many Blacks Jump Off the Corporate Job Ladder to Be Entrepreneurs," *Wall Street Journal* (August 2, 1984): 1. Also see Nick Feltovich and Chris Papageorgiou, "An Experimental Study of Statistical Discrimination by Employees," *Southern Economic Journal* 70 (April 2004): 837–49.

Equal Productivity Statistical discrimination may arise even if black and white or male and female workers have *equal* productivity. Two conditions have to be met for this to occur. The first is that predictors of individual productivity such as years of education or test scores must be less reliable for members of the minority group. As a real-world example, one study, using data from the personnel files of a large company, found that men's rate of absenteeism could be predicted more reliably than women's, and that the overall variance in absenteeism was greater for women than for men.[34] The second condition is that employers must be *risk averse* in choosing among job candidates—that is, when faced with two job candidates having equal credentials, the employer will select the one whose productivity is least uncertain.[35] A female worker of equal ability with a male worker may be passed over simply because the employer does not want to take the larger risk of hiring the woman. This practice leads to a vicious circle, since by not hiring women, the employer perpetuates the uncertainty about the actual performance of female workers.[36]

Earnings differentials due to statistical discrimination result from employers' imperfect information concerning the productivity of individual job candidates. What policies might be adopted to end such discrimination? One approach has been to enact civil rights and fairness-in-hiring laws that prohibit screening by background characteristics such as race, gender, or marital status. Whereas this will eliminate statistical discrimination, to the extent that race, gender, or other such group characteristics are correlated with productivity, it will also make it more difficult for firms to hire the best worker for the job. A second approach to ending statistical discrimination is to require that hiring tests used by firms measure people's ability without bias and that the scores on these tests be demonstrably related to performance on the job.[37] If hiring tests are not fair measures of ability, then the results of such tests might mistakenly indicate that the average level of productivity of minority workers was less than that of majority workers. In this case, the employer in Figure 9.4 would assume that $\overline{Q}_B < \overline{Q}_W$ when, in fact, this was simply the result of a poorly designed or poorly administered test. It is also important that differences in test scores be valid predictors of people's performance on the job. The results of a cognitive ability test might indicate, for example, that $\overline{Q}_B < \overline{Q}_W$ causing the employer to systematically favor group W workers. If a person's test score is unrelated to productivity on the job, however, group B workers will be unfairly passed over in the screening process. This issue of whether an employment test accurately measures performance of skills *necessary* for the job was a major focal point of the Civil Rights Act of 1991.

---

34 See Lawrence M. Kahn, "Comment on Sex Discrimination in Professional Employment: A Case Study," *Industrial and Labor Relations Review* 34 (January 1981): 273–75.

35 See Michael J. Orszag and Gylfi Zoega, "Hiring Risk and Labour Market Equilibrium," *Center for Economic Policy Discussion Paper #1314*, Birkbeck College (January 1996), for a formal derivation of this model and result.

36 See David Neumark, "Wage Differentials by Race and Sex: The Roles of Taste for Discrimination and Labor Market Information," *Industrial Relations* 38 (July 1999): 414–45, for empirical evidence of the importance of accurate information for improving the wages of women and minorities.

37 These issues are discussed in John E. Hunter and Frank L. Schmidt, "Ability Tests: Economic Benefits versus the Issue of Fairness," *Industrial Relations* 21, no. 3 (Fall 1982): 293–308.

IN THE NEWS

The Young and the Beautiful

A television journalist is fired because a viewer survey revealed that audiences perceived her as "unattractive." An over-60 screenwriter finds it necessary to include a younger partner on his projects in order to get his scripts through the producers' doors. In addition, recent research has found that attractive executives earn about 10 percent more (holding everything else, such as occupation, age, experience, etc., constant) than their less attractive counterparts; this result is most pronounced for women. Research has also found that unattractive people are 2 to 4 times more likely to be laid off from their jobs.

Have the workers in these examples been subjected to discrimination? The key to answering this question is determining whether a worker's appearance or age somehow affects his or her productivity.

There are some jobs, such as those in the glamour industries of movies and modeling, for which a premium on appearance has been ruled legal; beauty has a direct bearing on a worker's productivity in these industries. What about other jobs? Is it necessary to be beautiful to wait on tables efficiently? To manage workers effectively? To research and report news accurately? To create a captivating script? One economist points out that beautiful *children* generally receive more attention and praise from adults. If these early positive experiences transform these beautiful children into confident, highly motivated (and beautiful) adults, their greater earnings and employment opportunities may be as much a function of their confidence and motivation (productivity) as it is a function of their attractiveness.

But what about circumstances where a link between productivity and attractiveness is missing? Should the laws deny consumers their preferences to be served by attractive people, even if they don't report the news or wait tables any better than less attractive people? A cornerstone of the capitalist economy is that resources that are the most highly valued earn the rents associated with that valuation. So, if customers prefer to be served by beautiful people, and are willing to pay a premium to satisfy those preferences, employers are merely responding to the laws of supply and demand by paying a premium for appearance.

The problem with the above argument, however, is that it can be too easily extended to include characteristics other than a subjective measure of attractiveness, such as gender or race. We have decided as a society that employers are not allowed to indulge the (either perceived or real) prejudices of customers when it comes to race or gender. Just because a customer wants to be served by a man is not sufficient legal justification to discriminate in hiring or pay against women, for example. While one could provide a logical, profit-maximizing justification for treating employees differently based on physical characteristics, a society can decide to place limits on the circumstances in which it is legitimate to base employment decisions on appearance.

SOURCES: Patricia J. Williams, "The Beauty Myth," *Nation* 266 (1 June 1998): 10; Robert J. Barro, "So You Want to Hire the Beautiful. Well, Why Not?" *Business Week* (16 March 1998): 18; Suzanne Tregarthen, "In the Eye of the Beholder: How Beauty Affects Salaries," *The Margin* (November/December 1990): 44; NPR Morning Edition, *Hollywood Age Discrimination* (27 October 1998); Diane Stafford, "Our Bias for Beauty Is Showing" *Kansas City Star* (16 March 2000): workplace column; and Daniel S. Hamermesh, et al, "Dress for Success—Does Primping Pay?" *Labour Economics* 9 (2002): 361–73.

Discrimination and Life Cycle Earnings

The models of discrimination discussed so far are static in nature in that they provide only snapshots of the effects of discrimination at one particular point in time. Discrimination may lead not only to unequal wages among workers at a point in time, but also to a growing inequality in earnings over the life cycle from a variety of sources that will be explored here. Viewed from a lifetime perspective, the cumulative effect of discrimination may be much larger than that revealed by comparing two people at one point in their lives.

Research on life cycle earnings has found an extremely interesting pattern in black/white income differentials. Each year a new *cohort* of individuals (persons born in the same year) come into the labor market and begin their first year of work. Research evidence shows that from the early 1960s to the mid-1970s the gap between the wages of black and white men for each entering cohort became progressively smaller, implying that young black males in the mid-1970s started off in the "earnings race" with whites at a smaller disadvantage than did young blacks a decade earlier. After the mid-1970s, however, the wage gap between young black and young white men began to grow again, particularly during the 1980s.[38] During the 1990s, the gap seems to have held steady, with neither additional losses nor gains for young black men.[39]

Once each cohort of black and white males have entered the labor market and begun work, what then happens to the wage gap over the next 30 years of their working life? The research on this issue indicates that on average the wages of black men grow more slowly with years of experience than do the wages of white men.[40] Over the life cycle of a cohort of black and white men, therefore, the wage gap grows larger over time.

Another study finds that periods of self-employment can contribute to differences in life cycle earnings between men and women. Donald Williams finds that women suffer a penalty in terms of career wage growth for spells of self-employment, whereas men do not.[41]

Discrimination in Training

In attempting to explain how the wage gap might grow over time, economists have given particular attention to the process of on-the-job training. The more

---

38 Greg Duncan and Saul D. Hoffman, "A New Look at the Causes of the Improved Economic Status of Black Workers," *Journal of Human Resources* 18, no. 2 (Spring 1983): 268–82; James Smith and Finis Welch, "Black Economic Progress after Myrdal," *Journal of Economic Literature* 27, no. 2 (June 1989): 519–64; and John Bound and Richard Freeman, "What Went Wrong? The Erosion of Relative Earnings and Employment among Young Black Men in the 1980s," *Quarterly Journal of Economics* 107, no. 1 (February 1992): 201–32.

39 Evidence based on the authors' calculations using the March Supplements of the Current Population Survey.

40 See Bernt Bratsberg and Dek Terrell, "Experience, Tenure, and Wage Growth of Young Black and White Men," *Journal of Human Resources* 33 (Summer 1998): 658–82, and Gerald S. Oettinger, "Statistical Discrimination and the Early Career Evolution of the Black–White Wage Gap," *Journal of Labor Economics* 14 (January 1996): 52–78.

41 Donald R. Williams, "Consequences of Self-Employment for Women and Men in the United States," *Labour Economics* 7 (September 2000): 665–87.

TABLE 9.1

AMOUNTS OF ON-THE-JOB TRAINING RECEIVED BY RACE AND GENDER

Race–Gender Group	Proportion of Workers Who Received Training	Percentage of Workers Who Received "Company Training"
Gender		
Men	38.9	25.5
Women	37.1	21.9
Race		
White	39.1	24.9
Black	34.8	19.5

SOURCE: Based on information contained in Jonathan R. Veum, "Training among Young Adults: Who, What Kind, and For How Long?" *Monthly Labor Review* (August 1993): 27–32.

on-the-job training a person receives, the greater becomes his or her productivity to the firm, and the more rapidly earnings rise over the life cycle. One study estimates that each additional day of formal training increases a worker's salary at one company by 1 percent.[42]

Several studies have shown that, in the past, the wage gaps between men and women and between whites and blacks had a great deal to do with the fact that women and blacks were much less likely than white men to receive training.[43] More recent evidence indicates that the likelihood women and blacks receive training is much closer to that of white men. The *nature* of that training, however, still varies across race and gender. Table 9.1 presents evidence on these two points from a study by Jonathan Veum.[44] Veum's study asks, "Among 21–29-year-olds, who received training at any time over a 6-year period?" This study is noteworthy since it covers a longer period of time than other studies do, and it focuses on workers at an age when they are most likely to receive training and an age at which the

[42] Ann P. Bartel, "Training, Wage Growth, and Job Performance: Evidence from a Company Database," *Journal of Labor Economics* 13 (July 1995): 401–25. On average training amounts to a 4 percent higher salary overall since workers received about 4 days of training, on average. Also see Pal Schone, "Why Is the Return to Training So High?" *Labour* 18 (September 2004): 363–78, for evidence that previous estimates may be too large.

[43] See Greg J. Duncan and Saul D. Hoffman, "On-the-Job Training and Earnings Differences by Race and Sex," *Review of Economics and Statistics* 61 (November 1979): 594–603, for some early evidence on this point. More recent evidence that training is even more important for career advancement of women than for men is provided by Eduardo Melero, "Evidence on Training and Career Paths: Human Capital, Information, and Incentives," *IZA Discussion Paper No. 1377* (November 2004).

[44] Jonathan R. Veum, "Training among Young Adults: Who, What Kind, and For How Long?" *Monthly Labor Review* (August 1993): 27–32. Also see Harley Frazis, Maury Gittleman, Michael Horrigan, and Mary Joyce, "Results from the 1995 Survey of Employer-Provided Training," *Monthly Labor Review* (June 1998): 3–13. The BLS has not updated this survey.

training is most likely to have its greatest impact on wage growth. Table 9.1 presents the results of this study. Even though women and blacks were slightly less likely to receive training over this time period than men and whites, the differences in percentages are much smaller than they have been in the past. The pattern of women and blacks receiving a different *type* of training than men or whites, however, is evident from column 2 of Table 9.1. "Company training" can be thought of as training that is more likely to be firm-specific and more likely to lead to larger wage increases within the firm and greater chances for movement (promotions) within the firm as well. Women, and especially blacks, are found to be less likely to receive this type of training.

Do these differences in type of training reflect voluntary choices by the workers themselves and legitimate hiring and promotion decisions by employers, or are they due to discrimination? Part of the reason women and blacks receive less "company" or firm-specific training is that women have lower levels of job attachment and blacks have lower levels of education, both of which factors raise the costs of specific training to the firm. While these seemingly legitimate considerations help to explain the training advantage of white males, there is evidence that, at least in the past, employers have placed different values on the labor market experience of white males, women, and blacks.[45] For white males, a strong positive relationship has been shown to hold between years of employment with the firm and the chances of receiving additional training; for blacks and women, however, additional years of employment have brought only a small chance of acquiring additional training. One reason for these disparate outcomes might be that firms discriminate in offering training. Additional evidence of discrimination in who receives training is provided by Reed Olsen and Edwin Sexton.[46] They determined that women received 17 percent (0.16 years) less training just because they were women; this conclusion controls for the impact that experience, education, and other factors might have on determining who received training.

Discrimination in Promotion

Closely related to on-the-job training as a potential source of discrimination is promotion or advancement within the firm. Several factors determine a worker's probability of obtaining a promotion. One is the job structure of the firm. In some firms the technology of production gives rise to extended job ladders and

---

45 Robert W. White and Robert P. Althauser, "ILM's, Promotions, and Worker Skill: An Indirect Test of Skill ILM's," *Social Science Research* 13 (December 1984): 383–92. More evidence that employers reward the labor market experience of white men more than the labor market experience of black men can be found in Gerald S. Oettinger, "Statistical Discrimination and the Early Career Evolution of the Black–White Wage Gap," *Journal of Labor Economics* 14 (January 1996): 52–78.

46 Reed Neil Olsen and Edwin A. Sexton, "Gender Differences in the Returns to and the Acquisition of On-the-Job Training."

well-developed internal labor markets. Employees of such firms have much better promotion opportunities than workers at firms where job ladders are short or nonexistent. A second influence is the worker's job within the firm. Some jobs, such as those in the maintenance or clerical area, generally offer few promotion opportunities; other clusters, in the management or production area, for example, provide more room for vertical mobility. Jobs offering little opportunity for promotion within a firm are often referred to as dead-end jobs. Finally, a third factor determining a worker's promotion prospects is the criteria governing who is selected for promotion. If women or racial minorities are less frequently considered for promotions or if they are held to higher standards for promotion, the wage gap will continue to grow with experience.[47] This outcome is often referred to as a glass ceiling effect; women and minorities can see the top, and may be in line to get there, but they are held back through the promotion practices of their employers.

Women and Minorities in Dead-End Jobs Being in a dead-end job can hinder the earnings of a worker over his or her lifetime. First of all, workers from a particular race or gender group may be disproportionately concentrated in low-paying jobs that offer little opportunity for advancement. As a result, these workers begin their working life with lower earnings than comparable workers from other demographic groups. Second, movement from a dead-end job to a higher-paying, more promising job may be blocked. So, in addition to starting out with lower earnings, the growth of those earnings is slower than for other workers. Sixty-one percent of a sample of working women surveyed in 1994 indicated they have "little or no ability to advance [in the firm]."[48] In addition, 14 percent of white women and 26 percent of women of color indicate having lost a job or promotion because of their race or gender.

A study by Jeffrey Waddoups and Djeto Assane evaluates the concentration of men and women in three tiers of jobs that reflect different wage levels and opportunities for advancement.[49] The authors also compare the movement of men and women from lower-tier jobs to higher-tier jobs. What they find is that men are concentrated in jobs that offer the highest wages and the greatest amount of autonomy in work performance—jobs typically found to have longer job ladders, offering the best chances for advancement/promotion. Women, on the other hand, are found to be concentrated in second-tier jobs, which are characterized by "specific tasks linked to relatively narrowly defined job classifications" (p. 401); advancement in these positions is more closely tied to tenure with the firm than

47   See Deborah Cobb-Clark, "Getting Ahead: The Determinants of and Payoffs to Internal Promotion for Young U.S. Men and Women," *Research in Labor Economics* 20 (2001): 339–72.

48   U.S. Department of Labor, *Working Women Count! A Report to the Nation* (Washington, D.C.: U.S. Department of Labor, 1994).

49   Jeffrey Waddoups and Djeto Assane, "Mobility and Gender in a Segmented Labor Market: A Closer Look," *American Journal of Economics and Sociology* 52 (October 1993): 399–412.

TABLE 9.2

DISTRIBUTION OF RACE/GENDER GROUPS ACROSS OCCUPATIONS WITH VARYING PROMOTION OPPORTUNITIES, 2004

Sample of Job Classifications	Men	Women
First-Tier Jobs (managerial and craft)		
Engineers	3.30	0.61
Lawyers	0.93	0.45
Judges	0.04	0.06
Managers, administrators	12.77	8.49
Bakers	0.14	0.14
Brickmasons	0.33	0.00
Electricians	1.06	0.03
Auto Mechanics	1.28	0.02
TOTAL	**19.86**	**9.78**
Second-Tier Jobs		
Dietitians	0.01	0.12
Registered nurses	0.27	3.61
Drafters	0.22	0.08
Purchasing agents, buyers	0.18	0.25
Real estate agents, brokers	0.58	0.79
Retail salespersons	2.14	2.53
Bus drivers	0.43	0.46
TOTAL	**3.82**	**7.83**
Third-Tier Jobs		
Cashiers	0.98	3.59
File clerks	0.11	0.49
Telephone operators	0.01	0.07
Cleaning service workers	0.19	1.95
Bartenders	0.21	0.33
Guards	0.86	0.29
Typists	0.03	0.47
TOTAL	**1.28**	**3.04**

SOURCE: Occupation classification is made by Waddoups and Assane, "Mobility and Gender in a Segmented Labor Market: A Closer Look," appendix; distribution of workers across occupations from Bureau of Labor Statistics, *Employment and Earnings* (January 2005), table 11.

with job performance. In addition, a slightly greater proportion of women than men were found in third-tier jobs; these are jobs characterized by instability, poor pay, and poor working conditions. Table 9.2 shows the distribution of men and women in 2004 for a sample of occupations classified by Waddoups and Assane. Men are more heavily concentrated than women in first-tier jobs (19.86 percent of men versus 9.6 percent of women), whereas women are more heavily concentrated than men in second-tier jobs, and are about even with men in the third-tier jobs.

The research by Waddoups and Assane also documents that men are more likely than women to move from both third-tier and second-tier jobs into first-tier jobs. Movement from third-tier jobs to second-tier jobs is the same for men and women. Is the concentration of women in jobs that offer little chance of advancement and their lower probability of moving from a lower-tier job to a higher-tier job the result of women choosing certain occupations or of discriminatory treatment? While the result that women with children are less likely to move from a third-tier job to a first-tier job suggests that some of the observed immobility may be a matter of choice, other results suggest that discrimination may play a role as well. For example, the results of Waddoups and Assane suggest that the length of time a worker has been with his or her employer increases the chances of a man advancing from one tier to the next, but *decreases* the chances of a woman's movement. The authors also present evidence that education has a strong positive impact on the chances of a woman moving from one tier to the next, indicating that including education in attempts to improve the labor market outcomes of women will bear some fruit.[50]

So Close, and Yet So Far Away: The Glass Ceiling Effect The Federal Glass Ceiling Commission, chaired by the U.S. secretary of labor, was created in 1991 as part of the Civil Rights Act of 1991. The commission was directed to "conduct a study of opportunities for, and artificial barriers to, the advancement of minority men and all women into management and decision-making positions in Corporate America."[51] Table 9.3 highlights the findings of that study with today's statistics, which document the lack of representation of women and minority men in executive, decision-making positions.[52] In 1990, white men represented the greatest percentage of executives, managers, and administrators in every industry. In 2003, however, while men still dominate these positions across most industries, white women now make up the largest percentage of workers in these top positions in two industries, finance/insurance and retail trade. Given that white men made up only 42.7 percent of the overall labor force in 2003, they are overrepresented in decision-making occupations in all but two industries. The most sorely underrepresented in decision-making posts are black women, who made up 5.7 percent of the labor force in 2003, but who only represent from 1.1 to 5.0 percent of workers in Table 9.3.

---

50 Some additional support for this finding is provided by Lisa M. Lynch, "Entry-Level Jobs: First Rung on the Employment Ladder or Economic Dead End?" *Journal of Labor Research* 14 (Summer 1993): 249–63, who finds that women are more likely than men to change occupations after receiving general training.

51 U.S. Department of Labor, *Good for Business: Making Full Use of the Nation's Human Capital* (Washington, D.C.: U.S. Department of Labor, March 1995), 3. Many studies show that the glass ceiling phenomenon is not restricted to the United States; see Wiji Arulampalam, et al, "Is There a Glass Ceiling Over Europe? Exploring the Gender Pay Gay Across Wages Distribution," *IZA Discussion Paper No. 1373* (October 2004).

52 Also see "Glass Ceilings: The Status of Women as Officials and Managers in the Private Sector," *EEOC* (March 2004).

TABLE 9.3

PERCENTAGE OF EXECUTIVES, MANAGERS, AND ADMINISTRATORS REPRESENTED BY RACE AND GENDER GROUPS, BY INDUSTRY, 2003

Industry	White Men	Black Men	White Women	Black Women
Transportation and utilities	55.5	7.0	27.9	3.5
Wholesale trade	61.3	2.7	29.6	1.3
Manufacturing	64.0	2.7	26.5	1.1
Finance and insurance	43.6	3.9	42.6	3.9
Retail trade	46.7	2.3	42.7	2.1

SOURCE: Calculated from *Employment and Earnings* (January 2004), Table 17. Accessed through ftp://ftp.bls.gov/pub/special.requests/lf/aat17.txt.

While at any one time the representation of minority and female workers with decision-making roles can be disproportionate, it is also instructive to evaluate the promotion experience of workers over their careers. A study produced by Ellen Wernick for the Glass Ceiling Commission finds that the advancement experience of 1982 Stanford MBA graduates differed substantially by gender.[53] In 1993, 16 percent of the male graduates were CEOs, chairmen, or presidents of companies. Only 2 percent of the women of that same graduating class had attained the same status. In addition, greater percentages of the male graduates had attained positions just below the top posts than had the female graduates. Twenty-three percent of the men were vice-presidents (compared with 10 percent of the women), and 15 percent of the men were directors (compared with 8 percent of the women). More recently, in 2004, only eight Fortune 500 companies were headed by women CEOs.[54] A recent full-section focus by the *Wall Street Journal* on female executives point out that the women highlighted are different in many ways, but do have some things in common. For example, it was common among these women to have risen in the ranks of their firms by taking over troubled divisions and taking on greater risks than their male counterparts.

Another study of MBA students (from Georgia State University) found that the average starting salary of female graduates was 16 percent less than the men's.

---

[53] A copy of this study is on file at the U.S. Department of Labor, Glass Ceiling Commission, in Washington, D.C. Access to the report and background research papers can be found at http://www.eeoc.gov/stats/reports/glassceiling.

[54] Carol Hymowitz, "Through the Glass Ceiling," *Wall Street Journal* (8 November 2004): R1.

A considerable portion of this gap was explained by the fact that male graduates had accumulated more years of work experience than the women prior to enrollment in the MBA program. Five years later, the men's salaries had grown modestly faster than the women's, causing the average woman's salary to be 19 percent less than the average man's. Interestingly, however, when bonuses and commissions were added to salary, the wage gap widened considerably—to 26 percent. What accounted for this growing wage gap between men and women? One factor that negatively affected the growth of women's salaries was that they received somewhat fewer promotions than men. A second was that women tended to work in certain occupations and industries where salary growth was slower. A third factor explaining a modest amount of the difference in total compensation (but not salaries) among men and women was months spent out of the labor force.[55] A study of graduates in Germany finds that the timing of women's absences from the labor market also plays an important role of explaining differences in the career earnings of men and women.[56]

Still another study finds that among nurses, men and whites are significantly advantaged in terms of promotion. The promotion advantage translates into a career earnings difference of about $59,000 between male and female nurses and about $46,000 between white and black nurses.[57]

Do studies such as these, and the data in Table 9.3, provide evidence of discrimination against women and minorities in pay and promotions? The evidence is clear that over their work career, women's growth of earnings and promotions to higher job positions are slower than those of men. Whether this is due to outright discrimination, the effects of occupational segregation, voluntary choices made by women about career interruptions and industry of employment, or difference in work performance of women and men is extremely hard to disentangle. In addition, even though women are far from parity with men in position and promotion opportunities, progress of women moving into top management positions over time is reported by a study that found that the number of women in top jobs in U.S. companies nearly tripled between 1992 and 1997.[58] The study also found that once experience, age, and size of company were controlled for, the wage gap between male and female top executives fell to less than 5 percent.

55   Robert Eisenstadt, "Gender Differences in the Early Career Earnings of a Cohort of MBAs: An Intertemporal Analysis" (PhD dissertation, Georgia State University, 1991).

56   Astrid Kunze, "Gender Differences in Entry Wages and Early Career Earnings," *Annuales d'Economie et de Statistique* (July–December 2003): 245–65.

57   Stephen Pudney and Michael A. Shields, "Gender and Racial Discrimination in Pay and Promotion for NHS Nurses," *Oxford Bulletin of Economics and Statistics* (December 2000): 801–35. The study corresponds to the experience of British nurses. Dollar figures have been converted from pounds. Additional research finds evidence of a glass ceiling effect in the nonprofit sector in the United States as well. See Margaret Gibelman, "The Non-Profit Sector and Gender Discrimination: A Preliminary Investigation into the Glass Ceiling," *Nonprofit Management and Leadership* 10 (Spring 2000): 251–69.

58   Marianne Bertrand and Kevin Hallock, "The Gender Gap in Top Corporate Jobs," *Industrial and Labor Relations Review* 55 (October 2001): 3–21.

Discrimination and Labor Market Choices

Among the most important determinants of life cycle earnings are the early decisions one makes about schooling and occupational choice. These early choices impact on immediate earnings as well as on earnings potential for the rest of one's time in the labor market. If women and blacks observe that their investments in schooling reap lower rewards in the labor market than the same investments made by white men, women and blacks will be less likely to make those investments. This is a dangerous side of discrimination; its presence (or perceived presence) results in choices by the minority group that ensure that group's lower economic standing in the labor market. This is often referred to as "feedback." What evidence exists in support of this feedback effect, and what impact do the resulting choices have on life cycle labor market outcomes?

In a test of whether a woman's first-hand experience with discrimination affects her subsequent labor market decisions or outcome, David Neumark and Michele McLennan find little support for the feedback effect.[59] The authors find that women who reported experiencing discrimination on the job were more likely to change employers and subsequently to marry and to have children. The experience of discrimination, however, did *not* result in less accumulation of labor market experience, nor did it result in slower wage growth. So, while this study indicates that discrimination may affect some behavior, it does not severely impact long-term labor market outcomes. It is important to point out, however, that this study evaluates the experiences of women already attached to the labor market; it says nothing about how perceived discrimination might affect a woman's decision to enter the labor market in the first place or how it might affect a woman's occupational choices.

An additional test of the impact that actual or perceived discrimination has on behavior has been conducted by Michele McLennan, Susan Averett, and Megan Young.[60] These authors find two results that have implications for earnings over the life cycle for black men. First, the labor market rate of return to formal education is 10 percent for black men and 11 percent for white men. In addition, both blacks and whites are more likely to attend college when the estimated return from that investment is higher. Since, overall, blacks can expect lower rates of return on their investment in college, they will be less likely to attend college than whites. If some of that lower rate of return is the result of discrimination, then the presence of discrimination has negatively impacted the earnings of blacks over their entire life cycle through its impact on the decision to attend college. The second result of interest is that the higher the rate of return to whites for their investment in college, the less likely are *blacks* (in the same area) to attend college. While this result

---

59   David Neumark and Michele McLennan, "Sex Discrimination and Women's Labor Market Outcomes," *Journal of Human Resources* 30 (Fall 1995): 713–40.

60   Michele C. McLennan, Susan L. Averett, and Megan Young, "Do Higher Returns to College Education Encourage College Enrollments? An Analysis by Race," *Research in Labor Economics* 19 (2000): 63–82.

is difficult to explain, one possibility is that blacks perceive a particularly high rate of return to white men's education as an indication that the market places a high value on highly educated white labor, something a black man would have difficulty competing with.

Both of these studies indicate that the presence of discrimination may impact labor market and investment decisions of women and minorities that perpetuate their inferior labor market outcomes. The studies also indicate that eliminating the negative impact of discrimination will be complicated and slow.

The Measurement of Discrimination

Discrimination in all its various forms leads to one common result—lower income for the affected group. Figure 9.1 showed sizable disparities in the earnings of blacks and whites and women and men. An issue of tremendous economic and social importance is to what extent these earnings differentials are defensible as based on objective differences in education, experience, ability, and so on, and to what extent they are the indefensible result of discrimination. Whether discrimination is responsible for 10 percent or 90 percent of the earnings gap between blacks and whites, for example, makes a big difference in evaluating the pros and cons of both the efficiency of the market and the need for government intervention in the form of antidiscrimination and affirmative action laws. Over the past 30 years a large number of empirical studies have attempted to measure the portion of the earnings gap that is due to labor market discrimination. This section reviews this research, discussing first the technique used to estimate the discriminatory component of earnings differentials and, second, the estimates themselves.

The Residual Method

Many studies have tried to explain the source of the observed wage gap across race and gender; the majority of those studies find evidence of discrimination in the determination of wages.[61] One of the most recent studies, by Garey Durden and Patricia Gaynor, illustrates the issues and techniques involved in measuring discrimination in the labor market. Durden and Gaynor used 1990 census data on annual earnings, years of schooling, work experience, union representation, hours of work, sector (public versus private) of employment, geographic residence, and occupation and industry of employment to measure the degree to which discrimination can explain observed wage differences between white males and various other race, ethnic, and gender groups (see Table 9.4).

---

61 For example, see Mary Corcoran and Greg J. Duncan, "Work History, Labor Force Attachment, and Earnings Differences between the Races and Sexes," *Journal of Human Resources* 14 (Winter 1979): 3–20; Jeremiah Cotton, "On the Decomposition of Wage Differentials," *Review of Economics and Statistics* 70 (May 1988): 236–43; and Cordelia Reimers, "Labor Market Discrimination against Hispanic and Black Men," *Review of Economics and Statistics* 65 (November 1983): 570–79.

TABLE 9.4	MEAN VALUES OF WORKER CHARACTERISTICS AND PERCENTAGE OF WAGE GAP EXPLAINED					
	White Men	Black Men	Hispanic Men	White Women	Black Women	Hispanic Women
Years of formal education	13.4	12.4	10.0	13.3	12.7	10.9
Years of experience	19.4	19.0	17.8	19.0	18.7	17.6
Percent full-time employed	76.0	71.0	76.0	61.0	68.0	61.0
Percent represented by a union	3.9	5.0	3.6	2.5	3.7	2.3
Annual earnings[a]	$24,210	$17,802	$16,943	$14,566	$14,428	$12,442
Percentage of wage gap explained		81	99	72	70	78
Percentage of wage gap unexplained		19	1	28	30	22

[a]All dollar figures in the table have been converted to 2003 dollars. Annual earnings are approximated using reported log earnings and calculated wage gaps.

SOURCE: Based on Garey Durden and Patricia Gaynor, "More on The Cost of Being Other Than White and Male: Measurement of Race, Ethnic, and Gender Effects on Yearly Earnings," *American Journal of Economics and Sociology* 57 (January 1998), Table 1 and unpublished tables.

In this sample, the annual earnings of black men, Hispanic men, white women, black women, and Hispanic women were only 74 percent, 70 percent, 60 percent, 60 percent, and 51 percent, respectively, of the annual earnings of white men. There are two possible explanations for these earnings differentials. One is that white men earned more than the other groups because they had more of the characteristics associated with high productivity and high wages. Thus, one reason white men earned more than black men is because they had one more year of formal education than black men and women and about three years more of formal education than Hispanic men and women. The education of white men, however, is not appreciably different from the education of white women. A second explanation for the inequality in earnings in Table 9.4 is discrimination in the labor market. As discussed previously, market discrimination may take the form of unequal pay for equal work, fewer promotions in the firm, or segregation in low-paying occupations. This does not tell the whole story, however.

The challenge facing economists is to decompose the earnings gaps such as those in Table 9.4 into that part due to differences in productivity and that part due to ongoing discrimination in the labor market. In their study, Durden and Gaynor used an approach pioneered by Ronald Oaxaca known as the **residual method** of

FIGURE 9.5

THE RESIDUAL APPROACH TO MEASURING WAGE DISCRIMINATION

It is assumed that in the presence of discrimination, the earnings function of B workers $W(E_B)$ is flatter and lies below $W(E_W)$, the earnings function of W workers. Given an educational level of E_B and E_W, respectively, the wage of W workers is W_W and it is W_B for B workers. Of the total wage gap $W_W - W_B$, the portion $W_W - W_B^*$ is due to differences in years of education—assuming that in the absence of discrimination, B workers would have the earnings function $W(E_W)$; the residual or unexplained portion $W_B^* - W_B$ therefore, is attributable to discrimination.

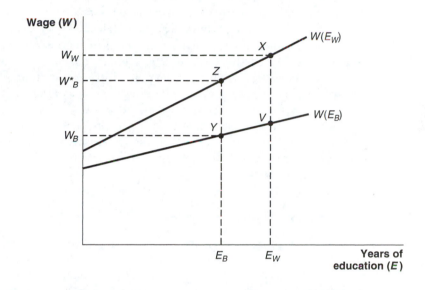

measuring market discrimination.[62] The basic idea behind the residual method is relatively simple and is illustrated in Figure 9.5. Assume that the only variable that determines a worker's productivity is years of education E, measured along the horizontal axis. The upward-sloping line $W(E_B)$ is the earnings function for, say, black workers; it shows the average wage W received by black workers possessing various years of schooling. The line $W(E_W)$ is the earnings function for white workers.

---

62 Ronald Oaxaca, "Male–Female Wage Differentials in Urban Labor Markets," *International Economic Review* 14 (October 1973): 693–709. For variations and extensions of this original methodology, see Jeremiah Cotton, "On the Decomposition of Wage Differentials," *Review of Economics and Statistics* 70 (May 1988): 236–43, and Ronald L. Oaxaca and Michael R. Ransom, "On Discrimination and the Decomposition of Wage Differentials," *Journal of Econometrics* 61 (March 1994): 5–21, and Shoshana Neuman and Ronald L. Oaxaca, "Gender Versus Ethnic Wage Differentials among Professionals: Evidence from Israel," *Annuales d'Economie et de Statistique* (July–December 2003): 267–92.

The line $W(E_B)$ has a flatter slope and lies below $W(E_W)$ on the assumption that discrimination results in blacks receiving a lower wage for any given level of education and a smaller monetary return for each additional year of education. To begin the analysis, assume that whites have an average level of schooling of E_W years while blacks, on average, have a smaller amount E_B. The earnings functions predict that the wage received by white workers is W_W (point X) and the wage received by black workers is W_B (point Y). The total wage gap between white and black workers is $W_W - W_B$, an amount corresponding to the observed wage gaps in Table 9.4.

Part of the wage gap $W_W - W_B$ is due to the fact that blacks have a lower level of education and productivity than whites; the other part is due to the fact that blacks are discriminated against and receive lower wages for any level of education. Using Oaxaca's residual approach, the wage gap can be decomposed into these two parts. The first step is to determine what wage black workers would have earned in the *absence* of discrimination, given their set of income-earning characteristics. Oaxaca assumed that in the absence of discrimination, blacks would receive the same returns to education as whites. Using the white earnings function $W(E_W)$, the average wage of blacks given an educational level of E_B would be W_B^* (point Z). Of the total wage gap of $W_W - W_B^*$ the portion $W_W - W_B^*$ is the result of the lower level of education and productivity of black workers. The unexplained or residual amount of the earnings gap $W_B^* - W_B$ is the amount that cannot be attributed to productivity differences and, thus, represents the portion of the earnings gap due to market discrimination.[63]

Estimates of Discrimination

The results obtained by Durden and Gaynor using the residual method are shown at the bottom of Table 9.4. For black men, differences in productivity (the "explained" portion) accounted for 81 percent of the wage gap, and the unexplained or residual portion due to discrimination was 19 percent. These estimates suggest that in the absence of discrimination, black men would have earned $19,020 per year, not $17,802. According to the statistics in Table 9.4, more of the wage differential between white men and all race/ethnicity combinations of women is left unexplained than for either category of minority men. Between 22 and 30 percent of the lower wage experienced by women cannot be explained by the characteristics controlled for in the study.

Using a variety of data sources and controlling for a variety of individual and job characteristics, studies using earlier data (mostly from the 1980s) have found that discrimination accounted for *at least* 30 percent of the total wage gap between

---

63 An alternative approach suggested by Oaxaca is to assume that in the absence of discrimination the returns to education for blacks and whites are given by the black earnings function. In this case, the vertical distance VX would measure the discriminatory part of the wage differential. This second approach yields a different (and in this case larger) estimate of discrimination than that obtained using the first approach.

white men and various race and gender groups.[64] One of the most recent of these other studies found that discrimination plays a larger role in the wage determination of workers with less education.[65] Discrimination was found to account for 45 percent of the wage gap between men and women high school graduates, whereas only 30 percent of the wage gap for college graduates was attributable to discrimination. One study also found that a rising unexplained portion of wage differentials between men and women can help explain the slowdown in earnings convergence between men and women during the 1990s.[66] If the estimates presented in these studies and others are accurate, discrimination is clearly a significant cause of earnings inequality.[67] For a number of reasons discussed in the next section, however, these estimates may be seriously in error.

An additional dimension of potential discrimination is explored in Empirical Evidence 9-1: how many hours workers from different demographic groups must work before receiving a "full-time wage premium."

⮕ SEE

Empirical Evidence 9-1: Discrimination in Full-Time Compensation, p. 500.

Sources of Bias

Some critics have charged that the residual approach overstates the true amount of labor market discrimination. Others have argued that it understates the full impact of discrimination on black and female earnings.

Why might the residual approach overstate the portion of the earnings gap that is due to market discrimination? Since discrimination is measured as the residual portion of the wage gap, if any factors that cause productivity differentials among people are omitted from the earnings functions, then the researcher will underestimate the explained portion due to productivity and overestimate the unexplained portion due to discrimination. For example, the Durden and Gaynor

---

64   For example, see William J. Carrington and Kenneth R. Troske, "Interfirm Segregation and the Black/White Wage Gap," *Journal of Labor Economics* 16 (April 1998): 231–60; and Paul Sicilian and Adam Grossberg, "Investment in Human Capital and Gender Wage Differences: Evidence from the NLSY," *Applied Economics* 33 (March 2001): 463–71.

65   See Charles Brown and Mary Corcoran, "Sex-Based Differences in School Content and the Male–Female Wage Gap," *Journal of Labor Economics* 15 (July 1997): 431–65. Also see Juame Garcia et al., "How Wide Is the Gap? An Investigation of Gender Wage Differences Using Quantile Regression," *Empirical Economics* 26 (March 2001): 149–67.

66   Francis D. Blau and Lawrence M. Kahn, "The U.S. Gender Pay Gap in the 1990s: Slowing Convergence," *NBER Working Paper No. 10853* (October 2004).

67   The residual (or direct regression) approach defines fairness as when men and women (or blacks and whites) with the same set of qualifications receive the same pay. Alternatively, Delores Conway and Harry Roberts ["Reverse Discrimination, Fairness, and Employment Discrimination," *Journal of Business and Economic Statistics* (January 1983): 75–85] have proposed that fairness be defined as when workers with the same level of pay have the same job qualifications. In this approach (called reverse regression) discrimination would arise if a man and a woman in a firm each earned the same salary, but the woman had higher qualifications than the man (implying that she must meet higher standards). One might expect this new reverse approach to give the same qualitative answer as the direct approach—if men are paid more than equally qualified women, then they are less qualified than equally paid women. Surprisingly, however, the two approaches often give conflicting answers as to the presence of discrimination. These issues are explored in Arthur Goldberger, "Reverse Regression and Salary Discrimination," *Journal of Human Resources* 19 (Summer 1984): 293–318, and Carole Green and Marianne Ferber, "Employment Discrimination: An Empirical Test of Forward versus Reverse Regression," *Journal of Human Resources* 19 (Fall 1984): 557–69.

study did not include any measures of IQ or scholastic ability. Since whites, on average, score higher than blacks on IQ tests and aptitude tests such as the SAT, and if such tests scores reflect ability, then omitting these scores from the earnings functions will give a downward bias to the estimated portion of the earnings gap due to productivity differences.

A second possible omitted variable is culture. Thomas Sowell argues that part of the economic success of Jewish and Japanese Americans and the relative lack of success of American Indians, Puerto Ricans, and blacks stems from cultural attitudes and values concerning work, family, and business.[68] If such cultural differences exist and are not controlled for in the earnings functions, the residual approach will again overestimate the true amount of the wage gap due to discrimination. Finally, a potential source of bias in comparison of earnings of men and women is neglect of differences between the sexes in their college major and occupational preferences. One study found that young men and women have substantially different job preferences (making money is a much more important factor for men) and choose quite different fields of study.[69] These differences were found to account for one-third of the gap in starting salaries between men and women college graduates.[70]

There are also reasons why the residual approach may underestimate the importance of discrimination. In the Durden and Gaynor study, for example, part of the explained or productivity-related portion of the wage gap is due to the concentration of women and nonwhite men in lower-paying occupations. If these workers are segregated by occupation due to discrimination, then Durden and Gaynor have underestimated the full impact of labor market discrimination on earnings. A related problem is whether blacks, for example, acquire fewer years of education because the payoff in the labor market is smaller due to discrimination. If so, part of the measured productivity differential between whites and blacks due to differences in education, therefore, really represents the indirect effect of discrimination. Finally, the residual approach attempts to measure only market discrimination, neglecting the portion of the productivity gap that arises from pre-market discrimination in quantity and quality of schooling and other such factors.

The Economic Progress of Blacks and Women

The evidence presented in the preceding section points to the presence of continuing discrimination in the labor market against blacks and women. According to most analysts, the extent of discrimination against these groups has lessened substantially in the past three decades. This section briefly examines this issue, looking first at the economic progress of blacks and, second, that of women.

---

68 Sowell, *Markets and Minorities* (New York: Basic Books, 1981). On this subject, also see Barry R. Chiswick, "The Earnings and Human Capital of American Jews," *Journal of Human Resources* 18, no. 3 (Summer 1983): 313–36.

69 See, for example, Peter Arcidiacono, "Ability Sorting and the Returns to College Major," *Journal of Econometrics* 121 (July–August 2004): 343–25.

70 Barry Gerhart, "Gender Differences in Current and Starting Salaries: The Role of Performance, College Major and Job Title," *Industrial and Labor Relations Review* 43, no. 4 (April 1990): 418–33. Also see Sarah Turner and William Bowen, "Choice of Major: The Changing (Unchanging) Gender Gap," *Industrial and Labor Relations Review* 52 (January 1999): 289–313.

Blacks

Few people would quarrel with the basic proposition that blacks as a group are in a far superior economic position today than they were 30 years ago. A fair amount of controversy remains, however, about how rapid and widespread the gains have been and the reasons for them.

Table 9.5 provides data between 1960 and 2000 on selected key indicators of the economic position of blacks in the American economy. The statistic that has been

TABLE 9.5 DIMENSIONS OF BLACK ECONOMIC PROGRESS, 1960–2000					
	1960	1970	1980	1990	2000
1 Black/White earnings ratio, male year-round, full-time workers	0.67	0.69	0.71	0.73	0.78
2 Median years of schooling[a]					
Blacks	8.2	10.1	12.2	12.5	12.6
Whites	10.8	12.2	12.5	12.7	12.9
3 Percentage in professional and managerial occupations					
Blacks	7.4	12.6	17.9	16.0	21.0
Whites	23.8	26.2	28.5	26.8	30.0
4 Employment/population ration (males)					
Blacks	67.9	71.5	60.4	62.6	67.6
Whites	79.4	76.8	73.4	73.3	74.5
5 Percentage of families with female head					
Blacks	20.9	28.3	40.0	44.0	44.0
Whites	8.1	9.0	12.0	13.0	12.7
6 Black/White family income ratio	0.60	0.65	0.63	0.62	0.66
7 Percentage of persons in poverty					
Blacks	55.1[a]	33.5	32.5	31.9	22.1
Whites	18.1[a]	9.9	10.2	10.7	9.4

[a]1959 statistics

SOURCES: Earnings: Bureau of the Census, *Money Income of Households, Families and Persons in the United States*, P-60 series, http://ferret.bls.census.gov/macro/032001/perinc/new05_032.htm. Education: National Center for Educational Statistics, U.S. Department of Education, Office of Educational Research and Improvement, *Digest of Educational Statistics*; education statistics calculated from the 2001 March Supplement of the Current Population Survey. Occupational representation: Bureau of the Census, *Statistical Abstract of the United States*, various issues. Employment/Population ratios: E. Jacobs, ed., *Handbook of Labor Statistics* (Lanham, Md.: Bernan Press, 1998) and Ferret extraction tool from http//ferret.bls.census.gov. Householder information: http://www.census.gov/population/www/socdemo/hh-fam.html. Family income statistics: http://dataferrett.census.gov. Poverty: Bureau of the Census *Poverty in the U.S. 2000* Current Population Reports Consumer Income Series, P-60, no. 214.

given the most attention by economists is the ratio of black/white median annual earnings for male year-round full-time workers, shown in row 1 of Table 9.5. For full-time workers a narrowing has taken place in black/white differences in earnings. Several factors lie behind this trend. One is the convergence among blacks and whites in various income-related background characteristics.[71] Probably most important in this respect is the narrowing of the schooling gap. This is shown in row 2; in 1960 the median level of education for blacks was nearly three years less than whites', but by 1990 the gap was nearly eliminated. Also important in this regard is the improvement in the quality of schooling received by blacks. David Card and Alan Krueger estimate that 20 percent of the narrowing of the black/white earning gap between 1960 and 1980 can be attributed to improvements in the relative quality of black schools.[72] Finally, the migration of blacks from the South to the North and from farm to city has also helped to equalize black/white incomes.

A second factor leading to a narrowing of the black/white earnings gap is a reduction in discrimination in the labor market. Empirical studies of black/white earnings in the 1950s and early 1960s uniformly found that the payoff to a high school or college education for blacks was substantially below that for whites. Research using more recent earnings data has found that rates of return to post-secondary education have equalized for blacks and whites and, in fact, that the payoff to a college degree for blacks is now larger.[73] Another result of lessening racial discrimination in the labor market is the crumbling of occupational segregation. As shown in row 3 of Table 9.5, in 1960 only 7.4 percent of blacks were employed in professional, technical, or managerial occupations, compared to 23.8 percent of whites. By 2000, this gap had narrowed significantly as the proportion of blacks in these white-collar occupations has almost tripled.

The data presented so far paint a basically optimistic picture of the economic progress of blacks. Counterbalanced against the positive trends, however, are two very worrisome developments. The first is the growing joblessness among black males. Some economists have charged that the statistics on earnings and occupational attainment in rows 1 and 3 overstate the gains made by blacks because they include only those blacks who actually have jobs.[74] A growing proportion of blacks are not employed, as shown by the **employment/population (E/P) ratio** in row 4. In 2000 only 67.6 percent of black males had jobs; the other 32.4 percent were either

71 See Richard B. Freeman, "Black Economic Progress after 1964: Who Has Gained and Why?" in Sherwin Rosen, ed., *Studies in Labor Markets* (Chicago: University of Chicago Press, 1981), 249–94.

72 David Card and Alan Krueger, "School Quality and Black–White Relative Earnings: A Direct Assessment," *Quarterly Journal of Economics* 107 (February 1992): 151–200. Also see Finis Welch, "Black–White Differences in Returns to Schooling," *American Economic Review* 63 (March 1973): 893–907.

73 James P. Smith and Finis R. Welch, "Black Economic Progress after Myrdal," *Journal of Economic Literature* 27 (June 1989): 519–64; Robert A. Margo, "Explaining Black–White Wage Convergence," *Industrial and Labor Relations Review* 48 (April 1995): 470–81; and Michele C. McLennan, Susan Averett, and Megan Young, "Do Higher Returns to College Education Encourage College Enrollments? An Analysis by Race."

74 William Darity Jr., "Illusions of Black Economic Progress," *Review of Black Political Economy* 10, no. 2 (Winter 1980): 153–68.

unemployed or not in the labor force. Although some improvement in the E/P ratio can be seen in recent years, the fact that one out of three working-age black males is either unemployed or out of the labor force is extremely worrisome because it suggests that for many of these men full-time gainful employment is no longer their primary activity.

A second development that threatens the economic progress of blacks is the breakup of the black family.[75] Among both whites and blacks the proportion of female-headed households is growing because of both higher divorce rates and greater numbers of single women having children. This trend is of economic concern, since the incidence of poverty among families headed by women is far greater than among married-couple families (27.9 percent versus 9.6 percent in 2000). As shown in row 5 of Table 9.5, female-headed households are far more common among blacks than among whites, to such an extent that more than two out of every five black families in 2000 was headed by a female. This development not only threatens black families of today with poverty, it also threatens disadvantage to future generations because the low income of female household heads reduces educational and cultural opportunities for their children.

The combined adverse impact of lower employment levels among black men and greater incidence of female-headed households is evident in the statistics on the black/white ratio of family income in row 6 of Table 9.5 and the percentage of blacks and whites in poverty in row 7. On the other hand, the black/white earnings ratio for full-time employed workers (row 1) has slowly, but steadily increased over time. In addition, after declining for decades, the black/white ratio of family income (row 6) has increased since 1990. Similarly, after a marked decline in the poverty rate among blacks (row 7), from 55.1 percent in 1960 to 33.5 percent in 1970, the poverty rate among blacks stagnated until a further decline during the 1990s, where it reached 22.1 percent. Taken together, the statistics in Table 9.5 give a mixed picture of the economic progress of blacks, with clear gains being made by the majority coupled with continuing distress on the part of a significant minority.[76]

Women

If the labor market picture for black Americans is mixed, what about the market for women? Here the evidence is more encouraging.

The statistic given the most emphasis by economists is the female/male earnings ratio for full-time, year-round workers. From the mid-1950s to 1980, this ratio actually declined—from 64 percent in 1955 to 60 percent in 1980. This downward trend was the subject of much controversy and debate. After all, during this period

---

75 See William John Bennett, "Reflections on the Moynihan Report: 30 Years Later," *The American Enterprise* 6 (January/February 1995): 28–32; Daniel Patrick Moynihan, "The Schism in Black America," *The Public Interest* no. 27 (Spring 1972) 3–24; and Gene E. Pollock and Atlee L. Stroup, "Economic Consequences of Marital Dissolution for Blacks," *Journal of Divorce and Remarriage* 26 nos. 1–2 (1996): 49–67.

76 The growing split in the black community into "haves" and "have-nots" is discussed in Martin Kilson, "Black Social Classes and Intergenerational Poverty," *The Public Interest* no. 64 (Summer 1981): 58–78; and William Julius Wilson, *The Truly Disadvantaged* (Chicago: University of Chicago Press, 1987).

The "Mommy Track": Fair or Unfair to Women?

One of the newest and most controversial innovations in corporate employment policy is the so-called mommy track. A description of this practice as well as the controversy that surrounds it follows.

Jobs in many managerial and professional occupations entail very long hours. It is not unusual for lawyers and accountants, for example, to work 70 or more hours per week. Although many people employed in these fields find such schedules burdensome, few demur because to do so almost guarantees they will not be promoted to "partner." (Typically promotion to partner depends significantly on the number of hours billed. Oftentimes, an employee who is not promoted to partner after a certain number of years must leave the firm and look for work elsewhere.)

Critics claim that the traditional system of employment in these firms works to the disadvantage of women workers, and particularly married women with children. In their view, women are forced into an unfair choice: either put in the long hours to advance one's career but forgo having children, or have children but give up one's career, at least in the large firms, which typically offer high salaries and prestige. It is not an accident, the critics say, that in 2003, only 13% of board seats at S&P 500 firms were held by women and only eight had female CEOs.

Business firms have been searching for a solution to this problem, as a way both to avoid possible sex discrimination charges and to retain valuable female employees. Some of the responses, as noted in the last chapter, have taken the form of more flexible work schedules (flex-time), telecommuting, and improved child-care arrangements. Another approach is the development of a mommy track in the firm.

It is not uncommon that junior executives are expected to work "full-time" (e.g., 70 hours per week). Those that cannot or will not are asked to leave. Some firms, however, have established two career paths or tracks. The first is the traditional track of full-time work. The second is a part-time track for those who desire for family reasons to take an extended leave of absence or to work, for example, only three days a week. Although in principle this part-time track is open to both male and female employees, in practice almost all employees choosing

the nation witnessed the entrance of millions of new female workers into the job market, the movement of women into once all-male occupations, and the passage of various antidiscrimination and affirmative action laws.

Why then did the gender earnings ratio decline? Several reasons have been cited.[77] One factor often alleged to have had a depressing effect on women's wages is occupational crowding. Between 1960 and 1980, 22 million new women workers entered the job market. Because the majority of jobs for women during this period

---

[77] See Francine Blau, "Discrimination against Women: Theory and Evidence," in William Darity Jr., ed., *Labor Economics: Modern Views* (Boston: Kluwer-Nijhoff, 1984), 53–90, and June O'Neill, "The Trend in the Male–Female Wage Gap in the United States," *Journal of Labor Economics* 3, no. 1 (January 1985): S91–S116.

continued

it are women with children; hence the name "mommy track." In some firms, persons on this part-time track can stay with the company indefinitely but give up the possibility of promotion, while others hold out the possibility of promotion, albeit only after a considerably longer period of employment. Many firms also allow persons on the part-time track to later switch back to the "fast track."

To its proponents, the mommy track is a significant advancement for working women because it allows them to have both a family and a professional career at the same time, with the possibility of resuming a full-time career once their children are older and in school. From this perspective, the mommy track is a plus because it provides working women with more options—those who want to concentrate on a professional career can get on the full-time track while those who want to combine children and a career can get on the part-time track.

Opponents of the mommy track, on the other hand, claim that it perpetuates women's second-class status by shunting them into dead-end jobs with lower pay and little chance for promotion. From the critic's point of view, the real solution to women's employment problems is to require men to shoulder an equal share of home and child-care responsibilities. If this were done, the track for "daddies" and "mommies" would become one and the same, and both men and women would compete for pay and promotions on an equal footing. Finally, critics note that firms generally create a mommy track for only their most valued female employees, implying that a mommy track creates two groups of second-class corporate citizens: women compared to men, and lower-level white and blue-collar women compared to executive and professional women.

SOURCES: "The Mommy Track," *Business Week* (March 20, 1989): 126–34; Marianne Bertrand and Kevin Hallock, "The Gender Gap in Top Corporate Jobs," *Industrial and Labor Relations Review* 55 (October 2001): 3–21; Carol Kleiman, "'Mommy Track': A Well-Worn Path Is Crumbling," *Chicago Tribune* (26 January 1999); "Study: Wage Penalties Tied to Flex Schedules," *Chicago Tribune* (12 February 2002): Carol Kleiman column; Anne Marie Chaker, "Luring Moms Back to Work," *Wall Street Journal* (30 December 2003): D1; and Carol Hymowitz, "In the United States, What Will It Take to Create Diverse Boardrooms?" *Wall Street Journal* (8 July 2003): B1.

were concentrated in a fairly narrow range of occupations, the flood of job seekers was funneled into only one part of the labor market, putting substantial downward pressure on wages in female-dominated occupations. A second and related factor is that the large inflow of new female job seekers also reduced the average experience level of the female workforce. Because earnings are positively related to experience, this, too, worked to hold down the female/male earnings ratio. Finally, a considerable body of empirical evidence suggests that women's earnings were held down in a number of firms by pay and employment practices that, whether consciously intended to be or not, were discriminatory.

During the 1980s and 1990s, however, women's progress in the labor market improved noticeably. The clearest indication was the rise in the full-time female/male median earnings ratio—from 60 percent in 1980 to 73 percent in

2000. What accounted for the substantial rise in women's relative earnings? Again, several factors most likely came into play.[78]

One positive event was the reduced barriers posed by occupational segregation. As shown in Chapter 8, during the 1980s women made substantial employment gains in a number of occupations that had once been primarily the preserve of men. Whereas in 1970 it was a rarity to find a female lawyer, engineer, or telephone line repairer, by the 1990s women composed a significant and growing proportion of the workforce in each of these jobs.

A second factor was the gain in work experience by women. During the 1960s and 1970s, millions of women entered the job market and took entry-level positions, often at relatively low pay due to their lack of prior experience. Although some of these women subsequently dropped out of the workforce, a large portion pursued full-time employment. The result was that the average level of job experience and seniority of women workers increased in the 1980s and 1990s, as did their access to higher-level job titles through the promotion process. Not unexpectedly, all of these developments were reflected in increased relative earnings for women.

Finally, there can be little doubt that the workplace is a more level playing field for women than it was 30 years ago. As an example, although it was common to find in the early 1970s that new female college graduates earned significantly less than similar male graduates, the bulk of evidence indicates that today within a particular occupation or industry men and women graduates are paid roughly similar salaries. Part of the reason, no doubt, is the revolution in corporate human resource policies toward women brought about by civil rights and affirmative action legislation (as reviewed in the next section).

Before ending this otherwise positive account, it must be pointed out that considerable gender inequalities in the labor market continue to exist. Even after the gains of the past two decades, for example, full-time working women still earn on average only 73 percent as much as men. Although a substantial portion of this gap may well be related to legitimate differences in productivity, such as differences in college major and years of expected job tenure, another portion no doubt arises from business policies, social customs, and family decisions that for one reason or another favor men over women. A prime example is the unequal sharing of child care and family responsibilities in most families. One study estimated that time spent at housework by married women accounts for about 9 percent of the gender wage gap.[79] The greater amount of time women tend to spend out of the workforce

78   Francine D. Blau and Lawrence M. Kahn, "Swimming Upstream: Trends in the Gender Wage Differential in the 1980s," *Journal of Labor Economics* 15 (January 1997): 1–42; Solomon Polachek and John Robst, "Trends in the Male–Female Wage Gap: The 1980s Compared with the 1970s," *Southern Economic Journal* 67 (April 2001): 869–88; and Jaume Garcia et al., "How Wide Is the Gap? An Investigation of Gender Wage Differences Using Quantile Regression."

79   Joni Hersch and Leslie Stratton, "Housework, Fixed Effects, and Wages of Married Workers," *Journal of Human Resources* 32 (Spring 1997): 285–307.

also means their lifetime earnings and retirement security is significantly lower than that of men.[80]

It is also true that while women workers are more likely to start out their careers at the same earnings level as men, over their working life the earnings of women advance at a slower rate than those of men. As indicated earlier, a significant reason for this problem is that women do not get promoted as fast as their male colleagues and more often have their careers stall out at the middle level of job titles in the firm or occupation.

Thus, while much has been accomplished in the 1980s and 1990s, more remains to be done for America's women workers.

Government Programs to Combat Discrimination

Beginning in the Kennedy administration, the federal government has enacted a wide range of legislation aimed at combating discrimination in the labor market. Several of the most important of these laws are discussed in this section.[81]

Federal Legislation

The cornerstone of federal policy in the employment area is the **Civil Rights Act of 1964.** Title VII of this act makes it an unlawful employment practice for an employer "to refuse to hire or to discharge any individual, or otherwise to discriminate against any individual with respect to his compensation, terms, conditions, or privileges of employment, because of such individual's race, color, religion, sex, or national origin." The act, as amended in 1972, applies to employers of 15 or more persons in an industry affecting interstate commerce, unions with 15 or more members, employment agencies, and employees of state and local governments.[82]

To administer the act, Congress created the Equal Employment Opportunity Commission (EEOC). The EEOC is an independent, five-member agency appointed by the president with the consent of the Senate. The activity of the EEOC was initially limited to investigation and persuasion in those cases that were

---

80 Stephen J. Rose and Heidi I. Hartmann, *Still a Men's Labor Market: The Long Term Earnings Gap* (Washington, D.C.: Institute for Women's Policy Research, 2004).

81 For a more detailed discussion, see Patrick J. Cihon and James Ottavio Castagnera, *Employment and Labor Law*, 4th ed. (Cincinnati, Oh.: West/Thomson, 2002), part 2.

82 Over the years, Title VII has been amended by Congress and interpreted by the courts to reflect the growing presence of women in the labor market and the subsequent rise in issues of concern to women. For example, Congress amended Title VII in 1978 to protect the rights of pregnant women through the **Pregnancy Discrimination Act.** In addition, the 1986 U.S. Supreme Court ruled that unwanted sexual advances at work can be the basis for a sex discrimination complaint under Title VII. See Charles J. Muhl, "The Law at Work: Sexual Harassment," *Monthly Labor Review* 121 (July 1998): 61–62, for an evaluation of several U.S. Supreme Court rulings in 1998 that further refined the implications of sexual harassment for discrimination cases.

brought to its attention. It could not force compliance with Title VII by issuing a cease and desist order, nor could it award back pay to a victim of discrimination. Amendments to the act in 1972 gave the EEOC more power by allowing it to pursue court action on behalf of complainants.

Since the passage of Title VII, the courts have wrestled with the question of what is and what is not discrimination. The Supreme Court's decision in 1971 in *Griggs v. Duke Power Company* established the basic guidelines that are still in use today. In this case, it was shown that prior to 1965, Duke Power Company had hired blacks only in the labor department of its power plants at jobs paying less than any of the jobs in the other four all-white departments. The day after the passage of the Civil Rights Act, the company dropped this exlusionary policy, but adopted a new regulation that required all new job applicants as well as existing employees who wished to transfer to new departments to have high school diplomas and satisfactory scores on two professionally designed aptitude tests. The company argued that this requirement was nondiscriminatory since it applied equally to both blacks and whites. In its decision, the Supreme Court said that for an employment practice to be discriminatory, two things must be shown: first, the person charging discrimination must show that the employment practice has a "disparate" (unequal) impact on the members of the minority group, and second, if there is a disparate impact, the burden of proof is on the company to show that the employment practice is related to a worker's successful performance of the job or is a matter of "business necessity" for the firm.

In the *Griggs* case, the court found the company guilty of discrimination. Evidence showed that the company's requirements disproportionately affected blacks (58 percent of whites but only 6 percent of the blacks were able to pass the aptitude test), and the company could not demonstrate that either the high school diploma or passing scores on the aptitude tests were necessary for successful performance of the jobs. This was suggested by the fact that many white employees had previously been hired even though they did not meet these qualifications.[83] The *Griggs* case did not outlaw the use of various screening devices such as aptitude tests; it *did* require that a firm's hiring standards be related in a demonstrable way to job performance.[84] Thus, in *Boyd v. Ozark Airlines*, the court ruled that a 5 foot 7 inch minimum height requirement for flight attendants was discriminatory against women, but a 5 foot 5 inch requirement was justified by the demands of the job.

---

83 Charles O. Gregory and Harold Katz, *Labor and the Law*, 3d ed. (New York: Norton, 1979), 551.

84 See Sheldon Zedeck and Mary L. Tenopyr, "Issues in Selection, Testing and the Law," in Leonard Hausman et al., eds., *Equal Rights and Industrial Relations* (Madison, Wis.: Industrial Relations Research Association, 1977), 167–96, and Hunter and Schmidt, "Ability Tests: Economic Benefits versus the Issue of Fairness." As discussed in the latter article, although ability tests were not outlawed by the Supreme Court, many companies dropped them because of the fear of court suits. In addition, economic research has shown that performance on cognitive tests does not accurately predict productivity levels, thus providing an additional reason for dropping them. See Peter Mueser and Tim Maloney, "Ability, Human Capital and Employer Screening: Reconciling Labor Market Behavior with Studies of Employer Productivity," *Southern Economic Journal* 57 (January 1991): 676–89.

Discrimination is prohibited not only in hiring, but in transfer, promotion, and other aspects of employment. A particularly thorny issue in this regard concerns seniority systems. It was common in industries such as steel, paper, and tobacco in the pre-Title VII days for blacks and whites to have separate seniority ladders with no transfer rights between them. Since blacks were generally hired only into menial, low-paying jobs, the seniority system continued to lock in the effects of discrimination long after the initial discrimination took place. The remedy for such discrimination has been controversial, however. Various court cases led to the development of the "rightful place" doctrine under which firms charged with discrimination are forced to merge departmental **seniority units** into one plantwide unit and then place black and white workers in a line of progression based on their previous years of seniority. This solution bumps some white workers into lower-level jobs by adding black workers of higher seniority who were formerly in the all-black unit. To black workers, this remedy is entirely justifiable as a means of rectifying past discrimination. The white workers who are demoted, however, see *themselves* as victimized since they are made to give up their jobs in order to correct an injustice they had no part in causing. To avoid this type of conflict, an alternative approach taken by the courts is to allow the seniority system to remain intact, but to award black workers back pay as compensation for discrimination. The problem with this remedy is that a black worker who transfers to a formerly all-white seniority unit gives up accumulated seniority rights and protection against layoff. There may be no way to correct past discrimination in seniority that does not hurt someone.

In *Wards Cove Packing Co. v. Antonio* in 1989, the Supreme Court, now with a more conservative majority, issued a ruling that changed the disparate impact standard of *Griggs* in ways that made it more difficult for employees to win discrimination charges against employers; Congress subsequently passed the **Civil Rights Act of 1991.** This act again made it incumbent upon employers to demonstrate that a disparate impact was a bona fide "business necessity."[85] It also amended Title VII to provide that an unlawful employment practice may be established by demonstrating that race, color, religion, sex, or national origin was a *motivating factor* for an adverse employment decision, even though other legitimate factors also entered into the decision. The act also allowed plaintiffs to sue not only for back pay and court costs, as under Title VII, but also for sizable punitive damages, thus substantially increasing the potential liability of employers for discrimination.

Next in importance among antidiscrimination laws is **Executive Order 11246,** signed in 1965 by President Johnson. The order requires every company

---

85   Further details on the business necessity standard can be found in Anonymous, "The Civil Rights Act of 1991: The Business Necessity Standard," *Harvard Law Review* 106 (February 1993): 896–913. The implication of the Civil Rights Act of 1991 for the ability to maintain class status in class-action lawsuits is explored by Daniel F. Piar, "The Uncertain Future of Title VII Class Actions after the Civil Rights Act of 1991," *Brigham Young University Law Review* (2001): 305–47.

doing business with the federal government to agree not to discriminate in any aspect of employment. To administer the order, the Office of Federal Contract Compliance Programs (OFCCP) was established within the Department of Labor.

The key provision promulgated by the OFCCP is that every contractor with $50,000 or more of business with the federal government must submit an **affirmative action program.** The program must include a statistical analysis of the contractor's workforce and of the available pool of qualified women or members of minority groups from which the firm could hire. If this analysis shows a significant deficiency of workers from a target group, the contractor is required to establish goals and timetables for increasing the employment of these workers. One well-known example of such an affirmative action program is the Philadelphia plan in construction, which mandates contractors to increase their hiring of blacks and women in the various skilled construction trades.

The affirmative action program of the OFCCP has been the center of much controversy.[86] Critics charge that it amounts to a de facto system of employment quotas, even though Title VII explicitly forbids quotas. A second criticism is that the affirmative action goals are unrealistic and force companies to hire unqualified members of minority groups. One study finds that lower hiring standards involved with recruiting more blacks reduced the quality of both minority and nonminority police officers hired.[87] The net result was higher crime in U.S. cities. Construction companies claim that it is impossible to meet affirmative action goals since few blacks or women have the training to be brickmasons or ironworkers. Affirmative action also has many supporters. In their view, affirmative action is necessary to break down hiring barriers and to force firms to upgrade minority workers into skilled jobs. It has also been argued that, even if some reverse discrimination is involved, it is justified as a compensation for past discrimination against blacks and women. In addition, one study finds that the increased screening and recruitment efforts that occur as a result of affirmative action more than offset the tendency of such policies to lead to hiring of less-qualified workers.[88]

A fourth antidiscrimination law is the **Equal Pay Act of 1963.** The Equal Pay Act, an amendment to the Fair Labor Standards Act, is the oldest federal legislation dealing with sex discrimination. The most important provision of the act is the mandate that men and women receive equal pay for equal work. The law describes

---

86   For example, see Roger Clegg, "Beyond Quotas," *Policy Review* (May/June 1998): 12–14; Joyce Jones, "Affirmative Action Onslaught Persists," *Black Enterprise* 29 (August 1998): 22; and Alexander Wohl, "Diversity on Trial," *The American Prospect* 12 (May 2001): 37–39.

87   John R. Lott Jr. "Does a Helping Hand Put Others at Risk?: Affirmative Action, Police Departments, and Crime," *Economic Inquiry* 38 (April 2000): 239–77. On the other hand, still another study finds that affirmative action hires typically are less qualified but are not found to perform at any lower levels than non-affirmative action hires. See Harry Holzer and David Neumark, "Are Affirmative Action Hires Less Qualified? Evidence from Employer-Employee Data on New Hires," *Journal of Labor Economics* 17 (July 1999): 534–69.

88   Harry J. Holzer and David Neumark, "What Does Affirmative Action Do?" *Industrial and Labor Relations Review* 53 (January 2000): 240–71.

SEE
Policy Application 9-1:
Comparable Worth,
p. 495.

equal work as that requiring equal skill, effort, and responsibility being performed under similar working conditions. The major impact of the act has been to outlaw the practice of direct wage discrimination where women in a firm are paid a lower wage than men for the same jobs. Efforts to amend the Equal Pay Act of 1963 to require equal pay for "comparable" work are discussed in Policy Application 9-1.

Additional antidiscrimination laws that deserve brief mention include the **Age Discrimination in Employment Act of 1967 (ADEA)** and the **Americans with Disabilities Act (ADA)**. The ADEA protects workers who are 40 years of age and older from discrimination in all aspects of employment based on age.[89] After complaints of age discrimination fell during the 1990s, they were up again in 2003.[90] In 2003, 19,124 age discrimination complaints were filed with the EEOC. In about 69 percent of the cases, the agency found no reason to suspect age discrimination, and about 15 percent (2,552) of the complaints were resolved in favor of the person bringing the charge. Passed in 1990 and implemented July 26, 1992, the ADA prohibits discrimination against "qualified" persons with physical or mental disabilities in regard to hiring, advancement, training, compensation, and other terms of employment in both private and public workplaces. Under ADA a "qualified" person is one who has a disability but with reasonable accommodation can perform the essential functions of the job. In 189,621 ADA cases resolved by the EEOC between 1992 and 2003, 81 percent were resolved in favor of the employer. Although the complaints were certainly well-intentioned and in many cases warranted, neither the ADEA nor the ADA have turned up rampant discrimination with respect to age or a worker's disability.

Effectiveness of Antidiscrimination Programs

Just because the government passes a law does not guarantee a corresponding change in human behavior. With respect to discrimination, the available evidence does suggest, however, that the antibias regulations in the Civil Rights Act and Executive Order 11246 have had a measurable impact on improving the pay and employment opportunities of blacks and women.

Two approaches have been used to test for the effects of government antidiscrimination laws. The first involves a time-series analysis of changes in the black/white or female/male earnings differential. For example, if antidiscrimination laws have been effective in increasing the pay of blacks, the black/white earnings ratio

---

89 See Richard A. Posner, "Employment Discrimination: Age Discrimination and Sexual Harassment," *International Review of Law and Economics* 19 (December 1999): 421–46, and David Neumark, "Age Discrimination Legislation in the United States," *Contemporary Economic Policy* (July 2003): 297–317.

90 Todd Ormsbee, "An Age-Old Story," *InfoWorld* 23 (13 August 2001): 40–41. The EEOC has also ruled on the growing number of ADEA waivers. The EEOC has ruled that requiring terminated workers to give up severance packages if they challenge their termination is not allowed. The commission cites the Older Workers Benefit Protection Act of 1990 in striking down this practice. See Thomas Scarlett, "EEOC Issues Rule Restricting Waiver of ADEA Rights," *Trial* 37 (May 2001): 95–96.

Discrimination and Sexual Orientation: The United Kingdom and United States Take Different Paths

At the end of 2003 the United Kingdom amended its antidiscrimination law to prohibit discrimination not only on the basis of race and gender but also religion and sexual orientation. American discrimination law also prohibits employment discrimination based on religious preference, so in this respect the British and American laws are now similar. Where the two differ, however, is in the highly controversial area of sexual orientation.

The British law forbids employers to treat heterosexual and homosexual people differently with regard to hiring, pay, and training. Efforts to amend American law at the federal level have aroused much debate but little progress. However, several individual states have followed the British and outlawed employment discrimination based on sexual orientation. For example, Minnesota has amended its Human Rights Act to also protect "gays, lesbians, and those whose gender identity is different than their biological maleness or femaleness." To date, less than 50 cases a year (about 3 percent of all discrimination claims) have been filed under the law with regard to sexual orientation.

A major argument advanced in favor of a capitalist economic system is that economic outcomes and rewards are determined by the impersonal market forces of demand and supply. But, of course,

behind demand and supply are real people, and these people all come to the labor market with personal likes and dislikes. A major philosophical and economic debate thus ensues around three points: (1) to what degree these personal likes and dislikes will actually affect the aggregate pattern of wages, employment and other outcomes; (2) to what degree market forces will subsequently erode these discriminatory (or preference-based) differentials; and (3) to what degree government has a legitimate mandate to overrule private choices and regulate labor markets in the "social interest."

Opinion in the American electorate and in the economics profession has slowly evolved on these matters. Whereas prohibiting gender and racial discrimination is now well-accepted, for example, up until the early 1960s such a policy did not receive widespread support and was viewed by many as socially radical. One can speculate that attitudes on discrimination on the basis of sexual orientation will also follow the same evolutionary pattern. Although anyone who watches cable TV news programs or reads the editorial pages of newspapers is well aware that at the present time the electorate is badly split on this issue.

One way economists can help inform and guide the public debate is by providing empirical evidence

should have grown more rapidly after the passage of the Civil Rights Act in 1964. In a detailed statistical study using data on various measures of black/white earnings for the years between 1948 and 1970, Richard Freeman found exactly this result, suggesting that government intervention has been an important cause of black economic progress in the labor market.[91] Freeman's conclusions were not

---

91   Richard B. Freeman, "The Changing Labor Market for Black Americans," *Brookings Papers on Economic Activity* 1 (1973): 67–120.

continued

on the existence and extent of discrimination against gays and lesbians. If gay and lesbian workers appear to suffer from significant discrimination in wages and other outcomes, such evidence would bolster the case for providing legal protection to these groups. If lack of such evidence is found, however, then the matter may have less practical urgency (although human rights arguments remain cogent). So, is there empirical evidence on the matter?

Economists are just beginning to investigate the effect of sexual orientation on labor market outcomes. Early and tentative findings in several studies, for example, find (using the wage decomposition technique) that gay and bisexual men suffer about a 30 percent wage penalty relative to heterosexual men, holding constant other measurable personal characteristics and determinants of productivity and skill. Interestingly, however, at least one study found that lesbian women enjoy a wage *advantage* of about 20 percent! Studies also find that employers are less likely to hire people known to be homosexual, while other studies find that homosexual employees may face a glass ceiling effect when it comes to promotion and advancement in the company.

Even if these differentials are real, caution has to be exercised in concluding that they reflect preference-based discrimination. It is possible, for example, that homosexual orientation is also correlated with other unobservable or unmeasured determinants of pay and productivity (e.g., occupational preference) and these factors account for the measured "discriminatory" differentials. Also, part of observed differentials between heterosexual and homosexual workers could arise from a form of statistical discrimination. For example, employers might systematically favor heterosexual job applicants over homosexual applicants (particularly males) if they believe the latter are more likely to have HIV/AIDS and that this medical condition will appreciably raise the company's health care costs.

SOURCES: Nathan Berg and Donald Lien, "Measuring the Effect of Sexual Orientation on Income: Evidence of Discrimination?" *Contemporary Economic Policy* 20 (October 2002): 394–414; John M. Blandford, "The Nexus of Sexual Orientation and Gender in the Determination of Earnings," *Industrial and Labor Relations Review* 56 (July 2003): 622–42; Jeff Frank, "Gay Glass Ceilings," *Department of Economics, University of London Discussion Paper 04/20* (April 2004); Doris Weichselbaumer, "Sexual Orientation Discrimination in Hiring," *Linz Economics Working Paper No. 00-21* (October 2001); Christopher Carpenter, "New Evidence on Gay and Lesbian Household Incomes," *Contemporary Economic Policy* 22 (January 2004): 78–94; Joan Harbison, "New Laws for More Equality," *Belfast News Letter* (23 March 2004): 11; and Lolita C. Baldor, "Lawmakers Want to Shore Up Civil Rights Laws," *Associated Press* (11 February 2004).

universally accepted, however.[92] Some argued that the black gains in the 1960s were primarily due to the economic boom associated with the Vietnam War. Others suggested that a growing number of blacks with the lowest incomes were

---

92 See, for example, Robert J. Flanagan, "Actual versus Potential Impact of Government Antidiscrimination Programs," *Industrial and Labor Relations Review* 29, no. 4 (July 1976): 486–507, and Richard Butler and James J. Heckman, "The Government's Impact on the Labor Market Status of Black Americans: A Critical Review," in Leonard Hausman et al., eds., *Equal Rights and Industrial Relations*, 235–81.

dropping out of the labor force, imparting an artificial upward bias to the black/white wage ratio. Finally, others argued that improvements in the quality of schooling received by blacks was the major source of black gains. In a study published in 1991, however, John Donahue and James Heckman surveyed the past research on this issue and concluded there was little doubt that passage and enforcement of civil rights legislation had been a major contributing factor to the economic gains of blacks.[93]

Several studies have examined the impact of the government's civil rights and affirmative action programs on women's earnings. The results found so far indicate that these programs have had a relatively small, positive effect on the earnings and employment of white women and a considerably larger impact on the earnings of black women.[94] There is even evidence that earnings and employment levels of black males benefitted substantially from affirmative action programs.[95]

A second approach to estimating the effect of government antibias programs involves a cross-sectional analysis of OFCCP affirmative action requirements on the employment of blacks and women in individual companies. If affirmative action programs were effective, it would be expected that firms that are federal contractors would have increased their employment of blacks and women more rapidly than firms that are not. A study by Jonathan Leonard did find this result; he estimated that between 1974 and 1980, the employment of black males, black females, and white females grew, respectively, 3.8 percent, 12.3 percent, and 2.8 percent faster in contractor firms than in noncontractor firms. He also found that affirmative action had resulted in significant gains in occupational attainment for black workers, but had given less help to white females.[96]

It would appear from these results that affirmative action has been effective in righting some of the wrongs of past discrimination. But has it? The answer, surprisingly, is not necessarily. If the purpose of affirmative action is to remove instances of discrimination among federal contractors, then presumably the OFCCP's compliance reviews would be targeted at those firms with the smallest

93 John Donahue III and James Heckman, "Continuous versus Episodic Change: The Impact of Civil Rights on the Economic Status of Blacks," *Journal of Economic Literature* 29, no. 4 (December 1991): 1603–43. Results consistent with Donahue and Heckman are also found by David Neumark and Wendy Stock, "The Effects of Race Discrimination Laws," *Public Policy Institute of California Working Paper No. 2003-13* (June 2003).

94 Jonathan S. Leonard, "The Impact of Affirmative Action Regulation and Equal Employment Law on Black Employment," *Journal of Economic Perspectives* 4 (Fall 1990): 47–63; Kenneth Y. Chay, "The Impact of Federal Civil Rights Policy on Black Economic Progress: Evidence from the Equal Employment Opportunity Act of 1972," *Industrial and Labor Relations Review* 51 (July 1998): 608–32; William J. Carrington et al., "Using Establishment Size to Measure the Impact of Title VII and Affirmative Action," *Journal of Human Resources* 35 (Summer 2000): 503–23; and David Neumark and Wendy A. Stock, "The Effects of Race and Sex Discrimination Laws," *Public Policy Institute of California Working Paper No. 2003-13* (June 2003).

95 James P. Smith, "Affirmative Action and the Racial Wage Gap," *American Economic Review* 83 (May 1993): 79–84.

96 Jonathan Leonard, "The Impact of Affirmative Action on Employment," *Journal of Labor Economics* 2 (October 1984): 439–63. Also see Thomas Hyclak, Larry W. Taylor, and James B. Stewart, "Some New Historical Evidence on the Impact of Affirmative Action: Detroit 1972," *Review of Black Political Economy* 21 (Fall 1992): 81–98; Harry Holzer and David Neumark, "Equal Opportunity and Affirmative Action," *Public Policy Institute of California Working Paper No. 2002-07* (December 2002).

proportion of minority workers. In a second study, Leonard examined this issue and found that such was not the case; a firm with a low proportion of minority workers was no more likely to be reviewed by the OFCCP than a firm with a large proportion of minority workers.[97] How, then, did the OFCCP target its compliance reviews?

The evidence indicated that they chose large companies with large numbers of white-collar employees, such as AT&T and IBM. Leonard concluded that these firms were selected for compliance reviews, not necessarily because they had committed the most blatant forms of discrimination (although they may have), but rather because they offered OFCCP officials the best opportunity to achieve a significant redistribution of jobs and income to minorities and women. Although this type of targeting strategy has succeeded in creating many new job openings for minorities and women in Fortune 500–type corporations, it has also made affirmative action susceptible to the claim that it has replaced one type of favoritism with another.

---

[97] Jonathan Leonard, "Affirmative Action as Earnings Redistribution: The Targeting of Compliance Reviews," *Journal of Labor Economics* 3 (July 1985): 363–84.

POLICY APPLICATION 9-1

Comparable Worth

A strong lobbying effort by women's groups, labor unions, and civil rights activists has been waged to amend the Equal Pay Act to incorporate a concept known as **comparable worth.** According to these groups, firms practice two types of wage discrimination against women and minorities. In the first, one class of people is paid less than another class for doing exactly or substantially the same job. A second type of wage discrimination occurs when the job structure within a firm is substantially segregated by sex or race and workers of one category are paid less than workers of another category, even though both groups are performing work that, although not the same, is of comparable worth or value to the employer. The Equal Pay Act declares the first type of wage discrimination illegal, but discrimination of the second type is not a violation of the act since the two groups of workers are employed in different jobs. To remedy this situation, the advocates of comparable worth propose changing the wording of the act from "equal pay for equal work" to "equal pay for jobs of equal value." Under this version of the law, employers would be required to pay similar wages to men and women not only for the same job, but for all jobs that are of the same value to the firm, regardless of the actual title or function.

According to the advocates of comparable worth, two central facts explain the gender gap in earnings: one is that men and women work in different jobs, and the second is that women's jobs almost always pay less than men's jobs, even when

FIGURE 9.6

RELATIONSHIP BETWEEN MONTHLY SALARY AND JOB WORTH POINTS FOR MEN AND WOMEN, WASHINGTON STATE, 1974

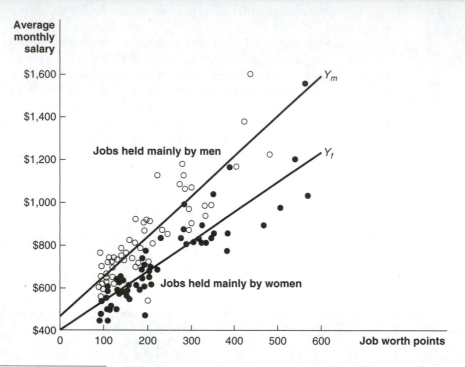

SOURCE: Donald J. Treiman and Heidi I. Hartmann, eds., *Women, Work, and Wages* (Washington, D.C.: National Academy Press, 1981): 61. Used with permission.

the actual type of work done is quite similar. A well-known example illustrates this contention.[1] In 1974 a consulting firm conducted a study of the rates of pay received by men and women in state government jobs in the state of Washington. In the 121 positions examined (representing approximately 13,600 workers) 59 were filled at least 70 percent by men, 62 were filled at least 70 percent by women. To assess the claim that women were paid substantially less than men for similar types of work, the consulting firm used the technique of job evaluation to rank each position in terms of its job content. As discussed in Chapter 6, job evaluation assigns points to job characteristics such as the

level of schooling, effort, skill, and responsibility required by the job, and the working conditions (amount of noise, heat, and so on) under which it is performed; the total number of points is then taken as a measure of the job's worth. The results of the study are shown in Figure 9.6. The solid dots show the combination of job worth points and average monthly salary for the predominantly female jobs; the hollow dots do the same for the predominantly male jobs. The line Y_m (Y_f) shows the relationship between an increase in job worth points for men

1   Described in "Pay Equity Is a Bad Idea," *Fortune* (May 14, 1984): 133–40.

(women) and the average increase in monthly salary associated with it. Two facts stand out. First, for jobs with equal evaluation scores, the women's jobs paid less than the men's—only about 80 percent as much on average. Second, the disparity in earnings increased with the worth of the job. As one example of the inequality in compensation, the study found that a Chemist II position (male) received 277 points and was paid at salary level 33, while a Registered Nurse IV position (female) received 573 points yet was paid only at salary level 31. With a comparable worth law, nurses would have been paid at salary level 39, six levels above the chemist.

Is a comparable worth law a good idea? Although the subject provokes considerable debate, it is fair to say that a large majority of economists oppose it. There are several reasons. At a conceptual level, the critics charge that an attempt to compare the worth of different jobs on the basis of a common set of traits is like trying to compare the value of apples and oranges on the basis of their nutritional content.[2] In the case of apples and oranges, it is clear that subjective consumer tastes obviously play a large part in determining the demand for, and therefore the prices of, the two fruits. Thus, even if oranges and apples were identical in their nutritional content, the price of apples might be much higher than that of oranges if consumers much preferred the taste of apples, or if they were in short supply. The same line of thinking applies equally well to different jobs in the labor market. Just because a job held by men has the same measured traits (skill requirements, etc.) as a job held by women, this does not imply they should necessarily command the same wage. If a large majority of women prefer certain jobs, and thus expand the supply of labor to them, it would be expected that the wage in the women's jobs would be lower.

Critics of comparable worth also raise a number of practical objections to such a law. Steven E. Rhoads highlights the "insurmountable" problems associated with implementing comparable worth policies.[3] First, the critics fear that if a comparable worth law were adopted, it would lead to serious inefficiencies in the labor market. Thus, job

evaluation might give carpenters and social workers in a city government an equal score and equal salaries. Since carpenters typically earn more than social workers, the result will be that the city government will lose all its carpenters to other employers while an excess supply of people will want social worker positions. Second, they argue that implementation of a comparable worth law will cause many women to lose their jobs by raising the relative wage of women, partly because of a general reduction in job opportunities, and partly because employers will substitute men for women in the production process. Third, if less occupational segregation is a legitimate goal, artificially raising the wages of predominantly female jobs gives women little incentive to pursue predominantly male jobs. Finally, the critics argue that it is impossible to use job evaluation techniques to determine the true worth of a job since the process is inherently subjective.[4] A job's evaluation score depends on what characteristics are included as compensable factors and the weight each characteristic is given in calculating the total score, considerations that are affected by the value system and beliefs of the evaluator.[5]

---

2   See Mark R. Killingsworth, "Economic Analysis of Comparable Worth and Its Consequences," *Proceedings of the Thirty-Seventh Annual Meeting* (Madison, Wis.: Industrial Relations Research Association, 1984): 183–89, and Mark Aldrich and Robert Buchele, *The Economics of Comparable Worth* (Cambridge, Mass.: Ballinger, 1986).

3   See Steven E. Rhoads, *Incomparable Worth: Pay Equity Meets the Market* (Cambridge: Cambridge University Press, 1993). Also see Mark R. Killingsworth, "Comparable Worth and Pay Equity: Recent Developments in the United States," *Canadian Public Policy* 28 (May 2002): 5171–86.

4   Empirical evidence on the lack of consistency in job evaluations across evaluators is provided by E. Jane Arnault et al., "An Experimental Study of Job Evaluation and Comparable Worth," *Industrial and Labor Relations Review* 54 (July 2001): 806–15.

5   The Washington state study, for example, used four broad job characteristics: knowledge and skills, mental demands, accountability, and work conditions. The weights assigned to these four characteristics were 47, 23, 27, and 3 percent, respectively. Aldrich and Buchele, *The Economics of Comparable Worth*, show that this weighting scheme tended to result in lower evaluation scores for men's jobs since men are more likely than women to work in blue-collar type jobs with adverse working conditions. When they recalculated the job worth points of male and female jobs using a 30 percent weight for working conditions, the relationship between pay and job worth points in Figure 9.6 changed substantially.

Canada's Experience with Comparable Worth

Comparable worth laws have been adopted in all but the three westernmost of Canada's provinces. As in the United States, most of these laws limit the applicability of the statutes to public sector employees. In 1987, the province of Ontario, however, went further and for the first time in North America extended the coverage of comparable worth to workers in both the public *and* private sectors.

The Ontario statute states that "work traditionally performed by women has been undervalued." It goes on to justify the implementation of comparable worth as a means to redress this situation through the elimination of the portion of the male–female earnings gap that is due to discrimination and occupational segregation.

Several aspects of the Ontario comparable worth law are noteworthy:

- The statute not only covers all nonfederal public sector employers in Ontario but also applies to all private sector employers with 10 or more workers.
- The law is proactive in that it requires all private sector employers with 100 or more workers to develop and implement a pay equity plan, regardless of whether any evidence exists that the company's pay practices result in underpayment of women or whether a complaint has been filed against the company alleging discriminatory behavior.
- The law requires that jobs performed primarily by women must be compared with jobs primarily performed by men, even if the jobs are completely dissimilar.
- Employers are required to use a gender-neutral system of comparison, but the law states only that this system should include a consideration of skill, effort, responsibility, and working conditions.
- The law stipulates that female-dominated jobs be upgraded to the pay of the lowest-paid male job found to be of comparable value and that the employer must commence making wage adjustments up to a maximum of 1 percent of payroll per year. If there are no male jobs in the establishment of comparable value to a female job, no adjustment is required.

Proponents of comparable worth either deny these charges or minimize their seriousness. First, they admit that in a competitive market, differences in supply and demand may give rise to legitimate differences in wages for jobs that have identical measured traits. The problem, however, is that real-world wage differentials between men and women do not arise from competitive market forces, but rather from the illegitimate crowding of women into certain occupations due to discrimination and outmoded sex roles and stereotypes.[6] An additional potential nonmarket source of pay differences stems from rigid pay structures instituted many years ago. One study traces pay differences in California state civil service jobs back to 1931, when California apparently deliberately lowered salaries for female-dominated jobs.[7] Thus, a comparable worth law would upset market-determined wage differentials, but this result is desirable since these wage differentials embody the effects of past and present discrimination.

---

6   See Richard Perlman and Maureen Pike, *Sex Discrimination in the Labour Market: The Case for Comparable Worth* (New York: St. Martin's Press, 1994); Elaine Sorensen, *Comparable Worth: Is It a Worthy Policy?* (Princeton: Princeton University Press, 1994); Barbara Bergman, "Does the Market for Women's Labor Need Fixing?" *Journal of Economic Perspectives* 3, no. 1 (Winter 1989): 43–60; and Paula England, "The Case for Comparable Worth," *Quarterly Review of Economics and Finance* 39 (Special 1999): 743–55.

7   Marlene Kim, "Inertia and Discrimination in the California State Civil Service," *Industrial Relations* 38 (January 1999): 46–68.

continued

- Even when jobs are found to be of comparable value, certain differences in pay are allowed, such as for seniority, merit pay, and skill shortages, but the employer must be ready to justify these differentials to the government agency in charge of administering the law.

One might expect that such a sweeping legislation would dramatically alter the experience of women in Ontario's labor market. This apparently has not been the case. Research has found rather modest and, in some cases, negative impacts of the legislation. Employers have found the administrative burden of the requirements overwhelming, which may account for the low levels of compliance, particularly by small firms. As a result, only 35 percent of working women and only 40 percent of working men are potentially impacted by the legislation.

Another reason for not finding an impact of the legislation is that there is rather low incidence of undervaluation of female jobs in Ontario's large union sector. In addition, it is estimated that as many as one-third of female jobs did not have appropriate male jobs to compare to. These difficulties have led to only modest improvements in female wages and slower *growth* of those wages for women in male-dominated jobs and slower growth of male wages in female-dominated jobs.

Besides all of the administrative and institutional difficulties standing in the way of a comparable worth policy showing results, one researcher points out, that the legislation also has market forces working against it over time as well.

SOURCES: "Ontario's Bold Pay Equity Law Hits Wage Gap," *HR News* (February 1992): C6–C7; Judith McDonald and Robert Thornton, "Private-Sector Experience with Pay Equity in Ontario," *Canadian Public Policy* 24 (June 1998): 185–208; Michael Baker and Nicole Fortin, "Comparable Worth Comes to the Private Sector: The Case of Ontario," *Econometric Society World Congress 2000* (August 2000); and Judith M. McDonald and Robert J. Thonton, "Comparable Worth in Amademe: Professors at Ontario Universities," *Canadian Public Policy* 27 (8 September 2001): 357–73.

Second, supporters of comparable worth tend to minimize the adverse impact of such a law on economic efficiency or the employment of women. They note, for example, that comparable worth laws have already been implemented in several states and cities, as well as in Australia and Great Britain, and have apparently not led to the dire consequences predicted by the law's opponents.[8] Finally, the proponents of the law argue that job evaluation can be done far more objectively than its critics would admit.

Sufficient empirical research has not yet been done on these issues to allow one to definitively decide in favor of the opponents or the supporters of a comparable worth law. Based on the evidence available, however, several conclusions can be drawn. First, implementation of a comparable worth law substantially raises women's wages. One study found, for example, that implementation of a comparable worth law among government workers in the state of Iowa caused the female/male earnings ratio to rise from 78.7 to 83.4 percent; a second study of government workers in the state of Washington found the earnings

---

8   See, for example, Morley Gunderson and Craig W. Riddell, "Comparable Worth: Canada's Experience," *Contemporary Policy Issues* 10 (July 1992): 85–94, and R. G. Gregory and R. C. Duncan, "Segmented Labor Market Theories and the Australian Experience of Equal Pay for Women," *Journal of Post-Keynesian Economics* 3 (Spring 1981): 403–28.

ratio increased from 80.2 to 85.6 percent.[9] A second impact of a comparable worth law is a significant increase in labor cost for business and government. Based on job evaluation studies for four states, one researcher estimated that a comparable worth law would increase payroll costs by an average of 8 percent.[10] A third result of a comparable worth law is a modest decrease in job opportunities for women, probably on the order of 2 to 3 percent.[11] Finally, evidence from several state governments that have implemented a comparable worth law indicates that the realignment of wages does lead to an exodus of male employees seeking higher-paying jobs in the private sector, whereas traditionally low-paying female jobs attract a significantly larger number of applicants (although most of these applicants continue to be women).[12]

9   Peter F. Orazem and J. Peter Mattila, "The Implementation Process of Comparable Worth: Winners and Losers," *Journal of Political Economy* 98, no. 1 (February 1990): 134–52. Also see June O'Neill, Michael Brien, and James Cunningham, "Effects of Comparable Worth Policy: Evidence from Washington State," *American Economic Review* 79, no. 2 (May 1989): 305–9, and Peter F. Orazem and J. Peter Mattila, "Male–Female Supply to State Government Jobs and Comparable Worth," *Journal of Labor Economics* 16 (January 1998): 95–121.

10 Elaine Sorensen, "Implementing Comparable Worth: A Survey of Recent Job Evaluation Studies," *American Economic Review* 76, no. 2 (May 1986): 364–67. Also see Lynda J. Ames, "Fixing Women's Wages: The Effectiveness of Comparable Worth Policies," *Industrial and Labor Relations Review* 48 (July 1995): 709–25.

11 Ronald G. Ehrenberg and Robert S. Smith, "Comparable-Worth Wage Adjustments and Female Employment in the State and Local Sector," *Journal of Labor Economics* 5 (January 1987): 43–62, and Aldrich and Buchele, *The Economics of Comparable Worth*, 168. Also see Mark Wooden, "The Employment Consequences of Comparable Worth Policies," *Australian Economic Review* 32 (September 1999): 286–91.

12 Orazem and Mattila, "Male–Female Supply to State Government Jobs and Comparable Worth."

EMPIRICAL EVIDENCE 9-1

Discrimination in Full-Time Compensation

As has been seen throughout this chapter, discrimination can take many forms. Differences in wage levels, training opportunities, and promotions across race and gender groups can all be evidence of discrimination if those differences are not caused by differences in productivity. One article identifies still another manifestation of potential discrimination: employers who set different wage-determining criteria for women versus men.[1] The research shows that men get a boost in their wages for agreeing to work at least 33 hours per week, but women have to work at least 37 hours (for white women) and 39 hours (for black women) before being paid the higher wage.

What Is a Full-Time Wage Premium?

It has long been observed that full-time workers receive a higher base wage than part-time workers. For example, if full-time workers earn, on average, $10 per hour, then comparable part-time workers will earn, on average, $8 per hour.[2] In this example,

1   Susan L. Averett and Julie L. Hotchkiss, "Discrimination in the Payment of Full-Time Wage Premiums," *Industrial and Labor Relations Review* 49 (January 1996): 287–301.

2   See Michael Lettau, "Compensation in Part-Time Jobs versus Full-Time Jobs: What If the Job Is the Same?," *Economics Letters* 56 (September 1997): 101–6; Mark Montgomery and James Cosgrove, "Are Part-Time Women Paid Less? A Model with Firm-Specific Effects," *Economic Inquiry* 33 (January 1995): 119–33; and Daniel Aaronson and Eric French, "The Effect of Part Time Work on Wages: Evidence from Social Security Rules," *Journal of Labor Economics* 22 (April 2004) 329–52. Estimates vary, but research suggests that full-time workers earn from 3 percent to 30 percent higher wages than part-time workers.

TABLE 9.6

NUMBER OF HOURS REQUIRED TO RECEIVE FULL-TIME WAGE PREMIUM BY RACE AND GENDER GROUPS

Race–Gender Groups	Number of Hours Person Must Work before Receiving a Full-Time Wage
White men	33 hours per week
Black men	33 hours per week
White women	37 hours per week
Black women	39 hours per week

SOURCE: Based on information contained in Susan L. Averett and Julie L. Hotchkiss, "Discrimination in the Payment of Full-Time Wage Premiums," *Industrial and Labor Relations Review* 49 (January 1996): 287–301, Tables 3a–3d.

then, workers earn a premium of $2 per hour for agreeing to work full-time. The generally accepted explanation for why full-time workers are offered higher wages than part-time workers is the presence of fixed employment costs.[3] For each new worker hired, the firm incurs some fixed costs (costs that do not vary with the number of hours worked) of orientation, training, and benefits provision. In addition, the first 800 hours (at a wage of $10 per hour) a worker works per year are more expensive for the firm than any hour after that, since unemployment insurance tax is only figured on the first $8,000 paid to each employee. So if a worker only works 20 hours per week, these fixed costs are spread over fewer hours, making the average cost of that worker much greater than if a worker works 40 hours per week; the employer passes some of those higher costs of part-time employment onto the worker in the form of a lower wage.

How Many Hours Is Full-Time?

The federal government, for purposes of data collection, considers a worker to be full-time employed when he or she works 35 hours or more per week. From the perspective of the employer, however, full-time might be defined as the number of hours a worker must work before being offered the full-time wage premium. The research by Susan Averett and Julie Hotchkiss indicates that employers define full-time differently for men and for women. As Table 9.6 shows, both white and black men must only work 33 hours per week before they start receiving the higher full-time wage, whereas white women must work 37 hours and black women must work 39 hours before they start receiving any full-time wage premium. Is this differential definition of full-time for women discriminatory? There is reason to expect that the fixed costs of employment are higher for women than for men. Women are more frequently absent from work than men and are more likely to quit their job at any given time than men. Both of these characteristics make hiring women (as a group) more expensive. However, as is the case in any instance of statistical discrimination, what may be true for the group may not be true for any individual woman. As a result, the employer may be using the number of hours a woman is willing to work as a signal about her attachment to the labor market; men are apparently able to signal that attachment at fewer hours of work. What may be needed to remedy this disparity is some clearer (nonhours) indication of women's labor market attachment before a woman is considered full-time (and receives the associated premium) at the same number of hours as a man.

3   Walter Oi, "Labor as a Quasi-Fixed Factor," *Journal of Political Economy* 70 (December 1962): 538–55.

Summary

Labor market discrimination occurs when two people of equal productivity are paid different wages, hired into different jobs, or given unequal training opportunities on the basis of some characteristic such as race, gender, religion, or nationality. The motive for discrimination may vary widely, as may the source of discrimination and the form it takes. In some cases, discrimination arises from prejudice or bigotry; in other cases, it stems from the drive for pecuniary gain or from imperfect information regarding a person's true productivity. Discrimination may originate with the employer, the workers of the majority group (and the unions that represent them), or consumers. Finally, discrimination may take the form of unequal wages for the same work, segregation into certain jobs or occupations, or unequal access to training and promotions.

Pronounced wage differentials separate men and women and blacks and whites. A portion of these differentials reflects differences in the average level of productivity of workers in each group; another portion reflects discrimination. The most common technique used by economists to estimate the portion of the wage gap due to discrimination is the residual method. Studies using the residual method typically find that one-half or more of the wage gap between race and sex groups is unexplained by measurable productivity differences among workers, suggesting that discrimination is both present and quantitatively significant. There are many potential sources of bias in such estimates, however.

Blacks have made considerable economic gains over the past 40 years in the United States. The gap in earnings between black and white workers has narrowed over time, as have racial differences in educational and occupational attainment. Not all segments of the black community have fared equally well, and some blacks remain quite disadvantaged economically. Particular sources of concern are the growing proportion of prime age males without jobs and the breakup of the black family. Women workers in the economy have also made substantial gains in terms of employment and occupational attainment. In addition, after decades of immobility of the ratio of women's earnings to men's, recent progress has been made in reducing the gap.

Since the early 1960s social policy in the United States has been actively directed at the elimination of discrimination in the labor market. The most important piece of legislation in this regard is the Civil Rights Act of 1964. Research has found that this and other forms of government antidiscrimination laws have been a significant factor behind the improvement in the economic status of minority workers. Some groups argue, however, that a comparable worth law is necessary to eliminate what they see as continuing inequities in the pay structure.

Review Questions

1. Discuss the impact that prejudice by employers, workers, and consumers will have on the wages and employment of minority workers.

2. Josh Gibson, the "Black Babe Ruth," earned around $8,000 a year playing baseball in the Negro leagues during the late 1930s. George Herman, the "real" Babe Ruth, earned around $80,000. Was there an incentive for one of the major league teams to hire Gibson? If so, why didn't any do it? In your answer, consider the possible role of prejudice by club owners, white baseball players, and the customers of

major league baseball. Could Gibson have been a victim of statistical discrimination?

3. Would the theory of monopsonistic discrimination offer a plausible explanation for the fact that male secretaries earn more, on average, than female secretaries? What about the lower relative earnings of female professors?

4. Two people are applying for the same job in a large bank in New York City. Both have comparable résumés in terms of degrees obtained, grade point average, prior work experience, and so on. The only difference is that one of the job candidates grew up in Boston and has a distinct Bostonian accent while the other grew up in Alabama and has a deep southern accent. Who do you think has the better chance of being hired? Why do you think this? Could prejudice play a role? What about statistical discrimination?

5. What are some alternative explanations for observing among MBA graduates that a greater percentage of men than women reach the highest ranks (e.g., president, CEO) within their firms?

6. A restaurant owner is charged with sex discrimination because he requires that all his wait staff weigh 130 pounds or less, a requirement with a disproportionate impact on men. In his defense he states, "Modeling agencies have similar requirements of their employees (models) which are not considered illegal and I'm just giving the customers what they want." Explain (a) why the case of the restaurant owner is different from the case of the modeling agency, and (b) how the requirements of the restaurant owner could be considered to be discriminatory.

7. A recent study used the residual approach to measure wage discrimination and concluded that 50 percent of the wage gap between black and white males was due to market discrimination. Discuss first what the residual approach is, and second why it might provide either an underestimate or an overestimate of the true amount of wage discrimination.

8. To be promoted to lieutenant, police officers in a city police department first have to pass a written aptitude test. This requirement was challenged in court by several black officers on the grounds that the test unfairly discriminated against blacks. To win the case, what did the black officers have to prove? What did the city have to prove, if anything, to be found innocent of discrimination?

9. What would a comparable worth law do? What are the arguments for and against such a law?

The Measurement of Discrimination

Chapter 9 gives a heuristic description of the residual method of estimating wage discrimination. This appendix shows how the residual method is operationalized in a regression context.

The basic tool used in measuring wage discrimination is the human capital earnings function discussed in the appendix to Chapter 7. To begin, assume as in Chapter 9 that there are group W and group B workers. The hourly earnings of workers in each group can then be expressed as:

$$\ln W^W = \alpha^W + \beta^W X^W$$
$$\ln W^B = \alpha^B + \beta^B X^B, \tag{9A.1}$$

where X is a vector of all those variables that affect worker productivity (for example, years of education, experience, and ability). The average difference in wages between the two groups can be determined by calculating:

$$\ln \overline{W}^W = \alpha^W + \beta^W \overline{X}^W$$
$$\ln \overline{W}^B = \alpha^B + \beta^B \overline{X}^B \tag{9A.2}$$

where $\overline{W}$ and $\overline{X}$ are average values of the relevant variables. The wage differential $\ln \overline{W}^W - \ln \overline{W}^B$ is the total wage gap between group W and group B workers (the distance $W_W - W_B$ in Figure 9.5). The objective is to decompose this difference in wages into the part due to productivity differences and the part due to discrimination.

On the assumption that in the absence of discrimination both group W and group B workers would be paid according to the W earnings function, the nondiscriminatory wage for group B workers $\hat{\overline{W}}^B$ is:

$$\ln \hat{\overline{W}}^B = \alpha^W + \beta^W \overline{X}^B. \tag{9A.3}$$

The wage gap $\ln \overline{W}^W - \ln \overline{W}^B$ can then be decomposed as follows:

$$
\begin{aligned}
\ln \overline{W}^W - \ln \overline{W}^B &= (\ln W^W - \ln \hat{\overline{W}}^B) + (\ln \hat{\overline{W}}^B - \ln \overline{W}^B) \\
&= [(\alpha^W + \beta^W \overline{X}^W) - (\alpha^W + \beta^W \overline{X}^B)] \\
&\quad + [(\alpha^W + \beta^W \overline{X}^W) - (\alpha^W + \beta^W \overline{X}^B)] \\
&= [\beta^W (\overline{X}^W - \overline{X}^B)] + [(\alpha^W - \alpha^B) + (\beta^W - \beta^B) \overline{X}^B]. \\
&\qquad\qquad (1) \qquad\qquad\qquad\qquad\qquad (2)
\end{aligned}
\tag{9A.4}
$$

The first part of Equation 9A.4 represents the nondiscriminating part of the wage differential (the difference in productivity characteristics) and part (2) represents the part due to discrimination (the difference in coefficients). In terms of Figure 9.5, part (1) equals the distance $W_W - W_B^*$; part (2) equals the distance $W_B^* - W_W$. Dividing part (2) by the total wage differential yields the proportion of the wage gap due to discrimination.

10

The Economics of Human Resource Management

This chapter takes a more in-depth look at the employment practices firms use to manage their workforces—an activity called **human resource management** (HRM). Previous chapters have examined facets of HRM, such as training (Chapter 7) and employee benefits (Chapter 8), while labor relations is covered in Chapters 11 and 12. In this chapter we focus on three other HRM practices: employee selection, compensation management, and employee involvement programs. Leading off, however, is a more fundamental issue—why firms hire employees instead of bidding out the work to independent contractors. Rounding out the chapter are four other topics—a Policy Application that examines the alleged shortfall of employee participation and representation in the economy and alternative methods suggested to close this gap, and three Empirical Evidence sections that examine, respectively, the pattern of HRM practices across firms, the impact of "advanced" HRM practices on firm performance, and the controversial subject of executive compensation.

The Pattern of HRM Practice

Among the many topics examined in this chapter, two stand out. The first is why firms have a human resource management function; the second is what determines the type and extent of their HRM practices. Figure 10.1 helps put these issues in perspective.

The data in Figure 10.1 come from a nationally representative survey of employees. The diagram plots the percentage of employees working in companies with alternative levels of "advanced human resource management practices" (AHRMP), where AHRMP ranges from "few" to "many" on the horizontal axis. The variable AHRMP is a composite measure derived by summing: (*a*) the presence (yes/no) of ten different HRM practices, and (*b*) the perceived effectiveness of each practice (rated on a 1 to 4 scale). Among the ten practices are these characteristics: company has a personnel/HR department; a bonus or gain-sharing compensation program; regular town-hall employee meetings; an employee involvement program; a grievance system with outside arbitrator; an employee stock ownership plan; and an "open-door" communication/dispute policy.

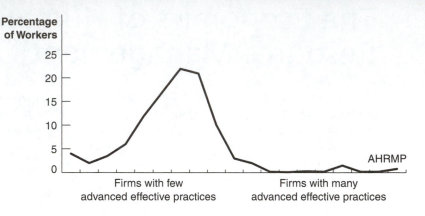

SOURCE: Reprinted from Richard B. Freeman and Joel Rogers, *What Workers Want* (Ithaca: Cornell University Press, 1999), 96. Copyright © 1999 by Russell Sage Foundation. Used by permission of the publisher, Cornell University Press.

Figure 10.1 reveals a wide dispersion of HRM practices in the American economy. Approximately one-quarter of employees (in the left-hand tail of the distribution) work in companies with very few advanced HRM practices (or very few effective practices). About three in ten employees report, for example, that their company does not have a personnel/HRM department. At the opposite end of the distribution is the 15 to 20 percent of people who work at firms with a very high AHRMP score. Included in this group are the 23 percent of employees that work at a company with a stock ownership plan and the 32 percent whose company has a formal grievance system. Between the two tails of the distribution is the bulk of the American workforce. The majority of employees work at companies with some but not many advanced HRM practices. These companies, for example, have a personnel/HRM department and perhaps several other advanced HRM practices, but a number of other practices are absent or of only low to modest effectiveness.

The Economic Basis of the Employment Relationship

The practice of human resource management presumes that firms have employees—otherwise there are no "human resources" to manage. It may seem self-evident that companies such as Ford Motor and Starbucks have to have employees, since if they did not, how would the cars and cappuccinos get produced? But economist Ronald Coase won a Nobel prize for showing that such is not necessarily the case.[1]

Coase's insight, later developed in much greater detail by Oliver Williamson, turns on the concept of transaction cost. The work of Coase and Williamson has spawned a school of thought called "new institutional economics," which builds on the "transaction" idea developed by "old institutional" economist John Commons (see Chapter 1).[2]

We know from the production function concept developed in Chapter 4 (labor demand) that if Ford Motor wants to produce more output it needs to use more labor inputs (capital being fixed in the short run). But there are two different ways Ford can acquire this labor input. One is to hire workers as *employees*, the other is to hire them as *independent contractors*.

The difference between an employee and an independent contractor is a legal one and turns on the issue of control. Both the employee and independent contractor enter into a contract, implicit or explicit, with the firm and agree to perform certain tasks in return for a sum of money. The difference is that the **independent contractor** retains control to perform the work as he/she sees fit, while the **employee** agrees to perform the tasks as directed by the employer. Stated another way, the firm's owner is the "boss" of the employee but a customer of the independent contractor. Typically, the independent contractor also provides the tools and equipment, while an employee uses those owned by the firm.

Firms thus have a choice of acquiring labor either as employees or as independent contractors. Which will they choose? According to Coase and Williamson, the decision hinges on a form of cost often neglected in traditional microeconomic theory—transaction cost. **Transaction cost** is the value of real resources used up to negotiate, implement, and enforce contracts between economic agents. Alternatively stated, it is the *ex ante* and *ex post* cost of exchanging ownership rights to tangible and intangible resources.

In standard microeconomic theory, transaction cost is implicitly assumed to be zero and thus is omitted. This fact arises because the model assumes economic agents have "unbounded rationality" and perfect information and, further, that government can costlessly and completely enforce all property rights and contract terms. The assumption of unbounded rationality means that economic agents have supercomputers for brains and can instantly process all information and calculate all future outcomes; the assumption of perfect information means they know all present and future actions of other people and the benefits and costs of all alternative choices. Combined with the assumption of complete and costless government enforcement of property rights, these conditions imply it is possible for economic

---

1   Ronald Coase, "The Nature of the Firm," *Economica* Vol. 4 (1937): 386–405.

2   Oliver Williamson, *The Economic Institutions of Capitalism* (New York: The Free Press, 1985). An overview of new institutional economics is provided in Eirik Furubotn and Rudolf Richter, *Institutions and Economic Theory: The Contribution of the New Institutional Economics* (Ann Arbor: University of Michigan Press, 1997); the contribution of Commons is discussed in Bruce E. Kaufman, "The Organization of Economic Activity: Insights from the Institutional Theory of John R. Commons," *Journal of Economic Behavior and Organization* 52 (1, 2003): 71–96.

agents to negotiate contracts and trade ownership rights at zero cost. A corollary of zero transaction cost is that it is possible for economic agents to negotiate, implement, and enforce *complete contracts*. A **complete contract** is a contract that stipulates in every detail and for every contingency what the two parties will do and for how much. In effect it removes all risk of nonperformance or other "surprises," since everything affecting the contract both at present and in the future is spelled out in minutest detail. In terms of labor, a complete contract means that the firm and the worker can devise an agreement that specifies exactly what the worker will deliver or perform, when it will be done, and how much compensation will be exchanged.

In a world of zero transaction cost, firms would have no reason to hire employees. The chief benefit for firms of having employees is *control*—the ability to tell the worker what to do and when to do it. But this benefit has no net value if transaction cost is zero, since the firm can without cost write and enforce a complete contract that also stipulates all these same conditions (e.g., what to do and when). Given the other nontransaction costs that go with having employees, such as tax payments for unemployment compensation and Social Security, firms would always find it advantageous to purchase labor from independent contractors. Note that this conclusion holds in theory for *all* types of labor services used by the firm, including senior-level management and technical/administrative personnel. Thus, with zero transaction cost, firms would continue to replace employees with independent contractors until there is only one person remaining—the owner/entrepreneur, such as Henry Ford or Starbucks' Howard Schultz. In this world of zero transaction cost, firms such as Ford Motor and Starbucks continue to exist, but as sole proprietorships that then contract with tens of thousands of other single-person firms for the supply of specialized labor services. For example, when Ford Motor needs someone to install windshields or serve as vice-president of marketing, it does not go to the labor market to hire new employees to do these jobs but goes instead to the product market, where it hires single-person firms (the workers-turned-independent contractors) to provide these services. In such an economy, labor markets disappear(!)—all labor services are traded in product markets just as wheat, computers, and consulting services are.[3]

In the real world, of course, transaction costs are nonzero. One reason is that economic agents have **bounded rationality**—i.e., they have limited mental and cognitive abilities to solve problems and process information. Agents also operate in an environment of imperfect information and fundamental uncertainty. Imperfect information means that information is costly to obtain, is often only partially known to one or both sides, and is sometimes deliberately hidden or distorted by others. **Fundamental uncertainty,** on the other hand, pertains to future events so indeterminate that economic agents cannot form even a roughly accurate estimate

---

[3] In this vein Coase states in *The Firm, the Market, and the Law* (Chicago: University of Chicago Press, p. 14), "In the absence of transaction costs, there is no economic basis for the firm." Also see Steven Cheung, "The Contractual Nature of the Firm," *Journal of Law and Economics* 26 (April, 1983): 1–21.

of their probability of occurrence. And, finally, enforcement of contracts is also imperfect and costly due to factors such as substantial costs of litigation, inadequate government regulatory and judicial personnel, and long time delays in court proceedings. As a result of these factors, the parties to a contract have to invest real resources in negotiating and drafting contracts, leading to positive transaction cost. Positive transaction cost also arises for one party when the other does not fully comply with agreed-upon contract terms, or when resources have to be devoted to litigation and court action. The corollary of positive transaction cost is that contracts are necessarily *incomplete*—they have unavoidable holes and gaps regarding each party's responsibilities, commitments, and duties and thus expose each side to the possibility of costly misunderstandings, disputes, and acts of opportunism and fraud.

Let us now return to the choice facing the firm: Should it hire labor as employees or as independent contractors? Both options entail a form of contract, one an employment contract and the other a "purchase of service" contract. According to Coase and Williamson, the decision rule the firm should follow is this: *Choose the contract form that minimizes transaction cost.* Since both options entail transaction cost, the challenge for the firm is to determine which one is the least costly.

Both methods of obtaining labor have transaction cost advantages and disadvantages. For example, the employment contract is, in general, cheaper to negotiate and draw up. For many types of jobs, the contract between employer and employee is an implicit one—it involves a handshake and an oral agreement or understanding about the terms and conditions of employment. Even where written employment contracts are used, they tend to be relatively brief and much less detailed than a purchase of service contract.

Likewise, the fact that the law gives the employer authority to direct the worker in the performance of the job means the employment contract does not have to be as detailed and comprehensive—the employer need not specify everything in writing up-front but can "fill in the details" through day-to-day instructions and discussions as the job progresses. Also, when hundreds or thousands of people work together in one interconnected production process (e.g., an assembly line), drafting individual purchase of service contracts that detail how each independent contractor should interact with all the others would be very time-consuming and complicated.

A third advantage is that the employment contract is in principle more easily terminated than a purchase of service contract, giving each party more flexibility. Once a purchase of service contract is agreed upon, both parties are legally obligated to carry out its provisions. Under the **employment-at-will doctrine,** however, either party to an employment contract can terminate the relationship "at will." This means the employer can fire the worker and the employee can quit the job at any time and for any reason. In recent years, however, a growing number of federal and state laws have restricted employers' freedom to unilaterally terminate workers. The best example is antidiscrimination legislation that prohibits companies from terminating employees on account of race or gender.

A fourth advantage of the employment contract for firms is that it reduces their exposure to *hold-up* problems and bargaining opportunism in situations where jobs require highly specialized or company-specific skills and qualifications. For example, companies often hire workers to start at entry-level jobs that require only basic, general skills readily attainable in the market. But over time these workers gain specialized skills and knowledge with the company that are not available elsewhere, or only at high cost. Independent contractors are in the same position—starting out in the entry-level jobs they get only market pay rates, but over time with the same firm they too acquire unique, hard-to-duplicate skills and knowledge. These skills and knowledge give both groups of workers a degree of monopoly power in the job market and, hence, give them leverage to "hold up" the firm for higher wages and benefits. The question is, Which group would be more likely to opportunistically exploit their monopoly power? Economists predict that it is the contractors, since they are more likely to view their relationship with the firm as a short-run, commercial "marriage of convenience," leading to a "get it while you can" mentality. After employees have developed a relationship with a firm, on the other hand, they are more likely to feel a part of an ongoing team and to have a stronger sense of organizational commitment and loyalty, motivating them to curb hold-up demands in favor of a more cooperative, long-run, "win-win" approach.

Employment contracts also have transaction cost disadvantages. The incomplete nature of employment contracts leads to a **principal–agent problem** (discussed in Chapter 6) and to the condition of "moral hazard." In the context of an employment contract, the firm is the principal and the worker is the agent. With the goal of maximizing profit, the firm desires that the employee exert maximum effort and diligence toward this end. But since the employee does not equally share in the profit and the firm cannot perfectly monitor the quantity and quality of work, the employee has room to pursue self-interested goals, such as working at a leisurely pace, taking long lunches, or doing personal business on company time. This form of behavior is called **moral hazard,** defined as actions of one party that harm another by taking advantage of holes or gaps in an incomplete contract. Independent contractors and firms also have divergent interests, and the contractors also cannot be perfectly monitored. But purchase of service contracts typically include more detailed work and performance specifications and, hence, provide less room for moral hazard. Also, many independent contractors are paid a lump sum to perform a task (as opposed to a wage per hour for an employee) and thus have greater incentives to work hard in order to complete the task and move on to another contract.

The independent contractor option also has transaction cost advantages and disadvantages. On the advantage side, firms typically avoid a number of costs that go with employees. One example is costs of employee benefits, such as pensions, vacations, and health insurance. A second is that it is often easier in practice to lay off an independent contractor than an employee. Although the employment-at-will doctrine gives firms the freedom to quickly terminate employees, many firms are loath to exercise this right because it hurts morale and productivity among the remaining workers (the "survivors"). Since independent contractors are typically not regarded as part of the corporate family, morale is less harmed when they are terminated. A third reason some companies prefer independent contractors is that labor law makes it far more difficult for them to organize a union and collectively bargain. On the disadvantage side, a major drawback of using independent contractors is that it is more difficult for firms to develop a positive, productivity-enhancing corporate culture and spirit of cooperation and teamwork. Employees more often feel they are a part of the corporate team than do contractors and, hence, they more easily develop a personal identification with and emotional commitment to the firm and its success.

The Firm's Demand for HRM Services

Those firms that choose to hire employees must give attention to the issue of human resource management. Among the most important HRM concerns are recruitment and selection, compensation, training and development, and employee relations. The problem facing each firm is to decide on the optimal amount of each of these HRM practices. At one extreme, the firm invests nothing in training and development of its employees and hires no specialized staff person(s) to handle recruitment and interviewing of job applicants. At the other extreme, it invests in a large-scale corporate university staffed by numerous full-time instructors and offering a wide range of classes and tutorials, as well as an employee selection assessment center staffed by professional psychologists skilled in administering employment tests and conducting job interviews. Or the firm can choose an in-between solution, such as sending certain employees to a one-week training course at a nearby technical school, or hiring one person to run the recruitment and selection function for the firm. Which level of training or recruitment/selection is best for the firm?

One way to answer this question is to use the theory of labor demand developed in Chapter 4.[4] From this perspective, an HRM practice such as employee recruitment or training is considered another form of factor input in the production process, like capital or labor. This can be represented in Equation 10.1 by the augmented production function,

$$Q = f[K, L \cdot e(HRM_i), HRM_i] \tag{10.1}$$

where K is capital input, L is hours of labor devoted to production, e is work effort, and HRM_i is the amount of the ith form of HRM practice (e.g., $HRM_a =$ recruitment, $HRM_b =$ training) used in producing this period's output Q.

Three things are different about this specification of the production function relative to earlier chapters (e.g., chapter 4). First, the amount of labor input in production is the product of work hours and work effort. Thus, for a given number of

---

4   This section is based on Bruce E. Kaufman, "Toward an Integrative Theory of Human Resource Management," in B. Kaufman, ed. *Theoretical Perspectives on Work and the Employment Relationship* (Champaign, IL: IRRA, 2004): 321–66.

Make or Buy HRM Services?

One of the most important developments of the past decade in human resource management is the outsourcing of traditional personnel programs to outside providers. Here is a revealing example, cited in a recent magazine article:

> Norstan Inc., a telecommunications company in suburban Minneapolis, has more than 2,000 employees in 30 states and a human resource department staff of just two people. For the past decade the company has off-loaded nearly every aspect of the HR function to a series of well-known vendors.

Before the outsourcing movement arrived, companies such as Norstan hired HR staff to conduct the full gamut of HRM activities, including staffing, compensation design and delivery, benefits administration, training, and employee assistance. Although the article does not state the size of Norstan's HRM department before outsourcing began, most companies its size have an HRM *staffing ratio* of roughly 1 to 100 (i.e., one HRM staff person per one hundred employees). If the company had not chosen to outsource, therefore, it would likely have an in-house HRM staff of approximately 20 people.

The Norstan case is a dramatic example of a shift from the "make" to the "buy" option in obtaining HRM services. What lies behind this shift? When should a company do one or the other?

Let's first answer the second question. The decision rule is to choose the option that provides the HRM service at the lowest per unit cost. If benefits administration, for example, can be produced in-house for each employee at $10 per month or purchased from a vendor for $8 per month, the company maximizes profit by choosing the "buy" option.

The per unit cost of "make or buy" for a good or service comprises two elements: transaction cost and production cost.[1] The transaction cost is the expense associated with contracting—negotiating, enforcing, and administering the contract; production cost is the expense of the inputs used to actually produce the good or service.

When a company like Norstan (call it Company A) chooses to "make" an HRM service, it incurs both kinds of cost. Company A incurs transaction cost when it contracts with people to work as employees and it incurs production cost equal to the expense of the labor (net of transaction cost), capital, and other resources used up in making each unit of the HRM good or service.

If Company A chooses the "buy" option, it also has to pay both kinds of cost, although in a different form. The company it buys the HRM service from (call it Company B) has to charge a price to cover its production cost, the transaction cost of obtaining employees, and a mark-up for profit. In addition, Company A also has to pay a per unit transaction cost—the expense of negotiating, administering, and enforcing the contract with Company B governing the purchase and delivery of the good or service.

If Company A chooses the "make" option, it incurs production cost and transaction cost from hiring labor; if it chooses the "buy" option it has to pay the per unit purchase price to Company B and the per unit transaction cost that goes along with the sales contract. As previously stated, it should choose the one that yields the lowest net per unit cost. Realistically, other factors besides monetary cost also have to be factored in, such as quality and timeliness.

Knowing this decision rule, we can consider the first question posed above—why firms such as Norstan have switched from making HRM services in-house to buying more of them in the market. Several reasons are important.

---

1 Our earlier discussion of the firm's choice between hiring an employee or an independent contractor involved only transaction cost because the only thing considered was the form in which the firm would contract for labor services (no good or service produced via a production function was involved). In this example, however, the "make or buy" decision involves a product produced with capital, labor, and other inputs, and thus both production and transaction cost must be considered. When Coase claims that firms disappear in a world of zero transaction cost (described in the text), he appears to omit production cost as a determinant of economic organization. Debate exists on the appropriateness of this omission, but is not discussed in more detail here. See Cheung, "The Contractual Nature of the Firm," and Kaufman, "The Organization of Economic Activity," for contrasting points of view.

- **New Computer and Telecommunications Technology.** Greater outsourcing of HRM activities has been made possible by the revolution in computer and telecommunications technology. Today, for example, a number of companies have outsourced benefits administration to an independent call center firm. Rather than have employees contact an in-house benefits administrator, firms now give them an 800 number that connects them to a benefits service center. When the employee calls with a question or problem, a computer is programmed to pull up the person's file. An employee of the vendor firm views it online and takes care of the issue, such as a change in beneficiary or insurance coverage. This new technology makes outsourcing possible by lowering both production cost and transaction cost. Production cost for vendor firms has fallen dramatically with the ability to communicate and process electronically, while the customer firm's transaction cost in using the market has also dropped because computers give it much better ability to monitor the vendor's performance (e.g., number of cases handled, turnaround time, etc.).

- **Economies of Scale.** A related benefit of computers is that vendors are able to automate and standardize many of the administrative or transactional parts of the HRM function, allowing them to serve numerous corporate clients with one system and thus achieve significant economies of scale. A company that specializes in payroll or 401K program administration and does it for many hundreds of client firms, for example, can produce the service at a much lower unit cost than can the individual firms doing it in-house.

- **Spread Investment Cost.** Another type of "scale" economy that favors outsourcing is that only a small number of vendor firms have to invest in the capital and technology to perform the task, while if each firm does the HRM activity in-house they all have to invest in it. Further, since technology is changing so fast, individual companies have difficulty keeping their people trained in the latest

skill sets and in financing the continual equipment and software upgrades. These tasks are less burdensome for a specialized vendor.

- **Shift Wage and Benefit Costs.** Some companies also find it profitable to contract out certain HRM activities and thus gain a production cost advantage because the vendor firms pay lower wages and benefits.

- **Focus on Core Competencies.** Companies have discovered that more profit is achieved when production is limited to only those goods or services for which they have a competitive advantage. Often top management decides that producing HRM services, such as interviewing job applicants and designing new pay programs, is not a core competency and hence they decide to outsource it to a specialized vendor.

Although many companies have outsourced a portion of their HRM function, few have gone as far as Norstan. These companies find there are production and transaction cost reasons for keeping part of their HRM activities in-house. Typically, companies keep HRM activities in-house for two reasons: to maintain greater control over delivery or because a particular activity is of strategic importance to the main part of the business. Thus, a company may outsource the administrative, or lower-end, of compensation management, such as payroll and 401K administration, but keep compensation design and performance evaluation in-house. It is more difficult to write a complete contract specifying a vendor's delivery and performance of, say, quarterly performance evaluations than to process monthly payroll checks, and the downside cost to most companies of poor delivery of performance reviews (e.g., multimillion-dollar court suits alleging discrimination) far outweighs the costs of poor payroll processing.

SOURCES: "Outsourcing: Getting It Right," *Human Resource Executive* (July 2000): 45–8; "The Bright Side of HR Outsourcing: Booming Job Growth at External Contractors," *HR Atlanta* (December 1997): 1.

work hours the greater the amount of worker effort the larger is the amount of labor input into the production function. Likewise, if effort is zero then labor input is zero. Second, the production function is now augmented to provide a role for HRM services to affect production, on the realistic view that HRM services help produce output and the greater the amount of HRM the larger will be the amount of output Q that is obtained by the firm.[5]

The third feature of this specification of the production function is that additional HRM services have both a direct and indirect affect on output. The direct effect is captured by the HRM term in the right hand part of the production function. It shows that holding constant the amount of capital and labor inputs, the addition of more HRM services increases output. Examples of the *direct HRM effect* are: investing more resources in an employee selection and recruitment program (thus obtaining a better employer–employee match) or an employee training program (upgrading the skills of the employees). The *indirect HRM effect* is captured by the term $e(HRM_i)$ in the production function. The idea is that more HRM services can increase output indirectly to the extent they increase employee work effort, which then increases total labor input to the production function ($L \cdot e$). The way HRM services affect employee work effort, in turn, is through motivation and morale. Thus, an employee training program might not only increase the skills of the workers (the direct effect) but also increase the morale of the workers (the indirect effect) because they feel more valued by the firm or like their jobs better, leading them to work harder and thereby increase output. Research shows that a large number of HRM services, particularly in the area of employee relations, are done precisely to maintain and boost employee morale and motivation.[6] Thus, firms invest considerable resources to conduct compensation, performance appraisal, and dispute resolution in ways that employees feel are fair and equitable, lest feelings of unfair or opportunistic treatment lead them to "get back" at the employer by withholding work effort. The adverse morale effect is also what makes many firms quite reluctant to cut wages in an economic downturn even when market conditions of excess labor supply make doing so an otherwise attractive and rational business decision.[7]

The goal of the firm is to maximize profit. It follows that additional units of each HRM practice should be devoted to production as long as the extra revenue generated is greater than or equal to the extra cost.

The revenue from an additional unit of an HRM practice is measured by the *marginal revenue product*, MRP_{HRM}. (To simplify things, for the time-being we drop the subscript i.) The *MRP*, in turn, is calculated as the marginal product of the HRM practice ($MP_{HRM} = \Delta Q / \Delta HRM$) multiplied by the marginal revenue ($MR = \Delta TR / \Delta Q$) received from each unit of output. For a competitive firm

---

5   For empirical evidence see Ann Bartel, "Human Resource Management and Organizational Performance: Evidence from Retail Banking," *Industrial and Labor Relations Review* 57 (January 2004): 181–203.

6   Robert Solow, *The Labor Market as a Social Institution* (Cambridge: Basil Blackwell, 1990); Ernst Fehr and Armin Falk, "Wage Rigidity in a Competitive Incomplete Contract Market," *Journal of Political Economy* 107 (February, 1999): 1106–34.

7   Truman Bewley, *Why Wages Don't Fall During a Recession* (Cambridge: Harvard University Press, 1999).

$MR = P$ (the product price), so MRP_{HRM} is thus $MP_{HRM} \cdot P$. The marginal product of HRM, MP_{HRM}, in turn, is determined by the size of the direct and indirect HRM effects. That is, $\Delta Q / \Delta HRM = [\Delta Q / \Delta e \cdot \Delta e / \Delta HRM + \Delta Q / \Delta HRM]$. If labor was a commodity like coal or steel (so that work effort is a "given"; this is similar to treating the number of BTUs or tensile strength in a particular grade of coal or steel as a "given"), the indirect (morale) effect would be zero and the marginal product of HRM would reflect only the direct effect (the right-hand term in the brackets). Because labor is embodied in human beings, however, an additional unit of HRM services can lead to higher output through both the direct and indirect effects, implying the larger the morale effect of HRM (the left-hand term in the brackets), the larger is HRM's marginal product (*ceteris paribus*).

A typical *MRP* schedule for an HRM practice is illustrated in Figure 10.2 by the line MRP_{HRM_1}. The position of the MRP_{HRM} line reflects the size of both the direct and indirect HRM effects—the larger are one or both, the larger is the MP_{HRM} and the further to the right in the diagram the *MRP* schedule will lie. The upward-sloping portion of the line shows that at first additional units of the HRM

FIGURE 10.2 THE DEMAND CURVE FOR HRM PRACTICES

In the region of diminishing returns, the marginal revenue product schedule (demand curve) for an HRM practice is downward sloping, such as MRP_{HRM_1}. At a price per unit of V_1, the firm demands HRM_1 units (point X); at a higher price of V_2 quantity demanded falls to HRM_2 (point Y). A technological improvement or increase in company sales and employment shifts the HRM demand curve rightward from MRP_{HRM_1} to MRP_{HRM_2}, leading to an increase in HRM input demand from HRM_1 (point X) to HRM_3 (point Z).

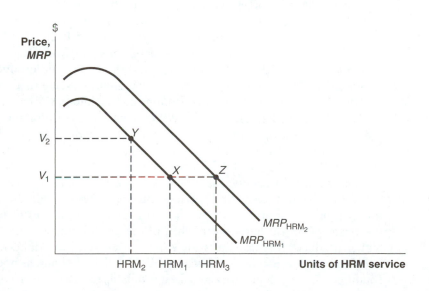

practice have a rising *MRP*, indicating that each extra unit of the HRM practice contributes a larger increment to output and revenue. This is the area of increasing returns in production. At some point the *MRP* schedule begins to slope downward, indicating that the use of additional units of the HRM practice is now subject to diminishing returns. One can well imagine, for example, that at some point adding additional training classes (or weeks of training) will, for a given size of workforce, yield successively smaller increments to production and revenue.

To determine the optimal amount of the HRM input, the firm also needs to know the input's *marginal cost* schedule. Let V denote the per unit cost (or price) of the HRM input. For simplicity, we assume that the firm can produce or buy additional units of the HRM practice at a constant cost of V_1. Hence, the profit-maximizing level of an HRM activity is where

$$V_1 = MP_{HRM} \cdot P. \tag{10.2}$$

In Figure 10.2, the optimal level of the HRM input is HRM_1 (point X), determined by the intersection of the marginal cost V_1 and the HRM demand curve (the MRP_{HRM} schedule).

Figure 10.2 shows that a firm's use of HRM practices follows the law of demand, just as it does for use of other factor inputs. Thus, a rise in the price of an HRM activity from V_1 to V_2 causes a movement up the HRM demand curve and a decline in quantity demanded from HRM_1 to HRM_2 (point X to point Y). If, for example, an occupational licensing law were passed that requires all HRM practitioners to have a university master's degree, firms would have to pay a higher wage (salary) to attract these more educated workers. This higher labor cost would in turn increase the marginal cost of each unit of employee recruitment activity, or other such HRM input, leading to a movement up the HRM demand curve and a decline in the firm's quantity demanded.

Firms' demand for HRM inputs is also influenced by all those variables that shift the HRM demand curve. Since the HRM demand curve is the marginal revenue product schedule, we know that a variable will shift the HRM demand curve only if it changes one or both of the determinants of MRP_{HRM}—the marginal product of the HRM input or the marginal revenue of the product/service produced (price P for a competitive firm). For example, assume that converting from an instructor-based to a web-based training format allows workers to learn a given set of skills in only half the time. This technological innovation increases the marginal product of training in the firm's production function, shifting the HRM input demand curve to the right. At a given cost V_1, the firm increases its use of training from HRM_1 (point X) to HRM_3 (point Z).

Or, as a second example, assume this firm is in an industry that is experiencing rapid growth, such as medical services. Increased demand for the product (other things equal) causes the product price to rise, leading to greater production and greater employment (a rightward shift of the firm's labor demand curve). But the higher product price also shifts the MRP_{HRM} curve to the right, making it profitable to now devote more resources to HRM activities. Thus, as booming demand conditions in the product market make it profitable to hire more production workers, so too do these conditions make it profitable to hire more HRM staff to conduct training, recruitment/selection, and other such activities.

The Equilibrium Level of Several HRM Inputs

Equation 10.2 defines the profit-maximizing level of one HRM input, but the firm has to simultaneously determine the level of the other HRM_i practices. To keep matters simple, let's work with only two HRM inputs, HRM_a and HRM_b (e.g., recruitment and training). The per unit cost of input HRM_a is V_a, the per unit cost of input HRM_b is V_b.

The profit-maximizing levels of HRM_a and HRM_b are analogous to Equation 10.2,

$$V_a = MRP_{HRM_a} \qquad \text{(10.3)}$$

$$V_a = MRP_{HRM_b}$$

In much the same way as consumers maximize total utility by equating the marginal utility per dollar spent on each item consumed, firms maximize profit by equating the marginal product per dollar cost of each input used in the production process. Thus, the equilibrium amount of multiple HRM inputs is given by Equation 10.4:

$$MRP_{HRM_a}/V_a = MRP_{HRM_b}/V_b \qquad \text{(10.4)}$$

This equation states that the firm should adjust the amount of inputs HRM_a and HRM_b until the "bang for the buck" is equal. Thus, if an additional dollar spent on employee recruitment yields an *MRP* of $10 and an additional dollar spent on training yields an *MRP* of only $6, the firm would increase profit by switching more resources to employee recruitment and away from training. This process of substitution should continue until the *MRP* per dollar of expenditure is equal.

Strategic HRM

A fast-growing area in management research in recent years is **strategic HRM.** One set of authors define it as "the pattern of planned human resource deployments and activities intended to enable an organization to achieve its goals."[8] The object of strategic HRM is to maximize firm performance, and its major propositions are twofold: first, performance is enhanced when HRM activities "fit" or "align" with the overall business strategy of the organization; and second, in putting together an HRM program it is important to choose individual practices that support each other and work together in a synergistic, integrated way to achieve the overall strategy.

Explicit in the first proposition is the assumption that different business strategies require different types of HRM programs to be successful. In terms of the theoretical model of HRM input demand developed above, this proposition is

---

8   P. Wright and G. McMahan, "Theoretical Perspectives for Strategic Human Resource Management," *Journal of Management* 18 (no. 2, 1992): 295–320.

equivalent to saying that the marginal revenue product of HRM practices is higher with one business strategy than with others. To illustrate, one strategic approach to competitive advantage is to be the low-cost producer in an industry; a second is to be #1 in customer service. Will the same HRM program serve both strategies equally well? Probably not. High employee morale is crucial to a customer service strategy, so firms pursuing this approach are more likely to pay above-market wages and benefits, have employee involvement programs, and provide extensive training. Firms pursuing the low-cost strategy, on the other hand, often emphasize volume production, tight supervision and control, and narrow job tasks, leading them to adopt a different set of HRM practices, such as strict job perfor-mance and absenteeism policies, wages and benefits that lag or only match the market, and hiring criteria that emphasize physical dexterity and sta-mina over "people" skills.[9] Additional evidence on this matter is provided in the Empirical Evidence 10-1 section at the end of this chapter.

➧ SEE

Empirical Evidence 10-1: The Configuration of Alternative Employment and HRM Systems, p. 548.

Explicit in the second proposition is the assumption that important comple-mentarities exist among individual HRM practices. In terms of the theoretical model developed above, this means that the marginal revenue product of one type of HRM practice is higher when a particular form of another HRM practice is used than it is with others. As an illustration, assume that a firm pursuing a customer ser-vice strategy determines that a profit-sharing program will boost employee morale. Will the effectiveness of the profit-sharing program be influenced by the type of job security program the firm adopts? Most likely. One option, for example, is a "hire and fire" employment-at-will program; a second is a "just cause" termination program where employees have assured job security except in cases of clear and egregious malperformance. It is reasonable to hypothesize that the profit-sharing program will be more effective with the just-cause program, given that employees have greater assurance they will be with the company in future years to reap the financial fruits of their hard work and loyal service.[10] Additional evidence on this matter is provided in Empirical Evidence 10-2.

➧ SEE

Empirical Evidence 10-2: The Link between HRM Practices and Firm Performance, p. 551.

Issues in Employee Selection

When firms decide to hire an employee, the challenge they face is finding the best person for the job. This issue is usually framed in terms of achieving the best "match" or "fit."

Maximizing the quality of the person/job match is a difficult but very impor-tant task. If done well, employee selection can provide a firm with a significant competitive advantage. One study, for example, estimates that the top 5 percent of

---

9   See Jeffrey Arthur, "The Link between Business Strategy and Industrial Relations Systems in American Steel Minimills," *Industrial and Labor Relations Review* 45 (April 1992): 488–506.

10   See Derek Jones, Takao Kato, and Jeffrey Pliskin, "Profit-Sharing and Gain-Sharing: A Review of Theory, Incidence, and Effects," in David Lewin, Daniel Mitchell, and Mahmood Zaidi, eds., *The Human Resource Management Handbook*, vol. 1 (Greenwich, JAI Press, 1997), 153–74.

a firm's employees are twice as productive as the bottom 5 percent.[11] Obviously, if the selection process is able to systematically identify the job applicants who have the potential to move into the top-performing group, firm-level productivity and performance will considerably increase.

The Employee Selection Process

Firms typically follow a five-step process in performing employee selection:[12]

1: Job Analysis   The first step is to use a procedure called "job analysis" to describe the content of a job and identify all the knowledge, skills, and abilities (KSA) a person must possess to perform it. Job analysis also considers systemwide attributes that influence performance, such as the leadership style, reward system, and culture of the company.

2: Criteria Determination   The second step is to identify the criteria that define successful job performance. Typically, these include variables related to quantity of output, quality of output, relations with workmates (e.g., is a team player), and contributions to broader organizational goals.

3: Choosing Predictors   The third step is to identify characteristics or attributes of individuals that are most closely associated with successful fulfillment of the criteria identified in step two and then devise "predictors" (e.g., interviews, physical exams, aptitude tests) that allow the company to differentiate among job applicants according to these desired characteristics and attributes.

4: Analyzing Predictor–Criterion Relationships   Once predictors are identified, the fourth step is to compare alternative predictors and determine which one(s) provide the most accurate information on matching up worker KSA and the criteria for successful job performance. This process, called predictor "validation," involves three separate aspects: *criterion-related validation*, *content validation*, and *construct validation*. The first measures the degree to which predictor scores and criterion scores are correlated (e.g., the degree to which a high score on a physical dexterity test correlates with the number of units of the good produced); the second measures the degree to which the predictor variable accurately captures the KSA needed for the job (e.g., the degree to which a physical dexterity test captures relevant job skills for a machine operator's position); and the third measures the degree to which the predictor variable actually measures what it purports to (e.g., the degree to which an intelligence test really measures native intelligence).

---

11   John Hunter and Frank Schmidt, "Ability Tests: Economic Benefits versus the Issue of Fairness," *Industrial Relations* 21 (Fall 1982): 293–308.

12   Cheri Ostroff and Teresa Rothausen, "Selection and Job Matching," in Lewin, Mitchell, and Zaidi, eds., *The Human Resource Management Handbook*, vol. 3, 3–52.

5: *Profitability and Usefulness* The fifth step is to determine whether use of the predictor leads to greater profit for the firm. If a predictor variable satisfies the three validity tests in step four, it will help the firm achieve a better job/person match. But the firm nevertheless must compare the extra benefits from using the selection predictor against the extra costs. If a predictor is quite costly to use (e.g., a two-day battery of psychological assessment tests) and yields only a modest improvement in fit, or if the improvement in fit yields only a modest improvement in job performance and revenue, the firm is better off not to use it. A related consideration, sometimes called "usefulness," concerns the job applicants' reaction to the selection method. When used, the selection method may increase profit, but if job applicants are averse to it (e.g., dislike participating in an "encounter group" to test interpersonal relations skills) and drop out of the interview process, then the selection method is not useful.

Employee Selection: An Economic Model

Several parts of the selection process described above (e.g., **job analysis**) are essentially administrative in nature and not of great interest or relevance to economists. Other parts, however, have been the subject of a good deal of research. The employee selection problem is a special case of a more general problem—optimal choice in situations of imperfect information. Imperfect information, in turn, entails both lack of information (the information set is incomplete or has holes) and **asymmetric information.** Asymmetric information occurs in a situation where the information set available to one party in a potential exchange relationship differs from that available to the other. Three economists, Michael Spence, Joseph Stiglitz, and George Akerlof, received Nobel prizes in 2001 for their path-breaking work in this area.

Imperfect and asymmetric information lie at the heart of the employee selection problem (steps 2–4 above). Employee selection would be trivial if the firm could determine with zero cost and complete accuracy the future job productivity of each candidate in the applicant pool. But the future productivity of each worker is in fact highly uncertain. One reason is lack of information—the firm lacks knowledge about all the KSA of each applicant. Another problem is asymmetric information— the applicants know more about their own skills, abilities, and knowledge than the firm does and, in a number of situations, will deliberately hide or selectively reveal information to maximize the probability of being selected.

Of the various models developed by economists concerning optimal choice in an environment of imperfect information, Michael Spence's theory of *job market signaling* is the most directly relevant to employee selection and ably illustrates the issues and challenges involved.[13] A brief and relatively simple exposition of the model follows.

---

13   Michael Spence, "Job Market Signaling," *Quarterly Journal of Economics* 87, no. 3 (August 1973): 355–74.

The Pay-off to Screening   The first thing Spence does is illustrate why it pays firms to spend resources on employee selection, or what he refers to as *employee screening*. To begin, assume there are two distinct, equal-sized groups of people in the firm's applicant pool: low-ability group A people and high-ability group B people. Because individuals in group A have a lower innate ability, their marginal revenue product for the firm will be, say, $10 per hour, while the marginal revenue product of higher-ability group B people is $20 per hour. If the firm possessed no data on the personal characteristics of each applicant, it would randomly select a worker from the applicant pool with a probability of 0.5 of getting a person from group A and group B, respectively. The expected value or average level of each worker's MRP_L, therefore, would be $0.5(\$10) + 0.5(\$20) = \$15$ per hour. Given that competition forces a firm to pay workers a wage commensurate with their marginal revenue product, the wage paid by the firm would also be $15 per hour.

The reason firms engage in screening is obvious from this example. At the going market wage of $15, any one firm could readily increase its profits if it could find some characteristic that distinguished a high-productivity group B person from a low-productivity group A person. It would reject all group A workers and hire only group B workers, paying a wage of only $15 (since this is what other firms are paying), yet reaping a MRP_L of $20. *All* firms, of course, have the same incentive to engage in screening. To the extent they are successful, wages in the market will move toward $10 for group A workers and $20 for group B workers, eroding the short-run profits that come from superior screening. As long as *any* uncertainty remains about the actual productivity of job applicants, however, the firm has an incentive to improve its employee selection process in order to obtain a workforce that is more productive relative to its competitors.

Given that it pays to engage in screening, how does a firm successfully do it? Each firm will attempt to identify characteristics or signals of workers that are correlated with employee performance on the job. There is a dynamic interaction in the screening process, however, since workers, realizing that a firm is using some characteristic such as years of education or veteran's status as a signal, will attempt to acquire more of it to improve their chances of being selected. Without some limit or constraint on the ability of both low- and high-productivity workers to acquire the signal, the firm will not be able to successfully screen workers of one group from another.

To illustrate under what conditions a worker characteristic will be able to serve as a successful screening device, the following discussion uses years of education as a case study. While firms use many other signals in the screening process (e.g., reference letters, number of previous jobs, leadership activities), years of education is undoubtedly one of the most important, as reflected by hiring standards at most firms that specify minimum years of educational attainment as a prerequisite for consideration for employment.

Education as a Screening Device   The conditions under which years of education serve as a successful screening device are illustrated in Figure 10.3. The horizontal axis measures the years of education (E) obtained by the job applicant, beginning

The hiring standard E^* successfully screens the applicant pool into low-productivity group A workers and high-productivity group B workers. Group A workers choose E_0 years of education since their net wage is $10, compared to only $6 if they choose E^*. Group B workers choose E^* years of education since their net wage is $13, compared to only $10 if E_0 is chosen.

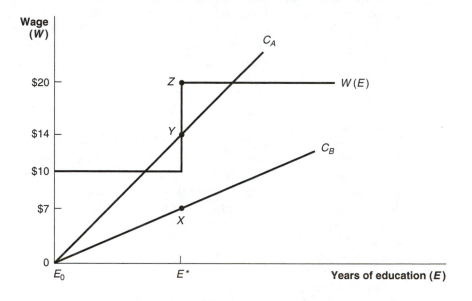

at the minimum level E_0 that each person is required by law to complete (eight years in the United States). As before, low-ability group A workers and high-ability group B workers are assumed to be in the applicant pool. The goal of each business firm is to use years of education as a screening device to separate group A workers from group B workers. Assume that based on past experience, firms believe that all workers with less than E^* years of education are the low-ability group A workers, with an MRP_L of $10 per hour, while workers with E^* or more years of education are the high-ability group B workers, with an MRP_L of $20 per hour. Since competition will force firms to pay a wage equal to the MRP_L of workers, the hiring standard of E^* gives rise to the discontinuous wage schedule $W(E)$. Workers with fewer than E^* years of education are presumed to be group A workers and are paid only $10; workers with E^* years or more of education are assumed to be group B workers and are paid $20.

Will E^* effectively screen group A from group B workers? The answer depends on the *costs* of acquiring the signal for persons in each group. If there were zero costs to obtaining E^* years of education, every worker would do so to earn a wage of $20. In this case, years of education would fail as a screening device since the firm would be unable to successfully differentiate between group A and group B workers. For any hiring standard to successfully sort group A from group B workers, the essential condition is that the cost of acquiring the signal be *negatively* correlated with the worker's productivity. This condition implies that it will be more costly for the less able workers in group A to obtain E^* than for the group B workers. Why might this be so? The costs of acquiring additional education involve direct money costs for tuition and books, indirect money costs in the form of forgone earnings from work, and "psychic" costs of stress and anxiety. An argument can be made that all three components of the costs of education will be greater for low-ability group A persons because of the extra time, expense, and difficulty they will face in mastering the subject matter. This may be particularly true at the college and postgraduate levels. Assuming that costs of education and ability are negatively correlated, this gives rise to the cost schedules C_A and C_B in Figure 10.3 (drawn as straight lines for convenience). Each line shows the dollar cost (prorated per hour of work) of acquiring various years of education for persons in groups A and B, respectively. It is assumed that the cost of obtaining the minimum E_0 level of education is zero for persons of both groups; as years of education increase, so do the costs. The line C_B lies below C_A on the assumption that the more able persons in group B can obtain a particular level of education at a lower cost than the less able workers in group A.

Given the wage schedule $W(E)$ and the cost schedules C_A and C_B, it can easily be shown that the hiring standard of E^* will, in fact, successfully separate the firm's applicant pool into group A and group B workers. To see this, determine the optimal level of education for the persons in each group. The optimal level of education is the one where the *net* wage (the wage W minus the cost of education C) is the greatest. For the low-ability workers in group A, the greatest net wage is at the education level E_0, where the wage is $10 and the cost of education is zero. Although group A workers could obtain a wage of $20 by acquiring E^* years of education, it would not pay them to do so because of the high costs—the wage is $20 (point Z), but the costs of obtaining E^* are $14 (point Y on C_A), yielding a net wage of $6. The optimal level of education for high-ability group B people can be determined in a similar fashion. If they were to choose E_0, their net wage would also be $10. Could they do better by acquiring E^* years of education? The answer is yes: their wage would be $20 (point Z), and the cost would be only $7 (point X on C_B), yielding a net wage of $13. While it pays group B workers to obtain E^*, it would not pay them to obtain more than E^*, since the wage remains constant but the costs rise. (For similar reasons it does not pay for group A workers to obtain more than E_0.) The conclusion is that the hiring standard E^* is a successful screening device because it correctly identifies or sorts the people in the firm's applicant pool into low-productivity group A workers and high-productivity group B workers.

Signaling Failures and the Optimal Signal   The hiring standard E^* is what Spence called a "signaling equilibrium," because it successfully identifies workers

FIGURE 10.4   SIGNALING FAILURES AND THE OPTIMAL SIGNAL

In graph (a), a relatively low hiring standard of E_1 fails to successfully screen between low- and high-productivity workers, since both groups A and B obtain a higher net wage at E_1 than E_0. Similarly, a relatively high standard of E_2 also fails as a screening device, since the net wage for both groups A and B at E_0 is higher than at E_2. In graph (b), the optimal hiring standard is the education level just to the right of E^*, since it successfully screens between low- and high-productivity workers at the lowest cost in terms of resources devoted to education.

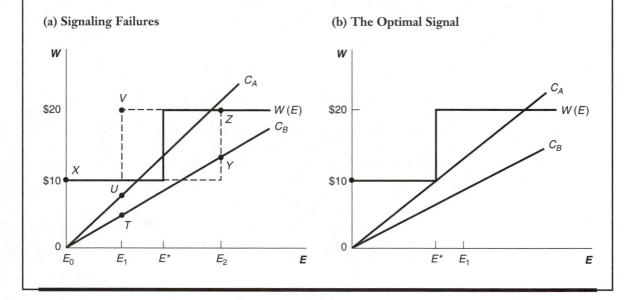

(a) Signaling Failures

(b) The Optimal Signal

as belonging to group A or group B. If it did not do so, employers would eventually discover, for example, that some workers thought to be high-productivity group B workers were actually low-productivity group A workers, and this information would cause the hiring standard E^* to be raised. It is a relatively easy task to identify the hiring standards that would *not* be a signaling equilibrium. This is shown in graph (a) of Figure 10.4.

Consider first if the hiring standard were lowered from E^* to E_1. The wage schedule $W(E)$ would rise from $10 to $20 at E_1, shown by the broken line at point V. Instead of maximizing their net wage at E_0, group A workers would find it profitable to invest in E_1 years of education since the distance between wages and costs (VU) now exceeds that at E_0 ($X0$). Group B workers would also select E_1, since the net wage VT is the largest that is obtainable.

In this situation, firms would be motivated to raise hiring standards in an attempt to separate group A from group B workers. What if the hiring standard were raised all the way to E_2? The wage schedule $W(E)$ would now become vertical along the broken line at point Z. Given this, it is easily seen that E_2 also fails as a signaling equilibrium since *neither* group A nor group B workers have an incentive to invest in this much education. At E_2, group A workers would suffer costs greater than the wage and would thus find E_0 more profitable; likewise, group B workers would also choose E_0 since the distance $X0$ exceeds ZY.

The final issue is whether there is an *optimal* hiring standard in this model. "Optimal" in this context means the level of the signal that is able to successfully differentiate between group A and group B workers at the least cost in terms of resources used in the screening process. There is, in fact, an optimal hiring standard and it is an educational level *just to the right* of E^* in graph (b) of Figure 10.4. A hiring standard of E^* or less would result in both group A and group B workers investing in the signal, and its screening value would be lost. If the hiring standard were increased beyond E^* to, say, E_1, individuals would still be accurately sorted into group A and group B workers, but the cost would be more than necessary since group B workers would be required to invest in E_1 years of education when slightly more than E^* years would fulfill the same screening function.

Issues in Compensation Management

Another functional area of HRM practice is *compensation management*. Compensation management is the task of determining and administering the pay structure of the firm. Viewed broadly, compensation management involves both direct and indirect forms of pay, where the former is a direct money payment (e.g., a wage per hour) and the latter is some type of indirect payment in the form of an employee benefit (e.g., health insurance). Since employee benefits were examined in Chapter 8, attention in this section is restricted to direct compensation.

The place to begin the analysis of compensation management is the model of wage determination in a competitive labor market. This model was presented at the beginning of Chapter 6 (see Figure 6.1), and the reader may wish to refer to that discussion. It is shown there that if the labor market satisfies all the assumptions of the perfect competition model—many buyers and sellers, utility-maximizing behavior, perfect information, zero costs of mobility, and homogeneous labor and jobs—competition among firms and workers leads to the emergence of a single going price (call it W_1) for every type of labor (legal secretaries, plumbers, etc.). We called this result the *law of one wage*. The essence of the law of one wage is that every firm has to pay at least W_1 or its workers will quit for higher-paying jobs elsewhere, while no firm would pay more than W_1 since its competitors would be getting equally productive workers but at less cost. In this scenario, labor markets resemble commodity and financial markets and, at a point in time, supply and demand determine the going price for legal secretaries and plumbers, just as they do for Winter No. 2 wheat and shares of IBM stock; while over time, shifts in supply and demand cause these market prices to rise and fall by the minute and hour.

In this theoretical world the task of compensation management is simple in the extreme. Market supply and demand completely determine the rate of pay for each type of labor and the firm need only look on a web site or in the daily newspaper to find the going price for labor, just as it would do to find the price of wheat or IBM shares.

Real-world labor markets do not, however, completely match the assumptions of the perfect competition model. As discussed in Chapter 6, the greater the number and significance of *market imperfections* (e.g., imperfect information, costs of mobility, heterogeneity in workers and jobs) the greater will be the divergence in pay rates and structure from that predicted by the competitive model. In particular, we noted that market imperfections create an *area of indeterminacy* in the wage structure (see Figure 6.3)—an area in which demand and supply establish the upper and lower bound on pay rates but within which firms have discretion as to the pay rate (and form of pay) they choose.

Administrative methods associated with the HRM function of compensation management are thus used by firms to "complete" or "fill in" the pay structure within the area of indeterminacy.[14] In labor markets that correspond relatively closely to the theoretical model of perfect competition, the area of indeterminacy will be small and market forces are the primary determinant of pay, leaving little room for compensation management to exert an independent force. In other labor markets where market imperfections bulk larger, however, the area of indeterminacy will be correspondingly larger, as will the latitude for firms to use compensation management methods to determine the pay structure. Firms with well-developed internal labor markets, as described in Chapter 6, exemplify this situation.

Two aspects of compensation management have particularly interested economists. The first concerns determining the appropriate pay *level* in the area of indeterminacy; the second concerns the best pay *form* (type of direct compensation). We briefly examine each.

Pay Level

A controversy in labor economics stretches back a half-century on the degree to which observed rates of pay are market determined by supply and demand or administratively determined by firms through their compensation management decisions. Some economists claim that market forces largely determine pay rates and that the compensation management practices of firms simply mimic or "ratify" what the market has decreed.[15] Others, however, claim that market forces leave a

---

14   George Milkovich and Jerry Newman, *Compensation Management*, 7th ed. (New York: McGraw-Hill Irwin, 2002).

15   Jonathan Leonard, "Wage Structure and Dynamics in the Electronics Industry," *Industrial Relations* 28 (Spring 1989): 251–75.

FIGURE 10.5

WAGE GRADIENT, FAST-FOOD RESTAURANTS IN ATLANTA, GEORGIA

The average restaurant wage increases with miles from the central business district (CBD), as indicated by the solid line. Within each mile interval, a dispersion of wage rates exists among restaurants, as indicated by the gap between the two dashed lines.

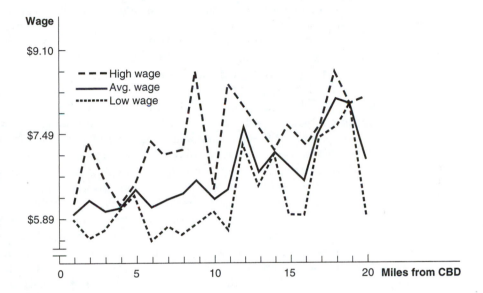

SOURCE: Madelyn V. Young and Bruce E. Kaufman, "Interfirm Wage Differentials in a Local Labor Market: The Case of the Fast-Food Industry," *Journal of Labor Research* 18 (Summer 1997): 475. The wage rates on the vertical axis have been rescaled to reflect 2004 prices.

large area of indeterminacy in pay rates, and firms' administrative decisions thus exert a considerable independent influence on the pay structure.[16]

The issues involved are better appreciated with reference to Figure 10.5. The figure comes from a study of wage rates paid in 1989 by 103 hamburger restaurants in metropolitan Atlanta, Georgia, to newly hired employees with no previous fast-food experience. Looking only at the raw data, it would appear that market forces

16   Erica Groshen, "Sources of Inter-Industry Wage Dispersion: How Much Do Employers Matter?" *Quarterly Journal of Economics* 106 (August 1991): 869–84, and Richard Freeman, "Does the New Generation of Labor Economists Know More Than the Old Generation?" in Bruce Kaufman, ed., *How Labor Markets Work: Reflections on Theory and Practice* by John Dunlop, Clark Kerr, Richard Lester, and Lloyd Reynolds (Lexington: Lexington Books, 1988), 205–32.

leave considerable latitude for firms to independently decide their rate of pay. The mean wage among these restaurants was $6.75 an hour (in 2004 dollars), but a sizable dispersion among restaurants existed. The lowest-paying restaurant offered $5.11 an hour to new hires; the highest-paying restaurant offered $7.64 an hour. Taken at face value, these data would seem to indicate a large area of indeterminacy (from $5.11/hour to $7.64/hour).

Such an inference would be a mistake, however. Statistical analysis revealed that much of this apparent random variation in pay rates among restaurants was in fact related in a commonsense way to demand and supply factors. The study found that the most important variable influencing a restaurant's pay level was the average family income in a three-mile radius around the restaurant—the higher the average family income, the higher the restaurant's pay level. The reason for this relationship is that teenagers are the largest component of the fast-food workforce and teens' reservation wage (the wage at which they are willing to seek market work) increases with family income (see Chapter 3, Figure 3.4). Thus, restaurants in low-income areas could offer a relatively low wage and yet attract teen workers (because their parents on average did not have money to give them for cars, clothes, etc.), while restaurants in affluent neighborhoods had to pay a significantly higher wage if they were to induce teens with much greater access to parent-provided funds to take a fast-food job (or to induce teens from poorer income neighborhoods to commute to these jobs). Taking this labor supply variable into account, it was possible to explain a large portion of the dispersion in restaurant wages. In particular, family income tended to rise (but not uniformly) with distance from the central business district (CBD) until well out into the suburbs, leading to an upward-sloping **wage gradient.** This wage gradient (the relationship between wage rates and distance from the CBD) is depicted in Figure 10.5 by the solid upward-sloping line.[17]

Other demand–supply variables also helped explain the dispersion of wages among restaurants (e.g., number of competing restaurants in a three-mile radius; accessibility to public transportation). But after all of these market-related factors were included, some unexplained dispersion in wage rates among restaurants remained. This dispersion is marked in Figure 10.5 by the upper and lower dashed lines. These lines show the highest- and lowest-paying restaurants within each mile interval from the CBD and effectively delineate the area of indeterminacy in this labor market. The average "spread" between the highest- and lowest-paying restaurants in these mile intervals was $0.72 an hour. Undoubtedly some of this dispersion was itself related to unmeasured demand–supply factors, but even restaurants across the street from each other paid wages to similar workers that varied by 5 to 10 percent. Studies of other types of labor markets, such as for manufacturing workers, find a much larger spread in wage rates across firms, presumably reflecting the fact the fast-food labor market corresponds more closely to the ideal of competitive theory.[18]

---

17 For additional discussion and evidence on wage gradients, see Keith Ihlanfeldt, "Intraurban Wage Gradients: Evidence by Race, Gender, Occupational Class, and Sector," *Journal of Urban Economics* 32 (July 1992): 70–91.

18 Groshen, "Sources of Inter-Industry Wage Dispersion."

In setting pay rates, firms have to achieve what is called in the literature of compensation management **external alignment** and **internal alignment**.[19] External alignment means that the firm's pay rates are aligned or consistent with pay rates for similar workers and jobs as determined in external labor markets. If firms do not achieve external alignment they suffer negative consequences, such as high employee turnover, numerous unfilled vacancies, or excessive labor cost and non-competitive product prices, that eventually force them to change their pay policy. Stated another way, external alignment is satisfied when the firm's pay rates are inside the area of indeterminacy.

Inside the area of indeterminacy, however, firms have discretion as to the wage level they choose to pay. They can choose one of three strategies: *lead the market* (stake out a pay position close to the top of the area of indeterminacy), *match the market* (pay the market average wage), or *lag the market* (pay close to the bottom wage rate in the area of indeterminacy). What strategy will firms choose? Economic research finds that several factors influence this decision.[20]

Efficiency Wages Firms may deliberately pay above-market wages in order to motivate employees to work harder or cut down on turnover. Called an "efficiency wage" by economists (see Chapters 6 and 13), this strategy is consistent with profit maximization since the firm expects to get a productivity gain or turnover cost saving that more than compensates for the higher wage cost.

Menu Costs Another reason firms may lead the market in pay rates is to reduce what are called **menu costs.** Menu costs are administrative and business costs associated with changing a firm's pay system/structure (the "menu" of rewards and incentives). If a firm matches the market, it may have to more frequently readjust its pay rates in order to maintain external alignment, while a market leader can hold pay rates steady for a longer period of time, avoiding menu costs.

Ability to Pay Considerable research finds that firms with above-average profits also pay above-average wages and salaries.[21] The converse is also true—firms that earn little or no profit also tend to lag the market. (For example, the lowest-paying restaurants in the Atlanta fast-food study discussed above were, on average, owned by the least-profitable of the hamburger chains.) Competitive market theory does not predict a link between profit and pay—pay is determined by the intersection of the labor demand and supply curves, and the level of a firm's profit does not itself affect either curve (as long as the firm stays in business). But when considerations of fairness and employee motivation are introduced, such a link is easily explained. Employees perceive that they contribute to a firm's financial performance and, as a

19 Milkovich and Newman, *Compensation Management.*

20 Erica Groshen, "Five Reasons Why Wages Vary among Employers," *Industrial Relations* 30 (Fall 1991): 350–81.

21 See, for example, David Levine, "Fairness, Markets, and Ability to Pay: Evidence from Compensation Executives," *American Economic Review* 83 (December 1993): 1241–59.

matter of fairness, deserve to share in it. Thus, to preserve employee motivation and good will, firms with above-normal profit (or "rents") will often share a portion with employees in the form of above-market wages (sometimes called "rent sharing"). Low-profit firms and new start-ups, on the other hand, have less ability to pay and thus either match or lag the market in pay. (In the case of start-ups, they often try to compensate for low base pay with stock option grants and other forms of deferred compensation.)

Internal Alignment   Another influence on pay levels across firms is "internal alignment." A firm has to align its pay rates not only with external market forces (external alignment), but also with regard to internal considerations of efficiency and fairness. Medium- and large-sized firms often have internal labor markets with relatively unskilled port of entry jobs at the bottom of the organization and jobs of increasing skill and responsibility connected to them in an ascending order along a "job ladder" (see Chapter 6). Pay rates need to be set for jobs along these ladders to provide sufficient incentive for employees to work hard and acquire the training needed to advance to higher-level positions. Seniority is also often a factor that determines movement up a job ladder, and employees typically feel as a matter of equity that workers with more years of seniority deserve higher pay. A common finding is that large-sized plants and firms pay higher wages than do smaller plants/firms.[22] One reason is that the former have more extensive internal labor markets and well-developed job ladders, causing them out of concern for internal alignment to pay higher average wages than other firms with a greater concentration of jobs at or near the port of entry level.

Union Avoidance   Pay levels also vary with the threat of unionization. When nonunion firms perceive they face a significant probability of being organized, they often choose a market-leader pay program to defuse the threat.[23]

Pay Form

The second aspect of compensation management examined in this section is the choice of pay form. By "pay form" we mean the alternative ways firms can pay people, such as a wage per hour, salary per year, piece rate, commission rate, profit-sharing bonus, or stock option. All these methods provide employees with money in exchange for their labor services, but they often differ greatly in their cost to the firm and motivational impact on workers.[24]

---

22   Charles Brown and James Medoff, "The Employer Size Wage Effect," *Journal of Political Economy* 97 (October 1989): 1027–59, and Walter Oi and Todd Idson, "Firm Size and Wages," in Orley Ashenfelter and David Card, eds., *Handbook of Labor Economics*, vol. 3B (New York: North-Holland: 1999): 2165–2214.

23   Daphne Gottlieb Taras, "Managerial Intentions and Wage Determination in the Canadian Petroleum Industry," *Industrial Relations* 36 (April 1997): 178–205.

24   See Beth Asch and John Warner, "Incentive Systems: Theory and Evidence," in Lewin, Mitchell, and Zaidi, eds., *The Human Resource Management Handbook*, vol. I, 175–216.

TABLE 10.1   ALTERNATIVE FORMS OF PAY

	Input-Based	Output-Based
Group-Based	**II** Annual company Christmas bonus	**IV** Gain-sharing Profit-sharing
Individual-Based	**I** Wage per hour Salary per year	**III** Piece-Rate Commission-Rate

Size Measure

Performance Measure

As illustrated in Table 10.1, pay form varies along two important dimensions. The first dimension is the *performance measure*. Two options exist: a measure based on employee *input* or a measure based on employee *output*. The typical input measure is amount of time worked (per hour, week, etc.); the output measure can take various forms, such as physical units of output or dollars of revenue or profit. The second dimension of pay form is the *size measure*. Two options exist here also: a measure based on individual performance (a size of 1) or group performance (a size of *N*).

The four cells of the table illustrate the possible permutations in pay form. Cell I is a pay form using an input performance measure and an individual size measure. Examples include a wage per hour or salary per year for individual workers. Cell II is an input performance measure and a group size measure. An example is a companywide bonus, say of $200 awarded each year to all employees at Christmas. Cell III is a form of pay based on an output performance measure and an individual size measure. Examples include a piece rate and commission (sales) rate. Cell IV is an output performance measure and a group size measure, such as a profit-sharing or gain-sharing pay plan. **Gain-sharing** is a compensation method that shares the gain from some agreed-upon performance improvement (e.g., reduction in per unit cost, increase in quality) with the workers.

The object of the firm is to choose the pay form (or mix of forms) that maximizes profit. In the theoretical world of perfect competition, the choice of pay form is simple. With perfect information and zero transaction cost, the firm can identify each worker's marginal product and write a complete contract that links the employee's pay directly to output produced per unit of time. We can speak of a "wage per hour" in the model of perfect competition, but in reality the worker's pay per hour is output-based—the greater the worker's marginal product per time period the greater the wage.

SEE

Empirical Evidence 10-3:
Executive Compensation:
Pay for Performance or
Skimming the Cream?,
p. 552.

In the presence of market imperfections and positive transaction cost, however, the firm's choice of pay form is more complicated. In this imperfect theoretical world, all pay forms have limitations and shortcomings, and the challenge facing the firm is to choose the one (or mix) that promotes maximum employee performance at least cost. One particularly complicated and controversial form of pay—executive compensation—is examined in more detail in Empirical Evidence 10-3 near the end of the chapter. Described below are some of the major considerations that influence this choice.[25]

Consider first the choice of an input or output performance measure. Ideally, the firm would prefer an output measure, as gaining additional output is the reason the firm hires the worker and is the true test of the worker's "worth" to the firm. But several problems can arise with an output performance measure that singly or collectively make it impractical to use. These include the following.

Measurement Difficulty For a variety of reasons a firm may not be able to identify a worker's individual contribution to production, making it difficult or impossible to base pay on output. One reason is that many production processes feature interdependencies and complementarities. An example is what economists call team forms of production, such as operation of a paper-making machine (typically requiring a seven-person crew) and flying a commercial jet (a pilot and copilot).[26] In all such production processes, one worker's output is dependent on everyone else's satisfactory performance; the individual's contribution is impossible to identify. A second reason is that many outputs are a service, such as teaching and legal counsel. Measurement of the intangibles in these processes is often difficult or impossible.

Unintended Consequences Even when output can be measured, it is often the case that not all dimensions of job performance can be included for reward. As an example, a firm may be able to count the number of windshields a worker installs on an assembly line, but it is much more difficult to monitor the quality of the installation. If output alone is rewarded, the firm will likely reap a gain in the number of windshields installed, but may then suffer the unintended consequence of a decline in quality. Another negative consequence of an output-based pay system is that workers sometimes decide to hold down production, fearing that if they go "all-out" their earnings will be so high that management will reduce the piece (or commission) rate. Likewise, workers put pressure on each other not to exceed a certain output level for fear that management will make the performance of the top person (the "rate-buster") the expected performance level for everybody. On the positive side, an indirect benefit of an output-based pay system is that it promises

---

25   See Asch and Warner, op. cit., and Edward Lazear, *Personnel Economics for Managers* (New York: Wiley, 1998).

26   The classic reference on team forms of production is Armen Alchian and Harold Demsetz, "Production, Information Costs, and Economic Organization," *American Economic Review* 72 (1972): 777–95. Measurement problems in compensation management are discussed in Patricia Zingheim and Jay Schuster, *Pay People Right: Breakthrough Reward Strategies to Create Great Companies* (San Franscisco: Jossey-Bass, 2000).

higher earnings to people of greater skill and motivation and, thus, the companies using these pay systems tend to attract better "quality" workers (sometimes called *positive sorting* or *self-selection*). Another benefit for firms—but quite possibly an unintended negative consequence for employees—from converting from an input (wage per hour) to an output-based pay system is that it provides a handy opportunity to increase overall performance expectations (the "effort bargain").[27]

Input-based reward systems also have serious limitations. The most important are the following.

Shirking The virtue of an input-based reward system, such as a wage per hour or salary per year, is that it is easy to measure and administer. But a major drawback is it encourages workers to **shirk**. Shirking means holding back on work effort, such as working at only half-speed or taking extra-long breaks when the boss is not looking. Shirking is a form of moral hazard and arises from the principal–agent problem.[28]

Increased Supervision Costs Not only does shirking lead to a productivity loss, it also gives rise to another form of cost—the cost of hiring additional people to act as monitors and contract enforcers. These people are called "foremen," "supervisors," and "team leaders." With a well-designed output-based pay system, this lower-level of the management hierarchy can be substantially reduced because the "pay for performance" nature of the reward system leads workers to self-monitor and self-police their level of work effort.

Next consider the second dimension in Table 10.1, the choice of an individual- or group-based form of compensation. Both forms of compensation have virtues and defects. Considered first is an individual-based system, then a group-based system.

Individual-Based Pay The virtue of an individual-based form of pay (e.g., a wage per hour or commission rate on individual sales) is that it tightly links the rewards an employee receives with the amount of work performed, creating the maximum motivation and work incentive. This virtue is sometimes said to arise from a "clear and short line of sight." The defect is that an individual-based pay method undercuts cooperation and teamwork. If the production process is characterized by a high degree of "divisibility" and "separability" (inputs and outputs can be broken down into small units and the contribution to production of one input is independent of that of the others), the firm gains little productivity advantage from emphasizing cooperation and teamwork. An individual-based pay form will do well in this situation. But where the production process contains significant indivisibilities and nonseparabilities, total output depends on a high level of cooperation and

27   David Marsden, "The Role of Performance-Related Pay in Renegotiating the "Effort Bargain": The Case of the British Public Service," *Industrial and Labor Relations Review* 57 (April 2004): 350–70.

28   See Haig Nalbantian, ed., *Incentive, Cooperation, and Risk Sharing* (Totowa, N.J.: Rowman and Littlefield, 1987).

teamwork among employees.[29] Here an individual-based pay system, by focusing employee attention only on self-interested, personal performance goals, will lead to significant inefficiency.[30]

Group-Based   The virtues and defects of a group-based pay system are the mirror opposite. A gain-sharing or profit-sharing system, for example, links self-interest to the performance of the work group and/or entire company. Obviously such a system does more to encourage teamwork and "good citizenship" behavior (e.g., going above and beyond the minimum requirements of the job) than does an individual-based method of pay. The defect of the group-based method of pay, however, is that it encourages individual workers to free-ride. When pay is evenly divided among members of a team or company, the link between individual performance and reward is weakened, leading self-interested workers to shirk or "free-ride" on the efforts of others. The incentive to free-ride becomes larger with the size of the group—a phenomenon called the **$1/N$ problem** (as the number of workers N gets larger, the observable impact of one person's free-riding gets smaller, leading to a greater incentive to shirk).[31] To encourage cooperation and teamwork, but limit the impact of the $1/N$ problem, firms often find that a more focused form of gain-sharing—such as a quarterly bonus to workers in a particular team or department for meeting a production or quality target—is more effective than a companywide program of profit-sharing.[32]

Issues in Employee Involvement and Participation

A third HRM function examined in this chapter is management-sponsored programs aimed at promoting greater **employee involvement and participation (EIP)** in the operation of the firm.

Few areas of HRM practice have grown more quickly in the last two decades than EIP programs. Under the influence of Frederick Taylor's theory and philosophy of *scientific management*, propounded in the early 1910s, most companies in earlier years believed a clear line should be established between the role and function of managers and workers. Taylor, an industrial engineer, sought to change the practice of management from an "art" into a science. He looked to the physical sciences for much of his inspiration, believing that the laws of science can

---

29   An example is piano moving—the piano cannot be divided into pieces, and the marginal product of one worker in moving the piano is dependent on the contribution of the other workers. Auto manufacturing using an assembly-line process is another example.

30   Gary Miller, *Managerial Dilemmas* (New York: Cambridge University Press, 1991).

31   Lazear, *Personnel Economics for Managers*, 317.

32   Jones, Kata, and Pliskin, "Profit-Sharing and Gain-Sharing."

be used to determine the "one best way" to organize production and manage employees.

One "law" that Taylor placed great stock in was the idea that efficiency is promoted by pursuing specialization and a greater division of labor. As Adam Smith had earlier explained in *The Wealth of Nations* in his famous example of pin manufacturing, the quantity of pins produced will be much greater when the manufacturing process is simplified by breaking production into numerous discrete tasks and then assigning a different person to specialize in the performance of each one. Taylor took this idea and applied it to the management of a business. He argued that the tasks of "managing" and "producing" should be clearly divided into separate jobs, and that the people most able and skilled at managing should be the "bosses" and those most able and skilled at production jobs, such as operating a machine or driving a truck, should be the "workers."

One consequence of Taylor's system was to transfer to industry the military model of top-down management—the CEO and top executives (the "generals") give the orders and the employees (the "soldiers") obey them. In this model, employee suggestions are viewed as "talking back" or bucking authority, and are not encouraged and often not welcomed. Knowing this, employees resign themselves to doing the job as ordered, even if they have ideas for how it might be done in a faster or more cost-effective way. In effect, although firms hire the whole person to report to work, they use only the person's labor and leave his or her heart and brain at the company door.

Viewed from today's perspective, Taylor's management model—while certainly based on some fundamentally correct insights—nonetheless is fatally flawed because it does not harness all the skills, ideas, and motivation of the employees to the task of production. Its ethos of authoritarianism in the workplace is also inconsistent with today's more democratic value system. Not surprisingly, some astute managers and academics recognized within a few years after Taylor that there were considerable gains to be had from fostering greater opportunities for employee involvement and participation.[33] This message was first propounded among academics by institutional labor economist John R. Commons in his book *Industrial Goodwill* (1919), which sought to convince employers that the worker was more than

SEE

Policy Application 10-1: The Employee Participation/ Representation Gap: How Large Is It and How Do We Solve It?, p. 542.

a machine and that they could gain competitive advantage by eliciting the worker's cooperation through fair treatment and providing opportunities for voice and involvement.[34]

Despite this message, for a half-century or more most firms were organized on the top-down model of management. Even today only a minority of firms provide extensive, formalized channels for voice and EIP. [See the Policy Application 10-1 regarding the gap between how much EIP workers want and how much they actually get from their employers.]

---

33 See Bruce E. Kaufman, "The Theory and Practice of Strategic HRM and Participative Management: Antecedents in Early Industrial Relations" *Human Resource Management Review* 11 (No. 4, 2001): 505–33.

34 John R. Commons, *Industrial Goodwill* (New York: McGraw-Hill, 1919).

Direct Forms of Employee Participation

Employee voice and involvement programs are of two basic types. The first is **direct participation.** With direct participation, the employee directly or "face-to-face" meets and confers with management. Forms of direct participation include the following.[35]

Open Door Policy   An employee is encouraged either individually or in a group to initiate a discussion with management by coming through the "open door" and saying what is on his or her mind. The issue may be related to a personal problem, a grievance, or a suggestion regarding the performance of work.

Production Team   In a number of companies the work process has been reorganized into production teams. These teams have been assigned responsibility for various tasks formerly done by foremen and supervisors, such as work scheduling, quality monitoring, and inventory resupply. This is a form of direct participation, since each employee in the work group is involved in the activity or the decision making. Typically the teams meet as a "group of the whole" when having discussions with management.

Feedback Session   Another way companies give employees voice is to hold periodic feedback sessions. As an example, on a once-a-month rotating basis the head of the human resources department holds a breakfast or lunch meeting with workers in a particular part of the plant or company and has a free-wheeling discussion concerning issues on the employees' minds. Sometimes these are brainstorming sessions with the management person soliciting employee ideas/opinions on a particular production issue or proposed change in company employment policy.

Quality Circle   With this concept, borrowed from Japan, a group of production employees in a particular department or work zone (e.g., dashboard assembly in an auto plant) meet "off line" (before or after work, or during some regularly scheduled break time) to confer among themselves or with a management representative about ways to improve product quality.

Town Hall Meeting   The employees of a company assemble in a meeting room or hall and the CEO or other top-level executive makes a presentation (e.g., last year's financial results and the outlook for the upcoming year) and fields employees' questions.

---

35   On direct and indirect participation, see John Cotton, *Employee Involvement* (Newbury: Sage, 1993). A number of companies use more than one of the EIP programs described in this section. Examples from American industry are provided in Bruce E. Kaufman, "Does the NLRA Constrain Employee Involvement and Participation Programs in Nonunion Companies? A Reassessment," *Yale Law and Policy Review* 17 (Spring 1999): 729–811.

Indirect Forms of Employee Participation

The second form of employee participation is **indirect participation.** In this type of participation the views and opinions of employees are presented to and discussed with management by a person or group selected or appointed to act as a representative for them. Forms of indirect participation include the following.

Ombud   An ombud is a person selected by the company to act as a neutral investigator and mediator of disputes. If an employee has a grievance or dispute with an manager, the ombud may represent the employee's position to a higher-level management person.

Safety Committee   Most manufacturing plants of medium to large size have some form of safety committee, usually composed of selected workers, supervisors, and an HR staff person. The workers on the safety committee represent the views and interests of the larger group employed in the plant.

Employee Council   Companies that want a more organized or formal method of learning the opinions and attitudes of employees form an employee council or forum. Council members are selected or elected by their peers, serve for a certain term of office, and meet and confer with management on a wide range of issues related to production, working conditions, community events, and so on.

Peer Review Panel   An increasingly popular method to resolve work-related disputes is a peer review panel. The panel has a small number of worker and management representatives, hears testimony from the parties to a dispute (e.g., a company's decision to terminate an employee for excessive absenteeism), and renders a recommendation or binding decision.

Employee Representatives on the Board of Directors   In some companies, employee representatives are appointed to sit in on board of directors meetings to provide the employees' perspective on major decisions facing the corporation. On occasion, labor unions have also demanded one or more seats on the board of directors for employee representatives as the quid pro quo for a wage concession or other "give back."

Labor Union   A labor union is also a form of indirect employee participation, although it is not typically chosen by companies as a part of their HRM program. The other forms of EIP listed above are typically established by the employer and, in the final analysis, are structured and run with the bottom-line interests of the firm in mind. Employees who feel that these programs do not give them enough say in workplace decisions may opt to form an independent labor union. A union gives workers both "muscle" and "voice" through collective bargaining, and greater protection from management retaliation for speaking up with unpopular opinions. Unions are sometimes a substitute for other forms of EIP (e.g., a plant-level employee council); in other cases they cooperate with management in setting-up EIP programs.[36] Some research suggests, in fact, that EIP programs are more effective and survive longer in unionized firms.[37]

The Benefits of EIP

As outlined in an earlier section of this chapter, employers demand EIP, like any other HRM practice, only to the extent that they perceive it contributes to greater profit. The extent and form of EIP activity across companies thus depend on the benefits and costs the employers expect from additional investments in it. Considered first are some of the most important benefits to companies.

Improved Two-Way Communication In large companies with thousands of employees scattered across numerous plants and facilities, it can be a daunting challenge to get timely and accurate information passed up and down the chain of command between the CEO at one end and the employees on the shop floor at the other. The severity of this problem can be reduced by an EIP council or forum, such as an employee committee that reports to the board of directors or to a divisional vice-president. This kind of committee allows "skip-level" reporting, so information and communication between the bottom and top of the company can bypass numerous levels of the bureaucracy and thus flow more quickly and with less filtering.[38]

Better Coordination/Control of Production The production of many goods and services, such as airline travel or the manufacture of semiconductor chips, requires a complex group of distinct tasks or processes to be performed on time and meshed together in exactly the right way. Because these processes and tasks are nonseparable (interdependent), if one fails to be performed well, all the others are negatively affected. Companies have found that these interdependencies are often more effectively controlled and coordinated by having EIP teams and committees monitor and respond to variances in performance instead of relying on supervisors and foremen.[39]

---

36 See Saul Rubinstein and Thomas Kochan, *Learning from Saturn* (Ithaca: Cornell University Press).

37 Adrienne Eaton, Paula Voos, and Dong-one Kim, "Voluntary and Involuntary Aspects of Employee Participation and Decision Making," in Lewin, Mitchell, and Zaidi, eds., *The Handbook of Human Resource Management*, 63–86, and David Weil, "Are Mandated Health and Safety Committees Substitutes or Complements to Labor Unions?" *Industrial and Labor Relations Review* 52 (April 1999): 339–60.

38 Patrick Boulton and Mathias Dewatripont, "The Firm as a Communication Network," *Quarterly Journal of Economics* 109 (no. 4, 1994): 809–39.

39 Roy Radner, "The Economics of Managing," *Journal of Economic Literature* 30 (September 1992): 1382–1415, and Eric Trist, *The Evolution of Socio-Technical Systems*, Occasional Paper No. 2 (Toronto: Ontario Quality of Working Life Center, 1981).

Higher Quality and Productivity Employee involvement is a central part of the *total quality management* (TQM) philosophy and *high-performance work system* (HPWS).[40] In a traditional production process, management delegates responsibility for quality to foremen, supervisors, and quality inspectors; in a TQM/HPWS enterprise, workers are formed into teams and committees and given responsibility for managing quality. While the traditional system uses tight supervision and threats of termination to motivate employees to produce quality products, a TQM/HPWS model relies on the positive power of peer monitoring and gain-sharing forms of compensation that tie employee pay to quality and productivity performance goals.

Higher Employee Morale, Commitment, and Job Satisfaction Employees report higher levels of morale, organizational commitment, and job satisfaction in companies that utilize EIP. Most workers like to be given more decision-making opportunity, greater access to information, and expanded opportunities for voice. When employees feel better about their jobs, companies gain a variety of benefits too, such as greater employee work effort, reduced absenteeism, improved customer service, and better "organizational citizenship" behavior.[41]

Better Management Employee involvement also leads to better, more professional management. In traditionally organized companies, foremen and supervisors often have considerable autonomy to manage operations and people as they please. Their actions and behaviors are also often hidden to some degree from the view of top management, given the numerous layers in the corporate hierarchy. EIP provides incentives and pressures for lower- and middle-level management to improve their job performance and to manage people in a more sensitive and equitable way, since employees have a formal channel for voice and are more likely to voice dissatisfaction as a group than they are as individuals.[42]

Reduced Employee Demand for Union Representation Research shows that employees who work in companies with a well-functioning EIP program express a reduced desire for union representation. Unions and nonunion EIP programs are alternative mechanisms for employee voice—if the latter works effectively employees are less motivated to seek the former. Since most companies prefer to

---

40 Warren Schmidt and Jerome Finnigan, *The Race without a Finish Line: America's Quest for Total Quality* (San Francisco, 1992), and David Nadler and Marc Gerstein, "Designing High-Performance Work Systems: Organizing People, Work, Technology, and Information," in David Nadler, Marc Gerstein, and Robert Shaw, eds., *Organizational Architecture* (San Francisco: Jossey-Bass, 1992), 110–31.

41 Peter Cappelli and Nikolai Rogovsky, "Employee Involvement and Organizational Citizenship: Implications for Labor Law and 'Lean Production,'" *Industrial and Labor Relations Review* 51 (July 1998): 633–53; and Bruce E. Kaufman, "High-level Employee Involvement at Delta Airlines," *Human Resource Management* 42 (Summer 2003): 175–90.

42 Daphne Taras, "Contemporary Experience with the Rockefeller Plan: Imperial Oil's Joint Industrial Council," in Kaufman and Taras, eds., *Nonunion Employee Representation*, 231–58.

operate without a union and a collective bargaining contract, they view this result of EIP as another benefit.[43]

The Costs of EIP

Looking at only the benefits, it would appear that all firms should invest in EIP programs. While many large firms have one or more forms of direct and/or indirect participation, surveys reveal that relatively comprehensive, in-depth EIP programs are found only among a minority of companies, and that numerous small- to medium-size companies have no formal EIP program.[44] Why is this? One part of the answer is that EIP programs also entail costs—sometimes significant costs. (Another part of the answer involves forms of market failure, which are discussed in the Policy Application section.) Thus, although an EIP program may bring benefits to a company, management may nonetheless conclude that the marginal cost of EIP is greater than the marginal gain and not adopt it. Here are some of the major forms of cost with EIP:

Forgone Production An EIP program diverts hundreds and often thousands of hours of employees' time into additional discussions, meetings, training sessions, and administrative matters, hours that could instead have been directly utilized for production. Some companies will conclude they get more value from the latter and thus forgo EIP.

Diversion of Management Time An EIP program also diverts managers' time from other duties and activities, and may require hiring additional management staff to coordinate and administer the program.[45] Particularly at the top executive level of companies, managers face many competing demands for their time and have numerous pressing issues that effect the growth and survival of the company. Taking time to meet with employees and discuss employees' concerns and issues may not yield as much value to the company as using that time in other areas, such as marketing, product development, or strategy formulation.

Slower, Less Flexible Decision Making In some cases EIP speeds decision making and improves operational flexibility; in others, however, EIP does just the opposite. Without EIP, management can unilaterally make a decision and implement it; with EIP management often must consult first with employees and obtain their sign-off.[46]

---

43   Daphne Taras, "Nonunion Representation: Complement or Threat to Trade Unions?" *Proceedings of the Fiftieth Annual Winter Meeting* (Madison, Wis.: Industrial Relations Research Association, 1998): 281–90.

44   Richard Freeman and Joel Rogers, *What Workers Want* (Ithaca: Cornell University Press, 1999), and Paul Osterman, "Work Reorganization in an Era of Restructuring: Trends in Diffusion and Effects on Employee Welfare," *Industrial and Labor Relations Review* 53 (January 2000): 179–96.

45   David Boone, "Operation of the Production District Joint Industrial Council, Imperial Oil," in Kaufman and Taras, eds., *Nonunion Employee Representation*, 457–62.

46   Rubinstein and Kochan, *Learning from Saturn*, and Joel Rogers and Wolfgang Streeck, eds., *Works Councils: Consultation, Representation, and Cooperation in Industrial Relations* (Chicago: University of Chicago Press, 1995).

Also, the decision that management wants may not be the one employees want, so with EIP a process of discussion and compromise has to take place. Management can find these constraints burdensome and costly for the firm, leading them to avoid EIP.

Higher Labor Cost Although workers in EIP programs do not formally negotiate or bargain with employers, the presence of an EIP program can lead the firm to pay higher wages and more generous benefits than it otherwise would.[47] One reason is the desire of firms to take distributive ("we versus them") issues, such as wages and salaries, "off the table" so the EIP meetings can focus on those things that directly promote firm performance (e.g., quality, customer service). Another factor is that EIP programs work best when both the management and the employee sides perceive that they lead to win-win or "mutual gain" outcomes. Thus, before employees will actively commit their heads and hearts to an EIP program, they must have confidence about job security and sharing in a portion of the gains in higher productivity, quality, and profits. But the costs associated with promises of job security and higher future wages and benefits may from management's perspective more than outweigh the prospective gains from EIP.

Loss of Management Power and Control Another cost of EIP to management is that it transfers power and control to employees. Empowering employees may increase organizational performance, but may also harm it if employees pursue goals that promote their interests over the interests of the firm and its shareholders.[48] Quite apart from issues of firm performance and profits, most people prefer more power and control to less, and managers are no different. Supervisors and foremen in particular often actively resist the introduction of an EIP program, and sometimes covertly work to subvert it, because the program directly threatens their power and authority over the people they direct.

Higher Probability of Unionization Although many companies adopt EIP programs to reduce the likelihood that their employees will want independent union representation, the actual impact may be just the opposite. When companies introduce an EIP program, they raise employee expectations about the amount of voice and involvement workers will have in the firm's operations. The employees also get greater experience working together as a group and thinking collectively. As long as the EIP program lives up to employee expectations, they infrequently desire union representation. But if the EIP program turns out to be largely window-dressing, or if the firm later backtracks on its commitment of job security or makes unilateral decisions without first consulting employees, the atmosphere of trust, cooperation, and mutual gain so critical to a successful EIP program quickly

47 Taras, "Contemporary Experience with the Rockefeller Plan," and John Addison Claus Schnabel and Joachim Wagner, "Nonunion Representation in Germany," in Kaufman and Taras, eds., *Nonunion Employee Representation*, 365–85.

48 Richard Freeman and Edward Lazear, "An Economic Analysis of Works Councils," in Rogers and Streeck, eds., *Works Councils*, 27–52.

evaporates. Feeling disillusioned and dissatisfied, employees may then be ripe for unionization.[49]

The Equilibrium Level of EIP

The breadth and depth of company-initiated EIP programs in industry reflect a comparison of marginal benefit and cost, as seen by corporate managers. Some managers will decide that the benefits are greater than the costs and adopt an EIP program. Of those that do, most will opt for a relatively small-scale program, featuring perhaps a safety committee, production teams in certain areas of plant operations, or a gain-sharing committee. Some will go much further, believing that the profit payoff justifies more formalized and widespread forums, councils, and teams. Many other companies, however, will look at EIP activities and conclude they do not contribute to profit, and thus will decide not to adopt them. Some of their employees will feel dissatisfied by lack of voice and involvement, but they have options. They can quit and seek employment at another company that does offer EIP or they can work with other employees to organize an independent union. Whether these mechanisms provide sufficient opportunity for employees to gain more voice is an interesting and hotly debated topic—a topic discussed further in Policy Application 10-1.

---

49 Reg Baskin, "My Experience with Unionization of Nonunion Employee Representation Plans in Canada," in Kaufman and Taras, *Nonunion Employee Representation*, 487–97.

POLICY APPLICATION 10-1

The Employee Participation/ Representation Gap: How Large Is It and How Do We Solve It?

In 1993 President Clinton appointed a ten-person commission, called the Commission of the Future of Worker–Management Relations (or Dunlop Commission, in honor of its chair, John Dunlop of Harvard University), to conduct a thorough review of the nation's labor law and provide recommendations for legislative action where needed. One of the areas the commission devoted considerable attention to was employee involvement and participation (EIP). In particular, the commission wanted to know whether American companies offer enough opportunities for EIP and, if not, how the shortfall could best be remedied.

To obtain information on the first question, the commission asked professors Richard Freeman and Joel Rogers to conduct a nationwide survey of workers and managers on the extent of EIP at their companies and their satisfaction with the programs. Freeman and Rogers (F&R in the following discussion) questioned several thousand people, assembled the data, and published the results in a book called *What Workers Want*.[1] Here, briefly, is what they found.

The central conclusion F&R reach is that employees want much more EIP than companies are providing. They say, for example, that their survey (p. 40) "shows as conclusively as any survey can that the vast majority of employees want more involvement and greater say in company decisions affecting their workplace." They call this shortfall of EIP the **participation/representation gap** (or P/R gap). One way they measure the size of the P/R gap is to compare the difference between two numbers in the survey: the first number is "the percentage of workers for whom it is very important to have a lot of influence" and the second number is "the percentage of workers who said they had a lot of direct influence and involvement." The average value for the first number ("wanting influence") is 55 percent, the average value for the second ("having influence") is 28 percent. Based on this calculation, F&R conclude that American workers want twice as much EIP as they actually have. (An alternative set of questions yields an even larger gap.)

Subsequent review of their survey and calculations reveals that they may have overstated the actual size of the P/R gap.[2] One reason is that they underestimate the actual amount of P/R that employees have in the workplace. (For example, the second survey question cited earlier asks workers if they had "a lot of *direct* influence," which tends to exclude all those workers who have *indirect* forms of EIP influence, thus leading to a larger measured P/R gap.) A second reason is that they overestimate employees' desired amount of P/R (for reasons discussed in the next section), which also leads to a larger measured P/R gap. But, these caveats aside,

most observers accept F&R's broad finding that a P/R gap exists, even if disagreement continues over its size and seriousness. The reason is that economic theory provides good grounds to believe that firms in a free market, competitive system will undersupply the socially optimal amount of EIP.

The Optimal Level of Participation and Representation

The socially optimal amount of P/R can be evaluated with respect to two criteria. The first is economic efficiency—using the nation's scarce factor inputs of labor, capital, and natural resources to produce the maximum amount of goods and services, given the state of technology and structure of consumer preferences and relative prices. When maximum efficiency is achieved, no reallocation of inputs can lead to an increase in one good without causing a decrease in another. The second criterion is ethical/moral beliefs about noneconomic goals, such as workplace democracy and social justice. We look first at the goal of economic efficiency.

Microeconomic theory shows that economic efficiency is promoted when firms use additional units of factor inputs as long as the marginal social benefit from the resulting production is greater than the marginal social cost of the input. When the two become equal, efficiency is maximized and usage of the input is optimal. As emphasized throughout this chapter, programs that provide employee participation and representation (or EIP) can be considered a factor input into production and thus the optimal amount of P/R can be calculated (in theory) by using the decision rule just described.

---

1   Freeman and Rogers, *What Workers Want* (Ithaca: Cornell University Press, 1999).

2   Bruce E. Kaufman, "The Employee Participation and Representation Gap: An Assessment and Proposed Solution," *University of Pennsylvania Journal of Labor and Employment Law* 3 (Spring 2001): 491–550.

Economic theory also shows that if product and labor markets are perfectly competitive then firms will be led by the price system to devote an optimal amount of resources—as measured by the goal of economic efficiency—to the supply (or "production") of P/R programs for employees. Just as firms are led by the invisible hand of competition to employ the optimal amount of capital and labor in production and provide employees with the optimal amount of work hours and safety protection, so too are firms led by competition to use the marginal decision rules described above to determine the profit-maximizing level of P/R. Furthermore, if all the conditions of perfect competition are met, the profit-maximizing level of P/R is exactly the amount that maximizes efficiency.

Freeman and Rogers report that employees in the United States desire much greater influence and say in the workplace than they have. Is this large P/R gap evidence that American labor markets significantly underproduce the efficient level of employee participation and representation? The answer is no, at least based on the evidence they provide. In addition to the measurement problems cited above, the second reason for taking their survey results with some caution is that the P/R gaps they report significantly overstate employees' "real" or "effective" demand for P/R.[3]

Why? Suppose a researcher calls several thousand people on the telephone and asks two questions: first, each person's desired number of annual vacation days in Europe and, second, the actual number of days the person had this year. What would the survey reveal? No doubt the answers would reveal the existence of a large "vacation gap," in that the desired amount of vacation time is far greater than the actual. Can we, however, take this evidence as a sign that the free market system is underproducing the socially optimal amount of vacation travel?

Clearly the answer is no, because it is a basic axiom of economics that people always desire more of all scarce goods than the nation can produce with the current state of technology and fixed supply of factor inputs. The problem with questions such as these is that they specify incorrectly the demand function for the good or service—they ask people their desired demand for something based only on their tastes (preferences) but omit consideration of *price*. If the price of vacation trips to Europe is presented to them, then it may well be that the measured vacation gap disappears. Indeed, this is the very result that is predicted to occur in a perfectly competitive market system—based on preferences, prices, etc., the market system will produce exactly the right amount of all goods and services, leading to a zero gap in terms of effective demand and supply.

So where does this leave us? F&R report that American employees want twice as much P/R as they have at work, but given the ambiguities in their survey methods how can we as citizens or policymakers determine whether the actual amount produced falls short of the economically efficient level? One way to approach this issue is to return to economic theory and see if it can help point us in the right direction.

Causes of Suboptimal P/R

Economic theory claims that if an economy meets all the conditions of a perfectly competitive market system then the price system will produce the efficient level of all economic goods, including employee P/R. But, obviously, the real economy does not fully match the assumptions of the competitive model—information is not perfect, mobility is not costless, etc. We may conjecture, therefore, that the greater are the market imperfections and failures in the real economy the more the actual supply of employee EIP will diverge from the optimal level. Further, as indicated below, consideration of various forms of market failure strongly suggests that the net effect is to lead to an *under*supply of participation and representation.

---

3   Ibid.

Here are some of the forms of market failure that may cause firms to underproduce the efficient amount of employee P/R.

Noncooperative Behavior The productivity and quality gains from P/R require cooperative behavior on the part of both firms and workers—firms have to invest in establishing trust with workers through job security and above-market wages, while employees have to work more diligently and provide better customer service in the expectation that firms will reciprocate and share part of the profits. But one or both sides, fearing that the other will behave opportunistically, may refuse to do their part to make P/R successful. For example, the firm may fear that once it provides job security and higher wages the employees will soon develop a feeling of "entitlement" and let their work effort and level of customer service drop back to a lower level, saddling the firm with higher costs but no productivity gain. The firm will thus rationally decide not to invest in P/R, even though the marginal gain to the firm and society would outweigh the marginal costs if both sides could be counted on to cooperate.

Bargaining Opportunism A related problem arises when management fears that even though employee P/R may increase productivity and profit, it will also increase the bargaining power of workers, who may use it opportunistically to capture most of the additional surplus. In effect, P/R creates a larger profit "pie" but employees use their newfound collective strength to take a larger "slice." This concern may cause a firm to forgo adoption of employee P/R.

Adverse Selection Firms that adopt employee P/R typically modify or attenuate the traditional "hire and fire" employment-at-will policies used at other firms. Because of the promise of fair dealing and increased job security, these firms will attract many job applicants. The problem for the P/R firms is that a disproportionate share of job applicants may be "lemon" employees who have a higher risk of dismissal for poor job performance—a process known as **adverse selection.** Given that a P/R employment policy leads to a lower-quality, poorer-performing pool of job applicants, firms may decide the benefits of P/R do not outweigh the costs.

Management Power and Control The principal–agent problem gives managers some slack to pursue self-interested goals. Although employee P/R may increase profit for shareholders, it may subtract from a "good" in the utility function of managers—power and control over subordinates—and hence they may choose not to implement it.

Unemployment and Macroeconomic Instability The presence of involuntary unemployment in labor markets and cyclical instability in the macroeconomy can also reduce the incentives for firms to adopt employee P/R. Involuntary unemployment, for example, provides firms with an alternative, often cheaper method to motivate the workforce—fear of dismissal. Likewise, extensive layoffs that go with frequent recessions and industry downturns reduce the incentives of firms to invest in the costly training necessary for successful employee P/R and, in addition, corrode the spirit of cooperation and trust between firms and workers.

All of these market imperfections cause firms to underinvest in the economically efficient level of employee participation and representation. Although the argument is not airtight, theory certainly suggests that Freeman and Rogers are right—the American economy produces a shortfall or gap in the optimal amount of P/R. If noneconomic goals of workplace democracy and social justice are brought into the analysis, this conclusion is only strengthened. The goal of firms is to maximize profit, and they will provide only the amount of workplace democracy and equitable treatment of employees that promotes this goal (abstracting from legal requirements). Although no definitive statement can be made, it is probable that the citizenry of most countries desire more of these "goods" in the workplace than most firms voluntarily provide. To the degree that employee P/R is a vehicle for delivering greater workplace democracy and fair treatment, we again conclude that a free market system will undersupply the socially optimal level of P/R.

Solving the P/R Gap

The survey evidence presented by Freeman and Rogers, along with the results of other research and testimony, convinced the members of the Dunlop Commission that the nation does face a significant shortfall in the socially optimal amount of EIP in the workplace.[4] The next issue is how to solve this problem. Three options are identifiable.

Greater Unionization The option that gained the most support by the commission is a change in labor law to promote greater unionization and collective bargaining in the American economy. The Freeman and Rogers survey found that one-third of American workers desire to be represented by a union at their workplace, yet in the private (non-government) sector of the economy less than one in ten workers actually have collective bargaining. The commission further concluded that the major reason so many workers who want union representation do not have it is that employers in various ways discourage or obstruct workers from successfully organizing. Methods include termination of union supporters, discrimination against union activists (e.g., assigning union activists to undesirable jobs), propaganda campaigns orchestrated by high-paid attorneys and consultants, and "stall" tactics (e.g., numerous legal appeals, extended litigation in the courts) to wear down union support.[5] To close the P/R gap, the commission thus recommended measures to strengthen the legal protection of the right to organize and speed up the union election process. So far, however, these proposals have not garnered enough political support to result in new legislation.

Works Councils A second option considered by the commission was a change in labor law to encourage or require firms to establish a plant- or company-level **works council.** The works council idea comes from Europe, where most countries mandate or highly encourage these organizations. A works council is an elected body of worker representatives in individual plants/companies that management is legally required to meet with to discuss and exchange information on workplace developments and issues that affect employees. Works councils are not unions, since they do not engage in bargaining or strikes, nor are they American-style EIP committees, which have no independent existence or rights other than those that companies choose to give them. Rather, they occupy a middle ground—works councils are independent of the employer and the employer has an obligation to seek the works council's concurrence on changes in personnel and employment policy, but the works council's power is limited to discussion and conference.[6] When disputes can not be resolved, they are typically adjudicated in a labor court.

The commission decided not to recommend the works council option for legislative action since it lacks political support from either employers or organized labor.[7] Most American companies oppose works councils, seeing them as overly bureaucratic and time-consuming, oriented more

4 Commission on the Future of Worker–Management Relations, *Fact-Finding Report* (1994) and *Final Report* (1994).

5 P. Wright and G. McMahan, "Theoretical Perspectives for Strategic Human Resource Management," *Journal of Management* 18 (no. 2, 1992): 295–320. Also see Richard Hurd and Joseph Uehlein, "Patterned Responses to Organizing: Case Studies of the Union-Busting Convention," in Sheldon Friedman, Richard Hurd, Rudolph Oswald, and Ronald Seeber, eds., *Restoring the Promise of American Labor Law* (Ithaca: ILR Press, 1994), 61–74, and Kate Bronfenbrenner, "Employer Behavior in Certification Elections and First-Contract Campaigns: Implications for Labor Law Reform," in Friedman et al., *Restoring the Promise*, 75–89.

6 Rogers and Streeck, *Works Councils*.

7 Thomas Kochan, "Using the Dunlop Report to Achieve Mutual Gains," *Industrial Relations* 34 (July 1995): 350–66.

toward implicit bargaining than productivity improvement, and too often a conduit for unionization. Paradoxically, most American labor unions also oppose the introduction of works councils, believing the councils unduly overlap with the purpose and function of collective bargaining. In Europe, unions tend to bargain industry- and region- wide contracts and do not have well-developed plant-level "locals." In the United States, on the other hand, union locals are well organized and often powerful, and thus are more likely to be in direct competition with a works council. Lacking a strong political constituency in this country, the works council option thus seems an unlikely means to close the employee P/R gap.

Encouragement of Nonunion Forms of P/R

The third option considered by the Dunlop Commission to close the employee P/R gap is liberalization of the labor law to give nonunion employers greater latitude to organize EIP forums and councils. Under provisions of the **National Labor Relations Act (NLRA)** enacted in 1935, nonunion employers are prohibited from organizing or supporting any kind of organization, committee, or plan that represents employees for the purpose of dealing with management over terms and conditions of employment (e.g., wages, hours, grievances, working conditions). The origin of this prohibition is the 1920s and early 1930s, when a number of nonunion American companies established *employee representation plans* (ERPs).[8] The plans allowed workers to elect employee representatives who met periodically with management to discuss workplace issues. Proponents considered the ERPs constructive vehicles for promoting greater cooperation, communication, and employee involvement; opponents charged that their main purpose was to help companies avoid unions. In the Great Depression the negative view won out, and provisions were inserted in the NLRA banning what the opponents derisively call *company unions.*

Employers testified before the Dunlop Commission that the company union restriction in the NLRA seriously obstructs their ability to offer more EIP in the workplace and, thus, to close the P/R gap. Nonunion companies can lawfully operate direct forms of EIP (e.g., self-managed teams) and indirect forms of EIP, such as committees, councils, and forums, but only as long as these bodies focus on production and quality issues and avoid dealing with wages, hours, and other such employment matters. But, say the employers, this restriction is burdensome and counterproductive because it means they cannot discuss issues employees want to discuss (e.g., a change in work schedules) or new initiatives that promote higher productivity (e.g., implementation of a skills-based compensation program).[9] American unions, however, strongly oppose liberalization of the NLRA's ban on ERPs, arguing that the purpose of these nonunion committees and councils remains largely one of union avoidance. The Dunlop Commission largely supported the union position. Several years later, Republicans passed legislation in both houses of Congress (called the *TEAM Act*) that opened the door for nonunion companies to operate ERPs, but President Clinton vetoed it.

The net result is that none of these three options to close the employee P/R gap have been implemented. Political stalemate continues to block progress on solving this problem, causing a shortfall in EIP for both employers and employees.

---

8   See Bruce E. Kaufman, "Accomplishments and Shortcomings of Nonunion Employee Representation in the Pre-Wagner Act Years," in Kaufman and Taras, eds., *Nonunion Employee Representation,* 21–60.

9   Kaufman, "Does the NLRA Constrain Employee Involvement and Participation Programs in Nonunion Companies?"

The Configuration of Alternative Employment and HRM Systems

A central idea in management thought is the concept of **contingency.** Contingency means there is no "one size fits all" approach to designing organizations and HRM systems. Stated another way, contingency means it is impossible to identify a set of "best practice" HRM policies that apply to all firms. The reason is that HRM practices are only effective when they fit each firm's particular business strategy, economic environment, technology of production, corporate culture, and other such variables. The "best practice" HRM system at Microsoft may be a disaster at General Motors.

The implication of contingency is that before designing and installing an HRM system in a new business, or revamping one in an existing business, top management must first identify the crucial features of the organization that determine the type(s) of HRM practices that are most appropriate for it. Whereas clear in theory, identifying the strategic contingencies in most organizations is difficult given their complex nature, large size, and continual change. Likewise, there is no one template for organizational design or people management, evidenced by the hundreds of books written by business executives and consultants each year touting their approach to running a business.

To shed light on this matter, three Stanford University professors—James Barton, Diane Burton, and Michael Hannan (BBH in the following discussion)—examined one hundred new business start-ups in Silicon Valley to see if there were any common patterns in what they call the organizational "employment system" or "employment model" adopted by the founding CEOs and whether, given the employment model, the founders utilized a particular set of HRM practices or an "HRM system" to go along with it.[1] Here is what they found.

Each business founder was asked if he or she had an "organizational model or blueprint" in mind when setting up the company. This is what BBH mean by an *employment model* or *system*. Two-thirds said yes. Analyzing these "yes" answers, BBH determined that the employment systems these founders described varied along three important dimensions:

- the primary basis of organizational attachment for employees,
- the primary means for controlling and coordinating the work, and
- the primary criterion to be emphasized in selecting employees.

Basis of Attachment   The first dimension on which the founders' models differed was "basis of attachment" of employees to the organization. Here there were also three distinct patterns: what BBH called *love, work,* and *money.* Some founders sought to attach employees to the organization by engendering intense emotional feelings of support and belongingness, or what they labeled "love." Others sought to attach employees by providing work opportunities that were exciting, cutting-edge, and challenging—an option they labeled "work." The third basis of attachment was "money"—or what one founder succinctly stated as the "you work, you get paid" model.

Basis of Control and Coordination   The second dimension contained in the founders' organizational blueprint was the means for controlling and coordinating work. Here, too, three distinct models appeared. The first model BBH call *peer* or *cultural control.* The idea here is to inculcate in employees

---

1   James Barton, M. Diane Burton, and Micahel Hannan, "The Road Taken: Origins and Evolution of Employment Systems in Emerging Companies," in Glenn Carroll and David Teece, eds., *Firms, Markets, and Hierarchies* (New York: Oxford University Press, 1999), 429–64.

through socialization, organizational culture, and peer pressure a dedication to hard work and willingness to collaborate for organizational goals. Other founders said they chose to rely on a second model of control and coordination, which BBH call *professional control*. Rather than rely on socialization, these founders sought to appeal to the professional goals and values of employees to attain cooperation and teamwork. For example, giving engineers exciting opportunities to practice their craft and then "getting out of the way" was part of this model. The third model was what they called *formal procedures and systems*. While these founders wanted to avoid hierarchy and bureaucracy, they nevertheless thought well-defined rules and procedures helped provide structure and guidance for "who does what, and when."

Basis of Selection   The third dimension in the founders' employment systems blueprint involved the criterion for selecting employees. Again three distinct models emerged. The first was a *skills and experience* (or *task*) model, with an emphasis on recruiting employees who had the skills and experience coming in the door to effectively accomplish concrete tasks and jobs. A second model identified by BBH is labeled *long-term potential*—the essence of which is captured by the statement of one founder that "if given a choice between an experienced employee and a smart one I'll always take the smart one." Finally, a third model is *values* or *cultural fit*. This model also has more of a long-term orientation, but puts heavier emphasis on recruiting employees who fit into the culture of the organization.

Relationship between Dimensions

The next interesting question is whether these three dimensions of the founders' organizational blueprints go together in any discernible pattern. That is, are there perceived synergies among different ways of attaching, controlling, and selecting employees? If the answer is yes, then achieving fit means that firms have to adopt the right package of employment design principles, rather than "mixing and matching" employment practices in some unsystematic way.

Given the three dimensions of attachment, control, and selection, and that each of these had three submodels to choose from, there are a total of 27 possible organizational combinations. Interestingly, the actual choices made by the CEOs clustered into only a few distinct bundles of organizational design characteristics or "employment systems." This fact suggests there are indeed strong complementarities and synergies in the choice of organizational design and employment practices.

Based on a clustering of the data, BBH identified four distinct employment systems. These four models are depicted in Table 10.2. They are:

Star   The first employment model is labeled "Star" by BBH. In this model the founder endeavors to attain competitive advantage by developing and retaining the best and brightest employees. Thus, employees are selected for *long-term potential*, the attachment to the organization is *challenging work*, and the control method is the *professional* model.

Engineering   The second employment system is labeled the "Engineering" model. It also utilizes *challenging work*, but instead seeks to control the work through *peer* or *cultural control* and selects employees on the basis of *skills and experience (task)*. Software development firms are often in this category.

Commitment   The third distinct employment system is called the "Commitment" model. It endeavors to gain competitive advantage by winning the "hearts and minds" of the employees. Thus, the basis of attachment is *love*, the basis of selection is *values* or *cultural fit*, and the method of control is *peer* or *cultural*.

Factory   The fourth model of employment systems—the "Factory" model—is the most traditional. It is predicated largely on monetary motivation as the basis of attachment, selects

TABLE 10.2   ALTERNATIVE EMPLOYMENT SYSTEMS

Three Dimensions of an Employment System

Three Sub-Dimensions	Attachment	Control	Selection
	Love	Peer	Task
	Work	Professional	Potential
	Money	Formal	Values

Four Alternative Employment Systems

Models				
Star	Work	Professional	Potential
Engineering	Work	Peer	Task
Commitment	Love	Peer	Values
Factory	Money	Formal	Task

SOURCE: James Barton, M. Diane Burton, and Michael Hannan, "The Road Taken: Origins of Employment Systems in Emerging Companies," in Glen Carroll and David Teece, eds., *Firms, Markets, and Hierarchies* (New York: Oxford University Press, 1999), 428–64.

employees on the basis of their ability to perform concrete tasks and jobs, and uses formal procedures and systems to control and coordinate work.

Patterns in HRM Practices

Given that founders and CEOs tended to gravitate toward one of four alternative employment systems, the next issue of interest is whether they also choose distinct patterns of HRM practices (or an HRM system) to fit with the employment model. The answer, BBH found, is a clear yes.

They found, for example, that within two years of its founding an organization using the Star model was far more likely to adopt stock options as part of the compensation program. Firms using a Commitment model, on the other hand, were much more likely to do thorough background and reference checks on new hires, do in-depth employee orientation sessions, and sponsor social events for employees. Engineering firms gave considerable emphasis to nonmonetary rewards programs, such as access to coveted skill-development opportunities. Firms using the Factory model, on the other hand, were much less likely to have adopted a mission statement within the first two years, to sponsor companywide meetings, or to do employee orientation sessions.

Implications

Three lessons emerge from this study. The first is that there are distinctly different models of organization and management that firms have the option of adopting. This study found four basic configurations—Star, Engineering, Commitment, and Factory—each entailing very different assumptions about how to maximize the contribution of employees and best control and coordinate the work process.

The second implication is that there are definite synergies among organizational design and HRM practices. For example, if a company chooses to pursue competitive advantage by adopting a Factory employment model, then to be successful this model has to be matched with the right set of HRM practices. The same applies to the other three models, each requiring a different set of HRM practices. This means that company founders and CEOs have to think in terms of systems and take contingency into account.

The third lesson from BBH's study is that once a particular employment model is adopted and is in place for a few years, it then becomes much harder to switch to a different one. To a significant degree, the die is cast when the founder of a start-up opts for one employment system versus another. Although employment systems can be altered—and often are in today's fast-changing economy—substantial change becomes more difficult as organizations age.

EMPIRICAL EVIDENCE 10-2

The Link between HRM Practices and Firm Performance

The theory of strategic HRM predicts that firms gain higher performance when they (1) use HRM practices that align with their business strategy and (2) adopt the package of HRM practices with the greatest amount of synergy among the constituent parts. Since the early 1990s, numerous empirical studies have been conducted to test the validity of these propositions. What is the verdict?

So far the evidence is mixed on both counts. A number of studies find evidence consistent with both hypotheses. One influential early study looked at the relationship between the extent of "advanced HRM practices" (AHRMP, such as discussed at the beginning of this chapter) at 855 firms and their performance, as measured by such things as productivity, employee turnover, and market value of the firm.[1] After holding constant a number of other factors (e.g., industry, degree of unionization, sales growth), the researcher found that a one standard deviation increase in AHRMP was associated with a 7 percent decrease in turnover, a $27,044 increase

in sales per employee, and a $3,814 increase in market value per employee.

Other studies arrive at broadly similar conclusions. For example, one researcher who examined 62 auto assembly plants located across the world found two different types of employment systems most prevalent—what he called the "mass production" and "flexible production" systems.[2] The former used traditional "command and control" HRM practices; the latter used more participative, team-oriented HRM practices. Both productivity and quality were higher in the assembly plants using the flexible production HRM system. This study also found that the positive impact of advanced HRM practices on productivity and quality was greater when they were used as a package rather than piecemeal.

1   Mark Huselid, "The Impact of Human Resource Management Practices on Turnover, Productivity, and Corporate Financial Performance," *Academy of Management Journal* 38 (1995): 635–72.

2   John Paul MacDuffie, "Human Resource Bundles and Manufacturing Performance: Organizational Logic and Flexible Production Systems in the World Auto Industry," *Industrial and Labor Relations Review* 48 (January 1995): 197–211.

Another researcher examined the impact of alternative HRM bundles on productivity and quality in customer call service centers operated by a large telecommunications company.[3] Three HRM approaches were identified: what she called a "mass production" model, a "total quality management" model, and a "self-managed team" model. Both sales and quality were higher in call centers using the "self-managed team" bundle of HRM practices. She also found evidence of significant synergy among HRM practices. For example, one reason the self-managed model generated higher productivity was that workers had more discretion and control over how they handled customer calls, but this resulted in higher productivity only when the employees were first given extensive training.

A cautionary note is warranted, however, before accepting at face value these apparently positive results for the strategic HRM theory. A more recent study published on this subject, and also the most thorough, finds no link between the adoption of advanced HRM practices and firm profitability.[4] This study looked at approximately 500 firms over the period 1977 and 1993, identified the year the firm switched to a system of AHRMP (some never switched), and calculated the impact on productivity and employee compensation. The authors found that adoption of AHRMP led to a sometimes small improvement in productivity, which by itself would increase firm profits (greater output per worker implies lower unit production cost). But adoption of AHRMP also led to higher wage and benefit cost (such as from gain-sharing and production pay bonuses). The net impact of AHRMP on profitability was thus approximately zero, since the lower cost from the productivity effect was offset by the higher cost from the compensation effect. This study also found only very weak evidence of positive synergy effects from "bundling" HRM practices.

We conclude, therefore, that the empirical evidence is suggestive but not conclusive with respect to the predictions of strategic HRM theory.

3   Rosemary Batt, "Work Organization, Technology, and Performance in Customer Service and Sales," *Industrial and Labor Relations Review* 52 (July 1999): 539–64.

4   Peter Cappelli and David Neumark, "Do 'High-Performance' Work Practices Improve Establishment-Level Outcomes?" *Industrial and Labor Relations Review* 54 (July 2001): 737–75.

EMPIRICAL EVIDENCE 10-3

Executive Compensation: Pay for Performance or Skimming the Cream?

Few subjects have stirred as much debate in corporate America in recent years as executive compensation.[1] Critics allege that executive compensation is out of control and that all too many CEOs are grossly overpaid. Defenders of the current system, on the other hand, claim the multimillion-dollar paychecks received by many corporate executives are in most cases a legitimate and deserved reward for topflight business skills, a crushing workload and set of responsibilities, and improved bottom-line results of shareholders.

What is the truth? The only undisputed facts are that CEO pay is quite high and growing rapidly. With regard to the level of executive pay, a survey of the annual compensation received by CEOs at

1   See John Abowd and David Kaplan, "Executive Compensation: Six Questions That Need Answering," *Journal of Economic Perspectives* 13 (Fall 1999): 145–68.

several hundred large companies in 2000 found that, on average, they earned $13.1 million, composed of $2.5 million in salary and the remainder in bonuses and stock options.[2] Some CEOs earn considerably less than this, but others earned considerably more. It is the latter group that most frequently captures the headlines. From 1995 to 2000, for example, Citigroup paid CEO Sanford Weil a total of $785 million in salary, bonuses, and stock options, while Michael Eisner at Disney garnered $738 million and Jack Welch at GE got $325 million.[3]

The second aspect of CEO pay that has come under scrutiny is its meteoric growth, particularly in relation to the pay of the average employee. Total CEO compensation rose by over 300 percent over the decade of the 1990s, compared to a 37 percent increase in average hourly pay for nonmanagerial employees. The result is that the average annual compensation of CEOs is over 300 times that of the employees who work for them. The disparity in pay is even more stark when one looks at pay rates in other countries. In Japan, for example, CEOs earn only about 16 times as much as the average employee.

Are CEOs worth this much money? The answer to this question remains in dispute, but two views exist. The basic dividing line between the two is the degree to which the wage determination process for CEOs is competitive and market-determined.

Defenders of CEO pay argue that the high and rising levels of executive compensation are a result of demand and supply conditions in the CEO labor market. Two features of demand and supply are particularly important. The first is that the demand for topflight CEO talent has increased substantially in recent years as companies confront ever greater competition in domestic and global product markets and pressure from shareholders and Wall Street for higher profits and stock prices. Effective leadership, companies believe, is one of the key strategic weapons in this battle, so competition for CEO talent has mushroomed. The other feature of the CEO labor market is that supply of topflight executive talent is very scarce and inelastic in supply. The result is rapidly rising CEO pay—a product of a large rightward shift of the CEO demand curve along an inelastic CEO supply curve.

The implication of the foregoing is that CEOs receive high pay because they produce an equivalent amount of value for shareholders (i.e., they are paid the value of their marginal product). Critics have long pointed to many examples, however, of CEOs who have been paid huge sums even when their companies' profitability sank during their tenure in the top job.

Economists have developed a second theory of executive compensation that sheds light on this apparent anomaly. It is known as **tournament theory.** Tournament theory looks at CEO pay, not as a reward for current job performance, but as a prize given to the winner of a sports-like competitive game. Economists Edward Lazear and Sherwin Rosen were among the first to point out the basic similarity in pay structures of executives and star athletes in certain professional sports, such as golf and tennis.[4] In a golf or tennis tournament, the winner often earns well over half of the total prize money, while the second-place winner earns much more than the third-place winner, and so on down the line. This highly skewed structure of rewards is illustrated in Figure 10.6, which shows winnings in two golf tournaments in 2000. The winner of the PGA (David Toms), for example, took home $956,000, compared to $562,000 for the second-place winner and $354,000 for the third-place winner. The hypothesized reason for structuring the winnings in this way is to elicit a higher quality and intensity of play; with such a huge prize at stake, the opportunity cost of *not* performing at one's absolute best is enormous.

---

2   "The Gravy Train Just Got Derailed," *Business Week* (November 19, 2001): 118–19.

3   "Share Scare," *Forbes* (May 14, 2001): 154.

4   Edward Lazear and Sherwin Rosen, "Rank-Order Tournaments as Optimum Labor Contracts," *Journal of Political Economy* 89 (October 1981): 841–64.

The payoffs in golf tournaments are structured so that the first-place winner goes home with a very large percentage of the entire purse. The rest of the players take home winnings in exponentially decreasing amounts.

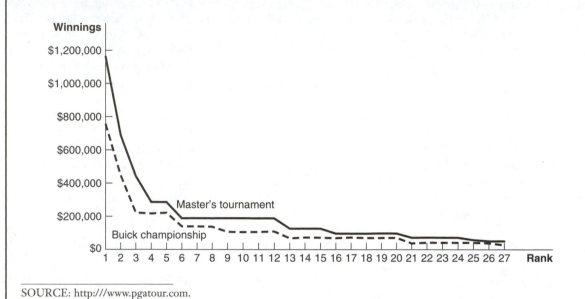

SOURCE: http:///www.pgatour.com.

Tournament theory suggests that exactly the same principle is involved in CEO compensation. By attaching an eye-catching multimillion-dollar prize to the top job, the company sets in motion a competitive process inside the organization that motivates people below the CEO level to perform at their highest level. One person will win and carry home the huge first prize; others get a consolation second or third prize (e.g., an executive vice-president's title and one-third the CEO's compensation), while others lower in the ranking may be asked to leave the company and seek employment elsewhere. Although the tournament leads to the "best" person being selected for the CEO job, once in office there is no guarantee the person will be successful in leading the company. Hence, high CEO pay and lackluster company performance may result.

Research finds evidence supportive of the predictions of tournament theory, although not uniformly so. The theory implies, for example, that (1) firms using a tournament pay system will stress promotion from within, (2) pay gaps increase with hierarchical level, (3) hierarchical levels serve as important determinants of pay, (4) large rewards (in present value terms) go with promotion, (5) the performance level of managers increases when they are offered higher rewards (prizes), and (6) the size of the CEO prize rises with the number of contestants in the organization. A recent study finds clear evidence that corporations structure pay for top-level executives in a way consistent with tournament theory, although not all the specific predictions listed above are supported.[5] Several of the predictions (e.g., the importance of promotion from within; the positive impact of larger prizes on performance), however, find empirical support in other studies.[6]

Critics of CEO compensation, while not necessarily rejecting the validity of tournament theory, nonetheless argue that a portion of CEO pay has no defensible explanation and represents an opportunistic "skimming the cream" at the expense of shareholders and employees.[7] From their point of view, the fact that CEO pay is so high is not because of competition but *lack* of competition. CEO pay, they note, is typically set by the board of directors of the company. In theory the people on the board of directors are supposed to be the watchdog of the shareholders' interests, but all too often, the critics charge, they have a self-interest in ratcheting the CEO's pay upward. Members of the board often include outside CEOs, lawyers, and investment bankers who do business with the company, all of whom stand to gain from granting higher pay to the CEO. The board of directors will also often hire an outside consulting company to make a recommendation on the size of the CEO's compensation, but the consulting company's recommendation may be biased in favor of higher

CEO pay by its desire to keep existing business with the company or to win new business.

One of the most recent and careful empirical studies on CEO pay found evidence that broadly supports *both* "pay for performance" and "skimming the cream" arguments.[8] The study examined the level and change in CEO pay at 600 firms over a seven-year period. The authors found that CEO pay varied in a positive direction with company performance, as the "pay for performance" hypothesis maintains, but that CEO pay also went up for reasons that had nothing to do with the person's job performance—as maintained by the cream-skimming hypothesis. The other conclusion of the study is that the extent of cream-skimming is well predicted by the nature of a company's corporate governance system. Where board oversight of the CEO is lax or membership is inbred, a larger portion of the CEO's pay appears to be a "gift."

5   Michael Bognanno, "Corporate Tournaments," *Journal of Labor Economics* 19 (April 2001): 290–315.

6   See Ronald Ehrenberg and Michael Bognanno, "Do Tournaments Have Incentive Effects? *Journal of Political Economy* 98 (December 1990): 1307–24, and John Fossum and Brian McCall, "Pay and Reward for Performance," in Lewin, Mitchell, and Zaidi, eds., *The Human Resource Management Handbook*, vol. 3, 111–43.

7   Graef Crystal, *In Search of Excess: The Over-Compensation of American Executives* (New York: Norton, 1991).

8   Marianne Bertrand and Sendhil Mulllainathan, "Agents with and without Principles," *American Economic Review* 90 (May 2000): 203–8.

Summary

Firms use human resource management (HRM) practices to control, coordinate, and motivate their workforces. From an economic perspective, these HRM practices are another input into the production process. This perspective allows economists to derive a demand curve for individual HRM practices, determine the equilibrium level of each HRM input, and demonstrate how the demand for HRM practices varies with changes in key variables. Examples include input price, the technology of production, the organizational structure of the firm, and the firm's business strategy.

Before firms have a demand for HRM practices, however, they have to have employees—otherwise there are no human resources to manage. The chapter demonstrated that firms may obtain labor in two ways—hire people to work as employees or as independent contractors. The choice turns on whichever mode minimizes transaction cost.

Three areas of HRM activities are examined in the chapter: employee selection, compensation management, and employee involvement. With respect to selection, the key problem facing the firm is that the productivity of job applicants is unknown due to imperfect and asymmetric information. Firms thus have to develop an employee selection system that identifies the key performance criteria of jobs and the knowledge, skills, and abilities needed by workers and then attempt to select the right people for the right jobs. To illustrate the issues involved, a model of job market signaling was presented. The model shows that successful employee screening depends on identifying an observable characteristic that (*a*) is positively correlated with job performance and (*b*) is more costly for low-ability people to obtain.

Two issues in compensation management are examined in the chapter. The first is a firm's choice of pay *level*, the second is choice of pay *form*. Because real-world labor markets contain various imperfections and impediments, pay rates are not completely determined by demand and supply, giving firms some discretion in their pay policies. They may lead the market, match the market, or lag the market. Several factors influence this decision, such as ability to pay, business strategy, concerns with turnover and employee morale, and union avoidance. With regard to pay form, firms have a variety of methods they can use to compensate employees, such as a wage per hour, salary per year, piece rate, commission rate, gain-sharing bonus, and stock options. These pay forms vary along two key dimensions: the *performance* measure (an input- or output-based form of pay) and the *size* measure (an individual- or group-based form of pay). Each has disadvantages and advantages related to ease of measurement, impact on individual work effort, and incentive for teamwork and cooperation.

The third HRM practice area examined in the chapter is employee involvement and participation (EIP). Firms can adopt either direct or indirect forms of EIP, the former using face-to-face methods of interaction and the latter various kinds of groups and committees in which certain workers represent the opinions and interests of other workers. Firms adopt EIP practices to the extent that the benefits exceed the costs. Benefits include improved two-way communication, higher employee morale and organizational commitment, and better control and coordination of production; disadvantages include loss of time from production, diversion of management time and attention, higher labor cost, and in some cases slower and less flexible decision making. The extent of EIP practices in industry is also influenced by various forms of market failure, such as principal–agent problems and fears of bargaining opportunism. We conclude that these problems most likely lead to an undersupply of EIP in the labor market and thus provide a rationale for public policy intervention to selectively encourage greater opportunities for employee participation and representation.

Review Questions

1. A restaurant can hire cooks and waiters as either employees or independent contractors. Most often they choose the former. Why do you think they prefer employees?

2. Explain the following observed patterns in HRM practice using the model of HRM input demand:

   a. Many small-sized firms do not have a HRM department.

   b. Improved computer technology often leads to a smaller HRM staffing ratio (e.g., from 1/100 to 1/200).

   c. Firms that pay psroduction employees on

a time basis (e.g., a wage per hour) tend to hire more supervisors and foremen (other things equal).

d. Firms that adopt a high-performance work system (HPWS) spend much more on employee training.

e. As the cost ("price") of administering employer-sponsored and employer-administered pension plans has increased, firms have increasingly opted for self-managed 401K retirement plans.

3. With regard to employee selection, answer these two questions:

a. If schools and universities changed from a letter grading system (A, B, C, D, F) to a pass-fail system, what impact would this most likely have on the usefulness of education as an effective employee screening device?

b. Are there jobs or occupations for which education would *not* serve as a useful screening device for employers? Name several and explain why.

4. It has been suggested that one way to raise the quality of teaching at colleges and universities is to link professors' pay to their performance in the classroom, say by making pay raises a positive function of the score they receive on end-of-semester student course evaluations. Evaluate the pros and cons of this suggestion.

5. Take the Star, Commitment, and Factory employment systems discussed in the chapter and discuss what would be the best pay system for each in terms of pay level and pay form (or mix of forms).

6. It has been proposed that a law be enacted requiring all workplaces with 50 or more employees to have a formal employee involvement and participation (EIP) committee that meets with management on a regular basis to discuss workplace issues. Evaluate the merits of this proposal based only on consideration of economic efficiency. Does introducing noneconomic considerations, such as workplace democracy and social justice, affect the conclusion?

7. Discuss the pros and cons of the ban on "company unions" in the National Labor Relations Act.

11

Union Membership and Collective Bargaining

The next two chapters are devoted to one of the most important subjects in labor economics—trade unionism and collective bargaining. The purpose of studying labor unions is to understand how unionism and collective bargaining affect the operation of the labor market and specific market outcomes such as wage rates, fringe benefits, and the level of productivity. The first step in this process is to examine the framework that governs or structures the process of collective bargaining. This covers a number of topics, such as why workers join labor unions, the legal framework within which collective bargaining operates, and the structure of bargaining between employers and unions. Each of these subjects is important because each helps to determine the objectives that labor unions and employers pursue in collective bargaining and the amount of power that each party can bring to the bargaining table to obtain these objectives.

The Pattern of Union Membership

Figure 11.1 charts the membership of five labor organizations between 1955 and 2002: the United Automobile Workers (UAW); the International Brotherhood of Electrical Workers (IBEW); the American Federation of State, County, and Municipal Employees (AFSCME); the American Federation of Teachers (AFT); and the International Association of Fire Fighters (IAFF).

A number of features depicted in Figure 11.1 are worth highlighting. One is the difference between a labor union and an employee association (all of the organizations shown in the figure are considered labor unions). The principal characteristic of a **labor union** is that it bargains on behalf of its members over the terms and conditions of employment and will strike the employer to achieve its objectives. Traditionally, an **employee association** has functioned more as a lobbying organization and professional society, eschewing both formal collective bargaining and strikes. During the 1970s, however, employee associations began to take on more and more of the activities of unions, until in 1980 the Bureau of Labor Statistics

FIGURE 11.1   MEMBERSHIP IN FIVE LABOR ORGANIZATIONS, 1955–2002

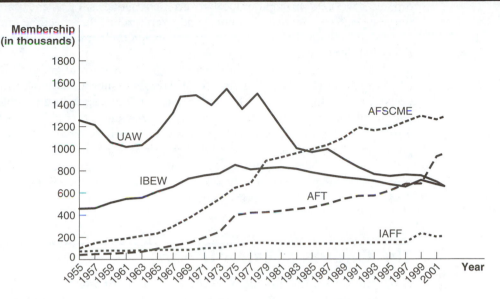

NOTE:

UAW: United Automobile Workers

IBEW: International Brotherhood of Electrical Workers

AFSCME: American Federation of State, County, and Municipal Employees

AFT: American Federation of Teachers

IAFF: International Association of Fire Fighters

SOURCE: Constructed from data found in Barry T. Hirsch and David A. Macpherson, *Union Membership and Earnings Data Book* (Washington D.C.: Bureau of National Affairs, 2004).

concluded that the difference between a labor union and an employee association was so blurred that it began calling both labor organizations.

A second feature of interest in Figure 11.1 is the difference between industrial unions and craft unions. Of the labor unions in Figure 11.1, the UAW and AFSCME are industrial unions, and the AFT and IAFF are craft unions; the IBEW is a combination of craft and industrial. A **craft union** is a union whose members include only workers from a specific occupation or craft, such as railway clerks, carpenters, plant guards, or truck drivers. Where craft unions are the dominant type of labor organization, the workers in a particular industry or in a single company may be split into a half-dozen or more separate unions. An **industrial union,** on the other hand, includes in its membership all the workers employed in a particular industry, regardless of their specific occupations. Thus, the UAW includes in its organizing jurisdiction any worker in the automobile industry, while the AFSCME organizes workers throughout local government agencies. In recent years, the distinction between industrial unions and craft unions has become increasingly blurred as individual unions have stepped outside their traditional jurisdictions in the search for new members.

A third feature of interest in Figure 11.1 is the pattern of growth of these five labor organizations. The AFT and AFSCME grew substantially over the past 40 years; membership in the IAFF grew modestly (all three are in the public sector); and membership in the UAW and the IBEW grew up to the mid-1970s but afterwards declined rather substantially (both are in the private sector). These divergent growth rates among unions raise several questions. First, how does each union organize new members? Second, why are some unions more successful in organizing than others? Finally, what are the future prospects for growth among these unions? These are some of the questions addressed in this chapter.

The Origins of Labor Unions

Labor unions are not a modern invention. The first unions in the United States date from about 1790; labor unions appeared in England at an even earlier time. Labor unions are also widespread across many cultures, economic systems, and political forms of government. Although the institutional details vary substantially, countries as diverse as Germany, Japan, Nigeria, Argentina, and Poland all have trade unions and labor movements of one form or another.

Scholars have debated for over a century about what forces or developments motivate workers to form and join labor unions. Although a number of different theories seek to explain the subject, it is possible to sift through them and identify certain fundamental conditions that are necessary for the growth and development of labor unions.[1]

The Divorce of Capital and Labor

In a classic study of trade unions in nineteenth-century England, Sidney and Beatrice Webb described what is still accepted today as the basic precondition for the development of labor unions.[2] They identified it as the **divorce of capital and labor** that accompanies the process of industrialization.

The Webbs observed that in a preindustrial economy most workers are self-employed as independent farmers, craftsmen, or artisans. In this situation, the individual worker is, in effect, a minibusiness firm in which the two functions of

---

1   See Mark Perlman, *Labor Union Theories in America: Background and Development* (Evanston, Ill.: Peterson, 1958), and Bruce Kaufman, "The Future of the Labor Movement: A Look at the Fundamentals," *Labor Law Journal* 48 (August 1997): 474–84.

2   Sidney and Beatrice Webb, *The History of Trade Unionism*, 2d ed. (London: Longmans, Green, 1896).

management and labor are combined in one person. The hallmark of industrialization is the replacement of the single producer with more complex, specialized, and large-scale forms of production. The individual shoemaker who produces and sells shoes, for example, can no longer compete with the capitalist entrepreneur who utilizes machinery and a complex division of labor. The result of industrialization is the demise of the single producer and the creation of a wage labor force that hires itself out to owners of capital.

The Webbs identify this separation of the worker from the ownership of the means of production (the divorce of capital and labor) as the necessary condition for trade unionism. The reason is that the divorce of capital and labor leads to a corresponding split in the functions of management and labor; with industrialization there emerges one group of people whose job is management (employers and their representatives) and a second group of people whose job is labor. When these two functions were united in the single producer, there was a harmony of interests between management and labor, since the same person shared equally in the profits and losses of production. The divorce of capital and labor brings the potential for an adversarial relationship between the two groups.[3] The basis of the adversarial relationship is the conflict of interests between management and labor over the two key variables of the employment relationship—the price of labor and the distribution of power in the business enterprise.[4]

Employers and Workers: Adversaries or Partners?

With the divorce of capital and labor, employers and workers enter into the employment relationship with different goals and objectives. The primary concern of the employer is profits and the survival and growth of the firm. Workers, on the other hand, enter into the employment relationship for two reasons: to obtain as high a wage or salary income as possible, and because work provides various forms of psychological gratification, such as a sense of accomplishment and an outlet for goal-directed behavior. These are often characterized, respectively, as "extrinsic" and "intrinsic" rewards from work.

Are the objectives of employers and workers necessarily in conflict? This question is a complex one and receives a range of answers from "always" to "generally not." In a capitalist economic system, the employment relationship embodies elements of both cooperation and conflict. The incentive for cooperation between workers and the employer comes from the fact that each side needs the other—

---

3   A recent illustration of this principle concerns doctors. Traditionally doctors have been self-employed, giving them little interest in unions. Today, however, an increasing number of doctors are being employed by health maintenance organizations (HMOs) as salaried workers. As described in Grace Bundays, *When Doctors Join Unions* (Ithaca: Cornell University Press, 1996), there is a newfound interest on the part of doctors in unionizing, yet they have had some difficulty convincing some judges that they are "employees" of the HMOs for which they work.

4   Jack Barbash, "Reflections on Positive Collective Bargaining," in James L. Stern and Barbara D. Dennis, eds., *Trade Unionism in the United States: A Symposium in Honor of Jack Barbash* (Madison, Wis.: IRRA, 1981), 201–11.

without a workforce the firm cannot operate and make a profit, and if the firm does not make a profit it will be unable to provide wages and jobs for the workers. The minimum profit requirements of the firm coupled with the minimum compensation requirements of the workers determine the boundaries within which the adversarial relationship must be confined if the employment relationship is to remain viable.

Given that some degree of cooperation is required if anything is to be produced, considerable room for conflict remains between management and labor. How serious will this conflict be? According to Marxists, the relationship between managers and workers in a capitalist system is inherently adversarial, since management's goal (higher profits) can only be obtained at the expense of the workers' goal (higher wages), and vice versa.[5] To strengthen their bargaining power and protect their class interests in the face of management's continual drive for greater profits, workers are inevitably led to form labor unions. From a Marxist perspective, however, labor unions are not the ultimate solution to the adversarial relationship. The ultimate solution is for workers to seize control of the state and substitute government ownership of capital for private ownership. Since the state will then be controlled by the workers, an adversarial relationship cannot exist because the workers will, in effect, be their own bosses. This line of thinking was used by the Polish government when it outlawed the independent union Solidarity in 1981. (If the state owns the means of production and operates them in the interests of the workers, why do workers need an independent union?) The continued buildup of labor unrest in Poland until the ouster of the Communist regime in 1989 suggests, however, that the goals of managers and workers in a socialist country may be in as much or even more conflict as those in a capitalist country.

Non-Marxists typically take a different point of view about the degree of conflict that exists in the employment relationship. While many workers and firms do have adversarial relationships, non-Marxists believe that it is also possible to have an employer/employee relationship that is built on cooperation.[6] This cooperation means not just the minimum necessary for the employment relationship to survive, but rather a relationship similar to that between two partners who pursue a common goal. In this view, the type of labor relations in a company is a subject of choice, not inevitability. Most companies' labor relations will contain elements of both cooperation and conflict, although the exact proportion will depend on the management philosophy of the employer and the firm's competitive position in the product market.

---

5   See, for example, Richard Hyman, *Industrial Relations: A Marxist Introduction* (London: Macmillan, 1975).

6   See Clark Kerr et al., *Industrialism and Industrial Man* (Cambridge, Mass.: Harvard University Press, 1960); and Edward Lawler, *The Ultimate Advantage: Creating the High-Involvement Organization* (San Francisco: Jossey-Bass, 1992); and Bruce E. Kaufman, "The Quest for Cooperation and Unity of Interest in Industry," in B. Kaufman, R. Beaumont, and R. Helfgott, eds., *Industrial Relations to Human Resource Management and Beyond* (Armonk: M.E. Sharpe), pp. 115–46.

Individual Action versus Collective Action

Workers in "high-standards" firms (i.e., well-run firms with good management, progressive personnel policies, generous wages and benefits), generally feel satisfied with the terms and conditions of employment and do not feel a need for or interest in a union. Workers in "low-standards" firms (i.e., poorly run firms with adversarial management styles, and poor working conditions), feel dissatisfied and taken advantage of by the employer. This worker actively seeks some mechanism to obtain the objectives of higher wages, control over the job, clean and pleasant working conditions, and respect and fair play from the boss.

Two avenues are open to the worker to improve his or her situation in the labor market. The first is **individual action.** This might involve quitting the present employer to find a better one, going back to school to get more education, or talking on a one-to-one basis with the employer or supervisor about a particular complaint or suggestion. The second option available to the worker is **collective action**—working through a group or organization to achieve a particular goal or objective. Thus, a worker could seek to improve his or her wages and working conditions or to gain some voice in the operation of the firm by joining a labor union. A worker could also attempt to improve his or her economic and social position through alternative forms of collective action such as joining a political party, lobbying group, or professional association.

Both individual and collective action have advantages and disadvantages. For workers to choose joining a labor union as the vehicle or instrument by which to achieve their work-related objectives, three conditions are necessary.

The first is that the worker's objectives not be obtainable through individual action. American culture has a strong credo of individualism and a corresponding lack of class identity or consciousness.[7] One of the core beliefs of most Americans is that through hard work and perseverance a person can get ahead in the economic system. Individual action is also appealing because it allows the worker the freedom and independence to find the job and working conditions that match his or her preferences without being encumbered by the rules or complex decision-making process of a larger group. Before the average American worker will seriously consider joining a union, therefore, he or she must feel unable to improve the situation at work through individual action.

For several reasons, individual action might fail in the labor market.[8] One reason is defects in the competitive market mechanism. An example would be the presence of persistent unemployment that prevented some workers from finding jobs at all and other workers from leaving low-standards employers in search of better jobs. Individual action might also fail if there are few other employers to choose from in the labor market. A third reason might be the worker's lack of mobility in the market due to specific on-the-job training, seniority or pension rights,

---

7   See Harry Triandis, *Individualism and Collectivism* (Boulder: Westview, 1995).

8   Also see Katherine Van Wezel Stone, "The Feeble Strength of One: Why Individual Worker Rights Fail," *American Prospect* (Summer 1993): 60–66.

limited financial resources, or marriage or other family ties. A fourth reason individual action might fail is if the person's progress in the labor market is blocked by discrimination or the forces of tradition and custom.

If a worker cannot achieve his or her goals through individual action, the person will consider alternative means, and one alternative is a labor union. Through the power of collective bargaining, a union can gain the higher wages, improved conditions, and voice in the firm that individual action sometimes cannot. Before the desire of an individual worker for a union can be realized, however, a second condition for collective action must be fulfilled: other persons at the workplace must also desire a union and share the same objectives or "community of interests." An individual cannot form a union alone; collective action requires the active participation of a group of people. For individual workers to find it in their self-interest to join a group, in turn, requires that they have a common, unifying set of objectives. With respect to labor unions, these common objectives arise out of the adversarial relationship that develops between workers and the management of low-standards firms.

The third condition for collective action is that it be permitted by law and that the group have a sufficient power base to pursue its objectives. Where public law or judicial rulings make labor unions illegal, workers cannot engage in collective bargaining even if they desire to do so. Likewise, if employers are allowed unrestrained freedom to thwart the formation of unions, or if government withholds the right to strike, the ability or incentive to form a labor union may be so small as to preclude effective collective action.

The Determinants of Union Membership: A Demand and Supply Model

The preceding discussion sketches the basic forces or motives that lead workers to form unions. This section explores these issues in more detail and, in particular, answers the question: Why is it that some workers join unions, while other workers do not? For example, today only about one in seven workers belongs to a union. The rate of unionization also varies widely among individual industries, occupations, and states of the country. What factors account for this pattern?

As with many other issues, economists have found it useful to analyze the determinants of why workers join or don't join unions in terms of supply and demand. In this theory, union membership is similar to an asset that provides its owner with a flow of services over time.[9] Like other assets, the amount of union membership that is provided in the market depends on both demand and supply. The demand for union services comes from individual workers; the supply of union

---

9   John Pencavel, "The Demand for Union Services: An Exercise," *Industrial and Labor Relations Review* 22, no. 2 (January 1971): 180–91.

services comes from labor unions. This section looks at both the demand and the supply of union services, discussing in more detail the specific variables that influence each.

The Demand for Union Services

The demand for union services may be likened to the demand for an asset such as a house. The amount of the asset that is demanded depends on its price, the net benefits of holding the asset, and the individual's income and preferences. With respect to union services, the influence of these factors can be represented graphically by a **demand curve for union services,** such as the demand schedule D_1 in Figure 11.2. The demand curve D_1 shows the amount of union services that workers desire to purchase at a given price. The price is generally of two kinds, monthly dues and one-time initiation fees. Monthly dues usually amount to one or two

---

FIGURE 11.2   THE DEMAND CURVE FOR UNION SERVICES

At a price of P_1, the demand for union services is U_1 (point A). A rise in the price results in a decline in the quantity demanded to U_2 (point B). An increase in the net benefits from belonging to a union or more favorable attitudes toward unions would shift the demand curve from D_1 to D_2. At the price P_1, the demand for union services would increase from U_1 to U_3 (point A to C).

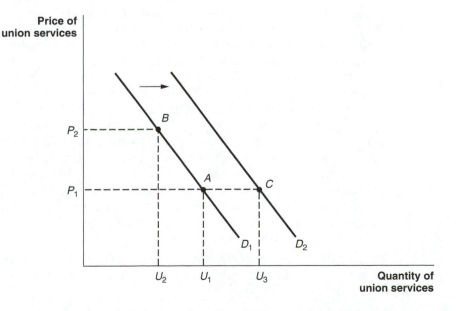

hours' pay per month; in 2004, for example, dues in the International Association of Machinists union were $40 per month. Some unions have considerably higher dues, and others have lower dues.[10] Most unions also charge new members a one-time initiation fee. A typical initiation fee is $5 or less, although in some craft unions, such as those in the building trades, initiation fees can be $300 or higher. A basic prediction of economic theory is that for a given level of benefits, the demand for union membership should be inversely related to its price. This is illustrated in Figure 11.2 by the negative slope of the demand curve D_1. At a low price of P_1, the quantity demanded of union services is U_1 (point A); as monthly dues and initiation fees are increased to P_2 the quantity demanded of union services falls to U_2 (point B). Given the assumption that each worker consumes one unit of union services, it is also possible to say that union membership itself declines from U_1 to U_2 as dues and fees go up.

The demand for union services is determined by more than its price. A second important variable is the *net benefits* that workers receive from union membership. Union membership carries both positive and negative attributes, or what can be called "benefits" and "costs." The benefits might be higher wages or improved working conditions, and the costs might include the loss of one's job or the loss of wages because of a strike. Note that the price of union membership (monthly dues) is distinct from these other elements of cost. The greater are the benefits of union membership relative to the costs, the greater will be the demand for union services at any given price. A third important variable is the worker's income; an increase in income would lead to an increase or decrease in union membership, depending on whether it is a normal or inferior good. Finally, the demand for union services is also influenced by individual preferences; the more favorable is a worker's attitude toward labor unions, the greater will be the demand for union services, and vice versa.

A change in the price of union membership is represented by a *movement* along a given demand curve. A change in the net benefits of union membership, income, or preferences, on the other hand, causes a *shift* in the demand curve. The demand curve D_1 in Figure 11.2 is drawn for a given level of net benefits, income, and preferences; should the net benefits of union membership increase, or should attitudes towards unions become more favorable, for example, the demand curve would shift to the right, from D_1 to D_2. At the price of P_1, the demand for union services and union membership would increase from U_1 (point A) to U_3 (point C). A shift to the left of the demand curve would cause a decrease in demand for union membership.

Differences in demand curves among workers are one reason some workers decide to join unions while others don't. Since a major determinant of the demand for union services is the net benefits derived from them, the exact nature of these benefits and costs must be examined more fully.

The Benefits of Union Membership   One benefit of a union is that it gives workers greater **bargaining power** vis-à-vis the employer, often allowing workers to

---

10   See John Raisian, "Union Dues and Wage Premiums," *Journal of Labor Research* 4, no. 1 (Winter 1983): 1–18.

gain better wages and conditions of employment than in a nonunion system of individual bargaining. The major source of the union's bargaining power is the threat of a strike. In a nonunion labor market, the potential cost to the employer of saying no to an individual worker is that the worker will quit. With a union, this potential cost is raised substantially, since all workers will walk off the job instead of just one. To avoid the lost production and profits that go with a strike, the employer will voluntarily pay a higher wage or provide greater fringe benefits and improved working conditions than it would in the absence of a union. To proponents of trade unionism, joining a union not only increases the bargaining power of workers, it also *equalizes* bargaining power. In this view, the individual worker and the large corporation do not approach the bargaining table on an equal footing, since the worker typically needs the job much more than the corporation needs the worker. Forming a union, therefore, is seen as a way to give workers equal strength in the determination of wages and other conditions of employment.[11]

A second benefit of a union is that it can help achieve a more *equitable pay structure* by eliminating the practice of arbitrary and discriminatory wage setting. Most people are concerned not only with the absolute amount in dollars and cents that they are paid, but also with their rate of pay relative to what other employees are making.[12] A person may consider $10 per hour fair until he or she discovers that a workmate earns $11 for the same work. Inequities in a firm's internal wage structure can arise from favoritism or discrimination, a lack of a centrally directed, formalized personnel policy, or the use of productivity or performance standards in wage determination that are not objective and consistent. One benefit of a union is that it can achieve equal pay for equal work by bargaining for uniform pay scales among job classifications and the use of objective criteria such as seniority in the award of pay increases and promotions. Similarly, workers may find a union attractive if their company's rate of pay lags behind what its competitors are paying for similar work.

A third benefit of a union is that it may provide workers with greater *job and income security*. This aspect of unionism was heavily emphasized by John R. Commons and Selig Perlman in their classic studies of the origins of trade unions.[13] According to Commons and Perlman, there is a basic conflict of interest between

---

11 This was one of the major justifications for passage of the National Labor Relations Act in 1935. The preamble to the act states, "The inequality of bargaining power between employees who do not possess full freedom of association . . . and employers who are organized in the corporate or other forms of ownership . . . tends to aggravate business depressions by depressing wage rates and the purchasing power of wage earners." For further discussion of this subject, see Howard Dickman, *Industrial Democracy in America: Ideological Origins of National Labor Relations Policy* (LaSalle, Ill.: Open Court Press, 1987), and Bruce E. Kaufman, "Labor's Inequality of Bargaining Power: Changes over Time and Implications for Public Policy," *Journal of Labor Research* 10, no. 3 (Summer 1989): 285–99.

12 Henry Farber and Daniel Saks, "Why Workers Want Unions: The Role of Relative Wages and Job Characteristics," *Journal of Political Economy* 88, no. 2 (April 1980): 349–69, and Albert Rees, "The Role of Fairness in Wage Determination," *Journal of Labor Economics* 11 (no. 1, part 1, 1993): 243–52.

13 John R. Commons, "American Shoemakers: A Sketch of Industrial Evolution, 1648–1895," *Quarterly Journal of Economics* 24, no. 1 (November 1909): 39–84, and Selig Perlman, *A Theory of the Labor Movement* (New York: Macmillan, 1928).

society and the individual worker over the benefits of competition. From society's point of view, competition is a virtue because it forces business firms to search constantly for ways to produce their products at lower cost. As seen by the individual worker, however, unrestrained competition is an evil to be avoided since it threatens his or her job and rate of pay. Competition, for example, may force the firm to speed up the work or tighten supervision. Competition may also lead the employer to replace higher-paid men with lower-paid women or part-time teenagers, or to move production to a low-wage area of the country or overseas. In the view of Commons and Perlman, an important benefit of a labor union is to protect workers from the insecurity of the competitive market system. One way unions do this is by organizing all the employers in the product market and then "taking wages out of competition" by establishing a uniform pay scale across firms. A second way is to restrict the employer's ability to lay off workers, subcontract out work, or hire nonunion workers.

A fourth benefit of a union is that it gives workers *protection from the unilateral authority of management.* In most American firms, the management system is a hierarchical chain of command with management at the top as "order givers" and workers at the bottom as "order takers." As the order givers, management has a wide degree of discretion in a nonunion firm over whom it hires, the wage it pays, the hours of work, job assignments, and matters related to discipline and discharge. In many nonunion firms, workers have few avenues of appeal to management decisions on these matters; the basic protection of the worker lies instead in the freedom to quit and go elsewhere or, alternatively, to seek legal redress before a court or government agency. A union gives workers an alternative form of protection from management power.

One way a union does this is by restricting or prohibiting certain management practices such as an arbitrary job reassignment or discharge without cause. A second way is by introducing a grievance system so that workers have an avenue to appeal management decisions. A third way is to give workers some input into the operation of the firm through the contract negotiation process. The Webbs called this benefit of unionism *industrial democracy*, and in more recent times Richard Freeman and James Medoff have popularized it as *worker voice.*[14]

An additional way workers gain from the voice provided by a union is the fifth benefit from union membership. Besides the level of wages and having a say on the job, working conditions are also of vital concern to employees. Many working conditions are what economists call **public goods.** A public good is some product or service that many people can consume together without reducing the total amount of it. A second feature of a public good is that it is difficult or impossible to deny people who have not helped to pay for it from consuming it. The classic example of a public good is national defense. Many working conditions are also public goods. One example is the speed of the assembly line, and a second is the

---

14   Sidney and Beatrice Webb, *Industrial Democracy* (London: Longmans, Green, 1920), and James Medoff and Richard Freeman, *What Do Unions Do?* (New York: Basic Books, 1984).

installation of an improved ventilation system. The problem with a public good is that each individual has an incentive to be a "free rider," hoping someone else will pay for the good and that he or she can then enjoy it for free. Thus, each worker may be concerned about safety in the plant, yet none will actually speak up, hoping someone else will do so. While this behavior is nonoptimal from the group's point of view, from the perspective of each worker it is entirely rational, since he or she would bear the cost of possible management retribution or displeasure while everyone else would reap the gain. As a result a system of individual bargaining may produce less than optimal working conditions. Where public goods are an important feature of work, a union may be quite attractive to workers.[15] In an organized firm, the union will speak to the employer in a collective voice through the union representative. Because each worker pays an equal amount of union dues, and because no one worker has to take the responsibility of speaking up, workers have a larger incentive to voice their true preference about working conditions.

The Costs of Union Membership A worker who buys union membership by paying the initiation fee and monthly dues gains certain benefits but also incurs certain costs. Among these costs or drawbacks of union membership are the following.

One cost of union membership is the *loss of wages during a strike*. The threat of a strike gives a union its ability to raise wages and benefits, but this extra bargaining power is not without cost, for sometimes the strike must actually be used. In 2003, 14 major (1,000 workers or more) strikes occurred, involving almost 129,000 workers. These strikes accounted for over 4.1 million days of idleness.[16] The loss in wages during a strike may be offset by strike benefits from the union, although not all unions pay them and those that do usually pay only 20 to 30 percent of regular earnings. There is also the possibility that the worker may never get the job back at all if the employer can successfully hire nonunion workers and break the strike. Finally, strikes lead to psychic costs for workers due to the conflict and ill feelings that strikes engender between union members and nonstriking workers and management personnel.

A second possible cost of union membership is the *loss of the job* due to layoffs or the closing of the plant. When a union wins higher wages, greater benefits, or restrictive work rules, the general result is to increase the employer's cost of labor per hour. An increase in labor cost leads to a decline in employment as the firm is forced to move up its labor demand curve; the more elastic is the demand curve, the greater the loss in jobs. Should labor costs increase to the point where the

---

15 See Robert Flanagan, "Workplace Public Goods and Union Organization," *Industrial Relations* 22, no. 2 (Spring 1983): 224–37, and David Weil, "Are Mandated Health and Safety Committees Substitutes for or Supplements to Labor Unions?" *Industrial and Labor Relations Review* 52 (April 1999): 339–60.

16 Bureau of Labor Statistics, "Major Work Stoppages in 2003," News Release, http://stats.bls.gov/news.release/wkstp.nr0.htm.

The Jungle—One Hundred Years Later

One envisions the modern-day workplace, protected by unions and regulated by OSHA, as being free from the nightmare conditions described in Upton Sinclair's *The Jungle* (an exposé of working conditions in the meatpacking industry published in 1906), which inspired early-twentieth-century labor reformers. Unfortunately, the conditions described by Sinclair can still be found in some modern workplaces. And these conditions are no longer just a blue-collar experience. This section describes two such employment environments and why workers are sometimes unable to make things better.

At a poultry-processing plant in rural Mississippi, workers dismantle and cut gizzards out of 90 chickens a minute flying past them on a swift steel shackle. Trips to the bathroom require approval from the foreman, whose attention is hard to get over the noise of the machinery. Safety training consists of a personnel worker reading a list of chemicals in use at the plant. Workers work close together along the line with knives and scissors, resulting in frequent cuts and scrapes. The floors are slick with wash water and chicken bits. The work is repetitive, monotonous, and strenuous; the industry ranks third for cumulative-trauma injuries (carpal tunnel syndrome). Over the past 15 years, processing-line speeds have increased from under 60 chickens per minute to 91 chickens per minute. Starting pay is between $6 and $8 an hour depending on the job.

In example number two, workers at what has been dubbed an "electronic sweatshop" process donations and perform other financial and clerical tasks contracted for by various nonprofit charities who used to do their own paperwork. Wages are also in the $6 to $8 range. Mail sorters are required to process three envelopes per minute. Keyboard operators have a quota of 8,500 strokes an hour. Talking is forbidden. Windows are covered. Workers' desks are barren of any personal items. Surveillance cameras and computers keep track of the workers' every move. The owner of the company admits that the environment he has created is stressful for workers; that's what keeps productivity high.

Both environments are models of an unbalanced employment relationship, both exhibiting conditions typically ripe for worker dissatisfaction and unionization. At the financial services company, however, a union representation vote has failed twice. And, roughly 80 percent of the workers in the poultry-processing industry are not unionized. Both businesses share characteristics that make union organizing particularly difficult. First, workers are afraid of employer retaliation. These jobs are typically the best alternative for workers with few skills and little mobility; they have a lot to lose if they are characterized as "troublemakers." For example, workers known to be in support of unionization at the poultry-processing plant have been observed being harassed, dismissed, or

revenues of the firm are less than its total variable costs of production, the employer will close the plant and all union members will lose their jobs.[17]

A third cost of union membership to the worker is *possible management retribution*. This retribution may take several forms; the employer might fire the worker,

---

17   See Charles Craypo and Bruce Nissen, eds., *Grand Designs: The Impact of Corporate Strategies on Workers, Unions, and Communities* (Ithaca, N.Y.: ILR Press, 1993), and Richard Freeman and Morris Kleiner, "Do Unions Make Enterprises Insolvent?" *Industrial and Labor Relations Review* 52 (July 1999): 510–22.

reassigned to the least-desirable jobs. In another plant, the management hung a sign in the break room that said "Democracies depend on the political participation of its citizens, but not in the workplace." Written in English and Spanish, the message was clear in any language.

A second barrier to organization is the lack of communication between workers. The work environments have prompted a "divide and conquer" strategy. Because of the high noise levels, workers at chicken-processing plants wear earplugs, making conversation difficult at the very least. Breaks are short and typically occupied with using the bathroom or eating a snack. The ban on any talking at the financial services company effectively eliminates any chance at conversation among workers there. If workers can't communicate and become of one mind regarding work conditions or at least about the desire to have a collective voice, unionization becomes more difficult.

High turnover also works against union organization. The working conditions and low wages themselves (the very issues that would typically motivate organization) are what drive workers away. Many poultry-processing plants experience a turnover of over 100 percent per year. In other white-collar "electronic sweatshops," the average length of employment is reported to be only 11 weeks. Workers do not feel like making the commitment to a union-

organizing effort (which, as described above, can be costly), if they don't anticipate staying with the company for very long.

A fourth, very effective, barrier against union organization is the aggressive management opposition to unionization. Both the poultry-processing industry and the financial service industry are very fast-growing industries, subjected to a lot of competitive pressures. Poultry processing is the second-fastest-growing factory job in the United States since 1980. And the outsourcing of the early 2000s has ensured the fast-pace growth of financial services. In the face of the competitive pressure that growth brings with it, and the resulting critical cost containment, management will put forth more than the average effort to defeat unionizing efforts.

All of these factors don't bode well for a shift in these industries from the current state of individual action to the more effective collective action through trade unions.

SOURCES: Steve Striffler, "Inside a Poultry Processing Plant: An Ethnographic Portrait," *Labor History* 43 (3, 2002): 305–13. Tony Horowitz, "Mr. Edens Profits from Watching His Workers' Every Move" and "9 to Nowhere: Blues on the Chicken Line," *Wall Street Journal* (1 December 1994): A1, and Dana Milbank, "'New-Collar' Work," *Wall Street Journal* (3 September 1993): A1.

reassign him to a less desirable job, or give her a smaller wage increase. While these types of antiunion practices by employers are illegal, employees recognize that the protection of the law is not ironclad. It is often difficult for the worker to prove that he or she was fired for union activities rather than for a legitimate cause such as insubordination or being habitually late to work. Court proceedings are also quite time-consuming and expensive, and in general, the employer has the greater staying power in such matters.

A fourth possible cost of union membership for a worker is a *loss of individualism and flexibility* in doing the job. In a unionized firm, personnel policies are generally more rigid, allowing workers less discretion in choosing work schedules or job assignments. Workers also have less room for exercising personal initiative in how the job is done. Another consideration is that the lines of communication between workers and management in a unionized firm are not as open and informal as in nonunion firms, cutting off the access of the worker to the employer. Finally, individual union members may feel they have no influence on the decision-making process in the union.

A fifth possible cost of union membership is a *loss in social status*. Many white-collar workers, for example, associate labor unions with lower-status factory workers or manual laborers and for that reason are reluctant to join a union. A second consideration is that many workers regard joining a union as a tacit admission that they can't get ahead on their own, an admission many Americans find very difficult to make.

The Supply Curve of Union Services

Union membership requires not only that workers desire union representation, but that a labor union be able and willing to supply union services to them. These services include such things as providing a union hall, negotiating collective bargaining agreements, representing workers in grievance hearings, organizing new members, and conducting strikes. The willingness and ability of a union to supply these services depends on the organizational goals of unions, the price unions can get for providing their services, the costs of organizing and representing workers, and the institutional and legal framework of collective bargaining.

The influence of these factors on the supply of union services can be shown graphically by a **supply curve of union services,** such as the supply curve S_1 in Figure 11.3. The supply curve of union services depicts the relationship between the price of union membership and the amount of union services labor unions are willing to provide. The supply curve is drawn with a positive slope, showing that labor unions are willing to supply more of their services at higher prices. If the price of union services is P_1, labor unions will supply U_1 amount of union services (point A); a higher amount of fees and dues of P_2 would lead to an increase in supply of union services to U_2 (point B).

The slope of the supply curve of union services is determined by two factors. The first is the nature of the *union services production function*. Union services such as organizing and bargaining are produced in a given technological environment by combining labor, capital, and entrepreneurial inputs. The supply curve in Figure 11.3 has a positive slope, on the assumption that the production of union services is subject to diminishing returns in the short run, and thus, increasing marginal costs. The slope of the supply curve of union services is also determined by the *organizational goals* of the union and its leadership. Unions do not have one particular goal, as firms do in maximizing profits. Most unions have multiple goals that include winning higher wages, increasing the number of members in the

FIGURE 11.3   THE SUPPLY CURVE OF UNION SERVICES

An increase in the price from P_1 to P_2 would cause unions to increase the supply of union services from U_1 to U_2 (point A to B). Higher costs of organizing or a more restrictive legal environment would shift the supply curve of union services from S_1 to S_2. At the price P_2, unions would reduce their supply of union services from U_2 to U_1 (point B to C).

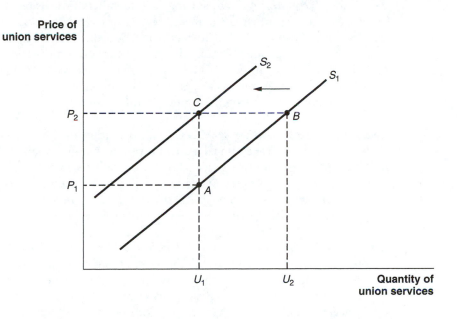

union, and maximizing the net income of the union.[18] Given the assumption of profit maximization, it is possible to derive one unique supply curve for a competitive firm. There is, however, a certain degree of indeterminacy in deriving the union's supply curve because the relationship between the price and quantity of services supplied depends on the goal or mix of goals of the union. If the dominant goal of unions is to increase the number of union members, the supply curve of union services will be relatively flat as unions try to keep dues and initiation fees as low as possible in their effort to expand union membership. If, on the other hand, the goal of unions is to maximize the net income of the union from fees and dues, the supply curve will probably have a steeper slope. Thus, rising marginal costs of

18 Alison Booth, *The Economics of the Trade Union* (Cambridge: Cambridge University Press, 1995), and Bruce E. Kaufman, "Models of Union Wage Determination: What Have We Learned since Dunlop and Ross?" *Industrial Relations* 41 (January 2002): 110–58.

producing union services ensure that the supply curve will be upward sloping, but the exact slope will depend on the goals and objectives of the union.

Whatever the exact slope of the supply curve, changes in the price of union services will cause a *movement* along the curve. A change in any other factor affecting the supply of union services will cause a *shift* in the supply curve. Some of the most important of these factors follow.

The Cost of Organizing   Organizing new members is an expensive activity for unions; one study estimated the marginal cost of organizing one new member to be between $784 and $2,994 in 2000 dollars.[19] Any factor that causes an increase in these costs of organizing will shift the supply curve of union services to the left, such as from S_1 to S_2 in Figure 11.3. Given the higher costs of organizing, at the prevailing level of fees and dues of, say, P_2, the union will be forced to reduce the supply of union services from U_2 (point B) to U_1 (point C).

The Costs of Representing Workers   The operation of a union is an expensive undertaking; the average annual expenditure per member is about $600 in 2004 dollars.[20] Approximately 45 percent of the operating expenses of a union go for salaries and wages of officers and staff, and 17 percent go for strike payments and pension benefits.[21] An increase in these costs of operating a union will shift the supply curve of union services to the left; a decrease will shift it to the right.[22]

Institutional Innovations and the Quality of Union Leadership   The supply curve of union services can also shift due either to innovations in the organizational structure of labor unions or changes in the quality of the union leadership. A particular type of organizational structure may allow the union to supply more of its services at a going price than others. For example, a switch from a craft union structure to an industrial union structure in a mass production industry such as steel or autos would shift the supply curve to the right. The supply of union services also depends on the organizational ability and personal drive of the union leaders. Dynamic and aggressive leaders such as Walter Reuther of the UAW or Cesar Chavez of the Farm Workers, for example, had dramatic effects on the supply of unionization in the auto industry in the 1930s and California agriculture in the 1970s, respectively.[23]

---

19   Paula B. Voos, "Union Organizing: Costs and Benefits," *Industrial and Labor Relations Review* 36, no. 4 (July 1983): 576–91.

20   Based on unpublished data provided by the International Association of Machinists.

21   Leo Troy, "American Unions and Their Wealth," *Industrial Relations* 14, no. 2 (May 1975): 134–44.

22   The size of the employer affects the cost of representing workers—the larger the employer, the lower the per member cost to the union of providing its services due to economies of scale. According to one study, for example, an important reason for the relatively low level of unionization among California farm workers is that the workers are scattered across several thousand different employers, making it quite expensive for a union to represent them. See Varden Fuller and John Mamer, "Constraints on California Farm Worker Unionization," *Industrial Relations* 17 (May 1978): 143–55.

23   Frank Carmier and William J. Easton, *Reuther* (Englewood Cliffs, N.J.: Prentice-Hall, 1970).

The Legal Environment The supply curve of union services will also shift with changes in labor legislation and court rulings. For example, a law that makes it easier for unions to organize new members would shift the supply curve to the right, as would legislation that permits public sector workers or foremen and supervisors to engage in collective bargaining. Adverse court rulings that restrict the union's ability to organize or its use of picketing, strikes, or boycotts would have the opposite effect, shifting the supply curve of union services to the left.[24]

The Equilibrium Level of Union Membership

The level of union membership is determined by the demand for union services on the part of workers and the supply of union services on the part of labor unions, as illustrated in Figure 11.4. Given the demand curve D_1 and supply curve S_1, the equilibrium amount of union services is U_1 and the equilibrium price is P_1 (point A). Given the assumption that each person consumes one unit of union services, U_1 is also the equilibrium level of union membership.

This model can be used to predict how changes in the factors underlying the demand and supply curves will affect the level of union membership. Any development that increases the net benefits of belonging to a union, for example, would shift the demand curve to the right, such as from D_1 to D_2 in Figure 11.4. More favorable attitudes toward unions would have the same result. In both cases, the equilibrium level of union membership would rise from U_1 to U_2 (point A to point B) and the equilibrium price from P_1 to P_2. Changes in the variables underlying the supply curve would also cause a change in union membership. More effective organizing techniques or the extension of bargaining rights to additional groups in the workforce would shift the supply curve to the right (not shown in Figure 11.4), causing union membership to increase from its original level.

This demand and supply model of union membership is a useful analytic device because it shows the major factors that determine why some workers are union mem-

⟐ SEE
Empirical Evidence 11-1:
Who Belongs to Unions, p. 604.

bers and others are not. Details regarding what group of workers are more likely to belong to unions are highlighted in Empirical Evidence 11-1. It also provides useful predictions about how union membership changes in response to various economic, historical, or political events. This model also has its defects. It is probably not very realistic in today's environment, for example, to assume that the amount of fees and dues charged by unions will rise or fall very quickly to restore equilibrium. (Unions in the early 1900s, however, did sometimes raise or lower dues and fees to balance the number of members and available jobs.) The assumption of market equilibrium is also unrealistic, because not all workers who desire union membership at the going price are actually able

---

24 For example, in January 1998, a director of the National Labor Relations Board's Philadelphia office ruled that doctors who worked with an HMO remained "skilled professionals with the characteristics of independent business people." As such, they were not allowed to organize. See Ronald Smothers, "Labor Board Orders Hearing on Doctor Union," *New York Times* (10 September 1998): B6. Since that ruling, the NLRB has decided to hold full-fledged hearings on the issue of whether doctors should be allowed to form unions.

FIGURE 11.4   THE EQUILIBRIUM LEVEL OF UNION MEMBERSHIP

The equilibrium level of union services is U_1 (point A) where demand and supply are equal. An increase in the net benefits of belonging to a union would shift the demand curve from D_1 to D_2, resulting in an increase in union services from U_1 to U_2 and a rise in the price from P_1 to P_2 (point A to B).

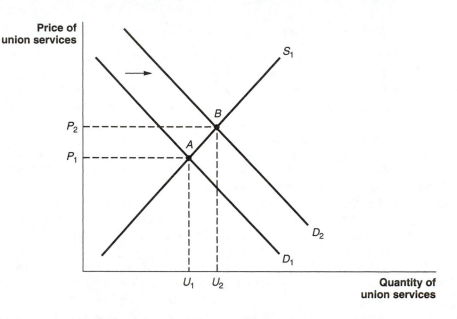

to purchase it, either because fellow workmates don't also want union membership, or the worker cannot get hired at a unionized firm.[25] One survey found, for example, that 32 percent of nonunion workers would vote for a union if given the opportunity.[26]

Union Membership over Time

The demand and supply model of union membership can be used to explain the pattern of union growth over time. As shown in Figure 11.5, the total number of union members in the United States grew tremendously over the past half-century,

25   See John Abowd and Henry S. Farber, "Job Queues and the Union Status of Workers," *Industrial and Labor Relations Review* 35, no. 3 (April 1982): 354–67, and Mary B. Hampton and John S. Heywood, "Reservation Wages and the Union Job Queue: A Sample Selection Approach," *Bulletin of Economic Research* 45 (October 1993): 315–28.

26   See Richard Freeman and Joel Rogers, *What Do Workers Want?* (Ithaca: Cornell University Press, 1999).

TOTAL UNION MEMBERSHIP AND MEMBERSHIP AS A PERCENTAGE OF EMPLOYMENT, 1930–2003

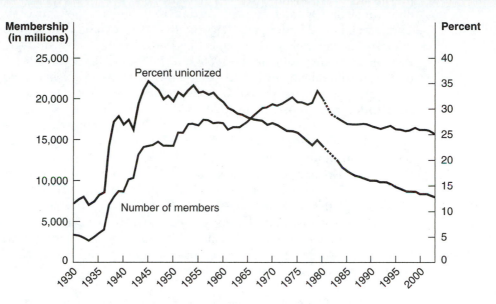

NOTE: Figures excluded Canadian membership. Percentage of nonagricultural employment, 1930–1976; percentage of total wage and salary employment, 1977–2003.

SOURCE: U.S. Department of Labor, Bureau of Labor Statistics, *Handbook of Labor Statistics* (December 1980): table 165; Eva E. Jacobs, ed. *Handbook of U.S. Labor Statistics* (Lanham, MD: Bernan Press, 1998: p. 321; Bureau of Labor Statistics, *Employment and Earnings* (January 2004).

from 3.4 million members in 1930 to 15.8 million members in 2003.[27] Another million workers in 2003 were represented by unions at their places of work although they were not themselves dues-paying members. The growth in union membership has not followed a smooth upward trend, but shows an irregular pattern of spurts, such as during 1935 to 1954 and 1965 to 1970, interspersed with periods of slow or stagnant growth, such as 1930 to 1934, 1955 to 1964, and 1970 to 1980. Since 1980, union membership in the United States has dropped sharply, registering a net decline of over 4.3 million members between 1980 and 2003.

A second way to look at union growth is by calculating the number of union members as a proportion of employment in the economy. These data are also

---

[27] The data in Figure 11.5 are not strictly comparable. Up to 1980 the data come from membership figures reported to the BLS by individual unions; after 1980 the data are from the *Current Population Survey*. The CPS membership estimates are substantially lower, partly because the earlier data included a large number of retirees.

shown in Figure 11.5. (For 1930 to 1980, nonagricultural employment is used as the base for comparison; for 1980 to 2003 the base is total wage and salary employment.) Union membership as a percentage of the workforce gives an entirely different picture of union growth. Starting from a unionization rate of slightly over 13 percent in 1935, the percentage of the nonagricultural workforce that was unionized nearly tripled, to 36 percent by 1945, declined slowly through 1954, and then fell off more rapidly in the 1960s and 1970s, until in 1980 only 24.7 percent of nonagricultural employees were union members. As a percentage of total wage and salary employment, the rate of unionization in the United States declined substantially, 23.0 percent in 1980 to 12.9 percent in 2003. Figure 11.5 reveals, therefore, that whereas the absolute number of union members continued to grow up to 1980, employment grew even faster, causing the percentage of the workforce unionized to steadily decline.

Economists have devoted considerable research attention to identifying the factors behind the pattern of union growth. Although space precludes an extensive discussion of this literature, the most important points are summarized below. Generally, when union membership grows, either the demand for union membership has increased (benefits to membership have increased and/or costs of membership have declined) or the supply of union services has increased (the cost of providing those services has declined), or both.

The 1930 to 1954 Period   The rise in union membership during this period was heavily influenced by a change in the legal environment. The **National Labor Relations Act (NLRA),** passed in 1935, prohibited various antiunion *unfair labor practices* by employers such as firing, demoting, or harassing workers for union activities. The NLRA decreased the cost of joining a union, shifting the demand for

SEE
Policy Application 11-1: The Legal Framework of Collective Bargaining, p. 599.

union services to the right. The NLRA also established the *union representation election* process, which required employers to bargain with a union whenever a majority of workers vote for union representation. This effectively reduced the cost of organizing for unions, shifting the supply of union services to the right. Policy Application 11-1 describes in greater detail the content and history of the legal framework for collective bargaining.

A structural change in union organization (i.e., institutional innovation) also influenced the growth in this period. In 1935 eight unions broke away from the **American Federation of Labor (AFL),** a federation of unions largely organized along craft lines, to form a new federation, the **Congress of Industrial Organizations (CIO),** which favored an industrial form of unionism (e.g., a union that represents all workers in an industry regardless of occupation or craft). This form of organization turned out to be much more efficient, causing a rightward shift in the supply of union services.

Workers in industries known for their monotony of tasks and for their potential job-related risks gain tremendously in terms of the public-goods nature of improvements that can be gained through collective action. The growth in manufacturing employment of 77 percent between 1930 and 1955 meant that many more workers were now employed in such an industry, resulting in a rightward shift in the demand for union services.

The potential of being involved in a strike or losing one's job can be strong deterrents to joining a union. The booming economy during World War II reduced the potential cost of losing one's job. In addition, the War Labor Board took an active role in settling disputes (thus reducing the chances of a costly strike) so that the war effort would not be interrupted. Both of these factors shifted the demand to the right.

The 1955 to 1980 Period   The factor most likely to have led to the slower growth in union membership, and the actual *decline* in percentage of workers unionized, during the 1955 to 1980 period was the shift from a goods-producing to a service-producing economy.[28] Between 1955 and 1980, employment in goods-producing industries (mining, construction, and manufacturing) increased only 25 percent, while employment in the service industries grew by 115 percent. Workers in service-producing industries don't gain as much from improving public-goods characteristics of the work environment and, coupled with the fact that white-collar workers have a long tradition of shunning unions, the demand for union services shifted left during this period of service-sector growth.

The shift of employment to the southern region of the United States resulted in a new legal environment in which it was more costly to organize. Employment in the South grew 142 percent between 1955 and 1980, compared with 79 percent growth for the entire United States. The South has a long tradition of **right-to-work** laws (which protect workers' right to keep the job even if they don't belong to the union), making it more costly to supply union services, which, in turn, shifts the supply of union services to the left.[29]

Many of the pay-equity and public-goods issues that drive workers to join unions started being provided for legislatively during this time period. For example, the Occupational Safety and Health Act, the Civil Rights Act, and pension reform laws have all supplanted many of the benefits workers gained from joining a union. As a result of additional legislative protections, the demand for union services shifted left.

While employers in the United States have always resisted the unionization of their workers, many observers felt that the degree of employer resistance to

---

28   One study concluded that 44 percent of the decline in the rate of unionization in the economy between 1956 and 1978 could be tied to the changing composition of employment among industries. See George R. Neumann and Ellen R. Rissman, "Where Have All the Union Members Gone?" *Journal of Labor Economics* 2 (April 1984): 175–92.

29   See Daphne Gottieb Jaras and Allen Ponak, "Mandatory Agency Shop Laws as an Explanation of Canada–U.S. Union Density Divergence," *Journal of Labor Research* 22 (Summer 2001): 541–68. One study documents the difficulty unions had in organizing new manufacturing firms in the South between 1975 and 1985. See Bruce E. Kaufman, Robert C. Eisenstadt, and Madelyn V. Young, "Union Organizing Successes in New Manufacturing Plants in Three Southern States," *Labor Law Journal* 37 (August 1986): 487–93. Also see William J. Moore, "The Determinants and Effects of Right-to-Work Laws: A Review of the Recent Literature," *Journal of Labor Research* 19 (Summer 1998): 445–69, for more recent evidence on the impact of right-to-work laws.

unionization increased noticeably during this time period.[30] One study concluded, for example, that while in the 1950s a number of companies expressed at least reluctant willingness to coexist with unions in the workplace, by the late 1970s keeping the firm nonunion had become "indisputably the highest priority objective in the employee relations area."[31] Increased management resistance increased the cost of membership to workers, shifting their demand curve left.

While most of the movement during this period was away from unions, a couple of factors helped maintain the overall growth in union numbers. President Kennedy's **Executive Order 10988** in 1962 allowed federal government workers to engage in collective bargaining; this was followed by similar provisions at the state and local levels. In addition, the development of employee associations (such as the American Association of University Professors) provided an alternative organizational structure for collective bargaining that better suits the needs of professionals and white-collar workers than the traditional industrial-type unions. Both of these factors had the effect of shifting the supply curve to the right.

The 1981 to 2003 Period While union membership continued to grow slowly up to 1980, in the next 24 years it suffered the worst declines since the 1920s. In the space of two decades organized labor lost over four million dues-paying members, with some of the most powerful unions, such as the United Automobile Workers and United Steel Workers, being particularly hard hit. This sharp decline in the power and influence of the labor movement has been accompanied by a debate over the future prospects of labor unions—are they a relic of the past that will continue to shrink in importance, or will unions rebound from their current difficulties with new programs and policies that appeal to the mass of the unorganized?

The decline in union membership since 1980 has a number of causes.[32] An important one is that employment in many unionized industries and firms dropped sharply due to large-scale plant closings and layoffs. Plant closings and layoffs result in a leftward shift of the demand curve for union services. One reason for the sharp decline in employment in unionized industries was the economic recessions of 1981 to 1982, 1990 to 1991, and 2001. A second factor was the deregulation of certain industries that had been union strongholds, such as airlines, telephone communication, and trucking.[33] Without the barrier to entry afforded by regulation, high-cost unionized firms soon felt great competitive pressure from new nonunion firms, resulting in bankruptcies and layoffs. A third factor was the growing inroads

---

30   Peter J. Pestillo, "Learning to Live without the Union," *Proceedings of the Thirty-First Annual Meeting* (Madison, Wis.: IRRA, 1978): 232–39. This resistance has extended into the 1990s as evidenced in U.S. Department of Labor, *OSBP Commission on the Future of Worker–Management Relations: Fact Finding Report* (May 1994).

31   See D. Quinn Mills, "Management Performance," in Jack Stieber et al., *U.S. Industrial Relations 1950–1980: A Critical Assessment* (Madison, Wis.: IRRA, 1980): 99–128.

32   See the collection of articles in James Bennett and Bruce Kaufman, eds., *The Future of Private Sector Unionism in the United States* (Armonk, N.Y.: M. E. Sharpe, 2001).

33   Michael Belzer, *Sweatshops on Wheels: Winners and Losers in Trucking Deregulation* (New York: Oxford University Press, 2000), and Barry Hirsch and David Macpherson, "Earnings, Rents, and Competition in the Airline Labor Market," *Journal of Labor Economics* 18 (January 2000): 125–55.

made by foreign competitors in domestic markets, symbolized by the Japanese invasion in the auto industry. Fourth, the sharp rise in the union/nonunion wage differential in the 1970s and the relative stability of this high differential in the 1980s and through the early 2000s caused many unionized companies in industries such as construction and mining to lose market share to lower-cost nonunion competitors.[34]

Other reasons identified for the leftward shift in demand for union services include (1) the ongoing change in the structure of the economy and the workforce, which has resulted in a greater proportion of female workers and workers in white-collar and service jobs;[35] (2) an improvement in human resource management practices in American firms and a decrease in the proportion of nonunion workers dissatisfied with their pay and job conditions; and (3) a decline in the confidence workers have in the effectiveness of unions.

In addition, the ability of employers to lawfully frustrate union organizing efforts in recent years has increased the cost of organizing, shifting the supply curve for union services to the left.[36]

So what does the future hold for union membership? While the trend from 1980 to 2003 looks fairly ominous, some hold out hope of reversal of this trend.[37] Among the factors union leaders predict will reverse the trend include a major shift of resources to new organizing by the AFL-CIO under president John Sweeny; innovative organizing methods utilizing the Internet, college students, and community activists; and persisting fears of job insecurity among a large segment of the workforce.

The Union–Management Bargaining Process

In unionized firms the levels of wages, fringe benefits, and other conditions of employment are determined through the process of collective bargaining. The preceding section sketched the institutional framework in which unions are formed

---

[34] Employees cited concerns about increased domestic competition as the most important factor influencing negotiations in the mid-1990s. See Joel Cutcher-Gershenfeld, Thomas A. Kochan, and James Calhoun Wells, "How Do Labor and Management View Collective Bargaining?" *Monthly Labor Review* (October 1998): 23–31. On the role of the union wage premium in union decline, see Barry Hirsch and Edward Schumacher, "Private Sector Union Density and the Wage Premium: Past, Present, and Future," *Journal of Labor Research* 22 (Summer 2001): 487–518.

[35] Women, typically being less attached to the labor market than men, and white-collar workers have long histories of low demand for union services. See C. Timothy Koeller, "Union Activity and Decline in American Trade Union Membership," *Journal of Labor Research* 15 (Winter 1994): 19–32, and Keith A. Bender, "The Changing Determinants of U.S. Unionism: An Analysis Using Worker-Level Data," *Journal of Labor Research* 18 (Summer 1997): 403–23.

[36] See Richard Rothstein, "Union Strength in the United States: Lessons from the UPS Strike," *International Labour Review* 136 (Winter 1997): 469–91, and Morris Kleiner, "Intensity of Management Resistance: Understanding the Decline of Unionization in the Private Sector," *Journal of Labor Research* 22 (Summer 2001): 519–40.

[37] Charles McDonald, "U.S. Union Membership in Future Decades: A Trade Unionist's Perspective," *Industrial Relations* 31 (Winter 1992): 13–30, and Nancy Mills, "New Strategies for Union Survival and Growth," *Journal of Labor Research* 22 (Summer 2001): 599–614.

FIGURE 11.6   THE TIME PATH OF WAGE DEMANDS IN A LABOR NEGOTIATION

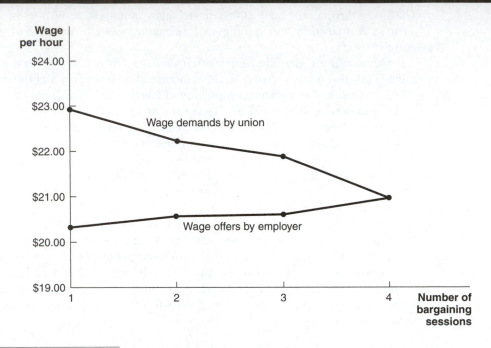

SOURCE: Based on Gary A. Hall and William R. Schriver, "Bluffing in the Bargaining Process: An Empirical Test," *Proceedings of the Thirtieth Annual Meeting* (Madison, Wis., IRRA, 1977): 286–93.

and in which collective bargaining takes place. This section examines the actual process of bargaining, focusing on such topics as a formal model of labor negotiations and alternative methods of dispute resolution. The topic of union bargaining goals is fully and formally developed in the appendix.

Several key features of the bargaining process are illustrated in Figure 11.6, which shows the results of an actual labor negotiation. The data come from a study by Gary Hall and William Schriver of the bargaining between the Tennessee Valley Authority (TVA) and the Tennessee Valley Trades and Labor Council (TVTLC). The TVTLC is an umbrella organization that coordinates the bargaining for the 16 unions that represent TVA workers. Hall and Schriver obtained information on the wage rate demanded by the unions and the average wage offered by the TVA in each of four formal sessions of bargaining.

The initial union demand was $22.92 per hour (in 2003 dollars), and the initial offer of the employer was $20.32 a difference of 11 percent. As the bargaining proceeded, the unions lowered their demand while the TVA raised its offer, until at the fourth bargaining session a settlement was reached at $20.98 an hour. Though both sides made concessions, the final outcome was much closer to the employer's initial offer than it was to the unions' (4 percent above the TVA's initial offer, 9 percent below the unions').[30]

These data illustrate three features of the bargaining process that the theory in this chapter will attempt to explain. The first is the size of the initial demands that the unions and the TVA put on the table. Why did the unions pick $22.92 as their initial demand and not a figure such as $23.00 or even $30.00? Similarly, what factors influenced the employer to start out with $20.32? The second feature is the process of concession. Given the wide distance separating the two sides at the beginning of the negotiations, both had to substantially reduce what they were asking to reach a settlement. To understand the bargaining process, it is necessary to discover what factors motivated the TVA and the unions to make concessions from their initial positions, and why it took four bargaining sessions for them to complete this process of offer and counteroffer. The third, and perhaps most important, feature of bargaining is the point of settlement. Why did the unions and the employer ultimately agree to $20.98 per hour, and not some other amount? Of equal interest, was it possible to reach a settlement without a strike? (In this case it was.)

A Model of the Bargaining Process

The relative bargaining power of the employer and the union determines in whose favor the settlement will go. Given this insight, is it possible to predict the wage rate the two sides will actually settle on? In an attempt to answer this question, economists have developed a number of formal models of union–management bargaining. This section briefly discusses some of the key features of these models and their implications for understanding the causes of strikes and the determination of wages in unionized labor markets.

The Contract Zone   Explicit or implicit in nearly every bargaining model is the concept of a **contract zone.** The contract zone defines the range of wage rates within which a settlement is possible. The upper limit of the contract zone is determined by the maximum wage rate that the union would desire to obtain; the lower limit of the contract zone is determined by the minimum wage rate that the firm would desire to have. Between the upper limit of the union and the lower limit of the firm is where the bargaining over wages will take place and where a settlement will be reached.

An example of a contract zone for a competitive firm is illustrated in Figure 11.7. It is assumed that the L_1 workers in the firm are ordered along the horizontal axis from left to right on the basis of seniority, the worker at L_1 being the least senior. The lower end of the contract zone is the market-determined wage

---

38   The same result was found in a study of 43 negotiations in the public sector. See Daniel Hamermesh, "Who 'Wins' in Wage Bargaining?" *Industrial and Labor Relations Review* 26, no. 4 (July 1973): 1146–49.

FIGURE 11.7 THE CONTRACT ZONE

The contract zone is the area between the wage rates W_1 and W_2. Below W_1 the firm would be unable to attract a workforce; above W_2 the majority of the union membership would lose their jobs.

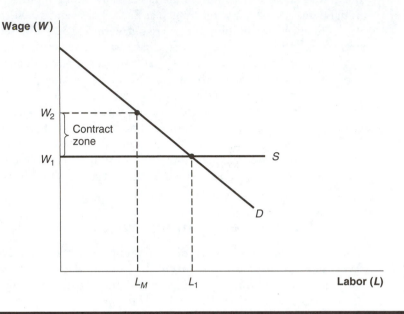

W_1. Even if the firm had unlimited bargaining power, it would not want to negotiate a wage below W_1, since all of its workers would quit and seek work elsewhere. It is evident that the union's demand for higher wages also has limits, since at some point a majority of the L_1 union members currently employed in the firm, denoted by person L_M, who is at the median point in the seniority distribution, will lose their jobs, and thus will vote to reject a proposed contract with any higher wage. This upper limit, accordingly, is the wage W_2. The contract zone or range of possible settlements, then, is the distance $W_2 - W_1$.

Union and Employer Reaction Functions The next task of bargaining models is to predict the actual wage rate in the contract zone to which the union and the employer agree at the end of the negotiations. Unfortunately, the nature of the bargaining process is such that it is quite difficult, because of the strategic interaction that takes place between the bargainers, to construct models that are realistic yet analytically tractable. Strategic interaction arises from the interdependency between the wage demands of the union and the company; the size of the company's wage offer, for example, influences the union's demand, which then causes the company

FIGURE 11.8   EMPLOYER AND UNION REACTION FUNCTIONS

The size of the contract zone is W_1 to W_4. The union's resistance curve $W_u(t)$ and the firm's concession curve $W_f(t)$ trace the time path of wage offers and counteroffers made by each side during the negotiations. The initial union demand is W_3, the initial offer by the company is W_2. Over the course of the bargaining the area of disagreement narrows, until at time $\bar{t}$ an agreement is reached at the wage $\overline{W}$.

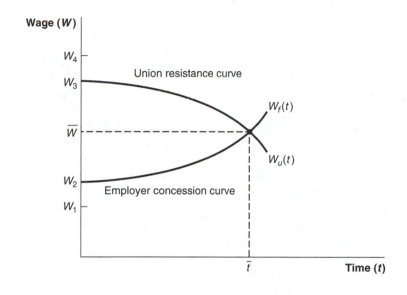

to modify its offer, which causes a further change in the union's position, and so on. This is exactly the same problem that confronts models of price determination under oligopoly.

Following on oligopoly theory, one approach to modeling union–management bargaining is to construct **reaction functions** for the company and the union.[39] Reaction functions are a pair of mathematical equations that predict the wage demands of each of the bargainers over the n rounds of the negotiations. A graphic representation of a set of reaction functions is given in Figure 11.8. The upper and lower limits of the contract zone are, respectively, W_4 and W_1; the horizontal axis measures days of lapsed bargaining time (t). The day $\bar{t}$ is the strike deadline. The curves $W_u(t)$ and $W_f(t)$ trace out the wage demands of the union and the wage offers of the firm, as predicted by the reaction functions. Following a famous bargaining

---

39   See Bruce E. Kaufman, "Bargaining Theory, Inflation, and Cyclical Strike Activity in Manufacturing," *Industrial and Labor Relations Review* 34, no. 3 (April 1981): 333–55.

model developed in the 1930s by J. R. Hicks, the curves $W_u(t)$ and $W_f(t)$ are called, respectively, the **union's resistance curve** and the **employer's concession curve**.[40] These curves show that at the beginning of the bargaining, the union's initial demand is a wage of W_3, and the firm's initial offer is W_2. Note that even at this first step of the negotiations, both sides have compromised by demanding wages that are inside the upper and lower limits of the contract zone. As the negotiations proceed, both the company and the union make further concessions, gradually narrowing the distance that separates their positions. Finally, at the strike deadline $\bar{t}$, the resistance and concession curves intersect, and an agreement is reached at a wage of $\overline{W}$.

To predict the actual time path of wage demands, it is necessary to specify the decision rule that each of the bargainers uses in modifying its position. One approach bases the decision rule on what is called **aspiration level theory**.[41] According to this theory, people have goals or aspirations that they seek to obtain. Studies in psychology have shown that a person's aspirations behave in a predictable way, rising with greater than expected success and falling with less than expected success. In calculating their optimal wage demands, both the union and the company negotiators implicitly estimate what the other side's demand will be and how fast the opponent will concede during the negotiations. Assume, for example, that the union negotiator believes that the company's initial offer will be $20 an hour and that this offer will then be increased to $21 in the second round. What happens to the union's wage demand if the company's initial offer is only $19 an hour and in the second negotiating session the company again offers only $19?

The failure of the company's wage offer to meet the union negotiator's expectations should cause a reevaluation of the union's demand. The union negotiator might conclude that he or she had overestimated the company's vulnerability to strike costs or underestimated the value the company places on holding down labor costs. If the union bargainer becomes convinced that the company's position is not a bluff but is, in fact, the firm's actual bargaining position, aspiration level theory predicts that the union negotiator will respond by lowering the union's demand from its initial position. Had the company's initial wage offer been more than the union anticipated, the opposite result will be predicted; the union bargainer will raise his or her expectations of what was attainable and will concede less than originally planned.[42]

Aspiration level theory provides several important insights into both the resistance and the concession curves in Figure 11.8 and the actual practice of collective bargaining. The first has to do with the process of concession and the convergence of the reaction functions. Earlier it was argued that often the union and the company

---

40 John R. Hicks, *The Theory of Wages*, 2d ed. (New York: St. Martin's Press, 1965). Although Hicks's concession and resistance curves resemble the reaction functions in Figure 11.8, analytically they are quite different.

41 See Walton and McKersie, *A Behavioral Theory of Labor Negotiations*, 42, and Reinhard Teitz, ed., *Aspiration Levels in Bargaining and Economic Decision Making* (Berlin: Springer-Verlag, 1983). This type of decision rule is often represented mathematically as an "error correcting" model.

42 Experimental evidence in support of this proposition is provided in G. A. Yukel, "Effects of Opponent's Initial Offer, Concession Magnitude, and Concession Frequency on Bargaining Behavior," *Journal of Personality and Social Psychology* 30 (1974): 332–35.

enter the negotiations with overly optimistic expectations of what they will be able to win—the union expects (or at least hopes) that the company will concede faster than it actually does, while the company hopes for moderate or "responsible" demands from the union. The result in most cases is that neither side gives in as much as the other expects, and as aspiration theory predicts, the two sides mutually lower their estimates of what is attainable, resulting in concessions and a movement along the resistance and concession curves toward the point of agreement.

A second insight provided by aspiration level theory concerns the optimal use of bluffing in labor negotiations. The usual purpose in bluffing is to give the negotiator some room to make concessions or to shift the opponent's estimates of what is most important to the negotiator. Bluffing can also work to a bargainer's disadvantage, however, since at some point the bluff (if it is truly a bluff) will have to be given away as a concession, and the larger that concession is, the more the other side is motivated to toughen its demands.[43]

Aspiration level theory also explains the incremental way labor negotiators move toward a settlement. One might imagine an exasperated company negotiator saying to his or her union counterpart, "Let's quit kidding around. You and I both know we're going to settle for a raise of $2 an hour so let's get it over with. That's my offer!" Unfortunately, for the company negotiator, "coming clean" like that usually results not in a settlement, but in an escalation of the union's demand—the company's immediate offer of $2 raises the union bargainer's aspiration level and its demand. This example also points out what is perhaps one of the most difficult tasks facing labor negotiators: how to make concessions without the other side reading them as signs of weakness.[44]

Not all labor negotiations exhibit the pattern of mutual concession and convergence to a settlement pictured in Figure 11.8. Probably the most famous exception is the style of bargaining used by the General Electric Co. in the 1950s and 1960s known as **Boulwarism,** named after the company vice-president who developed it.[45] In this approach, the company made one firm and final offer to the unions that they could either accept or reject. The company's offer was made only after considerable research and communication with the employees and was billed as a fair and equitable settlement that it would not improve upon. The unions that bargained with G.E. strongly opposed Boulwarism, since it gave them no active role

---

43 This is shown in John Cross, *The Economics of Bargaining* (New York: Basic Books, 1969), Chapter 8. Laboratory experiments show there is an inverse *U*-shaped relationship between a bargainer's initial demand and the ultimate outcome: a person who demands too little gets little; a person who demands too much also gets little. See John Magenau and Dean Pruitt, "The Social Psychology of Bargaining: A Theoretical Synthesis," in Geoffrey Stephenson and Christopher Brotherton, eds., *Industrial Relations: A Social Psychological Approach* (New York: John Wiley and Sons, 1979), 184.

44 An example of this type of behavior is revealed in the speeches by John Foster Dulles, secretary of state in the Eisenhower administration. Whenever the Russians made a concession, Dulles argued that they were weakening and the United States should toughen its position even further. See O. R. Holsti, "The Belief System and National Images: A Case Study," *Journal of Conflict Resolution* 6, no. 3 (September 1962): 244–52.

45 See Herbert R. Northrup, *Boulwarism: The Labor Relations Policies of the General Electric Company: Their Implications for Public Policy and Management Action* (Ann Arbor, Mich.: Bureau of Industrial Relations, University of Michigan, 1964).

in the wage determination process. After a 122-day strike in 1969, General Electric abandoned Boulwarism in favor of a more conventional style of bargaining.

Bargaining Power

The ability of the union to resist having to accept lower wages and the ability of the employer not to concede higher wages depend on the relative power position of each side. As one study on the subject has put it, *power* is the essence of collective bargaining.[46] Fundamental to understanding the process of wage determination in collective bargaining, therefore, is a consideration of bargaining power and the sources of power available to the union and the employer.[47]

Bargaining power may be defined as one's ability to induce an opponent to agree on one's own terms.[48] The origin of bargaining power is twofold. One determinant of bargaining power is the ability of party A to impose costs on party B if B does not agree to A's terms. The second determinant of party A's bargaining power is the ability to insulate itself from retaliatory cost-imposing sanctions by party B. This description of bargaining power suggests that one side's ability to win its demands depends on how costly it can make disagreement for the other while minimizing its own costs. Much of collective bargaining involves jockeying back and forth between the union and employer as each seeks ways either to strengthen its own sanctions against the other side or to protect itself from the cost-imposing ability of its opponent.

The Strike as a Source of Bargaining Power   The single most important source of bargaining power for the union is the threat of a strike; for the firm, it is the ability to resist a strike. A strike imposes costs on both sides, since the firm loses production and profits while the workers lose earnings from work. The relative bargaining power of the firm vis-à-vis the union hinges on whether the costs of a strike fall more heavily on the firm or the workers. A number of factors are important in determining the costs imposed on employers and workers by a strike.[49]

The financial loss imposed on a firm by a strike depends significantly on the type of product the firm produces. Companies that produce a durable good, such as coal or steel, are better able to take a strike because they can build up a large

---

46   Samuel B. Bacharach and Edward J. Lawler, *Bargaining: Power, Tactics, and Outcomes* (San Francisco: Jossey-Bass, 1981), 43.

47   Numerous case studies of the determinants of union bargaining power are presented in Charles Craypo, *The Economics of Collective Bargaining* (Washington, D.C.: Bureau of National Affairs, 1986). Also see Martin Roderick, *Bargaining Power* (New York: Oxford University Press, 1992), and Stanley Aronowitz, and Jonathan Cutler, "Can Unions Find a Strategy for Labor Market Strength?" *Working USA* 2 (May–June 1998): 51–64.

48   The concept of bargaining power is developed in much greater detail in Neil Chamberlain, *A General Theory of Economic Process* (New York: Harper and Row, 1955).

49   See Bruce Kaufman, "Research on Strike Models and Outcomes in the 1980s: Accomplishments and Shortcomings," and David Lewin, Olivia Mitchell, and Peter Scherer, eds., *Research Frontiers in Industrial Relations and Human Resources* (Madison, Wis.: IRRA, 1992), 77–130.

stockpile of the good prior to the walkout and then sell from the inventory during the strike. A firm that produces a perishable good or service, such as lettuce or airline travel, is much more vulnerable to a strike because its sales are immediately cut off and often cannot be made up after the strike is over. Similarly, a firm whose plants manufacture unrelated products also has more bargaining power than a firm that is vertically integrated (that is, when one plant produces a product used by another of the company's plants).

The balance of bargaining power in a strike is also affected by the firm's production technology. In labor-intensive industries, such as apparel or construction, a strike will quickly cripple the employer's ability to produce, since labor is crucial to the production process. The opposite is true in highly automated, capital-intensive industries, such as telephones or petroleum refining, where supervisory personnel can keep the operations going for several months and, in some cases, a year or more.

The overall state of the economy, as well as specific economic conditions in the industry or locality, can also have an important impact on the relative bargaining power of the union and firm. During prosperous economic periods, unions generally enjoy a relative power advantage since they are more likely to have built up some savings to withstand a strike, and they are also less likely to be replaced by strikebreakers. The firm is more vulnerable to a strike during prosperous economic times because of the much greater loss in sales it will suffer. During recessions, management may welcome a strike as a way to work off excess inventory, while workers are reluctant to strike out of fear of losing their jobs.

The **structure of bargaining** is of crucial importance in determining the relative power position of the union and the firm. In general, the negotiator who enjoys the advantage of relative size also enjoys a favorable power position. In an industry such as trucking, where a large union faces many small trucking companies, the union is much better able to stand the costs of a strike than the employer. The reverse is true in an industry such as chemicals, where large, multiplant companies face small, independent unions in single-plant bargaining.[50]

Bargaining power is based not only on objective factors such as the level of unemployment or the structure of bargaining, but also on subjective, psychological factors. The most important of these is the *militancy* and solidarity of the union membership and of the management of the firm. Militancy increases one side's bargaining power because the other side knows that it can prevail only if it is willing to accept a long and bitter strike. An employer facing a union whose members are unified and "ready to walk" will be likely to concede much more in bargaining than if the rank and file is apathetic or torn into competing factions. A union may also have second thoughts about striking when it faces an employer who is known for taking a hard-nosed, no-nonsense approach to bargaining.

---

50 See Lawrence Mishel, "The Structural Determinants of Union Bargaining Power," *Industrial and Labor Relations Review* 40 (October 1986): 90–104. Also see Marick F. Masters, "Union Wealth: The Bargaining Power Implications," *Journal of Labor Research* 18 (Winter 1997): 91–109, for an evaluation of the role that size and financial strength played in maintaining union strength between 1979 and 1993.

Other Sources of Bargaining Power   The threat of a strike is not the only source of power in collective bargaining. To impose costs on a company, a union can sponsor a **consumer boycott** of its product. A boycott attempts to increase the costs of disagreement for a firm by encouraging consumers to stop buying the company's products until it agrees to the union's demands. Consumer boycotts are generally rather ineffective, although the boycott of California lettuce and table grapes led by the United Farm Workers in the early 1970s is an exception.[51] A union can also increase its bargaining power through a **work-to-rule slowdown,** where workers scrupulously follow every regulation governing the performance of their jobs, substantially slowing down the rate of production. An example of this tactic was the work slowdown instigated by American Airlines pilots during the early part of 1999.[52] Finally, a source of bargaining power for unions that has lately gained considerable publicity are so-called **corporate campaign tactics.**[53] These tactics are typically used when the union's strike threat is too weak to be successful. The basic idea is to jeopardize the profits or public image of companies or individuals linked to the target employer—such as its institutional shareholders, creditors, or companies with common board members—through public demonstrations, shareholder elections, or shifts in pension funds, causing these companies to pressure the primary employer for a settlement.

Employers can also adopt various tactics to increase their bargaining power. One approach has been for companies to establish a system of **strike insurance.** Under such a plan, companies enter into a formal agreement that if one of the members is struck, the others will provide it with financial assistance.[54]

Outcomes of the Bargaining Process

The bargaining model, along with consideration of the balance of bargaining power, can be used to explain what are probably the two most important outcomes of the collective bargaining process: the determination of the wage rate and the occurrence of strikes. Wage determination is examined first.

Wage Determination   Shown in Figure 11.9, graph (a), are the demand and supply curves for labor for a competitive firm. In a nonunion labor market, competitive market forces are the main determinant of the wage at which labor services are

---

51   A recent example of a union-led boycott can be found in François Shalom, "Unions Rage at Kenworth," *The Gazette* (11 April 1996): D1. The Canadian Auto Workers Union called for a boycott across Canada of Kenworth products to protest the closing of a truck plant.

52   See Laurence Zuckerman, "U.S. Judge Orders Pilots in Sickout to Return to Job," *New York Times* (11 February 1999): A1. Also see Gary Slutsker, "What's Good for Caterpillar . . ." *Forbes* (7 December 1992): 108–11, for another example.

53   See Herbert R. Northrup, "Union Corporate Campaigns and Inside Games as a Strike Form," *Employee Relations Law Journal* 19 (Spring 1994): 507–49.

54   See Pierre-Yves Cremieux, "Does Strike Insurance Matter? Evidence from the Airline Industry's Mutual Aid Pact," *Journal of Labor Research* (Spring 1996): 201–17. Other examples are discussed in Laszlo Goerke, "Strike Pay and Employer's Strike Insurance," *Metroeconomics* 21 (August 2000): 284–303.

FIGURE 11.9

WAGE DETERMINATION IN A UNION AND NONUNION LABOR MARKET

The wage paid by a competitive firm—graph (a)—would be, in the absence of a union, the market-determined wage W_1. If the workers unionize, however, the contract zone becomes much larger, such as $W_3 - W_1$, since only at W_3 do a majority of union members lose their jobs.

The actual wage agreed to in collective bargaining is a product of the bargaining process—graph (b). Assuming this wage to be $\overline{W}$, the union raises the wage by $\overline{W} - W_1$.

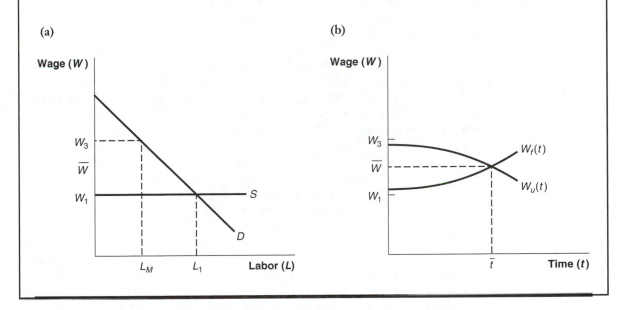

(a)

(b)

bought and sold. As was shown in Chapter 6, if the market fits the assumptions of the perfectly competitive model (zero mobility costs, perfect information, and so on), no individual firm has enough market power to pay less than the equilibrium wage of W_1, and no individual worker has the cost-imposing ability to force the firm to pay more than W_1. In this case, wage rates are completely market determined, much like the price of a bushel of wheat or a share of stock. In the presence of collective bargaining, however, the upper limit of the contract zone is much higher than the competitive market outcome, say the wage W_3 in graph (a), since it is only at W_3 that the majority of the union membership $L_1 - L_M$ lose their jobs. The range of potential wage outcomes in a unionized setting, therefore, is the distance $W_3 - W_1$.

The contract zone defines only the upper and lower limits to the wage bargain. The actual wage agreed upon by the firm and union is the outcome of the bargaining process. This outcome is illustrated in graph (b) of Figure 11.9. It shows the union's resistance curve $W_u(t)$ and the employer's concession curve $W_f(t)$. The initial wage demands of the employer and the union are relatively far apart; as the bargaining progresses, the threat of a strike induces both sides to compromise, until at the strike deadline $\bar{t}$ an agreement is reached setting the wage rate at $\overline{W}$.

Several points about the wage outcome $\overline{W}$ under collective bargaining should be noted. First, the union has been able to raise the wage rate considerably above the nonunion level. Relative to a perfectly competitive market, the bargaining power of the union has created a wage gain of $\overline{W} - W_1$ for its members. Not all union members share in the higher wage rate, however. As wages are pushed up to $\overline{W}$, the union forces the firm to move up its demand curve for labor, causing the least-senior members in the union to lose their jobs.

A second important point is that the negotiated wage rate $\overline{W}$ in graph (b) is still influenced by market forces in both direct and indirect ways. Market forces set the outer limits to the wage bargain by defining the contract zone. A more elastic demand curve in graph (a), for example, would cause the median union member to become unemployed at a lower wage than W_3, reducing the upper limit of the contract zone and the room for bargaining. Market forces also have an indirect influence on the determination of the wage $\overline{W}$ as they affect the bargaining power of the employer and the union. Higher unemployment, for example, depresses wage rates in both nonunion and union labor markets, in the former case because of competition among individual workers for scarce jobs, and in the latter case because higher unemployment tips the balance of bargaining power toward the company.

Finally, this analysis illustrates the crucial role that bargaining power plays in the wage determination process in a unionized labor market. The union is able to raise the wage to $\overline{W}$ because of its ability to impose costs on the employer through a strike; in effect, the employer concludes that it is cheaper to pay $\overline{W}$ than to take a strike to get a lower wage. It follows from this that the size of the union wage gain is directly related to the union's power position relative to the firm. In an industry such as construction or trucking, where the union's ability to weather a strike often far exceeds that of the companies it bargains with, the intersection of the resistance and concession curves will occur at relatively high wages. In industries such as textiles or chemicals, where the union's ability to strike is relatively limited, the resistance and concession curves will yield a wage settlement that exceeds the market level by only a small amount.

The Occurrence of Strikes   The second major outcome of the bargaining process that can be analyzed with bargaining models is the occurrence of strikes. Strikes are among the most visible and well-publicized aspects of collective bargaining. The actual negotiations between the company and the union generally take place behind closed doors, and the public remains unaware of the issues at stake or the positions of the parties. Should the negotiations break down and a strike occur, the dispute gains far more attention as picket lines go up, the planes are grounded or the assembly line grinds to a halt, and the media reports on the adverse impact of the strike for consumers and local communities.

Despite the public attention given to strikes, the preponderance of evidence suggests that strikes are the exception in collective bargaining, and when they do occur, they often impose relatively small costs on the public. The average amount of working time lost to strikes in 2003 was 0.01 percent, far less than the time lost to absenteeism or even coffee breaks. In some cases, strikes do impose considerable hardship on the general public; examples are strikes by city transportation workers, or nationwide truckers' strikes. This is particularly true (or so it is often alleged) for certain government services, such as police or fire protection, and is one reason the right to strike has been restricted for many public sector workers.[55] A possible second cost of some strikes may be large ripple effects as a shutdown in one industry, such as steel or railroads, leads to layoffs in other industries that are either suppliers to the struck companies or purchasers of their output. For several reasons, however, most strikes entail relatively limited economic disruption. One is that other firms in the industry typically increase their production to make up for the loss of output from the company that is struck. A second factor is the tendency of firms to carry large inventories of their products into the strike, or to work overtime after the strike to catch up with demand. One exception, however, was the 15-day strike of United Parcel Service during August 1997. UPS's product (delivery service) is about as "perishable" as it gets; there is no chance to store up "inventory." It proved difficult and costly for customers to find other means of delivery for the 12 million parcels normally delivered by UPS each day. Another example is the 10-day strike in 2002 by the International Longshore and Warehouse Union that closed the Pacific ports. The cost was estimated at $2 billion per day in lost production.

Even if most strikes impose relatively small costs on the public, they can result in serious losses for the company and the workers involved in the dispute. The 15-day UPS strike cost the company $650 million. In addition, UPS claimed during the negotiations it might have to lay off 15,500 workers (because of its increased labor costs and loss of market share).[56] It is precisely the desire of the union and the firm to avoid these costs that motivates them to compromise during the negotiations in an attempt to reach an agreement on or before the strike deadline. Why, then, do strikes still take place? The answer is that the bargainers believe the benefits they will get from striking outweigh the costs they will incur. Based on this line of reasoning, one influential theory of strikes holds that they represent "mistakes" in bargaining caused by faulty expectations of the union and company over the actual benefits and costs of the strike.[57] This theory is illustrated in Figure 11.10.

The resistance and concession curves show that at the strike deadline $\bar{t}$ the union and the company are still far apart in their wage demands; the union's demand is W_4, and the firm's offer is W_1. With the beginning of the strike only hours away, both negotiators have to make a crucial decision: would their utility be

---

55 Robert Hebdon, "Public Sector Resolution in Transition," in Dale Belman, Morley Gunderson, and Douglas Hyatt, eds., *Public Sector Employment in a Time of Transition* (Madison, Wis.: IRRA, 1996), 85–126.

56 See Mark Tram, "UPS Caves in after 15-day Teamsters Strike," *Guardian* (20 August 1997): Sec. 1, p. 18, and Chris Ready, "UPS Competitors May Profit from Strike but Delivery Giant Unlikely to Lose it Dominance, Analysts Say," *Boston Globe* (20 August 1997): E1.

57 Hicks, *The Theory of Wages.* Also see Martin J. Mauro, "Strikes as a Result of Imperfect Information," *Industrial and Labor Relations Review* 35, no. 4 (July 1982): 522–38, and Timothy Fisher, "An Asymmetric Information Model for Lockouts," *Bulletin of Economic Research* 53 (April 2001): 153–59.

FIGURE 11.10 **THE OCCURRENCE OF A STRIKE**

At the strike deadline, the union's final demand is W_4, the firm's final offer is W_1. A strike will occur if both sides believe they can gain more from striking than from giving in. Thus, the union may think that the firm will agree to W_3 (point A) after a strike of t^* days, while the firm expects the union to agree to W_2 (point B).

Based on these overoptimistic expectations, the two sides take a strike, finally agreeing to the wage W^*. Had both sides known that W^* would be the final settlement point, they could have settled there and avoided the strike altogether.

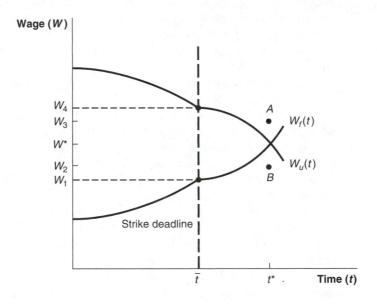

higher if they agreed to the other's terms and avoided a strike, or could they do better by striking in order to obtain more concessions from the other side? For a strike to take place, both sides must decide that they can achieve a higher level of utility by striking than by giving in. For example, the union bargainer at the strike deadline $\bar{t}$ concludes that the company cannot afford a long strike and would agree to a wage of W_3 (point A) after a strike of t^* days. Given this expected rate of concession, the union decides the benefit of striking (the increase in the wage from W_1 to W_3) exceeds the costs, and rejects the company's last offer. The company also has to estimate the benefits and costs of striking. Based on its assessment that the union membership does not want a lengthy strike, it concludes that the union would give in to a wage of W_2 (point B) after a strike of t^* days. From the company's point of view, the expected benefits (a decrease in the wage from W_4 to W_2) also outweigh the costs of the strike, and the company rejects the union's last offer.

The union and company begin the strike with mutually incompatible expectations of what they can gain. As the strike progresses, both the union and company negotiators realize that their expectations were overly optimistic and, as aspiration level theory suggests, begin to scale down their demands, resulting in a wage settlement of W^* after a strike of t^* days. With the advantage of hindsight, both sides realize that it would have been better to agree to W^* in the first place and save the costs of the strike. That they did not reflects a basic miscalculation over the actual benefits and costs of striking.

A basic implication of the view of strikes as mistakes in bargaining is that a strike could have been avoided if the bargainers had had sufficient information about each other's position. Although this conclusion has a large degree of validity, it does not fully explain why some strikes take place and why they sometimes last so long. A major factor in this regard is the role of *principle*, that is, the commitment of one or both sides to a particular position out of considerations of equity, moral or philosophical beliefs, or organizational survival. The company, for example, may believe that its long-run survival is contingent on preserving the wage concessions that it won from the union in earlier negotiations. The union negotiators, on the other hand, face growing pressure from the rank and file for "restore and more" wage increases. In effect, each side attaches a very high value to a specific outcome in the contract zone. A strike in this case is quite likely because the positions of both sides are so firm that there is little room for compromise. If a strike does occur, it is likely to be a very long one since the strike costs must be huge before they can outweigh the high value each party has attached to its position. A classic illustration of this type of strike is the pitched battles between companies and workers over the issue of union recognition in the pre-Wagner Act days.[58] A more recent example is the six-and-a-half year strike by the United Auto Workers against Caterpillar that ended in the spring of 1998 and the 139 day strike in 2004 among California grocery store chains over the issue of health care coverage.

Strikes also occur for a number of reasons related to internal political developments in the union or to interunion rivalries. Sometimes, for example, the candidates running for union president out-promise each other in terms of what they'll win from the company, leading to greater chance of a strike in the next negotiation. Also, workers sometimes defy their leaders and call a wildcat strike during the term of an existing contract in order to register their dislike for some development (for example, termination of a worker).[59] Interunion rivalries, such as jurisdictional disputes among craft unions in the construction industry, also cause strikes.

A more detailed look of when and why strikes might occur is found in the Empirical Evidence 11-2 box.

➤ **SEE**

Empirical Evidence 11-2:
The Pattern of Strike
Activity, p. 609.

---

58   Sidney Lens, *The Labor Wars* (New York: Anchor Books, 1974).

59   On wildcat strikes, see Victor Devinatz, "The Ideology of Wildcat Strikes and Shopfloor Governance Regimes," in David Lewin and Bruce Kaufman, eds., *Advances in Industrial and Labor Relations*, vol. 9 (Greenwich: JAI Press, 1999), 211–38.

Alternative Methods of Dispute Resolution

The strike has a number of virtues as a method of dispute resolution. It provides a powerful incentive to bargain and reach an agreement, and it results in a settlement to which both parties voluntarily agree. The strike also has several disadvantages as a means of dispute resolution, the major one being the costs it imposes on the economy, neutral third parties, and the bargainers themselves. The costs of strikes have motivated attempts to devise other means of dispute resolution that either lessen the probability of a strike or replace the strike altogether. This search for alternatives to the strike has been particularly strong in the public sector, where the right to strike is often either prohibited or heavily circumscribed by law. The most widely adopted approach is to introduce procedures for third-party intervention in bargaining. Three types of third-party intervention are most commonly used: mediation, fact-finding, and binding arbitration.

Mediation

Mediation is the most common form of third-party intervention in collective bargaining, and also the least intrusive. **Mediation** is a procedure in which an experienced neutral party joins the negotiations to assist the union and company in reaching an agreement. The mediator has no power to impose a settlement on the parties; the mediator facilitates the bargaining process by serving as a go-between in the negotiations.

The central purpose of the mediator is to help the parties reach an agreement. Because the mediator cannot impose sanctions or costs on the negotiators, the major influence the mediator can have on the speed with which an agreement is reached is by improving the flow of communication between the bargainers and suggesting possible areas of compromise. Mediation will usually be more effective in some types of disputes than others. For example, in a labor negotiation where one party has boxed itself into a "must strike" position through inexperienced or clumsy bargaining, a skillful mediator can suggest a compromise that allows an effective, face-saving retreat. Another important service the mediation can perform is facilitating concessions. As noted earlier, each negotiator must be careful not to convey weakness to the other side by "coming clean" too soon. A mediator can, therefore, suggest $\overline{W}$ as a point of settlement when neither of the parties would have dared to put it on the table themselves.

In other dispute situations, mediation may be relatively ineffective in bringing about a settlement. This is particularly true, for example, when matters of principle are involved or when the costs of disagreement are too low to induce the parties to compromise. This latter consideration is particularly important in many public sector disputes where no threat of a strike motivates the negotiators to search for a settlement.[60]

---

[60] See Dale Belman, Morley Gunderson, and Douglas Hyatt, eds., *Public Sector Employment in a Time of Transition* (Madison, Wis.: IRRA, 1996), for recent developments in public sector dispute resolution.

Fact-Finding

The next higher level of third-party intervention in bargaining is **fact-finding.** Fact-finding is most frequently used in the public sector and often begins when mediation has failed to bring about a settlement in the negotiations. Under fact-finding procedures, a neutral third party enters the negotiations and prepares a report that outlines the conditions surrounding the dispute and the positions of the parties. Fact-finding often goes beyond mere determination of the facts, because in many instances the fact finder is also empowered to prepare a set of recommendations as a suggested basis for a settlement of the dispute.

Proponents of fact-finding argue that it facilitates a settlement of collective bargaining disputes in three ways. First, fact-finding can resolve important disagreements between unions and employers over the truthfulness of the information with which each side buttresses its demands. Second, the fact-finder's recommendations can serve as a focal point around which a settlement can be reached. Finally, and perhaps most important, it is argued that fact-finding subjects the bargainer's demands to public scrutiny, inducing both sides to adopt more moderate positions than they would if the negotiations remained behind closed doors. Despite these claims in its favor, evidence suggests that, at least in the public sector, fact-finding has declined in its effectiveness as a means of dispute resolution. The major reason seems to be that fact-finding does not, contrary to its proponents' claims, arouse enough public pressure to move the parties to a settlement. Fact-finding does remain a viable option for some negotiations.[61]

Arbitration

The final form of third-party intervention in labor negotiations is **binding arbitration.** Under a system of binding arbitration, a neutral third party listens to both sides of the dispute and then issues a decision that the parties are committed to accept. Binding arbitration is the most intrusive form of third-party intervention because it allows an outsider to dictate the terms of the settlement.

There are several forms of binding arbitration. **Interest arbitration** is the use of arbitration to determine the terms and conditions of a new contract; **rights arbitration,** on the other hand, is used to adjudicate grievances or disputes over the interpretation or application of the terms of an existing contract. The use of binding arbitration to settle grievance disputes is quite common in this country and is one of the most distinctive features of collective bargaining in the United States. Virtually every collective bargaining agreement provides for a grievance process where workers can seek redress against company decisions or policies that are thought to violate the union contract. Most grievance procedures involve a series of hearings, culminating in binding arbitration if the dispute cannot be resolved at

---

61   See Mark D. Karper, "Fact Finding in Public Employment: Promise or Illusion, Revisited," *Journal of Collective Negotiations in the Public Sector* 23 (1994): 287–97.

an earlier stage. The major impetus behind the widespread adoption of rights arbitration is the desire of both unions and employers to replace the strike with an alternative form of dispute resolution that is less disruptive to the day-to-day employment relationship and that imposes lower costs on both sides. By 1980, over 90 percent of union contracts had imposed at least limited bans on strikes during the terms of the agreements.[62]

At least in the private sector, interest arbitration is much rarer. When it comes to the negotiation of a new contract, few unions or companies are willing to give up their right to strike or to place their future in the hands of an outside arbitrator. A notable exception was the **Experimental Negotiating Agreement (ENA)** in the steel industry.[63] Adopted in 1973, the ENA pledged both the steelworkers union and the major steel companies to submit all unresolved national issues in their contract negotiations to a panel of outside umpires for binding arbitration. The reason the parties adopted the ENA was because the threat of a strike in the industry every three years was causing a growing number of domestic steel users to turn to foreign producers in order to ensure reliable supplies of steel. The price of giving up the right to strike was quite high for the companies, as wage rates under the ENA shot up by 119 percent between 1973 and 1979.[64] For this and other reasons, the ENA was not renewed after 1980.

Interest arbitration is much more common in public sector bargaining, primarily because many public sector workers do not have the right to strike and an alternative form of dispute resolution is necessary. The positive side of interest arbitration is that it permits bilateralism between workers and employers in public sector negotiations without the threat of a strike. Interest arbitration also has several negative aspects. It is often alleged that interest arbitration has a **chilling effect** on the motivation of the employer and union to bargain and make concessions.[65] Without the prospective costs of a strike, neither side loses as much by being intransigent. Also, if both sides anticipate that the arbitrator will split the difference between their respective positions, they have a strong incentive to exaggerate their final positions in order to win a more favorable settlement. Interest arbitration may also lead to what is known as a **narcotic effect** in bargaining. The narcotic effect refers to the possibility that once the bargainers have used arbitration, they may automatically resort to arbitration in subsequent negotiations rather than reach a settlement on their own. The bargainers may, for example, find it easier to rely on a third party to resolve their dispute rather than undertake the hard work and political risks of fashioning an agreement within their own

---

62 Bureau of Labor Statistics, *Characteristics of Major Collective Bargaining Agreements, January 1, 1980*, Bulletin 2095 (Washington, D.C.: Government Printing Office, 1981): 114.

63 Garth L. Mangum and R. Scott McNabb, *The Rise, Fall, and Replacement of Industrywide Bargaining in the Basic Steel Industry* (Armonk, N.Y., and London: M. E. Sharpe, 1997).

64 See "When Steel Wages Rise Faster Than Productivity," *Business Week* (April 21, 1980): 144–48.

65 Thomas A. Kochan, "Dynamics of Dispute Resolution in the Public Sector," in Benjamin Aaron et al. (eds), *Public Sector Bargaining* (Madison, WI: Industrial Relations Research Association, 1979): 150–90.

organizations.[66] A final negative impact of interest arbitration, at least from the perspective of public officials and taxpayers, is that it seems to result in higher wages and benefits for workers relative to negotiated settlements.[67]

These negative side effects of interest arbitration have led to the development of **final offer arbitration.** Under final offer arbitration, the arbitrator chooses the final offer of one side or the other as the settlement. The hope is that the "all or nothing" nature of the award will provide a strong incentive to both sides to moderate their positions and reach a settlement on their own.[68] After a review of the empirical literature on the subject, Richard Freeman concluded that final offer arbitration does tend to reduce the chilling effect associated with conventional binding arbitration, but as a concomitant result, it also leaves a stronger residue of bad feelings between union and management because it produces a clear winner and loser. One proposed solution to this problem is issue-by-issue final offer arbitration.[69]

---

66 Evidence that the narcotic effect may not be too much of a concern can be found in Frederic Champlin et al., "Is Arbitration Habit Forming? The Narcotic Effect of Arbitration Use," *Labour* 11 (Spring 1997): 23–51.

67 See Peter Feuille and John Thomas Delaney, "Collective Bargaining, Interest Arbitration, and Police Salaries," *Industrial and Labor Relations Review* 39 (January 1986): 228–40.

68 Evidence to the contrary can be found in Orley Ashenfelter et al., "An Experimental Comparison of Dispute Rates in Alternative Arbitration Systems," *Econometrica* 60 (November 1992): 1407–33. Paul Pecorino and Mark Van Boening, "Bargaining and Information: An Empirical Analysis of Multi-Stage Arbitration Game," *Journal of Labor Economics* 19 (October 2001): 922–48, present evidence that allowing negotiation after final offers are made lowers dispute rates by 27 percentage points.

69 Richard B. Freeman, "Unionism Comes to the Public Sector," *Journal of Economic Literature* 24 (March 1986): 41–86.

POLICY APPLICATION 11-1

The Legal Framework of Collective Bargaining

An important determinant of the effectiveness of a union is the legal framework that governs collective bargaining. This framework is composed of statute law, common law, court rulings, and rulings of regulatory agencies that together define the rules of the game by which both employers and unions have to play. These rules are of paramount importance in collective bargaining because they define the rights and responsibilities of both sides and the amount of power that each brings to the bargaining table. Certain key pieces of legislation have had a fundamental impact on the practice and outcomes of collective bargaining in the past half-century.[1]

---

1 For more detail on this subject see Margaret Jasper, *Labor Laws* (New York: Ocean Publications, 1998).

The National Labor Relations Act

Without doubt, the single most important piece of legislation with respect to collective bargaining is the National Labor Relations Act (NLRA), also known as the **Wagner Act.** Prior to its enactment in 1935, public policy towards unionism and collective bargaining had been generally repressive and obstructive. The Wagner Act represented a fundamental shift in public policy because for the first time the power of the federal government was explicitly committed to the protection of the right to organize and the promotion of the process of collective bargaining.

The importance of the Wagner Act can be better judged by comparing it with the legal environment that existed prior to its adoption. The Wagner Act did not legalize either unions or the process of collective bargaining; these had been established in the nineteenth century by various court decisions. The Wagner Act protected the worker from discrimination or harassment for the *exercise* of that right. Prior to its passage, employers were free to fire, demote, or refuse to hire union members or persons suspected of union sympathies. To prevent unionism, employers frequently hired agents and spies to infiltrate a union organization to disrupt its activities and discover its leaders. Once discovered, the union activists faced the risk of being fired and blacklisted by the other employers in the area, making it impossible for these workers to find employment.[2]

A similar situation applied to the employer's legal obligation to recognize a union and bargain with it. Before the Wagner Act, the law did not forbid collective bargaining, but the employer was under no legal compulsion to accept it. Without a legal or administrative means by which to secure recognition and bargaining rights, unions had to strike to force the employer to accede to bargaining. Because the issue of union recognition and collective bargaining was often seen by both labor and management as a matter of principle and not subject to compromise, there occurred a number of bitter and drawn-out "recognition" strikes through-

out the late 1800s and the beginning decades of the twentieth century that resulted in considerable violence and a general radicalization of emotions on the issue of unionism.[3]

The Wagner Act covered all workers except those with supervisory or managerial roles or persons employed in government (local, state, and federal), agriculture, domestic service, and industries (railroads and airlines) covered under the Railway Labor Act. Three key provisions of the Wagner Act fundamentally altered the practice of collective bargaining and the balance of power between workers and employers.

Unfair Labor Practices To protect the right of workers to join and participate in unions, the Wagner Act prohibited certain **unfair labor practices** by the employer. An employer would commit an unfair labor practice should he or she attempt to interfere with, coerce, dominate, or discriminate against employees in the exercise of their right to organize and bargain. Examples of unfair labor practices are threatening discharge, demotion, or loss of job if an employee persists in union activity; interrogating prospective or present employees about their union sympathies or affiliations; and discriminating against an employee because of the filing of a grievance or unfair labor practice charge. A firm also commits an unfair labor practice if it refuses to bargain in "good faith" with the union in an attempt to reach a collective bargaining agreement.

A very fine line often separates what is and what is not an unfair labor practice by the employer. The law does not require that an employer remain neutral in a union organizing campaign. It is legal for an employer to explain and defend its labor policies and to present the advantages and disadvantages of unions in speeches and written

---

2   These and other antiunion tactics practiced by employers are described in Irving Bernstein, *The Lean Years: A History of the American Worker, 1920–1933* (Boston: Houghton Mifflin, 1960).

3   See Sidney Lens, *The Labor Wars* (New York: Anchor Books, 1974).

communications to its workers as long as it does not threaten reprisals or loss of benefits. Thus, an employer may legally publicize the fact that it is operating at a loss and that other unionized companies in its industry have recently gone out of business. It cannot state that if it is unionized it will close its doors and the workers will lose their jobs.

The National Labor Relations Board To administer and enforce the Wagner Act, a five-member **National Labor Relations Board** was established. The NLRB is an independent agency of the federal government. Its members serve for five-year terms and are nominated by the president and confirmed by the Senate. The NLRB's basic responsibility is to investigate and rule on charges of unfair labor practices that are brought before it and to conduct representation elections. Much of the actual casework is handled by staff persons of the NLRB at 51 regional, subregional, and resident offices. The law gives the NLRB the power to impose financial penalties and to issue cease and desist orders to end unfair labor practices. Although ostensibly neutral, evidence indicates that to some degree the rulings of the NLRB favor unions or employers depending on which political party is in power in Washington, D.C. and has the ability to appoint new members to the board.[4]

Union Representation Elections The second major provision of the NLRA was the establishment of the secret ballot **union representation election** to determine whether or not a group of workers desire union representation. A union representation election may be conducted by the NLRB whenever 30 percent or more of a group of workers sign *authorization cards* that state their desire for an election. Before the election can be held, the NLRB has to first determine the appropriate **election unit,** that is, the particular group in the plant or company that is to vote in the election. Once the election unit is decided on, the NLRB holds a secret ballot election in which all employees in the unit can vote for either "no union" or for one of the unions that are seeking representation

rights. If a majority of those voting choose a particular union, the union is certified as the exclusive bargaining representative for all the employees in the unit. The provision of **exclusive representation** requires that the union negotiate for and represent every employee in the unit, whether or not the person is actually a member of the union. Since the passage of the Wagner Act in 1935, over 30 million workers have voted in a union representation election.

The Taft-Hartley Act

When the **Taft-Hartley Act** was passed in 1947, collective bargaining in the United States bore little resemblance to the situation that prevailed when the NLRA was enacted in 1935. Union membership in 1935 was 3.5 million, concentrated heavily in a few industries such as construction, mining, railroads, and the needle trades. Thirteen years later, union membership stood at 14 million, and the mass production industries of autos, steel, rubber, and electrical equipment that had once been nearly devoid of unionism were solidly organized.

The success of organized labor set off a reaction among the American public. The public felt that the pendulum had swung too far; where labor was once the underdog, now it was too big and powerful. This sense of unease was heightened by a strike wave that hit the economy in 1946. As a result, in 1947 Congress enacted the Taft-Hartley Act, alternatively described by its proponents as a way to restore the balance of power between management and labor and by its critics as a "slave labor" law.

The Taft-Hartley Act did not repeal the Wagner Act, but it did amend the Wagner Act in some important ways. The Taft-Hartley Act contained four major provisions.

Unfair Labor Practices of Unions The Wagner Act had prohibited a series of unfair labor practices

---

4   See Michael Leroy, "The Formation and Administration of Labor Policy by the NLRB: Evidence from Economic and ULP Strike Rulings," *Journal of Labor Research* 22 (Fall 2001): 723–38.

by employers. The Taft-Hartley Act added a series of unfair labor practices that *unions* were prohibited from engaging in. The intent of Congress in passing the Wagner Act was to protect the right of workers to organize; with the Taft-Hartley Act, Congress moved to protect the right of workers *not* to organize. Unions were prohibited from coercing or discriminating against employees who chose not to be represented by a union. Unions were also placed under the same duty to bargain in good faith as employers were with the Wagner Act. Unions were also prohibited from engaging in a third unfair labor practice called a **secondary boycott.** In a secondary boycott, a union that has a dispute with one firm (the primary employer) involves neutral, secondary employers in the dispute, either by striking them or causing their workers to refuse to handle the goods of the primary firm.

Union Security   The second major provision of the Taft-Hartley Act concerned the issue of union security, which refers to various requirements written into collective bargaining contracts that specify who must join the union and under what conditions. Typical union security requirements have included, for example:

1. **Closed shops.** Workers must be a member of the union before they can be hired.
2. **Union shops.** Once hired, a worker must become a union member within 30 days as a condition of continued employment.
3. **Agency shops.** Workers do not have to join a union as a condition of employment, but they must pay a monthly fee in lieu of dues for the services that the union provides.

The Taft-Hartley Act made the closed shop illegal and gave individual states the option of prohibiting the union shop through so-called right-to-work laws. Under Section 14(b) of the act, the union shop is legal unless an individual state passes legislation expressly banning it. As of 2004, 22 states, mostly in the South and Midwest, had done so.

Proponents of right-to-work laws argue that the union shop is a form of compulsory unionism and that no one should be forced to join a union as a condition of employment. Opponents of right-to-work laws argue that the laws allow nonmembers to get a free ride since by law the union must represent every worker in the bargaining unit even if the worker does not financially support the union. One remedy to the free-rider problem has been the agency shop, which is legal in about half of the right-to-work states.[5]

Decertification Elections   A third important provision of the Taft-Hartley Act sought to balance the ability of workers to vote for a union with an equal ability to vote out a union. The act established the **decertification election,** in which the workers in a bargaining unit are allowed to vote on whether or not they want to stop being represented by a particular union. If a majority of the votes are in favor of decertification, the union loses its rights as sole bargaining agent for the workers.

Labor Disputes   A fourth set of provisions in the Taft-Hartley Act concern the settlement of strikes and prevention of labor/management conflict. Under the Taft-Hartley Act, the president is empowered to seek an injunction in a U.S. District Court to impose an 80-day back-to-work period in any **national emergency dispute,** that is, a strike that "imperils the national health or safety." The Taft-Hartley Act also created the Federal Mediation and Conciliation Service (FMCS). The act requires that 30 days prior to the expiration of any existing contract the parties must notify the FMCS that a potential labor dispute exists. This gives the FMCS an opportunity to make mediation and conciliation available to the bargainers before they reach a strike. The union and firm are not obligated, however, to accept the help of the FMCS.

---

5   Daniel Quinn Mills, *Labor–Management Relations*, 5th ed. (New York: McGraw-Hill, 1994), 479.

The Landrum-Griffin Act

In the decade after the Taft-Hartley Act, public attention turned to a new issue that was increasingly making the headlines. From 1957 to 1959 a lengthy series of congressional hearings held by the McClellan committee focused on union corruption and racketeering. Extensive testimony documented alleged cases of kickbacks, pension fraud, intimidation of dissident members by union officials, and undemocratic or fraudulent elections for union offices. While the bulk of the testimony focused on a handful of unions, most notably the Teamsters union, the hearings provided the impetus for general legislation to correct or prevent such abuses. This legislation was the **Labor Management Reporting and Disclosure Act of 1959,** commonly referred to as the **Landrum-Griffin Act.**

The Landrum-Griffin Act was an amendment to the original Wagner Act. It had several major provisions.

Bill of Rights for Union Members The Landrum-Griffin Act began with a bill of rights for union members that was intended to ensure the democratic operation of the union and to guarantee the individual member due process in meetings and disciplinary proceedings.

Financial Disclosure The Landrum-Griffin Act required that each national and local union file an annual financial disclosure statement listing its assets, liabilities, sources of income, expenditures, salaries and payments to union officials, and loans to businesses or individuals. The financial disclosure statements are available for inspection by any member of the public.

Trusteeships In certain situations a national union may take control of the administrative and financial affairs of a local union by placing it in a **trusteeship.** The McClellan committee found that in some cases a trusteeship was established not to protect union members from incompetent or corrupt officials in the local union, but to control the pension and dues money of the local or to stifle political dissent in the union. The Landrum-Griffin Act limited the ability of a national union to place a local under trusteeship and required the national to explain why a trusteeship that lasts more than six months has not been terminated.

Union Elections The Landrum-Griffin Act also sought to ensure that elections for union leadership positions were conducted in an open and democratic fashion. Every national union was required to hold elections at least once every five years, and elections in local unions were to be held at least once every three years. The act also required that elections be conducted by secret ballot and that every member have a right to vote.

Public Sector Labor Laws

One of the most important collective bargaining developments of the last decades has been the rapid spread of unionism among government workers. The initial impetus to unionism in the public sector came from Executive Order 10988 issued by President Kennedy in January 1962. The order guaranteed the right of federal employees to join unions, but it prohibited strikes by federal employees. It also prohibited various unfair labor practices by unions and employing agencies, much as the Wagner Act did. The executive order permitted collective bargaining between a union and the employing agency on a limited range of issues; major issues such as hiring, promotion, layoffs, wages, and fringe benefits were excluded. A grievance system was also established.

The most recent change in the legal framework of bargaining in the federal sector was the passage of the **Civil Service Reform Act of 1978 (CSRA).** The procedures of the Taft-Hartley Act governing union representation elections and unfair labor practices were incorporated into the CSRA, and a new agency, the Federal Labor Relations Authority (FLRA), was created to administer the law. The CSRA limits the scope of bargaining largely to matters concerning personnel practices and working conditions. Strikes are still prohibited.

One major group of federal employees, postal employees, is not covered by the CSRA. The Postal Reorganization Act of 1970 abolished the Post Office Department and established in its place an independent government corporation. The act placed postal employees under the jurisdiction of the Wagner Act, as amended, and also allowed bargaining over wages, hours, and working conditions. It prohibited strikes, however.

Perhaps the greatest area of ferment and change with respect to labor law is in state and local government. The introduction of limited collective bargaining rights in the federal sector forced a reevaluation of labor policy in many states and municipalities. By 2004, twenty-five states had enacted a comprehensive public sector bargaining law, and another fifteen had enacted more limited bargaining laws.

EMPIRICAL EVIDENCE 11-1

Who Belongs to Unions

The level of unionization among particular industries, demographic groups, and geographic areas varies widely. In this section the demand and supply model of union membership is used to explain these diverse patterns.

Industry

Table 11.1 shows that across all private sector industries, 7.9 percent of wage and salary workers were members of labor unions and 8.6 percent were represented by unions in 2004. Some industries, however, are much more highly unionized than others. The industries in Table 11.1 with the highest rate of unionization are communications and utilities, government, transportation, and construction. The least unionized industries include agriculture; finance, insurance, and real estate; services; and retail trade.

A number of factors account for this pattern. Among highly unionized industries, such as railroads, electric utilities, and autos, firms tend to be large in size and capital intensive; the product markets are regulated or oligopolistic; employment is subject to a great deal of cyclical instability; the workforce holds blue-collar, industrial-type jobs; and the jobs often involve dangerous or unpleasant working conditions. Construction firms are smaller but the jobs are very unstable and frequently dangerous, whereas governments have stable jobs but large and ponderous bureaucracies.

Each of these factors increases the benefits or reduces the costs to workers of union membership. First, the individual worker in a large firm or bureaucratic organization is more likely to feel at a bargaining disadvantage relative to the employer and less able to influence management decision making. Second, the capital intensity of production implies that the labor demand curve is likely to be relatively inelastic, allowing a union to raise wages without a large drop in employment. Third, since firms in these industries operate in regulated or oligopolistic product markets, larger potential profits are likely to be available for a union to capture for workers. Similarly, governments do not have a profit constraint and may be more willing to pay higher wages. Fourth, the large size of firms and

TABLE 11.1 — PERCENTAGE OF EMPLOYED WAGE AND SALARY WORKERS WHO ARE MEMBERS OF AND ARE REPRESENTED BY INDUSTRY, GENDER, AND RACE, 2004

Industry	Members of Unions (Percent)	Represented by Unions (Percent)	Gender and Race	Members of Unions (Percent)	Represented by Unions (Percent)
All industries			All Workers*	12.5	13.8
(private sector)	7.9	8.6	Men	13.8	15.0
Agriculture	2.2	2.9	White	13.6	14.7
Mining	11.4	11.7	Black	16.9	18.5
Construction	14.7	15.4	Hispanic	10.1	11.4
Manufacturing	12.9	13.9	Women	11.1	12.5
Durable	13.3	14.2	White	10.7	12.1
Nondurable	12.3	13.2	Black	13.6	15.2
Information	14.2	15.4	Hispanic	9.9	11.4
Transportation and utilities	24.9	26.3			
Wholesale trade	4.6	5.2			
Retail trade	5.7	6.1			
Finance, insurance, and real estate	2.0	2.5			
Services	4.6	5.3			
Government	36.4	40.7			

*Workers 16 Years and older.

SOURCE: Bureau of Labor Statistics, *Employment and Earnings* (January 2005, Tables 40 and 42). The Figures for communications and utilities and services are weighted averages calculated by the authors.

the cyclical sensitivity of employment tend to make workers more concerned about standardized personnel policies, particularly with respect to the allocation of job opportunities. Fifth, the blue-collar, industrial nature of the work reduces individualism on the job and helps foster a strong working-class identity among employees. Finally, the large size of firms and the dangerous or unpleasant characteristics of work in these industries make collective action to improve working conditions more important.

Certain industries, such as retail trade and finance, have low rates of unionization. Both of these industries contain a large number of white-collar jobs. White-collar workers typically do not perceive that a union would be effective in dealing with their employment problems or is consistent with their social status.[1] A second consideration,

---

[1] This may be changing, however. An issue of growing concern to clerical workers, for example, is the possible health hazards of working with video (CRT) terminals, particularly for pregnant women. This was a key issue leading to the first successful unionization drive among a group of clerical workers at the Equitable Life Assurance Co. Unionization is also increasing among white-collar professionals such as lawyers and doctors. The Union of American Physicians and Dentists, for example, has over 5,500 members.

particularly in retail trade, is that the high degree of turnover among many workers makes unions both more difficult to organize and less attractive to workers. Finally, in both retail trade and finance, the nature of the production process fragments workers into small groups with idiosyncratic tasks, hindering the development of a common group identity or community of interests.

Race

Table 11.1 also shows the rate of unionization among black, Hispanic, and white workers. A higher proportion of black men (16.9 percent) are members of unions than are white men (13.6 percent) or Hispanic men (10.1 percent). One explanation is that since blacks suffer the most from discrimination with respect to pay and promotion, they have the most to gain from a union. This explanation is, however, diluted to the extent that unions themselves discriminate against minority groups. A second explanation for the higher rate of unionization among blacks is that they are overrepresented in occupations most likely to be unionized, particularly blue-collar jobs. Finally, a nationwide survey found that blacks are twice as likely to state a preference for union representation as are whites.[2] This pro-union attitude probably reflects the fact that collective action has generally been a more effective means of economic and social gain for blacks than has individual action.

Gender

The rate of unionization also varies considerably between men and women. Table 11.1 shows that 13.8 percent of men but only 11.1 percent of women were members of labor unions in 2004. One important explanation for the lower level of unionization among women is their more intermittent nature of labor force participation. Workers with a long job tenure with one employer and a long-term commitment to work are more likely to actively seek a union if they feel dissatisfied with the conditions of employment than workers who

view their current job as only a temporary "way station" to some other job or nonmarket activity. A second factor explaining the lower rate of unionization among women is their concentration in white-collar or "pink-collar" jobs. Differences in attitudes between men and women with respect to the desirability of a union are apparently not an important factor, however, according to the survey mentioned earlier with respect to race.

State

A final characteristic of union membership is its distribution by state. The rate of unionization varies considerably in the United States, ranging from a low of 3.1 percent in North Carolina in 2003 to a high of 24.6 percent in New York. The 15 states with the highest levels of unionization are shown in Figure 11.11. The Middle Atlantic, North Central, and Pacific regions of the country are the most highly unionized; the states in the South, Midwest, and Mountain regions have below-average rates of unionization.

Regional differences in unionization arise from a number of factors. The lower rates of unionization in the South, for example, have been traced, in part, to the greater importance of nondurable manufacturing industries such as apparel, textiles, and furniture in the region's economy.[3] A second factor identified in several studies is the lower level of urbanization in southern states. Ray Marshall, perhaps the leading expert on labor in the South, has argued that in earlier years unionizing efforts were also adversely affected by the divisive effect of racial prejudice.[4]

---

2   Kochan, "How American Workers View Labor Unions." Also see Henry S. Farber, "Trends in Worker Demand for Union Representation," *American Economic Review* 79, no. 2 (May 1989): 166–71.

3   See William J. Moore and Robert J. Newman, "On the Prospects for American Trade Union Growth: A Cross-Sectional Analysis," *Review of Economics and Statistics* 57, no. 4 (November 1975): 435–45.

4   F. Ray Marshall, *Labor in the South* (Cambridge, Mass.: Harvard University Press, 1967).

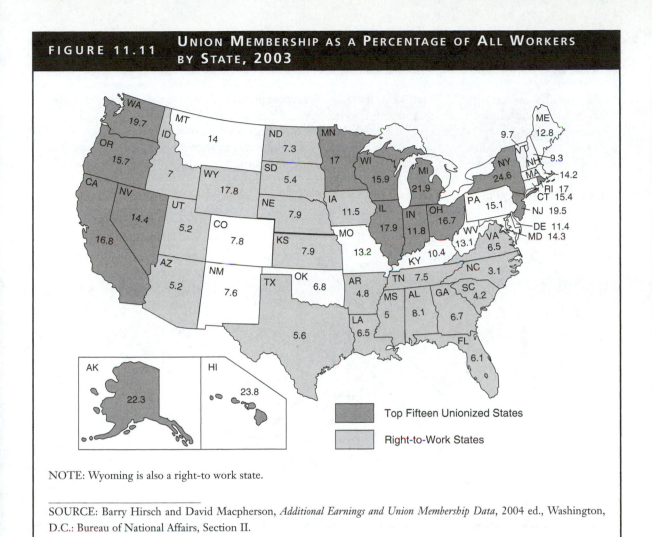

FIGURE 11.11 UNION MEMBERSHIP AS A PERCENTAGE OF ALL WORKERS BY STATE, 2003

WA 19.7	MT	ME 12.8
OR 15.7	ID 14	NY 24.6
	WY 7	NH 9.7

WA 19.7
MT 14
ID 7
OR 15.7
WY 17.8
ND 7.3
MN 17
WI 15.9
MI 21.9
ME 12.8
NY 24.6
VT 9.7
NH 9.3
MA 14.2
CA 16.8
NV 14.4
UT 5.2
SD 5.4
NE 7.9
IA 11.5
IL 17.9
IN 11.8
OH 16.7
PA 15.1
CT 17
RI 15.4
NJ 19.5
DE 11.4
MD 14.3
AZ 5.2
NM 7.6
CO 7.8
KS 7.9
MO 13.2
KY 10.4
WV 13.1
VA 6.5
TX 5.6
OK 6.8
AR 4.8
TN 7.5
NC 3.1
SC 4.2
MS 5
AL 8.1
GA 6.7
LA 6.5
FL 6.1

AK 22.3
HI 23.8

■ Top Fifteen Unionized States
▨ Right-to-Work States

NOTE: Wyoming is also a right-to work state.

SOURCE: Barry Hirsch and David Macpherson, *Additional Earnings and Union Membership Data*, 2004 ed., Washington, D.C.: Bureau of National Affairs, Section II.

Two additional considerations have been given considerable attention as explanations for the lower rate of unionization in the states of the South, Midwest, and Mountain regions. They are the role of right-to-work laws and attitudes. Under the Taft-Hartley Act, individual states were given the right to ban the union shop by passing so-called right-to-work laws. Under a union shop agreement, a new worker hired in a unionized firm is required as a condition of employment to join the union, usually within 30 days. A right-to-work law makes the union shop illegal and allows workers in unionized firms to remain nonmembers, enjoying the benefits of union membership without paying the costs of dues and initiation fees.

Currently 21 states have right-to-work laws, as shown in Figure 11.11. The level of unionization in right-to-work states is considerably below the national average—7 percent versus 13 percent in 2003. Is the reason traceable to the right-to-work

FIGURE 11.12   THE EFFECT OF A RIGHT-TO-WORK LAW
IN UNION MEMBERSHIP

One possible reason right-to-work states have lower levels of unionization is that unions find it more expensive to offer their services as a result of the "free rider" problem. This is represented by a leftward shift of the supply curve from S_1 to S_2, causing the amount of union services purchased to fall from U_1 to U_2 (point A to B).

A second possible reason is that a right-to-work law reflects adverse public attitudes toward unions. This is represented by the leftward shift of the demand curve from D_1 to D_2, causing the amount of union services also to fall from U_1 to U_2 (point A to C).

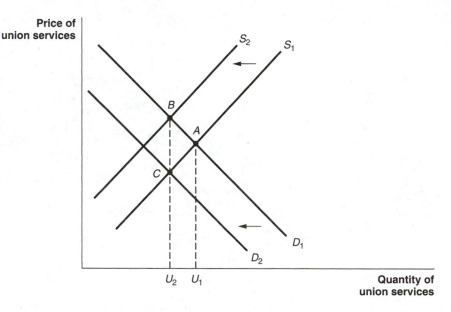

law, or are other factors responsible? There are two points of view on this.[5]

Some economists, and many union officials, argue that right-to-work laws result in a lower rate of unionization by shifting the supply curve of union services to the left, such as from S_1 to S_2 in Figure 11.12. The shift in the supply curve occurs because a right-to-work law makes it both more difficult and more expensive for a union to provide its services because of the free riders in the bargaining unit. The result is that union membership falls from U_1 to U_2 (point A to point B).

Other economists have taken a different view. Pointing out that a right-to-work law must have widespread public support to be passed in a state, they conclude that the major reason for low rates of unionization in right-to-work states is not the law itself but the public's negative attitude toward unions. This suggests that the real reason for low rates of unionization in right-to-work states is low

5   William J. Moore, "The Determinants and Effects of Right-to-Work Laws: A Review of the Recent Literature," *Journal of Labor Research* 19 (Summer 1998): 445–69.

demand for union services, represented by a shift in the demand curve from D_1 to D_2 in Figure 11.12. For a given supply curve such as S_1, the shift in the demand curve would reduce union membership from U_1 to U_2 (point A to point C) in the right-to-work states.

Is unionization low in right-to-work states because of the presence of the law or because of negative attitudes of workers toward unions? A recent review of the literature finds merit in both explanations.[6] Once public attitudes for and against

unions are taken into account (say by comparing political voting patterns in congressional elections across states), the author concludes that right-to-work laws reduce unionization in the long run by 3 to 8 percent. Free-riding among workers in right-to-work states is estimated to be 6 to 10 percent higher, and unions in those states also have more difficulty winning organizing campaigns.

---

6   Ibid.

EMPIRICAL EVIDENCE 11-2

The Pattern of Strike Activity

Figure 11.13 shows data on the number of strikes involving 1,000 workers or more in the United States between 1947 and 2003. The bars represent periods of recession. Several features about strike activity stand out. First, there is a good deal of volatility from one year to the next in the amount of strike activity in the economy. The smallest number of strikes was 15 in 2003, and the largest was 470 in 1952. Workers involved ranged from a low of 47,000 in 2002 to 2.7 million in 1952. Second, a fairly clear association emerges between strike activity and the business cycle, with the number of strikes increasing on the upswing of the business cycle and declining during recessions. And, third, after 1978, the number of work stoppages in the United States began a precipitous decline, falling to record low levels by 2001. A number of factors are important in explaining these trends.

The Bargaining Calendar

One important influence on the level of strike activity is the number of union contracts that come up for renegotiation each year, which is often referred to as the **bargaining calendar**. The majority of union contracts have three-year terms.[1]

This fact, coupled with the tendency for the major producers in an industry to bargain at the same time, gives rise to a three-year cycle or "round" of bargaining in a number of individual industries. Strikes in an industry are most likely to occur during the process of contract renegotiation, in part because most union contracts either restrict or ban altogether the right to strike during the term of an existing agreement.

Beginning in the 1950s, a distinct three-year cycle emerged for bargaining in the economy, characterized by two years of heavy bargaining activity followed by one year of light bargaining. The development of this three-year cycle not only imparted a similar movement to strike activity but also became an important factor in the development of pattern wage bargaining among certain key industries such as trucking, autos, and steel. This three-year bargaining cycle was seriously disrupted in the 1980s, partly because some major contracts were reopened ahead of schedule to incorporate wage concessions, and partly because some contracts

---

1   The reasons for long-term contracts and their historical evolution are discussed in Sanford M. Jacoby and Daniel J. B. Mitchell, "Employer Preferences for Long-Term Union Contracts," *Journal of Labor Research* 5, no. 3 (Summer 1984): 215–28.

FIGURE 11.13

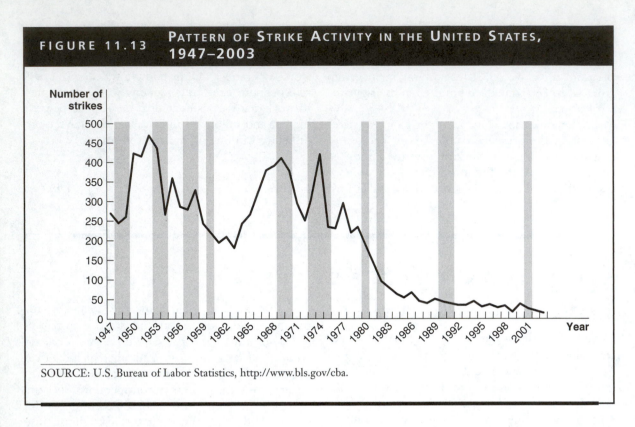

PATTERN OF STRIKE ACTIVITY IN THE UNITED STATES, 1947–2003

SOURCE: U.S. Bureau of Labor Statistics, http://www.bls.gov/cba.

were shortened to two years' duration as a hedge against the uncertain economic outlook. In the more stable economic environment of the 1990s and early 2000s the three-year bargaining cycle partially reappeared.

The Business Cycle

Nearly all studies have found that the single most important influence on the level of strike activity in the post-World War II period has been the expansion and contraction of economic activity over the business cycle.[2] The typical pattern for strike activity is *procyclical*, increasing on the upswing of the business cycle and falling off on the downswing. The major explanation for this pattern is the impact of changes in inflation and unemployment on bargaining.

Historically, a higher rate of inflation has almost always brought with it a higher level of strike activity. The reason can be seen in Figure 11.14.[3] Assume that the inflation rate is zero. The union's

resistance curve is $W_u(t)$, the employer's concession curve is $W_f(t)$, and a wage settlement of $\overline{W}$ is reached without a strike at time $\bar{t}$ (point A). After the wage settlement, inflation begins to accelerate as the economy enters the expansion phase of the business cycle. The problem for union workers in this situation is that their wages are locked into long-term contracts, and, unless the union negotiators accurately predicted the inflation, the workers' real wages will be eroded by the rise in prices. At the next bargaining round with the company, the

2   Orley Ashenfelter and George Johnson, "Bargaining Theory, Trade Unions, and Industrial Strike Activity," *American Economic Review* 50, no. 1 (March 1969): 35–49; Bruce E. Kaufman, "The Determinants of Strikes in the United States, 1900–1977," *Industrial and Labor Relations Review* 35, no. 4 (July 1982): 473–90; and Peter C. Cramton and Joseph S. Tracy, "The Determinants of U.S. Labor Disputes," Hoover Institute Working Papers in Economics: E-92-21 (September 1992).

3   Adapted from Kaufman, "Bargaining Theory, Inflation and Cyclical Strike Activity in Manufacturing."

FIGURE 11.14 AN INCREASE IN STRIKE ACTIVITY DUE TO INFLATION

Given the union's resistance curve $W_u(t)$ and the firm's concession curve $W_f(t)$, a settlement takes place at the wage $\overline{W}$ without a strike (point A). Assuming an inflation begins, the union will increase its wage demand in the next negotiations both to catch up with the rate of inflation over the term of the previous contract and to stay ahead of future inflation, shifting its resistance curve to $W_{u'}(t)$. The firm's concession curve also shifts upward, but only to $W_{f'}(t)$ since the firm will be unwilling to raise the wage by the full amount of the union's inflation forecast, fearing that the actual rate of inflation may be less. The result of inflation is to widen the distance separating the bargaining demands of the union and employer, causing a strike of $t^* - \bar{t}$ days (point B).

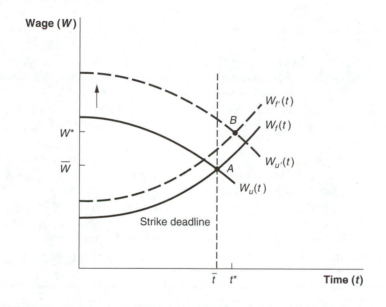

union's reaction function shifts upward to $W_{u'}(t)$ as the union increases its demand further, both to catch up with past inflation and to stay ahead of future inflation. The company will also raise its wage offer, knowing that a lengthy strike is a certainty if a pay increase at least equal to the past rate of inflation is not given. The problem for the firm is that the union also wants a pay increase equal to the expected rate of inflation over the next contract period. The firm will not agree to a wage increase of this amount because if the actual inflation rate is less than the union's forecast, the firm will be saddled with higher labor costs. The result is that the firm's concession curve shifts upward from $W_f(t)$ to $W_{f'}(t)$, an amount less than $W_u(t)$ to $W_{u'}(t)$. Because inflation has widened the gap between the union and company's demands, the concession process is more difficult and takes longer, resulting in a strike of $t^* - \bar{t}$ days (point B).[4]

---

4   For empirical evidence on this point, see Cynthia Gramm, Wallace Hendricks, and Lawrence Kahn, "Inflation Uncertainty and Strikes," *Industrial Relations* 27 (Winter 1988): 114–29; and Peter C. Cramton and Joseph S. Tracy, "The Determinants of U.S. Labor Disputes," Hoover Institute Working Papers in Economics: E-92-21 (September 1992).

Factors behind the Drop in Strikes

One of the most notable developments of the last 25 years in collective bargaining has been the sharp drop in strike activity. As shown in Figure 11.13, the number of major strikes (those involving 1,000 or more workers) in the United States between 1981 and 2003 dropped to the lowest level since the end of World War II. In addition to the reasons established in the academic literature explaining this trend, the popular press has put forth its own theories in a number of newspaper articles.

According to these articles, the drop-off in strike activity in the 1980s and 1990s reflected far-reaching economic and political shifts that fundamentally tipped the balance of power in favor of employers. Specific factors often cited include:

- High levels of unemployment in the 1980s and fears of job insecurity in the 1990s and early 2000s, particularly among workers in the basic industries that have been traditional union strongholds, made unions leery of calling a strike.
- Unions feared that higher wage demands would drive more employers to close plants or declare

bankruptcy, costing thousands of additional jobs.
- The Reagan administration was perceived to be antiunion because of its dismissal of the air traffic controllers. This action was widely interpreted as a signal to employers that it was all right to get tough with unions. Although not explicitly anti-union, the republican administrations of George H. Bush and George W. Bush have, in general, continued the Reagan policies toward organized labor.
- New technology and increased automation undercut union bargaining power by making it easier for companies to continue operating during a strike.
- Public support of unions was thought to have declined significantly, with the result that strikes did not have the community support they once had.

Most experts agree, however, that the most important factor behind the decline in strikes in the post-1980s period is the increased willingness of employers to hire strikebreakers, and the greater willingness of workers to cross union picket lines and take these jobs. In earlier years, a widespread "gentlemen's agreement" in American industry prevented

---

In an effort to keep up with inflation in the 1970s, many unions bargained for **cost-of-living allowance (COLA) clauses** in their contracts. COLA clauses provide for automatic increases in the level of wages, usually on a quarterly basis, based on the percentage increase in the Consumer Price Index (CPI). Only 25 percent of workers covered under major union contracts in 1970 had some form of COLA protection, but by 1980 this figure had risen to 60 percent. As inflation receded in the 1980s and 1990s, many unions elected to trade away COLA protection for other benefits.

Empirical studies have also found a strong link between strike activity and the level of unemployment in the labor market. During periods of high unemployment there are usually substantially fewer strikes. The major reason has to do with tactical considerations on the part of the union. During periods of high unemployment, the balance of power tips in the employer's favor, causing the union to store up its grievances rather than risk a potentially disastrous strike.[5] When improved

---

5   Albert Rees, "Industrial Conflict and Business Fluctuations," *Journal of Political Economy* 60, no. 5 (October 1952): 371–82.

employers from trying to operate during a strike or hiring replacements for striking employees. Under intense pressure to reduce costs, and aided by several favorable rulings of the NLRB, many companies abandoned this policy and fired strikers, replacing them with new recruits who often worked at wages substantially below the union rate. After companies such as Phelps-Dodge Copper Co., Continental Airlines, Hormel Meatpacking Company, and Caterpillar successfully broke strikes by hiring replacement workers, other unions became very cautious about calling strikes lest their members suffer the same fate.

In response to the tougher bargaining tactics of employers, unions attempted to buttress their strike threat in several ways. One was to maneuver the employer into initiating the strike, transforming the impasse from a work stoppage called by the union into an employer-initiated "lockout." Under the nation's labor law, during a lockout strikers cannot be permanently replaced, while they can in a union-initiated "economic strike" (a strike called by the union over economic issues such as wages). Also, in

a lockout, workers are eligible for unemployment compensation benefits while in most states strikers are not.

A second way unions attempted to reduce the employers' ability to replace strikers was to call "unfair labor practice strikes" (a strike alleging violations of the National Labor Relations Act) rather than an economic strike. Employers cannot hire permanent replacements for strikers during an unfair labor practice strike. A number of unions have also experimented with work slowdowns and various corporate campaign tactics in an attempt to find a viable substitute for the strike.

A third tactic, and the one being pursued most aggressively by unions, is to lobby Congress to pass legislation banning permanent striker replacements. To date, these efforts have been futile.

SOURCES: "Why Labor Unions Have Grown Reluctant to Use the 'S' Word," *Wall Street Journal* (December 19, 1999), and Del Jones, "Usually, Everybody Loses in a Lockout," *USA Today* (7 January 1999): 3B.

economic times arrive, the tactical advantage in bargaining shifts toward the union. At this point the union's backlog of demands gets put on the table, causing a wide gap between what the union thinks is its due and what the company thinks is reasonable. The result is more difficult bargaining and a greater number of strikes.

Political Events

Bargaining and strikes are also influenced by political events.[6] The most obvious example is the outbreak of war. In World War II and the Korean

War, wage–price controls were imposed, and some type of war labor board was created with the power to intervene in labor disputes. These actions had a paradoxical effect on strikes. Wage–price controls reduced incentives for unions to call strikes, since a ceiling limited the allowable rate of wage increase. Government intervention in bargaining worked to increase strikes, however, because the unions found that calling a strike was a sure way to bring government pressure on the employer to quickly reach

6   Kaufman, "The Determinants of Strikes in the United States, 1900–1977."

a compromise and restore production. Once wage–price controls are lifted, strike activity usually rebounds as unions seek to make up for lost gains. This seems to be partly responsible for the surge in strikes in 1974 that followed the expiration of the Nixon wage–price controls.

Another type of political event that can affect strike rates is new labor legislation. After the passage of the Wagner Act in 1935, strikes increased substantially as unions sought to exercise their newfound bargaining and organizing rights. Some evidence also suggests that strike rates increased after the passage of the Landrum-Griffin Act in 1959 as union leaders came under more political pressure in the union to bargain for contracts that would ensure their reelection to office.[7] A final form of political influence on strikes is executive action, such as President Reagan's decision to fire the air traffic controllers who illegally went on strike in 1981. This action seemed to have a chilling effect on the willingness of other unions to strike, since both labor and management widely interpreted the act as a signal that it was now permissible for firms to replace workers who strike.[8]

7   Ashenfelter and Johnson, "Bargaining Theory, Trade Unions, and Industrial Strike Activity."

8   Also see Peter C. Cramton, Morley Gunderson, and Joseph S. Tracy, "The Effect of Collective Bargaining Legislation on Strikes and Wages," *Review of Economics and Statistics* 81 (August 1999): 475–87.

Summary

Labor unions are one of the most important institutions in the labor market. Currently about one out of seven American workers belongs to a labor union, a percentage that has declined rather steadily over the past 30 years. Workers choose to join labor unions because they perceive that a union will improve their position in the labor market. The precise benefits of union membership take many forms, such as higher wages, improved working conditions, more equitable wage structures, or influence on how the job is done. Joining a union also entails costs, which have to be balanced against the benefits. These costs include the possibility of job loss, fear of management retribution, loss of social status, and possible forgone income from a strike. Before a worker can actually become a union member, a union also has to be willing and able to supply its services. The supply of union services depends on factors such as the cost of organizing, the institutional structure of unions, and the legal environment. From this interaction of the demand for union services by workers and the supply of union services by labor unions arises the level and distribution of union membership in the economy.

Collective bargaining is heavily influenced by the large body of law that defines the rules of the game by which labor and management must play. The most important piece of labor legislation is the National Labor Relations Act. This law outlawed various unfair labor practices by employers, established the union representation election, and set up the National Labor Relations Board to administer the act. Other important pieces of labor legislation are the Taft-Hartley Act and the Landrum-Griffin Act. One of the most significant developments in collective bargaining in the past 30 years has been the growth of unionism in the public sector.

In unionized firms the levels of wage, fringe benefits, and other conditions of employment are determined through the process of collective bargaining. The extent to which the union and the company achieve their objectives in bargaining depends to a large degree on their relative power positions. The origin of bargaining power is the ability of one party to impose costs on the other and to shield itself from the cost-imposing sanctions of its opponent. In collective bargaining, the most important source of bargaining power for the union is its ability to shut the firm down with a strike. The company's bargaining power comes from its ability to withstand a strike. Both sides have other sources of bargaining power in the form of consumer boycotts, corporate campaign tactics, strike insurance, and so on.

Economists have constructed formal models of the bargaining process in an attempt to predict the wage rate that the union and the company will agree to and whether or not a strike will take place. The particular model considered in this chapter involved a pair of reaction functions that yield the time path of offers and counteroffers by both sides from the start of bargaining to the ultimate point of agreement. This model shows that the union's ability to raise the wage above the market level depends critically on the right to strike. This model also shows why strikes take place. The fundamental factors are that both sides have overly optimistic expectations of what they can gain from a strike, or that considerations of principle prevent either side from making the concessions necessary to reach an agreement.

Because strikes may impose large economic costs on third parties that are not themselves involved in the dispute, attempts have been made to replace the strike with alternative methods of dispute resolution. Three such alternatives are mediation, fact-finding, and arbitration. Because workers in the public sector are often denied the right to strike, binding arbitration is one means that is frequently used to break a bargaining impasse involving them. Due to the chilling effect and the narcotic effect, binding arbitration may actually make it less likely that the parties will voluntarily reach an agreement without outside intervention.

Review Questions

1. A common saying is, "A union organizer's best friend is bad management." What does this mean? If a union succeeds in organizing a firm, is this necessarily a sign of management failure?

2. Unionization among nurses and schoolteachers increased substantially in the 1980s and 1990s. Among bank employees, on the other hand, unions made few inroads. Can you explain what factors might account for this difference?

3. What do you think are the growth prospects for labor unions in the next 10 years? Briefly explain the reasons for your answer.

4. In a number of respects the Teamsters union has a poor public image. Each year, however, more workers vote to join the Teamsters than any other union. Can you offer an explanation for this paradox?

5. Explain the major provisions of the National Labor Relations Act and the Taft-Hartley Act.

6. How does bargaining power affect the size of the wage increase that the union is able to win from the company? What factors increase the union's bargaining power? What factors increase the company's?

7. A common finding is that a company and a union that have bargained together for many years are less likely to experience a strike than a union and company that are new to each other. Can you explain this observation?

8. Some economists have argued that strikes are irrational forms of behavior. According to this line of reasoning, if after a strike of S days the two sides agree to a wage W, wouldn't both the union and the company have been better off to agree to W in the first place and avoid the costs of the strike? What do you say to this?

9. How might mediation be able to lessen the probability of a strike occurring? In what situations might mediation be more successful than in others? Answer these same questions for fact-finding.

A Comparison of Monopoly, Efficient Contract, and Median Voter Models of Union Wage Determination

This appendix provides a more in-depth analysis of models of union wage determination and introduces several new theoretical approaches not covered earlier. These include the monopoly, efficient contract, and median voter models of unions. All three have received considerable attention in recent years.[1]

The Monopoly Model

The first analytical model of union wage determination was put forward by John Dunlop in the mid-1940s. Dunlop hypothesized that union wage policy is directed toward the maximization of some particular objective, such as the wage bill or net economic rents of the membership. William Fellner suggested, however, that a more general approach is to assume that the objective of the union is to maximize the total utility of the membership.[2] He argues, in turn, that the two key variables of interest to each union member are the wage rate W and the level of employment L in the firm. Assuming it is possible to aggregate over the preferences of individual union members with respect to W and L, a union utility function of the form can be obtained. This function can be used to derive union indifference curves, such as I_1, I_2, and I_3 in Figure 11A.1. Because both the wage rate and employment level are "goods" to the union, each indifference curve has a negative slope. (To keep utility constant, a higher wage must be offset by a lower level of employment.) The indifference curves are also convex, indicating a diminishing willingness on the union's part to further substitute W for L, and vice versa. Finally, higher indifference curves represent higher levels of utility for the union.

Given the union's indifference curves, what wage will the union seek in bargaining? Assume that to begin with, the firm is nonunion and pays the going market wage W_1 in Figure 11A.1. The monopoly model presumes that the union sets the wage and the firm then adjusts employment to the profit-maximizing level on its demand curve. The labor demand curve, therefore, represents all the various combinations of W and L that the union can choose from. The utility-maximizing wage/employment combination for the union in this situation is clearly at point X in Figure 11A.1, where the indifference curve I_2 is tangent to the labor demand

---

1   This selection is based on Bruce E. Kaufman, "Models of Union Wage Determination: What Have We Learned since Dunlop and Ross?" *Industrial Relations* 41 (January 2002): 110–58.

2   William Fellner, *Competition among the Few* (New York: Knopf, 1949). Dunlop's model is in John Dunlop, *Wage Determination under Trade Unions* (New York: Macmillan, 1944).

The union's indifference curves are I_1, I_2, and I_3, and the employer's demand curve is D. The nonunion wage/employment combination is W_1/L_1. If the workers organize a union, it will use its bargaining power to raise the wage to W_2 (point X) where the labor demand curve D is tangent to the indifference curve I_2. This model assumes that the firm remains free to set the level of employment. At the wage of W_2, therefore, the firm will reduce employment to L_2.

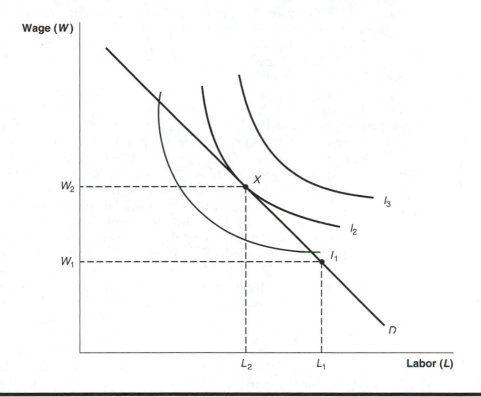

curve D.[3] The union's bargaining power results in a wage increase from W_1 to W_2, but employment falls from L_1 to L_2. Note that this result closely resembles the impact on price and quantity demanded by a monopolistic firm in the product market. Although the trade-off of a higher wage W_2 for a lower level of employment L_2 is optimal for this union, another union with different preferences regarding

---

3   The simple version of these models assumes that the union has sufficient bargaining power to set the wage at whatever level maximizes its utility. More complex models bring in the bargaining process, often in the form of game theory. See Alison Booth, *The Economics of Trade Unions* (Cambridge: Cambridge University Press, 1995).

wages versus employment (and, thus, differently shaped indifference curves) would choose some other point on the labor demand curve.

The Efficient Contract Model

A number of economists have suggested that the predictions of the monopoly model of unions are suspect because its optimal wage/employment combination is not an "efficient" or "Pareto optimal" contact.[4] A labor contract is efficient or Pareto optimal if it is not possible to find any other combination of W and L that makes at least one of the bargaining parties better off without making the other worse off. The fact that the monopoly outcome is inefficient is important, the critics say, because it means *some other* bargaining outcome exists that would yield the union and the firm a higher level of utility and that they would, therefore, have a strong incentive to adopt.

The nature of this argument is more easily understood by looking at Figure 11A.2, which reproduces the firm's labor demand curve D and the union's indifference curve I_1 and I_2. What is new is the series of concave *isoprofit curves* P_1 and P_2. Each curve is the locus of wage/employment combinations along which the firm's profits are unchanged. They represent indifference curves for the employer. Each isoprofit curve slopes upward on either side of the labor demand curve until a maximum is reached where the two curves intersect.

The reason they have this particular shape is straightforward. Given a wage rate W_4 such as in Figure 11A.2, the firm maximizes profit by hiring L_4 workers, given by point X on the demand curve. Clearly, if the firm either expands or contracts employment from L_4, the only way profit will not decline is if the wage is also lowered. Plotting all the resulting wage/employment combinations for which profit remains unchanged yields the isoprofit curve P_1. Finally, note that a lower isoprofit curve such as P_2 represents a higher level of profit for the firm than P_1 because the wage associated with any given level of employment is smaller along P_2.

As before, let W_1 be the going market wage. Given the union's indifference curves, the monopoly wage outcome is W_4 with an employment level of L_4 (point X). It is easy to show that the monopoly union outcome is an inefficient contract. Consider the alternative wage/employment combination of W_2/L_2 (point Y), for example. Compared to the monopoly outcome, the union is equally well off since it remains on the indifference curve I_1, but the firm is better off because it earns a higher level of profit by being on the isoprofit curve P_2. Alternatively, consider the wage/employment combination of W_3/L_3 (point Z). This outcome is also superior to point X since the firm's profits remain the same, but the union has reached a higher level of utility.

It can be seen that there is in fact an entire set of contracts that the union and firm will find at least as good as the monopoly contract. These superior outcomes are given by the shaded area in Figure 11A.2. Among this set, those that are Pareto

---

4   This point was first made by Wassily Leontief in "The Pure Theory of the Guaranteed Annual Wage Contract," *Journal of Political Economy* 54 (February 1946): 76–79. His insight was further developed and popularized in Ian McDonald and Robert Solow, "Wage Bargaining and Employment," *American Economic Review* 71 (December 1981): 896–908.

The monopoly union outcome is W_4/L_4 (point X). This outcome is not efficient or Pareto optimal, however, because other wage/employment combinations to the right of labor demand curve D can make at least one side better off without reducing the utility of the other. One such efficient contract outcome is W_2/L_2 (point Y) because, relative to the monopoly outcome of W_3/L_3, the employer is able to earn a higher level of profit (by moving from the isoprofit curve P_1 to P_2) while the union's utility remains constant along the indifference curve I_1. The contract curve that connects points Y and Z represents the locus of efficient contract outcomes.

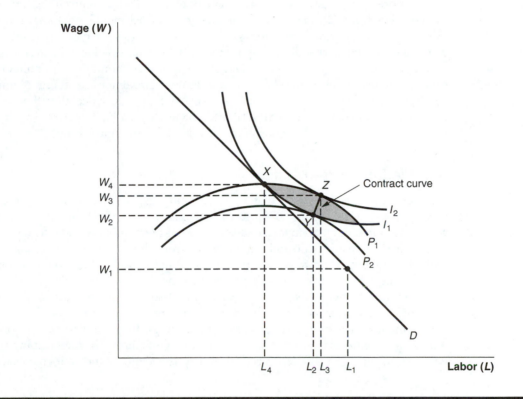

optimal or efficient contracts are where an isoprofit curve and an indifference curve are tangent to each other. Two such efficient contracts are points Y and Z. Observe that for each outcome, there is no alternative wage/employment combination that will not make one of the bargainers worse off.

Points Y and Z are only two of many possible efficient contracts. The locus of efficient contracts is given by the line that connects points Y and Z, a line often called the "contract curve." The contract curve may be upward sloping, vertical, or negatively sloped, depending on the precise shape of the isoprofit and indifference curves. Although each point on the contract curve is an efficient bargain, this does *not* mean that the firm and union are indifferent to where along the line YZ they reach a settlement. The union would clearly prefer to locate on the contract curve as close to point Z as possible where both wages and employment are higher, while the firm would prefer moving toward point Y where its profits are the greatest. The efficient contract model predicts, therefore, that the bargained outcome will be somewhere on the contract curve. The precise point of settlement will reflect the relative bargaining power of the two sides.

Compared to the monopoly union outcome of W_4/L_4, the predicted outcome in the efficient contract model entails a lower wage, but a higher level of employment. Also, the firm is no longer on its labor demand curve, but rather has agreed to hire more workers at the bargained wage than it would hire if given the freedom to maximize profits. Proponents of the efficient contract model argue that this result offers a ready explanation for why unions desire various types of restrictive work rules or "featherbedding" requirements such as narrow job classifications or minimum crew sizes. In each case, the net effect of these contract requirements is to force the firm to hire more labor than it desires. Two empirical studies of union contract settlements in the printing industry did find evidence that the wage/employment outcomes were off the labor demand curve, a finding at odds with the monopoly union model, but consistent with the efficient contract model.[5]

The Median Voter Model

Another study has suggested that *both* the monopoly and the efficient contract models are critically flawed because each neglects the political nature of union wage determination.[6] An important assumption of the monopoly and efficient contract models is that it is possible to construct from the underlying preferences of individual rank-and-file members an aggregate union utility function and union indifference curves. Economists that have used these models generally justify such an assumption by hypothesizing that each union member has the same probability of layoff or, alternatively, that all union members equally share a reduction in employment by working fewer hours (work-sharing). In actual practice, however, most union contracts mandate that the order of layoff among the membership is by inverse seniority.[7] If layoff depends on seniority, it becomes impossible to construct

---

5   See Thomas McCurdy and John Pencavel, "Testing between Competing Models of Wage and Employment Determination in Unionized Markets," and James Brown and Orley Ashenfelter, "Testing the Efficiency of Labor Contracts," *Journal of Political Economy* 94, part 2 (June 1986): S3–S39 and S40–S87. Data from the Swedish construction sector provide predictions about union behavior consistent with both the monopoly union model and the efficient contract model, depending on the statistical model specified. See Thomas Aronsson et al., "Monopoly Union versus Efficient Bargaining: Wage and Employment Determination in the Swedish Construction Sector," *European Journal of Political Economy* 9 (August 1993): 357–70.

6   Bruce E. Kaufman and Jorge Martinez-Vazquez, "Monopoly, Efficient Contract, and Median Voter Models of Union Wage Determination: A Critical Comparison," *Journal of Labor Research* 11 (Fall 1990): 401–23.

7   For evidence see Andrew Oswald, "Efficient Contracts Are on the Labour Demand Curve: Theory and Facts," *Labour Economics* 1 (June 1993): 85–113.

a well-defined union utility function, since the preference of the least-senior worker for wage versus employment is likely to be quite different from the preference of a relatively senior worker.

One way around this problem posed by heterogeneity of preferences among the rank and file is to analyze union wage determination in the context of the median voter model. A layoff-by-seniority rule creates a distribution of most preferred wage/employment outcomes among the membership. The nature of this preference ranking is illustrated in Figure 11A.3 for two representative union members.

FIGURE 11A.3 THE PREFERRED WAGE OF THE MEDIAN VOTER

The union membership is arrayed along the horizontal axis on the basis of seniority, with worker L_1 having the lowest seniority and worker L_M being in the median position. As long as employment remains L_1 or greater, the utility for worker L_1 rises with increases in the wage rate, as represented by the upward shift of the indifference curves from $I_{1,1}$ to $I_{1,2}$ and so on. At an employment level less than L_1, this worker is laid off and utility falls to zero along the broken vertical line. The same type of preference ordering applies to worker L_M, except that utility only falls to zero when employment is less than L_M. Given the demand curve D, the optimal wage for worker L_1 is W_1 (point X); for worker L_M it is W_M (point Y).

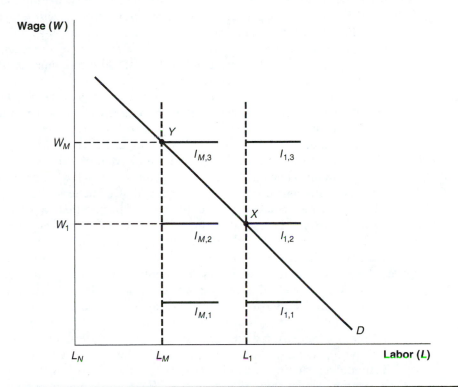

The union membership is ordered along the horizontal axis from left to right, with the L_{1st} worker being the least senior, the L_{Mth} being the median, and the L_{Nth} being the most senior. For the least-senior union member L_1, as long as employment is L_1 or greater his or her utility increases with the wage, represented by the upward movement from indifference curve $I_{1,1}$ to $I_{1,2}$ to $I_{1,3}$. The indifference curves are horizontal to the right of L_1 on the assumption that each union member's utility is a function of only his or her employment, and not the total level of employment. To the left of the broken line at L_1, however, the utility of the L_{1st} member falls to zero (neglecting the possibility of alternative employments). The same type of preference ordering applies to the median member, except that utility only falls to zero when employment is less than L_M.

Given these preference orderings, each union member's most preferred wage rate is at the point where their highest indifference curve intersects the firm's labor demand curve. Thus, the L_{1st} member's optimal wage is W_1 (point X) and the median member's is W_M (point Y). At any higher wage, these workers would lose their jobs and utility would fall to zero.

Given this distribution of preferred wage rates among the membership, what wage will the union demand from the employer? Figure 11A.4 provides the answer. This diagram incorporates the union indifference curves, employer isoprofit curves, and labor demand curve from Figure 11A.2 with a portion of the indifference curves of the median voter from Figure 11A.3. The convex union indifference curves I_1 and I_2 no longer represent the preferences of the entire union, however, but rather those of the union leadership. The union leadership's indifference curves are convex on the reasonable assumption that the leadership values both higher wages and greater employment and is willing to substitute more of one for less of the other. As before, I_2 is preferred to I_1.

The market wage is W_1. The wage that the union demands from the employer depends on the political system within the union with respect to the election of officers and ratification of contracts. Two polar cases will be considered. The first is a perfectly democratic union where the rank and file have a costless and unobstructed ability to vote in repeated referenda on the election of officers and ratification of contracts. In this situation, the union's bargaining demands will be the most preferred wage of the **median voter** among the rank and file. The reason is that a vote on any wage/employment combination will not garner the required 51 percent approval to pass until the wages are as high as they can go without the median member being laid off. The median member will vote no for any higher wage because he or she would get laid off. The median member would vote no for any lower wage because he only cares about his job and would still keep his job at a higher wage. In Figure 11A.4, the median voter's preferred wage, given the labor demand curve D, is W_M (point X).

If the union leadership were completely free to choose, they also would prefer an alternative wage to W_M. Given the tangency point between the leadership's indifference curve I_1 and the demand curve, their preferred wage is W_3 (point Y). With perfect democracy, however, the leadership is constrained to choose W_M as the union's bargaining demand since it is the only wage that will win a majority vote among the membership. A lower wage of W_3, for example, would be opposed by a

In a perfectly democratic union, the wage outcome is W_M (point X) where the median voter's difference curve $I_{M,1}$ is tangent to the labor demand curve D. In a nondemocratic union, the wage outcome is W_3 (point Y) where the union leader's indifference curve I_1 is tangent to the demand curve. Assuming that the convex indifference curves I_1 and I_2 belong to the entire union rather than just the leadership, the median voter model's wage outcome is W_M, the monopoly union's wage outcome is W_3, and one of the efficient contract wage outcomes is W_2.

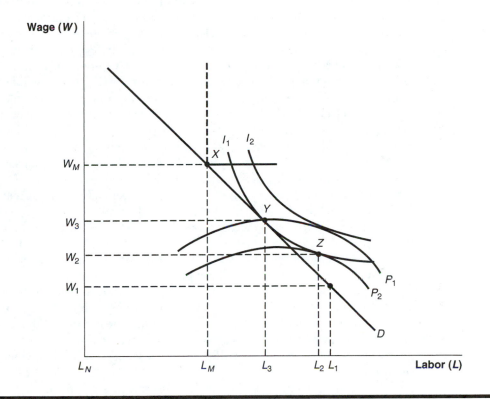

majority of union members comprising all workers with seniority greater than L_3, while a wage above W_M would be opposed by a majority including the median voter and all workers of lower seniority.

The polar opposite of a perfectly democratic union is a dictatorial union where the rank and file have no effective voice in the choice of leaders or the approval of contracts. In this case, the union leadership is free to pursue a wage policy that maximizes its own utility, at least within fairly wide limits. The preferred wage of the union leadership may be above W_M or below it, depending on where the union leadership's indifference curve is tangent to the labor demand curve. In Figure 11A.4 the leadership's preferred wage is W_3 (point Y), a lower wage than W_M.[8] A majority of the union membership oppose this wage and would vote down such a contract in favor of one paying the higher wage W_M. Since the union members cannot vote they grudgingly accept W_3 since it is still superior to the alternative wage of W_1 available at other, nonunion firms.

A Comparison of the Three Models

It is possible to depict in Figure 11A.4 the wage/employment outcomes in the monopoly, efficient contract, and median voter models. Assuming I_1 and I_2 are indifference curves for the aggregate union (instead of the leadership), the monopoly outcome is W_3/L_3 (point Y), an efficient contract outcome is W_2/L_2 (point Z), and the median voter outcome under perfect democracy is W_M/L_M (point X).

Figure 11A.4 can also be used to illustrate two significant drawbacks to the efficient contract model. First, layoff by seniority makes it impossible to derive a unique set of efficient contracts. In the efficient contract model, the outcome W_2/L_2 is considered to be an efficient contract since the union membership is, as a group, no worse off relative to the monopoly outcome of W_3/L_3, but the firm is on a higher isoprofit curve. Heterogeneous preferences among the union rank and file, however, mean that the movement from W_3/L_3 to W_2/L_2 clearly results in gains for some in the union, but losses for others. In particular, the outcome of W_2/L_2 would represent a utility gain for the $L_2 - L_3$ union members who are laid off at the wage W_3 but have a job at W_2, while a utility loss would be suffered by the $L_2 - L_3$ workers of higher seniority who take a wage cut from W_3 to W_2 with no corresponding benefit of increased employment.

The same conclusion holds starting from any other point on the labor demand curve, suggesting that no unique union indifference curve and, thus, contract curve of efficient bargains exists. Even if they did, in a democratic union there is strong reason to doubt that an efficient contract outcome such as W_2/L_2 would gain approval by a majority of the membership since a large number of the rank and file $L_N - L_3$ are, in effect, being asked to accept a wage cut of $W_3 - W_2$ in order to provide additional jobs for a small minority ($L_2 - L_3$) of union members of low seniority.

A second problem with the efficient contract model is that it leads to the expectation that most union contracts will contain featherbedding requirements or

---

8 Some evidence suggests that union leaders are less militant than the rank and file, while other evidence points to the opposite conclusion. As an example of the former, following the passage of the Landrum-Griffin Act in 1959 (with its provisions for greater union democracy) a growing number of contracts negotiated by the leadership were rejected by the rank and file. See William E. Simkin, "Refusals to Ratify Contracts," *Industrial and Labor Relations Review* 21 (July 1968): 518–40. Evidence in support of the latter interpretation is presented in another study [Jack Fiorito and Wallace Hendricks, "Union Characteristics and Bargaining Outcomes," *Industrial and Labor Relations Review* 40 (July 1987): 569–584], which found that negotiated wage levels among manufacturing firms were lower when more democratic unions were involved.

restrictive work rules. In bargaining an efficient contract, the most straightforward tactic for the union would be simply to require that the firm employ a certain number of workers, such as L_2 in Figure 11A.4. The problem with this approach is it is generally not practical, since every firm needs the flexibility to reduce its workforce in the event of a slowdown in business activity.[9] Without some type of contractual safeguard, however, the union has good reason to refuse to move from the monopoly outcome of W_3/L_3 to the efficient contract outcome of W_2/L_2, since the firm has the opportunity to cheat on the agreement once it is signed by claiming that sales are slower and employment needs to be cut back to the demand curve.

One way out of this dilemma is for the union to bargain for various "make-work" requirements such as minimum crew sizes. Such restrictive work rules have the advantage that they force the firm to have more workers than desired, thus moving the firm off the demand curve, and at the same time are more easily policed by the union for potential cheating on the part of the employer.[10] If the efficient contract model is a valid representation of union wage determination, therefore, it should be expected that most union contracts would contain such restrictive work rules. The evidence, however, is that featherbedding practices are prevalent in only a minority of unionized industries, principally in declining industries such as railroads or in industries where craft unions such as the printers are threatened by technological change.[11] The reason for this anomaly is easily explained with the median voter model.

To obtain a make-work requirement in the contract, a union generally has to give up something else, such as higher wages. Thus, the firm would willingly trade the monopoly outcome of W_3/L_3 (point Y) on the isoprofit curve P_1 in Figure 11A.4 for the efficient contract outcome on the isoprofit curve P_2 with a lower wage of W_2 but a larger level of employment of L_2 (point Z) associated with some type of featherbedding requirement. The problem with this trade-off, however, is that a majority of the rank and file have no incentive to vote for it. They suffer a cut in wages from W_3 to W_2 but reap none of the benefits from the additional jobs created. The implication, therefore, is that most unions do not bargain for make-work requirements since obtaining them would not benefit the majority of the union's members. In certain industries, however, where a majority of the rank and file feel their job security is threatened by technological change or some other such development, make-work policies are much more likely to be an attractive bargaining issue for the union.

---

9   This is evident in the historic 1987 Ford–UAW contract, for example, where the company pledged to avoid layoffs for all currently employed UAW members *except* when a decline in sales made layoffs necessary.

10 See George Johnson, "Work Rules, Featherbedding, and Pareto-Optimal Union Management Bargaining," *Journal of Labor Economics* 8, no. 1, pt. 2 (January 1990): S237–S259.

11 See Sumner Slichter, James Healy, and E. Robert Livernash, *The Impact of Collective Bargaining on Management* (Washington, D.C.: The Brookings Institution, 1960).

The Economic Impact of Unions

Bargaining theory predicts that the level of wages in a unionized labor market should be higher than in a similar nonunion market. This chapter looks at the empirical evidence on this issue. The first topic is the measurement of union–nonunion wage differentials. The chapter then turns to a review of various estimates of the union wage effect, first at the aggregate level and then for specific demographic, industry, and occupational groups. The chapter ends with a discussion of the impact of unions on three important nonwage outcomes in the labor market: fringe benefits, productivity, and profits.

Do Unions Raise Wages?

The central question addressed in this chapter is whether unions raise their members' wage rates above what they would have earned in an otherwise comparable nonunion setting, and if so, by how much. Some of the issues involved are illustrated in Table 12.1.

Column 1 of Table 12.1 shows the percentage of full-time wage and salary workers in each industry or occupation who were represented by a labor union. Columns 2 and 3 show the median weekly earnings of full-time wage and salary workers in 2004, classified by industry, occupation, and whether or not the worker was represented by a labor union.[1] The data in column 4 represent what this chapter calls the **unadjusted union–nonunion wage differential** (U), calculated as the percentage differential between the reported earnings (hourly, weekly, or annual) of union workers, W_u, and the reported earnings of nonunion workers, W_n:

$$U = \frac{W_u - W_n}{W_n} \times 100. \tag{12.1}$$

---

1   Median earnings are the level of earnings that half the workers earn more than and half the workers earn less than.

TABLE 12.1

UNADJUSTED UNION-NONUNION EARNINGS DIFFERENTIALS, 2004

	Percentage Represented by a Union	Median Weekly Earnings, Union Workers	Median Weekly Earnings, Nonunion Workers	Unadjusted Earnings Differential
National Average	13.8	$734.00	$604.00	21.5
Industry				
Construction	15.4	884	588	50.3
Manufacturing	13.9	692	654	5.8
Transportation and Utilities	26.3	850	662	28.4
Retail and Wholesale Trade	5.9	590	547	7.9
Services	5.3	713	609	17.1
Government	40.7	827	683	21.1
Occupation				
Professional	20.9	907	875	3.7
Office	11.9	671	519	29.3
Construction and Extraction	20.5	852	555	53.5
Installation and Maintenance	20.7	880	662	32.9
Transportation	20	689	491	40.3
Services	12.3	647	389	66.3

SOURCE: Bureau of Labor Statistics, *Employment and Earnings* (January 2005): Tables 42 and 43.

Do unionized workers earn higher wages? Based on the data in Table 12.1, the answer would appear to be yes. The first row shows that for workers across all industries and occupations, unionized workers earn approximately 21.5 percent more than nonunion workers. Note, however, that the union differential is only 3.7 percent for professional occupations. In addition, in several cases not shown in this table's broad aggregates the unionized workers in highly organized industries or occupations actually earn less than their nonunion counterparts. Does this mean that unions in a weakly organized industry, such as services, are able to raise wages more than unions in strongly organized industries, such as manufacturing?

The answer is no. For obvious and not so obvious reasons, the unadjusted wage differentials reported in Table 12.1 give a very biased estimate of the true impact of unions on wage rates in the labor market. The purpose of this chapter is to explain the nature of these biases and show how economists adjust the reported wage differentials in Table 12.1 to isolate the pure union wage effect.

Measuring the Union–Nonunion Wage Differential

Previous chapters have shown that the earnings of individual workers will differ for a host of reasons related to age, race, gender, level of education, industry, and occupation, as well as union status. The problem for empirical studies is to disentangle the pure, isolated effect of unions on wages from the influence of all these other variables. In effect, the question is: What would be the difference in the wage rates for two people who are identical in every other respect, if one was a union member and one was not?

The unadjusted estimate U in Equation 12.1 will not, in general, yield an accurate answer for two reasons. First, the union status of workers is correlated in a systematic way with many of the other factors causing earnings differentials. For example, the higher wage of union members may be due to their union membership, or it may reflect the fact that union members are more than proportionately male or that they tend to work in high-wage industries, such as steel or construction. The second reason is that the positive effect of union status on the earnings of union workers may itself change the earnings of nonunion workers, making it impossible to disentangle the direct effect of union status on W_u from its indirect effect on W_n.[2] For example, nonunion employers may raise their wages in line with the wage gains won by union workers in order to keep from being organized.

The reported earnings data for union and nonunion workers must be adjusted to standardize or hold constant all these other influences on wage rates. Letting $W_u{}^*$ and $W_n{}^*$ stand for these standardized wage rates, the **adjusted union–nonunion wage differential** U^* can be calculated as:

$$U^* = \frac{W_u^* - W_n^*}{W_n^*} \times 100. \qquad \textbf{(12.2)}$$

> ➲ **SEE**
> **Empirical Evidence 12-1:**
> Estimates of the Union
> Wage Effect, p. 653.

It is this adjusted estimate U^* that measures the pure, isolated effect of unionism. Detailed estimates of U^* are presented and discussed in Empirical Evidence 12-1.

The Problem of Other Things Equal

For two basic reasons, the unadjusted value of U given in Equation 12.1 will yield inaccurate estimates of the true union wage effect U^*. The first is the fact that the earnings of union workers are systematically correlated with other determinants of

---

2   See Lawrence M. Kahn, "Unionism and Relative Wages: Direct and Indirect Effects," *Industrial and Labor Relations Review* 32, no. 4 (July 1979): 520–32, and C. Jeffrey Waddoups, "Unions and Wages in Nevada's Hotel–Casino Industry," *Journal of Labor Research* 21 (Spring 2000): 345–62.

earnings, leading to what might be called the **problem of other things equal.** There are at least five major sources of bias in this regard.[3]

Demographic Characteristics   One source of bias in the unadjusted estimate U arises from systematic differences between union and nonunion workers in various demographic characteristics. Union members, for example, are more likely to be male, black, and older than nonunion workers. Since male workers and older workers have higher earnings, on average, than female or younger workers, part of the positive union–nonunion wage differential measured by U is actually a result of these variables, not of union status.[4] An opposite conclusion would apply to the influence of race.

Productivity Differences   If unionized firms pay higher wages, one result should be a long queue of job applicants for them to choose from, allowing unionized firms to "skim the cream" of the workforce.[5] It may be that by paying a higher wage, the unionized firm also obtains workers who are more productive and who would have commanded higher wages even without a union (sometimes called a "positive selection effect"). This greater productivity may be associated with demographic characteristics such as age, race, gender, or years of education. It may also arise from factors such as longer tenure with the firm or unmeasured characteristics such as motivation and work effort. Whatever the source, if union workers are more productive than nonunion workers, the unadjusted union–nonunion wage differential U will mistakenly attribute all of the difference between W_u and W_n to the effect of unionism when, in reality, part of it is due to productivity differences among workers.

Job-Related Characteristics   The characteristics of the jobs held by union and nonunion workers may also cause U to overstate the true union wage effect U^*. Union workers, for example, are more likely to be employed in blue-collar, goods-producing jobs than are nonunion workers. These jobs frequently have more disagreeable features, such as monotony of work, risk of injury and illness, more physical exertion, or less flexible work schedules. It has been argued that part of the higher wage rate W_u paid to union members is not the result of union status, but

---

3   For the sake of simplicity, a sixth source of bias is not discussed in the text. This involves the possible simultaneous relationship between wages and unionism that, if uncontrolled for in regression analysis, will bias the estimate of U^*. For a comprehensive discussion of this and other issues involved in measuring union wage effects, see H. G. Lewis, *Union Relative Wage Effects: A Survey* (Chicago: University of Chicago Press, 1986). Also see Alison Booth, *The Economics of Trade Unions* (Cambridge: Cambridge University Press, 1995).

4   See, for example, Phanindra Wunnava and Noga Peled, "Union Wage Premiums by Gender and Race: Evidence from PSID 1980–1992," *Journal of Labor Research* 20 (Summer 1999): 415–24.

5   Empirical evidence is provided in Gauthier Lanot and Ian Walker, "The Union/Nonunion Wage Differential: An Application of Semiparametric Methods," *Journal of Econometrics* 84 (June 1998): 327–49.

rather represents a market-determined compensating differential for disagreeable job characteristics.[6]

Structure of the Firm's Product Market   The earnings of union and nonunion workers may also differ because of the varying degrees of competition their employers face in the product market. Unionized firms tend to be in oligopolistic or regulated industries where barriers to entry allow firms to earn above-average profits. A number of studies have found that more-profitable firms also pay higher wages, other things being equal. This could be due to satisficing behavior or a desire to attract a particular type of worker. Whatever the reason, if part of the higher wage W_u earned by unionized workers is actually due to the more generous compensation policy of their employers, the unadjusted estimate U will again overstate the true union wage effect U^*.

Employee Benefits   A fifth source of bias in estimating the union wage effect will result if fringe benefits are omitted from the analysis. Studies have found that unionized workers receive not only higher wages, but also more employee benefits. Since employee benefits are an alternative form of earnings for workers and another form of labor cost for firms, the unadjusted estimate U will understate the true effect of unions on earnings since it includes only wages and ignores fringe benefits.[7]

The Problem of Mutual Interdependence

The second major problem in estimating U^* is that a change in the wage rate of unionized workers may also cause a change in the wage of nonunion workers. This might be called the **problem of mutual interdependence.** It occurs for two reasons.

The Spillover Effect   One source of bias in the unadjusted wage effect U is due to the **spillover effect,** as illustrated in Figure 12.1. Graph (a) is the union sector; graph (b) is the nonunion sector. Assume that jobs and other such factors are identical in both sectors and that neither sector is organized. Mobility in the labor market will bring about an equilibrium such that wages are equal in both

6   See Greg Duncan and Frank Stafford, "Do Union Members Receive Compensating Wage Differentials?" *American Economic Review* 70, no. 3 (June 1980): 355–71, and Peter F. Kostiuk, "Compensating Differentials for Shift Work," *Journal of Political Economy* 98 (October 1990): 1054–75.

7   One article estimates that unionized employers spend from 15 to 93 percent more on health insurance and from 33 to 168 percent more on pensions than nonunionized employers do. See Augustin Kwasi Fosu, "Nonwage Benefits as a Limited-Dependent Variable: Implications for the Impact of Unions," *Journal of Labor Research* 14 (Winter 1993): 29–43. Another study hypothesizes that unionized firms are able to provide more benefits because they use production technologies that yield higher work productivity, or because unionized firms prefer to pay their workers economic rents in the form of higher benefits. See Edward Montgomery and Kathryn Shaw, "Pensions and Wage Premia," *Economic Inquiry* 35 (July 1997): 510–22.

FIGURE 12.1   THE SPILLOVER AND THREAT EFFECTS

The union is able to raise the wage in the union sector—graph (a)—from the competitive level W_1 to W_u. The size of the union wage effect U^* is $(W_u - W_1)/W_1$. Since W_1 is unobservable, the comparison used in calculating U^* is between W_u and the wage in the nonunion sector—graph (b). Both the spillover and threat effects, however, bias this estimate of U^*. With the spillover effect, the expansion of labor supply in the nonunion sector drives the wage from W_1 to W_n; the threat effect, on the other hand, causes nonunion firms to pay to avoid unionization. In the former case, $(W_u - W_n)$ overstates U^*, in the latter case $(W_u - W_n^2)/W_n^2$ understates U^*.

(a) Union Sector

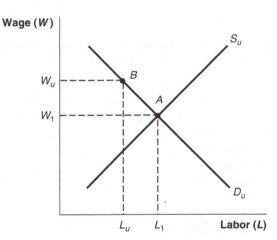

(b) Nonunion Sector

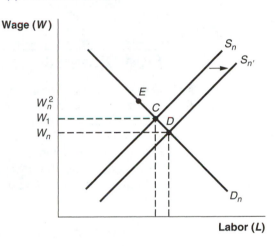

sectors, shown in graphs (a) and (b) by the common wage W_1 at points A and C, respectively.

What if a union succeeds in organizing the workers in the first sector and, because of its bargaining power, is able to raise the wage in graph (a) to W_u (point B)? The pure union wage effect would be measured as $U^* = (W_u - W_1)/W_1 \cdot 100$. Unfortunately, the estimate of U using reported earnings data for both sectors will not equal U^*. In the union sector, $L_1 - L_u$ workers lose their jobs at the higher wage of W_u, causing some of the unemployed to spill over into the nonunion sector in search of work. The increase in the supply of labor in the nonunion sector results in a rightward shift in the supply curve from S_n to S'_n and a decline in the nonunion wage rate to W_n (point C to point D). Calculating the unadjusted union–nonunion wage differential results in $U = (W_u - W_n)/W_n \cdot 100$. U overstates the true union wage effect U^* because it captures the effect of both the union's bargaining power and the market response to an increase in labor supply.[8]

The Threat Effect The spillover effect causes U to overstate U^*. A second form of interdependency between W_u and W_n, the **threat effect,** leads to the opposite result. To forestall the unionization of their workers, nonunion employers may voluntarily pay wage rates higher than the market level.[9] Such a wage rate might be W_n^2 (point E) in graph (b). The unadjusted union wage effect in this case is $U = (W_u - W_n^2)/W_n^2 \times 100$. The threat effect causes U to understate U^*. One study estimates that wages for nonunion registered nurses in a unionized labor market will be 2.5 percent higher than if they were employed in a labor market that was not heavily unionized.[10] In some cases, to remain nonunion a firm will pay a wage higher than the union wage. In this situation the unadjusted wage effect U will be negative.

Five Dimensions of the Union Wage Effect

In addition to taking care of other things being equal and the problem of mutual interdependence when comparing union and nonunion wages, there are five additional dimensions of the union wage effect worth considering. These include how the percentage of the workforce that is unionized impacts the wage effect, how the union wage effect has changed over time, how the structure of the product market impacts the wage effect, how the presence of a union impacts wage inequality, and the influence unions have in the public sector.

Percentage of the Workforce Organized

An important determinant of the union wage effect for workers in a particular industry or geographic area is the percentage of the workforce that are union members. Several reasons support the supposition that as the rate of unionization increases among firms in a given product market, so does the wage rate that a union

---

8   Evidence of spillover effects within industries (as unionization in an industry increases, the nonunion wage in that industry declines) can be found in David Neumark and Michael L. Wachter, "Union Effects on Nonunion Wages: Evidence from Panel Data on Industries and Cities," *Industrial and Labor Relations Review* 49 (October 1995): 20–38.

9   Evidence indicates that the impact of the threat effect on wages depends on the size of the firm, with larger firms being much more likely than smaller ones to raise wages to avoid unionization. One reason may be that smaller firms have less profit; a second may be that they are less attractive targets for unions because the per-member costs of representing their workers are higher. See, for example, "Unions, Firm Size and Wages," *The Economic Record* 72 (June 1996): 138–53. Also see Giacomo Corneo and Claudio Lucifora, "Wage Formation under Union Threat Effects: Theory and Empirical Evidence," *Labour Economics* 4 (September 1997): 265–92.

10   Barry T. Hirsch and Edward J. Schumacher, "Union Wages, Rents, and Skills in Health Care Labor Markets," *Journal of Labor Research* 19 (Winter 1998): 125–47.

is able to win in bargaining. For one thing, the labor demand curve becomes more inelastic, allowing the union greater latitude to push up wages without a significant employment effect. This result stems from both the first and second laws of derived demand, discussed in Chapter 5. A greater degree of union organization among firms in the product market reduces the ability of consumers to switch from higher-priced union-made products to lower-priced nonunion products, making the product demand curve of unionized firms more inelastic and, thus, making their labor demand curve more inelastic (the first law). Greater unionization of firms in a given market may also make the labor demand curve more inelastic if it reduces the ability of employers to substitute nonunion for union labor (the second law). Finally, a greater percentage organized will increase the union's bargaining power by allowing it to shut down more of the firms in a strike.

The relationship between the percentage unionized in an industry or locality and the union wage effect U^* is illustrated in Figure 12.2. The union wage effect increases with the degree of organization in a nonlinear fashion. At low levels of unionization, the union's bargaining power is weak because, if it raises wages very far, it will put the few firms it has organized at a serious competitive disadvantage. The result is only a slight union wage effect. Over the middle range of percentage

---

FIGURE 12.2   **THE RELATIONSHIP BETWEEN THE PERCENTAGE ORGANIZED AND THE SIZE OF THE UNION WAGE EFFECT**

The union wage effect U^* varies with the percentage of the workforce organized among firms in the product market. At low levels of unionization, U^* is small, rises rapidly in the middle range, and then increases slowly again at high levels of unionization.

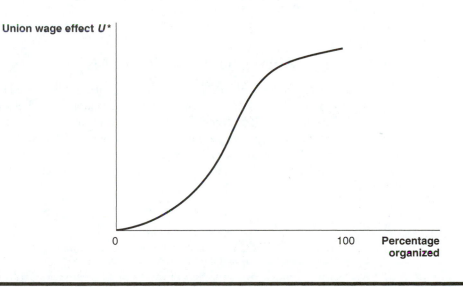

organized, the union's wage-raising ability increases relatively rapidly as its strike threat becomes more potent. Beyond some upper limit, the union has squeezed much of its potential gain from employers, and further increases in the percentage organized up to 100 percent raise U^* only slightly more.

In estimating the relationship between U^* and the percentage organized, it is necessary to consider the effect that the percentage organized has not only on the union wage rate, but also on the nonunion wage rate. The observed nonunion wage W_n may increase or decrease as the percentage organized becomes larger, depending respectively on whether the threat effect or the spillover effect is quantitatively more significant. Evidence on this issue presents a seemingly mixed picture. A study of the hospital industry found clear evidence for the existence of threat effects—the greater the percentage of health care workers unionized in metropolitan areas, the greater were the wages of both union and nonunion health care workers.[11] A study by David Neumark and Michael Wachter, on the other hand, found evidence of significant spillover effects within a variety of industries.[12]

Although these two examples seem to contradict each other—one finding a threat effect, the other a spillover effect—they are not incompatible. Within a particular industry, such as hospitals, airlines, or construction, greater unionization will boost the wages of nonunion workers in that industry because of the threat effect. Nonunion wages in other industries will be depressed as workers displaced by higher wages in the union sector add to the competition for jobs in the nonunion sector. In fact, Neumark and Wachter found that in comparing union wage effects across occupations, there is evidence for spillover effects in blue-collar occupations (a 1 percentage point increase in percentage of workers unionized results in a 0.3 percent decrease in the wage of nonunion blue-collar workers), and threat effects in white-collar occupations (a 1 percentage point increase in percentage of workers unionized results in a 0.2 percent increase in the wage of nonunion white-collar workers).[13]

The Union Wage Effect over Time

The union wage effect also varies considerably over time, as illustrated in Figure 12.3, which shows estimates of U^* for consecutive five-year periods between 1920 and 2002. The union wage effect reached its highest level (38 percent) in the Depression years, fell to practically zero (2 percent) in the late 1940s, and then gradually increased from 1950 to the early 1980s (25 percent). From 1985 to 2002 the union wage differential trended modestly downward, reaching a level of 18 percent in the early 2000s.

---

11   Ibid.

12   David Neumark and Michael L. Wachter, "Union Effects on Nonunion Wages: Evidence from Panel Data on Industries and Cities," *Industrial and Labor Relations Review* 49 (October 1995): 20–38.

13   Also see Dale Belman and Paula Voos, "Wage Effects of Increased Coverage: Methodological Considerations and New Evidence," *Industrial and Labor Relations Review* 46 (January 1993): 368–80.

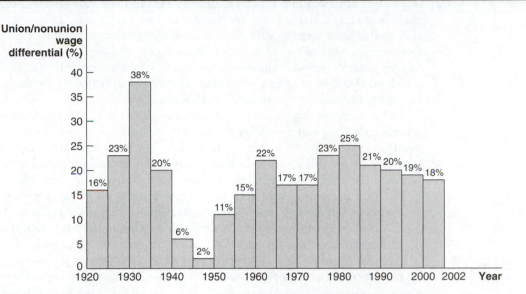

FIGURE 12.3 THE UNION–NONUNION WAGE DIFFERENTIAL OVER TIME, 1920–2002

SOURCES: George E. Johnson, "Changes over Time in the Union–Nonunion Wage Differential in the United States," in Jean-Jacques Rosa, ed., *The Economics of Trade Unions: New Directions* (Boston: Kluwer Nijhoff, 1984): 5. The data for 1990 to 2000 are from Barry Hirsch and Edward Schumacher, "Private Sector Union Density and the Wage Premium: Past, Present, and Future," *Journal of Labor Research* 22 (Summer 2001): Figure 6; the data from 2000–2002 are from David Blanchflower and Alex Bryson, "What Effect Do Unions Have on Wages Now and Would Freeman and Medoff be Surprised?" *Journal of Labor Research* 25 (Summer): Table 4.

The major explanation for this pattern has been called the **wage rigidity hypothesis**.[14] In this view, long-term union contracts make union wages less sensitive to aggregate demand conditions in the economy. When unemployment increases, for example, nonunion firms react to the growing amount of slack in the labor market by scaling back wage increases rather quickly. Wage growth in the unionized sector exhibits much more inertia since wages are typically established for the two- to three-year duration of the contract.[15] This line of argument predicts that in periods of high unemployment the union–nonunion differential should

14   See Wallace Hendricks, "Unionism, Oligopoly, and Rigid Wages," *Review of Economics and Statistics* 63, no. 2 (May 1981): 198–205.

15   Evidence that unions have adverse effects on a variety of economic growth measures is provided by Lou Pantuosco et al., "The Effect of Unions on Labor Markets and Economics Growth: An Analysis of State Data," *Journal of Labor Research* 22 (Winter 2001): 195–205.

widen, as borne out by the increase in U^* in the Depression years and the early 1960s.

Long-term contracts also make union wages less sensitive to inflation. During periods of rapid inflation, nonunion firms increase their wages at least annually so that workers can keep up with the cost of living; the wages of unionized workers, however, are locked in by a long-term contract and cannot adjust upwards as quickly. During periods of inflation, therefore, the union–nonunion wage differential should become smaller, a prediction seemingly confirmed by the decline in U^* in the high-inflation years of the mid-1940s and late 1960s.

The decade of the 1970s appears to represent something of an anomaly for the wage rigidity hypothesis—inflation reached double-digit figures in several years, yet the union–nonunion wage differential widened noticeably. There are two explanations for this aberrant behavior.[16] The first is the widespread introduction of cost-of-living allowance (COLA) clauses into union contracts in the 1970s. As noted in the preceding chapter, COLA clauses automatically increase wage rates by a formula tied to the Consumer Price Index, usually on a quarterly basis. Although COLA clauses typically offer only partial protection against inflation, the extent of unanticipated inflation in the 1970s was so great that the wage gains of nonunion workers fell significantly behind those of workers in the union sector, who received regular quarterly cost-of-living increases.[17] The second explanation for the more rapid growth of union wages in the 1970s was the combination of inflation with high unemployment—stagflation. Even as COLA clauses kept union wages growing with inflation, the relatively high levels of unemployment in the economy held back nonunion wages, giving a one-two punch to the union–nonunion wage differential.

The union–nonunion wage differential has declined since the mid 1980s. One study attributes this decline to two primary factors.[18] First, many highly unionized industries lost some of their protection from competitive forces. Foreign competition affected manufacturing industries, such as automobiles and steel, while deregulation added competitive pressures to transportation industries, such as trucking and airlines. Second, the pay of white-collar workers, who are much less likely to be unionized, rose more sharply during the 1980s than that of blue-collar workers. The union–nonunion wage differential might have declined even further in the 1990s had it not been for the recession in 1990–1991. As in earlier periods, the growth in nonunion wages slowed more quickly than did union wage growth, temporarily arresting the narrowing of the gap. Since then, nonunion wages have

---

16   Moore and Raisian, "The Level and Growth of Union/Nonunion Wage Effects," and Bruce E. Kaufman and Paula E. Stephan, "Determinants of Interindustry Wage Growth in the Seventies," *Industrial Relations* 26 (Spring 1987): 186–94.

17   This is shown in Wallace E. Hendricks and Lawrence M. Kahn, "Cost of Living Clauses in Union Contracts: Determinants and Effects," *Industrial and Labor Relations Review* 36, no. 3 (April 1983): 447–60. In 1978, COLA clauses increased wages, on average, by 57 percent of the increase in prices.

18   Albert Schwenk, "Trends in the Differences between Union and Nonunion Workers in Pay Using the Employment Cost Index," *Compensation and Working Conditions* (September 1996): 27–33.

again outpaced union wages, according to the Employment Cost Index, causing the gap to again narrow, albeit very modestly, so that by the year 2002 the union–nonunion wage differential was approximately 18 percent.[19]

The Union Wage Effect and the Structure of the Product Market

Does it affect the ability of a union to raise wages if the firm is in a highly competitive industry or in a concentrated industry (one with only a few firms)? This question has intrigued economists for several decades. The evidence is contradictory. In the manufacturing sector, a positive relationship seems to hold between concentration and union bargaining power. The strongest unions are found in oligopolistic industries, such as autos, steel, and rubber, while unions in more competitive industries, such as textiles and shoes, have generally been quite weak. This generalization breaks down in the nonmanufacturing sector, where in certain industries, such as construction, mining, and trucking, the union wage gain has been quite large, yet the employer side is made up of dozens and even hundreds of individual companies.

Harold Levinson offered one resolution to this puzzle.[20] According to Levinson, the key requirement for a union if it is to be successful is to organize all the major producers in the product market. The reason for this was alluded to in the discussion of the relationship between union wage gains and the percentage of the workforce organized. If a union organizes only some of the firms in the product market, its ability to raise wages is severely restricted because of the constant threat that the unionized segment of the industry will be driven out of the market by its lower-cost nonunion rivals. Should the union organize all the firms in the market, its ability to raise wages is increased considerably, since labor costs and product prices will go up equally at each firm, preventing any one firm from getting a competitive advantage.

What role does product market structure play in this? Levinson argues that the union's ability to organize all the producers in the product market depends critically on the existence of either barriers to new firms' entry into the market or restrictions on the ability of already unionized firms to move outside the union's control. A barrier to entry is some such factor as high capital requirements, large advertising costs, or government regulation that impedes the ability of new firms to enter the product market. In the manufacturing sector, concentration and union

---

19   Evidence from the Employment Cost Index indicates that wages and salaries of nonunion workers grew (in real terms) an average of 10.3 percent between 1995 and 2003, whereas union wages and salaries grew at a rate of only 6.5 percent (Bureau of Labor Statistics, Data Selective Access, http://www.bls.gov/ncs/ect/#data. The modest decline in the union wage premium is also documented in Dale Belman abd Paula Voos, "Change in Union Wage Effects by Industry: A Fresh Look at the Evidence," *Industrial Relations* 43 (July 2004): 491–519.

20   See Harold Levinson, "Unionism, Concentration and Wage Changes: Toward a Unified Theory," *Industrial and Labor Relations Review* 20, no. 2 (January 1967): 198–205.

power seem to go together because concentration is itself the result of substantial entry barriers in the form of large economies of scale in production and the billions of dollars of capital investment that such economies require. In the textile and shoe industries, for example, economies of scale are quite small and many individual firms exist, so entry into the market by new firms is relatively easy. In this case, should the union raise wages, new, lower-cost nonunion firms could easily enter the market and undercut the unionized firms. In oligopolistic industries such as steel or autos, however, economies of scale are quite large, resulting in only a handful of firms. Because of their size, these firms may be difficult to organize, but once organized the union has more latitude to raise wages since entry is impeded by the huge capital requirements.

In nonmanufacturing, concentration and union power do not always go hand in hand, because barriers to entry into the market take different forms. One important type of entry barrier has been government regulation. In the trucking, airline, and intercity bus industries prior to deregulation, for example, firms were assigned specific routes and could not enter new markets without the permission of the Interstate Commerce Commission (ICC) or the Civil Aeronautics Board (CAB). Such permission was often quite difficult to obtain, with the result that there were a number of firms in the industry but only limited competition within individual markets. In other nonmanufacturing industries, such as construction, mining, or longshoring, a different factor explains the coexistence of many employers and substantial union power. In each of these industries there are distinct geographical limitations to the area in which production can take place. Mining companies, for example, must locate where the mineral deposits are, and shipping companies must locate where harbor facilities are. Spatial limitations to the area of production help a union in its organizing efforts because firms cannot evade the union by moving to a different part of the country. Perhaps the classic example of how the geographic migration of firms can break a union's bargaining power is the movement of textile firms from the heavily organized states in the Northeast to the relatively nonunion states of the South.

This analysis suggests that it is not market structure per se that affects the ability of a union to raise wages, but the existence of entry barriers or spatial limitations to the area of production. Most empirical studies on this subject have examined a cross section of manufacturing industries to see if there is a positive relationship between the size of the union–nonunion wage differential and the degree of concentration in the product market. The results of these studies, however, seem to refute the theory. Most studies find that the effect of unionization on wages becomes *smaller* in more concentrated industries.[21] How can this be explained? The key to this puzzle has two

---

21 See David B. Audretsch and J.-Matthias Graf von der Schulenburg, "Union Participation, Innovation, and Concentration: Results from a Simultaneous Model," *Journal of Institutional and Theoretical Economics* 146 (June 1990), and Barry T. Hirsch, "Market Structure, Union Rent Seeking, and Firm Profitability," *Economics Letters* 32 (January 1990): 75–79. Inasmuch as firm size can be used as a proxy for industry concentration (the larger the firm the lower the concentration), Paul Miller and Charles Mulvey, "Unions, Firm Size, and Wages," *Economic Record* 72 (June 1996): 138–53, find that industry concentration is associated with union strength.

parts. First, unionization and concentration tend to go together (the strongest unions are found in the most concentrated industries). Second, concentrated industries pay higher wages than competitive industries even in the absence of unions. Thus, unionized workers in concentrated industries *do* receive substantially higher wages than similar workers in competitive industries; the reason unionization has a small effect is because wages were *already* much higher than elsewhere.[22]

A second way to judge the importance of entry barriers is to look at what happens to wages, employment, and unionization in industries when these barriers are removed.[23] Consider the experience of deregulation in four industries—in trucking, railroad, airline, and telecommunications. Each experience is a bit different and has a lot to do with the natural barriers that remained after the artificial barrier of regulation was removed, with technological advancements in the industries, and with growth in demand for the products produced by the industries.

After deregulation (which began in 1977), the trucking industry experienced a decline in union membership by half and a drop in average real hourly earnings by 26 percent between 1978 and 2000. Given that the trucking industry has relatively low capital requirements to enter, it is not surprising that many nonunion trucking firms were able to enter the market and erode the power of the union in that industry.[24]

The railroad industry, on the other hand, is much more difficult for firms to enter because of the high capital requirements. The difficulty of entry for low-cost nonunion competitors meant that union membership in this industry remained high after deregulation. The unions were also able to retain their wage levels between 1978 and 2000, although employment declined by more than half during the same time period. Economist James Peoples suggests that it was the consolidation of services (through mergers and acquisitions) and the ability of employers to negotiate more efficient work rules after deregulation that led to the employment decline.

While union membership fell in both the airline and telecommunications industries after deregulation, countervailing factors actually led to a growth in overall employment and wages for both these industries. For the airline industry, the tremendous increase in the number of people flying during the past 30 years led the way for employment and wage growth in that industry.[25] After the breakup

---

22   Evidence of this can be found in Erling Barth and Josef Sweimüller, "Labour Market Institutions and the Industry Wage Distribution: Evidence from Austria, Norway and the U.S.," *Empirica* 19 no. 2 (1992): 181–201.

23   See James Peoples, "Deregulation and the Labor Market," *Journal of Economic Perspectives* 12 (Summer 1998): 111–30.

24   See Michael H. Belzer, "Collective Bargaining after Deregulation: Do the Teamsters Still Count?" *Industrial and Labor Relations Review* 48 (July 1995): 636–55, for further analysis of union strength in the trucking industry after deregulation. Also see Dale L. Belman and Kristen A. Monaco, "The Effects of De-unionizations, Technology, and Human Capital on the Work and Work Lives of Truck Drivers," *Industrial and Labor Relations Review* 54 (March 2001): 502–24.

25   See Pierre-Yves Cremieux, "The Effect of Deregulation on Employee Earnings: Pilot, Flight Attendants, and Mechanics, 1959–1992," *Industrial and Labor Relations Review* 49 (January 1996): 223–42, for further analysis of earnings in the airline industry after deregulation.

German Unions Feeling the Pain of Economic Integration

Effective in 1992, the countries of the European Common Market agreed to eliminate many barriers to the movement of labor and goods across national borders. Then in 2002 the EU countries converted to a single currency. The clearest winners from economic integration will be consumers, who should be able to purchase a wider assortment of goods and services at lower prices. A second group of winners, on net, will be European business firms, who will gain lower costs of production due to the greater economies of scale made possible by a larger market. The most likely losers from trade liberalization, on the other hand, are unionized workers, particularly in high-wage countries such as Germany.

German labor unions have been extraordinarily successful in gaining generous wages, benefits, and improved working conditions for their members. Wage and benefit payments per hour in Germany, for example, are the highest in Europe and exceed hourly Japanese and American labor costs by 30 percent. Not only are German workers highly paid, they also work fewer hours per year than do workers in almost any other country. Most German union contracts, for example, strictly forbid work on Saturdays and Sundays, and in 1989 the German Metal Workers Union successfully negotiated a 35-hour workweek. By comparison, the average Portuguese worker earns less than one-sixth as much per hour as a German worker, works 18 percent more hours per year, and is protected by far less stringent safety and dismissal regulations.

The removal of barriers to the free flow of goods and labor has undermined the bargaining power of German unions and their ability to maintain high labor standards. Union membership is also in decline. Trade liberalization leads to weaker unions for a number of reasons. First, the heretofore sheltered German domestic market has been opened up to greater competition from lower-cost producers in low-wage countries such as Spain and Poland. Second, German companies now have incentives to shift production to low-wage countries, shutting down high-wage plants in Germany and opening up new plants in southern Europe. And, third, the reduced barriers to labor mobility, in conjunction with high German wages, will result in an influx of millions of new immigrants into the German labor market, providing employers with a cheaper alternative to union labor.

The unions in Germany have undertaken a number of different strategies to counteract the threats from free trade. Some strategies are clear signs of the weaker bargaining position of the unions, but are necessary for their survival. For example, wage concessions agreed to by IG Chemie, the chemical workers union, the adoption by the IG Metall (metalworkers) union at Volkswagen of a two-tier wage system that allows temporary workers to earn wages 10 percent lower than permanent workers, and a negotiated increase in the workweek at the Hanover tire plant are all signs that German unions are definitely feeling the pressures of greater competition in both the product and the labor markets.

Other strategies are designed to proactively counter threats to the union position. For example, six German unions have decided to merge into one large union. The unions participating in the merger include the independent German Employees' Union, the Union for Public Service, the Postal Workers' Union, the teaching and science union, the banking and insurance union, and the media workers' union. The strategy is to provide each union additional leverage in negotiating future wage levels and working conditions. A political strategy of protest and lobbying is also being used. In May 2003, unions across Germany staged massive protests against proposed legislation that would try to reduce labor costs by cutting job security protections and employer benefit costs.

SOURCE: "In Germany, Unions' Power Faltering," *Philadelphia Inquirer* (September 4, 2004); "German Unions Vent Anger," *BBC News Worldwide* (May 1, 2003); and Matt Marshall, "Six German Unions Are Merging Ranks to Boost Leverage," *Wall Street Journal* (25 February 1998): A19.

of AT&T in 1984, expansion of services in the telecommunications industry and the technological advancements requiring workers with higher skills offset losses resulting from a weaker bargaining position.

Unions and Wage Inequality

A fourth dimension of the union wage effect is the impact of unions on the inequality of earnings among wage and salary workers. The relative degree of inequality in earnings is measured by the variance or relative spread of the earnings distribution; the greater the gap between the highest-paid and lowest-paid workers, and the more workers at either of these extremes, the greater will be the degree of inequality.

Union wage effects have a contradictory impact on the degree of wage inequality in the labor market, working in some ways to increase inequality, but in other ways to decrease it. The empirical question is to determine which predominates. A thorough evaluation of the effect of unions on wage inequality has been performed by Thomas Lemieux.[26] He provides evidence on four ways unions affect wage inequality.

Wage Dispersion within Firms   One source of inequality in wages among workers arises from the variance in wages among the workers within each firm. Lemieux found that the variance in wages among blue-collar workers in unionized firms was approximately one-third less than in nonunion firms, reflecting the influence of several forces. One is the political pressure on the union leadership to pursue a wage policy that reflects the preferences of the median union member. If, as is likely, the mean wage is above the median wage in a firm or plant, the union leadership will come under pressure to redistribute pay from the relatively small group of workers at the high end of the wage scale to the larger group of workers in the middle and at the lower end of the wage scale. Also, nonunion firms generally have more freedom to pay different wages to individual workers based on merit and personal characteristics such as education, race, or gender, giving rise to a good deal of wage dispersion among individual workers. A central goal of union wage policy is to remove personal characteristics as a determinant of pay, basing wages instead on *job* characteristics. The usual practice is to group specific jobs into a relatively small number of job categories (36 in steel, for example). By including diverse jobs in one category and making the range of pay rates within each category fairly narrow, unions substantially reduce the dispersion of wages among workers in a firm. Lemieux found that among nonunion firms, wages of the highest-skill workers were 66 percent higher than those of the lowest-skill workers, whereas wages of skilled workers were only 28 percent higher in union firms.

---

26   Thomas Lemieux, "Unions and Wage Inequality in Canada and the United States," in David Card and Richard B. Freeman, eds., *Small Differences That Matter: Labor Markets and Income Maintenance in Canada and the United States* (Chicago and London: University of Chicago Press, 1993), 69–107. Also see David Card, "The Effect of Unions on Wage Inequality in the U.S. Labor Market," *Industrial and Labor Relations Review* 54 (January 2001): 296–315, and Richard B. Freeman, "Unionism and the Dispersion of Wages," *Industrial and Labor Relations Review* 34 (October 1980): 3–23.

Wage Dispersion between Firms   Even if every worker in each individual firm received the same wage, inequality in wages would still occur among these workers if different firms paid different wages. When he examined this source of wage inequality, Lemieux found that the presence of a union reduced wage dispersion by 15 percent among low-skill workers. The primary explanation for this result rests with the goal of union wage policy to take wages out of competition by establishing a common wage scale that applies to all firms in a given product market. The advantage to the union is that the competitive threat to its members from lower-wage firms is eliminated.

The White-Collar/Blue-Collar Wage Differential   A third source of wage inequality arises from pay differences between blue-collar and white-collar workers. The average white-collar worker is more highly paid than the average blue-collar worker; any policy that reduces the white-collar/blue-collar differential will reduce overall wage inequality. Because the majority of union members are blue-collar workers, unionism should narrow the white-collar/blue-collar pay gap. Lemieux finds that 44 percent of the lower wage dispersion found in union firms is due to smaller differences between the highest-paid workers and the lowest-paid workers.

The Blue-Collar Union–Nonunion Wage Differential   A fourth source of wage inequality that unions unambiguously increase is the greater wages that blue-collar union workers receive relative to blue-collar nonunion workers, as measured by the estimates of U^*. In this regard, critics of labor unions have labeled union members the "labor aristocracy" because they are highly paid and also make up a relatively small share of the total labor force. Critics further note that union wage gains increase wage inequality not only by pushing up union wages, but also by depressing nonunion wages through the spillover effect.

Lemieux concluded that, on balance, unionism reduces the overall dispersion of wages in the labor market, lowering wage inequality by about 6.3 percent.[27] Whether this reduction is good or bad depends first, on one's views about the optimal degree of equality and second, on the competitive nature of the economy. Persons who believe that the market mechanism is relatively efficient will probably regard the leveling of wages by unions as undesirable because it distorts the price signals in the labor market, resulting in a misallocation of resources. Persons who give more weight to imperfections and noncompetitive elements in the labor market will probably regard the leveling of wages as a desirable removal of arbitrary or discriminatory differentials.

---

27   David Card, "Falling Union Membership and Rising Wage Inequality: What's the Connection?" *NBER Working Paper* 6520 (April 1998), estimates that the presence of unions lowers the overall labor market wage inequality by about 4 percent (using 1993 data). Thomas Lemieux, "Estimating the Effects of Unions on Wage Inequality in a Panel Data Model with Comparative Advantage and Nonrandom Selection," *Journal of Labor Economics* 16 (April 1998): 261–91, estimates, for the labor market in Canada, an overall reduction in inequality due to the presence of unions of between 7.1 and 17.3 percent. David G. Blanchflower and Richard B. Freeman, "Unionism in the United States and Other OECD Countries," *Industrial Relations* 31 (Winter 1992): 56–79, find similar results for other industrialized countries.

The Union Wage Effect in the Public Sector

A final dimension of the union wage effect is the impact of collective bargaining on wages and labor costs in the public and nonprofit sectors of the economy. Union membership and collective bargaining activity among government workers expanded quite rapidly after the mid-1960s. Some observers feared that collective bargaining in the public sector would result in excessive wage increases outstripping even the wage gains of private sector unions.[28] There were four reasons for this concern. First, public sector employers do not face the critical constraint of having to make a profit as private business firms do, perhaps weakening the motivation of government officials to resist union demands. Second, the strike threat of unions in the public sector is often greater than in the private sector due to the essential nature of many government services such as sanitation and police protection. It was feared, for example, that rather than risk a shutdown of the city's hospitals or transportation system, government officials would capitulate and agree to excessive union wage demands. A third factor is the inelasticity of labor demand for government workers. Empirical studies have found that the labor demand curve for various types of government workers, with the exception of teachers, is relatively inelastic, giving unions more freedom to raise wages without the fear of large declines in employment.[29] The inelasticity stems from the poor substitution possibilities that face consumers of government services (the first law of derived demand), both because many government services are essential and because few alternative suppliers of the good exist in the relevant market area. A controversial policy that contributes to poor substitution possibilities is the Davis-Bacon Act, which is discussed in detail in Policy Application 12-1. Finally, a fourth area of concern was that public sector unions have both economic and political weapons to pressure government officials for higher wages.[30] The economic weapon is the threat of a strike; the political weapon is the ability of the unions to threaten the reelection of government officials through their campaign endorsements and financial contributions.

SEE

Policy Application 12-1:
The Davis-Bacon Act,
p. 652.

Against this backdrop it is surprising that the bulk of the evidence suggests that, on average, unions in the public sector have raised wages less than in the private sector. The gap, however, has gradually closed over time. Table 12.2 shows

---

28 Harry H. Wellington and Ralph K. Winter, *The Unions and the Cities* (Washington, D.C.: The Brookings Institution, 1971). Also see Richard B. Freeman, "Unionism Comes to the Public Sector," *Journal of Economic Literature* 24 (March 1986): 41–86.

29 One study estimates that whereas the demand for police is inelastic (−0.24), demand for firefighters is elastic (−1.449). See Stephen J. Trejo, "Public Sector Unions and Municipal Employment," *Industrial and Labor Relations Review* 45 (October 1991): 166–80. In addition, another study, using longitudinal data, of a variety of municipal employees (firefighters, sanitation workers, police, streets and highways employees, and finance and control personnel) suggests that public sector workers are not nearly as effective at raising wages without much loss in employment as we once thought they were. See Robert G. Valletta, "Union Effects on Municipal Employment and Wages: A Longitudinal Approach," *Journal of Labor Economics* 11 (July 1993): 545–74.

30 See Linda C. Babcock et al., "Wages and Employment in Public-Sector Unions," *Economic Inquiry* 35 (July 1997): 532–43.

TABLE 12.2   UNION WAGE EFFECTS IN THE PUBLIC SECTOR, 1996–2001

Group	Wage Gap
Private Sector	17%
Public Sector	15
Registered Nurses	6
Teachers	21
Social Workers	12
Lawyers	17
Firefighters	19
Polics	18

SOURCE: David Blanchflower and Alex Bryson, "What Effect Do Unions Have on Wages Now and Would Freeman and Medoff be Surprised?" *Journal of Labor Research* 25 (Summer 2004), Table 3.

the estimate of U^* for all private and public sector workers and six public sector occupations. Measured over 1996–2001, the wage gap for private sector union workers was 17 percent and 15 percent for public sector workers. The lowest estimate of U^* is for nurses (6 percent), and the highest is for teachers (21 percent). By way of comparison, the estimate of U^* for private sector workers is 15 to 20 percent.

Why have public sector unions apparently had a modestly smaller wage effect than private sector unions? One reason is that public sector unions tend to include a greater proportion of white-collar workers, a group for which union bargaining power has traditionally been less effective in securing large wage gains. Second, for reasons to be discussed shortly, public sector unions have apparently been quite successful in winning improved fringe benefits, implying that their impact on total labor cost may be greater than is suggested by looking at wages alone.[31] A third factor is that the right to strike is still restricted or denied to a large number of government workers. Where the right to strike is permitted, government leaders have shown an increasing willingness to take strikes as the price for obtaining moderate wage settlements. This latter trend reflects, in part, the apparent ability of communities to weather hospital or sanitation strikes more easily than once thought possible. Finally, the larger impact of private sector unions on wages may simply reflect the fact that they have had many more years over which to push up wages than have their public-sector counterparts.

[31] See H. Gregg Lewis, "Union/Nonunion Wage Gaps in the Public Sector," *Journal of Labor Economics* 8 (January 1990): S260–328.

The Union Effect on Nonwage Outcomes

Even though economists have traditionally focused on the effect of unions on wage rates, unions also have an important impact on nonwage aspects of the employment relation, especially employee benefits, productivity, and profits.

Unions and Employee Benefits

Unions affect the provision of employee benefits by changing the amount and the mix of employee benefits received by workers. Table 12.3 shows the amount of total compensation that union and nonunion firms paid in the form of employee benefits, as well as the distribution of expenditure by type of benefit in 2004. The data reveal that unionized firms paid 37 percent of their total compensation in the form of benefits, compared to 27 percent for nonunion firms. Part of these benefits are required by law (for example, Social Security and unemployment compensation premiums), and the remainder are voluntarily supplied by the firm. There is little difference between union and nonunion firms in the required portion

TABLE 12.3	EMPLOYEE BENEFITS RECEIVED BY UNION AND NONUNION PRIVATE SECTOR WORKERS, 2004	
	Share of Total Compensation	
	Union	**Nonunion**
Total compensation per hour ($32.04 for union, $22.38 for nonunion)	1.00	1.00
Straight-time pay (wages and salaries)	0.63	0.73
Required fringes	0.09	0.09
Voluntary fringes		
Vacation	0.03	0.03
Holiday	0.02	0.02
Sick leave	0.01	0.01
Life insurance	0.00	0.00
Health insurance	0.10	0.06
Disability insurance	0.03	0.02
Pensions	0.07	0.03
Bonuses	0.01	0.02

Note: Sum may not equal 1 due to rounding.

SOURCE: U.S. Bureau of Labor Statistics, *News: Employer Costs for Employee Compensation* (2004) http://www.bls.gov/news.release/ecec.t07.htm.

The Crisis in Union Health and Pension Programs

Three of the traditional union strongholds in the American economy are the airline, auto, and steel industries. Unions in each industry over the last four decades have been remarkably successful in bargaining for higher wages and benefits for their members. Traditionally, most of the attention in the news media and academic research community has been on the union wage effect. By 1980, for example, unionized steel workers were the highest paid industrial workers in the country, while by the year 2000 senior airline pilots at the major carriers were earning $250,000 a year or more for a flying time of forty hour a *month*.

While these unions were successfully pushing up wages, they also secured much-desired but less-publicized gains in benefits for their members. Principal among these were extensive health insurance packages and pension programs. One reason these benefit gains were less publicized is they did not have a large immediate impact on either corporate profit and loss statements or the standard of living of union families. Two factors accounted for this small short-term effect. The first was that when these new benefit programs were first negotiated in the 1960s–1980s the bulk of the workforce in unionized companies was still relatively young. Being young, the workers were still 20–25 years from retiring and thus corporate pension payments seemed far in the future; also younger workers and their families have relatively moderate health care needs. The second factor was that these companies were typically quite large and prosperous and, if they remained so in the future, would have the financial ability to honor their benefit promises.

In the early 2000s things looked dramatically different and more dire. A classic example is the Bethlehem Steel Company. In the 1950s to 1960s Bethlehem was the number two steelmaker in the United States and employed over 300,000 workers. It supplied the steel for the Golden Gate Bridge, over 1,200 Liberty ships during World War II, and nearly every bridge and tunnel in the New York–New Jersey area. A half a century later, in 2001, Bethlehem declared bankruptcy and its workforce had fallen to 11,000. A major reason the company declared bankruptcy was the gargantuan size of its health care and pension costs. The company, with a decrease in size and profits, was faced with health care and pension costs for 95,000 retirees— nearly ten retirees for every currently employer worker! By declaring bankruptcy, Bethlehem was able to shed nearly $5 billion of pension costs and its hugely expensive retiree health care program. Retired workers, who had put in 30 years in the mills with the expectation of an assured monthly pension payment (typically in the $1,500–$2,000 a month range) and health care protection, suddenly found themselves with no health insurance and much-reduced monthly pension checks. (The pension obligations of bankrupt companies are taken over by the U.S. government's Federal Pension Guarantee Corporation, but it typically cuts the size of the pension check by one-third to one-half.)

This scenario is being played out in other industries and companies. General Motors, for example, has 142,000 hourly workers who contribute to its pension plan but 360,000 retired workers who draw

of employee benefits; the major difference is in the voluntary component. After adjusting for worker quality and other such factors, one study found that benefits in unionized firms are approximately 20 percent higher than those of comparable nonunion firms.[32]

---

32   William E. Even and David A. Macpherson, "The Impact of Unionism on Fringe Benefit Coverage," *Economics Letters* 36 (May 1991): 87–91.

continued

on the plan. These retired workers also qualify for a generous health care program. The total cost of the pension and health care payments for the company in 2003 was $6.2 billion or $1,784 per vehicle. Not only is this a huge cost burden in itself but the situation is doubly onerous because the company's foreign competitors have much smaller health care and pension costs. Toyota's American auto plants, for example, have a much younger workforce and pension costs per vehicle are only $200. As a result, Toyota is able to offer lower car prices, gain market share, and earn higher profits.

This situation clearly puts General Motors in a vicious cycle: the company's higher costs cause it to gradually lose market share; as employment and production fall the unit cost of health care and pension costs rise; to cover these higher average overhead costs the company is again forced to raise car prices; but market share again falls while pension and health care costs again rise (since layoffs lead to more early retirements); and the process repeats itself. The net effect is that the high and rising pension and health care costs have caused General Motors to gradually move up its product demand and labor demand curves, leading the company to progressively shrink over time (absent one or more developments that shifts the company's product demand and labor demand curves to the right, such as a booming macro-economy or hotter styling and higher car quality). If allowed to continue long enough, General Motors—once the largest industrial corporation in the world—could find itself in the same situation as Bethlehem. Lest this forecast seem overly dramatic, consider that United Airlines—once the world's largest air carrier—filed for bankruptcy in 2003. Among the reasons the company cited was the need to get out from underneath $8 billion of pension obligations.

Clearly the nation faces a difficult problem and one that appears only to be getting worse. Many hundreds of thousands of workers find that the pension and health care programs they had been promised suddenly disappear. For many families this represents a major hardship. For the companies, these pension and health care obligations agreed upon two and three decades ago now imperil their survival. From the unions' point of view, every retired worker in an advanced country such as the United States deserves a decent company-provided pension and health care package—particularly since retirement payments from Social Security are very modest and the nation does not have a national system of health insurance. But the federal government is currently running very large budget deficits and has little fiscal room to take on new obligations in the health care and pension area, while the Federal Pension Guarantee Corporation is itself in serious risk of insolvency. Clearly some hard choices lay ahead.

SOURCES: "United's Pension Woes: Sign of Bigger Issue," *Christian Science Monitor* (October 4, 2004): 1; "The Benefits Trap," *Business Week* (July 19, 2004): 64–72; "Is Bethlehem Steel the Canary in the Economic Mine Shaft?" www.econlib.org/library/columns/robertssteel.html, 2004.

Why do unionized firms pay more of their compensation in the form of benefits? One reason is that the union's bargaining power is able to induce the employer to pay not only higher wages but also more employee benefits—union members get more of both![33] The positive correlation between wages and benefits suggests,

---

33 See Peter Feuille, Wallace E. Hendricks, and Lawrence M. Kahn, "Wage and Nonwage Outcomes in Collective Bargaining: Determinants and Tradeoffs," *Journal of Labor Research* 2, no. 1 (Spring 1981): 39–54.

therefore, that studies of the union wage effect U^* that ignore benefits underestimate the total increase in labor compensation received by union members.[34]

A second reason union members receive more benefits is that collective bargaining gives greater weight to the preferences of older workers, who generally desire a larger proportion of benefits.[35] A nonunion firm offers the amount of employee benefits necessary to attract and keep the "marginal" worker, the one just on the margin of indifference between working for the firm and going elsewhere. This worker is likely in most firms to be relatively young with little seniority and often with fewer family responsibilities. The preference of this worker is usually to receive more in wages and less in benefits, particularly retirement-related benefits such as pensions. In a unionized firm, the union's bargaining demands reflect the preferences of the median employee in the seniority distribution, who is likely to be considerably older than the marginal worker. As a result, the union's bargaining demands will give more weight to securing benefits in place of wages.

Table 12.3 shows that unionism also affects the mix of benefits in the firm's compensation package. A greater proportion of benefits in unionized firms go toward pensions; life, accident, and health insurance; and vacation and holiday pay. Each of these benefits is likely to be more desired by senior than by junior workers, again pointing to the greater influence that the preferences of the median worker play in union wage policy. Finally, unions also discourage some types of employee benefits. One example is bonus payments that, from the point of view of a union, provide an undesirable opportunity for management to pay some workers differently than others.

Unions and Productivity

A second nonwage outcome of considerable importance is the effect of labor unions on productivity. Productivity measures the amount of output produced per employee hour of labor input. According to most observers of collective bargaining, unions have both beneficial and harmful effects on productivity in the economy.

Probably the most harmful effect of unions on productivity comes from **restrictive work rules** or "featherbedding" requirements that force business firms to use more labor than they otherwise would.[36] Restrictive work rules come from the workers' concern for job security. The effort of management to increase productivity in the firm may entail two costs for workers. One cost is that new technology or improved production methods may result in layoffs of some workers. A second cost is that a greater intensity of work effort may be required of each

---

34 Paul Miller and Charles Mulvey, "Trade Unions, Collective Voice and Fringe Benefits," *The Economic Record* 68 (June 1992): 125–41, for example, estimate that the compensation (wages plus fringes) differential between union and nonunion workers in Australia is one and a half percentage points larger than the wage difference alone.

35 Freeman and Medoff, *What Do Unions Do?*; John Budd, "Nonwage Forms of Compensation," *Journal of Labor Research* 25 (Fall 2004): 597–622.

36 See John T. Addison, "Trade Unions and Restrictive Practices," in Jean-Jacques Rosa, ed., *The Economics of Trade Unions: New Directions* (Boston: Kluwer Nijhoff, 1984), 83–124.

worker—the assembly line may be run at a faster speed, discipline may be tightened, or break time may be reduced.[37]

To shield workers from these costs of increased productivity, unions have bargained for a variety of work rules that limit management's discretion in the use of labor. One approach establishes rules concerning crew size that specify how many workers must be in the cockpit of the airplane, attending a particular machine, or in a longshoring gang to unload a ship. Unionized airlines, for example, are generally required to use three people to guide a plane from the loading ramp at an airport, but most nonunion airlines use just two. A more blatant form of featherbedding was the long-standing requirement that railroads use firemen on diesel locomotives.

A second type of restrictive work rule limits management's ability to introduce new technology.[38] Unions, in some cases, have a long history of fighting technological advancements, primarily out of fear of labor displacement. Recognizing the inevitability of progress, however, many unions have adopted a strategy of participating with management in the decisions regarding content and process of the technological change.[39]

A third type of restrictive work rule requires the employer to use only workers of a particular craft or occupation for a specific task. This rule is quite common in the construction trades, where an electrician can install a wall outlet, but a carpenter must first cut the opening in the wall. In manufacturing, a unionized auto parts plant will often have 75 or more job classifications detailing the precise type of work each employee may perform.

The discussion of productivity and the demand for labor in Chapter 5 provides an important insight into the benefits and costs to union members from restrictive work rules. In the short run, restrictive work rules preserve employment, and thus work to the benefit of union members. By forcing the firm to use more labor than necessary, however, restrictive work rules also raise the costs of production, placing unionized firms at a competitive disadvantage relative to lower-cost nonunion firms. In the long run, therefore, restrictive work rules lead to fewer jobs for union workers because unionized firms are gradually driven out of business.[40] A number of empirical studies have found clear evidence that employment growth (and capital

---

37 An example of the negative impact of work rules on productivity can be found in Dennis Byrne et al., "Unions and Police Productivity: An Econometric Investigation," *Industrial Relations* 35 (October 1996): 566–84.

38 One study estimated that restrictions on technology use (or combination of factor use) in public schools increased production costs of unionized schools by 8 percent. See Randall W. Eberts and Joe A. Stone, "Unionization and Cost of Production: Compensation, Productivity, and Factor-Use Effects," *Journal of Labor Economics* 9 (April 1991): 171–85.

39 See Robert J. Thomas, "Technological Choice and Union–Management Cooperation," *Industrial Relations* 30 (Spring 1991): 167–92. Also see Bart D. Finzel and Steven E. Abraham, "Bargaining over New Technology: Possible Effects of Removing Legal Constraints," *Journal of Economic Issues* 30 (September 1996): 777–95.

40 The railroad industry provides a classic example. Between 1955 and 1962, employment on the Florida East Coast Railway (FEC) fell from 3,741 to 2,128. In 1963, the FEC took a strike and broke the unions. As a nonunion company, the FEC eliminated union work rules, allowing it to run a freight train from Jacksonville to Miami with one two-man crew instead of three five-man crews. The short-run result was that employment dropped to 600 in 1963; the long-run result, however, was that the cost savings made the FEC more competitive, and by 1980 employment had grown to 1,136. By comparison, employment on unionized railroads fell by 30 percent between 1963 and 1980, primarily due to competition from lower-cost truckers.

investment) are indeed notably lower at unionized firms, although another study found no evidence that unions lead to move firm "deaths."[41]

Unions may hurt productivity in other ways as well. One often-cited method is by forcing company management to adopt inefficient personnel practices. Examples of such practices include promotion by seniority rather than merit, preventing the firing of poorly performing workers, and restricting the use of incentive pay plans. A recent study of the steel industry indicates that the structure of employment practices, or personnel policies, can have a significant impact on the productivity of workers.[42]

Restrictive work rules and inefficient personnel practices are among the most objectionable aspects of union behavior to management and the public. Less noticed are the ways in which unions benefit productivity. One way is by forcing management to be more efficient in operating the firm (sometimes referred to as a "shock effect"). One study of the construction industry found that productivity on a construction site increased 38 percent with the presence of a union.[43] Cavalluzzo and Baldwin conclude that up to one-third of that productivity differential may be attributed to more efficient management styles on the union sites.

A second reason why unionized firms may have higher productivity is lower employee turnover. This argument has been developed by Freeman and Medoff in their **exit/voice theory of unionism**.[44] According to Freeman and Medoff, workers in a nonunion and a union firm have two different options for expressing dissatisfaction with their conditions of employment. The major alternative for a nonunion worker is to quit or exit the firm in the search for a better job; a worker in a unionized firm, however, can voice dissatisfaction to the employer through the union. An implication of the exit/voice model is that unionized firms should have fewer quits among their workers. Freeman and Medoff found that quits were 31 to 65 percent lower among unionized workers after standardizing for differences in wage rates, firm size, and so on, and that unionized firms gained an increase in productivity of 1 to 2 percent.[45] Similar results have been found in other countries and in earlier historical periods.[46]

41 See John Addison and Clive Belfield, "Unions and Employment Growth: The One Constant?" *Industrial Relations* 43 (April 2004): 305–23; and Richard Freeman and Morris Kliener, "Do Unions Make Enterprises Insolvent?" *Industrial Labor and Relations Review* 52 (July 1999): 510–27.

42 Casey Ichniowski et al., "The Effects of Human Resource Management Policies on Productivity: A Study of Steel Finishing Lines," *American Economic Review* 87 (June 1997): 291–313, estimated that one production line experienced an increase in operating profits by over $10 million (over a 10-year period) merely as the result of changes they made in employment practices.

43 Linda Cavalluzzo and Dennis Baldwin, "Unionization and Productive Efficiency," in Harold O. Fried et al., eds. *The Measurement of Productive Efficiency: Techniques and Applications* (New York and Oxford: Oxford University Press, 1993), 210–20.

44 Freeman and Medoff, *What Do Unions Do?* Chapters 6, 11.

45 The flip side of a lower quit rate is that union workers should also have much longer average job tenure. This is shown to be true in John T. Addison and Alberto C. Castro, "The Importance of Lifetime Jobs: Differences between Union and Nonunion Workers," *Industrial and Labor Relations Review* 40 (April 1987): 393–405.

46 See David Fairris, "From Exit to Voice in Shopfloor Governance: The Case of Company Unions," *Business History Review* 69 (Winter 1995): 494–529, and Paul W. Miller and Charles Mulvey, "Australian Evidence on the Exit/Voice Model of the Labor Market," *Industrial and Labor Relations Review* 45 (October 1991): 44–57.

Given that unions can have both beneficial and harmful effects on productivity, what is the net effect? Studies on the subject have found mixed evidence. The study by Cavalluzzo and Baldwin estimated that productivity on union construction sites was 38 percent higher than on nonunionized construction sites. A study of the impact of unionization on minority student test scores estimates that the presence of a teachers' union increases standardized test scores of the students by 2 percent.[47] Another study, however, found that the presence of a union *reduced* the productivity of police officers (in terms of arrests for minor crimes) by 26 percent.[48] In addition, one tabulation of union productivity effects found that unions reduced productivity in 11 of the 18 industries evaluated, amounting to an average 8 percent reduction in productivity among unionized firms across all industries.[49] Finally, Freeman and Medoff argue that positive union effects on productivity are most likely in those firms that have good labor relations climates, since only then will both sides gain from the voice aspect of unionism. A study of productivity at 18 General Motors plants found evidence in support of this proposition; the plants with lower rates of grievances filed by workers had higher levels of productivity.[50]

Unions and Profits

From a management perspective, the impact of unionism on wages, fringe benefits, and productivity is of secondary concern; what really matters is what unionism does to *profits*. The strength with which most firms resist the unionization of their workers provides circumstantial evidence that employers think unions are bad for profits. But are they? Several recent studies have examined this issue and reached a unanimous conclusion: Unionized firms earn lower profits than similar nonunion firms.[51] Hirsch finds that firms' profits (measured by the rate of return on capital) are, on average, 14 percent lower in union firms than in nonunion firms. In

---

47 Martin Milkman, "Teachers' Unions, Productivity, and Minority Student Achievement," *Journal of Labor Research* 18 (Winter 1997): 137–50.

48 Dennis Byrne et al., "Unions and Policy Productivity: An Econometric Investigation," *Industrial Relations* 35 (October 1996): 566–84. Another study finds *very weak* support for higher productivity among a broader range of unionized public sector workers. See Linda N. Edwards and Elizabeth Field-Hendrey, "Unions and Productivity in the Public Sector: The Case of Sanitation Workers," in Solomon W. Polachek, ed., *Research in Labor Economics*, vol. 15 (Greenwich, Conn., and London: JAI Press, 1996), 305–28.

49 Barry T. Hirsch, *Labor Unions and the Economic Performance of Firms* (Kalamazoo, Mich.: W. E. Upjohn Institute, 1991), Chapter 6.

50 Harry C. Katz, Thomas A. Kochan, and Kenneth R. Gobeille, "Industrial Relations Performance, Economic Performance, and QWL Programs: An Interplant Analysis," *Industrial and Labor Relations Review* 37, no. 1 (October 1983): 3–17.

51 See Barry T. Hirsch, *Labor Unions and the Economic Performance of Firms* (Kalamazoo, Mich.: W. E. Upjohn Institute, 1991), Chapter 4; Brian Becker and Craig Olson, "Unions and Firm Profits," *Industrial Relations* 31 (Fall 1992): 395–415; and Damien J. Neven et al., "Union Power and Product Market Competition: Evidence from the Airline Industry," Working Paper, Université de Lausanne-Cashiers de Recherches Economique #9810 (1998).

addition, he finds that the risk-adjusted market value of firms' stock is 20 percent lower in union firms than in nonunion firms.[52]

From a purely dollars and cents point of view, employers seem to have a good reason to resist the unionization of their workers. It is also possible that consumers have good reason to oppose unionization if in reaction to union wage gains, firms attempt to recoup some of their lost profits by raising prices. So far the evidence indicates, however, that it is employers, not consumers, who are the biggest losers from unionism. Several studies have found, for example, that unions reduce profits only slightly or not at all for firms in highly competitive product markets, but significantly reduce the profits of firms in oligopolistic or concentrated markets.[53] Others find that the union wage gain comes largely from capturing the financial returns earned by firms on long-lived capital investments and R&D expenditures.[54]

---

52 Some evidence exists that suggests these lower rates of return to the value of unionized firms' stock may have disappeared by the late 1980s. See Barry T. Hirsch and Barbara A. Morgan, "Shareholder Risk and Returns in Union and Nonunion Firms," *Industrial and Labor Relations Review* 47 (January 1994): 302–18. In addition, Naercio Aquino Menezes-Filho, "Unions and Profitability over the 1980s: Some Evidence on Union–Firm Bargaining in the United Kingdom," *The Economic Record* 107 (May 1997): 651–70, finds that the negative union effect on profits has declined in recent years for British firms.

53 See Thomas Karier, "Unions and Monopoly Profits," *Review of Economics and Statistics* 67 (February 1985): 34–43; Paula B. Voos and Lawrence R. Mishel, "The Union Impact on Profits: Evidence from Industry Price–Cost Margin Data," *Journal of Labor Economics* 4 (January 1986): 105–133; and, Stephen J. Machin, "Unions and the Capture of Economic Rents: An Investigation Using British Firm Level Data," *International Journal of Industrial Organization* 9[2] (1991): 261–74.

54 See Brian Becker and Craig Olson, "Unions and Firm Profits," *Industrial Relations* 31 (Fall 1992): 395–415, and William F. Chappell et al., "Union Rents and Market Structure Revisited," *Journal of Labor Research* 12 (Winter 1991): 35–46.

POLICY APPLICATION 12-1

The Davis-Bacon Act

Unions affect wage rates directly through the process of collective bargaining and indirectly through the political process as they lobby Congress and state legislatures for various types of protective labor legislation. One law that has become the center of considerable controversy is the **Davis-Bacon Act.**[1] Passed in 1931, the act requires that contractors working on federally financed construction projects must pay wage rates and fringe benefits at least equal to those prevailing in the locality of the project. Prevailing wage rates are determined on a case-by-case basis by the Department of Labor (DOL) according to several criteria. In practice, the prevailing wage rate chosen by the DOL usually equals the union wage rate in the area.

Unions actively lobbied for passage of the act, and continue to strenuously support it. Its purpose

---

1 See John P. Gould and George Bittlingmeyer, *The Economics of the Davis-Bacon Act* (Washington, D.C.: American Enterprise Institute, 1980), and A. J. Thieblot, "A New Evaluation of Impacts of Prevailing Wage Law Repeal," *Journal of Labor Research* 17 (Spring 1996): 297–322.

is to prevent cutthroat competition from depressing wage rates in the construction industry to undesirably low levels. The government awards construction projects to the company submitting the lowest bid. The resulting competition among companies puts downward pressure on all elements of cost but, according to the proponents of the act, particularly on wage rates. One reason is that labor is a variable cost while, in the short run, much of a contractor's capital cost is fixed. A second factor is the relatively high level of unemployment common in the construction industry. The shortage of job opportunities, coupled with the ongoing financial obligations of workers (mortgage payments, food and clothing expenses, and so on), results in intense competition for work and a bidding down of wages in an unregulated market, as occurred in the Depression. Finally, the downward pressure on wages is exacerbated by the high degree of labor mobility in the industry. A specific complaint that led to passage of the act was that fly-by-night contractors with cheap imported labor would enter a local area and underbid the established contractors for the government project. Supporters of the act claim that the law is socially desirable because it takes wages out of competition and forces contractors to compete on the basis of nonlabor cost and management efficiency.

Opponents of the Davis-Bacon Act present a much different view. According to them, the purpose of the act is to prevent downward pressure on artificially high union wage rates. Union wage rates are often 20 to 60 percent above those paid by nonunion contractors. Without some form of protection, unionized contractors would be unable to win government construction contracts because nonunion companies could underbid them, resulting in substantial unemployment of union members. Critics charge that the act has several negative consequences. First, because the DOL defines the prevailing wage rate as equal to the union wage rate in most cases, the cost of government construction projects is increased between 5 and 20 percent. Second, the act discriminates against nonunion contractors because they pay lower wages and are often unwilling to disrupt their pay scales in order to bid on a government project. Third, by protecting the monopoly power of construction unions, the act also results in higher costs in nongovernment construction projects.

The 1990s has seen much heated debate on the Davis-Bacon Act in Congress. In both 1995 and 1996, the act came close to being repealed. The most recent attempt, in 1996, did result in some minor modifications, such as establishing a minimum contract size to which Davis-Bacon applied. Court decisions have also limited the reach of the act. In December 1996, a federal court of appeals ruled that only employees physically working on a job site were eligible for the prevailing wage under Davis-Bacon. In spite of fierce opposition of many policymakers, Davis-Bacon appears to have become the sacred cow of labor.

Estimates of the Union Wage Effect

Given the pitfalls associated with measuring the union–nonunion wage differential, what do the estimates of U^* look like?

Cross-Sectional Estimates

The standard approach to calculating U^* involves estimating cross-sectional wage equations with the statistical tool of linear regression. The technical aspects of this method are explained in more detail

TABLE 12.4	ESTIMATES OF THE UNION IMPACT ON WAGES USING CROSS-SECTIONAL DATA				
	United States			**Great Britain**	
	1983	1993	1996–2001	1983	1993
Data Set	Current Population Survey	Current Population Survey	Current Population Survey	General Household Survey	Labour Force Surveys
Number of observations	173,404	171,439	546,823	7,951	16,159
Percentage gain in wages due to collective bargaining	15.5%	15.5%	17.0%	11.2%	9.8%

SOURCE: Constructed from David G. Blanchflower, "Changes over Time in Union Relative Wage Effects in Great Britain and the United States," *NBER Working Paper 6100* (July 1997): Tables 1, 2, 4, and 5, and David Blanchflower and Alex Bryson, "What Effect do Unions Have on Wages Now and Would Freeman and Medoff be Surprised?" *Journal of Labor Research* 25 (Summer 2004), Table 2.

in the appendix to this chapter; the basic idea, however, is relatively simple. To estimate U^*, economists typically use cross-sectional survey data that provide information on the earnings of workers; their demographic characteristics such as age, race, gender, and education; and job-related characteristics such as industry, occupation, and working conditions. The researcher then specifies a wage equation; the dependent variable is the individual's wage rate, and the independent or explanatory variables are the individual's union status and all the other demographic, human capital, and job-related variables that affect earnings. With the help of a computer, linear regression sorts out or decomposes the variation in hourly earnings among the sample of individuals into the separate parts due to each of the independent variables, including union status. If the wage equation includes all the explanatory variables that are correlated with union status and affect earnings, and if the researcher is able to control for spillover and threat effects, the estimated effect of union status obtained from the regression will give an unbiased

estimate of the true or adjusted union–nonunion wage differential U^*. Unfortunately, few studies are able to fully accomplish this task.

Shown in Table 12.4 are cross-sectional estimates of the union wage effect U^* calculated from five samples of workers by David Blanchflower.[1] Blanchflower was able to control for a wide range of demographic, industry, and occupational differences among workers, although other factors, such as employee benefits, working conditions, and threat and spillover effects, could not be accounted for. Table 12.4 shows that union workers in the United States receive approximately 15 to 17 percent higher pay than nonunion workers, and that the union wage gap was relatively stable between 1983 and 2001. Interestingly, an earlier study by H. G. Lewis also found a 15 percent union wage premium in the United States, but for the years

---

1   David G. Blanchflower, "Changes over Time in Union Relative Wage Effects in Great Britain and the United States," *NBER Working Paper 6100* (July 1997).

1967 and 1979.[2] Blanchflower found that in Great Britain the union wage effect is modestly smaller—about 10 percent, a result also obtained in other studies.[3]

The estimates of U^* in Table 12.4 suggest the size of the union wage effect for the average worker. Figure 12.4, which again comes from Blanchflower, illustrates the value of U^* for specific demographic and occupational groups.

The size of the union wage effect varies inversely with a worker's level of education; the least educated workers gain the most from union membership, the most educated gain relatively little, especially in the United Kingdom. It is reasonable that the bargaining power of a union would have the biggest impact on the earnings of those persons who, due to lack of job market skills, had the least individual bargaining power. Union wage polices also tend to have a leveling influence on a firm's internal wage structure, holding down earnings for workers with more education or job skills. This influence arises in part from the practice of unions of negotiating across-the-board cents-per-hour wage increases that, on a percentage basis, raise wage rates in the lowest labor grades more than in the higher grades.[4] The same explanation helps explain why the union wage effect is greater for part-time workers.[5] Another part of the explanation is that political pressure on the union leadership, coming from the need to win reelection to office and ratification of new contracts, motivates them to follow a wage policy that appeals to a majority of the rank and file. If highly educated workers are a minority in the union's membership, the leadership has an incentive to bargain for the larger wage increases for the less educated.[6]

Figure 12.4 also shows the relationship between a worker's age and the size of the union wage gap. The leveling influence of union wage policy causes a flattening of the inverse U-shaped age/earnings profile commonly observed for nonunion workers.[7] By substantially raising entry-level salaries in the firm, unions increase the earnings of young, inexperienced workers considerably above what they could obtain in a similar nonunion company. The flip side of wage leveling is that earnings in a unionized firm grow more slowly with experience, resulting in a gradual narrowing of the union wage effect as workers reach middle age. Other studies have found the union wage effect widening again after age 55 or so as seniority provisions in union contracts protect older workers from the decline in relative earnings that typically occurs after they pass their peak productivity years.[8]

A third important feature of Figure 12.4 is the size of the union wage effect by race and gender. Holding other things constant, Blanchflower found that unionism results, on average, in significantly larger increases in earnings for British women and nonwhite workers, but American women and nonwhite workers do not earn a greater union wage premium. These differences could be explained either by structural differences in the two labor

---

2 H. G. Lewis, *Union Relative Wage Effects: A Survey* (Chicago: University of Chicago Press, 1986). David Blanchflower and Richard B. Freeman, "Unionism in the United States and Other Advanced OECD Countries," *Industrial Relations* 31 (Winter 1992): 56–79, provide estimates ranging from a low of 4 percent in Sweden to a high of 18 percent in the United States.

3 Alison Booth, *The Economics of the Trade Union* (Cambridge: Cambridge University Press, 1995); see Table 6.1.

4 Evidence is offered by Barry T. Hirsch and Edward J. Schumacher, "Unions, Wages, and Skills, *Journal of Human Resources* 33 (Winter 1998): 201–19, that the differential in the union wage premium by skill is the result of low-skill workers being overrepresented in unions. The difference between union and nonunion wages for low-skill workers was found to be greater than the union wage differential among high-skill workers. Also see P. D. Murphy et al., "The Effects of Trade Unions on the Distribution of Earnings: A Sample Selectivity Approach," *Oxford Bulletin of Economics and Statistics* 54 (November 1992): 517–42.

5 Also see Brian G. M. Main and Barry Reilly, "Women and the Union Wage Gap," *Economic Journal* 102 (January 1992): 49–66.

6 For empirical evidence on this point, see Michael D. White, "The Intra-Unit Wage Structure and Unions: A Median Voter Model," *Industrial and Labor Relations Review* 35 (July 1982): 565–77.

7 See Richard Freeman and James Medoff, *What Do Unions Do?* (New York: Basic Books, 1984), 131. Alison L. Booth and Jeff Frank, "Seniority, Earnings and Unions," *Economica* 63 (November 1996): 673–86, however, find a systematic transfer of earnings from less senior to more senior workers in British contracts that explicitly specify pay scales based on seniority.

8 See Alison L. Booth and Jeff Frank (1996).

FIGURE 12.4

THE UNION WAGE EFFECT AMONG DEMOGRAPHIC AND OCCUPATIONAL GROUPS, UK AND THE USA, 1993

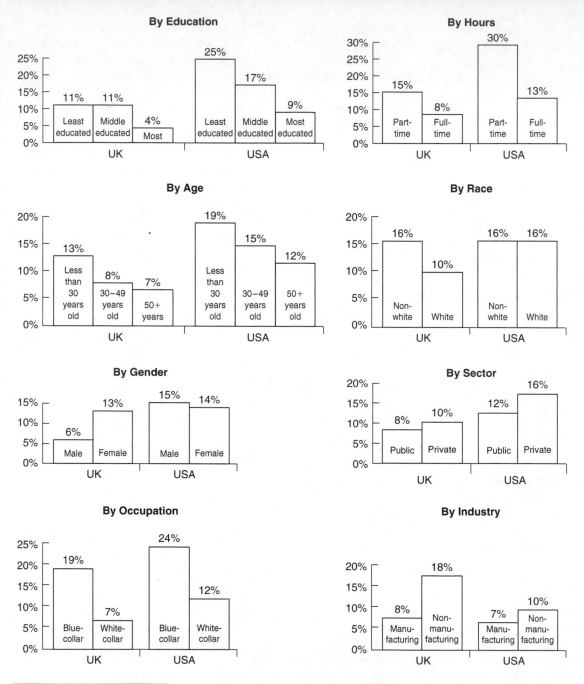

SOURCE: Constructed from statistics provided in Blanchflower, "Changes over Time in Union Relative Wage Effects in Great Britain and the United States."

markets or by organizational structures of the unions.[9]

The last three comparisons in Figure 12.4 are wage differentials by sector, occupation, and industry. Results across these categories are similar for both the United Kingdom and the United States. Unions in the private sector appear to be more successful in raising wages relative to unions in the public sector. This may be because there are more rents to capture in the private sector than in the public sector.[10] Both blue-collar and nonmanufacturing workers enjoy a larger union wage premium than their white-collar and manufacturing counterparts. This may be because there are greater threat effect in the manufacturing sector (thus reducing the measured union wage again) and because of the sorting of low-skill workers into unions (increasing the measured wage effect for blue-collar workers).[11]

Longitudinal Estimates

The estimates of U^* presented above suggest that unions have a sizable impact on earnings in the labor market. This conclusion hinges on the assumption that the explanatory variables included in the cross-sectional wage equations were able to control for all the factors identified earlier as possible sources of bias in measuring U^*.

One source of bias for which it is difficult to control is the differences in the characteristics of jobs held by union and nonunion workers. One study estimated that up to 50 percent of the union–nonunion wage differential in the trucking industry was actually a compensating wage differential.[12]

A more troublesome source of bias in the cross-sectional estimates of U^* arises from unobservable or unmeasured productivity differentials between union and nonunion workers. As noted previously, because unionized firms pay high wages they should be able to hire the most-productive workers. Some determinants of productivity, however, such as manual dexterity, motivation and work effort, and innate mental ability, are not captured in cross-sectional survey data. To the extent that these unmeasured productivity traits of union workers are omitted or uncontrolled for in the wage equations, the estimates of U^* will still overstate the true wage impact of unionism.

In recent years, economists have devised an ingenious approach to overcome this problem with the help of **longitudinal (panel) survey data.** In a longitudinal survey, data are collected on earnings, union status, education, and so on, for several thousand individuals for a number of successive years. Rather than estimating U^* by comparing the earnings of different individuals at a point in time, longitudinal data allow one to calculate U^* by examining the change in earnings over time as specific individuals in the survey move from nonunion to union jobs and vice versa. The great advantage of this approach, assuming that a given individual's unmeasured or unobservable productivity traits do not change as the person switches union status, is that the resulting change in earnings should reflect the pure, isolated effect of union membership.

---

9   This result is consistent with that presented in Orley Ashenfelter, "Racial Discrimination and Trade Unionism," *Journal of Political Economy* 80 (May/June 1971): 435–64. He finds that discrimination within the union structure can work to the detriment of black workers resulting in a lower union wage premium than earned by white workers.

10   For more on the public versus private union wage gap, see H. Gregg Lewis, "Union/Nonunion Wage Gaps in the Public Sector," *Journal of Labor Economics* 8 (January 1990): S260–328.

11   See John Driffill and Meloria Meschi, "Unions and Wages in 1984 and 1990: Evidence from Cross Sections of the Establishments in the UK," University of Southampton Discussion Paper in Economics and Econometrics: 9643 (October 1996), and Barry T. Hirsch and Edward J. Schumacher, "Unions, Wages, and Skills," *Journal of Human Resources* 33 (Winter 1998): 201–19.

12   Barry T. Hirsch, "Trucking Deregulation and Labor Earnings," *Journal of Labor Economics* 11 (April 1993): 279–301. Hirsch identifies the differential he measures as a "worker quality" wage premium. However, considering the alternatives available to low-quality workers, this compensation wage differential based on unmeasured *worker* characteristics can be treated qualitatively the same as any compensating differential associated with a characteristic of the *job*, such as risk. Also see Greg J. Duncan and Frank Stafford, "Do Union Members Receive Compensating Wage Differentials?" *American Economic Review* 70 (June 1980): 355–71, and J. Paul Leigh, "Are Unionized Blue-Collar Jobs More Hazardous Than Nonunion Blue-Collar Jobs?" *Journal of Labor Research* 3 (Summer 1982): 349–57.

	Estimates of Union Impact on Wages Using Longitudinal Data	
TABLE 12.5		

	Estimate Wage Gain from Belonging to/Joining a Union	
Sample	Low-Skill Workers	High-Skill Workers
(a) National sample of young workers		
Cross-sectional estimate	0.178	0.022
Longitudinal estimate	0.060	0.106
(b) Health industry workers		
Cross-sectional estimate	0.108	0.032
Longitudinal estimate	0.033	0.011

SOURCES: (a) Barry T. Hirsch and Edward J. Schumacher, "Unions, Wages, and Skills," *Journal of Human Resources* 33 (Winter 1998): 201–19. (b) Barry T. Hirsch and Edward J. Schumacher, "Union Wages, Rents, and Skills in Health Care Labor Markets," *Journal of Labor Research* (Winter 1998): 125–47.

Table 12.5 presents two sets of estimates of U^* calculated by Barry Hirsch and Edward Schumacher using two different longitudinal data sets.[13] The table presents union wage effects obtained for low-skill and high-skill workers using both cross-sectional and longitudinal data. The longitudinal estimates result from asking the question, "What will happen to a worker's wage if he or she joins a union?" Two features of these results warrant comment. First of all, the longitudinal estimates are much smaller than the cross-sectional estimates for low-skill workers. This suggests that the U^* estimates reported in Table 12.4 are artificially high because the low-skill workers in unions earn more not only because of the union's bargaining power but also because they are more productive due to unmeasured factors such as work effort and innate ability.[14]

The second feature of interest is that for both samples, the union wage effect declined by a greater percentage among low-skill workers than among high-skill workers; the union wage effect even became *larger* for high-skill workers in the first (national) sample. The implication of these results is that the most productive low-skill workers are drawn to (or hired into) unions, whereas the most productive high-skill workers are drawn to the nonunion sector.[15]

Before we accept the "true" U^* to be on the order of 6 to 10 percent (for the national sample of young workers in Table 12.5) rather than the 15 to 20 percent typically estimated from cross-sectional

13   Barry T. Hirsch and Edward J. Schumacher, "Unions, Wages, and Skills," *Journal of Human Resources* 33 (Winter 1998): 201–19, and "Union Wages, Rents, and Skills in Health Care Labor Markets," *Journal of Labor Research* (Winter 1998): 125–47.

14   George Jakubson, "Estimation and Testing of the Union Wage Effect Using Panel Data," *Review of Economic Studies* 58 (October 1991): 971–91, finds similar results. Contrary evidence is provided in Steven Raphael, "Estimating the Union Earnings Effect Using a Sample of Displaced Workers," *Industrial and Labor Relations Review* 53 (April 2000): 503–21, which finds that the longitudinal estimate of U^* is close to the cross-sectional estimate.

15   This result is consistent with the finding by others that the returns to education are smaller in the union sector than in the nonunion sector. See Phanindra V. Wunnava and Albert A. Okunade, "Cross-sectional Versus Panel Estimates of Union Wage Effects: Evidence from the PSID," *Economics Letters* 35 (January 1991): 105–10.

studies, there is another source of error that has been identified with using longitudinal data. David Card (among others) has found that some of the workers recorded as changing from nonunion to union status never did; they were simply misclassified through various reporting or measurement errors.[16] Although this may not seem like much of a problem, Card found that these measurement errors bias the longitudinal estimates of U^* downward, because a worker would not voluntarily make the switch unless the nonunion job paid a higher wage than the union one. Card estimated that correcting for the misclassification, the union wage effect increased from 10 to 28 percent for low-skill workers, and from 5 to 11 percent for high-skill workers.

Somewhere in the range of the low longitudinal estimates and the high cross-sectional estimates lies that elusive value of U^* for which economists continue to search.

---

16   David Card, "The Effect of Unions on the Structure of Wages: A Longitudinal Analysis," *Econometrica* 64 (July 1996): 957–79. Also see Richard B. Freeman, "Longitudinal Analysis of Trade Union Effects," *Journal of Labor Economics* 2 (January 1984): 1–26.

Summary

Bargaining theory predicts that wages in a unionized market should be higher than in a nonunion market. Estimating the actual size of the wage gain attributable to unionism is difficult, however, for several reasons. One is the problem of other things equal. Because the union status of workers is correlated with a number of other factors that affect rates of pay, it is difficult to separate out the true effect of unionism from the influence of these other variables. The second problem is the mutual interdependence between union and nonunion wage rates. One form this interdependence takes is the spillover effect; a second form is the threat effect.

Several dozen studies have attempted to estimate U^*, the adjusted union–nonunion wage differential. Estimates from cross-sectional survey data typically estimate U^* to be on the order of 15 percent, while studies using longitudinal data estimate U^* to be in the neighborhood of 6 to 10 percent. Because both approaches are subject to error, the true value of U^* probably lies somewhere between these two estimates.

Besides the level of the aggregate union–nonunion wage differential, five other dimensions of the union wage effect are of interest. It was shown that the union wage effect increases with the percentage of the workforce organized in the market, during periods of higher unemployment, and with barriers to entry in the product market. Unionism also seems to reduce the amount of inequality in earnings in the economy. Finally, union wage gains in the public sector have tended to be smaller than in the private sector.

Unions attempt to gain higher wages through the passage of various types of protective labor legislation. One example is the Davis-Bacon Act. The act requires contractors on federal construction projects to pay prevailing wages in the locality. Proponents of the act argue that it prevents substandard wages in construction; opponents argue that it protects inflated union wage rates.

Labor unions also have a significant effect on nonwage outcomes in the labor market. One of these is fringe benefits. In unionized firms a larger proportion of employee compensation takes the form of employee benefits relative to nonunion firms. Unionism also changes the mix of benefits offered by the firm. A second nonwage outcome influenced by unions is productivity. Unions have both beneficial and harmful effects on productivity. The harmful impact comes from restrictive work rules that force companies to use more labor than they really need. The beneficial effect comes from the fact that unionism both reduces employee quits and forces management to be more efficient in its operation of the firm. A third nonwage impact of unions is on company profits. The evidence is unambiguous that unions reduce the profits of business firms below what they otherwise would be.

Review Questions

1. In a survey of business firms in the Chicago area, workers who belonged to a union earned $110 more a week than nonunion workers. Does this $110 earnings differential represent the true amount by which union bargaining power was able to raise wages? Discuss the reasons why or why not.

2. It is commonly observed that many nonunion companies in a particular city or industry pay higher wages and fringe benefits than their unionized competitors. Does this mean that unions are ineffective in gaining higher wages and benefits? Why or why not?

3. Why might estimates of the adjusted union–nonunion wage differential U^* obtained from cross-sectional data be either an understatement or an overstatement of the true impact on wages? What about estimates of U^* from longitudinal data?

4. The United Automobile Workers union has lobbied Congress to adopt a "domestic content" bill that would require auto companies to buy most of their parts and components from U.S. suppliers (many of whom are organized by the UAW). Why does the UAW desire such a bill? What effect would it have on the wages of their members and why?

5. Do public sector unions have an advantage or disadvantage relative to unions in the private sector in winning higher wages for their members?

6. Why would a unionized firm be likely to pay a greater proportion of hourly compensation in the form of employee benefits, such as pensions and life insurance, than a nonunion firm?

7. In the 1980s, newspaper publishers desired to install computers and video terminals as a way to increase productivity in composing and copyediting. The printing unions tried to either block or slow down the introduction of this new equipment, fearing the loss of jobs that would result. Discuss the benefits and costs in the short run and long run to the union and its members from such a policy. Can you think of any policies that the company could adopt that would reduce the union's resistance to improvements in productivity?

Estimating Union–Nonunion Wage Differentials

Chapter 12 gives a brief heuristic explanation of the technique by which economists estimate the adjusted union–nonunion wage differential, U^*. This appendix explains this technique in more detail.

The typical approach in estimating U^* is to estimate a cross-sectional wage equation. In some cases, the data are grouped so that the comparison is between the wage rate and the percentage of the workforce unionized across a set of individual industries, states, or occupations. In other cases, the data are for individual workers, allowing the researcher to compare directly the earnings of two workers who are similar except for their union status. In general, the latter approach is preferable and is focused on here.[1]

The adjusted union wage gain U^* is the percentage by which a union is able to raise the wage rate above what it would have been in the absence of unionism. Assuming the labor market is competitive, U^* can be written as:

$$U^* = \frac{W_u - W_c}{W_c}, \qquad \text{(12A.1)}$$

where W_u = the wage the worker receives if a union member and W_c = the competitive wage the worker would have received in the absence of unionism. Two problems arise in measuring U^*. The first is that the desired comparison is the effect on wages of a change in union status for the *same* worker, holding everything else constant. Apart from several recent longitudinal data sets, such information is generally unavailable. The alternative is to compare the wages of *different* individuals who are as alike as possible except for their union status. This comparison may yield a biased measure of U^*, however, if all other determinants of earnings differentials are not controlled for (the problem of "other things equal"). The second problem is that the competitive wage W_c that would have existed in the absence of unionism is unobservable. In its place is used W_n, the wage of workers who do not belong to a union. This may also bias U^*, because W_n may either understate or overstate W_c to the extent of any spillover or threat effects, respectively.

With these caveats in mind, based on the human capital earnings function discussed in the appendix to Chapter 7, the nonunion wage can be specified as:

$$\ln W_n = \alpha_1 + \alpha_2 S + \alpha_3 EXP + \alpha_4 EXP^2 + \alpha_5 Z, \qquad \text{(12A.2)}$$

where S = years of schooling, EXP = years of labor force experience, $EXP^2 = (EXP) \cdot (EXP)$, and Z = a vector of all other variables (ability, race, gender, and so on) that affect an individual's wage rate. Assuming the relative wage gain to

---

1   See H. Gregg Lewis, "Union Relative Wage Effects: A Survey of Macro Estimates," *Journal of Labor Economics* 1, no. 1 (January 1983): 1–27.

union membership is the same for all workers, the wage rate for the unionized worker can be written as:

$$W_u = (1 + U^*)^M W_n, \qquad\qquad (12A.3)$$

where $M = 0$ if the worker is nonunion, and $M = 1$ if the worker is a union member. Equation 12A.3 can be rewritten (taking logs and substituting in Equation 12A.2) as:

$$\ln W_u = \ln(1 + U^*)M + \ln W_n$$
$$= \alpha_1 + \beta M + \alpha_2 S + \alpha_3 EXP + \alpha_4 EXP^2 + \alpha_5 Z, \qquad (12A.4)$$

where $\beta = \ln(1 + U^*)$. The regression equation will yield an estimate of β, say, $\hat{b}$. For small values of U^* (for example, 0.1), U^* and $\hat{b}$ will be quite similar, but for larger values of U^* the value of $\hat{b}$ will understate U^*. To obtain the exact value of U^*, it is necessary to calculate the antilog of $\hat{b}$, that is, $U^* = e^{\hat{b}} - 1$.

The discussion presented above can be made more concrete by considering an actual example of an estimate of U^* obtained from a cross-sectional wage equation. The study was done by Barry Hirsch and Edward Schumacher. Their data set was drawn from the May Current Population Surveys for 1973 through 1981 and the outgoing rotation group earnings files of the monthly Current Population Surveys for January 1983 through December 1994. Their emphasis was on union wage premia in the health services sector, so three samples were constructed; one of registered nurses (38,555 people), one of health technicians (29,594 people), and one of other health services occupations (45,044 people).

The basic form of the wage equation estimated by Hirsch and Schumacher was:

$$\ln W = \alpha_1 + \beta UNION + \alpha_2 S + \alpha_3 EXP + \alpha_4 EXP^2/100$$
$$+ \alpha_5 BLACK + \alpha_6 MALE + \alpha_7 HOSP \qquad (12A.5)$$
$$+ \alpha_8 MSA + \alpha_9 PT,$$

The estimated regression coefficients, t-ratios, and the R^2 are reported in Table 12A.1 for each of the three samples, as is the definition of each variable. The regressions show that, other things equal, persons who had more years of education, who were white, who were male, who worked for a hospital, and who lived in a large metropolitan area had higher weekly earnings than otherwise similar workers. The positive coefficient on the variable EXP and the negative one on the variable $EXP^2/100$ together give rise to a conventionally shaped age/earnings profile that peaks in midlife and then declines. The regression coefficient on the union status variable for registered nurses is 0.032 and is significantly different from zero. To obtain the value of U^*, it is necessary to take the antilog of the regression coefficient, obtaining $U^* = e^{.032} - 1 = 0.033$. This indicates that holding all other factors in Equation 12A.5 constant, registered nurses who were union members received a wage that was, on average, 3.3 percent higher than that received by nonunion workers. Performing the same calculation indicates that union health technicians earned 5.0 percent more and workers in other health service occupations earned 12.1 percent more than their nonunion counterparts.

Sample	Dependent Variable	Independent Variable									
		UNION	S	EXP	$EXP^2/100$	BLACK	MALE	HOSP	MSA	PT	R^2
Registered nurses	ln W	0.032 (6.4)	0.033 (33.0)	0.013 (13.0)	−0.027 (−27)	−0.095 (−14)	0.028 (3.5)	0.159 (39.8)	0.102 (25.5)	0.007 (1.75)	0.187
Health technicians	ln W	0.049 (7.0)	0.074 (74.0)	0.018 (18.0)	−0.033 (−33)	−0.055 (−7.9)	0.070 (11.7)	0.067 (16.8)	0.099 (19.8)	0.002 (0.4)	0.222
Health service occupations	ln W	0.114 (22.8)	0.041 (41.0)	0.011 (NA)	−0.021 (−21)	−0.078 (19.5)	0.045 (7.5)	0.146 (36.5)	0.115 (28.8)	−0.029 (7.25)	0.216

Definition of variables:

ln W = natural logarithm of weekly earnings

UNION = 1 if person is a union member, 0 otherwise

S = years of schooling

EXP = potential experience (person's age minus schooling minus 6)

$EXP^2/100$ = potential experience squared divided by 100

BLACK = 1 if person is black, 0 otherwise

MALE = 1 if person is male, 0 otherwise

HOSP = 1 if person works in a hospital, 0 otherwise

MSA = 1 if person's job is in a large metropolitan area, 0 otherwise

PT = 1 if person is part-time employed, 0 otherwise

SOURCE: Adapted from Barry T. Hirsch and Edward J. Schumacher, "Union Wages, Rents, and Skills in Health Care Labor Markets," *Journal of Labor Research* 19 (Winter 1998): 125–47. *T*-ratios are in parentheses. Regressions also included a control for marital status, employment sector (public v. private), and an intercept term.

Hirsch and Schumacher go on in their analysis to estimate the union wage effect using longitudinal data (individuals are observed more than once over time). One problem with the cross-sectional estimates is that unions may attract more-productive workers, so workers in unions will be earning higher wages not (only) because they are in unions, but because they are more productive than similarly skilled nonunion workers. By observing the same individuals over a period of time, one can control not only for observable levels of education, experience, and so forth, but also for unobservable levels of productivity. This unobservable level of productivity is referred to as a fixed effect, because it is a determinant of wages that remains fixed for each person over a period of time. The relationship between earnings and other variables for person i at time t, say 1993, becomes:

$$\ln W_{i,93} = \beta UNION_{i,93} + \alpha_2 S_{i,93} + \alpha_3 EXP_{i,93}$$
$$+ \alpha_4 EXP_{i,93}^2/100 + \alpha_5 Z_{i,93} + F_i \qquad \text{(12A.6)}$$

F_i corresponds to person i's (unobserved) fixed effect. The same relationship is expected to hold at time $t + 1$, say 1994:

$$\ln W_{i,94} = \beta UNION_{i,94} + \alpha_2 S_{i,94} + \alpha_3 EXP_{i,94}$$
$$+ \alpha_4 EXP_{i,94}^2/100 + \alpha_5 Z_{i,94} + F_i \qquad \text{(12A.7)}$$

By subtracting the 1993 equation (Equation 12A.6) from the 1994 equation (Equation 12A.7), one is left with a regression equation in which the variables are in difference (or change) form and the fixed effect (F_i) disappears because it does not change over time ($F_{i,93} = F_{i,94}$). The actual equation estimated is:

$$\Delta \ln W_i = \beta \Delta UNION_i + \alpha_2 \Delta S_i + \alpha_3 \Delta EXP_i$$
$$+ \alpha_4 \Delta EXP_i^2/100 + \alpha_5 \Delta Z_i \qquad \text{(12A.8)}$$

TABLE 12A.2   UNION–NONUNION WAGE EFFECTS; LONGITUDINAL DATA

Sample	Sample Size	Dependent Variable	UNION
Registered nurses	7,583	$\Delta \ln W$	0.011 (1.10)
Health technicians	4,743	$\Delta \ln W$	0.014 (1.00)
Health service occupations	5,856	$\Delta \ln W$	0.033 (2.75)

SOURCE: Adapted from Barry T. Hirsch and Edward J. Schumacher, "Union Wages, Rents, and Skills in Health Care Labor Markets," *Journal of Labor Research* 19 (Winter 1998): 125–47. *T*-ratios are in parentheses.

Table 12A.2 presents Hirsch and Schumacher's results from estimating Equation 12A.8. Any union wage effect essentially disappears for registered nurses and for health technicians. This suggests that most (if not all) of the union wage effect identified for these workers was really a wage differential associated with differences in unobserved productivity levels; union workers are more productive than nonunion workers and *that* is why the union workers earn higher wages. A 3.4 percent wage differential persists among workers in other health service occupations, suggesting that even though most of the wage differential even in this group is attributable to productivity differences, workers in these occupations do still enjoy a premium for belonging to a union. This result is consistent with the literature discussed in the text indicating that unions do more to enhance wages of low-skill workers (which this group represents) than more highly skilled workers.

Unemployment

There is little question that unemployment has been and continues to be one of the most serious and pervasive economic problems in the labor market. Low wages, discrimination, substandard working conditions, and other types of labor market pathologies are all threats to the economic security and well-being of significant numbers of workers, but few approach the impact of unemployment as a cause of both economic hardship and wasted resources.

The causes of unemployment are myriad and complex. For some people, unemployment is relatively short-term, associated with the normal process of moving between jobs or from school to work. For others, unemployment may last for months because of inability to find a job. The fact that unemployment has multiple causes and very disparate impacts on the workers who experience it leads to controversy about how serious a social and economic problem unemployment is and what policies would be best to combat it. This chapter explores these issues, examining different theoretical explanations for the occurrence of unemployment and the empirical evidence for and against these different points of view.

The Pattern of Unemployment

Figure 13.1 shows the rate of unemployment for the total economy for the years 1950 through 2004, as well as for three specific groups in the labor force: adult white males, blacks, and teenagers. The bars in Figure 13.1 denote periods of recession.

These data illustrate four facts about unemployment. First, even in the tightest labor markets some minimum amount of unemployment always remains. During the Korean War and the Vietnam War, for example, the economy was producing at close to full capacity, yet unemployment remained at or above 3 percent. A second feature of unemployment is its relationship to the business cycle. The unemployment rate exhibits a distinct countercyclical movement, falling during periods of business expansion and then rising quite rapidly with the onset of recession. This pattern is revealed in Figure 13.1 by comparing the level of unemployment in the shaded bars (recessions)

FIGURE 13.1 — PATTERN OF UNEMPLOYMENT RATES OVER TIME AND ACROSS DEMOGRAPHIC GROUPS, 1950–2004

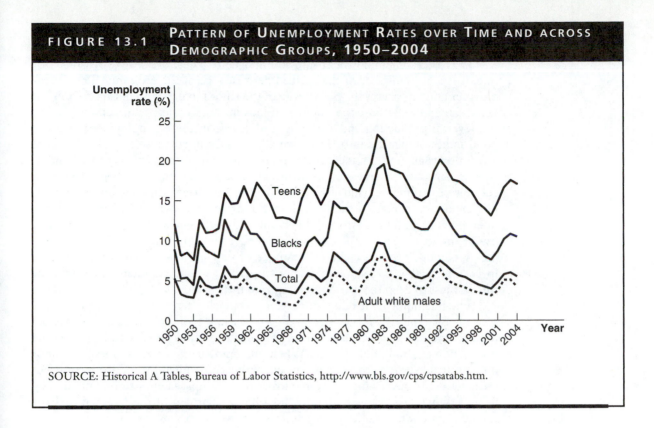

SOURCE: Historical A Tables, Bureau of Labor Statistics, http://www.bls.gov/cps/cpsatabs.htm.

and white areas (expansions). A third feature of unemployment is its uneven distribution across demographic groups in the labor force. During both business cycle expansions and recessions, the unemployment rate among blacks tends to be roughly double the national average, and for teenagers, two and one-half to three times as much. The unemployment rate among adult white males, on the other hand, is consistently the lowest among the various age, race, and gender groups in the labor force. Finally, a fourth feature of unemployment revealed in Figure 13.1 is its long-term trend, marked by a gradual increase from 1950 to 1982 and then a gradual decrease from 1983 to the present.

Why Worry about the Unemployment Rate?

The importance of unemployment is clear from the public attention it receives. Few economic statistics are given more news coverage and figure more heavily in political debates than the unemployment rate. For example, on the first Friday of each month the Bureau of Labor Statistics (BLS) announces the unemployment rate for the previous month. Whatever the figure is, it is sure to be the subject of comment from the president, members of Congress, and economic analysts on Wall Street.

Why is the unemployment rate so important? There are several reasons. For one, it is a key indicator of the cyclical performance of the economy. The unemployment rate measures the percentage of the labor force that do not have a job but are seeking one. Because the number of jobs in the economy is directly related to the level of production and spending, a decrease in the unemployment rate is a good indicator that business firms are adding jobs in response to rising levels of sales and production. An increase in the unemployment rate, on the other hand, is often a harbinger of recession as firms cut back on new hiring or begin layoffs in response to falling demand. Paradoxically, however, *both* employment and unemployment may increase at the same time. For example, between 2000 and 2004, the unemployment rate rose from 4.0 percent to 5.5 percent while employment grew by 2.3 million persons. The explanation is that the growth in the number of new jobs was more than offset by the number of new job seekers entering the labor force. Given labor force growth of about 1 percent a year, employment has to grow this fast just to keep the unemployment rate from rising.

The unemployment rate also receives so much attention because it is a measure of economic efficiency. A central goal of every economic system is to use the limited amounts of land, labor, and capital as efficiently as possible to maximize the production of goods and services. When unemployment occurs, some of the labor input available to the economy is unused, with a consequent loss of production. An estimate of the size of the economic loss from unemployment can be obtained by using **Okun's law** (named after Arthur Okun, chairman of the Council of Economic Advisers for the Johnson administration). According to Okun's law, every percentage point rise in the unemployment rate is equal to a 2 percent drop in GNP.[1] Thus, the rise in the unemployment rate from 4.0 percent to 4.8 percent in the early period of the 2001 recession cost the economy approximately 1.6 percent of GDP, or $173 billion in goods and services per year (in 2004 dollars).

A third reason for the attention given to unemployment is that it imposes substantial costs on individual workers and their families. These costs take at least three forms. The first is the loss in income that goes with unemployment. Since earnings from work are the principal source of income for most people, a prolonged period of joblessness can impose a significant hardship on workers and their families. A second potential cost to workers from unemployment stems from the *scarring effect* that a prolonged period of joblessness may have on their chances of getting new jobs and resuming their movement up a career or training ladder.[2] For

---

1   See David Romer, *Advanced Macroeconomics* (New York: McGraw-Hill, 2001). Also see Donald G. Freeman, "Panel Tests of Okun's Law for Ten Industrial Countries." *Economic Inquiry* 39 (October 2001): 511–23. Jesus Crespo Cuaresma, "Okun's Law Revisited," *Oxford Bulletin of Economics and Statistics* 65 (September 2003): 439–51, presents evidence that the relationship between unemployment and loss in GNP is nonlinear and is more severe during recessionary time periods.

2   Maura Sheehan and Mike Tomlinson, "Unemployment Duration in an Unemployment Blackspot," *Labour* 12 (Winter 1998): 643–73, find that employers regard long spells of unemployment as a negative "signal" about a worker's potential productivity.

many workers, a short spell of unemployment has little adverse effect on their future success in the labor market, but the depreciation in skills and job contacts for those who remain out of work for months may make a successful transition from unemployment to work increasingly difficult. Unemployment also imposes significant psychological and emotional costs on workers and their families, as revealed by the positive association between increased unemployment and higher frequencies of mental illness, suicide, and divorce.[3] Finally, society must bear substantial economic costs because unemployment can lead to heightened levels of crime, drug addiction, and other social maladies.[4]

The Measurement of Unemployment

The concept of unemployment is intuitively easy to understand—unemployment occurs when a person doesn't have work but wants it. Underneath this simple definition lurk a number of practical difficulties, however. For example, if a person who professes to want a job is offered one but turns it down, should he or she still be considered unemployed? Similarly, should a person be considered unemployed if he or she states a desire for a job but makes no observable effort to find one for six months? What about the person who wants to work 40 hours per week but can't find more than a 20-hour part-time job—should this individual be counted as one-half unemployed?

The definition of unemployment is important because it has a large bearing on how much joblessness is reported in the official statistics and, thus, on people's evaluation of the economy's performance and the social and economic costs imposed by unemployment. The current approach by which the BLS measures unemployment is illustrated in Figure 13.2. As discussed in Chapter 3, the data on unemployment are obtained on a monthly basis through the Current Population Survey (CPS). The civilian noninstitutional population includes persons 16 years of age or older who are not residents of a prison, mental hospital, or other institution, and are not in the armed forces. The civilian noninstitutionalized population is then broken down into two groups: those who are employed or unemployed are counted as "in the labor force"; those who do not have jobs and have not looked for one are counted as "not in the labor force." To be classified as "employed" a person must have worked in the survey week for at least one hour for pay, or for a minimum of 15 hours without pay in a family-run business. A person who has a job

---

3   One study provides evidence that being unemployed does impact a person's potential to abuse alcohol. See John Mullahy and Jody Sindelar, "Employment, Unemployment, and Problem Drinking," *Journal of Health Economics* 15 (August 1996): 409–34.

4   See M. Harvey Brenner, "Influence of the Social Environment on Psychopathology: The Historical Perspective," in James E. Barrett et al., eds., *Stress and Mental Disorder* (New York: Raven Press, 1979); W. Kip Viscusi, "Market Incentives for Criminal Behavior," in Richard B. Freeman and Harry J. Holzer, eds., *The Black Youth Employment Crisis* (Chicago: University of Chicago Press, 1986), 301–46; and Roy Ralton, "Economy and Race: Interactive Determinants of Property Crime in the United States, 1958–1995: Reflections on the Supply of Property Crime," *American Journal of Economics and Sociology* 58 (July 1999): 405–34.

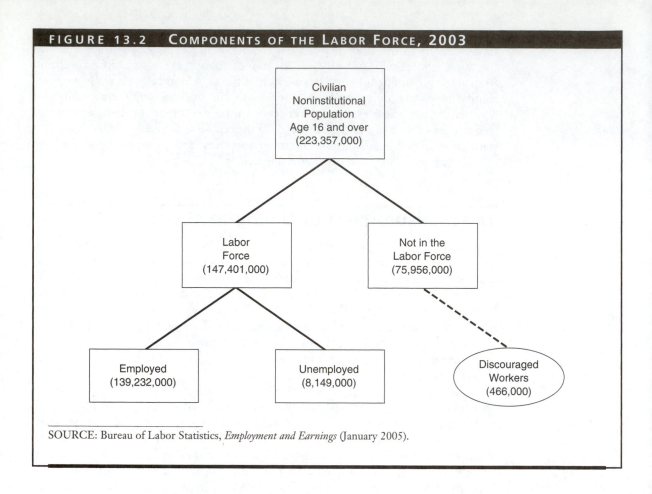

FIGURE 13.2   COMPONENTS OF THE LABOR FORCE, 2003

Civilian
Noninstitutional
Population
Age 16 and over
(223,357,000)

Labor
Force
(147,401,000)

Not in the
Labor Force
(75,956,000)

Employed
(139,232,000)

Unemployed
(8,149,000)

Discouraged
Workers
(466,000)

SOURCE: Bureau of Labor Statistics, *Employment and Earnings* (January 2005).

but is temporarily absent from work due to vacation, illness, bad weather, or a strike is also counted as employed. To be counted as "unemployed," a person must satisfy three criteria: (1) he or she is without a job, (2) he or she would be able to take a job if it were offered, and (3) he or she has looked for work in the preceding four weeks. The **unemployment rate** is then calculated as the number of persons unemployed divided by the number of persons in the labor force. In 2004, the annual rate of unemployment was 5.5 percent.

The government's measures of employment and unemployment have been criticized on a number of grounds.[5] One is that the data on unemployment provide a poor and possibly misleading indicator of the economic costs and hardship imposed by unemployment. On one hand, it can be persuasively argued that the

[5]   An excellent set of articles that discusses unemployment and its measurement is contained in *How the Government Measures Unemployment*, prepared by John F. Stinson Jr. for the Bureau of Labor Statistics, U.S. Department of Labor (Report 864, February 1994).

conventional labor force statistics *understate* the true costs of unemployment. The most obvious example is the exclusion of discouraged workers from the count of the unemployed. **Discouraged workers** are persons who desire work, have looked for work sometime during the past year, but have made no effort in the past four weeks to find work, either because of a perceived lack of jobs or a perceived inability to land a job due to a personal factor such as age, race, or lack of skills. Since discouraged workers have made no overt job search efforts, they are counted as outside the labor force and do not enter into the unemployment rate (see Figure 13.2). In 2004, an average of 466,000 people were discouraged workers; had they been counted as unemployed, the official unemployment rate would have risen from 5.5 percent to 6.2 percent.

A second reason why the conventionally measured unemployment rate understates the costs of unemployment is that it fails to reflect persons who are underemployed. In 2004, for example, 3.3 million of the employed reported that they involuntarily worked part-time, either because employers had cut back their hours of work or, in the case of new job seekers, because they could not find full-time work. Even though these people could not find as much work as they desired, as long as they worked even one hour they were counted as employed, just as is the person holding down a full-time, 40-hour-a-week job.

There are valid arguments, on the other hand, that the official unemployment rate *overstates* the economic costs imposed by unemployment. For example, it is frequently alleged that the unemployment insurance program inflates the measured unemployment rate because recipients can afford to remain out of work for a longer time. In a similar vein, welfare programs such as Temporary Assistance for Needy Families (TANF) and food stamps may artificially increase unemployment because of their requirement that applicants register for work as a condition for the receipt of benefits. Even if these income transfer programs do not lead to higher unemployment, they reduce for workers and their families the economic hardship associated with unemployment. A second source of upward bias in the unemployment rate is the changing demographic composition of the labor force. The growing share of teenagers and women in the workforce, for example, is said to exaggerate any slack in the economy because persons in both groups enter and exit the labor force frequently and, thus, are more often counted as unemployed. Similarly, the growth of two-earner families has reduced the financial pressure on individual family members to cut short their job searches and take the first job that comes along, also leading to an increase in measured unemployment.

As one response to the critics, Congress in 1976 established the National Commission on Employment and Unemployment Statistics to systematically examine the methods of data collection and the measurement of various labor force concepts. In late 1979 the commission reported its recommendations to the secretary of labor.[6] The commission recommended that the official measures of

---

[6]   These are summarized in Robert L. Stein, "National Commission's Recommendations on Labor Force Statistics," *Monthly Labor Review* 103, no. 4 (April 1980): 11–21.

employment and unemployment remain unchanged, with the exception of certain technical adjustments and data improvements. Perhaps most controversial, the commission argued that discouraged workers should not be included in the count of unemployed, principally because the majority of these workers have a very tenuous attachment to the labor force.[7]

Ten years later, yet another review was undertaken of the employment and unemployment statistics. This time a decision was made to significantly revise several of the questions in the Current Population Survey—the first such change in 25 years. Careful parallel surveying (using both the old and the new surveys at the same time to discern any differences in outcomes) indicated that the redesign of the CPS did not significantly alter the measured unemployment rate for any demographic group except for workers between the ages of 55 and 64. The redesign did impact the measure of other factors, however. For example, the proportion of the unemployed classified as new entrants into the labor market increased, women's employment-to-population ratio increased, the proportion of the employed classified as part-time workers increased, and those not in the labor force classified as discouraged workers decreased.[8] The change in the proportion of workers classified as part-time employed arises from the new way the CPS distinguishes between "full-time" workers (one job of 35 or more hours) and "multiple part-time" workers (several jobs that together equal 35 or more hours). Previously, this latter category would have been classified as full-time employed. In 2003 1.7 million workers held more than one part-time job.

Types of Unemployment

Economists usually distinguish between three different types of unemployment: frictional, structural, and cyclical.[9]

Frictional Unemployment

Frictional unemployment arises because of the constant flow of people between jobs and into and out of the labor force, because information in the job market is imperfect, and because it takes time for unemployed workers and employers with

---

7   A study found that more than half of the people classified as discouraged workers had not looked for a job in over a year. See Paul O. Flaim, "Discouraged Workers: How Strong Are Links to Job Market?" *Monthly Labor Review* 107, no. 8 (August 1984): 8–11.

8   See Anne E. Polivka, "The Redesigned Current Population Survey," *Journal of Economic Perspectives* 10 (Summer 1996): 169–80, for a summary of the motivation behind the survey redesign, the measures taken to estimate its impact on measured statistics, and the outcomes of those tests. Also see John Haltiwanger et al., eds., *Labor Statistics Measurement Issues* (Chicago: University of Chicago Press, 1998), for the most recent adjustments to be used for comparing old and new survey outcomes.

9   Some economists distinguish seasonal unemployment as a fourth type. Since it is relatively short term, it is included here as part of frictional unemployment.

job vacancies to find each other. Even when the demand and supply situation in the labor market is in balance, some unemployment will always occur as workers and firms search for the best matches. If information were perfect and mobility were costless, this process could be done instantaneously, and no unemployment would occur. Since neither condition is met in the real world, an inevitable by-product of a dynamic labor market is a certain amount of frictional unemployment. The exact amount depends on the frequency of turnover and the speed and efficiency with which job seekers and job vacancies are matched.

Frictional unemployment has several distinctive characteristics. First, it affects a relatively large number of people across all demographic groups, industries, and areas of the country. The incidence of frictional unemployment is not the same for everyone, however, since turnover is greater in some industries, such as construction or retail trade, and among particular demographic groups, such as teenagers. A second important feature of frictional unemployment is that it tends to be of relatively short duration. Many people who change jobs or seek work for the first time experience no unemployment at all; for those who do, the length of time spent looking for work is frequently a month or less. A third feature is that a certain amount of frictional unemployment is unavoidable. Because of the large flows of people into and out of the labor force and the continual process of job changing, even in the tightest of labor markets it is impossible to reach a zero unemployment rate. Finally, more than other types of unemployment, frictional unemployment entails not only economic costs but also some tangible economic benefits. For an individual worker, a short spell of unemployment may be a worthwhile investment if it allows a more intensive and wide-ranging job search; for the economy a certain amount of frictional unemployment is necessary if the process of labor mobility is to efficiently reallocate labor from one industry or area of the country to another. Not all frictional unemployment is beneficial, however, as illustrated by persons who frequently hop from one dead-end job to another.

The nature of frictional unemployment suggests several ways public policy could reduce it. An obvious avenue of attack would be to improve the flow of job information in the labor market, such as with a computerized job bank, an improved public employment service, or job fairs where prospective job candidates talk with representatives of different companies. One study suggests that recently passed state policies encouraging firms to provide references for former employees (improving the flow of information to potential new employers) would reduce frictional unemployment.[10] Public policy could also reduce the level of frictional unemployment by eliminating undesirable causes of turnover. One frequent suggestion is reform of the unemployment insurance system. Another policy that had been debated for years is the federal Family Medical Leave Act, which went into effect in 1993. The effect of this policy should be to reduce frictional unemployment by allowing a worker to take a leave from his or her job for a limited amount

10   Miles B. Cahill, "Truth or Macroeconomic Consequences: Theoretical Implications of the Decline and Rise of Job References in the United States," *Journal of Post Keynesian Economics* 22 (Spring 2000): 451–75.

of time rather than requiring the person to quit. If a person takes a leave, he reenters the labor force as employed. If a worker has to quit, reentrance almost assuredly means a spell of unemployment while looking for a new job.

Structural Unemployment

Structural unemployment arises from a basic mismatch between the types of jobs that are available and the types of people who are seeking jobs. This mismatch may be related to skill, education, geographic area, or age.[11] For example, structural unemployment occurs if the job openings in the economy are in skilled occupations, such as computer programmer, aerospace engineer, or office manager, while the persons seeking jobs are either young people without much education or experience or adults who have been laid off from unskilled jobs such as truck driver. Structural unemployment can also result if the job openings are in California or the Sunbelt while the job seekers are in the North or Midwest. Unemployment in this case arises not from imperfect information, but from barriers to mobility between labor markets that impede or prevent unemployed workers from competing for available jobs. With structural unemployment, job vacancies and unemployed workers coexist in the market and, even in the long run, are not easily matched.

Structural unemployment has several distinctive features. Unlike frictional unemployment, it tends to be concentrated among certain groups that have been adversely affected by technological change, the decline of a major industry, or the movement of jobs to another part of the country. Also, structural unemployment tends to be long-lasting. Workers who are displaced by new technology or a plant closing may find few alternative sources of employment in the area, and the job search process may continue for a number of months. This suggests that a fine line frequently divides frictional unemployment and structural unemployment, since both involve the process of job search. The major difference is the speed with which the job search process is completed—relatively quickly with frictional unemployment, but slowly for the structurally unemployed.

The nature of structural unemployment suggests several ways in which public policy might work to reduce it. One solution is government provision or subsidization of training programs. An example of the former is federal government programs such as the Job Corps that attempt to give hard-to-employ young people marketable skills; an example of the latter is tax incentives given to companies that offer training to workers from targeted groups. A second approach would be to encourage the movement of unemployed workers out of depressed areas, say by providing relocation allowances. A third possibility is to make the government the employer of last resort by offering public service jobs to workers who suffer persistent unemployment.

---

11   See, for example, Bradford F. Mills, "Unemployment Duration in Non-metropolitan Labor Markets," *Growth and Change* 32 (Spring 2001): 174–92.

Cyclical Unemployment

Cyclical unemployment (sometimes called **demand-deficient unemployment**) is the result of insufficient aggregate demand in the economy to generate enough jobs for those who seek one. With frictional and structural unemployment, the problem is inability to match job openings with job seekers. With cyclical unemployment, there are not enough jobs to go around. Cyclical unemployment is closely linked to the movement of the economy up and down the business cycle. On the upswing of the cycle, the unemployment rate gradually declines as growth in spending and production in the economy induces firms to increase employment, both by calling back laid-off workers and hiring new employees. With the onset of recession, the pattern reverses—the decline in sales prompts firms to lay off some existing employees and cut back on new hires, leading to a shortfall of available jobs in the economy and a rise in unemployment. Demand-deficient unemployment may have a noncyclical component as well if the economy suffers from chronic low growth, a condition referred to as "secular stagnation."

Cyclical unemployment has several distinctive characteristics. Compared to frictional and structural unemployment, cyclical unemployment exhibits much greater year-to-year variation as the economy expands and contracts. Cyclical unemployment, like frictional unemployment, also tends to be widespread throughout the economy, although workers in durable goods industries and in the northern industrial states are generally hit harder than others during recessions. There is also evidence that more-educated workers are less likely to bear the brunt of cyclical unemployment.[12] Finally, the length of unemployment for the cyclically unemployed falls in between the short spell of joblessness of the frictionally unemployed and the long-term joblessness of the structurally unemployed.

Public policy might reduce the extent of cyclical unemployment in several ways. The most direct approach is to adopt fiscal and monetary policies that ensure stable and healthy rates of economic growth. Once a recession does begin, timely intervention in the form of tax cuts or easier monetary policy can limit the severity of the economic downturn and resulting unemployment. An alternative approach might time public works projects, such as highway construction or urban renewal, to begin with periods of recession. Hours reduction through work-sharing has also been suggested as a way to moderate the pain of cyclical downturns.[13]

Distinguishing between Types of Unemployment

Although the concepts of frictional, structural, and cyclical unemployment are clear enough in theory, it is not always easy in practice to distinguish one type of

---

[12]   See Yona Rubenstein and Daniel Tsiddon, "Born to Be Unemployed: Unemployment and Wages over the Business Cycle," Tel Aviv Foerder Institute for Economic Research and Sackler Institute for Economic Research Working Paper 99/39 (1999).

[13]   Jennifer Hunt, "Hours Reduction as Work Sharing," *Brookings Papers on Economic Activity* 0.1 (1998): 339–69. Also see Nuri Erbas and Chera Sayers, "Can a Shorter Work Week Induce Higher Employment? Mandatory Reductions in the Workweek and Employment Subsidies," *International Tax and Public Finance* 8 (August 2001): 485–509.

How Many Jobs Are Enough to Keep Unemployment in Check?

Coming out of the 2001 recession, the United States experienced what many people have dubbed a "jobless recovery." Before the economic decline, there were 132 million jobs in the total U.S. (non farm) economy. As of the third quarter of 2004, employment had recovered to only 131 million jobs. This amounts to a net loss from the beginning of the recession to the end of 2004 of just over one million jobs. The graph that follows depicts the number of jobs in the U.S. economy indexed to the employment level in the quarter before the recession began. Where the solid line falls below 100, the total number of jobs in the economy is below the level seen in the 4th quarter of 2000. The graph also plots the unemployment rate as an index value. The unemployment rate rose

from the beginning of the recession and has not declined to pre-recession levels. This graph makes the relationship between job creation and the unemployment rate clear: as more jobs are created, the lower the unemployment rate goes (and vice versa).

Every month the Bureau of Labor Statistics (BLS) reports the number of jobs that have been created in the previous month. To estimate this number, they survey establishments across the United States to see how many workers were employed during the previous month. This survey is commonly referred to as the Establishment Survey, and it is distinct from the Current Population Survey (discussed earlier in the chapter) from which we calculate the unemployment rate. The Establishment Survey is believed to provide

EMPLOYMENT GROWTH AND CHANGE IN THE UNEMPLOYMENT RATE SINCE THE 2001 RECESSION

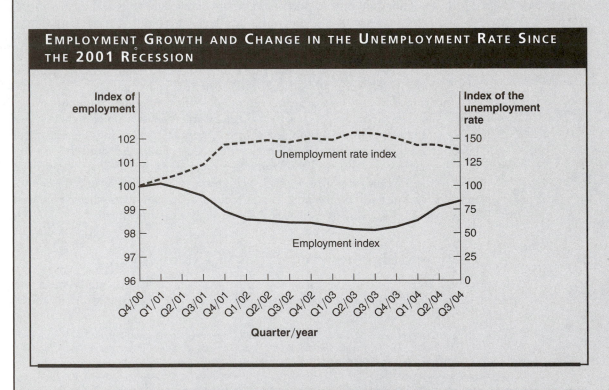

the best estimate available of the total number of jobs in the economy at any given time. Since the end of the recession through 2004, the popular press (and politicians) have lamented this slow job growth. Indeed, jobs have never taken so long to regain their pre-recession levels as they have after the 2001 recession. Headlines in newspapers have ranged from, "Jobs Report Disappoints," to "Job Growth Lags," to "Less-than-Robust Job Growth." These headlines were followed by explanations that the U.S. economy needs to create a certain number of jobs each month to absorb the growing population. If enough jobs are not created, those looking for jobs will not find them and the unemployment rate will rise. So, how many jobs are the newspapers, economists, and politicians looking for? How many jobs are enough to keep the unemployment rate from rising?

In calculating the number of jobs needed to keep the unemployment rate in check, it is typical to assume that job creation needs to grow at the same rate as the population. Between 2000 and 2003 the U.S. non-institutional population experienced an average annual growth rate of 1.35 percent. Furthermore, in 2003 there were approximately 130 million jobs in the economy. Applying the population growth rate to this employment base means the economy needs to create 1.76 million jobs per year, or an average of about 146,000 jobs per month (146,000 = (0.0135*130,000,000)/12), to at least keep unemployment from going up.

This calculation assumes that the percent of the population that wants a job (the labor force participation rate) stays constant over time. If the labor force participation rate declines over time (or the labor force grows more slowly than the population), then the economy does not have to create as many jobs to absorb those who want them. Between 2000 and 2003, the labor force participation rate actually

did decline from 67.1 percent in 2000 to 66.3 percent in 2003. This small change in the percent of the population that wants a job means that the economy only has to create 98,000 jobs per month to keep unemployment in check.

This relationship between job creation levels and the unemployment rate is illustrated by looking at a specific period of time. Between June 2003 and June 2004 the unemployment rate experienced a fairly steady decline (see Figure 13.1) from 6.3 percent to 5.6 percent. Over this same time period, the U.S. economy created an average of 107,000 jobs per month, which is more than the 98,000 estimated above, meaning that the decline in the unemployment rate over this time period is expected since more jobs on average were created than were needed to absorb the growing labor force.

So, although the rate of job creation may have been less than what the economy has experienced coming out of previous recessions, it appears, at least in the short-run, to have been enough to absorb the labor force. If the labor force participation rate had not been declining over this time period, the creation of only 107,000 per month would have resulted in a rise in the unemployment rate. In addition, faster job growth would have lowered the unemployment rate even further, which may have been what reporters and politicians were hoping for.

SOURCES: Aeppel, Timothy, "Turn of the Screw: In Tepid Job Scene, Certain Workers Are in Hot Demand—'Swiss-Style' Machinists Doing Ultra-Precise Tasks Typify Shortage of Skills—Mr. Schrader Gets Courted," *The Wall Street Journal* (17 August 2004): A1; Andrews, Edmund L. "A Growing Force of Non-workers," *The New York Times* (18 July 2004): Sect 3: 4; Lowenstein, Roger, "Help Wanted," *The New York Times Magazine* (5 September 2004); and Porter, Eduardo, "In Trying Time, Scaling Down Expectations of Job Growth," *The New York Times* (6 September 2004): 1.

FIGURE 13.3 DISTINGUISHING BETWEEN TYPES OF UNEMPLOYMENT

Along the 45° line the number of job vacancies equals the number of job seekers, which is one common definition of full employment. An increase in frictional or structural unemployment is represented by a shift in the Beveridge curve from B_1 to B_2 (point J to K); an increase in cyclical unemployment is represented by a movement down a particular Beveridge curve, such as from point J to M on curve B_1.

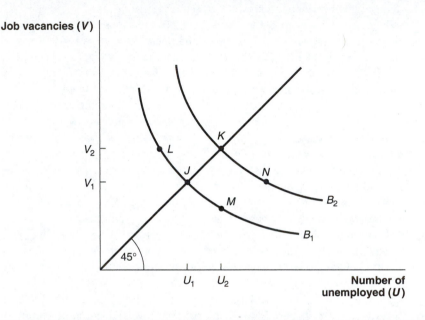

unemployment from another. One useful approach to resolving this problem is illustrated in Figure 13.3.[14] The vertical axis measures the number of job vacancies in the economy, and the horizontal axis measures the number of unemployed workers. Along the 45-degree line the number of job vacancies equals the number of people looking for work—one commonly accepted definition of **full employment**. A point above the 45-degree line represents excess demand for labor; a point below the line represents excess supply.

Even at full employment a positive amount of unemployment will still exist, due to both frictional and structural causes. This is illustrated by point J on the 45-degree line where full employment prevails, yet U_1 unemployment persists. Is this unemployment frictional or structural? From Figure 13.3 it is impossible to

---

14 See J. C. R. Dow and L. A. Dicks-Mireaux, "The Excess Demand for Labor: A Study of Conditions in Great Britain, 1945–56," *Oxford Economic Papers* 10, no. 1 (February 1958): 1–33.

tell. Job vacancies V_1 are, in the aggregate, equal to the number of job seekers U_1, but the diagram does not show whether the vacancies and unemployed will be quickly matched up, in which case U_1 is frictional unemployment, or whether they will simply coexist over time, implying that U_1 is structural unemployment. The most likely possibility is that U_1 is a combination of both types of unemployment. Note, moreover, that U_1 is only one of many possible levels of unemployment that are consistent with full employment. The greater the amount of frictional or structural unemployment, the farther out on the 45-degree line the economy will be. Thus, at point K the unemployment rate has risen to U_2, yet equality between job seekers and job vacancies remains. The increase in both vacancies and unemployment could reflect a greater amount of turnover in the labor force, a longer period of job search by the unemployed, or a greater structural imbalance between the skills desired by employers and the skills possessed by the unemployed. A reduction in frictional or structural unemployment through government workforce and training programs or improved job placement services would cause a movement down the 45-degree line.

Through each point on the 45-degree line passes a convex curve, such as B_1 and B_2, known as a **Beveridge curve** after Sir William Beveridge, a British economist. For any given structure of the labor market, the Beveridge curve shows how job vacancies and unemployment vary over the business cycle. Starting from some position of full employment such as point J, on the upswing of the cycle the economy moves up the curve B_1 to a spot such as point L. At point L demand for labor exceeds supply, shown by the excess of job vacancies relative to unemployment. (Even the tightest labor market will have some unemployment due to turnover.) Conversely, with the onset of recession the number of job vacancies declines as firms cut back on hiring, while layoffs swell the number of unemployed, reflected by a movement down the curve B_1 to a spot such as point M. At point M, the unemployment rate is U_2. Had the economy been at full employment (point J), the unemployment rate would have been U_1. The difference $U_2 - U_1$, therefore, measures the amount of cyclical unemployment, the remainder being due to frictional and structural unemployment. Beveridge curves using actual data on unemployment and vacancies between 1960 and 1996 are presented and discussed in the Empirical Evidence 13-1 section later in this chapter.

➡ SEE

Empirical Evidence 13-1: The Beveridge Curve in the US, p. 703.

If the unemployment rate increases over time, is it possible to identify the cause? Conceptually, at least, the answer is yes, although the lack of statistics in the United States on unfilled job vacancies makes it difficult in practice. An increase in cyclical unemployment would be evidenced by an increase in unemployment but a decrease in job vacancies, shown by a movement down a particular Beveridge curve, such as B_1, from point J to M. An increase in frictional or structural unemployment, on the other hand, would be revealed by an increase in both job vacancies and unemployment, represented by a shift in the Beveridge curve from B_1 to B_2 (point J to point K).

There are several ways to determine if the movement from point J to K is due to frictional or to structural causes. One method is to look at the dispersion of job vacancies and unemployment. A widespread growth in job vacancies and unemployment across industries and states would indicate frictional unemployment; a concentration of job vacancies in one area of the economy and unemployment in another would point to structural unemployment. A second method is to look at statistics on the duration of unemployment. An increase in the proportion of the unemployed who experience long spells of joblessness would suggest that structural problems were becoming more important.

An increase in unemployment may also stem from a combination of demand-deficient and structural unemployment. This would occur, for example, with widespread plant closings in the auto industry, with no offsetting increase in vacancies elsewhere in the economy. This would be represented by a horizontal movement from point J to point N. Part of the high unemployment among auto workers could be cured by an increase in aggregate demand. This would help to revive the auto industry, resulting in some of the laid-off workers being called back to their old jobs. A second impact would be to create new job openings throughout the rest of the economy that these workers might apply for. Even if the economy were to return to full employment (point K), however, structural unemployment will still show a net increase of $U_2 - U_1$. The implication is that aggregate demand can whittle down pockets of structural unemployment, but it cannot completely eliminate them.[15]

Causes of Unemployment

The distinction between frictional, structural, and cyclical unemployment provides a number of insights into the causes of unemployment. Further insight can be gained by examining three of the most important theories of frictional, structural, and cyclical unemployment—job search, rigid wages, and efficiency wages.

Job Search

The process of job search provides an important theoretical explanation for the existence of unemployment. Regardless of whether the person seeking a job is a new entrant to the labor force, a victim of a plant closing, or a worker who wants to change jobs, imperfect information forces the job seeker to go from firm to firm in search of job openings and information regarding the rates of pay, working conditions, and so on. For young workers who are already employed, the search for a better job involves a spell of unemployment only about 50 percent of the time.[16] In this situation, the worker is usually able to search for a new job during off-work

---

15 On this issue, see Mark D. Partridge and Dan S. Rickman, "Regional Differences in Chronic Long-Term Unemployment," *Quarterly Review of Economics and Finance* 38 (September 1998): 193–215.

16 Donald O. Parsons, "The Job Search Behavior of Employed Youth," *Review of Economics and Statistics* 73 (November 1991): 597–604.

FIGURE 13.4   HYPOTHETICAL FREQUENCY DISTRIBUTION OF WAGE OFFERS

The curve $f(W)$ shows the frequency distribution of wage offers facing an unemployed worker. The probability of obtaining a job paying W_1 is π_1. During a recession, the distribution of wage offers will shift to the left, such as from $f(W)$ to $f'(W)$.

If the worker sets W_1 as the minimum acceptance wage, all wage offers below that amount will be rejected. Clearly, the higher the minimum acceptance wage, the longer will be the period of search until an acceptable job is found.

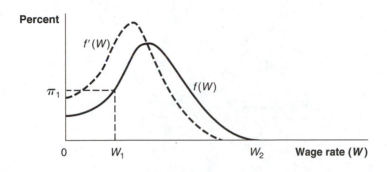

hours and, after finding a satisfactory job, make the switch with no intervening spell of joblessness. In 1999, an average of 4.5 percent of all workers were actively searching for a different job while employed.[17] For workers who are laid off or just entering the labor market, however, the process of job search usually involves periods of unemployment as they check want ads, fill out application forms at personnel offices, and interview with employers. Two questions about this process are of particular interest. The first is how long the person will remain unemployed as he or she searches for a job, and second, what factors influence the length of search.

To make the discussion of job search more concrete, consider the case of person A, who has just received an MBA degree from a well-known university. Person A enters the job market knowing that N different firms hire MBAs, although the exact wage rate each pays is unknown. Based on the experience of friends, last year's starting salaries, and so on, person A will, however, have an idea of the distribution of wage offers. Such a distribution is shown in Figure 13.4. The curve $f(W)$ is the frequency distribution of wage offers; it shows, for example, that the probability of obtaining a wage offer of W_1 is π_1, while the probability of obtaining an offer above W_2 is zero. For those firms from which no job offer is received, the wage rate is zero.

---

17   Joseph R. Meisenheimer II and Randy E. Ilg, "Looking for a 'Better Job': Job Search Activity of the Employed," *Monthly Labor Review* (September 2000): 3–14.

FIGURE 13.5   THE STIGLER MODEL OF JOB SEARCH

The marginal cost of search curve MC_A slopes upward, showing that additional days of job search entail rising marginal costs. The marginal benefit of search curve MB_A, on the other hand, slopes downward, illustrating that the additional monetary gain from successive days of search declines. The optimal amount of job search is N_2 where $MC_A = MC_B$ (point X).

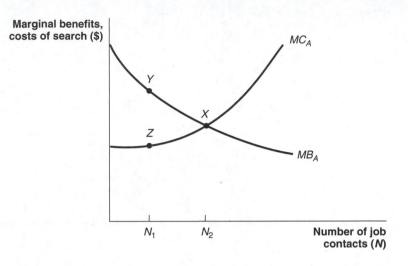

With perfect information, person A would know which firm paid the wage W_2, and no search process would be necessary. Since this is unknown, person A will spend a certain amount of time unemployed, hunting for the best (assumed here to mean highest-paying) job. How long will this period of unemployment last? Two different theories of job search have been developed to answer this question.

The Stigler Model   The first formalized model of job search was developed by George Stigler in the early 1960s.[18] According to Stigler, the optimal amount of job search can be calculated by the same type of marginal decision rule that applies to all other economic problems: Keep on contacting additional firms as long as the marginal benefit of further search exceeds the marginal increase in costs; when the two are equal, the optimal number of job contacts has been reached. This idea is illustrated in Figure 13.5, which shows the marginal benefit of a search curve for person A, MB_A, and the marginal cost of search curve MC_A.

---

18   George Stigler, "Information in the Labor Market," *Journal of Political Economy* 70, part 2 (October 1962): 94–105.

The marginal cost of a search curve slopes upward and to the right, implying that additional search is subject to increasing marginal costs. Search costs have two components. The first is direct costs, such as gas, postage, fees paid to an employment agency, and so on. The second is in the form of opportunity costs. As person A continues to interview with additional firms, the income that could have been earned if earlier job offers had been accepted is forgone. The size of these opportunity costs depends on whether or not job offers are "storable." Should previous job offers be quickly lost if a person continues to search, the marginal cost of search will be much higher than if the person can accumulate job offers and then choose the best among them. In either case, continued search is likely to involve an increase in both direct and opportunity costs, because of the widening area over which the search must be conducted and the growing loss of income from forgone job opportunities.

The marginal benefits of search, on the other hand, are subject to diminishing returns. This is shown by the marginal benefit of search curve MB_A, which slopes downward and to the right. The marginal benefit of additional search is the present value of the increase in income that person A realizes from contacting one more employer (the discounted value over the life of the job of the higher wage that is gained by additional search). Since person A is likely to interview with the most promising prospects first, the chances of finding a still better paying job diminish with additional search, giving a negative slope to the marginal benefit curve.

How many job contacts should person A undertake? The answer is N_2 contacts, where $MB_A = MC_A$ (point X). It is quite possible that person A could have ended his or her job search (and unemployment) much earlier by contacting only a few firms (say N_1) and accepting the best offer received. To do so, however, would not maximize income since the marginal benefit of additional search (point Y) outweighs the marginal cost (point Z). It is also possible that person A could have found a still better job by contacting more than N_2 firms. This also would be nonoptimal, however, since the probability of a higher wage offer is too small to justify the extra expense of continued search.

The McCall Model A second model of the job search process was developed by John McCall.[19] In Stigler's model, workers estimate the optimal length of search and then select the best job offer they receive in that time. Empirical research has found that workers frequently pursue an alternative strategy, making job contacts in sequential order, and accepting the first offer that exceeds their minimum aspiration levels. This alternative strategy is developed in McCall's theory.

McCall's model of job search can be illustrated with Figure 13.4 and the example of the MBA graduate, person A. The key feature of McCall's model is the concept of a **minimum acceptance wage.** The minimum acceptance wage is the

19 John J. McCall, "Economics of Information and Job Search," *Quarterly Journal of Economics* 84, no. 1 (February 1970): 113–126. A similar model is presented in Dale T. Mortensen, "Job Search, the Duration of Unemployment, and the Phillips Curve," *American Economic Review* 60 (December 1970): 847–62.

lowest wage that the unemployed worker will consider accepting. In the case of person A, the minimum acceptance wage might be W_1 in Figure 13.4; a job offer with a wage equal to or greater than W_1 would be accepted, a job offer below W_1 would be rejected. The length of search depends on the level of the minimum acceptance wage relative to the frequency distribution of wage offers. If person A sets a relatively low acceptance wage, a suitable job offer will be received quickly and the period of unemployment will be short; a high acceptance wage will result in a lengthy period of search.

What determines the worker's minimum acceptance wage—why is it W_1 rather than some other wage rate? In deciding upon an acceptance wage, person A has to balance the benefits versus the costs of each possible choice. The marginal benefit of a higher acceptance wage is that once such a job is found, the worker receives a higher rate of pay than in other jobs. A higher acceptance wage entails additional costs, however, since a longer period of unemployment will be necessary, on average, before a job paying that wage can be found. The optimal level of the acceptance wage occurs where the marginal benefit and marginal cost of a higher demand are equal. Realistically speaking, factors such as the person's pay on the previous job, the customary standard of living, and the job offers received by friends or acquaintances also influence the minimum acceptance wage.

Person A uses the acceptance wage as a benchmark by which to accept or reject job offers, anticipating that after a certain time a satisfactory job will be obtained. What if after that time person A has not received any job offers at all? Person A may conclude that he or she is the victim of bad luck and has contacted firms that happen to be in the left-hand tail of the frequency distribution $f(W)$ in Figure 13.4. A second possibility is that the job market for MBAs is worse than person A anticipated, and the distribution of wage offers, instead of being $f(W)$, is really the broken line $f'(W)$. If this is the case, the job offers person A expected to receive will increasingly diverge over time from the ones actually received. According to McCall, this divergence should lead the job searcher to gradually revise downward the estimate of $f(W)$ and the minimum acceptance wage.[20] At some point when the acceptance wage has fallen far enough, an acceptable job will be found, although the period of search and unemployment will have been longer than if $f(W)$ had been correctly estimated in the first place.[21]

Implications   These models of job search have a number of implications regarding unemployment. First, note that job search is, in essence, another type of human capital investment that workers make to improve their positions in the labor market. As

20   Evidence that the prediction of a declining reservation wage is consistent with human behavior can be found in James C. Cox and Ronald L. Oaxaca, "Direct Tests of the Reservation Wage Property," *Economic Journal* 102 (November, 1992): 1423–32.

21   There is some evidence that even with counseling as to what $f(W)$ looks like, the long-term unemployed will not substantially adjust their minimum acceptance wage. See Peter Dolton and Donald O'Neill, "The Impact of Restart on Reservation Wages and Long-Term Unemployment," *Oxford Bulletin of Economics and Statistics* 57 (November 1995): 451–70.

with education or on-the-job training, job search is an investment that entails a current cost in the form of a spell of unemployment but also yields future benefits in the form of a better-paying, more attractive job.[22] In these models, job search and the unemployment that goes with it are seen as a voluntary and productive use of one's time to produce a valuable economic good—job market information.

Second, these models also can explain why the length of job search varies among individuals in the workforce and why some labor force groups have higher unemployment rates than others. In 2001, the typical prime-aged (25–64 years) male worker who had been unemployed at least one month had used an average of 2.01 job search methods.[23] By contrast, prime-aged women used an average of 1.91 search methods, and teens used an average of 1.54 methods. In addition, there is evidence that the most effective method of job search is using friends and relatives, and both women and blacks are less likely to use this method of search.[24] One reason given for men searching more intensively than women is that they are planning to stay in the labor force, or with any one particular employer, longer than the average women. In addition, whites may use friends and relatives more often than blacks to find jobs because on average white workers have better access to and knowledge of promising employment situations that they are able to pass on. In a similar vein, a 1979 survey revealed that the minimum acceptance wage averaged $4.30 per hour for unemployed white youths and $4.22 per hour for unemployed black youths. The wages actually received by these respondents in their most recent jobs averaged $4.63 per hour for whites and $3.90 per hour for blacks. A likely explanation for the higher unemployment rate of black youths, therefore, is that their reservation wage was much higher relative to the actual wage they were likely to be offered than was the case for white youths.[25]

Third, these models suggest that any factor that reduces the costs of unemployment will increase the length of job search and duration of unemployment. A prime consideration is the unemployment compensation program. Under this program, workers who are laid off and meet the eligibility requirements are entitled to

---

22   Evidence on this can be found in Christian Belzil, "Relative Efficiencies and Comparative Advantages in Job Search," *Journal of Labor Economics* 14 (January 1996): 154–73. Belzil reports that among prime-aged males, workers that were laid off or quit their jobs both experienced higher earnings, on average, in their subsequent jobs.

23   The job search methods included in the CPS survey include (1) contacted the employer directly, (2) sent out resumes or filled out applications, (3) placed or answered ads, (4) checked with relatives and friends, (5) used a public employment agency, and (6) used a private employment agency.

24   See Steven M. Bortnick and Michelle Harrison Ports, "Job Search Methods and Results: Tracking the Unemployed, 1991," *Monthly Labor Review* (December 1992): 29–35. Evidence on the use of the Internet as a job search method is provided by Peter Kuhn and Mikal Skuterud, "Job Search Methods: Internet versus Traditional," *Monthly Labor Review* (October 2000): 3–11.

25   See Harry J. Holzer, "Reservation Wages and Their Labor Market Effects for Black and White Male Youth," *Journal of Human Resources* 21 (Spring 1986): 157–77. A replication of this study using slightly more recent data found that while blacks were found to have higher reservation wages (relative to what they could expect to obtain in the labor market) than whites, this higher reservation wage does *not* account for higher unemployment rates among blacks. See Stephen M. Petterson, "Black–White Differences in Reservation Wages and Joblessness: A Replication," *Journal of Human Resources* 33 (Summer 1998): 758–70.

weekly payments for at least 26 weeks, typically amounting to 50 percent or more of after-tax earnings received from work. Job search theory predicts that the higher the benefit payment, or the longer the period over which benefits can be received, the higher will be the person's minimum acceptance wage and likelihood of remaining unemployed.

Finally, search theory also offers an explanation for the countercyclical movement of unemployment over the business cycle.[26] On the upswing of the business cycle, the distribution of job offers $f(W)$ in Figure 13.4 will improve (shift to the right), resulting in a greater likelihood that job searchers will obtain a wage offer that exceeds their minimum acceptance level. In this case, both the number of unemployed and the duration of unemployment should decline. With the onset of recession, the opposite takes place as the distribution of wage offers worsens (shifts to the left) in a slack market. Since the first few job offers during a recession are likely to be relatively unattractive, unemployed workers will choose to continue their job search, leading to a higher amount of measured unemployment. Note that in this scenario unemployment is seen as largely a voluntary phenomenon—there are job openings even during the worst recession, but the unemployed turn them down in order to find something better.

Rigid Wages

In addition to job search, the existence of downwardly inflexible money wage rates in the labor market offers a second major explanation for unemployment. In the theory of job search, unemployment arises not so much from a lack of jobs, but from a lack of information about where to find these jobs and how much they pay. Unemployment caused by rigid wages is fundamentally different. The basic problem is not imperfect information but an insufficient number of jobs for the number of people who want one.

The problem caused by rigid money wage rates is illustrated in Figure 13.6. The vertical axis measures the *real wage*, w, defined as the money wage W divided by the price level P. Up to this point prices have been treated as a given, making it possible to analyze labor demand and supply in terms of the money wage rate (if P is constant, a change in W implies an equal change in w). As the analysis moves to more macroeconomic-type issues, however, it is necessary to explicitly incorporate both wages and prices into the model of the labor market. In Figure 13.6, the labor demand curve D_1 and labor supply curve S_1 are drawn as functions of the real wage. Equilibrium in the market occurs at the real wage w_1 and level of employment L_1 (point A). The employment level L_1 is a point of full employment in that the number of people wanting to work is just matched by the number of people firms wish to hire, although there will be some frictional unemployment due to turnover and job search.

---

26   See Mortensen, "Job Search, the Duration of Unemployment, and the Phillips Curve."

FIGURE 13.6 UNEMPLOYMENT CAUSED BY RIGID WAGES

A decrease in production in the economy causes the labor demand curve to shift to the left from D_1 to D_2. In a perfectly competitive market, the real wage would decline from w_1 to w_2, restoring equilibrium by stimulating additional labor demand and causing a cutback in labor supply until $D_2 = S_1$ (point C). If the real wage is inflexible downward, however, at the prevailing wage of w_1 involuntary unemployment arises, since firms desire to hire only L_3 (point B) while L_1 workers (point A) desire employment.

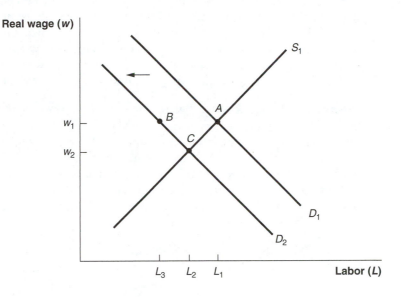

To see how rigid money wages cause unemployment, assume that consumer spending decreases, either in the entire economy or for the major product of one industry or area of the country (such as coal or steel). The initial effect is to cause firms to reduce their desired level of employment, represented in Figure 13.6 by the leftward shift of the labor demand curve to D_2. At the prevailing real wage of w_1, employment falls to L_3 (point A to point B), leading to $L_1 - L_3$ amount of demand-deficient unemployment (in a particular industry it would more closely resemble structural unemployment). If money wages were flexible downward, the excess supply of labor in the market should result in a bidding down of money wage rates until a new equilibrium is established at the real wage rate of w_2, where the demand and supply of jobs are again equal (point C). The fall in the money wage eliminates the $L_1 - L_3$ amount of unemployment both by inducing firms to increase their hiring and by causing some of the unemployed to drop out of the labor force to pursue more attractive nonmarket activities, such as attending school, working in the home, or consuming leisure.[27] Should money wages be rigid in the downward direction, this equilibrating process will not take place, and the labor market will remain at the real wage of w_1 with $L_1 - L_3$ amount of involuntary unemployment. Even if money wages did fall as envisioned in the competitive model, prices might fall an equal or greater amount, leaving the real wage at or above the initial value of w_1. This happened in the Depression as money wages fell by 19 percent between 1929 and 1933, but prices fell 24 percent.[28]

It is a commonplace observation that in a modern economy, money wage rates generally do not decline even in the face of substantial unemployment, short-circuiting the ability of the labor market to automatically return to full employment.[29] This downward inflexibility of wages offers an explanation for both cyclical and structural unemployment. In either case, if wage rates would fall in response to an excess supply of labor, eventually a new equilibrium would be restored in the market. The question, then, is, why are money wage rates so inflexible downward?

Unions and Minimum Wage Laws   One source of wage rigidity is labor unions and government minimum wage laws. Since many union contracts have three-year terms, wages in unionized industries cannot readily respond to short-run increases in unemployment in the market. Even in the long run, union bargaining power, coupled with the commitment of many union members to a policy of "no backward step," may prevent any outright cut in wage rates. Federal and state minimum wage laws have the same effect as union contracts in that they impose an artificial floor below which wage rates cannot fall.

Implicit Contracts   Wage rates also exhibit a marked downward inflexibility in markets unaffected by either unions or minimum wage laws. One attempt to

---

27   This idea that a cyclical drop in the real wage will cause some people to voluntarily give up paying jobs in favor of alternative uses of time is known as the "intertemporal substitution" hypothesis. According to one survey article, little evidence exists that explains much of the cyclical change in employment and unemployment. See Thomas J. Kniesner and Arthur H. Goldsmith, "A Survey of Alternative Models of the Aggregate U.S. Labor Market," *Journal of Economic Literature* 25 (September 1987): 1241–80. More recent research, however, finds evidence connecting intertemporal substitution of labor supply and cyclical labor market fluctuations. See Richard Rogerson and Peter Rupert, "On Testing the Intertemporal Substitution Theory of Labor Supply," *Journal of Economic Dynamics and Control* 17 (January–March 1993): 37–50, and Donald H. Dutkowsky and Robert M. Dunsky, "Intertemporal Substitution, Money, and Aggregate Labor Supply," *Journal of Money, Credit, and Banking* 28 (May 1996): 216–32.

28   See Martin N. Bailey, "The Labor Market in the 1930s," in James Tobin, ed., *Macroeconomics, Prices, and Quantities: Essays in Memory of Arthur M. Okun* (Washington, D.C.: The Brookings Institution, 1983), 21–61. The actual movement of the real wage over the business cycle is subject to considerable controversy. Some studies find the real wage does not exhibit any systematic variation over the business cycle, while others find the real wage exhibits a procyclical pattern. For a selective survey and attempt at reconciliation of the conflicting evidence, see Katherine G. Abraham and John C. Haltiwanger, "Real Wages and the Business Cycle," *Journal of Economic Literature* 33 (September 1995): 1215–64. They conclude that there is no systematic evidence for either pro- or counter-cyclicality of real wages, nor can we expect the cyclicality (or lack thereof) to be stable over time. Also see Paul J. Devereax, "The Cyclicality of Real Wages within Employer–Employee Matches," *Industrial and Labor Relations Review* 54 (July 2001): 835–50.

29   See, for example, Horst Siebert, "Labor Market Rigidities: At the Root of Unemployment in Europe," *Journal of Economic Perspectives* 11 (Summer 1997): 37–54.

explain wage rigidity in nonunion markets is implicit contract theory.[30] According to proponents of this theory, workers have a strong preference for a stable stream of income. When a recession occurs, a firm has two options to reduce its labor costs: It can cut employment through layoffs but maintain the hours and wage rates of the remaining employees, or it can maintain the original level of employment but reduce everyone's hours and rate of pay. The preference of a majority of workers would no doubt be for the former, since the brunt of adjustment is borne by the least experienced workers, who are laid off. Among unionized workers, the preference for a layoff policy over a wage-cut policy is revealed by the provisions in union contracts that call for a combination of rigid wage scales and layoff by seniority. Although nonunion firms are not bound by any explicit, written agreement to follow a layoff policy over a policy of wage cuts, some economists argue that an unwritten, tacit understanding or **implicit contract** does exist between workers and firms that such a policy will be followed. One author has called such implicit contracts the "invisible handshake."[31] Because implicit contracts are unwritten, it is difficult to directly confirm this theory. Empirical research has shown, however, that layoffs are the primary method by which firms, particularly unionized firms, reduce labor costs.[32]

Transfer Programs   The growth in government transfer programs may also have imparted a greater downward rigidity to wages. In the days before unemployment insurance, Social Security, food stamps, and other such programs, unemployed workers were forced by economic necessity to find work at whatever wage they could get. To the extent that the growth in transfer payments has reduced the costs of unemployment, workers have less incentive to lower their acceptance wage and take a job that pays less than they desire.[33]

---

30   See Costas Azariadis, "Implicit Contracts and Underemployment Equilibria," *Journal of Political Economy* 83, no. 6 (December 1975): 1103–1202, and Martin Bailey, "Wages and Employment under Uncertain Demand," *Review of Economic Studies* 41, no. 1 (January 1974): 37–50.

31   Arthur Okun, *Prices and Quantities: A Macroeconomic Analysis* (Washington, D.C.: The Brookings Institution, 1981). In Okun's theory substantial turnover costs induce both workers and firms to enter into long-term implicit contracts. A very readable account of his theory is given in "The Invisible Handshake and the Inflationary Process," *Challenge* (January/February 1980): 5–12. In the theories of Azariadis and Bailey, implicit contracts essentially represent an insurance contract that risk-averse workers purchase from risk-neutral firms. In return for a promise by the firm of stable wages and employment (at least for the majority of workers), the employees agree to work for a wage that is sufficiently low to pay the firm to accept the risk to profits such a promise implies.

32   See Susan N. Houseman and Katharine G. Abraham, "Labor Adjustment under Different Institutional Structures," in Friedrich Buttler et al., eds., *Institutional Frameworks and Labor Market Performance: Comparative Views on the U.S. and German Economies* (London and New York: Routledge, 1995), 285–315, and Peter A. Groothuis, "Turnover: The Implication of Establishment Size and Unionization," *Quarterly Journal of Business and Economics* 33 (Spring 1994): 41–53.

33   See Paul T. Decker, "Work Incentives and Disincentives," in Christopher J. O'Leary and Stephen A. Wandner, eds., *Unemployment Insurance in the United States* (Kalamazoo, Mich.: W. E. Upjohn Institute, 1997), 285–320. Also David Autor and Mark Duggan trace a more liberal disability benefit system to a level of unemployment that is two-thirds of a percentage point lower than it would be in a less generous setting; workers drop out of the labor force when they lose their jobs rather than become employed. See their paper, "The Rise in Disability Recipiency and the Decline in Unemployment," *NBER Working Paper* W8336 (June 2001).

Relative Wage Comparisons   Another source of wage rigidity comes from the importance that workers attach to their relative position in the income distribution.[34] According to J. M. Keynes, workers are far more likely to resist a reduction in real wages due to a cut in money wage rates than if the same thing is achieved by a rise in prices.[35] Since both events lead to an equivalent fall in the real wage, it may seem irrational for workers to resist one more than the other. Keynes argued that this distinction was not irrational at all. The money wage rate determines each person's position in the distribution of income. Because relative income comparisons are important to people, workers will resist a reduction in money wages out of fear that it will lower their position in the income distribution. An equivalent decline in real wages brought about by a rise in prices, on the other hand, leaves everyone's relative position in the income distribution the same and is accepted much more readily.

Turnover and Training Costs   The bidding down of wage rates in a slack labor market may also be hindered by substantial turnover and training costs. Even if unemployed workers offer to work for less than present employees are earning, firms may find it unprofitable to hire them. Substantial turnover costs are incurred when new workers are hired and old ones let go, including expenses associated with interviewing and testing, additional payments for various fringe benefit programs, and substandard production from new hires. A second reason relates to the specific training that firms have invested in their present workers. To the extent that on-the-job training is firm specific, employers are restrained from substituting unemployed workers for present employees both by the cost of training the new workers and the capital loss from dismissing workers whom the firm has already spent money to train.

Efficiency Wages

A third and relatively recent explanation for unemployment is based on **efficiency wage theory.**[36] The key assumption behind this theory is that employee work effort, or "efficiency," is a positive function of the wage rate—the higher the wage the firm pays, the harder its employees work (although probably at a diminishing rate). This idea has a large element of common sense, but leads to some unexpected

---

34   See Robert H. Frank, "Does Growing Inequality Harm the Middle Class?" *Eastern Economic Journal* 26 (Summer 2000): 253–64, on the importance of relative incomes in one's level of overall satisfaction.

35   John Maynard Keynes, *The General Theory of Employment, Interest and Money* (New York: Harcourt, 1936).

36   See George A. Akerloff and Janet L. Yellen, eds., *Efficiency Wage Models of the Labor Market* (Cambridge, Eng.: Cambridge University Press, 1986), and George A. Akerloff and Janet L. Yellen, "The Fair Wage–Effort Hypothesis and Unemployment," *Quarterly Journal of Economics* 105, no. 2 (May 1990): 255–84. Although the efficiency wage explanation for unemployment is relatively new, the more general idea that worker productivity is influenced by the size of the wage goes back many years among more institutionally oriented economists. See Bruce E. Kaufman, "The Postwar View of Labor Markets and Wage Determination," in *How Labor Markets Work: Reflections on Theory and Practice by John Dunlop, Clark Kerr, Richard Lester, and Lloyd Reynolds* (Lexington, Mass.: Lexington Books, 1988), 145–203.

consequences. One of them is that a firm can actually make more profit by paying its employees a wage higher than that mandated by demand and supply in the market. A second result follows from the first: Even with flexible wage rates, a competitive labor market is likely to experience some amount of involuntary unemployment.

The link between efficiency wage theory and unemployment is relatively straightforward. It is evident that the amount of output produced by an employee is a function not only of the amount of time worked, but also of the level of effort devoted to the task. Most employees are paid at some type of time rate, such as a wage per hour or salary per year. Although time rates are easy to administer, one of their defects is that they reward only the first component of labor input, the time put in at the job, and not the second, the level of effort. Firms must, therefore, employ supervisory staff such as foremen and line managers to monitor employees to prevent shirking and malingering on the job. Even this is not a totally satisfactory solution, however. It is, in general, impossible to fully monitor every employee's performance. Also, the threat of being fired for shirking is not credible in a competitive labor market because, by assumption, the worker can easily get another job at the same wage with another firm.

How, then, can the firm induce its employees to put forth more than a minimum amount of effort? One possibility is to base employee pay directly on the amount of output or sales produced. In many firms, however, piece rates or commission-type compensation schemes are impractical or too expensive to administer. Carl Shapiro and Joseph Stiglitz have suggested that an alternative approach is for firms to deliberately pay employees a wage above the going market rate, inducing a greater work effort in two ways.[37] First, they argue, a higher wage elicits greater work effort because employees value their jobs more and have higher morale. Second, by increasing wages above the market level the firm raises the cost of being fired for loafing on the job. What one firm has an incentive to do, however, all firms will have an incentive to do. The net result is that each firm pays a wage above the market level, leading to an excess of labor supply relative to demand and, hence, unemployment.[38]

Several points should be noted about this result. First, from the perspective of each firm, some degree of unemployment is optimal since it creates work incentives for employees. From a more Marxist perspective, a "reserve army of the unemployed" is created in the labor market which serves essentially as a worker discipline

---

37 Carl Shapiro and Joseph E. Stiglitz, "Equilibrium Unemployment as a Worker Discipline Device," *American Economic Review* 74 (June 1984): 433–44.

38 Evidence on firms' incentives to pay an efficiency wage can be found in Sushil B. Wadhwani and Martin Wall, "A Direct Test of the Efficiency Wage Model Using UK Micro-data," *Oxford Economic Papers* 43 (October 1991): 529–48; David I. Levine, "Can Wage Increases Pay for Themselves? Tests with a Production Function," *Economic Journal* 102 (September 1992): 1102–15; Arthur H. Goldsmith et al., "Working Hard for the Money?: Efficiency Wages and Worker Effort," *Journal of Economic Psychology* 21 (August 2000): 351–85. Evidence of the payment of efficiency wage across international boundaries can be found in Sushil Wadwani and Abid A. Burki, "Efficiency Wages in Pakistan's Small Scale Manufacturing," *Lahore Journal of Economics* 4 (January–June 1999): 1–22, and Sebastien Ringuede, "An Efficiency Wage Model for Small Firms: Firm Size and Wages," (using French data), *Economics Letters* 59 (May 1998): 263–68.

device. Second, the unemployment that emerges in this model is involuntary unemployment because the workers who are unemployed would willingly take jobs at the market wage if such jobs were available. This type of unemployment might be called "wait" unemployment, as opposed to search unemployment, because with a deficiency of job openings, each unemployed worker must bide his or her time until a vacancy opens up.[39] Third, efficiency wage theory offers an explanation for the seeming downward rigidity of money wage rates. Even if unemployed workers offer to work at lower wages, a firm may well lose money by cutting wages and taking the workers on, since employee effort and productivity will also decline. Finally, the efficiency wage model does *not* predict that the bulk of those unemployed at any one time are necessarily shirkers or loafers. If the threat of unemployment is effective, little or no shirking and sacking of employees will actually take place. Instead, the unemployed are a rotating pool of individuals who have quit jobs for personal reasons, who are new entrants to the labor market, or who have been laid off by firms due to declining sales.

The Composition of Unemployment

The incidence of unemployment varies widely among persons of different demographic groups. This is illustrated by the data in Table 13.1. In 1998, the economy was very close to full employment, with an overall unemployment rate of 4.5 percent. Among demographic groups, the unemployment rate varied from a low of 2.4 percent for married men to a high of 27.6 percent for black teenagers. The unemployment rate of married women (2.9 percent) was higher than that of married men (2.4 percent), the unemployment rate of blacks (8.9 percent) was more than double that of whites (3.9 percent), and the unemployment rate of white teenagers (12.6 percent) was almost four times as large as that of white adult men (3.2 percent). Although blacks and teenagers accounted for only 17 percent of the labor force, they made up 42 percent of the unemployed.

A distinct structure of unemployment rates also characterizes occupations and industries. In 1998, for example, the unemployment rate among blue-collar workers (5.6 percent) was double that of white-collar workers (2.8 percent). Among industries, the unemployment rate varied from 1.8 percent for government workers to 5.9 percent for construction workers.

Another feature of unemployment revealed in Table 13.1 is the different impact of cyclical unemployment on particular labor force groups. In March 2001 the economy entered a recession after many years of growth. As the data in Table 13.1 illustrate, in a recession year unemployment is higher in every sector of the labor force (except for black women, in this instance)—a sure sign of cyclical unemployment.

---

39 See Lori Kletzer, "Industry Wage Differentials and Wait Unemployment," *Industrial Relations* 31 (Spring 1992): 250–69, for evidence of wait unemployment behavior among blue-collar workers but not among white-collar workers.

TABLE 13.1

UNEMPLOYMENT RATES BY DEMOGRAPHIC GROUP, OCCUPATION AND INDUSTRY, 1998 AND 2001

Selected Categories	1998	2001
Demographic Group		
Total, 16 years and over	4.5%	4.8%
White, total	3.9	4.2
Both Sexes, 16 to 19	12.6	12.7
Men, 20 years and older	3.2	3.7
Women, 20 years and older	3.4	3.6
Black, total	8.9	8.7
Both Sexes, 16 to 19	27.6	29
Men, 20 years and older	7.4	8
Women, 20 years and older	7.9	7
Married Men, spouse present	2.4	5.5
Married women, spouse present	2.9	4.9
Occupation		
White-collar workers	2.8	2.3
Blue-collar workers	5.6	4.6
Service workers	6.4	5.9
Industry		
Construction	5.9	7.3
Manufacturing	3.8	5.2
Wholesale and Retail	5.2	5.6
Government	1.8	2.1

SOURCE: Bureau of Labor Statistics, *Employment and Earnings* http://www.bls.gov/cps/cpsatabs.htm.

Some groups, however, are affected much more than others. The unemployment rate of white men in 2001, for example, exceeded that of white women (3.7 percent versus 3.6 percent), whereas in a nonrecession year such as 1998, the reverse is true. This largely reflects the fact that men are disproportionately employed in industries and occupations that are the most sensitive to the business cycle. Similarly, in 2001 the unemployment rate among blue-collar workers and in the construction and manufacturing industries was substantially higher than in 1998, whereas the unemployment rate among service workers and in industries such as finance, services, and government was only modestly higher in 2001 than in 1998. Not only are men more affected by cyclical unemployment than women, so too are blacks relative to whites. Among black teenagers, the unemployment rate in 2001 was an astronomical 29 percent. In addition, the change in the unemployment rate

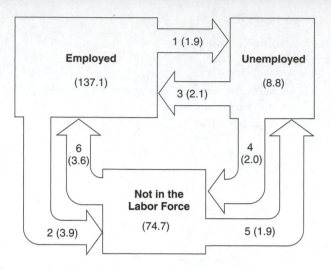

Note: Numbers in parentheses are millions of persons.

SOURCE: Bureau of Labor Statistics, unpublished data.

between the prosperous year of 1998 and the recession year of 2001 was larger for blacks than for whites.

Unemployment Flows

The data in Table 13.1 show who is unemployed; they do not, however, explain why certain groups have higher unemployment rates. This issue can be better understood with the help of Figure 13.7. Every person in the noninstitutional population is in one of three categories: employed, unemployed, or not in the labor force, represented by the boxes in the diagram. The number in parentheses in each box shows how many millions of persons were in each labor force category in a typical month in 2003; the number in each arrow shows how many people (in millions) changed from one category to another. These data illustrate the tremendously dynamic nature of the labor market, as literally millions of people each month are hired, fired, or laid off, enter and exit the labor force, and so on.[40] The particular

40   For a discussion of the merits and the limitations of gross-flow data, see Anthony J. Barkume and Francis W. Horvath, "Using Gross Flows to Explore Movements in the Labor Force," *Monthly Labor Review* (April 1995): 28–35.

paths or transitions from one category to another are denoted by the arrows, numbered from 1 to 6. These are as follows:

1. Loss of a job (layoff or quit) with a transition to unemployment.
2. Loss of a job with an exit from the labor force (for example, school or retirement).
3. Finding of a job, ending a period of unemployment.
4. Movement from unemployment to not being in the labor force (for example, the discouraged worker).
5. Movement from outside the labor force to unemployment.
6. Movement from outside the labor force to immediate employment.

Figure 13.7 shows two routes to unemployment (arrows 1 and 5) and two routes out of unemployment (arrows 3 and 4). A relatively high unemployment rate for a particular labor force group, such as blacks or teenagers, may occur for one of two reasons (or a combination of both). The first is a *long duration* of unemployment as a few persons in the affected group remain in the unemployment box a considerable time before finding employment (arrow 3) or leaving the labor force (arrow 4). A second reason is *frequent spells* of unemployment as many people in the group pass through the unemployment box for a short while, due to a high propensity either to enter or reenter the labor force (arrow 5) or to quit or be laid off (arrow 1). Persons in a group may experience both frequent spells of unemployment and a long duration of unemployment.[41]

Two Sources of High Unemployment Rates

Given this conceptual framework, what explains the different unemployment rates among the various age, race, and gender groups? Over the past 20 years, two different points of view have emerged.[42] The first school of thought might be called the **turnover view of unemployment.** Underlying this view of unemployment are two major premises: first, the bulk of unemployment arises not from a lack of jobs, but from high rates of job turnover among members in the labor force; second, much of the higher unemployment rates experienced by women, blacks, and teenagers is frictional in nature, reflecting their tendency to move frequently from

---

41   The unemployment rate for a particular labor force group can be calculated as $U = S \cdot D$, where S is the average number of spells of unemployment experienced by each worker and D is the fraction of the year that each spell lasts. If each worker experiences two spells, each lasting two weeks (or 3.85 percent of the year), $U = (2) \cdot (3.85) = 7.7$ percent. An increase in either S or D will increase U.

42   For a review, see David M. Lillien and Robert E. Hall, "Cyclical Fluctuations in the Labor Market," in Orley Ashenfelter and Richard Layard, eds., *Handbook of Labor Economics*, vol. 2 (Amsterdam: North-Holland, 1986), 1001–35.

job to job or in and out of the labor force.[43] The turnover view has been challenged by a second school of thought, which might be labeled the **lack of jobs view of unemployment.** The major premises underlying this view of unemployment are, first, that the bulk of unemployment, even in tight labor markets, is accounted for by relatively few persons who are out of work a large part of the time, and, second, that much of the higher unemployment rates experienced by women, blacks, and teenagers is traceable to a lack of jobs in the market, both because of inadequate aggregate demand in the economy and a structural imbalance between the people firms want to hire and the people seeking jobs.[44]

The turnover view of unemployment was prominent during the early 1970s,[45] but came under attack in the late 1970s by proponents of the lack of jobs view of unemployment.[46] What do current statistics have to say about the relative importance of turnover and job access in the determination of the high unemployment rates of certain groups of workers? Table 13.2 yields some answers. It shows the unemployment rate of each demographic group in 2004. Each unemployment rate is then decomposed into the part due to one of four reasons: (1) lost a job, either from being fired or laid off; (2) voluntarily quit a job; (3) reentered the labor force to look for work after a period of nonparticipation; and (4) entered the labor force for the first time to look for a job. The table also reports the length of the most recent unemployment spell, in weeks, experienced by the average person in each demographic group.

Several features of these data lend credence to the turnover view of unemployment. The bulk of the unemployment for women, teens, and blacks (the groups experiencing the highest rates of unemployment) was due to the voluntary movement between jobs or into and out of the labor force, a pattern quite unlike that for men. The large degree of turnover among women can be traced to marriage and family roles, as women quit jobs to move with their families to different cities or reenter the labor force after their children have begun school. Among teenagers, first-time entrants into the labor force account for a large share of that group's unemployment rate.[47] Turnover among teenagers is high, as they alternate

---

43   Lawrence F. Katz and Alan B. Krueger, "The High-Pressure U.S. Labor Market of the 1990s," Princeton Industrial Relations Section Working Paper 416 (1999), find that demographic changes among labor force participants, primarily age, help explain unemployment declines of the 1990s.

44   Recent evidence of this source can be found in Katherine G. Abraham and Robert Shimer, "Changes in Unemployment Duration and Labor Force Attachment," *NBER Working Paper* W8513 (October 2001).

45   See, for example, George L. Perry, "Unemployment Flows in the U.S. Labor Market," *Brookings Papers on Economic Activity* 2 (Washington, D.C.: The Brookings Institution, 1972): 245–78, and Robert E. Hall, "Turnover in the Labor Force," *Brookings Papers on Economic Activity* 3 (Washington, D.C.: The Brookings Institution, 1972): 709–86.

46   See, for example, Kim B. Clark and Lawrence H. Summers, "Labor Market Dynamics and Unemployment: A Reconsideration," *Brookings Papers on Economic Activity* 1 (Washington, D.C.: The Brookings Institution, 1979): 13–60. Also see Kim B. Clark and Lawrence H. Summers, "The Dynamics of Youth Unemployment," in Richard B. Freeman and David Wise, eds., *The Youth Labor Market Problem: Its Nature, Causes, and Consequences* (Chicago: University of Chicago Press, 1982), 199–234.

47   Reentrants actually make up the largest component of teenagers' unemployment; this is a relatively recent phenomenon, as teenagers are entering the labor force at earlier and earlier ages.

Unemployment Statistic	Total	Males, 20 years and Over	Females, 20 Years and Over	Both Genders, 16-19 Years	Whites	Blacks
Total Unemployment Rate	5.5	5	4.9	17	4.8	10.4
Job loser rate	2.8	3.3	2.4	2.3	2.6	5
Job leaver rate	0.6	0.5	0.6	1.1	0.5	0.9
Reentrant rate	1.6	1	1.7	7.2	1.4	3.5
New entrant rate	0.5	0.1	0.2	6.4	0.4	1
Mean Duration of Unemployment (weeks)	19.6	18.88	10.9	12.6	18.5	23

SOURCE: Bureau of Labor Statistics, *Employment and Earnings* (January 2005), Tables 27, 28, and 31.

between school and work. In June of every year, for example, the teenaged labor force expands by 30 to 40 percent as high school and college students enter the labor force in search of summer jobs.[48] The data in Table 13.2 for blacks reveal that their unemployment rate is higher than that for whites for all four reasons. Not only do blacks experience higher rates of voluntary movement into and out of the labor force than whites, they are also more likely to lose their jobs, perhaps for reasons of discrimination.

In looking at the average length of unemployment in Table 13.2, one can see that not only do blacks experience less labor market stability, but each spell of unemployment also lasts, on average, longer (23 weeks) than the average spell for whites (18.5 weeks). These longer spells seemingly provide support for the lack of jobs view of unemployment; black workers have a harder time finding new jobs, perhaps due to discrimination or lack of skills. Looking at the data for teens, however, one might be tempted to conclude that the higher unemployment rates of this group can be explained by spells of unemployment that are shorter, but perhaps occur more frequently, than those experienced by the average adult male. There is

[48] For analysis of teenage unemployment see Martin Feldstein and David T. Ellwood, "Teenage Unemployment: What Is the Problem?" in Richard B. Freeman and David Wise, eds., *The Youth Labor Market Problem: Its Nature, Causes, and Consequences* (Chicago: University of Chicago Press, 1982), 17–33. The problem of youth unemployment is not unique to the United States. See, for example, Suresh Aggarwal and J. K. Goyal, "Trends in Youth Unemployment in India: An Empirical Analysis," *Indian Journal of Labour Economics* 43 (October–December 2000): 641–55, and Morley Gunderson et al., "Youth Unemployment in Canada, 1976–1998," *Canadian Public Policy* 26 (Supplement July 2000): S85–100.

a problem with this interpretation, however.[49] While the average unemployment spell for teens might be shorter than for adults, there is evidence that within that group of teens (especially very hard-to-employ groups, such as black teens) there is a small core of the unemployed that experience very long spells of unemployment. For example, the 1.2 percent of the labor force who experienced more than six months of unemployment in 2004 accounted for over 21.8 percent of the total amount of unemployment. In addition, another reason long-term unemployment may be more serious than recognized by the turnover theory is because the *actual* spell of unemployment experienced by many persons is much longer than the *measured* spell calculated from the official unemployment statistics. For example, as illustrated in Figure 13.7, 2.0 million people flowed from unemployment to out of the labor force, meaning that a fair number of unemployment spells do not end with a job.

Why is it important to distinguish which theory is right concerning the source of unemployment? If the main source of unemployment among women and teens is frequent turnover as they move back and forth between market and nonmarket activities, and they have relatively little difficulty finding jobs (evidenced by short unemployment spells), there is little cause for concern. If, on the other hand, a large share of the total days of unemployment in each demographic group is accounted for by a relatively few persons who are out of work for extended periods of time, there

➲ SEE

Policy Application 13-1: Government Employment and Training Programs, p. 698.

is call for policy intervention to improve the job market chances of the hard-core unemployed, such as training programs, wage subsidies to private firms, or public sector jobs. (These different government programs are discussed in detail in the Policy Application 13-1 section.) Neither side of the debate suggests that the other has no merit; the dispute, therefore, is largely a matter of emphasis.

---

49 These problems are well articulated and illustrated empirically in Kim B. Clark and Lawrence H. Summers, "Labor Market Dynamics and Unemployment: A Reconsideration," in Lawrence H. Summers, ed., *Understanding Unemployment* (Cambridge, Mass.: The MIT Press, 1990), 3–47.

POLICY APPLICATION 13-1

Government Employment and Training Programs

As a reaction to the mass unemployment of the Depression years, Congress passed the Employment Act of 1946, mandating the federal government to purposely pursue policies that would maintain the economy at full employment. In carrying out this mandate, the federal government has adopted a multipronged approach. One strategy has been to attack demand-deficient unemployment through expansionary fiscal and monetary policies. A second strategy has been to attack frictional unemployment through the expansion of the federally funded, state-operated Employment Service. Begun in the 1930s, the Employment Service (through its 2,000 local job placement offices) between July 1, 2003, and June 30, 2004, registered 14.9 million job seekers, listed 7.0 million job openings, and placed 61 percent of job seekers. An additional program designed to reduce frictional unemployment is the **Worker Adjustment and Retraining Notification Act (WARN),** which became effective in February 1989. WARN requires employers with 100 or more employees to notify workers 60 days in advance of a plant closing or mass layoff. This notification allows workers to begin looking for alternative employment, reducing the likelihood that they experience a spell of unemployment. A third approach has been to attack structural unemployment through a series of government-sponsored employment and training programs, sometimes referred to as "manpower" or "human resource development" programs. This third approach to reducing unemployment is examined here.

Certain groups, such as disadvantaged youth, low-skill adults, and residents of economically depressed areas, suffer persistently high levels of unemployment. The best example is black teenagers, a group whose unemployment rate (27.6 percent) in the prosperous year of 1998 was more than six times the national average (4.5 percent). To some degree the high unemployment rates of these groups can be alleviated through expansionary aggregate demand policies. In a buoyant economy, the scarcity of labor will cause employers to hire persons at the bottom of the labor queue whom in a slack economy they would pass by. The use of aggregate demand to reduce the number of hard-core unemployed is heavily constrained, however, by the threat of inflation. The basic dilemma is that before economic growth can significantly reduce the unemployment rate among the hard-to-employ groups, the economy encounters serious shortages of skilled blue-collar and professional white-collar workers, leading to a bidding up of wages and prices.

Because of the selective nature of structural unemployment, the federal government has attempted to complement aggregate demand policies with employment and training programs specifically targeted at the hard-core unemployed. Employment and training programs can be categorized as follows.[1]

Training Programs for Jobs in the Private Sector

These programs aim to provide unemployed workers with the skills necessary to obtain unsubsidized jobs in the private sector. The first program of this sort was the **Manpower Development and Training Act (MDTA),** passed in 1962. It was created to provide retraining for heads of households who had been displaced from their jobs by technological change. Although some on-the-job training was furnished, the great bulk of expenditures was used for classroom instruction in vocational skills and remedial education. A second training program was the **Job Corps,** created in 1964. Under this program, disadvantaged youths are placed for at least six months in residential centers where they receive the employment training, basic education, and social skills needed to function in a private sector job. Since 1964, through 2000, the Job Corps has trained 1.9 million youth.

By the early 1970s the variety of programs providing training led to a growing problem of

---

1   For additional description and economic evaluation of government-sponsored employment and training programs see Daniel Friedlander et al., "Evaluating Government Training Programs for the Economically Disadvantaged," *Journal of Economic Literature* 35 (December 1997): 1809–55, and Robert J. LaLonde, "The Promise of Public Sector–Sponsored Training Programs," *Journal of Economic Perspectives* 9 (Spring 1995): 149–68.

If You Pay, They Will Come . . . Maybe

One appealing approach to reducing structural unemployment among residents of inner-city areas is to induce business to locate there through the provision of various tax incentives. This idea of establishing enterprise or empowerment zones gained new momentum during the 1990s, with 87 new zones established by the federal government between 1994 and 1998. In addition, in November 2004 the House approved $10 million in new funding for 15 empowerment zones across the country. Although some locations have enjoyed the predicted renewal from such attention, many firms apparently find that the additional cost of doing business in economically depressed areas is not worth the tax savings being offered, making an inner-city business an unattractive investment.

Some potential entrepreneurs and well-established corporations cite high crime, decayed buildings, lack of access to public transportation and utilities, and a dearth of well-trained workers as deterrents to locating in empowerment zones.

Several examples of inner-city plants illustrate the problems of doing business in a ghetto area. One is an Aerojet General Co. tent-making plant in the Watts section of Los Angeles. The plant's management was unprepared to deal with a totally unskilled workforce. Many new hires had never held jobs before and had to be coaxed to get to work on time. The company even tried giving new employees alarm clocks. To make matters worse, workers used job experience at the plant as a ticket out of the ghetto, leaving the company with a constant stream of new, inexperienced workers. After four years of losses, the company decided to sell the plant.

The experience of IBM with its computer parts plant in the Bedford-Stuyvesant area of Brooklyn, New York, shows what it takes for a business to survive in a tough neighborhood. When IBM opened the 400-employee plant, absenteeism exceeded 18 percent and the plant ran at a substantial loss. Most companies would have given up after several years, but not IBM. The company instituted special in-plant

---

duplication and wasted resources. In response, in 1973 Congress enacted the **Comprehensive Employment and Training Act (CETA).** The act consolidated the supervision of most training programs under the Department of Labor. The actual planning and operation of the training programs was transferred from federal control to state and local officials designated as "prime sponsors." Funding under CETA was also decategorized so that local officials had more flexibility in targeting the training to specific problem groups in the local economy.

The CETA program became a center of controversy in the late 1970s and was allowed to expire in 1982. The Job Corps was retained, but significantly reduced in size. In place of CETA, Congress enacted the **Job Training Partnership Act (JTPA).** Under the JTPA, federal funds (at a significantly reduced level relative to expenditures under CETA) flow to states via block grants and from states to services deliverers via a system of private industry councils (PICs), on which a majority of seats are held by local business representatives. This approach reflected the belief that, because the decisions of the PICs would be controlled by business representatives, the graduates would be better prepared to work in the private sector.

The entire structure of the workforce development and job training section of the U.S.

continued

training courses to teach basic job skills and after-hours education courses in remedial reading and writing. It also urged employees to attend local vocational and training schools and offered to pay their tuition. The company also found that many workers suffered from significant health problems due to a chronic lack of medical care, so it set up a special medical facility near the plant. Two years after implementing these measures the plant became profitable, but not profitable enough for IBM to try the experiment again.

It appears that tax inducements are by themselves generally an ineffective method to bring jobs to inner-city areas. Some states have sweetened the deal for potential businesses in a variety of ways. After not attracting a single business to the Capital Heights community empowerment zone of Washington, D.C., the county upped the ante by offering to refund the sales tax paid for construction materials used to build in the area. The city of Crosstown, Massachusetts, has resorted to renovating the dilapidated downtown buildings itself, after trying unsuccessfully to lure private businesses into the area; they are hoping to break the inertia of nonactivity.

The lesson seems to be that promotion of economic development is an expensive and complicated endeavor. What works in one location may not be enough of an incentive in another. It is also clear that if businesses have better trained workforces that they could count on, locating in an empowerment zone would be seen as a better investment.

SOURCES: "Enterprise Zones—Or Twilight Zones?" *Business Week* (27 February 1989); Andrew Caffrey, "Selling Roxbury's Crosstown; Despite a Robust Real Estate Market, There Are Problems Attracting New Businesses," *Boston Globe* (12 April 1998): F1; Dee-Ann Durbin, "Zones Draw 59 Projects: But Developers Need More Incentives to Move In, Report Finds," *Detroit News* (20 November 1998): C8; Jackie Spinner, "Upping the Ante in Enterprise Zones; Prince George's Legislators Propose Bigger Incentives to Lure Business to Poor Areas," *Washington Post* (14 March 1999): C05; and "House Approves New Round of Funding for Empowerment Zones," *US FedNews* (20 November 2004).

Department of Labor was reorganized under the **Workforce Investment Act (WIA) of 1998**, which was signed into law in August of 1998. Under the WIA, all separate JTPA programs were to be phased out by July 1, 2000. The WIA emphasizes the "one-stop" approach to job assistance delivery, where customers have easy access to the employment, education, training, and information services they need at a single location in their neighborhoods. In addition, under the WIA, all adults (not just disadvantaged adults) aged 18 years and older are now eligible for core services. Recipients of public assistance and other low-income individuals, however, will have priority for receiving intensive training assistance.

Private Sector Employment Incentives

In addition to providing training directly to low-skill workers, the government provides incentives to employers to hire and train these workers. These incentives typically take the form of tax credits, theoretically providing at least the difference between what the employer has to pay the workers and their initial level of (lower) productivity. The idea is that the workers will gain experience and training, making them more productive and marketable on their own.

The **New Jobs Tax Credit (NJTC)** was the first incentive provided to private sector employers designed to increase overall employment levels. The NJTC offered a tax credit up to $2,100 per employee for employment increases of more than 2 percent over the past year. The NJTC was replaced by the **Targeted Jobs Tax Credit (TJTC)** in 1979, and this program remained in place until 1994. The TJTC differed from the NJTC in that it targeted specific groups of (typically, economically disadvantaged) workers rather than employment in general. The TJTC was also more generous, providing for tax credits of initially up to $6,000. The evidence of the effectiveness of these wage subsidy programs is mixed.[2]

Two of the most recent examples of tax credits offered to employers include the **Work Opportunity Tax Credit (WOTC)** and the **Welfare-to-Work Tax Credit.** The WOTC was designed to reduce an employer's federal tax liability by as much as $2,400 for *each* new hire from any one of eight targeted groups. Also administered under the WOTC, the Welfare-to-Work Tax Credit reduces an employer's federal tax liability by as much as $8,500 for each new hire of a long-term welfare recipient. During the first nine months of its existence, this program issued 46,000 certifications for tax credit. Both of these programs were relatively short-lived, with the WOTC originally scheduled to be in effect for one year and the Welfare-to-Work Tax Credit initially authorized to last only 18 months.

Public Sector Job Creation Programs

The idea that government should be the employer of last resort has a long history. In America, the concept was invoked in the 1930s when agencies such as the Works Project Administration (WPA) and Civilian Conservation Corps (CCC) were created to provide jobs for the unemployed during the Depression. In more recent years, as part of CETA, Congress enacted a **Public Service Employment (PSE)** program. This program provided temporary federally funded jobs to persons who were cyclically or structurally unemployed. At its peak in 1978, the PSE program funded more than 750,000 persons (about 10 percent of all those unemployed at the time) through an expenditure of approximately $5.6 billion. PSE workers were employed by local governments in a variety of clerical, service, and maintenance jobs.

Proponents of the PSE program listed several arguments in its favor. For one, it provided direct on-the-job training for workers. A second was that it directly attacked the problem of structural unemployment by creating jobs for people who otherwise could not find work. Finally, expenditures on public service employment were seen as a more effective way to reduce unemployment than other types of expansionary fiscal policies such as tax cuts.

Arrayed on the other side were a number of criticisms of the program. A basic complaint was that most of the public sector jobs were "make-work" jobs that offered little training to workers. Critics also argued that the PSE program created far fewer jobs than claimed because of "fiscal substitution"—the cutback in local government employment that took place as CETA workers were substituted for existing employees. Finally, the CETA program, and the PSE component in particular, were widely regarded as excessively costly because of poor management and fraud in the delivery of services. For these and other reasons, the Reagan administration terminated the CETA program in 1982.

As part of the **Personal Responsibility and Work Opportunity Reconciliation Act** of 1996,

---

2   John Bishop, "Employment in Construction and Distribution Industries: The Impact of the New Jobs Tax Credit," in Sherwin Rosen, ed., *Studies in Labor Markets* (Chicago: University of Chicago Press, 1981), 209–46, concluded that the NJTC was responsible for generating as many as one-third of all new jobs in the construction and retail industries in 1977 and 1978. Lawrence F. Katz, however, concludes that wage subsidy programs must contain a training component to be effective in improving the labor market outcomes of disadvantaged workers; "Wage Subsidies for the Disadvantaged," in Richard Freeman and Peter Gottschalk, eds., *Generating Jobs: How to Increase Demand for Less-Skilled Workers* (New York: Russell Sage, 1998), 21–53.

stricter work requirements were placed on recipients of welfare. Although the emphasis is on finding employment and training for welfare recipients in the private sector, many states have made provisions for subsidized public sector employment. So, although not officially a "job creation" program, the structure of welfare reform in the 1990s sustains the role of government as the employer of last resort.

Economic Development Programs

A third type of employment program aims to foster the development of firms likely to hire disadvantaged workers. The Economic Development Administration (EDA) of the Department of Commerce, for example, provides a variety of grants, loans, and loan guarantees to encourage the development of private firms in areas with persistently high unemployment. In addition, an idea, born in the early 1980s, of encouraging businesses to locate in economically depressed areas gained new momentum and grew into the **Empowerment Zone and Enterprise Community (EZ/EC) Initiative.** Between 1994 and 2004, 121 urban and 57 rural communities have been designated as empowerment zones or enterprise communities, making them eligible for more than $1.5 billion in performance grants and more than $2.5 billion in tax incentives. In addition to other tax write-offs, employers in the designated areas receive $3,000 for every employee hired who lives within the empowerment zone boundaries. The advantage of economic development programs like this is that it creates jobs in the private sector without requiring direct government expenditures or the expansion of government bureaucracy. The evidence has been mixed regarding the effectiveness of EZ/EC designation in promoting economic growth and employment. Even though the potential is fairly widely recognized, many areas with long-term experience with enterprise zones have not seen the predicted outcomes.[3]

---

3   See Wei Ge, "The Urban Enterprise Zone," *Journal of Regional Science* 35 (May 1995): 217–31, for an analysis of the potential of enterprise zones for promoting urban renewal and economic growth. Disappointing outcomes in New Jersey are analyzed by Marlong G. Boarnet and William T. Bogart, "Enterprise Zones and Employment: Evidence from New Jersey," *Journal of Urban Economics* 40 (September 1996): 198–215, and Leslie E. Papke, "What Do We Know About Enterprise Zones?" in *Tax Policy and the Economy* James Poterba, ed. (Cambridge, Mass.: MIT Press, 1993): 37–72. Marlon G. Boarnet suggests ways to better assess the impact of enterprise zones in "Enterprise Zone and Job Creation: Linking Evaluation and Practice," *Economic Development Quarterly* 15 (August 2001): 242–54.

EMPIRICAL EVIDENCE 13-1

The Beveridge Curve in the United States

Figure 13.1 at the beginning of the chapter shows the long-term trend in the unemployment rate in the United States since 1950. Abstracting from the short-run rise and fall in the unemployment rate due to the business cycle, it appeared that until the 1990s the unemployment rate was on a relentless upward path. In the 1950s, for example, the 10-year average unemployment rate was 4.5; in the 1960s it was 4.7; in the 1970s it rose to 6.2 percent, and in the 1980s it rose still further to 7.2 percent. The average between 1990 and 2001, however, was at 5.5 percent, lower even than in the 1970s. For certain groups, however, the upward trend doesn't

FIGURE 13.8 THE BEVERIDGE CURVE, 1970–2003

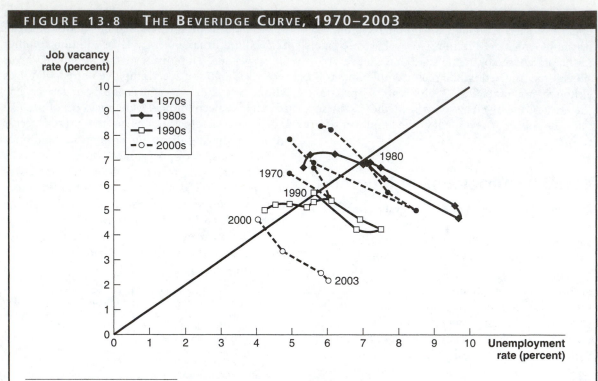

SOURCE: Conference Board and the Bureau of Labor Statistics. Job vacancy rate is the number of newspaper advertisements divided by the number employed.

seem to have abated as much. The teen unemployment rate, for example, lowered only slightly during the 1990s, from 17.7 percent between 1970 and 1989 to 16.5 percent between 1990 and 2003.

As with other aspects of unemployment, the exact reasons for the long-term trends identified in Figure 13.1, and whether the trends are caused by frictional, structural, or demand-deficient factors, inspire a good deal of dispute. Earlier in the chapter, it was suggested that one way to help distinguish whether an increase in unemployment is due to frictional, structural, or demand-deficient factors is to examine the Beveridge curves for the economy. This is done in Figure 13.8, which plots the unemployment rate and the job vacancy for the years 1970 to 2003.

These data illustrate changes in all three types of unemployment. First, a purely cyclical component of unemployment is clearly evident in Figure 13.8 by the movement of the economy up and down a particular Beveridge curve.

Observations at the top of each Beveridge curve correspond to peak economic years (see the observations that correspond to 1970 and 2000, relatively prosperous years), and observations at the bottom of the curve correspond to trough years (see the observation for 2003, a recession year). Each of the time periods identified in the figure contains both types of economic conditions. Second, certain time periods appear to have been plagued by deficient demand. The preponderance of observations between 1979 and 1986, for example, show up in the southeast portion of the diagram (few vacancies and high unemployment), suggesting that the high unemployment during that time period was due to a more general lack of aggregate demand.[1] And, third, the rightward shift of the Beveridge curves over the period of 1960 through the mid-1980s is evidence of the growth of frictional and/or structural unemployment during this time period. However, the dramatic shift *back* of the Beveridge curve during the 1990s suggests a decrease in frictional and structural unemployment factors. The years of 1987–1989 are clearly transition years.

Economists Hoyt Bleakley and Jeffrey Fuhrer identify three candidates to explain this leftward shift in the Beveridge curve during the 1990s: the increased efficiency with which workers and jobs find each other, a slowdown in the growth of the labor force, and reduced turnover in the labor market.[2]

Job-Matching Efficiency

There could be several reasons for the matching of workers and jobs to be hindered. Simple lack of information may be one reason. If firms are not well informed about the willingness of workers to supply their labor at certain wages, it may take some time of not filling a vacancy to figure out that they have to raise the wage to attract workers. If workers are not well informed about job openings, it will take longer for them to find the jobs than if they had better information. Another reason is a structural imbalance in either geographic distance between workers and job openings or differences in skills needed by firms and skills possessed by workers. Improvement in the flow of information and geographic or skill matching will increase the efficiency with which jobs and workers find each other. While they are not able to identify the *source* of greater efficiency, Bleakley and Fuhrer estimate that over the period of the late 1980s and the early 1990s, the process of matching of workers and jobs became 13 percent more efficient. Another potential source of increased efficiency is the greater availability and reliance on use of temporary or contingent workers during this time period than in the past; use of temporary workers allows firms to fill vacancies much more quickly.

Growth of the Labor Force

Another potential source of the leftward shift in the Beveridge curve is a slowdown in the rate at which workers are entering the labor force. As the rate of entry into the labor force declines, the unemployment rate will decline because there are fewer workers looking for jobs at any one time.

Bleakley and Fuhrer find some evidence that flows into the labor market declined during the time in which the Beveridge curve shifted leftward. For instance, the labor force grew at a rate of 2.5 percent per year between the late 1970s and the late 1980s, whereas the following period saw a growth rate of the labor force of only 1.5 percent per year. Bleakley and Fuhrer attribute this slowdown in labor force growth to two factors: entry of the generation of workers following the baby boom (often referred to as the "baby bust") and the leveling-off of female labor force participation. While certainly quantifiable, this reduction in labor force entry rates likely resulted in only a modest decline in the unemployment rates. Bleakley and Fuhrer figure that, at most, this decline in labor force growth resulted in a decline in the unemployment rate of less than half a percentage point.

---

1   For supporting evidence, see Katherine G. Abraham, "Structural/ Frictional versus Demand-Deficient Unemployment: Some New Evidence," *American Economic Review* 73 (September 1983): 708–24.

2   Hoyt Bleakley and Jeffrey C. Fuhrer, "Shifts in the Beveridge Curve, Job Matching, and Labor Market Dynamics," *New England Economic Review* (September/October 1997): 3–19. For evaluation of unemployment sources prior to the 1990s, see Katharine G. Abraham and Lawrence F. Katz, "Cyclical Unemployment: Sectoral Shifts or Aggregate Disturbances?" *Journal of Political Economy* 94 (June 1986): 507–22, and Lawrence H. Summers, "Why Is the Unemployment Rate So Very High near Full Employment?" *Brookings Papers on Economic Activity* 2 (Washington, D.C.: The Brookings Institution, 1986): 339–83.

Turnover

Bleakley and Fuhrer also find that lower rates of churning in and out of employment help explain the leftward shift of the Beveridge curve. Lower turnover reflects greater attachment to jobs. Although the conventional wisdom of the nineties was that downsizings and corporate restructurings led to massive layoffs and the disappearance of job security, the data suggest otherwise. Bleakley and Fuhrer document, for example, that the proportion of people in the labor force moving in and out of employment actually decreased significantly since the mid-1980s. This leads to the conclusion that for the overall economy there was actually more stability in jobs than existed in the 1970s, although certain firms and certain groups of workers experienced the opposite.[3]

---

3   Hoyt Bleakley and Jeffrey C. Fuhrer, "Shifts in the Beveridge Curve, Job Matching, and Labor Market Dynamics," Figure 6. Also see Anthony J. Barkume and Francis W. Horvath, "Using Gross Flows to Explore Movements in the Labor Force," *Monthly Labor Review* (April 1995): 28–35.

Summary

Unemployment is perhaps the most serious economic problem in the labor market. Devising policies to reduce unemployment is a complicated task because it arises from a number of distinct causes. Economists distinguish between three types of unemployment: frictional, structural, and cyclical (demand-deficient). Frictional unemployment is associated with turnover in the labor market, while structural unemployment stems from a basic mismatch between workers and jobs. Cyclical unemployment is related to fluctuations in aggregate demand in the economy.

In accounting for these three types of unemployment, economists have focused on the roles of job search, rigid wages, and efficiency wages. From a job search perspective, workers use a period of unemployment to gather information from firms on the availability of jobs and rates of pay. Seen in this way, unemployment has a large voluntary component and represents a form of human capital investment. A second explanation for unemployment focuses on the downward inflexibility of money wage rates due to factors such as hiring and training costs, unions, and implicit contracts. A third explanation is that employers pay wage rates above the market clearing level, creating both unemployment and an incentive for employees to work diligently to avoid being fired and forced into the ranks of the jobless.

Some groups in the labor force, such as teenagers, blacks, and women, have relatively higher rates of unemployment than other demographic groups. Of the two contrasting explanations for this pattern, one is the turnover view. According to this theory, the higher unemployment rates of people in these groups reflect frequent spells of unemployment as they move from job to job or in and out of the labor force. The problem is not lack of jobs, but instability in employment. The second explanation is the lack of jobs view. According to this theory, the bulk of unemployment is concentrated among relatively few persons who experience very long periods of joblessness. The reason for the high unemployment rate among teenagers, blacks, and women is a lack of job opportunities due to structural imbalances and a deficiency of aggregate demand.

Until the 1990s, the average level of unemployment in the economy exhibited an upward trend. Since the early 1990s, however, unemployment has fallen back to its pre-1970s levels. This trend reversal is due to both frictional and structural factors, including reduced labor market turnover, a slowdown in the growth of the labor force, and increased efficiency with which workers and jobs find each other.

The federal government has undertaken a number of policies to reduce unemployment. One is the establishment of various employment and training programs. These programs fall into four categories: training programs for jobs in the private sector, private sector employment incentives, public service employment programs, and economic development programs.

Review Questions

1. Discuss the arguments for and against broadening the official definition of unemployment to include discouraged workers.

2. In 2003 the unemployment rate was 6.0 percent. Is it possible to decompose it into the parts due to frictional, structural, and cyclical causes? How would you go about this? What information would help you distinguish among these three types of unemployment?

3. In a typical month in 2003, over 8 million people claimed to be unemployed, yet each Sunday's edition of the *New York Times* had, on average, 20 or more pages of help-wanted ads. How would you explain this seeming inconsistency?

4. During the Depression many economists recommended that a general cut in wages was the best policy to cure unemployment in the economy. What was the rationale behind this recommendation? Would it work?

5. What effect would extending the maximum term of unemployment insurance from 26 to 39 weeks have on the measured unemployment rate? Use a model of job search to answer this question.

6. What demographic groups have the highest unemployment rates? What are the explanations for this? Should policymakers be concerned?

7. Evidence shows that women and teenagers have more frequent spells of unemployment than adult men, but that each spell is of significantly shorter duration. What does this suggest about the role of turnover as a cause of unemployment for these two groups? Why might this evidence be misleading?

8. Over the past 40 years the unemployment rate in the economy has gradually crept upwards. What are the reasons for this? Is this increase in the jobless rate due primarily to greater cyclical, structural, or frictional unemployment? What are the policy implications of your answer to the last question?

International Unemployment Statistics

The level of unemployment is a popular indicator of the health of an economy. Every country is concerned about its level of unemployment both from a social perspective (in terms of the numbers of people without a job, thus more likely to be in poverty) and from an efficiency perspective (the more people unemployed, the more resources being wasted and the lower is an economy's potential overall productivity). From an international perspective, high unemployment in one country means less demand for imports, potentially affecting the economy in other countries. The purpose of this appendix is to offer a picture of what unemployment looks like in countries other than in the United States. The International Labor Statistics Section of the U.S. Department of Labor collects data on a wide range of economic developments in other countries, including prices, productivity, earnings, and unemployment. These data can be accessed via the Internet at http://stats.bls.gov/fls, and some are provided in Tables 13A.1–13A.3 of this appendix.

Figure 13A.1 illustrates the path of unemployment rates for four countries from 1959 to 2003: the United States, the United Kingdom, France, and Japan.

FIGURE 13A.1   UNEMPLOYMENT RATES FOR FOUR COUNTRIES, 1959–2003

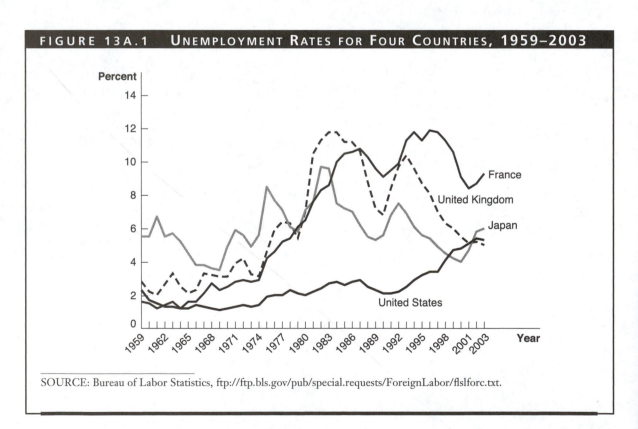

SOURCE: Bureau of Labor Statistics, ftp://ftp.bls.gov/pub/special.requests/ForeignLabor/flslforc.txt.

		TABLE 13A.1	UNEMPLOYMENT IN TEN COUNTRIES, 1959–2003 (IN THOUSANDS, APPROXIMATING U.S. CONCEPTS)							

	US	Canada	Australia	Japan	France	Germany	Italy	Nether-lands	Sweden	United Kingdom
1959	3,740	350	(a)	980	290	510	1,000	(a)	60(3)	660
1960	3,852(b)	420	(a)	750	270	280	760	(a)	63(3)	530
1961	4,714	439	(a)	660	230	160	670	(a)	55	480
1962	3,911(b)	368	(a)	590	270	150	580	(a)	55	670
1963	4,070	351	(a)	590	300	120	480	(a)	62	830
1964	3,786	306	63	540	240	100	540	(a)	58	620
1965	3,366	263	61	570	310	70	690	(a)	44	540
1966	2,875	251	76	650	320	70	730	(a)	59	570
1967	2,975	296	94	630	420	340	670	(a)	80	830
1968	2,817	358	94	590	550	290	700	(a)	85	810
1969	2,832	362	96	570	480	170	680	(a)	73	770
1970	4,093	476	91	590	530	140	640	(a)	59	770
1971	5,016	535	107	640	580	160	640	(a)	101	980
1972	4,882(b)	553	150	730	610	190	740	(a)	107	1,070
1973	4,365(b)	515	136	680	590	190	720	160	98	820
1974	5,156	514	162	730	630	420	620	190	80	790
1975	7,929	690	302	1,000	910	890	690	270	67	1,180
1976	7,406	711(b)	298	1,080	1,020	890	790	290	66	1,540
1977	6,991	829	358	1,100	1,160	900	840	270	75	1,660
1978	6,202(b)	890	405	1,240	1,220	870	850	280	94	1,650
1979	6,137	827	408	1,170	1,390	780	920	290	88	1,420
1980	7,637	849	409	1,140	1,490	770	920	350	86	1,850
1981	8,273	883	394	1,260	1,760	1,090	1,040	540	108	2,790
1982	10,678	1,289	495	1,360	1,930(b)	1,560	1,160	630	137	3,000
1983	10,717	1,428	697	1,560	2,020	1,900(b)	1,270	700(b)	151	3,140
1984	8,539	1,370	641	1,610	2,360	1,970	1,280	710	136	3,200(b)
1985	8,312	1,309	603	1,560	2,470	2,010	1,310	600	125	3,078
1986	8,237(b)	1,209	601(b)	1,670	2,520	1,860	1,680(b)	640	117	3,081
1987	7,425	1,122	612	1,730	2,570	1,800	1,760	650	97(b)	2,990
1988	6,701	998	558	1,550	2,460	1,810	1,790	460(b)	84	2,469
1989	6,528	982	490	1,420	2,320	1,640	1,760	430	72	2,064
1992	9,613	1,505	897	1,420	2,430(b)	2,615	1,680	370	255	2,760(b)
1993	8,940	1,539	914	1,660	2,770	3,113	2,300(b)	440	416	2,916
1994	7,996(b)	1,373	829	1,920	2,920	3,318	2,510	490	426	2,716
1995	7,404	1,246	739	2,100	2,800	3,200	2,640	480	404	2,439
1996	7,236	1,289	751	2,250	2,970	3,505	2,650	440	440	2,297
1997	6,739(b)	1,252	759	2,300	2,960	3,907	2,690	370	445	1,985
1998	6,210(b)	1,169	721	2,790	2,870	3,693	2,750	300	368	1,783
1999	5,880(b)	1,080	652	3,170	2,740	3,333(b)	2,670	250	313	1,721
2000	5,692(b)	962	602	3,200	2,380	3,065	2,500	240	260	1,580
2001	6,801	1,031	661(b)	3,400	2,210	3,110	2,270	210	227	1,483
2002	8,378	1,150	636	3,590	2,310	3,396	2,160	230	234	1,520
2003	8,774(b)	1,159	611	3,500	2,480	3,661	2,100	320	264	1,479

(a) Not available

(b) Break in series

SOURCE: Bureau of Labor Statistics, ftp://ftp.bls.gov/pub/special.requests/ForeignLabor/flslforc.txt.

UNEMPLOYMENT RATES IN TEN COUNTRIES, 1959–2003
(PERCENT, APPROXIMATING U.S. CONCEPTS)

	US	Canada	Australia	Japan	France	Germany	Italy	Nether-lands	Sweden	United Kingdom
1959	5.5	5.6	2.1	2.3	1.6	2	4.8	(a)	1.7	2.8
1960	5.5(b)	6.5	1.6	1.7	1.5	1.1	3.7	(a)	1.7	2.2
1961	6.7	6.7	3	1.5	1.2	0.6	3.2	(a)	1.5	2
1962	5.5(b)	5.5	2.9	1.3	1.4	0.6	2.8	(a)	1.5	2.7
1963	5.7	5.2	2.3	1.3	1.6	0.5	2.4	(a)	1.7	3.3
1964	5.2	4.4	1.4	1.2	1.2	0.4	2.7	(a)	1.6	2.5
1965	4.5	3.6	1.3	1.2	1.6	0.3	3.5	(a)	1.2	2.1
1966	3.8	3.4	1.6	1.4	1.6	0.3	3.7	(a)	1.6	2.3
1967	3.8	3.8	1.9	1.3	2.1	1.3	3.4	(a)	2.1	3.3
1968	3.6	4.5	1.8	1.2	2.7	1.1	3.5	(a)	2.2	3.2
1969	3.5	4.4	1.8	1.1	2.3	0.6	3.5	(a)	1.9	3.1
1970	4.9	5.7	1.6	1.2	2.5	0.5	3.2	(a)	1.5	3.1
1971	5.9	6.2	1.9	1.3	2.8	0.6	3.3	(a)	2.6	3.9
1972	5.6(b)	6.2	2.6	1.4	2.9	0.7	3.8	(a)	2.7	4.2
1973	4.9(b)	5.5	2.3	1.3	2.8	0.7	3.7	3.1	2.5	3.2
1974	5.6	5.3	2.7	1.4	2.9	1.6	3.1	3.6	2	3.1
1975	8.5	6.9	4.9	1.9	4.2	3.4	3.4	5.1	1.6	4.6
1976	7.7	6.8(b)	4.8	2	4.6	3.4	3.9	5.4	1.6	5.9
1977	7.1	7.8	5.6	2	5.2	3.4	4.1	4.9	1.8	6.4
1978	6.1(b)	8.1	6.3	2.3	5.4	3.3	4.1	5.1	2.2	6.3
1979	5.8	7.3	6.3	2.1	6.1	2.9	4.4	5.1	2.1	5.4
1980	7.1	7.3	6.1	2	6.5	2.8	4.4	6	2	7
1981	7.6	7.3	5.8	2.2	7.6	4	4.9	8.9	2.5	10.5
1982	9.7	10.6	7.2	2.4	8.3(b)	5.6	5.4	10.2	3.1	11.3
1983	9.6	11.5	10	2.7	8.6	6.9(b)	5.9	11.4(b)	3.5	11.8
1984	7.5	10.9	9	2.8	10	7.1	5.9	11.5	3.1	11.8(b)
1985	7.2	10.2	8.3	2.6	10.5	7.2	6	9.6	2.8	11.2
1986	7.0(b)	9.2	7.9(b)	2.8	10.6	6.6	7.5(b)	10	2.6	11.2
1987	6.2	8.4	7.9	2.9	10.8	6.3	7.9	10	2.2(b)	10.7
1988	5.5	7.3	7	2.5	10.3	6.3	7.9	7.3(b)	1.9	8.8
1989	5.3	7.1	6	2.3	9.6	5.7	7.8	6.7	1.6	7.2
1992	7.5	10.6	10.5	2.2	9.9(b)	6.7	7.3	5.3	5.6	9.7(b)
1993	6.9	10.8	10.6	2.5	11.3	8	10.2(b)	6.3	9.4	10.4
1994	6.1(b)	9.5	9.4	2.9	11.8	8.5	11.2	6.9	9.6	9.6
1995	5.6	8.6	8.2	3.2	11.3	8.2	11.8	6.7	9.1	8.7
1996	5.4	8.8	8.2	3.4	11.9	9	11.7	6	9.9	8.1
1997	4.9(b)	8.4	8.3	3.4	11.8	9.9	11.9	4.9	10.1	7
1998	4.5(b)	7.7	7.7	4.1	11.3	9.3	12	3.9	8.4	6.3
1999	4.2(b)	7	6.9	4.7	10.6	8.5(b)	11.5	3.2	7.1	6
2000	4.0(b)	6.1	6.3	4.8	9.1	7.8	10.7	2.9	5.8	5.5
2001	4.7	6.4	6.8(b)	5.1	8.4	7.9	9.6	2.5	5	5.1
2002	5.8	7	6.4	5.4	8.7	8.6	9.1	2.8	5.1	5.2
2003	6.0(b)	6.9	6.1	5.3	9.3	9.3	8.8	3.8	5.8	5

(a) Not available

(b) Break in series

SOURCE: Bureau of Labor Statistics, ftp://ftp.bls.gov/pub/special.requests/ForeignLabor/flslforc.txt.

UNEMPLOYMENT RATES IN TEN COUNTRIES BY GENDER, 1990–2003 (PERCENT, APPROXIMATING U.S. CONCEPTS)

	US	Canada	Australia	Japan	France	Germany	Italy	Nether-lands	Sweden	United Kingdom
Male										
1990	5.7	7.9	6.6	1.9	7	4.2	4.8	4.2	1.8	7.1
1991	7.2	10.5	9.7	1.8	7.5	4.6	4.9	3.9	3.4	9.3
1992	7.9	11.6	11.2	1.8	8	5.5	5.3	4.1	6.7	11.6
1993	7.2	11.5	11.3	1.9	9.7	6.7	7.6	5.5	11	12.4
1994	6.2	10.2	9.8	2.3	10.2	7.3	8.7	6.2	11	11.4
1995	5.6	9.1	8.6	2.5	9.6	7.3	9.1	5.5	9.9	10.1
1996	5.4	9.3	8.5	2.8	10.2	8.4	9.1	4.7	10.4	9.5
1997	4.9	8.7	8.5	2.8	10.3	9.4	9.1	3.7	10.4	7.8
1998	4.4	8.1	8	3.2	9.7	8.9	9.2	3	8.7	6.9
1999	4.1	7.3	7.1	3.9	9.1	8.1	8.9	2.2	7.4	6.6
2000	3.9	6.3	6.5	4.3	7.6	7.6	8.3	2.1	6.2	6
2001	4.8	6.8	7	4	7	7.8	7.5	2.1	5.3	5.6
2002	5.9	7.5	6.6	4.7	7.7	8.8	7.1	2.6	5.6	5.7
2003	6.3	7.3	6	4.5	8.2	9.7	6.9	3.7	6.3	5.6
Female										
1990	5.5	7.4	6.8	2.7	11.6	6.1	10.8	8.5	1.8	6.5
1991	6.4	8.9	8.7	2.4	12	7	10.4	7.9	2.8	7.2
1992	7	9.4	9.5	2.5	12.3	8.4	10.8	7.2	4.5	7.4
1993	6.6	9.8	9.7	3	13.2	9.6	14.7	7.7	7.6	7.7
1994	6	8.7	9	3.4	13.8	10.1	15.4	7.8	8.2	7.4
1995	5.6	8	7.7	3.3	13.4	9.4	16.3	8	8.1	6.9
1996	5.4	8.2	7.8	3.7	13.7	9.6	16.2	7.8	9.3	6.4
1997	5	7.9	7.9	3.8	13.5	10.6	16.2	6.6	9.7	5.9
1998	4.6	7.2	7.4	3.7	13.1	9.8	16.3	4.9	8	5.4
1999	4.3	6.5	6.7	4.7	12.4	8.9	15.7	4.4	6.7	5.2
2000	4.1	5.8	6.1	4.9	10.9	8.1	14.6	3.7	5.3	4.9
2001	4.7	5.9	6.5	4.6	10.1	7.9	13	3.1	4.7	4.5
2002	5.6	6.4	6.2	5.4	9.9	8.3	12.3	3	4.7	4.5
2003	5.7	6.4	6.1	5.2	10.5	8.8	11.7	4.1	5.2	4.4

SOURCE: Bureau of Labor Statistics, ftp://ftp.bls.gov/pub/special.requests/ForeignLabor/flslforc.txt.

Each of these countries' experience is quite varied. While exhibiting a great deal of cyclical variation, unemployment in the United States actually appears to have been the most stable over the time period (among these countries), while France's employment situation demonstrated the greatest amount of deterioration. The growing unemployment in Europe beginning in the late 1960s has been the source of much speculation and research.[1] One reason offered for Europe's rise in unemployment is the increase in nonwage labor costs. A rise in social insurance and

1   Much of the following discussion is inspired by Melvin M. Brodsky, "Labor Market Flexibility: A Changing International Perspective," *Monthly Labor Review* (November 1994): 53–60.

other labor taxes provides employers with an incentive to rely on overtime work and to employ labor-saving technologies. Of the four countries depicted in Figure 13A.1, nonwage labor costs are the highest in France.

A related reason often cited for the rise in European unemployment is the generosity of social insurance programs. When workers receive high unemployment benefits (as they do in France and Germany), they have little incentive to leave unemployment.[2] Minimum wage laws and inflexible employment relationships are also cited as reasons for high unemployment in Europe. While the general trend in the 1980s (particularly in the United States) was for the real value of the minimum wage to decline, France was, once again, the exception. In addition, some of the strongest unions exist in Germany and France, allowing workers in these countries to win employment protections and high wages, reducing the flexibility firms have to make adjustments.[3]

Some degree of cyclicality seems to be shared by all countries, with Japan's troughs being the most shallow. In addition, each of the countries, except the United States, seems to be continuing on its long-term upward trend in the unemployment rate.[4]

---

2 Additional evidence on this point can be found in Stefano Scarpetta, "Assessing the Role of Labour Market Policies and Institutional Settings on Unemployment: A Cross-Country Study," *OECD Economic Studies* (1996): 43–98.

3 Additional evidence of the impact of employment protection policies on unemployment can be found in Kjell G. Salvanes, "Market Rigidities and the Labour Market Flexibility: An International Comparison," *Scandinavian Journal of Economics* 99 (June 1997): 315–33.

4 For a discussion of this phenomenon, see Olivier J. Blanchard and Lawrence H. Summers, "Hysteresis and the European Unemployment Problem," in Stanley Fischer, *NBER Macroeconomics Annual 1986* (Cambridge, Mass.: The MIT Press, 1986): 15–77.

Added worker effect   This effect causes the labor force to grow during recessions as other family members seek work to make up for the drop in family income due to the loss of job by the primary earner.

Adjusted union–nonunion wage differential   The percentage differential between the wage rate of union workers and nonunion workers, where both wage rates have been adjusted to eliminate the problem of other things equal and the problem of mutual interdependence.

Adverse selection   A situation where "lemon" employees are attracted to a firm by some positive aspect of its HRM policy or practice.

Affirmative action program   A program in which companies doing business with the federal government must analyze the demographic composition of their work forces and try to recruit persons of underrepresented minority groups.

Age Discrimination in Employment Act of 1967 (ADEA)   Legislation which protects workers 40 years and older from discrimination in all aspects of their employment.

Age/earnings profile   The relationship between age and earnings among a cross-section of individuals of the same educational level.

Age/participation profile   The relationship between age and labor force participation rate for a cross-section of persons.

Agency shop   A form of union security in which workers do not have to join the union but must pay a fee in lieu of dues for services provided by the union.

Aid to Families with Dependent Children (AFDC)   A welfare program begun in 1935 that provides income to poor families with children who are in need because of the death, incapacitation, or absence of one of the parents.

American Federation of Labor (AFL)   A federation of national craft unions founded in 1886.

Americans with Disabilities Act (ADA)   A law passed in 1990 that prohibits discrimination against handicapped people if, with a reasonable accommodation on the part of the firm, they can adequately perform the essential functions of the job.

Area of indeterminacy   The range of wage rates within which demand and supply allow firms discretion as to their pay policies.

Aspiration level theory   A psychological theory that a person's aspirations rise with greater than expected success and fall with less than expected success.

Asymmetric information   A situation where one party to an exchange relationship possesses information unavailable or unknown to the other party.

Average Product of Labor (AP_L)   Measured as output per worker, or total product divided by the number of workers.

Backward-bending supply curve   A labor supply curve that has a positively sloped segment at low wage rates and a negatively sloped segment at high wage rates.

Bargaining calendar   The schedule of union contract negotiations.

Bargaining power   One's ability to induce an opponent to agree on one's own terms.

Barriers to entry   Factors that impede the ability of new firms (workers) to enter a product (labor) market.

Beveridge curve   A curve that shows the inverse relationship between the number of job vacancies and the number of unemployed workers in the economy as aggregate demand expands and contracts over the business cycle.

Binding arbitration   A form of dispute resolution in labor negotiations in which both sides agree to accept the decision of a neutral third party.

Block grant   A fixed sum of money based on the *projected* welfare needs of a state; these funds are administered by the state for the welfare program as they see fit.

Boulwarism   A bargaining strategy in which the company makes one firm and final offer to the union which it can accept or reject.

Bounded rationality   A model of the human actor that presumes problem solving and information processing are impeded by emotional states and cognitive limitations.

Break-even point (BE)   The level of earned income for a family at which it no longer qualifies for a welfare payment.

Budget constraint The line that shows all the combinations of hours of work and income available to a person, given the wage rate and amount of nonlabor income.

Chilling effect The adverse effect of binding arbitration on the incentive of the union and employer to make concessions because of the small costs to continued intransigence and the assumption that the arbitrator may split the difference between the two sides' demands.

Civil Rights Act of 1964 A law that prohibits discrimination in employment on the basis of race, color, religion, gender, or national origin.

Civil Rights Act of 1991 A law passed that effectively overturns several recent Supreme Court decisions. It reaffirms that business firms must prove that any personnel policies that have a disparate impact on minorities must be justified as a business necessity.

Civil Service Reform Act of 1978 (CSRA) The CSRA limits the scope of bargaining in the federal government largely to matters concerning personnel practices and working conditions and still prohibits strikes. It also incorporates the procedures of the Taft-Hartley Act governing union representation elections and unfair labor practices.

Closed shop A form of union security in which workers must belong to the union before a firm can hire them.

Collective action Action an individual undertakes by working through a group or organization to achieve a particular goal or objective.

Comparable worth A method of determining employee compensation based on the principle that jobs of equal value should pay equal wages.

Compensating wage differentials Wage differentials that equalize the net attractiveness of occupations.

Complete contract A contract that stipulates in every detail and for every contingency what the two parties will do and for how much.

Comprehensive Employment and Training Act (CETA) A law passed in 1973 that funded a variety of job training programs and a program of public sector employment.

Congress of Industrial Organizations (CIO) A labor federation of industrial unions formed in 1935.

Consolidated Omnibus Budget Reconciliation Act—COBRA An amendment to the Employee Retirement Income Security Act of 1974 (ERISA), passed by Congress in 1985, which requires employers to allow workers the opportunity to continue health insurance coverage for up to 18 months after leaving their jobs.

Consumer boycott A cost-imposing sanction by the union in which it encourages consumers to boycott the company's products until the company agrees to the union's demands.

Contingency A management concept stating that the best HRM practice depends on various contingent factors, such as the nature of the firm's product, the technology of production, the state of the economy, the characteristics of the workforce, and so on.

Contract zone The range of wage rates within which a settlement between the union and the firm is possible.

Corporate campaign tactics An attempt by a union to jeopardize the profits or the public image of other companies or individuals associated with the target firm so that they will pressure it to settle the dispute.

Cost-of-living allowance (COLA) clause A clause in union contracts that provides for an automatic cents per hour wage increase for each percentage point rise in the price level.

Craft union A union that represents workers in a particular occupation or skill group.

Cross-sectional data Data collected at a point in time for a number of separate individuals.

Cross-substitution effect The change in one family member's hours of work given a change in the wage rate of another family member, holding total income of the family constant.

Current Population Survey (CPS) A nationwide survey of 60,000 households conducted each month to obtain data on the size and characteristics of the labor force.

Cyclical (or demand deficient) unemployment Unemployment that occurs because there are not enough jobs for everyone who seeks work due to insufficient aggregate demand in the economy.

Davis-Bacon Act A law passed in 1931 that requires all contractors working on federal construction projects to pay workers the prevailing wage rate in the locality.

Decertification election An election in which workers vote on whether they continue to desire union representation.

Demand curve for human capital A curve that shows the marginal rate of return earned from each additional dollar spent on human capital.

Demand curve for union services A curve showing the amount of union services demanded at a given price.

Derived demand The demand for labor by the firm that is derived from the demand for its product.

Direct participation A form of workplace participation where employees voice opinions or views directly or "face-to-face" with the employer or manager.

Discouraged worker   A person who gives up searching for work due to discouragement over the prospects of obtaining employment.

Discouraged worker effect   This effect causes the labor force to shrink during recessions because some of the unemployed give up searching for work.

Discrimination coefficient   A measure of the amount of psychic disutility received from contact with a person of a minority group.

Divorce of capital and labor   The separation of the worker from the ownership of the means of production.

Economic rent   A payment above a factor input's minimum supply price.

Efficiency wage theory   A theory that assumes employee work effort is positively related to the size of the wage rate the firm pays.

Elasticity of labor demand (E_D)   A measure of the sensitivity of employment to changes in the wage rate. It is defined as the percentage change in employment divided by the percentage change in the wage rate.

Election unit   The particular group in the plant or company that is to vote in an (NLRB) union representation election.

Employee   A person hired by a firm who agrees to provide labor services in a manner and timing as directed by the owner or manager in return for an agreed-upon amount of compensation.

Employee association   An organization of workers that promotes its members' interests through lobbying and public relations.

Employee Retirement Income Security Act of 1974 (ERISA)   Federal legislation which provided for regulation of benefit provisions by private employers, including vesting rules and the establishment of individual retirement accounts (IRAs).

Employer concession curve   A curve that shows the timepath of wage offers made by the firm to the union over the course of the negotiations.

Employment-at-will   A legal doctrine the gives both the employer and employee the right to terminate the labor contract "at will."

Employment/population (E/P) ratio   The percentage of the noninstitutional population who are employed.

Empowerment Zone and Enterprise Community (EZ/EC) Initiative   An Economic development program encouraging businesses through tax incentives to locate in economically depressed areas.

Equal Pay Act of 1963   An amendment to the Fair Labor Standards Act that requires that men and women doing the same job be paid equal wages.

Exclusive representation   A provision of the NLRA that a union must represent all workers in an election unit even if he or she does not belong to the union.

Executive Order 10988   President Kennedy's 1962 order that allowed federal government workers to engage in collective bargaining.

Executive Order 11246   An executive order that requires every company doing business with the federal government to agree not to discriminate in any aspect of employment.

Exit/voice theory of unionism   A theory that hypothesizes that workers have two options for expressing dissatisfaction; in a nonunion firm workers can quit, while in a union firm the workers can voice their grievances through the union.

Experimental Negotiating Agreement (ENA)   An agreement adopted in the steel industry in which the union and companies agreed to submit all unresolved issues in their contract negotiations to a neutral third party for binding arbitration.

External alignment   A situation where pay rates are structured or "aligned" so that they are consistent with pay rates for similar workers and jobs in the external labor market.

External labor market   The labor market external to the firm where workers compete for entry level jobs.

Fact-finding   A form of dispute resolution where a third party enters the negotiations and prepares a public report on the issues in the dispute and the position of the union and the employer.

Factor market   A market where a factor of production such as land, labor, or capital is bought and sold.

Fair Labor Standards Act (FLSA)   Passed in 1938, this law sets minimum wage and overtime standards for employers covered by the act.

Family and Medical Leave Act of 1993   A Federal law passed in 1993 that requires employers of 50 or more workers to provide eligible employees with 12 weeks of unpaid leave following the birth of a child, their own serious illnesses, or the illness of a child, spouse, or parent.

Final offer arbitration   A form of binding arbitration in which a neutral third party chooses either the union's or the employer's final offer as the terms of the settlement.

Fixed costs of employment   Costs of employment that do not vary with hours worked. Examples are hiring, training, and certain fringe benefit costs.

Four laws of derived demand Four specific factors that determine the size of the elasticity of labor demand.

Frictional unemployment Unemployment that occurs because of the movement of people between jobs and in and out of the labor force.

Full employment A situation where the number of job vacancies equals the number of people looking for work.

Fundamental uncertainty Future events that are so uncertain that it is impossible to assign reliable probabilities to their occurrence.

Gain-sharing A compensation system that bases at least a portion of employee pay on improvements in the firm's profits, productivity, or cost reduction.

General on-the-job training Training that increases a worker's productivity not only in the firm providing the training, but also in other firms in the labor market.

Health Insurance Portability and Accountability Act of 1996 (HIPAA) An amendment to the Employee Retirement Income Security Act of 1974 (ERISA) that provides for a limit on how long someone may be denied health insurance coverage on a new job for a pre-existing health condition.

Human Resource Management (HRM) The employment staff function in business firms and the strategies and practices managers use to coordinate and allocate labor for production.

Implicit contract A tacit, unwritten agreement between the firm and its workers that the adjustment to a fall in labor demand will take the form of layoffs rather than cuts in wages.

Implicit tax rate (*t*) The amount by which a welfare payment is reduced for each additional dollar of earnings beyond the level of disregard.

Income effect The change in hours of work resulting from a change in income, holding the wage rate constant.

Income guarantee (*G*) The amount of welfare payment received by a family if it has zero earnings from work.

Income maintenance program An income transfer program which bases eligibility and the size of payments on financial need.

Independent contractor A person doing business as an independent supplier who is hired by a firm to perform pre-agreed tasks or services. The independent contractor retains authority to perform and organize the work and often provides the capital equipment.

Indifference curve A curve that plots all the combinations of income and leisure that yield the same level of utility.

Indirect participation A form of workplace participation where the opinions or views of the employees are presented to management by a person or group selected or appointed to act as their representative.

Individual action Action taken by an individual such as quitting the firm or talking to the supervisor in order to improve the person's position in the labor market.

Industrial union A union that organizes all workers in an industry regardless of occupation.

Input–output coefficients The coefficients of the input–output model. The *labor input–output coefficient* is the amount of labor required per unit of output; the *capital input–output coefficient* is the amount of capital required per unit of output.

Institutional forces The influence that organizations such as unions, corporations, and government have on the pricing and distribution of labor.

Institutional school A school of thought in labor economics that emphasizes imperfections in the market mechanism and the importance of institutional and sociological forces.

Interest arbitration The use of arbitration to determine the terms and conditions of a new collective bargaining contract.

Internal alignment A situation where pay rates inside a firm are structured or "aligned" in a manner that best promotes employee motivation, training, and allocation among jobs.

Internal labor market The group of jobs in the firm that are filled through internal promotion rather than hiring from the external market.

Internal rate of return The discount rate that equalizes the net present value of the income streams from two alternative human capital investments.

Isocost line A line that shows all the various combinations of labor and capital that a firm can purchase with a particular amount of money expenditure, given the wage rate and cost of capital.

Isoprofit curve A curve showing all the combinations of the wage rate and some job amenity or disamenity that yield the same total labor cost per hour (meaning profit is the same).

Isoquant A curve that shows all the various combinations of capital and labor that a firm can use to produce a particular level of output.

Job analysis A technique used by firms to establish an internal wage structure that ranks jobs on the basis of various attributes such as skill, responsibility, and so on.

Job cluster Jobs related to a common activity in the firm.

Job Corps   An ongoing residential training program for youth providing employment training, basic education, and social skills to function in a private sector job.

Job ladder   A vertical hierarchy of jobs in the firm that workers move up as they acquire training at each rung.

Job lock   The constraint placed on mobility as a result of the risk of losing health insurance.

Job structure   The set of jobs in terms of skill and function required by a firm.

Job Training Partnership Act (JTPA)   A federal law passed in 1982 that provides for job training financed by block grants to states which then are allocated by private industry councils.

Labor demand curve   A curve that illustrates the inverse relationship between the wage rate and the quantity of labor demanded by business firms, holding other factors constant.

Labor force participation rate   The percent of the noninstitutional population that is employed or looking for work.

Labor Management Reporting and Disclosure Act of 1959   A law that provides a bill of rights for union members and requires financial disclosure of union assets, liabilities, and income. *See also* Landrum-Griffin Act.

Labor market   The area within which demand and supply determine the price for a particular type of labor.

Labor market outcomes   The observed events, developments, or trends in the labor market.

Labor market process   The mechanics of the labor market—how it works, the nature of the cause and effect relationships, and the major actors and institutions.

Labor market segmentation   A development that impedes the mobility of workers between labor markets because of barriers to entry such as internal labor markets and occupational licensing laws.

Labor productivity   The amount of output produced per employee-hour.

Labor supply curve   A curve that illustrates the positive relationship between the wage rate and the quantity of labor supplied by workers, holding other factors constant.

Labor union   An organization of workers that engages in collective bargaining with the employer.

Lack of jobs view of unemployment   A theory that the high unemployment rate of certain demographic groups is due to a lack of jobs in the labor market.

Landrum-Griffin Act   A law that provides a bill of rights for union members and requires financial disclosure of union assets, liabilities, and income. *See also* Labor Management Reporting and Disclosure Act of 1959.

Law of diminishing returns   An economic law that states holding one factor of production constant, as additional units of another factor are added, output will increase but eventually at a diminishing rate.

Law of one wage   An economic law that states that in a perfectly competitive labor market all firms will pay the same wage rate for a particular type of labor.

Level of disregard (D)   The amount of earnings a welfare recipient is allowed to earn before his or her benefits start being reduced.

Long-run demand curve for labor   A curve that depicts the relationship between the wage rate and the firm's desired level of employment, assuming both labor and capital are variable.

Longitudinal (panel) survey data   Data collected on the same set of individuals over a number of years.

Manpower Development and Training Act (MDTA)   A law passed in 1962 to provide retraining for heads of households who had been displaced from their jobs by technological change.

Marginal cost of labor (MCL) schedule   A line that shows the change in the firm's total cost of labor per hour for each additional worker hired.

Marginal product of labor (MP_L)   The change in total output resulting from a one unit change in labor input, holding capital constant.

Marginal rate of substitution (MRS)   The rate at which a person is psychologically willing to trade leisure for income.

Marginal rate of technical substitution ($MRTS$)   The rate at which capital can be substituted for labor, holding output constant.

Marginal revenue product (MRP_L)   The additional dollars of revenue earned by the firm from the output produced by the last worker hired. Calculated by multiplying the marginal product of labor times the marginal revenue.

Market discrimination   Discrimination that occurs in the labor market when individuals of equal capability are given unequal job assignments, wage rates, or promotions.

Market equilibrium   A state of balance in the labor market where demand and supply are equal.

Market forces   The influence that the market forces of demand and supply have on the pricing and distribution of labor.

Market imperfection   Factors such as imperfect information or nonmaximizing behavior that cause labor markets to diverge from the perfectly competitive model.

Median voter   The person who occupies the median position in the electorate with respect to the desired amount of the good or service.

Mediation   A form of dispute resolution in which a neutral third party enters the negotiations as a go-between in order to improve the communications between the union and the employer.

Menu costs   Administrative and business costs associated with changing a firm's pay system/structure (the "menu" of rewards and incentives).

Minimum acceptance wage   The lowest wage for a job that an unemployed worker will consider accepting.

Monopoly rent   A wage rate that is higher than the competitive level because of a restriction on the supply of labor or some other form of market power.

Monopsonistic discrimination   Discrimination that results when a monopsonistic employer is able to pay different wage rates because one group of workers has a more inelastic labor supply curve than another.

Monopsonistic exploitation   The difference between the dollar value of the output produced by labor and the wage labor is paid by a monopsonistic firm.

Monopsony   A labor market with only one buyer of labor.

Moral hazard   Actions of one party that harm another by opportunistically taking advantage of holes or gaps in an incomplete contract.

Narcotic effect   The tendency that once the union and the employer have used binding arbitration, they will increasingly come to rely on it rather than make the concessions necessary to reach agreement.

National emergency dispute   A strike the president, under the Taft-Hartley Act, can seek by court injunction to suspend if it threatens national health or safety.

National Labor Relations Act (NLRA)   A law passed in 1935 which outlaws various unfair labor practices by employers and provides for union representation elections. *See also* Wagner Act.

National Labor Relations Board   A five-member board responsible for administration of the NLRA.

Neoclassical school   A school of thought in labor economics that bases its theory on the twin assumptions of competitive markets and the model of economic man.

New Jobs Tax credit (NJTC)   A federal incentive provided to private sector employers designed to increase overall employment levels by offering a tax credit for employment increases of more than 2 percent over the past year.

Noncompeting groups   Socioeconomic groups among which there is little competition in the labor market due to differences in family background, class, or skills.

Normative economics   The study of economics based on value judgments of what ought to be.

North American Industry Classification System (NAICS)   A system of classifying firms into industry groups; the classification system is shared by the United States, Canada, and Mexico.

Occupational Safety and Health Administration (OSHA)   The agency that operates under the jurisdiction of the Department of Labor to administer the Occupational Safety and Health Act of 1970. The purpose of the act is to reduce injuries and illnesses at the workplace through the enforcement of detailed health and safety standards.

Occupational segregation   The division of the occupational structure into jobs that primarily employ workers of only one gender or race group.

Okun's Law   An economic law that states that each percentage point rise in the unemployment rate is equal to a 2.5 percent decline in gross national product.

Participation/representation Gap   The difference (or gap) between the amount of voice and influence business firms actually give employees and the amount of voice and influence that the employees desire.

Personal Responsibility and Work Opportunity Reconciliation Act   A federal law passed in 1996 placing stricter work requirements on recipients of welfare.

Port of entry   The entry level position on a firm's job ladder where hiring is done from the external market.

Positive economics   The study of economics based on objective facts or logic.

Pregnancy Discrimination Act   A 1978 amendment to Title VII of the 1964 Civil Rights Act which protects the rights of pregnant women against prejudice and work restrictions based on a woman's pregnancy.

Premarket discrimination   Discrimination that occurs prior to a person's entrance in the labor market. Examples are discrimination in education, housing, and health services.

Present value   The value in the present time period of a sum of money to be received in a future time period.

Primary labor market   The sector in the economy that contains the desirable jobs with high wages, good promotion prospects, and employment stability.

Principal–agent problem   The difficulty the stockholders of the firm (the principal) have in ensuring that the managers (the agent) operate the business in order to maximize profit.

Private rate of return   The yield on an investment in education that is received by the person making it.

Problem of mutual interdependence   A potential source of bias in measuring the union–nonunion wage differential that arises from the effect that a change in the union wage has on the nonunion wage.

Problem of other things equal   A potential source of bias in measuring the union–nonunion wage differential that arises from the correlation between a worker's union status and other factors that affect employee compensation, such as demographic characteristics.

Production function   A mathematical equation that states the amount of output that can be produced given the amount of factor inputs and the state of technology.

Productivity-adjusted wages   The wage rate per unit of output produced.

Public good   A good or service for which consumption by one person does not reduce the amount available for another, and which it is difficult to exclude people from using.

Public Service Employment (PSE) program   A program enacted under CETA in which local governments were provided funds to create jobs for persons who were cyclically or structurally unemployed.

Rational Actor Model   A theory of human behavior that assumes persons maximize their level of well-being, exercise rational choice, and are individualistic.

Reaction functions   A pair of mathematical equations that predict the wage demands of the union and firm over the n rounds of negotiations.

Reservation wage   The wage rate at which a person would just be willing to work the first hour at market employment.

Residual method   A statistical technique that separates the wage gap between persons of two groups into the parts due to productivity differences and discrimination, respectively.

Restrictive work rules   Rules negotiated by unions such as crew size limits or detailed job classifications, that force a firm to hire more labor than necessary.

Right-to-work   A state law that protects workers' right to be hired even if they don't belong to a union.

Rights arbitration   Arbitration to adjudicate disputes over the interpretation or application of the terms of an existing collective bargaining contract.

Scale effect   The change in labor demand that results from the change in the firm's optimal level of production due to a wage increase or decrease.

Scientific management   A theory of management advanced by Frederick Taylor that holds there is a "one best way" to organize work and manage employees, and that this one best way is discoverable through scientific analysis.

Secondary boycott   A boycott or strike by a union against a secondary employer in the hope of bringing additional pressure on the primary employer to settle.

Secondary labor market   The sector in the economy that contains the undesirable jobs with low wages, few promotion prospects, and unstable employment.

Seniority unit   The group of jobs in which a worker's seniority must be given weight by an employer in making decisions about promotions and layoffs.

Shirking   Shirking occurs when an employee deliberately holds back on work effort or in some other way provides less than agreed-upon labor services to the employer.

Shock effect   The positive impact on management efficiency of an increase in the minimum wage or other such factor.

Short-run demand curve for labor   A line that depicts the relationship between the wage rate and the firm's desired level of employment, holding capital and all other factors constant.

Social insurance program   An income transfer program which bases eligibility and the size of payments on loss of income from an identifiable problem and the amount of past contributions into the program.

Social rate of return   The yield to society on the resources devoted to education.

Sociological forces   The influence that social groups and norms have on the pricing and distribution of labor.

Specific on-the-job training   Training that increases a worker's productivity only in the firm providing the training.

Spillover effect   An effect that occurs when workers laid off in the union sector because of a wage increase migrate to the nonunion sector, increasing the supply of labor and forcing down the nonunion wage rate.

Standard Industrial Classification (SIC)   A classification system in which each firm in the nonagricultural economy is assigned to a particular group based on the type of product produced.

Statistical discrimination   Discrimination that occurs when employers use group characteristics such as race or gender to screen job applicants.

Strategic HRM   The pattern of planned human resource deployments and activities intended to enable an organization to achieve its goals.

Strategic interaction   The interdependency that exists in the bargaining process as the wage demand by one party influences the demand of the second party, which then affects the demand of the first party, and so on.

Strike insurance   A formal agreement among companies that if one company is struck, the others will provide it financial support.

Structural unemployment   Unemployment that occurs because of a mismatch between the types of jobs available and the types of people looking for work.

Structure of bargaining   The determination of who bargains with whom and who is covered under the collective bargaining agreement.

Substitution effect (of labor demand)   The change in labor demand that results from the substitution of capital for labor (or vice versa) in response to a change in the wage rate.

Substitution effect   The change in hours of work resulting from a change in the wage rate, holding income constant.

Supply curve of investable funds   A curve that shows the marginal interest cost that must be paid to obtain an additional dollar of funds for human capital investment.

Supply curve of labor   The relationship between the wage rate and the hours of work supplied to the market.

Supply curve of union services   A curve showing the amount of services provided by unions at a given price.

Taft-Hartley Act   An amendment to the NLRA passed in 1947 that prohibited union unfair labor practices and provided for decertification elections.

Targeted Jobs Tax Credit (TJTC)   Federal program created in 1979 to replace the New Jobs Tax Credit (NJTC) differing in that it targeted specific groups of (typically, economically disadvantaged) workers rather than employment in general.

Temporary Assistance for Needy Families (TANF)   A block-grant welfare program which replaced AFDC and was created by The Personal Responsibility and Work Opportunity Reconciliation Act of 1996.

Threat effect   An effect that occurs when non-union employers increase their wage rates above the competitive level in response to the threat of unionization.

Time-series   A format for data which show the change over time in a statistical series.

Tournament Theory   A theory about internal wage structures that suggests that workers' performances will be improved if they are in competition for a "prize," which is typically manifested in promotion to the top CEO position within the firm.

Transaction cost   The value of real resources used up in negotiating, implementing, and enforcing contracts.

Trusteeship   An action taken by a national union to take control of the administration of a local union.

Turnover view of unemployment   A theory that the high unemployment rate of certain demographic groups is due to frequent movement of people between jobs and in and out of the labor force.

Two-tier employment systems   A system composed of "core" groups of permanent employees and larger groups of "contingent" workers with little or no job security.

Unadjusted union–nonunion wage differential   The percentage differential between the wage rate of union and nonunion workers, where neither wage rate has been adjusted to control for possible biases in reported earnings data.

Unemployment Insurance (UI) program   A state-administered program that provides weekly cash payments for 26 weeks or more to eligible workers who are unemployed.

Unemployment rate   The percent of the labor force counted as unemployed.

Unfair labor practices   Illegal actions by an employer or a union that interfere with rights guaranteed workers under the NLRA.

Union representation election   An election in which workers in a designated election unit vote on whether they desire to be represented by a union.

Union resistance curve   A curve that shows the time-path of the union's wage demands over the course of the negotiations.

Union shop   A form of union security in which a new employee has 30 days to join the union as a condition of continued employment.

Wage bill   The firm's total money outlay for labor, calculated by multiplying the average wage rate times the number of employees.

Wage gradient   The relationship between the average level of wages rates in a metropolitan area and the distance of the area from the central business district.

Wage rigidity hypothesis   A hypothesis that maintains long-term contracts make union wages less sensitive than nonunion wages to changes in unemployment and inflation.

Wagner Act   A law passed in 1935 that outlaws various unfair labor practices by employers and provides for union representation elections. *See also* National Labor Relations Act.

Welfare-to-Work Tax Credit An incentive that reduces an employer's federal tax liability for each new hire of a long-term welfare recipient. The incentive is administered under the WOTC.

Work Opportunity Tax Credit (WOTC) A federal tax incentive designed to reduce an employer's federal tax liability for *each new* hire from any one of eight targeted groups.

Work-to-rule slowdown A cost-imposing tactic used by a union where the workers follow every regulation governing the performance of their job, substantially slowing down the rate of production.

Worker Adjustment and Retraining Notification Act (WARN) The 1989 federal law requiring employers of 100 or more employees to give 60 days' notice to employees who are to be laid off because of plant shutdowns or relocations.

Workforce Investment Act (WIA) of 1998 A federal law passed in August 1998 that consolidates the programs of and phases out the JTPA; an emphasis of the reorganization is on "one-stop" assistance delivery.

Works council A European system of workplace representation where a plant- or enterprise-level council of elected employee representatives meets with management to consult and advise on employment matters.

1/N Problem A situation in a work group where as the number of workers N gets larger the observable impact on output of one person's shirking gets smaller, leading to a greater incentive to free-ride in the provision of work effort.

Note: Page numbers followed by "f" indicate figures; "n" indicate notes; "t" indicate tables.

Riall, William, 249n
Rickey, Branch, 446n
Rickman, Dan S., 680n
Riddell, Craig W., 498n
Rindfuss, Ronald R., 24n, 146n
Riney, Bobye J., 143n
Ringuede, Sebastien, 270n, 691n
Rizzo, John A., 92n
Roberts, Mark J., 231n
Robinson, Jackie, 456n
Robinson, James C., 402n, 436n
Robinson, Jean, 448n
Robinson, Joan, 275–276, 275n
Robinson, John P., 72n
Robinson, Michael D., 305n
Robst, John, 486n
Rodgers, Robert C., 364n
Rodriguez, Daniel, 251n
Rogers, Joel, 506f, 540n,
    543–544, 543n
Rogovsky, Nikolai, 539n
Roma, Martin, 292n
Romer, David, 668n
Romienko, Lisiunia, 304n
Rose, Elaine, 127n
Rose, Karen, 76n
Rose, Stephen J., 487n
Rosen, Sherwin, 28, 209n, 397–398,
    397n, 553–554, 553n
Rosenzweig, MArk, 460n
Ross, Arthur, 31–35
Rothausen, Teresa, 519n
Rothstein, Richard, 339, 581n
Rottenberg, Simon, 415n
Rowan, Richard L., 82n
Rubenstein, Yona, 675n
Rubin, Rose M., 143n
Rubinstein, Saul, 538n
Ruggles, Nancy D., 261n
Ruggles, Richard, 261n
Ruhm, Christopher J., 251n
Rush, Kimberly, 425n
Ryder, Karl E., 133n

S
Saks, Daniel, 567n
Saltzman, Amy, 82n
Salvanes, Kjell G., 712n
Sami, Daniel, 22n

Sampson, Anthony A., 461n
Sanberg, Joanne, 144, 144n
Sandy, Robert, 397n, 401n
Sass, Tim R., 427n
Sattinger, Michael, 270n, 463n
Sauer, Robert, 418n
Sawhill, Elizabeth, 90n
Sayers, Chera, 675n
Sazanami, Yoko, 211n
Scarpetta, Stefano, 712n
Schady, Norbert R., 353n
Schapiro, Morton Owen, 336n
Scheuer, Markus, 357
Schmidt, Christoph, 270n
Schmidt, Frank L., 465n
Schmidt, Warren, 539n
Schnable, John Addison Claus, 541n
Scholz, John Karl, 153n, 155n–156n
Schone, Pal, 358n
Schor, Juliet, 129n
Schriver, William R., 582–583, 582f
Schultz, Howard, 508
Schultz, T. Paul, 140n, 142n
Schultz, Theodore, 28, 328–329
Schumacher, Edward J., 13f, 391n,
    632n, 635f, 659n, 659t,
    662–665, 663t–664
Schurr, Any, 411
Schuster, Jay, 532n
Schweitzer, Mary M., 151n
Schwenk, ALbert, 636n
Seldon, Barry J., 419n
Seligman, Daniel, 463n
Sewell, William, 379n
Sewimüller, Josef, 639n
Sexton, Edwin A., 365n, 468, 468n
Shackett, Joyce R., 351n
Shalom, F., 589n
Shapiro, Carl, 142n, 691n
Shapiro, David, 362n
Shapiro, Isaac, 430n
Sharpe, M. E., 26n
Shaw, Katherine, 142n, 408n, 412n
Sheehan, Maura, 668n
Sheilds, Michael A., 473n
Shellenberger, Sue, 84n
Shepherd, Lawrence, 418n
Shimda, Haruo, 147n
Sholz, John K., 155n

Shoven, Bruce, 136n, 368n
Showalter, Mark H., 93n
Shuguang, Zhang, 211n
Shultz, George P., 271, 271n
Shultz, James H., 306n
Sicherman, Nachum, 74n,
    138n, 423n
Siebert, Horst, 688n
Siegel, Donald S., 237n
Silber, Jacques, 442n
Silverman, B., 300n
Simkin, William E., 624n
Simon, Herbert, 33, 33n,
    188n, 268n
Simon, Julian L., 185n
Simpson, Wayne, 92n, 94n
Slemrod, Joel, 87n, 91n
Slichter, Summer, 625n
Slottje, D. J., 351n
Slutsky, M., 96
Smelser, Neil, 26n
Smith, Adam, 20–21, 20n, 29, 139n,
    328–329, 328n, 389–393,
    389n–390n, 397n, 441
Smith, Geri, 213n
Smith, James P., 161n, 379n, 482n
Smith, Michael R., 213n
Smith, Ralph E., 161n
Smith, Robert S., 27n, 31n, 405n,
    430n, 434n–435n
Smith Conway, Karen, 74n, 92n
Smulders, Sjak, 244n
Smyth, David J., 203n
Snow, Arthur, 91n
Solow, Robert W., 514n, 617n
Sorensen, Elaine, 371n, 499n–500n
Sousa-Poza, Alfonso, 72n
Sowell, Thomas, 25, 25n, 452–453,
    453n, 480n
Spalter-Roth, Roberta M., 151n
Spellman, William, 307n
Spence, Michael, 530–531, 530n
Spinner, Jack, 701
Spletzer, James R., 157n
Stafford, Diane, 465
Stafford, Frank P., 129n, 132n,
    133n, 630n
Staudohar, Paul, 27n
Stein, Robert L., 671n

Note: Page numbers followed by "f" indicate figures; "n" indicate notes; and "t" indicate tables.

Overview and summary topics (*contd.*)
unemployment, 666, 706–707
union membership and collective bargaining, 558, 614–615
wage determination, 260, 317
work hours, 44, 94–95

P

P-R (participation-representation) gaps, 542–547, 718
Paid time off patterns, 84
Panel (longitudinal) survey data, 657–659
Paper chase concept, 353–354, 353n
Parenting impacts, 140–142
Part-time *vs.* full time work hour patterns, 46
Participation-related concepts, 114–171, 542–547, 718
labor force participation, 114–171. *See also* Labor force participation
participation-representation (P-R) gaps, 542–547, 718
Partner *vs.* adversary relationships, 561–562
Passive wage takers, 458
Patterns. *See also under individual topics*
capital-labor substitution, 219–221, 220f
consumer expenditure, 204–205, 205f
education and earnings, 326–328
employment, 173–174, 173f
human capital theory, 326–328
human resource management (HRM), 550–551
labor force participation, 118–119, 119f
practice, 505–506, 506f
short-run labor demand, 173–174, 173f
unemployment, 666–667, 667f
union membership and collective bargaining, 558–560, 559f
wage, 260–263, 261t
work hours, 44–46, 45f, 79–86, 80f
age profiles, 86

consumption, 86
cross-sectional, 44–46, 45f
full time *vs.* part-time, 46
hours reduction processes, 81–83
increases *vs.* decreases, 83–87
institutional forces roles, 82–83
market force roles, 81–82
moonlighting, 86
overviews, 44–46
paid time off, 84
time series, 45f, 46, 79–86, 80f
Pay forms, 530–534
Pay levels, 526–530, 527f
Pecuniary gains, 458
Peer review panels, 536
Pension plan impacts, 133–137, 134f, 404, 646
Per hour compensation costs, 261
Perfect elasticity, 193
Perfectly competitive markets, 283–287, 284f
Performance measures, 531
Personal prejudice, 450–458
Personal Responsibility and Work Opportunity Act of 1996, 63–64, 70–71, 702–703, 718
PICs. *See* Private industry councils (PICs)
Policy applications. *See* Public policy applications
Ports, entry, 21, 298–299, 718
Positive economies, 718
Positive sorting concept, 533
Practice patterns, 505–506
Pragmatism, 34–35
Predictor-criterion relationship analyses, 519–520
Preferences curves, 47–51
Pregnancy Discrimination Act, 718
Prejudice, 450–458. *See also* Discrimination, labor market
consumer, 457–458
employer, 451–454
personal prejudice, 450–458
union, 461
worker prejudice, 454–457

Premarket *vs.* market discrimination, 450
Present values, 331–332, 718
Price-related concepts, 22, 28n
price takers, 22
price theory *vs.* choice theory, 28n
Primary labor markets, 301, 718
Principal-agent problem, 268–269, 510, 719
Private industry councils (PICs), 700–701
Private rates of return, 333–335, 373–379, 719
Private sector-related concepts, 699–702
employment incentives, 701–702
job training programs, 699–701
Problems. *See also under individual topics*
1/N, 534, 721
hold-up, 509–510
mutual interdependence, 630–632, 631f, 719
other things equal, 628–630
principal-agent, 268–269, 510, 719
Processes, labor market. *See* Labor market processes
Procyclical patterns, 610–611
Product demand, 183–184, 197–205
increases, 183–184
labor demand relationships, 197–205, 198f–199f, 202f, 205f
Product of labor, marginal *vs.* average, 176–178, 713
Production-related concepts, 175–176, 221–224, 536, 538
production control and coordination, 538
production functions, 175–176, 176t, 719
production teams, 536
production technology, 221–224, 222f, 224f
Productivity-related concepts, 174–191, 245–246, 462–464, 648–651, 719
equal productivity, 464

Union Membership

All Workers

Year	Number (thousands)	As Percent of Employed
1930	3,401	11.6
1935	3,584	13.2
1940	8,717	26.9
1945	14,322	35.5
1950	14,267	31.5
1955	16,802	33.2
1960	17,049	31.4
1965	17,299	28.4
1970	19,381	27.3
1975	19,611	25.5
1980	20,095	23.0
1983	17,717	20.1
1984	17,340	18.8
1985	16,996	18.0
1986	16,975	17.5
1987	16,913	17.0
1988	17,002	16.8
1989	16,980	16.4
1990	16,740	16.1
1991	16,568	16.1
1992	16,390	15.8
1993	16,598	15.8
1994	16,748	15.5
1995	16,360	14.9
1996	16,269	14.5
1997	16,110	14.1
1998	16,211	13.9
1999	16,477	13.9
2000	16,258	13.5
2001	16,275	13.5
2002	16,145	13.3
2003	15,776	12.9

Union Members as Percent of Employed in Occupation, Industry, or Group, 1990, 1995, 2003

Occupation/Industry	1990	1995	2003
Occupation			
Managerial and Professional	14.3%	13.8%	13.0%
Sales	5.0	13.5	4.2
Clerical	13.6	13.4	11.1
Service	9.9	13.5	11.5
(not private household or protective)			
Farming, Forestry, Fishing	4.9	4.9	3.5
Operators, Fabricators, and Laborers	26.4	23.0	18.7
Industry			
Agriculture	1.9%	2.1%	1.6%
Mining	18.0	13.8	9.1
Construction	21.0	17.7	16.0
Manufacturing	20.6	17.6	13.5
Transportation	29.3	26.9	25.8
Communication & Public Utilities	34.6	27.3	28.2
Wholesale and Retail Trade	6.3	6.1	6.2
Finance, Insurance, and Real Estate	2.5	2.1	2.1
Public Administration	36.5	37.8	37.2

Demographic Group	1990	1995	2003
Gender			
Male	19.3%	17.2%	14.3%
Female	12.6	12.3	11.4
Race			
Whites	15.5	14.2	12.5
Males	18.8	16.6	14.0
Females	11.7	11.4	10.8
Blacks	21.1	19.9	16.5
Males	24.4	22.5	18.3
Females	18.0	17.6	15.0
Asians	14.8	13.0	11.4
Males	16.3	14.0	11.0
Females	12.5	11.6	10.9
Age			
16–24 year olds	4.6	5.6	5.1
25–54 year olds	18.8	17.1	14.2
55 years old and older	15.3	13.4	15.1
Education[a]			
0–11 years of school	13.5	10.5	7.3
12 years of school (high school)	18.5	16.5	13.5
13–15 years of school	14.8	14.4	14.3
16+ years of school (college)	15.6	15.5	16.5

SOURCE: U.S. Department of Labor, Bureau of Labor Statistics, Handbook of Labor Statistics (December 1980): table 165; Eva E. Jacobs, ed. *Handbook of U.S. Labor Statistics* (Lanham, MD: Bernan Press, 1998): p. 321; Bureau of Labor Statistics, *Employment and Earnings* (January 1996): table 40. Bureau of Labor Statistics, *Employment and Earnings* (January 2004): tables 40 and 42. Barry T. Hirsch and David A. Macpherson, Union Membership and Earnings Data Book: Compilations from the Current Population Survey (2004 edition) (Washington, D.C.: Bureau of National Affairs, March 2004): tables 3a, 3b, 3c (Education Membership Data). Data in Table 3 is discussed in Chapter 11, "Union Membership and Collective Bargaining."

[a]2001 education statistics usually correspond to the year 2000.